The
DIRECTORY
of
POETRY
PUBLISHERS

16th Edition, 2000–2001

Len Fulton, Editor

★ **Dustbooks** ★

■CONTENTS

Dustbooks would like to thank the many people who by advice and criticism have helped make this Directory a more useful and readable publication.

▶▶DIRECTORY OF POETRY PUBLISHERS◀◀

PAPER: $22.95/copy ISBN 0-916685-80-2
$72.00/4-year subscription

email: dustbooks@dcsi.net
web page address: http://www.dustbooks.com

Published annually by Dustbooks, P.O. Box 100, Paradise, CA 95967, also publishers of the *International Directory Of Little Magazines & Small Presses*, *The Small Press Record of Books in Print*, *The Directory Of Editors & Publishers*, and the *Small Press Review/Small Magazine Review* (bimonthly). Systems design, typesetting format and computer programming by Neil McIntyre, 3135 Prince Henry Dr., Sacramento, CA 95833.

Pressure sensitive or cheshire labels are available from the International Directory data base. These can be sorted alphabetically or by Zip Code.

Cover Photo of Mama Nancy

ESCHAR PUBLICATIONS ● P.O. Box 1196 ● Waynesboro, VA 22980

THE
MOUNT DORANS

African American History Notes Of A Florida Town

Vivian W. Owens

Meet people who journeyed far beyond the stereotypical barriers of racism, even poverty and under-education, to make zenith contributions to small town living and the masses of humanity.

$18.95
ISBN: 0-9623839-8-8
Fax: (540) 942-3650

SWEEPSTAKES 2000

One of the things I ask editors in the annual survey from which this directory of poetry publishers is compiled is to name five poets whom that editor has published recently. There are 6,560 such entries contained in the 2,000 poetry publisher listings in this directory. Of course there are many ways to measure a poet's popularity. This is just one of them.

I've been compiling this list and calling it the "Sweepstakes" for thirteen years now and each year the list comes out slightly different from the year before.

This frequency curve of statistical distribution, if you will, continues to reflect the very populism of poetry in this age. The curve is a long, flat one with the poet named most often (Lyn Lifshin) getting 71 entries (out of the 6,560). As far as this directory and these responses are concerned, no single poet holds the international attention.

The top ten (actually sixteen) entries go like this:

Rank	Poet	Entries
1	Lyn Lifshin (71)	
2	Simon Perchik (25)	
2	Walter MacDonald (25)	
3	Richard Kostelanetz (21)	
4	John Grey (20)	
5	Robert Cooperman (19)	
6	Marge Piercy (18)	
6	A.D. Winans(18)	
7	Gerald Locklin (17)	
8	Robert Bly (15)	
8	John M. Bennett (15)	
9	Errol Miller (14)	
10	Albert Goldbarth (13)	
10	Seamus Heaney (13)	
10	Sherman Alexie	
10	B.Z. Niditch	

If you would like a count for any given poet write to me and I will be happy to provide it.

--Len Fulton, 2000

NUMBER SIXTEEN

This **Directory of Poetry Publishers** is an annual companion volume to Dustbooks' "Small Press Information Library," which includes the **International Directory of Little Magazines & Small Presses,** the **Directory of Small Magazine/Press Editors & Publishers,** and the **Small Press Record of Books In Print,** as well as the bimonthly **Small Press Review/Small Magazine Review.**

In the original **International Directory** in 1965 there were a scant 250 total listings covering all subjects. While poetry was then, and is now, the largest single subject category, the sheer volume of poetry publishing today exceeds that of thirty six years ago by a magnitude of perhaps **ten.**

Hence this directory which we started in 1985 and is now in this sixteenth edition. There are more than 2,000 book and magazine publishers listed here who use poetry of one kind or another. The Subject Index for this directory has grown since the first edition to several dozen subject categories of poetry.

The information here does not duplicate that in the **International Directory,** but supplements it. The idea is to broaden and deepen the description of the poetry publishers' programs in terms of needs, biases and contributors. Listings are of two basic kinds: those for **magazines** (periodicals) and those for **presses** (book publishers). A complete **magazine** listing includes, in the following order: name of magazine, general address, telephone number, name(s) of poetry editor(s), address for poetry submissions (if different from general address), founding year, additional comments about poetry publishing policies, circulation, frequency, number of poems published in 1999, number expected in 2000 and 2001, subscription price, sample copy price, average number of pages per issue, size, rights purchased, percent of submissions published, deadlines, reporting time, payment, interest in previously unpublished poets, policy on simultaneous submissions, recent contributors, policy on submission quantity, and special interests.

A complete **press** listing includes, in the following order: name of press, general address, telephone number, name(s) of poetry editor(s), address for poetry submissions (if different from general address), founding year, additional comments about poetry publishing policies, average press run, number of poetry titles published in 1999, number expected in 2000 and 2001, average copy price for cloth, paper and other bindings, average number of pages, rights purchased, percent of submissions published, reporting time, royalty and payment arrangements, interest in previously unpublished poets, policy on simultaneous submissions, recent contributors, policy on submission quantity, and special interests.

A listing preceded by a bullet (●) is a new listing to this edition.

For publishers who wish to list a magazine or press in future editions of this (or any other Dustbooks') directory, we provide a special form. Please write to us for it. Once you have filled that out and returned it to us further forms and requests for information will be sent automatically. A "proof sheet" is sent in February of each year for updating listings in all directories. Deadline is July 1st for inclusion in that September's editions.

■Len Fulton

Keep Your Directory Updated!
With
Small Press Review
Bi-Monthly

The bi-monthly **Small Press Review**, now including the **Small Magazine Review**, is published in an expanded format with two sections, one for books, one for magazines. All the features of both periodicals are still included – news and notes on editorial needs and contests, reviews, guest editorials, copious listings of new publishers, letters, columns by Laurel Speer, Bob Grumman and others. Also every issue: the popular "Free Sample Mart," offering free copies of some thirty books and magazines.

$25 / yr.❖ $33 / 2 yrs❖ $36 / 3yrs

DUSTBOOKS
THE LEADER IN THE SMALL PRESS INFORMATION FIELD
P.O. Box 100, Paradise, CA 95967-0100

A

A & U AMERICA'S AIDS MAGAZINE, 25 Monroe Street, Suite 205, Albany, NY 12210, 518-426-9010, fax 518-436-5354, mailbox@aumag.org. Christopher Hewitt. 1991. "Always include telephone numbers" circ. 150M. 12/yr. Pub'd 30 poems 1999; expects 40 poems 2000, 50 poems 201. sub. price: $24.95, $80.00 Library; sample: $5. 80pp; 8⅛×10½; Rights purchased: First North American Serial Rights. Publishes 2-5% of poems submitted. Deadlines: varies. Reporting time: 6 months. Payment: copies plus small honorarium. Interested in new or unpub'd poets: yes. Simultaneous submissions accepted: yes. Recent contributors: John Asnbery, Gwendolyn Brooks, Eileen Myles, William Dickey, Mark Doty. Submission quantity: 5 or less. Special interests: all formats encouraged.

A.L.I., 20 Byron Place, Bristol, B58 1JT, England, E-mail: DSR@maths.bath.ac.uk. 1990. circ. 200. 4/yr. sub. price: $10; sample: $5. 12pp; 8×11½.

A.R.A. JOURNAL, American Romanian Academy, Dr. Ion Manea-Manoliu, 3328 Monte Vista Avenue, Davis, CA 95616, 916-758-7720. 1975. circ. 500. 1/yr. sample price: $20. 300pp; 5½×8½.

AABYE (formerly New Hope International Writing), New Hope International, 20 Werneth Avenue, Gee Cross, Hyde, Cheshire SK14 5NL, United Kingdom, 061-351-1878, newhope@iname.com. Gerald England. 1970. "Name/address on each sheet; short covering letter; International Reply Coupons (US stamps NOT accepted by UK Post Office). Guidelines for contributors available for IRC." circ. 500-1M. 1/yr. Pub'd 50 poems 1999; expects 50 poems 2000, 50 poems 2001. sub. price: £10 for 3 issues (UK); £13 sterling only. 60pp; size A5; Rights purchased: first British serial rights. Publishes 1% of poems submitted. Deadlines: anytime. Reporting time: 6 months max. but usually not more than 5 weeks. Payment: copies. Interested in new or unpub'd poets: yes. Simultaneous submissions accepted: not encouraged. Recent contributors: David Cobb, Eamer O'Keeffe, Lucien Stryk, Frances Nagle, Kenneth C. Steven. Submission quantity: 3-6. Special interests: all styles from haiku to long poems, traditional to avant-garde.

AAIMS Publishers, 11000 Wilshire Boulevard, PO Box 241777, Los Angeles, CA 90024-9577, 213-968-1195, 888-490-2276, fax 213-931-7217, email aaims1@aol.com. 1969.

Aardvark Enterprises (A Division of Speers Investments Ltd.), 204 Millbank Drive S.W., Calgary, Alta T2Y 2H9, Canada, 403-256-4639. J. Alvin Speers, Editor-Publisher. 1977. "Prefer rhyme. No porn or obscenity. Annual contest closed March 31, 1991 to be reviewed regarding continuance depending on interest. Illustrated anthology August 1987 well received. 1992 anthology published." avg. press run 100. Pub'd 3 poetry titles 1999; expects 3 poetry titles 2000, 3 poetry titles 2001. 5½×8½; avg. price, paper: $15. 65pp; Publishes 50% of poetry manuscripts submitted. Reporting time: fast and friendly, 30 days or less. Payment: publish for hire, plus own volumes for participants buying book. Interested in new or unpub'd poets: yes, on sample basis initially. Simultaneous submissions accepted: yes, with advice thereof. Recently published poets: J. Alvin Speers, Annette Jung, Jim Elliott. Submission quantity: 5. Special interests: Free verse without discipline of rhyme, punctuation, etc. leaves us cold. For that, try elsewhere.

ABBEY, White Urp Press, 5360 Fallriver Row Court, Columbia, MD 21044. David Greisman. 1971. "Poetry should give the same tingle that I get from an iced mug of Molson Ale!" circ. 200. 3-4/yr. Pub'd 80 poems 1999; expects 80 poems 2000, 80 poems 2001. sub. price: $2; sample: 50¢. 28pp; 8½×11; Rights purchased: none. Publishes 10% of poems submitted. Deadlines: continuous. Reporting time: 2 weeks-2 months. Payment: none. Interested in new or unpub'd poets: yes. Simultaneous submissions accepted: no. Recent contributors: D.E. Steward, Wayne Hogan, Carol Hamilton, Joan Payne Kincaid, Harry Calhoun. Submission quantity: no more than 6. Special interests: Experimental—NO! Satire—NO! No poems dealing with social issues! Prefer poems with surface and symbol, am predisposed to poems about Shakespeare, running, and/or taverns, but please don't stereotype the magazine for this bias. Give *Abbey* your best work on any theme and we'll see if it has 'it', although I haven't got the slightest idea what that means.

Abiko Literary Press (ALP Ltd.) (see also THE ABIKO QUARTERLY WITH JAMES JOYCE FW STUDIES), 8-1-8 Namiki, Abiko, Chiba 270-1165, Japan, 011-81-471-69-7319. Tatsuo Hamada, Laurel Willis, Annie Bilton. 1988. "Thelma & Charlie Willis Memorial Award Contest: First prize $1,000. Up to 3 poems. We accept translations. I like poetry in the vein of Ted Hughes and T.S. Eliot" avg. press run 200. Pub'd 1 poetry title 1999. 13×5; avg. price, cloth: $20 US dollars; paper: $20; other: $20. 350pp; Publishes 10% of poetry manuscripts submitted. Reporting time: 2 weeks. Payment: 1 free copy, you pay $15 postage due to high cost of handling and dispatching abroad. Interested in new or unpub'd poets: yes. Simultaneous submissions accepted: no. Recently published poets: George Kalamaras, Eileen Malone, James Fairhall, Daneeta Lorella Saft, Stephen Malone. Submission quantity: up to 10.

THE ABIKO QUARTERLY WITH JAMES JOYCE FW STUDIES, Abiko Literary Press (ALP Ltd.), 8-1-8 Namiki, Abiko-shi, Chiba-ken 270-1165, Japan, 011-81-471-69-7319, alp@mil.net.ne.jp. Tatsuo Hamada. 1989. "We do not retype manuscripts for publication. Send camera-ready copy designed as creatively or experimentally as you want. We have the Thelma & Charlie Willis Poetry Award contest each year. First prize $1,000." circ. 200. Irregular. Pub'd 60 poems 1999. sub. price: $20 for reservation copy only; sample: $20 to handle high cost of s/h costs. 342pp; size B5; Rights purchased: 1st Serial Rights. Publishes 20% of poems submitted. Deadlines: Sept. 1. Reporting time: 2 weeks. Payment: contributor's copy, you must pay $15 for p/h. Interested in new or unpub'd poets: only if they're accompanied by 2 IRCs (American postage doesn't work in Japan), and SA for response. Simultaneous submissions accepted: no. Recent contributors: George Kalamaras, Eileen Malone, James Fairhall, Daneeta Loretta Saft, Stephen Malone. Submission quantity: up to 10. Special interests: we like poetry in the vein of T.S. Eliot and Ted Hughes.

ABILITY NETWORK, PO Box 24045, Dartmouth, Nova Scotia B3A 4T4, Canada, 902-461-9009; FAX 902-461-9484; e-Mail: anet@fox.nstn.ca. Spencer Bevan-John. 1992. circ. 35M-50M. 4/yr. Pub'd 12 poems 1999; expects 14 poems 2000, 16 poems 2001. sub. price: $15; sample: free. 48-64pp; 8½×10⅞; Rights purchased: none. Publishes 10% of poems submitted. Deadlines: Feb. 10/May 10/Aug. 10/Nov. 10. Reporting time: 3 months. Payment: small honorarium. Interested in new or unpub'd poets: yes, interested in submissions from persons with disabilities, in particular. Simultaneous submissions accepted: yes. Recent contributors: Maxine Tynes, Gille Legacey, Jim Scrimshaw, Christine Kania, Michelle Amerie. Special interests: Contributors should be disabled or topics of poems should be disabilities.

●**ABORIGINAL, DNA Publications, Inc.,** PO Box 2449, Woburn, MA 01880. sample price: $6.

ABRAXAS, PO Box 260113, Madison, WI 53726-0113, 608-238-0175, irmarkha@students.wisc.edu, www.litline.org/html/abraxas.html, www.geocities.com/Paris/4614. Ingrid Swanberg, Editor-in-Chief. 1968. "*Abraxas* will announce submission guidelines as projects arise. We no longer accept unsolicited poems. Please include an SASE with all submissions and inquiries. We are not able or willing to read book-length sumissions" circ. 500+. Irregular. Expects 70 poems 2000, 140 poems 2001. sub. price: $16/4 issues, $20/4 issues foreign; sample: $8 double issues, $4 single issue. 80pp, 144pp double issues; 6×9; Rights purchased: none. Publishes 2%-5% of poems submitted. Deadlines: announced as projects arise. Reporting time: 2 weeks to 5 months, often longer; we currently have a very great backlog. Payment: copies, 40% author's discount. Interested in new or unpub'd poets: yes, upon announcement of project only, no unsolicited mss. Simultaneous submissions accepted: no. Recent contributors: Ivan Arguelles, Denise Levertov, Andrea Moorhead, prospero saiz, Cesar Vallejo. Submission quantity: 5. Special interests: We are interested in poetry which attends to language and to rhythm, and have a particular interest in the lyric mode.

ABSOLUTE MAGNITUDE, DNA Publications, Inc., PO Box 2988, Radford, VA 24143-2988, 540-763-2925, dnapublications@iname.com. Warren Lapine. 1993. "We want poetry about people not about novas or nebulas etc." circ. 9M. 4/yr. Pub'd 1 poem 1999; expects 2 poems 2000, 4 poems 2001. sub. price: $16; sample: $5. 64pp; 8½×11; Reporting time: 2-4 weeks. Payment: $10 per poem, 2 contrib. copies. Interested in new or unpub'd poets: yes. Recent contributors: Mike Allen, Matt Deoden. Submission quantity: no more than 3. Special interests: SF poetry.

AC, Alternating Crimes Publishing, 306 Parham Street, Suite 200, Raleigh, NC 27601, 919-834-5433; Fax 919-834-2449; E-mail gstudios@mindspring.com. Katherine Boone. 1985. "Send for a sample issue, we frequently comment on poems submitted, previously published poets preferred, list all/most outstanding publishing/professional credentialsm but we read/consider all submissions" circ. 2M. 2/yr. Pub'd 15 poems 1999; expects 15 poems 2000, 15 poems 2001. sub. price: $7/postage; sample: $3.50 w/postage. 32pp; 6¾×10; Rights purchased: 1st North American. Publishes 5% of poems submitted. Deadlines: continuous. Reporting time: 16 weeks. Payment: copies. Interested in new or unpub'd poets: yes. Simultaneous submissions accepted: no. Recent contributors: Charles Bukowski, Michael S. Reynolds, M. Kettner, Kat Meads, Carol Collier. Submission quantity: 1-4, 12 max.

Acclaim Publishing Co. Inc., PO Box 3918, Grand Junction, CO 81502-3918, 719-784-3712. 1992. 5½×8½, 8½×11.

ACM (ANOTHER CHICAGO MAGAZINE), 3709 N. Kenmore, Chicago, IL 60613, 312-248-7665, www.anotherchicagomag.com. Barry Silesky. 1976. "SASE required." circ. 2.5M. 2/yr. Pub'd 50 poems 1999; expects 50 poems 2000, 50 poems 2001. sub. price: $15; sample: $8. 220pp; 8½×5½; Rights purchased: first serial. Publishes 5% of poems submitted. Deadlines: none. Reporting time: 10 weeks. Small cash payment + copy + 1 year subscription. Interested in new or unpub'd poets: yes. Simultaneous submissions accepted: yes. Recent contributors: Diane Wakoski, Michael McClure, Wanda Coleman, Jack Anderson, Albert Goldbarth. Submission quantity: 3. Special interests: Translations, long poems, socio-historical.

2

THE ACORN, Hot Pepper Press, PO Box 1266, El Dorado, CA 95623, theacorn@visto.com. Joy Burris, J.K. Colvin, Harlon Stafford. 1993. "Focus is on the geography, environment, history and society of the western slope of the Sierra Nevada. Maximum length 30 lines; shorter poems prefered" circ. 250. 4/yr. Pub'd 40 poems 1999; expects 40 poems 2000, 40 poems 2001. sub. price: $12; sample: $4. 48pp; 5¼×8½; Rights purchased: one-time. Publishes 16% of poems submitted. Deadlines: 2/1, 5/1, 8/1, 11/1. Reporting time: less than 1 month after deadlines. Payment: 2 copies. Interested in new or unpub'd poets: yes. Simultaneous submissions accepted: yes, if so informed. Recent contributors: Taylor Graham, Carmela Ruby, Anselm Brocki, Edward Lynskey, Joyce Odam. Submission quantity: 3-5. Special interests: Regional poetry.

ACORN WHISTLE, 907 Brewster Avenue, Beloit, WI 53511. Fred Burwell, Editor. 1994. circ. 500. 1-2/yr. Pub'd 40 poems 1999; expects 40 poems 2000, 40 poems 2001. sub. price: $14 for 2 issues; sample: $7. 75-100pp; 8½×11; Rights purchased: First North American Serial Rights. Publishes 1% or less of manuscripts submitted. Reporting time: 1 week to 3 months. Payment: 2 copies. Interested in new or unpub'd poets: yes. Simultaneous submissions accepted: yes. Recent contributors: Denise Pendleton, Daniel Smith, Ruth Daigon, Roseann Lloyd, Allison Joseph. Submission quantity: 1-10. Special interests: We seek narrative and lyrical poetry. No length limits. Not interested in experimental.

Acre Press (see also FELL SWOOP), 3003 Ponce De Leon Street, New Orleans, LA 70119. X.J. Dailey. 1980. "Sample copies are available for $3 postpaid. Purchase is necessary to enlist editorial consideration for submitted mss. We like poetry with a twist or a twist-off." avg. press run 200. Pub'd 1 poetry title 1999; expects 1 poetry title 2000, 1 poetry title 2001. 5½×8½; avg. price, paper: $3. 20pp; Reporting time: quick. Payment: copies. Interested in new or unpub'd poets: yes. Simultaneous submissions accepted: yes. Recently published poets: Gordon Anderson, Richard Martin, Elizabeth Thomas, Anselm Hollo, Pat Nolan. Submission quantity: 20 pg. mss. Special interests: We revel in sustained verse eruptions which lead to a higher airplane of consciousness. Happy landings!

Adastra Press, 16 Reservation Road, Easthampton, MA 01027-1227. Gary Metras, Editor and Publisher. 1978. "All books are hand-set letterpress printed and hand-sewn with flat spine paper wrapper. Each book is individually designed with the poetry in mind. I pay attention to the craft and art of printing and expect poets to pay attention to their art. Interested authors should query first. The poetry should have some bite to it and be grounded in experience. Poem cycles, thematic groups and long poems are alwlays nice to produce in chapbook format. Reading period for manuscripts is during the month of February only. Send queries with samples in the fall; if I like the sample, I'll ask you to send the manuscript in February. Manuscripts should have 12 to 18 pages; nothing longer; no full-length manuscripts will be considered. Accepted authors can expect to help with publicity. Payment is copies. *Adastra Press* is a one man operation, paying for itself as it goes without grants of any kind, and I am always overworked and booked in advance. Chances of acceptance are slim, but there's no harm in trying. Some titles to date are: *Antonio & Clara,* David Gianinni; *Niagara Falls,* Jim Daniels; *Millrat,* Michael Casey; *Suspended Knowledge,* Geoffrey Jacques; *Beautiful Wreckage: New and Selected Poems,* W.D. Ehrhart. Send $6 for a sample chapbook" avg. press run 200+. Pub'd 4 poetry titles 1999; expects 4 poetry titles 2000, 3 poetry titles 2001. 5×8; avg. price, cloth: $30; paper: $7-$10; other: $15-$30 cloth/signed and numbered. 20pp; Publishes less than 1% of poetry manuscripts submitted. Reporting time: 2 months. Initial payment in copies, approx. 10% of print run. Interested in new or unpub'd poets: yes. Simultaneous submissions accepted: yes. Recently published poets: W.D. Ehrhart, Richard Jones, Geoffrey Jacques, Linda Lee Harper, Tom Sexton. Submission quantity: 5 poems from a chapbook manuscript if a query.

The Advocado Press (see also THE DISABILITY RAG & RESOURCE), PO Box 145, Louisville, KY 40201, 502-459-5343. 1981. 5¼×8¼.

THE ADVOCATE, HCR 2, Box 25, Panhandle, TX 79068, 806-335-1715. 1986. "Please only peace and justice subject matter." circ. 1M. 4/yr. Pub'd 5 poems 1999; expects 6 poems 2000, 6 poems 2001. sub. price: $5; sample: $1. 4pp; 8½×11; Rights purchased: none. Publishes 10% of poems submitted. Payment: none. Interested in new or unpub'd poets: yes. Simultaneous submissions accepted: yes. Recent contributors: Terry Fox, Phyllis McKenzie, Paul Weinam, Ellen Gruver, Cindy Breeding. Submission quantity: 2.

Aegina Press, Inc., 1905 Madison Avenue, Huntington, WV 25704, 304-429-7204; fax 304-429-7234. Ira Herman, Managing Editor. 1984. "*Aegina Press* was established to publish worthy work by new or emerging authors. This includes authors who have never before had work published in book form as well as those who have already had several books published. *Aegina Press* will give careful consideration to each manuscript submitted, and when time permits, its editor will comment on the work presented. *Aegina Press* will publish works of all types, including experimental poetry, free verse, haiku, and rhymed poetry. Our bias is toward no particular school of poetry. All manuscripts and queries should be accompanied by a self-addressed, stamped envelope or mailer sufficient to return the material. *Aegina Press* is currently publishing single-author collections and poetry books experimental in design and content. *Aegina Press* seeks to find, encourage, and establish new poets." avg. press run 500-1M. Pub'd 15 poetry titles 1999; expects 15 poetry titles 2000, 15 poetry titles 2001. 5½×8½; avg. price, cloth: $7; paper: $5. 64-128pp; Publishes 15-20% of poetry manuscripts

3

submitted. Reporting time: 1 month for manuscripts, 1 week for queries. Payment: varies, depending on book and author; most are subsidized. Interested in new or unpub'd poets: yes. Simultaneous submissions accepted: yes. Recently published poets: David Herrstrom, Marek Kedzierski, Riyad Hamzah. Submission quantity: a sampling of 10 or so representative poems or the complete manuscript. Sending the complete manuscript sometimes speeds consideration for publication. Special interests: Translations, bilingual editions, and regional poetry will also be considered for publication.

AERIAL, P.O. Box 25642, Washington, DC 20007, 202-362-6418; aerialedge@aol.com. Rod Smith, Editor. 1984. "Stockhausen said, 'I demand one of two things from a composer: invention or that he astonish me.' That is what is needed in writing today, we must work for a change in our systems of thought before their application destroys this planet." circ. 1M. Irregular. Pub'd 50-100 poems 1999. sub. price: $25/2 issues; sample: $15.00. 200pp; 6×9; Rights purchased: We reserve the right to reprint in anthology format. All other rights revert to author. Publishes .1% of poems submitted. Reporting time: 1 week - 2 months. Payment: copies. Interested in new or unpub'd poets: not right now. Simultaneous submissions accepted: no. Recent contributors: John Cage, Melanie Neilson, Lyn Hejinian, Jean Donnelly, Rachel Blau DuPlessis. Submission quantity: 2-10 pages. Special interests: Also open to prose on poetry, translations, interviews, theoretical statements/speculations.

AFFABLE NEIGHBOR, Affable Neighbor Press, PO Box 3635, Ann Arbor, MI 48106. Leigh Chalmers, Joel Henry-Fisher. 1994. circ. 25-1M. Irregular. sub. price: $20 (includes prizes and extras). 50pp; 8½×11; Publishes 5-10% of poems submitted. Deadlines: none. Reporting time: varies. Payment: personal negotiation. Interested in new or unpub'd poets: yes. Simultaneous submissions accepted: yes. Recent contributors: Huervo Sanchez, Mohamed Mensch, Robin Clenard, Sheila Manson, David Noven. Submission quantity: How ever many are their best/favorite.

Affable Neighbor Press (see also AFFABLE NEIGHBOR), PO Box 3635, Ann Arbor, MI 48106. 1994. size varies. Reporting time: as soon as we get around to it. Payment: per individual. Interested in new or unpub'd poets: yes. Simultaneous submissions accepted: yes. Recently published poets: Huervo Sanchez, Mohamed Mensch, Robin Clenaro, Sheila Manson, David Noven. Submission quantity: How ever many are their best/favorite. Special interests: must be gripping enough to make me like it (editor-in-chief) so I can't put it down.

THE AFFILIATE, 777 Barb Road, #257, Vankleek Hill, Ontario K0B 1R0, Canada, 613-678-3453. Peter Riden, Publisher and Editor. 1987. "When submitting, we want to know clearly who you are, so send picture along with basic port-folio. We really want to uncover the deserving, so if it's you, contact us." circ. as requested, can be as much as 10M. 6/yr. Pub'd 18+ poems 1999; expects 18+ poems 2000, 18+ poems 2001. sub. price: $75 US/North America, $100 anywhere else; sample: $10 N. America, $15 elsewhere. 52-60pp; 8½×11; Rights purchased: it remains author's right with mutual agreement. Publishes 20% of poems submitted. Deadlines: 15th of the month prior to upcoming issue. Payment: complimentary copy and an opportunity of acceptation rather than rejection. Interested in new or unpub'd poets: definitely! How do we expect anyone to be recognized if not first given this initial chance? Simultaneous submissions accepted: it is often done with our regulars. Recent contributors: Ben G. Price, Gerald D. England, Los Farley, Patricia Sutton, George Gott. Submission quantity: 4 to 6 is best for a good yet easy evaluation. Special interests: All subjects of positive interest and due awareness are most welcome. No insipidities, inanities will ever make our pages. We want to hear of all the positive vibes out there. Make it fit on 8½ X 11 page.

AFRICAN AMERICAN REVIEW, Indiana State University, Dept. of English, Terre Haute, IN 47809, 812-237-2968. Sterling Plumpp, Poetry Editor; Thadious M. Davis, Poetry Editor; Pinkie Gordon Lane, Poetry Editor; E. Ethelbert Miller, Poetry Editor. 1967. "Only poetry by African-Americans included" circ. 4068. 4/yr. Pub'd 17 poems 1999; expects 30 poems 2000, 30 poems 2001. sub. price: $24 individuals, $48 institutions (foreign add $7); sample: $8. 176pp; 7×10; Rights purchased: one time serial. Publishes 8% of poems submitted. Reporting time: 3 months. Payment: 1 copy and offprints; honorarium. Interested in new or unpub'd poets: yes. Simultaneous submissions accepted: no. Recent contributors: Amiri Baraka, Gwendolyn Brooks, Wanda Coleman, Clarence Major, Sterling Plumpp. Submission quantity: no more than 6.

AFRO-HISPANIC REVIEW, Romance Languages, Univ. of Missouri, 143 Arts & Science Building, Columbia, MO 65211, 573-882-5040 or 573-882-5041. 1982. "All poems must be on Afro-Hispanic condition. Can be in English or Spanish" circ. 500. 2/yr. Pub'd 2-4 poems 1999; expects 2-4 poems 2000, 2-4 poems 2001. sub. price: $15 indiv., $20 instit.; sample: $7.50. 60pp; 8½×11; Rights purchased: none. Publishes a variable % of poems submitted. Deadlines: anytime. Payment: 3 copies of issue containing contribution. Interested in new or unpub'd poets: yes, but must be on subject of Afro-Hispanic condition. Simultaneous submissions accepted: yes. Recent contributors: Jose Emilio Cardoso, Beatriz Santos, Georgina Herrera, Nancy Morejon, Cristina Rodriguez Cabral. Submission quantity: any number. Special interests: Translations of poems by Afro-Hispanic authors most welcomed.

AGADA, 2020 Essex Street, Berkeley, CA 94703, 510-848-0965. Reuven Goldfarb, Editor. 1981. "We are looking for poetry with Jewish-related themes and subject matter, of high literary quality. Themes emerge for each issue as the editor reads manuscript submissions; sometimes a perfectly satisfactory piece of work will be excluded from an upcoming issue because it does not fit thematic criteria just developed. Where possible, such work will be held over to a subsequent issue, where it may become the core for a new conceptual framework. Future issues will explore such themes as 'Jewish Spirituality' and 'Varieties of Jewish Experience''' circ. 1M. 1/yr. Pub'd 12 poems 1999; expects 12 poems 2000, 12 poems 2001. sub. price: $12/double issue; sample: $6.50. 64pp; 7×10; Rights purchased: 1st North American Serial, reprint rights revert to poet upon publication. Publishes minimal % of poems submitted. Deadlines: no fixed times. Reporting time: 3-4 months, more or less. Payment: 2 copies of the issue in which their contribution appears, and a reduced rate on purchase of additional copies. Interested in new or unpub'd poets: yes. Simultaneous submissions accepted: yes, but please notify me if the work is accepted elsewhere or has been published elsewhere. Recent contributors: Robert Stern, Roger White, Yoel Mesinai, Edith Goldenhar, Shulamith Surnamer. Submission quantity: 1-6. Special interests: We have a special interest in new translation of 'Classical' Jewish poetry, Scriptural, Kabbalistic, or other, whether originally written in Hebrew, Aramaic, Yiddish, Ladino, or any other languages used by Jews at home or in the Diaspora. Singable English versions of Hebrew prayers might also be a consideration here. Original restatements of Biblical themes and motifs also rate more than a passing glance. However, cliche-riddled, maudlin, or primarily sentimental and most didactic work will not withstand scrutiny.

AGNI, Boston University, 236 Bay State Road, Boston, MA 02215, 617-353-7135. Askold Melnyczuk, Editor; Eric Grunwald, Managing Editor. 1972. "Our poetry selections are eclectic; however, reading in previous issues gives a good idea of our range. We read mss from Oct. 1 to April 30 only. In the past we have shortened the reading period due to increased submissions. Check magazine for current dates" circ. 1.8M. 2/yr. Pub'd 145 poems 1999. sub. price: $15; sample: $9. 200-270pp; 5⅜×8½; Rights purchased: first serial. Publishes .5% of poems submitted. Deadlines: Oct. 1 to April 30. Reporting time: 1-4 months. Payment: $10 per page ($150 max, $20 minimum). Interested in new or unpub'd poets: yes. Simultaneous submissions accepted: yes. Recent contributors: Sharan Strange, Olena Kalytiak Davis, Derek Walcott, Mark Strand, Ha Jin. Submission quantity: 3-5 optimum. Special interests: Translations.

THE AGUILAR EXPRESSION, 1329 Gilmore Avenue, Donora, PA 15033, 724-379-8019. Xavier F. Aguilar. 1986. "Please send for writer's guidelines before submitting (SASE required)" circ. 150. 2/yr. Pub'd 10 poems 1999; expects 25 poems 2000, 30 poems 2001. sub. price: $11; sample: $6. 8-14pp; 8½×11; Rights purchased: none, all rights remain authors. Publishes 10% of poems submitted. Deadlines: none. Reporting time: 1 month. Payment: byline, free issue. Interested in new or unpub'd poets: All-ESP. New Poets. Simultaneous submissions accepted: no. Recent contributors: B.Z. Niditch, Jonathan M. Berkowitz. Submission quantity: 1-3.

AHA Books, PO Box 767, Gualala, CA 95445, 707-882-2226. Jane Reichhold. 1986. "Since this summer (1996) we have been working to establish a place for poets on the Internet with a Web site. We are in the final phases of completing that work. Through this new venture we have decided not to publish, for a time, any more paper books. Through our Web site we offer authors several options about how to share what they have written. We hope that there you can pick the method that is best for your book." Pub'd 7 poetry titles 1999; expects 8 poetry titles 2000, 7 poetry titles 2001. 5×8; avg. price, cloth: $12; paper: $10. 80-200pp; Publishes 25% of poetry manuscripts submitted. Reporting time: 1 month. Payment: second printing as agreed upon individually. Interested in new or unpub'd poets: yes. Simultaneous submissions accepted: yes. Recently published poets: Geraldine C. Little, David Elliott, Charles B. Dickson, N.H. Lawrence. Special interests: Tanka, renga, haibun.

Ahsahta, Boise State University, Department of English, Boise, ID 83725, 208-426-1999; orders 1-800-526-6522; www.bsubkst.idbsu.edu/. Tom Trusky, Editor. 1975. "We're interested in contemporary poetry of the American West. Note we ask for poetry samplers (approximately 15 representative poems) to be sent SASE Jan-Mar. If we like a sampler, we request a complete manuscript be sent. Spare us dull coyote poems, Jesus-in-the-sagebrush, buckaroo ballads, etc. We're looking for original voices and visions in and of the West. Not reading samplers until Jan. 2000" avg. press run 500. Pub'd 3 poetry titles 1999; expects 3 poetry titles 2000, 3 poetry titles 2001. 6×8½; avg. price, paper: $9.95 postpaid; other: $9 Ahsahta Cassette Sampler postpaid. 60pp; Publishes 1% of poetry manuscripts submitted. Reporting time: samplers (15 poems) read Jan-Mar. If we like sampler, we ask for complete MS within 1 month. Send SASE. We report on MSS within 2 months. Payment: author's copies for first two printings; royalties of 25% commence with 3rd printing sales; our titles remain in print eternally. Interested in new or unpub'd poets: yes (but samplers, first—not complete MSS). Simultaneous submissions accepted: yes. Recently published poets: Linda Bierds, Miriam Sagan, Leo Romero, Thomas Hornsby Ferril, Gary Short. Submission quantity: 15 with SASE. Special interests: We're interested in poetry of the American West: its history, cultures, ecology, peoples.

AIM MAGAZINE, PO Box 1174, Maywood, IL 60153-8174. Mark Boone. 1973. "We prefer poetry that addresses social issues." circ. 7M. 4/yr. Pub'd 16 poems 1999. sub. price: $12; sample: $5. 48pp; 8½×11; Rights purchased: 1st. Publishes 15% of poems submitted. Deadlines: 1st of September, December, March,

June. Reporting time: 6 weeks. Payment: $3. Interested in new or unpub'd poets: yes. Simultaneous submissions accepted: yes. Recent contributors: David Appell, Dr. Scott Mandel, Damien Filer, Caroline Tuley. Submission quantity: 2. Special interests: 10%.

Airplane Books, PO Box 111, Glenview, IL 60025. 1994. 5½×8.

ALABAMA LITERARY REVIEW, Smith 253, Troy State University, Troy, AL 36082, 334-670-3307;FAX 334-670-3519. Ed Hicks. 1987. "Deadlines are not that important. We are reading all year long." circ. 800+. 1/yr. Pub'd 12 poems 1999; expects 20 poems 2000, 25 poems 2001. sub. price: $10; sample: $5. 100pp; 7×10; Rights purchased: first pub.; return all rights. Publishes 10% of poems submitted. Deadlines: April 1, Nov. 15. Reporting time: 1-3 months. Payment: 2 copies and honorarium of $5-10 per printed page when available. Interested in new or unpub'd poets: yes. Simultaneous submissions accepted: yes. Recent contributors: Roald Hoffman, Paul Grant, Coleman Barks, Larry McLeod, Elizabeth Dodd. Submission quantity: 2-3.

ALARM CLOCK, PO Box 1551, Royal Oak, MI 48068, 313-593-9677. 1990. circ. 200. 4/yr. sample price: $2. 32pp; 5½×8½.

ALASKA QUARTERLY REVIEW, University of Alaska-Anchorage, 3211 Providence Drive, Anchorage, AK 99508, 907-786-6916. Ronald Spatz, Executive Editor. 1981. "We publish both experimental and traditional forms of poetry." circ. 2.2M. 2/yr. Pub'd 50 poems 1999; expects 50 poems 2000, 50 poems 2001. sub. price: $10; sample: $5. 264pp; 6×9; Rights purchased: First North American. Publishes 2% of poems submitted. Deadlines: unsolicited manuscripts can only be read between August 15 and May 15. Reporting time: 6-12 weeks. Payment: 1 contributor's copy and a one-year subscription; additional payment depends on the terms of our grant. Interested in new or unpub'd poets: yes. Simultaneous submissions accepted: yes if indicated in cover letter. Recent contributors: Pattiann Rogers, Dorianne Laux, Nancy Eimers, Jane Hirshfield, Billy Collins. Submission quantity: 3-5. Special interests: No light verse.

The Aldine Press, Ltd. (see also HELLAS: A Journal of Poetry & the Humanities), 304 South Tyson Avenue, Glenside, PA 19038. Gerald Harnett. 1988. "We will occasionally publish a first book of poems for an author whose poems have appeared previously in *Hellas.* Submitters should therefore start out by submitting poems to the journal, and afterward inquire about sending us full-length book manuscripts. The Lycidas Award for the best chapbook of metrical verse is offered annually. Annual deadline December 31, max. length 24 pages plus title page. Fee $10. The award is $100 plus 50 copies of the chapbook" avg. press run 500. Expects 1 poetry title 2000. 6×9; avg. price, cloth: $18; paper: $12. 80pp.

THE ALEMBIC, Department of English, Providence College, Providence, RI 02918-0001. revolving editors. 1920. "Manuscripts between September and December 15. Interested in any length poems, explorations of genre. Translations (with originals). No light verse" circ. 4M. 1/yr. Pub'd 70 poems 1999. sub. price: $15/2 years. 200pp; 7×9; Publishes 10% of poems submitted. Deadlines: Dec. 15. Reporting time: 4 months. Payment: 1 copy. Interested in new or unpub'd poets: yes. Simultaneous submissions accepted: no. Recent contributors: Mark Rudman, William Matthews, Ai, Laura Mullen, Martha Collins. Submission quantity: up to 5.

Alice James Books, University of Maine at Farmington, 98 Main Street, Farmington, ME 04938-1911. Peg Peoples, Program Director. 1973. "The Alice James Poetry Cooperative offers two book competitions each year: The New England/New York Competition and the Beatrice Hawley Award. The winners of the New England/New York Competition become active members of the Alice James Poetry Cooperative. (Poets must live in New England or New York.) Authors agree to a three-year work commitment during which they participate in the running of a small press (grant-writing, mss. selection, editing, marketing, etc.). The Beatrice Hawley Award is a national prize that offers $1,000 and publication. There is no work commitment with the cooperative. All new AJB poets work with AJB-affiliated designers, active cooperative members, and the Director to produce and market their book. In 1997, Alice James Books offered the first Jane Kenyon Chapbook Award, a chapbook series established to honor and remember poet and cooperative member Jane Kenyon. This biannual award is offered in odd years (2001) and awards the winner $300 and 25 copies. Alice James Books does not read manuscripts year round. Please send SASE for complete guidelines and reading periods for all awards." avg. press run 1.2M. Pub'd 4 poetry titles 1999; expects 5 poetry titles 2000, 4 poetry titles 2001. 5½×8½; avg. price, paper: $9.95. 72pp; Publishes 1% of poetry manuscripts submitted. Reporting time: 2-3 months. Payment: each author receives cash award; no royalties. Interested in new or unpub'd poets: yes. Simultaneous submissions accepted: yes, if we are notified of other submissions. Recently published poets: Laura Kasischke, Eric Gamalinda, B.H. Fairchild, Matthea Harvey, Suzanne Wise. Submission quantity: book length manuscripts, 64pp minimum. Special interests: Alice James Books does not publish light or inspirational poetry, nor does it publish children's poetry. We are looking for the highest literary poetry we can find. No restrictions or preferences in form.

ALLEGHENY REVIEW, Box 32, Allegheny College, Meadville, PA 16335, 814-332-6553. Errin Fisher. 1983. "The poem judged by the Editors to be the most outstanding will receive a $50 prize. Submissions should be sent with SASE and brief cover letter" circ. 1M. 1/yr. Pub'd 35 poems 1999; expects 40 poems 2000, 40 poems 2001. sub. price: $6; sample: $5. 100pp; 6×9; Rights purchased: none, book is copyrighted. Publishes 5% of poems submitted. Deadlines: early February; exact date fluctuates yearly. Reporting time: 2½ months following deadline. Payment: $50 to 1st place submission; contrib. copies (2) to pub. poets. Interested in new or unpub'd poets: yes, exclusively. Simultaneous submissions accepted: no. Submission quantity: 3-5. Special interests: The *Allegheny Review* is an annual volume, devoted solely to the publication of undergraduate works of creative literature (poetry, short fiction, and short drama) in an effort to fill the need for a national outlet for the undergraduate writer.

●**Alligator Press**, PO Box 49158, Austin, TX 78765, 512-454-0496; Fax 512-380-0098; www.alligator-press.com. 1999. 5½×8½.

Alms House Press, PO Box 218, Woodbourne, NY 12788-0218. Alana Sherman, Lorraine DeGennaro. 1985. "We seek variety and excellence in many styles. Chapbooks published from submissions during reading periods." avg. press run 200. Pub'd 5 poetry titles 1999; expects 3-4 poetry titles 2000, 3-4 poetry titles 2001. 5½×8½; avg. price, paper: $5. 20pp; Publishes 10% of poetry manuscripts submitted. Reporting time: 3 months. Payment: authors receive 15 copies; we copyright for author. Interested in new or unpub'd poets: yes. Simultaneous submissions accepted: prefer not to. Recently published poets: William Vernon, Stephen R. Roberts, Evelyn Sharenov, Martin Anderson, Lenore Balliro. Submission quantity: 16-24 chapbook. Special interests: Manuscripts must be accompanied by a reading fee. Send SASE for complete guidelines.

Alpha Beat Press (see also ALPHA BEAT SOUP; BOUILLABAISSE), 31 Waterloo Street, New Hope, PA 18938, 215-862-0299. Dave Christy. 1987. "Beat Generation, post-Beat independent and modern writings" avg. press run 200 to 500. Pub'd 4 poetry titles 1999; expects 4 poetry titles 2000, 6 poetry titles 2001. size varies; avg. price, paper: $10; other: $5. 50-150pp; Publishes 35% of poetry manuscripts submitted. Reporting time: immediately. Payment: copies. Interested in new or unpub'd poets: yes. Simultaneous submissions accepted: yes. Recently published poets: A.D. Winans, Ana Christy, Daniel Crocker, Joseph Verrilli, Pradip Choudhuri. Submission quantity: 5.

ALPHA BEAT SOUP, Alpha Beat Press, Alpha Beat Press, 31 Waterloo Street, New Hope, PA 18938. David Christy. 1987. "Currently planning two issues a year. At least half of each issue of Alpha Beat Soup is devoted to little known on previously unpublished poets. In addition to the magazine, 4 booklets of poetry are published each year." circ. 600. 2+. Pub'd 75-100 poems 1999. sub. price: $15; sample: $10. 75pp; 7×8½; Rights purchased: none. Publishes 50% of poems submitted. Deadlines: 1 month prior to issue. Reporting time: immediately. Payment: copy of issue. Interested in new or unpub'd poets: yes. Simultaneous submissions accepted: yes. Recent contributors: Pradip Choudhuri, Jack Micheline, Ralph Haselmann, Steve DeFrance, Ana Christy. Submission quantity: maximum 5. Special interests: Interested in work relaying the Beat spirit, also haiku and translations.

Alternating Crimes Publishing (see also AC), 306 Parham St. Ste 200, Raleigh, NC 27601, 919-834-5433; fax 919-834-2449; e-mail 6studios@mindspring.com. Katherine Boone. 1985. "We publish a select few poetry manuscripts and are taking at least 1 year after manuscript acceptance until actual publication" avg. press run 500. Expects 2 poetry titles 2001. 6½×10; avg. price, paper: $6. 32pp; Publishes 5% of poetry manuscripts submitted. Reporting time: 16 weeks. Payment: 50% of net profit. Interested in new or unpub'd poets: yes. Simultaneous submissions accepted: no. Recently published poets: Kat Meads. Submission quantity: entire manuscript.

AMARANTH, PO Box 184, Trumbull, CT 06611, 203-452-9652. Becky Rodia, Co-editor; Christopher Sanzeni, Co-editor. 1995. "Potential contributors must be avid readers of contemporary poetry, including literary journals. People who don't read poetry simply don't write the kind of poetry we publish." circ. 1M. 2/yr. Pub'd 40 poems 1999; expects 40 poems 2000, 40 poems 2001. sub. price: $10; sample: $6. 40pp; 5½×8½; Rights purchased: rights revert upon publication. Publishes 10% of poems submitted. Deadlines: ongoing. Reporting time: rejects are returned almost immediately, serious contenders are held 3-6 months. Payment: 2 free copies with an option to purchase more at a discount. Interested in new or unpub'd poets: We have published a few " first-timers"-quality is our main criterion, regardless of publication history. Simultaneous submissions accepted: Yes, but please notify us. Recent contributors: Charles H. Webb, Joyce Peseroff, Gary Young, Denise Duhamel, Walt McDonald. Submission quantity: 3-5. Special interests: Formal verse, especially prose poems.

AMBIT, 17 Priory Gardens, London, N6 5QY, England, 0181-340-3566. Carol Ann Duffy, Henry Graham, Martin Bax. 1959. circ. 3M. 4/yr. Pub'd 250 poems 1999; expects 250 poems 2000, 250 poems 2001. sub. price: £24 UK, £26 ($52) USA and overseas; sample: £6 UK, £8 overseas. 96pp; 9½×7½; Rights purchased: first serial rights only. Publishes 1% of poems submitted. Reporting time: 3-4 months. Payment: usually £5 per page. Interested in new or unpub'd poets: yes. Simultaneous submissions accepted: no. Recent contributors: Carole Satyamurti, Peter Porter, Satyendra Srivastava, Fred Voss, Lance Lee. Submission quantity: not more than 6. Special interests: Translations, experimental poetry, regional poetry, longpoems.

AMELIA, Amelia Press, 329 'E' Street, Bakersfield, CA 93304, 661-323-4064. Frederick A. Raborg, Jr., Editor. 1983. *"Amelia* awards more than $3,000 in prizes to poets annually in the following contests: The Anna B. Janzen Romantic Poetry Award; The Bernice Jennings Traditional Poetry Award; The Kate Smith Award; The Georgie Starbuck Galbraith Light/Humorous Verse Awards; The Charles William Duke Longpoem Award (winner published in chapbook format); The Lucille Sandberg Haiku Awards; The Grace Hines Narrative Poetry Prize; The Johanna B. Bourgoyne Poetry Prizes; The Douglas Manning Smith Epic/Heroic Poetry Prize; The Hildegarde Janzen Prizes for Oriental Forms of Poetry; The Eugene Smith Prizes for Sonnets; The A & C Limerick Contest; The Montegue Wade Lyric Poetry Award; The Amelia Awards and The Amelia Chapbook Award." circ. 1.75M. 4/yr. Pub'd 224 poems 1999; expects 260 poems 2000, 300 poems 2001. sub. price: $30; sample: $10.95 ppd. 288-300pp; 5½x8½; Rights purchased: 1st North American serial rights. Publishes 2% of poems submitted. Deadlines: none, except for contests; consideration is ongoing. Reporting time: 2 weeks-3 months (occasionally longer in special circumstances). Payment: $2-$25 per poem on acceptance plus 2 copies. Interested in new or unpub'd poets: yes. Simultaneous submissions accepted: no. Recent contributors: Pattiann Rogers, Walter Griffin, David Ray, John Millett, Maxine Kumin, Charles Edward-Eaton. Submission quantity: 3-10; no one poem should exceed 100 lines, except longpoem contest entries, which have no length limit. Special interests: We use excellent translations, but a copy of the original must accompany each submission; we use experimental and ultra avant-garde poetry, longpoems, light verse, but not of the newspaper category, and satire. I look for strong imagery and strong concepts. I want the poem to say something. Sonnets should go beyond the 'moon, June, spoon' situations, i.e. my favorite Shakespearean sonnet is #29 and I do not object to experimentation such as Updike did in *Midpoint*. I like good blank verse and heroic verse when they tell stories or take stands. Regional poetry should not be maudlin and 'sappy'. I like to read work in which the poet obviously has some pride—neatly presented work with good spelling and punctuation correct when used. I like black ribbons on typewriters, though I will read neat handwriting. I do not want to waste my time reading work that already has been published; *Amelia* uses only first rights. I like to read the work of poets who have done their homework by reading a copy of *Amelia*. Such poets know the quality of material *Amelia* seeks and finds. I will publish a newcomer just as quickly as I will publish a 'name'. I will not shy away from strong issues, though I do not want to see the patently religious or the overtly political. I publish high quality ethnic poetry and gay/lesbian, too, but such poetry ought to enhance both the subject and the reader and not be written solely for shock value. I will publish that occasial erotic poem, but not the offensively pornographic. I also look for good pen and ink sketches and fine line drawings to supplement poetry used and pay according to size and use. We're always in need of excellent nude studies—female or male (biggest need is always the male, since most artists draw females. I love nature, but 9 out of 10 poems submitted have nature as their themes. Remember, there's truth in that expression...Give me strength—of purpose. Every poem used must justify its existence.

Amelia Press (see also AMELIA; CICADA; SPSM&H), 329 'E' Street, Bakersfield, CA 93304, 661-323-4064. Frederick A. Raborg Jr., Editor. 1983. "Write for guidelines, SASE." avg. press run 500. Pub'd 4 poetry titles 1999; expects 4 poetry titles 2000, 4 poetry titles 2001. 5½x8; avg. price, paper: $6.95. 16-80pp; Publishes 1% of poetry manuscripts submitted. Reporting time: 3 months. Payment: varies. Interested in new or unpub'd poets: yes. Simultaneous submissions accepted: yes. Recently published poets: Michael Lassell, Michael J. Bugeja, June Qwens, David Ray, Sharon E. Martain. Submission quantity: 5-10. Special interests: Eclectic interests for predominantly college-educated readership.

AMERICA, 106 West 56th Street, New York, NY 10019, 212-581-4640. Paul Mariani, Poetry Editor. 1909. *"America* is a weekly journal of opinion devoted largely to religious, social, political, and cultural themes. Single poems (preferably between 10 and 30 lines long) are included in 10 issues a year. A sufficiently stamped return envelope must be included with each submission, which should be addressed to the Poetry Editor. Poems may be submitted throughout the year. Poets should not write detailed explanations of their work; and we prefer that they send no more than 2 or 3 poems at a time. For a poem to be published in a quality Catholic magazine like America, it should actually be harder rather than easier than being published in a "secular" magazine. A Catholic poem should be at least as good technically as poems elsewhere, and then on top of that display a religious or—better— sacramental vision of things that would draw at least imaginative assent from readers of a wide cast of backgrounds and faiths." circ. 40M. 41/yr. Pub'd 37 poems 1999; expects 25 poems 2000, 10 poems 2001. sub. price: $43; sample: $2.25. 32pp; 8¼x10½; Rights purchased: first, reprint and on web. Publishes 1% of poems submitted. Reporting time: within 3 weeks. Interested in new or unpub'd poets: yes. Simultaneous submissions accepted: no. Recent contributors: Doris Donnelly, Larry Rubin, Fredrick Zydek, William Stafford, Daniel Berrigan. Submission quantity: preferably not more than 2 or 3. Special interests: We do not use translations and prefer not to see haiku or other forms of verse best suited to the literature of non-English-speaking countries. Imitations of the style of well-known poets are not welcome, and regularly rhymed poems sounding as if they were written in the 19th or early 20th centuries do not appeal to us. Obscurity for its own sake, as well, does not serve our purposes. Poems that seize the reader's attention from the first line and hold it to the end are most likely to be accepted.

American Canadian Publishers, Inc., PO Box 4595, Santa Fe, NM 87502-4595, 505-983-8484, fax

505-983-8484. 1972. "At this time, unfortunately, we cannot accept unsolicited manuscripts. P.S. Please note: The 'language' you are used to is corporate supported and corporate defended. The corporations will not allow pleasurable and much-needed changes in language because it interrupts *their profits*! See us if you agree-disagree. Thanks." 6×9. Special interests: Prose-poetry, a horribly neglected form in America; one that was and is cherished in Europe. We have therefore published poetic novels—that is, a form of the novel that combines poetry and prose—a prose-poetry form. If you will send an SASE, we will forward our catalog of publications in this area. We categorically reject realism in the novel simply because it is by now a bankrupt form. We reject orthodox story because it generally tortures the truth to fit the formula. We support the novel that investigates inner consciousness, that is multi-dimensional and open structured in language and thought: the novel for the year 2000! Thanks for reading this.

THE AMERICAN DISSIDENT, 1837 Main Street, Concord, MA 01742, enmarge@aol.com. G. Tod Slone. 1998. "I want personal, tough poems centered around dissidence, corruption, falsity, etc." circ. 200. 2/yr. Pub'd 100 poems 1999; expects 100 poems 2000, 100 poems 2001. sub. price: $14; sample: $7. 56pp; 5½×8½; Rights purchased: First North American, reverts back to poet upon publication. Publishes 5-10% of poems submitted. Deadlines: none. Reporting time: 1 week to 2 months. Payment: 1 copy. Interested in new or unpub'd poets: sure. Simultaneous submissions accepted: yes. Submission quantity: 3. Special interests: Looking for poems in Spanish and French.

AMERICAN INDIAN CULTURE AND RESEARCH JOURNAL, 3220 Campbell Hall, Box 951548, Los Angeles, CA 90095-1548, 310-825-7315; Fax 310-206-7060; www.sscnet.ucla.edu/esp/aisc/index.html. 1972. circ. 1.2M. 4/yr. sub. price: $25 individuals, $60 institutions. 300pp; 6×9.

AMERICAN JONES BUILDING & MAINTENANCE, Missing Spoke Press, PO Box 9569, Seattle, WA 98109, 206-443-4693; von@singspeak.com. Von G. Binuia, Editor. 1997. circ. 400. 4/yr. Expects 90 poems 2000. sub. price: $12; sample: $3. 128pp; 5½×8½; Rights purchased: one-time/all rights. Publishes 1% of poems submitted. Deadlines: none. Reporting time: 4 months. Payment: various and copies (10%). Interested in new or unpub'd poets: yes. Simultaneous submissions accepted: yes. Recent contributors: Greg Kosmicki, Cynthia Gallaher, Elizabeth Ann James, Charles Potts. Submission quantity: no limit. Special interests: long poems, narrative poems, short short fiction.

AMERICAN LETTERS & COMMENTARY, 850 Park Avenue, Suite 5B, New York, NY 10021, fax 212-327-0706, e-mail rabanna@aol.com, www.amleters.org. Anna Rabinowitz. 1988. "Seek innovative, challenging work" circ. 1.5M. 1/yr. sub. price: $6; sample: $6. 160pp; 7×8; Rights purchased: none. Deadlines: Reading period 6/1-10/31. Reporting time: 2 weeks - 4 months. Payment: copies. Interested in new or unpub'd poets: yes. Simultaneous submissions accepted: yes, if notified. Recent contributors: Barbara Guest, C.D. Wright, Paul Hoover, David Lehman, Susan Wheeler. Submission quantity: 3-4. Special interests: Experimental, innovative, translations, longpoems.

American Literary Press Inc./Noble House, 8019 Belair Road #10, Baltimore, MD 21236, 410-882-7700; fax 410-882-7703; e-mail amerlit@erols.com; www.erols.com/amerlit. Kimberly Barker, Managing Editor. 1991. "Submission typed upper and lower case, one poem per page, we specialize in publishing poetry for new and/or unknown poets" avg. press run 500 or 1M. Pub'd 15 poetry titles 1999; expects 17 poetry titles 2000, 20 poetry titles 2001. 5½×8½; avg. price, cloth: $19.95; paper: $9.95; other: $6.50 saddle stitched. 112pp; Publishes 25% of poetry manuscripts submitted. Reporting time: 2-3 weeks. Payment: 45% (available with Noble House imprint only). Interested in new or unpub'd poets: yes. Simultaneous submissions accepted: yes. Recently published poets: Dumas F. Frick, Ingrid B. Pope, Jackie Hall, Jane Hwa Hu, Craig Burgess. Submission quantity: minimum of 60 for paperback binding.

AMERICAN LITERARY REVIEW, Dept of English, University of North Texas, Denton, TX 76203-6827, 817-565-2127. Bruce Bond. 1990. circ. 900. 2/yr. Pub'd 40 poems 1999; expects 40 poems 2000, 40 poems 2001. sub. price: $15 individual, $25 institution; sample: $8. 128pp; 7×10; Rights purchased: First American Serial. Deadlines: September 1 to May 1. Reporting time: 8-12 weeks. Payment: 2 copies. Interested in new or unpub'd poets: yes. Simultaneous submissions accepted: yes, if indicated. Recent contributors: Pattiann Rogers, Eric Pankey, William Logan, David St. John, Erin Page. Submission quantity: 3-5.

American Living Press (see also WEIRD POETRY), PO Box 901, Allston, MA 02134, 617-522-6196. Michael Shores. 1982. "Currently not accepting submissions." avg. press run 250-500. Pub'd 2 poetry titles 1999. 5½×8½; avg. price, cloth: $5; paper: $5. 30-50pp; Publishes 50% of poetry manuscripts submitted. Reporting time: 3-6 weeks. Payment: copies of book. Interested in new or unpub'd poets: yes. Recently published poets: Richard Hay, David Roscoes, Tyanna Lei, Mary Winters, Ray McNiece. Submission quantity: 5.

AMERICAN POETRY REVIEW, 1721 Walnut St., Philadelphia, PA 19103, 215-496-0439. Steven Berg, David Bonanno, Arthur Vogelsang. 1972. circ. 18M. 6/yr. Pub'd 250 poems 1999. sub. price: $18; sample: $3.95. 52pp; 9¾×13¾; Rights purchased: 1st serial. Publishes 1% of poems submitted. Deadlines: none.

Reporting time: 10 weeks. Payment: $2 per line. Interested in new or unpub'd poets: yes. Simultaneous submissions accepted: no. Recent contributors: John Ashbery, Brenda Hillman, Gerald Stern, Adrienne Rich, Allen Ginsberg. Submission quantity: 5 or less.

American Romanian Academy (see also A.R.A. JOURNAL), University of California, Dept. of French & Italian, Davis, CA 95616, 916-758-7720. 1975. 6×9.

AMERICAN TANKA, PO Box 120-024, Staten Island, NY 10312-0024, email editor@americantanka.com, website www.americantanka.com. Laura Maffei, Editor. 1996. "We are dedicated exclusively to English-language tanka poetry." circ. 100. 2/yr. Pub'd 200 poems 1999; expects 250 poems 2000, 250 poems 2001. sub. price: $16; sample: $8. 120pp; 5½×8½; Rights purchased: 1st N. American serial, rights revert to author upon publication. Publishes 15-20% of poems submitted. Deadlines: February 15 (spring), August 15 (fall). Reporting time: 4-6 weeks. Payment: 1 copy. Interested in new or unpub'd poets: yes. Simultaneous submissions accepted: no. Recent contributors: Sanford Goldstein, Anna Holley, Marianne Bluger, Nasira Alma, James Tipton. Submission quantity: 5. Special interests: Concrete and focused poems evoking a single, present-tense moment.

THE AMERICAN VOICE, 332 West Broadway, #1215, Louisville, KY 40202, 502-562-0045. Frederick Smock. 1985. *"The American Voice* is a pan-American quarterly, interested in vigorously original work by new and established poets—nothing sexist, racist, homophobic, or classist. Manuscripts read year-round." circ. 2M. 3/yr. Pub'd 40 poems 1999; expects 40 poems 2001. sub. price: $15; sample: $7. 150pp; 6×9; Rights purchased: 1st North American serial. Publishes 2% of poems submitted. Deadlines: none. Reporting time: 6 weeks. Payment: varies. Interested in new or unpub'd poets: yes. Simultaneous submissions accepted: no. Recent contributors: Olga Broumas, Ursula LeGuin, Mark Doty, Sophie Cabot Black, Jorge Luis Borges. Submission quantity: 5. Special interests: Women poets and South American poets.

AMERICAS REVIEW, PO Box 72466, Davis, CA 95617. Gerald Gray, Karen Joy Fowler, Mary Hower, Glenn Keyser, Kieran Ridge, Hannah Stein. 1985. "Contest: each winter we have a poetry contest (submission dates announced by ads) with several $100 prizes. Each entrant is charged a $7 reading fee, and is sent one copy of AR. All those published receive a copy of the issue in which their work appears. We earnestly request that writers put their name, address, and phone number on each page of their submission, and enclose a SASE with return postage" circ. 1M. 1/yr. Pub'd 35 poems 1999; expects 35 poems 2000, 35 poems 2001. sub. price: $7 individual, $10 institution; sample: $5 indiv., $7 institution. 75pp; 6×9; Rights purchased: first serial. Publishes 5% of poems submitted. Deadlines: open. Reporting time: 5 months. Payment: 1 copy of mag. Interested in new or unpub'd poets: yes. Simultaneous submissions accepted: yes. Recent contributors: Kevin Clark, Oscar Hahn, Adrian Oktenberg, Rebecca Baggett, Susan Kelly-DeWitt. Submission quantity: 3-5. Special interests: Excellent poetry of a political nature.

Amethyst & Emerald, 1556 Halford Avenue, Suite 124, Santa Clara, CA 95051-2661, 408-296-5483; fax 408-249-7646. Cathyann Ortiz, Editor-Publisher. 1997. avg. press run 50. Expects 1 poetry title 2000, 2 poetry titles 2001. 5½×8½; avg. price, paper: $10. 60pp; Reporting time: 2 months. Interested in new or unpub'd poets: yes. Simultaneous submissions accepted: yes.

THE AMETHYST REVIEW, 23 Riverside Avenue, Truro, N.S. B2N 4G2, Canada, 902-895-1345. Penny Ferguson, Editor. 1992. "Annual contest, write for guidelines. Contest deadline: January 31." circ. 150-200. 2/yr. Pub'd 50 poems 1999; expects 50 poems 2000, 50 poems 2001. sub. price: $12CAN; sample: $6CAN. 84pp; 6¾×8½; Rights purchased: 1st N.A. serial. Publishes 10% of poems submitted. Deadlines: Jan 31 and Aug 31. Reporting time: 6 months max. Payment: 1 copy. Interested in new or unpub'd poets: yes. Simultaneous submissions accepted: no. Recent contributors: Edith Van Beek, Virgil Suarez, M. Travis Lane, John B. Lee, Brian Burke. Submission quantity: 3-5. Special interests: Quality contemporary.

Amherst Writers & Artists Press, Inc. (see also PEREGRINE), PO Box 1076, Amherst, MA 01004, 413-253-7764 phone/fax; e-mail awapress@javanet.com. Pat Schneider, Editor. 1981. "We publish only books which we solicit. Annual contests in poetry & fiction, $500 prize & publication in *Peregrine*. Send for guidelines." avg. press run 500-1M. Pub'd 2 poetry titles 1999; expects 2 poetry titles 2000, 3 poetry titles 2001. 6×9; avg. price, paper: $7 *Peregrine); $12 books.* 70pp, chapbooks 34pp, *Peregrine* 90pp; Interested in new or unpub'd poets: no. Recently published poets: Carol Edelstein, Steven Riel, Barbara Van Noord, Frances Balter, Mary-Beth O'Shea-Noonan. Submission quantity: 3.

THE AMICUS JOURNAL, 40 West 20th Street, New York, NY 10011, 212-727-2700. Brian Swann, Poetry Editor. 1979. "We publish only poems rooted in nature, up to one manuscript page in length." circ. 150M. 4/yr. Pub'd 16 poems 1999; expects 16 poems 2000, 16 poems 2001. sub. price: $10; sample: $4.00. 56pp; 7½×10½; Rights purchased: 1st North American Serial. Publishes 2% of poems submitted. Deadlines: none. Reporting time: 2 months. Payment: $50 per poem. Interested in new or unpub'd poets: yes. Simultaneous submissions accepted: no. Recent contributors: Reg Saner, Mary Oliver, Pattiann Rogers, Aimee Grunberger, John Haines. Submission quantity: up to 10.

AMNESIA, PO Box 661441, Los Angeles, CA 90066. 1989. "International artist audience" circ. 500. 2/yr. Pub'd 20 poems 1999; expects 20 poems 2000, 20 poems 2001. sample price: $3 U.S., $4 overseas. 50pp; 8×11; Rights purchased: none. Publishes 5% of poems submitted. Deadlines: cyclical. Payment: 1 copy of publication. Interested in new or unpub'd poets: yes. Simultaneous submissions accepted: yes. Recent contributors: Jack Skelley, Robin Carr, Michelle T. Clinton, Jerome Sala, Bob Flanagan. Submission quantity: 3-5. Special interests: Shorter work: poetry, prose, experimental.

●**anabasis,** PO Box 216, Oysterville, WA 98641, anabasis@willapabay.org. 1976. *"Living in the Document* chapbook series seeks post disjunkt semi-reformalist poetry and poetics characterized by spiritual accuracy." 5×8. Reporting time: quick. Payment: to be arranged. Simultaneous submissions accepted: yes. Recently published poets: Leonard Cirino, Heidi Andrea Rhodes, Jesse Freeman, Lewis LaCook, David Campiche.

Anamnesis Press, PO Box 51115, Palo Alto, CA 94303-0688, 415-255-8366, Fax 415-255-3190, anamnesis@compuserve.com, website ourworld.compuserve.com/homepages/anamnesis/. Keith Allen Daniels. 1990. "Anamnesis Press sponsors an annual poetry chapbook contest. We're looking for poetry with intellectual and emotional depth that avoids cliches and has an ear for sound and music, although formal structure is not necessary. Submissions must be postmarked by March 15. Reading fee: $15 per manuscript. Write for more details, or visit our website. Award: $1,000 + 20 copies of winning chapbook and award certificate." avg. press run 500. Pub'd 3 poetry titles 1999; expects 4 poetry titles 2000, 3 poetry titles 2001. 5½×8½; avg. price, cloth: $29.95; paper: $12.95; other: $6.95 chapbooks, $3 poetry on disk. 80pp; Publishes 2% of poetry manuscripts submitted. Reporting time: 1 month. Payment: 10% of gross. We are interested in manuscripts from new or previously unpublished poets only for our annual contest. We accept simultaneous submissions for our annual contest only. Recently published poets: James Blish, Joe Haldeman, Robert Frazier, David R. Bunch, David Lunde. Submission quantity: 20-30 (for chapbook contest). Special interests: Highly imaginative poetry with an ear for sound and music—visionary, science fiction, fantasy, horror, science, non-traditional subject matter.

Androgyne Books, 930 Shields, San Francisco, CA 94132, 415-586-2697. Ken Weichel. 1971. "Submissions are welcome but query before sending longer fiction. Catalog of titles available on request." avg. press run 500. Pub'd 2 poetry titles 1999; expects 2 poetry titles 2000, 2 poetry titles 2001. 5×7½; avg. price, paper: $12. 80pp; Publishes 5% of poetry manuscripts submitted. Reporting time: 1 month. Payment: 10% press run. Interested in new or unpub'd poets: yes. Simultaneous submissions accepted: yes. Recently published poets: Allen Cohen, Fred Pietarinerc, Mel Clay, Steve Abbott, Rebekha Whetstyne. Submission quantity: 5 poems. Special interests: Translations, Dutch poets in translations, surrealism and dada, experimental poetry, prose poetry.

ANGELFLESH, Angelflesh Press, PO Box 141123, Grand Rapids, MI 49514. Jim Buchanan. 1994. "Please send SASE w/submissions" circ. 100-200. 3/yr. Pub'd 150 poems 1999; expects 150 poems 2000, 150 poems 2001. sub. price: $10 for 3 issues; sample: $4. 50pp; 5½×8½; Publishes 2%-5% of poems submitted. Deadlines: none. Reporting time: about 1 month. Payment: 1 copy. Interested in new or unpub'd poets: yes. We accept simultaneous submissions but prefer not to. Recent contributors: John Sweet, Juliet Cook, Elizabeth Florio, Joseph Shields, Martin Vest. Submission quantity: 3-7.

Angelflesh Press (see also ANGELFLESH), PO Box 141123, Grand Rapids, MI 49514. Jim Buchanan. 1994. "Please send a SASE with submissions" avg. press run 100-200. Pub'd 3 poetry titles 1999; expects 2 poetry titles 2000, 2 poetry titles 2001. 5½×8½; avg. price, other: $3-5. 30-50pp; Publishes 2%-5% of poetry manuscripts submitted. Reporting time: 2 months. Interested in new or unpub'd poets: yes. We accept simultaneous submissions but prefer not to. Recently published poets: Juliet Cook, Martin Vest, Gerald Locklin, Todd Balazic, Elizabeth Florio. Submission quantity: 3-7.

Anhinga Press, PO Box 10595, Tallahassee, FL 32302, 850-521-9920; Fax 850-442-6323; info@anhinga.org; www.anhinga.org. Van Brock, Rick Campbell, Director. 1973. "Send a #10 SASE for details." avg. press run 2M. Pub'd 2 poetry titles 1999; expects 3 poetry titles 2000, 3 poetry titles 2001. 6×9; avg. price, cloth: $21; paper: $11. 96pp; Publishes 1% of poetry manuscripts submitted. Reporting time: varies greatly, 4-6 months. Payment: percentage of press run; occasional cash payments;royalty. Interested in new or unpub'd poets: yes, if they are any good. Simultaneous submissions accepted: yes. Recently published poets: Frank Gaspar, Judith Kitchen, Robert Dana, Keith Ratzlaff, Michael Mott. Submission quantity: query-10 pages. Special interests: Each year Anhinga Press awards the Anhinga Prize for Poetry for a book-length manuscript of original poetry in English. The winner is chosen in an open competition, and the final decision is made by a poet of outstanding achievement. $2000 goes to the winning poet, and the winning manuscript is published by Anhinga Press. Winners of the prize include Ricardo Pau-Llosa, Judith Kitchen, Earl S. Braggs, Jean Monahan, Janet Holmes. Donald Hall, Marvin Bell, William Stafford, and Hayden Carruth have been our judges. For contest guidelines, send a pre-addressed, stamped #10 envelope. In addition to the prize winners, we occasionally publish other books we discover among contest entries.

ANT ANT ANT ANT ANT, PO Box 16177, Oakland, CA 94610, www.home.earthlink.net/~antfive. Chris

Gordon. 1994. "A haiku-biased collusion of words and images preoccupied with fragmentary investigations into the secret meanings of everyday life. Mostly poems 1-5 lines in length, some up to 10 lines, a few longer (sequences, assemblages, microscopy, etc.), photographs, collages, calligraphy, abstract art, text as image, varying format. Magazine as art rather than magazine about art: no articles, letters, reviews, table of contents, index, or page numbers. Lo-fi web simulcast." circ. 200. 1/yr. Pub'd 170 poems 1999; expects 170 poems 2000, 170 poems 2001. sub. price: $8; sample: $8. 68pp; 5½x8½; Rights purchased: none. Publishes 5% of poems submitted. Deadlines: none. Reporting time: 1-3 months. Payment: none. Interested in new or unpub'd poets: yes. Simultaneous submissions accepted: yes. Recent contributors: Robert Creeley, Hiroaki Sato, Dennis Saleh, Dorothy Howard, M. Kettner. Submission quantity: 10-20.

THE ANTHOLOGY OF NEW ENGLAND WRITERS, PO Box 483, Windsor, VT 05089, 802-674-2315, newvtpoet@aol.com. Frank Anthony, Editor; Susan C. Anthony, Associate Editor. 1989. "Each issue a contest with Robert Penn Warren Awards ($300, $200, $100). Open to all poets." circ. 400. 1/yr. Pub'd 33 poems 1999. sub. price: $3.95; sample: $3.50. 44pp; 5½x8½; None-We return all rights (after first publishing) to the author. Publishes approx. 10% of poems submitted. Deadlines: June 15th annually. Reporting time: 6 weeks after deadline (June 15th). Payment: 1 copy. Interested in new or unpub'd poets: Yes. Simultaneous submissions accepted: No. Recent contributors: Katherine LeRoy, Vivian Shipley, Gregory Donovan, Mary Sue Koeppel, Nola Perez. Submission quantity: 3-9 poems. Special interests: Free verse poetry only; 30 lines or less.

ANTIETAM REVIEW, 41 S. Potomac Street, Hagerstown, MD 21740-5512, 301-791-3132. Ethan Fischer. 1982. "We look for excellent literary quality poems, tightly structured, with attention to language and sound. *AR* is a regional publication of the Washington County Arts Council. We take work from writers who live in or come from Maryland, Virginia, West Virginia, Pennsylvania, DE or Washington D.C. Annual *Writer's Day Workshop* in October in MD." circ. 2K. 1/yr. Pub'd 14 poems 1999; expects 20-22 poems 2000, 20-22 poems 2001. sub. price: $5.25; sample: $3.15/$5.25. 72pp; 8½x11; Rights purchased: 1st North American, copyright reverts to author. Publishes 3-4% of poems submitted. Deadlines: September 1-February 1. Reporting time: 2 weeks to several months, we send a card if it's being seriously considered. Payment: $20 per poem. Interested in new or unpub'd poets: yes. Simultaneous submissions accepted: reluctantly. Recent contributors: James Harms, Elisabeth Murawski, Michael Glaser, Rick Cannon, Barbara Hurd. Submission quantity: max. of 5. Special interests: We look for strong literary work—well-crafted poems.

THE ANTIGONISH REVIEW, St Francis Xavier University, PO Box 5000, Antigonish, Nova Scotia B2G 2W5, Canada. Peter Sanger. 1970. "Poets should not submit more than 6 or 7 poems. Authors should write for guidelines" circ. 800. 4/yr. Pub'd 350 poems 1999; expects 340 poems 2000, 350 poems 2001. sub. price: $24; sample: $5 accompanied by postage. 150pp; 9x6; Rights purchased: rights retained by authors. Publishes 20% of poems submitted. Deadlines: none. Reporting time: 3 months. Payment: 2 free copies. Interested in new or unpub'd poets: yes. Simultaneous submissions accepted: no. Recent contributors: Zenovia Sadoway, Anne Blonstein, Robert Cooperman, Stewart Donovan, Robert Stern. Submission quantity: 6-8. Special interests: Translations from Hungarian, Chinese, Serbo-Croatian, Icelandic. No erotica.

THE ANTIOCH REVIEW, PO Box 148, Yellow Springs, OH 45387, 937-767-6389. Judith Hall, Poetry Editor. 1941. "No 'light' or inspirational verse, please." circ. 5M. 4/yr. Pub'd 64 poems 1999. sub. price: $35 ($45 foreign), $65 institutional ($75 foreign); sample: $6. 128pp; 9x6; Rights purchased: 1st serial rights; rights revert upon publication. Publishes 1% of poems submitted. Deadlines: we do not read between May 1 and September 1. Reporting time: 8-12 weeks. Payment: $10/published page, payable on publication. Interested in new or unpub'd poets: yes. Simultaneous submissions accepted: no. Recent contributors: Cal Bedient, Collette Inez, Sandra McPherson, David Wojahn, James Cummins. Submission quantity: 3-6.

APHRODITE GONE BERSERK, 233 Guyon Avenue, Staten Island, NY 10306. 1995. "AGB is a semi-annual journal of erotic art dedicated to publishing the best work reflecting the homosexual, lesbian, heterosexual or bi-sexual experience" circ. 250. 2/yr. Expects 14 poems 2001. sub. price: $12; sample: $7. 48pp; 5 1/2x8 1/2; Rights purchased: 1 time rights. Publishes 5% of poems submitted. Reporting time: immediately - 2 month. Payment: 1 copy. Interested in new or unpub'd poets: yes. Recent contributors: Gerrard Malanga, Lyn Lifshin, Mariko Nagai.

APKL Publications, 42-07 34th Avenue #4-D, Long Island City, NY 11101-1115. Stephen Mark Rafalsky. 1977. "APKL is an acronym of the Greek *apokalypsis*, which means uncovering or revelation. We find buried in the collective consciousness of the human race the central archetype of existence; we declare this to be Jesus Christ the resurrected and living Creator, and we publish those works that illuminate the human condition in this light. We are not religious, but creators of consciousness. No unsolicited manuscripts, please. Inquiries w/SASE accepted" avg. press run 10-200. Pub'd 1 poetry title 1999; expects 1 poetry title 2000, 1 poetry title 2001. 5½x8½; avg. price, paper: $2. 4-100pp; Payment: none.

APOSTROPHE: USCB Journal of the Arts, 801 Carteret Street, Beaufort, SC 29902, 803-521-4158; FAX

803-522-9733; E-Mail ibfrt56@vm.sc.edu. Sheila Tombe. Address poetry submissions to: e-mail sjtombe@gwm.sc.edu. 1996. circ. 700. 2/yr. Pub'd 15 poems 1999; expects 15 poems 2000, 15 poems 2001. sub. price: $15; sample: $3. 65pp; 5½×8; Publishes 3% of poems submitted. Deadlines: none. Reporting time: too long, could be 6 months. Payment: 2 copies. Interested in new or unpub'd poets: yes. Simultaneous submissions accepted: yes, with immediate notification of acceptance elsewhere. Recent contributors: Lyn Lifshin, D.C. Miller, Jay Paul, Edward Butscher, Jorn Ake. Submission quantity: 3-5.

APPALACHIA JOURNAL, 5 Joy Street, Boston, MA 02108, 617-523-0636. Parkman Howe. 1877. circ. 13M. 2/yr. Pub'd 12 poems 1999; expects 12 poems 2000, 12 poems 2001. sub. price: $10; sample: $5. 160pp; 6×9; Publishes 25% of poems submitted. Deadlines: Feb. 1- August 1. Reporting time: 4-6 weeks. Interested in new or unpub'd poets: yes. Simultaneous submissions accepted: yes. Recent contributors: Mary Oliver, Warren Woessner, Thomas Reiter, Maxwell Corydon Wheat, Jr. Submission quantity: 2-3. Special interests: We look for poems on mountaineering, nature, and outdoor activities such as canoeing and hiking.

Appalachian Consortium Press, University Hall, Appalachian State University, Boone, NC 28608, 704-262-2064, fax 704-262-6564. 1971. avg. press run 500-1M. Pub'd 1 poetry title 1999. 6×9¼; avg. price, cloth: $15.95; paper: $7.95. 150pp; Publishes a very small % of poetry manuscripts submitted. Reporting time: 6 months. Payment: 5%. Interested in new or unpub'd poets: yes, but this is not a priority for our press (moratorium until 6/01/92). Simultaneous submissions accepted: no. Recently published poets: Jim Wayne Miller, Francis P. Hulme, Bettie M. Sellers. Special interests: Appalachian regional poetry.

APPALACHIAN HERITAGE, Appalachian Center, Berea College, Berea, KY 40404, 859-985-3140, jim-gage@berea.edu. James Gage, Editor. 1973. *"Appalachian Heritage* is a Southern Appalachian literary magazine. All material should relate to Appalachia in some fashion." circ. 1050. 4/yr. Pub'd 12 poems 1999. sub. price: $18; sample: $6. 80pp; 6×9; Rights purchased: first printing rights only. Publishes 5% of poems submitted. Deadlines: seasonal material should arrive quarter before specific season mentioned, or inquire. Reporting time: 4 weeks. Payment: contributor's copies. Interested in new or unpub'd poets: yes if regional. Simultaneous submissions accepted: yes. Recent contributors: James Still, Jim Wayne Miller, Bennie Lee Sinclair, Bettie Sellers, Albert Stewart. Submission quantity: 2-5. Special interests: Regional poetry.

Appalachian Log Publishing Company (see also THE SOUTHERN JOURNAL), PO Box 20297, Charleston, WV 25362, 304-342-5789. 1991. 5½×8½. Simultaneous submissions accepted: yes.

AQUARIUS, Flat 4, Room B, 116 Sutherland Avenue, London W9, England. 1968. "We publish no more than 3 poems per issue. John Heath-Stubbs is (Co Editor Equarius)" circ. 1.5M. 2/yr. sub. price: $40; sample: £5 - $12. 120pp; Rights purchased: coyrights belong to authors. Deadlines: anytime. Payment: by agreement. Interested in new or unpub'd poets: yes. Simultaneous submissions accepted: yes. Special interests: John Heath-Stubbs—Schalon + Poet. Born in London, 9th July 1918. Educated Queen's College, Oxford. Published various volumes of verse, drama, criticism. His recent volume of verse include *Artorius* (1972), for which he received the Queen's Gold Medal for Poetry in 1974. His recent volume are *Cats Parnassus* (1987) Time Pieces (1988) and on June 16th 1988 his *Collected Poems* will be published. His other books in print are *Immolation of Aleph* and *Naming the Beasts*. Has just been made by Queen in (English Honours) 1989-OBE. Eddie Linden, the Editor. Born in Ireland in 1935, brought up in Scotland, has worked as miner, went to Oxford in 1964. Studied economics for two years. Biographer on his life published in 1979 *First A Book*. His poems, *City of Razar's*—1980. The Best of Scottish Poetry. (1989 Chambers-Edinbugh) Edited by Robin Bell. The Penguin Book of Homosexual Verse. Edited by Stephen Coote; 1983. (Life Doesn't Frighten Me At All) Edited by John Agard.

AQUATERRA, METAECOLOGY & CULTURE, 5473 Highway 23N, Eureka Springs, AR 72631. Jacqui Froelich. 1986. "All submissions should include water and water-related subjects." circ. 3M. 1/yr. Pub'd 4 poems 1999; expects 4 poems 2000, 4 poems 2001. sub. price: $9.95; sample: $9.95. 140pp; 8×5; Rights purchased: none. Publishes 50% of poems submitted. Payment: none. Interested in new or unpub'd poets: yes, water-related only. Simultaneous submissions accepted: yes. Recent contributors: Evi Seidman, Coco Gordon, Barbara Helen Harmony, Caryn Goldberg, Douglas Dobbyns. Submission quantity: 1+.

ARARAT, 55 E 59th Street, New York, NY 10022-1112. Leo Hamalian, Editor. 1960. circ. 2.2M. 4/yr. Expects 30 poems 2001. sub. price: $24; sample: $4. 74pp; 9×12; Rights purchased: 1st. Deadlines: 3 months. Reporting time: 3 months. Payment: $10-$20. Interested in new or unpub'd poets: only if Armenian. Simultaneous submissions accepted: yes. Recent contributors: Harold Bond, Helene Pilibosian, Diana Der HoVanessian, Sylva Gaboudikian, Jerry Renjilion.

ARBA SICULA, Legas, c/o Modern Foreign Languages, St. John's University, Jamaica, NY 11439-0002. G. Cipolla, Editor. 1979. "We generally solicit. We publish only poetry written in Sicilian. We also publish translations from the Sicilian." circ. 2M. 2/yr. Pub'd 15 poems 1999; expects 15 poems 2000, 15 poems 2001. sub. price: $20; sample: $10. 90pp; 5½×8½; Deadlines: none. Payment: we cannot pay.

ARCHIPELAGO, PO Box 2485, Charlottesville, VA 22902-2485, editor@archipelago.org, www.archipelago.org. Katherine McNamara, Editor and Publisher. 1997. circ. via the world wide web. 4/yr. Pub'd 15-20 poems 1999. 95-100pp; 8×11; Rights purchased: first serial. Publishes a small % of poems submitted. Reporting time: 4-6 months. Payment: none. Simultaneous submissions accepted: yes. Recent contributors: Errol Miller, David Cooper, Rachel Eshed, Dannie Abse, Sandor Kanyade.

Arctos Press, PO Box 401, Sausalito, CA 94966, 415-331-2503, Fax 415-331-3092, runes@aol.com, http://members.aol.com/runes/index.html. CB Follett, Editor. 1996. "Calls for submissions and theme will be announced in *Poets & Writers* and similar venues. Always include SASE. Poetry is not returned but recycled. We look for quality poems, originality of language, well-crafted attention to theme." avg. press run 1.5M. Pub'd 1 poetry title 1999; expects 3 poetry titles 2000, 1 poetry title 2001. 6×9, 8×10; avg. price, paper: $15. 130pp; Reporting time: 2-3 months. Payment: 1 copy of book. Interested in new or unpub'd poets: no, except in response to anthology calls. Simultaneous submissions accepted: yes. Recently published poets: Robert Hass, Jane Hirshfield, Kay Ryan, Brenda Hillman, Susan Terris. Submission quantity: up to 5.

ARIEL—A Review of International English Literature, The University of Calgary, 2500 University Drive NW, Calgary, Alberta T2N 1N4, Canada, 403-220-4657. V.J. Ramraj. 1970. "Submit 2 copies and submit your best poems because *Ariel* has limited space and competition is very keen." circ. 925. 4/yr. Pub'd 24 poems 1999; expects 24 poems 2000, 24 poems 2001. sub. price: $33 institution, $23 individual; sample: G.S.T. Canada. 140pp; 6×9; Rights purchased: contact editor. Publishes less than 10% of poems submitted. Deadlines: none. Reporting time: 3 months. Payment: none. Interested in new or unpub'd poets: yes, both. Simultaneous submissions accepted: no. Recent contributors: Edward Baugh, Wayne Keon, Dennis Cooley, Allison Childs, Heather Brown. Submission quantity: less than 10. Special interests: pluralistic approach used by *Ariel*. Also accepts original translations.

Arjuna Library Press (see also JOURNAL OF REGIONAL CRITICISM), 1025 Garner Street, D, Space 18, Colorado Springs, CO 80905-1774. Count Prof. Joseph A. Uphoff Jr., Director. 1983. "Arjuna Library publishes extremely limited edition prototype volumes in the nature of advertising and solicitation for patronage. We request options to buy copyrights upon notice and acceptance of terms unless previously sold. Publications include introductions with illustrative mathematical/theoretical presentations. While personal computers continue to grow more capable of visual and dynamic forms for poetics, the poetry of letters and typeprogramming, derived from typesetting, has been consolidated as a system capable of handling advanced solutions in mathematical theory for literature, philosophy, and the arts in general." avg. press run 1-25. Pub'd 18+ poetry titles 1999; expects 36+ poetry titles 2000, 36+ poetry titles 2001. 5×7; avg. price, cloth: none; paper: $3. 35pp; Reporting time: indefinite. Payment: notice of acceptance, copy of anthology or broadside (in an issue). Interested in new or unpub'd poets: yes. Simultaneous submissions accepted: no, exceptional cases. Recently published poets: Daniel Suders, Uzeik Sidetski, Dane Cervine, Marianne Aweagon Broyles, A.M. Bauers. Submission quantity: 1 or more, complete manuscripts. Special interests: Current anthologies are being developed as a mixture of commentary, criticism, and biography with illustrative material, theoretical equations, and poetry (surrealist and dreamlike prose poetry suitable for a general audience). Since we use xerography we can handle experimental visual poetics and scientific illustration. Material submitted will also appear through *The Journal of Regional Criticism*.

The Ark, 176 Centre Street, East Sullivan, NH 03445-4111, 603-847-3028, anarkiss@mindspring.com. Geoffrey Gardner. 1970. "Publication is now primarily by invitation and occasional as economies allow. We will consider poetry of any form or style. Depth, power and excellence are what we want. We are especially interested in new translation of poetry from all languages and periods. Query before submission. Stringent finances have made it very unlikely that we will be able to take on any new publishing ventures over the next several years. We will continue to read all that comes to us. It is less likely than ever we will accept any new, unsolicited work for publication." avg. press run 1.5M. Pub'd 1 poetry title 1999; expects 1 poetry title 2000. 5½×8½; avg. price, cloth: $10; paper: $5. 116pp; Publishes 1% or less of poetry manuscripts submitted. Reporting time: at once to 3 months. Payment: 10% of press run and 10% of gross. Interested in new or unpub'd poets: yes, provided they query first and submit work of the highest quality. Simultaneous submissions accepted: no. Recently published poets: Kenneth Rexroth, David Budbill, Linda Hogan, John Haines, Paul Mann. Submission quantity: 10 pages. Special interests: Work as good as the masters of world poetry, translation, regionally based poetry.

Armadillo Books, PO Box 2052, Georgetown, TX 78627-2052, 512-863-8660. 1997. "Pleas submit poems as one file." avg. press run 100. Pub'd 1 poetry title 1999; expects 1 poetry title 2000. 5¼×8; avg. price, paper: $9.95. 75pp; Payment: self-publishing. Interested in new or unpub'd poets: yes, on disk. Simultaneous submissions accepted: no. Recently published poets: Don Snell, Marshall Thomas. Submission quantity: ~75.

ARNAZELLA, 3000 Landerholm Circle SE, Bellevue, WA 98007, 206-641-2373. 1976. "Please submit only 3 entries in each category of prose, poetry, art and photography." circ. 300. 1/yr. Pub'd 20 poems 1999; expects 20 poems 2000, 20 poems 2001. sample price: $10. 80pp; 8½×9; Rights purchased: North American first rights.

Publishes 10-15% of poems submitted. Deadlines: end of January. Reporting time: 2-4 months. Payment: copies of magazine. Interested in new or unpub'd poets: yes. Simultaneous submissions accepted: no. Submission quantity: 3.

ART TIMES, PO Box 730, Mount Marion, NY 12456-0730, 914-246-6944, email arttimes@alster.net. Raymond J. Steiner, Editor. 1984. "Up to 20 lines. All topics, all forms. High literary quality sought. Readers of *Art Times* are generally over 40, affluent and art conscious. Articles in *Art Times* are general pieces on the arts written by staff *and are not solicited.* General tone of paper governed by literary essays on arts—no journalistic writing, press releases. Always include SASE. Sample copy: SASE, 3 first-class stamps. Guidelines: business size envelope, one 1st-class stamp." circ. 21M. 11/yr. Pub'd 35-40 poems 1999; expects 35-40 poems 2000, 35-40 poems 2001. sub. price: $15, $25 foreign; sample: SASE + 3 first class stamps. 20pp; 10×14½; Rights purchased: first serial. Publishes 1% of poems submitted. Deadlines: none. Reporting time: 12-24 weeks. Payment: 6 copies of issue + 1 year's subscription. Interested in new or unpub'd poets: yes. We do not encourage simultaneous submissions. Recent contributors: Mary Francis, R. Scott Yarbrough, Philip A. Waterhouse, Sinann, Kelly R. Thompson. Submission quantity: 1-5.

ART-CORE, PO Box 49324, Austin, TX 78765. Patty Puke, Pistol Pete. 1989. "Send SASE for guidelines, deadlines and special theme material we need. Always list submitted material by title with signed note granting *Art-Core* permission to publish. Adult subject matter, include age statement." circ. 400. 3/yr. Pub'd 30 poems 1999; expects 40 poems 2000, 40 poems 2001. sample price: $4 ppd. 24pp; 8×10; Rights purchased: none; copyright remains with author. Publishes 10% of poems submitted. Deadlines: Feb. 15, June 15, Oct. 15. Reporting time: 6-8 weeks max. Payment: free copy. Interested in new or unpub'd poets: yes. Recent contributors: Cheryl Townsend, Paul Weinman. Submission quantity: 5 maximum.

Arte Publico Press, University of Houston, Houston, TX 77204-2090, 713-743-2841. Nicolas Kanellos, Publisher. 1980. "We publish original books of poetry by U.S. Hispanic authors in English or Spanish. Bilingual publications are desirable" avg. press run 1.5M-3M. Pub'd 4 poetry titles 1999. 5½×8½; avg. price, paper: $3.95-$16.00. 80-160pp; Publishes less than 8% of poetry manuscripts submitted. Reporting time: 4 months. Payment: by individual contract. Interested in new or unpub'd poets: yes. Simultaneous submissions accepted: no. Recently published poets: Pat Mora, Evangelina Vigil, Leo Romero, Gloria Vando, Rafael Campo. Submission quantity: complete manuscript.

ARTFUL DODGE, Department of English, College of Wooster, Wooster, OH 44691. Daniel Bourne, Editor. 1979. "*Artful Dodge* takes a strong interest in poets who are continually testing 'what they can get away with' in regards to subject, rhetoric, perspective, language, etc., but who also show mastery of current American poetic technique—its varied textures and its achievement in the illumination of the particular. *AD* also has a sustained commitment to translation, especially from Poland and Eastern Europe, and we feel that the interchange between the American and foreign works on our pages is important to our readers. We are starting a special ongoing feature of poets as translators, bringing together both the translations and original poetry of a number of prominent American poets. We often offer encouragement to writers whose work we find promising, but *Artful Dodge* is more a journal for the already emerging writer than for the one just starting out. Current issues are $7." circ. 1M. 2/yr. Pub'd 45 poems 1999; expects 50-60 poems 2000, 50-60 poems 2001. sub. price: indiv. $14, instit. $120; sample: current issues are available for $7. Older sample copies are $5. 100pp; 5½×8½; Rights purchased: 1st North American serials rights. Publishes less than 1% of poems submitted. Deadlines: none. Reporting time: 6 months. Payment: 2 copies, plus at least $5 per page honorarium, thanks to Ohio Arts Council support. Interested in new or unpub'd poets: depends on quality—*Artful Dodge* is not a place to 'break in' Simultaneous submissions accepted: no. Recent contributors: Naomi Shihab Nye, Tim Seibles, Julia Kasdorf, Charles Simic, Ronald Wallace. Submission quantity: 3-6 poems, or one longpoem or poem-cycle of any length. Special interests: Translations (especially from Eastern European and Third World countries); longpoems.

ARTHUR'S COUSIN, 6811 Greycloud, Austin, TX 78745, 512-445-7065. Joshua Handley. 1993. "No historical fiction from the 1800-era old west, no 'sappy' love poetry, no poems on roses. I want pain, tears, and blaring emotion. Please send copies only, no SASE. I won't send them back because I may need them later on." circ. 100. 4/yr. Pub'd 33 poems 1999; expects 33 poems 2000. sample price: $1. 24-30pp; 8½×11; Publishes 75% of poems submitted. Deadlines: no deadlines. Interested in new or unpub'd poets: yes. Simultaneous submissions accepted: yes. Recent contributors: Larry Oberc, Jim DeWitt, Terence Bishop, Robert Harrington, Dennis Gulling. Submission quantity: no limit. Special interests: Experimental poetry, dark, gothic, but realistic poetry.

Artifact Press, Ltd., 900 Tanglewood Drive, Concord, MA 01742, 978-287-5296; Fax 978-287-5299; hershey@tiac.net. Connie Hershey. 1991. "We are currently publishing anthologies, not individual poets. We will call for manuscripts. No unsolicited submissions." avg. press run 1M. Pub'd 1 poetry title 1999; expects 1 poetry title 2001. 6×9; avg. price, paper: $12.95. 215pp; Interested in new or unpub'd poets: no.

ART/LIFE, Art/Life Limited Editions, PO Box 23020, Ventura, CA 93002, 805-648-4331. Joe Cardellia, Publisher & Editor. 1981. "We seek well-crafted poetry and short prose in which there is a sense of discovery, fresh language, use of concrete imagery over abstract, and which has a compelling yet comfortable voice. Include self-addressed stamped envelope with each submission. We encourage brief cover letters" circ. 500-1M. 11/yr. Pub'd 110 poems 1999; expects 110 poems 2000, 110 poems 2001. sub. price: $450; sample: $50. 50pp; 8½×11; Publishes 65% of poems submitted. Deadlines: first each month, work will be held over. Reporting time: 1-6 weeks. Payment: a copy of the issue in which work appears. Interested in new or unpub'd poets: yes. Simultaneous submissions accepted: yes. Recent contributors: Jeffrey Skinner, Barry Spacks, Malcolm Glass, Elaine Mott, Peter Wild. Submission quantity: 5.

Art/Life Limited Editions (see also ART/LIFE), PO Box 23020, Ventura, CA 93002, 805-648-4331. Joe Cardellia, Editor & Publisher. 1981. "We seek well-crafted poetry and short prose in which there is a sense of discovery, fresh language, use of concrete imagery over abstract, and which has a compelling yet comfortable voice. Include self-addressed stamped envelope with each submission. We encourage brief cover letters" avg. press run 150. Expects 110 poetry titles 2000. 8½×11; avg. price, other: $50. 10pp; Publishes 65% of poetry manuscripts submitted. Reporting time: 1-6 weeks. Payment: a copy of the issue in which work appears. Interested in new or unpub'd poets: yes. Simultaneous submissions accepted: yes, but prefer not to. Recently published poets: Jeffrey Skinner, Barry Spacks, Malcolm Glass, Elaine Mott, Peter Wild. Submission quantity: 5. Special interests: Translations are okay, with English version.

ART:MAG, PO Box 70896, Las Vegas, NV 89170, 702-734-8121. Peter Magliocco, Editor. 1984. "Limited Editions Press chapbooks &/or *ART:MAG* issues for 1998-99 will primarily contain the works of solicited writers, poets, and artists only. However, there will be some exceptions, and the following guidelines pertain to any unsolicited individual contributors: We strive to expel the superficiality of our factitious culture, in all its drive-thru, junk-food-brain, and commercial-ridden extravagances" circ. 100+. 2/yr. Pub'd 50+ poems 1999; expects 50+ poems 2000, 50+ poems 2001. sub. price: $10; sample: $5. 35-90pp; 8½×11, 8½×7; Rights purchased: first time North American. Publishes 5-10% of poems submitted. Deadlines: query suggested during winter. Reporting time: 1-3 months. Payment: 1 copy of magazine. Interested in new or unpub'd poets: yes. Simultaneous submissions accepted: yes. Recent contributors: T. Anders Carson, Dave Michalak, Donald Ryburn, B. Chown, Laurie Calhoun. Submission quantity: 5. Special interests: Will consider all special interests.

●**ARTS & LETTERS JOURNAL OF CONTEMPORARY CULTURE,** Georgia College & State University, Campus Box 89, Milledgeville, GA 31061-0490, 912-445-1289, al@mail.gcsu.edu, http://al.gcsu.edu. Martin Lammon. 1998. "We sponsor a spring contest where our winner gets $1,000 and publication. Deadline for submissions: April 30th. Past judges include Alice Fulton and Frances Mayes. Send SASE for guidelines." circ. 1.5M. 2/yr. Pub'd 38 poems 1999; expects 35 poems 2000, 40 poems 2001. sub. price: $15. 200pp; 7×10; Rights purchased: First time (rights revert back to author). Publishes .5% of poems submitted. Deadlines: we accept manuscripts from Sept. 1st through April 30th. Reporting time: 3 months. Payment: 1-5 pages $50 + $10 a page over 5 pages. Interested in new or unpub'd poets: yes. Simultaneous submissions accepted: no. Recent contributors: Jean Valentine, Donald Hall, Maxine Kumin, Margaret Gibson, Stuart Lishan. Submission quantity: no more than 8. Special interests: Translations - inquire first for guidelines, essays on contemporary culture.

Arts End Books (see also NOSTOC MAGAZINE), Box 162, Newton, MA 02468. Marshall Brooks. 1979. "Potential contributors might want to examine our catalogue. To secure catalogue, mail us an SASE." avg. press run 500-600. Pub'd 1 poetry title 1999; expects 1 poetry title 2001. size varies; avg. price, cloth: $15; paper: $4. 30pp; Publishes a small % of poetry manuscripts submitted. Reporting time: 2-3 weeks, ideally. Payment: worked out on an individual basis. Interested in new or unpub'd poets: yes. Simultaneous submissions accepted: no. Recently published poets: Herschel Silverman, Les Whitten, Bern Porter. Submission quantity: query only w/a brief sample. Special interests: Translations.

ARTWORD QUARTERLY, PO Box 760, Minneapolis, MN 55414-2411, 612-378-3261. Karen Kraco, Editor; Sherry Kempf, Editor. 1995. "Prefer submissions in #10 business size envelope with mss. and cover letter folded together. Include SASE with adequate postage and brief bio." circ. 200. 4/yr. Pub'd 140 poems 1999; expects 140 poems 2000, 140 poems 2001. sub. price: $15; sample: $4. 40pp; 5½×8½; Publishes 10% of poems submitted. Deadlines: Mar.1, Jun.1, Sep.1, Dec.1. Reporting time: 1-4 months. Payment: 1 copy. Interested in new or unpub'd poets: yes. Simultaneous submissions accepted: no. Recent contributors: Rosemary Hildebrandt, Dennis Saleh, Matt Welter, Paul Anderson, Joe Paddock. Submission quantity: no more than 5. Special interests: Quality is key!

ASCENT, Department of English, Concordia College, Moorhead, MN 56562, E-mail Ascent@cord.edu. 1975. circ. 500. 3/yr. sub. price: $9; sample: $4. 85pp; 6×9.

The Ashland Poetry Press, Ashland University, Ashland, OH 44805, 419-289-5110, FAX 419-289-5329.

Stephen H. Haven. 1969. "Unsolicited manuscripts are not read. For the past four decades, we have published the histories of the decades as seen through poetry" avg. press run 1M. Pub'd 1 poetry title 1999; expects 2 poetry titles 2000, 2 poetry titles 2001. 8½×5; avg. price, paper: $9. 85pp; Payment: 10%. Interested in new or unpub'd poets: yes, if we ask for them. Simultaneous submissions accepted: yes, but only solicited manuscripts. Recently published poets: William Sylvester, David Ray, Alberta T. Turner, Wendy Battin, Philip Brady. Special interests: Good poetry.

THE ASIAN PACIFIC AMERICAN JOURNAL, 37 Saint Marks Place, New York, NY 10003-7801, 212-228-6718. 1992. "Interested in works from all segments of the Asian Pacific American community" circ. 2M. 2/yr. Pub'd 50 poems 1999; expects 50 poems 2000, 75 poems 2001. sub. price: $35, includes membership to the Asian American Writers' Workshop; sample: $12. 200pp; 7×8¼; Rights purchased: Non-exclusive one-time rights. Publishes 20% of poems submitted. Deadlines: May 1 and November 1. Payment: 2 free copies. Simultaneous submissions accepted: yes, but please let us know. Recent contributors: Cathy Song, Koon Woon, Kimiko Hahn, R. Zamora Linmark. Submission quantity: 4-6.

●**Aspermont Press,** 1251 Hayes Street, San Francisco, CA 94117.

ASSEMBLING, Assembling Press, Box 444 Prince Street, New York, NY 10012-0008. Charles Doria. 1970. "We are interested primarily in innovative work that tests the limits of the form and the artist's imagination. By invitation only" circ. 200. 1/yr. sub. price: $30; sample: $10 for a sample. 300pp; size varies; Rights purchased: none. Deadlines: none. Reporting time: infinity. Payment: copies. Interested in new or unpub'd poets: by invitation only. Simultaneous submissions accepted: no. Recent contributors: Rochelle Owens, Rose Drachler, Charles Doria, Richard Kostelmotz, Tim Reynolds. Special interests: Translations, experimental poetry, regional poetry, longpoems, light verse, satire, etc.

Assembling Press (see also ASSEMBLING), Box 444 Prince Street, New York, NY 10012-0008. Charles Doria, Editor & Publisher. 1970. avg. press run 300. Pub'd 2 poetry titles 1999. size varies; avg. price, cloth: $20; other: $3. 30pp; Publishes few to 0% of poetry manuscripts submitted. Reporting time: a long time. Interested in new or unpub'd poets: by invitation only. Simultaneous submissions accepted: no. Submission quantity: 0.

Astro Black Books, P O Box 46, Sioux Falls, SD 57101, 605-338-0277. C. Luden. 1976. "Currently we are a limited operation. Hopefully this will change in the future. At present, only solicited manuscripts are accepted." avg. press run 1M. Expects 2 poetry titles 2000. 5½×8½; avg. price, cloth: $15; paper: $5. 80pp; Payment: negotiable. Recently published poets: David Hellwig, Charles Luden, Jeffrey Reetz. Special interests: We publish contemporary poetry of any kind if it has strong mental impact.

Asylum Arts, 5847 Sawmill Rd., Paradise, CA 95969, 530-876-1454, asyarts@sunset.net. 1990. "Manuscripts by invitation only" avg. press run 1M. Pub'd 1 poetry title 1999; expects 5 poetry titles 2000, 2 poetry titles 2001. 5½×8½; avg. price, paper: $10. 80pp; Payment: varies. Interested in new or unpub'd poets: no. Simultaneous submissions accepted: no. Recently published poets: Robert Peters, Elliot Richman, Carolyn Stoloff, Kenneth Bernard. Submission quantity: query.

ATELIER, 8 Holton Street, Allston, MA 02134-1337. Sarah Jenson. 1990. "Must include SASE for response" circ. 250. 4/yr. Pub'd 100 poems 1999; expects 100 poems 2000, 100 poems 2001. sub. price: $18; sample: $5. 48pp; 5½×8½; Rights purchased: None. Publishes 10% of poems submitted. Deadlines: Continuously reading. Reporting time: 3 months. Payment: copies. Interested in new or unpub'd poets: Yes. Simultaneous submissions accepted: yes. Recent contributors: Andrew Schelling, Susan Smith Nash, Ed Sanders, Vincent Ferrini. Submission quantity: At least 5. Special interests: Experimental poetry, haiku, language.

ATLANTA REVIEW, PO Box 8248, Atlanta, GA 31106. Poetry Editor. 1994. "AR seeks quality poetry of genuine human appeal." circ. 4M. 2/yr. Pub'd 120 poems 1999; expects 120 poems 2000, 120 poems 2001. sub. price: $10; sample: $5. 120pp; 6×9; Publishes 1% of poems submitted. Deadlines: June 1 and December 1. Reporting time: 1 month. Payment: 2 copies. Interested in new or unpub'd poets: yes. Simultaneous submissions accepted: yes. Recent contributors: Seamus Heaney, Derek Walcott, Maxine Kumin, Naomi Shihab Nye, R.T. Smith. Submission quantity: up to 5. Special interests: Each spring issue features a different country or region, but is still open to all topics.

ATOM MIND, PO Box 22068, Albuquerque, NM 87154. Gregory Smith. 1992. circ. 1M+. 4/yr. Pub'd 150 poems 1999; expects 200 poems 2000. sub. price: $20; sample: $6. 120pp; 8½×11; Rights purchased: First North American. Less than 1% of unsolicited material is accepted for publication. Deadlines: accepted year round. Reporting time: 1-2 months. Payment: contributor's copies, with some cash awards. Interested in new or unpub'd poets: definitely; very much enjoy "discovering" new talent. Simultaneous submissions accepted: yes. Recent contributors: Judson Crews, Lawrence Ferlinghetti, Lyn Lifshin, Edward Field, Tony Moffeit. Submission quantity: 6-8.

AUFBAU, 2121 Broadway, New York, NY 10023, 212-873-7400, fax 212-496-5736. Henry Marx, Executive

Editor. 1934. circ. 20M. 26/yr. Pub'd 30 poems 1999. sub. price: USA $58.50; sample: free. 24pp; 10½×13¼; Rights purchased: only in German. Publishes 5% of poems submitted. Payment: $10-$15.

AURA LITERARY/ARTS REVIEW, HUC 135, 1530 3rd Avenue South, Birmingham, AL 35294, 205-934-3216. Tina Harris. 1974. "It is helpful if a short biographyis included in a cover letter. I submission is accepted, the biography will be published issue" circ. 500. 2/yr. Pub'd 50 poems 1999; expects 50 poems 2000. sub. price: $12; sample: $6. 120pp; 6×9; Publishes 5% of poems submitted. Deadlines: none. Reporting time: 1-3 months. Payment: 2 copies. Interested in new or unpub'd poets: yes. Simultaneous submissions accepted: no. Recent contributors: G.E. Murray, Andrew Glaze, Theodore Haddin, Steven Ford Brown, Virgil Suarez. Submission quantity: 8-10.

THE AUROREAN, A POETIC QUARTERLY, PO Box 219, Sagamore Beach, MA 02562-0219, 508-833-0805 phone/fax, phone before faxing. Cynthia Brackett-Vincent, Publisher, Editor. 1995. "New and widely published welcome! Inspirational (not religious), meditational, positive poetry. Request guidelines." circ. 450. 4/yr. Pub'd 180 poems 1999; expects 220 poems 2000, 220 poems 2001. sub. price: $17,$21 international; sample: $5,$6 international. 41pp; 5½×8½; Rights purchased: one-time only. Publishes 15% of poems submitted. Deadlines: Feb. 15, May 15, Aug. 15, Nov. 15. Reporting time: 3½ months, maximum. Payment: 3 copies per poem, 10 plus one-year sub. to featured poet. Interested in new or unpub'd poets: absolutely. Simultaneous submissions accepted: only if noted. Recent contributors: Anne Dewees, John Grey, Michael Keshigian, Ed Meek. Submission quantity: 3-5. Special interests: Very regional focus (New England); page devoted to Laiku in each issue. Acknowledges mss; sends proofs. Publishes bios of all poets. Has a 'Markets' section.

Avocet Press Inc., 19 Paul Court, Pearl River, NY 10965, 212-754-6300, email oopc@interport.net, www.avocetpress.com. 1997.

AVON LITERARY INTELLIGENCER, 20 Byron Place, Bristol, BS8 1JT, United Kingdom, 44-225-826105. 1992. circ. 200. 4/yr. sub. price: $10; sample: $5. 10pp; 8½×11.

AXE FACTORY REVIEW, Cynic Press, PO Box 40691, Philadelphia, PA 19107. 1986. circ. 100. 2-3/yr. Pub'd 50 poems 1999; expects 20 poems 2001. sub. price: $20/5 issues; sample: $3. Pages vary; 8½×11; Rights purchased: copyright for author/poet. Reporting time: 2 weeks. Payment: 2 copies. Interested in new or unpub'd poets: yes, if good. Simultaneous submissions accepted: yes. Recent contributors: Normal, John Sweet, Xu Juan, Adrian Manning. Submission quantity: 5. Special interests: readable. Prefer under 70 lines.

THE AZOREAN EXPRESS, Seven Buffaloes Press, PO Box 249, Big Timber, MT 59011. 1985. circ. 500. 2/yr. sub. price: $10; sample: $7.75. 80pp; 5½×8½.

B

Baba Yoga Micropress, 430 N. Main Street, Herkimer, NY 13350. 1994. 8×10.

BABYSUE, PO Box 8989, Atlanta, GA 31106, 404-320-1178. Don W. Seven, Editor. 1985. "The only type of poetry we're interested in is bizarre and unsettling stuff." circ. 5M. 2/yr. Pub'd 5-10 poems 1999. sub. price: $12; sample: $3. 32pp; 8½×11; Rights purchased: none. Publishes 5% of poems submitted. Deadlines: none. Reporting time: 1 month, if we are able to use something. Payment: 1 free copy in which their poem appears. Interested in new or unpub'd poets: certainly. Simultaneous submissions accepted: yes. Recent contributors: S. Fievet, Angela Peterson, Bob Andrews, Easy Bub. Submission quantity: doesn't matter. Special interests: Experimental poetry is our favorite.

The Bacchae Press, c/o The Brown Financial Group, 10 Sixth Street, Astoria, OR 97103-5315, 503-325-7972; FAX 503-325-7959; 800-207-4358; E-mail brown@pacifier.com. Robert Brown, Editor & Publisher. 1992. "Bacchae Press chapbook competition: Deadline April 15. Write for guidelines" avg. press run 500. Pub'd 5 poetry titles 1999; expects 4 poetry titles 2000, 4 poetry titles 2001. 5½×8½; avg. price, paper: $8; other: $5 chapbooks. 70pp; Publishes less than 1% of poetry manuscripts submitted. Reporting time: 3 months. Payment: 10%. Interested in new or unpub'd poets: no. Simultaneous submissions accepted: yes, if informed. Recently published poets: Julia Wendell, Hal Sirowitz, Karen Braucher, Bart Baxter, Robert J. Levy. Submission quantity: 5. Special interests: Especially interested in translations, NW poems, and experimental work.

BACKSPACE: A QUEER POETS JOURNAL, 25 Riverside Avenue, Gloucester, MA 01930-2552, e-mail bkspqpj@aol.com. Kimberley J. Smith, Editor. 1991. 3/yr. sub. price: $10 includes postage; sample: $2. 28+pp; 5½×8½; Rights purchased: none. Deadlines: per issue. Reporting time: 2 months. Payment: none. Interested in new or unpub'd poets: yes. Simultaneous submissions accepted: yes. Recent contributors: Mark Sonnerfeld, Jameson Currier, Mary Leary, Annette Dubois, David Matthew Barnes. Submission quantity: up to 8.

Backspace Ink, 561 Paloma Avenue, Pacifica, CA 94044-2438, 650-355-4640, FAX 650-355-3630, joski@ix.netcom.com. Thomas A. Ekkens, Editor. 1985. "We do *not* want to receive unsolicited manuscripts/poems. We are not soliciting others' poetry at this time" avg. press run 200. Expects 1 poetry title 2001. 5½x8½; avg. price, cloth: $12. 96pp; Payment: none.

The Backwaters Press, 3502 North 52nd Street, Omaha, NE 68104-3506, 402-451-4052. Greg Kosmicki. 1997. "Anthology of writing of prairie women with submission deadline of Dec. 31, 2000. SASE for details" avg. press run 300-600. Pub'd 3 poetry titles 1999; expects 3 poetry titles 2000, 3 poetry titles 2001. 5½x8½; avg. price, paper: $12. 78-90pp; Publishes 1% of poetry manuscripts submitted. Reporting time: varies, for contest 2 months after deadline. Payment: varies, discounts, copies. Interested in new or unpub'd poets: yes, for contests, all other ms. by invitation only. Simultaneous submissions accepted: if so noted. Recently published poets: Jack Collom, Kevin Griffith, Marjorie Saiser, Laura Towhee, Greg Kuzma. Submission quantity: send SASE for contest guidelines. Special interests: Tend not to be 'moved' by academic poems. Prefer poems written with psychological depth, and insight into the human condition. Like humorous poems as well as serious. Want to see poems that were written to survive, not as exercises.

THE BAFFLER, PO Box 378293, Chicago, IL 60637. Damon Krukowski, Jennifer Moxley. 1988. "We do not accept unsolicited poetry." circ. 30M. 3/yr. Pub'd 10 poems 1999; expects 10 poems 2000, 10 poems 2001. sub. price: $20/4 issues; sample: $6. 128pp; 6x9; Rights purchased: all. Publishes 0% of poems submitted. Payment: yes. Interested in new or unpub'd poets: no. Simultaneous submissions accepted: no. Recent contributors: Charles Simic, Rosmarie Waldrop, Michael Warr. Submission quantity: 5.

BAKER STREET GAZETTE, Baker Street Publications, 577 Central Avenue, Box 4, Jefferson, LA 70121-1400, E-mail sherlockian@mailcity.com, sherlockian@england.com, www2.cybercities.com/z/zines/. Sharida Rizzuto, Editor; Harold Tollison, Associate Editor; Ann Hoyt, Assistant Editor; Rose Dalton, Assistant Editor. 1983. "This publication is devoted to Sherlock Holmes and Victoriana. All submissions must be double-spaced and typewritten" circ. 500. 2/yr. Pub'd 10-20 poems 1999. sub. price: $13.80; sample: $6.90. 80pp; 8½x11; Rights purchased: one-time rights, first serial rights, or second serial rights. Publishes 30% of poems submitted. Deadlines: always open to submissions. Reporting time: 2-6 weeks. Payment: free copy only. Interested in new or unpub'd poets: yes. Simultaneous submissions accepted: yes. Recent contributors: Bruce E. Newling, Tom Galusha, Walter P. Armstrong, Carl Buchanan, Robert R. Hentz. Submission quantity: 1-5. Special interests: We are willing to look at any type of poetry. No length requirements.

Baker Street Publications (see also BAKER STREET GAZETTE; SLEUTH JOURNAL; JACK THE RIPPER GAZETTE; PEN & INK WRITERS JOURNAL), 577 Central Avenue, Box 4, Jefferson, LA 70121-1400, E-mail sherlockian@mailcity.com, sherlockian@england.com, www2.cybercities.com/z/zines/. Sharida Rizzuto, Senior Editor; Harold Tollison, Associate Editor; Ann Hoyt, Assistant Editor; Rose Dalton, Assistant Editor. 1983. "Approximately 5-10 pages per issue of each of our quarterly journals is devoted to poetry. Our publications cover mystery and Sherlock Holmes, Victoriana, Jack the Ripper. All submissions must be double-spaced and typewritten. A SASE must be included. We also publish poetry chapbooks. Always open to submissions" avg. press run 300-800. Pub'd 20 poetry titles 1999; expects 20 poetry titles 2000, 20 poetry titles 2001. 8½x11; avg. price, paper: $4.90-$7.90. 50-60pp; Publishes 30% of poetry manuscripts submitted. Reporting time: 2-6 weeks. Payment: negotiable fee plus free copy/s for non-fiction, free copy/s only for poetry and fiction. Interested in new or unpub'd poets: yes. Simultaneous submissions accepted: yes. Recently published poets: Margarita Perez Beltran, John Youril, George Chadderdon, Leilah Wendell, Kim Elizabeth. Submission quantity: 1-5. Special interests: We are willing to look at any type of poetry. There are no length requirements.

THE BALTIMORE REVIEW, PO Box 410, Riderwood, MD 21139, 410-377-5265, Fax 410-377-4325, E-mail hdiehl@bcpl.net. 1996. "Read year-round, no themes, material suitable for a literary journal and not better suited elsewhere. Our poetry editor varies, we have 2-3 reviewers per issue." 2/yr. Pub'd 40 poems 1999; expects 40 poems 2000, 40 poems 2001. sub. price: $14; sample: $8 incl. p/h. 128pp; 6x9; Rights purchased: first-time. Deadlines: March 1st for summer issue, September 1st for winter issue. Payment: 2 copies and reduced rate for add'l copies. Recent contributors: Julia Wendell, Clarinda Harriss, Lyn Lifshin, Simon Perchik, Gary Stein. Submission quantity: 1-5.

BAMBOO RIDGE, Journal of Hawai'i Literature and Arts, Bamboo Ridge Press, PO Box 61781, Honolulu, HI 96839-1781. Eric Chock. 1978. "We welcome unsolicited submissions for our regular issues which alternate with special issues—focusing on specific themes, or individual writers or groups of writers. Submissions should be typed, accompanied by SASE." circ. 600-1M. 2/yr. Pub'd 30 poems 1999; expects 30 poems 2000, 30 poems 2001. sub. price: $20 individual, $25 institutions; sample: $10. 125-200pp; 6x9; Rights purchased: none. Publishes 10% of poems submitted. Deadlines: varies, submissions are considered for next appropriate issue. Reporting time: 3-6 months. Payment: 2 copies of the issue, $10 per poem. Interested in new or unpub'd poets: yes. Simultaneous submissions accepted: no. Recent contributors: Juliet Kono, Wing Tek Lum, Lois-Ann Yamanaka, Joseph Stanton, Albert Saijo. Submission quantity: 1-5. Special interests: Emphasis on poetry by and/or about Hawaii's people.

Bamboo Ridge Press (see also BAMBOO RIDGE, Journal of Hawai'i Literature and Arts), PO Box 61781, Honolulu, HI 96839-1781, 808-626-1481 phone/Fax, brinfo@bambooridge.com. Eric Chock. 1978. avg. press run 1M. Pub'd 1 poetry title 1999. 6×9; avg. price, paper: $10. 90pp; Reporting time: 6 months. Interested in new or unpub'd poets: no, recommend poets send material to *Bamboo Ridge, Journal of Hawaii's Literature and Arts*. Simultaneous submissions accepted: no. Recently published poets: Wing Tek Lum, Juliet Kono, Eric Chock, Albert Saijo, Lois-Ann Yamanaka. Submission quantity: 1-5 poems. Special interests: Poetry by and/or about Hawaii's people.

Bank Street Press, 24 Bank Street, New York, NY 10014, 212-255-0692. Mary Bertschmann. 1984. avg. press run 300. Pub'd 2 poetry titles 1999; expects 2 poetry titles 2000, 2 poetry titles 2001. 5½×8½; avg. price, paper: $6. 96pp; Reporting time: 3 weeks. Payment: negotiable. Interested in new or unpub'd poets: yes. Simultaneous submissions accepted: yes. Recently published poets: Mary York Sampson, Maurice Hart, Isabelle Kellogg, Luc van Wambeke. Submission quantity: 3.

THE BANNER, 2850 Kalamazoo SE, Grand Rapids, MI 49560, 616-224-0819. 1865. "We are a denominational biweekly published by the Christian Reformed Church in North America" circ. 30M. 26/yr. Pub'd 5 poems 1999; expects 5 poems 2000, 5 poems 2001. sub. price: $36.95. 39pp; 8½×11; Rights purchased: first. Publishes a very small % of poems submitted. Deadlines: none. Reporting time: 8 weeks. Payment: $40/poem. Interested in new or unpub'd poets: yes. Simultaneous submissions accepted: no. Recent contributors: James Pecquet, Peg De Boer, Margaret Wiedyke, Sylvia Cooper, Mike Vanden Bosch. Submission quantity: 2-3.

Banshee Press (see also ONE TRICK PONY), PO Box 11186, Philadelphia, PA 19136-6186. Louis McKee. 1997. "Manuscripts are by invitation" avg. press run 400. Pub'd 1 poetry title 1999. 5½×8½; avg. price, paper: $6. 32pp; Interested in new or unpub'd poets: no. Recently published poets: Harry Humes, Vivian Shipley, Tom Devaney.

Bard Press (see also WATERWAYS: Poetry in the Mainstream), 393 St. Paul's Avenue, Staten Island, NY 10304-2127, 718-442-7429. Richard Spiegel. 1974. avg. press run 300. Pub'd 1 poetry title 1999; expects 1 poetry title 2000, 1 poetry title 2001. 4×5½; avg. price, paper: $5. 32pp; Publishes 10% of poetry manuscripts submitted. Reporting time: 2 months. Payment: 100 copies + 10% of cover price. Interested in new or unpub'd poets: no, acceptance is by invitation. Simultaneous submissions accepted: no. Recently published poets: Ilsa Gilbert, Albert Huffstickler, Ida Fasel, Joanne Seltzer, Joy Hewitt Mann. Submission quantity: 0.

Bardsong Press, PO Box 775396, Steamboat Springs, CO 80477, 970-870-1401, fax 970-879-2657. Ann Gilpin. 1997. "All poetry should have Celtic themes" avg. press run 500. Expects 1 poetry title 2000, 1 poetry title 2001. 6×9; avg. price, paper: $11.95. 64pp; Publishes 1% of poetry manuscripts submitted. Reporting time: 4 weeks. Payment: varies. Interested in new or unpub'd poets: yes. Simultaneous submissions accepted: yes. Submission quantity: poet's discretion.

THE BAREFOOT POET: Journal of Poetry, Fiction, Essays, & Art, Writers House Press, PO Box 52, Pisgah, IA 51564-0052, 712-456-2132; stmike-press@saint-mike.org. John-Paul Ignatius, O.L.S.M., Publisher & Editor. 1994. "Not accepting manuscripts at this time. *The Barefoot Poet* welcomes new and unestablished poets. Fiction, essays and art accepted, too. All manuscripts will be critiqued and returned unless you are uninterested in feedback. Even if your poem is rejected at first, after critique and revision a second or third draft may be accepted, thus providing a sort of mini poetry workshop experience. No light verse or haiku. Barefoot Poet and Writers House Press has been acquired by St. Michael's Press" 1/yr. Expects 30 poems 2000, 30 poems 2001. sub. price: $15; sample: $15. 64pp; 5½×8½; Rights purchased: one-time. Publishes 5-10% of poems submitted. Reporting time: 3 minutes to 3 months. Interested in new or unpub'd poets: yes. Simultaneous submissions accepted: yes. Submission quantity: 5-10.

●**BARK!**, PO Box 738, New York, NY 10025. 2000. circ. ca. 500. 4/yr. sub. price: $6; sample: free. 12pp; 7×8½.

Barking Dog Books, Centro De Mensajes, A.P. 48, Todos Santos, B.C.S. 23300, Mexico, fax 011-52-114-50288. 1996. 5½×8½.

BARNABE MOUNTAIN REVIEW, PO Box 529, Lagunitas, CA 94938. Gerald Fleming. 1995. "Seek directness, passion, craft, and music" circ. 500. 1/yr. sub. price: $10; sample: $10. 200+pp; 5½×8½; Deadlines: May 1 annually. Reporting time: 3 weeks. Payment: 2 copies. Interested in new or unpub'd poets: yes. Recent contributors: Diana O'Hehir, Peter Kunz, Lawrence Fixel, Bill Edmondson, Gillian Conoley. Special interests: Contemporary translations, accessible experimental prose poems.

BARNWOOD, The Barnwood Press, PO Box 146, Selma, IN 47383. Tom Koontz, Editor; Thom Tammaro, Editor. 1980. "SASE required. Good idea to buy a sample copy of magazine ($5.00). Our criterion is artistic excellence, but that does not rule out innovation; the fact that we have room for only 18 poems each year helps us maintain high standards. We want our subscribers to smile with anticipation when they find *Barnwood* in their mail" circ. 500. 3/yr. Expects 18 poems 2000, 18 poems 2001. sub. price: $15; sample: $5. 16pp; 8½×7; Rights purchased: First U.S. magazine only. Publishes 2% of poems submitted. Deadlines: September 1 through May 15. Reporting time: 1 month. Payment: $25 per poem + 5 copies. Interested in new or unpub'd poets: yes. Simultaneous submissions accepted: yes. Recent contributors: Robert Bly, Jared Carter, Siv Cedering, Marge Piercy, William Stafford. Submission quantity: 1-3. Special interests: This magazine does not offer room for a very long poem.

The Barnwood Press (see also BARNWOOD), PO Box 146, Selma, IN 47383. Tom Koontz, Editor; Thom Tammaro, Editor. 1975. "SASE required. Submit only September 1 through May 15. We have a chapbook series designed especially for the single long poem or sequence of closely related poems. Our criterion is artistic excellence, but that does not rule out experimentation or innovation. On the other hand, we have been saddened by the number of submissions that show no awareness of anything that has been done in American poetry" avg. press run 1M. Expects 2 poetry titles 2001. 6×9; avg. price, paper: $8; other: $15. 64pp; Publishes 5% of poetry manuscripts submitted. Reporting time: 1 day to 3 months. Payment: 10% of run, others available at cost. Interested in new or unpub'd poets: yes. Simultaneous submissions accepted: yes, if we are informed. Recently published poets: Robert Bly, Jared Carter, William Stafford, Patricia Goedicke, Alice Friman. Submission quantity: 3. Special interests: None.

BATH AVENUE NEWSLETTER (BATH), Vincent Laspina, 1980 65th Street #3D, Brooklyn, NY 11204, 718-331-5960; Fax 718-331-4997; E-mail Laspina@msn.con, VLaspina@wow.con. 1996. circ. 3M+. 12/yr. sub. price: $24; sample: $2.50. 16pp; 8½×11.

BATHTUB GIN, Pathwise Press, PO Box 2392, Bloomington, IN 47402, 812-323-2985. Christopher Harter, Tom Maxedon. 1997. "We read July 1-September 15: January 1-March 15. No confessions (nobody cares about your family) no unrequited love rantings (ditto). Include cover letter with bio." circ. 150. 2/yr. Pub'd 10 poems 1999; expects 20-25 poems 2000, 20-25 poems 2001. sub. price: $8; sample: $5. 60pp; 5½×8½; Publishes 10% of poems submitted. Deadlines: July 1st and January 1st. Reporting time: 1-2 months. Payment: one contributor's copy + discounts. Interested in new or unpub'd poets: yes. Simultaneous submissions accepted: yes. Recent contributors: Taylor Graham, Ken Waldman, Lyn Lifshin. Submission quantity: 3-5. Special interests: We are electic and use a wide range of styles.

William L. Bauhan, Publisher, PO Box 443, Dublin, NH 03444-0443, 603-563-8020. 1960. avg. press run 750-1M. Pub'd 3 poetry titles 1999; expects 4 poetry titles 2000, 5 poetry titles 2001. 5½×8½; avg. price, cloth: $12.95; paper: $8.95. 80pp; Publishes 10% of poetry manuscripts submitted. Reporting time: 6 weeks-2 months. Payment: varies, depending on market; straight royalty or purchase agreement. Interested in new or unpub'd poets: no. Simultaneous submissions accepted: yes. Recently published poets: May Sarton, Francis Blessington, Morris Earle, Sarah Singer, Jane Gillespie. Submission quantity: 6-8. Special interests: Emphasis on New England regional poets.

Bay Area Poets Coalition (see also POETALK), POETALK, PO Box 11435, Berkeley, CA 94712-2435, 510-272-9176. Dale Hermann. 1974. "Sufficiently stamped SASE/SASP insures communication. SASE required for notification. Shorter poems preferred, 40 lines maximum. Name and address on each page. No hand-printed or hand-written submissions accepted" avg. press run 400. Pub'd 600 poetry titles 1999; expects 600 poetry titles 2000, 600 poetry titles 2001. avg. price, paper: yearly anthology free to members. Write for price for extras; other: $15 membership, $6 subscription to *POETALK*, a bimonthly. Publishes 20-30% of poetry manuscripts submitted. Reporting time: 2-4 months. Payment: copy of issue in which poem is published. Interested in new or unpub'd poets: yes. Simultaneous submissions accepted: yes. Recently published poets: Carol Bardoff, James Garvey, Joyce Odam, J. Speer, John Elsberg. Submission quantity: Open: SASE with sufficient postage required. Special interests: Broad variety of styles and subjects. No doggerel, no prose poetry (no room). Will look at anything, but show some effort and talent.

BAY WINDOWS, 631 Tremont Street, Boston, MA 02118, 617-266-6670, X211. Rudy Kikel, Poetry Editor. 1983. circ. 60M. 51/yr. Pub'd 51 poems 1999; expects 51 poems 2000, 51 poems 2001. sub. price: $50; sample: $3 (includes p/h). 80pp; 10⅛×15½; Rights purchased: first. Publishes 10% of poems submitted. Deadlines: none, we publish every week. Reporting time: 2-3 months. Payment: copies. Interested in new or unpub'd poets: yes. Simultaneous submissions accepted: yes, if it's stated. Recent contributors: Judith Saunders, Walter Holland, Dennis Rhodes, Ron Mohring, Chrstina Hutchins. Submission quantity: 3-5 is ideal. Special interests: We're looking for short poems (1-36 lines) on themes of interest to gay men and lesbians.

BAYBURY REVIEW, 40 High Street, Highwood, IL 60040, e-mail baybury@flash.net. Janet (general and poetry editor) St. John. 1997. circ. 500. 1/yr. Pub'd 26 poems 1999; expects 19 poems 2000, 22 poems 2001.

sub. price: $8; sample: $7.25 (including p/h). 80-100pp; 5½×8½; Rights purchased: first serial. Publishes 5% of poems submitted. Deadlines: reading period is 6/1 to 12/1. Reporting time: 2-3 months. Payment: 2 copies. Interested in new or unpub'd poets: yes, if high quality. Simultaneous submissions accepted: if indicated. Recent contributors: Lyn Lifshin, Mark Halperin, Mary Crow, Patrick Lawler, Mikhammad Abdel-Ishara. Submission quantity: 3-5.

BB Books (see also GLOBAL TAPESTRY), 1 Spring Bank, Longsight Road, Copster Green, Blackburn, Lancs BB1 9EU, England, 0254 249128. Dave Cunliffe. 1963. "Poets whose work I like, but I'm unable or unwilling to publish their book manuscript, are asked to submit to *Global Tapestry Journal* magazine or one of our specialized irregular anthologies." avg. press run 600. Pub'd 4 poetry titles 1999; expects 4 poetry titles 2000, 4 poetry titles 2001. 8×6; avg. price, paper: $5. 40pp; Publishes 2% of poetry manuscripts submitted. Reporting time: as soon as possible. Payment: 10 copies per 100, half cover price for extra. Interested in new or unpub'd poets: yes. Simultaneous submissions accepted: sometimes. Recently published poets: Bill Wyatt, George Dowden, Michael Kelly. Submission quantity: book manuscript. Special interests: Beat to New Wave high energy work.

●**Beacon Light Publishing (BLP),** PO Box 1612, Thousand Oaks, CA 91358, 805-583-2002, toll free 888-771-1197. 1999. 5½×8½.

THE BEAR DELUXE, PO Box 10342, Portland, OR 97296, 503-242-1047, Fax 503-243-2645, bear@teleport.com. Steven Babcock, Regina Weaver. 1993. "Send SASE for guides and themes. One theme per year. 50 lines max." circ. 17M. 3/yr. Pub'd 10 poems 1999; expects 15 poems 2000, 20 poems 2001. sub. price: $16; sample: $3. 56pp; 11×14; Rights purchased: first time. Publishes 3% of poems submitted. Deadlines: none. Reporting time: 3-6 months. Payment: $10 per poem published, subscription, contributors copies and invitations to events. Interested in new or unpub'd poets: yes. Simultaneous submissions accepted: yes, but should be noted. Recent contributors: Judith Barrington, Robert Pyle, Brian Christopher Hamilton, Leann Grabel. Submission quantity: 3-5.

Bear Star Press, 185 Hollow Oak Drive, Cohasset, CA 95973, 530-891-0360, www.bearstarpress.com. Beth Spencer. 1996. "Good stuff early on in the manuscript keeps us reading" avg. press run 300-500. Pub'd 3 poetry titles 1999; expects 2 poetry titles 2000, 2-3 poetry titles 2001. 5½×8¼; avg. price, paper: $7-$12. Publishes 2% of poetry manuscripts submitted. Reporting time: 3-4 months. Payment: cash and copies. Interested in new or unpub'd poets: yes. Simultaneous submissions accepted: yes. Recently published poets: George Keithley, Deborah Woodard, Terri Drake, Gary Thompson, Muriel Nelson. Submission quantity: manuscript per contest guidelines.

Bearhouse Publishing (see also LUCIDITY), 398 Mundell Rd., Eureka Springs, AR 72631-8906, 501-253-9351, E-mail tbadger@ipa.net. Ted O. Badger, Editor. 1985. "We view our effort as co-operative publication: we try to get poets into print at minimum cost to them. We are primarily a press for self-publishing, but we do some promotion." avg. press run 100. Pub'd 17 poetry titles 1999; expects 12 poetry titles 2000, 10 poetry titles 2001. 5½×8½; avg. price, paper: $5-6. 40-50pp; Publishes 90% of poetry manuscripts submitted. Reporting time: 30 days. Interested in new or unpub'd poets: yes, but write for guidelines first. Simultaneous submissions accepted: yes. Recently published poets: Ann Talley Kinnaird, Marge Rogers, Marlene Meehl. Submission quantity: query first.

BEGINNINGS - A Magazine for the Novice Writer, PO Box 92-R, Shirley, NY 11967, 516-924-7826, scbeginnings@juno.com, www.scbeginnings.com. 1998. "Looking for poetry, 30 lines max." circ. 1M. 2/yr. sub. price: $9; sample: $3. 54pp; 8×10.

THE BELLINGHAM REVIEW, Signpost Press Inc., Mail Stop 9053, WWU, Bellingham, WA 98225, 360-650-3209. Bruce Beasley, Suzanne Paola. 1977. "We sponsor, annually, the 49th Parallel Poetry Contest. The prizes are $500, $250, and $150. Send SASE for details. We also sponsor the Tobias Wolff Award in Fiction and the Annie Dillard Award in nonfiction. Prizes $1000, $250, $150. Send SASE." circ. 2.5M. 2/yr. Pub'd 32 poems 1999; expects 50 poems 2000, 50 poems 2001. sub. price: $10/2 issues, $19/4 issues, $25/6 issues; sample: $5. 120pp; 5½×8½; Rights purchased: 1st N.A. serial rights. Publishes 5% of poems submitted. Deadlines: from October 1st to May 1st. Reporting time: 1-4 months. Payment: copy of issue and one year subscription. Interested in new or unpub'd poets: yes. Simultaneous submissions accepted: yes. Recent contributors: Albert Goldbarth, Timothy Liu, Cyrus Cassells, Charles Wright, Tess Gallagher. Submission quantity: 3-6.

BELLOWING ARK, Bellowing Ark Press, PO Box 55564, Shoreline, WA 98155, 206-440-0791. Robert R. Ward. 1984. "*Bellowing Ark* prefers truth to polish, honesty to gloss. We are interested in long poems, narrative poems, and are not averse to well-executed formal poems." circ. 1M+. 6/yr. Pub'd 240 poems 1999; expects 240 poems 2000, 240 poems 2001. sub. price: $15; sample: SASE (9 X 12 please) with $1.25 postage, or $3. 32pp; 11½×16; Rights purchased: first reprint. Publishes .5% of poems submitted. Deadlines: continuous. Reporting time: 6-10 weeks. Payment: 2 copies of issue containing contribution. Interested in new or unpub'd poets: yes. Simultaneous submissions accepted: NO!! Recent contributors: Elizabeth Biller Chapman, Muriel Karr, P.F. Allen, Rita Ott, Irene Culver. Submission quantity: 3-5. Special interests: *Bellowing Ark* is interested in poetry which explores the human, the affirmative, poetry which transcends pain and opposition. We are particularly interested in long narrative poems.

Bellowing Ark Press (see also BELLOWING ARK), PO Box 55564, Shoreline, WA 98155, 206-440-0791. Robert R Ward. 1987. "Not presently interested in unsolicited submissions." avg. press run 500. Pub'd 5 poetry titles 1999; expects 5 poetry titles 2000, 5 poetry titles 2001. 6×9; avg. price, paper: $4-$20. 48-192pp; Payment: at present, 10% of net. Interested in new or unpub'd poets: no. Simultaneous submissions accepted: no. Recently published poets: Margaret Hodge, L.L. Ollivier, Rachael Dacus, Suey Irvine, David Athey. Special interests: Autobiographical poetry, long + narrative poems, nature poetry.

BELOIT POETRY JOURNAL, 24 Berry Cove Road, Lamoine, ME 04605, 207-667-5598. Marion K. Stocking. 1950. "We are looking for strong poems on the growing tip of contemporary poetry. Poets should be familiar with the magazine. Advice for contributors available for SASE or with sample copy." circ. 1.2M. 4/yr. Pub'd 75 poems 1999; expects 63 poems 2000, 70 poems 2001. sub. price: $18; sample: $5. 48pp; 6×9; Rights purchased: first serial. Publishes .7% of poems submitted. Deadlines: none. Reporting time: immediately to 4 months. Payment: 3 copies. Interested in new or unpub'd poets: yes. Simultaneous submissions accepted: no. Recent contributors: Lola Haskins, Albert Goldbarth, Bei Dao, A.E. Stallings, Sherman Alexie. Submission quantity: as many as will go for 33¢, more or less. Special interests: We have wide-ranging tastes and no taboos. We will consider translations, experimental poetry, regional poetry, long poems, light verse, satire, etc., but it should be first-rate of its kind.

Bennett & Kitchel, PO Box 4422, East Lansing, MI 48826. 1990. avg. press run 600. Expects 2 poetry titles 2000. 5½×8½; avg. price, cloth: $10. 68pp; Publishes 2% of poetry manuscripts submitted. Reporting time: 2 weeks. Payment: negotiable. Interested in new or unpub'd poets: yes. Simultaneous submissions accepted: yes. Recently published poets: Anthony Lombardy, Rhina P. Espaillat, Troxey Kemper. Submission quantity: 8-12, fewer or more.

BERKELEY POETRY REVIEW, 201 MLK Student Union, University of California, Berkeley, CA 94720. Patricia Johnson, Editor. 1973. "We accept submissions Sept. 1-March 1. Reporting time, however, is dependent on when we receive manuscripts in relation to when most recent issue was published" circ. 750. 1/yr. Pub'd 100+ poems 1999. sub. price: $10. 120-150pp; 5½×8½; Publishes roughly 10% of poems submitted. Reporting time: 120-180 days. Payment: contributor's copies. Interested in new or unpub'd poets: yes. Simultaneous submissions accepted: yes. Recent contributors: Czeslaw Milosz, Robert Hass, Robert Pinsky, Thom Gunn, Leonord Nathan. Submission quantity: 5 or less. Special interests: Our interests are relatively broad. In the past, we have published many types of poetry, including translations, 'experimental' works and occasional 'longpoems'. We have not, to my knowledge, published any 'light verse' or any poems running over 7 printed pages.

THE BERKELEY REVIEW OF BOOKS, 1731 10th Street, Apt. A, Berkeley, CA 94710, 415-528-8713. H.D. Moe, Editor; Florence Windfall, Publisherz & Managing Editor. 1988. "No contests, no themes, clearly typed or written poems, stories, reviews will be read year around" circ. 500-1M. 1/yr. Pub'd 2 poems 1999. sub. price: $20/4 issues; sample: $10. 100-150pp; 8½×11; Rights purchased: copyright reverts to author. Publishes 1% of poems submitted. Deadlines: open year round. Reporting time: 3 months. Payment: none. Interested in new or unpub'd poets: yes. Simultaneous submissions accepted: yes. Recent contributors: Judith Tannen, Stanley McNail, Geoffrey Cook, Phyllis Stowell, Nanos Valaoritis. Submission quantity: 10. Special interests: all schools, kinds, forms of poetry including translations.

BGB Press, Inc. (see also THE PANNUS INDEX), 160 King Street, Northampton, MA 01060-2336, www.home.earthlink.net/~bgbpress. Vincent Bator, Leonard Anno. 1996. "We will be changing our format to an online journal, see website for info." avg. press run 500. Pub'd 25 poetry titles 1999. 5½×8½; avg. price, paper: $8. 104pp; Publishes 2% of poetry manuscripts submitted. Reporting time: 4 months. Payment: comp. copy. Interested in new or unpub'd poets: sure. Simultaneous submissions accepted: no. Recently published poets: Errol Miller, Richard Kostelanetz, David Catron, Fernand Roqueplan, Alan Britt. Submission quantity: 2-3.

●**BIBLIOPHILOS,** 200 Security Building, Fairmont, WV 26554, 304-366-8107. Gerald J. Bobango, Editor. 1982. "We read submissions Sept. 1 through April 1; query for guidelines and send for sample issue *before* sending material. Annual poetry contest." circ. 300-400. 4/yr. Pub'd 24 poems 1999; expects 60 poems 2000, 60 poems 2001. sub. price: $18, $35/2 years; sample: $5.25. 72pp; 5¾×8½; Rights purchased: 1st North American rights. Publishes 25% of poems submitted. Deadlines: Sept. 1 through March 1. Reporting time: 30 days. Payment: $5-$20, free copy, offprints. Interested in new or unpub'd poets: yes. Simultaneous submissions accepted: yes. Recent contributors: Lenore M. Coberly, Conrad Geller, Louis Phillips, Lois Greene Stone, Jodi Varon. Submission quantity: 5. Special interests: We welcome translations, regional or 'local color' work, poems with anti-state, anti-political correctness; no vulgarity or drug culture stuff. Poems celebrating individualism, animals, scholarship and academics.

BIG SCREAM, Nada Press, 2782 Dixie S.W., Grandville, MI 49418, 616-531-1442. David Cope. 1974. "Objectivist bias; prefer short 10-30 line works. Poetry written on the street and that retains concern for the planet and its occupants. Publish in January; submit after July." circ. 100. 1/yr. Pub'd 30 poems 1999; expects 30 poems 2000, 30 poems 2001. sub. price: $5; sample: $5. 35pp; 8½×11; Publishes maximum of 5% of poems submitted. Reporting time: 1 day - 1 month. Payment: copies. Interested in new or unpub'd poets: yes. Simultaneous submissions accepted: yes. Recent contributors: Marcia Arrieta, Allen Ginsberg, Anne Waldman, Jim Cohn, Antler. Submission quantity: 10.

Big Star Press, 1770 48th Avenue, #2-D, Capitola, CA 95010, 408-464-3625 ph/fax. 1996. 5½×8½.

Bilingual Review/Press (see also BILINGUAL REVIEW/Revista Bilingue), Hispanic Research Center, Arizona State Univ., Box 872702, Tempe, AZ 85287-2702, 602-965-3867. 1976. avg. press run 2M. Pub'd 2 poetry titles 1999; expects 3 poetry titles 2000, 3 poetry titles 2001. 5½×8½; avg. price, paper: $9. 96pp; Publishes 5% of poetry manuscripts submitted. Reporting time: 2 months. Payment: 10% royalty on net sales price, with advance on royalties; this applies to single-authored books; royalty is divided if multi-authored book and paid in October. Interested in new or unpub'd poets: yes. Simultaneous submissions accepted: no. Recently published poets: Marjorie Agosin, Leroy V. Quintana, Alurista, Gustavo Perez Firmat, Judith Ortiz Cofer. Submission quantity: 5. Special interests: Our interest is limited to poetry by United States Hispanics and, very occasionally, bilingual editions of Latin American poets of interest to United States Hispanics.

BILINGUAL REVIEW/Revista Bilingue, Bilingual Review/Press, Hispanic Research Center, Arizona State Univ., Box 872702, Tempe, AZ 85287-2702, 602-965-3867. 1974. circ. 1M. 3/yr. Pub'd 10 poems 1999; expects 10 poems 2000, 10 poems 2001. sub. price: $35 institutions, $21 individuals; sample: $13 institutions; $7 individuals. 96pp; 7×10; Rights purchased: we don't buy anything; we publish only previously unpublished poems and copyright in our name. Publishes 5% of poems submitted. Deadlines: none. Reporting time: 2 months. Payment: 2 complimentary copies of issue. Interested in new or unpub'd poets: yes. Simultaneous submissions accepted: no. Recent contributors: Martin Espada, Marjorie Agosin, Alberto Rios, Judith Ortiz Cofer, Demetria Martinez. Submission quantity: 5. Special interests: Our interest is limited to poetry by or about United States Hispanics. We do not publish translations. The *Bilingual Review* is a scholarly/literary journal that contains a section of creative literature; occasionally we publish special issues devoted exclusively to creative literature.

Birch Brook Press, PO Box 81, Delhi, NY 13753, 212-353-3326 editorial messages only, Phone & Fax orders & sales inquiries 607-746-7453, birchbrkpr@prodigy.net, www.birchbrookpress.com. Tom Tolnay. 1982. "Birch Brook Press operates a letterpress print shop and uses monies from typesetting/printing/designing for other publishers to bring out a few books of quality poetry and fiction on a co-op basis. Our anthologies are done on a project-by-project basis, and we solicit material for each." avg. press run 250-1M. Pub'd 3 poetry titles 1999; expects 2 poetry titles 2000, 3 poetry titles 2001. 5½×8½, 6×9; avg. price, cloth: $25-30; paper: $12-$19; other: $35-$100 limited edition. 56-164pp; Reporting time: 3-8 weeks. Payment: varies. Simultaneous submissions accepted: if indicated as such. Recently published poets: Joel Chace, Jesse Glass, Stanley Nelson, Elisabeth Stevens, Jeffrey Thomson. Submission quantity: inquiry letter plus 4-6 poems. Special interests: The very best we can find.

BIRMINGHAM POETRY REVIEW, English Department, University of Alabama-Birmingham, Birmingham, AL 35294, 205-934-8573. Robert Collins, Co-Editor; Adam Vines, Co-Editor. 1988. "No cover letters please. We are not impressed by publication history. No resumes." circ. 600. 2/yr. Pub'd 70-80 poems 1999; expects 70-80 poems 2000, 70-80 poems 2001. sub. price: $4; sample: $2. 50pp; 6×9; Rights purchased: first only. Publishes less than 1% of poems submitted. Deadlines: November 1st and May 1st, but we read all year round. Reporting time: 3-6 months. Payment: 2 copies plus a one year subscription. Interested in new or unpub'd poets: yes. Simultaneous submissions accepted: no. Recent contributors: Richard Hague, Walter McDonald, D.C. Berry, Joanne Lowery, Ron Wallace. Submission quantity: 3-5. Special interests: Regional poetry.

BIRTHKIT NEWSLETTER, PO Box 2672, Eugene, OR 97402, 503-344-7438. 1994. 4/yr. sub. price: $20. 12pp; 8½×11.

BITTER OLEANDER, 4983 Tall Oaks Drive, Fayetteville, NY 13066-9776, FAX 315-637-5056, E-mail bones44@ix.netcom.com. Paul B. Roth, Editor and Publisher. 1974. "Contest: Francis Locke Poetry Award (send SASE for guidelines) $500 award" circ. 1500. 2/yr. Expects 150 poems 2000, 150 poems 2001. sub. price: $15; sample: $8. 128pp; 6×9; Publishes 1% of poems submitted. Deadlines: every month but July. Reporting time: 1-3 months. Payment: 1 copy. Interested in new or unpub'd poets: yes. Simultaneous submissions accepted: no. Recent contributors: Robert Bly, Simon Perchik, Silvia Scheibli, Duane Locke, Alan Britt, Charles Wright. Submission quantity: 5-8. Special interests: Translations.

24

BkMk Press, University of Missouri-Kansas City, 5100 Rockhill, University House, Kansas City, MO 64110, 816-235-2558; FAX 816-235-2611; freemank@smtpgate.ssb.umkc.edu. James McKinley, Editor-in-Chief. 1971. "Manuscripts should be accompanied by a SASE. We publish poetry of the highest literary quality. We're interested in Midwestern writers, but we do not limit ourselves to publishing only Midwesterners" avg. press run 750. Pub'd 2 poetry titles 1999; expects 4 poetry titles 2000, 4 poetry titles 2001. 5½x8½; avg. price, cloth: $10; paper: $7; other: $3 chapbooks. 64pp; Publishes 5% of poetry manuscripts submitted. Reporting time: 16 weeks. Payment: varies. Interested in new or unpub'd poets: yes. Simultaneous submissions accepted: yes, if poet specifies this. Recently published poets: John Knoepfle, Peter Simpson, Bruce Cutler, Harry Martinson, Mbembe Milton Smith. Submission quantity: 10 poems, up to 20 pages. Special interests: Publish a translation series, regional as well as non-regional poetry.

Blacfax, Midtown Station, PO Box 542, New York, NY 10018.

Black Bear Publications (see also BLACK BEAR REVIEW), 1916 Lincoln Street, Croydon, PA 19021-8026, BBReview@earthlink.net, http://home.earthlink.net/~BBReview. Ave Jeanne, Editor. 1984. "We suggest that poets read current issues to stay abreast with chapbook needs and submissions for the review. Please keep introductory letters brief and use SASE. Make sure name and address appear clearly on each submission page. Handwritten cover letters are not read if they are not legible. Submissions should be sent via e-mail." avg. press run 500. Pub'd 2 poetry titles 1999. 5½x8½; avg. price, paper: $5. 34pp; Publishes 5% of poetry manuscripts submitted. Reporting time: 2 weeks. Payment: copy. Interested in new or unpub'd poets: yes. Simultaneous submissions accepted: no. Recently published poets: John Grey, Rick Duffey, David Stone, Livio Farallo, A.D. Winans. Submission quantity: 5. Special interests: Social/political.

BLACK BEAR REVIEW, Black Bear Publications, Black Bear Publications, 1916 Lincoln Street, Croydon, PA 19021, E-mail BBReview@earthlink.net, http://home.earthlink.net/~BBReview. Ave Jeanne, Editor; Ron Zettlemoyer, Associate Editor. 1984. "Submissions by e-mail only. We like to see poetry that is potent and brief. Forms used are avant-garde, free verse and haiku. We would like to see artwork in black & white, signed by author. Artists published: Wayne Hogan, Robert Bixby, George Myers, Jr.We have a poetry contest annually" circ. 500. 2/yr. Expects 150 poems 2000, 150 poems 2001. sub. price: $12; sample: $6. 64pp; 5½x8½; Rights purchased: first rights. Publishes 5% of poems submitted. Deadlines: continuous. Reporting time: 1 week. Payment: contributor copy. Interested in new or unpub'd poets: yes. Simultaneous submissions accepted: no. Recent contributors: A.D. Winans, Robert King, R.M. Host, John Sullivan, Sean Thomas Dougherty. Submission quantity: 5. Special interests: We are partial to topics on: the environment, social concern, war/peace & human gut emotion, but read all submissions with objectivity. Degrees and past publications do not sway us. It's not enough to send the correct topic; study style and format. Wide poems are usually passed over. No traditional poems are considered. Nothing religious. No bumper stickers.

BLACK BOUGH, 188 Grove Street #1, Somerville, NJ 08876. Charles Easter, Editor. 1991. circ. 200. 3/yr. Pub'd 225 poems 1999; expects 225 poems 2000, 225 poems 2001. sub. price: $16.50; sample: $6. 30pp; 4¼x5½; Rights purchased: first rights only. Publishes 5% of poems submitted. Deadlines: none. Reporting time: 1-3 months. Payment: $1 for each verse, up to $4 for sequence or long poem. No contributor's copies, except in cases of financial hardship. Interested in new or unpub'd poets: yes. Simultaneous submissions accepted: no. Recent contributors: Jim Kacian, Emily Romano, Lee Gurga. Submission quantity: 10. Special interests: Haiku and related poetry.

Black Buzzard Press (see also VISIONS-INTERNATIONAL, The World Journal of Illustrated Poetry; BLACK BUZZARD REVIEW), 1007 Ficklen Road, Fredericksburg, VA 22405. Bradley R. Strahan. 1979. "We publish only by prior arrangement, after we have developed a working relationship with the poet (usually our solicitation). We only publish poets whose work has often appeared in our magazine *Visions*. Costs of publication are usually shared." avg. press run 450. Expects 1 poetry title 2001. 5½x8½; avg. price, paper: $5. Pages vary; Publishes .05% of poetry manuscripts submitted. Reporting time: 2-4 weeks. Payment: poet usually receives 75% of the books printed if costs are shared. Interested in new or unpub'd poets: yes, but only by prior arrangement. Simultaneous submissions accepted: no. Recently published poets: Karlis Freivalds, Lane Jennings, Larry Couch, Michael Mott, Deborah Tannen. Submission quantity: 5-8 but must query first and should read a copy of one of our books. Special interests: We only publish unified, mature work that is deep and yet accessible. No regional or experimental work. No poems in excess of 4 double-spaced, typed pages. No sentimental, purely religious or light verse. No dry academic word games.

BLACK BUZZARD REVIEW, Black Buzzard Press, 1007 Ficklen Road, Fredericksburg, VA 22045. Bradley R. Strahan. 1988. "Please don't send us sentimental, old fashioned, religious or commonplace poems. Prefer not more than 30 lines per poem, *no more* than 6 poems." circ. 300. 1/yr. Pub'd 150 poems 1999; expects 155 poems 2000, 155 poems 2001. sub. price: $3.50 when added to a subscription to *Visions-International* (no separate subscription); sample: $4. 32pp; 8½x11; Rights purchased: 1st only. Publishes 5% of poems submitted. Reporting time: 2 weeks - 2 months. Payment: 1 copy. Interested in new or unpub'd poets: no. Simultaneous submissions accepted: no. Recent contributors: Laurel Speer, Diane Glancy,

Barbara Lefcowitz, Gerald Locklin, Elizabeth Bartlett. Submission quantity: 3-6. Special interests: All kinds from rhyme to 'far out' but no so-called 'typographical' or concrete poems.

BLACK CROSS, 3121 Corto Place #2, Long Beach, CA 90803, 562-987-4305; wstien@csulb.edu. Jim Guess, Erik Jensen. 1995. "Our website recently was voted best poetry website, we are planning an issue devoted to love poems, cute poet chicks send nude photos with submissions." circ. 250-300. 2/yr. Pub'd 150 poems 1999; expects 200 poems 2000. sub. price: $4; sample: $2. 70pp; 4¼×5½; Rights purchased: first time. Publishes 5% of poems submitted. Deadlines: no deadlines, we accept year round. Reporting time: 1 week to 6 months, depending on how much coffee we have. Payment: 1 copy. Interested in new or unpub'd poets: yes. Simultaneous submissions accepted: no. Recent contributors: Patrick Mackinnon, Antler, Daniel Crocker, R. Eirik Ott, Caron Andregg. Submission quantity: 2-5. Special interests: We pretty much like anything that kicks ass, rock n' rolls, or involves sodomy or lesbianism.

Black Dress Press (see also SPINNING JENNY), PO Box 213, Village Station, New York, NY 10014, website www.blackdresspress.com. C.E. Harrison, Editor. 1994. avg. press run 1M. Pub'd 1 poetry title 1999; expects 1 poetry title 2000, 2 poetry titles 2001. 5¼×9½; avg. price, paper: $6. 70pp; Publishes 5% of poetry manuscripts submitted. Reporting time: 8 weeks. Payment: complimentary copies. Interested in new or unpub'd poets: yes. Simultaneous submissions accepted: no. Recently published poets: Matthew Lippman, Renee Sedliar, m loncar, Sarah Messer, Michael Morse. Submission quantity: 5. Special interests: experimental poetry.

Black Hat Press (see also RAG MAG), Box 12, Goodhue, MN 55027, 651-923-4590. Beverly Voldseth, Editor. 1989. "We work closely with poets. They have contact with process from beginning to end. Just remember a high quality finished ms. + SASE. We have books planned for this year. We're not soliciting any book ms. for the time being, but queries are always in order." avg. press run 500-1M. Pub'd 1 poetry title 1999; expects 2 poetry titles 2000. 5½×8½; avg. price, paper: $10. 50pp; Publishes 1% of poetry manuscripts submitted. Reporting time: 1 month. Payment: negotiable. Interested in new or unpub'd poets: not until further notice. Simultaneous submissions accepted: yes. Recently published poets: Patrick McKinnon, Pierre Garnier, Diane Glancy, Ellen Kort, Tom Hennen. Special interests: I would be thrilled with translations, especially from Norwegian women poets. I'm open to anything vivid, alive. Poems that tell stories.

BLACK JACK & VALLEY GRAPEVINE, Seven Buffaloes Press, Box 249, Big Timber, MT 59011. Art Coelho. 1973. "A lot of the time a poet sends a stamp with an envelope, but he or she might have from 8-10 pages of poems - and one stamp won't cover that. Four pages for one stamp; nine pages for the second ounce is a good rule of thumb. I am doing a yearly anthology issue on the Southern Appalachian Mountains." circ. 750. 1/yr. Pub'd 100 poems 1999; expects 100 poems 2000, 100 poems 2001. sample price: $7.75. 80pp; 5½×8½; Rights purchased: first serial rights. Publishes 10% of poems submitted. Deadlines: none. Reporting time: 1 day-2 weeks. Payment: copies. Interested in new or unpub'd poets: yes. Simultaneous submissions accepted: no. Recent contributors: Jim Wayne Miller, Simon Ortiz, Laurel Speer, Steven Levi, Bob Warden. Submission quantity: 4-12. Special interests: I publish rural poetry, farm and ranch, especially material from the Southern Appalachian region. In the case of the Appalachias, I publish Hill and Holler poems. In other words, my focus is on land and people themes; heritage, the working man, The American Indian and The American Hobo. Poets with a Dustbowl heritage.

BLACK LACE, BLK Publishing Company, PO Box 83912, Los Angeles, CA 90083, 310-410-0808, fax 310-410-9250, e-mail newsroom@blk.com. Alycee J. Lane. 1991. "*Black Lace* is currently on hiatus." circ. 9M. 4/yr. Expects 20 poems 2000, 20 poems 2001. sub. price: $20; sample: $7. 48pp; 8⅛×10⅞; Publishes 10% of poems submitted. Reporting time: 4 weeks. Payment: varies. Interested in new or unpub'd poets: yes. Simultaneous submissions accepted: yes, if told. Submission quantity: 5. Special interests: black lesbian.

BLACK MOON, 233 Northway Road, Reisterstown, MD 21136, 410-833-9424. Alan Britt, Editor& Publisher; Silvia Scheibli, West Coast Editor. 1994. "Socially aware poetry" circ. 2M. 1/yr. Pub'd 100 poems 1999. sub. price: $8.95 + $1.75(S & H); sample: $8.95 + $1.75(S & H). 224pp; 6×9; Rights purchased: none. Publishes 5% of poems submitted. Deadlines: Reading: year round. Reporting time: 2 months. Payment: contributor's copy. Interested in new or unpub'd poets: yes. Simultaneous submissions accepted: yes. Recent contributors: Robert Bly, Duane Locke, Colette Inez, Louis Simpson, Ira Sadoff. Special interests: Translations, surrealism, experimental, long poems, Dada.

Black Sparrow Press, 24 Tenth Street, Santa Rosa, CA 95401. Michele Filshie. 1966. "Black Sparrow Press publishes avant garde poetry, prose, and literary critism. Please request our catalogue and be familiar with the authors we publish if you care to submit a manuscript" avg. press run 4M. Pub'd 4 poetry titles 1999; expects 4 poetry titles 2000, 4 poetry titles 2001. 6×9; avg. price, cloth: $17.50; paper: $9; other: (signed) $27.50. 190pp; Publishes 2% of poetry manuscripts submitted. Reporting time: 60 days. Interested in new or unpub'd poets: yes, if they understand our publishing program. Simultaneous submissions accepted: yes. Recently published poets: Diane Wakoski,Charles Bukowski, Clayton Eshleman, David Bromige, John Wieners.

●**Black Spring Press (see also BLACK SPRING REVIEW),** 63-89 Saunders Street #6G, Rego Park, NY

11374. 1997. 5½×8½.

●BLACK SPRING REVIEW, Black Spring Press, 63-89 Saunders Street #6G, Rego Park, NY 11374. 1997. circ. 100. 4-5/yr. sub. price: $20; sample: $5. 28pp; 5½×8½.

Black Thistle Press, 491 Broadway, New York, NY 10012, 212-219-1898. 1990. ''We are very small, very limited, but very dedicated'' avg. press run 1000. Pub'd 2 poetry titles 1999. 7×9, varies; avg. price, paper: $12. 150pp; Reporting time: 2 months. Payment: individual, book by book. Simultaneous submissions accepted: yes with SASE. Recently published poets: Jonas Mekas, Judith Morley, Vyt Balcaitis. Submission quantity: 5-10.

Black Tie Press, PO Box 440004, Houston, TX 77244-0004, 713-789-5119 fax. Peter Gravis, Publisher-Editor; John Dunivent, Art Consultant; Harry Burrus, Associate Editor & Designer. 1986. ''We want to see dynamic, exciting writing. If it is narrative, it must be unusual. It should disturb, shock, or certainly provoke. We like surreal, sensual, erotic lingerings. The work may be opaque or abstract, it must rivit the reader. We are not interested in the academic. We prefer writers who have experienced life, who have traveled and whose job record is layered. We like to use photographs and artwork of our authors. Send artwork with manuscript. Manuscripts should be 30-50+ poems. We don't want to receive rhymed poetry. We are not like a university press or the commercial presses. This pleases us.'' avg. press run 250-2M. Pub'd 1 poetry title 1999; expects 3 poetry titles 2000, 3-4 poetry titles 2001. 6×9, 5½×8½; avg. price, cloth: $19.95, signed limited edition are more $30, $45 with a photo by the author; paper: $10.50-$20; other: $28 lettered limited edition. 40-112pp; Publishes less than 1% of poetry manuscripts submitted. Reporting time: right away, but may not be able to read the ms. for 2 months depending on backlog. Payment: percentage of press run. Interested in new or unpub'd poets: yes. Simultaneous submissions accepted: yes. Recently published poets: Craig Cotter, Donald Rawley, Jenny Kelly, Laura Ryder, Steve Wilson. Submission quantity: complete ms., 30-60 poems.

THE BLACK WARRIOR REVIEW, PO Box 862936, University of Alabama, Tuscaloosa, AL 35486-0027, 205-348-4518. Mark Neely. 1974. circ. 2M. 2/yr. Pub'd 45 poems 1999; expects 45 poems 2000, 45 poems 2001. sub. price: $14; sample: $8. 180pp; 6×9; Rights purchased: 1st North American. Publishes 1% of poems submitted. Deadlines: we read all year. Reporting time: 2-12 weeks. Payment: varies; most recently $40 per poem. Interested in new or unpub'd poets: yes. Simultaneous submissions accepted: yes. Recent contributors: Yusef Komunyakaa, Bob Hicok, C.D. Wright, Nicole Cooley, W.S. Merwin. Submission quantity: 3-5.

BLACKBOX, 77-44 Austin Street #3F, Forest Hills, NY 11375. 1996. circ. 100. 2/yr. sample price: $6. 25pp; 8×11.

BLACKFIRE, BLK Publishing Company, PO Box 83912, Los Angeles, CA 90083, 310-410-0808, fax 310-410-9250, e-mail newsroom@blk.com. 1992. circ. 12M. 6/yr. Expects 18 poems 2000, 25 poems 2001. sub. price: $30; sample: $7.00. 48pp; 8⅛×11⅞; Publishes 40% of poems submitted. Interested in new or unpub'd poets: yes. Simultaneous submissions accepted: yes, if told. Submission quantity: 5. Special interests: Black gay.

BLADES, Poporo Press, 335 Paper Mill Road, Newark, DE 19711-2254. Francis Poole, JoAnn Balingit. 1977. ''Blades accepts submissions continuously. Poetry should be short; poems occasionally accepted up to 60 lines, but Blades's small format may prevent a longer poem from being published immediately. Need more women to submit!'' circ. 175. 2/yr. Pub'd 10 poems 1999; expects 20 poems 2000, 20 poems 2001. sub. price: $1 or exchange of publications, and SASE; sample: $1,or for exchange, enclose SASE. 36pp; 4¼×3¾; Rights purchased: rights revert to author upon publication. Publishes 5% of poems submitted. Deadlines: none. Reporting time: 8 weeks maximum. Payment: copies. Interested in new or unpub'd poets: yes. Simultaneous submissions accepted: yes. Recent contributors: John M. Bennett, Ivan Arguelles, Robert Peters, Franz Wright, Andrei Codrescu. Submission quantity: 3 or 4. Special interests: Short translations, travel poems, surrealism, satire, visual/graphic poetry, mail-art.

BLAST, PO Box 3514, Manuka, Act. 2603, Australia. 1987. circ. 1M. 4/yr. Pub'd 25 poems 1999. sub. price: $A30; sample: free. 30pp; Publishes 5% of poems submitted. Deadlines: 1 March, 1 June, 1 September, 1 December. Reporting time: 3-10 months. Simultaneous submissions accepted: no. Recent contributors: Geoff Page, Bruce Dawe, Anne Edgeworth. Submission quantity: 1-3.

Bleeding Heart Press (see also THE BLIND HORSE REVIEW), PO Box 15902, Beverly Hills, CA 90209-1902. 1992.

Blind Beggar Press, Box 437 Williamsbridge Station, Bronx, NY 10467, 914-683-6792. Gary W. Johnston. 1976. ''Annual anthology, 'New Rain' series. Sponsor book parties, readings and workshops'' avg. press run 1M. Pub'd 2 poetry titles 1999; expects 3 poetry titles 2000, 3 poetry titles 2001. 5½×8½, 6×9; avg. price, paper: $6.95-$15. 48-200pp; Publishes 20%-35% of poetry manuscripts submitted. Reporting time: 2-3 months. Payment: copies. Interested in new or unpub'd poets: yes. Simultaneous submissions accepted: yes. Recently published poets: Judy Simmons, Fatisha, Americo Casiano, Catherine Sanders, Ruby Dee. Submission quantity: 5-10 poems. Special interests: Publish work relevant to third-world people and will consider all forms of poetry

27

from experimental to long poems.

THE BLIND HORSE REVIEW, Bleeding Heart Press, PO Box 15902, Beverly Hills, CA 90209-1902. Todd Kalinski. 1992. ''I perfer a healthy batch to choose from, say 10 poems from each poet. It gives a better feel of their work'' circ. 200-300. Irregular. Pub'd 100 poems 1999; expects 100 poems 2000. sub. price: $16; sample: $6. Pages vary - (46-54) about 15 writers an issue; size varies; Publishes less than 10% of poems submitted. Deadlines: no deadlines. Reporting time: 0-2 months. Payment: 1 copy. Interested in new or unpub'd poets: yes. Simultaneous submissions accepted: no. Recent contributors: Steve Richmond, A.D. Winans, Hugh Fox, Barbara Peck, Chris Mortenson. Submission quantity: 10-15 poems. Special interests: Not afraid of the wildly experimental or the long poem, as long as it's their best.

BLITHE SPIRIT, Hill House Farm, Knighton, Powys LD7 1NA, United Kingdom, 0154-752-8542, Fax 0154-752-0685. Caroline Gourlay. 1991. circ. approx. 400-500. 4/yr. Pub'd 400 poems 1999; expects 400 poems 2000, 400 poems 2001. sub. price: £12 Britain, £16 elsewhere; sample: £4. 64pp; 5½×8½; Rights purchased: None. Publishes 20%-25% of poems submitted. Deadlines: Feb. 1, May 6, Aug. 6, Nov. 6. Reporting time: 1 month. Payment: none. Interested in new or unpub'd poets: only if members of British Haiku Society, or if in original lanuguage + English, French, or German. Simultaneous submissions accepted: no. Recent contributors: David Cobb, Brian Tasker, Stephen Gill, Martin Lucas, Ken Jones. Submission quantity: 12. Special interests: Haiku, senryn, renga (renku), tanka-originals or translations, haibun.

BLK, BLK Publishing Company, PO Box 83912, Los Angeles, CA 90083, 310-410-0808, fax 310-410-9250, e-mail newsroom@blk.com. Alan Bell, Mark Haile. 1988. circ. 22M. 12/yr. sub. price: $18; sample: $2.95. 60pp; 8⅛×10⅞; Deadlines: Features lead time 4 weeks, news lead times 2 weeks, adv. lead time 2 weeks. Interested in new or unpub'd poets: no. Simultaneous submissions accepted: yes. Submission quantity: 5.

BLK Publishing Company (see also BLACK LACE; BLACKFIRE; KUUMBA; BLK), PO Box 83912, Los Angeles, CA 90083, 310-410-0808, Fax 310-410-9250, newsroom@blk.com. 1988.

BLOCK'S MAGAZINE, 1419 Chapin Street, Beloit, WI 53511, 608-364-4893. Alan J. Block. 1993. ''no trite poems, no religious dogma, include a cover letter, DONT use a submission service.'' circ. 100. 4/yr. Pub'd 120 poems 1999; expects 150 poems 2000, 150 poems 2001. sub. price: $20; sample: $6. 60pp; 5½×8½; Rights purchased: first time. Publishes 3% of poems submitted. Reporting time: 3 months. Payment: 1 copy per poem. Interested in new or unpub'd poets: yes. Simultaneous submissions accepted: no. Recent contributors: Robert Bunzel, Corrine DeWinter, John Grey, Jonathan Falk, Graham Duncan. Submission quantity: No more than 5. Special interests: short poems with more imagery and less message, i.e., don't pound the reader over the head.

BLOOD & FEATHERS: Poems of Survival, 36495 Vine Street, Suite I, Willoughby, OH 44094-6347, 440-951-1875. Jennifer Helms. 1995. ''B&F is a magazine that reflects the beauty and sorrow that comes from everyday life. Subject matter is open and I prefer free verse to structured. Being a published poet myself, I've tried to keep this a friendly forum for beginners as well as more experienced poets. Cover letters are preferred, but not lists of credits. Impress me with your poetry, not your profile. No SASE, no response. I comment on work when asked to, although response time will take longer if I do so. Contest for the Blood & Feathers Chapbook Series has $5 entry fee. Deadline Nov. 31, 1998. Each entry receives current issue of the magazine. Send SASE for more info. I also publish 1-2 chapbooks of my choice throughout the year. Those are by invitation only, usually from past contributors.'' circ. 100. 4/yr. Pub'd 128 poems 1999; expects 80 poems 2000, 80 poems 2001. sub. price: $12; sample: $3. 30pp; 5½×8; Rights purchased: all rights returned. Publishes 16% of poems submitted. Deadlines: none. Reporting time: 2 weeks - 1 month. Payment: copies and/or cash; Agreed upon between editor and author. Interested in new or unpub'd poets: yes. Simultaneous submissions accepted: yes. Recent contributors: John Sweet, Greg Watson, Christopher Presfield, Lyn Lifshin, W. Gregory Stewart. Submission quantity: 3-5. Special interests: I prefer strong image to surrealism, concrete to experimental, and free verse to structured. Poems no longer than 1 page typed. Subject matter is open as long as there is some aspect of survival to it. For instance, what inspires us to write, what gets us up in the morning, what makes life worth living despite all the little slings and arrows that hit us daily?

Bloody Someday Press, 3721 Midvale Avenue, Philadelphia, PA 19129, 610-667-6687; FAX 215-951-0342; E-mail poettes@erols.com; website http://www.libertynet.org/bsomeday. T.H. Cornell, Stan Heleva. 1996. avg. press run 500. Pub'd 1 poetry title 1999; expects 1 poetry title 2000, 1 poetry title 2001. 7×4¼, 8½×5½, 5⅜×8½; avg. price, paper: $12. 70pp; Publishes 3% of poetry manuscripts submitted. Reporting time: 3 months. Payment: 25% of list price after printing cost. Interested in new or unpub'd poets: yes, but only as a submission to our annual manuscript contest, deadline 7/31. Simultaneous submissions accepted: yes. Recently published poets: Sheila King, Cy K. Jones, Rochelle Theo Pienn. Submission quantity: Minimum 48 page manuscript (enclose $12 payable to Bloody Someday) annually, deadline 7/31. Special interests: Poetry with originality that contributes to the traditions of literature.

THE BLOOMSBURY REVIEW, 1553 Platte Street, Suite 206, Denver, CO 80202, 303-455-3123, Fax 303-455-7039. Ray Gonzalez. 1980. ''Send copies only.'' circ. 50M. 6/yr. Pub'd 20 poems 1999. sub. price:

$16; sample: $4. 24pp; 10½×15¼; Rights purchased: 1st time, then reverts to writer. Publishes 5% of poems submitted. Deadlines: ongoing. Reporting time: 3 months. Payment: $5. Simultaneous submissions accepted: no. Recent contributors: Judith Infante, Nan Cuba, Michael Hogan, Greg McNamee, Margaret Randall. Submission quantity: 2-4. Special interests: No light verse.

THE BLOWFISH CATALOG, Blowfish Press, 2261 Market Street #284, San Francisco, CA 94114, 415-864-0880; fax 1-415-864-1858; e-Mail blowfish@blowfish. rom. Staff. 1994. circ. 4M. 3/yr. Pub'd 6 poems 1999; expects 8 poems 2000, 8 poems 2001. sub. price: $10; sample: $3. 48+pp; 8½×11; Rights purchased: one-time only. Publishes 5% of poems submitted. Deadlines: June 15th/September 30th. Reporting time: 2 months. Payment: $10-25. Interested in new or unpub'd poets: yes. Simultaneous submissions accepted: yes. Submission quantity: 2-5.

Blowfish Press (see also THE BLOWFISH CATALOG), 2261 Market Street #284, San Francisco, CA 94114, 415-864-0880; fax 1-415-864-1858; e-Mail blowfish@blowfish. com. 1993. 5½×8½.

BLU, PO Box 517, New Paltz, NY 12561, 1-800-778-8461; e-mail revcenter@hotmail.com; website www.revolutioncenter.org. 1998. circ. 4M. 6/yr. sub. price: $27; sample: free. 24pp; 7½×13.

BLUE BEAT JACKET, Blue Jacket Press, 1-5-54 Sugue-cho, Sanjo-shi, Niigata-ken 955-0832, Japan, 0256-32-3301. Yusuke Keida. 1971. "Independent Beat and Post-Beat magazine. Need translators of Japanese poetry." circ. 50-100. 2/yr. Expects 20 poems 2000, 20 poems 2001. sub. price: $5; sample: $2. 50-60pp; size A5; Publishes 70% of poems submitted. Deadlines: always. Payment: no money but 2 copies. Interested in new or unpub'd poets: yes. Simultaneous submissions accepted: yes. Recent contributors: Steve Dalachinsky, Sam Hamill, Gerald Nicosia, Hersch Silverman, A.D. Winans. Submission quantity: 2 or 3.

BLUE COLLAR REVIEW, Partisan Press, PO Box 11417, Norfolk, VA 23517, 757-627-0952; e-mail redart@pilot.infi.net. A. Markowitz, Mary Franke. 1997. "Best to see an issue before submitting. Contest: Working Peoples Poetry Competition = $15 per entry. Prize $100 and subscription. Deadline May 1st" circ. 253. 4/yr. Pub'd 100 poems 1999; expects 100 poems 2000, 100 poems 2001. sub. price: $10 - to A. Markowitz (BCR); sample: $5. 40-60pp; 5½×8½; Rights purchased: none, rights return to poet upon publishing. Publishes 10-20% of poems submitted. Reporting time: 3-6 weeks. Payment: copies. Interested in new or unpub'd poets: yes. Simultaneous submissions accepted: yes. Recent contributors: Tim Hoppey, Alan Harawitz, Jay Griswold, Martin Espada, Katherine Kirkpatrick. Submission quantity: 2-5.

Blue Jacket Press (see also BLUE BEAT JACKET), 1-5-54 Sugue-cho, Sanjo-shi, Niigata-ken 955-0832, Japan, 0256-32-3301. Yusuke Keida. 1971.

BLUE MESA REVIEW, Department of English, Humanities Building, Albuquerque, NM 87131, 505-277-6347, fax 277-5573, bluemesa@unm.edu. Paticia Lynn Sprott. 1989. "Theme for next issue: On the border (effects on culture, technology, relationships, etc.)" circ. 1,200. 1/yr. Pub'd 50 poems 1999. sub. price: $10 + $2 postage; sample: $10 + $2 postage. 220pp; 6×9; Publishes 25% of poems submitted. Deadlines: October 31. Reporting time: by December 31. Payment: 2 copies of published review. Interested in new or unpub'd poets: yes. Simultaneous submissions accepted: no. Recent contributors: Lyn Lifshin, Thomas Swiss, Kathleen Spivack, Roberta Swann. Submission quantity: 5-10. Special interests: multi-cultural, esp, Native American, Hispanic American.

●**Blue Night Press (see also PRECHELONIAN),** 1003 Lakeway, Kalamazoo, MI 49001. 1991. 5½×8½.

The Blue Oak Press, HC10 Box 621, Lakeview, OR 97630-9704, 916-994-3397. Morris Campbell, Editor. 1967. "By invitation only." avg. press run 500-1M. Pub'd 1-3 poetry titles 1999. 6×9; avg. price, cloth: $15-$30; paper: $10. 80-100pp; Interested in new or unpub'd poets: not at this time. Recently published poets: Hotchkiss, Everson, Hoyt, Berutti.

Blue Star Press, PO Box 645, Oakville, WA 98568, 360-273-7656. 1995. 6×9.

BLUE UNICORN, 22 Avon Road, Kensington, CA 94707, 510-526-8439. Ruth G. Iodice, Martha E. Bosworth, Fred Ostrander. 1977. "We want to publish the best that can be found in contemporary poetry. We accept well-crafted poetry of all kinds, in form and free verse, and also expert translations. We shun the trite, the inane, the soft-centered, the contrived poem. We prefer submissions on 8½ X 11 sheets, typed in standard form. Fancy packaging or elaborate enclosure letters do not impress us; the poem must stand on its own. In addition to publishing *Blue Unicorn*, we sponsor an annual *BU* Poetry Contest, with prizes of $100, $75, and $50, plus honorable mentions. For details send SASE after October for contest with deadline March 1 the following year." circ. 500. 3/yr. Pub'd 200 poems 1999; expects 250 poems 2000, 250 poems 2001. sub. price: $14, $20 foreign; sample: $5; $7 foreign. 48-60pp; 4¼×5½; Rights purchased: first rights. Publishes .5% of poems submitted. Deadlines: we read and accept/reject year round. Reporting time: 1-3 months. Payment: 1 copy of the magazine in which the writer's poem appears. Interested in new or unpub'd poets: yes. Simultaneous submissions accepted: no. Recent contributors: Josephine Miles, Charles Edward Eaton, William

Stafford, James Schevill, Beth Bentley. Submission quantity: 3-5 preferably. Special interests: We use translations, experimental poetry, regional poetry, longpoems, light verse, satire, etc., provided it is excellent. We can use shorter poems more easily than longer ones due to limited space.

Blue Unicorn Press, Inc., PO Box 40300, Portland, OR 97240-3826, 503-775-9322. Wanda Z. Larson. 1990. "We have a strong history interest, women, metaphysical" avg. press run 200-300. Pub'd 1+ poetry titles 1999; expects 2+ poetry titles 2000, 7 poetry titles 2001. 5½×8½; avg. price, paper: $4.95-$8.95. 20-150pp; Publishes 1% of poetry manuscripts submitted. Reporting time: 6 months. Payment: percentage, sometimes advance. Interested in new or unpub'd poets: very little. Simultaneous submissions accepted: yes. Recently published poets: Wanda Z. Larson. Submission quantity: 10. Special interests: Longpoems, metaphysical.

BLUE VIOLIN, PO Box 1175, Humble, TX 77347-1175. Mary Agnes Dalrymple. 1995. "I can not respond if SASE is not provided. Also, please provide and SASE that is large enough for the return of your manuscript." circ. very small, but growing. 2/yr. Pub'd 60 poems 1999. sub. price: $10; sample: $5. 40pp; 5½×8½; Rights purchased: one time. Reporting time: 2 weeks-1 month. Interested in new or unpub'd poets: yes. Simultaneous submissions accepted: yes. Recent contributors: Barbara F. Lefcowitz, William Greenway, Lyn Lifshin, Simon Perchik. Submission quantity: 3-7. Special interests: I tend to publish people oriented poems over poems dealing with issues or abstract ideas.

BLUEBOOK, 766 Valencia Street, San Francisco, CA 94110, 415-437-3450, Fax 415-626-5541. 1998. circ. 400. 4/yr. sub. price: $15; sample: $5. 100pp.

BLUELINE, State University College, English Dept., Potsdam, NY 13676, 315-267-2043. Stephanie Deghett, Editor. 1979. "*Blueline* reads poetry manuscripts between September 1 and December 1. We are seeking original, unpublished work. Xerox copies are acceptable if neat and legible; the poet's name and address should be written on each manuscript and all submissions must be accompanied by a SASE. Refer to *Small Press Review* and other newletters for announcements of reading times and occasional theme issues." circ. 600. 1/yr. Pub'd 100 poems 1999; expects 100 poems 2000, 100 poems 2001. sub. price: $10; sample: $10. 180-200pp; 6×9; Rights purchased: first rights, rights revert to author after publication. Publishes 5% of poems submitted. Deadlines: December 1. Reporting time: 2-10 weeks. Payment: 1 copy. Interested in new or unpub'd poets: yes. Simultaneous submissions accepted: no. Recent contributors: Roger Shepper, Hugh Ogden, June F. Baker, Eric Ormsby. Submission quantity: 5 or less. Special interests: *Blueline*'s special focus is on the Adirondack Mountains of northern New York. Poems should be of a rural nature and relevant to the Adirondacks, if not in geography, in spirit. We prefer poems under 75 lines (but more than 4 lines); sometimes we publish longer poems. We are not interested in effusive descriptions of the scenery. We are looking for realistic approaches to the environment and poetry that shows imagination, reflection and insight. Humor and irony are quite acceptable. *Blueline* is indexed in the *Index Of American Periodical Verse*.

BOA Editions, Ltd., 260 East Avenue, Rochester, NY 14604, 716-546-3410. A. Poulin, Jr., Publisher. 1976. avg. press run 3M. Pub'd 6 poetry titles 1999; expects 6 poetry titles 2000, 6 poetry titles 2001. 6×9; avg. price, cloth: $20; paper: $12.50. 100pp; Publishes 1% of poetry manuscripts submitted. Reporting time: 8 weeks. Payment: advance and royalty. Interested in new or unpub'd poets: yes. Simultaneous submissions accepted: yes. Recently published poets: Anne Hebert, Lucille Clifton, Dorianne Laux, Li-Young Lee, Peter Makuck. Submission quantity: sample of 10 pages. Special interests: open to all.

BOGG, Bogg Publications, 422 N Cleveland Street, Arlington, VA 22201. John Elsberg, Editor (U.S.); George Cairncross, Editor (U.K.); Sheila Martindale, Editor (Can.); Wilga Rose, Editor (Aus.). 1968. "U.K. address: 31 Belle Vue St., Filey, N. Yorks, UK YO14 9HU. Canadian address: PO Box 23148, 380 Wellington St., London, ON N6A 5N9. Australian address: 13 Urara Road, Avalon Beach, NSW 2107. Please read the magazine first, it has a quite distinctive tone. Always looking for good humorous/wry short poems as balance. Plus a certain amount of 'experimmatical' poetry and prose" circ. 850. 2-3/yr. Pub'd 120-150 poems 1999; expects 120-150 poems 2000. sub. price: £5 ($12)/3 issues; sample: $3.50. 68pp; 6×9; Rights purchased: one-time. Publishes 1% of poems submitted. Deadlines: open. Reporting time: 1 week. Payment: 2 copies. Interested in new or unpub'd poets: yes. Simultaneous submissions accepted: no. Recent contributors: Ann Menebroker, Miriam Sagan, Jim Kacian, Charles Bukowski, John Millett. Submission quantity: 6. Special interests: All forms, but preference for "modernist" diction, distinctive poetic voice, humor & satire, American work with a British setting or reference, and innovative experimental forms.

Bogg Publications (see also BOGG), 422 North Cleveland Street, Arlington, VA 22201. John Elsberg, Editor (U.S.); George Cairncross, Editor (U.K.); Sheila Martindale, Editor (Can); Wilga Rose, Editor (Aus.). 1968. "U.K. address: 31 Belle Vue St., Filey, N. Yorks, UK YO14 9HU. Canadian address: PO Box 23148, 380 Wellington St., London ON N6A 5N9. Australian address: 13 Urara Road, Avalon Beach, NSW 2107. By invitation only. Unsolicited MSS are not read. Invitations are extended to poets who have previously appeared in *Bogg* magazine." avg. press run 300. Pub'd 3 poetry titles 1999; expects 2 poetry titles 2000, 2 poetry titles 2001. size varies; avg. price, paper: free-for-postage or $3 (successive reprintings). 20pp; Reporting time:

immediately. Payment: 25% of print run. Interested in new or unpub'd poets: no. Simultaneous submissions accepted: no. Recently published poets: Laurel Speer, Derrick Buttress, Ann Menebroker, Tina Fuller, Joan Payne Kincaid. Submission quantity: 30-50.

Bolchazy-Carducci Publishers, Inc., 1000 Brown Street, Wauconda, IL 60084, 847-526-4344; fax 847-526-2867. 1981.

BOMB MAGAZINE, 594 Broadway, Suite 905, New York, NY 10012, 212-431-3943, FAX 212-431-5880. Betsy Sussler, Editor-in-Chief. 1981. *"Bomb* publishes new art, writing, poetry, short fiction and interviews. *Bomb* has published translations of Central American, Sri Lankan, and Filipino poetry. *Bomb* is interested in regional poetry (oral-histories), experimental poems, translations, interested in serious efforts." circ. 60M. 4/yr. Pub'd 20 poems 1999; expects 20 poems 2000, 20 poems 2001. sub. price: $18; sample: $6 (includes p/h). 112pp; 8⅞×10⅞; Rights purchased: rights revert to author. Publishes 8% of poems submitted. Reporting time: 4 months. Payment: $50-$100. Interested in new or unpub'd poets: maybe. Simultaneous submissions accepted: no. Recent contributors: Willie Perdomo, Sandra Cisneros, Harold Pinter, David Mawer, Vijay Seshadrn. Submission quantity: 4-5.

Bombshelter Press (see also ONTHEBUS), P.O Box 481266, Bicentennial Station, Los Angeles, CA 90048, 213-651-5488. Jack Grapes, Michael Andrews. 1975. "No unsolicited submissions. Send query letter. We publish L.A. & So. Calif. poets." avg. press run 800. Pub'd 3 poetry titles 1999; expects 3 poetry titles 2000, 3 poetry titles 2001. 5½×8½; avg. price, paper: $9. 72pp; Payment: free copies (50) plus 10% profits from sales. Interested in new or unpub'd poets: no—query first. Simultaneous submissions accepted: yes. Recently published poets: John Oliver Simon, Lee Rossi, Jack Grapes, Charles Bukowski, Michael Andrews. Submission quantity: 3 to 6.

BONE & FLESH, PO Box 349, Concord, NH 03302-0349. Lester Hirsh, Frederick Moe, Amy Shea, Monica Nagel, Susan Bartlett. 1988. "We are a small, independent publication in the true sense of the word. We do not publish large quantities of poetry, but we do publish what we feel is an eclectic blend of literary styles. We prefer cordial cover letters, and are not impressed by publishing credits. Good writing has impact and will stand on its own. We accept submissions from Feb. to May, would prefer not to get volumes of mail around the holidays. We encourage poets to send for guidelines before submitting work—SASE essential." circ. 350+. 2/yr. Pub'd 75 poems 1999; expects 75 poems 2000, 60 poems 2001. sub. price: $14(includes 1 main issue, 1 chapbook, occasional inserts or newsletter) or supplemental issue; sample: $6. 50-70pp; 7×8, 8×10; Rights purchased: first rights. Publishes 10% of poems submitted. Deadlines: Feb. 1 - May 1. Reporting time: 2-3 months. Payment: 1 copy. Interested in new or unpub'd poets: yes, if quality work. Simultaneous submissions accepted: no. Recent contributors: Gayle Elen Harvey, Mary Winters, Ellen Hersh, Albert Russo. Submission quantity: no more than 6. Special interests: Prose poems, concrete, experimental, as well as traditional verse. We publish work that is thought provoking and aesthetic. Themes should focus on the substance of our lives, or the link with other lives and times. We are oriented towards inner journeys but emphasize the literary heritage or universal themes. Themes that are of historical propotion, that touch the current state of world affairs are also accepted for perusal by the editorial staff. Example: Bosnia, the Holocaust, relations of the East and West.

The Book Department, 107 White Rock Drive, Windsor, CT 06095-4348. 1978. 8¼×5¼.

The Bookman Press, PO Box 1892, Sag Harbor, NY 11963, 516-725-1115. 1994.

THE BOOMERPHILE, PO Box 17446, Boulder, CO 80308-0446, 303-444-3363, www.delphi.com/boomer. Dan Culberson, Editor, Publisher. 1992. circ. 150. 12/yr. Pub'd 3 poems 1999; expects 5 poems 2000, 5 poems 2001. sub. price: $20; sample: $1. 8pp; 8½×11; Rights purchased: First North American serial rights. Publishes 5% of poems submitted. Deadlines: First of every month. Reporting time: 1-2 weeks. Payment: 2 copies. Interested in new or unpub'd poets: yes. Simultaneous submissions accepted: yes. Recent contributors: Sharon Rose Schibig, Deborah Dixon, Peter Fogo. Submission quantity: 1-5.

BORDERLANDS: Texas Poetry Review, PO BOX 33096, Austin, TX 78764, fax 512-499-0441; e-mail cemgilbert@earthlink.net; website http://www.fastair.com/borderlands. Robert Lee, Ramona Cearley. 1992. "We have a special interest in poetry that is outward-looking as opposed to introspective or personal. Always send SASE with submissions and inquiries." 2/yr. Pub'd 124 poems 1999; expects 124 poems 2000, 124 poems 2001. sub. price: $17 includes p/h; sample: same. 100pp; 5½×8½; Rights purchased: first serial rights. Publishes 5% of poems submitted. Deadlines: We read ongoing submissions. See journal for upcoming dates. Reporting time: up to 4 months, but may vary. Payment: 1 copy. Interested in new or unpub'd poets: yes. Simultaneous submissions accepted: no. Recent contributors: Sylvia Manning, L.L. Oilivier, Carol Coffee Reposa, Bill Sweeney, Mario Susko. Submission quantity: up to 5. Special interests: Political poetry, regional poetry (southwest), bilingual poetry (not translations of another's work), poetry about the outer world (society, cultures, environment, history).

Borealis Press Limited, 110 Bloomingdale Street, Ottawa, Ont. K2C 4A4, Canada, 613-798-9299, Fax

613-798-9747. Glenn Clever, Managing Editor. 1972. "We publish material that is by Canadian authors or specifically Canadian in content" avg. press run 500. Pub'd 2 poetry titles 1999; expects 1 poetry title 2000, 1 poetry title 2001. 5½×8½; avg. price, cloth: $29.95; paper: $14.95. 80-100pp; Publishes 2% of poetry manuscripts submitted. Reporting time: 5 months. Payment: 10% of retail, paid once yearly. Interested in new or unpub'd poets: only after inquiry. Simultaneous submissions accepted: no. Recently published poets: Cogswell, Rowdon, Dawber, Welch. Submission quantity: at least enough for a book of 50+ pages. Special interests: Must have interest to Canadian readers and critics.

Bosck Publishing House, 1474 Dodson Drive, Atlanta, GA 30311, 404-755-8170. 1991. "We are committed through 1998 and are not seeking submissions." avg. press run 2M. Pub'd 2 poetry titles 1999. 5⅜×8⅜; avg. price, cloth: $14.95; paper: $9.95. 58-85pp; Interested in new or unpub'd poets: not at this time. Simultaneous submissions accepted: yes. Submission quantity: 4.

THE BOSTON BOOK REVIEW, 30 Brattle Street, 4th floor, Cambridge, MA 02138, 617-497-0344, BBR-info@BostonBookReview.org, www.BostonBookReview.org. 1993. circ. 10M. 10/yr. sub. price: $24 domestic, $50 international; sample: $5. 44-60pp; 11½×14½.

BOSTON REVIEW, 30 Wadsworth Street, MIT, Cambridge, MA 02139, 617-253-3642, fax 617-252-1549. 1975. "We don't publish long poems or light verse. Otherwise, we are open-minded regarding style—though we are extraordinarily selective because we publish so few poems per issue. We strongly urge writers to familiarize themselves with the *Boston Review* before they submit poems." circ. 20M. 6/yr. Pub'd 35 poems 1999; expects 35 poems 2000, 35 poems 2001. sub. price: $15 individuals, $18 institutions; sample: $4.50. 40pp; 11⅜×14½; Rights purchased: one-time. Publishes .5% of poems submitted. Deadlines: none. Reporting time: up to 4 months. Payment: varies, generally around $40. Interested in new or unpub'd poets: yes. Simultaneous submissions accepted: no. Recent contributors: Robert Pinsky, Yusef Komunyakaa, Rachel Hadas, Hayden Carruth, David Ferry. Submission quantity: no more than 5.

BOTH SIDES NOW, 10547 State Highway 110 North, Tyler, TX 75704-3731, 903-592-4263. Elihu Edelson, Editor. 1969. "*BSN* has few pages, uses little poetry, so keep it short and heed our interests." circ. 200. 4 double issues/year. sub. price: $9/10 issues, $6/6 issues; sample: $2 (double issue). 20pp; 8½×11; Rights purchased: authors retain rights. Reporting time: varies. Payment: copies/subscription. Interested in new or unpub'd poets: yes. Simultaneous submissions accepted: yes, and we'd reprint good stuff that deserves more exposure. Submission quantity: varies according to length. Special interests: *BSN* is a New Age magazine in the broadest sense, covering such diverse areas as the occult/metaphysics, progressive strains in traditional religion, ecology, appropriate technology, and "green politics" (nonviolence, eco-spirituality, grassroots democracy, social responsibility). We *strongly* prefer poetry which reflects these interests. Moods may vary considerably from mystical and lyrical through expository, satirical, and humorous, but preferably not downbeat or pessimistic.

Bottom Dog Press, c/o Firelands College of BGSU, Huron, OH 44839, 419-433-5560, http://members.aol.com/lsmithdog/bottomdog. Larry Smith, Editor. 1984. "We do a combined chapbook series stressing full units of work, not a loose selection of poems. Focus and cohesiveness are a must. We stress Ohio and Midwest writers, but would consider others on a co-op basis. Most of our books have a strong sense of place and a synthesis of head and heart. We have gone to publishing chapbooks in a set of two-three perfectbound, in one book form. We like working class writing" avg. press run 350. Pub'd 3 poetry titles 1999; expects 3 poetry titles 2000, 3 poetry titles 2001. 5½×8½, 6×9; avg. price, cloth: $20; paper: $10; other: $9. 90-120pp; Publishes 10% of poetry manuscripts submitted. Reporting time: 2-3 months. Payment: royalties co-op or in copies. Interested in new or unpub'd poets: yes. Simultaneous submissions accepted: yes, if notified. Recently published poets: Ann Townsend, Alberta Turner, David Shevin, Jim Daniels. Submission quantity: chapbook of 40-60 poems. Special interests: We like the long journal poem and sense of place writing. We are open to all forms and styles, but content is essential. Write well about what moves you as a full person. Find a full voice and express it clearly. Work must be of the Midwest.

BOUILLABAISSE, Alpha Beat Press, 31 Waterloo Street, New Hope, PA 18938, 215-862-0299. Dave Christy, Ana Christy. 1991. circ. 700. 2/yr. Pub'd 160 poems 1999; expects 200 poems 2000, 200 poems 2001. sub. price: $17; sample: $10. 160pp; 8½×11; Rights purchased: none. Publishes 35% of poems submitted. Deadlines: none. Reporting time: immediately. Payment: copies. Interested in new or unpub'd poets: yes. Simultaneous submissions accepted: yes. Recent contributors: Antler, Frank Moore, elliott, A.D. Winans, Joseph Verrilli. Submission quantity: up to 3. Special interests: Beat, post-Beat, and modern writings.

●**BOULDER HERETIC,** PO Box 17446, Boulder, CO 80308-0446, 303-444-3363, danculberson@juno.com. 1999. circ. 25-30. 12/yr. sub. price: $20; sample: $1. 6pp; 8½×11.

BOULEVARD, 4579 Laclede Avenue, #332, St. Louis, MO 63108-2103, 215-568-7062. Richard Burgin. 1985. "Send a reasonable amount of poetry, not a whole book. We're eclectic in our tastes believing only in the school of talent. We are open potentially to any style and like poetry written with both the head and heart" circ.

3.5M. 3/yr. Pub'd 54 poems 1999; expects 77 poems 2000, 112 poems 2001. sub. price: $12; sample: $8. 200-225pp; 5⅜×8½; Rights purchased: first serial, one-time publication. Publishes 1% of poems submitted. Deadlines: none. Reporting time: 2 months. Payment: small honoraria, usually $25-$75, sometimes up to $300 depending on length of poem. Interested in new or unpub'd poets: yes. Simultaneous submissions accepted: yes. Recent contributors: W.S. Merwin, Donald Hall, John Updike, Ruth Stone, James Tate. Submission quantity: 3, no more than 5.

THE BOUND SPIRAL, 72 First Avenue, Bush Hill Park, Enfield, Middlesex, EN1 1BW, England. 1988. circ. 100-200. 2/yr. sub. price: £6; sample: £2.50. 35-40pp; 5¾×8¼.

Box Turtle Press (see also MUDFISH), 184 Franklin Street, New York, NY 10013. Jill Hoffman, Editor; Jennifer Belle, Associate Editor; Doug Dorph, Associate Editor; Stephanie Emily Dickenson, Associate Editor; Rob Cook, Associate Editor; David Lawrence, Associate Editor; Charlotte Rindvi, Associate Editor. 1983. "A brief cover letter is appreciated. Send SASE for Mudfish Poetry Prize guidelines" avg. press run 1.2M. 6⅞×8¼; avg. price, paper: $10. 168-178pp; Reporting time: immediately to 2 months. Payment: 1 copy. Interested in new or unpub'd poets: yes. Simultaneous submissions accepted: no. Recently published poets: Charles Simic, Richard Garcia, Stephen Sandy, Barbara O'Dair, John Ashbery. Submission quantity: 4-6.

Branch Redd Books (see also BRANCH REDD REVIEW), 9300 Atlantic Avenue, Apt. 218, Margate City, NJ 08402-2340. William Sherman. 1976. "No unsolicited manuscripts. Letters of inquiry and correspondence welcome." avg. press run 400. Pub'd 1 poetry title 1999; expects 1 poetry title 2000. size varies; avg. price, paper: $10.00. Payment: by agreement. Recently published poets: Hanne Bramness, Shreela Ray, Asa Benueniste, Eric Mottram, Alexandra Grilikhes.

BRANCH REDD REVIEW, Branch Redd Books, 9300 Atlantic Ave, Apt 218, Margate City, NJ 08402-2340. Bill Sherman. 1976. "Branch Redd Books incorporates *Branch Redd Review* (5 issues so far) and Branch Redd poetry chapbooks (5 chapbooks so far). The first Branch Redd book is *She Wants To Go To Pago-Pago*, a new sequence of poems by Bill Sherman (48 pages, printed by Jim Pennington in London, 1986). The second Branch Redd book is translations of Norwegian poet Dagny Juel by Hanne Bramness, published in late 1987. *No unsolicited manuscripts*" circ. 400. Irregular. sub. price: No subscriptions available; sample: none. Pages vary; size varies; Rights purchased: copyright remains with authors. Payment: copies. Recent contributors: Allen Fisher, Kate Ruse-Glason, Asa Benueniste, Eric Mottram, Shreela Ray. Special interests: Postmodern poetry.

Brandylane Publishers (see also PLEASANT LIVING), PO Box 261, White Stone, VA 22578, 804-435-6900; Fax 804-435-9812. 1985. 6×9.

BRAVO, THE POET'S MAGAZINE, John Edwin Cowen/Bravo Editions, 1081 Trafalgar Street, Teaneck, NJ 07666, 201-836-5922. Jose Garcia Villa, Founding Editor; John Edwin Cowen, Publisher & Editor. 1980. *"Read Bravo before submitting. 'Bravo* believes: poetry must have formal excellence; poetry must be lyrical; poetry is not prose.'" circ. 500. 1/yr. Expects 48 poems 2000, 48 poems 2001. sample price: $10. 50pp; 6×9; Publishes (unsolicited) 1% of poems submitted. Deadlines: none. Reporting time: 2 months maximum. Payment: 2 free copies. Interested in new or unpub'd poets: yes. Simultaneous submissions accepted: no. Recent contributors: Gloria Potter, Nick Joaquin, Virginia Moreno, John Edwin Cowen, Mort Malkin. Submission quantity: 5-6. Special interests: Lyrical poetry, experimental lyrical poetry. Some poets *Bravo* respects: E.E. Cummings, Dylan Thomas, Marianne Moore, Elinor Wylie, Emily Dickinson, Walt Whitman, Gerald Manley Hopkins, John Donne, George Barker, Richard Eberhart, and Gwendolyn Brooks.

BREAKFAST ALL DAY, 43 Kingsdown House, Amhurst Road, London E8 2AS, United Kingdom, 0171-923-0734. 1995. circ. 500. 4/yr. sub. price: £5. 36pp; 8×11½.

BRICK, Box 537, Station Q, Toronto, ON M4T 2M5, Canada, www.brickmag.com. 1977. 2/yr. sub. price: US$41/2 years. 160pp; 8×8.

BrickHouse Books, Inc., 541 Piccadilly Road, Baltimore, MD 21204, 410-828-0724, 830-2938. Clarinda Harriss, Editor-in-Chief. 1970. "BrickHouse Books prints single-author books (from 42-112 pages) of poetry and artistic prose. Writers may submit complete mss. (not samples) directly to BHB, Inc., or to one of BHB's 2 non-subsidized divisions. *New Poets Series* accepts mss. from writers who have established a track record of magazine publication but have not previously had a collection of their work published in book form. *Stonewall* publishes poetry and prose with a lesbian, gay, or bisexual emphasis. *Chestnut Hills Press*, BHB's third division, allows the top 10% of mss. which the other divisions had to reject, for budgetary reasons, the option to be published with the author paying production costs. Authors do not submit to *CHP* directly, but only by invitation." avg. press run 1M. Pub'd 6 poetry titles 1999; expects 6 poetry titles 2000, 6 poetry titles 2001. 6×9, 7×10; avg. price, paper: $10; other: illustrated broadsheets: $2 numbered; $5 signed. (limited ed.). 80pp; Publishes 5% of poetry manuscripts submitted. Reporting time: 10 months to 1 year. Payment: 25 copies, all sales proceeds revert to NPS to finance next book. Interested in new or unpub'd poets: 1st books a major interest, but must demonstrate high professional level with prior publications in mags. Simultaneous submissions accepted: yes, definitely (Life is short!). Recently published poets: Rane Arroyo, Jeff Mann, Chester Wickwire, Edward McCrorie, Sharon White. Submission quantity: 50-64pp. Special interests: No 'light verse' though wit & satire are not unwelcome, by any means. Only criterion: excellence. Any form (from traditional to experimental) is welcome, as is any subject NPS books have been nominated for Nat'l Book Awards. Jan Sherrill's was a finalist, having been nominated by Pulitzer laureate, Anne Tyler. *Stonewall* publishes book by gay or lesbian writers.

THE BRIDGE: A Journal of Fiction and Poetry, 14050 Vernon Street, Oak Park, MI 48237, 313-547-6823. Mitzi Alvin, Poetry Editor. 1990. "Poems must make literal sense." circ. 700. 2/yr. Pub'd 70 poems 1999. sub. price: $10, $15/2 year; sample: $5. 192pp; 5½x8; Rights purchased: first serial. Publishes 3% of poems submitted. Reporting time: 3 months. Payment: none right now. Interested in new or unpub'd poets: yes. Simultaneous submissions accepted: no. Recent contributors: Ruth Whitman, Ruth Feldman, John Tagliabue, Patricia Hooper, Barri Armitage. Submission quantity: 5-7. Special interests: no translation, very little experimental.

BRIDGES: A Journal for Jewish Feminists and Our Friends, PO Box 24839, Eugene, OR 97402, 541-343-7617, E-mail ckinberg@pond.net. Ruth Abrams, Enid Dame. 1990. circ. 3M. 2/yr. Pub'd 20 poems 1999; expects 20 poems 2000, 20 poems 2001. sub. price: $15; sample: free. 128pp; 7x10; Rights purchased: none. Publishes 5% of poems submitted. Reporting time: 6 months. Payment: 3 copies of issue plus $50-75 per poetry selection of 1-6 poems upon publication. Interested in new or unpub'd poets: yes. Simultaneous submissions accepted: no. Recent contributors: Kathryn Hellerstein, Adrienne Rich, Margaret Randall, Robin Becker, Susan Sherman. Submission quantity: 3-6. Special interests: Translations from Hebrew and Yiddish.

Bright Hill Press, PO Box 193, Treadwell, NY 13846, Fax 607-746-7274; E-mail wordthurs@aol.com. 1992. "SASE for guidelines. We do one Anthology a year, each with different themes. SASE for theme." avg. press run 1,000. Pub'd 3 poetry titles 1999; expects 3 poetry titles 2000, 3 poetry titles 2001. 5½x8½; avg. price, cloth: $11.00; paper: $11.00; other: chapbook $6.00. 64pp; Publishes 1% of poetry manuscripts submitted. Reporting time: 6 months. Payment: Cash Award and copies; discount on additional copies. Interested in new or unpub'd poets: rarely. Yes, if poet notifies us if ms. accepted elsewhere. Recently published poets: Regina O'Melveny, Ruth Stone, Graham Duncan, Judith Neeld. Submission quantity: None. Send ms. for competions only (write w/ SASE for guidelines).

BRILLIANT STAR, Baha'i National Center, 1233 Central Street, Evanston, IL 60201. 1969. "Themes lists available on request. Please know that this magazine is aimed at children 5-12 years old. Long narratives are rarely accepted. All poems are illustrated." circ. 3M. 6/yr. Pub'd 6 poems 1999; expects 6 poems 2000, 6 poems 2001. sub. price: $18; sample: $3 with 9 X 12 SASE with postage for 5 oz. 32pp; 8½x11; Rights purchased: none. Publishes 2% of poems submitted. Deadlines: none—we accept poetry on its merit and applicability to theme of issue. Reporting time: 8-12 weeks. Payment: we give no money for anything we publish. Interested in new or unpub'd poets: yes, we prefer to publish poems written by children. Simultaneous submissions accepted: yes, but please indicate so. Recent contributors: Linda Taylor, Susan Engle, Barbara LeMay, Linda Mui, Erin Daugherty. Submission quantity: 1 or 2.

THE BROBDINGNAGIAN TIMES, 96 Albert Road, Cork, Ireland, (214311227). Giovanni Malito. 1996. "SASE is required but trade will be accepted in lieu of postage. We are also looking for poetry on an ongoing basis for our single-author palmtop series of books." circ. 500. 4/yr (plus occasional themed supplements). Pub'd 40 poems 1999; expects 40 poems 2000, 40 poems 2001. sub. price: £2, $4; sample: 2 IRC's for postage. 8pp; 6x8½; Rights purchased: first time only. Publishes 6-10% of poems submitted. Deadlines: none. Reporting time: 2-6 weeks. Payment: copies. Interested in new or unpub'd poets: yes. Simultaneous submissions accepted: yes. Recent contributors: Miroslav Holub, Steven Sneyd, Leonard J. Cirino, Richard Kostelanetz, Albert Huffstickler. Submission quantity: 4-8. Special interests: We will look at anything from anywhere at any time but would like to see more translations and haiku.

Broken Boulder Press (see also GESTALTEN), PO Box 172, Lawrence, KS 66044-0172, E-mail paulsilvia@excite.com, website www.brokenboulder.com. Paul Silvia. 1996. "Send cover letter and brief bio with submission - be prepared to send ms on floppy disk or by e-mail if accepted." avg. press run 200. Pub'd 4 poetry titles 1999; expects 6 poetry titles 2000, 6 poetry titles 2001. 5½x8½; avg. price, paper: $3. 20-80pp; Publishes 5% of poetry manuscripts submitted. Reporting time: 4 weeks. Payment: negotiated case-by-case. Interested in new or unpub'd poets: yes. Simultaneous submissions accepted: no. Recently published poets: Glenn Ingersoll, Kreg Wallace, W.B. Keckler, Errol Miller. Submission quantity: up to 50. Special interests: Interested in experimental and visual poetry of all kinds.

Broken Jaw Press (see also NEW MUSE OF CONTEMPT), PO Box 596 Stn A, Fredericton, NB E3B 5A6, Canada, ph/fax 506-454-5127, jblades@nbnet.nb.ca, www.brokenjaw.com. Joe Blades, Publisher. 1985. "*New Muse of Contempt*, experimental visual concrete poetry, mail art magazine 2 times/yr (subs. $12; sample $6).

Dead Sea Physh Products and Book Rat chapbooks, Broken Jaw Press: prefers Atlantic Canadian literary writers.'' avg. press run 500. Pub'd 11 poetry titles 1999; expects 10 poetry titles 2000, 10 poetry titles 2001. 6×9; avg. price, paper: $14; other: $3.95-$4.95 chapbooks. Chapbooks 24-40pp; books 80pp; Publishes 1% of poetry manuscripts submitted. Reporting time: 3-12 months. Payment: 10% of list. Interested in new or unpub'd poets: no. Simultaneous submissions accepted: no. Recently published poets: R.M. Vaughan, Rob McLennan, Nela Rio, Allan Cooper, Eric Miller. Submission quantity: not accepting unsolicited mss. Special interests: Canadian authored experimental.

Broken Shadow Publications, 472 44th Street, Oakland, CA 94609-2136, 510-450-0640. Gail Ford. 1993. ''We are not accepting manuscripts'' avg. press run 500. Expects 2 poetry titles 2000. 5½×8¼; avg. price, paper: $10. 75pp; Recently published poets: Tom Quontamatteo/ Larry Beresford. Special interests: Material we publish is honest, accessible and deeply felt. Contributing authors place an emphasis on communication, and participate in regular peer reveiw to insure the clarity and power of their work.

Brooding Heron Press, Bookmonger Road, Waldron Island, WA 98297. Sam Green, Co-Publisher; Sally Green, Co-Publisher. 1984. ''Because of heavy commitments we are not accepting unsolicited manuscripts at this time'' avg. press run 300. Pub'd 1 poetry title 1999; expects 3 poetry titles 2000, 3 poetry titles 2001. size varies; avg. price, cloth: $25-$125; paper: $10; other: $40-$275 limited edition. Pages vary; Publishes 1% of poetry manuscripts submitted. Reporting time: 1-2 weeks. Payment: 10% of press run. Interested in new or unpub'd poets: no. Simultaneous submissions accepted: no. Recently published poets: Denise Levertov, James Laughlin, Gary Snyder, Ted Genoways, Hayden Carruth. Submission quantity: chapbook-size.

The Brookdale Press, 566 E. Shore Rd., Jamestown, RI 02835, 203-322-2474. 1976.

Brooks Books (see also MAYFLY), 4634 Hale Dr, Decatur, IL 62526-1117, 217-877-2966. Randy Brooks, Co-Editor; Shirley Brooks, Co-Editor. 1976. ''Chapbook submissions (40 to 100 short poems) should be the sustained effort of several years as a writer. Minichapbooks are of tightly unified small collections or sequences (15 to 30 short poems). They are *by invitation only.* We also publish a reference book on haiku books and haiku publishing in English—please send haiku books for review and news of essays on haiku in English. Probably 85% of our publishing is haiku in English. Subscribers may submit haiku to our magazine, *Mayfly.*'' avg. press run 500. Pub'd 6 poetry titles 1999; expects 2 poetry titles 2000, 2 poetry titles 2001. 4¼×5½; avg. price, cloth: $20; paper: $10 chapbook; other: $5 for perfectbound paperbacks / $20 for fullsize cloth books. 24-40pp; Publishes .01% of poetry manuscripts submitted. Reporting time: 2-4 months. Payment: after publication expenses are met, authors receive 15% royalty on profits; before that, author receives copies and a 40% discount. Interested in new or unpub'd poets: no. Simultaneous submissions accepted: we're not interested in this shotgun approach. Recently published poets: Lee Gurga, Elizabeth S. Lamb, Eric Aman, George Swede, Michael Dudley. Submission quantity: 25-50. Special interests: We are committed to evocative, concise poetry based on empirical awareness. We are not interested in metaphors nor abstract symbolism, but pefer exact literalness derived from direct, immediate sense perceptions. We are not interested in careless chatter, rambling thoughts, philosophical ideology, word games, poetic conceits nor complex poetic tropes. We don't care what something reminds you of, or what something is like; we want to know the way things ARE and what it IS to be alive.

Browder Springs, PO Box 823521, Dallas, TX 75382, 214-368-4360. 1996. ''I publish only authors who live or have lived in Texas.'' 5½×8½.

Brownout Laboratories, 103 East 4th Street, Brooklyn, NY 11218. 1994. ''Submissions may be made in English, French, German, Spanish, or Croation/Bosnian. For other languages send an inquiry letter first. Greeting card verse and 'expression of the poet's deepest soul' poesy should be sent elsewhere.'' avg. press run 50. Expects 1 poetry title 2000. size usually 5½×8½ but also other formats; avg. price, paper: $5. 24pp; Publishes less than 5% of poetry manuscripts submitted. Reporting time: 6 days to 6 months. Payment: author receives 20% royalty on all copies sold. Interested in new or unpub'd poets: only if they are printed on reused or recycled paper. Simultaneous submissions accepted: yes. Recently published poets: Kurt Hemmer. Submission quantity: 3 max.

THE BROWNSTONE REVIEW, 335 Court St. #114, Brooklyn, NY 11231-4335. Aaron Scharf, Poetry Editor. 1995. circ. 100. 2/yr. sub. price: $10; sample: $6. 64pp; 5½×8½.

Brunswick Publishing Corporation, 1386 Lawrenceville Plank Road, Lawrenceville, VA 23868, 804-848-3865; Fax 804-848-0607; brunspub@jnent.com. Dr. Walter J. Raymond. 1973. avg. press run 500-1M. Pub'd 8 poetry titles 1999; expects 8 poetry titles 2000, 10 poetry titles 2001. 5¼×8¼, 6×9, 8½×11; avg. price, cloth: $22; paper: $12. 130pp; Publishes 10% of poetry manuscripts submitted. Reporting time: 2-3 weeks. Payment: send for Statement of Philosophy and Purpose. Interested in new or unpub'd poets: yes. Simultaneous submissions accepted: yes. Recently published poets: Kei Kunihiro, Henry Willis, David Thomas. Submission quantity: 5-6 samples or complete manuscript.

BRUTARIAN, PO Box 25222, Arlington, VA 22202-9222, 703-360-2514. Dominic Salemi. 1991. "Just work hard on your verse." circ. 3M. 4/yr. Pub'd 10-15 poems 1999. sub. price: $12; sample: $6. 84pp; 8½×11; Rights purchased: only the right to publish/copyright reverts to author on publication. Publishes 10% of poems submitted. Deadlines: 1 week before the 1st day of each season (winter, spring, summer, fall). Reporting time: 30 days. Payment: $20 per poem. Interested in new or unpub'd poets: always. Simultaneous submissions accepted: sometimes, it depends on the circulation of the other zine. Submission quantity: as many as they would like. Special interests: all areas.

●**BUCKLE &**, PO Box 1653, Buffalo, NY 14205. 1998. "No inspirational verse. Send 3-5 poems or poetry translations. No previously published poems, please." circ. 200. 2/yr. sub. price: $9; sample: $5. 56pp; 5½×8½; Simultaneous submissions accepted: no. Submission quantity: 3-5 poems.

Buddhist Text Translation Society, 1777 Murchison Drive, Burlingame, CA 94010-4504, phone/fax 415-692-9286, e-mail drbabtts@jps.net. 1970. "Our publications are based on traditional Buddhist ideals. In addition to translations of ancient texts from the Buddhist canon, we also periodically publish commentarial works which may include collections of poetry" avg. press run 2M. Expects 1 poetry title 2000. 5½×8½; avg. price, paper: $8. 200pp; Publishes 10% of poetry manuscripts submitted. Reporting time: 3 months. Payment: none, all are free contributions. Interested in new or unpub'd poets: yes, if relevent to traditional Buddhism. Simultaneous submissions accepted: yes. Recently published poets: Master Hua, Heng Sure, Master Yung Chia. Submission quantity: several. Special interests: translation works from classical Buddhist Chinese texts would be of particular interest.

The Bunny & The Crocodile Press/Forest Woods Media Productions, Inc, PO Box 416, Hedgesville, WV 25427-0416, 304-754-8847. 1976. 5½×8½.

BurnhillWolf, 321 Prospect Street, SW, Lenoir, NC 28645, 704-754-0287; FAX 707-754-8392. 1995. "Please query before sending submissions." 5½×8½.

Burning Books, PO Box 2638, Santa Fe, NM 87505, Fax 505-820-6216, E-mail brnbx@nets.com. 1979. "We will not be accepting any new manuscripts for two years. Query first" avg. press run 1M. Pub'd 1 poetry title 1999. 8×10; avg. price, cloth: $10. 84pp; Publishes a very, very small % of poetry manuscripts submitted. Payment: copies. Recently published poets: Barbara Golden, John Cage, Yoko Ono, Charles Amirkhanian, Melody Sumner Carnahan. Submission quantity: 1. Special interests: Composers who use words with their music, writers whose words go with musical - musical prose. Opera librettos and lyrics.

Burning Bush Publications, PO Box 9636, Oakland, CA 94613-0636, 510-482-9996, www.bbbooks.com. Abby Bogomolny, Editor-in-Chief; Amanda Majestie, Submissions Coordinator. 1996. avg. press run 1M. Expects 1 poetry title 2000, 1 poetry title 2001. 5½×8½, 6×9; avg. price, paper: $9.95. 98pp; Reporting time: 2 months. Payment: negotiable. Interested in new or unpub'd poets: yes. Simultaneous submissions accepted: no. Recently published poets: Morton Marcus, Opal Palmer Adisa, Lyn Lifshin, David Kherdian, Aya de Leon. Submission quantity: 6. Special interests: Burning Bush is a press committed to social and economic justice. We seek poetry that dramatizes and illustrates personal experiences that will lead readers to work for a more harmonious and equitable world. Interested in womanist vision.

THE BURNING CLOUD REVIEW, 225 15th Avenue N, St. Cloud, MN 56303-4531, E-mail ERhinerson@aol.com. 1996. circ. 150. 6/yr. sub. price: $18; sample: same. 36pp; 8½×5½.

Burning Deck Press (see also SERIE D'ECRITURE), 71 Elmgrove Avenue, Providence, RI 02906. Rosmarie Waldrop, Keith Waldrop. 1962. "Potential contributors would do well to buy a sample book to get an idea what kind of work we respond to." avg. press run 500-1M. Expects 1 poetry title 2000, 1 poetry title 2001. 6×9; avg. price, cloth: $20; paper: $10; other: chapbooks $5-8. 40-60pp; Publishes 1% of poetry manuscripts submitted. Reporting time: 2 months. Payment: copies only (10% of edition). Interested in new or unpub'd poets: yes, unless we are backlogged. Simultaneous submissions accepted: no. Recently published poets: Berssenbrugge, Yau, Gizzi, Einzig, Silliman. Submission quantity: manuscript. Special interests: Experimental.

Burning Llama Press (see also THE IMPLODING TIE-DYED TOUPEE; THE NEW SOUTHERN SURREALIST REVIEW), 82 Ridge Lake Drive, Columbia, SC 29209-4213. Keith Higginbotham, Editor; Tracy R. Combs, Editor. 1993. "Always include SASE and cover letter or we will not consider" avg. press run varies. Pub'd 1 poetry title 1999; expects 1 poetry title 2000, 1 poetry title 2001. size varies; avg. price, paper: varies. 1-40pp; Publishes .01% of poetry manuscripts submitted. Reporting time: immediate to 3 months. Payment: negotiable. Interested in new or unpub'd poets: no. Simultaneous submissions accepted: no. Submission quantity: 5. Special interests: Dada, surreal, experimental, visual.

BUTTON, PO Box 26, Lunenburg, MA 01462, E-mail buttonx26@aol.com. Delia Ellis Bell. 1993. "We like wit, brevity, poetry that might have a rhyme scheme, but isn't a rhyme scheme that's abab or aabb or anything really obvious, true moments carefully preserved. We don't like whining, cheap sentimentality, egregious profanity, vampires, neuroses for neuroses' sake, most song lyrics passing as poetry, anything overlong, overdull or overreaching.'' circ. 1M. 2/yr. Pub'd 7 poems 1999; expects 12 poems 2000, 12 poems 2001. sub. price: $5; sample: $2. 28pp; 4×5; Rights purchased: 1st American serial rights. Publishes 7% of poems submitted. Deadlines: quarterly, we read all year. Reporting time: 12 weeks. Payment: 2 copies plus 3 year subscription; 2 2yrs subscribtion to give away-$ in 1997. Interested in new or unpub'd poets: yes. Simultaneous submissions accepted: no. Recent contributors: Brendan Galvin, Stephen Sandys, William Corbett, Amanda Powell,Diana Der-Hovanessian. Submission quantity: 3-4. Special interests: translations, experimental poetry, regional poetry.

BYLINE, PO Box 130596, Edmond, OK 73013, 405-348-5591. Sandra Soli, Poetry Editor. 1981. ''Study the magazine before submitting; all poems must be about writing or the creative process. We use both light verse and serious poetry. We're tired of poems on writer's block and 'the muse''' circ. 3.5M. 11/yr. Pub'd 110 poems 1999; expects 110 poems 2000, 110 poems 2001. sub. price: $22; sample: $4. 36pp; 8½×11; Rights purchased: 1st. Publishes 5% of poems submitted. Deadlines: continuous. Reporting time: 6-8 weeks. Payment: $10. Interested in new or unpub'd poets: yes. Simultaneous submissions accepted: no. Recent contributors: John Engle Jr., Kathryn Howd Machan, Robert Brimm, Henry Stobbs. Submission quantity: 1-3. Special interests: Want thoughtful but lean poems about the creative experience.

C

●**C & G Publishing, Inc.**, PO Box 5199, Greeley, CO 80634, 970-356-9622, ccgcook@aol.com. 1989.

Cadmus Editions, PO Box 126, Belvedere Tiburon, CA 94920-0126. Jeffrey Miller. 1979. ''Poet should write first, enclosing an SASE, before making submission. Do not send unsolicited MSS'' avg. press run 500-1M. Pub'd 1 poetry title 1999; expects 1 poetry title 2000, 1 poetry title 2001. 6×9; avg. price, cloth: $30 (signed); paper: $15. 75pp; Publishes .001% of poetry manuscripts submitted. Reporting time: 60-90 days. Payment: varies. Interested in new or unpub'd poets: no. Simultaneous submissions accepted: no. Recently published poets: Ed Dorn, Tom Clark, Carol Tinker, Cid Corman, Gustaf Sobin. Submission quantity: none.

CAESURA, San Jose Museum of Art, 110 S. Market, San Jose, CA 95113, FAX 408-624-7432. Lequita Watkins-Vance. Address poetry submissions to: PO Box 221847, Carmel, CA 93922. 1976. ''Annual competition, $500-prize, leading poet as judge. Susan Terris 1995 winner, Carolyn Kizer judge. Contributors: Richard Tillinghast, Elisabeth Marshall, Jane Hirshfield, Lynne McMahon, Donald Hall.'' circ. 900. 4/yr. Pub'd 10-16 poems 1999. sub. price: $12; sample: $2. 24pp; 8½×11; Rights purchased: First/reverts to author. Payment: 3 issues of journal. Simultaneous submissions accepted: no. Recent contributors: Galway Kinnell, Jachie Osherow, Miroslav Holub, Anna Mortal, Sherod Santos. Special interests: We publish a wide range of highest quality work.

THE CAFE REVIEW, c/o Yes Books, 20 Danforth Street, Portland, ME 04101, e-mail seegerlab@aol.com, www.thecafereview.com. Wayne Atherton, Editor; Steve Luttrell, Editor-in-Chief; Alex Fisher, Editor. 1989. ''Included: Best American Poetry 1998'' circ. 300-500. 4/yr. Expects 300+ poems 2000, 180+ poems 2001. sub. price: $24; sample: $6 includes p/h. 60-70pp; 5½×8½; Rights purchased: none as yet. Publishes 10% of poems submitted. Deadlines: none. Reporting time: 2 months average. Payment: 1 copy. Interested in new or unpub'd poets: yes. Simultaneous submissions accepted: no. Recent contributors: Michael McClure, Anne Waldman, Charles Bukowski, Lawrence Ferlinghetti, Diane DiPrima. Submission quantity: 3-5. Special interests: Well-crafted free verse leaning towards a beat sensibility, but will consider academic poetry that is not too stuffy or pretentious; translations, regional poetry, Beat influenced.

CALAPOOYA, School of Arts and Sciences, Eastern Oregon University, La Grande, OR 97850, 541-962-3633. Jodi Varon, David Axelrod. 1981. ''Please include sufficient postage for the return of all materials.'' circ. 1.5M. 1/yr. Pub'd 100 poems 1999. sub. price: $5; sample: $5. 44pp; 11¼×17½; Rights purchased: none. Publishes 3% of poems submitted. Deadlines: reading period March and April only. Reporting time: 4-6 weeks. Payment: copies. Interested in new or unpub'd poets: yes. Simultaneous submissions accepted: no. Recent contributors: Robert Bly, Joseph Bruchac, Roland Flint, Patricia Goedicke, William Stafford. Submission quantity: 5 max. Special interests: translations, prose poems.

CALIFORNIA QUARTERLY (CQ), CSPS/CQ, PO Box 7126, Orange, CA 92863, 805-543-8255, 949-854-8024, jspalley@aol.com. Julian Palley, Managing Editor. Address poetry submissions to: 21 Whitman Court, Irvine, CA 92612, 949-854-8024, jspalley@aol.com. 1973. ''CQ publishes the best submissions received during a 3 month period. Write for guidelines (SASE)'' circ. 400. 4/yr. Pub'd 200-220 poems 1999; expects 200-220 poems 2000, 200-220 poems 2001. sub. price: $20; sample: $5. 64pp; 5½×8½; Rights purchased: first publication rights, copyright then reverts to poet. Publishes 2-5% of poems submitted. Deadlines: none, poems received all year. Reporting time: 1-4 months. Payment: 1 copy of magazine. Interested in new or unpub'd poets: yes. Simultaneous submissions accepted: yes. Recent contributors: Pearl Karrer, Julian Palley, Robert Cooperman, Paul Willis, Deanne Bayer. Submission quantity: 3-6. Special interests: Poems should be one or two pages. Translations, experimental poetry.

CALLALOO, English Dept., Univ. of Virginia, PO Box 400121, Charlottesville, VA 22904-4121, 804-924-6637, Fax 804-924-6472, callaloo@virginia.edu. Charles H. Rowell, Editor. 1976. *"Callaloo* is a journal of African-American and African Diaspora arts and letters" circ. 1M. 4/yr. Pub'd 75 poems 1999; expects 75 poems 2000, 150 poems 2001. sub. price: $35.50 individuals, $86 institutions; sample: $11. 280pp; 6⅞×10; Publishes 10% of poems submitted. Deadlines: none. Reporting time: 6 months. Payment: 2 free copies of journal/offprints. Interested in new or unpub'd poets: yes. Simultaneous submissions accepted: yes. Recent contributors: Rita Dove, Lucille Clifton, Natasha Tretheway, Carl Phillips, Michael Harper. Submission quantity: 5 or fewer.

Calypso Publications, 5810 Osage Avenue #205, Cheyenne, WY 82009. Susan Richardson. 1989. "Each project requires different submissions. Submissions are not accepted open-endedly. Please watch writers magazines for guidelines" avg. press run 250-500. 6×9; avg. price, paper: $8. Publishes 5% of poetry manuscripts submitted. Reporting time: 3 months. Payment: copies. Interested in new or unpub'd poets: yes. Simultaneous submissions accepted: depends on project. Recently published poets: Tam Neville, William Kloefkorn, Jean Nordhaus, William Dickey, Barbara Crooker. Submission quantity: 5.

CALYX: A Journal of Art and Literature by Women, Calyx Books, PO Box B, Corvallis, OR 97330, 541-753-9384, Fax 541-753-0515, calyx@proaxis.com. Margarita Donnelly, Director; Beverly McFarland, Senior Editor; Micki Reaman, Managing Editor. 1976. "Please be familiar with our editorial policy by reading *Calyx.* Always include a SASE and brief biographical statement! Please include phone number with bio. data." circ. 3.5M. 2/yr. Pub'd 100 poems 1999; expects 100 poems 2000, 100 poems 2001. sub. price: $19.50 indiv., institutional & library $25 (subs are 3 issues but take 18 months to complete); sample: $9.50. 128pp; 6×8; Publishes around 5% of poems submitted. Deadlines: 10/1-12/15 annually. Reporting time: 6-12 months. Payment: in copies and subscriptions. Interested in new or unpub'd poets: yes. Simultaneous submissions accepted: yes. Recent contributors: Jane Glazer, Eleanor Wilner, Judith Ferguson, Diane Glancy, Marjorie Agosin. Submission quantity: up to 6 poems (only). Special interests: We are interested in translations of contemporary women writers whose work is not easily available in the US in English. Include copy of work in original language with translation submissions. We are interested in finding book reviewers. Query *Calyx* with SASE, writing sample, and resume with publishing credits for review guidelines and a review list. We're also interested in critical essays and journals.

Calyx Books (see also CALYX: A Journal of Art and Literature by Women), PO Box B, Corvallis, OR 97330, 541-753-9384, Fax 541-753-0515, calyx@proaxis.com. 1986. "Please do not submit book mss. without querying with SASE for book submission guidelines. We will only be publishing one book annually. We are closed until further notice for book submissions" avg. press run 2M. Pub'd 2 poetry titles 1999; expects 1 poetry title 2000, 1 poetry title 2001. 6×9; avg. price, cloth: $23; paper: $12. 80pp; Publishes a very small % (01%) of mss received, we only do 1 poetry book a year. Reporting time: 18 months. Payment: individually contracted. Interested in new or unpub'd poets: yes. Simultaneous submissions accepted: yes. Recently published poets: Frances Payne Adler, Judith Sornberger, Haunani-Kay Trask, Cortney Davis, Sandra Kohler. Submission quantity: query for book submission guidelines with SASE. Special interests: translations of Latin American women writers.

Cambric Press dba Emerald House, 208 Ohio Street, Huron, OH 44839-1514, 419-433-5660; 419-929-4203. Joel Rudinger. Address poetry submissions to: 6039 Zenobia Road, Wakeman, OH 44889. 1975. "Please query first to indicate awareness of self-publishing process." avg. press run 500. Pub'd 1 poetry title 1999; expects 2 poetry titles 2000, 3 poetry titles 2001. 5½×8½, 4¼×6⅞; avg. price, paper: $8.95. 64-80pp; Publishes 80% of poetry manuscripts submitted. Reporting time: 2 weeks to 1 month. Payment: self-publishing; author receives 100%. Interested in new or unpub'd poets: yes. Simultaneous submissions accepted: yes. Recently published poets: Michael Joseph Phillips, Joel Rudinger, Mary Ann Henning, Laura Dennison, Susan Osterman. Submission quantity: query first. Special interests: open to all points of view.

Camel Press (see also DUST (From the Ego Trip)), Box 212, Needmore, PA 17238, 717-573-4526. Katharyn Howd Machan. 1984. "All work must be carefully crafted" avg. press run 700. Expects 1 poetry title 2000, 1 poetry title 2001. 4¼×5¾; avg. price, paper: $1-3; other: $1 sample copy. 20pp; Publishes 5% of poetry manuscripts submitted. Reporting time: 2 weeks. Payment: 50 copies. Simultaneous submissions accepted: yes. Recently published poets: Sheryl Nelms, Elizabeth Hahn, Paul Humphrey, Virgil Suarez, Rochelle Lynn Holt. Submission quantity: a few. Special interests: poems should tell a story or create an unambiguous mental image.

CANADIAN LITERATURE, University of British Columbia, 167-1855 West Mall, Vancouver, B.C. V6T 1Z2, Canada, 604-822-2780. Jain Higgins. 1959. "Include return postage. We publish Canadian poets only.

We're more likely to accept short poems than long ones, but have published and will consider publishing excerpts from longer poems (whether the excerpting is done by author or editor)." circ. 1.5M. 4/yr. Pub'd 30-40 poems 1999; expects 30-40 poems 2000, 30-40 poems 2001. sub. price: indiv. $40, institution $55 plus $15 postage (outside Canada); sample: $15-25. 192-208pp; 6×9; Rights purchased: first Canadian. Publishes a very small % of poems submitted. Deadlines: none. Reporting time: approx. 1 month. Payment: none. Interested in new or unpub'd poets: yes, provided return postage is included. Simultaneous submissions accepted: no. Recent contributors: Zoe Landale, Bert Almon, Dale Zieroth, Tom Wayman. Submission quantity: no limits. Special interests: We will consider translations made from the work of Canadian poets dealing with languages other than English (please submit both original and translation in such circumstances).

CANADIAN WOMAN STUDIES/les cahiers de la femme, 212 Founders College, York Univ., 4700 Keele Street, New York, Ontario M3J 1P3, Canada, 416-736-5356, fax 416-736-5765, e-mail cwscf@yorku.ca. Marlene Kadar. 1978. "We are a thematic journal and, although not necessary, give consideration to poetry that is relevant to the theme of a particular issue." circ. 3M. 4/yr. Pub'd 40-50 poems 1999. sub. price: $38.52 indiv. (Cdn), $53.50 instit. (Cdn), add $12 outside Canada; sample: $5. 156pp; 8½×11; Rights purchased: none. Publishes 10% of poems submitted. Deadlines: vary with each issue. Reporting time: 6 months. Payment: complimentary copy of issue in which work appears. Interested in new or unpub'd poets: no. Simultaneous submissions accepted: no. Submission quantity: 3-5.

CANDELABRUM POETRY MAGAZINE, Red Candle Press, 9 Milner Road, Wisbech PE13 2LR, England, tel: 01945 581067. M.L. McCarthy. 1970. "Overseas authors: please (on bended knees) *don't* put stamps of your own country on your SAE; IRCs (please). *Candelabrum Poetry Magazine* Volume X 2000-02: subscription to the whole volume US$13 in bills. If you like traditional-style poetry, this is your kind of poetry magazine." circ. 1M. 2/yr. Pub'd 160 poems 1999; expects 160 poems 2000, 160 poems 2001. sub. price: One year subs. no longer accepted. Subscription to volume 10 (2000-2002) £13.50 or $27 (bills only, don't accept checks). 40pp; 8½×5½; Rights purchased: none. Publishes up to 5% of poems submitted. Deadlines: poems may be submitted any time. Reporting time: about 8 weeks. Payment: contributors receive 1 complimentary copy. Interested in new or unpub'd poets: yes. Simultaneous submissions accepted: no. Recent contributors: Leo Yankevich, Andrea Abraham, William Ayot, Terence Gallagmer, Alice Evans. Submission quantity: about 4-6, but there's no rigid rule. Special interests: Metrical and rhymed poetry chiefly welcome, but good quality, rhythmic, free verse is also considered. Any length, up to approx. 70 lines, any subject, but racist, ageist or sexist matter is not accepted. We particularly welcome imaginative work and skillful use of metaphor, metre, and rhyme.

Canterbury Press, 5540 Vista Del Amigo, Anaheim, CA 92807, Fax 714-998-1929. 1979. size varies.

THE CAPE ROCK, English Dept, Southeast Missouri State, Cape Girardeau, MO 63701, 314-651-2500. Harvey Hecht. 1964. "We do not read poetry submissions April through August." circ. 600. 2/yr. Pub'd 100 poems 1999; expects 100 poems 2000, 100 poems 2001. sub. price: $7; sample: $3. 64pp; 5½×8¾; Rights purchased: all rights, reprints allowed on request with acknowledgement. Deadlines: none. Reporting time: 2-4 months. Payment: $200 best poem each issue; all contributors receive 2 copies. Interested in new or unpub'd poets: yes. Simultaneous submissions accepted: yes. Submission quantity: 3-7.

THE CAPILANO REVIEW, 2055 Purcell Way, North Vancouver, B.C. V7J 3H5, Canada, 604-984-1712. Ryan Knighton, Editor. 1972. "Always include SAE with IRC's" circ. 800. 3/yr. Pub'd 60 poems 1999; expects 25 poems 2000, 40 poems 2001. sub. price: $25; sample: $9. 120pp; 6×9; Rights purchased: 1st North American serial. Publishes 1-5% of poems submitted. Deadlines: none. Reporting time: 4 months. Payment: $50-$200. Interested in new or unpub'd poets: yes. Simultaneous submissions accepted: no. Recent contributors: John Pass, bill bissett, Don MacKay, Erin Moure. Submission quantity: 5-10 depending on length. Special interests: innovative poetry, avant-garde, long poems, min 5-6.

THE CARIBBEAN WRITER, RR 2, Box 10,000, Univ of Virgin Islands, Kingshill, St. Croix, VI 00850, 340-692-4152; fax 340-692-4026; e-mail ewaters@uvi.edu or qmars@uvi.edu. Erika Waters, Editor. 1987. "*The Caribbean Writer* is an international magazine with a Caribbean focus. The Caribbean should be central to the work or the work should reflect a Caribbean heritage, experience or perspective." circ. 1M. 1/yr. Pub'd 33 poems 1999; expects 36 poems 2000. sub. price: $10 + $1.50 postage; sample: $5 + $1.50 p/h. 288pp; 6×9; Rights purchased: one time use only. Publishes 15% of poems submitted. Deadlines: Sept. 30. Reporting time: authors of accepted mss are notified in December/January. Payment: 2 copies of magazine. Interested in new or unpub'd poets: yes. Simultaneous submissions accepted: yes, if we are notified. Recent contributors: Cecil Gray, Elaine Savory, Thomas Reiter, Opal Palmer Adiga, Lorna Goodison. Submission quantity: 5 maximum. Special interests: Anonymous submissions only. Place name, address and phone, and title of manuscript on separate sheet. Title only on manuscript.

THE CAROLINA QUARTERLY, CB# 3520 Greenlaw Hall, Univ of N. Carolina, Chapel Hill, NC 27599-3520, 919-962-0244, fax 919-962-3520. Christopher Windolph, Poetry Editor. 1948. "We read submissions year round. Pls. include SASE with submissions. Wood Award ($500) is given to author of best short story or poem *The Carolina Quarterly* publishes each year. Only writers without major publications are eligible.'' circ. 1.1M. 3/yr. Pub'd 44 poems 1999; expects 45 poems 2000, 45 poems 2001. sub. price: $12 indiv., $15 instit.; sample: $5 (postage paid). 88-100pp; 6×9; Rights purchased: 1st North American serial. Publishes 1% of poems submitted. Deadlines: none. Reporting time: 2-4 months. Payment: 2 copies. Interested in new or unpub'd poets: yes. Simultaneous submissions accepted: no. Recent contributors: William Harmon, Charles Wright, Robert Morgan, Albert Goldbarth, Angela Shaw. Submission quantity: 4-6. Special interests: None - though we enjoy long poems and do publish translations.

Carolina Wren Press/Lollipop Power Books, 120 Morris Street, Durham, NC 27701, 919-560-2738. David Kellogg. 1976. avg. press run 1M. Expects 1 poetry title 2000, 2 poetry titles 2001. 6×9; avg. price, cloth: $25; paper: $12.50. 80-100pp; Publishes 1% of poetry manuscripts submitted. Reporting time: 4 months. Payment: 10% of all print runs, cash for this when possible. Interested in new or unpub'd poets: yes. Simultaneous submissions accepted: no. Recently published poets: Jaki Shelton Green, C. Eric Lincoln, George Elliott Clarke, Andrea Selch. Submission quantity: complete ms.

Carpenter Press, PO Box 14387, Columbus, OH 43214. Robert Fox, Publisher. 1973. ''No longer interested in chapbooks.'' avg. press run 500. 6×9; avg. price, paper: $3-$7. 32-96pp; Payment: varies. Recently published poets: Steve Kowit, Jane Teller, David Shevin.

Carrefour Press, Saddle Fold, Hawkins Lane, Rainow, Macclesfield, Cheshire, England. 1929. size varies.

CASTAWAYS, c/o Derek Davis, 3311 Baring Street, Philadelphia, PA 19104. 1996. circ. 100+. 2/yr. sub. price: $15 for 3 issues; sample: $5. 60pp; 8½×11.

Castle Peak Editions, PO Box 277, Murphy, OR 97533, 503-846-6152. Judith Shears. 1971. ''No unsolicited manuscripts, please.'' avg. press run 500. Expects 2-3 poetry titles 2000. 5×7, 7×9, 8×11; avg. price, cloth: $15; paper: $25. 100-200pp; Recently published poets: Richard Berger, James B. Hall, Bill Hotchkiss, William Everson.

Catamount Press (see also COTYLEDON), 2519 Roland Road SW, Huntsville, AL 35805, 205-536-9801. Georgette Perry. 1992. ''We frequently use short poems, 10 lines or less'' avg. press run 150-200. Pub'd 1 poetry title 1999; expects 2 poetry titles 2000, 2 poetry titles 2001. 5½×8½; avg. price, paper: $6; other: $3 chapbook. Chapbooks 24pp; Publishes 5% of poetry manuscripts submitted. Reporting time: 1-3 months. Payment: copies. Interested in new or unpub'd poets: yes. Simultaneous submissions accepted: yes. Recently published poets: James Miller Robinson, Virginia Gilbert, Jeanne Shannon, Tim Scannell. Submission quantity: 6. Special interests: Nature and environmental subjects, use of scientific themes.

CAVEAT LECTOR, 400 Hyde Street, Apt. 606, San Francisco, CA 94109, 415-928-7431. 1989. ''Include SASE'' circ. 300. 2-3/yr. Pub'd 50 poems 1999; expects 50 poems 2000, 50 poems 2001. sub. price: $10; sample: $3. 48pp; 4¼×11; Rights purchased: 1st North American serial rights. Publishes 1% of poems submitted. Reporting time: 1 month. Payment: 3 copies of issue containing work. Interested in new or unpub'd poets: yes. Simultaneous submissions accepted: yes. Recent contributors: Les Murray, Simon Perchik, Joanne Lowery, Deanne Tayer, Aldred Robinson. Submission quantity: 6 or fewer. Special interests: We publish long poems (up to 300 lines) of unusual merit. We like poems of any style and idiom, that are tightly organized, well thought-out, and strongly felt.

Wm Caxton Ltd, PO Box 220, Ellison Bay, WI 54210-0220, 414-854-2955. Kubet Luchterhand. 1986. ''Our only iron-clad criteria for publishing a given book of poetry are two: First, the editor of the press (Kubet Luchterhand) has to like it well enough to pass it on for review to outside readers, and at least one outside reader must like it well enough to give an enthusiastic report; second, we have to believe that it will sell enough copies that we can get our printing cost investment out of it. We believe that one cannot consider oneself a *real* publisher until one has lost money on a poetry book, and we have.'' avg. press run 500-700. Pub'd 1 poetry title 1999; expects 1 poetry title 2000, 2 poetry titles 2001. 5½×8½, 6×9, 8½×11; avg. price, cloth: $10; paper: n/a so far; we issue poetry initially only in casebound editions. 75-100pp; Publishes 20% of poetry manuscripts submitted. Reporting time: 1-3 months, depending on season. Payment: varies widely; prefer subvention for printing costs tied to much higher than average royalty for author. We guarantee to keep the books we publish in print for a minimum of five years. Interested in new or unpub'd poets: certainly. Simultaneous submissions accepted: yes, but we want to know that they are being sumbitted elsewhere, and we prefer single submissions. Recently published poets: David Koenig, Carolyn Sibr, William Olson, Marily Taylor. Submission quantity: enough to make a book, preferably. Special interests: No restrictions beyond above comments.

CAYO, A MAGAZINE OF LIFE IN THE KEYS, P.O. Box 4516, Key West, FL 33040, 305-296-4286. Kirby Congdon. 1995. ''Clean copy, our editor is a stickler'' circ. 1M. 4/yr. Pub'd 50 poems 1999; expects 20 poems 2000, 20 poems 2001. sub. price: $16; sample: $4. 48pp; 8½×11; Publishes 5% of poems submitted. Reporting time: 4 months. Payment: copies. Interested in new or unpub'd poets: yes. Simultaneous submissions accepted: yes. Recent contributors: James Merrill, Dan Gerber, Kirby Congdon, Marion Smith, Lawrence Ferlinghetti. Submission quantity: 1-3.

CC. Marimbo Communications, PO Box 933, Berkeley, CA 94701-0933. Randy Fingland, Editor. 1996. "CC. Marimbo fashions hand-made minichaps (4¼ X 5½), smythe-sewn, to encourage attention for new and underpublished poets" avg. press run 26-250. Pub'd 1 poetry title 1999; expects 3 poetry titles 2000. 4¼x5½; avg. price, paper: $4.95. 40pp; Publishes 5% of poetry manuscripts submitted. Reporting time: 4-6 weeks. Payment: 10% of cover price. Interested in new or unpub'd poets: yes. Simultaneous submissions accepted: yes, if they're up front about it. Recently published poets: Tom Plante, Errol Miller, Arthur Winfield Knight, Don A. Hoyt. Submission quantity: perhaps 20-25 according to length of poem. Special interests: Poems mostly under 20 lines, well-written short collections.

Cedar Hill Publications (see also CEDAR HILL REVIEW), 3722 Highway 8 West, Mena, AR 71953, 501-394-7029. Christopher Presfield, Editor. Address poetry submissions to: E-91632 Box 5246, Corcoran, CA 93212. 1997. "Accomplished work only" avg. press run 300. Pub'd 10 poetry titles 1999; expects 10 poetry titles 2000, 10 poetry titles 2001. 5½x8½; avg. price, paper: $9. 80pp; Publishes 2% of poetry manuscripts submitted. Reporting time: 30 days. Payment: 50% press run. Interested in new or unpub'd poets: yes. Simultaneous submissions accepted: yes. Recently published poets: Leonard Cirino, Maggie Jaffe, Alan Britt, James Doyle, William Doreski. Submission quantity: varies. Special interests: socially engaged work.

CEDAR HILL REVIEW, Cedar Hill Publications, 3722 Highway 8 West, Mena, AR 71953, 501-394-7029. Maggie Jaffe, Poetry Editor. Address poetry submissions to: 3438 Villa Terrace, San Diego, CA 92104-3424. 1997. "All forms considered. Quality the standard. Work that is racist, sexist, or anti-environment will not be considered." circ. 300. 2/yr. Pub'd 60 poems 1999; expects 180 poems 2000, 120 poems 2001. sub. price: $10; sample: $4. 80pp; 5½x8½; Rights purchased: one time rights. Publishes 2% of poems submitted. Deadlines: 1/1; 7/1. Reporting time: 30 days. Payment: 1 copy plus 1 year subscription. Interested in new or unpub'd poets: yes/yes. Simultaneous submissions accepted: yes. Recent contributors: Hayden Carruth, David Budbill, Sharon Doubiago, Alan Britt, Yannis Ritsos. Submission quantity: varies. Special interests: Actively seeks Mentor Poet and Master Poet submissions. Must demonstrate a major contribution to the poetic arts over many years to qualify.

CELEBRATION, 2707 Lawina Road, Baltimore, MD 21216-1608, 410-542-8785, wsullivan@freeww-web.com. William J. Sullivan. 1975. "ISSN: 0883-9174 — Work submitted with hand written corrections or typed over correction fluid or any other thing which tends to make the work even slightly difficult to read is not given much attention." circ. 300. Occasional. Pub'd 30 poems 1999; expects 30 poems 2000, 30 poems 2001. sub. price: $8/4 issues; sample: $2. 30pp; 5½x8½; Rights purchased: none. Publishes 2-5% of poems submitted. Reporting time: 4-8 months depending on the number of works submitted in a quarter. Payment: 2 copies of magazine. Interested in new or unpub'd poets: yes. Simultaneous submissions accepted: no. Recent contributors: Lisa Yount, Sheila E. Murphy, Robert K. Rosenburg, Harrold Fleming, Ivan Arguelles. Submission quantity: 4-6. Special interests: We seldom publish rhymed verse, nor do we publish poems of more than about two pages in length.

Celestial Otter Press (see also MAGIC CHANGES), 237 Park Trail Court, Schaumburg, IL 60173. John Sennett, Editor. 1978. "Illustrated works invited." avg. press run 200. Expects 1 poetry title 2001. 5½x8½; avg. price, paper: $5. 64pp; Publishes 1% of poetry manuscripts submitted. Reporting time: 2-3 months. Payment: negotiable. Interested in new or unpub'd poets: yes. Simultaneous submissions accepted: Yes. Recently published poets: Donald Bullen, John Sennett. Submission quantity: 6. Special interests: imagistic, musical poems, songs.

Celo Valley Books, 346 Seven Mile Ridge Road, Burnsville, NC 28714, 828-675-5918. 1989. avg. press run 50-300. Pub'd 1 poetry title 1999; expects 3 poetry titles 2000, 5 poetry titles 2001. size varies; avg. price, cloth: $12; paper: $8. 96pp; Publishes 5% of poetry manuscripts submitted. Reporting time: 1 month. Payment: so far all our titles are paid for by the author; within 5 years, though, we hope to do some titles in a more traditional way. It is unlikely that poetry will be published except under subsidy terms. Interested in new or unpub'd poets: yes, as long as they understand we do subsidized only. Simultaneous submissions accepted: yes. Recently published poets: Namaya, Halon, Adams, Warlick, Flumerfelt. Submission quantity: full ms.

THE CELTIC PEN, 36 Fruithill Park, Belfast, BT11 8GE, Ireland, 01232-232608. Diarmuid Breaslain, General Editor. 1993. "Poetry must be written originally in a celtic language under celtic translation who published." circ. 900. 4/yr. Pub'd 40 poems 1999; expects 40 poems 2000, 40 poems 2001. sub. price: $15.00; sample: $3. 28pp; Recent contributors: Derick Thompson, Nuala Ni Dhomhneill, Gabriel Resenstock.

THE CENTENNIAL REVIEW, 312 Linton Hall, Mich. State Univ., E. Lansing, MI 48824-1044, 517-355-1905. R.K. Meiners. 1955. "We tend to publish good free verse, organic form poems about contemporary themes and interests." circ. 1M. 3/yr. Pub'd 10 poems 1999; expects 10 poems 2000, 10 poems 2001. sub. price: $12; sample: $6. 200pp; 6×9; Publishes 1% of poems submitted. Deadlines: none. Reporting time: 3 months. Payment: copies and a year's subscription to journal. Interested in new or unpub'd poets: yes. Simultaneous submissions accepted: no. Recent contributors: David Citino, Susan Fromberg Schaeffer, Lyn Lifshin, David Ignatow, Herbert Scott. Submission quantity: group (3-5). Special interests: Women's writing.

Center for Japanese Studies, 202 S. Thayer Street, University of Michigan, Ann Arbor, MI 48104-1608, 734-998-7265, FAX 734-998-7982. 1947. "We publish only translations of Japanese poets and poetry." Pub'd 2 poetry titles 1999; expects 1 poetry title 2001. 6×9, 8½×11. Simultaneous submissions accepted: no. Recently published poets: Oguma Hideo, Kurihara Sadako.

Center Press, PO Box 17897, Encino, CA 91416-7897. Gabriella Stone, Publisher. 1980. "Do submit clean, edited copies without spelling errors, etc. Do not submit saccharine, droll, lifeless, or cliche, etc. Do submit fresh, evocative, carefully constructed lines, etc. We are not interested in simply good, but only great or near great" avg. press run 3.5M. Pub'd 4 poetry titles 1999; expects 4 poetry titles 2000, 6 poetry titles 2001. 5½×8½; avg. price, cloth: $19.95; paper: $9.95. 112pp; Publishes .002% of poetry manuscripts submitted. Reporting time: 4-6 weeks. Payment: standard. Interested in new or unpub'd poets: yes. Simultaneous submissions accepted: yes. Recently published poets: Federico Garcia Lorca, Lee Tae Bok, Scott Sonders. Submission quantity: 2-4. Special interests: experimental, narrative, longpoems, satire.

CHACHALACA POETRY REVIEW, English Department, Univ. of Texas - Brownsville, Brownsville, TX 78520, 956-544-8239; Fax 956-544-8988; E-Mail mlewis@b1.utb.edu. Marty Lewis, Editor. 1997. circ. 500. 1-2/yr. Expects 50 poems 2000, 60-100 poems 2001. sub. price: $15/2 issues; sample: $3. 60pp; 6×9; Publishes 3-5% of poems submitted. Reporting time: 3 weeks to 3 months, depending on when submitted (summer is slow). Payment: 2 copies. Interested in new or unpub'd poets: yes. Simultaneous submissions accepted: yes, with notification. Recent contributors: Susan Weston, Michael Blumenthal, Vivian Shipley. Submission quantity: 5. Special interests: length-long poems not likely to be published, we're looking for thoughtful content (not just novelty) solid work with language, control of line/meter, no intrusive rhymes or arbitrary typography.

CHAFFIN JOURNAL, Department of English, 467 Case Annex, Eastern Kentucky University, Richmond, KY 40475-3140. 1998. circ. 500. 1/yr. sub. price: $5. 100pp; 5½×8½.

Chandelier Books, PO Box 7610, Tacoma, WA 98407-0610. 1999. 6×9.

CHANTEH, the Iranian Cross Cultural Qu'ly, PO Box 703, Falls Church, VA 22046, 703-533-1727. 1992. "No sentimentality, grandiloquence" circ. 1.2M. 4/yr. Pub'd 8 poems 1999; expects 8 poems 2000, 8 poems 2001. sub. price: $20; sample: $5. 50pp; 8½×11; Rights purchased: first. Publishes 10% of poems submitted. Deadlines: all year. Reporting time: 6-8 weeks. Payment: 2 copies. Interested in new or unpub'd poets: yes. Simultaneous submissions accepted: yes. Submission quantity: 3 or more.

CHAOS FOR THE CREATIVE MIND, PO Box 633, Tinley Park, IL 60477. Rich Carpenter. 1998. "All submissions must be typed, one poem per sheet" circ. 100. 12/yr. Expects 8 poems 2000, 40 poems 2001. sub. price: $9; sample: free. 24pp; 8½×11; Rights purchased: author retains rights. Publishes 90% of poems submitted. Deadlines: 15th of month. Reporting time: 2-3 weeks. Payment: 3 copies. Interested in new or unpub'd poets: yes. Simultaneous submissions accepted: yes. Recent contributors: Reid Karris, Jeanene Beauregard, Chris Koczot. Submission quantity: 1-4. Special interests: I like poems that have a message to them. I also like experimental poems. I look at all poetry types.

CHAPMAN, 4 Broughton Place, Edinburgh EH1 3RX, Scotland, 0131-557-2207. Joy M. Hendry. 1970. "Potential contributors are strongly recommended to buy a sample copy before submitting. Submissions MUST be accompanied by return postage or International Reply Coupons. Please fax proof for the new additions to the list: our fax number is listed." circ. 2M. 4/yr. Expects 500 poems 2000. sub. price: £16 (£21 overseas, US$35); sample: £3.30 ($6) + 50p ($1) postage. 104pp; 6×8½; Rights purchased: first serial rights. Publishes 1% or less of poems submitted. Reporting time: 2 months. Payment: copies of magazine. Interested in new or unpub'd poets: yes. Simultaneous submissions accepted: no. Recent contributors: Norman MacCaig, Dilys Rose, Jenny Robertson, Sorley MacLean, Edwin Morgan. Submission quantity: 6-8.

THE CHARIOTEER, Pella Publishing Co, 337 West 36 Street, New York, NY 10018, 212-279-9586. Carmen Capri-Karka. 1960. circ. 1M. 1/yr. Pub'd 2 poems 1999; expects 6 poems 2001. sub. price: $15 US indiv., $20 US instit., $20 foreign indiv., $25 foreign instit.; sample: free. 160pp; 5½×8½; Rights purchased: none. Publishes 1% of poems submitted. Deadlines: none. Reporting time: 6 months. Payment: none. Interested in new or unpub'd poets: no. Simultaneous submissions accepted: no. Recent contributors: Seferis, Ritsos, Pagoulatou, Bagliore, Cavafy. Special interests: Translations from the Greek.

CHARITON REVIEW, Truman University, Kirksville, MO 63501, 660-785-4499. Jim Barnes, Editor. 1975. "We are interested in only the best poetry, regardless who writes it. Nothing persuades us, but the poetry itself. SASE required please!" circ. 650+. 2/yr. Pub'd 40-45 poems 1999; expects 40-50 poems 2000, 40-50 poems 2001. sub. price: $9/yr, $15 2/yr; sample: $5. 104pp; 6×9; Rights purchased: first NA serial. Publishes .05% of poems submitted. Deadlines: none. Reporting time: 2 weeks. Payment: $5 per page. Interested in new or unpub'd poets: yes. Simultaneous submissions accepted: no. Recent contributors: Laurence Lieberman, Lee Perron, Samuel Maio, Phyllis Stowell. Submission quantity: 4-7. Special interests: Experimental poetry, translations, longpoems, and traditional types as well.

THE CHATTAHOOCHEE REVIEW, Georgia Perimeter College, 2101 Womack Road, Dunwoody, GA 30338-4497, 404-551-3019. Collie Owens, Poetry Editor. 1980. "We look for vivid imagery, unique point of view and voice, freshness of figurative language, and attention to craft. All themes, forms, and styles are considered as long as they impact the whole person: heart, mind, intuition, and imagination." circ. 1.3M. 4/yr. Pub'd 35 poems 1999; expects 35 poems 2000, 35 poems 2001. sub. price: $16/yr or $30/2 yrs; sample: $6. 120pp; 6×9; Rights purchased: first rights. Publishes 3% of poems submitted. Deadlines: manuscripts are read year round. Reporting time: 3-4 months. Payment: $50 per poem on publication. Interested in new or unpub'd poets: yes. Simultaneous submissions accepted: no. Recent contributors: Robert Dana, Ron Rash, Wendy Bishop, A.E. Stallings, Virgil Suarez. Submission quantity: 5 maximum. Special interests: We are especially interested in interviews with and informal essays about poets.

CHELSEA, PO Box 773, Cooper Station, New York, NY 10276-0773. Richard Foerster, Editor. 1958. "We look for intelligence and sophisticated technique in both experimental and traditional forms. $1000 Chelsea Award for poetry is given in alternate issues; send SASE for guidelines." circ. 2.2M. 2/yr. Pub'd 100 poems 1999; expects 100 poems 2000, 100 poems 2001. sub. price: $13/2 consecutive issues as published or one double issue, $16 foreign; sample: $7. 224pp; 6×9; Rights purchased: first North American serial & one-time non-exclusive reprint rights. Publishes less than 1% of poems submitted. Deadlines: continuous, unless we are preparing a special issue. Reporting time: immediately to 3 months. Payment: 2 copies plus $20 per printed page. Interested in new or unpub'd poets: yes. Simultaneous submissions accepted: no. Recent contributors: Susan Aizenberg, Terrance Hayes, Timothy Liu, Ruth Schwartz, Reginald Shepherd. Submission quantity: 5-6. Special interests: superior translations.

THE CHEROTIC (r)EVOLUTIONARY, PO Box 11445, Berkeley, CA 94712, 510-526-7858, FAX 510-524-2053, fmoore@eroplay.com. Frank Moore. 1991. "I publish anything I like" circ. 500. Irregular. Pub'd 18 poems 1999; expects 18 poems 2001. sample price: $5. 28pp; 8½×11; Rights purchased: none. Publishes 10% of poems submitted. Deadlines: none. Reporting time: 1-2 months. Payment: free copy. Interested in new or unpub'd poets: yes. Simultaneous submissions accepted: yes. Recent contributors: Karen Finley, Jack Foley, Ana Christy, Frank Moore, Robert Howington.

CHICAGO REVIEW, 5801 South Kenwood, Chicago, IL 60637, 773-702-0887, chicago-review@uchicago.edu. Eric Elshtain. 1946. circ. 2900. 4/yr. Pub'd 50 poems 1999; expects 50 poems 2000, 50 poems 2001. sub. price: $18 individuals, $42 institutions, add $5/yr postage to foreign countries; sample: $6. 144pp; 6×9; Rights purchased: We don't pay authors. Publishes 1% of poems submitted. Deadlines: none. Reporting time: 2 months average. Payment: 3 free copies and year subscription. Interested in new or unpub'd poets: yes. Simultaneous submissions accepted: yes. Recent contributors: Susan Howe, Brenda Hillman, Derek Mahon, Peter Riley, Michael Palmer. Submission quantity: no more than 5.

Chicken Soup Press, Inc., PO Box 164, Circleville, NY 10919, 914-692-6320, fax 914-692-7574, e-mail poet@warwick.net. 1995.

Chicory Blue Press, Inc., 795 East Street North, Goshen, CT 06756, 860-491-2271, FAX 860-491-8619. Sondra Zeidenstein. 1987. "Poetry by women over 60" avg. press run 500-1M. Pub'd 3 poetry titles 1999; expects 1 poetry title 2000, 1 poetry title 2001. 6×9; avg. price, paper: $15. Publishes 2-3% of poetry manuscripts submitted. Reporting time: 6 months. Payment: negotiable. Interested in new or unpub'd poets: only query letters with samples. Simultaneous submissions accepted: yes. Recently published poets: Honor Moore, Nellie Wong, Joan Swift. Submission quantity: 6.

CHILDREN, CHURCHES AND DADDIES, A Non Religious, Non Familial Literary Magazine, Scars Publications, Attn: Janet Kuypers, 8830 West 120th Place, Palos Park, IL 60464, E-ail ccandd96@aol.com, www.members.aol.com/scarspub/scras.html. Janet Kuypers, Editor. 1993. "Look for strong, narrative poetry. Writing that makes the reader feel like they are there. Electronic submissions (e-mail or disk-text ormat, Macintash prefered) appreciated" circ. varies. 12/yr. Pub'd 120 poems 1999; expects 300 poems 2000, 300 poems 2001. sub. price: $36; sample: $4.25, $3. Pages vary; 8½×11; Rights purchased: none. Publishes 40% of poems submitted. Deadlines: none. Reporting time: about 1 week, include SASE. Payment: electronic copy. Interested in new or unpub'd poets: yes. Simultaneous submissions accepted: yes. Recent contributors: Cheryl Townsend, C. Ra McGuirt, Mary Winters, Ben Ohmart, Paul Weinman. Submission quantity: as many as you want, as often as you want. Special interests: Feminist work; work about family; or work about struggle (which ususally entails feminism and family).

Chili Verde, 736 E. Guenther Street, San Antonio, TX 78210, 210-532-8384. 1993. 5½×11.

CHINESE LITERATURE, Chinese Literature Press, 24 Baiwanzhuang Road, Beijing 100037, People's

Republic of China, 892554. Xu Shengui. 1951. "All poems are chosen from various publications by our own editor for translation" circ. 50M. 4/yr. Pub'd 32 poems 1999; expects 30 poems 2000, 30 poems 2001. sub. price: $10.50. 200pp; 21.5×14cm; Interested in new or unpub'd poets: no. Simultaneous submissions accepted: no. Recent contributors: Feng Zhi, Zhou Tao, Li Ying, Zhao Kai, Li Xiaoyu.

Chinese Literature Press (see also CHINESE LITERATURE), 24 Baiwanzhuang Road, Beijing 100037, People's Republic of China. Xu Shengui. 1951. Pub'd 32 poetry titles 1999; expects 30 poetry titles 2000, 30 poetry titles 2001. 21.5×14cm. Interested in new or unpub'd poets: no. Simultaneous submissions accepted: no. Recently published poets: Feng Zhi, Zhou Tao, Li Ying, Zhao Kai, Li Xiaoyu.

CHIRON REVIEW, Chiron Review Press, 702 North Prairie, St. John, KS 67576-1516, 316-549-6156, 316-786-4955, chironreview@hotmail.com, www.geocities.com/soho/nook/1748. Michael Hathaway, Editor; Shon Fox, Assistant Editor; Gerald Locklin, Contributing Editor. 1982. "Presents the widest possible range of contemporary creative writing—fiction and non-fiction, traditional and off-beat—in an attractive, professional tabloid format, including artwork and photographs of featured writers. All submissions are invited; no taboos. Be sure to include self-addressed, stamped envelope with all correspondence and submissions." circ. 2.5M. 4/yr. Pub'd 200 poems 1999; expects 200 poems 2000, 200 poems 2001. sub. price: $12 ($24 overseas), $28 instit.; sample: $5 ($10 overseas), $7 instit. 48pp; 10×13; Rights purchased: one-time. Publishes 10% of poems submitted. Deadlines: Spring Jan.1, Summer Apr.1, Fall July 1, Winter Oct.1; read year-round. Reporting time: 1-4 weeks. Payment: 1 copy. Interested in new or unpub'd poets: yes. Simultaneous submissions accepted: no. Recent contributors: Charles Bukowski, Marge Piercy, Jack Micheline, Leslea Newman, Geezus Lee. Submission quantity: 3-6; no more than 10.

Chiron Review Press (see also CHIRON REVIEW), 702 North Prairie, St. John, KS 67576-1516, 316-549-6156, chironreview@hotmail.com, www.geocities.com/soho/nook/1748. Michael Hathaway. 1987. avg. press run 100-200. Pub'd 2 poetry titles 1999; expects 1 poetry title 2001. 8½×5½; avg. price, paper: $10. 48pp; Publishes 5% of poetry manuscripts submitted. Reporting time: 1-4 weeks. Payment: 25% of press run, no royalty. Interested in new or unpub'd poets: yes. Simultaneous submissions accepted: no. Recently published poets: Scott Heim, Wilma Elizabeth McDaniel, Belinda Subraman, Jon Forrest Glade, Robert Penick. Submission quantity: entire ms and SASE.

CHRISTIANITY & THE ARTS, PO Box 118088, Chicago, IL 60611, 312-642-8606. Robert Klein Engler. Address poetry submissions to: 901 S. Plymouth Court #1801, Chicago, IL 60605. 1994. "Poetry—religion and christianity" circ. 5M. 4/yr. Pub'd 20 poems 1999. sub. price: $21; sample: $7. 72pp; 8½×11; Rights purchased: First—rights revert to author. Publishes 10% of poems submitted. Deadlines: all the time—no deadlines. Reporting time: 1-2 weeks. Payment: 2 copies. Interested in new or unpub'd poets: yes. Simultaneous submissions accepted: yes. Recent contributors: Judith Deem Dupree, Pat Schneider, Jacki Bartley. Submission quantity: no limit.

CHRONICLES OF DISORDER, 20 Edie Road, Saratoga Springs, NY 12866-5425. Thomas Christian, Editor. 1996. "Upcoming and re-occuring themes: The Beat Generation, Patti Smith, Arthur Rimbaud, Rolling Stones, James Joyce, Lou Reed." circ. 500. 2/yr. Pub'd 20 poems 1999; expects 40 poems 2000, 40 poems 2001. sample price: $2.95. 48pp; 5½×8½; Rights purchased: copyrighted, rights retained by author. Publishes 20% of poems submitted. Deadlines: ongoing. Reporting time: 1 month. Payment: 2 copies of issue. Interested in new or unpub'd poets: yes. Simultaneous submissions accepted: yes. Recent contributors: Thurston Moore, Patti Smith, Arthur Winfield Knight, John Gilmore, Ron Whitehead. Submission quantity: 3. Special interests: Always seeking introspective, personal creations in any style.

CICADA, Amelia Press, 329 'E' Street, Bakersfield, CA 93304, 661-323-4064. Frederick A. Raborg, Jr., Editor. 1985. "*Cicada* uses haiku, senryu, tanka, haibun, sequences or garlands—traditional or experimental, including one-liners and English haiku using 22 syllables. We enjoy translations from all languages, but especially from the Japanese when accompanied by a copy of the original with calligraphy when appropriate. We also need essays on the form, and will consider fiction which incorporates the form or centers on the Japanese culture (see Marsh Cassady's work in a recent issue). We look for intensity, imagery, essence, of course, but also for that haiku that reaches to extend the form. I believe that haiku, particularly in English, ought not to be limited to creeping, crawling things, fluffy or angry clouds, tree boughs and snow. Oriental artwork, for which we pay a modest honorarium, is always considered—black and white only, any medium. We also use a few reviews, and welcome books of, or about, the form." circ. 800. 4/yr. Pub'd 412 poems 1999; expects 440 poems 2000, 440 poems 2001. sub. price: $18; sample: $6 ppd. 44pp; 5½×8½; Rights purchased: first North American Serial Rights only. Publishes 12% of poems submitted. Deadlines: ongoing consideration, no specific deadline. Reporting time: 1-2 weeks. Payment: 3 "best of issue" poets each receive $10 on publication; no other payment. Interested in new or unpub'd poets: yes. Simultaneous submissions accepted: no. Recent contributors: H.F. Noyes, Roger Ishii, David Ray, Ryokufu Ishizaki, Francine Porad. Submission quantity: 6-12. Special interests: We enjoy humor and wit in the senryu used.

Cider Mill Press, PO Box 211, Stratford, CT 06497. 1966.

CIMARRON REVIEW, 205 Morrill Hall, Oklahoma State University, Stillwater, OK 74078-0135, 405-744-9476. James Cooper, Lisa Lewis, Doug Martin, Todd Fuller. 1967. "Please type name and address of author in *upper right hand* corner of each poem submitted" circ. 500. 4/yr. Pub'd 56 poems 1999; expects 60-65 poems 2000, 60-65 poems 2001. sub. price: $16 ($20 in Canada), $45/3 years ($55 Canada); sample: $5. 96-128pp; 6×9; Rights purchased: all with liberal reprint policy. Publishes under 3% of poems submitted. Deadlines: none (published chronologically as accepted). Reporting time: 3 months. Payment: 1-year subscriptions, $15 per poem. Interested in new or unpub'd poets: yes, if of high quality writing. Simultaneous submissions accepted: no. Recent contributors: William Stafford, Tess Gallagher, Albert Goldbarth, Michael Bugeja, Ann Fletcher. Submission quantity: 3-5. Special interests: We look for grace and strength in writing.

City Lights Books, Attn: Bob Sharrard, Editor, 261 Columbus Avenue, San Francisco, CA 94133, 415-362-8193. Lawrence Ferlinghetti, Nancy Peters, Robert Sharrard. 1955. "Manuscripts must be accompanied with a stamped, self-addressed envelope" avg. press run 2M. Pub'd 3 poetry titles 1999; expects 5 poetry titles 2000, 5 poetry titles 2001. size varies; avg. price, paper: $5.95. 96pp; Reporting time: 4-6 weeks. Interested in new or unpub'd poets: yes. Simultaneous submissions accepted: yes. Recently published poets: Andrei Codrescu, Allen Ginsberg. Submission quantity: 10-15 pages.

CITY PRIMEVAL, PO Box 30064, Seattle, WA 98103, 206-440-0791. David Ross. 1995. "Be useful to write for guidelines before submitting. Since *City Primeval* is primarily fiction, we don't use more than 2 or 3 poems per issue, usually." circ. 100+. 4/yr. Pub'd 10 poems 1999; expects 25 poems 2000, 25 poems 2001. sub. price: $18; sample: $6 + $1.01 postage. 72pp; 6×9; Rights purchased: 1 time. Deadlines: continuous. Reporting time: 2-3 months. Payment: 1 copy. Interested in new or unpub'd poets: yes. Simultaneous submissions accepted: no. Recent contributors: Robert R. Ward, Paula Milligan, P.F. Allen.

CLACKAMAS LITERARY REVIEW, 19600 South Molalla Avenue, Oregon City, OR 97045. Jeff Knorr. 1996. "*CLR* promotes the work of emerging writers and established writers of fiction, poetry, and creative nonfiction. Submission deadline (postmark) for Spring issue: September 25th. Submissions received after the posted deadlines will not be held for the next issue. Manuscripts must be typed or produced on a letter-quality printer—clean photocopies are acceptable. Send poetry and prose separately. We cannot respond to submissions unless they are accompanied by a SASE. We have previously published work by Naomi Shihab Nye, Pamela Uschuk, George Kalamaras, Greg Sellers, Ron Carlson, H. Lee Barns, and Milissa Pritchard." circ. 1M. 1-2/yr. sub. price: $10. 128pp; 6×9; Reporting time: 2 months. Interested in new or unpub'd poets: yes. Simultaneous submissions accepted: yes, please inform us if work is accepted elsewhere. Submission quantity: 6 poems maximum.

Clamp Down Press, PO Box 7270, Cape Porpoise, ME 04014, 207-967-2605. Joshua Bodwell. 1997. "I am very interested in the 'book' as an entire project. Clamp Down Press is not one to slap together some words and just throw it out there. A book is like a poem, it takes time to grow and become all that it can be. I work with poets whose poetry affects me with such intensity that I can't get the words out of my head. I almost have to give the poems a 'boat to float on.' A book." avg. press run varies. Pub'd 2 poetry titles 1999; expects 4 poetry titles 2000. 5½×8½ and others; avg. price, cloth: $14; paper: $25; other: $50. 60pp; Reporting time: varies. Payment: special to each project. Interested in new or unpub'd poets: always willing to read work and advise on it, though my publishing schedule is *very* full. Recently published poets: Mark Weber, Gerald Locklin, David Heminway, Tom Sexton, Gary Metras.

Clamshell Press, 160 California Avenue, Santa Rosa, CA 95405. D. L. Emblen. 1973. "Regularity and consistency are not among our virtues (or vices, depending upon how you look at those traits). We publish 1) that which strongly takes hold of our fancy 2) when we can find the time to set it in type. We have just brought out a bilingual, retrospective edition of the poems of the Swedish poet, Werner Aspenstrom, the first substantial collection of his work to appear in English. Our most recent publication is *Cock Robin and Other Bird Poems*, by D.L. Emblen. We do issue a series of Clamshell Poetry Broadsides, anywhere from 6 to 10 of those a year. We also publish the Clamshell Sampler series, 2-5 per year. We are primarily interested in poetry, translations, and criticism, in that order. Our publications are handsomely printed, but we're not very good (nor very interested, it would seem) in distribution" 5½×8½.

THE CLASSICAL OUTLOOK, Department of Classics, The University of Georgia, Athens, GA 30602, 706-542-9257, fax 706-542-8503, mricks@arches.uga.edu. David Middleton, David Slavitt. 1923. "*The Classical Outlook* publishes original poems in English *on classical themes*, verse translations from Greek and Roman authors, and original Latin poems. Submissions should, as a rule, be written in traditional poetic forms and should demonstrate skill in the use of meter, diction, and rhyme if rhyme is employed. Original poems should be more than mere exercise pieces or the poetry of nostalgia. Translations should be accompanied by a photocopy of the original Greek or Latin text; Latin originals should be accompanied by a literal English rendering of the text. Submissions should not exceed 50 lines. Submit two annonymous copies. Poetry not returned without a SASE.'' circ. 4M. 4/yr. Pub'd 29 poems 1999; expects 38 poems 2000, 35 poems 2001. sub. price: $35 ($37 Canada, $40 overseas); sample: $10. 40pp; 8½×11; Rights purchased: none. Publishes 11% of poems submitted. Deadlines: none. Reporting time: 6 months. Payment: 2 complimentary copies. Interested in new or unpub'd poets: yes. Simultaneous submissions accepted: no. Recent contributors: Robert Cooperman, Paul Murgatroyd, Lisa Barnett, Victor Howes. Submission quantity: 50 lines, no more than 5 poems. Special interests: Translations from Latin and classical Greek, original verse along classical themes. Light verse and satire published in the "Facetiae" column.

Cleveland State Univ. Poetry Center, 1983 East 24th Street, Cleveland, OH 44115-2400, 216-687-3986; Fax 216-687-6943; poetrycenter@popmail.csuohio.edu. Ted Lardner, Co-Director; Ruth Schwartz, Co-Director. 1962. "Send only Nov. 1st thru Feb 1st. Mss. should be typed or letter-quality print; clear photocopies acceptable. We publish both full-length books (50-100 pp.) and chapbooks (50 or fewer pages). CSU Poetry Center prize, $1,000 plus publication in the CSU Poetry Series. Entry fee for prize, $20. CSU Poetry Series books selected from manuscripts submitted for prize. Reading fee for chapbooks, $15. No reading fee for Cleveland Poets series (Ohio poets only). For detailed guidelines, send SASE. Send $2 for 64 page catalogue." avg. press run 1M. Pub'd 4 poetry titles 1999; expects 4 poetry titles 2000, 4 poetry titles 2001. size varies; avg. price, cloth: $17.50; paper: $10; other: chapbooks $5. 80pp; Publishes .5% of poetry manuscripts submitted. Reporting time: 5-7 months. Payment: CSU Poetry Series (nationally advertised & distributed)—50 copies + $300, Cleveland Poets Series and other books—100 copies. Interested in new or unpub'd poets: yes. Simultaneous submissions accepted: yes, but they should be identified as such. Recently published poets: Jared Carter, Marilyn Krysl, Frankie Paino, Anthony Vigil, Judith Vollmer. Submission quantity: 50+ pages (at least 20 for chapbooks). Special interests: We try to remain receptive to a variety of styles and approaches, including experimental poetry. We have published volumes that include translations, but none that are exclusively translations. No light verse, no devotional verse, or verse in which rhyme and meter seem to be of major importance.

THE CLIMBING ART, 6390 E. Floyd Dr., Denver, CO 80222-7638. Ron Morrow. 1986. "We are about the literature, poetry, art for and about the spirit of climbing" circ. 1M. 2/yr. Pub'd 50 poems 1999. sub. price: $18; sample: $4.50. 160pp; 7½×5½; Reporting time: 2 months. Payment: up to $50. Interested in new or unpub'd poets: yes. Simultaneous submissions accepted: yes. Recent contributors: Reg Sander, Terry Gifford, Paul Wills, Ralph Mitchell. Special interests: We are interested in all types of poetry.

CLUBHOUSE, Your Story Hour, PO Box 15, Berrien Springs, MI 49103, (616) 471-9009. Krista Hainey. 1951. "Not currently accepting. Try again in the Spring of 1999. All submissions should be made in April of each year. Prefer short mood or humor pieces that children would enjoy." circ. 4M. 12/yr. Pub'd 12-15 poems 1999; expects 12-15 poems 2000, 10-12 poems 2001. sub. price: $5; sample: free with SASE for 3 oz. 8pp; 8½×11; Rights purchased: first, second or reprint. Publishes 2-5% of poems submitted. Deadlines: send in April of each year. Reporting time: 8 weeks. Payment: $10-$20. Interested in new or unpub'd poets: yes. Simultaneous submissions accepted: yes. Submission quantity: no more than 10.

CLUTCH, 147 Coleridge Street, San Francisco, CA 94110. Dan Hodge, Lawrence Oberc. 1991. "We invite both new and previously published poetry. Please indicate if work has been previously published and where. Rights revert to authors. Please do not submit work more than once a year. Work accepted for publication may take up to two years for printing." circ. 400-500. 1/yr. Pub'd 20-40 poems 1999; expects 20-40 poems 2000, 20-40 poems 2001. sub. price: $5/issue, payment must be made in cash or check payable to Dan Hodge; sample: $5. 65pp; 5½×8½; Publishes 7% of poems submitted. Reporting time: approx. 1-6 months. Payment: free copy. Interested in new or unpub'd poets: yes. Simultaneous submissions accepted: yes. Recent contributors: Charles Bukowski, Lorri Jackson, Simon Perchik, Todd Moore, Robert Peters. Submission quantity: no more than 7. Special interests: No preconceived subject specialties. Non-academic writing with an edge emphasized. We publish both tried and unheard-from voices.

CLWN WR, PO Box 2165 Church Street Station, New York, NY 10008-2165. 1972. circ. 300-500. Irregular. sample price: #10 SASE w/2oz. postage. 10-14pp; 8½×11.

COBBLESTONE: Discover American History, 30 Grove Street, Suite C, Peterborough, NH 03458, 603-924-7209, Fax 603-924-7380, custsvc@cobblestone.mv.com. 1980. "*Cobblestone* is thematic; all poems must relate to the theme. Poets are advised to request *upcoming themes and guidelines* before submitting material" circ. 36M. 9/yr. sub. price: $29.95 + $8/yr for foreign and Canada, Canadian subs add 7% GST; sample: $4.95. 52pp; 7×9; Rights purchased: all. Payment: up to $1.50/line. Interested in new or unpub'd poets: no, queries only. Simultaneous submissions accepted: yes.

Coffee House Press, 27 N. 4th Street, Minneapolis, MN 55401, 612-338-0125, Fax 612-338-4004, jim@coffeehousepress.org. Allan Kornblum, Publisher; Christopher Fischbach, Managing Editor. 1984. avg. press run 2M. Pub'd 4 poetry titles 1999; expects 4 poetry titles 2000, 4 poetry titles 2001. poetry 7×10, fiction 5½×8½; avg. price, cloth: $15.95; paper: $13.95. 128pp; Publishes 1% of poetry manuscripts submitted.

Reporting time: 8-12 weeks. Payment: 10% of sales or press run. Interested in new or unpub'd poets: yes. Simultaneous submissions accepted: no. Recently published poets: Linda Hogan, Marjorie Welish, Kenward Elmslie, Wang Ping, Victor Hernandez Cruz. Submission quantity: 15.

COKEFISH, Cokefish Press, 31 Waterloo Street, New Hope, PA 18938. Ana Christy, Publisher-Editor. 1990. "Want legible poems, not too long. Do not want to see religion, rhyme, silly stuff about butterflies or unnecessary sunsets" circ. 500. 6/yr. Pub'd 900 poems 1999. sub. price: $17; sample: $6. 50-60pp; 8½×11; Rights purchased: none. Publishes 50% of poems submitted. Deadlines: none. Reporting time: immediately to 1 week. Payment: free copy. Interested in new or unpub'd poets: yes. Simultaneous submissions accepted: yes. Recent contributors: David Whitacre, Joan Reid, Laurence Lasky, George Dowden, Dave Christy. Submission quantity: unlimited. Special interests: Want to see poetry that will raise my eyebrows, arouse my interest, make me forget to cook dinner and let the dogs out. Want to see social issues, sex, avant-garde and humor.

Cokefish Press (see also COKEFISH), 31 Waterloo Street, New Hope, PA 18938. Ana Christy. 1990. "We publish chapbooks dealing with everyday life and situations. Stimulating avante-garde and modern poetry. Also offer co-operative publishing" avg. press run 200. Expects 2 poetry titles 2001. 5×8½; avg. price, paper: $5. 30-50pp; Publishes 20% of poetry manuscripts submitted. Reporting time: immediately to 1 week. Payment: copies. Interested in new or unpub'd poets: yes. Simultaneous submissions accepted: yes. Recently published poets: Steve DeFrance, Margaret Crocker, George Schaeffer, Gary Jurechka, Golda Fried. Submission quantity: 20-30.

COLD-DRILL, Cold-Drill Books, 1910 University Drive, Boise, ID 83725, 208-426-3862. Mitch Wieland, Faculity Editor. 1970. "Open to poems of high quality." circ. 500. 1/yr. Pub'd 40 poems 1999. sub. price: $15 (inc. p/h); sample: $15 (inc. p/h). 150pp; 6×9; Rights purchased: first. Publishes 10% of poems submitted. Deadlines: December 1 each year. Reporting time: you will be notified by January 15th of each year. Payment: author's copy of magazine. Interested in new or unpub'd poets: yes. Simultaneous submissions accepted: yes. Submission quantity: no limit.

Cold-Drill Books (see also COLD-DRILL), Dept. of English, Boise State University, Boise, ID 83725. 1980. "Prior publication in *Cold-Drill Magazine* required." size varies.

COLLEGE ENGLISH, Dept. of English, U Mass/Boston, 100 Morrissey Boulevard, Boston, MA 02125-3393. Thomas O'Grady, Poetry Editor. 1939. "Please send submissions directly to Thomas O'Grady at the University of Massachusetts. Include a short biography and a telephone number" circ. 16M. 8/yr. Pub'd 64 poems 1999. sub. price: $40, includes membership in NCTE, student rate $10.50; sample: $6, $6.25 from NCTE in Urbana, IL. 100pp; 7½×9½; Rights purchased: none. Deadlines: submissions accepted all year. Reporting time: 8 weeks. Payment: none. Interested in new or unpub'd poets: yes. Simultaneous submissions accepted: no. Recent contributors: Sherman Alexie, Catherine Phil MacCarthy, W.D. Ehrhart. Submission quantity: 1-3. Special interests: Wide variety of interests.

COLORADO REVIEW: A Journal of Contemporary Literature, 359 Eddy, English Dept., Colorado State University, Fort Collins, CO 80523, 303-491-5449. Jorie Graham, Donald Revell. 1966. "We prefer poems that are highly imaginative, that transform rather than observe or describe, that explore alternative visions. See our issues Vol. IX, #2, Vol. X, #1 to get an idea of what we mean. We are probably less focused on magical realism in the upcoming issues, but for the most part that statement still holds. Mere description, mere observation, poems without a sense of compelling imagery & rhythm, these do not interest us here. We want fiction that engages the reader with immediately presented experience in depth, with themes that are ambitious, with language that achieves levels. *Colorado Review* also sponsors the Colorado Prize for Poetry. Deadline for the 2001 prize is Jan. 8, 2001. Send SASE for guidelines." circ. 1.8M. 3/yr. Pub'd 40-50 poems 1999; expects 40-50 poems 2000, 40-50 poems 2001. sub. price: $24/1 year, $45/2 years, $65/3 years; sample: $10. 200pp; 6⅛×9¼; Rights purchased: 1st North American serial. Publishes 5-10% of poems submitted. Deadlines: each year Sept. thru April 30. Reporting time: 4-6 months. Payment: $5 per printed page. Interested in new or unpub'd poets: we still are, though editorial pressures do not permit comments on poems except rarely. Simultaneous submissions accepted: no. Recent contributors: John Ashbery, Lyn Hejinian, Susan Wheeler, Cal Bedient, Rebecca Wolff. Submission quantity: 3-6. Special interests: *Colorado Review* publishes three issues each year that contain short fiction, poetry, translations from around the world, articles on literary culture, interviews with significant contemporary authors, and reviews of recent works of the literary imagination.

COMMON LIVES / LESBIAN LIVES, 1802 7th Ave. Ct., Iowa City, IA 52240-6436. 1981. "No exclusions except poetry must be accessible to a broad audience of lesbians-i.e. not academic, abstruse, abstract" circ. 3M. 4/yr. Pub'd 16-20 poems 1999; expects 16-20 poems 2000, 16-20 poems 2001. sub. price: $15; sample: $5. 128pp; 5½×8½; Rights purchased: copyrights revert to authors, *no simultaneous publication*. Publishes 10% of poems submitted. Deadlines: ongoing. Reporting time: 3-6 months. Payment: 2 copies. Interested in new or unpub'd poets: yes, lesbians only. Simultaneous submissions accepted: no. Recent contributors: Sandra Lundy, Kris Hill, flying thunder cloud, Lisa Palmer, Sapphire. Submission quantity: 5 max.

A COMPANION IN ZEOR, 307 Ashland Ave., Egg Harbor Township, NJ 08234-5568, 609-645-6938, fax 609-645-8084, Klitman323@aol.com, www.simegen.com/sgfandom/rimonslibrary/cz. Karen Litman. 1978. "Our publication is based on the science fiction universes of Jacqueline Lichtenberg and work should be based on her creations. Any poetry related to any book she has written is welcomed, and it is suggested strongly that the contributor be familiar with the Lichtenberg work. Now limited to only Lichtenberg creations." circ. 100. Irregular. Pub'd 3 poems 1999; expects 3 poems 2000, 3 poems 2001. 60pp; 8½×11; Rights purchased: first rights with copyright release form signed by the poetry contributor. We will try to eventually publish all poems submitted; usually 2-4 an issue depending on length. Deadlines: none, since we publish irregularly. Reporting time: 1 month for all submissions. Payment: contributor's copy (or copies if asked). Interested in new or unpub'd poets: yes. Simultaneous submissions accepted: if submitted to the 'sister fanzines' in our group, this is acceptable. Usually we have non-simultaneous material. Recent contributors: Lisa Calhoun, Gail Ray Barton, Rhonda K. Marsh. Submission quantity: no set limit. Special interests: Occasional long poems, satire ok, light verse, or most any item is considered. Any poetry style such as rhyme, open verse, etc.

Company of Words Publishing, 2082 Shannon Lakes Blvd., Kissimmee, FL 34743-3648, 617-492-7930; FAX 617-354-3392; e-mail wordspub@aol.com; web page www.wordspublishing.com. 1996. 5½×8½.

THE COMPLEAT NURSE, Dry Bones Press, PO Box 597, Roseville, CA 95678-0597, 415-707-2129 phone/Fax, www.drybones.com. J. R.N. Rankin, MSN. 1991. circ. 500. 12/yr. Expects 8 poems 2000. sub. price: $12; sample: SASE. 4-6pp; 8½×11; Rights purchased: single publish. Deadlines: monthly. Reporting time: ASAP. Payment: glory, being published, copies. Interested in new or unpub'd poets: yes. Simultaneous submissions accepted: yes. Recent contributors: J. Rankin, Anon patient, Miller Williams. Submission quantity: As desired, but our areas of interest, only 2-3 poems used per issue.

THE COMSTOCK REVIEW, Comstock Writers' Group, Inc., 4958 St. John Drive, Syracuse, NY 13215. Peggy Sperger Flanders, Managing Editor. 1987. "No tasteless pointless poetry; no heavily religious poetry. Prefer poetry that is grammatically correct and clearly understandable. No greeting-card verse or rhymes-for-rhyme's-sake. Yearly contest $1,300 in prizes. $3 per poem, 40 lines. SASE for complete guidelines." circ. 500. 2/yr. Pub'd 200+ poems 1999; expects 200+ poems 2000, 200+ poems 2001. sub. price: $15/2 issues; sample: $6. 105pp; 5½×8½; Rights purchased: 1st N. American. Publishes 2% of poems submitted. Deadlines: 2 reading periods (Jan.1-Feb.28 & July 1-Aug.31). Reporting time: within 6 weeks of reading period. Payment: copy. Interested in new or unpub'd poets: Yes. Simultaneous submissions accepted: No. Recent contributors: Susan Terris, Virgil Suarez, Charles Atkinson, Carolyne Wright, Vivian C. Shipley. Submission quantity: 4-6. Special interests: We enjoy both traditional formal poetry and well-done free forms, including humorous poems. We like metaphor and fresh imagery and poems dealing with issues, ideas, feelings and beliefs common to us all.

CONCHO RIVER REVIEW, English Department, Angelo State University, San Angelo, TX 76909, 915-942-2273, james.moore@angelo.edu. Jerry Bradley. Address poetry submissions to: English Dept., West Texas A&M University, Canyon, TX 79016-0001, 806-656-2455, jbradley@wtamu.edu. 1986. "We read poems all year. Don't send big manila envelopes; fold poems in legal-sized envelope. Include SASE and don't send your only copy. All styles are welcomed" circ. 300. 2/yr. Pub'd 28 poems 1999; expects 35 poems 2000, 35 poems 2001. sub. price: $14; sample: $5. 115pp; 6×9; Rights purchased: 1st rights, revert to author. Publishes 10-15% of poems submitted. Deadlines: continuous. Reporting time: 2-6 months. Payment: copy. Interested in new or unpub'd poets: yes. Simultaneous submissions accepted: yes. Recent contributors: Albert Huffstickler, Carol C. Reposa, Wendy Barker, Peter Wild, Walter McDonald. Submission quantity: 3-5. Special interests: poems of one page have an advantage, but we occasionally use longer (2-3 pages) poems. We do not accept trite, didactic pieces, but we are not afraid of sentiment. We are always looking for good humorous verse, and we would like to see strong poems in traditional form. Free verse is fine, but we like poems that read well. We do not publish poems in bad taste or poems that romanticize suicide, drugs, or the occult.

CONDUIT, 510 Eighth Avenue NE, Minneapolis, MN 55413. Brett Astor, William D. Waltz. 1993. circ. 1M. 2/yr. Pub'd 75 poems 1999; expects 75 poems 2000, 75 poems 2001. sub. price: $11 individuals, $20 institutions; sample: $5. 64pp; 5⅛×10; Rights purchased: none. Publishes 1% of poems submitted. Deadlines: none. Reporting time: 6 weeks-6 months. Payment: copies. Interested in new or unpub'd poets: yes. Simultaneous submissions accepted: yes. Recent contributors: James Tate, Mary Jo Bang, Russell Edson, Amy Gerstler, Dara Wier. Submission quantity: 3-5. Special interests: Experimental, traditional, open to all forms.

CONFLICT OF INTEREST, Proper PH Publications, 4701 East National Road, Springfield, OH 45505-1847, 330-630-5646 phone/Fax; E-mail PHartney@aol.com. 1994. circ. 250+. 4/yr. sub. price: $20; sample: $5. 100pp; 11×17.

CONFLUENCE, PO Box 336, Belpre, OH 45714, 304-422-3112; e-mail dbprather@prodigy.net. James S. Bond, Poetry Editor; David B. Prather, Poetry Editor. 1989. "Always include biographical infromation and SASE" circ. 500. 1/yr. Pub'd 27 poems 1999; expects 25-30 poems 2000, 25-35 poems 2001. sub. price: $5 +

$1.24 S&H; sample: $4 + $1.24 S&H. 112pp; 5½×8½; Rights purchased: 1st Am. rights/revert to author on pub. Publishes 1-2% of poems submitted. Deadlines: Sept. 1 - March 1 annually. Reporting time: 1-3 months. Payment: copy. Interested in new or unpub'd poets: yes. Simultaneous submissions accepted: no. Recent contributors: Richard Hague, Pamela Kircher, Walt McDonald, and Valerie Martinez. Submission quantity: 3-7 max. Special interests: translations.

Confluence Press, Inc., Lewis-Clark State College, 500 8th Avenue, Lewiston, ID 83501-2698, 208-799-2336. James R. Hepworth. 1975. avg. press run 1.5M. Pub'd 2 poetry titles 1999; expects 2 poetry titles 2000, 2 poetry titles 2001. 5½×8½, 6×9; avg. price, cloth: $14.95; paper: $8.95. 70pp; Publishes 1-2% of poetry manuscripts submitted. Reporting time: 6-8 weeks. Payment: negotiated on an individual basis. Interested in new or unpub'd poets: yes. Simultaneous submissions accepted: yes. Recently published poets: James Welch, John Daniel, Sherry Rind, William Stafford. Submission quantity: 10 for a sample, 36-50 for a complete manuscript. Special interests: work from poets who live and write in the interior of the western United States.

CONFRONTATION, English Department, C.W. Post of Long Island Univ., Greenvale, NY 11548, 516-299-2720. Katherine Hill-Miller. 1968. "We print thematic issues from time to time. We do not read during June, July, August" circ. 2M. 2/yr. Pub'd 100 poems 1999; expects 100 poems 2000, 100 poems 2001. sub. price: $10; sample: $3. 295pp; 6×9; Rights purchased: first serial rights. Publishes 10% of poems submitted. Deadlines: open. Reporting time: 6-8 weeks. Payment: $10-$50. Interested in new or unpub'd poets: yes. Simultaneous submissions accepted: yes, reluctantly. Recent contributors: David Ignatow, Joseph Brodsky, Molly Peacock, David Ray, Irving Feldman. Submission quantity: no more than 6. Special interests: Open to all forms and style.

CONJUNCTIONS, 21 East 10th Street #3E, New York, NY 10003-5924. General Editors. 1981. "Potential contributors are invited to read several issues of the magazine itself in order to best determine whether their work might be appropriate—otherwise, no policies, as such, are indicated" circ. 7.5M. 2/yr. Pub'd 25-30 poems 1999; expects 25-30 poems 2000, 25-30 poems 2001. sub. price: $18 indiv., $25 instit. and overseas; $32/2 yrs indiv., $45/2 yrs instit. and overseas; sample: $12. 400pp; 6×9; Rights purchased: first serial. Publishes 1% of poems submitted. Deadlines: June 15 for Fall issue, December 15 for Spring issue. Reporting time: 3-4 weeks. Payment: varies. Interested in new or unpub'd poets: yes. Simultaneous submissions accepted: no. Recent contributors: Leslie Scalapino, Charles Stein, John Ashbery, Ann Lauterbach, Jorie Graham. Submission quantity: up to 5.

THE CONNECTICUT POETRY REVIEW, PO Box 818, Stonington, CT 06378. J. Claire White, Editor; Harley More, Editor. 1981. circ. 400. 1/yr. Pub'd 25-30 poems 1999. sub. price: $3.50; sample: $3.50. 40-45pp; 4¼×8½; Rights purchased: none. Publishes 5% of poems submitted. Deadlines: October 1. Reporting time: 3 months. Payment: $5 per poem plus contributor's copy. Interested in new or unpub'd poets: yes. Simultaneous submissions accepted: no. Recent contributors: Robert Peters, Peter Wild, Odysseus Elytis, Claudia Buckholts, Margaret Randall. Submission quantity: 3 poems. Special interests: We accept anything of quality!

CONNECTICUT REVIEW, SCSU, 501 Crescent Street, New Haven, CT 06515, 203-392-6737, Fax 203-392-5748. Vivan Shipley. 1967. circ. 3M. 2/yr. Pub'd 90 poems 1999. sub. price: $12. 176pp; 6×9; Rights purchased: 1st. Publishes 1% of poems submitted. Deadlines: September 1 and February 1. Reporting time: 3-4 months. Interested in new or unpub'd poets: yes. Simultaneous submissions accepted: no. Recent contributors: Maria Mazotti Gillan, Walt McDonald, Colette Inez, Pattiann Rogers, Alberto Rios. Submission quantity: 3-5. Special interests: Translations.

CONNECTICUT RIVER REVIEW: A National Poetry Journal, PO Box 4053, Waterbury, CT 06704-0053, http://pages.prodigy.net/mmwalker/cpsindex.html. Kevin Carey. 1978. "Looking for original, honest, diverse, vital, well-crafted poetry. Poetry, poetry translations, long-poems" circ. 500. 2/yr. Pub'd 60-100 poems 1999; expects 60-100 poems 2000, 60-100 poems 2001. sub. price: $12, $20/2 years; sample: $6 + $1 p/h. 35-50pp; 6×9; Rights purchased: none. Publishes 5% of poems submitted. Deadlines: none, continuous reading schedule. Reporting time: 6-8 weeks. Payment: 1 copy of magazine. Interested in new or unpub'd poets: yes. Simultaneous submissions accepted: no. Recent contributors: Walt McDonald, Alvin Laster, Fileman Waitts, Kathryn Rantala, Thomas Michael McDade. Submission quantity: no more than 3.

CONSCIENCE, 1436 U Street NW, Washington, DC 20009. Andrew Merton, Poetry Editor. 1980. "The magazine is published by Catholics For a Free Choice, a prochoice organization. No polemics, please. Poetry need not specifically address abortion but can be broadly related to social, physical, sexual, religious thinking, and experience." circ. 10M. 4/yr. Pub'd 12 poems 1999; expects 12 poems 2000, 12 poems 2001. sub. price: $10; sample: free to writers w/$1.01 9x12 SASE. 40pp; 8×10½; Rights purchased: first. Publishes 10% of poems submitted. Deadlines: anytime. Reporting time: 2 months. Payment: $10 plus 5 copies. Interested in new or unpub'd poets: yes. Simultaneous submissions accepted: no. Recent contributors: Angela M. Mendez, Alice Brooks-Smith, Andrew Wulf, Sallie Bingham.

CONTEXT SOUTH, Box 4504, Schreiner College, Kerrville, TX 78028, 512-896-7945. David Breeden,

Editor; Paul Hadella, Assistant Poetry Editor. 1989. "Be an artist not a sycophant" circ. 500. 2-3/yr. Pub'd 30 poems 1999; expects 50 poems 2000, 50 poems 2001. sub. price: $10; sample: $5. 65pp; 4¼×5½; Rights purchased: first. Publishes 1% of poems submitted. Deadlines: continuous. Reporting time: 4-6 weeks. Payment: 1 copy. Interested in new or unpub'd poets: yes. Simultaneous submissions accepted: yes. Recent contributors: Wayne Dodd, Richard Kostelanetz, Andrea Hollander Budy, Peter Drizal, Gloria Mindock. Submission quantity: 2-5. Special interests: experimental poetry.

THE COOL TRAVELER, 196 Bowery Street, Frostburg, MD 21532-2255, 215-440-0592. Mary Beth Feeney. 1988. "We like material that emphasizes what is a cool traveler?" circ. 1M. 6/yr. Pub'd 10 poems 1999; expects 10 poems 2000, 10 poems 2001. sub. price: $10; sample: $2. 12pp; 8½×11; Rights purchased: simultaneous, North American First Rights. Publishes 10% of poems submitted. Deadlines: no deadlines—kept for next issue. Reporting time: 4 weeks. Payment: usually in copies. Interested in new or unpub'd poets: yes. Simultaneous submissions accepted: yes. Recent contributors: Anne Louis Huffman, John J. Koller. Submission quantity: 3. Special interests: We accept a limited number of poems per year.

Copper Beech Press, P O Box 2578, English Department, Providence, RI 02906, 401-351-1253. Randy Blasing. 1973. avg. press run 1M. Pub'd 4 poetry titles 1999; expects 3 poetry titles 2000, 3 poetry titles 2001. size varies; avg. price, paper: $9.95. 64pp; Reporting time: 1 month. Payment: 5% copies. Interested in new or unpub'd poets: no. Simultaneous submissions accepted: yes. Recently published poets: Jeffrey Harrison, Phillis Levin, Kay Ryan, Robert B. Shaw, Len Roberts. Submission quantity: 5.

Copper Canyon Press, PO Box 271, Port Townsend, WA 98368. Sam Hamill. 1972. "We do not publish chapbooks. We almost never accept unsolicited manuscripts because we remain committed to many of the poets we publish and will continue to publish accordingly. Our tastes are feminist, engaged, and multicultural. We also are interested in translations from almost any language (and which should be queried with bi-lingual texts)." avg. press run 2.5M. Pub'd 6 poetry titles 1999; expects 6 poetry titles 2000, 7 poetry titles 2001. 6×9; avg. price, cloth: $22; paper: $12. 80pp; Publishes .5% of poetry manuscripts submitted. Reporting time: 1 month. Payment: standard contracts. Simultaneous submissions accepted: no. Recently published poets: Pablo Neruda, Carolyn Kizer, Olga Broumas, Hayden Carruth, Lucille Clifton. Submission quantity: 7 pages. Special interests: No light verse, no "experimental" poetry, and no "concrete" poetry.

Coreopsis Books, 1384 Township Drive, Lawrenceville, GA 30243, 404-995-9475. Lee Passarella, Publisher. 1993. "Coreopsis hopes to have an annual chapbook contest with a deadline in October. The winner of the first annual contest will appear in May 1995. Coreopsis will also maintain a chapbook series" avg. press run 300. Expects 3-4 poetry titles 2000, 3-4 poetry titles 2001. avg. price, paper: $7. 50pp; Publishes 10% or less of poetry manuscripts submitted. Reporting time: 1 month for queries; 3-4 months for manuscripts. Payment: varies. Interested in new or unpub'd poets: yes. Simultaneous submissions accepted: yes. Submission quantity: Query with 10.

CORNERSTONE, 939 W. Wilson Avenue, Chicago, IL 60640, 773-561-2450 ext. 2080; fax 773-989-2076. 1972. circ. 38M. 3-4/yr. Pub'd 3 poems 1999; expects 10 poems 2000, 15 poems 2001. sub. price: donation; sample: SASE with 5 first class stamps. 64-72pp; 8½×11; Rights purchased: first rights, reprint rights. Publishes 1% of poems submitted. Reporting time: 6-8 weeks. Payment: varies. Interested in new or unpub'd poets: yes. Simultaneous submissions accepted: yes. Submission quantity: 3-10.

CORONA, Dept. of Hist. & Phil., Montana State Univ., PO Box 172320, Bozeman, MT 59717, 406-994-5200. 1980. "Open to a variety of approaches. Next issue: The BOOK" circ. 2M. Occasional. Pub'd 18 poems 1999; expects 15 poems 2000, 15-20 poems 2001. sub. price: $7; sample: $7. 130pp; 10×7; Rights purchased: 1st rights, then they revert to author. Publishes .05% of poems submitted. Deadlines: none. Reporting time: 1 week-6 months. Payment: $10 upon publication. Interested in new or unpub'd poets: yes. Simultaneous submissions accepted: no. Recent contributors: Philip Dacey, James Dickey, Richard Hugo, Wendy Battin, Charles Edward Eaton. Submission quantity: a handful. Special interests: Everything; no translations, no greeting cards.

Cosmic Trend (see also PARA*PHRASE), Sheridan Mall, Box 47014, Mississauga, Ontario L5K 2R2, Canada. George Le Grand, Jiri Jirasek. 1984. "Send $1 for submission conditions and fees. No US postal stamps!" avg. press run 100. Pub'd 3 poetry titles 1999; expects 3 poetry titles 2000, 3 poetry titles 2001. 8½×11; avg. price, paper: $8 ($12 incl. audio cassette). 70pp; Reporting time: usually less than 1 month. Payment: discount copy of book (& cassette). Interested in new or unpub'd poets: yes. Simultaneous submissions accepted: yes. Recently published poets: Susan Benischek, Heather Fraser, Joanna Nealon, Charles David Rice, Charles Tuck. Submission quantity: 10. Special interests: Non-rhyming short peotry exploring human soul through love and sex.

Coteau Books, 401-2206 Dewdney Avenue, Regina, Sask. S4R 1H3, Canada, 306-777-0170; e-Mail coteau@coteau.unibase.com. Editorial Board. 1975. avg. press run .5M-1.5M paper. Pub'd 2 poetry titles 1999; expects 4 poetry titles 2000, 3 poetry titles 2001. 6×9, 4¼×7, 8×8, 8½×11; avg. price, paper: $9.95. 100pp;

Publishes 1% of poetry manuscripts submitted. Reporting time: 2-6 months. Payment: 12% royalty usually. Interested in new or unpub'd poets: yes, must be Canadian. Simultaneous submissions accepted: no. Recently published poets: Elizabeth Philips, Anne Szumigalsk, Bruce Rice, Kristjana Gunnars, Tonja Gunvaldsen Klaassen. Submission quantity: an entire collection.

COTTONWOOD, Cottonwood Press, 400 Kansas Union, Box J, University of Kansas, Lawrence, KS 66045, 785-864-2528. Philip Wedge. 1965. "We read continuously. An SASE is required. We appreciate a small selection of a poet's best work. We have established the Alice Carter Awards (annual) for the best poetry and fiction published each year in our magazine." circ. 500-600. 2/yr. Pub'd 15 poems 1999; expects 30 poems 2000, 30 poems 2001. sub. price: $15, $18 overseas; sample: $4. 112pp; 9×6; Rights purchased: 1st publication rights revert to author. Publishes 1% of poems submitted. Deadlines: none. Reporting time: 2-5 months. Payment: 1 copy. Interested in new or unpub'd poets: yes. Simultaneous submissions accepted: yes. Recent contributors: Wanda Coleman, Victor Contoski, Denise Low, Walter McDonald, Rita Dove. Submission quantity: no more than 7. Special interests: We publish what, in our opinion, is the best poetry received, regardless of region, style or length. But we're generally not too interested in translations and longpoems. We look for fresh images, controlled narratives, effective metaphors and a control of language without losing sight of the poem's content.

Cottonwood Press (see also COTTONWOOD), 400 Kansas Union, Box J, Univ. of Kansas, Lawrence, KS 66045, 785-864-2528. Philip Wedge. 1965. avg. press run 500. Pub'd 1 poetry title 1999; expects 1 poetry title 2001. 9×6; avg. price, paper: $10. 80pp; Interested in new or unpub'd poets: no. Simultaneous submissions accepted: no. Recently published poets: Michael Johnson, Edgar Wolfe, Denise Low, Victor Contoski. Submission quantity: solicited.

COTYLEDON, Catamount Press, 2519 Roland Road SW, Huntsville, AL 35805, 205-536-9801. 1997. 5/yr. Pub'd 130 poems 1999; expects 150 poems 2000, 150 poems 2001. sub. price: $3; sample: $1 or 3 unattached 33¢ stamps. 12 or 16pp; 3½×4¼; Publishes 5% of poems submitted. Deadlines: read all year. Reporting time: 1-2 months. Payment: copies. Interested in new or unpub'd poets: both, but must be good. Recent contributors: Christopher Presfield, Don Wentworth, Patricia G. Rourke, Jeanne Shannon, Carolyn Foster Segal. Submission quantity: 6. Special interests: The size of the magazine means I'm looking for *very short* poems.

COUNTERMEASURES, Creative Writing Program, College of Santa Fe, St. Michael's Drive, Santa Fe, NM 87505. Greg Glazner, Jon Davis. 1994. circ. 2M. 2/yr. Pub'd 5 poems 1999; expects 5 poems 2000, 5 poems 2001. sub. price: $5; sample: $2.50. 40pp; 8½×11; Publishes 1% of poems submitted. Deadlines: Sept.-April. Reporting time: 2 months. Payment: none. Interested in new or unpub'd poets: yes. Simultaneous submissions accepted: yes. Recent contributors: Dana Levin, Cort Day, Sandra Kohler, Stephen Berg. Submission quantity: 3-5.

COUNTRY CHARM MAGAZINE, Box 696, Palmerston, ON N0G 2P0, Canada, 519-343-3059. Denise Friedel, Publisher. 1993. "No more than 20 lines per poem; no religion, politics, sex and/or violence" circ. 1.5M. 12/yr. Pub'd 24 poems 1999; expects 24 poems 2000, 24 poems 2001. sub. price: $14; sample: $1. 24pp; 8½×11; Publishes 40-50% of poems submitted. Deadlines: 15th of the preceding month. Reporting time: 1 month. Interested in new or unpub'd poets: no. Simultaneous submissions accepted: yes. Recent contributors: Pat Korell, Cathy Nichol, Bud Blakeslee, Shirley Millingen, Karen Nelson. Submission quantity: 2-3. Special interests: Rural oriented, rhyming poetry preferred.

Courtyard Publishing Company, 3725 May Street, Los Angeles, CA 90066. 1992. 5½×8½.

COVER MAGAZINE, Hard Press, 632 East 14th Street, #18, New York, NY 10009, 212-673-1152, Fax 212-253-7614. Cliff Fyman, Lita Hornick, Arnold Falleder. 1987. circ. 25M. 6/yr. sub. price: $10; sample: $5 with submission also. 64pp; 10×11½; Publishes 4% of poems submitted. Reporting time: 3 months. Payment: none. Interested in new or unpub'd poets: yes. Simultaneous submissions accepted: no. Recent contributors: John Ashbery, Anne Waldman, Tom Clark, Clark Coolidge, Elaine Equi.

John Edwin Cowen/Bravo Editions (see also BRAVO, THE POET'S MAGAZINE), 1081 Trafalgar Street, Teaneck, NJ 07666. John Edwin Cowen, Publisher & Current Editor; Jose Garcia Villa, Founding Editor. 1977. "Do not send full-length ms. Send a letter of inquiry with 5-6 poems. 'Bravo belives that poetry must have formal excellence; poetry must be lyrical; poetry is not prose.' (Publisher: John Edwin Cowen)" avg. press run 1M. Pub'd 1 poetry title 1999; expects 1 poetry title 2000, 1 poetry title 2001. 6¼×9½; avg. price, cloth: $20; paper: $10. 70pp; Reporting time: 2 months maximum. Payment: to be negotiated. Interested in new or unpub'd poets: yes. Simultaneous submissions accepted: no. Recently published poets: Jose Garica Villa, Arthur Vanderborg. Submission quantity: 5-6. Special interests: Lyrical, contemporary poetry is desired. John Edwin Cowen/Bravo Editions publications or *Bravo, The Poet's Magazine* should be read before submitting ms.

Coyote Books, PO Box 629, Brunswick, ME 04011. James Koller. 1964. avg. press run 200-1000. 5½×8½; avg. price, cloth: none. Publishes a small % of poetry manuscripts submitted. Reporting time: varies. Payment:

copies - percentage. Interested in new or unpub'd poets: query. Simultaneous submissions accepted: query. Recently published poets: Bob Arnold, Philip Whalen. Submission quantity: query.

Coyote Publishing, PO Box 1854, Yreka, CA 96097, 916-842-5788. 1991. "Coyote Publishing is solely a self-publishing organization that helps writers/authors self-publish - from manuscript through marketing - or parts thereof" avg. press run short runs 100+. Pub'd 2 poetry titles 1999. 5½×8½; avg. price, paper: $15. 150-200pp; Interested in new or unpub'd poets: only those interested in self-publishing. Recently published poets: Jesse Hamaker, Chrek Dixon, B.G.

COZY DETECTIVE MYSTERY MAGAZINE, Meager Ink Press, 686 Jakes Court, McMinnville, OR 97128, 503-435-1212; Fax 503-472-4896; e-mail papercapers@yahoo.com. 1993. circ. 500. 4/yr. sub. price: $10.50; sample: $2.95 + $1.50 p/h. 68pp; 5½×8½.

CRAB CREEK REVIEW, 1115 35th Avenue, Seattle, WA 98122-5210, 206-772-8489; http://www.drizzle.net/nccr. Kimberly Allison, Harris Levinson, Laura Sinai, Terri Stone. 1983. "Include SASE. Type name and address on each poem. Read the magazine first, but don't clone what you find there. Watch *Poets & Writers* for specific call for next anthology's submissions." circ. 400. 2/yr. Pub'd 30 poems 1999; expects 70 poems 2000, 70 poems 2001. sub. price: $15 per anthology 1996; $10-2 semiannual issues; sample: $6; $5 for anniversary 1994, $5 for Bread for the Hunger (1996). 80pp; 6×9; Rights purchased: 1st North American. Publishes 5% of poems submitted. Deadlines: reading all year. Reporting time: 10-12 weeks. Payment: 2 copies. Interested in new or unpub'd poets: yes. Simultaneous submissions accepted: no. Recent contributors: David Lee, Naomi Shihab Nye, Yedhuda Amichai, Joanne Clark, Kevin Miller. Submission quantity: up to 5. Special interests: Prefer poems under 40 lines. Interested in translations; please include copy in original language and letter indicating you have author's permission to translate if original is under copyright.

CRAB ORCHARD REVIEW, Dept. of English, Southern Illinois University, Carbondale, IL 62901, 618-453-6833. Allison Joseph, Poetry Editor. 1995. "Please query with SASE for info. about thematic issues. Please send SASE with all submissions. No electronic submissions." circ. 1.4M. 2/yr. Pub'd 60 poems 1999; expects 60 poems 2000, 60 poems 2001. sub. price: $10; sample: $6. 280pp; 5½×8½; Rights purchased: First North American Serial Rights. Publishes less than 10% of poems submitted. Deadlines: Sept. to Dec. for yearly thematic issue, Jan. to April for general issue. Reporting time: 3 weeks to 5 months. Payment: $5 per page/$50 minimum, plus a year's subscription, 2 contributor copies. Interested in new or unpub'd poets: yes. Simultaneous submissions accepted: yes, if informed that they are. Recent contributors: Billy Collins, Colleen J. McElroy, Kyoko Mori, Maura Stanton, Virgil Suarez. Submission quantity: 3-5 poems, no more. Special interests: translations welcome, as is a range of poetic forms and styles.

The F. Marion Crawford Memorial Society (see also THE ROMANTIST), Saracinesca House, 3610 Meadowbrook Avenue, Nashville, TN 37205. 1975. 8½×11.

CRAZYHORSE, 2801 S. University, Dept. of English, Univ. of Arkansas-Little Rock, Little Rock, AR 72204, 501-569-3161. Ralph Burns. 1960. circ. 1M. 2/yr. Pub'd 60 poems 1999; expects 60 poems 2000, 60 poems 2001. sub. price: $10; sample: $5. 150pp; 6×9; Rights purchased: 1st North American serial rights. 1 in 250 poems is published. Deadlines: none. Reporting time: 2-12 weeks. Payment: $10 per printed page; also annual $500 poetry award. Interested in new or unpub'd poets: yes. Simultaneous submissions accepted: no. Recent contributors: Richard Cecil, Khaled Mattawa, Yusef Komunyakaa, Maura Stanton. Submission quantity: 2-5.

THE CREAM CITY REVIEW, PO Box 413, English Dept, Curtin Hall, Univ. of Wisconsin, Milwaukee, WI 53201, 414-229-4708. Brent Gohde, Poetry Editor; Karen Howland, Poetry Editor. 1975. "The deadline for *The Cream City Review*'s annual poetry contest is April 30. First place $100 plus publication; other winners published. 3-5 poems per entry, under 100 lines per poem. Entry fee $5, payable to *The Cream City Review*. Submit with SASE for results only; specify Poetry Contest on first line of address" circ. 2M. 2/yr. Pub'd 100 poems 1999; expects 100 poems 2000, 100 poems 2001. sub. price: $12; sample: $5. 200pp; 5½×8½; Rights purchased: 1st N.A. serial rights and reprints rights, rights revert to author after publication. Deadlines: none. Reporting time: 4 months; we read from Sept. 1st - April 30th only. Payment: copies of magazines or subscriptions. Interested in new or unpub'd poets: yes. Simultaneous submissions accepted: yes. Recent contributors: Audre Lorde, Albert Goldbarth, Tess Gallagher, Adrienne Rich, Cathy Song. Submission quantity: 1-5. Special interests: We'll consider any well-crafted poem free verse or formal.

Creative Arts & Science Enterprises (see also STARBURST), 341 Miller Street, Abilene, TX 79605-1903. Charles J. Palmer, Jacqueline Palmer. 1989. "Contest deadlines: Feb 28/ April 30/June 30/Aug 31/Oct 31/Dec. Poetry: 32 lines or less. Any subject suitable for a general reading audience. Winners of contest and other selected works of high quality, produced in one of three hardcover anthologies each year. (No reading fees, no purchase necessary to enter and win contest.) Guidelines available, send SASE." Pub'd 4 poetry titles 1999; expects 3 poetry titles 2000, 3 poetry titles 2001. 8½×11; avg. price, cloth: $39.95. 230pp; Publishes 8% of poetry manuscripts submitted. Reporting time: 90 days. Payment: contest cash winners 45 days from end of contest. Interested in new or unpub'd poets: yes. Simultaneous submissions accepted: yes. Recently published poets: C. David Hay, Diane Krueger, William McDaniel, John Haney, Barry Sherer. Submission quantity: (1-10 is average) limit 10 SASE required.

●**Creative Arts Book Company**, 833 Bancroft Way, Berkeley, CA 94710, staff@creativeartsbooks.com. Donald S. Ellis, Publisher. 1968. avg. press run 2.5M. Pub'd 2 poetry titles 1999; expects 3 poetry titles 2000, 6 poetry titles 2001. 6×9; avg. price, cloth: $23.50; paper: $14.95. 80-100pp; Reporting time: 12 weeks. Payment: yes. Interested in new or unpub'd poets: yes. Simultaneous submissions accepted: yes. Recently published poets: Stephen Kessler, Sandy Diamond, Gloria Frym, Al Young, Lawrence Ferlinghetti. Submission quantity: 10.

●**Creative Book Company**, 13920 Roscoe Boulevard, Panorama City, CA 91402-4213, Fax 818-894-5282. 1952. 5½×8½.

Creative With Words Publications (CWW) (see also THEECLECTICS), PO Box 223226, Carmel, CA 93922-3226, Fax: 831-655-8627; e-mail: cwwpub@usa.net; http://members.tripod.com/~creativewithwords. Brigitta Geltrich. 1975. "SASE is a must; poems dealing with folklore must be accompanied by an information sheet (available upon request and SASE); already published poems are not accepted; CWW follows its guidelines (available upon request and SASE or on our website) and not those set by indiviual poets/writers; all rights revert to author after publication by CWW, however, CWW must be given due credit. *No SASE, no response. CWW prefers cover letters with submission. If child submits, age must be given (up to 19)" Pub'd 12-14 poetry titles 1999; expects 12-14 poetry titles 2000, 12-14 poetry titles 2001. 7×8½; avg. price, cloth: $10-12.50, specials $15-$20; paper: $10-12.50, specials $15-$20. 50-80pp; Publishes 80% of poetry manuscripts submitted. Reporting time: 2 weeks to 1 month; 2 months after set deadline. Payment: 20% deduction on purchase price. Interested in new or unpub'd poets: yes; however, ms must be quality writing. Simultaneous submissions accepted: no. Recently published poets: Gideon Green, Jamie M. Olson, Rachel Roth, Jimmy J. George, Jordan Moelis. Submission quantity: if sufficient return postage is on SASE, there is no limit. We do limit length of poetry to 20 lines or less, 46 characters per line or less. Poet must state for what project he submits. Special interests: Poetry of folkloristic nature, thematic poetry (inquire with SASE), satire, short poems, light and serious poems, poetry for children (inquire with SASE), poetry by children (accepted at all times), poetry by senior citizens (inquire with SASE). Four important words: Brevity - Quality - Inquire - SASE.

THE CREATIVE WOMAN, 126 East Wing Street #288, Arlington Heights, IL 60004, 708-255-1232; FAX 708-255-1243. 1977. circ. 1M. 4/yr. Pub'd 24 poems 1999; expects 25-30 poems 2000, 20-25 poems 2001. sub. price: $16; sample: $5. 52pp; 8½×11; Publishes 5% of poems submitted. Reporting time: varies, depending on time available. Payment: 3 copies. Interested in new or unpub'd poets: yes. Simultaneous submissions accepted: no. Recent contributors: Susan Terris, Olivia Diamond, Joan Siegel, Sarah Whitney. Submission quantity: 2 or 3. Special interests: Poetry by and about women.

Crescent Moon (see also PAGAN AMERICA; PASSION), PO Box 393, Maidstone, Kent ME14 5XU, United Kingdom. Jeremy Robinson. 1988. "Non-rhyming poetry preferred. SAE + International Reply Coupons essential. Do not send whole manuscripts." avg. press run 100-200. Pub'd 6 poetry titles 1999. avg. price, paper: $9.99. 50-60pp; Publishes 3% of poetry manuscripts submitted. Reporting time: 3 months. Payment: to be negotiated. Interested in new or unpub'd poets: yes. Simultaneous submissions accepted: yes. Submission quantity: 6.

CRICKET, PO Box 300, Peru, IL 61354, 815-224-6656. Marianne Carus, Editor-in-Chief; Deborah Vetter, Senior Editor; John Allen, Executive Editor; Julia Messina, Assistant Editor. 1973. "SASE is required for response." circ. 71M. 12/yr. Pub'd 53 poems 1999; expects 45 poems 2000, 45 poems 2001. sub. price: $35.97; sample: $5. 64pp; 8×10; Rights purchased: first publication rights in the English language. Publishes 1% of poems submitted. Reporting time: approx. 3 months. Payment: up to $3 per line. Interested in new or unpub'd poets: only their best efforts. Simultaneous submissions accepted: yes, notify immediately if used somewhere else. Recent contributors: Carl Sandburg, Chitra Banerjee Divakaruni, J. Patrick Lewis, Marion Dane Bauer, Diane Siebert. Submission quantity: no more than 5.

CRIPES!, 110 Bement Avenue, Staten Island, NY 10310. Jim Tolan, Aimee Record. 1994. "We're on hiatus until further notice. We want poetry that melds passion and divine frenzy with craft and the well made. No soulless academic verse of uncrafted impulses played for shock" circ. 300. Irregular. Pub'd 18 poems 1999; expects 18 poems 2000, 18 poems 2001. sub. price: $13/3 issues; sample: $5. 48-60pp; 5½×8½; Publishes 1% of poems submitted. Deadlines: none. Reporting time: 2 weeks-2 months. Payment: copies. Interested in new or unpub'd poets: yes. Simultaneous submissions accepted: yes. Recent contributors: John Grey, Larissa Szporluk, Martin Vest, Erika Murphy. Submission quantity: 3-5.

CRONE CHRONICLES: A Journal of Conscious Aging, PO Box 81, Kelly, WY 83011, 307-733-5409. Ann Kreikamp. 1989. circ. 6M. 4/yr. Pub'd 20 poems 1999; expects 20 poems 2000, 20 poems 2001. sub. price: $21 in US; sample: $6.50. 80pp; 8½×11; Rights purchased: none bought, one time rights. Publishes 1% of poems submitted. Deadlines: Aug. 1, Nov. 1, Feb. 1, May 1. Reporting time: varies. Payment: none. Interested in new or unpub'd poets: yes. Simultaneous submissions accepted: prefer not.

CROSS CURRENTS, College of New Rochelle, New Rochelle, NY 10805-2339, 914-235-1439; fax: 914-235-1584; aril@ecunet.org. Beverly Coyle. 1950. "We are a quarterly magazine and publish only 1 or 2 poems per issue." circ. 4.5M. 4/yr. Pub'd 9 poems 1999; expects 6 poems 2000. sub. price: $40, libraries $50, outside US $5 additional postage; sample: $7.50. 144pp; 6×9; Deadlines: none. Reporting time: asap. Payment: none. Interested in new or unpub'd poets: yes. Simultaneous submissions accepted: yes. Submission quantity: no limit. Special interests: Interreligious.

CROSSCURRENTS, A QUARTERLY, 24440 Valencia Blvd. #3101, Valencia, CA 91355-1811, 818-991-1694. Elizabeth Bartlett, Poetry Editor. 1980. "We are looking for quality, literary poetry. We have had problems, recently, with submittors who omit the basics: SASE, clean, professional submissions. A potential contributor should study a sample copy of *CROSSCURRENTS* to determine whether or not his or her work is the type of poetry we publish. We publish two special editions each year, and one or two open collections. For example, in 1986, we published *Many Voices*, a celebration of the ethnic diversity of American literary culture, and *Literary Profiles*, a cross-section of work, selected and introduced by scholars, by Margaret Atwood, Saul Bellow, Joyce Carol Oates and Gary Snyder. Our 1987 special collections will include *California Writers*, a tribute to our home state, and *New York by Award Winners II*, a collection of poetry and short fiction by authors who have recently won literary awards. Our remaining issues are open to unsolicited submissions" circ. 3M. Irregular. Expects 110 poems 2000, 150 poems 2001. sample price: $6. 176pp; 6×9; Rights purchased: 1st North American serial rights. Publishes 5% of poems submitted. Deadlines: we review unsolicited submissions of poetry between June 1 and November 30 each year. Reporting time: 3-6 weeks. Payment: $15/poem, plus 1 contributor's copy. Interested in new or unpub'd poets: if they are brilliant, yes! Simultaneous submissions accepted: no. Recent contributors: Linda Pastan, Yannis Ritsos, Jaroslav Seifert, Ron Wallace, Hollis Summers. Submission quantity: no more than 5, please. Special interests: We use translations, and when possible, include original language text. We do not use much experimental work, long poems, light verse. High quality literary poetry.

CRUCIBLE, English Department, Barton College, Wilson, NC 27893, 252-399-6456. Terrence L. Grimes, Editor. 1964. "We read all submissions between late April and June. We have 2 poetry contests (1st prize $150, 2nd prize $100 for one and one prize of $150 for Sam Ragan Poetry Competition). All submissions for publication are automatically considered for the contest. Three copies of each manuscript should be submitted without the author's name. A brief biography should be included." circ. 300. 1/yr. Pub'd 32 poems 1999; expects 35 poems 2000, 35 poems 2001. sub. price: $6; sample: $6. 70pp; 6×9; Rights purchased: none. Publishes 9% of poems submitted. Deadlines: April 30. Reporting time: 2-4 months. Payment: 2 complimentary copies. Interested in new or unpub'd poets: yes. Simultaneous submissions accepted: no. Recent contributors: Anthony Abbott, R.T. Smith, Ronald Bayes, Erroll Miller. Submission quantity: maximum of 5.

CUMBERLAND POETRY REVIEW, Poetics, Inc., PO Box 120128 Acklen Station, Nashville, TN 37212, 615-373-8948. Eva Touster, Bob Darrell, Jeanne Gore, Alison Touster-Reed, John Gibson, Sherry Bevins Darrell, Joyce Sommer, Bard Young, Elizabeth Hahn. 1981. "*Cumberland Poetry Review*, a semi-annual publication devoted to poetry and poetry criticism, presents poets of diverse origins to a widespread audience. We place no restrictions on form, subject, or style. Manuscripts will be selected for publication on the basis of the writer's perspicuous and compelling means of expression. We welcome translations of high quality poetry. Our aim is to support the poet's effort to keep up the language. We accept special responsibility for reminding American readers that not all excellent poems in English are being written by U.S citizens. Must include SASE. Interested in translations and critical articles. Send poems on standard 8½ X 11 & typed" circ. 500. 2/yr. Pub'd 100 poems 1999. sub. price: $18 (individuals), $24 (institutions), $28 (overseas); sample: $10. 75-100pp; 6×9; Rights purchased: reverts to author. Publishes 2-5% of poems submitted. Deadlines: April 15, Oct. 15. Reporting time: 6 months. Payment: 2 copies of magazine in which their poem appears. Interested in new or unpub'd poets: yes. Simultaneous submissions accepted: no. Recent contributors: R.T. Smith, X.J. Kennedy, Seamus Heaney, Laurence Lerner, Dana Gioia. Submission quantity: 1-5. Special interests: translations and articles on poetry.

CURARE, c/o Whalen, 20 Clinton Street #1G, New York, NY 10002, 212-533-7167. Charlene Cambridge. 1993. "No return of submitted material without SASE with sufficient postage" circ. 200. 2/yr. Pub'd 50 poems 1999; expects 50 poems 2000, 50 poems 2001. 50pp; 8½×11; Rights purchased: none. Publishes 25% of poems submitted. Deadlines: none. Reporting time: 3-6 months. Payment: one copy. Interested in new or unpub'd poets: yes. Recent contributors: Larry Jones, J.D. Rage, Mike Halchin, Susan Sherman, Jurado. Submission quantity: 3-4.

Curbstone Press, 321 Jackson Street, Willimantic, CT 06226, 203-423-5110; fax 203-423-9242; e-Mail TAYLORAL@ECSUC.CTSTATEV.EDU. Alexander Taylor, Co-Director. 1975. avg. press run 3M. Pub'd 3 poetry titles 1999; expects 4 poetry titles 2000, 3 poetry titles 2001. 6×9, 5½×8½; avg. price, paper: $12. 96pp;

Publishes 1% of poetry manuscripts submitted. Reporting time: 2-3 months. Payment: 12% net sales, generally payable in copies of the book for first edition. Interested in new or unpub'd poets: no. Simultaneous submissions accepted: yes. Recently published poets: Leo Sonnellan, Roberto Sosa, Martin Espada, Kevin Bowen, Cheryl Savageau. Submission quantity: 10. Special interests: Translations and committed poetry/Latin American Literature.

CUTBANK, English Dept., University of Montana, Missoula, MT 59812. 1973. "All accepted submissions eligible for the Richard Hugo Memorial Poetry Award; must enclose SASE." circ. 600. 2/yr. Pub'd 40 poems 1999; expects 40 poems 2000, 40 poems 2001. sub. price: $12; sample: $4. 120+pp; 5½×8½; Rights purchased: rights returned to author upon publication. Publishes 1% of poems submitted. Deadlines: We accept submissions from Aug. 15 until March 15. Dealine for the fall issue is Novermber 15; deadline for the spring issue is March 15. Reporting time: 8-12 weeks. Payment: 2 copies. Interested in new or unpub'd poets: yes. Simultaneous submissions accepted: we prefer not to receive simultaneous submissions. Recent contributors: Seamus Heaney, Amiri Baraka, Gerald Stern, James Tate, David Baker. Submission quantity: 3-5. Special interests: Although we publish poetry from across the country, we still see ourselves, at least in part, as a regional journal, and encourage Western and Northwest poets to send their best work.

Cynic Press (see also AXE FACTORY REVIEW), PO Box 40691, Philadelphia, PA 19107. Joseph Farley. 1996. avg. press run 100-600. Pub'd 1 poetry title 1999; expects 1 poetry title 2000, 1 poetry title 2001. size varies; avg. price, paper: $8. Publishes 1% of poetry manuscripts submitted. Reporting time: 1 month. Payment: copies or special arrangement. unsolicited poetry book manuscripts must come with $10 reading fee, check made payable to Joseph Farley. Simultaneous submissions accepted: yes. Recently published poets: Xu Juan, Jeff Vetock, Joe Banford, Louis McKee, Michael Hafer. Submission quantity: send entire manuscript with reading fee. Special interests: Selective tastes, all styles. Interested in narrative and oriental work.

D

THE DALHOUSIE REVIEW, Dalhousie University, Halifax, Nova Scotia B3H 3J5, Canada, 902-494-2541, fax 902-494-3561, email dalhousie.review@dal.ca. Ronald Huebert, Editor. 1921. "Preferred length of poems is less than forty lines. Return of manuscripts cannot be expected unless accompanied by an addressed envelope and return postage in Canadian stamps or International Reply Coupons" circ. 750. 4/yr. Pub'd 20 poems 1999; expects 30 poems 2000, 30 poems 2001. sub. price: institutional: $32.10 within Canada, outside $40 includes GST; individual: $22.50 within Canada, $28 outside; sample: $10 + mailing and handling ($12 double issue). 144pp; 9×6; Rights purchased: we sell reprint rights. Publishes 1% of poems submitted. Deadlines: none. Reporting time: 1-3 months. Payment: 2 complimentary copies of issue and 10 offprints. Interested in new or unpub'd poets: yes. Simultaneous submissions accepted: yes. Recent contributors: Terry Watada, Stan Rogal, Edward Locke, Julie Leibrich, Elizabeth Brewster. Submission quantity: 5-7.

DANDELION ARTS MAGAZINE, Fern Publications, Casa Alba, 24 Frosty Hollow, E. Hunsbury, Northants NN4 0SY, England, 01604-701730. Jacqueline Gonzalez-Marina. 1978. "We do not publish political, religious or offensive material" circ. 1M. 2/yr. Pub'd 40-50 poems 1999; expects 40-50 poems 2000, 40-50 poems 2001. sub. price: £9 UK, £18 Europe incl. postage + packing, £20 USA and the rest of the world (money could be sent in dollars but add extra for transaction); sample: £5 UK, £10 Europe incl. postage + packing, £10 USA and the rest of the world. 20-30pp; size A4; Rights purchased: none. Percentage of poetry published depends upon the quality of the submissions. Deadlines: no deadlines unless submitting for competitions but it can alter. Reporting time: around 2 weeks. Payment: none. Interested in new or unpub'd poets: yes. Simultaneous submissions accepted: yes. Recent contributors: J. Gonzalez-Marina, Marlene J. Bennetts, Andrew Duncan, Gerald Denley, Jeanne Monk. Submission quantity: Max. 6, min. 3 accompanied by a SAE and cover letter about their work. Special interests: Anything considered that could have an international appeal - even educational. Modern approach preferred but old fashion sonnets not ruled out, if of quality. Also illustrations and clear photographs considered for publication.

John Daniel and Company, Publishers, PO Box 21922, Santa Barbara, CA 93121, 805-962-1780, fax 805-962-8835, email dand@danielpublishing.com. John Daniel, Publisher. 1980. "Alas, we have a difficult time marketing poetry. Hence we can afford to publish very few titles, and we must be *very* selective. However, our only criteria are the poet's quality and our intuition." avg. press run 1M. Pub'd 1 poetry title 1999; expects 1 poetry title 2000, 1 poetry title 2001. 5½×8½; avg. price, cloth: $15; paper: $10. 80pp; Publishes less than 5% of poetry manuscripts submitted. Reporting time: 6 weeks. Payment: 10% of net receipts, no advance. Interested in new or unpub'd poets: yes. Simultaneous submissions accepted: yes. Recently published poets: John Finlay, Kingsley Tufts, Judson Jerome, Daniel Haberman, Perie Longo. Submission quantity: 12+/-.

DARK REGIONS: The Years Best Fantastic Fiction, 30 Canyon View Drive, Orinda, CA 94563. Bobbi-Sinha Morey. 1987. circ. 3M. 2-4/yr. Pub'd 25 poems 1999. sub. price: $14/3 issues; sample: $4 first time sample copy. 80-150pp; 11×17; Rights purchased: NASR. Publishes 5% of poems submitted. Deadlines: none. Reporting time: 2-3 weeks. Payment: $2.50 a poem, plus 1 contributor copy. Interested in new or unpub'd poets: yes. Simultaneous submissions accepted: no. Recent contributors: Bruce Boston, William John Watkins, Mary Turzillo, W. Gregory Stewart, Wendy Ruthbone. Submission quantity: no more than 5 at a time. Special interests: Light and dark horror, science fiction, and fantacy.

DAUGHTERS OF SARAH, 2121 Sheridan Road, Evanston, IL 60201. Elizabeth Anderson. 1974. "Prefer short poems because we have a small magazine. Must be both Christian and feminist. Please no rhymed couplets" circ. 5M. 4/yr. Pub'd 17 poems 1999; expects 14 poems 2000, 14 poems 2001. sub. price: $22; sample: $6.25. 64pp; 5½×8½; Rights purchased: one-time first N.A. rights. Publishes 5% of poems submitted. Deadlines: May 31 for summer issue; August 31 for fall; November 30 for winter; February 28 for spring issue. Reporting time: up to 2 months. Payment: $10-$25. Interested in new or unpub'd poets: open to it. Simultaneous submissions accepted: no. Recent contributors: Maren Tirabassi, Mary Cartledge-Hayes, Aliene Pylant, Geri Lynn Baumblatt, Louie Crew. Submission quantity: prefer no more than 2-3.

DAYS AND NIGHTS OF A SMALL PRESS PUBLISHER, 577 Central Avenue, Box 4, Jefferson, LA 70121-1400, e-mail popculture@popmail.com, publisher@mailexcite.com; www2.cybercities.com/z/zines/. Sharida Rizzuto. 1983. circ. 500. 3/yr. Pub'd 30 poems 1999; expects 30 poems 2000, 30 poems 2001. sub. price: $12; sample: $4. 40-50pp; 8½×11; Rights purchased: one-time rights, first serial rights, or second serial rights. Publishes 30-35% of poems submitted. Deadlines: always open. Reporting time: 2-6 weeks. Payment: free copy only. Interested in new or unpub'd poets: yes. Simultaneous submissions accepted: yes. Recent contributors: J.M. Cox, Jim DeWitt, Lucinda MacGregor. Submission quantity: 1-5.

Dead Metaphor Press, PO Box 2076, Boulder, CO 80306, 303-417-9398. Richard Wilmarth. 1985. avg. press run 100-500. Pub'd 2 poetry titles 1999; expects 2 poetry titles 2000, 2-4 poetry titles 2001. 6×9, 7×9; avg. price, paper: $4.95; other: $7.95. 24-60pp; Payment: varies. Interested in new or unpub'd poets: yes. Simultaneous submissions accepted: yes. Recently published poets: Jack Collom, Aimee Grunberger, Richard Wilmarth, Tree Bernstein, Tracy Davis. Submission quantity: Complete ms. with bio., acknowledgements and SASE and $10 contest fee. Special interests: Poems about what goes on between people.

DEANOTATIONS, 11919 Moss Point Lane, Reston, VA 20194, 703-471-7907, fax 703-471-6446, e-mail blehert@aol.com, website www.blehert.com. Dean Blehert. 1984. "I publish only my own work in *Deanotations*" circ. 300. 6/yr. Pub'd 240 poems 1999; expects 240 poems 2000, 240 poems 2001. sub. price: $10, $17.50/2 yrs, $35/3 yrs; sample: free with SASE. 4pp; 8½×11; Rights purchased: none. Publishes 0% of poems submitted. Recent contributors: Blehert, Dean. Special interests: Poems mostly short, often humorous, including parody, satire, aphorism, and some lyrical works.

DeeMar Communications, PMB 320, 6325-9 Falls of Neuse Rd., Raleigh, NC 27615, 919-870-6423, postmaster@deemar.com, www.deemarcommunications.com, www.deemar.com. Diane Tait, Owner. 1995. "Submissions accepted January through April only. No electronic submissions. Need to have social/historical theme." avg. press run 100. Pub'd 1 poetry title 1999; expects 1 poetry title 2001. 5½×8½; avg. price, paper: $7.95. 80pp; Publishes 50% of poetry manuscripts submitted. Reporting time: 1 month. Payment: 10% and 10 copies. Interested in new or unpub'd poets: no. Simultaneous submissions accepted: no. Recently published poets: Neca Stoller. Submission quantity: entire manuscript equal to at least 50 pages.

Manya DeLeon Booksmith, 940 Royal Street, Suite 201, New Orleans, LA 70116, 504-895-2357. 1993. "Please include SASE with all submissions. Short biography of prior publications helpful. Letters are always welcome, however, please no phone calls to publisher or staff." avg. press run 500-2M. Expects 1 poetry title 2000, 1 poetry title 2001. 8½×6½; avg. price, cloth: $13; paper: $10. 100pp; Reporting time: 4-6 weeks. Payment: negotiable; expect standard royalty after costs met; authors to receive maximum possible authors' copies of work(s) plus other titles, no advances on royalties. Interested in new or unpub'd poets: yes. Simultaneous submissions accepted: yes, if indicated in query letter. Recently published poets: Magus Magnus, Skye Kathleen Moody, Lisa Kahn, Robert Phillips. Submission quantity: maximum of 5; do not send books or full mss. - query first. Special interests: Interested in contemporary translations of international work and new translations of classic poetry.

●**Delta Press,** 27460 Avenue Scott, Valencia, CA 91355, 661-294-2208. 1999. 5½×8½.

DENVER QUARTERLY, University of Denver, Denver, CO 80208, 303-871-2892. Bin Ramke, Editor. 1966. "We do not subscribe to any set of rules nor do we try to align ourselves with a particular school of poetry. As much as possible, we try simply to respond to what we find on the page. Or to put it another way, we're looking only for the best work we can find, regardless of genre or affiliation. We do not read during the summer months (May 15 to Sept 15). All manuscripts received during that time will be returned unread." circ. 1M. 4/yr. Pub'd 100-130 poems 1999. sub. price: $24/institutions, $20/individuals; sample: $6. 144pp; 6×9; Rights purchased:

1st North American. Publishes 5-10% of poems submitted. Deadlines: Sept. 15-May 15. Reporting time: 4-5 months. Payment: $5 a page at present; financial problems may force us to cease payments. Interested in new or unpub'd poets: yes. Simultaneous submissions accepted: yes, if told. Recent contributors: Joshua McKinney, James Tate, Jorie Graham, Rosmarie Waldrop. Submission quantity: no more than 5. Special interests: We would prefer not to define our poetry publishing in the belief that the best writing cannot be defined or categorized.

Depth Charge, 1352 Hardeman, 1st Floor, Macon, GA 31201, 708-733-9554;800-639-0008; fax 708-733-0928. Eckhard Gerdes. 1986. "Please familiarize yourself with our publications before submitting" avg. press run 500-1M. Expects 1 poetry title 2001. 5½×8½; avg. price, paper: $9.95-16.95. 76-154pp; Reporting time: 6-8 weeks, query first. Payment: 8% of list. Interested in new or unpub'd poets: yes. Simultaneous submissions accepted: yes. Recently published poets: Richard Kostelanetz, Arthur Winfiel Knight, Tim W. Brown. Submission quantity: 73 pages (one poem). Special interests: We are especially interested in typographically unusual book-length experimental poetry that borders on prose and concrete poetry.

DESCANT, English Department, TCU, Box 297270, Fort Worth, TX 76129. Dave Kuhne. 1955. "Poems 60 lines or fewer. *descant* specifies no particular subject matter or style. Named for *descant*'s founding editor, the Betsy Colquitt Award for Poetry ($500) is awarded annually to the best poem or series of poems by a single author in a volume. A SASE must be included to guarantee return, reply or acknowledgement." circ. 500. 1 double issue published each summer. Expects 35 poems 2000. sub. price: $12, $18 foreign; sample: $6. 64pp; 6×9; Rights purchased: none. Publishes .5% of poems submitted. Deadlines: none. Reporting time: 6 weeks. Payment: in copies. Interested in new or unpub'd poets: yes. Simultaneous submissions accepted: no. Recent contributors: Beth Houston, Francis Blessington, Mary Gran Hughes, Ralph J. Mills Jr., William Virgil Davis. Submission quantity: no more than 5 at one time.

DESCANT, PO Box 314, Station P, Toronto, Ontario M5S 2S8, Canada. Karen Mulhallen. 1970. "Standards for acceptance are high. We advise reading at least one issue of *Descant* before submitting." circ. 1M. 4/yr. Pub'd 90 poems 1999; expects 100 poems 2000. sub. price: Ind.: $25 - one year $40 two years instit.: $35 one year $70 two years add $6 per year outside Canada; sample: $8.50 + $2 outside Canada. 120pp; 6×8; Rights purchased: first serial. Publishes 3% of poems submitted. Deadlines: none. Reporting time: 4 months. Payment: $100. Interested in new or unpub'd poets: yes. Simultaneous submissions accepted: no. Recent contributors: Lorna Crozier, Steven Heighton, Tim Lilburn, Brian Henderson, Jan Zwicky. Submission quantity: at least 5 or 6. Special interests: We publish all types of quality poetry.

DESIRE STREET, 257 Bonnabel Boulevard, Metairie, LA 70005-3738, 504-835-3419, Fax 504-834-2005, ager80@worldnet.att.net. Jonathan Laws, Alan Mossy. 1984. "ASI II disk test format on disk, please. Any subject: no pornography, no hunting themes, no abuse of women, children, dogs, any abuse. No traditional religious themes" circ. 1.2M. 4/yr. Pub'd 200 poems 1999; expects 200 poems 2000, 200 poems 2001. sub. price: $25, also entitles subscribers to one free critique of one 1-page original poem and all 50 weekly Weds. night 3-hour workshops when/if in New Orleans, LA; sample: $5. 8pp; 8½×11; Rights purchased: none. Publishes 45% of poems submitted. Deadlines: monthly, ongoing. Reporting time: 6 months. Payment: copies. Interested in new or unpub'd poets: yes. Simultaneous submissions accepted: yes. Recent contributors: Beverly Matherne, Jonathan Laws, Andrea Saunders Gereighty, Lee Meitzengrue, Martha McFerran. Submission quantity: 5. Special interests: no poems longer than 1- 8½ X 11 page; author must sign works. No light verse, and no long poems.

THE DESK, PO Box 50376, Washington, DC 20091. 1996. "Focus: reviews of spoken word, poet's audio, video, and theater, and other non-printed dimensions of poetic practice." circ. 350. 4/yr. sub. price: free. 8pp; 8×11.

Desk-Drawer Micropress, 209 W. Ann Street, Milford, PA 18337. 1997. 5×8.

Desktop, Ink., PO Box 548, Archer, FL 32618-0548, 352-486-6570 phone/Fax; E-mail dktop@aol.com.

DEVIL BLOSSOMS, PO Box 5122, Seabrook, NJ 08302. 1997. circ. 500. 1-2/yr. sub. price: $8/3 issues; checks payable to John C. Erianne; sample: $3. 24pp; 8½×11.

THE DEVIL'S MILLHOPPER, The Devil's Millhopper Press (TDM Press), USC - Aiken, 471 University Parkway, Aiken, SC 29801-6399, Fax/Phone 803-641-3239 e-mail Gardner@vm.sc.edu. Stephen Gardner, Editor. 1976. "Please send SASE for submission guidelines and contest information." circ. 600. 1/yr. Pub'd 25 poems 1999; expects 25 poems 2000, 25 poems 2001. sub. price: $6, $10 for 2 years; sample: $4.50. 40pp; 5½×8½; Rights purchased: 1st North American Serial. Publishes 1% of poems submitted. Deadlines: Sept. 1-Oct. 31. Reporting time: 3 months. Payment: 2 copies, Kudzu contest—$150, $100, $50 prizes. Interested in new or unpub'd poets: yes. Simultaneous submissions accepted: no. Recent contributors: Susan Ludvigson, Jeff Worley, Stephen Corey, Richard Frost, Walter McDonald. Submission quantity: 5+/-.

The Devil's Millhopper Press (TDM Press) (see also THE DEVIL'S MILLHOPPER), USC - Aiken, 471 University Parkway, Aiken, SC 29801-6399, phone/fax 803-641-3239; e-Mail gardner@vm.sc.edu. Stephen Gardner, Editor. 1984. "We are a poetry chapbook press—we run an annual contest with a Feb. 28 deadline. Manuscripts should be well organized with title, acknowledgements, contents, etc., and may be no longer than 24 pages of poetry. All inquiries and submissions must include SASE. Fees: Chapbook Contest, $10 includes one-year subcription; Kudzu Contest: $3 per poem. Non-contest submissions (no fee) considered Sept. and Oct. of each year." avg. press run 600. Pub'd 2 poetry titles 1999; expects 2 poetry titles 2000, 2 poetry titles 2001. 5½x8½; avg. price, paper: $4.50 magazine; $5 chapbook. 32-48pp; Publishes less than 1% of poetry manuscripts submitted. Reporting time: chapbook contest—3 months after Feb. 28 deadline of each year; Kudzu contest—2 months after Oct. 31 deadline of each year. Payment: chapbook, minimum of $50 up front + 50 copies of book; poetry issue, Kudzu Contest—3 cash prizes, $150, $100, $50. Interested in new or unpub'd poets: yes. Simultaneous submissions accepted: yes (chapbook contest only). Recently published poets: Susan Ludvigson, Stephen Corey, Richard Frost, Jeff Worley, Walter McDonald. Submission quantity: chapbook contest - up to 24 pages, 1 poem per page; Kudzu Contest - any number, 50 line length limit. Special interests: Open to all forms, styles, and subjects.

DIALOGOS: Hellenic Studies Review, Dept. of Byzantine & Modern Greek, Attn: David Ricks, King's College, London WC2R 2LS, United Kingdom, fax 020-7848-873-2830. Dr. David Ricks. 1994. "All material must be related to the Greek world" circ. 500. 1/yr. Pub'd 3 poems 1999; expects 2 poems 2000, 2 poems 2001. sub. price: $59.50 cloth, $29.50 paper; sample: $59.50 cloth, $29.50 paper. 150pp; 5¾x8½; Publishes 5% of poems submitted. Deadlines: none. Reporting time: 1 month. Payment: none. Interested in new or unpub'd poets: yes. Simultaneous submissions accepted: no. Recent contributors: Homer, Haim Gouri, Warren Hope, Yannis Ritsos. Submission quantity: 5. Special interests: Translation.

Paul Dilsaver, Publisher, PO Box 1621, Pueblo, CO 81002. 1974. size varies.

DIONYSIA, Box 1500, Capital University, Columbus, OH 43209, 614-236-6563. 1980. circ. 500. 1/yr. sub. price: distributed free. 20pp; 5½x8½.

DIRIGIBLE, 101 Cottage Street, New Haven, CT 06511, email dirigibl@javanet.com. David Todd, Editor; Cynthia Conrad, Co-Editor. 1994. "Please enclose an SASE with sufficent return postage." circ. 500. 4/yr. Pub'd 50 poems 1999; expects 60 poems 2000, 60 poems 2001. sub. price: $7 ppd, $10 outside US; sample: $3 ppd. 40-48pp; 4¼x7; Rights purchased: first rights; all rights return to author upon publication. Publishes less than 10% of poems submitted. Reporting time: 1-4 months. Payment: 2 copies. Interested in new or unpub'd poets: yes. Simultaneous submissions accepted: no. Recent contributors: Sheila E. Murphy, W.B. Keckler, J.M. Bennett, Ron Padgett, Richard Kostelanetz. Submission quantity: 8 poems maximum. Special interests: We like wit, charm and inventive, exploratory language. We're interested in a phenomenological lyricism which recreates the texture and logic of interior experience. We're not interested in social issue, inspirational, scatological, beat, emotional/moral exhibitionism. Due to format, our magazine does not publish concrete poetry.

THE DIRTY GOAT, Host Publications, Inc., 2717 Wooldridge, Austin, TX 78703, 512-482-8229, E-mail jbratcher3@aol.com. Joe Bratcher III, Elizbieta Szoka. 1988. circ. 500. 2/yr. Pub'd 50 poems 1999. sub. price: $20; sample: $2. 100pp; 8x10; Publishes 20% of poems submitted. Reporting time: long. Interested in new or unpub'd poets: no. Simultaneous submissions accepted: yes. Recent contributors: Gerald Nicosia, Anna Frajlich, Urszula Koziol, Milan Fust, Helena Poswiatowska. Special interests: translations.

THE DISABILITY RAG & RESOURCE, The Advocado Press, PO Box 145, Louisville, KY 40201, 502-459-5343. Anne Finger, Poetry Editor. 1980. "General themes for issues are announced in the magazine usually three issues in advance, but poetry and other articles do not necessarily have to fit the theme" circ. 4M. 6/yr. Pub'd 15 poems 1999; expects 15 poems 2000, 15 poems 2001. sub. price: $17.50 individuals; $35 organizations; $42 international; sample: free. 48pp; 8x10½; Rights purchased: First North American serial rights. Publishes 10% of poems submitted. Deadlines: no particular deadline, but we currently have an 8-10 month backlog of acceptances. Reporting time: 1-2 months. Payment: $25 per poem + 2 copies of magazine. Interested in new or unpub'd poets: yes. Simultaneous submissions accepted: yes. Recent contributors: Kenny Fries, Cheryl Marie Wade, Margaret Robison, Nancy Gigelow Clark, Katherine M. Simpson. Submission quantity: no restrictions. Special interests: We are interested in poetry growing out of the disability experience, and more in the social theme than in the personal effects.

DNA Publications, Inc. (see also ABSOLUTE MAGNITUDE; DREAMS OF DECADENCE: Vampire Poetry and Fiction; FANTASTIC STORIES; WEIRD TALES; ABORIGINAL), PO Box 2988, Radford, VA 24143-2988, 540-763-2925, dnapublications@iname.com. 1993. 8x5.

Doctor Jazz Press, 119 Pintail Drive, Pelham, AL 35124, 205-663-3403. A.J. Wright. 1979. avg. press run 100. Pub'd 5 poetry titles 1999; expects 5 poetry titles 2000, 5 poetry titles 2001. 8½x11; avg. price, paper: $1. 1 page; Publishes 1% of poetry manuscripts submitted. Reporting time: 1-2 months. Payment: 50% of press run.

Interested in new or unpub'd poets: yes. Simultaneous submissions accepted: yes. Recently published poets: A.J. Wright. Submission quantity: 5-10.

Dolphin-Moon Press, PO Box 22262, Baltimore, MD 21203. James Taylor, President; Richard Byrne, Managing Editor. 1973. "Press concentrates on poetry and prose with publication often in unique format/design; *Signatures* series runs twice yearly, each run comprised of 3 separate poetry pamphlets by different poets; press issues a major poetry or prose collection per year. Publication by invitation and unsoliticed outside submissions; underground/newave comix are also published by the press periodically, as are record albums, note cards, and other printed/recorded objects" avg. press run 500-1M. Pub'd 1 poetry title 1999; expects 7 poetry titles 2000, 7 poetry titles 2001. size varies; avg. price, cloth: $16; paper: $8 ppd; other: $1.50 pp (pamphlets). 100pp; Publishes 1% of poetry manuscripts submitted. Reporting time: 1 month. Payment: in copies. Interested in new or unpub'd poets: yes. Simultaneous submissions accepted: prefer not to. Recently published poets: Josephine Jacobsen, Judson Jerome, Michael Weaver, Daniel Mark Epstein, John Strausbaugh. Submission quantity: 6+/-. Special interests: Press does not favor any one writing style over another but *quality* of the work (regardless of genre) must be high; press has published virtually every type of work from formal sonnets to concrete poems to poems on records to poems coupled with photographs to cartoons to etc. & etc.

DOOR COUNTY ALMANAK, 10905 Bay Shore Drive, Sister Bay, WI 54234, 414-854-2742. 1982. "There are no current plans for another issue in the near future" Irregular. Expects 15-25 poems 2000. sample price: $9.95. 300pp; 6×9; Rights purchased: one-time. Publishes 2% of poems submitted. Reporting time: 2-3 months. Payment: $1-$2 plus copy. Simultaneous submissions accepted: yes. Special interests: We prefer poetry related to each issue's theme and preferably related to the region.

●**Double SS Press**, PO Box 1450, Wimberley, TX 78676, 512-847-5173, Fax 512-847-9099, dorey@sspress.com, www.sspress.com. 1987. 5½×8½.

DOWN UNDER MANHATTAN BRIDGE, 224 E. 11th Street #5, New York, NY 10003-7329, 212-388-7051, lizard.evny@msn.com. Elizibeth Morse, Daniel Freeman. 1979. "Very important: enclose SASE. Save poets forget to do this" circ. 1M+. 2/yr. Expects 15-35 poems 2000. sub. price: $8; sample: $4.89. 32pp; 6×9; Rights purchased: All rights revert to author after publication. Publishes 5% of poems submitted. Reporting time: 6 months. Payment: copies. Interested in new or unpub'd poets: yes. Simultaneous submissions accepted: yes. Recent contributors: Tom Savage, Sparrow, Vyt Bsakaitis, Wanda Plipps, Enid Dame. Submission quantity: 1-5. Special interests: No light verse. We like gritty, courageious material.

DREAM INTERNATIONAL QUARTERLY, 411 14th Street #H1, Ramona, CA 92065-2769. Carmen M. Pursifull, Senior Poetry Editor. Address poetry submissions to: 809 W. Maple, Champaign, IL 61820-2810. 1980. "Checks/money orders and overseas drafts to be made payable to Charles Jones rather than DIQ." circ. 65-80. 2-3/yr. Pub'd 60 poems 1999; expects 80 poems 2000, 100 poems 2001. sub. price: US $50 (domestic rate); sample: Outside US: $10. Consult US Editor for postage and handling costs. 140-180pp; 8½×11; Rights purchased: rights revert to author upon publication. Publishes 35-40% of poems submitted. Deadlines: none. Reporting time: 8-10 weeks. Payment: contributors' copies; contributor must pay s/h costs of $3 US; foreign, contact Editor-in-Chief for s/h. Interested in new or unpub'd poets: yes. Simultaneous submissions accepted: yes. Recent contributors: C.A. Gelrin, John Grey, Kathleen Youmans, Julia Duncan, Margaret Boe, Carmen M. Pursifull. Submission quantity: 4-6. Special interests: dream/fantasy poetry, satire, humor, translations, non-fiction scientific papers on dreaming. 'How-to' articles on dreaming, health benefits, etc.

DREAM NETWORK JOURNAL, PO Box 1026, Moab, UT 84532-3031, 435-259-5936; dreamkey@la-sal.net; http:dreamnetwork.net. H. Roberta Ossana, Editor. 1982. "Dream and myth related poetry only." circ. 4M. 4/yr. Pub'd 12-15 poems 1999. sub. price: $22 USA; $30 Canada, Mexico, libraries; $38 foreign airmail; sample: $5.95. 52pp; 8½×11; Publishes 50% of poems submitted. Deadlines: 2/28, 5/31, 8/31, 11/30. Reporting time: 6 weeks-2 months. Payment: 5 issues in which poetry appears and/or 1-year subscription. Interested in new or unpub'd poets: yes. Simultaneous submissions accepted: yes. Recent contributors: Christina Pacosz, John Ashbaugh, David Spalenburg, Jill Gregory. Submission quantity: 2.

DREAM WHIP, PO Box 53832, Lubbock, TX 79453, 806-794-9263. Dirk Wanaghbalghe. 1992. "Dream Whip Poet Festival/Rock-o-Roma every June 19th" circ. 44. 4/yr. Pub'd 500 poems 1999. sub. price: $4. 30pp; 5½×4¼; Rights purchased: none. Publishes .002% of poems submitted. Deadlines: none. Reporting time: none. Payment: none. Interested in new or unpub'd poets: yes. Simultaneous submissions accepted: no. Recent contributors: Jen Doolightly, Pete Reamdip, John Tripream. Submission quantity: 1. Special interests: Road trips, lonely late nights, draw bridges and iron works.

DREAMS AND NIGHTMARES, 1300 Kicker Road, Tuscaloosa, AL 35404, 205-553-2284, e-Mail dragontea@earthlink.net. David C. Kopaska-Merkel, Editor. 1986. "Generally poems should fit, single-spaced, on 8½ X 11 paper. I print some longer ones. Don't like gory or trite poems, but gore and sex is ok if not gratuitous. *Any* format is fine. I do publish prose poetry and visual poetry" circ. 200. 3/yr. Pub'd 46 poems

1999; expects 46 poems 2000, 46 poems 2001. sub. price: $12/6 issues inside N. America and $15/6 issues elsewhere.; sample: $3. 24pp; 5½×8½; Rights purchased: First N. Am. Serial. Publishes 5% of poems submitted. Deadlines: anytime. Reporting time: 2-4 weeks. Payment: $5 on publication plus 2 copies. Interested in new or unpub'd poets: yes. Simultaneous submissions accepted: no. Recent contributors: Ann K. Schwader, Robert Frazier, Charlee Jacob, Bruce Boston, J.W. Donnelly. Submission quantity: 3-6. Special interests: short poems.

DREAMS OF DECADENCE: Vampire Poetry and Fiction, DNA Publications, Inc., PO Box 2988, Radford, VA 24143-2988, dnapublications@iname.com. Angela Kessler. 1994. circ. 5M. 4/yr. Pub'd 50 poems 1999. sub. price: $16/4 issues; sample: $5. 64pp; 8½×11; Rights purchased: FNASR. Publishes 5% of poems submitted. Reporting time: 1 month. Payment: $5-$20. Interested in new or unpub'd poets: yes. Simultaneous submissions accepted: yes. Recent contributors: Charlie Jacobs, Tippi Blevins, Wendy Rathbone.

THE DRIFTWOOD REVIEW, PO Box 700, Linden, MI 48451, E-mail midrift@aol.com. Jeff Vande Zonde. 1996. "We publish *Michigan* poets only." circ. 100. 1/yr. Pub'd 25 poems 1999; expects 25 poems 2000, 25 poems 2001. sub. price: $6; sample: $6. 100pp; 6×9; Rights purchased: First North American Serial. Publishes 5% of poems submitted. Deadlines: Oct. 1. Reporting time: 2-3 months. Payment: 1 copy. Interested in new or unpub'd poets: yes. Simultaneous submissions accepted: no. Recent contributors: Anca Vlasopolos, Joseph Sheltraw, David Watson, Elizabeth Socolow. Submission quantity: 3-5.

THE DROPLET JOURNAL, 19 Pine Street, Great Barrington, MA 01230-1417, 413-232-0052; E-mail droplet@bcn.net. 1995. circ. 300. 12/yr. sub. price: $10; sample: $1. 16pp; 8½×11.

Drum, 40 Potter Street, Concord, MA 01742. Craig Ellis. 1995. "No unsolicited mss, queries welcome, with SASE" Expects 2 poetry titles 2000, 6 poetry titles 2001. Reporting time: 2 months. Payment: negotiable, usually copies. Recently published poets: Creeley, Eigner, Enslin, Jonathan Williams.

DRUMVOICES REVUE, Southern Illinois University, English Dept., Box 1431, Edwardsville, IL 62026-1431, 618-650-2060; Fax 618-650-3509. Eugene B. Redmond, Jeffrey Skoblow. 1990. circ. 1.5M. 1-2/yr. Pub'd 60 poems 1999. sub. price: $10; sample: $5. 132pp; 6×9; Rights purchased: none. Publishes 30% of poems submitted. Deadlines: continual. Reporting time: 2-4 weeks. Payment: 2 copies of mag. Interested in new or unpub'd poets: yes. Simultaneous submissions accepted: yes. Recent contributors: Darlene Roy, Eric Stinus, Raymond Patterson, Pamela Plummer, Quiincy Troupe. Submission quantity: 3-5. Special interests: Translations, experimental poetry, regional poetry.

Dry Bones Press (see also THE COMPLEAT NURSE), PO Box 597, Roseville, CA 95678-0597, 415-707-2129 phone/Fax, jrankin@drybones.com, www.drybones.com. J. Rankin. 1992. Pub'd 3-4 poetry titles 1999. 8½×5½; avg. price, paper: $14.95. Less than 20pp; Publishes 50% of poetry manuscripts submitted. Reporting time: ASAP. Payment: glory, being published, sample, freedom to order directly from printer. Interested in new or unpub'd poets: yes. Simultaneous submissions accepted: yes. Recently published poets: J. Rankin. Submission quantity: representative sample. Special interests: Actually quite open if related to our themes.

DRY CRIK REVIEW, PO Box 44320, Lemon Cove, CA 93244, 209-597-2512; fax 209-597-2103. John C. Dofflemyer. 1990. "Must—SASE, poetic insight, whether free or structured, must speak in terms of the livestock business or the experience of the range livestock culture. Not interested in barnyard rhyme about pets. Especially intrigued by verse that relates to today's cultural dilemmas with honesty, openness and passion." circ. 400. 4/yr. Pub'd 100 poems 1999; expects 100 poems 2000. sub. price: $20; sample: $7 - some more. 72pp; 5½×8½; Rights purchased: one-time publishing. Publishes 10% of poems submitted. Deadlines: 30 days prior to printing—Jan. 20, Apr. 20, July 20, Oct. 20. Reporting time: 30-60 days. Payment: in copy. Interested in new or unpub'd poets: yes. Simultaneous submissions accepted: no. Recent contributors: Wilma McDaniel, Kenneth Brewer, Keith Wilson, Linda Hussa, Bruce Embree. Submission quantity: 5-7 max. Special interests: Environmental rural poetry which celebrates a healthy, bio-diversified mind; hands-on experience.

Duende Press, Box 571, Placitas, NM 87043, 505-867-5877. Larry Goodell. 1964. avg. press run limited. 120pp; Interested in new or unpub'd poets: no. Simultaneous submissions accepted: no. Recently published poets: Bill Pearlman.

Dufour Editions Inc., PO Box 7, Chester Springs, PA 19425-0007, 610-458-5005, FAX 610-458-7103. Thomas Lavoie. 1949. "SASE must be enclosed or material will be destroyed if rejected. We are primarily co-publishers of British poetry" avg. press run 250-500. Pub'd 1 poetry title 1999. size varies; avg. price, cloth: $30; paper: $15. Pages vary; Publishes less than 1% of poetry manuscripts submitted. Reporting time: 6 months. Payment: negotiable. Interested in new or unpub'd poets: no. Simultaneous submissions accepted: yes. Recently published poets: Osip Mandelstam, Miroslav Holub, Brendan Kennelly, Georges Bataille. Submission quantity: 20-50 if possible. Special interests: translations.

DUST (From the Ego Trip), Camel Press, Box 212, Needmore, PA 17238, 717-573-4526. Katharyn Howd

Machan. 1984. "all work must be carefully crafted. No stream of consiousness writing" circ. 700. Irregular. Pub'd 10 poems 1999; expects 10 poems 2000, 10 poems 2001. sub. price: $1-3 per issue on standing order; sample: $1. 20pp; 4¼×5¾; Rights purchased: none. Publishes 5% of poems submitted. Deadlines: none. Reporting time: 2 weeks. Payment: 50 copies. Interested in new or unpub'd poets: ok. Simultaneous submissions accepted: yes. Recent contributors: Katharyn Howd Machan, Elizabeth Hahn, Paul Humphrey, Virgil Suarez, Rochelle Lynn Holt. Submission quantity: a few. Special interests: poems should tell a story or create an unambiguous mental image.

DWAN, Box 411, Swarthmore, PA 19081, e-mail dsmith3@swarthmore.edu. 1993. circ. 1M. Irregular. sample price: $2. 38pp; 5½×8½.

E

THE EAR, Irvine Valley Coll., School of Humanities, 5500 Irvine Center Drive, Irvine, CA 92620, 714-541-5341. Marie Conners, Editor. 1983. *"The Ear* is a community journal of South Orange County. We occasionally publish work from other areas but must give consideration to local writing first. Manuscripts must be submitted in duplicate and will be accepted until December 15; writers should submit a cover sheet with name, address, and phone number. No manuscripts will be returned unless accompanied by SASE" circ. 2.5M. 1/yr. Pub'd 16 poems 1999. 150pp; 6×9; Publishes 6% of poems submitted. Deadlines: Dec. 15, 1997. Reporting time: 1-5 months. Payment: copies. Interested in new or unpub'd poets: yes, if they reside in Orange County, California. Simultaneous submissions accepted: yes. Recent contributors: Marcia Cohee, Michele Mitchell-Foust, Allyson Shaw, Allison Benis. Submission quantity: 5. Special interests: *The Ear* is most interested in publishing the well-crafted poem. We do not print light verse.

EARTH'S DAUGHTERS: Feminist Arts Periodical, PO Box 41, Central Park Station, Buffalo, NY 14215-0041, 716-627-9825, http://bfn.org/~edaught. Kastle Brill, Co-Editor. 1971. "We are a collective of 7 women, editorship rotates among members. Members of the collective are: Kastle Brill, Bonnie Johnson, Robin Willoughby, Ryki Zuckerman,Pat Colvard, Joyce Kessel, Joan Ford. We are dedicated to producing good work, and to continuing the publication of what we believe to be the longest-lived feminist magazine extant. For current topics, send SASE to Earth's Daughters, address above. IMPORTANT! Per each issue, authors are limited to a total of 6 poems or 1500 word prose. We also accept b/w graphics. Photocopies and dot matrix ok if clearly legible. Please SASE for writer's guidelines" circ. 1M. 2-3/yr. Pub'd 120 poems 1999; expects 120 poems 2000, 120 poems 2001. sub. price: $18/3 issues, instit. $22/3 issues; sample: $6. 60pp; size varies; Rights purchased: first rights only. Publishes 5+% of poems submitted. Deadlines: open issues anytime, special issues announced. Reporting time: 3-4 weeks except for special issues. Payment: 2 copies, additional copies available at half price. Interested in new or unpub'd poets: yes. Simultaneous submissions accepted: yes, but we must be notified *immediately* if work is accepted elsewhere. Recent contributors: Marge Piercy, Lyn Lifshin, Len Roberts, Denise Levertov, Olga Broumas. Submission quantity: no more than 6. Special interests: Translations, experimental poetry, unusual work is well received. We require work of technical skill and artistic intensity; our focus is the experience and creative expression of women. We welcome submissions from "unknown" contributors, and critique when we have time. We do special topical issues which are announced in *Poets & Writers Magazine, COSMEP* newsletter, *Small Press Review* and other small press newsletters, please no "greeting card" verse. We accept very little work which is written in traditional verse and/or rhyme.

EASTGATE QUARTERLY REVIEW OF HYPERTEXT, Eastgate Systems Inc., 134 Main Street, Watertown, MA 02172, 617-924-9044, Fax 617-924-9051, info@eastgate.com. sub. price: $49.95.

Eastgate Systems Inc. (see also EASTGATE QUARTERLY REVIEW OF HYPERTEXT), 134 Main Street, Watertown, MA 02172, 617-924-9044, Fax 617-924-9051, info@eastgate.com. "Hypertextual poetry only-please visit www.eastgate.com to learn more." Expects 1-2 poetry titles 2000, 1-2 poetry titles 2001. avg. price, other: $19.95. Interested in new or unpub'd poets: yes. Simultaneous submissions accepted: yes. Recently published poets: Edward Falco, Stephanie Strickland. Special interests: The editor is interested in translations. Everything we publish could be construed as 'experimental.' No light verse, *nothing* sentimental - there is nothing worse than going for unearned emotional effect.

ECLIPSE, General Delivery, Brownsville, MD 21715-9999, E-mail Kiirenza@aol.com. 1992. "Typewritten work only, please read guidelines or buy a sample issue to make sure submitted work is appropriate in theme." circ. 200. 4/yr. Pub'd 150 poems 1999; expects 150 poems 2000, 150 poems 2001. sub. price: $15; sample: $5. 52pp; 8½×11; Rights purchased: 1st time. Publishes 5% of poems submitted. Deadlines: none. Reporting time: up to 4 months. Payment: 1 copy per issue included. Interested in new or unpub'd poets: yes. Simultaneous submissions accepted: no. Recent contributors: Charlee Jacob, Ryan G. Van Cleave, John Grey, G.O. Clark. Submission quantity: no more than 5.

EDDIE THE MAGAZINE, PO Box 199, Newtown, N.S.W. 2042, Australia, phone 61-2-211-2339; fax 61-2-211-2331. 1991. circ. 3M. 3/yr. sub. price: $US20; sample: $6. 100pp; size A4 trimmed.

THE EDGE CITY REVIEW, 10912 Harpers Square Court, Reston, VA 20191, E-mail terryp17@aol.com. 1994. circ. 500+. 3/yr. sub. price: $15; sample: $5/ppd. 48pp; 8½×11.

Edgewise Press, 24 Fifth Avenue #224, New York, NY 10011, 212-982-4818, FAX 212-982-1364. 1995. "We do not accept unsolicited mss." avg. press run 1M. Pub'd 1 poetry title 1999. 4¼×7¼; avg. price, paper: $10. 64pp; Interested in new or unpub'd poets: no. Simultaneous submissions accepted: no. Recently published poets: Alan Jones, Nanni Cagnone, Cid Corman.

EDITION KEY SATCH(EL), 93 Main Street, Florence, MA 01062, 413-587-0776 phone/Fax, keysatch@quale.com. 1997. "Do not send verse. Focus is on prose poetry only. In 2000 mag shifts to publishing chapbook collections of prose poetry solicited only." circ. 200. 4/yr. Pub'd 96 poems 1999; expects 96 poems 2000, 96 poems 2001. sub. price: $16; sample: $5. 24pp; 5½×8½; Rights purchased: first serial. Payment: 25 copies. yes, with note that it is simultaneous. Recent contributors: Morton Marcus, Maxine Chernoff, Joseph Torra.

The Edwin Mellen Press (see also Mellen Poetry Press), PO Box 450, Lewiston, NY 14092, 716-754-2266. H. Richardson, Director; Patricia Schultz, Poetry Editor. 1974. "We are willing to reprint previously published poems so long as more than half the poems in our volume have not been previously published. Send for guidelines." avg. press run 200. Pub'd 25 poetry titles 1999; expects 50 poetry titles 2000. 6×9; avg. price, paper: $14.95. 64-84pp; Publishes 30-50% of poetry manuscripts submitted. Reporting time: 2 months. Payment: no royalties. Interested in new or unpub'd poets: yes. Simultaneous submissions accepted: no. Recently published poets: Albert Cook, W.R. Elton, Emery George, Lisa Kahn, Peter Ulisse. Submission quantity: 30-50. Special interests: Translations, serious poetry, light verse, lyric.

1812, Box 1812, Amherst, NY 14226-7812, http://1812.simplenet.com. Rick Lupert. 2/yr. Expects 10 poems 2000. sub. price: free; sample: free. Rights purchased: 1st Times. Publishes 1% of poems submitted. Reporting time: 1-4 months. Payment: varies. Interested in new or unpub'd poets: yes. Simultaneous submissions accepted: yes. Submission quantity: 5.

EKPHRASIS, Frith Press, PO Box 161236, Sacramento, CA 95816-1236, 916-451-3038, http://members.aol.com/ekphrasisl. Laverne Frith, Editor; Carol Frith, Editor. 1997. "We consider submissions year round. we specialize in poetry based on individual works from and artistic genre. We are looking for well-crafted poetry the main content of which is based on individual works form any artistc genre. Please identify the specific work that is the focus of the poem. Because the source work will not be reproduced, the poem should stand on its own. Acceptable ekprastic verse transcends mere description." circ. 100+. 2/yr. Pub'd 85 poems 1999; expects 71 poems 2000, 76 poems 2001. sub. price: $12; sample: $6. 50pp; 5½×8½; Publishes 5%-7% of poems submitted. Deadlines: ongoing. Reporting time: up to six months. Payment: 1 issue of the journal in which they appear. Interested in new or unpub'd poets: yes. Simultaneous submissions accepted: no. Recent contributors: Joseph Stanton, Rhina Espaillat, William Greenway, Stephanie Strickland, Peter Cooley. Submission quantity: 3-7.

●**ELEMENTS,** 2820 Houston Street, Alexandria, LA 71301, 318-445-5055. 1979. circ. 800. 6/yr. sub. price: $25; sample: $1.75. 20pp; 8×11.

THE ELEVENTH MUSE, a publication by Poetry West, PO Box 2413, Colorado Springs, CO 80901. J.R. Thelin, Editor. 1982. circ. 300. 2/yr. Pub'd 64 poems 1999; expects 80 poems 2000, 88 poems 2001. sub. price: $8 for 2 issues; sample: $4.50. 48-56pp; 8½×5½; Rights purchased: 1st. Publishes 7-10% of poems submitted. Deadlines: none. Reporting time: 4 days to 4 months. Payment: 1 copy per poem accepted. Interested in new or unpub'd poets: yes. Simultaneous submissions accepted: no. Recent contributors: Jack Myers, Lois Hayna, Kathy Shorr, Leslie Ullman, Joan Stone. Submission quantity: no more than 5, no less than 3. Special interests: Anything with a strong, original vision; many styles acceptable. We read all submissions aloud.

ELF: ECLECTIC LITERARY FORUM (ELF MAGAZINE), PO Box 392, Tonawanda, NY 14150, 716-693-7006. C.K. Erbes, Editor. 1990. "Read year round, write for guidelines (SASE) and sample copy (Ruth Cable memurial prize for poetry). Annual poetry competition March 31st deadline, SASE for guidelines. ELF: Eclectic Literary Forum welected by Writer's Digest as one of the top mainstream markers for poetry." circ. 4M. 3/4. Pub'd 100 poems 1999. sub. price: $16 (foreign rate: add $8); sample: $5.50. 56-64pp; 8½×11; Rights purchased: First North American Serial Rights. Publishes 10%-15% of poems submitted. Deadlines: none. Reporting time: 6-8 weeks. Payment: 1 copy of magazine. Interested in new or unpub'd poets: yes. Simultaneous submissions accepted: yes, if notified. Recent contributors: Lucien Styk, Rachel Hadas, Elise Paschen, David Mason, Mark Jarman. Submission quantity: 3. Special interests: All poetry is reviewed that is not obscene or exhibits graphic violence.

ELLIPSE, Univ. de Sherbrooke, Box 10, Faculte des Lettres et Sciences Humaines, Sherbrooke, Quebec J1K 2R1, Canada, 819-821-7238. 1969. *"Ellipse* doesn't accept unsolicited material." circ. 750. 2/yr. sub. price: $12; sample: $7. 120pp; 5½×8½; Interested in new or unpub'd poets: no. Simultaneous submissions accepted: no. Recent contributors: Gustafson, Avison, McEwn, Lane, Moure' Special interests: Translations of anglophone and francophone poets in the other language. Two poets per issue.

Embassy Hall Editions (see also THE GALLEY SAIL REVIEW), PO Box 665, Centralia, IL 62801-0665. Stanley McNail, General Editor. 1985. "Embassy Hall is extremely limited in scope and for the present uses only solicited material" avg. press run 500. Pub'd 2 poetry titles 1999; expects 2 poetry titles 2000, 3 poetry titles 2001. 5½×8½; avg. price, paper: $6; other: $3 chapbooks. 60pp; Reporting time: 2-3 months. Payment: subject to negotiation with individual author. Interested in new or unpub'd poets: not if unsolicited. Simultaneous submissions accepted: no. Recently published poets: Skip Robinson, Leslie Woolf Hedley, Stanley McNail, H. David Moe. Submission quantity: 3-5. Special interests: Not limited in this respect—we use good contemporary poetry and are eclectic in choices.

EMERGING VOICES, 1722 N. 58th Street, Milwaukee, WI 53208-1618, 414-453-4678. Lucille Tamin. 1995. "No publication without our permission form first! Write for guidelines and agreement. We are a vanity press." Irregular. Pub'd 5 poems 1999; expects 50 poems 2000, 100 poems 2001. sample price: $10. 20pp; 8½×11; Rights purchased: one-time. Publishes 100% of poems submitted. Reporting time: 5-10 days. Interested in new or unpub'd poets: yes, author must be/have been 18. Submission quantity: unlimited. Special interests: Must be written prior to author's 18th birthday.

EMPLOI PLUS, 1256 Principale N. St., Ste. #203, L'Annonciation, Quebec, J0T 1T0, Canada, 819-275-3293 phone/Fax. Daniel Reid. 1990. "No submissions accepted, private press" circ. 500. Occasional. sample price: $5. 12pp; 7×8½; Recent contributors: Robert Ott, Robert Biro, Claire Moquin, Julie Herbst, C. Mulrooney.

THE EMSHOCK LETTER, Randall Flat Road, PO Box 411, Troy, ID 83871, 208-835-4902. Steven E. Erickson, Publisher. 1977. "Poetry submissions are accepted *only* from subscribers to *The Emshock Letter.* After reading 3 or 4 issues of our publication, the poet will know whether or not his/her material might be appropriate to the context of the publication. This, in fact, is our only guideline; aside from the certainty that all poetry appearing in *The Emshock Letter* has been, and ever will be generated by subscribers to the publication" circ. 1M. 3-12/yr. Pub'd 20 poems 1999; expects 15 poems 2000, 20 poems 2001. sub. price: $25; sample: none, *one issue cannot adequately depict a publication of this nature.* 5-7pp; 8½×11; Rights purchased: one time rights. No deadlines. Reporting time: varies (with no promise to return unsolicited material). Payment: usually copies. Interested in new or unpub'd poets: yes, but only from subscribers to *The Emshock Letter.* Simultaneous submissions accepted: yes. Submission quantity: any number. Special interests: Poetry containing intensity, depth, meaning.

En Passant Poetry Press (see also EN PASSANT/POETRY), 2 Whirlaway Court, Hendersonville, NC 28792-8552. Jim Costello. 1981. "Send $4 for format issue entitled *The Underbelly Poems,* by Jim Costello" 5½×8½; avg. price, other: $4. 44pp; Reporting time: prompt. Interested in new or unpub'd poets: yes. Simultaneous submissions accepted: no.

EN PASSANT/POETRY, En Passant Poetry Press, 2 Whirlaway Court, Hendersonville, NC 28792-8552. Jim Costello. 1975. "We like incantatory poetry represented by lines like the following by Jim Costello: "Bahlia, did you know the victim painted blue/ Who was tied to a cross, whose penis was cut,/ Whose blood was smeared on the idols?/ Did you know the lords who circled him/ Dancing, chanting, sending their arrows into/ That blue body, making of it a porcupine of death?/ Bahlia, did you know your turn would come?/ That they would fill your mouth with corn and/ Jade, and bury you in Quintana Roo?"" circ. 300. Irregular. sample price: $3. 40pp; 5½×8½; Rights purchased: first and share remaining rights. Publishes less than 5% of poems submitted. Deadlines: none. Reporting time: prompt. Payment: copies. Interested in new or unpub'd poets: yes. Simultaneous submissions accepted: no. Recent contributors: Daniel Berrigan, Joe Bruchac, Robert Desnos, Vicente Huidobro, Herbert Morris. Submission quantity: 5 or 6.

ENDING THE BEGIN, Headveins Graphics, PO Box 4774, Seattle, WA 98104-0774, 206-726-0948. 1992. "No long poetry. We are partial to cynicism, humor, fivolity ans melanchlia" circ. 100. Irregular. sub. price: $2/3 issues; sample: $1 postpaid. 17-24pp; 2¾×4; Submission quantity: 2-3. Special interests: experimental poetry, different forms, visual text.

●**ENIGMA,** 402 South 25th Street, Philadelphia, PA 19146, 215-545-8496, sydx@att.net. Syd Bradford. 1989. circ. 50. 4/yr. Pub'd 30 poems 1999; expects 30 poems 2000, 30 poems 2001. sub. price: none; sample: $5. 100pp; 8½×11; Rights purchased: none. Publishes 25% of poems submitted. Reporting time: 3 weeks. Payment: 1 free copy. Interested in new or unpub'd poets: yes. Simultaneous submissions accepted: no. Recent contributors: Diana K. Rubin, Arthur Schuler, Phil Winter, Salvatore Galioto, Verma Grego. Submission quantity: 3.

Enitharmon Press, 36 St George's Avenue, London N7 OHD, England, 0171-607-7194; FAX 0171-607-8694. Stephen Stuart-Smith. 1969. avg. press run 500. Pub'd 10 poetry titles 1999; expects 12 poetry titles 2000. size 8V0; avg. price, cloth: £15; paper: £7.95; other: £25 signed limited edition cloth. 70pp; Publishes 2% of poetry manuscripts submitted. Reporting time: 4 weeks. Payment: royalties vary according to contract; authors able to buy copies at trade discount. Interested in new or unpub'd poets: yes, but only if introductory letter sent first. Simultaneous submissions accepted: no. Recently published poets: Jeremy Hooker, Neil Curry, David Gascoyne, Jeremy Reed, C.H. Sisson. Submission quantity: 10.

ENTELECHY MAGAZINE, 2363 Jackson Street #4, San Francisco, CA 94115-1345, e-mail shorn@entelechy.org; website www.entelechy.org. Steven Horn, Poetry Editor. 1993. "We tend to publish new or sparsely published poets...to give voice to an unheard group of writers, a forum for richness in language. The Internet site of our publication publishes about six to eight poems every two weeks" circ. 1M. 2/yr. Expects 100 poems 2000, 100 poems 2001. sub. price: $15.90; sample: $8. 208pp; 6×9; Rights purchased: FNASR. Publishes 10% of poems submitted. Reporting time: 6-8 weeks. Payment: 3 complimentary copies. Interested in new or unpub'd poets: yes. Simultaneous submissions accepted: yes. Recent contributors: Lyn Lifshin, Stacy Smith, Marlys West, Andrew Urbanus, Marilyn Kallet. Submission quantity: up to 12, preferable 6.

EPOCH, 251 Goldwin Smith Hall, Cornell Univ., Ithaca, NY 14853, 607-255-3385. 1947. "We suggest that writers examine an issue or 2 of *Epoch* before submitting. Don't send work between May & August" circ. 1M+. 3/yr. Pub'd 20-25 poems 1999. sub. price: $11; sample: $5. 128pp; 6×9; Rights purchased: usual. Publishes less than 1% of poems submitted. Deadlines: 15 September, 15 April only. Reporting time: 4-6 weeks. Payment: $5-$10 per printed magazine page. Interested in new or unpub'd poets: yes-very interested. Simultaneous submissions accepted: no. Recent contributors: Robert Creeley, Wanda Coleman, Thylias Moss, Robert Morgan, Leslie Scalapino. Submission quantity: 3-5. Special interests: We're an eclectic magazine. We try to publish the best writing from different schools and persuasions.

●**Epona Publishing,** 12 Clearview Avenue #1, Gloucester, MA 01930, http://kathywer.homepage.com/index.html. 1999. 8½×11.

Erespin Press, 304 Mountain View Lane, Laurel, MT 59044-2047. D. L. Kent. 1980. "Letterpress equipment; all work done in-house, including binding. Limited editions (i.e., 150-200 copies) only. Types and mouldmade or handmade papers suited to content" avg. press run 100. Pub'd 1 poetry title 1999; expects 1 poetry title 2000, 1 poetry title 2001. 6×9. 36pp; Publishes 10% of poetry manuscripts submitted. Reporting time: 1 week. Payment: negotiable. Interested in new or unpub'd poets: yes. Simultaneous submissions accepted: yes, but should be so informed. Recently published poets: Robert Lambert, Anita Sharp, Don D. Wilson. Submission quantity: 1 could be enough; no more than 10. Special interests: Historical translations only.

●**Essex Press,** PO Box 914, North Andover, MA 01845, sxpress@banet.net. 1998. 6×9.

Etaoin Shrdlu Press (see also PABLO LENNIS), Fandom House, 30 N. 19th Street, Lafayette, IN 47904. John Thiel, General Editor. 1976. "I accept only science fiction and fantasy poetry and prefer these not be of an irreverant nature" avg. press run 200. Expects 1 poetry title 2000. 8½×11; avg. price, paper: $5. 90pp; Publishes 99% of poetry manuscripts submitted. Reporting time: 2 weeks or less. Interested in new or unpub'd poets: yes. Simultaneous submissions accepted: no. Recently published poets: Keith Allen Daniels, Lloyd Michael Lohr, Jerry Rea Ellis, Michael Pendragon, Peter Zenger. Submission quantity: as many as wished. Special interests: Science fiction, fantasy, and science.

EUROPEAN JUDAISM, Leo Baeck College, 80 East End Rd., Sternberg Centre for Judaism, London N3 2SY, United Kingdom, 44-181-349-4525; Fax 44-181-343-2558; leo-baeck-college@mailbox.ulcc.ac.uk; www.lb-college.demon.co.uk. Ruth Fainlight. 1966. "We are not primarily a poetry magazine, but always include a few poems in each issue. Most of our published poems are by established poets." circ. 400. 2/yr. Pub'd 18 poems 1999; expects 20 poems 2000, 18 poems 2001. sub. price: £18 ($27); sample: gratis from Berghahn Books. 156pp; 9×6; Publishes 20% of poems submitted. Reporting time: variable. Payment: 1 free copy. Interested in new or unpub'd poets: yes. Simultaneous submissions accepted: no. Recent contributors: Linda Pastan, Grace Shulman, Daniel Weissbort, Gaby Morris, Charles Fishman. Submission quantity: 1-3. Special interests: Short poems of Jewish interest.

EVANSVILLE REVIEW, Univ. of Evansville, English Dept., 1800 Lincoln Avenue, Evansville, IN 47714, 812-488-1042. Jennifer Giffin, Benjamin Vogt. 1991. "We read manuscripts from May until December 5th, please include an SASE for reply only; we recycle all manuscripts. A brief bio or list of previous publication is helpful as we print contributors notes." circ. 3M. 1/yr. Pub'd 70 poems 1999. sample price: $5. 200pp; 6×9; Rights purchased: none. Publishes 1% of poems submitted. Deadlines: December 5th. Reporting time: We notify in late February. Payment: 2 copies. The majority of our poetry is authored by nonestablished writers. yes, with notification. Recent contributors: John Updike, Marge Piercy, Lucien Stryk, David Ignatow, Charles

Wright. Submission quantity: 1-6. Special interests: We publish a wide variety of poetry including translations, regional poetry, and satire. All subjects welcome.

EVENT, Douglas College, PO Box 2503, New Westminster, B.C. V3L 5B2, Canada, 604-527-5293, Fax 604-527-5095, event@douglas.bc.ca. Gillian Harding-Russell. 1971. "We are interested in narrative and lyrical poems, in which cadence always makes an important contribution to the work. See 28/3 for 'Creative Non-Fiction' contest upcoming, which may be of interest to poets writing in a different genre: deadline April 15. Write for details." circ. 1.2M. 3/yr. Pub'd 68 poems 1999; expects 60 poems 2000, 60 poems 2001. sub. price: US$20, US$30/2 years; sample: current $7. 136-160pp; 6×9; Rights purchased: first. Publishes 5% of poems submitted. Deadlines: ongoing. Reporting time: 2-4 months, depending on how long we consider the poem. Payment: $22/page, min. payment $25. Interested in new or unpub'd poets: yes. Simultaneous submissions accepted: no. Recent contributors: Tom Wayman, Lorna Crozier, Sue Wheeler, Harold Rhenisch, Patricia Young. Submission quantity: 5 or 6 at least, no more than 10.

THE EVER DANCING MUSE, Who Who Who Publishing, PO Box 7751, East Rutherford, NJ 07073. 1993. "I will gladly send a prospective contributor a free copy to familiarize them with this project" circ. 50-100. 2/yr. sub. price: $8/3 issues; sample: $3. 20pp; 8½×5½; Reporting time: 1-4 weeks. Payment: copies. Interested in new or unpub'd poets: yes. Simultaneous submissions accepted: yes, if specified. Recent contributors: Duane Locke, Lyn Lifshin, Sparrow, Mary Winters, Simon Perchik. Submission quantity: 3-5.

THE EVERGREEN CHRONICLES, PO Box 8939, Minneapolis, MN 55408-8939, 612-823-6638; e-mail evgrnchron@aol.com. Susan Raffo, Managing Editor; Louisa Castner. 1985. "We intend to appeal first and foremost to a lesbian/gay/bisexual/transgender audience. Poems submitted may be in a wide range of styles and subject matter, but they should be specific enough to be attractive and interesting to this readership. Send 4 copies and short bio." circ. 1M. 3/yr. Pub'd 48 poems 1999; expects 45-50 poems 2000, 45-50 poems 2001. sub. price: $20 individual, $40 institution, $25 international; sample: $7.95 + $1 postage. 90pp; 5½×8½; Rights purchased: first time serial rights. Publishes 15-20% of poems submitted. Deadlines: Jan. 1, July 1. Reporting time: 2 months from deadline. Payment: in copies and honoranium. Interested in new or unpub'd poets: yes. Simultaneous submissions accepted: yes, but like to be told that in a cover letter. Recent contributors: Jim Elledge, Leslea, Newman, Sima Rabinowitz, Alfrerd Corn, Djola Branner. Submission quantity: no more than 10 poems or 10 pages. Special interests: tranlations, experimental poetry.

EX FILLAPIO IN PENUSIO, Pen-Dec Press, 2526 Chatham Woods, Grand Rapids, MI 49546. 2000. "Lusts for b&w art, uses no fiction. Seeking climactic harangues" Irregular. Pub'd 30 poems 1999; expects 30 poems 2000, 30 poems 2001. sample price: $4. 24pp; 8½×5½; Publishes 15% of poems submitted. Interested in new or unpub'd poets: yes. Simultaneous submissions accepted: yes. Recent contributors: Phyllis Settles, Marion Smith, Cassius, Rachael Houseman. Submission quantity: 8-10.

●**Excelsior Publishing,** PO Box 8122, Reston, VA 20195-2022, lsheet@alum-mit.edu, www.excelsiorpublishing.com. 1999. 5½×8½.

Exhorter Publications International, 323 W. High Street, Elizabethtown, PA 17022-2141. 1995.

EXIT 13 MAGAZINE, P O Box 423, Fanwood, NJ 07023. Tom Plante, Editor-in-Chief. 1987. "There's an *Exit 13* in every state—this one celebrates life, love, travel, work, and the wonder that poets bring to their pens. Poets everywhere are welcome at *Exit 13*." circ. 500. 1/yr. Expects 65 poems 2000, 65 poems 2001. sub. price: $7; sample: $7. 64pp; 5½×8½; Rights purchased: rights revert to author, but *Exit 13* keeps anthology rights. Publishes 5-10% of poems submitted. Reporting time: 3-5 months. Payment: 1 copy, photos of Exit 13 road signs earn a free magazine. Interested in new or unpub'd poets: yes. Simultaneous submissions accepted: yes. Recent contributors: D.E. Steward, Madeline Hoffer, Errol Miller, Adele Kenny, Gerald Stern. Submission quantity: 4-5. Special interests: *Exit 13* is the successor of *Berkeley Works*—experimental. Poems with heart and a sense of place. A poetic view of the terrain is always welcome as is a love of geography and nature.

Expanded Media Editions, PO Box 190136, Prinz Albert Str. 65, 53AA3 Bonn 1, Germany, Germany, 0228/22 95 83, FAX 0228/21 95 07. Pociao. 1969. avg. press run 1M. 21×14; avg. price, paper: DM 14; other: DM 20. 100pp; Publishes 1% of poetry manuscripts submitted. Reporting time: 4 weeks. Payment: 10%. Interested in new or unpub'd poets: no. Simultaneous submissions accepted: yes. Recently published poets: Ginsberg, Bowles, Malanga, Plymell. Submission quantity: 10.

●**EXPERIMENTAL FOREST,** 223 A. Bosler Avenue, Lemoyne, PA 17043, 717-730-2143, xxforest@yahoo.com, www.geocities.com/paris/salon/9699. Jeanette Trout, Kevyn Knox. 1999. "No sappy love poetry, please." circ. 250+. 6/yr. Pub'd 150 poems 1999; expects 200 poems 2000, 200 poems 2001. sub. price: $18; sample: $4. 60pp; 5½×8½; Rights purchased: one-time only. Publishes 10-15% of poems submitted. Deadlines: accept all year round. Reporting time: 2-4 months. Payment: 1 copy and discounts on extra copies. Interested in new or unpub'd poets: yes. Simultaneous submissions accepted: no. Recent contributors: Richard Kostelanetz, John Taggart, Marty Esworthy, Kerry Shawn Keys, Deborah Ryder. Submission quantity: up to 5.

EXPLORATIONS, English Dept., Alaska Univ. Southeast, 11120 Glacier Highway, Juneau, AK 99801. Art Petersen, Editor; Alice Tersteeg. 1981. "Best to send for complete guidelines. Reader/entry fee of $6 for 2 poems (ea. 60 lines max.) and $3 per poem to 5, and for prose, $6 each for limit of 2 (3000 words maximum). The editors respond favorably to 'language really spoken by men' and women. Standard form as well as innovation are encouraged as well as appropriate and fresh aspects of imagery (allusion, metaphor, simile, symbol...). Deadline for submissions: May 15 of each year." circ. 650. 1/yr. Pub'd 35 poems 1999; expects 35 poems 2000, 30-35 poems 2001. sub. price: $6/1 issue, $11/2 issues, $10/3 issues; sample: $5. 60pp; 5½x8½; Rights purchased: one-time publication. Publishes 2.5% of poems submitted. Deadlines: December through May 15; notification in July. Reporting time: June. Payment: 2 contributor's copies, $1700 in prizes: $1000, $500, 2 X $100. Interested in new or unpub'd poets: yes. Simultaneous submissions accepted: yes. Recent contributors: Charles Bukowski, Bill Hotchkiss, Johnathan Russell, Joanne Townsend. Submission quantity: no more than 5, 60 lines maximum.

F

●Face to Face Press, 3322 12th Avenue, Suite 2, Brooklyn, NY 11218, 718-436-2331, Fax 419-828-4684, slevart@face2facepress.com, www.face2facepress.com. 1999. 5×7.

FAG RAG, Fag Rag Books, Good Gay Poets Press, Box 15331, Kenmore Station, Boston, MA 02215, 617-426-4469. E. Carlotta. 1970. "Gay male poetry welcome. We reject all poems containing the following: 'God', 'Fire Island', 'ice cream', and vicious put downs of people in struggle." circ. 5M, readership 20M. 1/yr. Pub'd 100 poems 1999; expects 100 poems 2000. sub. price: US $10 for 4 issues, international $15 for 2 issues; sample: $5. 32pp; 11×17; Rights purchased: all rights reside with author. Publishes 20% of poems submitted. Deadlines: continuous. Reporting time: 1 week to 6 months. Payment: in issues. Interested in new or unpub'd poets: yes. Simultaneous submissions accepted: no. Recent contributors: John Wieners, Paul Mariah, Walta Borouski, Ron Schreiber. Submission quantity: 5 maximum. Special interests: The Revolutionary both in form and in impulse is especially welcome.

Fag Rag Books (see also FAG RAG), PO Box 15331, Boston, MA 02215.

FANTASTIC STORIES, DNA Publications, Inc., PO Box 329, Brightwaters, NY 11718-0329, E-mail pwpubl@aol.com. 1992. circ. 7M. 4/yr. sub. price: $16; sample: $5. 64pp; 8½x11.

Far Corner Books, PO Box 82157, Portland, OR 97282. 1991. "SASE must be provided. Query first if we are open to submission. Include one poem, publication history, and query letter" avg. press run 2M. Expects 1 poetry title 2000, 1 poetry title 2001. 6×9; avg. price, cloth: $15; paper: $8. 72-122pp; Publishes 1% or less of poetry manuscripts submitted. Reporting time: 2-3 months. Payment: depends on author and mss. Interested in new or unpub'd poets: moderately interested. Simultaneous submissions accepted: no. Recently published poets: M. Simms, J. Kaplinski, N.S. Nye, W. Greenway, A. Douglas. Submission quantity: query first with acknowledgement and publication history, with SASE.

FAT TUESDAY, 560, Manada Gap Road, Grantville, PA 17028, 717-469-7159. F.M. Cotolo, Editor; B. Lyle Tabor, Assistant Editor; Lionel Stevroid, Assistant Editor; Thom Savion, Assistant Editor; Kristen Vonoehrke, Luxurious, Sacred Editor. 1981. "Know our magazine. The best way to do that is to obtain an issue and absorb it. We also produce audio magazines. Our first Fat Tuesday's Cool Noise, ($5) features 20 artists reading with original music and sound collage in stereo. We originally described ourselves as eclectic, but in the ten years we've published things have changed. We will not accept just any good poem. Well constructed or not, we want true statements from the author as an individual. Relevant or irreverant, we want each piece to be the quintessential voicing of the author. Remember: to us, your work is your signature. And we can tell forgery, even if we don't know you!" circ. 350-500. 1+. Pub'd 50 poems 1999; expects 50 poems 2000, 50 poems 2001. sample price: $5. 45pp; 5½x8½, 8½x11; Rights purchased: one-time, copyright reverts to author after publication. Publishes 5% of poems submitted. Deadlines: reading all year. Reporting time: 2 weeks, sometimes less. Payment: 1 comp. copy in which contribution appears. Interested in new or unpub'd poets: both, as long as the material has never appeared anywhere else. Simultaneous submissions accepted: no. Recent contributors: Mary Lee Gowland, Chuck Taylor, G.K. Rimpau, Charles Bukowski, Gerald Locklin. Submission quantity: as many as one feels may fit our genre. Special interests: Translations are fine. Experiment all you wish. Regional is fine as long as it doesn't get esoteric. No real longies, please—we've limited space. Besides, it shouldn't take that long to reveal yourself. Light verse is fine, but nothing Hallmarky. Satire is terrific, everything will work as long as the author speaks from within.

FATHOMS, PO Box 62634, Tallahassee, FL 32313. Rex West, Poetry Editor. 1991. "When submitting label envelope 'poetry editor''' circ. 800. 2/yr. Pub'd 40 poems 1999. sub. price: $8; sample: $4.50. 40pp; 5½×8½; Rights purchased: first serial. Deadlines: year-round - best in summer. Reporting time: 1-5 months. Payment: 2 copies. Interested in new or unpub'd poets: yes. Simultaneous submissions accepted: yes. Recent contributors: William Greenway, Ronald Wallace, Jennifer Wootton, J.L. Haddaway. Submission quantity: 3-5.

FC-Izdat Publishing, 3 Cottage Avenue, Winchester, MA 01890, 617-776-2262; vvv@tiac.net. 1982. 5½×8½.

The Feathered Serpent, 55 Galli Drive #C, Novato, CA 94949-5715, 415-499-8751. 1952.

FELL SWOOP, Acre Press, 3003 Ponce de Leon Street, New Orleans, LA 70119. X.J. Dailey. 1983. *"Fell Swoop* is a gorilla/guerilla adventure rampage. We embrace the Aberrant in vision + cinemascope hope - hope you like the Coming Detractions!'' circ. 300. 3/yr. Pub'd 30 poems 1999; expects 30 poems 2000, 30 poems 2001. sub. price: $8; sample: $3. 20pp; 8½×11; Publishes 50% of poems submitted. Deadlines: ongoing. Reporting time: 1 month or better. Payment: copies. Interested in new or unpub'd poets: yes. Simultaneous submissions accepted: no. Recent contributors: Anselm Hollo, Randall Schroth, Elizabeth Thomas, Ed Dorn. Submission quantity: 5.

FEMINIST STUDIES, c/o Women's Studies Program, University of Maryland, College Park, MD 20742, 301-405-7413. Shirley Geok-Lin Lim. 1972. circ. 6M. 3/yr. Pub'd 7 poems 1999; expects 12 poems 2000, 12 poems 2001. sub. price: $85 institutions, $30 individuals; sample: $25 inst., $12 indiv. 200-250pp; 6×9; Publishes 10% of poems submitted. Deadlines: May 1 and December 1. Reporting time: 5 months. Payment: none. Interested in new or unpub'd poets: yes. Simultaneous submissions accepted: no. Recent contributors: Toi Derricotte, Lorrie Sprecher, Audre Lorde, Cherrie Mcraga. Submission quantity: no limit. Special interests: Experimental poetry. All poetry that focuses on women or gender. Feminist perspective.

FEMINIST VOICES NEWSJOURNAL, 1630 Bultman Road #106, Madison, WI 53704-3676, 608-251-9268. Xanda Fayeh. 1987. *"Feminist Voices* is a women's newspaper with 1-2 pages per issue featuring artwork, poetry and very short stories. Poem length should generally not exceed two double-spaced pages. We accept poetry from women only. Some issues have themes; write to FV for information on upcoming themes'' circ. 7M. 10/yr. Pub'd 40 poems 1999; expects 30-40 poems 2000, 30-40 poems 2001. sub. price: $15/yr. Free to females in prison, $25 institution; sample: $1. 12-16pp; 9¾×16; Rights purchased: rights remain with writer. Publishes 70% of poems submitted. Deadlines: open. Reporting time: varies, up to 2 months. Payment: copies of issue in which work appears. Interested in new or unpub'd poets: yes. Simultaneous submissions accepted: yes. Recent contributors: Cedar Marie, Marie Iglesias-Cardihale, Kathleen A. Kelly, Mimi LaGrange, Tatyana Mamanova. Submission quantity: up to 5.

FENICE BROADSHEETS, New Broom Private Press, 78 Cambridge Street, Leicester LE3 0JP, England, 547419. Toni Savage. 1994. "My broadsheets are printed on a small handpress in editions of 2-300 copies. These are given away free of charge to folk, jazz, or theatre audiences—no payment is given to the poets. 25-30 copies. Mostly I print new poetry—at times a re-print takes my fancy. I enjoy receiving from writers, but am too often inundated. To fill in the above would be false. My output is limited by time—sometimes 10-15 titles are published a year—often less. Poets published this way include: Edward Murch (Yennadon Plays), Spike Milligan (poet, playwright, actor & goon), Charles Ackerman Berry (poet, writer & hobo), Geoffrey Shovelton (opera singer), Charles Causley (poet), Brian Patten (poet), Boyd Lichfield (poet), Sue Mackrell (poet).'' circ. 2-300. Pub'd 14 poems 1999; expects 15 poems 2000, 15-20 poems 2001. sub. price: free plus postage; sample: free plus postage (to America, $1) ICRs only please. 1 page; 9×5 approx.; Payment: 30 copies. Interested in new or unpub'd poets: yes. Recent contributors: Chris Challis, Sue Mackrell, Alix Weisz, Jane Lord Bradbury, Spike Milligan. Submission quantity: 4-8.

●**Fern Publications (see also DANDELION ARTS MAGAZINE),** Casa Alba, 24 Frosty Hollow, E. Hunsbury, Northants NN4 0SY, England, 01604-701730. 1978. size A4.

THE FIDDLEHEAD, Campus House, PO Box 4400, University of New Brunswick, Fredericton, NB E3B 5A3, Canada, 506-453-3501. Lynn Davies, Poetry Editor. 1945. "Submissions should be typed and accompanied by *Canadian*-stamped, self-addressed envelopes or *International Reply Coupons*. Submissions accompanied by American-stamped envelopes cannot be returned.'' circ. 1.1M. 4/yr. Pub'd 120 poems 1999; expects 120 poems 2000, 120 poems 2001. sub. price: $20 Canada, U.S. $20US + $6 postage; sample: $8 + postage Can. and US. 128-200pp; 6×9; Rights purchased: 1st N.A. serial rights. Publishes less than 5% of poems submitted. Deadlines: none. Reporting time: 10-20 weeks. Payment: $12/printed page. Interested in new or unpub'd poets: yes. Simultaneous submissions accepted: no. Recent contributors: Eric Ormsby, Eric Miller, Dan Zwicky. Submission quantity: 6-10 poems. Special interests: None, quality alone remains the criterion.

FIELD: Contemporary Poetry and Poetics, Oberlin College Press, 10 N. Professor Street, Oberlin College, Oberlin, OH 44074-1095, 440-775-8408, Fax 440-775-8124, oc.press@oberlin.edu. David Walker, Co-Editor; David Young, Co-Editor; Pamela Alexander, Co-Editor; Martha Collins, Co-Editor; Alberta Turner, Co-Editor. 1969. "Many people don't include sufficient return postage—we cannot respond to those submissions. Contact us for details of annual Field Poetry Prize for previously unpublished manuscripts.'' circ. 1.5M. 2/yr. Pub'd 100 poems 1999. sub. price: $14, $24/2 years; sample: $7 ppd. 100pp; 5¼x8½; Rights purchased: first. Publishes .25%-.50% of poems submitted. Deadlines: none. Reporting time: 4-6 weeks. Payment: $15-$25 a page. Interested in new or unpub'd poets: yes. Simultaneous submissions accepted: no. Recent contributors: Carl Phillips, Lee Upton, Billy Collins, Franz Wright, Sandra McPherson. Submission quantity: 5-8. Special interests: Translations must include proof of right to translate.

FIGMENTS, Figments Publishing, 14 William Street, Donaghadee, Co. Down NI BT21 0HP, United Kingdom, 01247-884267. 1995. circ. 750. 12/yr. sub. price: £18 + p/h; sample: £1.50 + p/h. 24pp; 9×11½.

Figments Publishing (see also FIGMENTS), 14 William Street, Donaghadee, Co. Down N.I. BT21 0HP, United Kingdom, 01247-884267. 1995. size A5.

The Figures, 5 Castle Hill Avenue, Great Barrington, MA 01230-1552, 413-528-2552. Geoffrey Young, Editor. 1975. ''We are small, publish few books (especially lately, w/o NEA funding), and have plans to publish several new books by the same poets we've already published. Because of this, we are not as eager to see unsolicited material as other publishers. It would be useful if those poets who are interested in sending work would read some of our books first.'' avg. press run 1M. Pub'd 4 poetry titles 1999; expects 7 poetry titles 2000, 1 poetry title 2001. 5½x8½; avg. price, paper: $12.50. 96pp; Publishes 1% of poetry manuscripts submitted. Reporting time: 3 weeks. Payment: (copies) 10% of the edition. Interested in new or unpub'd poets: no. Simultaneous submissions accepted: yes. Recently published poets: Clark Coolidge, Lyn Hejinian, Bill Luoma, Elaine Equi, Michael Gizzi. Submission quantity: 3. Special interests: Interested in art, language, music, geology, flora and fauna, food, cut-up, irony, vernacular, painting, urban decay, pastoral, frankness, as well as natural clarity.

FINE MADNESS, PO Box 31138, Seattle, WA 98103-1138. Sean X. Bentley, John Q. Malek, Anne Pitkin, Al Wald. 1982. ''No xeroxes or dot-matrix please. We have no restrictions as to form, though if you use a traditional form we hope it works for the poem and not against it. A sense of humor, exacting vocabulary, and original imagery are appreciated. No pious verse. We are looking for intelligence, not just words.'' circ. 800. Irregular. Pub'd 50 poems 1999; expects 50 poems 2000, 100 poems 2001. sub. price: $9/2 issues; sample: $4. 62pp; 5½x8; Rights purchased: 1st North American serial, first anthology. Publishes 6% of poems submitted. Deadlines: none. Reporting time: 4 months. Payment: subscription and 1 copy. Interested in new or unpub'd poets: yes, but don't send us poems if you don't *read* poetry! We recommend buying a sample copy before submitting. Simultaneous submissions accepted: no! Recent contributors: Pattiann Rogers, Albert Goldbarth, Melinda Mueller, Caroline Knox. Submission quantity: 3-6. Special interests: Translations (please send originals too).

FIRE, Field Cottage, Old Whitehill, Tackley, Kidlington OXON OX5 3AB, United Kingdom. 1994. circ. 250+. 3/yr. sub. price: £7. 150pp; size A5.

The Fire!! Press, 241 Hillside Road, Elizabeth, NJ 07208, 908-289-3714, Fax 908-688-9330, firepres@injersey.com. Thomas H. Wirth. 1981. avg. press run 2M. Pub'd 1 poetry title 1999. 5½x8½; avg. price, paper: $13. 120pp; Interested in new or unpub'd poets: no. Recently published poets: Abba Elethea, James W. Thompson.

THE FIREFLY (A Tiny Glow In a Forest of Darkness), 300 Broadway #107, St. Paul, MN 55101. Jon Lurie, Jane Kirby. 1990. ''We are open to any themes that have social or political relevance'' circ. 500. 4/yr. Pub'd 5 poems 1999; expects 1 poem 2000, 4 poems 2001. sub. price: $10/6 issues; sample: $1+stamp. 8-12pp; 8½×11; Rights purchased: none. Publishes less than 25% of poems submitted. Deadlines: 30 days in advance. Reporting time: 30-60 days. Payment: copies for family and friends. Interested in new or unpub'd poets: yes. Simultaneous submissions accepted: yes. Recent contributors: Tashunka Raven, Linae Enockson, Philip Hensel, Marianne Aweagon Broyles. Submission quantity: up to 5. Special interests: Prose poetry prefered, rhyme and lyric not necessary.

Fireweed Press, PO Box 75418, Fairbanks, AK 99707-2136, 907-452-5070 or 907-488-5079. Joe Ensweiler, Jane Hixon, Karen Randlev. 1976. ''Please, no submissions—poets are invited to submit. Our New Alaskan Poetry Series issues 3 books annually; submission is by solicitation only. Yearly anthologies are usually regional and advertised heavily within the state'' avg. press run 1M. Pub'd 1 poetry title 1999; expects 3 poetry titles 2000, 4 poetry titles 2001. 6×9; avg. price, paper: $5.95. 95pp; Payment: varies. Interested in new or unpub'd poets: no. Simultaneous submissions accepted: no. Recently published poets: Warren Woessner, Joe Ensweiler, Patricia Monaghan, Frank Keim, Bob Weeden. Special interests: Regional poetry; Alaska only.

FIRM NONCOMMITTAL: An International Journal of Whimsy, 5 Vonda Avenue, Toronto, ON M2N 5E6, Canada, e-mail firmnon@idirect.com; webhome.idirect.com/~firmnon. Brian Pastoor, Editor; Vince Cicchine, Artistic Director. 1995. ''Reads in May and June, publishes July; No American stamps, se comprende!'' circ. 200. 1/yr. Pub'd 45 poems 1999; expects 45 poems 2000, 45 poems 2001. sub. price:

$7CAN; sample: $5CAN. 48pp; 6×8; Rights purchased: none. Publishes 10% of poems submitted. Deadlines: May and June submissions only. Reporting time: 2 months. Payment: none yet. Interested in new or unpub'd poets: yes. Simultaneous submissions accepted: yes, please inform. Recent contributors: bill bissett, David Holliday, Coral Hull, Francine Porad, K.V. Skene. Submission quantity: 6, more for haiku. Special interests: Humor: light verse, experimental poetry, concrete, haiku. All forms to 40 lines.

FIRST CLASS, Four-Sep Publications, PO Box 12434, Milwaukee, WI 53212, E-mail chriftor@execpc.com, www.execpc.com/~chriftor. Christopher M. 1996. circ. 200-400. 3/yr. Pub'd 60 poems 1999; expects 70 poems 2000, 70 poems 2001. sub. price: $14/3 issues; sample: $1 sampler, $5 issue. 50pp; 8½×11; Rights purchased: none, 1st. Publishes 5-10% of poems submitted. Deadlines: continuous. Reporting time: 1 week. Payment: 1 copy. Interested in new or unpub'd poets: yes. Simultaneous submissions accepted: yes. Recent contributors: Alan Catlin, Gerald Locklin, Robert Ruden, B.Z. Niditch, Susanne Bowers. Submission quantity: 3-6.

FIRST DRAFT, 3636 Fieldston Road, Apt. 7A, Riverdale Bronx, NY 10463-2041, 718-543-5493. Dorian Tenore-Bartilucci. 1992. "FD is not a typical magazine, but an Amateur Press Assn./Alliance. It's a writers' workshop that meets by mail. Only the 15 members of FD (and folks requesting spec. copies) receive issues, hence the small circulation and limited number of copies printed." circ. 20. 6/yr. Pub'd 12 poems 1999. sub. price: $18 for one year of spec copies; sample: $3. 250pp; 8½×11; Publishes 100% of poems submitted. Deadlines: Last day of every even-numbered month (Feb., April, June, Aug., Oct., Dec.). Reporting time: 2 months for members. Payment: copies. Interested in new or unpub'd poets: only if they're members of FD. Recent contributors: Anna Deborah Ackner, Georg Patterson, Jim Downard, de la rosa, Thomas A. Roe. Submission quantity: As many as she/he wants, as long as she/he is member of FD.

FIRST INTENSITY, First Intensity Press, PO Box 665, Lawrence, KS 66044-0713, e-mail leechapman@aol.com. Lee Chapman. 1993. "Enclose SASE; include bio/publishing history" circ. 300. 2/yr. sub. price: $17; sample: $9. 180pp; 6×9; Rights purchased: none. Reporting time: 8 weeks. Payment: 2 copies. Interested in new or unpub'd poets: Yes. Simultaneous submissions accepted: no. Recent contributors: Theodore Enslin, Robert Kelly, Kenneth Irby, Duncan McNaughton, Diane di Prima. Submission quantity: No more than five.

First Intensity Press (see also FIRST INTENSITY), PO Box 665, Lawrence, KS 66044, e-mail leechapman@aol.com. Lee Chapman. 1993. "We do not consider unsolicited poetry book manuscripts" avg. press run 300-500. Pub'd 2 poetry titles 1999. 6×9; avg. price, paper: $10-$12. Payment: copies of book. Interested in new or unpub'd poets: no. Simultaneous submissions accepted: no. Recently published poets: James Thomas Stevens, Patrick Doud, Duncan McNaughton, Barry Gifford, Kristin Prevallet.

FISH DRUM MAGAZINE, PO Box 966, Murray Hill Station, New York, NY 10156, www.fishdrum.com. Suzi Winson. 1988. "Fish Drum prefers West Coast poetry, the exuberant 'continuous nerve movie' that follows the working of the mind and has a relationship to the world and the reader. Philip Whalen's work, for example, and much of *Calafia, The California Poetry,* edited by Ishmael Reed. Also magical-tribal-incantatory poems, exemplified by the future/primitive *Technicians of the Sacred,* ed. Rothenberg. Personal material that sings and surprises, OK?" circ. 2M. 1-2/yr. Pub'd 80 poems 1999; expects 80 poems 2000, 80 poems 2001. sub. price: $24/4 issues; sample: $6. 80pp; 6×9; Rights purchased: first serial rights. Publishes 2-5% of poems submitted. Deadlines: none. Reporting time: 2 months. Payment: 2 or more copies. Interested in new or unpub'd poets: no. Simultaneous submissions accepted: no. Recent contributors: Philip Whalen, Miriam Sagan, Alice Notley, Leslie Scalapino, Jessica Hagedorn. Submission quantity: 3-5. Special interests: Zen and lyric poems.

FISH STORIES, 3540 N. Southport Avenue #493, Chicago, IL 60657-1436, 773-334-6690. Amy G. Davis, Editor in Chief; Kelli Kaufmann, Poetry Editor. 1994. "We are open to a diverse selection of poetry but look for quality work that has been revised and crafted with an understanding of form and content. Our magazine makes special effort to publish the work of both new and established poets" circ. 1.2M. 1/yr. Pub'd 15 poems 1999; expects 18 poems 2000, 18 poems 2001. sub. price: $10.95; sample: $10.95. 224pp; 5½×8½; Rights purchased: one - time. Publishes 4% of poems submitted. Deadlines: Dec. 1. Reporting time: 6-9 months. Payment: copies. Interested in new or unpub'd poets: yes. Simultaneous submissions accepted: yes. Recent contributors: Maureen Seaton, Jorie Graham, Yusef Komunyakaa, Li-Young Lee, Christopher Buckley. Submission quantity: up to 5 poems (a maximum of 3 pages each).

Fithian Press, PO Box 1525, Santa Barbara, CA 93102, 805-962-1780, Fax 805-962-8835, e-mail dandd@danielpublishing.com. John Daniel, Editor. 1985. "Fithian Press is a creative co-publisher. Authors contribute production costs in exchange for a high royalty and unlimited free copies." avg. press run 500. Pub'd 7 poetry titles 1999; expects 7 poetry titles 2000, 7 poetry titles 2001. 5½×8½; avg. price, paper: $9. 80pp; Publishes 10% of poetry manuscripts submitted. Reporting time: 6 weeks. Payment: 60% of net receipts. Interested in new or unpub'd poets: yes. Simultaneous submissions accepted: yes. Recently published poets: Jeanne Lohman, W.R. Wilkins, Francis Fike, Julie Cunningham, Tom Smith. Submission quantity: 12.

Five Corners Publications, Ltd., Old Bridgewater Mill, PO Box 66, Bridgewater, VT 05034-0066,

802-672-3868; Fax 802-672-3296; e-mail don@fivecorners.com. 1990. 8½×11, 6×9.

Five Fingers Press (see also FIVE FINGERS REVIEW), PO Box 12955, Berkeley, CA 94712-3955. Jaime Robles. 1984. avg. press run 1M. Pub'd 2 poetry titles 1999. 6×9; avg. price, paper: $9 + $3 postage. 75pp; Reporting time: 3-5 months. Interested in new or unpub'd poets: yes. Simultaneous submissions accepted: yes. Recently published poets: Peter Gizzi, Rosmarie Waldrop, Fanny Howe, Forrest Gander, Lyn Hejinian. Submission quantity: 5-8. Special interests: Writing with a sense of experimentation, an awareness of tradition, and a willingness to explore the boundaries of genre and form.

FIVE FINGERS REVIEW, Five Fingers Press, PO Box 12955, Berkeley, CA 94712-3955. Jaime Robles. 1984. "SASE always. Writing with a sense of experimentation, an awareness of tradition, and a willingness to explore the boundaries of genre and form" circ. 1M. 1/yr. Pub'd 60 poems 1999; expects 60 poems 2000, 60 poems 2001. sub. price: $16/2 issues; sample: $6 + $1 postage. 200pp; 6×9; Rights purchased: 1st publication, North America. Publishes 2-5% of poems submitted. Deadlines: ongoing. Reporting time: 1-2 months. Payment: 2 copies, cash payment depends upon funding. Interested in new or unpub'd poets: yes. Simultaneous submissions accepted: yes. Recent contributors: Rosmarie Waldrop, Fanny Howe, Barbara Einzig, Rafael Camp, Robert Kelly. Submission quantity: 5-8. Special interests: Language poetry, narrative poetry, experimental poetry, translations, prose poems, etc. All welcome. We want distinct text and voices, a wide range of approaches.

FIVE POINTS, Georgia State University, University Plaza, Atlanta, GA 30303-3083, 404-651-0071, Fax 404-651-3167. David Bottoms. 1996. circ. 6M. 3/yr. Pub'd 30+ poems 1999. sub. price: $20; sample: $6. 170pp; 6½×9; Rights purchased: First American Serial. Publishes 5% of poems submitted. Deadlines: Sept. 1-April 30. Reporting time: 3-4 months. Payment: $50 per poem. Interested in new or unpub'd poets: yes. Simultaneous submissions accepted: no. Recent contributors: Charles Wright, Barbara Hamby, W.S. Merwin, Linda Pastan, Sam Hamill. Submission quantity: 3 (no more than 50 lines each).

Floating Bridge Press, PO Box 18814, Seattle, WA 98118, 206-860-0508. Peter Pereira, T. Clear, Jeff Crandall, Ted McMahon. 1994. "We publish at least 1 poetry chapbook and 1 poetry anthology per year, from manuscripts submitted to our annual contest series. We are committed to producing a high-quality book, printed on acid-free, archival-quality paper, with cardstock cover and engaging cover art. We also produce a local reading for the winnnng poet(s). Send SASE for guidelines; $6 ppd. for sample book. We have a variety of tastes, but tend to prefer manuscripts that hold together thematically as a collection. We sometimes publish broadsides and recently produced an audio-CD." avg. press run 200-400 chapbook; 500-1000 anthology. Pub'd 2 poetry titles 1999; expects 2 poetry titles 2000, 2 poetry titles 2001. 5½×8½, 6×9, varies; avg. price, paper: $6-$8. 24-32pp; Reporting time: 3-6 months. Payment: honorarium plus copies. Interested in new or unpub'd poets: yes. Simultaneous submissions accepted: yes. Recently published poets: Joannie Kervran, Nance Van Winkel, Molly Tenenbaum, James Gurley, Bart Baxter. Submission quantity: chapbook manuscripts only. Special interests: Washington State poets.

FLOATING ISLAND, Floating Island Publications, PO Box 2347, Brewster, MA 02631, 508-896-4572. Michael Sykes, Editor. 1976. "*Floating Island IV* is editorially complete. Not accepting any new poetry until further notice. The first series (4 volumes) ends with the current volume and the format and scope of the second series has yet to be determined." circ. 1M. Publish 1 every 3-4 years. Pub'd 60 poems 1999; expects 10 poems 2001. Standing orders only - full price; sample price: full-price. 160pp; 8½×11; Rights purchased: none. Publishes less than 1% of poems submitted. Deadlines: none. Reporting time: 2-4 weeks. Payment: copies. Interested in new or unpub'd poets: no. Simultaneous submissions accepted: no. Recent contributors: Robert Bly, Joanne Kyger, Frank Stewart, Michael McClure, Cole Swensen. Submission quantity: 6-10. Special interests: No preferences. All forms considered. The magazine is very eclectic, wide-ranging, unpredictable. Strong emphasis on typography and design, graphic illustration, photography.

Floating Island Publications (see also FLOATING ISLAND), PO Box 2347, Brewster, MA 02631, 508-896-4572. Michael Sykes, Editor. 1976. "I'm not currently accepting any new poetry manuscripts, either for book publication or for the anthology, *Floating Island*. I am currently engaged in the completion of a publishing program that will include the first series of *Floating Island* (4 volumes) and approximately 50 additional titles." avg. press run 1M. Expects 1 poetry title 2001. 6×9, 5½×8½; avg. price, cloth: $25; paper: $8; other: $15 for anthologies. 64pp; Publishes 0% of poetry manuscripts submitted. Reporting time: 2-4 weeks. Payment: 10% of press run. Interested in new or unpub'd poets: no. Simultaneous submissions accepted: no. Recently published poets: Cole Swensen, Frank Stewart, William Witherup, Robert Bly, Stephan Torre. Submission quantity: 6-10, or chapbook. Special interests: Strong emphasis on typography and design. Generally solid full-length collections or chapbooks that have a tight focus. If anything, I prefer more poetry in the future that has a broader acceptance rather than the exclusive appreciation of other poets. So much poetry that is published today is completely incomprehensible outside the rarified atmosphere of its practitioners.

THE FLORIDA REVIEW, PO Box 25000, English Department, University of Central Florida, Orlando, FL

32816, 407-823-2038. Pat Rushin, Poetry Editor. 1972. "Include SASE and brief bio. Enjoy poems that have concrete images, evocative metaphors, and strong narrative vein." circ. 1M. 2/yr. Pub'd 20 poems 1999; expects 20 poems 2000, 20 poems 2001. sub. price: $10; sample: $6. 140pp; 6¾×9¾; Rights purchased: first rights. Publishes approx. 1% of poems submitted. Deadlines: none. Reporting time: 12 weeks. Payment: occasional honoraria; 3 copies. Interested in new or unpub'd poets: yes. Simultaneous submissions accepted: yes. Recent contributors: William Stafford, Karen Fish, William Hathaway, Philip Dacey, Stuart Friebert. Submission quantity: maximum of 5. Special interests: No axes to grind.

FLYING HORSE, PO Box 1029, Ellsworth, ME 04605-1029. 1996. circ. 1M. 2/yr. Pub'd 150+ poems 1999. sub. price: $7; sample: $4. 100+pp; 6×9; Rights purchased: 1st rights. Publishes 15% of poems submitted. Payment: $10/poem. Interested in new or unpub'd poets: yes. Simultaneous submissions accepted: yes. Submission quantity: 1-5.

FLYWAY, 206 Ross Hall, Iowa State University, Ames, IA 50011, 515-294-8273, FAX 515-294-6814, flyway@iastate.edu. Debra Marquart, Poetry Editor. 1995. circ. 600. 3/yr. Pub'd 60 poems 1999; expects 60 poems 2000, 60 poems 2001. sub. price: $18; sample: $8. 64pp; 8½×11; Rights purchased: rights revert to author. Publishes 2% of poems submitted. Deadlines: we don't read June - August. Reporting time: 4 weeks. Payment: 1 copy and additional copies at cost. Interested in new or unpub'd poets: yes. Simultaneous submissions accepted: no. Recent contributors: Neal Bowers, Lola Haskins, Ray A. Younger Bear, Walter McDonald, Mary Swander. Submission quantity: 3-4.

FOLIO: A Literary Journal of American University, Dept. of Literature, American University, Washington, DC 20016, 202-885-2971. Editors change yearly. 1984. "$100 prize for best poem among those selected for the Fall and Spring issue." circ. 400. 2/yr. Pub'd 30 poems 1999; expects 30 poems 2000, 30 poems 2001. sub. price: $12; sample: $6. 64pp; 6×9; Rights purchased: first serial rights. Publishes 2-3% of poems submitted. Deadlines: Nov. 1 (Winter/Spring), March 15 (Summer/Fall). Reporting time: 2-4 months. Payment: 2 copies. Interested in new or unpub'd poets: yes. Simultaneous submissions accepted: yes. Recent contributors: William Stafford, Jean Valentine, Henry Taylor, Colette Inez, Roland Flint. Submission quantity: less than 5.

FOREVER ALIVE, PO Box 12305, Scottsdale, AZ 85267-2305, 602-922-0300; fax 602-922-0800; e-Mail HERBBOWIE@AOL.COM. Herb Bowie. 1989. "Must speak of aliveness, immoutality, etc" circ. 3M. 4/yr. Pub'd 8 poems 1999; expects 8 poems 2000, 8 poems 2001. sub. price: $24; sample: $6. 52pp; 8½×11; Rights purchased: one-time. Publishes 10% of poems submitted. Reporting time: 90 days. Payment: magazine issues. Interested in new or unpub'd poets: yes. Simultaneous submissions accepted: yes. Recent contributors: Joe Bardin, Shereena Smith, Danny Callen, Injy Tawil. Submission quantity: 1-5.

THE FORMALIST, 320 Hunter Drive, Evansville, IN 47711-2218. William Baer, Editor. 1990. "*The Formalist: A Journal of Metrical poetry* publishes contemporary, *metrical* verse written in the great tradition of English-language poetry. The editors suggest submitting 3-5 poems at one time. We're looking for well-crafted poetry in a contemporary idiom which uses meter and the full range of traditional poetic conventions in vigorous and interesting ways. We're especially interested in sonnets, couplets, tercets, ballads, the French forms, etc. We also consider metrical translations of major formalist non-English poets — from the ancient Greeks to the present. We're not, however, interested in haiku (or syllabic verse of any kind) or sestinas. Only rarely do we accept a poem over 2 pages, and we do not publish any type of erotica, blasphemy, vulgarity, or racism. We suggest that those wishing to submit become familiar with the journal beforehand. Submissions are considered throughout the year; a brief cover letter is recommended, and an SASE is necessary for a reply and the return of the MSS. No simultaneous submissions, previously published work, or disk submissions. *The Formalist* also sponsors the annual Howard Nemerov Sonnet Award of $1,000; deadline June 15th; entry fee $3/sonnet; past judges were Richard Wilbur, Mona Van Duyn, Anthony Hecht, and Donald Justice. Send SASE for rules." 2/yr. Pub'd 120 poems 1999; expects 120 poems 2000, 120 poems 2001. sub. price: $12, foreign $16; sample: $6.50. 128pp; 6×9; Rights purchased: 1st North American Serial Rights. Publishes 5% of poems submitted. Deadlines: we consider poems throughout the year. Reporting time: 4-8 weeks. Payment: 2 copies. Interested in new or unpub'd poets: yes. Simultaneous submissions accepted: no. Recent contributors: Derek Walcott, Richard Wilbur, Mona Van Duyn, Maxine Kumin, Donald Justice. Submission quantity: 3-5.

Fort Dearborn Press, 245 Bluff Court (LBS), Barrington, IL 60010, 312-235-8500. 1993. 6×9.

●Fouque Publishers, 150 Fifth Avenue, Suite 845, New York, NY 10011, 646-486-1061, Fax 646-486-1091, fouquepublishers@earthlink.net. Thomas Thornton, Thomas Stoelger. 1999. "Anthologies and contests forthcoming" avg. press run 700. Expects 2 poetry titles 2000, 5 poetry titles 2001. 5½×8½; avg. price, paper: $6. 80pp; Publishes 5% of poetry manuscripts submitted. Reporting time: 4 weeks. Payment: 8-30%. Interested in new or unpub'd poets: yes. Simultaneous submissions accepted: yes. Recently published poets: 10. Special interests: We're open-minded, no category is excluded.

Four Seasons Publishers, PO Box 51, Titusville, FL 32781, E-mail fourseasons@gnc.net. Frank Hudak. 1996. avg. press run 1M. Expects 2 poetry titles 2001. 5½×8½; avg. price, paper: $6.95. 120pp; Reporting time: 1

month. Interested in new or unpub'd poets: yes. Simultaneous submissions accepted: yes. Submission quantity: 6.

Four Way Books, PO Box 607, Marshfield, MA 02050. Martha Rhodes, Dzvinia Orlowsky. 1992. avg. press run 1.5M. Expects 5 poetry titles 2000, 5 poetry titles 2001. size varies; avg. price, paper: $10.95. 50pp; Reporting time: asap. Payment: standard. Interested in new or unpub'd poets: yes. Simultaneous submissions accepted: yes.

4*9*1, PO Box 91212, Lakeland, FL 33804, stompdncr@aol.com, www.fournineone.com. Donald Ryburn, Editor. 1997. "Visit the website" circ. infinite. Ongoing. Pub'd 80 poems 1999; expects 80-100 poems 2000, 80-100 poems 2001. sub. price: free; sample: free. Pages vary; Rights purchased: none. Publishes less than 1% of poems submitted. Deadlines: none. Reporting time: varies. Payment: cash (discretionary). Interested in new or unpub'd poets: absolutely. Simultaneous submissions accepted: yes. Recent contributors: Donald Ryburn, Stephen Sleboda, Rhonda Roszell. Submission quantity: 3-5.

Four-Sep Publications (see also FIRST CLASS), PO Box 12434, Milwaukee, WI 53212, E-mail chriftor@execpc.com, www.execpc.com/~chriftor. Christopher M. 1996. avg. press run 200-400. Pub'd 8 poetry titles 1999; expects 12 poetry titles 2000, 15 poetry titles 2001. 8½×11; avg. price, paper: $5. 32pp; Publishes 10-15% of poetry manuscripts submitted. Reporting time: 1 week initial response. Payment: varies, personal. Interested in new or unpub'd poets: yes. Simultaneous submissions accepted: yes. Recently published poets: Gerald Locklin, Alan Catlin, Errol Miller, A.D. Winans, Robert Ruden. Submission quantity: 4-10.

FOURTEEN HILLS: The SFSU Review, Creative Writing Dept., SFSU, 1600 Holloway Avenue, San Francisco, CA 94132, 415-338-3083, fax 415-338-0504, E-mail hills@sfsu.edu. 1994. "We do our best to achieve a diversity of voice in each issue of our magazine. We publish quite a bit of experimental poetry but are also interested in seeing fresh uses of more traditional forms." circ. 600. 2/yr. Pub'd 54 poems 1999; expects 50 poems 2000, 50 poems 2001. sub. price: $12; sample: $5. 160pp; 6×9; Rights purchased: rights revert back to author on publication. Publishes less than 5% of poems submitted. Deadlines: Fall issue: September 1, Spring issue: Febuary 1. Reporting time: 2-4 months. Payment: 2 contributor's copies. Interested in new or unpub'd poets: yes. Simultaneous submissions accepted: no. Recent contributors: Alice Notley, August Kleinzahler, Amiri Baraka, Amy Gerstler, Gustaf Sobin. Submission quantity: up to 5.

FRANK: AN INTERNATIONAL JOURNAL OF CONTEMPORARY WRITING AND ART, 32 rue Edouard Vaillant, 93100 Montreuil Sous Bois, France, (33) 1 48596658, e-mail david@paris-anglo.com. David Applefield, Editor. 1983. "For translations, send also poem in original language if possible" circ. 4M. 2/yr. Pub'd 50 poems 1999; expects 70 poems 2000, 70 poems 2001. sub. price: $38 (4 issues), $60 instit.; sample: $9. 224pp; 8×5; Rights purchased: first serial world rights, reverts to poet on publication. Publishes 10% of poems submitted. Deadlines: Feb. 1 for Summer issue, June 1 for Winter issue. Reporting time: 12 weeks. Payment: 2 copies of journal, plus $5/printed page. Interested in new or unpub'd poets: absolutely. Simultaneous submissions accepted: only if notified. Recent contributors: Derek Walcott, Rita Dove, Duo Duo, W.S. Merwin, Jim Morrison. Submission quantity: 1-10. Special interests: All styles—translations, especially from languages rarely read by anglophones. Innovative *and* committed.

FREE LUNCH, PO Box 7647, Laguna Niguel, CA 92607-7647. Ron Offen, Editor. 1988. "Accept submissions only between 9/1 and 5/31. Those received at other times will be returned unread. Prefer poets to send for guidelines (with SASE) before submitting." circ. 1.1M. Irregular. Pub'd 70 poems 1999; expects 70 poems 2000, 70 poems 2001. sub. price: 3issues/$12 US, $15 foreign; sample: $5 US, $6 foreign. 32pp; 5½×8½; Rights purchased: we copyright each issue; rights revert to poets upon written request. Publishes 10% of poems submitted. Deadlines: none, but no submissions accepted 6/1 to 8/31. Reporting time: 1-3 months. Payment: 1 copy of appearance issue and free subscription. Interested in new or unpub'd poets: yes. Simultaneous submissions accepted: yes. Recent contributors: Neal Bowers, Thomas Carper, Jared Carter, Russell Edson, Charles H. Webb. Submission quantity: no more than 3. Special interests: Experimental, long poems okay, no light verse, also looking for good Brechtian political poetry. No haiku, please.

FREEDOM ISN'T FREE, Temporary Vandalism Recordings, PO Box 6184, Orange, CA 92863-6184. Robert Roden, Barton Saunders. 1994. circ. 500. 2/yr. Pub'd 40 poems 1999; expects 40 poems 2000, 40 poems 2001. sample price: $1. 32pp; 5½×4¼; Publishes 5% of poems submitted. Reporting time: 3-6 months. Payment: 2 copies. Interested in new or unpub'd poets: yes. Simultaneous submissions accepted: yes. Recent contributors: Gerald Locklin, Lyn Lifshin, Daniel McGinn, Mary Punza. Submission quantity: 3-5.

FREEFALL, Alexandra Writers Centre Society, 922 9th Avenue S.E., Calgary, AB T2G 0S4, Canada, fax 403-264-4730, e-mail awcs@writtenword.org, website www.writtenword.org/awcs. 1990. circ. 300. 2/yr. sub. price: $12 Canada; $14 US; sample: $7.50 Canada; $8.50 US. 40pp; 8×11½; Recent contributors: 2-5 poems, 6 pages maximum.

French Bread Publications (see also PACIFIC COAST JOURNAL), PO Box 23868, San Jose, CA 95153, e-mail paccoastj@bjt.net. Stillson Graham, Editor. 1992. "Usually publish writers we are already familiar with" avg. press run 200. Pub'd 1 poetry title 1999; expects 1 poetry title 2000, 1 poetry title 2001. 5½×8½; avg. price, other: $4. 28pp; Reporting time: 6 months. Payment: varies. Interested in new or unpub'd poets: yes. Simultaneous submissions accepted: yes, if they let us know. Submission quantity: 5-10. Special interests: Experimental, visual, The Creative Process.

Frith Press (see also EKPHRASIS), PO Box 161236, Sacramento, CA 95816-1236, 916-451-3038, http://members.aol.com/ekphrasisl. Laverne Frith, Editor; Carol Frith, Editor. Address poetry submissions to: PO Box 161236, Sacramento, CA 95816-1236, 916-451-3038. 1995. "Most projects considered through annual chapbook competition: 16-24 pages of poetry; cover sheet with poet's name, address and phone; acknowledgment list, $8 reading fee (US funds) payable to Laverne E. Frith; SASE for winners' list; no poems pending publication; no manuscripts will be returned; deadline: Oct. 31 of each year." avg. press run 200. Pub'd 4 poetry titles 1999; expects 4 poetry titles 2000, 4 poetry titles 2001. 5½×8½; avg. price, paper: $6. 50pp; Publishes 2-7% of poetry manuscripts submitted. Reporting time: annual competition; could take up to a year. Payment: variable on chapbooks; annual contest winner: $100 & 50 books. Interested in new or unpub'd poets: should submit to annual competition. Simultaneous submissions accepted: no. Recently published poets: Joyce Odam, William Doreski, Martha Modena Vertreace, Susan Kelly-DeWitt, Patricia M. Bindert. Submission quantity: 16-24 pages for chapbook competition.

THE FROGMORE PAPERS, The Frogmore Press, 42 Morehall Avenue, Folkestone, Kent CT19 4EF, United Kingdom. Jeremy Page. Address poetry submissions to: 18 Nevill Road, Lewes, East Sussex BN7 1PF, United Kingdom. 1983. "Annual poetry prize, closing date 30 June." circ. 500. 2/yr. Pub'd 80 poems 1999; expects 80 poems 2000, 80 poems 2001. sub. price: $20; sample: $5 (dollar bills only). 40pp; 6×8; Rights purchased: none. Publishes 2%-3% of poems submitted. Deadlines: none. Reporting time: 3 months. Payment: 1 copy. Interested in new or unpub'd poets: yes. Simultaneous submissions accepted: no. Recent contributors: Pauline Stainer, Myra Schneider, Geoffrey Holloway, John Latham, Mary Maher. Submission quantity: up to 5.

The Frogmore Press (see also THE FROGMORE PAPERS), 42 Morehall Avenue, Folkestone, Kent. CT19 4EF, United Kingdom. Jeremy Page. 1983. "Do not send unsolicited manuscripts." avg. press run 250. Pub'd 2 poetry titles 1999; expects 4 poetry titles 2000, 1 poetry title 2001. 6×8; avg. price, paper: $10. 44pp; Publishes 5% of poetry manuscripts submitted. Reporting time: 3 months. Payment: 12 copies. Interested in new or unpub'd poets: no. Simultaneous submissions accepted: no. Recently published poets: Robert Etty, Geoffrey Holloway, Sophie Hannah, David Lightfoot, Michael Paul Hogan. Submission quantity: up to 5.

FROGPOND: Quarterly Haiku Journal, Red Moon Press, PO Box 2461, Winchester, VA 22604, 540-722-2156, redmoon@shentel.net. Jim Kacian, Editor. 1978. "Publication of the Haiku Society of America. Publish haiku/senryu, sequences, haibun, and renju. Open to traditional and modern North American haiku in 1-4 lines, and 'concrete' haiku. Contests (send SASE for rules and deadlines): Harold D. Henderson Haiku Award; Gerad Brady Senryu Award; Bernard Lionel Einbond Memorial Renku Contest; Nicholas A. Virgilio Memorial Haiku Competition for High School Students, Merit Book Awards. Best-of-issue awards given through a gift from the Museum of Haiku Literature, Tokyo" circ. 800. 4/yr. Pub'd 600 poems 1999; expects 600 poems 2000, 600 poems 2001. sub. price: $28 USA, $30 Canada, $35 Europe, $45 elsewhere; sample: $8 USA, $10 Canada, $12 elsewhere. 96pp; 5½×8½; Rights purchased: 1st publication rights. Publishes less than 1% of poems submitted. Deadlines: ongoing. Reporting time: 2 weeks whenever possible. Payment: $1/published item. Interested in new or unpub'd poets: yes. Simultaneous submissions accepted: no. Recent contributors: Dimitar Anakiev, Yu Chang, Dee Evetts, M. Kettner, Matthew Louviere. Submission quantity: prefer 5-10.

From Here Press (see also XTRAS), PO Box 2740, Santa Fe, NM 87504-2740, 505-438-3249. William J. Higginson, Penny Harter. 1975. "No unsolicited work" avg. press run 200-1M. Expects 1 poetry title 2000, 2 poetry titles 2001. 5½×8½, 8½×11; avg. price, paper: $2.50-$12. 40-100pp; Payment: varies with book. Interested in new or unpub'd poets: no. Simultaneous submissions accepted: no. Recently published poets: Elizabeth Searle Lamb, Ruth Stone, Dee Evetts, Yatsuka Ishihara.

FROM THE MARGIN, 50 E. 1st Street, Storefront West, New York, NY 10003-9311. 1997. circ. 150. 4/yr. sub. price: $12; sample: $3. 16pp; 8½×11.

FRONTIERS: A Journal of Women Studies, Women's Studies, PO Box 644007, Washington State University, Pullman, WA 99164-4007, 509-335-7268. 1975. "Type poems; include SASE; leave name OFF manuscript; be patient; DO NOT double submit." circ. 1M. 3/yr. Pub'd 14 poems 1999; expects 12 poems 2000, 12 poems 2001. sub. price: $24 indiv., $45 instit.; sample: $15. 208pp; 6×9; Rights purchased: 1st North American serial rights. Publishes less than 5% of poems submitted. Deadlines: accepted year round. Reporting time: 3-6 months. Payment: 2 copies of issue. Interested in new or unpub'd poets: yes. Simultaneous submissions accepted: NO! Recent contributors: Marsha Connell, Shirley Ho, Rachel Lockard, Janine DeBaise, Lan Duong. Submission quantity: 2-5. Special interests: Poems of interest to a general feminist audience.

Frozen Waffles Press/Shattered Sidewalks Press; 45th Century Chapbooks, The Writer's Group, 329 West 1st Street #5, Bloomington, IN 47403. Rick Fox. 1980. "No gimmicks. No 'contests'. We publish when and whom we can, when able — when patronage or grants can be obtained...or editors' own cash contributions." avg. press run often as high as 1M. Expects 1 poetry title 2001. size varies; avg. price, cloth: $25-$35; paper: varies; other: pamphlets - circa $5. 25-80pp; Publishes up to 5% of poetry manuscripts submitted. Reporting time: 1 week to 1 year. Payment: poets are paid in rather generous amounts of copies of their books. Interested in new or unpub'd poets: we solicit, at present. Simultaneous submissions accepted: no. Recently published poets: Shohei Kiyama, Toshiko Takata, David Wade, Bro. Dimitrios, Michael Joseph Phillips. Submission quantity: none, wait for approach from us. Special interests: We love good translations, especially from modern Far Eastern poets (Japanese, Chinese (both Chinas), including Buddhist-meditationally-oriented poets, Korean, et al) modern Slavic poets, modern Latino/Latina and East European poets. Also would consider experimental and visual poetry — but, again, patronage and "angels" standing in the wings are a necessity. We desire to remain as unattached as possible to governments and establishments. *Still selling Michael J. Phillips' *Underworld Love Poems* and Teresinka Pereira's *The Falcons Swoop In*. Please do not forget them. These books are sold thru and associated with 45th Century Chapbooks and Frozen Waffles Press & Tapes/Shattered Sidewalks Press. In near future, we hope to do 'poetry videos' of Wade's, Phillips'—and *others'*—poetry, short dramas, etc. Any help from people in Midwest area, or elsewhere, will be greatly appreciated (distribution, sales, marketing, film, video equipment).

FUCK DECENCY, 5960 S. Land Park Drive #253, Sacramento, CA 95822. Andrew Roller. 1986. "Mostly I just post poems now on usenet newsgroups, such as rec.arts.poems, but I follow a special format I created in posting them, so back issues can be searched for and found. It is a professional-style Internet-only zine. All contributors are welcome. I publish occasionally, when I have the time to type people's poems into the computer" circ. Internet only. 10/yr. Pub'd 25 poems 1999. sub. price: Free by e-mail; sample: Free. 1 page; 8½×11; Rights purchased: 1st N. American Serial. Publishes 50% of poems submitted. Deadlines: any time. Reporting time: 4 weeks or longer. Payment: free over the internet. Interested in new or unpub'd poets: any *good quality* poems will be considered. Simultaneous submissions accepted: sure. Recent contributors: William Dockery, Allan Freer, P.D. Wilson, Andrew Roller. Submission quantity: 2-3. Special interests: Erotica, general weirdness, SF.

FUGUE, Brink Hall, Room 200, Engl. Dept., University of Idaho, Moscow, ID 83844-1102, 208-885-6156. Ryan Witt, Managing Editor. 1989. "Submit poetry and prose separately" circ. 300. 2/yr. Pub'd 10 poems 1999; expects 25 poems 2000, 25 poems 2001. sub. price: $10; sample: $5. 100pp; 6×9; Publishes less than 2% of poems submitted. Reporting time: 12 weeks. Payment: $10 per poem. Interested in new or unpub'd poets: yes. Simultaneous submissions accepted: no. Recent contributors: Stephen Dunn, Roberta Hill, Virgil Suarez, Sharon Olds, Georgia Tiffany. Submission quantity: 3-6.

●**FULLOSIA PRESS,** 299-9 Hawkins Avenue, PMB 865, Ronkonkoma, NY 11779, Fax 631-588-9428, deanofrpps@aol.com, www.angelfire.com/bc2/FULLOSIAPRESS/. JD Collins. 1971. "Submit on dixk or by e-mail embedded in text." circ. 100. 12/yr. Pub'd 4 poems 1999. sub. price: free online, $25 in print; sample: $2 + SASE. Rights purchased: first North American. Publishes 15% of poems submitted. Payment: none. Interested in new or unpub'd poets: yes. Simultaneous submissions accepted: yes. Recent contributors: D.G. Deman. Special interests: Say what you want, but make it short, simple and to the point.

●**THE FUTURE PHATNESS,** 4902 University Drive, Wilmington, NC 28403-2922, 910-793-3362; kingpsycho@visinton.net. 1996. circ. 300. Published every 6 weeks. sub. price: $10; sample: free. 22pp; 8½×11.

The Future Press, Box 444 Prince Street, New York, NY 10012-0008. Richard Kostelanetz. 1976. "Be familiar with what we have already published before you submit; otherwise, you will be wasting your own time as well as ours." avg. press run 500. Pub'd 1 poetry title 1999. size varies; avg. price, cloth: $16; paper: $6; other: $10 (audiotapes). 64pp; Reporting time: 1 month. Payment: 10% of the edition. Interested in new or unpub'd poets: yes. Simultaneous submissions accepted: yes. Recently published poets: Ian Tarnman, Bob Heman, Loris Essary, Carl D. Clark, Paul Nagy. Submission quantity: as many as necessary to impress us with the specialness of what you are doing. Special interests: *Extremely* experimental poetry only.

G

Gaff Press, PO Box 1024, 114 SW Willow Lane, Astoria, OR 97103, 503-325-8288; e-mail gaffpres@pacifier.com. 1987. 4¼×5½.

•**GaiaQuest,** PO Box 3065, Branford, CT 06405, 203-481-8747 phone/fax, gaiaquest@snet.net. Ana Davis. 1999. "No unsolicited ms. until June 2001. Include SASE for return; typed ms., one poem per page" avg. press run 50-100. Pub'd 1 poetry title 1999; expects 1-2 poetry titles 2000, 2-3 poetry titles 2001. 6×9; avg. price, paper: $12.95; other: $9.95 tapes. 72pp; Publishes 15% of poetry manuscripts submitted. Reporting time: 3 months. Payment: varies, % copies and/or royalty. Interested in new or unpub'd poets: yes. Simultaneous submissions accepted: no. Recently published poets: Sally Belenardo, Sue Holloway. Submission quantity: 5 with query. Special interests: Interested in nature poetry, New England, birds.

Galaxy Press, 71 Recreation Street, Tweed Heads, N.S.W. 2485, Australia, (07) 5536-1997. Lance Banbury. 1979. avg. press run 150. Pub'd 5 poetry titles 1999; expects 5 poetry titles 2000, 3 poetry titles 2001. 6×8½; avg. price, paper: $4. 14pp; Publishes 0% of poetry manuscripts submitted. Reporting time: 1 month. Payment: exchange copies. Interested in new or unpub'd poets: yes. Simultaneous submissions accepted: yes. Special interests: no criteria.

The Galileo Press Ltd., 3637 Black Rock Road, Upperco, MD 21155-9322. Julia Wendell, Editor-in-Chief. 1980. "It is best to request submission guidelines before submitting." avg. press run 1M. Pub'd 3 poetry titles 1999; expects 6 poetry titles 2000, 5 poetry titles 2001. size varies; avg. price, cloth: $15.95; paper: $9.95. 60pp; Publishes 2% of poetry manuscripts submitted. Reporting time: 3-6 months. Payment: 10% royalties. Interested in new or unpub'd poets: yes. Simultaneous submissions accepted: yes. Recently published poets: Matthew Graham, Steven Cramer, Mark Irwin, Robert Long, Jim Simmerman.

THE GALLEY SAIL REVIEW, Embassy Hall Editions, PO Box 665, Centralia, IL 62801-0665. Stanley McNail, Editor. 1958. "We publish, in addition to poetry, reviews and comment on books of or relating to poetry, trends in poetry, etc. *The Galley Sail Review* values both sincerity and craftsmanship. It seeks poetry that is compassionate and responsive to the human condition. It encourages a certain individuality of voice and style. There is room for humor and satire in *GSR*. The proverbial 'four letter words' may occasionally be employed, when context justifies their use. Indiscriminate pornography is not welcome. Neither is trite, cliche-ridden 'sewing circle' verse, or verse that wallows in self-pity. An SASE should be enclosed with the submission. Please do not submit material requiring long, involved annotations or explanations to the reader. Poetry should stand or fall on its own merit" circ. 500. 3/yr. Pub'd 87 poems 1999; expects 300 poems 2000. sub. price: 2-year $15 (add $2 outside US & CAN); sample: $3. 40-44pp; 5½×8½; Rights purchased: 1st N.A. serial, copyright reverts to author on publication. Deadlines: submissions should be in about 2 months before publication of Spring, Summer, or Fall-Winter issue. Reporting time: 1-3 months, earlier if possible. Payment: each contributor receives 2 or more copies, depending on scope of contribution. Interested in new or unpub'd poets: yes. Simultaneous submissions accepted: they are discouraged; they are not entirely ruled out, but we must have assurance that material is not being published elsewhere. Recent contributors: Thom Gunn, Ursula LeGuin, Walter McDonald, James Schevill, Diane Wakoski. Submission quantity: at least 3, preferably 5 or more. Special interests: *The Galley Sail Review* is eclectic, with no special axes to grind except poetry, which may be traditional, experimental, avant-garde, lyrical, humorous, or what have you.

Garden St Press, PO Box 1231, Truro, MA 02666-1231, 508-349-1991. Naomi Feigelson Chase, Co-Director. 1993. "Contest: 100 copies plus publication of an original poetry manuscript; author bio, acknowledgements, reading fee $15, deadline June 31. SASE for guidelines. Judges announced at end of contest. Typed, paginated ms of 64-68 pages. We are not yet accepting unsolicited mss." avg. press run 1M-2M. Pub'd 1 poetry title 1999; expects 3 poetry titles 2000, 3 poetry titles 2001. 5½×8½; avg. price, paper: $11. 64-70pp; Payment: varies. Interested in new or unpub'd poets: yes. Simultaneous submissions accepted: yes. Recently published poets: Eve Merriam, Denise Duhamel, Miriam Goudman. Submission quantity: for contest, 64pp.

GARGOYLE, Paycock Press, 1508 U Street NW, Washington, DC 20009, 202-667-8148; e-mail atticus@radix.net. Richard Peabody, Lucinda Ebersole, M. Maja Praqusnitz. 1976. "Poets should make an effort to see at least one issue of the magazine before submitting." circ. 3M. 1-2/yr. Pub'd 80 poems 1999; expects 100 poems 2000, 80 poems 2001. sub. price: $25 universities (2 Issues); sample: $10. 350pp; usually 8½×11, but format varies, sometimes cassette; Rights purchased: 1st N. American serial rights. Publishes .1% of poems submitted. Deadlines: none. Reporting time: 1 month. Payment: 1 copy. Interested in new or unpub'd poets: yes. Simultaneous submissions accepted: no. Recent contributors: Nicole Blackman, John Cooper Clarke, Wayne Koestenbaum, Minnie Bruce Pratt, Jeremy Reed. Submission quantity: 5. Special interests: We are interested in translations, particularly of contemporary East & West German poetry. Prefer shorter poems (1 page or less) but will consider longer work. Satire, regional poetry, and traditional forms are all possibilities, as is 'experimental' work, though our selections are generally difficult to categorize.

A GATHERING OF THE TRIBES, PO Box 20693, Tompkins Square, New York, NY 10009, 212-674-3778, Fax 212-674-5576, info@tribes.org, www.tribes.org. Steve Cannon, Publisher; Amy Ouzoonian, Associate Editor; Jennifer Seymore, Associate Editor. 1991. "Accept few unsolicited submissions, return only with SASE. Interested in non-traditional, non-academic work, multicultural perspective." circ. 3M. 2/yr. Pub'd 30 poems 1999; expects 30 poems 2000, 30 poems 2001. sub. price: $20; sample: $12.50. 96pp; 8½×11; Rights purchased: none. Publishes 5% of poems submitted. Deadlines: June 30 for Fall issue, Jan. 31 for Spring issue. Reporting time: 3 months. Payment: copies. Interested in new or unpub'd poets: yes. Simultaneous submissions accepted: yes. Recent contributors: Jayne Cortez, Victor Hernandez Cruz, Paul Beatty, Lorenzo Thomas, Susan Lee Yung. Submission quantity: 10, with SASE. Special interests: accept translations, print in both original and translation—Spanish, Hebrew, Chinese, Japanese, etc.

Gay Sunshine Press, Inc., PO Box 410690, San Francisco, CA 94141, 415-626-1935; Fax 415-626-1802. Winston Leyland. 1970. "We publish only poetry on gay male themes. We do not publish individual poemsor chapbooks of poems, only poems as parts of anthologies. Poets should not submit their work unless they have appeared in at least five literary magazines during the preceding two or three years. We want innovative, pioneering work; no trite emotings. Do not send unsolicited book-length manuscript. We prefer that you send query letter giving biographical details, along with five poems and a SASE. 12 titles over past 15 years." avg. press run 2M. 6x9, 5½x8½; avg. price, paper: $10. 96pp; Reporting time: 8 weeks. Payment: royalties to author, or negotiable. Interested in new or unpub'd poets: yes, but only material from poets whose work has already appeared in literary magazines. Simultaneous submissions accepted: no. Recently published poets: Allen Ginsberg, Jean Genet, Luis Cernuda, E.A. Lacey, Jim Everhard. Submission quantity: about 5, with SASE. Special interests: Translations.

Gearhead Press, 565 Lincoln, Northwest, Grand Rapids, MI 49504, 459-7861 or 459-4577. Bruce Rizzon, Barbara Rizzon. 1975. "So far we have put to print only poems, etc., by Bruce Rizzon. Like—*I am The Lonely Sea, Hermit, Out to Lunch, Diamond Ice Skies, Dago Red, For Sale, Dean Lake Poems, Ninth Street Poems, The Road, Ashoult Shadows, Blow on the Moon, Black Cloud Hanging Over My Head, BAR, Lonely are the Brave.* Right now Bruce Rizzon and I are taking a different path. Bruce Rizzon is working on a Hot Rod How-to Book and Building a Modern Day Hot Rod book." 5½x8½; avg. price, cloth: $4-10; paper: $1; other: $1. 8-100pp; Reporting time: 4 minutes - 4 years. Interested in new or unpub'd poets: yes. Simultaneous submissions accepted: yes. Recently published poets: Bruce Rizzon. Submission quantity: 4-10.

Geekspeak Unique Press (see also PLOPLOP), PO Box 11443, Indianapolis, IN 46201, 317-849-6227; www.ploplop.com. 1991. avg. press run 100. Pub'd 4 poetry titles 1999; expects 6 poetry titles 2000, 4 poetry titles 2001. 4x5; avg. price, paper: $5. 25pp; Publishes 5% of poetry manuscripts submitted. Reporting time: 6-8 weeks. Payment: negotiable. Interested in new or unpub'd poets: yes. Simultaneous submissions accepted: yes. Recently published poets: Kit Andis, Antler, Hal Sirowitz, Richard Kostelanetz, Wanda Coleman. Submission quantity: 10-15.

THE GENRE WRITER'S NEWS, 30 Canyon View Drive, Orinda, CA 94563, 510-254-7442. circ. 300. 2/yr. sub. price: $25; sample: $3.95. 43pp; 7¾x10¾.

THE GENTLE SURVIVALIST, General Delivery, Arroyo Seco, NM 87514. 1991. circ. 250+. 11/yr. Pub'd 24 poems 1999. sub. price: $20; sample: $2. 8pp; 8½x11; Rights purchased: none. Publishes 20% of poems submitted. Deadlines: none. Reporting time: 2 months. Payment: none. Interested in new or unpub'd poets: yes. Simultaneous submissions accepted: yes. Recent contributors: Keith Moore, C.S. Churchman, Laura Martin-Buhler, David Sparenburg. Submission quantity: 4.

GEORGE & MERTIE'S PLACE: A Microzine, PO Box 10335, Spokane, WA 99209-1335, 509-325-3738. George Thomas, Mertie Duncan. 1995. "We like a cover letter that personalizes the submission. A bit of bio., a recent publication or award, maybe something about the submitted material itself (its roots)" 11/yr. Pub'd 15 poems 1999; expects 50 poems 2000, 60 poems 2001. sub. price: $15; sample: $2. 4-8pp; 8½x11; Rights purchased: first rights. Publishes 5% of poems submitted. Deadlines: none. Reporting time: 1-2 months. Payment: 1¢/word, $2 minimum, we offer a $25 "Richard Diver best of issue" award each month. Interested in new or unpub'd poets: yes. Simultaneous submissions accepted: no. Recent contributors: Simon Perchik, Eric Howard, Dennis Saleh, Geoff Peterson, Madeline Defrees. Submission quantity: 1-5.

THE GEORGIA REVIEW, Univ. of Georgia, Athens, GA 30602-9009, 706-542-3481. Stephen Corey, Acting Editor; Janet Wondra, Assistant Editor. 1947. "We do not read unsolicited manuscripts during the months of June, July, and August. We suggest that potential contributors read the poetry in a few recent issues of *The Georgia Review* before submitting." circ. 6M. 4/yr. Pub'd 71 poems 1999; expects 75 poems 2000, 75 poems 2001. sub. price: $18 in US, $23 outside US; sample: $6. 208pp; 7x10; Rights purchased: 1st North American serial rights. Publishes .25% of poems submitted. Deadlines: none. Reporting time: 1-3 months. Payment: $3 per line. Interested in new or unpub'd poets: yes. Simultaneous submissions accepted: no. Recent contributors: Rita Dove, Stephen Dunn, Charles Simic, Linda Pastan, Albert Goldbarth. Submission quantity: 3-5. Special interests: We rarely publish translations and discourage their submission.

GERBIL: Queer Culture Zine, PO Box 10692, Rochester, NY 14610, 716-262-3966, gerbil@rpa.net. Tony Leuzzi, Brad Pease. 1995. "Lively, personal material that pays attention to musical language, poetical." circ. 3M. 4/yr. Pub'd 25 poems 1999. sub. price: $10; sample: $3. 32pp; 7½x9½; Rights purchased: none. Publishes 5% of poems submitted. Deadlines: rolling. Reporting time: 3-5 months. Payment: 3 copies. Interested in new or unpub'd poets: yes. Simultaneous submissions accepted: no. Recent contributors: Rane, Arroyo, David Trinidad, Beth Bailey, Glenn Sheldon, Deb Owen-More. Submission quantity: 2-6. Special interests: We'll take anything good!

GESAR-Buddhism in the West, 2910 San Pablo Avenue, Berkeley, CA 94702, 415-548-5407. Leslie Bradburn. 1973. "We publish only poetry translated from Tibetan" circ. 3.5M. 4/yr. Pub'd 10 poems 1999; expects 10 poems 2000, 10 poems 2001. sub. price: $12; sample: $2. 48pp; 7×9¼; Rights purchased: none. Publishes 1% of poems submitted. Reporting time: indefinite. Payment: none. Interested in new or unpub'd poets: no. Simultaneous submissions accepted: yes. Recent contributors: Paltrul Rinpoche, Lama Mipham.

GESTALTEN, Broken Boulder Press, PO Box 172, Lawrence, KS 66044-0172, www.brokenboulder.com. Paul Silvia. 1996. circ. 1M. 1/yr. Pub'd 40 poems 1999; expects 40 poems 2000, 40 poems 2001. sub. price: $3; sample: $3. 40pp; 11×14; Rights purchased: one-time. Publishes 10% of poems submitted. Deadlines: none. Reporting time: 3 weeks. Payment: 5 copies. Interested in new or unpub'd poets: yes. Simultaneous submissions accepted: no. Recent contributors: John M. Bennett, Jim Leftwich, Tim Gaze. Submission quantity: 5-25. Special interests: Only experimental work, especially visual texts.

THE GETTYSBURG REVIEW, Gettysburg College, Gettysburg, PA 17325, 717-337-6770. Peter Stitt, Editor. 1988. "Be sure to enclose a SASE when submitting. Have patience concerning reporting time. The editors are interested in publishing both long and shorter poems. Potential contributors should be familiar with *The Gettysburg Review*." circ. 4M. 4/yr. Pub'd 93 poems 1999; expects 85-90 poems 2000, 85-90 poems 2001. sub. price: $24, $32 foreign; sample: $6 + $1 p/h. 184pp; 6×9½; Rights purchased: First North American Serial Rights. Publishes approx. 1% of poems submitted. Deadlines: read poetry September-May. Reporting time: 1-3 months. Payment: $2 per line. Interested in new or unpub'd poets: yes. Simultaneous submissions accepted: no. Recent contributors: Linda Pastan, Pattiann Rogers, Rita Dove, Donald Hall, Charles Wright. Submission quantity: 3-5. Special interests: No particular special interests. *Quality* is the watchword. Special theme issues are announced from time to time.

Ghost Pony Press, PO Box 260113, Madison, WI 53726-0113, 608-238-0175, irmarkha@students.wisc.edu, www.litline.org/html/abraxas.html, www.geocities.com/Paris/4614, www.thing.net/~grist/l&d/dalevy/da-levy.htm, www.thing.net/~grist/ld/saiz/saiz.htm. Ingrid Swanberg, Editor. 1980. "No contests. Some emphasis on first books. *Inquire before sending MSS.* Please include sample poems and/or description of book and SASE." avg. press run 500. Expects 2 poetry titles 2000, 3 poetry titles 2001. 6×9, 7×10, varies; avg. price, paper: $20; other: $23 special editions; $1 broadsides. 60-120pp; Publishes 2% of poetry manuscripts submitted. Reporting time: 3 months, sometimes longer (please send inquiries, not mss!). Payment: arrangements made per project. Interested in new or unpub'd poets: yes. Simultaneous submissions accepted: yes. Recently published poets: Ivan Arguelles, Peter Wild, d.a.levy, Gerald Locklin, prospero saiz. Submission quantity: 5. Special interests: We are interested in contemporary occurrences of the lyric poem.

GINOSKO, PO Box 246, Fairfax, CA 94978, 415-460-8436. Robert Cesaretti. 1993. circ. 1M. 1/yr. sub. price: free; sample: free. Page number undetermined; 4×5½; Rights purchased: none. Deadlines: none. Reporting time: 3-4 weeks. Payment: copy. Interested in new or unpub'd poets: yes. Simultaneous submissions accepted: yes. Submission quantity: 12. Special interests: Experimental: Strong on style; prophetic/apocalyptic/mythic: revealing the sacred in the common.

●**Gival Press,** PO Box 3812, Arlington, VA 22203, 703-351-0079 phone/Fax, givalpress@yahoo.com, www.givalpress.com. 1998. 5½×8½.

THE GLASS CHERRY, The Glass Cherry Press, 901 Europe Bay Road, Ellison Bay, WI 54210-9643, 414-854-9042. Judith Hirschmiller, Editor. 1994. "Send for guidelines and sample issue prior to submitting" circ. 500. 4/yr. Pub'd 500 poems 1999; expects 500 poems 2000, 500 poems 2001. sub. price: $15; sample: $6. 50pp; 5½×8½; Rights purchased: one time only. Publishes 10% of poems submitted. Deadlines: none. Reporting time: 30 days. Payment: none, copy of issue published in. Interested in new or unpub'd poets: yes. Simultaneous submissions accepted: no. Recent contributors: Lyn Lifshin, Simon Perchik, Martin J. Rosenblum, Duane Locke, Hugh Fox. Submission quantity: at least 5. Special interests: Tasteful writing of quality. No pornography.

The Glass Cherry Press (see also THE GLASS CHERRY), 901 Europe Bay Road, Ellison Bay, WI 54210, 414-854-9042. Judith Hirschmiller, Editor. 1994. "Individual poetry ms read from January thru April. Send for guidelines + sample issue prior to submitting. Ms will be returned only if SASE is enclosed." avg. press run 500. Expects 3 poetry titles 2000, 3 poetry titles 2001. size varies; avg. price, cloth: $15; paper: $10; other: $20. 50pp; Publishes 5% of poetry manuscripts submitted. Reporting time: up to 3 months for individual manuscripts. Payment: negotiated individually with each author. Interested in new or unpub'd poets: yes. Simultaneous submissions accepted: no. Recently published poets: Lyn Lifshin, Simon Perchik, Hugh Fox. Submission quantity: for individuals, entire ms; when submitting for magazine, send 5 poems. Special interests: Tasteful writing of quality. Writers of all cultures and lifestyles welcomed. No pornography. Interested in

Japanese translations.

GLB Publishers, 1028 Howard Street #503, San Francisco, CA 94103, 415-621-8307, www.GLBpubs.com. John Hanley, Associate Editor for Poetry. 1990. "Established for cooperative publishing work by gay, lesbian, and bisexual writers; can be explicit or not explicit. Vanity publishing considered. Also PO Box 78212, San Francisco, CA 94107. Also sponsor 'perpubpoetry' for e-books on Internet with special formatting and presentational innovations (Web address above)." avg. press run 2M. Pub'd 2 poetry titles 1999; expects 2 poetry titles 2000, 2 poetry titles 2001. 5½x8½, 6x9; avg. price, cloth: $20; paper: $12; other: E-book editions are under study ($2.50-$5). 110pp; Publishes 20% of poetry manuscripts submitted. Reporting time: 2 months. Payment: variable. Interested in new or unpub'd poets: yes. Simultaneous submissions accepted: no. Recently published poets: Thomas Cashet, Robert Peters, Paul Genega, Winthrop Smith, William Tarvin. Submission quantity: 10. Special interests: Experimental and erotic poetry considered seriously.

GLOBAL TAPESTRY, BB Books, Spring Bank, Longsight Road, Copster Green, Blackburn, Lancs BB1 9EU, England, 0254 249128. Dave Cunliffe. 1971. "A specialized bohemian and counter-culture publication, with a readership ranging from academics to New Wave punks. Only present UK magazine of its kind. Use poetry of all kinds but prefer avant-garde, experimental and alternative work." circ. 1.3M. 4/yr. Pub'd 250 poems 1999; expects 250 poems 2000, 250 poems 2001. sub. price: $20/4 issues; sample: $3. 72pp; size A5; Rights purchased: none. Publishes 12% of poems submitted. Deadlines: none. Reporting time: as soon as possible. Payment: 1 copy. Interested in new or unpub'd poets: yes. Simultaneous submissions accepted: yes. Recent contributors: Tina Morris, Billy Childish, Jeff Cloves, Jay Findlay, Bill Lewis. Submission quantity: 2-10 poems. Special interests: Beat to New Wave high energy work.

Goats & Compasses, PO Box 524, Brownsville, VT 05037, 802-484-5169. 1991.

god is DEAD, publications, 910 North Martel, Suite #207, Los Angeles, CA 90046, 213-850-0067. 1995.

THE GODDESS OF THE BAY, PO Box 8214, Warwick, RI 02888, E-mail Belindafox@aol.com. 1998. circ. 200. 4-6/yr. sub. price: $15/4 issues; sample: $4. 40pp; 8½x11.

Golden Isis Press (see also PAGAN PRIDE), PO Box 4263, Chatsworth, CA 91313. Gerina Dunwich, Editor. 1980. "A one-time reading fee of $10 (refunded upon publication of the work) plus return postage is required with each chapbook submission. Query first with SASE or send complete manuscript with brief cover letter and reading fee. Sample chapbooks are available for $9.95 (postpaid)." avg. press run 1M. Pub'd 5 poetry titles 1999; expects 5 poetry titles 2000, 5 poetry titles 2001. 5x8; avg. price, paper: $9.95. 52pp; Reporting time: 1-2 months. Payment: 10% royalties on all copies sold for as long as the book remains in print, plus 10 free copies of the book. Interested in new or unpub'd poets: yes. Simultaneous submissions accepted: yes. Submission quantity: complete manuscript (80 pgs. maximum).

Good Gay Poets Press (see also FAG RAG), Box 277, Astor Station, Boston, MA 02123. 1973. "Please send letter of inquiry before submitting any mss." avg. press run 500. Pub'd 1 poetry title 1999; expects 1 poetry title 2000, 1 poetry title 2001. 5½x8½; avg. price, paper: $5. 64pp; Publishes 10% of poetry manuscripts submitted. Payment: 1/2 net profits. Interested in new or unpub'd poets: not now. Simultaneous submissions accepted: no. Recently published poets: John Wieners, Ruth Weiss, Pat Kuras, Walter Borawski.

●Goose River Press (see also NORTHWOODS JOURNAL, A Magazine for Writers), 3400 Friendship Road, Waldoboro, ME 04572, 207-832-6665, Fax 207-832-5348, dbenner@ime.net. 2000. 5½x8½.

GORHAM, 30-32 Macaw Avenue, PO Box 279, Belmopan, Belize, 501-8-23284. Daniel Gorham. 1981. circ. 3M. 4/yr. Pub'd 12 poems 1999. sub. price: $15; sample: $2. 24pp; 8½x11; Rights purchased: first. Publishes 5% of poems submitted. Deadlines: 3 months before issue. Reporting time: 5 months. Payment: free subscription. Interested in new or unpub'd poets: yes. Simultaneous submissions accepted: yes. Recent contributors: Gilder, Ture, Gorham, Hampton, Smith. Submission quantity: 5. Special interests: Must have meaning! No sex!

Gothic Press, 4998 Perkins Road, Baton Rouge, LA 70808-3043, 504-766-2906. 1979. 5½x8½.

GOTTA WRITE NETWORK LITMAG, 515 East Thacker Street, Hoffman Estates, IL 60194-1957, FAX 847-296-7631; e-mail Netera@aol.com. 1988. circ. 200. 2/yr. sub. price: $12.75; sample: same. 48-72pp; 8½x11.

GRAFFITI OFF THE ASYLUM WALLS, 1002 Gunnison Street #A, Sealy, TX 77474-3725. 1991. "No minors" circ. varies. Published whenever I have enough material. sub. price: $10/4 issues; sample: $3. 20pp; 8½x5½; Rights purchased: One time. Publishes an unknown % of poems submitted. Deadlines: anytime. Reporting time: varies. Payment: contributors get $2/copy discount price. Interested in new or unpub'd poets: sure. Simultaneous submissions accepted: yes. Submission quantity: no more than 5.

GRAIN, Saskatchewan Writers Guild, Box 1154, Regina, Sask. S4P 3B4, Canada, 306-244-2828, e-mail grain.mag@sk.sympatico.ca. Sean Virgo, Poetry Editor. 1973. "Submissions will be considered only if accompanied by a self-addressed envelope with sufficient Canadian postage or International Reply Coupons. 'We strive for artistic excellence, seek material that is accessible as well as challenging to our readers. Ideally, a *Grain* poem or story (like visual art) should be well-crafted, imaginatively stimulating, distinctively original.' Please read a recent issue of our magazine before submitting.'' circ. 1M. 4/yr. Pub'd 65 poems 1999; expects 65 poems 2000, 65 poems 2001. sub. price: $26.95; USA $26.95 + $4 p/h; foreign $26.95 + $6 p/h; sample: $7.95. 128pp; 6×9; Rights purchased: one-time only. Publishes 5% of poems submitted. Reporting time: 3 months maximum. Payment: $30-$100. Interested in new or unpub'd poets: yes, provided they research our magazine first. Simultaneous submissions accepted: no. Recent contributors: Jan Zwicky, Aislinn Hunter, Don Domanski, Sylvia Legris, David Zieroth. Submission quantity: no more than 10 pages.

GRAND STREET, 214 Sullivan Street #6C, New York, NY 10012, 212-533-2944. 1981. circ. 4M. 4/yr. Expects 32 poems 2000. sub. price: $40 individual, $50 institutions, $55 foreign; sample: $15 all issues after grand sheet #52. 256pp; 7×9; Rights purchased: one-time use, copyright reverts to author on publication. Publishes 1% of poems submitted. Deadlines: none. Reporting time: 60 days. Payment: yes. Interested in new or unpub'd poets: yes. Simultaneous submissions accepted: no. Recent contributors: W.S. Merwin, James Merrill, Amy Clampitt, John Hollander, Elisabeth Murawski. Submission quantity: 5.

GRASSLANDS REVIEW, PO Box 626, Berea, OH 44017. Laura B. Kennelly, Editor. 1989. "We read only material postmarked in March or October. Send no more than 5 poems or 1 short story with a SASE. We are looking for (and favor) new talent. Contest: Editors' Prize. Up to 5 poems. $12 (includes sub.) Deadline: April 30." circ. 300. 2/yr. Pub'd 40-50 poems 1999; expects 40-50 poems 2000, 40-50 poems 2001. sub. price: $10 individual, $20 libraries; sample: $4. 80pp; 6×8; Rights purchased: 1st. Publishes 10% of poems submitted. Deadlines: postmarked in March or October *only*. Reporting time: up to 3 months. Payment: 1 copy plus discount on more. Interested in new or unpub'd poets: yes. Simultaneous submissions accepted: no. Recent contributors: Lauren Bower Smith, John Jenkinson, Stfn Comack, Lynne Martin Bowman, Linda Roth. Submission quantity: 3-5. Special interests: We are open to suggestion.

Gravity Presses (Lest We All Float Away), Inc. (see also NOW HERE NOWHERE), 27030 Havelock, Dearborn Heights, MI 48127, 313-563-4683, e-mail mikeb5000@yahoo.com. 1998.

Graywolf Press, 2402 University Avenue #203, St. Paul, MN 55114, 651-641-0077, 651-641-0036. Fiona McCrae, Jeffrey Shotts. 1974. avg. press run 2M-3.5M. Pub'd 4 poetry titles 1999; expects 4 poetry titles 2000, 4 poetry titles 2001. size varies; avg. price, cloth: $24.95; paper: $12.95. 92pp; Publishes less than 1% of poetry manuscripts submitted. Reporting time: 12 weeks. Payment: 7½%, advance negotiated. Interested in new or unpub'd poets: no. Simultaneous submissions accepted: no. Recently published poets: Tony Hoagland, Carl Phillips, William Stafford, Sandra Alcosser, Eamon Grennan. Submission quantity: 5-10.

THE GREAT IDEA PATCH, 110 Jeffery Street, Shelburne, ON L0N 1S4, Canada. S.P. Bragg. 1990. "Please include IRC on SASE, Canadian postage please if you wish your material returned" circ. 500. 6/yr. sub. price: $15; sample: $2.25. 10pp; 8½×11; Rights purchased: none. Deadlines: No deadlines. Poems will be used as space becomes available. Reporting time: 1-3 months. Payment: 1 copy of newsletter. Interested in new or unpub'd poets: yes. Simultaneous submissions accepted: yes. Submission quantity: no limit. Special interests: The poetry that I am looking for must tell a story! Also interested in hiliday themes. A new version of The Night Befor Christmas would deffinitely catch my attention.

GREAT RIVER REVIEW, PO Box 406, Red Wing, MN 55066, Fax 612-388-2528, E-mail acis@pressenter.com. Robert Hedin, Richard Broderick. 1977. circ. 500. 2/yr. Pub'd 50 poems 1999; expects 50 poems 2000, 50 poems 2001. sub. price: $14; sample: $6. 120pp; 5½×7; Rights purchased: none. Publishes 2% of poems submitted. Deadlines: open. Reporting time: 1-2 months. Payment: copies. Interested in new or unpub'd poets: yes. Simultaneous submissions accepted: no. Recent contributors: Philip Levine, Marvin Bell, Linda Pastan, Maggie Anderson, Ted Kooser. Submission quantity: 3-5. Special interests: Poetry, fiction, essays, translations.

Great Western Publishing Company, PO Box 2355, Reston, VA 20195-0355. 1987. 5½×8½, 8½×11.

Green Bean Press, PO Box 237, Canal Street Station, New York, NY 10013, phone/fax 718-302-1955, e-mail gbpress@earthlink.net. Ian Griffin. 1995. "Don't send full mss, send sample w/SASE and we will say whether or not we want to see the whole thing. We almost never publish full-length collections by writers who we haven't been in contact with before or published a chap by." avg. press run 600. Pub'd 3 poetry titles 1999; expects 4 poetry titles 2000, 4 poetry titles 2001. 6×9; avg. price, paper: $12; other: $3 for chapbooks. 150pp; Publishes 1% of poetry manuscripts submitted. Reporting time: 1 month. Payment: varies. Interested in new or unpub'd poets: yes. Simultaneous submissions accepted: no. Recently published poets: Joe R., Daniel Crocker, A.D. Winans, Nathan Graziano. Submission quantity: 3-5. Special interests: Realism, dark humor, no nature or religion.

GREEN EGG, 212 S. Main Street #22B, Willits, CA 95490-3535, 707-456-0332; Fax 707-456-0333; e-mail admin@greenegg.org. Maeriam Morris, Poetry Editrix. 1968. circ. 11M. 6/yr. Pub'd 10 poems 1999. sub. price: $28; sample: $6 (includes p/h). 76pp; 8½×11; Rights purchased: 1st pub. Publishes 5% of poems submitted. Deadlines: 3 months before cover date. Reporting time: 1 month. Payment: copies of issue. Interested in new or unpub'd poets: sure. Simultaneous submissions accepted: no. Recent contributors: Tom Williams, Holly Tannen, P.E.I. Bonewits, Bill Beattie, Gwydion Pendderwen. Submission quantity: 1-6. Special interests: Sacred, mythological, prayers, invocations, ritual poetry, metaphysical, songs.

GREEN FUSE POETRY, 3365 Holland Drive, Santa Rosa, CA 95404, 707-544-8303. Brian Boldt. 1984. "We don't read submissions during February-March and August-September, and we can't return submissions without SASE." circ. 700. 2/yr. Pub'd 100 poems 1999; expects 100 poems 2000, 100 poems 2001. sub. price: $11, $16/3 issues; sample: $4. 64pp; 5½×8½; Rights purchased: none. Publishes 2% of poems submitted. Deadlines: January 15 and July 15. Reporting time: within 12 weeks. Payment: copies. Interested in new or unpub'd poets: yes, if the work is accomplished. Simultaneous submissions accepted: no. Recent contributors: Antler, Laurel Speer, Elliot Richman, Dorianne Laux, Donald Hall. Submission quantity: 3 or fewer. Special interests: We seek accessible, contemporary free verse concerned with peace, social justice and the environment—70 lines or less.

THE GREEN HILLS LITERARY LANTERN, PO Box 375, Trenton, MO 64683, 660-359-3948 x324. Joe Benevento, Poetry Editor. Address poetry submissions to: Truman State Univ., Div. of Language and Lit., McClain Hall 310, 100 East Normal, Kirksville, MO 63501-4221. 1990. "Don't want haiku, simple rhyme that isn't ironic, poems more than two pages long. Most poems taken are probably within 14 to 50 line limit, with exceptions of course." circ. 500. 1/yr. Pub'd 66 poems 1999; expects 65 poems 2000, 65-70 poems 2001. sub. price: $7; sample: $7. 200pp; 6×9; Rights purchased: one-time. Publishes less than 10% of poems submitted. Deadlines: Jan. 1. Reporting time: 3 months. Payment: 2 copies. Interested in new or unpub'd poets: yes. yes, but prefer not to. Recent contributors: R. Nikolas Macioci, Jim Thomas, Francine Tolf, Philip Dacey, Philip Miller. Submission quantity: 4-7.

The Green Hut Press, 1015 Jardin Street East, Appleton, WI 54911, 414-734-9728. 1972. "We will consider the work of poets when it is suitable to accompany artwork by Fritz Faiss (German-American artist, 1905-1981)." size varies.

GREEN MOUNTAINS REVIEW, Johnson State College, Johnson, VT 05656, 802-635-1350. Neil Shepard, Poetry Editor. 1987. "*GMR* is interested in quality writing from well-known writers and promising newcomers. Interested in essays by poets which address new poetics or define new literary movements at home or abroad." circ. 1.7M. 2/yr. Pub'd 72 poems 1999; expects 72 poems 2000, 72 poems 2001. sub. price: $14; sample: $5. 192pp; 6×9; Rights purchased: 1st North American Serial Rights. Publishes 2% of poems submitted. Deadlines: read from Sept. 1.-March 1. Reporting time: 2-4 months. Payment: free copy of magazine + 1 year subscription. Interested in new or unpub'd poets: yes. Simultaneous submissions accepted: yes. Recent contributors: Yusef Komunyakaa, Mary Oliver, James Tate, David St. John, Maxine Kumin. Submission quantity: no more than 5 poems at a time. Special interests: *GMR* is interested in multi-cultural writing in America as well as translations of foreign poets.

GREEN PRINTS, "The Weeder's Digest", PO Box 1355, Fairview, NC 28730, 704-628-1902. 1990. circ. 10M. 4/yr. Pub'd 4 poems 1999; expects 4 poems 2000, 4 poems 2001. sub. price: $17.97; sample: $4.50. 80pp; 6×9; Rights purchased: first. Publishes 5% of poems submitted. Reporting time: 3 months. Payment: $25.

●**Green River Press,** PO Box 6454, Santa Barbara, CA 93160, 805-964-4475, Fax 805-967-6208, 75364.3643@compuserve.com. 1999. "Current topic of interest is with all members of the adoption triangle." avg. press run 3M. Pub'd 1 poetry title 1999. 6×9; avg. price, other: $19.95. Reporting time: 6 months. Payment: copies and 40% discount. Interested in new or unpub'd poets: yes. Simultaneous submissions accepted: yes. Recently published poets: John Heldebiddle, Norbert Kempf, Karen Braucher, Ellen Bass, Penny C. Partridge. Submission quantity: 5.

Green River Writers, Inc./Grex Press, 11906 Locust Road, Middletown, KY 40243, 502-245-4902. Mary O'Dell. 1993. avg. press run 1.5M. Pub'd 1 poetry title 1999; expects 1 poetry title 2000, 1 poetry title 2001. avg. price, cloth: $18; paper: $11. 60pp; Payment: on individual basis. Interested in new or unpub'd poets: only if solicited. Recently published poets: Tom Gatus, Lee Pennington, Jim Wayne Miller.

GREEN WORLD: News and Views For Gardening Who Care About The Earth, 12 Dudley Street, Randolph, VT 05060-1202, E-mail: gx297@cleveland.freenet.edu. Cathy Czapla. 1994. "Prefer Poetry submissions by email" circ. 200. 6/yr. Pub'd 3 poems 1999; expects 12 poems 2000, 15 poems 2001. sub. price: $15; sample: $3. 40pp; 8½×11; Publishes 10% of poems submitted. Reporting time: immediate. Payment: contributors copy. Interested in new or unpub'd poets: yes. Simultaneous submissions accepted: no. Recent contributors: Walt Franklin, Suzanne Smith, Gypsy Brown. Submission quantity: 2-3.

The Greenfield Review Press/Ithaca House, PO Box 308, Greenfield Center, NY 12833-0308, 518-584-1728. Joseph Bruchac, Carol Bruchac. 1970. "No unsolicited manuscripts." avg. press run 2M. Pub'd 3 poetry titles 1999; expects 3 poetry titles 2000, 3 poetry titles 2001. 5½×8½; avg. price, paper: varies according to size from $9.95 to $14.95. 40-120pp, anthologies 400+pp; Publishes less than 5% of poetry manuscripts submitted. Payment: 10% royalty on cover price, $250 advance on royalties, payments yearly; author also receives 2% of press run plus a 50% discount on copies purchased. Simultaneous submissions accepted: no. Recently published poets: Kimberly Blaeser, Tiffany Midge, Charles Ballard. Special interests: Our primary interests are Native American and Asian American writing.

Greenhouse Review Press, 3965 Bonny Doon Road, Santa Cruz, CA 95060, 831-426-4355. Gary Young, Editor. 1975. avg. press run 250. Pub'd 3 poetry titles 1999. size varies; avg. price, cloth: $50; paper: $20. 25pp; Publishes 5% of poetry manuscripts submitted. Reporting time: 1 month. Payment: copies. Interested in new or unpub'd poets: yes. Simultaneous submissions accepted: yes. Recently published poets: Brad Crenshaw, Yannis Ritsos, Christopher Buckley, Philip Levine. Submission quantity: 3. Special interests: We publish finely printed limited editions, usually with illustrations, and focus on single poem broadsides and short, self-contained manuscripts.

GREEN'S MAGAZINE, Box 3236, Regina, Saskatchewan S4P 3H1, Canada. David Green. 1972. "We generally carry a variety in each issue. No jingly greeting card stuff unless for definite irony or humor effect." circ. 300. 4/yr. Pub'd 160 poems 1999; expects 160 poems 2000, 160 poems 2001. sub. price: $15; sample: $5. 96pp; 5¼×8½; Rights purchased: 1st North American. Publishes 5% of poems submitted. Deadlines: reading continually. Reporting time: 8 weeks. Payment: 2 contributor copies. Interested in new or unpub'd poets: yes. Simultaneous submissions accepted: no. Recent contributors: Robert D. Hoeft, Robert Cooperman, Mary Balazs, B.Z. Niditch, Gerald Zipper. Submission quantity: 3-6. Special interests: Like a variety, therefore, generally open on subject so long as it is suitable for 'family' reading.

THE GREENSBORO REVIEW, PO Box 26170, Dept. of English, Univ. of North Carolina-Greensboro, Greensboro, NC 27402-6170, 336-334-5459, fax 336-334-3281, e-mail jlclark@uncg.edu, www.uncg.edu/eng/mfa. 1966. "Prefer to read late August-mid February; work submitted after deadlines may be held until next deadline for consideration. Send SASE. Literary Awards deadline September 15; guidelines for SASE. No restrictions on length of poetry. We like to see the best being written regardless of theme, subject, form. Publish new talent beside established writers." circ. 800. 2/yr. Pub'd 35-40 poems 1999; expects 35-40 poems 2000, 35-40 poems 2001. sub. price: $10; sample: $5. 128pp; 6×9; Rights purchased: 1st North American serial rights, copyright transferred to author upon request. Publishes 2% of poems submitted. Deadlines: February 15, September 15. Reporting time: 3-6 months. Payment: 3 copies. Interested in new or unpub'd poets: yes. Simultaneous submissions accepted: no. Recent contributors: Brendan Galvin, Michael McFee, Adrienne Su, Stanley Plumly, Ira Sadoff. Submission quantity: 3-5. Special interests: No restrictions except that we normally do not publish translations.

Greensleeve Editions (see also URBAN GRAFFITI), PO Box 41164, Edmonton, AB T6J 6M7, Canada. 1988. 5½×8½.

Griffon House Publications, 1401 Pennsylvania Avenue, Suite 105, Wilmington, DE 19806, 302-656-3230. 1974. 6×9.

The Groundwater Press, PO Box 704, Hudson, NY 12534, 516-767-8503. Roseanne Wasserman. 1974. "About 99% of the time, we publish poets we have contacted first. No unsolicited material returned without SASE; it takes a year to report, at least" avg. press run 500. Pub'd 2 poetry titles 1999; expects 1-2 poetry titles 2000, 1-2 poetry titles 2001. 5½×8½, 6×9; avg. price, paper: $10. 80pp; Publishes 1% of poetry manuscripts submitted. Payment: dependent on grants and sales. Interested in new or unpub'd poets: no. Simultaneous submissions accepted: no. Recently published poets: Pierre Martory, Edward Barrett, Marc Cohen, Star Black, Tomoyuki Iino. Submission quantity: no booklength MSPS. Special interests: translations, New York School poets and artists.

GRUE MAGAZINE, Hell's Kitchen Productions, PO Box 370, Times Square Station, New York, NY 10108, e-mail nadramia@panix.com. Peggy Nadramia. 1985. "We are primarily a magazine of horror fiction. Shorter poems of the macabre are most desirable. Do not submit E.A.P. ripoffs. Think Apocalypse Culture." circ. 3M. 1/yr. Pub'd 15 poems 1999; expects 20 poems 2000, 20 poems 2001. sub. price: $14; sample: $5. 96pp; 5½×8½; Rights purchased: 1st N.A. serial. Publishes 5% of poems submitted. Reporting time: 3-6 months. Payment: $5. Interested in new or unpub'd poets: yes. Simultaneous submissions accepted: no. Recent contributors: Denise Dumars, T. Winter-Damon, G. Sutton Breiding, Steve Sneyd, Andy Darlington. Submission quantity: 3-4. Special interests: Neo-Baudelairean Cyber-Sade.

Guernica Editions, Inc., PO Box 117, Station P, Toronto, Ontario M5S 2S6, Canada, 416-658-9888, FAX 416-657-8885, guernicaeditions@cs.com. Antonio D'Alfonso. 1978. "We publish poetry that offers a new view of the world we live." avg. press run 1M-2M. Pub'd 3 poetry titles 1999; expects 10 poetry titles 2000, 6 poetry titles 2001. 4½×7½, 5×8, 4¼×7; avg. price, paper: $12. 96pp; Publishes 1% of poetry manuscripts submitted. Reporting time: 2-4 weeks if definitely not interested, 3 months otherwise. Payment: 10%. Interested in new or unpub'd poets: only on query. Simultaneous submissions accepted: no. Recently published poets: Gianna Patriarca, Mario Luzi, Tonino Guerra, Diane Raptosh, Giose Rimanelli. Submission quantity: 6-10 pages. Special interests: Translations from international poetry. Must have rights cleared first.

Guildford Poets Press (see also WEYFARERS), 9 White Rose Lane, Woking, Surrey, GU22 7JA, England. Jeffery Wheatley, Margaret Pain, Martin Jones. 1972. "At the moment, we have (hopefully temporarily) ceased considering poems for booklets, and are concentrating on *Weyfarers Magazine*. Our booklet publication will be very limited. Booklets, if any, would be largely confined to poets who have published frequently in *Weyfarers* and are familiar to our readers. In these cases we do our best with notes in our newsletter, reviews, etc. to promote sales, although the poet must be responsible for a large part of his own distribution. Individual booklet publication temporarily suspended. *No unsolicited poems will be considered.*" avg. press run 200. 8×6; avg. price, paper: £1.60 (overseas, £2 sterling or cash, or $5 cheque). 28pp; Reporting time: from return mail to several months in suitable cases. Payment: co-operative basis; poet pays printing costs and small nominal contribution to expenses, poet and press share distribution, press provides all editorial services, poet takes profits. Interested in new or unpub'd poets: no. Simultaneous submissions accepted: no. Recently published poets: Susan James, Jeffery Wheatley, John Emuss, Paddy Stevens. Submission quantity: when appropriate, at least 50 poems would be expected, but *no unsolicited work without prior arrangement*. Special interests: High-standard poetry with lift-off, not too experimental, but original.

GULF COAST, Dept. of English, University of Houston, Houston, TX 77204-3012. Matt Otremba, Michael Theune, Julie Chisholm. 1987. circ. 1M. 2/yr. Pub'd 30 poems 1999; expects 30 poems 2000, 30 poems 2001. sub. price: $12; sample: $7. 144pp; 9×6; Rights purchased: rights revert to author on publication. Publishes 5% of poems submitted. Deadlines: read year-round, except May and June. Reporting time: 4 months. Payment: copies, sometimes small monetary reimbursement. Interested in new or unpub'd poets: yes. Simultaneous submissions accepted: yes. Recent contributors: Rafael Campo, W.S. Merwin, Amy Gerstler, Lisa Lewis, John Yau. Submission quantity: 3-5. Special interests: We are interested inproviding a forum for new and emerging writers who are producing well-crafted work that takes risks: writing that intensifies the accepted conventions for poetry or that seeks, in whatever sense, to get beyond them. While we don't necessarily value clarity, the poems must be recognizably human: rambunctious, sullen or subtle. We hope to feature an eclectic selection each issue—poems that, because they move according to their own sturctural necessity, do so forcefully, vidly, with ease and grace. Submissions should be typed with the poet's name, address and phone number on the first page of each.

Gut Punch Press, PO Box 105, Cabin John, MD 20818. 1988. avg. press run 1M. Pub'd 1 poetry title 1999; expects 1 poetry title 2001. 5½×8½; avg. price, paper: $7.95. 64pp; Reporting time: 2 months. Payment: 50 copies of 1st printing. Interested in new or unpub'd poets: no. Simultaneous submissions accepted: no. Recently published poets: Jared Hendrickson, Richard Peabody, Reuben Jackson, Sunil Freeman, Rose Solari.

H

H & C NEWSLETTER, PO Box 24814 GMF, Barrigada, GU 96921-4814, 671-477-1961. Richard E. Mezo. 1996. "Not a poetry magazine, but interested in publishing poetry of literary quality" circ. 150. Irregular. sub. price: $10 (includes full membership in AASHC). 8-10pp; 8½×11; Reporting time: 1-3 months. Payment: 3 copies of magazine. Submission quantity: 3. Special interests: Would like to see short imagistic poems. Space is limited.

●**H.A.K.T.U.P.!, Osric Publishing**, PO Box 4501, Ann Arbor, MI 48106, haktup@osric.com; www.osric.com/haktup/. 1999. circ. varies, about 100. 12/yr. sub. price: $36; sample: $3. 24pp; 5½×8½.

HABERSHAM REVIEW, PO Box 10, Demorest, GA 30535, 706-778-3000 Ex 132. Whited Stephen R. 1991. 2/yr. Pub'd 25 poems 1999; expects 25 poems 2000, 25 poems 2001. sub. price: $12; sample: $6. 96pp; 6×9; Rights purchased: 1st time. Publishes 10% of poems submitted. Payment: 5 copies of issue.

HAIGHT ASHBURY LITERARY JOURNAL, 558 Joost Avenue, San Francisco, CA 94127. Indigo Hotchkiss, Co-Editor; Alice Rogoff, Co-Editor; Conyus, Co-Editor. 1980. "Please enclose SASE and name and address on every page. We are interested in 'socially conscious' poetry, and would like a multi-cultural publication. We also welcome any type of poetry. Prefer poems under 2 pages long" circ. 3M. 1-3/yr. Pub'd 120 poems 1999; expects 120 poems 2000, 120 poems 2001. sub. price: $35, includes 3 back issues and 9 future issues, $6 for 2 issues, $12 for 4 issues; sample: $3 (with postage). 16pp; 11½×17½; Rights purchased: all rights return to the author. Publishes 5% of poems submitted. Deadlines: Oct. 2000. Reporting time: 2-3 months to notify that we are considering a poem, up to 6 months for a final decision. Payment: copies of the issue, "center" writers paid. Interested in new or unpub'd poets: yes. Simultaneous submissions accepted: yes. Recent contributors: Edgar Silex, Tony Vaughan, Opal Palmer Adisa, Molly Fisk, Saint Teresa Stone. Submission quantity: up to 6 poems. Special interests: Our editors have a variety of tastes in poetry. Translations and the original (especially in Spanish), haikus and poems about the Haight Ashbury would be interesting additions to the magazine.

Halbar Publishing (see also SHARING & CARING), 289 Taylor Street, Wills Point, TX 75169-9732. Bill Halbert, Mary Barnes. 1994. "We publish names, addresses and try to make writers sell. We run free ads on books we publish, do book reviews on those we publish and others for subscribers, have a quarterly newsletter, give helpful hints for being successful in the field." avg. press run 100. Pub'd 400 poetry titles 1999. 5¼x7½; avg. price, paper: varies. 30pp; Publishes with sub., 98% of poetry manuscripts submitted. Reporting time: 2 weeks. Interested in new or unpub'd poets: yes. Simultaneous submissions accepted: yes. Recently published poets: Terri Warden, Marian Ford Park, Jani Johe Webster, Linda Creech, Linda Hutton. Submission quantity: 4. Special interests: Publish all genres of poetry except porn, libel, slander.

Haley's, PO Box 248, Athol, MA 01331, haleyathol@aolcom. Marcia Gagliardi. 1989. "Financing may be creative; we do a poetry/art collaborative" avg. press run 650. Pub'd 4 poetry titles 1999; expects 4 poetry titles 2000, 4 poetry titles 2001. 8½x11, 6x9, 7x10; avg. price, paper: $10.95. 100pp; Publishes 5% of poetry manuscripts submitted. Reporting time: 10 weeks. Payment: varies. Interested in new or unpub'd poets: not particularly. Simultaneous submissions accepted: with prior agreement. Recently published poets: Doug Anderson, Doris Abramson, John Hodgen, Candance Curran, Julia Penelope.

HALF TONES TO JUBILEE, English Dept., 1000 College Blvd., Pensacola Jr. College, Pensacola, FL 32504, 904-484-1000 ext. 1400. Walter Spara, Senior Editor. 1986. "No bias, no theme issues, we select the best from submissions. Reading all year. SASE a must." circ. 500. 1/yr. Pub'd 50 poems 1999; expects 50-60 poems 2000, 50-60 poems 2001. sub. price: $4; sample: $4. 100pp; 6x9; Rights purchased: First. Publishes 10% of poems submitted. Deadlines: May 15. Reporting time: 1-3 months. Payment: copies. Interested in new or unpub'd poets: yes. Simultaneous submissions accepted: no. Recent contributors: Gayle Elen Harvey, Larry Rubin, R.T. Smith, Peter Wild. Submission quantity: 3-5.

Handshake Editions, Atelier A2, 83 rue de la Tombe-Issoire, Paris 75014, France, 4327-1767. Jim Haynes. 1971. "I prefer face to face discussions with all individuals I elect to publish." avg. press run 1M first printing, but I aim to keep all titles in print. Expects 4-5 poetry titles 2000. avg. price, paper: $10. 80pp; Payment: copies. Interested in new or unpub'd poets: no. Simultaneous submissions accepted: no. Recently published poets: Ted Joans, Bill Levy, David Day. Special interests: Sexual freedom, one-world sense of responsibility, anti-automobile in cities, love of life, a positive 'we-can-do-anything' attitude.

HANGING LOOSE, Hanging Loose Press, 231 Wyckoff Street, Brooklyn, NY 11217. Robert Hershon, Dick Lourie, Mark Pawlak, Ron Schreiber. 1966. "Each issue is 80-90% poetry. *Hanging Loose* is interested in work by new poets and poets who have been unjustly neglected." circ. 2M. 3/yr. sub. price: $17.50/3 issues (individuals); sample: $8.50 (incl. postage). 128pp; 7x8½; Rights purchased: first serial. Deadlines: we read throughout the year. Reporting time: up to 3 months. Payment: 2 copies and small cash payment. Interested in new or unpub'd poets: yes. Simultaneous submissions accepted: absolutely not. Recent contributors: Sherman Alexie, Jack Anderson, Paul Violi, Donna Brook, D. Nurkse. Submission quantity: 4-6 suggested. Special interests: We hate getting poems from people who have clearly never seen the magazine and advise writers to send for a sample copy.

Hanging Loose Press (see also HANGING LOOSE), 231 Wyckoff Street, Brooklyn, NY 11217. Robert Hershon, Dick Lourie, Mark Pawlak, Ron Schreiber. 1966. "*Hanging Loose* is able to consider book manuscripts *only* by invitation. No exceptions." avg. press run 1.5M. Pub'd 6 poetry titles 1999; expects 6 poetry titles 2000, 6 poetry titles 2001. 5½x8½, varies; avg. price, cloth: $20; paper: $13. 96pp; Interested in new or unpub'd poets: not books. Simultaneous submissions accepted: no! Recently published poets: Ron Overton, Donna Brook, Paul Violi, Kimiko Hahn, Gary Lenhart.

Hannacroix Creek Books, Inc, 1127 High Ridge Road #110, Stamford, CT 06905, 203-321-8674; Fax 203-968-0193; E-mail hcbbooks@aol.com. Jan Yager. 1996. avg. press run 1M. Pub'd 1 poetry title 1999; expects 1 poetry title 2000, 1 poetry title 2001. avg. price, cloth: $21.95. 96pp; Recently published poets: Priscilla Orr.

Hard Press (see also COVER MAGAZINE), 632 East 14th Street, #18, New York, NY 10009, 212-673-1152. Jeffrey C. Wright. 1976. "*Hard Press* occasionally accepts unsolicited work for its postcard series. I suggest ordering samples before submitting. A cover letter and SASE necessary for submission, but not for order. For order enclose $5 or request catalog" avg. press run 500. Expects 4 poetry titles 2000, 4 poetry titles 2001. 5½x4¼; avg. price, paper: $4; other: $2.50 (per set of postcards). 4pp (postcards) or 24pp; Publishes

5% of poetry manuscripts submitted. Reporting time: 10 weeks. Payment: 10%. Interested in new or unpub'd poets: yes. Simultaneous submissions accepted: yes. Recently published poets: Robert Creeley, Alice Notley, Pedro Pietri, Maureen Owen, William Matthews. Submission quantity: 5. Special interests: I am interested in expanding the audience for poetry. The utilitarian aspect of postcards appeals to the pragmatism of Americans. The cards are attractive and use various elements of design such as colored inks, collage, typography, and photography. Sometimes the poet designs the card with poem; usually I match the poem with a design. We are seeking the popular but profound, the meaningful and mysterious. We publish the celebrated beside the promising.

Hard Press, Inc. (see also LINGO), PO Box 184, West Stockbridge, MA 01266, 413-232-4690. 1993.

HARMONY: Voices for a Just Future, PO Box 210056, San Francisco, CA 94121-0056, 415-221-8527. Rose Evans, Managing Editor. 1987. "We are interested in poetry about peace, justice and reverence for life." circ. 1.4M. 6/yr. Pub'd 12 poems 1999; expects 12 poems 2000, 12 poems 2001. sub. price: $12; sample: $2. 28pp; 8½×11; Rights purchased: 1st N. American rights only. Publishes .05% of poems submitted. Deadlines: ongoing. Reporting time: 2 months. Payment: copies only. Interested in new or unpub'd poets: yes. Simultaneous submissions accepted: yes. Recent contributors: Jean Blackwood, Tom Keene, Paul Truttman, R.L. Cook, Mary R. Stanko. Submission quantity: 3.

HARP-STRINGS, PO Box 640387, Beverly Hills, FL 34464. Madelyn Eastlund, Editor; Sybella Beyer Snyder, Associate Editor. 1989. "2 contests a year" circ. 100. 2/yr. Pub'd 60 poems 1999; expects 60-70 poems 2000, 60-70 poems 2001. sub. price: $11; sample: $6. 40-44pp; 5½×8½; Rights purchased: one time. Publishes 2% of poems submitted. Deadlines: No deadlines. Reporting time: 3 weeks. Payment: contributors copy. Interested in new or unpub'd poets: yes. Simultaneous submissions accepted: no. Recent contributors: Helen Mar Cook, Marilyn Hogan, Ralph Hammond, Evelyn Ritchie. Submission quantity: 3-5. Special interests: Narratives. *Harp-Strings* wants "poetry to remember"—poetry that will haunt the reader, that will be read over and over again! Some kinds of poetry that we like: crown of sonnets, sestinas, blank verse, rhymn royal.

THE HARVARD ADVOCATE, 21 South St., Cambridge, MA 02138, 617-495-0737. Lucy Ives, Poetry Editor. 1866. "We regret we can only accept submissions by past or present Harvard University students, faculty, officers, and alumni" circ. 4M. 4/yr. Pub'd 20 poems 1999; expects 24 poems 2000, 28 poems 2001. sub. price: $25 for 4 issues; sample: $5. 40pp; 9×12; Rights purchased: first. Publishes 10% of poems submitted. Reporting time: varies. Payment: none. Interested in new or unpub'd poets: Harvard affiliates only. Simultaneous submissions accepted: yes. Submission quantity: no specification. Special interests: All types, genres of poetry.

THE HAUNTED JOURNAL, 577 Central Avenue, Box 4, Jefferson, LA 70121-1400, e-mail fullmoon@edoramail.com or haunted@rocketmail.com; www.spaceports.com/~haunted, www.eclecticity.com/ zines/, www.members.xoom.com/blackie or http://www.angelfire.com/la/hauntings/index.htm/, www2.cybercities.com/z/zines. Sharida Rizzuto, Editor; Harold Tollison, Associate Editor; Ann Hoyt, Assistant Editor; Rose Dalton, Assistant Editor. 1983. "This publication covers the entire horror genre. All submissions must be double-spaced and typewritten. Occult matter also included" circ. 1M-1.2M. 2/yr. Pub'd 60 poems 1999. sub. price: $15.80; sample: $7.90. 100pp; 8½×11; Rights purchased: one-time rights, first serial rights, or second serial rights. Publishes 35% of poems submitted. Deadlines: always open to submissions. Reporting time: 2-6 weeks. Payment: free copies. Interested in new or unpub'd poets: yes. Simultaneous submissions accepted: yes. Recent contributors: Holly Day, Leilah Wendell, Chris Friend, Janet Reedman. Submission quantity: 1-5. Special interests: We are willing to look at any type of poetry. No length requirements.

HAWAII PACIFIC REVIEW, 1060 Bishop Street, Honolulu, HI 96813, 808-544-1107. Patrice Wilson, Editor. 1987. "The *Hawaii Pacific Review* is looking for poetry, short fiction, and personal essays that speak with a powerful and unique voice. We encourage experimental narrative techniques and poetic styles. While we occasionally accept work from novice writers, we publish only work of the highest quality. We will read one submission per contributor consisting of one prose piece of up to 5000 words or 5 poems. Please include a cover letter with a 5-line bio and an SASE. Experimental works, translations and long poetry (up to 100 lines) are all welcome." circ. 500-750. 1/yr. Pub'd 30 poems 1999; expects 33 poems 2000, 30 poems 2001. sub. price: $7; sample: $4. 100pp; 6×9; Rights purchased: First North American. Publishes 5% of poems submitted. Deadlines: Our reading period is Sept. 1 to Dec. 31. Reporting time: 10-12 weeks. Payment: 2 copies. Interested in new or unpub'd poets: yes, but we are *highly* selective. Simultaneous submissions accepted: yes. Recent contributors: Wendy Bishop, Willie James King, B.Z. Niditch, Barbara Hamby. Submission quantity: up to 5.

HAWAI'I REVIEW, c/o Dept. of English, 1733 Donaghho Road, Honolulu, HI 96822, 808-956-3030. Katherine Santiago. 1973. "Must send SASE with sufficient postage for return of submissions" circ. 1M. 2/yr. Pub'd 130 poems 1999; expects 125 poems 2000, 130 poems 2001. sub. price: $20, $30/2 years; sample: $10. 150-250pp; 5½×8½; Rights purchased: 1st, rights revert to author upon publication. Publishes 5% of poems submitted. Deadlines: submit all year round. Reporting time: 3-6 months. Payment: 4 copies. Interested in new or unpub'd poets: yes. Simultaneous submissions accepted: yes. Recent contributors: Susan M. Schultz, Juliana Spahr, Joe Balaz, Lois-Ann Yamanaka, Zachary Chartkoff. Submission quantity: 5 or less. Special interests: Translations, experimental poetry, regional poetry, multicultural, Hawaiian (with English version attached).

Hawk Publishing Group, 6420 S. Richmond Avenue, Tulsa, OK 74136, 918-492-3854, fax 918-492-2120, wb@hawkpub.com, www.hawkpub.com. William Bernhardt, Publisher. 1999.

HAYDEN'S FERRY REVIEW, Box 871502, Arizona State University, Tempe, AZ 85287-1502, 602-965-1243. Editors are chosen for 1-year terms only. 1986. circ. 1M. 2/yr. Pub'd 50 poems 1999; expects 50 poems 2000, 50 poems 2001. sub. price: $10; sample: $6. 128pp; 6×9; Rights purchased: North American Serial Rights. Publishes 2% of poems submitted. Deadlines: February 28 and September 30. Reporting time: 8-10 weeks after deadline. Interested in new or unpub'd poets: yes. Simultaneous submissions accepted: yes, with notification. Recent contributors: Raymond Carver, Maura Stanton, Rita Dove, Norman Dubie, David St. John. Submission quantity: no more than 6.

Headveins Graphics (see also ENDING THE BEGIN), PO Box 4774, Seattle, WA 98104-0774, 206-726-0948. Brad Angell. 1984. "No long poetry. We are partial to cynicism, hunor, frivolity and melanchlia"

Heat Press, PO Box 26218, Los Angeles, CA 90026, 213-482-8902, chpeditt@cdrewu.edu. Christopher Natale Peditto, Publisher & General Editor; Barbara Romain, Associate Editor; Terry D'Ovido, Art Director; Harold Abramowitz, Associate Editor. 1993. "Not currently accepting unsolicited manuscripts. Queries are welcomed" avg. press run 1500. Expects 1 poetry title 2000, 1 poetry title 2001. 5×8; avg. price, paper: $9.95. 100pp; Payment: negotiated. Recently published poets: Charles Bivins, Eric Priestley, Elliott Levin, Wil Perkins.

HEAVEN BONE MAGAZINE, Heaven Bone Press, PO Box 486, Chester, NY 10918, 914-469-9018. Steven Hirsch, Gordon Kirpal, Contributing Editor. 1986. "We like work that is deeply rooted in nature and image yet inspired by cosmic visions and spiritual practice. Current issues tending toward the surreal and eidetic. Editor loves work by Rilke. Where are his followers? Nothing turns us off more than artificially forced end-line rhyming; however, rhymed verse will be considered if obviously excellent and showing careful work." circ. 2.5M. 1/yr. Pub'd 60 poems 1999; expects 50 poems 2000, 50 poems 2001. sub. price: $10; sample: $10. 96-144pp; 8½×11; Rights purchased: 1st North American serial. Publishes less than 5% of poems submitted. Deadlines: none, reading all year. Reporting time: 1 week to 6 months. Payment: 2 copies, discount (30%) on add. copies. Interested in new or unpub'd poets: yes. Simultaneous submissions accepted: yes, if notified. Recent contributors: Charles Bukowski, Marge Piercy, Ed Mycue, Kirpal Gordon, Stephen-Paul Martin. Submission quantity: 3-10. Special interests: Experimental, esoteric, spiritual, surrealism.

Heaven Bone Press (see also HEAVEN BONE MAGAZINE), PO Box 486, Chester, NY 10918, 914-469-9018. Steve Hirsch. 1986. avg. press run 500. Pub'd 2 poetry titles 1999. 5½×8½; avg. price, paper: $5.95. 32pp; Publishes 2% of poetry manuscripts submitted. Reporting time: 3-36 weeks. Payment: varies. Interested in new or unpub'd poets: yes, query first. Simultaneous submissions accepted: yes if advised. Recently published poets: Diane DiPrima, Janine Pommy Vega, Kirpal Gordon, Marge Piercy, Antler. Submission quantity: no more than 5. Special interests: Surrealism.

HECATE, P.O. Box 99, St. Lucia, Queensland 4067, Australia. 1975. circ. 2M. 2/yr. sub. price: $25/yr (ind), $100 (inst), please pay in Australian $; sample: $6 (ind); $10 (inst). 180pp; 4×6½; Reporting time: varies. Payment: $40 per poem.

HEELTAP/Pariah Press, Pariah Press, c/o Richard D. Houff, 604 Hawthorne Ave. East, St. Paul, MN 55101-3531. Richard David Houff. 1996. "Always include SASE. I read year round. No special issues etc. as yet. With enough appoprriate material, each issue should form itself into a thematic collage on it's own" circ. 200. 2/yr. Expects 100 poems 2000. sub. price: $18/4 issue sub.; sample: $4. 48pp; 5½×8½; Rights purchased: 1st only/revert back. Publishes 5% of poems submitted. Deadlines: on-going. Reporting time: 2 weeks to 1 month. Payment: copies. Interested in new or unpub'd poets: yes. Simultaneous submissions accepted: yes. Recent contributors: Antler, Greg Bachar, Tom Clark, Paul Dickinson, Dave Etter. Submission quantity: 5.

Heidelberg Graphics, 2 Stansbury Court, Chico, CA 95928-9410, 530-342-6582. Larry S. Jackson, Editor. 1972. "Most poets published by Heidelberg Graphics are either by invitation or are the result of personal contact. We also offer complete services to self-publishers." avg. press run 500. Pub'd 1 poetry title 1999; expects 1 poetry title 2000, 1 poetry title 2001. 6×9; avg. price, paper: $12.95. 112pp; Publishes 1% of poetry manuscripts submitted. Reporting time: 6 months. Payment: negotiable. Interested in new or unpub'd poets: no. Simultaneous submissions accepted: no. Recently published poets: Eliabeth Revere, Maurice Kenny, Alison Zier. Submission quantity: the whole book.

Helicon Nine Editions, Box 22412, Kansas City, MO 64113, 816-753-1095, Fax 816-753-1016, helicon9@aol.com, www.heliconnine.com. Patty Seyburn, Editor-in-Chief. Address poetry submissions to: 3607 Pennsylvania Avenue, Kansas City, MO 64111. 1977. "We conduct an annual poetry contest (The Marianne Moore Poetry Prize) and publish the winning manuscripts (write for details). We're small but dedicated, and promote our authors." avg. press run 800-2M. Pub'd 1 poetry title 1999; expects 3 poetry titles 2000, 3-4 poetry titles 2001. 6×9; avg. price, paper: $9.95-$11.95. 55-84pp; Publishes 1% of poetry manuscripts submitted. Reporting time: query first. Payment: varies according to individual contracts. Interested in new or unpub'd poets: query first. Simultaneous submissions accepted: yes, but we don't encourage it. Recently published poets: David Ray, Christopher Seid, Elizabeth Goldring, Marjorie Stelmach, Susan Gubernat. Submission quantity: query first. Special interests: No light or inspirational verse.

Helikon Press, 120 West 71st Street, New York City, NY 10023. 1972. "We cannot encourage submissions. We publish only a few books of poems in the English verse tradition—works built around poems we have read in magazines or heard in public readings." no standard size (each book is designed to suit the particular poems & poet). Interested in new or unpub'd poets: no. Recently published poets: Helen Adam, George Barker, Thom Gunn, John Heath-Stubbs, Michael Miller.

HELIOTROPE: A Writer's Summer Solstice, PO Box 20037, Spokane, WA 99204-0037, 509-624-0418. Jan Strever, Iris Gribble-Neal, Tom Gribble. 1997. "Submissions are read only during the summer (June 21-Sept 21)" circ. 200. 1/yr. Pub'd 40 poems 1999; expects 50 poems 2000, 50 poems 2001. sub. price: $6.50; sample: $5. 75pp; 5½×8½; Publishes 10% of poems submitted. Deadlines: June 21-Sept 21. Reporting time: 1 month. Payment: 1 copy. Interested in new or unpub'd poets: yes. Simultaneous submissions accepted: no. Recent contributors: James Grabill, Kris Christensen, Jon Fischer, Nance Van Winckel, Christopher Howell. Submission quantity: five. Special interests: Criticism - 800-1,000 words, Flash Fiction 1,000 words.

HELLAS: A Journal of Poetry & the Humanities, The Aldine Press, Ltd., 304 South Tyson Avenue, Glenside, PA 19038, 215-884-1086. Gerald Harnett, Editor. 1988. "Any verse welcome, but we prize elegance and formality in verse. We especially welcome metrical verse, and advise submitters to avoid meaninglessness and prosaism." 2/yr. Pub'd 70 poems 1999. sub. price: $16; sample: $9 postpaid. 180pp; 6×9; Rights purchased: First N.A. Serial. Publishes 3% of poems submitted. Deadlines: none. Reporting time: 2-4 months. Payment: 1 copy. Interested in new or unpub'd poets: yes. Simultaneous submissions accepted: no. Recent contributors: Steele, Megaw, Gioia, Butler, Moore. Submission quantity: 4-5, not more.

HELLP!, Hellp! Press, PO Box 38, Farmingdale, NJ 07727. Rick Silvani, Joe Musso. 1997. circ. 150. 6-12/yr. Pub'd 200 poems 1999; expects 200 poems 2000, 200 poems 2001. sub. price: $25; sample: $3. 40+pp; 5½×8; Rights purchased: first. Publishes 25% of poems submitted. Reporting time: 1-2 months. Payment: copies. Interested in new or unpub'd poets: yes. yes, if notified. Recent contributors: Rich Quatrone, Lyn Lifshin, John Sweet, Koon Woon, Melody Rose Robins. Submission quantity: 3-5. Special interests: Our only interests are good writing. We're very open minded.

Hellp! Press (see also HELLP!), PO Box 38, Farmingdale, NJ 07727. Rick Silvani, Joe Musso. 1997. avg. press run 50. Expects 10 poetry titles 2000, 20 poetry titles 2001. size varies; avg. price, paper: $3. 20-48pp; Publishes 10% of poetry manuscripts submitted. Reporting time: 1-2 months. Payment: copies. Interested in new or unpub'd poets: yes. yes, if notified. Recently published poets: Rich Quatrone, Lyn Lifshin, John Sweet, Koon Woon, Melody Rose Robins. Submission quantity: entire manuscript.

Hermes House Press (see also KAIROS, A Journal of Contemporary Thought and Criticism), 113 Summit Avenue, Brookline, MA 02446-2319, 617-566-2468. Richard Mandell, Alan Mandell. 1980. "Not currently accepting poetry submissions. Individual poems may be sent to *Kairos*, c/o Mandell, 450 E. 63rd Street, New York, NY 10021." avg. press run 500. Expects 2 poetry titles 2001. 5½×8½, 4¼×7; avg. price, paper: $5. Pages vary; Publishes 10% of poetry manuscripts submitted. Reporting time: 4-8 weeks. Payment: a percentage of sales income, arranged with the author. Interested in new or unpub'd poets: yes. Simultaneous submissions accepted: no. Recently published poets: Stanley Diamond. Submission quantity: 5-10. Special interests: All types of poetry, including translations (bilingual publications especially), experimental poetry, and longpoems, as long as the writing is well crafted with a sensitivity for the ear.

Heyday Books, PO Box 9145, Berkeley, CA 94709, 510-549-3564, FAX 510-549-1889. Joyce Jenkins, Series Editor, California Poetry Series. 1974. "California poets only! Any style accepted." avg. press run 3.5M. Pub'd 4 poetry titles 1999; expects 4 poetry titles 2000, 4 poetry titles 2001. 6×9; avg. price, paper: $12.50. 80pp; Interested in new or unpub'd poets: yes. Simultaneous submissions accepted: yes. Recently published poets: Dan Ballm, Suzanne Lummis, Steve Kowit, Molly Fisk, Priscilla Lee. Submission quantity: manuscript.

The Heyeck Press, 25 Patrol Court, Woodside, CA 94062, 650-851-7491; Fax 650-851-5039; heyeck@ix.netcom.com. 1976. size varies.

●**HIDDEN OAK POETRY JOURNAL,** PO Box 2275, Philadelphia, PA 19103, hidoak@att.net. Louise Larkins. 1999. circ. 100. 3/yr. Expects 180-200 poems 2000. sub. price: $11; sample: $3. 65pp; 5½×8½; Rights purchased: none. Publishes 40% of poems submitted. Deadlines: Mar. 1, Aug. 1, Nov. 1. Reporting time: 2 weeks. Payment: 1 copy. Interested in new or unpub'd poets: yes. Simultaneous submissions accepted: no. Submission quantity: 4.

●**Higganum Hill Books**, PO Box 666, Higganum, CT 06441, rcdebold@connix.com. 1999. 6×8.

THE HIGGINSVILLE READER, PO Box 141, Three Bridges, NJ 08887, 908-788-0514, hgvreader@yahoo.com. Amy Finkenaur, Frank Magalhaes, Kathe Palka. 1991. "Please indicate your interests and background with a cover letter. We like work rich in imaginative language. We do not want poems that wander without aim, overt sentimentality, assaultive negativism." circ. 150. 4/yr. Pub'd 60 poems 1999; expects 60 poems 2000, 60 poems 2001. sub. price: $5; sample: $1.50. 16pp; 7×8½; Rights purchased: none. Publishes 8-10% of poems submitted. Deadlines: open. Reporting time: 8 weeks. Payment: 1 copy upon publication. Interested in new or unpub'd poets: we are interested, we are always more concerned with quality than name. Simultaneous submissions accepted: yes. Recent contributors: D.E. Steward, Taylor Graham, David Chorlton, Joan Payne Kincaid, Bertha Rodgers. Submission quantity: 3-6. Special interests: All types of poetry interest us—experimental, regional, longpoems, light verse, etc. The editors welcome all styles and forms.

HIGH PLAINS LITERARY REVIEW, 180 Adams Street, Suite 250, Denver, CO 80206, (303) 320-6828. Connie Orhring, Ray Gonzalez, Michael Leiberman. 1986. circ. 1150. 3/yr. Pub'd 30 poems 1999; expects 25 poems 2000, 25 poems 2001. sub. price: $20; sample: $4. 140pp; 6×9; Rights purchased: 1st Anerican. Publishes 5% of poems submitted. Reporting time: 12-15 weeks. Payment: $10/published page. Interested in new or unpub'd poets: yes. Simultaneous submissions accepted: yes. Recent contributors: Fred Dings, Joseph Hutchison, Leonard Edgerly, Elizabeth Edge. Submission quantity: up to 4.

High Plains Press, Box 123, Glendo, WY 82213, 307-735-4370, Fax 307-735-4590, 800-552-7819. Nancy Curtis, Editor. 1984. "Book-length manuscripts only. *The Red Drum* by Jane Candia Coleman won 1994 Western Heritage Award in poetry." avg. press run 1M. Pub'd 1 poetry title 1999; expects 1 poetry title 2000, 1 poetry title 2001. 5½×8½, 6×9, etc.; avg. price, paper: $11.95. 50pp; Publishes 1% of poetry manuscripts submitted. Reporting time: 2-6 weeks. Payment: advance outright purchase or advance and 10% royalty. Interested in new or unpub'd poets: yes. Simultaneous submissions accepted: yes. Recently published poets: Linda Hasselstrom, Robert Roripaugh, Charles Levendosky, Jane Candia Coleman, Laurie Wagner Buyer. Submission quantity: book-length ms only, around 50 poems. Special interests: Regional poetry, West-related but not "cowboy" poetry.

THE HIGHWAY POET, PO Box 1400, Brewster, MA 02631. Colorado T. Sky, National Secretary. 1990. "Seeking short, concise, powerful poetry and essays" circ. 200. Intermittent frequency. sub. price: $10/6; sample: $2. 12pp; 8½×11; Rights purchased: one-time. Publishes 10% of poems submitted. Deadlines: none fixed. Reporting time: 3-5 weeks with SASE. Payment: $10 plus subscription. Interested in new or unpub'd poets: select submissions or (chap)books for review only. Simultaneous submissions accepted: yes. Recent contributors: Flynch Thompson, Ogar, Peddiar MacMillan, Aeric Smith, Randy Black. Submission quantity: 2-8.

●**HIP Inc. (see also HIPPYLAND HIPPIE MAGAZINE)**, PO Box 13665, La Jolla, CA 92039-3665, 505-534-9476; skip@hippy.com; www.hippy.com. 1996. 5½×8½.

HIP MAMA, Attn: Ariel Gore, PO Box 9097, Oakland, CA 94613, 510-658-4508. Lara Candland, Poetry Editor. 1993. "Include a short bio. Especially receptive to poetry related directly to parenting" circ. 5M. 4/yr. Pub'd 8 poems 1999; expects 24 poems 2000, 24 poems 2001. sub. price: $12-$22 sliding scale; sample: $3.95. 28pp; 8½×11; Rights purchased: writers retain copyright. Publishes 50% of poems submitted. Deadlines: March 30, June 30, September 30, December 30. Reporting time: 3 months. Payment: 1-2 copies, subscription. Interested in new or unpub'd poets: yes. Simultaneous submissions accepted: yes, tell us. Recent contributors: Rae Cole, Opal Palmer Adisa, Donna Weir, Joan Jobe Smith. Submission quantity: 3-5. Special interests: Shorter poems (2 pages max, some exceptions), experimental.

Hippopotamus Press (see also OUTPOSTS POETRY QUARTERLY), 22 Whitewell Road, Frome, Somerset BA11 4EL, England, 0373-466653. Roland John. 1974. "We are interested in new or neglected poets, particularly those that have had the usual magazine and pamphlet publications and now have a larger collection to place. We wish to see work written in recognisable English from those who have learned from the Modernist movement of Pound/Eliot. We are not interested in experimental work or other glimpses into the workshop." avg. press run 750 paper, 250 cloth. Pub'd 2 poetry titles 1999; expects 5 poetry titles 2000. size varies; avg. price, cloth: £12, $24; paper: £6, $12. 80pp; Publishes 1% of poetry manuscripts submitted. Reporting time: 2 weeks U.K., 4 weeks overseas. Payment: royalty. Interested in new or unpub'd poets: yes. Simultaneous submissions accepted: yes. Recently published poets: Peter Dale, John Greening, Lotte Kramer, Shaun McCarthy, Peter Dent. Submission quantity: 20-40. Special interests: We publish original poetry and translations. We are not bound by any rules other than those of quality. We are interested in work that has technical merit.

●**HIPPYLAND HIPPIE MAGAZINE, HIP Inc.**, PO Box 13665, La Jolla, CA 92039-3665, 505-534-9476; skip@hippy.com; www.hippy.com. 1996. circ. 35M. Updated weekly. sub. price: free. Over 15,000pp on website.

HIRAM POETRY REVIEW, Box 162, Hiram, OH 44234, 330-569-5330, Fax 330-569-5449. Hale Chatfield. 1967. "Very interested in high literary quality from new poets." circ. 500. 1/yr. Pub'd 50-55 poems 1999; expects 50-55 poems 2000, 50-55 poems 2001. sub. price: $15, $35 for 3 yrs; sample: free. Rights purchased: 1st N.A. serial. Publishes 1% or less of poems submitted. Deadlines: none. Reporting time: 2-6 months. Payment: 2 copies. Interested in new or unpub'd poets: yes. Simultaneous submissions accepted: no. Recent contributors: Robert Cooperman, William Virgil Davis, Steve Kowit, Barbara Moore, Elizabeth Rees. Submission quantity: 4 or 5. Special interests: New poets, computers.

Hobblebush Books, 17-A Old Milford Road, Brookline, NH 03033, voice/fax 603-672-4317; E-mail shall@jlc.net; website http:www.jlc.net/~hobblebush/. 1993.

HOBO POETRY & HAIKU MAGAZINE, PO Box 166, Hazelbrook NSW 2779, Australia. Dane Thwaites, Janice Bostok. 1993. "SASE and name on each page is essential." circ. 700. 4/yr. Pub'd 160 poems 1999; expects 160 poems 2000, 160 poems 2001. sub. price: $20; sample: $5.50. 64pp; 160×200mm; Rights purchased: authors retain copyright. Publishes 2% of poems submitted. Reporting time: 4-8 weeks. Payment: $14 per page. Interested in new or unpub'd poets: yes. Simultaneous submissions accepted: yes.

Hochelaga Press, 4982 Connaught Avenue, Montreal, BC H4V 1X3, Canada, 514-484-3186; Fax 514-484-8971; hochelaga@sympatico.ca. 1995.

THE HOLLINS CRITIC, PO Box 9538, Hollins University, VA 24020. Cathryn Hankla. 1964. "No formal guidelines, but poems that are relatively short, unhackneyed, and at least as well written as the poems we print." circ. 400. 5/yr. Pub'd 31 poems 1999; expects 25 poems 2000, 25 poems 2001. sub. price: $6 U.S.; $7.50 elsewhere; sample: $1.50 U.S. 24pp; 7½×10; Rights purchased: first. Publishes 4% of poems submitted. Deadlines: none. Reporting time: approx. 2 months. Payment: $25. Interested in new or unpub'd poets: yes. Simultaneous submissions accepted: yes, SASE required. Recent contributors: George Garrett, John Engels, Lyn Lifshin, Dara Wier, R.T. Smith. Submission quantity: 1-5.

HOLLYWOOD NOSTALGIA, 577 Central Avenue, Box 4, Jefferson, LA 70121-1400, e-mail: publisher@mailexcite.com or blackie@talkcity.com; Websites www.home.talkcity.com/SunsetBlvd/blackie, www.wbs.net/homepages/b/l/a/blackkie.htm/, www2.cybercities.com/z/zines/. Sharida Rizutto, Harold Tollison, Ann Hoyt, Rose Dalton. 1983. circ. 500. 2/yr. Pub'd 20 poems 1999; expects 20 poems 2000, 20 poems 2001. sub. price: $15.80; sample: $7.90. 100pp; 8½×11; Rights purchased: one-time rights, first serial rights, or second serial rights. Publishes 30% of poems submitted. Deadlines: always open. Reporting time: 2-6 weeks. Payment: free copy only. Interested in new or unpub'd poets: yes. Simultaneous submissions accepted: yes. Recent contributors: Carl Brennan, Lucinda MacGregor, Ona Hill, Jimmy Skinner, Lyndia Glover. Submission quantity: 1-5.

Holy Cow! Press, PO Box 3170, Mount Royal Station, Duluth, MN 55803, 218-724-1653 phone/Fax. Jim Perlman. 1977. "Please query first before sending manuscripts. We publish, from time to time, anthologies centered around important themes and will solicit work for these. Please include SASE." avg. press run 1.5M. Pub'd 3 poetry titles 1999; expects 2 poetry titles 2000, 3 poetry titles 2001. 6×9; avg. price, cloth: $15; paper: $7.95. 72pp; Publishes 5% of poetry manuscripts submitted. Reporting time: 2-3 months. Payment: negotiable with each author. Interested in new or unpub'd poets: yes. Simultaneous submissions accepted: yes, if notified. Recently published poets: Roberta Hill Whiteman, Kate Green, Jeanie Thompson, Anya Achtenberg. Submission quantity: 6-10.

HOME PLANET NEWS, Home Planet Publications, P.O. Box 415 Stuyvesant Station, New York, NY 10009, 718-769-2854. Enid Dame, Donald Lev. 1979. "We don't take poems which, in our opinion, are racist, anti-semitic, anti-woman, or otherwise limit or denigrate the human spirit." circ. 3M. 3-4/yr. Pub'd 65 poems 1999; expects 95 poems 2000, 95 poems 2001. sub. price: $10; sample: $3. 24pp; 10×15; Rights purchased: first only, all rights revert to poet. Publishes 3% of poems submitted. Deadlines: none. Reporting time: 3-4 months. Payment: 4 copies plus 1 year's gift subscription. Interested in new or unpub'd poets: yes. Simultaneous submissions accepted: no. Recent contributors: Lyn Lifshin, Robert Peters, Denise Duhamel, Richard Kostelanetz, Leslea Newman. Submission quantity: 3-6. Special interests: Shorter poems have a better chance with us, for reasons of space, though we occasionally take longpoems. We like humor, concrete images, an urban sensibility—but are not dogmatic about any of these.

Home Planet Publications (see also HOME PLANET NEWS), PO Box 415 Stuyvesant Station, New York, NY 10009, 718-769-2854. Enid Dame, Donald Lev. 1991. 5×8.

Homeward Press, PO Box 2307, Berkeley, CA 94702, 412-526-3254. John Curl. 1980. avg. press run 200. 5½×8½; avg. price, paper: $5. 60pp; Payment: cooperative arrangement. Special interests: Publishing oral poetry in book/tape combinations.

HORIZONS, 577 Central Avenue, Box 4, Jefferson, LA 70121-1400, e-mail: horizons@altavista.net or publisher@mailexcite.com; Website www2.cybercities.com/z/zines/. 1983. circ. 300-500. 2/yr. sub. price: $15.80; sample: $7.90. 100pp; 8½×11.

HORIZONS BEYOND, 577 Central Avenue, Box 4, Jefferson, LA 70121-0517, e-mail fullmoon@eudora-mail.com or haunted@rocketmail.com; Websites www.members.xoom.com/blackie, www2.cybercities.com/z/zines/, www.eclecticity.com/zines/, www.spaceports.com/~haunted/. Sharida Rizzuto, Editor; Harold Tollison, Ann Hoyt. 1983. "This publication includes science fiction and fantasy, and sword and sorcery. Poetry submissions should be suitable. All submissions must be double-spaced and typewritten" circ. 300. 2/yr. Pub'd 20-28 poems 1999. sub. price: $15.80; sample: $7.90. 100pp; 8½×11; Rights purchased: one-time rights, first serial rights, or second serial rights. Publishes 30% of poems submitted. Deadlines: always open to submissions. Reporting time: 2-6 weeks. Payment: free copies. Interested in new or unpub'd poets: yes. Simultaneous submissions accepted: yes. Recent contributors: Chris Friend, Dwight E. Humphries, Lucinda MacGregor. Submission quantity: 1-5. Special interests: We are willing to look at any type of poetry. No length requirements.

The Hosanna Press, 203 Keystone, River Forest, IL 60305, 708-771-8259. Catherine Ruggie Saunders. 1974. avg. press run 75. Pub'd 1 poetry title 1999; expects 1 poetry title 2000, 1 poetry title 2001. size varies. Pages vary; Reporting time: 6 weeks. Payment: a percentage of the edition. Interested in new or unpub'd poets: yes. Simultaneous submissions accepted: no. Recently published poets: Jack L. Bryan, Gerald Lange, Diane Ruggie. Submission quantity: 6 (minimum). Special interests: Interested in imagistic poetry whose content and spirit might be visually expressed in the conceptual and physical format of the Handmade Book.

Host Publications, Inc. (see also THE DIRTY GOAT), 2717 Wooldridge, Austin, TX 78703-1953, 512-482-8229, Fax 512-482-0580, jbratcher3@aol.com. Joe Bratcher. 1988. avg. press run 1M. Pub'd 2 poetry titles 1999; expects 2 poetry titles 2000. 5½×8½; avg. price, cloth: $30; paper: $15. 150pp; We publish 5% or less of poetry manuscripts submitted. Reporting time: 6 months to 1 year. Payment: pre-publication payment, no royalties. Interested in new or unpub'd poets: no. Simultaneous submissions accepted: yes. Recently published poets: Pablo Neruda, Enrique Lihn. Submission quantity: 5. Special interests: Interest is in translations, will publish books bilingualy.

Hot Pepper Press (see also THE ACORN), PO Box 39, Somerset, CA 95684. 1991. Simultaneous submissions accepted: no.

HQ POETRY MAGAZINE (The Haiku Quarterly), 39 Exmouth Street, Swindon, Wilshire, SN1 3PU, England. 1990. circ. 1.2M. 3-4/yr. sub. price: £12 overseas; £9 UK; sample: £2.60. 56pp; size A5.

H2SO4, PO Box 423354, San Francisco, CA 94142, 415-431-2135, h2so4@socrates.berkeley.edu. Jill Stauffer. 1992. "We do not believe in having an ornately bordered 'poetry ghetto' page. If a work can stand on its own and assert itself, send it in" circ. 1M. 2/yr. Pub'd 6 poems 1999; expects 6 poems 2000, 6 poems 2001. sub. price: $8, $18/5 issues; sample: $4. 48pp; 8½×11; Publishes 15% of poems submitted. Deadlines: Mar 15 and Aug 15. Reporting time: 4 months. Payment: copies. Interested in new or unpub'd poets: yes. Simultaneous submissions accepted: no. Recent contributors: Jeff Gburek, Nanos Valaoritis, Stephen Ellis, Halliday Dresser, Franetta McMillian. Submission quantity: 1-5. Special interests: Obtain a sample copy for more information.

HUBBUB, 5344 S.E. 38th Avenue, Portland, OR 97202, 503-775-0370. Lisa Steinman, Jim Shugrue. 1983. "We are slower in responding during the summer; we do on occasion get 'backed up.' However, we will read manuscripts whenever they come in. We will not read multiple submissions or book-length manuscripts. Also, we cannot respond unless a SASE is enclosed. Beyond that, we look for poems that are strong—well crafted and with something to say." circ. 350. 1/yr. Pub'd 30 poems 1999; expects 40 poems 2000, 40 poems 2001. sub. price: $5; sample: $3.75. 70pp; 5½×8½; Rights purchased: copyright reverts to author. Publishes 5% of poems submitted. Deadlines: continuous. Reporting time: 1-3 months. Payment: 2 contributor copies. Interested in new or unpub'd poets: yes. Simultaneous submissions accepted: no. Recent contributors: Madeline DeFrees, Patricia Goedicke, Henri Cole, C.S. Giscombe, Shara McCallum. Submission quantity: no more than 6, preferably 3-4. Special interests: We do not rule out long poems, translations, etc. Though we are probably less likely to take light verse and satire, nothing is, in principle, ruled out.

THE HUDSON REVIEW, 684 Park Avenue, New York, NY 10021, 212-650-0020, fax 212-774-1911. 1948. circ. 4.5M. 4/yr. Pub'd 30 poems 1999. sub. price: $28 domestic, $32 foreign; sample: $8. 176pp; 4½×7½; Rights purchased: first. Deadlines: we read poetry from April 1 through July 31. Reporting time: 6-8 weeks. Payment: 50¢ per line. Interested in new or unpub'd poets: yes. Simultaneous submissions accepted: no. Recent contributors: David Mason, Dana Gioia, Maxine Kumin, Robert McDowell, Emily Grosholz. Submission quantity: no more than 8.

Hug The Earth Publications, 42 Greenwood Avenue, Pequannock, NJ 07440. Kenneth Lumpkin. 1980. "I am interested in doing broadsides for poets who want certain poems showcased. I have done a one-shot literary journal called *Hug the Earth, a Literary Journal of Land and Life*. Am accepting poetry and prose on the environment, nature, mythos, geography, land and life, etc. Same thing with the broadsides. Stylized broadsides with line art, pen & ink, prof. design, original art, etc., choice of fonts and stock, from helvetica to pepita to rice paper. The poetry could be called regional, since I am and always will be an ardent follower of Charles Olson. I am looking for poetry of place. I will publish unknown poets, but I am really seeking the work of established poets who want a real nice presentation made. I am also interested in poems on Magick and the occult'' avg. press run 500. Pub'd 2 poetry titles 1999; expects 2 poetry titles 2000, 2 poetry titles 2001. 4¼×5½; avg. price, paper: $5; other: $2.50 broadside. 40pp; Publishes 70% of poetry manuscripts submitted. Reporting time: 6 weeks. Payment: by arrangement. Interested in new or unpub'd poets: yes. Simultaneous submissions accepted: yes. Recently published poets: Kenneth Lumpkin, Charles Olson, Gary Snyder, E. Durling Merrill, Flavia Alaya. Submission quantity: at least 4, no more than 12.

●HUNGER, Hunger Press, PO Box 505, Rosendale, NY 12472, 914-658-9273, hungermag@aol.com, www.hungermagazine.com. J.J. Blickstein, Publisher & Editor; Susan G. McKechnie, Assitant Editor. 1997. *"Hunger* has no school/stylistic limit but has a preference or bent for forms of image/language experiments. We like translations and book reviews.'' circ. 300-600. 2/yr. sub. price: $14, $20 foreign; sample: $7, $10 foreign. 90pp; 8½×11; Publishes 10-15% of poems submitted. Reporting time: 3 days to 3 months depending on backlog. Payment: varies. Simultaneous submissions accepted: yes. Recent contributors: Clayton Eshleman, Paul Celan, Robert Kelly, Lyn Lifshin, Amiri Baraka. Submission quantity: 3-10 pages or poems.

●Hunger Press (see also HUNGER), PO Box 505, Rosendale, NY 12472, hungermag@aol.com, www.hungermagazine.com. J.J. Blickstein, Publisher & Editor; Susan G. McKechnie, Assistant Editor. 1997. "Hunger has no school/stylistic limits but has a preference or bent for forms of image/language experiments. We like translations and book reviews.'' avg. press run 300-600. Expects 2-3 poetry titles 2000, 2-3 poetry titles 2001. 4¼×5½; avg. price, paper: $4-$6. 24-40pp; Publishes 10-15% of poetry manuscripts submitted. Reporting time: 3 days - 3 months depending on backlog. Payment: varies. Simultaneous submissions accepted: yes. Recently published poets: Clayton Eshleman, Paul Celan, Robert Kelly, Lyn Lifshin, Amiri Baraka. Submission quantity: 3-10 pages or poems.

THE HUNTED NEWS, The Subourbon Press, PO Box 9101, Warwick, RI 02889, 401-739-2279. Mike Wood. 1991. ''My only suggestion is for the author to make sure he/she doesn't try to bullshit the audience. Conceit shows. Shock, be cool, be morbid, but only if it's relevant. If you *need* to write it, we'll *need* to read it.'' circ. 500+. 3-4/yr. Pub'd 60 poems 1999; expects 100 poems 2000. sub. price: free. 30-50pp; 8½×11; Publishes 15-20% of poems submitted. Deadlines: none. Reporting time: 1 month. Payment: copies. Interested in new or unpub'd poets: yes. Simultaneous submissions accepted: yes. Recent contributors: Thomas Vaultonburg, Mike Blake, Hal Sirowitz, Steve Richmond, Charles Bukowski. Submission quantity: 15-20. Special interests: Minimalist poetry, narrative poetry, prose poems, translations.

Huntsville Literary Association (see also POEM), c/o English Department, University of Alabama, Huntsville, AL 35899. Nancy F. Dillard, Editor; Olga Lavan, Assistant Editor. 1967. "In continuous publication since 1967, *Poem* welcomes all submissions of good poetry. We are open to traditional as well as non-traditional forms and we have no bias as to length so long as the work has the expected compression and intensity of good poetry. We have no bias as to subject matter or theme; however, we generally do favor poems that are about inspired sentiments earned from within the poem itself. We favor poems that have a high degree of verbal and dramatic tension, and that transpire from the particular to the universal. We welcome equally submissions from established poets as well as from less known and beginning poets. We do not accept translations or previously published works, nor do we consider simultaneous submissions. We have no requirements as to format, except that we prefer to see a sample of three to five poems at a submission and we require that all submissions be accompanied by a self-addressed, stamped envelope for response or return of manuscript. We generally respond within a month. We are a non-profitmaking organization and can pay only in copy to contributors. Sample copies are available at $5. Thank you for your interest.'' avg. press run 500. Pub'd 180 poetry titles 1999; expects 180 poetry titles 2000, 180 poetry titles 2001. 4½×7⅓; avg. price, paper: $5. 70pp; Publishes 10% of poetry manuscripts submitted. Reporting time: 1 month. Payment: 1 copy. Interested in new or unpub'd poets: yes. Simultaneous submissions accepted: no. Recently published poets: Charles Edward Eaton, Norman Nathan, Ronald Wallace, Michael McFee, Stephen Lang. Submission quantity: 3-5. Special interests: Do not publish translations or prose poems.

HURRICANE ALICE, Dept. of English, Rhode Island College, Providence, RI 02908. Joan Dagle, Submission Manager. 1983. "We are interested in poems written from a feminist perspective.'' circ. 1M. 4/yr. Pub'd 8 poems 1999; expects 8 poems 2000, 8 poems 2001. sub. price: $12; sample: $2.50. 16pp; 11×17; Rights purchased: First North American serial rights. We publish 10% or less of poems submitted. Deadlines: none. Reporting time: 6 months. Payment: 6 copies of the issue in which poem appears. Interested in new or unpub'd poets: yes. Simultaneous submissions accepted: yes, if noted. Recent contributors: Cathleen Calbert,

Marjorie Roemer, Nancy Harvey, Sarah Miller. Submission quantity: no more than 3.

Hutton Publications (see also MYSTERY TIME ANTHOLOGY; RHYME TIME POETRY NEWSLETTER), Po Box 2907, Decatur, IL 62524. Linda Hutton. 1983. "Do *not* telephone us—send poems with an SASE." 8½×11. Publishes 10% of poetry manuscripts submitted. Reporting time: 1 month. Interested in new or unpub'd poets: yes. Simultaneous submissions accepted: yes. Recently published poets: Jane Sherwood, Penny Hurley Turner, Melinda Weber. Submission quantity: 3-4.

I

●**IBBETSON ST. PRESS, Ibbetson St. Press**, 33 Ibbetson Street, Somerville, MA 02143, e-mail p99264@hotmail.com. Doug Holder, Dianne Robitaille, Richard Wilhelm, Art Director. 1999. "Please tell us something about yourself" circ. 100. 4/yr. Pub'd 160 poems 1999. sub. price: $7; sample: $4. 20pp; Rights purchased: 1st time. Publishes 40% of poems submitted. Deadlines: May, Aug., Nov. Reporting time: 1-3 months. Payment: 1 copy. Interested in new or unpub'd poets: yes. Simultaneous submissions accepted: yes. Recent contributors: Dianne Robitaille, Don DiVecchio, Robert K. Johnson, Joanne Holdridge, Sue Sullivan. Submission quantity: 3-5. Special interests: Free verse that deals with character study, urban scenes, but we look at everything.

Ibbetson St. Press (see also IBBETSON ST. PRESS), 33 Ibbetson Street, Somerville, MA 02143, e-mail p99264@hotmail.com. 1999.

IBEX Publishers, PO Box 30087, Bethesda, MD 20824, 301-718-8188, FAX 301-907-8707. 1979. "Poetry published is in Persian, translated from Persian or by Iranian author." Interested in new or unpub'd poets: no.

IBIS REVIEW, PO Box 133, Falls Village, CT 06031, 203-824-0355. 1995. "Address poetry submissions 'Attn: Poetry Editor.'" circ. 500. 1/yr. Pub'd 40 poems 1999; expects 50 poems 2000, 60 poems 2001. sub. price: $8.95; sample: $8.95. 116pp; 5½×8½; Rights purchased: Single publication-author maintain copyright-acknowledgement in succeeding publications. Publishes 15% of poems submitted. Deadlines: Jan-April 30. Reporting time: end of June. Payment: 2 copies. Interested in new or unpub'd poets: yes. Simultaneous submissions accepted: yes. Recent contributors: James Laughlin, Simon Perchik, Brian A Connelly, John Briggs, Dorthy Blackcrow Mack. Submission quantity: up to 5. Special interests: New and established poets, conemporary-formalist-we're open!

ICARUS WAS RIGHT, Itidwitir Publishing, PO Box 13731, Salem, OR 97309-1731, 619-461-0497; icaruswas@pobox.com. 1995. circ. 3M. 4/yr. sub. price: $8; sample: $3. 120pp; 8⅛×10¾.

ICON, KSU-TC, 4314 Mahoning Avenue NW, Warren, OH 44483, 330-847-0571. Rachel Mathis. 1966. "Submissions should be typed or word processed in a standard typeface. We do not read during the summer. We host a local reading series." circ. 1M. 2/yr. Pub'd 60 poems 1999; expects 60 poems 2000, 60 poems 2001. sub. price: $6; sample: $3. 50pp; 5½×8½; Rights purchased: first international. Publishes 5-10% of poems submitted. Deadlines: April 1 for Spring, November 1 for Fall. Reporting time: 3-6 months. Payment: 1 copy. Interested in new or unpub'd poets: yes. Simultaneous submissions accepted: Yes.Withdrawals must be made 1 week prior to press date. Recent contributors: Yvonne V. Sapia, Robert Cooperman, Carolyn Moore, Erroll Miller.

THE ICONOCLAST, 1675 Amazon Road, Mohegan Lake, NY 10547-1804. Phil Wagner. 1992. "Revision is as important as inspiration. Please no more than one submission per month" circ. 600-3M. 8/yr. Pub'd 80 poems 1999; expects 90 poems 2000, 90 poems 2001. sub. price: $13/8 issues; sample: $2. 40pp; 5½×8; Rights purchased: one-time serial. Publishes 2% of poems submitted. Deadlines: none. Reporting time: 2 weeks - 2 months. Payment: 1 copy, additional copies 40% off (subscribers receive $2-5/poem on acceptance). Interested in new or unpub'd poets: yes, if conforming to submission practices. Simultaneous submissions accepted: yes, if noted. Recent contributors: Reeves M. Marcus, Anselm Brocki, Nelson James Dunford, Ben Wilensky, Gerald Kaminski. Submission quantity: 3-4.

IDIOM 23, Central Queensland University, Rockhampton, Queensland, 4702, Australia, 0011-079-360655. Geof. Donoher. 1988. circ. 500. 2/yr. Pub'd 40 poems 1999. sub. price: Aus $10. 90pp; 8¾×11¾; Rights purchased: none. Publishes 33% of poems submitted. Reporting time: 1 month. Payment: $10 (Aust.) per poem. Interested in new or unpub'd poets: yes. Simultaneous submissions accepted: yes. Recent contributors: Silvana Gardiner, Jena Woodhouse, Bill Scott, R.J. Hay, Anne Lloyd. Submission quantity: 2-3. Special interests: Experimental poetry, regional poetry, light verse, satire.

IDIOT WIND, PO Box 87, Occoquan, VA 22125, 703-494-1897 evenings. Douglas Carroll, Chief Editor. 1984. "We frequently describe ouselves as National-Lampoon-esque. But only because people hat it when we turn a word or phrase into an adjective by tacking-esque on the end of it. We've even started doing theme issues, so write us for a schedule upcoming issue themes. We prefer poems that rhyme or parody other poetry that stays on topic with whatever theme we are doing for that particular issue. We can be reached by email at idiotwind@radix.net" circ. 100-200. 4/yr. Pub'd 3 poems 1999; expects 4 poems 2000, 4 poems 2001. sub. price: free; sample: free. 16+pp; 5½x8½; Deadlines: Mar 15, June 15, Sept 15, Dec 15. Reporting time: 4 weeks. Payment: copies. Interested in new or unpub'd poets: yes. Simultaneous submissions accepted: yes. Submission quantity: up to 10. Special interests: Satire and parodies on current events and subjects on topic with whatever theme we're tackling that issue. Write or email for details on future themes.

IGNIS FATUUS REVIEW, 18 Yuma Trail, Bisbee, AZ 85603. Nadine McInerney. 1991. "Editor does not like rhyme" circ. 150. 4/yr. Pub'd 80-100 poems 1999; expects 80-100 poems 2000, 80-100 poems 2001. sub. price: $16; sample: $4. 24pp; 8½x11; Rights purchased: one time use. Publishes 10% of poems submitted. Deadlines: none. Reporting time: 90 days. Payment: 1 copy of issue they are in. Interested in new or unpub'd poets: yes, but nothing amataur. Recent contributors: Nadine Kachur, Dick Bakken, Margueritte, August Schafer, Tod McCartney. Submission quantity: 4-6. Special interests: Not light verse.

ILLINOIS ARCHITECTURAL & HISTORICAL REVIEW, 202 South Plum, Havana, IL 62644, 309-543-4644. Gene Fehler, Poetry Editor. Address poetry submissions to: 106 Laurel Lane, Seneca, SC 29678. 1993. "Poems must relate to Illinois, especially its history, architecture, and/or historical figures. Maximum length: 40 lines." circ. 12M. 4/yr. Pub'd 16-20 poems 1999. sub. price: $20; sample: free. 96-104pp; 8½x11; Rights purchased: none. Deadlines: Feb. 1, May 1, Aug. 1, Nov. 1. Payment: copies. Interested in new or unpub'd poets: yes. Simultaneous submissions accepted: yes. Recent contributors: Kennette H. Wilkes, Gus Wentz, Sheryl Minter, Kate Buckley, Dianne Henderson. Submission quantity: 5. Special interests: regional poetry.

ILLUMINATIONS, English Dept., 66 George Street, College of Charleston, Charleston, SC 29424-0001. Simon Lewis, Editor. 1982. "*Illuminations* attempts to assist new and unestablished writers by publishing them with more recognized writers. But we are looking for serious writers. Recent issues have featured writings from South and East Africa." circ. 500. 1/yr. Pub'd 60 poems 1999; expects 60 poems 2000, 60 poems 2001. sub. price: $20/3 issues; sample: $10. 60pp; 6½x9, 5x8; Rights purchased: none. Publishes 1% of poems submitted. Deadlines: 2 months prior to publication of each issue. Reporting time: 2-3 months. Payment: none, save in subscription. Interested in new or unpub'd poets: yes. Simultaneous submissions accepted: no. Recent contributors: Seamus Heaney, Joseph Brodsky, James Dickey, Charles Wright, James Merrill. Submission quantity: no more than 6, at least 2-3. Special interests: Especially interested in translations from any language. The poetry of new writers, and unestablished writers. We like poems with something worthwhile to say, but pre-eminent is an acute awareness of the possibilities of sound and language.

ILLYA'S HONEY, PO Box 225435, Dallas, TX 75222. Members of the Dallas Poets Community. 1994. "Do include cover letter with brief bio and SASE for notification." circ. 125. 4/yr. Pub'd 80 poems 1999; expects 80 poems 2000, 80 poems 2001. sub. price: $18; sample: $5 + $1 p/h. 24pp; 5½x8½; Rights purchased: none. Publishes 5% of poems submitted. Deadlines: none. Reporting time: 3-5 months. Payment: 1 copy. Interested in new or unpub'd poets: no. Simultaneous submissions accepted: no. Recent contributors: Lyn Lifshin, Lisa Yun, Nancy McGovern, Clebo Rainey. Submission quantity: 3-5. Special interests: We are partial to free verse.

IMAGO, Queensland Univ Technology, School of Media and Journalism, PO Box 2434, Brisbane Q1D 4001, Australia, (07)864 2976, FAX (07)864 1810. Philip Neilsen, Associate Professor; Helen Horton. 1988. circ. 500. 3/yr. Pub'd 61 poems 1999; expects 60 poems 2000, 60 poems 2001. sub. price: $A40 (includes airmail postage overseas). 140-160pp; 7x9¾; Rights purchased: First Australian serial rights. Publishes a variable % of poems submitted. Deadlines: none. Reporting time: 3-6 months. Payment: at editor's discretion. Interested in new or unpub'd poets: yes. Simultaneous submissions accepted: no. Recent contributors: Bruce Dawe, Chris Mansell, Thomas Shapcott, Geoff Page. Submission quantity: up to 6.

IMPETUS, Implosion Press, 4975 Comanche Trail, Stow, OH 44224, 216-688-5210 phone/Fax, E-mail impetus@aol.com. Cheryl A. Townsend, Editor-in-Chief. 1984. "Annual *female* only issue and *erotica* issue. Know the magazine first. *I do not* publish nature poetry or the like. Send the sugar elsewhere! Would appreciate knowing where referral came from. Do not fold poems separately and make sure that name and address are on each page!" circ. 1M. 4/yr. Pub'd 500 poems 1999; expects 600 poems 2000, 800 poems 2001. sub. price: $15, $20; sample: $5. 100pp; 7x8½; Rights purchased: first. Publishes 5% of poems submitted. Deadlines: ongoing. Reporting time: 4 months. Payment: copy of issue of appearance. Interested in new or unpub'd poets: yes. Simultaneous submissions accepted: no. Recent contributors: Lyn Lifshin, Sherman Alexie, Ron Androla. Submission quantity: no limit. Special interests: Social protest, radical, energetic, odd, erotica, experimental, what general markets usually find/hold taboo, poetry that is driven.

THE IMPLODING TIE-DYED TOUPEE, Burning Llama Press, 82 Ridge Lake Drive, Columbia, SC 29209-4213. Keith Higginbotham, Editor; Tracy R. Combs, Editor. 1993. "SASE and cover letter required" circ. 100-300. 1-2/yr. Pub'd 100 poems 1999; expects 100 poems 2000, 100 poems 2001. sub. price: $7; sample: $4. 40pp; 5½x8½; Publishes 1% of poems submitted. Deadlines: ongoing. Reporting time: immediate to 3 months. Payment: copies. Interested in new or unpub'd poets: yes. Simultaneous submissions accepted: no. Recent contributors: John M. Bennett, Sheila E. Murphy, Susan Smith Nash, Dan Raphael. Submission quantity: 3-10. Special interests: Dada, surreal, experimental.

Implosion Press (see also IMPETUS), 4975 Comanche Trail, Stow, OH 44224, 216-688-5210 phone/Fax, E-mail impetus@aol.com. Cheryl A. Townsend, Editor-in-Chief. 1984. "I generally only invite for my chapbook series, but wouldn't want to miss out on a good book, so I am always open for new writers." avg. press run 500. Pub'd 4 poetry titles 1999; expects 4 poetry titles 2000, 4 poetry titles 2001. 8½x7; avg. price, paper: $4. 24pp; Publishes 2% of poetry manuscripts submitted. Reporting time: within 4 months. Payment: 20 copies of chapbook, discount on additional orders (1/2 price). Interested in new or unpub'd poets: yes. Simultaneous submissions accepted: no. Recently published poets: Lyn Lifshin, Belinda Subraman, Lonnie Sherman, Ron Androla, Bill Shields. Submission quantity: up to 10. Special interests: I am into more radical writing, social protest and strong emotions.

INDEFINITE SPACE, PO Box 40101, Pasadena, CA 91114. Marcia Arrieta, Kevin Joy. 1992. circ. 2M. 1/yr. sub. price: $8; sample: $5. 40pp; 5½x8½; Rights purchased: poets retain rights. Publishes an unknown % of poems submitted. Reporting time: 1-2 months. Payment: 1 copy. Simultaneous submissions accepted: yes. Recent contributors: John Perlman, Harry Polkinhorn, Sheila Murphy, Marton Koppany, Dan Campion. Submission quantity: 5-7.

THE INDIAN WRITER, 1-A, 59 Ormes Road, Chennai 600010, India, 6261370, 6284421. Dr. P.K. Joy, Editor. 1986. "We publish short poems and articles on mechanics of writings and news about national and international literary activities" circ. 750. 4/yr. Pub'd 48 poems 1999. sub. price: $20; sample: free. 16pp; size A4; Rights purchased: rights remain with authors. Publishes 10% of poems submitted. Deadlines: none. Reporting time: 2 months. Payment: none. Interested in new or unpub'd poets: yes. Simultaneous submissions accepted: yes. Submission quantity: 3-5.

INDIANA REVIEW, Ballantine Hall 465, Indiana Univ., 1020 E. Kirkwood Avenue, Bloomington, IN 47405, 812-855-3439. 1976. "We read manuscripts through the entire year. All manuscripts must be accompanied by proper SASE for reply. Please submit to Poetry Editor. Manuscripts read slower in summer." circ. 1.7M. 2/yr. Pub'd 80 poems 1999; expects 80 poems 2000, 80 poems 2001. sub. price: $14, institutions $18, please add $6 for overseas; sample: $8. 200pp; 6x9; Rights purchased: 1st North American. Publishes less than 5% of poems submitted. Deadlines: ongoing. Reporting time: 2 weeks to 2 months. Payment: $5 per page of poetry, $10 minimum. Interested in new or unpub'd poets: yes. Simultaneous submissions accepted: yes. Recent contributors: Heather McHugh, Lucia Perillo, Bob Hicok, Dean Young, Belle Waring. Submission quantity: 3-5. Special interests: Lyrical poems, prose poems, and some long poems. Mainly, however, we are most interested in the quality of language.

The Infinity Group, PO Box 2713, Castro Valley, CA 94546, 510-581-8172; kenandgenie@yahoo.com. 1987. 4¼x6¾.

INKY TRAIL NEWS, 70 Macomb Place, #226, Mt. Clemens, MI 48043, e-mail inkytrails@prodigy.net. 1993. circ. 1M. 6/yr. sub. price: $15; sample: $3. 24pp; 11x13.

INNER VOICES: A New Journal of Prison Literature, PO Box 4500 #219, Bloomington, IN 47402. Williams. 1993. "Poetry and other creative writing by prisoners. (Please help us to ensure that *Inner Voices* will be available to other prisoners by avoiding censorable material.) Short personal or biographical statements are welcome; Pen names OK." circ. 200. 2/yr. Pub'd 70 poems 1999. sub. price: $10 institutions, $8 individuals, $5 prisoners, free to contributors; sample: $5. 50pp; 5½x8½; Rights purchased: one-time publication. Reporting time: varies. Payment: copies. Interested in new or unpub'd poets: yes. Simultaneous submissions accepted: no. Submission quantity: 1-5.

Insomniac Press, 393 Shaw Street, Toronto, ON, M6J 2X4, Canada, 416-536-4308. Mike O'Connor. 1992. "Looking for new, hip poetry that works with graphic design" avg. press run 1M. Pub'd 2 poetry titles 1999; expects 4 poetry titles 2000, 4 poetry titles 2001. 6x9; avg. price, paper: $9.99-$10.99. 96-128pp; Reporting time: 8 weeks. Payment: royalty. Interested in new or unpub'd poets: yes. Simultaneous submissions accepted: yes. Recently published poets: Jill Battson, Stan Rogal, Tatiana Lizaman, Matthew Remski, Noah Leznoff. Submission quantity: 10-12. Special interests: Canadian - performance poetry - prose poetry.

INTERBANG, PO Box 1574, Venice, CA 90294, 310-450-6372. Heather Hoffman. 1995. "Please write your name and address on each page of your submission. 'In literature, we require distinction, charm, beauty, and imaginative power'- Oscar Wilde" circ. 2M. 4/yr. Pub'd 24 poems 1999; expects 48 poems 2000, 48 poems

2001. sub. price: $8; sample: $2. 28pp; 8½×7; Rights purchased: none. Publishes 25% of poems submitted. Deadlines: always accepting submissions. Reporting time: 3-4 months. Payment: multiple copies of issue and an *Interbang* t-shirt. Interested in new or unpub'd poets: yes. Simultaneous submissions accepted: yes. Recent contributors: Allison Lubas, Rob Lipton, David Centorbi. Submission quantity: 10-15. Special interests: *Interbang* places no restrictions on length or content. Writers interested in submitting can request a free issue of *Interbang*.

INTERIM, Department of English, University of Nevada, Las Vegas, Las Vegas, NV 89154-5011, 702-895-3172. James Hazen, Editor; Timothy Erwin, Associate Editor; Claudia Keelan, Associate Editor; John Heath-Stubbs, English Editor. 1944 (now revived 1986 with Vol. 5, No. 1). "We want the best poetry we can get (no limitations on form). Old copies from earlier *Interim* amd individuals on sale for libraries on request." circ. 700. 1/yr. Pub'd 80-100 poems 1999. sub. price: $7/yr; $12/2 yrs; $15/3 yrs; sample: $7. 100pp; 6×9; Rights purchased: first serial rights. Publishes 2% of poems submitted. Deadlines: none. Reporting time: 2 months. Payment: contributor's copies plus a 2-year subscription. Interested in new or unpub'd poets: yes. Simultaneous submissions accepted: no. Recent contributors: X.J. Kennedy, Robert Cooperman, Walter McDonald, Anca Vlasopolus, Stephen Stepanchev. Submission quantity: 3-6; never just 1, unless it is a long poem.

Interim Press, 3 Thornton Close, Budleigh Salterton, Devon EX9 6PJ, England, (0395) 445231. Peter Dent. 1975. "Strongly image based, concise modern poetry." avg. press run 250. Expects 1 poetry title 2000. 5¾×8¾; avg. price, paper: £3. 24-40pp; Publishes 10% of poetry manuscripts submitted. Reporting time: 2 weeks. Payment: copies. Interested in new or unpub'd poets: no. Simultaneous submissions accepted: no. Recently published poets: Daud Kamal, Lorine Niedecker, Allen Upward, Tom A. Clark, George Oppen. Submission quantity: 6-12. Special interests: Lyrics, translations, versions.

INTERNATIONAL OLYMPIC LIFTER, 3562 Eagle Rock Boulevard, Los Angeles, CA 90065-2827, 213-257-8762. Dale Rhoades. 1973. "Poets have to know our magazine. (The Olympic sport of weight lifting). We do not publish poems about muscle flexing, pumping iron, power lifting, physique, weight training. ONLY - Olympic style weight lifting, lifters, their trials, tribulations, etc. Prefer rhyming verse but do publish some free verse. Don't exceed 40 lines" circ. 3M. 6/yr. Pub'd 1-2 poems 1999; expects 1-2 poems 2000, 1-2 poems 2001. sub. price: $28 1st class, $40 foreign air; sample: $4. 36pp; 8½×11; Rights purchased: only publication. Publishes 80% of poems submitted. Deadlines: none. Reporting time: when published. Payment: $10-$25. Interested in new or unpub'd poets: yes. Simultaneous submissions accepted: yes. Recent contributors: Herb Glossbrenner, Dale Rhoades, Keith Cain, Amy Hazelton, Ron Hall. Submission quantity: up to 3.

INTERNATIONAL POETRY REVIEW, Dept of Romance Languages, The University of North Carolina at Greensboro, Greensboro, NC 27412-5001, 336-334-5655. Mark Smith-Soto, Editor. 1975. "Reading period: Sept. 1-April 30" circ. 400. 2/yr. Pub'd 100 poems 1999; expects 100 poems 2000. sub. price: $10 individuals; $15 libraries, institutions; sample: $5. 100pp; 5½×8½; Publishes 2% of poems submitted. Reporting time: 3 months. Payment: copies. Interested in new or unpub'd poets: yes. Simultaneous submissions accepted: yes, but poet must so indicate. Recent contributors: Ana Istaru, Alexis Levitin, Jorge Teillier, Mary Crow, Fred Chappell. Submission quantity: 5. Special interests: We print primarily translations of contemporary poetry in any language. Send originals for bilingual format. Original English - language poetry should perferably have a cross-cultural or international: Moral dimension.

INTERNATIONAL QUARTERLY, PO Box 10521, Tallahassee, FL 32302-0521, 904-224-5078. Andrea Kelly, Poetry Editor. 1993. "Sponsor an annual contest called Crossing Boundaries with four categories, $500 prize in each category: fiction, essay, poetry, Crossing Boundaries. Send SASE for guidelines. Upcoming themes for Volume 3: Surrealism, the Artist & the Secret Police, Unity/Disunity, Food & Hunger." circ. 2M. 4/yr. Pub'd 66 poems 1999. sub. price: $30 worldwide; sample: $6 postpaid. 160pp; 7½×10; Rights purchased: first serial (for English) or first English translation serial rights. Publishes 5% of poems submitted. Deadlines: open, unless designated for special issues. Reporting time: 2-4 months. Payment: subscription and extra copies of issue published in. Interested in new or unpub'd poets: yes. Simultaneous submissions accepted: yes. Recent contributors: Bei Dao, Anna Akhmatora, Angles Gergeley, David Bottoms. Submission quantity: 3-6. Special interests: translations, experimental, short genres, multi-cultural, and regional. Work with a personal flair.

Intertext, 149 Water Street #35, Norwalk, CT 06854. Sharon Ann Jaeger, Editor. 1982. "1. We are looking for poetry with intensity, striking insight, vivid imagery, fresh and compelling metaphor, simplicity and elegance, musical use of language in both word sounds and rhythm. The work must make the world come alive for the readers. 2. The poets whose work I most respect and admire include Louis Hammer, William Stafford, Wallace Stevens, A.R. Ammons, Antonio Ramos Rosa, Rainer Maria Rilke, and Sarah Kirsch. 3. Submissions without SASE will not be returned—no matter how 'famous' the writer. Do not submit an entire MS unless asked to do so, please. As we have several projects in progress, we will not be able to consider unsolicited material until 2001." avg. press run 300-1M. Pub'd 2 poetry titles 1999; expects 2 poetry titles 2000. avg. price, cloth: $25; paper: $15; other: Limited editions, about $25. Poems needed, 48-96; Publishes less than 1% of poetry manuscripts submitted. Reporting time: 3-6 months. Payment: in copies only in future; 10% of print run. No, we're only interested in receiving manuscripts from excellent writers with a track record. Simultaneous submissions accepted: no, but simultaneous queries OK with SASE, please. Recently published poets: James Hanlen, Louis Hammer, Brenda Jaeger, Kyi May Kaung. Submission quantity: 3-5 only in a 1st-Class envelope with SASE, cover letter optional. Special interests: Prefer metaphorically rich poetry, whether surrealist or realist. No political satire or light verse. Cannot use religious verse.

INTUITIVE EXPLORATIONS, PO Box 561, Quincy, IL 62306-0561, 217-222-9082. 1987. circ. 1M+. 6/yr. sub. price: $15; sample: $3. 12-24pp; 8½×11.

IOTA, 67 Hady Crescent, Chesterfield, Derbyshire S41 0EB, Great Britain, 01246-276532. David Holliday. 1988. "Looking for good, well-crafted verse that says something; light verse appreciated; concrete (no facilities) and scatological (no time) out, otherwise anything goes." circ. 450. 4/yr. Pub'd 284 poems 1999; expects 280 poems 2000, 280 poems 2001. sub. price: $15 (add $10 if by cheque); sample: $2. 48pp; 5¾×8¼ (A5); Rights purchased: First British serial. Publishes 5% of poems submitted. Deadlines: any time. Reporting time: first assessment, usually a couple of weeks; but a final decision may take months. Payment: 2 complimentary copies. Interested in new or unpub'd poets: yes. Simultaneous submissions accepted: yes. Recent contributors: Ian Caws, Edmund Harwood, Edmund Prestwich, K.V. Skene, Marcus Smith. Submission quantity: up to half a dozen. Special interests: Almost anything goes, but shorter poems preferred (for reasons of space).

THE IOWA REVIEW, 308 EPB, Univ. Of Iowa, Iowa City, IA 52242, 319-335-0462. David Hamilton, Mary Hussmann, Editor. 1970. circ. 1.5M. 3/yr. Pub'd 85-100 poems 1999. sub. price: instit. $20 (+$3 outside US), indiv. $18 (+$3 outside US); sample: $6 for most recent issue. 192pp; 6×9; Rights purchased: rights revert to author upon publication, first North American serial rights and nonexclusive electronic. Publishes between 2%-3% of poems submitted. Deadlines: read from September 1 through January 31. Reporting time: 6-10 weeks. Payment: $25 minimum or $1 per line. Interested in new or unpub'd poets: yes. Simultaneous submissions accepted: yes. Recent contributors: Gary Soto, James Laughlin, James Tate, Chase Twichell, Frankie Paino. Submission quantity: 4-6.

IPSISSIMA VERBA/THE VERY WORDS: Fiction & Poetry in the First Person, 32 Forest Street, New Britain, CT 06052, fax 860-832-9566; e-mail: ipsiverba@aol.com. P.D. Jordan. 1989. "All poetry *must* be written in the first person singular!" 2/yr, with occasional "special" issues. Expects 16 poems 2000, 25-30 poems 2001. sub. price: $15; sample: $6. 60pp; 8½×11; Rights purchased: one time. Reporting time: 1 month. Payment: copies now, will go to $ in future. Interested in new or unpub'd poets: yes. Simultaneous submissions accepted: no. Recent contributors: Laurel Speer, Ron Watson, Tony Lewis-Jones. Submission quantity: up to 10.

IRIS: A Journal About Women, Box 323, HSC, University of Virginia, Charlottesville, VA 22908, 804-924-4500; iris@virginia.edu. Margo Figgins, Poetry Editor. 1980. "Upcoming themes: Money, the South (poetry need not relate to themes)." circ. 4M. 2/yr. Pub'd 24 poems 1999. sub. price: $9; sample: $5. 72pp; 8½×11; Rights purchased: 1st rights only, copyright reverts to author. Publishes 5% of poems submitted. Deadlines: we read all year long. Reporting time: 3 months. Payment: 1 year subscription. Interested in new or unpub'd poets: yes. Simultaneous submissions accepted: yes. Recent contributors: Liliana Ursu, Naomi Shihab Nye, Gregory Orr, Linda Pastan, Lisel Mueller. Submission quantity: 5 or less. Special interests: poetry by or about or of interest to women.

IRISH JOURNAL, 577 Central Avenue, Box 4, Jefferson, LA 70121-1400, e-mail irishrose@cmpnet-mail.com, rose.dalton@edmail.com; websites www.fortunecity.com/bally/harp/189/, www2.cybercities.com/z/zines/. Sharida Rizzuto, Rose Dalton. 1983. "All poems must be about the Irish, culturally, historically, etc." circ. 300-500. 2/yr. Pub'd 30 poems 1999; expects 30 poems 2000, 30 poems 2001. sub. price: $11.80; sample: $5.80. 60pp; 8½×11; Rights purchased: one-time rights, first serial rights, or second serial rights. Publishes 30-35% of poems submitted. Deadlines: always open. Reporting time: 2-6 weeks. Payment: free copy only. Interested in new or unpub'd poets: yes. Simultaneous submissions accepted: yes. Recent contributors: Rose Dalton, Ann Hoyt, Lucinda MacGregor.

Irish Studies, 2592 N Wading River Road, Wading River, NY 11792-1404, 516-929-0224.

●**IRON HORSE LITERARY REVIEW,** Texas Tech University, English Dept., PO Box 43091, Lubbock, TX 79409-3091, 806-742-2500 X234. William Wenthe, Poetry Editor. 1999. "We read from August 1 - May 1. Please include SASE" circ. 500. 2/yr. Expects 40 poems 2000, 40 poems 2001. sub. price: $12; sample: $5. 180pp; 6×9; Rights purchased: 1st time NA serial. Publishes 1% of poems submitted. Reporting time: 3 months. Payment: $40 per poem. Interested in new or unpub'd poets: yes. Simultaneous submissions accepted: yes. Recent contributors: Henry Taylor, Kelly Cherry, David Wagoner, Robert Cooperman, Sydney Lea. Submission quantity: 3-5.

Irvington St. Press, Inc., 3439 NE Sandy Boulevard #143, Portland, OR 97232, E-mail; pdxia@aol.com. Tami Parr, Ce Rosenour. Address poetry submissions to: 3439 NE Sandy Boulevard #174, Portland, OR 97232. 1992. Pub'd 2 poetry titles 1999; expects 2 poetry titles 2000, 2 poetry titles 2001. Reporting time: 1-2 months. Payment: per author. Simultaneous submissions accepted: no. Recently published poets: Walt Curtis, Laura Winter, Peter Sears, Susan Denning, Tim Barnes. Submission quantity: 6 max.

Island Publishers, Box 201, Anacortes, WA 98221-0201, 206-293-3285/293-5398. Thelma Palmer, Delphine Haley. 1985. "The *Sacred Round* is our first book. Our second book will probably be a book on sea mammals. We may or may not publish more poetry. At the present we are not soliciting poetry manuscripts." avg. press run 1M. Pub'd 1 poetry title 1999. avg. price, paper: $7.95. 66pp; Reporting time: 1 month. Payment: inquire. Interested in new or unpub'd poets: yes. Simultaneous submissions accepted: yes.

ISRAEL HORIZONS, 114 W. 26th Street #1001, New York, NY 10001-6812, 212-868-0377; FAX 212-868-0364. Rochelle Ratner, Poetry Consultant; Jonathan Shevin, Poetry Consultant. 1952. "Judaism and contemporary Jewish identity, culture and ethics, Israel, women, 3rd world issues, democratic socialism are topics we cover in our articles and poetry should in some way be connected. Poems should be no longer than 1 page!" circ. 3M-5M. 4/yr. Pub'd 12 poems 1999; expects 8 poems 2000, 12 poems 2001. sub. price: $15; sample: $4. 36pp; 8½×11; Publishes 10% of poems submitted. Deadlines: none. Reporting time: open. Payment: 5-10 free copies of issue. Interested in new or unpub'd poets: yes. Simultaneous submissions accepted: yes, if notified. Recent contributors: Carole Glickfeld, Willa Schneberg, Leah Goldberg, Alex Cigale, Joseph Benari. Submission quantity: 1-5. Special interests: Translations (with original versions), longpoems, satire.

ISSUES, PO Box 424885, San Francisco, CA 94142-4885, 415-864-4800 X136. Susan Perlman. 1978. circ. 40M. 6/yr. Pub'd 6 poems 1999; expects 8 poems 2000, 8 poems 2001. sub. price: free; sample: 50¢. 8-12pp; 8½×11; Rights purchased: 1st publication. Publishes 10% of poems submitted. Reporting time: 2-3 weeks. Payment: varies. Interested in new or unpub'd poets: yes. Simultaneous submissions accepted: yes. Recent contributors: Sheldon Sher, Melissa Moskowitz, Gary Gach, Stewart Henderson. Submission quantity: up to 3. Special interests: Poetry using Judaic imagery dealing with spiritual matters from a Jewish/Christian perspective and Jewish holiday themes.

ITALIAN AMERICANA, University of Rhode Island, 80 Washington Street, Providence, RI 02903-1803. Dana Gioia, Poetry editor. 1974. "No nostalgia poetry" circ. 2.5M. 2/yr. Pub'd 8 poems 1999; expects 30 poems 2000, 30 poems 2001. sub. price: $20 indiv., $22.50 instit., $15 student, $35 foreign; sample: $7. 150pp; 6×9; Rights purchased: first rights. Publishes 15% of poems submitted. Deadlines: none; none read during July, August, September. Reporting time: 4-6 weeks. Payment: free copy. Interested in new or unpub'd poets: yes. Simultaneous submissions accepted: no. Recent contributors: Peggy Rizza Ellsberg, Ned Condini, Lewis Turco, Cynthia Tedesco, Felix Stefanile. Submission quantity: 3 poems.

Italica Press, Inc., 595 Main Street, #605, New York, NY 10044, 212-935-4230; fax 212-838-7812; inquiries@italicapress.com. Ronald G. Musto, Eileen Gardiner. 1985. "We specialize in publishing English translations of Italian (and Latin) authors from Middle Ages to present." avg. press run 1M. Expects 1 poetry title 2000, 1 poetry title 2001. 5½×8½; avg. price, paper: $15. 200pp; Publishes 5% of poetry manuscripts submitted. Reporting time: 6 weeks. Payment: approx. royalty 10% net sales. Interested in new or unpub'd poets: no. Simultaneous submissions accepted: yes. Recently published poets: Guido Cavalcanti, Gaspara Stampa. Special interests: Italian and medieval and Renaissance Latin literature.

Itidwitir Publishing (see also ICARUS WAS RIGHT), PO Box 13731, Salem, OR 97309-1731, 619-461-0497; icaruswas@pobox.com. 1994.

J

J & J Consultants, Inc. (see also NEW ALTERNATIVES), 603 Olde Farm Road, Media, PA 19063, 610-565-9692, Fax 610-565-9694, wjones13@juno.com, www.members.tripod.com/walterjones/. 1997. 5½×8½.

THE J MAN TIMES, 2246 Saint Francis Drive #A-211, Ann Arbor, MI 48104-4828, E-mail TheJMan99@aol.com. J. Rassoul. 1994. circ. 100. 3/yr. Pub'd 15 poems 1999; expects 15 poems 2000, 15 poems 2001. sub. price: $3; sample: $1. 20pp; 5½×8½; Rights purchased: none. Publishes 35% of poems submitted. Reporting time: 1 week. Payment: 1 copy of issue published in. Interested in new or unpub'd poets: yes. Simultaneous submissions accepted: yes. Recent contributors: Holly Day, Dan Buck, Amy Ware.

Submission quantity: 1-5.

J. Mark Press (see also POETS' VOICE), Box 742-052, Boynton Beach, FL 33474-7902, website www.worldtv3.com/jmark.htm. 1963. 7×8½.

JACARANDA, English Department, California State Univ—Fullerton, Fullerton, CA 92634, 714-773-3163. Laurence Roth, Poetry Editor. 1984. "We have two poetry contests per year, one for each issue, each judged by a major poet. $500 worth of prizes are available for each contest. Contestants may send as may poems as they like. There is a $3 reading fee per poem. With 4 poems entered, the contestant receives a free year's subscription to *Jacaranda*" circ. 1.5M. 2/yr. Pub'd 70 poems 1999; expects 60 poems 2000, 60 poems 2001. sub. price: $10; sample: $6. 160pp; 5½×8; Rights purchased: rights revert to author upon publication. Publishes 1-2% of poems submitted. Deadlines: Spring/Summer issue 3/15, Fall/Winter 10/31. Reporting time: 10-12 weeks. Payment: 3 copies plus 20% discount on additional copies. Interested in new or unpub'd poets: yes. Simultaneous submissions accepted: yes. Recent contributors: Carolyn Forche, Heather McHugh, Charles Bukowski, David St. John, Wanda Coleman. Submission quantity: no more than 6.

JACK MACKEREL MAGAZINE, Rowhouse Press, PO Box 23134, Seattle, WA 98102-0434. Greg Bachar, Editor. 1994. "We publish serializations of ongoing long poems, chapbooks and mini chapbooks, books of poetry, and occasional poetry posters which are put up all over town" circ. 500-1M. 4/yr. sub. price: $12; sample: $5. 40-60pp; 8½×11; Rights purchased: none. Deadlines: ongoing. Reporting time: 1 month or less. Payment: copies. Interested in new or unpub'd poets: yes. Simultaneous submissions accepted: no. Recent contributors: David Berman, William D. Waltz, Carl Faucher, Katie J. Kurtz, Ann Miller. Submission quantity: As many as author sees fit if SASE is included.

JACK THE RIPPER GAZETTE, Baker Street Publications, 577 Central Avenue, Box 4, Jefferson, LA 70121-1400, sherlockian@england.com, sherlockian@mailcity.com, www2.cybercities.com/z/zines/. Sharida Rizzuto, Harold Tollison, Ann Hoyt, Rose Dalton. 1983. "The publication is devoted to Jack the Ripper and other villians of the victorian era" circ. 500. 2/yr. Pub'd 10 poems 1999; expects 14 poems 2000. sub. price: $10; sample: $5. 40-45pp; 8½×11; Rights purchased: One-time rights, first or second time rights. Publishes 30% of poems submitted. Deadlines: Always open to submissions. Reporting time: 2-6 weeks. Payment: free copy only. Interested in new or unpub'd poets: yes. Simultaneous submissions accepted: yes. Recent contributors: George Chadderdou, Madeline Hoffer, Margarita Perez Beltran, Holly Day, Gregory E. Harrison. Submission quantity: 1-5. Special interests: We are willing to look at any type of poetry.

Jackson Harbor Press, RR 1, Box 107AA, Washington Island, WI 54246. William Olson. 1993. "We presently do not accept unsolicited manuscripts" avg. press run 300. Pub'd 3 poetry titles 1999; expects 1 poetry title 2000, 1 poetry title 2001. 5½×8½; avg. price, other: $4. 48pp; Interested in new or unpub'd poets: no. Simultaneous submissions accepted: no.

JAFFE INTERNATIONAL, Jaffe Publishing Management Service, Kunnuparambil Buildings, Kurichy, Kottayam 686549, India, 91-481-430470; FAX 91-481-561190. 1975. circ. 3M. 4/yr. sub. price: $10; sample: same. 48pp; 8½×11.

Jaffe Publishing Management Service (see also JAFFE INTERNATIONAL), Kunnuparambil Buildings, Kurichy, Kottayam 686549, India, phone/fax 91-481-430470. 1985. 8½×11.

JAMES DICKEY NEWSLETTER, 1753 Dyson Drive, Atlanta, GA 30307, 404-373-2989 phone/FAX. Joyce M. Pair, Editor. 1984. "*JDN* publishes long and short poems, particularly poems about nature, about nature of universe, about innerconnectedness of man to nature. Will read poems any time, but we want poems of high degree of intelligence, use of compact, dense language, excellent grammar, preferably poems with a narrative — a story line." circ. 200. 2/yr. Pub'd 6 poems 1999; expects 4-6 poems 2000, 3 poems 2001. sub. price: $12 USA individuals, $14 institutions, outside USA: $12 indiv., $15 instit.; sample: $8. 30pp; 8½×11; Rights purchased: first publication rights. Publishes 10-20% of poems submitted. Deadlines: August/February. Reporting time: 2-3 weeks. Payment: 3 copies. Interested in new or unpub'd poets: yes, if and only if poems contain high level in content and form. Simultaneous submissions accepted: no. Recent contributors: Linda Roth, Jes Simmons, Paula Goff, Arthur Madson. Submission quantity: 1-3. Special interests: We have room for only a few poems, and we use our space for especially excellent, metaphor narrative poems. When people send us a whole bunch of poems—and poems unlike those we normally publish—we return them unread. We will comment and edit good poems and correspond with the poet.

JAMES JOYCE BROADSHEET, School of English, University of Leeds, West Yorkshire LS2 9JT, England, 0113-233-4739. Dr. Richard Brown, Editor-in-Chief. 1980. "We do not pay contributors and only print poems very occasionally and only those connected with James Joyce. Our publication is primarily a vehicle for reviewing scholarly books on James Joyce" circ. 800. 3/yr. Pub'd 1 poem 1999; expects 1 poem 2000, 1 poem 2001. sub. price: £7.50 Europe (£6 for students)/$18 ($15 for students elsewhere); sample: £2/$4. 4-6pp; 11.7×16.5; Rights purchased: none. Publishes 35% of poems submitted. Deadlines: December 1, April 1,

September 1. Reporting time: 1 month. Payment: none. Interested in new or unpub'd poets: yes. Simultaneous submissions accepted: yes. Recent contributors: Seamus Heaney, Edwin Morgan, Derek Mahon, Gavin Ewart. Special interests: We will accept and publish any verse of quality as long as we deem it pertinent to Joyce or to be influenced by Joyce's works.

JAMES WHITE REVIEW; A Gay Men's Literary Quarterly, PO Box 73910, Washington, DC 20056-3910, 612-339-8317. Clif Mayhood, Poetry Editor. 1983. "We are interested in any expressions from gay men. We are now also interested in reviewing poetry and desire the right to reprint from reviewed books." circ. 4.5M. 4/yr. Pub'd 48 poems 1999; expects 48 poems 2000, 48 poems 2001. sub. price: $14 (institutions $14, foreign $20); sample: $4. 24pp; 13×18; Rights purchased: return rights to authors. Publishes 12% of poems submitted. Deadlines: Aug. 1, Nov. 1, Feb. 1, May 1. Reporting time: 1-2 months. Payment: $25 per poet per issue. Interested in new or unpub'd poets: yes. Simultaneous submissions accepted: no. Recent contributors: James Broughton, Jonathan Williams, Carl Morse, Mark Doty, Robert Peters. Submission quantity: up to 10. Special interests: We are interested in all forms of poetry whether it is metered, rhymed or experimental.

JAPANOPHILE, Japanophile Press, 6602 14th Avenue W, Bradenton, FL 34209-4527. Earl Snodgrass, Editor. 1974. "We use tanka, haiku and other Japanese forms—in English on any subject. We use any form of poetry if the subject is Japanese culture anywhere." circ. 1M. 4/yr. Pub'd 50-60 poems 1999. sub. price: $14; sample: $4. 56pp; 5¾×8½; Rights purchased: usually first. Publishes 5% of poems submitted. Deadlines: one month before first day of each season. Reporting time: 3 months. Payment: $1 for a haiku, more for longer poems. Interested in new or unpub'd poets: yes. Simultaneous submissions accepted: yes. Recent contributors: Mimi Hinman, George Ralph, Fred C. Holmberg, Edna Kovacs. Submission quantity: prefer 2 or more. Special interests: Translations, light verse, satire—all forms considered.

Japanophile Press (see also JAPANOPHILE), 6602 14th Avenue W, Bradenton, FL 34209-4527, 517-669-2109; E-mail japanlove@aol.com. Earl Snodgrass. 1974. avg. press run we have yet to publish a book of poetry.

JB Press, 1130 North Cabrillo, San Pedro, CA 90731, 310-832-7024. James S. Benedict. 1992. avg. press run 250. Pub'd 1 poetry title 1999; expects 1 poetry title 2000, 2 poetry titles 2001. 5½×8½; avg. price, cloth: $15; paper: $10; other: $5. 100pp; Publishes 50% of poetry manuscripts submitted. Reporting time: 1 month. Payment: negotiable. Interested in new or unpub'd poets: yes. Simultaneous submissions accepted: yes. Submission quantity: 25-30. Special interests: Conventional, contemporary, rhyme or non-rhyme.

JEJUNE: america Eats its Young, PO Box 85, Prague 1, 110 01, Czech Republic, 42-2-96141082; Fax 42-2-24256243. Vincent Farnsworth, Managing Editor; Gwendolyn Albert, Editor. 1994. "Extremism in the name of poetry is no vice, timidity in the name of publication is no virtue." circ. 700. 2/yr. Pub'd 50 poems 1999; expects 52 poems 2000, 94 poems 2001. sub. price: $10; sample: $5. 70pp; 6½×10½; Publishes 22% of poems submitted. Deadlines: ongoing. Reporting time: 2-12 weeks. Payment: copies. Interested in new or unpub'd poets: yes. Simultaneous submissions accepted: yes. Recent contributors: Eileen Myles, A.D. Winans, Robert Bove, Jules Mann, Jack Hirschman. Submission quantity: 5+. Special interests: open to suggestions.

Jessee Poet Publications (see also POETS AT WORK), Box 113, VAMC, 325 New Castle Road, Butler, PA 16001. Jessee Poet. 1985. "Keep poetry under 21 lines. I have constant contests; always some free ones. I publish *every* subscribing poet who submits poetry in good taste. I have many unusual fun, poetry related activities. I have poets in all levels of accomplishment from the novice to the very excelled poet." avg. press run 350. Pub'd 1800 poetry titles 1999. 5½×8½, 7×8½; avg. price, cloth: $20 for six bimonthly issues; paper: $3.50 (sample). 36-40pp; Publishes 100% of poetry manuscripts submitted. Reporting time: about 2 weeks. Payment: none. Interested in new or unpub'd poets: only if they are willing to subscribe. Simultaneous submissions accepted: yes. Recently published poets: Ann Gasser, Ruth McDaniels, Ralph Hammond, William Middleton, Dr. Karen Springer. Submission quantity: 5. Special interests: I accept all poetry that is in good taste and under 21 lines.

Jesus Pinata Press, PO Box 26692, San Francisco, CA 94126, E-mail elfool@aol.com. 1995. 6×9.

JEWISH CURRENTS, 22 E. 17th Street, Suite 601, New York, NY 10003, 212-924-5740. Morris U. Schappes. 1946. "We are a secular, not a religious, Jewish magazine. At the moment we are so heavily supplied with poems awaiting publication that we have had to declare a temporary moratorium on all submissions in this category" circ. 2M. 11/yr. Pub'd 12-15 poems 1999; expects 12-15 poems 2000, 12-15 poems 2001. sub. price: $30; sample: $3. 36pp—except Dec., 52pp (average); 8¼×10¾; Publishes 10% of poems submitted. Reporting time: 2 months. Payment: 1 year subscription. Interested in new or unpub'd poets: yes. Simultaneous submissions accepted: no. Recent contributors: David Bittner, Rade Panich, Khane Kheytin. Submission quantity: 1. Special interests: Translations from Yiddish or Hebrew.

JEWISH LIFE, 577 Central Avenue, Box 4, Jefferson, LA 70121-1400, E-mail publisher@jewishmail.com, jewishlife@newyorkoffice.com; www.world.up.co.il/jewishlife, www2.cybercities.com/z/zines/. Sharida Rizzuto, Elaine Wolfe. 1983. "All poems must pertain to Jews." circ. 300-500. 2/yr. Pub'd 30 poems 1999; expects 30 poems 2000, 30 poems 2001. sub. price: $15.80; sample: $7.90. 100pp; 8½×11; Rights purchased: one-time rights, first serial rights, or second serial rights. Publishes 30-35% of poems submitted. Deadlines: always open. Reporting time: 2-6 weeks. Payment: free copy only. Interested in new or unpub'd poets: yes. Simultaneous submissions accepted: yes. Recent contributors: Elaine Wolfe, Ann Stein, David Stone, David Rosen, Deborah Shapiro.

Jewish Publication Society, 2100 Arch Street, Philadelphia, PA 19103-1308, 215-564-5925; Fax 215-564-6640. 1888.

J-Mart Press, PO Box 8884, Virginia Beach, VA 23450, 757-498-4060 (phone/fax), e-mail jmartpress@aol.com. Art Hiene. 1990. avg. press run 2M. size varies; avg. price, paper: $3.95. 32-64pp; Publishes 5% of poetry manuscripts submitted. Reporting time: 30 days. Payment: trade. Interested in new or unpub'd poets: no. Simultaneous submissions accepted: no. Recently published poets: Edna May Foeckler. Submission quantity: 5.

THE JOURNAL, OSU Dept. of English, 164 W. 17th Avenue, 421 Denney Hall, Columbus, OH 43210-1370, 614-292-4076, fax 614-292-7816, e-mail thejournal05@pop.service.ohio-state.edu. Kathy Fagan, Co-Editor. 1973. circ. 1.6M. 2/yr. Pub'd 100 poems 1999; expects 100 poems 2000, 100 poems 2001. sub. price: $12; sample: $7. 140pp; 6×9; Rights purchased: 1st serial. Publishes 2% of poems submitted. Deadlines: poetry read year-round, though we are slower to respond during the summer months. Reporting time: 6-10 weeks. Payment: 2 copies + small stipend, when funds are available. Interested in new or unpub'd poets: yes. Simultaneous submissions accepted: yes. Recent contributors: Linda Bierds, Carl Phillips, Bob Hicok, Brenda Hillman, Larissa Szporluk. Submission quantity: no more than 5. Special interests: We are open to all kinds of poems and translations. We seek to achieve a mix of styles and sensibilities and voices. We are open to work of both new and established writers, and look for poetry and fiction with a sense of craft, and a strong sensibility. Our sole criterion is excellence.

THE JOURNAL OF AFRICAN TRAVEL-WRITING, PO Box 346, Chapel Hill, NC 27514. Carrie Blackstock. 1996. "Please do not send us work that has been published previously" circ. 600. 2/yr. Pub'd 3 poems 1999; expects 15 poems 2000, 10 poems 2001. sub. price: $10; sample: $6. 96pp; 7×10; Rights purchased: First publication rights. Publishes 5% of poems submitted. Deadlines: none. Reporting time: 4-6 weeks. Payment: copies. Interested in new or unpub'd poets: yes. Simultaneous submissions accepted: no. Recent contributors: Theresa Sengova, Jose Craveirinha, Sonia Gomez, Charles Hood. Submission quantity: 1-6. Special interests: Translations, long and short poems, poetry related to African travel.

JOURNAL OF ALASKA WOMEN, HCR 64 Box 453, Seward, AK 99664, 907-288-3168. 1990. Irregular. sub. price: none. 36-40pp; 8½×11; Rights purchased: One time. Publishes 10% of poems submitted. Reporting time: 2 weeks with SASE. Payment: $10. Interested in new or unpub'd poets: yes. Simultaneous submissions accepted: yes. Submission quantity: 2-3.

JOURNAL OF CONTEMPARARY ANGLO-SCANDINAVIAN POETRY, Original Plus, 11 Heatherton Park, Bradford on Tone, Taunton, Somerset TA4 1EU, England, 01823-461725; e-mail smithsssj@aol.com. 1994. circ. 150. 2/yr. sub. price: $11 US, £7 UK; sample: £3. 72pp; 5¾×8.

•JOURNAL OF CURRICULUM THEORIZING, 4154 State Street Drive, New Orleans, LA 70125. circ. 500. 4/yr. sub. price: $75 ind., $125 inst. 160pp; 6×9.

JOURNAL OF NEW JERSEY POETS, 214 Center Grove Road, County College of Morris, Randolph, NJ 07869, 201-328-5471, e-mail szulauf@ccm.edu. Sander Zulauf, Editor; Sara Pfaffenroth, Associate Editor; North Peterson, Associate Editor; Wendy Jones, Associate Editor. 1976. "Publish work by present and former New Jersey residents—we are seeking the best poems we can find, by poets who have done time here. SASE please. Typed or LQ processed MSS only." circ. 1M. 2/yr. Pub'd 70 poems 1999; expects 70 poems 2000, 70 poems 2001. sub. price: $10/2 issues, $16/4 issues, $10/4 issues students and seniors (please specify); sample: $5. 64-72pp; 8½×5½; Rights purchased: 1st. Publishes 7%-10% of poems submitted. Deadlines: ongoing. Reporting time: 6 months-1 year. Payment: 5 copies plus 2 issue subscription. Interested in new or unpub'd poets: yes. Simultaneous submissions accepted: yes, with notice and withdrawal if accepted elsewhere. Recent contributors: Amiri Baraka, Gerald Stern, X.J. Kennedy, Brigit-Pegeen Kelly, Madeline Tiger. Submission quantity: 1-3. Special interests: Planning to review books by New Jersey poets in future issues.

JOURNAL OF REGIONAL CRITICISM, Arjuna Library Press, 1025 Garner Street, Box 18, Colorado Springs, CO 80905-1774. Count Prof. Joseph A. Uphoff Jr., Director. 1979. "*The Journal Of Regional Criticism* is an ongoing manuscript copy of a research document in theoretical and mathematical fine arts. Submitted poetry is published in an illustrative and surrealist (paradoxical) context. One or two pages of a submission will be published in any single issue. Where possible the document is presented to interested parties with solicitation concerning possible transactions." circ. open. 6-12/yr. Pub'd 18 poems 1999; expects 18 poems 2000, 18 poems 2001. sample price: at cost. 4pp; 8½×11; Reporting time: indefinite. Payment: notice of acceptance, eventual copy of anthology. Interested in new or unpub'd poets: yes. Simultaneous submissions accepted: no, exceptional cases. Recent contributors: Henry Tokarski, Donette Faure, Harry Samuel Watnik, Deborah Hotchkiss, Jack Shadoian. Submission quantity: 1 or more, complete manuscripts. Special interests: The document is presented in a strategic fashion on an arbitrary basis, including universities, libraries, and foreign countries. Therefore, material should be suitable for a general audience. We have a censorship policy for willing authors. Please submit author's biography or resume. We are interested in surrealist and dreamlike prose poetry, and collections of poems. We use Xerography and can handle experimental visual poetics or esoteric symbolism.

Journey Books Publishing, 3205 Highway 431, Spring Hill, TN 37174, 615-791-8006. Edward Knight. 1997. "We accept nothing containing sexual content or profanity." avg. press run 250. Expects 2 poetry titles 2000, 2 poetry titles 2001. 5½×8½; avg. price, paper: $8.99. 64pp; Publishes less than 1% of poetry manuscripts submitted. Reporting time: 3 months. Payment: flat fee per poem or 10% royalty on entire volume. Interested in new or unpub'd poets: yes. Simultaneous submissions accepted: yes. Recently published poets: John Richards. Submission quantity: 1-3. Special interests: We are interested in imaginative poetry and poems about nature and the human spirit.

Juggernaut, PO Box 3824, Chicago, IL 60654-0824, 773-583-9261. 1992. 6×9.

Junction Press, PO Box 40537, San Diego, CA 92164-0537, 619-702-4607. Mark Weiss. 1991. avg. press run 1M. Pub'd 3 poetry titles 1999; expects 2 poetry titles 2000, 3 poetry titles 2001. 5½×8½; avg. price, paper: $9. 80pp; Reporting time: 3 months. Payment: 10% of copies run. Interested in new or unpub'd poets: yes. Simultaneous submissions accepted: yes. Recently published poets: Mervyn Taylor, Susie Mee, Richard Elman, Stephen Vincent. Special interests: Modernist/post modernist poetry, non-academic. Long, even book-length poems welcomed.

Jungle Man Press, 211 W. Mulberry Street, 3rd Floor, Baltimore, MD 21201. R. Monroe-Smith. 1993. avg. press run 50-100. Pub'd 1 poetry title 1999; expects 4 poetry titles 2000, 2 poetry titles 2001. 5½×8½; avg. price, paper: $3.50. 30pp; Publishes 5% of poetry manuscripts submitted. Reporting time: immediate. Payment: copies. Interested in new or unpub'd poets: yes. Simultaneous submissions accepted: no. Submission quantity: 20-30.

K

K.T. Publications, 16, Fane Close, Stamford, Lincs., PE9 1HG, England, (07180) 754193. Kevin Troop. 1987. "No obscenity. SASE essential for each submission. Please make names, instructions, titles, addresses clear on each letter or page" Pub'd 6 poetry titles 1999; expects 6 poetry titles 2000, 6 poetry titles 2001. size A5. 40-50pp; Publishes up to 10% of poetry manuscripts submitted. Reporting time: as quickly as humanly possible. Payment: none. Interested in new or unpub'd poets: yes. Simultaneous submissions accepted: no, not really. Recently published poets: John C. Desmond, Michael Newman, Christine Billington, Pauline Kirk, Isabel Cortan. Submission quantity: up to 6. Special interests: Experimental poetry is welcome, word-play, traditional, rhyming is, was, and always will be popular with readers, as long as it is not 'false' or 'forced.'

KAIROS, A Journal of Contemporary Thought and Criticism, Hermes House Press, 113 Summit Avenue, Brookline, MA 02446-2319. Alan Mandell, Richard Mandell. 1981. "Not currently reading unsolicited work. We read poetry throughout the year. Each of issue of *Kairos* focuses on a specific theme, mentioned in previous issues, though the poetry does not necessarily need to pertain to any specific theme. Always send SASE." circ. 500. 2/yr. Pub'd 2 poems 1999; expects 7 poems 2000, 8 poems 2001. sub. price: $11 individual, $15 institutions; sample: $6 + $1 p/h. 120pp; 5½×8½; Publishes 25% of poems submitted. Deadlines: open submissions. Reporting time: 4-6 weeks. Payment: copies. Interested in new or unpub'd poets: yes. Simultaneous submissions accepted: no. Recent contributors: Stanley Diamond, Ivan Arguelles, Emily Grosholz, Marie Luise von Kaschnitz. Submission quantity: 1-10. Special interests: None, though we welcome translations and experimental poetry in addition to any other well crafted poems.

KALDRON, An International Journal Of Visual Poetry, PO Box 7164, Halcyon, CA 93421-7164, 805-489-2770; Website http://www.thing.net/~grist/l&d/kaldron.htm. Karl Kempton, Editor; Karl Young, Harry Polkinhorn, Klaus Peter Dencker, Thalia. 1976. "*KALDRON* is North America's Longest Running Visual Poetry Magazine. Its on-line version opened on Bastille Day, 1997. Sections include 1) Selections from the Kaldron Archive: Number 21/22 and First Visualog Show, 1979; 2) Volume Two continuing on-line issue of the magazine: samples from fall, 1997 for Kaldron Wall Archives; 3) A Kaldron Wall Ancestor: Chumash Rock

Painting showing a solar eclipse. 4) Surveys: A - Individual Poets: Avelino de Araujo; Doris Cross; Klaus Peter Dencker; Scott Helmes; D.A. Levy (includes visual poetry, book art, paintings, lexical poetry: a- holistic approach to this major figure); Hassan Massoudy; bpNichol (includes a wide variety of poems, continuation of TTA project, and commentary); Kenneth Patchen; Marilyn R. Rosenberg; Alain Satie; Carol Stetser; thalia; Edgardo Antonio Vigo (first instalments of a joint memorial to this great and typically unrecognized) Argentine polymath, shown in conjunction with Postypographika; B- Group Surveys: Lettriste Pages: A collective effort of Australian visual poets; a workshop with Hungarian visual poets; U.S. and Canadian pages for Nucleo Post Arte's VI Biennial: Festival of Experimental Art and Literature, Mexico City, November, 1998; Free Graphz: Meeting place for graffiti art and visual poetry. Much more including numerous essays by Karl Young who is also the site Webmaster.'' circ. web-www. sub. price: donations accepted; sample: all back issues are $10 each, limit of 4 per order. Rights purchased: all rights remain with contributor. Deadlines: open. Reporting time: 1 week to 2 month. Payment: none-web. Interested in new or unpub'd poets: yes. Simultaneous submissions accepted: yes. Recent contributors: Hassan Massoudy, Alain Satie, Kenneth Patchen Jalevy, Klaus Peter Dencker. Submission quantity: no limits, but if return desired, then return self addressed and correct postage envelope necessary.

KALEIDOSCOPE: International Magazine of Literature, Fine Arts, and Disability, United Disability Services, 701 S. Main Street, Akron, OH 44311-1019, 330-762-9755, 330-379-3349 (TDD), Fax 330-762-0912, mshiplett@udsakron.org, pboerner@udsakron.org. Sandra Lindow. 1979. ''*Kaleidoscope* is a forum for disability-related literature. We avoid the stereotypical and sentimental. We seek fresh language and imagery and thought-provoking subject matter.'' circ. 2M. 2/yr. Pub'd 20 poems 1999; expects 20 poems 2000, 20 poems 2001. sub. price: $9 indiv., $14 instit., add $8 Int'l and $5 Canada; sample: $4 to cover p/h. 64pp; 8½×11; Rights purchased: first serial right, all rights returned to author upon publication. Publishes 5% of poems submitted. Deadlines: March 1, August 1. Reporting time: acknowledgement of submissions 2 weeks, final acceptance within 2 weeks of deadline dates, March 1 and August 1. Payment: $25 (max.), $10 (min.). Interested in new or unpub'd poets: yes. Simultaneous submissions accepted: yes. Recent contributors: Sheryl L. Nelms, Charles Tinkham, Patricia Ranzoni, Sandra J. Lindow. Submission quantity: 1-6. Special interests: We publish the best of what we receive of all types of poetry in an effort to make a substantive contribution in the field of disability studies.

KALLIOPE, A Journal of Women's Literature and Art, 3939 Roosevelt Blvd, Florida Community College at Jacksonville, Jacksonville, FL 32205, 904-381-3511. Mary Sue Koeppel, Editor. 1979. ''Please include address and phone number on each ms page. Send SASE and contributor's note at time of submission. Work must be by women, but not necessarily about women. We like to publish a wide range of voices, but nothing sexist, racist, or homophobic.'' circ. 1.6M. 3/yr. Pub'd 60-75 poems 1999; expects 60-75 poems 2000, 60-75 poems 2001. sub. price: $15; sample: $4 pre-1987 issues, $7 recent issues. 80pp; 8¼×7¼; Rights purchased: first, copyright reverts to author upon request. Publishes 5-10% of poems submitted. Deadlines: we read mss. Sept. to May. Reporting time: 3 months. Payment: 2 copies or 1-yr subscription. Interested in new or unpub'd poets: extremely interested. Simultaneous submissions accepted: no. Recent contributors: Marge Piercy, Elisavietta Ritchie, Enid Shomer, Joy Harjo, Tess Gallagher. Submission quantity: 3-7. Special interests: We are interested in experimental poetry; finely crafted poetry. Any topic women write about is appropriate.

KARAMU, Department of English, Eastern Illinois Univ., Charleston, IL 61920, 217-581-6297. Olga Abella, Editor; Lauren Smith, Co-Editor. 1966. ''We like poetry that builds around real experiences, real images and real characters, and that avoids abstraction, overt philosophizing and political rhetoric. Any subject matter can be appropriate if skillfully treated. Some issues are thematic, announced by ads and flyers; inquire. In terms of form, we prefer well-structured free verse, poetry with an inner, sub-surface structure as opposed to the surface structure of rhymed quatrains. It is advisable to send for sample issue ($7.50, $6) and examine the poetry in it to see what we like; mention in your order that *poetry* is your specific interest. We sometimes accept two of a poet's submissions for the same issue, if we like the work.'' circ. 400. 1/yr. Pub'd 40 poems 1999; expects 40 poems 2000, 45 poems 2001. sub. price: $7.50; sample: $7.50. 128pp; 5½×8; Rights purchased: 1st rights. Publishes 5% of poems submitted. Deadlines: Sept.1-April 1. Reporting time: initial screening, 6-8 weeks; promising material may be kept up to 4 months for final decision; for thematic issue or contests, specific date for decisions as announced. Payment: 1 copy of issue in which poetry appears, extra copies at half price. Interested in new or unpub'd poets: yes. Simultaneous submissions accepted: yes, but prefer not. Recent contributors: James Sallis, Tiff Holland, Robert Manaster, M. Rebecca Ransom, Janet St. John. Submission quantity: 5. Special interests: Experimental, regional poetry, poetry from the special consciousness of minorities and women; however, the poet's use of language and sense of form impresses us more than any subject matter per se.

KARAWANE, 402 S. Cedar Lake Road, Minneapolis, MN 55405, 612-381-1229, karawane@prodigy.net, http://pages.prodigy.net/fluffysingler. Laura Winton. 1996. ''We are focused on people involved in spoken word communities around the country. You will get a quicker response if you tell me that you read/perform and where.'' circ. 600. 2/yr. Pub'd 100 poems 1999; expects 40 poems 2000, 75 poems 2001. sub. price: $10/4 issues; sample: $1. 16-20pp; 8½×11; Rights purchased: one time. Publishes 50% of poems submitted. Deadlines: ongoing; May/October. Reporting time: 6 months. Payment: copies. Interested in new or unpub'd poets: yes, if your perform your work in public. Simultaneous submissions accepted: yes. Recent contributors: Terrence J. Folz, Danielle Billington, Jim Dewitt, Dave Okar, Susan P. Stein. Submission quantity: 3-6. Special interests: We don't like narrative/story telling poems. Show, don't tell, use image/metaphor, language/form to elucidate your meaning. After that, anything goes.

Katydid Books, 1 Balsa Road, Santa Fe, NM 87505. Thomas Fitzsimmons, Editor-Publisher. 1973. "Concentrating at present on translations of Japanese poets. Publishing only solicited mss." avg. press run 1.5M. Pub'd 3 poetry titles 1999; expects 3 poetry titles 2000, 3 poetry titles 2001. 5×8, 6×9, 7×9; avg. price, cloth: $28; paper: $12. 200pp; Payment: 10%.

●**Kaya Press,** 373 Broadway, Suite E2, New York, NY 10013, 212-343-9503, Fax 212-343-8291, kaya@kaya.com, www.kaya.com. 1994. 5¼×7¼.

THE KELSEY REVIEW, Mercer County, Community College, PO Box B, Trenton, NJ 08690, 609-586-4800 ext. 3326, e-mail kelsey.review@mccc.edu. G. Robin Schore. "No kittens, no autumn leaf sadness, no 'my grandmother'." circ. 2M. 1/yr. Pub'd 10 poems 1999; expects 10 poems 2000, 10 poems 2001. sub. price: free. 84pp; 7×11; Publishes 10% of poems submitted. Deadlines: May 1. Reporting time: 30 days. Payment: 5 copies of journal. Interested in new or unpub'd poets: yes. Simultaneous submissions accepted: no. Recent contributors: Valerie Egar, Betty Lies, Jim Richardson. Submission quantity: 6. Special interests: Contributors limited to people living or working in Mercer County, New Jersey.

Kelsey St. Press, 50 Northgate Avenue, Berkeley, CA 94708-2008, 510-845-2260; FAX 510-548-9185, e-mail kelseyst.@sirius.com; www.kelseyst.com. Rena Rosenwasser, Editor; Patricia Dienstfrey. 1974. "All manuscripts submitted should be in the completed form of a book of poems with special emphasis on the unity and integrity of it as a composed book." avg. press run 750-1M. Pub'd 2 poetry titles 1999; expects 3 poetry titles 2000, 3 poetry titles 2001. 5½×8½; avg. price, paper: $10. 58pp; Reporting time: 2-6 months. Payment: 10%, can be taken in dollars or books. Interested in new or unpub'd poets: yes. Simultaneous submissions accepted: yes. Recently published poets: Erica Hunt, Myung Mi Kim, Barbara Guest, Mei-Mei Berssenbrugge. Submission quantity: 25-40 poems. Special interests: Translations of works by women, experimentalist women's poetry, West Coast women writers, women of color.

Kenyette Productions, 20131 Champ Drive, Euclid, OH 44117-2208, 216-486-0544. Kenyette Adrine-Robinson, Editor-Publisher. 1976. "Coop publishing is what we are doing. Any interested parties should write to us. There is also a need for producing anthologies with minority publishers. If interested, please notify us" avg. press run 750. Expects 1 poetry title 2000, 2 poetry titles 2001. 5½×8½; avg. price, cloth: $15; paper: $10.95. 48pp; Publishes 20% of poetry manuscripts submitted. Reporting time: 2 months. Payment: 60-40, also negotiable. Interested in new or unpub'd poets: yes. Simultaneous submissions accepted: yes. Recently published poets: my students, Kenyette Adrine-Robinson. Submission quantity: 5-10 with cover letter. Special interests: Short, direct, sharp poems are our forte. We are also looking for poetry that relates to the Diaspora or African worldview from middle school through graduate school.

THE KENYON REVIEW, Kenyon College, Gambier, OH 43022, 740-427-5208, Fax 740-427-5417, e-mail kenyonreview@kenyon.edu. David Baker, Poetry Editor. 1939. "Have backlog of accepted manuscripts. Not accepting new work until Oct. 2000." circ. 4M-5M. 3/yr. Pub'd 130 poems 1999; expects 150 poems 2000, 150 poems 2001. sub. price: $25 individuals, $35 libraries; sample: $9 includes postage. 200pp; 7×10; Rights purchased: 1st North American Serial. Publishes 1% of poems submitted. Reporting time: 3 months. Payment: $15/ printed page. Interested in new or unpub'd poets: yes—We strongly suggest they be familiar with the magazine as readers, and be aware that we receive close to 3,000 poetry submissions a year. Simultaneous submissions accepted: no. Recent contributors: Rachel Hadas, Yusef Komunyakaa, Rebecca McClanahan, W.S. Merwin, Cathy Song. Submission quantity: not more than 10 pages. Special interests: We are interested in all poetry forms and translations.

KEREM: Creative Explorations in Judaism, 3035 Porter Street, NW, Washington, DC 20008, 202-364-3006; fax 202-364-3806; e-mail srh@udel.edu; www.kerem.com. Gilah Langner, Sara R. Horowitz, Kathryn Hellestein. 1992. "1999 vol.6 issue: theme is "parenting"." circ. 2M. 1/yr. Pub'd 7 poems 1999; expects 5 poems 2000, 5 poems 2001. sub. price: $8.50; sample: $8.50. 128pp; 6×9; Rights purchased: one-time. Publishes 10% of poems submitted. Deadlines: anytime. Reporting time: 3-5 months. Payment: none. Interested in new or unpub'd poets: yes. Simultaneous submissions accepted: yes. Recent contributors: Marge Piercy, Richard Chess, Jay Liveson, Leo Haber, Sheila Freeman. Special interests: Jewish content.

THE KERF, 883 W. Washington Boulevard, Crescent City, CA 95531, 707-464-6867. Ken Letko. 1995. "The editors especially encourage themes related to humanity and/or environmental consciousness, but are open to diverse subjects" circ. 275. 1/yr. Pub'd 33 poems 1999; expects 33 poems 2000, 33 poems 2001. sub. price: $5; sample: $5. 49pp; 8½×5½; Rights purchased: First North American serial rights. Publishes 5% of poems

102

submitted. Deadlines: March 31. Reporting time: 2 months. Payment: 1 copy. Interested in new or unpub'd poets: yes. Simultaneous submissions accepted: no. Recent contributors: Susan Thomas, Ray Gonzalez, Meg Files, Susan Clayton-Goldmor, Philip Dacey. Submission quantity: up to 7. Special interests: None really, the editors are rather open to new things.

KESTREL: A Journal of Literature and Art, PO Box 1797, Clarksburg, WV 26302-1797, 304-367-4815, Fax 304-367-4896, e-mail kestrel@mail.fscwv.edu. Mary Dillow Stewart. 1993. circ. 600. 2/yr. sub. price: $10; sample: $6. 100pp; 6×9; Reporting time: 3-4 months. Payment: 5 copies of issue. Interested in new or unpub'd poets: yes. Simultaneous submissions accepted: no. Recent contributors: Shara McCallum, Debra Kang Dean, Lucille Clifton, Seamus Heaney, E. Etherlbert Miller. Submission quantity: 5-10. Special interests: Translation, longpoems. We are interested in presenting a substantial selection of contributors work—3 to 7 poems, a longpoem, translations with the original on facing pages.

Kettle of Fish Press, PO Box 364, Exeter, NH 03833.

KICK IT OVER, Kick It Over Collective, PO Box 5811, Station A, Toronto, Ontario M5W 1P2, Canada. 1981. "We're a political magazine. Poetry doesn't have to be overly political, but a social/political consciousness should inform the work" circ. 1.5M. 4/yr. Pub'd 1 poem 1999; expects 10-15 poems 2000, 10-15 poems 2001. sub. price: $14; sample: $3.50. 68pp; 8½×10½; Reporting time: up to 3 months. Payment: 3 copies. Interested in new or unpub'd poets: yes. Simultaneous submissions accepted: yes, pleas inform us. Submission quantity: up to 6.

KID'S WORLD, 1300 Kicker Road, Tuscaloosa, AL 35404, 205-553-2284. Morgan Kopaska-Merkel, Editor. 1993. circ. 75. 4/yr. sub. price: $5; sample: $2. 16pp; 5½×8½; Rights purchased: 1st National Serial Rights. Publishes 10% of poems submitted. Deadlines: anytime. Reporting time: 1-3 months. Payment: 1 copy per piece published. Interested in new or unpub'd poets: yes. Simultaneous submissions accepted: no. Recent contributors: Aubry Hopkins, Raena Steffen, Stephanie Howard, Justin Howell. Submission quantity: 1-6. Special interests: Fantasy, rhyming poems are especially good, ice cream, etc.

Kings Estate Press, 870 Kings Estate Road, St. Augustine, FL 32086, 800-249-7485, kep@aug.com. Ruth Moon Kempher. 1993. "Can't really consider manuscripts anytime soon" avg. press run 200. Pub'd 3 poetry titles 1999. 7×8½; avg. price, other: $13. 80pp; Payment: negotiated. Interested in new or unpub'd poets: no. Recently published poets: Gerald Locklin, Joan Payne Kincaid, Kyle Lacos, Tony Moffeit.

Knightraven Books, PO Box 100, Collinsville, IL 62234, 314-725-1111, Fax 618-345-7436. Wayne A. Reinagel. 1980. avg. press run 2M. Pub'd 1 poetry title 1999; expects 2 poetry titles 2000, 3 poetry titles 2001. 5½×8½; avg. price, paper: $12.95. 256pp; Publishes 5% of poetry manuscripts submitted. Reporting time: 3 months. Payment: negotiable. Interested in new or unpub'd poets: no. Simultaneous submissions accepted: no. Recently published poets: Susan Sheild, Barb Wilson, Barbara Heilig, Nan Mayse, Carol Miller.

KOJA, 7314 21 Avenue #6E, Brooklyn, NY 11204, email mikekoja@aol.com. Mikhail Magazinnik, Editor. 1996. "Unsolicited submissions must be accompanied by $7 for a sample copy. Submissions w/o $7 will be returned unread. No reading deadlines - submissions can be sent all year long." circ. 200. 1-2/yr. Pub'd 15 poems 1999; expects 30 poems 2000, 30 poems 2001. sub. price: not available; sample: $7. 64pp; 5½×8½, 8½×11; Rights purchased: rights revert to authors upon publication. Publishes 5% of poems submitted. Deadlines: none. Reporting time: 6-9 months. Payment: 1 issue. Interested in new or unpub'd poets: yes. Simultaneous submissions accepted: no. Recent contributors: E. Myles, W. Austin, R. Kostehanetz, B. Andrews, A.D. Coleman. Submission quantity: as many as one wishes. Special interests: experimental poetry, visual/concrete poetry, sound poetry.

Konocti Books, 23311 County Road 88, Winters, CA 95694. Noel Peattie. 1973. "Presently inactive. We're not interested in unasked mss. While our doors are not entirely shut, *query before sending*. We don't have the finances to enter into a big-time poetry publishing program." avg. press run 250-500. Pub'd 1 poetry title 1999. avg. price, paper: $2-$8. 20-40pp; Reporting time: 2 months. Payment: contributor's copies. Interested in new or unpub'd poets: only if they send 2-10 pages with SASE. Simultaneous submissions accepted: no. Recently published poets: Ramona Weeks, Gloria Bosque, Doc Dachtler, Karl Kempton, Jane Blue. Submission quantity: 10. Special interests: Regional poetry.

THE KOSCIUSZKO PORTFOLIO, 405 Madison Avenue, Albany, NY 12210. circ. varies. 4/yr. sub. price: $20; sample: $5. Pages vary; 8½×11.

Kosmos, 20 Millard Road, Larkspur, CA 94939. Kosrof Chantikian. 1974. "We have established a *Modern Poets in Translation Series* to introduce poets of other parts of this planet to the reading public in the United States. We are interested in publishing translations of contemporary works by poets from outside of the United States, as well as new interpretations of significant poetic works of the past. Each work contains the original poetic text with facing English translation. Publications include: *The Other Shore* by Rafael Alberti (vol I); *Transparent God* by Claude Esteban (vol II); *The Beaches of Thule* by Jean Laude (vol III); *Conjuncture of*

103

Body and Garden/Cosmogony by Claude Esteban (vol IV). A letter of inquiry (along with a SASE) giving an outline of your proposed project should be sent to the editor before submission of a manuscript." avg. press run 1.2M. 6×9; avg. price, cloth: $17; paper: $7.95. 88-256pp; Publishes a small % of poetry manuscripts submitted. Reporting time: 4 weeks. Payment: arranged with author. Interested in new or unpub'd poets: no. Simultaneous submissions accepted: no. Recently published poets: Octavio Paz, Rafael Alberti, Claude Esteban, Jean Laude.

●**Kota Press (see also KOTA PRESS POETRY JOURNAL)**, 2237 NW 62nd, Suite 2, Seattle, WA 98107, editor@kotapress.com, www.kotapress.com. Kara L.C. Jones. 1999. "Please see and follow full contest guidelines on our website" avg. press run 250 for anthologies. Pub'd 2 poetry titles 1999; expects 2 poetry titles 2000, 2 poetry titles 2001. 5×8; avg. price, paper: $10-$15. approx. 170pp; Reporting time: 1-2 months. Payment: 14 copies of anthology author is in. Interested in new or unpub'd poets: yes. Simultaneous submissions accepted: no. Recently published poets: Carla T. Griswold, Tim Hulley, Dana Gerringer, Sandra Bailey, Heidi Sauer. Submission quantity: min. 15 pages, max. 25 pages for anthology contest.

●**KOTA PRESS POETRY JOURNAL**, Kota Press, 2237 NW 62nd, Suite 2, Seattle, WA 98107, editor@kotapress.com, www.kotapress.com/framejournal.htm. Kara L.C. Jones. 1999. "Please see full guidelines for the journal at our website." circ. 10M+. 4/yr. Pub'd 120 poems 1999; expects 120 poems 2000, 120 poems 2001. sub. price: free. 30pp; Rights purchased: one-time electronic rights. Publishes 25% of poems submitted. Deadlines: see guidelines on website. Reporting time: 1-2 months. Interested in new or unpub'd poets: yes. Simultaneous submissions accepted: no. Recent contributors: Charles Fishman, Ruth Daigon, Seana Sperling, Claudia Mauro. Submission quantity: up to 4 via e-mail.

Kozmik Press, 134 Elsenham Street, London SW18 5NP, United Kingdom, 44-81-874-8218. 1975. Expects 2 poetry titles 2000. Payment: 10%. Interested in new or unpub'd poets: no.

KRAX, 63 Dixon Lane, Leeds, Yorkshire LS12 4RR, England. Andy Robson. 1971. "We have a permanent backlog of material, hence topical themes are out. Name desired to be attached to work even where pseudonym/anon. requested. Issues are compiled from accepted material and specific publication dates cannot be given." 2/yr. Pub'd 150 poems 1999; expects 220 poems 2000, 180 poems 2001. sub. price: £10 ($20); sample: $1. 64pp; size A5; Rights purchased: none. Publishes 1% of poems submitted. Deadlines: continuous. Reporting time: 6-8 weeks. Payment: none. Interested in new or unpub'd poets: yes. Simultaneous submissions accepted: occasionally. Submission quantity: up to 10 if only 3-6 lines long—no more than 6 if longer. Special interests: Humorous viewpoints, original ideas, encourage enthusiastic, new writers—inspiration scores over craftmanship.

KUMQUAT MERINGUE, PO Box 736, Pine Island, MN 55963-0736, e-mail moodyriver@aol.com; Website Http://www.geostar.com/kumquatcastle. Christian Nelson. 1990. "Like mostly short poetry. We're dedicated to the memory of Richard Brautigan, so let that be the guidelines." circ. 600. 1-2/yr. Expects 150 poems 2000, 150 poems 2001. sub. price: $10; sample: $5. 40pp; 5½x8½ (digest size); Rights purchased: one time. Publishes less than 1% of poems submitted. Deadlines: none. Reporting time: 30-60 days. Payment: 1 copy. Interested in new or unpub'd poets: yes. Simultaneous submissions accepted: yes—but let us know. Recent contributors: Lyn Lifshin, Mark Weber, Lynne Douglass, Ianthe Brautigan. Submission quantity: as many as they want. Special interests: Richard Brautigan-Related either in tone or in content.

KUUMBA, BLK Publishing Company, PO Box 83912, Los Angeles, CA 90083, 310-410-0808, fax 310-410-9250, e-mail newsroom@blk.com. 1991. circ. 1M. 2/yr. Pub'd 80 poems 1999; expects 80 poems 2000, 100 poems 2001. sub. price: $7.50; sample: $5.50. 48pp; 8⅛x10⅞; Publishes 10% of poems submitted. Interested in new or unpub'd poets: yes. Simultaneous submissions accepted: yes, if told. Submission quantity: 5.

L

La Alameda Press, 9636 Guadalupe Trail NW, Albuquerque, NM 87114. 1991. avg. press run 1M. Pub'd 3 poetry titles 1999; expects 2 poetry titles 2000. size varies; avg. price, paper: $12. 96pp; Interested in new or unpub'd poets: no. Recently published poets: John Brandi, Mirian Sagan, Joan Logghe, Larry Goodell, Penny Harter.

La Jolla Poets Press, PO Box 8638, La Jolla, CA 92038, 619-457-1399. Kathleen Iddings, Publisher & Editor. 1985. "This press was originated in 1985 to publish worthy individual poets' books. Editor/Publisher/Poet Kathleen Iddings was the originator of the press. In 1996, the press was founded the 'National Poetry Book

Series' contests. The winner receives a $500 award and the publishing of his/her manuscript. This contest is for a poet who has published any number of books. Watch the *Small Press Review* and other poetry magazines for announcements of future contests. They are not held every year." avg. press run 500. Pub'd 2 poetry titles 1999; expects 3 poetry titles 2000. 5½x8½; avg. price, cloth: $18; paper: $10. 75-100pp; Publishes 5% of poetry manuscripts submitted. Reporting time: 2 months. Payment: usually in books. Interested in new or unpub'd poets: no. Simultaneous submissions accepted: yes. Recently published poets: Kevin Pilkington, Susan Terris, Edward G. Moll, Melissa Morphew. Submission quantity: prefer poets watch for contest submission information in poetry publications before submitting. Special interests: Excellent poetry is the No. 1 criteria. Leanings are toward contemporary style versus end-rhyme and formal verse.

LADYBUG, the Magazine for Young Children, 315 5th Street, PO Box 300, Peru, IL 61354, 815-224-6656. Paula Morrow, Editor. 1990. "Submissions should be age appropriate but not condescending. Our audience is children ages 2-6" circ. 132M. 12/yr. Pub'd 30 poems 1999; expects 30 poems 2000, 30 poems 2001. sub. price: $35.97; sample: $5. 36pp; 8x10; Rights purchased: 1st publication rights in the English language. Publishes less than 1% of poems submitted. Deadlines: none. Reporting time: 12 weeks. Payment: on publication, pay up to $3/line with 20 line max. Interested in new or unpub'd poets: yes. Simultaneous submissions accepted: yes. Recent contributors: Aileen Fisher, Alan Benjamin, Lee Bennett Hopkins, Mary Ann Hoberman, Gwendolyn Lavert. Submission quantity: no more than 5. Special interests: Finger plays and action rhymes.

Lakes & Prairies Press, 15774 S. LaGrange Road #172, Orland Park, IL 60462-4766, website www.lakesprairies.com. Ned Haggard. 1998 (incorporation); 1974-75 as a literary journal; later, press. avg. press run 1-1.5M. Expects 2 poetry titles 2000, 2 poetry titles 2001. size varies. Publishes a very select % of poetry manuscripts submitted. Reporting time: 2-4 months. Payment: negotiated as per circumstances. Interested in new or unpub'd poets: yes. Simultaneous submissions accepted: yes, with notice. Submission quantity: entire manuscript. Special interests: We like poetry that has the weight of conviction, well executed. We have no interest in the expression of egotists or narcissists.

THE LANGSTON HUGHES REVIEW, Box 2006, Univ. of Georgia, Athens, GA 30612-0006, 401-863-1815. 1982. "No editorial assistance in office during July and August; poetry published is related to Langston Hughes only." circ. 300-325. 2/yr. Expects 11 poems 2000. sub. price: $10 ($12 foreign). 40-60pp; 6x9; Rights purchased: none. Publishes 40% of poems submitted. Deadlines: none. Reporting time: 2 months maximum. Payment: in copies (5). Interested in new or unpub'd poets: if poems are related to Langston Hughes, his life and/or work. Simultaneous submissions accepted: yes. Recent contributors: Naomi Long Modgett, Samuel Allen, Leonard Moore, Julius Thompson, Carole Boston Weatherford. Submission quantity: 3 only. Special interests: Langston Hughes, Blues, Jazz poems.

Laocoon Books, PO Box 20518, Seattle, WA 98102, 206-323-7268; erotica@laocoonbooks.com. M. Kettner, Co-Editor; Kathleen K., Co-Editor. 1980. "No unsolicited manuscripts at this time. Most recent title: *Beneath a Naughty Moon* by M. Kettner, $5." avg. press run 300. Expects 4 poetry titles 2000, 1 poetry title 2001. size varies; avg. price, paper: $4. 28-40pp; Interested in new or unpub'd poets: no.

Latin American Literary Review Press, 121 Edgewood Avenue, 1st Floor, Pittsburgh, PA 15218-1513, 412-371-9023; FAX 412-371-9025. Yvette E. Miller, Editor. 1977. "We request a clean manuscript. We publish anthologies" avg. press run 1M. Pub'd 3 poetry titles 1999; expects 2 poetry titles 2000, 3 poetry titles 2001. 5½x8½; avg. price, cloth: $12; paper: $8.50. 96-160pp; Publishes 75% of poetry manuscripts submitted. Reporting time: 6 months. Payment: 10% press run. Interested in new or unpub'd poets: yes. Simultaneous submissions accepted: no. Recently published poets: Fernando Alegria, Marco Antonio Montes de Oca, Isabel Fraire, Jose Emilio Pacheco, Raul Zurita. Submission quantity: 10. Special interests: Translations; also original poetry submissions in Spanish and Portuguese. We are especially interested in poetry by Latin American Women writers, in bilingual format, Spanish/English.

LATINO STUFF REVIEW, LS Press, Inc., PO Box 440195, Miami, FL 33144, www.ejl@lspress.net. 1990. circ. 1M. 2/yr. sub. price: $4; sample: $3. 24pp; 8½x11.

LAUREATE LETTER, 899 Williamson Trail, Eclectic, AL 36024. Brenda Williamson, Editor. 1981. "Any style of poetry, 20 words maximum." circ. 1M. 1/yr. sub. price: $3.95; sample: $3.95. 24pp; 5½x8½; Simultaneous submissions accepted: yes.

THE LAUREL REVIEW, Department of English, Northwest Missouri State University, Maryville, MO 64468, 816-562-1265. William Trowbridge, Editor; David Slater, Editor; Beth Richards, Editor; Catie Rosemurgy, Editor; Randall R. Freisinger, Associate Editor; Steve Heller, Associate Editor; Nancy Vieira Couto, Associate Editor; Jim Simmerman, Associate Editor. 1960. "We read Sept through May. We have no regional, political, ethnic, or religious bias. We seek well-crafted poems with fresh, vigorous imagery, precise use of language, and an awareness that poetry should be accessible to a wide range of serious readers, not merely to the poet and his/her immediate family. We would be delighted to find poems capable of making a reader laugh; we do not especially want poems that seek to persuade a reader of much of anything. Good poems are more important to us than are impressive reputations." circ. 900. 2/yr. Pub'd 100 poems 1999; expects 100 poems 2000, 100 poems 2001. sub. price: $8; sample: $5. 128pp; 6×9; Rights purchased: first rights. Publishes 1% of poems submitted. Deadlines: Sept through May. Reporting time: 1 week to 4 months. Payment: 2 copies of magazine and 1 year subscription. Interested in new or unpub'd poets: yes. Simultaneous submissions accepted: no. Recent contributors: Patricia Goedicke, David Citino, Brendan Calvin, Albert Goldbarth, Katherine Soniat. Submission quantity: 3-6 poems. Special interests: no translations.

LEAPINGS LITERARY MAGAZINE, 2455 Pinercrest Drive, Santa Rosa, CA 95403, E-mail 72144.3133@compuserve.com. Susan Warner. 1998. "Annual poetry competition with deadline of May 1." circ. ~200. 2/yr. Pub'd 70 poems 1999; expects 70 poems 2000, 70 poems 2001. sub. price: $10; sample: $5 (back issue). 60pp; 5½×8½; Rights purchased: First North American Serial Rights. Publishes 5% of poems submitted. Deadlines: ongoing. Reporting time: 1 month. Payment: 2 contributor copies. Interested in new or unpub'd poets: yes. Simultaneous submissions accepted: yes, if noted. Recent contributors: G.E. Coggshall, Vince Scalese, John Bush, Janet Buck. Submission quantity: 3-6. Special interests: open to anything really.

Ledero Press, U. T. Box 35099, Galveston, TX 77555-5099, 409-772-2091. 1990. 6×9.

THE LEDGE, 78-44 80th Street, Glendale, NY 11385. Timothy Monaghan, Editor. 1988. "*The Ledge* sponsors an Annual Poetry Chapbook Contest, and an Annual Poetry Contest. Send SASE for details" circ. 1M. 2/yr. Pub'd 100 poems 1999; expects 100 poems 2000, 100 poems 2001. sub. price: $13 2 issues or $24/4 issues or $32/6 issues. For subscriptions outside North America, please add $3 per issue; sample: $7. 144pp; 5½×8½; Rights purchased: none, all revert to author upon publication. Publishes 5% of poems submitted. Deadlines: Reading period: Sept. through May. Reporting time: 4-6 months. Payment: 2 contributor's copies. Interested in new or unpub'd poets: yes. Simultaneous submissions accepted: yes. Recent contributors: Sherman Alexie, Brooke Wiese, Elton Glaser, Kurt Brown, Tony Gloeggler. Submission quantity: Please limit submissions to 5 poems or fewer. Special interests: Our purpose is to publish outstanding poetry. We have no restrictions on form or content. Excellence is our only criterion.

LEFT CURVE, PO Box 472, Oakland, CA 94604, E-mail: leftcurv@wco.com. Csaba Polony, Jack Hirschman. 1974. "*Left Curve* is an artist produced open, critical journal that addresses the problem(s) of cultural forms emerging from the crises of modernity that strive to be independent from the control of dominant institutions. We publish original work by individuals, as well as cultural work that is an integral, organic part of emancipatory movements. Our general orientation is the recognition of the destructiveness of commodity (capitalist) systems to all life, and the need to build a non-commodified culture that could potentially create a more harmonious relationship among people, and between the human and natural world" circ. 2M. Irregular. Pub'd 32 poems 1999; expects 25 poems 2000, 25 poems 2001. sub. price: $30 indiv, $45 instit (3 issues); sample: $8. 112-144pp; 8½×11; Publishes 5% of poems submitted. Deadlines: open. Reporting time: 3-6 months. Payment: 3 copies of issue. Interested in new or unpub'd poets: yes. Simultaneous submissions accepted: no. Recent contributors: Jack Hirschman, Sarah Menefe, Paul Laraque, Luis J. Rodriguez, P.J. Laska. Submission quantity: 1-5.

Left Hand Books, Station Hill Road, Barrytown, NY 12507, 914-758-6478; FAX 914-758-4416. Bryan McHugh. 1990. "Generally, submissions are made at the express invitation of publisher or through recommendation of certain people" avg. press run 750. Pub'd 2 poetry titles 1999; expects 1 poetry title 2000, 1 poetry title 2001. size varies; avg. price, paper: $10. 68pp; Publishes 1% of poetry manuscripts submitted. Reporting time: cannot respond to unsolicited manuscripts. Payment: arrangements vary. Interested in new or unpub'd poets: by recommendation only. Simultaneous submissions accepted: no. Recently published poets: Dennis Barone, Jeremy Sigler, George Economou, Rillo, Susan Smith Nash. Special interests: Full-spectrum.

Legal Information Publications, 18221 East Park Drive, Cleveland, OH 44119-2019. 1990. 1×9¼.

Legas (see also ARBA SICULA; SICILIA PARRA), PO Box 040328, Brooklyn, NY 11204. Gaetano Cipolla. 1987. "We specialize in Italian/Sicilian poetry in translation" avg. press run 1M. Pub'd 1 poetry title 1999; expects 1 poetry title 2000. 5½×8½; avg. price, paper: $16-20. 200pp; Reporting time: 3 weeks. Interested in new or unpub'd poets: yes. Simultaneous submissions accepted: yes. Submission quantity: 2.

L'Epervier Press, 1326 NE 62nd Street, Seattle, WA 98115. Robert McNamara, Editor; Bridget Culligan, Managing Editor. 1977. "Do query before sending a submission. Do enclose SASE or postcard with above" avg. press run 500. Pub'd 2 poetry titles 1999; expects 4 poetry titles 2000, 4 poetry titles 2001. 5½×8½; avg. price, cloth: $12; paper: $6. 80pp; Publishes 8% of poetry manuscripts submitted. Reporting time: 6 months, query first. Payment: 10% of the press run. Interested in new or unpub'd poets: yes. Simultaneous submissions accepted: yes. Recently published poets: Albert Goldbarth, Lorrie Goldensohn, Christopher Howell, Jack Myers, Frederick Will. Submission quantity: 5. Special interests: N.W. poets, experimental poetry, and longpoems.

●**LETHOLOGICA**, 710 Arch Street, Salem, OH 44460, lethicon@juno.com, www.geocities.com/lethicon. Ben Lybarger, Editor; William Oesch, Associate Editor. 1999. circ. 500. 1/yr. Pub'd 18 poems 1999; expects 12 poems 2000, 15 poems 2001. sample price: $4. 40pp; 8½×11; Publishes 10% of poems submitted. Deadlines: none. Reporting time: 2 weeks to 2 months. Payment: 2 copies. Interested in new or unpub'd poets: yes. Simultaneous submissions accepted: no. Recent contributors: Jill Nagle, Thomas Hartl, Bob Riedel, Jeff Bush, Craig Paulenich.

THE LETTER PARADE, PO Box 52, Comstock, MI 49041. Bonnie Jo. 1985. circ. 100 or so. 4/yr. Pub'd 6 poems 1999; expects 6 poems 2000, 6 poems 2001. sub. price: $6; sample: $1. 6pp; 8½×14; Rights purchased: none-just let us print it. Publishes 10% of poems submitted. Payment: subscriptions. Interested in new or unpub'd poets: Yes. Simultaneous submissions accepted: Yes. Submission quantity: 3. Special interests: We like poems that make us laugh.

LFW Enterprises, PO Box 370234, Denver, CO 80237-0234, 303-750-1040. 1995. 6×9.

LIBERTY, PO Box 1181, Port Townsend, WA 98368, 360-379-0242. Stephen Cox. Address poetry submissions to: Humanities 0306, 1512 Galbraith Hall, University of California SD, La Jolla, CA 92093. 1987. circ. 15M. 6/yr. Pub'd 2 poems 1999; expects 2 poems 2000, 2 poems 2001. sub. price: $19.50; sample: $4. 72pp; 8½×11; Rights purchased: first N. American serial, non-exclusive right to anthologize. Publishes 5% of poems submitted. Deadlines: none. Reporting time: 1-2 months. Payment: none. Interested in new or unpub'd poets: yes. Simultaneous submissions accepted: no. Recent contributors: Joanne Lowery, Brett Rutherford, Don Mager, Marc Ponomareff, Richard Kostelanetz. Submission quantity: 1-5.

LIBIDO: The Journal of Sex and Sensibility, PO Box 146721, Chicago, IL 60614, 773-275-0842. Marianna Beck, Jack Hafferkamp. 1988. "*Libido*'s goal is exploration of sexual themes—funny, painful, honest. Strong emphasis on humor—no limericks, please. Automatic rejections: Lower case i poetry, the phrase 'waves of pleasure,' or the words 'big tits'" circ. 10M. 4/yr. Pub'd 15 poems 1999. sub. price: $30; sample: $9. 88pp; 6½×9½; Rights purchased: 1st. Publishes 2% of poems submitted. Deadlines: none. Reporting time: 5 months. Payment: $10-$25. Interested in new or unpub'd poets: ok. Simultaneous submissions accepted: yes, with notice. Recent contributors: Joy Schneiders, Stacie M. Kirer. Submission quantity: 2-3.

Libra Publishers, Inc., 3089C Clairemont Dr., Suite 383, San Diego, CA 92117, 619-571-1414. William Kroll, Editor & Publisher. 1960. "We publish two professional journals and books that are mainly in the behavioral sciences, but we do publish some general nonfiction and fiction as well as poetry." avg. press run 500. Expects 4 poetry titles 2000. 5½×8½; avg. price, cloth: $10.95; paper: $7.95. 96pp; Publishes 20% of poetry manuscripts submitted. Reporting time: 2-3 weeks. Payment: we had been publishing books of poetry on a standard royalty basis, but due to our limited budget and relatively small sales, primarily we offer to publish on the basis of an author investment in the production costs. In this case we pay a 40% royalty as compared with 10% on the standard basis. This does not preclude the possibility of acceptance on the standard basis if we 'fall in love' with a particular work and think it has exceptional sales potential. Or we can provide all services necessary to help an author to self-publish. Interested in new or unpub'd poets: yes. Simultaneous submissions accepted: yes. Recently published poets: William Blackwell, John C. Anderson, C. Margaret Hall, Sydney Davis, Gwen Jamsma. Submission quantity: manuscript, but will accept 12 poems or so. Special interests: We have no special preferences.

THE LICKING RIVER REVIEW, Department of Literature and Language, Northern Kentucky University, Highland Heights, KY 41099. Poetry Editor. 1989. "Submissions read from Aug.-Dec. We welcome crafted work that leaves a memorable impression" circ. 1-1.5K. 1/yr. Expects 15 poems 2000, 20 poems 2001. sub. price: $5; sample: $5. 96pp; 7×10; Rights purchased: first rights. Publishes 18% of poems submitted. Reporting time: 1-9 months. Payment: 2 contributors copies. Interested in new or unpub'd poets: yes. Simultaneous submissions accepted: no. Recent contributors: Rhonda Pettit, Joni Lang, Judi A. Rypma, Kenneth Pobo, Leatha Kendrick. Submission quantity: 5 poems maximum. Special interests: No poems over 70 lines.

LIES MAGAZINE, 1308 Shawnee, Durham, NC 27701, 505-268-7316; email okeefine@aol.com; www.cent.com/abetting/. 1994. circ. 2M+. 4/yr. sub. price: $12/6 issues; sample: $3. 44pp; 8¼×10¾.

LIFTOUTS, Preludium Publishers, 1414 S. 3rd Street-#102, Minneapolis, MN 55454, 612-321-9044, Fax 612-305-0655. Barry Casselman, Editor; Frederic Will, Editor. 1983. "*Liftouts* does not accept unsolicited submissions of poetry at this time." circ. 5M. 1/yr. sub. price: $5; sample: $5. 40-75pp; 5×8½; Rights purchased: 1st North American rights. Reporting time: prompt. Simultaneous submissions accepted: no. Special interests: Experimental poetry in English; translations of new poetry from around the world.

LIGHT: The Quarterly of Light Verse, PO Box 7500, Chicago, IL 60680. John Mella, Editor. 1992. "Send SASE for guidelines" circ. 1M. 4/yr. Pub'd 240 poems 1999; expects 240 poems 2000, 240 poems 2001. sub. price: $18/4 issues, $30/8 issues, $28/4 issues international; sample: $4 + $2 1st class mail. 64pp; 6×9; Rights purchased: 1st American Serial. Publishes 5-10% of poems submitted. Reporting time: 2-4 months. Payment: 2

copies domestic, 1 copy foreign. Interested in new or unpub'd poets: yes. Simultaneous submissions accepted: no. Recent contributors: X.J. Kennedy, Tom Disch, Reed Whittemore, David R. Slaritt, Barbara Goldberg. Submission quantity: 1-6. Special interests: Translations, light verse, satire, metrical poems, humorous poems.

Light, Words & Music, 16710 16th N.W., Seattle, WA 98177, 206-546-1498, Fax 206-546-2585; sisp@aol.com. 1995. 8½×11.

LIGHTHOUSE STORY COLLECTIONS, Lighthouse Publications, PO Box 48114, Watauga, TX 76148-0114. Joyce Parchman, Doris Best. 1986. "All submissions must be 'G-Rated.' Each poem on separate sheet for evaluating purposes" circ. 300+. 4/yr. Pub'd 6 poems 1999; expects 12 poems 2000, 12 poems 2001. sub. price: $14.95/4 issues, $16.95 outside USA; sample: $4.50 (includes writers' guidelines, p/h). 52-56pp; 5½×8½; Rights purchased: first & first North American serial. Publishes 1% of poems submitted. Deadlines: none. Reporting time: 1-3 months, longer indicates interest. Payment: up to $5. Interested in new or unpub'd poets: yes. Simultaneous submissions accepted: no. Submission quantity: 5 or less. Special interests: traditional and free verse—light-hearted to inspirational.

LIGHTNING & ASH, 3010 Hennepin Avenue South #289, Minneapolis, MN 55408. 1996. circ. 500. 2/yr. sub. price: $10. 100pp; 8½×5½.

LILITH, 250 West 57th, #2432, New York, NY 10107, 212-757-0818. Marge Piercy, Poetry Editor. 1976. "We generally don't publish poems that have already appeared in other publications" circ. 10M. 4/yr. Pub'd 5 poems 1999; expects 4 poems 2000, 6 poems 2001. sub. price: $18; sample: $6, includes postage. 48pp; 8⅛×10⅞; Rights purchased: all. Publishes 5-10% of poems submitted. Deadlines: continuous; poetry will be read twice a year, submit by March 1 or Oct. 1. Reporting time: 8-12 weeks. Payment: issues. Interested in new or unpub'd poets: yes, provided the quality is high and the subject matter appropriate. Simultaneous submissions accepted: do not like to, but want authors to inform us if they are doing so. Recent contributors: Andrea Adam Brat, Netta Blatt, Zelda, Carol Davis, Davi Walders. Submission quantity: 3-5. Special interests: we look for poetry with Jewish feminist content, and poetry of interest to Jewish women.

LILLIPUT REVIEW, 282 Main Street, Pittsburgh, PA 15201. Don Wentworth. 1989. "All poems must be 10 lines or *less*. All styles and forms considered. SASE or in the trash, period. 3 poem maximum per submission. Any submission beyond the maximum will be returned unread. Currently, every fourth issue is a broadside featuring the work of one particular poet" circ. 225-300. Irregular. Pub'd 230 poems 1999; expects 230 poems 2000, 230 poems 2001. sub. price: $12; sample: $1 or SASE. 16pp; 4.25×3.6; Rights purchased: one time rights, all rights revert. Publishes 5% of poems submitted. Deadlines: continuous. Reporting time: 1-12 weeks. Payment: 2 copies. Interested in new or unpub'd poets: all manuscripts considered. Simultaneous submissions accepted: no. Recent contributors: Linda Zeiser, Lyn Lifshin, Lonnie Sherman, David Chorlton, Jennifer Besemer. Submission quantity: 3 maximum.

Limberlost Press, 17 Canyon Trail, Boise, ID 83716. Rick Ardinger, Editor. 1976. "Limberlost Press publishes poetry chapbooks in fine letterpressed editions. Recent titles include: *Have a Heart* by Robert Creeley, *The Canticle of Jack Kerouac* by Lawrence Ferlinghetti, *The Only Light We Read By* by Margaret Aho, and *Mind Writing Slogans* by Allen Ginsberg, with chapbooks forthcoming from Sherman Alexie, and Bruce Embree. Limberlost also publishes letterpressed broadsides and postcards. Poets considering submitting manuscripts should be familiar with the quality of the work Limberlost currently publishes." Pub'd 22 poetry titles 1999; expects 12 poetry titles 2000. size varies. Reporting time: 2 months. Payment: copies. Interested in new or unpub'd poets: yes. Simultaneous submissions accepted: yes, if specified. Recently published poets: Lawrence Ferlinghetti, Allen Ginsberg, Margaret Aho, William Studebaker, Sherman Alexie. Special interests: No restrictions on style or form. Special interest in poets from the Northwest and in Western writers generally.

LIME GREEN BULLDOZERS (AND OTHER RELATED SPECIES), PO Box 4333, Austin, TX 78765. Lainie Duro. 1986. "Will read unsolicited, but publication is invitation only project" circ. 300. 2/yr. Pub'd 50 poems 1999. sample price: $3. 50pp; 8½×11; Rights purchased: none. Publishes 25% of poems submitted. Deadlines: as answered. Reporting time: 2-6 months. Payment: none. Interested in new or unpub'd poets: yes. Simultaneous submissions accepted: yes. Recent contributors: Sigmund Weiss, Judson Crews, Lyn Lifshin. Submission quantity: 3-5.

LIMESTONE: A Literary Journal, English Dept., Univ. of Kentucky, 1215 Patterson Office Tower, Lexington, KY 40506-0027. M.J.W. O'Hara, Senior Literary Editor. 1979. "All submissions to *Limestone* should be made from August thru February. Please enclose a brief biographical statement with any submission including information on previously published work. We evaluate work on merit, not by subject" circ. 1M. 1/yr. Pub'd 45 poems 1999; expects 50 poems 2000, 45 poems 2001. sub. price: $5 individual, $10 institution; sample: $5 individual, $10 institution. 140-170pp; 5½×8½. Rights purchased: none. Publishes 5-10% of poems submitted. Deadlines: Early Feb. of each year. Reporting time: up to 6 months. Payment: 2 copies. Interested in new or unpub'd poets: yes. Simultaneous submissions accepted: yes. Recent contributors: Guy Davenport, James Baker Hall, Nikky Finney, Wendell Berry. Submission quantity: 1-5. Special interests: experimental poetry, regional, satire.

Lincoln Springs Press, 40 Post Avenue, Hawthorne, NJ 07506-1809. M. Gabrielle. 1987. "We have ceased accepting unsolicited poetry manuscripts for the time being. Do not send entire manuscript. Interested in sample and bio, but please include SASE for all." avg. press run 1M. Pub'd 2 poetry titles 1999. 5½×8½; avg. price, paper: $5.95. 72pp; Publishes 1% of poetry manuscripts submitted. Reporting time: 3 months. Payment: 15%. Interested in new or unpub'd poets: yes. Simultaneous submissions accepted: yes. Recently published poets: Arthur L. Clements, Lois Van Houten, James T. McCartin. Submission quantity: 5 poems and bio with SASE. Special interests: High-quality poetry of all types. Order a copy of one or two of our books to get an idea of the poetry we have selected.

LINGO, Hard Press, Inc., PO Box 184, West Stockbridge, MA 01266, 413-232-4690. 1993. circ. 3.5M. 2/yr. sub. price: $20; sample: $12.50. 172pp; 8½×11.

LINKS, 'Bude Haven' 18 Frankfield Rise, Tunbridge Wells TN2 5LF, United Kingdom, 01892-539800. Bill Headdon. 1997. circ. 200. 2/yr. Pub'd 60-75 poems 1999. sub. price: £4 (£5 ex UK); sample: £2 (£3 ex UK). 28pp; 5.5×8.3; Publishes 6% of poems submitted. Reporting time: 2-3 weeks. Interested in new or unpub'd poets: yes. Simultaneous submissions accepted: no. Recent contributors: Shuttle, Bartlett, Gross, Guest, Holloway. Submission quantity: up to 6.

LINQ, School of Humanities, James Cook Univ.-North Queensland, Townsville 4811, Australia, e-mail jcu.linq@jcu.edu.au. 1971. "send SAE and IRC" circ. 350. 2/yr. Pub'd 45 poems 1999; expects 45 poems 2000, 45 poems 2001. sub. price: $30 indiv.; $40 instit. including postage, Australian, Overseas $50 Australian. 140pp; 5½×8½; Rights purchased: first publication rights. Publishes 10% of poems submitted. Deadlines: June and November each year. Reporting time: 2 months. Payment: $20 per poem. Interested in new or unpub'd poets: yes. Simultaneous submissions accepted: yes. Recent contributors: Coral Hull, Ouang Yu, Peter Porter. Submission quantity: 5 or fewer. Special interests: Good quality poetry.

Lintel, 24 Blake Lane, Middletown, NY 10940, 212-674-4901. Walter James Miller. 1978. "We are not interested in traditional or 'greeting card' verse but only in the finest available poetry. One of our books, by Judy Light Ayyildiz, is illustrated with line drawings; its success means we shall hope for similar submissions, joint submissions by poet and artist working together. Most of our poets—Edmund Pennant, Walter James Miller, et al—help with sales by giving regular readings. Pennant's *Dream Navel* is our first book to go into a second printing; it won a P.S.A. award. We have been praised by *Motherroot* in a review of Leah Paransky's work, for our typographical perfection. Sample book, to potential authors only, at $1 plus $1.25 postage and handling; we send a recent volume rather than guidelines to any poet considering us as publisher and submitting that $2.25." avg. press run 1M. Pub'd 2 poetry titles 1999; expects 1 poetry title 2000, 3 poetry titles 2001. 5¾×9, 5×8; avg. price, cloth: $14.95; paper: $9.95. 70pp; Publishes about .5% of poetry manuscripts submitted. Reporting time: 60-90 days. Payment: negotiable. Interested in new or unpub'd poets: of course. Simultaneous submissions accepted: yes, if author notifies us at once of acceptance elsewhere. Recently published poets: Sue Elkind, Leah Paransky, Samuel Exler, Adrienne Wolfert, Nathan Teitel. Submission quantity: 5-6 with SASE.

Lion Press, Ltd., 108-22 Queens Boulevard, #221, Forest Hills, NY 11375, 718-271-1394. 1994. 6×9.

LIONESS EGGS RAGING, Pen-Dec Press, 2526 Chatham Woods, Grand Rapids, MI 49546. 2000. "Lusts for b&w art. Uses no fiction. Seeking barnstorming invectives" Irregular. Pub'd 30 poems 1999; expects 30 poems 2000, 30 poems 2001. sample price: $4. 24pp; 8½×5½; Publishes 15% of poems submitted. Interested in new or unpub'd poets: yes. Simultaneous submissions accepted: yes. Recent contributors: Phyllis Settles, Marion Smith, Cassius, Rachael Houseman. Submission quantity: 8-10.

LITERAL LATTE, 61 East 8th Street, Suite 240, New York, NY 10003, 212-260-5532. Jenine Gordon Bockman, Editor and Publisher. 1994. "Annual Literal Latte Poetry Awards (close in July)" circ. 25M. 6/yr. Pub'd 30 poems 1999. sub. price: $15 institution; $11 individual, $25 intern; sample: $3 incl. postage. 24pp; 11×17; Rights purchased: 1st pub, one time rights. Publishes 1-2% of poems submitted. Deadlines: ongoing; annual poetry awards close in July. Reporting time: 3 months. Payment: copies and subscriptions + $25. Interested in new or unpub'd poets: yes. Simultaneous submissions accepted: yes. Recent contributors: Allen Ginsberg, John Updike, John Tobias, Carol Muske, Lynne Sharon Schwartz. Submission quantity: up to 6. Special interests: All styles, quality only determining factor.

●**LITERALLY HORSES,** 116 Fellows Avenue, Kalamazoo, MI 49001, 616-345-5915. Laurie Cerny. Address poetry submissions to: PO Box 51554, Kalamazoo, MI 49005. 1999. "Submissions need to have a horse/rider, cowboy, or western lifestyle theme. Inspirational, upbeat pieces preferred. No off-color, sexual, racist themed poems wanted. Sponsors an annual contest. $75 1st place poem and 2 honorable mentions. Deadline: May 15 of each year. Submit up to 3 poems (under 35 lines), SASE, bio, $9.95 entry fee (includes a 1-year subscription to *Literally Horses*)." circ. 1M. 4/yr. Pub'd 15 poems 1999; expects 25 poems 2000, 40+ poems 2001. sub. price: $7.95; sample: $2.50. 20pp; 5½×8½; Rights purchased: one-time. Publishes 75% of poems submitted.

Deadlines: none, accepts poetry all year. Reporting time: 1 month. Payment: $3 poem + 3 copies. Interested in new or unpub'd poets: yes. Simultaneous submissions accepted: yes. Recent contributors: Tena Bastian. Submission quantity: up to 3 at a time.

LITERARY MOMENTS, PO Box 30534, Pensacola, FL 32503-1534, 850-857-0178. Larnette Phillips. 1999. "Always include SASE; tel. # and complete address and SSN" circ. 500. 4/yr. Pub'd 4 poems 1999; expects 4-8 poems 2000. sub. price: $65; sample: $12.50 US, $17.50 foreign. 20-50pp; 8½×11; Rights purchased: one-time rights. Publishes 90% of poems submitted. Deadlines: included under writing competitions. Reporting time: 1-2 months max. Payment: 2 copies, byline, author's bio, unless they win a competition—$500 1st, $250 2nd, $100 3rd, SASE for dates/guidelines. Interested in new or unpub'd poets: only new or unpublished poets. Simultaneous submissions accepted: yes. Recent contributors: Kevin Sanders, Lindsey Kelley, Frances Robinson. Submission quantity: 1-3.

THE LITERARY REVIEW, Fairleigh Dickinson University, 285 Madison Avenue, Madison, NJ 07940, 973-443-8564, Fax 973-443-8364. Walter Cummins, Editor-in-Chief; Martin Green, Co-Editor; Harry Keyishian, Co-Editor; William Zander, Co-Editor. 1957. "Our tastes are eclectic, but we assume all poems will have sophistication of form and control of language and technique." circ. 2M-2.5M. 4/yr. Pub'd 60-75 poems 1999; expects 60-75 poems 2000, 60-75 poems 2001. sub. price: $18 U.S., $21 foreign; sample: $5 recent issues. 128-152pp; 6×9; Rights purchased: we ask authors to approve reprints and give automatic approval or reversion of rights for reprinting in authors' book length collections. Publishes 5% of poems submitted. Deadlines: Sept. through May. Reporting time: 3-4 months. Payment: 2 copies. Interested in new or unpub'd poets: yes. Simultaneous submissions accepted: yes. Recent contributors: Beth Houston, Gary Fincke, Tom Hansen, Barbara Orton, Elisabeth Murawski. Submission quantity: no more than 6. Special interests: We use many translations and will consider long poems.

LITERARY ROCKET, PO Box 672, Water Mill, NY 11976-0672, e-mail RocketUSA@delphi.com. Darren Johnson, Editor. 1993. "Don't forget the SASE, cover letter" circ. 2M. 4/yr. Pub'd 20 poems 1999; expects 40 poems 2000, 50 poems 2001. sub. price: $5; sample: as low as 55¢ for issue #6 - send 2 unlicked stamps. 20pp; 4¼×11, 11×8½; Rights purchased: one time. Publishes 1-2% of poems submitted. Deadlines: rolling. Reporting time: 1-3 months. Payment: none. Interested in new or unpub'd poets: yes. Simultaneous submissions accepted: yes. Recent contributors: Lyn Lifshin, Ben Ohmart, Cheryl Townsend. Special interests: Experimental poetry, erotic verse, avante garde - nothing trite or 'old'. Streamlined poetry, if you know what I mean.

LITRAG, PO Box 21066, Seattle, WA 98111-3066, www.litrag.com. A.J. Rathbun. 1997. "We favor well crafted poems that show an interest in contemporary poetry; if you aren't actually reading contemporary poetry, we're probably not for you" circ. 1M. 3/yr. Pub'd 18 poems 1999; expects 18 poems 2000, 18 poems 2001. sub. price: $12; sample: $3. 40pp; 11×17; Rights purchased: First N. American Serialization Rights. Publishes 5% of poems submitted. Deadlines: on-going. Reporting time: 6-8 weeks. Payment: 2 copies, special gift, per diam when possible. Interested in new or unpub'd poets: yes. Simultaneous submissions accepted: yes. Recent contributors: Ed Skoog, Mark Halliday, Derick Burlson, Malena Morling. Submission quantity: 3. Special interests: translations, long poems.

Little Bayou Press, 1735 First Avenue North, St. Petersburg, FL 33713-8903, 813-822-3278. 1982. 7½×5½.

●**Little Leaf Press, Inc.,** PO Box 187, Milaca, MN 56353, 1-877-548-2431, Fax 320-556-3585, littleleaf@maxminn.com, www.maxminn.com/littleleaf. 1998. 8½×11.

THE LITTLE MAGAZINE, English Department, State Univ. of New York at Albany, Albany, NY 12222, website www.albany.edu/~litmag. Manny Savopoulos, Ted Fristrom. 1965. "We have no set guidelines, we're open to both experimental and traditional work, that is conceived of or lends itself to hypermedia publication. We'd like to see more hypertexts, prose poems, language poems, avante garde poems, poems by minorities." circ. 2M. 1/yr. Pub'd 56 poems 1999; expects 50 poems 2000. sub. price: $15 (for the CD-Rom); sample: $15 (for the CD-Rom). Rights purchased: 1st North American serial rights. Publishes 2% of poems submitted. Deadlines: We do not read from May to August. Reporting time: 2-8 weeks. Payment: 2 copies of mag. Interested in new or unpub'd poets: yes. Simultaneous submissions accepted: yes. Submission quantity: 3 or 4.

Little River Press, 10 Lowell Avenue, Westfield, MA 01085, 413-568-5598. Ronald Edwards. 1976. avg. press run 50-150. Pub'd 2 poetry titles 1999; expects 3 poetry titles 2000, 3 poetry titles 2001. 7½×6¼; avg. price, cloth: $5. 20pp.

Livingston Press (see also Swallow's Tale Press), Station 22, University of West Alabama, Livingston, AL 35470. Joe Taylor. 1984. avg. press run 1M. Pub'd 2 poetry titles 1999; expects 1 poetry title 2000, 1 poetry title 2001. 5½×8½; avg. price, cloth: $20.95; paper: $9.95. 75pp; Publishes 2% of poetry manuscripts submitted. Reporting time: 6 months. Payment: 15% of run. Interested in new or unpub'd poets: no. Simultaneous submissions accepted: yes. Recently published poets: R.T. Smith, Stephen Corey, Eugene Walter. Submission quantity: book length.

LO STRANIERO: The Stranger, Der Fremde, L'Etranger, Via Chiaia 149, Napoli 80121, Italy, ITALY/81/426052. 1985. circ. 10M. 2/yr. sub. price: $50; sample: $20. 32pp; 8½×13; Rights purchased: none. Payment: none. Interested in new or unpub'd poets: yes. Recent contributors: W. Bronk, A. Yasusada, S. Smith, R. Johnson, R. Kostelanetz. Special interests: ''On estrangement''

Lockhart Press, Inc., Box 1366, Lake Stevens, WA 98258, fax 206-335-4818, ral@halcyon.com, www.ralockhart.com. Russell A. Lockhart. 1982. ''Our books are limited editions entirely handmade with the finest materials available and therefore, are suitable only for special editions of work of exceptional merit.'' avg. press run 120-200. Pub'd 1 poetry title 1999; expects 1 poetry title 2000, 1 poetry title 2001. 6×9, 9×12; avg. price, cloth: $75; paper: $10-$12. 80pp; Publishes 1% of poetry manuscripts submitted. Reporting time: 90 days. Payment: 15% net sales, 10 copies at time of publication. Interested in new or unpub'd poets: yes. Simultaneous submissions accepted: yes. Recently published poets: Janet Dallet, Marc Hudson, Peter Levitt. Submission quantity: 5. Special interests: We are especially interested in poetry originating in dreams—all kinds of material open to consideration.

Logodaedalus (see also LOGODAEDALUS), PO Box 14193, Harrisburg, PA 17104. Paul Weidenhoff, W.B. Keckler. 1993. ''Don't send poetry that could have been written in 1820. Don't send poetry that a computer could have written'' avg. press run 100-150. Pub'd 2 poetry titles 1999; expects 1 poetry title 2000, 1 poetry title 2001. size varies; avg. price, paper: $3.50. 24-110pp; Publishes less than 1% of poetry manuscripts submitted. Reporting time: under 6 months. Payment: flexible, usually in copies. Interested in new or unpub'd poets: rarely. Simultaneous submissions accepted: no. Recently published poets: Celestine Frost, Steve Carll. Submission quantity: 5-10. Special interests: Experimental poetry with an understanding of the literary past.

LOGODAEDALUS, Logodaedalus, PO Box 14193, Harrisburg, PA 17104. Paul Weindenhoff, W.B. Keckler. 1991. circ. 100+. 1-2/yr. sample price: $5. 32-40pp; 8½×11; Rights purchased: none. Publishes 20% of poems submitted. Reporting time: 3-6 weeks. Payment: copies. Interested in new or unpub'd poets: yes. Simultaneous submissions accepted: no. Recent contributors: Celestine Frost, Jeff Vetock, Steve Carll, Richard Kostelanetz. Submission quantity: SASE included, send as many as you want. Special interests: Experimental poetry, postmodern and L=A=N=G=U=A=G=E writing.

LONDON REVIEW OF BOOKS, 28-30 Little Russell Street, London WC1A 2HN, England, 020-7209-1141, fax 020-7209-1151. Jean McNicol, Deputy Editor. 1979. ''Please include SAE.'' circ. 34.9M. 24/yr. Pub'd 30 poems 1999. sub. price: $42; sample: $3.95 + postage. 40pp; 330×246mm; Rights purchased: first serial. Payment: negotiable. Interested in new or unpub'd poets: yes. Simultaneous submissions accepted: no. Recent contributors: Tony Harrison, Craig Raine, Frederick Seidel, Les Murray, Seamus Heaney. Submission quantity: up to 5.

LONE STARS MAGAZINE, 4219 Flinthill, San Antonio, TX 78230-1619. Milo Rosebud. 1992. ''Poetry must have feeling and be coherent'' circ. 200. 3/yr. Pub'd 500+ poems 1999. sub. price: $15; sample: $5. 24pp; 8½×11; Rights purchased: One-time publications, all rights revert to author. We publish a large % of quality works submitted. Reporting time: 4-6 weeks. Interested in new or unpub'd poets: yes. Simultaneous submissions accepted: yes. Recent contributors: Terry Lee, Marian F. Park, Jan Brevet, Sandra Wangbichler, Virginia Gomez. Submission quantity: 3-5. Special interests: All forms welcomed; partial to well rhymed lyric forms that have a train of thought, tell a story, and hold the readers interest.

Lone Willow Press, PO Box 31647, Omaha, NE 68131-0647. Dale Champy. 1994. ''If you don't send a SASE - I chuck the typescript. Write for guidelines'' avg. press run 200. Pub'd 2 poetry titles 1999; expects 2 poetry titles 2000, 2 we'll do 3 in 1998- 3 more in 1999 poetry titles 2001. 5½×8½; avg. price, paper: $7.95. 25-40pp; Publishes 2% of poetry manuscripts submitted. Reporting time: 2 months. Payment: 25 copies as payment, royalty when expenses met. Interested in new or unpub'd poets: Manuscripts are uaually invited but I have accepted some sent in over the transom. Simultaneous submissions accepted: yes, if I am informed. Recently published poets: Fredrick Zydek, Brian Bengtson, Marjorie Power, Philip Arnold, Carolyn Riehle. Submission quantity: complete typescript. Special interests: We're open to anything. Publish only collections with a single theme.

LONG SHOT, PO Box 6238, Hoboken, NJ 07030. Nancy Mercado, Danny Short, Andy Clausen. 1982. ''Don't send query letters, just send work and we'll get to it.'' circ. 2M. 2/yr. Pub'd 100-150 poems 1999; expects 100-150 poems 2000, 100-150 poems 2001. sub. price: $12; sample: $8. 160pp; 5×8; Rights purchased: all rights reserved by individual contributors. Publishes 2% of poems submitted. Reporting time: 10-12 weeks. Payment: copies. Interested in new or unpub'd poets: sure. Simultaneous submissions accepted: as long as it doesn't wind up being simultaneously published. Recent contributors: Amiri Baraka, Pedro Pietri, Sherman Alexie, Peg E. Gaines, Eileen Myles. Submission quantity: doesn't matter. Special interests: We like exciting stuff.

LONGHOUSE, Longhouse, 1604 River Road, Guilford, VT 05301, e-mail poetry@sover.net; www.sover.net/~poetry. Bob Arnold, Editor, Publisher. 1973. ''*Longhouse* is always looking for the independent, serious working poet." circ. 200. 1/yr. Pub'd 50 poems 1999; expects 50 poems 2000, 50 poems 2001. sub. price: $12 (includes bookshop catalog of new and used books); sample: $10. 35pp; 8½×14, 8½×11; Reporting time: 2 weeks. Payment: copies. Interested in new or unpub'd poets: yes—please be familiar with the publication. Simultaneous submissions accepted: no. Recent contributors: Lorine Niedecker, Eduardo Roditi, Robert Creeley, Antler, Jonathan Greene. Submission quantity: 3-5. Special interests: Translations, regional poems, long poems, political poems.

Longhouse (see also LONGHOUSE), 1604 River Road, Guilford, VT 05301, e-mail poetry@sover.net; www.sover.net/~poetry. Bob Arnold, Editor, Publisher. 1973. "Basically a very limited and homespun policy-much like our *Longhouse* magazine-much of our interested are (solicited) but we never close the door to new voices." avg. press run 25-100. Pub'd 1 poetry title 1999; expects 1 poetry title 2000, 1 poetry title 2001. size varies; avg. price, other: $10. 16-50pp; Reporting time: 1 month. Payment: copies. Interested in new or unpub'd poets: yes. Simultaneous submissions accepted: no. Recently published poets: Janine Pommy-Vega, Ian Hamilton Finlay, Franco Beltrametti, Bill Deemer, Gael Turnbull. Submission quantity: 5. Special interests: Translations, regional poetry, long poems.

Longleaf Press, Methodist College, English Dept., 5400 Ramsey Street, Fayetteville, NC 28311, 910-822-5403. Robin Greene, Poetry Editor. 1997. "Annual fall chapbook contest, write for guidelines" avg. press run 500. Expects 1 poetry title 2000, 2 poetry titles 2001. 5½×8½; avg. price, paper: $6. 30pp; Publishes 2% of poetry manuscripts submitted. Reporting time: 4 months. Payment: honorarium to authors and 50 copies. Interested in new or unpub'd poets: yes. Simultaneous submissions accepted: yes. Recently published poets: Barbara Presnell. Submission quantity: 20 pages. Special interests: no light verse or religious.

THE LONSDALE - The International Quarterly of The Romantic Six, Trash City 3rd Floor, 6-18-16 Nishi-Gotanda, Shinagawa-ku, Tokyo 141, Japan, 03(5434)0729. 1994. circ. 30M. 4/yr. sub. price: $12, $20/2 years; sample: free. 12pp; 8½×11.

Loom Press, Box 1394, Lowell, MA 01853. Paul Marion, Publisher. 1978. avg. press run 500-1M. Pub'd 1 poetry title 1999; expects 2 poetry titles 2000, 2 poetry titles 2001. 6×9; avg. price, paper: $10 book. Pages vary; Reporting time: 12-16 weeks. Payment: negotiable. Interested in new or unpub'd poets: yes. Simultaneous submissions accepted: yes. Recently published poets: Tom Sexton, Juan Delgado, Doug Flaherty, Susan April, Marie Louise St. Onge. Submission quantity: 5. Special interests: Contemporary poetry; arts and culture.

LOONFEATHER: A magazine of poetry, short prose, and graphics, Loonfeather Press, PO Box 1212, Bemidji, MN 56619, 218-751-4869. Betty Rossi, Marsh Muirhead, Elmo Heggie. 1979. "We're a regional magazine and use material primarily from or about northern MN, but not exclusively. Often use special emphasis or theme. Writers unfamiliar with magazine should write for sample copy and guidelines." circ. 300. 2/yr. Pub'd 61 poems 1999; expects 55 poems 2000, 55 poems 2001. sub. price: $7.50; sample: $5 postpaid. 48pp; 5½×8½; Rights purchased: one-time rights. Publishes 15% of poems submitted. Deadlines: July 31, Jan. 31 for Nov. and May publication. Reporting time: 1 month following publication date. Payment: 2 copies. Interested in new or unpub'd poets: yes. Simultaneous submissions accepted: no. Recent contributors: Marilyn Boe, Melanie Richards, Michael Moos, Bradley Steffens. Submission quantity: no more than 10.

Loonfeather Press (see also LOONFEATHER: A magazine of poetry, short prose, and graphics), PO Box 1212, Bemidji, MN 56619, 218-751-4869. Betty Rossi, Marsh Muirhead, Elmo Heggie. 1979. "We are not interested in light verse." avg. press run 1M. Expects 1 poetry title 2000. 5½×8½; avg. price, paper: $9.95. 60pp; Reporting time: 3-6 months. Payment: 10% royalties, copies, payment. Interested in new or unpub'd poets: Yes. Simultaneous submissions accepted: No. Recently published poets: William Borden, Carol Ann Russell, Philip Dancey. Submission quantity: unrestricted.

Lorien House, Attn: David Wilson, PO Box 1112, Black Mountain, NC 28711, 828-669-6211. David Wilson, Editor. 1969. "Poetry can only be done as a 'subsidy' arrangement at this time. I keep the cost as low as possible" avg. press run 100-200. Pub'd 1 poetry title 1999; expects 1 poetry title 2000, 1 poetry title 2001. 5½×8½; avg. price, paper: $8. 100pp; Publishes 1% of poetry manuscripts submitted. Reporting time: 1 month. Payment: individually determined. Interested in new or unpub'd poets: yes. Simultaneous submissions accepted: no. Recently published poets: Diana Goure, Al Beck, Charles Baar, Martha Anderson. Submission quantity: 10.

LOS, 150 North Catalina Street #2, Los Angeles, CA 90004. Virginia M. Geoffrey, Editor; I.B. Scrood, Editor; P.N. Bouts, Editor. 1991. Recent contributors: Ed Orr, Peter Layton, Ahmed Balfouni.

LOST AND FOUND TIMES, Luna Bisonte Prods, 137 Leland Ave, Columbus, OH 43214. John M. Bennett. 1975. "Interested in experimentation, surrealism, visual poetry, craziness. Would like to see more experimental material in Spanish." circ. 300. Irregular. Pub'd 100 poems 1999; expects 100 poems 2000, 100 poems 2001. sub. price: $25/5 issues; sample: $6 for sample. 56pp; size varies; Rights purchased: rights revert to author upon publication. Publishes a small % of poems submitted. Deadlines: none. Reporting time: 1 week.

Payment: copies. Interested in new or unpub'd poets: yes. Simultaneous submissions accepted: no. Recent contributors: John M. Bennett, Jim Leftwich, Sheila Murphy, Ivan Arguelles, Peter Ganick. Submission quantity: some.

Lost Coast Press, 155 Cypress Street, Fort Bragg, CA 95437.

LOST GENERATION JOURNAL, Route 5 Box 134, Salem, MO 65560, 314-729-2545; 729-5669. Deloris Gray Wood, Editor. 1973. ''Send only poems about Paris in the twenties and the American expatriates who were there. Short, 20 lines or less'' circ. 400. 1/yr. Pub'd 9 poems 1999; expects 10 poems 2000, 10 poems 2001. sub. price: $10; sample: $10. 32pp; 8½×11; Rights purchased: 1st N.A. Publishes 10% of poems submitted. Deadlines: accept anytime. Reporting time: 6 weeks, need SASE. Payment: 1¢ per word or 2 issues when poem is published. Interested in new or unpub'd poets: yes. Simultaneous submissions accepted: yes. Recent contributors: L.E. Ward, Joan Auer Kelly, Deloris Gray Wood, Deborah A. Casty, Robert W. Lewis. Submission quantity: unlimited. Special interests: Light verse on the topic.

Lost Horse Press, 9327 South Cedar Rim Lane, Spokane, WA 99224, 509-448-4047; e-mail losthorse@ior.com. 1998. 8¼×5½.

Lost Prophet Press (see also THIN COYOTE), 2657 Grand Street NE, Mineapolis, MN 55418-2603, 612-781-6224, Fax 612-333-5800. 1992. ''Cover letters appreciated, exhaustive publishing histories not.'' 5½×8½. Reporting time: 1 month. Interested in new or unpub'd poets: yes. Simultaneous submissions accepted: yes. Recently published poets: Jonis Agee, Simon Perchik, Patrick McKinnon, Joseph Shields, Sappho. Submission quantity: 5-10 pages.

Lost Roads Publishers, 351 Nayatt Road, Barrington, RI 02806-4336, 401-245-8069. C. D. Wright, Co-Editor; Forrest Gander, Co-Editor. 1977. ''Most acceptances from solicited mss. Query 1st with small sample. Always include SASE. Familiarize yourself with the press prior to submitting. Support presses from whom you want support; buy books'' avg. press run 1M. Pub'd 4 poetry titles 1999; expects 4 poetry titles 2000, 4 poetry titles 2001. 6×9; avg. price, paper: $12. 48-64pp; Publishes 5% of poetry manuscripts submitted. Reporting time: 30 days. Payment: $300 to author, standard royalty contract with editions subsequent to the 1st run. Interested in new or unpub'd poets: query first please. Simultaneous submissions accepted: yes. Recently published poets: Frances Mayes, John Taggart, Josephine Foo, Sam Truitt, J.L. Jacobs. Submission quantity: query with sample of 5-8 pages; ms upon request, 40 pages or more. Special interests: Work in translation, experimental poetry, long poems - all favored.

Lotus Press, Inc., PO Box 21607, Detroit, MI 48221, 313-861-1280, fax 313-861-4740, lotuspress@aol.com. Naomi Madgett, Editor. 1972. ''We are a tax-exempt company under IRS Code 501(c)(3) and some of our poets (as well as the general public) choose to make contributions, but they are not required and do not in any way determine our selections. We are not subsidy publishers. We specialize in poetry by black American authors. We are not concerned about message or ideology, but we are concerned about literary excellence. Those still hung up in the Sixties have often not studied their craft. 'Black poetry' grows out of the uniqueness of individual and collective African-American experiences and is therefore sometimes different from 'mainstream' European poetry. But black poetry does not need to apologize for its differences, when they occur—unless its only value is its blackness. A good poet, of whatever ancestry, does not excuse sloppiness in writing skills with the tired argument that any mention of literary standards is automatically racist, or that black poets need not be concerned with 'white standards.' (Racism, of course, does exist in literature, as well as elsewhere in the American scheme of values, and is as evident in the sentimental raving, by some critics, over work that should be considered distinctly inferior by any standards, as in the caustic attacks [or complete indifference] by others on superior writing, simply because of its racial content or the critics' ignorance.) Good poetry can be as political as it needs to be, as long as its message is conveyed effectively. It deserves to be called *art* when its creator begins to think of him/herself as an artist and trains him/herself accordingly. Unfortunately, much poetry that is mediocre or just plain bad has found its way into print, and the novice may be deceived into imitating the worst examples. Entries for the annual Naomi Long Madgett Poetry Award are received Apr. 1 to June 1 each year. Winners must be African-American. Interested persons should send SASE after Jan. 1, 2000 for guidelines or request them by e-mail. Winner receives $500 cash and Lotus Press publishes the manuscript.'' avg. press run 500-2M. Pub'd 2 poetry titles 1999; expects 3 poetry titles 2000, 2 poetry titles 2001. 5½×8½; avg. price, cloth: $25; paper: $12; other: $21 set of 7 laminated broadsides. 72-120pp; Publishes 1% of poetry manuscripts submitted. Reporting time: 6 weeks. Payment: copies, additional copies may be ordered at a discount (no requirement that this be done), see info on award. Interested in new or unpub'd poets: yes, if poets have studied craft. Simultaneous submissions accepted: no. Recently published poets: Robert Chrisman, Ruth Ellen Kocher, Sybil Kein. Submission quantity: 5-10. Special interests: We are interested in serious poetry that demonstrates a knowledge of what poetry is and how it operates. 'Blackness' in content is no excuse for sloppiness, and we are impartial in terms of subject matter.

THE LOUISIANA REVIEW, Division of Liberal Arts, Louisiana State Univ., PO Box 1129, Eunice, LA

70535. 1999. circ. 300-600. 1/yr. sub. price: $3. 48-72pp; 8½×11.

Louisiana State University Press, Baton Rouge, LA 70893, 504-388-6294. L. Phillabaum, Director. 1935. "Query first." avg. press run 750 cloth, 1M paper. Pub'd 6 poetry titles 1999; expects 8 poetry titles 2000, 8 poetry titles 2001. avg. price, cloth: $15.95; paper: $8.95. 64pp; Publishes small % of poetry manuscripts submitted. Reporting time: 2-3 months. Payment: varies. Interested in new or unpub'd poets: yes. Simultaneous submissions accepted: yes. Recently published poets: Susan Ludvigson, Elizabeth S. Morgan, Margaret Gibson, David R. Slavitt, Anthony Petrosky. Submission quantity: 5-10.

THE LOUISVILLE REVIEW, Spalding University, 851 S. 4th Street, Louisville, KY 40203, 502-585-9911. David Garrison, Kathleen Driskell. 1976. circ. 500. 2/yr. Pub'd 30 poems 1999; expects 30 poems 2000, 30 poems 2001. sub. price: $8; sample: $4. 96pp; 5½×8½; Rights purchased: 1st North American rights. Publishes 10% of poems submitted. Deadlines: read year round. Reporting time: 3 months. Payment: 1 copy of magazine. Interested in new or unpub'd poets: yes. Simultaneous submissions accepted: no. Recent contributors: Maura Stanton, Greg Pape, Jeffrey Skinner, Stuart Dybek, Maureen Morehead. Submission quantity: 3-5.

L'OUVERTURE, PO Box 8565, Atlanta, GA 30306, 404-572-9141. 1996. "We want only poems of political or sociological content. No love poems." circ. 500. 6/yr. Pub'd 30 poems 1999; expects 30 poems 2000, 30 poems 2001. sub. price: $15; sample: $3.50. 44pp; 8½×11; Rights purchased: rights revert back to poet. Publishes 10% of poems submitted. Reporting time: 6-8 weeks. Payment: 2 contributors copies. Interested in new or unpub'd poets: yes. Simultaneous submissions accepted: yes. Recent contributors: Dr. Juba, Stephanie Siegel, B.Z. Niditch, David Burch. Submission quantity: 1-6 poems. Special interests: We are very sympathetic to satirical and experimental poetry. We would also like to see more translations. Longer pieces would have a tougher time being placed within our pages.

THE LOWELL REVIEW, 3075 Harness Drive, Florissant, MO 63033-3711, E-mail rita@etext.org; website http://www.etext.org/Zines/LowellReview. 1994. circ. 200. 1/yr. Pub'd 22 poems 1999; expects 19 poems 2000. sub. price: $7; sample: $5. 70pp; 5½×8½; Rights purchased: FNASR. Publishes 1-2% of poems submitted. Deadlines: May 1st. Reporting time: 1 week-4 months. Payment: 1 copy. Interested in new or unpub'd poets: yes. Simultaneous submissions accepted: yes. Recent contributors: Jim Daniels, Lola Haskins, Naomi Feigelson Chase, Sam Cornish, Stephen Frech. Special interests: Premarily interested in the narrative form. We're most interested in labor issues/working class life. We love the occasional humorous poem!

LOWLANDS REVIEW, 6109 Magazine, New Orleans, LA 70118. Tom Whalen. 1974. "Due to economic and temporal factors, *LR* is in a long-term holding pattern and is not accepting unsolicited manuscripts." circ. 400. 2/yr. sub. price: $6; sample: $3. 48pp; 6×9; Recent contributors: Christopher Middleton, Leon Stokesbury, Karl Krolow, Henri Michaux, Gunter Eich.

Low-Tech Press, 30-73 47th Street, Long Island City, NY 11103, 718-721-0946. Ron Kolm. 1981. "I don't use unsolicited mss." avg. press run 500. Pub'd 1 poetry title 1999; expects 1 poetry title 2000, 1 poetry title 2001. 5½×8½; avg. price, paper: $5. 36-50pp; Reporting time: 2 weeks. Payment: percentage of copies (i.e. 25 copies out of a print run of 500). Interested in new or unpub'd poets: I like to see new work, but I usually only use solicited mss. Simultaneous submissions accepted: yes. Recently published poets: Hal Sirowitz, Max Blagg, Janet Hamill, Richard Kostelanetz, Mike Topp. Submission quantity: 5. Special interests: I'm especially interested in short, image-oriented work—and I like to couple words and graphics.

LS Press, Inc. (see also LATINO STUFF REVIEW), PO Box 440195, Miami, FL 33144, 305-262-1777; fax 305-447-8586; www.ejl@lspress.net. 1993. size varies.

LUCIDITY, Bearhouse Publishing, 398 Mundell Rd., Eureka Springs, AR 72631-9505, 501-253-9351, E-mail tbadger@ipa.net. Ted O. Badger, Editor & Publisher. 1985. "Do not submit without first securing guidelines for SASE. We are now paying poets for most selections." circ. 300. 2/yr. Pub'd 285 poems 1999; expects 300 poems 2000, 300 poems 2001. sub. price: $6; sample: $2.75. 68pp; 5½×8½; Rights purchased: one time rights only. Publishes 10-12% of poems submitted. Deadlines: none, entries missing one issue held for the next. Reporting time: 120-150 days. Payment: cash & copies plus 3 awards each issue of $15/$10/$5. Interested in new or unpub'd poets: yes, but query first. Simultaneous submissions accepted: yes. Recent contributors: Mary M. Carlisle, Winnie Fitzpatrick, Mickey Huffstutler, Mary Gribble, Barbara Kaplan. Submission quantity: 1-5 *but only according to guidelines.* Special interests: Any style or subject but written in comprehensible diction. We seek lucid poems dealing with the whole spectrum of human relationships, experiences. Please, no political, nature or religious poems.

LUCKY HEART BOOKS, Salt Lick Press, 1900 West Highway 6, Waco, TX 76712. James Haining. 1939. "Open. No particular bias toward content, form, or muse." circ. 1M. Irregular. Expects 40 poems 2000. sub. price: $15, $1 samplers. 68pp; 8×10½, 9×6; Rights purchased: all rights released after publication. Publishes 1-2% of poems submitted. Deadlines: none. Reporting time: 2-5 weeks. Payment: copies. Interested in new or unpub'd poets: yes. Simultaneous submissions accepted: yes. Recent contributors: Michael Lally, Gerald Burns,

114

Robert Trammell, Julie Siegel, David Searcy.

LULLWATER REVIEW, Box 22036, Emory University, Atlanta, GA 30322, 404-727-6184. Rotating editors. 1990. "Always include cover letter and SASE; watch *Poets & Writers* for information about national contests; we prefer submissions from September to April" circ. 2M-3M. 2/yr. Pub'd 50 poems 1999; expects 70 poems 2000, 70 poems 2001. sub. price: $12; sample: $5. 110pp; 6×9; Publishes 5% of poems submitted. Deadlines: We accept throughout the year. Reporting time: 6-8 weeks, longer during summer. Payment: 3 copies of issue. Interested in new or unpub'd poets: yes. Simultaneous submissions accepted: yes, if we are notified. Recent contributors: Colette Inez, Charles Edward Eaton, Vivian Shipley, Lyn Lifshin, Jaroslaw Seifert. Submission quantity: 6 or fewer. Special interests: we publish translations.

LUMMOX JOURNAL, Lummox Press, PO Box 5301, San Pedro, CA 90733-5301, 562-439-9858, e-mail lumoxraindog@earthlink.net. Raindog, Editor. 1995. "Lummox accepts articles on the creative process-poetry is published once a year in special issue (April)" circ. 200. 12/yr. Pub'd 20 poems 1999; expects 30 poems 2000, 30 poems 2001. sub. price: $20; sample: $2 or trade. 20-24pp; 5½×8½; Rights purchased: none. Publishes 10% of poems submitted. Deadlines: 20th of each month. Reporting time: 1-3 months. Payment: contributor's copy. Interested in new or unpub'd poets: yes. Simultaneous submissions accepted: yes. Recent contributors: Scott Wannberg, Gerry Locklin, Todd Moore, Rene Diedrich, A.D. Winans. Submission quantity: 2-3. Special interests: Geo-political or social commentary poetry, poetry written without pretense - from the heart.

Lummox Press (see also LUMMOX JOURNAL), PO Box 5301, San Pedro, CA 90733-5301, 310-521-9642, e-mail lumoxraindog@earthlink.net. RD Armstrong. 1994. "$5 reading fee on unsolicited mss, cover letter w/bio (short)" avg. press run 100-300. Pub'd 16 poetry titles 1999; expects 12 poetry titles 2000, 12 poetry titles 2001. 4¼×5½; avg. price, paper: $5; other: $8-$10. 48pp; Publishes 20% of poetry manuscripts submitted. Reporting time: 2-3 months. Payment: after 2nd printing, author receives 10% profit. Interested in new or unpub'd poets: yes. Simultaneous submissions accepted: no. Recently published poets: Scott Wannberg, Todd Moore, Hugh Fox, A.D. Winans, Linda Lerner. Submission quantity: 30-40. Special interests: Experimental poetry, longpoems. Occasional themed anthologies: jazz, blues, gay, AIDS, homeless, the road.

Luna Bisonte Prods (see also LOST AND FOUND TIMES), 137 Leland Ave, Columbus, OH 43214, 614-846-4126. John M. Bennett. 1974. "Interested in experimentation, surrealism, visual poetry, craziness." avg. press run 300. Pub'd 2 poetry titles 1999; expects 2 poetry titles 2000, 2 poetry titles 2001. size varies; avg. price, paper: $5; other: $15 (signed and lettered). 30-40pp; Publishes a small % of poetry manuscripts submitted. Reporting time: 1 week. Payment: copies. Interested in new or unpub'd poets: yes. Simultaneous submissions accepted: no. Recently published poets: John M. Bennett, Sheila E. Murphy, Peter Ganick, Bob Heman, Ivan Arguelles. Submission quantity: 10 approx.

Lunar Offensive Publications (see also RAG SHOCK), 1910 Foster Avenue, Brooklyn, NY 11230-1902. Stephen Fried. 1994. "No unsolicited mss for chapbooks." avg. press run 200. Pub'd 5 poetry titles 1999; expects 8 poetry titles 2000, 12 poetry titles 2001. 5½×8½; avg. price, cloth: none; paper: $5. 32pp; Payment: 30 copies from first run, sales split 50/50 on agreed chap price. Interested in new or unpub'd poets: yes. Simultaneous submissions accepted: yes. Recently published poets: Alan Gold, Vito Ricci, Letta Neely, David Mark Speer, Thea Hillman. Submission quantity: 5 or less. Special interests: Need authors to go over their edges, into the realms of the disturbing and disturbed.

●LUNGFULL! MAGAZINE, 126 East 4th Street #2, New York, NY 10003, 212-533-9317, lungfull@interport.net. 1995. circ. 1M. 2/yr. sub. price: $15.90; sample: $9.50. 200pp; 7×8½.

LUNO, 31960 SE Chin Street, Boring, OR 97009, 503-663-5153. 1984. circ. 200+ network. 9/yr. sub. price: $10; sample: $1 + stamp. 10pp; 8½×11.

LUZ EN ARTE Y LITERATURA, 5008 Hazeltine Avenue #16, Sherman Oaks, CA 91423. Veronica Miranda, Editor. 1992. "The magazine has different topics in each issue. Please contact editor for information about theme issues" circ. 1M. 1/yr. Pub'd 80 poems 1999; expects 80 poems 2000, 80 poems 2001. sub. price: $25; sample: $8. 100-120pp; 6½×8½; Rights purchased: one time rights. Publishes 10% of poems submitted. Deadlines: six months before publication date. Reporting time: 6-12 months. Payment: 1 copy. Interested in new or unpub'd poets: yes. Simultaneous submissions accepted: yes. Recent contributors: Carlota Caulfield, Angela McEwan, Joan Peternel, Isaac Goldenberg, Laureano Albam. Submission quantity: no less than ten. Special interests: We publish bilingually. We are interested in translations English/Espanish Spanis/English. We make our own translation sometimes. We are very interested in spanish written poetry.

Lycanthrope Press, PO Box 9028, Metairie, LA 70005-9028, 504-866-9756. Rev. Laurence Talbot. 1993. "Inquiry letter first. Will not accept without." avg. press run 1M. avg. price, cloth: $9.95; paper: $5.95. 85pp; Publishes 10% of poetry manuscripts submitted. Reporting time: 6 months. Payment: standard. Interested in new or unpub'd poets: yes. Simultaneous submissions accepted: yes. Recently published poets: Victor Klein, Laurence Talbot, W. von Lafourche. Submission quantity: 5. Special interests: experimental.

LYNX EYE, 1880 Hill Drive, Los Angeles, CA 90041, 323-550-8522. Pam McCully, Kathryn Morrison. 1994. "Well crafted work is our only specification" circ. 500. 4/yr. Pub'd 80 poems 1999; expects 80 poems 2000, 80 poems 2001. sub. price: $25; sample: $7.95. 120pp; 5½×8; Rights purchased: FNASR. Publishes 5% of poems submitted. Reporting time: 12 weeks. Payment: $10 per piece plus 3 comp. copies. Interested in new or unpub'd poets: yes, each issue features a previous unpublished writer/artist. Simultaneous submissions accepted: yes, if specified as such. Recent contributors: A.D. Winans, Alicia Vogl Saenz, Don Mager, Dawn Zapletal, R. Kimm. Submission quantity: 6 or less preferable.

THE LYRIC, 307 Dunton Drive SW, Blacksburg, VA 24060-5127. Leslie Mellichamp, Editor. 1921. "We use rhymed verse in traditional forms, for the most part; 40 lines usual limit. We print poetry only—no reviews, ads, etc. We do not seek to shock, embitter, or confound readers; avoid contemporary political or social problems; accessible on 1st or 2nd reading as a rule. Work must be original, unpublished and not under consideration elsewhere. Send SASE if a reply is expected." circ. 650. 4/yr. Pub'd 250 poems 1999; expects 250 poems 2000, 250 poems 2001. sub. price: $12 a year, $22 for 2 years $30 for 3 years, Canada and other foreign add $2 per year postage; sample: $3. 36pp; 5⅜×7½; Rights purchased: 1st North American. Publishes 5% of poems submitted. Deadlines: seasonal poems should be submitted 6 months in advance of publication. Reporting time: 2 months. Payment: contributors receive 1 copy of the issue containing their work and are eligible for quarterly and annual prizes (cash) totaling $800. Interested in new or unpub'd poets: yes. Simultaneous submissions accepted: we read all submissions. Recent contributors: Rhina P. Espaillat, Alfred Dorn, Gail White, John R. Quinn, R.H. Morrison. Submission quantity: 5 max. Special interests: No translations.

M

THE MAC GUFFIN, Schoolcraft College, 18600 Haggerty Road, Livonia, MI 48152, 313-462-4400, ext. 5292 or 5327. Arthur J. Lindenberg. 1983. "We are interested in quality work. Since we publish year round, we will read and consider poems at any time. We hope to be able to pay contributors within the next few years. Sponsors a national POET HUNT. Send an SASE for rules" circ. 600. 3/yr. Pub'd 100 poems 1999; expects 80 poems 2000, 100 poems 2001. sub. price: $18; sample: $6. 160+pp; 6×9; Rights purchased: 1st. Publishes 15-20% of poems submitted. Deadlines: We read year around. Reporting time: 10-12 weeks. Payment: 2 copies and occasional honoraria. Interested in new or unpub'd poets: yes. Simultaneous submissions accepted: no. Recent contributors: Barbara Lefcowitz, Tom Sheehan, Rustin Larson, Patricia Hooper, Virgil Suarez. Submission quantity: up to 5. Special interests: No biases on form or genre. Light verse, however, must be exceptional. But so must all poems.

MACHINEGUN MAGAZINE: New Lit. Quarterly, 601 S. Washington, Suite 281, Stillwater, OK 74074, E-mail chinaski00@aol.com. 1997. circ. 100. 4/yr. sub. price: $12; sample: $5. 46pp; 8½×11.

MAD POETS REVIEW, PO Box 1248, Media, PA 19063-8248. Eileen D'Angelo, Co-Editor; Camelia Nocella, Co-editor. 1990. "No pornography, although tasteful sensual poetry is published, no gore or violence. We hold an annual competition, Mad Poets' Review Competition, usually in the fall, winners are published, and small cash prizes." 1/yr. Pub'd 50-60 poems 1999. sub. price: $8; sample: $8. 70pp; 5½×8½; Rights purchased: all rights revert back to the author after we publish the poem once. Deadlines: ongoing. Reporting time: 6-8 weeks. Payment: contributor's copies. Interested in new or unpub'd poets: yes. Simultaneous submissions accepted: yes. Recent contributors: Louis McKee, C.A. Conrad, Bill Shields, Ray Greenblatt, James Freeman. Submission quantity: 6. Special interests: Last issue we published Russian Poet Steven Duplis in Russian and English; also Spanish poet Emileano Martin in Spanish and Englishu.

Mad River Press, State Road, Richmond, MA 01254, 413-698-3184. Barry Sternlieb, Maureen Sternlieb. 1986. "Work is solicited." avg. press run 125-500. Pub'd 3 poetry titles 1999; expects 3 poetry titles 2000, 3 poetry titles 2001. 5½×8, 6×9; avg. price, paper: $7-$25; sample $8; other: broadsides $15-$100. 20-28pp; Payment: 10%-20% of press run. Interested in new or unpub'd poets: no. Recently published poets: Linda Gregg, Gary Snyder, W.S. Merwin, Hayden Carruth, Cortney Davis.

THE MADISON REVIEW, Dept of English, H.C. White Hall, 600 N. Park Street, Madison, WI 53706, 263-3303. Erin Hanusa. 1978. "Felix Pollak Poetry Prize: $500 for the best group of 3 unpublished poems. Manuscripts for prize must arrive during September. Please write in advance for rules, SASE must be included with all inquiries and correspondence. We like poems that are serious, tough and tight. Poems over 6 pages are discouraged." circ. 500. 2/yr. Pub'd 12 poems 1999; expects 23 poems 2000, 18 poems 2001. sub. price: $8; sample: $2.50. 80-150pp; 6×9; Rights purchased: rights revert to author on publication. We publish 5% or less of poems submitted. Deadlines: Winter issue Oct. 1, Spring March 1. Reporting time: 2 months. Payment: 2 copies. Interested in new or unpub'd poets: yes. Simultaneous submissions accepted: no. Recent contributors: Lisa Goett, Maura Stanton, Kelly Cherry, Jim Daniels, Richard Tillinghast. Submission quantity: minimum of 3/max. of 6. Special interests: No light verse, love poems, religious tract poems, please!

MAGIC CHANGES, Celestial Otter Press, 237 Park Trail Court, Schaumburg, IL 60173. John Sennett, Editor. 1978. "Upcoming themes: myths, mysteries, music, time. Make checks payable to John Sennett." circ. 500. 1 issue every 2 years. Expects 40 poems 2001. sample price: $5. 100pp; 8½×11; Rights purchased: 1st North American. Publishes 1% of poems submitted. Deadlines: anytime. Reporting time: 2-3 months. Payment: contributor's copies or cash. Interested in new or unpub'd poets: yes. Simultaneous submissions accepted: no. Recent contributors: Sri Chinmoy, Margaret Kaminsky, D.M. Jones, A.D. Winans, Sue Standing. Submission quantity: 3. Special interests: Short poems preferred.

MAGIC REALISM, Pyx Press, PO Box 922648, Sylmar, CA 91392-2648. C. Darron Butler, Editor. 1990. circ. 1M + Spanish version (200 projected). 4/yr. Pub'd 25 poems 1999; expects 25 poems 2000, 25 poems 2001. sub. price: $19.50; sample: $5.95. 76pp; 5½×8½; Rights purchased: first or one-time rights and nonexclusive reprint rights. Publishes .2% of poems submitted. Reporting time: 3 months, occasionally longer. Payment: 1 copy + $3 per magazine page. Interested in new or unpub'd poets: yes. Simultaneous submissions accepted: yes. Submission quantity: 3-8.

MAIN STREET JOURNAL, 29 Princes Road, Ashford, Middlesex TW15 2LT, United Kingdom, 44-171-378-8809. 1992. circ. 1.5M. 1/yr. sub. price: £6; sample: educational institutions only. 96pp; 8×8.

MAIN STREET RAG, PO Box 25331, Charlotte, NC 28229-5331, 704-535-1918, E-mail mainstrag@mindspring.com. M. Scott Douglass. 1996. "We like people to have at least read one copy of the magazine before sending something." circ. 350-500. 4/yr. Pub'd 300+ poems 1999; expects 125+ poems 2000, 125+ poems 2001. sub. price: $15; sample: $5. 76pp; 5½×8½; Rights purchased: 1st time. We publish 10% or less of poems submitted. Reporting time: 1-4 weeks. Payment: 1 copy. Quality is our criteria, not point of origin. Simultaneous submissions accepted: no. Recent contributors: A.D. Winans, David Chorlton, Robert Cooperman, Cheryl Townsend, Jennifer B. MacPherson. Submission quantity: no more than 6 pages. Special interests: We're open to all forms and subjects. Prefer grittier, blue-collar poets as well as satire.

Maisonneuve Press, PO Box 2980, Washington, DC 20013-2980, 301-277-7505; FAX 301-277-2467. 1987. 6×9.

Majestic Books, PO Box 19097D, Johnston, RI 02919. 1991. "We are currently searching for quality poetry from writers under the age of 18 for an anthology. There are no restrictions in regards to genre." 5½×8½.

Malafemmina Press, 4211 Fort Hamilton Parkway, Brooklyn, NY 11219. Rose Sorrentino. 1990. "Don't spell accents" avg. press run 200. Pub'd 1 poetry title 1999; expects 3 poetry titles 2000. 5½×8½; avg. price, paper: $2. 20pp; Reporting time: 3 months. Payment: 50 copies & 50% discount. Interested in new or unpub'd poets: yes. Simultaneous submissions accepted: no. Recently published poets: Eileen Spinelli, Anna Bart, Jennifer Lagier, Rose Romano. Submission quantity: 15-20. Special interests: Work that combines feminist issues with Italian-American culture, bilingual Italian/English poetry.

THE MALAHAT REVIEW, PO Box 1700, Stn. CSC, Victoria, British Columbia V8W 2Y2, Canada. Marlene Cookshaw, Editor. 1967. "Must include sufficient Canadian postage for returning ms. Biennial Long poem competition, deadline March 1 (1997, 99...). Write for info" circ. 1.2M. 4/yr. Pub'd 120 poems 1999; expects 120 poems 2000, 120 poems 2001. sub. price: $30 in Canada, $40 other; sample: $10. 135pp; 9×6; Rights purchased: first world serial rights. Publishes 3% of poems submitted. Deadlines: none. Reporting time: 1-3 months. Payment: $30 per magazine page plus year's free subscription. Interested in new or unpub'd poets: yes. Simultaneous submissions accepted: no. Recent contributors: P.K. Page, Don Coles, Michael Redhill, Kate Braid. Submission quantity: 6-10. Special interests: translations.

Mandala Publishing Group, 1585A Folsom Street, San Francisco, CA 94103-3728, 541-688-2258, 800-688-2218; Fax 541-461-3478; E-mail gvs@efn.org. 1995.

MANGROVE MAGAZINE, Dept. of English, Univ. of Miami, PO Box 248145, Coral Gables, FL 33124, 305-284-2182. Poetry Editor. 1994. "Submitted materials should be top quality copies to facilitate reading and computer scanning" circ. 500. 1/yr. Pub'd 50 poems 1999; expects 2000 poems 2000. sub. price: $6; sample: $6. 125pp; 6×9; Rights purchased: 1st serial. Publishes 3% of poems submitted. Deadlines: accepted August 1 through December 1. Reporting time: 1-6 months, report Dec. thru April. Payment: 2 free copies. Interested in new or unpub'd poets: yes. Simultaneous submissions accepted: yes. Recent contributors: Campbell McGrath, Jamaica Kincaid, David Kirby, Carolyn Kizer, Carolyne Wright. Submission quantity: no more than 5. Special interests: At this time we accept a broad variety. Also interested in work with a multicultural focus. We like to print both formal and free verse, but contemporary, nothing archaic, no "thee" and "thous" please!

THE MANHATTAN REVIEW, c/o Philip Fried, 440 Riverside Drive, #45, New York, NY 10027. Philip Fried. 1980. "Submit 3-5 poems with a short bio. Prefer ambitious work." circ. 500. 1/yr. Expects 25 poems 2000, 25 poems 2001. sub. price: 1 volume (2 issues) $10 individuals (U.S. and Canada), $15 libraries (U.S. and Canada), $19 libraries elsewhere; sample: $5 individuals, $7.50 libraries. 64pp; 5½×8½; Rights purchased: 1st North American. Publishes .33% of poems submitted. Reporting time: 12-14 weeks. Payment: 2 copies. Interested in new or unpub'd poets: yes. Simultaneous submissions accepted: no. Recent contributors: Ana Blandiana, D. Nurkse, Baron Wormser, Bei Dao, Edmond Jabes. Submission quantity: 3-5. Special interests: Catholic taste, translations of Eastern European poetry, Irish poets, Chinese poets, French poets.

MANKATO POETRY REVIEW, Box 53, Mankato State University, Mankato, MN 56001, 507-389-5511. Roger Sheffer, Editor. 1984. "Name and address in top left-hand corner of each sheet. We'll look at any style, any length under 60 lines." circ. 200. 2/yr. Pub'd 50 poems 1999; expects 50 poems 2000, 45 poems 2001. sub. price: $5; sample: $2.50. 35pp; 7×8; Publishes about 5% of poems submitted. Deadlines: November 15 and April 15. Reporting time: up to 3 months. Payment: 2 copies. Interested in new or unpub'd poets: yes. Simultaneous submissions accepted: no. Recent contributors: Walter Griffin, Jane Varley, Judith Skillman. Submission quantity: 3-8. Special interests: None, not likely to accept light verse or religious, unless very good.

MANOA: A Pacific Journal of International Writing, English Department, University of Hawaii, Honolulu, HI 96822, 956-3070, fax 956-7808, E-mail mjournal-l@hawaii.edu. Frank Stewart, Editor. 1988. "Please see our Web site at http:..www2.hawaii.edu/mjournal for information on the journal, our guidelines, and issues" circ. 2.5M. 2/yr. Pub'd 70 poems 1999; expects 70 poems 2000, 70 poems 2001. sub. price: $22; sample: $12. 220pp; 7×10; Rights purchased: 1st serial. Publishes 1-5% of poems submitted. Deadlines: none. Reporting time: 4-6 weeks. Payment: competitive. Interested in new or unpub'd poets: yes. Simultaneous submissions accepted: no. Recent contributors: Walter Pavlich, Martha Zweig, Arthur Sze, John Haines, Nguyen Quang Thieu. Submission quantity: 3-5.

MANUSHI - a journal about women & society, C-174 Lajpat Nagar - I, New Delhi, New Delhi 110024, India, 6833022 or 6839158. Madhu Kishwar. 1978. 6/yr. Pub'd 15-20 poems 1999; expects 15-20 poems 2000, 15-20 poems 2001. sub. price: $25 (USA), Rs 90 (India), $36 Rs 120 (instit); sample: $4 (includes airmail postage). 44pp; 7×9; Rights purchased: any reprinting from *Manushi* requires prior written permission. Publishes 20% of poems submitted. Reporting time: 1 month. Payment: we send complimentary copies to the author. Interested in new or unpub'd poets: yes. Simultaneous submissions accepted: yes. Recent contributors: Kishwar Naheed, Devi Prasad Mishra, Indu Sena, Saeeda Gazdar, Nirupma Duut. Submission quantity: no restrictions. Special interests: Women's experience, poetry relating to life in the Indian subcontinent; and in translations into English of poems (ancient, medieval or modern) in languages of the subcontinent, women's rights, human rights, art, literature, sociology.

MANY MOUNTAINS MOVING, 420 22nd Street, Boulder, CO 80302, 303-545-9942, Fax 303-444-6510. Alissa Reardon Norton, Poetry Editor. 1994. "Open to poets of all cultures. Sponsoring an annual poetry award ($200 prize)." circ. 2.5M. 3/yr. Pub'd 33 poems 1999; expects 90 poems 2000, 90 poems 2001. sub. price: $18; sample: $6.50. 250pp; 6×8¾; Rights purchased: First North American serial rights & anthology rights. Publishes 1% of poems submitted. Deadlines: May through August. Reporting time: usually within 1 month, but if we are seriously considering a submission, it may take longer. Payment: contributors' copies. Interested in new or unpub'd poets: yes. Simultaneous submissions accepted: yes. Recent contributors: Sherman Alexie, Adrienne Rich, Ursula K. LeGuin, Robert Bly, Lorna Dee Cervantes. Submission quantity: 3-10. Special interests: open.

March Street Press (see also PARTING GIFTS), 3413 Wilshire Drive, Greensboro, NC 27408-2923. Robert Bixby. 1988. "Unsolicited manuscripts should be accompanied by a $10 reading fee." avg. press run 100. Pub'd 8 poetry titles 1999; expects 6 poetry titles 2000, 6 poetry titles 2001. 5½×7½; avg. price, paper: $5-$7. 40pp; Publishes 5-10% of poetry manuscripts submitted. Reporting time: 2-3 months. Payment: copies. Interested in new or unpub'd poets: sure. Simultaneous submissions accepted: no. Recently published poets: Elizabeth Kerlikowske, Russ Thorburn, Stephen Dunning, Kelly Cherry, William Greenway. Submission quantity: 50-60.

THE MARLBORO REVIEW, PO Box 243, Marlboro, VT 05344. Ellen Dudley, Editor; Ruth Anderson:Poetry Editor Barnett. 1995. "SASE with adequate postage. Prefer not to read in August. Annual Marlboro Prize in Poetry. Absolutely no submissions via e-mail" circ. 1M. 2/yr. Expects 100 poems 2000, 100+ poems 2001. sub. price: $16; sample: $8 + 75¢ postage. 100pp; 6×9; Rights purchased: none. Publishes 6% of poems submitted. Deadlines: ongoing. Reporting time: 3 months or less. Payment: copies. Interested in new or unpub'd poets: yes. Simultaneous submissions accepted: yes, if notified. Recent contributors: William Matthews, Brenda Hillman, Stephen Dobyns, Jean Valentine, Carl Phillips. Submission quantity: 3-5. Special interests: Long poems, translations, essays, interviews and reviews.

●**MARYLAND POETRY REVIEW,** 99 Smithwood Avenue, Baltimore, MD 21228, http://marylandpoetry.org. 1986. circ. 500. 1/yr. sub. price: $20/2 issues; sample: $5 + $1 p/h. 70pp; 7×9.

●**Marymark Press**, 45-08 Old Millstone Drive, East Windsor, NJ 08520, 609-443-0646, www.experimental-poet.com. Mark Sonnenfeld, Editor. 1994. "I prefer to be sent only experimental writing, artwork, photography" avg. press run 300-350. Pub'd 12 poetry titles 1999. 16-20pp; Reporting time: 1 month max. Payment: none. Interested in new or unpub'd poets: yes. Simultaneous submissions accepted: yes. Recently published poets: Carpentier Pascal, Steve Andrews, Pete Lee, Colin Cross, Kevin Hibshman. Submission quantity: 3. Special interests: experimental.

THE MASONIA ROUNDUP, 200 Coolwell Road, Madison Heights, VA 24572-2719. Richard Mason, Poetry Editor. 1991. "Do type, double space, always enclose SASE, line limit 50 but exceptions made" circ. 150. 4/yr. Pub'd 8 poems 1999; expects 8 poems 2000, 8 poems 2001. sub. price: $5; sample: $1.50. 16pp; 7×8½; Rights purchased: one-time. Publishes 25% of poems submitted. Deadlines: none. Reporting time: 6-8 weeks. Payment: 2 complimentary copies. Interested in new or unpub'd poets: yes. Simultaneous submissions accepted: yes. Recent contributors: Jim Dewitt, Dainis Hazners. Submission quantity: 1-20. Special interests: We look for satire, humor and parody reflecting family life.

THE MASSACHUSETTS REVIEW, South College, Univ. of Mass/Box 37140, Amherst, MA 01003-7140, 413-545-2689. Paul Jenkins, Anne Halley, Martin Espada. 1959. circ. 2M+. 4/yr. Pub'd 80 poems 1999. sub. price: $18; sample: $7. 172pp; 6×9; Rights purchased: first publication. Publishes .8% of poems submitted. Deadlines: none. Reporting time: 1 month. Payment: $10-$50, depending on length. Interested in new or unpub'd poets: yes. Simultaneous submissions accepted: yes. Recent contributors: Adelia Prado, Brigit Pegeen Kelly, Agha Shahid Ali, Tony Hoagland, Carol Frost. Submission quantity: 4-6.

MATCHBOOK, 242 North Broad Street, Doylestown, PA 18901, 215-489-7755, Fax 215-340-3965, www.matchbookpress.com. Stevens DeBrie. 1995. circ. internet. 4/yr. Pub'd 50 poems 1999; expects 100 poems 2000, 100 poems 2001. sub. price: on internet. 64-128 web pages; Rights purchased: 1st, revert to author on publication. Publishes 5% of poems submitted. Deadlines: irregular. Reporting time: 2-4 weeks. Interested in new or unpub'd poets: yes. Simultaneous submissions accepted: yes, if noted. Recent contributors: Hugh Fox, Diana DerHovanession, Jesse Glass Jr., Vivian Shipley, John Elsberg. Submission quantity: 5-6. Special interests: Also accepts translations, query before sending. Review copies accepted of poetry books, chapbooks, small press magazines.

MATI, Ommation Press, 5548 N. Sawyer, Chicago, IL 60625. Effie Mihopoulos. 1975. "Please include SASE with sufficient return postage." circ. 500. Irregular. sub. price: $2; sample: $1.50 + $1.05 bookrate postage. 40pp; 8½×11; Publishes 30% of poems submitted. Deadlines: none. Reporting time: as soon as possible. Payment: contributor's copy. Interested in new or unpub'd poets: no. Simultaneous submissions accepted: yes (please note). Recent contributors: Susan Fromberg Schaeffer, Eugene Wildman, Will Inman, Lyn Lifshin, Ted Berrigan, Alice Notley. Submission quantity: up to 10. Special interests: Open to all kinds of poetry, but rhyming poetry does not usually interest me.

Maxima New Media, 2472 Broadway #195, New York, NY 10025, 212-439-4177, Fax 212-439-4178, e-mail aronst@ibm.net. 1995.

Mayapple Press, PO Box 5473, Saginaw, MI 48603-0473, 517-793-2801, kerman@mayapplepress.com, www.mayapplepress.com. Judith Kerman. 1978. "Please send inquiries, not full MS. At this point, we do chapbooks, max 32 pp., not full-size books. Clear xeroxes ok. Name and address on every page. No returns without SASE. We expect poets, esp. unknowns, to take major responsibility for distribution (terms are negotiable, but concept is, alas, inevitable!)." avg. press run 200-500. Pub'd 1 poetry title 1999; expects 1 poetry title 2000, 1 poetry title 2001. 5½×8½, 7×8, 8½×11; avg. price, paper: $4-$7. 24pp; Reporting time: up to 4 months. Payment: 5% of run as royalty, 50% discount on purchase of copies. Interested in new or unpub'd poets: only when I'm seeking a manuscript—watch *Poets & Writers*, not open except when advertising. Simultaneous submissions accepted: simultaneous inquiries are recommended, not full mss. Recently published poets: Judith Minty, Toni Ortner-Zimmerman, Evelyn Wexler. Submission quantity: 4-6. Special interests: Great Lakes poets, women's poetry, prose poems.

MAYFLY, Brooks Books, 4634 Hale Drive, Decatur, IL 62526-1117. Randy Brooks, Shirley Brooks. 1985. "Include SASE" circ. 350. 2/yr. Pub'd 48 poems 1999; expects 48 poems 2000, 48 poems 2001. sub. price: $8/2 copies; sample: $3.50. 16pp; 3½×5; Rights purchased: first-time only. Publishes .005% of poems submitted. Deadlines: November, July. Reporting time: 6 months. Payment: $20 per haiku. Interested in new or unpub'd poets: yes. Simultaneous submissions accepted: no. Recent contributors: Michael Dudley, Jean Jorgensen, Frederick Gasser, Lee Gurga. Submission quantity: no more than 5. Special interests: Haiku.

McGregor Publishing, 4532 W. Kennedy Blvd., Tampa, FL 33609-2042, 813-681-0092; FAX 813-254-2665; Toll-free 888-405-2665. 1994. 6×9.

MCS Publishing, 5212 Chicago SW #2, Tacoma, WA 98499, 253-984-1345. Mia Sillanpoa. Address poetry submissions to: 937 NW 56th Avenue, Seattle, WA 98107. 1994. "Send your best!" Pub'd 5 poetry titles 1999; expects 5 poetry titles 2000, 5 poetry titles 2001. 5×7; avg. price, paper: $9.95+. 64+pp; Percent of poems published is subsidy dependent. Reporting time: 2 weeks - 1 month. Payment: 8% wholesale. Interested in new or unpub'd poets: yes. Simultaneous submissions accepted: yes. Recently published poets: Mia Sillanpoa. Submission quantity: full manuscript. Special interests: Educational works.

ME MAGAZINE, Pittore Euforico, PO Box 182, Bowdoinham, ME 04008, 207-666-8453. Carlo Pittore. 1980. "In order to publish a poet, the poetry has to overwhelm me, but the poet has to overwhelm me too. I only publish friends. Some friends I know only in the mails but still they are friends. Poetry is also the UNSEEN spirit." circ. 2M. Published at editor's discretion. Expects 1 poem 2000. sub. price: $20; sample: $5. 8pp; 8½×11; Rights purchased: none, only to publish once. Publishes less than 1% of poems submitted. Reporting time: 6 weeks. Interested in new or unpub'd poets: absolutely and preferably. Simultaneous submissions accepted: sure. Recent contributors: Bern Porter, Jeff Wright, Mark Melnicove, Bob Holman, Steve Petroff. Special interests: Only interested in poems about *ME*, as an idea. Art is not self-promotion, but it is self-involvement & manifestation. Poems about the "me", the subjective. Also, love poems, erotic poems. Poems written to *ME*.

Meager Ink Press (see also COZY DETECTIVE MYSTERY MAGAZINE), 686 Jakes Court, McMinnville, OR 97128, 503-435-1212; detectivemag@onlinemac.com. 5½×8½.

MEANJIN, 131 Barry Street, Carlton, Victoria 3053, Australia, 613-9344-6950. Peter Minter. 1940. "Enclose SASE" circ. 2.5M. 4/yr. sub. price: Individuals: $65AUD overseas, $45AUD + GST Australia; Institutions: $95AUD overseas, $75AUD + GST Australia; sample: $16.25AUD overseas, $12AUD Australia. 208pp; 5½×8¼, 212×136mm; Rights purchased: 1%. Deadlines: anytime. Reporting time: 12 weeks. Payment: $50/poem minimum. Interested in new or unpub'd poets: yes. Simultaneous submissions accepted: yes. Recent contributors: John Kinsella, John Tranter, Brian Henry, Louis Armand, Emma Lew. Special interests: Emphasis on Australian poetry and poets or Australian themes.

MEDIPHORS, PO Box 327, Bloomsburg, PA 17815, e-mail mediphor@ptd.net, website www.mediphors.org. Eugene D. Radice, M.D. 1992. "Prefer previously unpublished poems to 30 lines." circ. 1M. 2/yr. Pub'd 70 poems 1999; expects 75 poems 2000, 90 poems 2001. sub. price: $15; sample: $6. 72pp; 8×11; Rights purchased: 1st NA Serial Rights. Publishes 10% of poems submitted. Deadlines: none. Reporting time: average 4 months. Payment: 2 copies. Interested in new or unpub'd poets: yes. Simultaneous submissions accepted: no. Submission quantity: max 6. Special interests: Any type of poetry related to medicine and health.

MEDUSA'S HAIRDO, 2631 Seminole Avenue, Ashland, KY 41102, 606-325-7203, medusashairdo@yahoo.com. Beverly Moore. 1995. "Cover letter required" circ. 50. 2/yr. Pub'd 12 poems 1999; expects 12 poems 2000, 12 poems 2001. sub. price: $8.70; sample: $4.50. 16-24pp; 8½×11; Rights purchased: FNASR. Publishes 5% of poems submitted. Deadlines: none; open to submissions year-round. Reporting time: 2-4 weeks. Payment: 1 copy. Interested in new or unpub'd poets: yes. Simultaneous submissions accepted: yes, if so noted. Recent contributors: Jane Stuart, Lyn Lifshin, Gary Every, Michael Mina. Submission quantity: up to 5.

Mellen Poetry Press (see also The Edwin Mellen Press), PO Box 450, 415 Ridge Street, Lewiston, NY 14092-0450, 716-754-2266, Fax 716-754-4056, E-mail mellen@wzrd.com, www.mellenpress.com. Patricia Schultz. 1974. avg. press run 200. Pub'd 25 poetry titles 1999; expects 50 poetry titles 2000. 6×9; avg. price, paper: $14.95. 64-72pp; Publishes 30-50% of poetry manuscripts submitted. Reporting time: 2-3 months. Payment: 5 free copies, no royalties. Interested in new or unpub'd poets: yes. Simultaneous submissions accepted: no, prefer not. Submission quantity: 30-60.

MEMO, PO Box 1497, Mendocino, CA 95460. W.J. Kovanda. Address poetry submissions to: Box 1375, Mendocino, CA 95460. "All poetry should be neatly hand written or typed. Send 4 or 5 poems at a time, if you like. Please keep your own copies. Please include a self-addressed, stamped envelope with all submissions. Put your name and mailing address on every page of poetry. In the Mendocino County, find MEMO in a store close to you. Wherever you live, buy a subscription. It's the supportive thing to do, as there's no advertising in Route One and MEMO must pay the printer. Send $25 to Memo, box 1497, Mendocino, CA 95460, and say goodbye to dull care. I prefer these types of poetry: nature poetry, romantic, risque, sarcastic, humorous, sensual. Send your poetry today! Mail all poetry to Route One, C/O Poetry Ed., William James Kovanda, Box 1375, Mendocino, CA 95460" circ. 4.5M. 20/yr. sub. price: $25. 16pp; 11×17; Rights purchased: none. Payment: none. Simultaneous submissions accepted: yes. Submission quantity: 2-5.

The Menard Press, 8 The Oaks, Woodside Avenue, London N12 8AR, England. A. Rudolf. 1969. "N.B. Menard rarely accepts unsolicited material" avg. press run 1.5M. Expects 2 poetry titles 2000. demi octavo; avg. price, paper: $10. 56pp; Recently published poets: Ra'hel, Plath, G.F. Dutton. Special interests: Translation.

Meridien PressWorks, PO Box 640024, San Francisco, CA 94164, 415-928-8904. 1996. 5½×8½.

MERLYN'S PEN: Fiction, Essays, and Poems By America's Teens, Merlyn's Pen, Inc., PO Box 910, East Greenwich, RI 02818-0964, 401-885-5175, www.merlynspen.com. R. Jim Stahl, Editor & Publisher. 1985. "Work only by students in grades 6 through 12 is considered. Write for guidelines on 'How to Submit.' See our website for our cover sheet: www.merlynspen.com" circ. 5M. 1/yr. Pub'd 20 poems 1999; expects 20 poems 2000, 20 poems 2001. sub. price: $29 + $9 for foreign orders; sample: catalog=free. 100pp; 8½×10⅞; Rights purchased: all rights. Publishes 2% of poems submitted. Deadlines: none. Reporting time: 9 weeks. Payment: 1 complimentary copy of magazine and $20-$50. Interested in new or unpub'd poets: yes, only from students grades 6-12. Simultaneous submissions accepted: no. Recent contributors: students, not professional authors. Submission quantity: 3 maximum. Special interests: any and all.

Merrimack Books, PO Box 80702, Lincoln, NE 68501-0702, e-mail wedwards@infocom.com. 1989. 5½×8½.

MESECHABE: The Journal of Surre(gion)alism, 1539 Crete Street, New Orleans, LA 70119, 504-944-4823. Dennis Formento. 1988. "I prefer to read poetry submissions at midnight. Typed submissions are better than handwritten at that hour, unless I need a handwriting sample to cast a spell for more poetry" circ. 500. 2/yr. Pub'd 30 poems 1999; expects 30 poems 2000, 30 poems 2001. sub. price: $25/5 issues, $35 institutions; sample: $5. 40pp; 8 1/2×11; Publishes 10% of poems submitted. Reporting time: 2-6 weeks. Payment: 2 copies. Interested in new or unpub'd poets: yes. Simultaneous submissions accepted: only if you tell me so. Recent contributors: A. Michele, Robert Creeley, Eileen Myles, Kalamuya Salaam, John Sinclair. Submission quantity: 5-10. Special interests: Translations and experiments are fine, satire too. Neo-nothing, we want straight-up rebel, blues and jazz poetry (Sun-Ra was a surregionalist). Would like to do Caribbean issue, w/New Orleans as Northernmost point of Carib mythoregions.

●**A MESSAGE FROM THE HEART NEWS/MAGAZINE, Messenger Publishing Inc.,** PO Box 373424, Decatur, GA 30037, 770-961-2900, Fax 770-961-1711, kphilli4@bellsouth.net, www.messengerp.com. Kimberly Phillips. 1999. "All poems submitted must be motivational with a message" circ. 1M. 2-4/yr. sub. price: $20; sample: free. 14pp; 8½×11; Rights purchased: none, author retains the rights. Publishes 80% of poems submitted. Deadlines: Aug. 15th to March 15th. Reporting time: 5-10 days. Payment: contributors volunteer their time. Interested in new or unpub'd poets: yes. Simultaneous submissions accepted: yes. Submission quantity: 1.

●**Messenger Publishing Inc. (see also A MESSAGE FROM THE HEART NEWS/MAGAZINE),** PO Box 373424, Decatur, GA 30037, 770-961-2900, Fax 770-961-1711, kphilli4@bellsouth.net, www.messengerp.com. 1998. 5½×8.

META4: Journal of Object Oriented Poetics (OOPS), c/o Jurado, 1793 Riverside Drive #3F, New York, NY 10034. 1994. "Internet website for zine: http//triveca.ios.com/insomnia/meta4" circ. 250. 2/yr. sub. price: $6; sample: $5. 40pp; Publishes 2% of poems submitted. Deadlines: 10-31-96, 02-28-97. Reporting time: 4-6 months. Interested in new or unpub'd poets: yes. Simultaneous submissions accepted: no. Recent contributors: Eric Docherty, Willard Gellis, Ron Price, William Huhn, Tsaurah Litzky. Submission quantity: 3-4.

Miami University Press, English Dept., Miami University, Oxford, OH 45056, 513-529-5110, Fax 513-529-1392, E-mail reissja@muohio.edu. "Miami University Press regrets that it can no longer consider unsolicited manuscripts right now because of a backlog of books already under contract. Thank you for thinking of the press." 5½×8½.

Mica Press, 113 Cambridge Road, Madison, WI 53704-5909, 608-246-0759; Fax 608-246-0756; E-mail jgrant@bookzen.com; website www.bookzen.com. 1990.

MICHIGAN QUARTERLY REVIEW, 3032 Rackham Bldg., University of Michigan, Ann Arbor, MI 48109, 734-764-9265. Laurence Goldstein, Editor. 1962. "*MQR* is an academic journal that publishes mainly essays and reviews, and therefore our choice of poems is highly selective. This is not a good journal for beginners to try, but we are receptive to poets whose work is original and thoughtful and well-crafted. A sample copy will help you understand what kind of poetry we publish." circ. 1.8M. 4/yr. Pub'd 32 poems 1999; expects 32 poems 2000, 32 poems 2001. sub. price: $18; sample: $2.50 + 2 1st class stamps. 160pp; 6×9; Rights purchased: first only. Publishes 1% of poems submitted. Deadlines: none. Reporting time: 4-6 weeks. Payment: $8-$10 per printed page. Interested in new or unpub'd poets: yes. Simultaneous submissions accepted: no. Recent contributors: Robert Hass, Carolyn Kizer, Maxine Kumin, Cathy Song, Wole Soyinka. Submission quantity: 3-5. Special interests: We publish no light verse. We are open to all other types and forms so long as the poem is intelligently arrived at and worked over.

MICROPRESS YATES, 29 Brittainy Street, Petrie, Queensland 4502, Australia, 07-32851462; gloriabe@powerup.com.au. Gloria B. Yates. 1992. circ. 4-500. 10/yr. Pub'd 400 poems 1999; expects 400 poems 2000. sub. price: $10 AUS; $20 overseas; $17 US; sample: 50¢. 12pp; size A4; Rights purchased: don't buy. Publishes 20% of poems submitted. Deadlines: none. Reporting time: 1 month. Payment: none. Interested in new or unpub'd poets: yes. Simultaneous submissions accepted: yes. Recent contributors: Watha Lambert USA, Catherine Mair NZ, Jeff Guess AUS, Rob Bishop FRG, Janice Boston AUS. Submission quantity: 4-6.

MID-AMERICAN REVIEW, Dept of English, Bowling Green State University, Bowling Green, OH 43403, 419-372-2725. David Hawkins, Poetry Editor. 1980. circ. 1M. 2/yr. Pub'd 60 poems 1999; expects 65 poems 2000. sub. price: $12; sample: $5. 160pp; 5½×8½; Rights purchased: rights revert to author on publication. Publishes 5% of poems submitted. Deadlines: none. Reporting time: 4-6 weeks (except during the summer months, a bit slower then). Payment: $10 per page. Interested in new or unpub'd poets: yes. Simultaneous submissions accepted: no. Recent contributors: Stephen Dunn, Greg Pape, Naomi Shihab Nye, Dionisio D. Martinez, Frankie Paino. Submission quantity: 3-5. Special interests: Each issue includes a chapbook (10-15 poems) translation of original contemporary poetry in any language. Recent issues have featured translations of Eugenio de Andrade, Ana Maria Fagundo, Sandor Csoori, Claudio Rodriguez, and three Bengali women poets.

Middlebury College (see also NEW ENGLAND REVIEW), Middlebury College, Middlebury, VT 05753, 802-443-5075, Fax 802-443-2088, E-mail nereview@middlebury.edu. Stephen Donadio, Editor. 1978. "See *New England Review*" 7×10.

Mid-List Press, 4324 12th Avenue South, Minneapolis, MN 55407-3218, 612-822-3733, Fax 612-823-8387, guide@midlist.org, www.midlist.org. Lane Stiles, Senior Editor. 1989. "We publish serious, literary poetry only; and only book-length original collections by individual poets" avg. press run 500-1M. Pub'd 2 poetry titles 1999; expects 2 poetry titles 2000, 2 poetry titles 2001. 5½×8½, 6×9; avg. price, paper: $11. 80pp; Publishes less than 1% of poetry manuscripts submitted. Reporting time: 1-4 months. Payment: by contract. Interested in new or unpub'd poets: yes. Simultaneous submissions accepted: yes. Recently published poets: Donald Morrill, Neil Shepard, Jennifer O'Grady, Renny Golden, Adam Sol. Submission quantity: write or visit our website for guidelines.

Midmarch Arts Press, 300 Riverside Drive, New York City, NY 10025, 212-666-6990. Sylvia Moore. 1975. "Please send query letter first." avg. press run 3M. Pub'd 1 poetry title 1999; expects 1 poetry title 2000, 1 poetry title 2001. 5½×8½, 6×9, 8½×11; avg. price, paper: $12. 100pp; Publishes 20% of poetry manuscripts submitted. Reporting time: 3-6 months. Payment: standard arrangements after expenses of production are paid. Interested in new or unpub'd poets: yes, only with accompanying original illustrations, only interested in poetry and images. Simultaneous submissions accepted: no. Recently published poets: Adrienne Rich, Muriel Rukeyser, W.C. Williams, Suzanne Noguere, Charlotte Mandel. Submission quantity: only book ms considered. Special interests: Focus is on women. Must be related to or in combination with visual arts.

MIDWEST POETRY REVIEW, PO Box 20236, Atlanta, GA 30325-0236, 404-350-0714. Joan Ottley. 1980. "Midwest Poetry review is committed to quality, accessible poetry. If we don't understand your poem on first or second reading, we'll ask you to share it with another publication. We do no fiction or other prose. We'll do our best to deliver a knowledgeable, friendly, and entertaining quarterly which will encourage and inspire you ro produce more and better poetry. We are not a vanity market. You must have talent to get in, but we're open to new poets. Our primary sources of income are subscriptions and contest entry fees. We need, and depend on, our subscribers' loyalty. We know we have to earn it. We don't publish glitzy anthologies. We won't try to sell you anything whether or not we accept your work. In selecting poetry, we give the edge ot our subscribers, but we welcome work from others. We choose on the basis of quality (as we subjectively define it). Your subscription doesn't guarantee publication. We publish only work that has not appeared elsewhere. We accept no second printings, simultaneous submissions, or anything that isn't your own work. Violate these simple requirements and you severely compromise your chances of being considered again, ever. SASE must accompany all correspondence to which you expect a reply. We don't pay postage due" circ. 246. 4/yr. Pub'd 300 poems 1999; expects 300 poems 2000, 300 poems 2001. sub. price: $20; sample: $5. 40pp; 5½×8½; Rights purchased: 1st. Publishes 5-10% of poems submitted. Reporting time: 4-6 weeks. Payment: $5-$20, contest $25-$500. Interested in new or unpub'd poets: yes. Simultaneous submissions accepted: no. Recent contributors: Kimberly Courtright, Patricia Hutson, William Lamb, Anna-Margaret O'Sullivian, Jeanne Shaw. Submission quantity: 5 limit. Special interests: No translations. We are looking for quality, accessible poetry...Thrashing that grabs you by the throat...Or mists your eyes...Sensory verbs and nouns. We want to feel you feelings, not learn about them intellectually.

THE MIDWEST QUARTERLY, Pittsburg State University, History Department, Pittsburg, KS 66762, 316-235-4369. Stephen Meats. 1959. "*MQ* welcomes submissions from all serious writers of poetry. Include SASE." circ. 1M. 4/yr. Pub'd 60 poems 1999; expects 60 poems 2000, 60 poems 2001. sub. price: $12 within U.S., otherwise $17; sample: $5. 110pp; 6×9; Rights purchased: first publication, then rights revert to author. Publishes 2% of poems submitted. Deadlines: year round. Reporting time: 8 weeks. Payment: 2 copies of the issue. Interested in new or unpub'd poets: yes. Simultaneous submissions accepted: yes. Recent contributors: Walter McDonald, Lyn Lifshin, Jeanne Murray Walker, Patricia Traxler, William Kloefkorn. Submission quantity: 10 or fewer, 60 lines or less preferred. Special interests: Well-crafted, though not necessarily traditional poems that explore the inter-relationship of the human and natural worlds in bold, surrealistic images of a writer's imaginative, mystical experience.

MIDWIFERY TODAY, Box 2672, Eugene, OR 97402, 503-344-7438. 1985. circ. 6M. 4/yr. sub. price: $50; sample: $12.50. 72pp; 8½×11.

Milkweed Editions, 1011 Washington Ave. S., Ste. 300, Minneapolis, MN 55415, 612-332-3192, Fax 612-215-2550, www.milkweed.org. Emilie Buchwald, Publisher & Editor. 1984. "Please include return postage for manuscripts submitted. Please check previous poetry collections published by Milkweed Editions to get a sense of our editorial choices. Send $1 for catalog. Send SASE for guidelines or see them online. *Only read poetry in June and January.*" avg. press run 1.5M. Pub'd 1 poetry title 1999; expects 1 poetry title 2000, 2 poetry titles 2001. 6×9; avg. price, cloth: $18.95; paper: $12.95. 96pp; Publishes 1% of poetry manuscripts submitted. Reporting time: up to 6 months. Payment: small advance and six month royalty reports and payments. Interested in new or unpub'd poets: yes. Simultaneous submissions accepted: yes. Recently published poets: John Caddy, Pattiann Rogers, Marilyn Chin, Harry Humes, Ralph Black. Submission quantity: whole manuscript. Special interests: poetry with an ecological slant.

Mille Grazie Press, PO Box 92023, Santa Barbara, CA 93190, 805-963-8408. David Oliveira. 1992. "The editors invite poets whose work they are interested in publishing to submit mss. No unsolicited mss. will be considered" avg. press run 100. Pub'd 5 poetry titles 1999; expects 4 poetry titles 2000, 4 poetry titles 2001. 5½×8½; avg. price, other: chapbooks $8. Chapbooks 40pp; Reporting time: We do not read unsolicited submissions. Payment: copies. Interested in new or unpub'd poets: no. Simultaneous submissions accepted: no. Recently published poets: Wilma Elizabeth McDaniel, Will Inman, Paul Willis, Kevin Patrick Sullivan, Joyce La Mers. Special interests: The editors are primarily interested in poets who live and work along California's Central Coast, though subject matter is not limited or restricted to California themes.

MIM NOTES: Offcial Newsletter of the Maoist Internationalist Movement, PO Box 3576, Ann Arbor, MI 48106. 1984. circ. 10M. 12/yr. sub. price: $12; sample: $1. 12pp; 11½×15.

MINAS TIRITH EVENING-STAR, W.W. Publications, PO BOX 7871, Flint, MI 48507-0871, 813-585-0985 phone/Fax. Philip Helms. 1967. "Must be related to J.R.R. Tolkien or middle-earth." circ. 350+. 4/yr. Pub'd 50 poems 1999; expects 40 poems 2000, 20 poems 2001. sub. price: $10 U.S., $15 foreign, $12.50 Canada & Mexico; sample: $2. 24pp; 5½×8½; Rights purchased: copyrights for journal and then turned over to authors. Publishes 50% of poems submitted. Deadlines: 1st of every third month (March/June/Sept./Dec.). Reporting time: 1 month, SASE please. Payment: free issues of journal. Interested in new or unpub'd poets: yes. Simultaneous submissions accepted: no. Recent contributors: Thomas M. Egan, Anne Etkin, Nancy C. Pope, Lee Garig, Marthe Benedict. Submission quantity: no more than 5. Special interests: Fantasy, Tolkien, middle-earth.

●**MINDFIELD MAGAZINE: Your Mental Weapons Manual,** PO Box 14114, Berkeley, CA 94712-5114, 510-433-7945; mindfld@dnai.com; www.dnai.com/mindfld.

THE MINDFULNESS BELL, 14200 Fountain Lane, Charlotte, NC 28278, 510-527-3751; e-mail parapress@aol.com. 1990. circ. 3M. 3/yr. Pub'd 12-15 poems 1999. sub. price: $18; sample: $6. 40pp; 8½×11; Rights purchased: none. Publishes 25% of poems submitted. Deadlines: 6 weeks before pub. date. Payment: none. Interested in new or unpub'd poets: fine. Simultaneous submissions accepted: yes. Recent contributors: Claude Thomas, Thich Nhat Hanh, Sarah Rohrs, Svein Myreng. Submission quantity: 2-5. Special interests: buddhist poetry.

●**MINESHAFT,** 16 Johnson Pasture Drive, Guilford, VT 05301. Everett Rand. 1999. "*Mineshaft* is an independent international art magazine with very diverse contributors. No magazine 'policy.' The best way to see if you want to contribute to this mag is to read a copy and see if you like it." circ. 350. 3/yr. Pub'd 20 poems 1999; expects 45 poems 2000, 45 poems 2001. sub. price: $12; sample: $4. 48pp; 5½×8½; Publishes 15% of poems submitted. Reporting time: 1-2 weeks. Payment: contributors copies. Interested in new or unpub'd poets: yes. Simultaneous submissions accepted: no. Recent contributors: Tommy Trantino, Irving Stettner, Jeremy Reed, Charles Bukowski, A.D. Winan. Special interests: *Mineshaft* believes it is important to look at all poetry submissions with an open mind.

MINIMUS, 2245 N. Buchanan Street, Arlington, VA 22207. 1989. circ. 200. 1/yr. sub. price: $9.75; sample: $9.75. 84pp; 5½×8½.

THE MINNESOTA REVIEW, English Dept., Univ. of Missouri, 107 Tate Hall, Columbia, MO 65211. Jeff Williams, Editor. 1960. "Future issue themes include 'Academostars' and Fifties culture." circ. 1.5M. 2/yr. Pub'd 43 poems 1999; expects 45 poems 2000, 45 poems 2001. sub. price: $12 individual, $36 institutions and/or overseas; sample: $7.50. 180-260pp; 8½×5½; Rights purchased: rights to first publication only; upon publication, all rights released to author again (though we expect acknowledgement upon republication). We publish 2% or less of poems submitted. Deadlines: we read poetry submissions year-round. Reporting time: 1-4 months. Payment: 2 copies. Interested in new or unpub'd poets: yes, of course. Simultaneous submissions accepted: yes; with the proviso that we be immediately notified if a poem has been accepted elsewhere. Recent contributors: Alvin Greenburg, Martin Espada, Jim Daniels, Katherine Lederer, Denise Duhamel. Submission quantity: not more than 5 or 6. Special interests: We describe *the minnesota review* as a journal of 'committed writing'—that is, of writing which is socially engaged in radical, progressive ways. That means, among other things, that we are not ordinarily much interested in the poem that is about purely personal or abstract experience, or about itself; but we are very interested indeed in work which uses either traditional or experimental means to satisfy the demands of both social and political commitment and of art.

Minor Heron Press, 5275 NDCBU, Taos, NM 87571, 505-758-1800. Anne MacNaughton. 1982. avg. press run 500-1M. Pub'd 6 poetry titles 1999; expects 6 poetry titles 2000, 6 poetry titles 2001. 5×8; avg. price, paper: $12; other: $29, videotapes. 100pp; Reporting time: 90 days. Payment: standard. Interested in new or unpub'd poets: no. Simultaneous submissions accepted: no. Recently published poets: Peter Rabbit, Victor Henandez Cruz, Anne Waldman, Ntozake Shange, Quincy Troupe. Submission quantity: N.A. Special interests: SW regional, translations, languages other than English (specifically Spanish, Native American), northern New Mexico & southern Colorado region, primarily Western U.S. writers.

MIP Company, PO Box 27484, Minneapolis, MN 55427, 763-544-5915, Fax 952-544-6077, mp@mipco.com, www.mipco.com. 1984. "Poetry in Russian." Pub'd 2 poetry titles 1999. 80pp; Simultaneous submissions accepted: yes. Recently published poets: M. Armalinsky, A. Shelvakh. Special interests: Erotic poetry in Russian.

Missing Spoke Press (see also AMERICAN JONES BUILDING & MAINTENANCE), PO Box 9569, Seattle, WA 98109, 206-443-4693; von@singspeak.com. Von G. Binuia. 1997. avg. press run 200. Expects 5 poetry titles 2000. 5½×8½; avg. price, paper: $12. 90pp; Publishes 20% of poetry manuscripts submitted. Reporting time: 4 months. Payment: 10% of copies. Interested in new or unpub'd poets: yes. Simultaneous submissions accepted: no. Recently published poets: Cynthia Gallaher, Greg Kosmicki, Kirby Congdon. Submission quantity: 6-20. Special interests: neighborhoods, family, work, experimental.

MISSISSIPPI REVIEW, USM, Box 5144, Southern Station, Hattiesburg, MS 39406-5144, 601-266-4321. Angela Ball, Poetry Editor. 1971. circ. 1.5M. 2/yr. Pub'd 10 poems 1999; expects 10 poems 2000, 10+ poems 2001. sub. price: $15; sample: $8. 125-200pp; 5½×8¾; Reporting time: 2-4 months. Payment: copies, small fee. Interested in new or unpub'd poets: yes. Simultaneous submissions accepted: yes. Recent contributors: Lisa Zeidner, James Tate, Norman Dubie, W. Bishop, Bin Ramke.

THE MISSOURI REVIEW, 1507 Hillcrest Hall, University of Missouri-Columbia, Columbia, MO 65211, 573-882-4474; Fax 573-884-4671; e-mail umcastmr@missouri.edu. Greg Michalson. 1978. "We currently publish a poetry 'feature' format exclusively consisting of 6-12 pages of poems by each of 3 to 5 poets per issue" circ. 6.5M. 3/yr. Pub'd 60 poems 1999; expects 60 poems 2000, 60 poems 2001. sub. price: $19, $35/2 years, $45/3 years, $22 foreign yearly; sample: $7. 224pp; 6×9; Rights purchased: 1st N. American. Publishes 5% of poems submitted. Reporting time: 10 weeks. Payment: $120-$250 for a 6-12 page feature. Interested in new or unpub'd poets: yes. Simultaneous submissions accepted: no. Recent contributors: Jeffrey Levine, Robert Wrigley, Susan Terris, Davis McCombs, Laura Kasischke. Submission quantity: 6-12pp.

MR. COGITO, Mr. Cogito Press, 2518 NW Savier Street, Portland, OR 97210, rjdavies@gte.net, barbala@teleport.com. Robert A. Davies, Co-Editor; John M. Gogol, Co-Editor; Barbara La Morticella, Co-Editor. 1973. "Poems should be submitted via e-mail. Will be accepted or rejected by same." Continuous. sub. price: free. Rights purchased: 1st publication and our anthology rights. Publishes 10% of poems submitted. Reporting time: 1 month. Interested in new or unpub'd poets: yes. Simultaneous submissions accepted: yes. Recent contributors: Barbara LaMorticella, William Ferrell, Norman H. Russell, Marcelijus Martinaitis, Jerzy Ficowski. Submission quantity: 4 or 5. Special interests: *Translations, graphics,* image, conceits, wit, heightened language: *poems that move us.*

Mr. Cogito Press (see also MR. COGITO), 2518 N.W. Savier, Portland, OR 97210, 503-233-8131, 226-4135, rjdavies@gte.net. John M. Gogol, Co-Editor; Robert A. Davies, Co-Editor. 1978. "Invitation only. Anthology (12 year anniversary available. Translation award (publication) possible" avg. press run 500. 5½×8½; avg. price, paper: $10. 35pp; Publishes (by invitation) 90% of poetry manuscripts submitted. Reporting time: 1-2 months. Payment or copies, copies-10% of total copies. Interested in new or unpub'd poets: by invitation. Simultaneous submissions accepted: no. Recently published poets: Gray, Napora, Chandonnet, Russell. Special interests: We like translations, image, conceit, wit, heightened language: *poems that move us.* East-European poetry in translation.

MIXED BAG, 577 Central Avenue, Box 4, Jefferson, LA 70121-1400, e-mail: publisher@mailexcite.com, zines@theglobe.com, zines@rsnmail.com; Websites www.members.tripod.com/~literary/index.htm/, www.members.the globe.com/zines/default.htm/, www2.cybercities.com/z/zines/, www.zines.freeservers.com. Sharida Rizzuto, Editor; Harold Tollison, Associate Editor; Ann Hoyt, Assistant Editor. 1992. "We are willing to look at any type of poetry. No length requirements." circ. 800-1M. 2/yr. Pub'd 20-25 poems 1999; expects

35-50 poems 2000, 35-50 poems 2001. sub. price: $15.80; sample: $7.90. 100pp; 8½×11; Rights purchased: one-time rights, first serial rights, second serial rights, or simultaneous rights. Publishes 30-40% of poems submitted. Deadlines: always open to submissions. Reporting time: 2-6 weeks. Payment: fee for non-fiction plus free copies, free copies only for poetry and fiction. Interested in new or unpub'd poets: yes. Simultaneous submissions accepted: yes. Recent contributors: Jeanett M. Cox, Holly Day, Jim DeWitt, Paul A. Hanson. Submission quantity: 1-5. Special interests: Avant garde, beat experimental, free verse, light verse, long poems, prose poems, satire, regional.

MOCCASIN TELEGRAPH, 5813 E. Saint Charles Road, Columbia, MO 65202-3025, 573-817-3301. Lee Francis. 1992. "Accept material from Wordcraft Circle of Native Writers & Storytellers members, and other Native American Indian writers." circ. 500-1M. 6/yr. Pub'd 20 poems 1999; expects 36 poems 2000, 36 poems 2001. sub. price: $40; sample: $8. 30-32pp; 8×11; Rights purchased: none. Deadlines: Jan. 10, March 10, May 10, July 10, Sept. 10, Nov. 10. Reporting time: 1 month. Payment: none. Interested in new or unpub'd poets: yes. Simultaneous submissions accepted: yes. Submission quantity: 4 maximum.

MOCKINGBIRD, PO Box 761, Davis, CA 95617. C.G. MacDonald, Joe Aimone. 1994. "Robert Francis Memorial poetry prixe, July 4 - October 31, $2 p. poem; one year subscription with four poems entry $350 in prizes. Annie Finch, Judge 1996" circ. 250. 2/yr. Pub'd 55 poems 1999. sub. price: $7; sample: $4. 38pp; 8½×5½; Rights purchased: First Serial. Publishes 2% of poems submitted. Deadlines: year round. Reporting time: 2-3 weeks. Payment: 1 copy, 2 copies to poets who attend reading. Interested in new or unpub'd poets: yes. Simultaneous submissions accepted: no. Recent contributors: Sandra McPherson, Barry Spacks, Barbara A. Henderyson, Francisco X. Alarcon, Annie Finch. Submission quantity: 3-5. Special interests: We are especially keen on formal poems using contemporary language, West Coast writers, and other marginalized voices - lively writing - clarity.

MODERN HAIKU, PO Box 1752, Madison, WI 53701. Robert Spiess. 1969. "We like haiku that follow Daisetz T. Suzuki's definition: 'A haiku does not express ideas, but puts forward images reflecting intuitions.' We do not publish an individual's book of poetry, only an individual's poems (haiku only) in our magazine." circ. 675. 3/yr. Pub'd 850 poems 1999; expects 900 poems 2000, 900 poems 2001. sub. price: $18.50; sample: $6.25. 124-136pp; 5½×8½; Rights purchased: 1st North American. Publishes 5% of poems submitted. Deadlines: continuous acceptance. Reporting time: 2 weeks. Payment: $1 a haiku, $5 page for articles. Interested in new or unpub'd poets: yes. Simultaneous submissions accepted: no. Recent contributors: Cor van den Heuvel, Bruce Ross, Lee Gurga, Carol Montgomery, David Lanoue. Submission quantity: no limit. Special interests: We publish haiku, senryu, haibun, and articles on haiku; also reviews of haiku books. No tanka or other forms. Also translations of foreign haiku.

MOODY STREET IRREGULARS: A Jack Kerouac Magazine, Moody Street Irregulars, Inc., 2737 Dodge Road, East Amherst, NY 14051-2113. Joy Walsh. 1977. "On Jack Kerouac and the literature of the fifties." circ. 500-1M. 2-3/yr. Pub'd 20 poems 1999; expects 20 poems 2000, 20 poems 2001. sub. price: $10; sample: $5. 50pp; 8½×11; Rights purchased: none. Publishes 50% of poems submitted. Deadlines: none. Reporting time: 1 month. Payment: copies. Interested in new or unpub'd poets: yes. Simultaneous submissions accepted: no. Recent contributors: Ted Joans, Carl Solomon, Jack Micheline, Tom Clark, Tony Moffeit. Submission quantity: 6. Special interests: Concrete rather than abstract!!!

Moody Street Irregulars, Inc. (see also MOODY STREET IRREGULARS: A Jack Kerouac Magazine), 2737 Dodge Road, East Amherst, NY 14051-2113. Joy Walsh. 1977. "Include SASE." avg. press run 300. Pub'd 3 poetry titles 1999. 8½×11; avg. price, paper: $3.50; other: same. 30pp; Publishes 3% of poetry manuscripts submitted. Reporting time: 1 month. Payment: copies. Interested in new or unpub'd poets: yes. Simultaneous submissions accepted: no. Recently published poets: Marion Perry, Harry Polkinhorn, Morris Soronow, Joy Walsh, Michael Hopkins. Submission quantity: 3-6. Special interests: All forms on the work and for life of Jack Kerouac (for Moody Street Irregulars)- for textile Bridge Press. Concrete rather than abstract.

MOONRABBIT REVIEW, 2525 Arapahoe Avenue, Ste. E4-230, Boulder, CO 80302, 303-439-8860; Fax 439-8362; JHLee@ucsub.Colorado.edu. Mary Courney Ning. 1994. "Enclose a brief cover letter and biolong with SASE. Our annual poetry/fiction contest deadline is Oct 1, 1997." circ. 2M. 2/yr. Pub'd 50 poems 1999. sub. price: $17; sample: $7. 144pp; 6×9; Rights purchased: First North American Rights. Publishes 10% of poems submitted. Deadlines: Oct 1, 1997. Reporting time: 1-3 months. Payment: 3 copies of issue. Interested in new or unpub'd poets: yes. Simultaneous submissions accepted: yes. Recent contributors: Eileen Tabios. Submission quantity: 3-5. Special interests: We're expecially interested in experimental translations, satire as well as regional poetry.

MOOSE BOUND PRESS JOURNAL/NEWSLETTER, PO Box 111781, Anchorage, AK 99511-1781, 907-333-1465 phone/FAX e-mail mbpress@alaska.net; Website http://www.alaska.net/~mbpress. Sonia Walker, Editor; Robert Walker, Publisher. 1995. "We accept wholesome uplifting and entergetic writing. Something the entire family can enjoy. We are kind to beginning writers. Editor's award (announced in current journal)" circ. 350. 4/yr. Pub'd 200 poems 1999; expects 200 poems 2000, 200 poems 2001. sub. price: $24; sample: $3. 100pp; 8½×11; Rights purchased: one-time rights. Publishes 80% of poems submitted. Reporting time: 3-6 months. Payment: none, publication is payment. Interested in new or unpub'd poets: yes. Simultaneous submissions accepted: yes. Recent contributors: Lyn Lifshin, Diana Kwiatkowski Rubin, Marian Ford Park, Michael Lizza. Submission quantity: 5. Special interests: Narritive poetry; family type material; poems on nature/great outdoors anything in good taste.

Morris Publishing, 3212 E. Hwy 30, Kearney, NE 68847, 800-650-7888. 5½×8½ or 8½×11. Interested in new or unpub'd poets: yes. Simultaneous submissions accepted: yes.

Mortal Press, 2315 North Alpine Road, Rockford, IL 61107-1422, 815-399-8432. Terry James Mohaupt, Editor, Publisher. 1975. "*Mortal Press* now publishes the works of one poet exclusively. It is possible that may change in the future, but there are no definite plans for it. Cash advance, retail sales only, by direct mail order." avg. press run 250. Expects 1 poetry title 2001. 5½×8½; avg. price, cloth: $12; paper: $6. 80pp; Publishes 0% of poetry manuscripts submitted. Reporting time: 3 months to 1 year. Payment: negotiable. Interested in new or unpub'd poets: no. Simultaneous submissions accepted: no. Recently published poets: Terry James Mohaupt aka Morpheus. Submission quantity: 0. Special interests: The poetry *Mortal Press* publishes is more lyric and philosophic—rather than epic or pastoral—introspective emotional content expressed in strong rhythmic styles.

MOTHER EARTH JOURNAL: An International Quarterly, Uniting the World Press, Inc., c/o National Poetry Association, 934 Brannan Street, 2nd Floor, San Francisco, CA 94103, 415-552-9261; fax 415-552-9271. Herman Berlandt, Publisher; Editor, Maureen Hurley, Co-Editor. 1990. "Eco poetry or international interest" circ. 1450. 4/yr. Pub'd 600 poems 1999. sub. price: $18; sample: $3. 40pp; 11×15; Rights purchased: none. Publishes 10-15% of poems submitted. Deadlines: none. Reporting time: 6 weeks with SASE. Payment: 2 copies for author and translator. Interested in new or unpub'd poets: yes. Simultaneous submissions accepted: yes. Recent contributors: Kof. Awoonor, Frank Chipasula, Gary Snyder, Zindzi Maudela, Maya Angelou. Submission quantity: 3 poems. Special interests: Translations especially of poems dealing with environmental and other contemporary political and cultural issues.

THE MOTHER IS ME: Profiling the Cultural Aspects of Motherhood, Amer. Cons. HCMC PSC 461 Box #500, FPO, AP 96521-0002, 603-743-6828; E-mail zoey455@aol.com. 1996. circ. 3M. 4/yr. sub. price: $15.95; sample: $4. 36pp; 8½×11.

Mount Olive College Press (see also MOUNT OLIVE REVIEW), Mount Olive College, 634 Henderson Street, Mount Olive, NC 28365. Pepper Worthington, Editor. 1990. avg. press run 300-500. Pub'd 4 poetry titles 1999; expects 4 poetry titles 2000, 4 poetry titles 2001. avg. price, paper: $10-$15. 65-94pp; Publishes 5% of poetry manuscripts submitted. Reporting time: 6 months to 1 year. Payment: negotiated. Interested in new or unpub'd poets: yes. Simultaneous submissions accepted: no. Recently published poets: Sam Barbee, Peggy Gambill, Annette Allen, Eddie Williams, Richard Zyne. Submission quantity: 3-5.

MOUNT OLIVE REVIEW, Mount Olive College Press, Department of Language and Literature, 634 Henderson Street, Mount Olive, NC 28365, 919-658-2502. Pepper Worthington, Editor. 1987. 1/yr. sub. price: $25; sample: $25. 394pp; 8×11; Publishes 20% of poems submitted. Reporting time: 6 months. Interested in new or unpub'd poets: yes. Simultaneous submissions accepted: no. Submission quantity: 3-5.

Mountain State Press, c/o University of Charleston, 2300 MacCorkle Avenue SE, Charleston, WV 25304-1099, 304-357-4767, mspl@newwave.net. 1978. avg. press run 500. Pub'd 1 poetry title 1999. 5½×8½; avg. price, cloth: $14.95; paper: $10.95. 120pp; Publishes 5% of poetry manuscripts submitted. Reporting time: 4 months. Payment: 10% after publishing costs recovered. Interested in new or unpub'd poets: yes. Simultaneous submissions accepted: yes. Recently published poets: Sydney M. Kleeman, Shirley Klein, Jean Battlo.

Moving Parts Press, 10699 Empire Grade, Santa Cruz, CA 95060-9474, 408-427-2271. Felicia Rice. 1977. "Moving Parts Press is a limited edition letterpress publishing effort. All books edited, designed, typeset, and printed on the spot. Marketing, other than local authors, is limited to distributors and direct mail flyers." avg. press run 350. Pub'd 1 poetry title 1999; expects 1 poetry title 2000, 1 poetry title 2001. 6×9; avg. price, cloth: $35; paper: $10. 56pp; Publishes 1% of poetry manuscripts submitted. Reporting time: 3 months. Payment: 10% copies. Interested in new or unpub'd poets: no. Simultaneous submissions accepted: no. Recently published poets: W.P. Root, Christopher Buckley, Robert Lundquist, Katharine Harer, Lucille Clifton. Submission quantity: 4 plus tape. Special interests: Women's and feminist poetry, Chicano, Latino poetry (Sp./Eng), 20th century lives d'artiste poetry (Fr/Eng).

MUDFISH, Box Turtle Press, 184 Franklin Street, New York, NY 10013, 212-219-9278. Jill Hoffman, Poetry Editor. 1983. "A brief cover letter is appreciated. The MUDFISH POETRY PRIZE deadline is usually in the late fall of each year. The contest, which offers a significant cash prize to the winner, is judged by and internatally renowned poet. Send SASE in September for guidelines" circ. 1.2M. 1/yr. Pub'd 150 poems 1999;

expects 150 poems 2000, 150 poems 2001. sub. price: $20 for 2 year subscription; sample: $10 + $2.50. 200pp; 6⅞×8¼; Publishes 5% of poems submitted. Deadlines: ongoing. Reporting time: immediately to 2 months. Payment: 1 copy. Interested in new or unpub'd poets: yes. Simultaneous submissions accepted: no. Recent contributors: Charles Simic, Tom Lux, Malena Morling, Peggy Garrison, Timothy Monaghan. Submission quantity: 4-6.

MUDLARK, English Department, University of N. Florida, Jacksonville, FL 32224, 904-620-2273, Fax 904-620-3940, E-mail mudlark@unf.edu, www.unf.edu/mudlark. William Slaughter. 1995. "As our full name, *Mudlark: An Electronic Journal of Poetry & Poetics,* suggests, we will consider accomplished work that locates itself anywhere on the spectrum of contemporary practice. We want poems, of course, but we want essays, too, that make us read poems (and write them?) differently somehow. Although we are not innocent, we do imagine ourselves capable of surprise. *Mudlark* has an ISSN (1081-3500), is refereed, copyrighted, archived and distributed free on the World Wide Web, by e-mail, and on disk. *Mudlark* is "never in and never out of print."" circ. 500/week. Irregular but frequent. sub. price: free (online); sample: free. 16-100pp; Rights purchased: First North American Serial Rights. Deadlines: year-round. Reporting time: we answer our mail soon. Payment: In *Mudlark* poetry is free. Our authors give us their work and we, in turn, give it to our readers. What is the coin of poetry's realm? Poetry is a gift economy. One of the things we can do at *Mudlark* to pay our authors for their work is point to it here and there, wherever else it is. We can tell our readers how to find it, how to subscribe to it, and how to buy it if it is for sale. Interested in new or unpub'd poets: Yes, but do read *Mudlark* before submitting. After all, it is free. Simultaneous submissions accepted: we'd rather not. Recent contributors: Henry Gould, Sheila E. Murphy, Mike O'Connor, Diane Wald, Andrw Schelling. Submission quantity: *Mudlark* publishes in three distinct formats: single-author issues (electronic chapbooks), posters (electronic broadsides), and 'flash' poems (poems that feel like current events, poems that have 'news' in them. Submissions vary, accordingly, from small groups of poems to small collections of poems, from sequences of short poems to individual long poems...to 'flash' poems. Special interests: *Mudlark* is interested in that rare thing: the personal essay that is also critical, the critical essay that is also personal, and that has everything to do with poetry.

MurPubCo, 3335 Chisholm Trail #206, Boulder, CO 80301. 1985. "MurPubCo is dedicated to humor—publishes prose-poetry and poetry. Write for details."

●**Muse World Media Group,** PO Box 55094, Madison, WI 53705, 608-238-6681. Ron Louis. "We do many co-publishing and subsidary publishing projects" avg. press run 200-1M. Pub'd 5-10 poetry titles 1999. 8½×5½; avg. price, cloth: $8.95-$10.95; paper: $8.95. 50-150pp; Publishes 5-10% of poetry manuscripts submitted. Reporting time: 2 months. Payment: 25% royalty. Interested in new or unpub'd poets: yes. Simultaneous submissions accepted: yes. Recently published poets: Ron Louis, Tony Jarvis, Paul Graff, Trader X. Submission quantity: 10+. Special interests: experimental poetry.

MUSHROOM DREAMS, 14537 Longworth Avenue, Norwalk, CA 90650-4724. Jim Reagan, Editor. 1997. circ. 110. 2/yr. Pub'd 12 poems 1999; expects 12 poems 2000. sub. price: $2; sample: $1. 32pp; 5½×8½; Rights purchased: First Rights. Publishes 5% of poems submitted. Deadlines: Oct.1, Apr.1. Reporting time: 2 months. Payment: $10 per poem published. Interested in new or unpub'd poets: yes. Simultaneous submissions accepted: yes. Recent contributors: Nancy Dodrill, Kenn Mitchell, Sheila Glen Bishop, Georgia Axtell, Lyn Lifshin. Submission quantity: 2 each no more than 30 lines. Special interests: Literary.

THE MUSING PLACE, 2700 Lakeview, Chicago, IL 60614, 312-281-3800. 1983. circ. 500. 1/yr. sub. price: $4; sample: free. 32pp; 8½×11.

MYSTERY TIME ANTHOLOGY, Hutton Publications, PO Box 2907, Decatur, IL 62524. Linda Hutton, Editor. 1983. "We prefer humorous poems about detectives or about mystery writers; poetry must relate to mystery or suspense." circ. 150. 2/yr. Pub'd 8 poems 1999; expects 8 poems 2000, 8 poems 2001. sub. price: $10; sample: $4. 44pp; 8½×11; Rights purchased: one-time rights. Publishes 50% of poems submitted. Deadlines: year-round. Reporting time: 1 month. Payment: 1 copy plus $5 per poem. Interested in new or unpub'd poets: yes. Simultaneous submissions accepted: yes. Submission quantity: 4-5.

N

Nada Press (see also BIG SCREAM), 2782 Dixie S.W., Grandville, MI 49418, 616-531-1442. David Cope. 1974. "Obejctivist bias; prefer short 10-30 line works. Poetry written on the street and that retains concern for the planet and its occupants. Publish in January; submit after July." avg. press run 100. Pub'd 1 poetry title 1999; expects 1 poetry title 2000, 1 poetry title 2001. 8½×11; avg. price, paper: $5. 35pp; Publishes a maximum of 5% of poetry manuscripts submitted. Reporting time: 1 day - 1 month. Payment: copies. Interested in new or unpub'd poets: yes. Simultaneous submissions accepted: yes. Recently published poets: Marcia Arrieta, Allen Ginsberg, Anne Waldman, Jim Cohn, Antler. Submission quantity: 10.

NANNY FANNY, 2524 Stockbridge Drive #15, Indianapolis, IN 46268-2670, 317-329-1436, nightpoet@prodigy.net. Lou Hertz, Editor. 1998. "Guidelines available for SASE. Submit anytime. If submission was previously published, please notify me. Always send SASE with submission. Put name and address on every page, please. Guidelines available via e-mail, submissions via 'snail mail' only" circ. 100. 3/yr. Pub'd 75 poems 1999; expects 75 poems 2000, 75 poems 2001. sub. price: $9; sample: $3.50. 32pp; 5½x8½; Rights purchased: one-time rights. Publishes 7-10% of poems submitted. Deadlines: none. Reporting time: 2 weeks to 2 months. Payment: contributor's copy. Interested in new or unpub'd poets: yes. Simultaneous submissions accepted: yes, but this is discouraged. Recent contributors: B.Z. Niditch, Lamar Thomas, John Grey, Ella J. Cvancara, A.D. Winans. Submission quantity: 3-8. Special interests: Not too light and not too heavy. I want poems of substance—light but not too cute, serious but not self-centered.

Nashville House, PO Box 111864, Nashville, TN 37222, 615-834-5069. Steve Eng. 1991. "Chapbooks by query only." avg. press run 300. Pub'd 1 poetry title 1999; expects 1 poetry title 2000. 5x8; avg. price, cloth: $8; paper: $4. 50pp; Publishes 20% of poetry manuscripts submitted. Reporting time: 4 weeks. Payment: negotiable. Interested in new or unpub'd poets: by query only. Simultaneous submissions accepted: no. Recently published poets: Lucile Coleman, John Gawsworth, Gary William Crawford. Submission quantity: query letter and sample (5).

National Poetry Association Publishers (see also POETRY USA), Fort Mason Center, Building D, Room 270, San Francisco, CA 94123, 415-776-6602. Herman Berlandt, Editor + Publisher. 1985. "We are planning to publish *single poets* tabloid of 200 copies to sell for $2 per copy." avg. press run 1M. Expects 2 poetry titles 2000. 5½x8½; avg. price, cloth: $10; paper: $5, $3. 60-102pp; Publishes 15% of poetry manuscripts submitted. Reporting time: send xeroxes; no returns, no SASE's. Payment: 3 complimentary copies. Interested in new or unpub'd poets: yes. Simultaneous submissions accepted: yes. Recently published poets: Bob Kaufman, Robert Bly, Diane Di Prima, Julia Vinograd, Denise Levertov. Submission quantity: 3 poems, preferably under 1 page in length (double-spaced). Special interests: A bold and compasinate overview of the contemporary human condition and planetary survival as well as a private world.

●**National Writers Press,** 3140 S. Peoria Street, PMB 294, Aurora, CO 80014, 720-851-1944, Fax 303-841-2607, www.nationalwriters.com. 1970. 5½x8½.

NATURAL BRIDGE, English Dept., Univ. of Missouri, 8001 Natural Bridge Road, St. Louis, MO 63121, E-mail natural@jinx.umsl.edu. Steven Schreiner, Howard Schwartz. 1999. 2/yr. Expects 100 poems 2000. sub. price: $15; sample: $6. 200pp; 6x9; Deadlines: July 1-Aug. 31; Nov. 1-Dec. 31. Reporting time: 1-4 months. Payment: 2 copies. Interested in new or unpub'd poets: yes. Simultaneous submissions accepted: yes. Recent contributors: Eric Pankey, Greg Pape, Jennifer Atkinson, Steve Orlen, Diane Wakoski. Submission quantity: 4-6. Special interests: Translations are a special interest.

NATURE SOCIETY NEWS, Purple Martin Junction, Griggsville, IL 62340, 217-833-2323, Fax 217-833-2123, natsoc@adams.net, www.naturesociety.org. Karen E. Martin. 1966. 12/yr. Pub'd 36 poems 1999; expects 36 poems 2000, 36 poems 2001. sub. price: $15; $20 US funds in Canada; sample: no charge. 32pp; 61x15½; Rights purchased: one time only. Publishes +/-50% of poems submitted. Deadlines: 10th of each month. Payment: none. Interested in new or unpub'd poets: yes. Simultaneous submissions accepted: yes. Recent contributors: Ann Sherwood, Paul E. Snider. Special interests: Bird/nature appreciation poems.

NEBO, Department of English, Arkansas Tech University, Russellville, AR 72801, 501-968-0256. Paul Lake, Poetry Editor. 1982. circ. 300. 1-2/yr. Pub'd 53 poems 1999; expects 70 poems 2001. sub. price: $10; sample: $5. 48-60pp; 5x8; Rights purchased: first serial rights. Publishes 1% or less of poems submitted. Deadlines: open all year. Reporting time: 2 weeks-3 months. Payment: 1 copy. Interested in new or unpub'd poets: yes. Simultaneous submissions accepted: yes. Recent contributors: Timothy Steele, Dana Gioia, Brenda Hillman, Richard Martin, Richard Kostelanetz. Submission quantity: 3-5. Special interests: The editors of *Nebo* have a continuing interest in high quality formal or experimental poetry. We seek writing that—without archaisms, poetic diction or stilted syntax—uses traditional poetic devices such as meter, rhyme, syllabics, and stress count to create memorable poems. We also publish free verse if its language and rhythms are sufficiently controlled and interestng. In addition, we print articles and brief reviews concerning new poetry and have a special interest in publishing new poets who have taken the trouble to learn their craft.

THE NEBRASKA REVIEW, FA 212, University of Nebraska-Omaha, Omaha, NE 68182-0324, 402-554-3159. Susan Aizenberg, Poetry Editor. 1972. "Control of technique is a necessary starting point in our evaluations, though we are looking for more: a personal relationship to people, place, and to the language, for instance. We read throughout our submission period, we read for the TNR awards in poetry and fiction from September 1-November 30. Open submissions are read from January 1-April 15." circ. 1M. 2/yr. Pub'd 50 poems 1999; expects 50 poems 2000, 50 poems 2001. sub. price: $11; sample: $3. 108pp; 6×9; Rights purchased: 1st N.A. serial. Publishes 5% of poems submitted. Deadlines: offices closed between April 1 and Aug. 30. Reporting time: 3-5 months. Payment: 2 copies and 1 yr subscription. Interested in new or unpub'd poets: yes. Simultaneous submissions accepted: no. Recent contributors: Mary Swander, Roger Weingarten, Kelly Cherry, Patricia Goedicke, Jim Barnes. Submission quantity: 3-6.

NEDGE, PO Box 2321, Providence, RI 02906. Henry Gould, Janet Sullivan, Editors. 1994. "Include SASE" circ. varies. Irregular. Pub'd 40 poems 1999; expects 40 poems 2000, 40 poems 2001. sub. price: $12/2 issues; sample: $4 ppd. 100pp; 5½×7½; Publishes 2% of poems submitted. Reporting time: 1-3 months. Payment: 1 copy of the magazine. Interested in new or unpub'd poets: yes. Simultaneous submissions accepted: no. Recent contributors: Edwin Honig, Elena Shvarts, Rosmarie Waldrop, Susan Wheeler, Leslie Scalapino. Submission quantity: 5. Special interests: Interested in original, experimental poetry with a sense of tradition; translations; longpoems.

NEGATIVE CAPABILITY, Negative Capability Press, 62 Ridgelawn Drive East, Mobile, AL 36608, 205-460-6146. 1981. "Annual Eve of St. Agnes poetry contest. 1988 judge - Leo Connellan. Winning poems including Honorable Mentions published in subsequent issue." circ. 1M. 3/yr. Pub'd 500 poems 1999; expects 500 poems 2000, 500 poems 2001. sub. price: $18; sample: $6. 184pp; 5½×8½; Rights purchased: one time rights. Publishes 10% of poems submitted. Deadlines: no submissions from June-August, we do not read during the summer. Reporting time: 4-6 weeks. Payment: 1 copy of journal in which poem(s) appear. Interested in new or unpub'd poets: yes. Simultaneous submissions accepted: no. Recent contributors: Diane Wakoski, Richard Moore, Karl Shapiro, Marge Piercy, Jimmy Carter. Submission quantity: 3-5. Special interests: Translations, experimental poetry, longpoems.

Negative Capability Press (see also NEGATIVE CAPABILITY), 62 Ridgelawn Drive East, Mobile, AL 36608, 334-460-6146. 1981. "We publish hardbacks, paperbacks, chapbooks, broadsides, and poetscards." avg. press run 1M. Expects 1 poetry title 2000, 1 poetry title 2001. 6×9; avg. price, paper: $10; other: $19. 86pp; Publishes a very small % of poetry manuscripts submitted. Reporting time: 6 weeks. Payment: by negotiation. Simultaneous submissions accepted: no. Recently published poets: Karl Shapiro, Vivian Shipley, Pat Schneider, John Brugaletta, Marge Piercy. Submission quantity: 3-5. Special interests: We prefer to be open, and our interests in this area are quite varied.

NEOLOGISMS, Box 869, 1102 Pleasant Street, Worcester, MA 01602. Jim Fay, Editor & Publisher. 1996. "No 'love-mush.'" circ. 80. 4/yr. Pub'd 75 poems 1999. sub. price: $20; sample: $5. 65pp; 8½×11; Rights purchased: 1st. Publishes 40% of poems submitted. Deadlines: continuous. Reporting time: 1-3 months. Payment: copy. Interested in new or unpub'd poets: yes. Simultaneous submissions accepted: yes, but this is frowned upon. Recent contributors: Vincent Ferrini, Greg St. Thomasino, Julian Bernick, Jenny Curtis. Submission quantity: whatever.

NERVE COWBOY, PO Box 4973, Austin, TX 78765, www.onr.com/user/jwhagins/nervecowboy.html. Joseph Shields, Jerry Hagins. 1995. circ. 250. 2/yr. sub. price: $7; sample: $4. 64pp; 7×8½; Rights purchased: first rights. Publishes 5% of poems submitted. Deadlines: read year round. Reporting time: 6-8 weeks. Payment: 1 copy. Interested in new or unpub'd poets: yes. Simultaneous submissions accepted: no. Recent contributors: Fred Voss, Gerald Locklin, Serena Fusek, Susanne R. Bowers, Joan Jobe Smith. Submission quantity: 5-6 poems.

Neshui Publishing, 1345 Bellevue, St. Louis, MO 63117, 314-725-5562, e-mail info@neshui.com, website www.neshui.com. 5×7.

Network 3000 Publishing, 3432 Denmark Avenue #108, St. Paul, MN 55123-1088, 612-452-4173. 1992. 5½×8½.

NEW ALTERNATIVES, J & J Consultants, Inc., 603 Ole Farm Road, Media, PA 19063, 610-565-9692, Fax 610-565-9694, wjones13@juno.com, www.members.tripod/walterjones. Walter Jones. 1993. circ. 250. 6/yr. Pub'd 10 poems 1999. sub. price: $12. 8pp; 8½×11; Publishes 10% of poems submitted. Deadlines: none. Reporting time: 2 months. Payment: none. Interested in new or unpub'd poets: yes, only interested in new writers. Simultaneous submissions accepted: yes. Recent contributors: Najua Tayo Sabur, Janet Burgents. Submission quantity: unlimited.

NEW AMERICAN WRITING, 369 Molino Avenue, Mill Valley, CA 94941, 415-389-1877 phone/Fax. Paul Hoover, Editor; Maxine Chernoff, Editor. 1971. "Writers are advised to read our magazine first. Do not send entire mss. #4: Australian poetry issue; #5: Censorship and the arts; #9: New poetry from Great Britain; #12 special supplement - 12 Brazilian poets." circ. 6M. 1/yr. Pub'd 100 poems 1999. sub. price: $21 three issues individuals, $27/3 issues institutions, $7 postal surcharge foreign mail; sample: $8. 150pp; 5½×8½; Rights purchased: first serial rights. Publishes 1-5% of poems submitted. Deadlines: open. Reporting time: 1-6 months. Payment: 2 copies. Interested in new or unpub'd poets: yes. Simultaneous submissions accepted: no. Recent contributors: Robert Creeley, Lyn Hejinian, Charles Simic, Ann Lauterbach, John Ashbery. Submission quantity: no more than 5.

New Broom Private Press (see also FENICE BROADSHEETS), 78 Cambridge Street, Leicester, England. Cynthia A. Mas Savage. 1994. "The broadsheets are printed on a 10 x 8 handpress and are given away. The poets recieve 25-30 copies but no payment. I like poetry to rhyme and make sense, points which frequently seem to be ignored. The press is a hobby—no exact times for publication can be expected. I took over the press on the death of my husband, Toni Svage, Oct. 4, 1994. I am still practicing and for this reason, the only book I have printed so far was one of my own poems. Thus I could not offend a *real* poet. The broadsheets are now titled *Fenice Broadsheets*." avg. press run 100-120. Pub'd 1 poetry title 1999. 8x5; avg. price, paper: £6. 20pp; Publishes 50% of poetry manuscripts submitted. Payment: 6 copies. Interested in new or unpub'd poets: yes. Recently published poets: Neil Hall, Paul Humphrey, Dean Juniper, Alix Weisz, Cynthia A. Savage. Submission quantity: 4-8.

New Canaan Publishing Company Inc., PO Box 752, New Canaan, CT 06840, 203-966-3408 phone/Fax. 1995. size varies.

NEW COLLAGE MAGAZINE, New Collage Press, 5700 N. Tamiami Trail, Sarasota, FL 34243-2197, 813-359-4360. A. McA. Miller, General Editor. 1970. "We welcome submissions year-round, including summer. A word of advice to those sending computer-printed text: cute doodles and enormous headings do little for us, and some fonts are definitely more attractive than others. We have nothing against readable dot-matrix script—but please, make it legible. It's tough to give an unbiased reading to an eyesore." circ. 500. 3/yr. Pub'd 60-70 poems 1999. sub. price: $9, $17/2 years; sample: $3. 32pp; 5½x8½; Rights purchased: 1st North American serial rights. Publishes 7.5% of poems submitted. Deadlines: rolling. Reporting time: 6 weeks. Payment: 2 copies. Interested in new or unpub'd poets: yes. Simultaneous submissions accepted: no. Recent contributors: Peter Meinke, Stephen Corey, Malcolm Glass, Lola Haskins, Peter Klappert. Submission quantity: 3-5.

New Collage Press (see also NEW COLLAGE MAGAZINE), 5700 North Trail, Sarasota, FL 34234, 813-359-4360. A. McA. Miller, General Editor. 1970. "Manuscripts by solicitation only." avg. press run 500-1M. Expects 1 poetry title 2000, 1 poetry title 2001. 5½x8½; avg. price, paper: $3. 32pp; Payment: by negotiation. Interested in new or unpub'd poets: Yes. Simultaneous submissions accepted: No. Recently published poets: Carol Flint, Harry Brody, Willie Reader, Terri Drake, Elisa Wilson.

THE NEW CRITERION, 850 Seventh Avenue, New York, NY 10019, 212-247-6980. Robert Richman. 1982. circ. 7M. 10/yr. Pub'd 50 poems 1999; expects 50 poems 2000, 50 poems 2001. sub. price: $36; sample: $5. 90pp; 7x10; Rights purchased: one-time. Publishes 5% of poems submitted. Deadlines: none. Reporting time: 2-3 months. Payment: $2.50 per line, $75 minimum. Interested in new or unpub'd poets: yes. Simultaneous submissions accepted: no. Recent contributors: Donald Justice, Theodore Weiss, John Frederick Nims, Jane Kenyon, Elizabeth Spires. Submission quantity: 3 or 4.

NEW DELTA REVIEW, c/o Dept. of English, Louisiana State University, Baton Rouge, LA 70803-5001, 504-388-4079. Nat Hardy, Poetry Editor 2000-2001. 1984. "Each issue features a poetry award, the Eyster Prize, for $50. Judges are established poets, which vary from issue-to-issue. We read year-round and urge new writers to submit" circ. 500. 2/yr. Pub'd 25 poems 1999; expects 17 poems 2000, 25 poems 2001. sub. price: $12; sample: $4 issue, $10 for 3. 150pp; 6x9; Rights purchased: First North American serial. Publishes 1-5% of poems submitted. Deadlines: March 1, September 1. Reporting time: 2-4 months. Payment: 2 copies. Interested in new or unpub'd poets: yes. Simultaneous submissions accepted: no. Recent contributors: Virgil Suarez, Georgann Eubanks, George Looney, Mary Leader, David Trinidad. Submission quantity: 1-3. Special interests: Translations (if translator has obtained rights).

New Earth Publications, 1921 Ashby Ave, Berkeley, CA 94703, 510-549-0176. Clifton Ross. 1990. "Publisher of Latin American poetry anthologies with progressive political slant in bilingual editions, world and local poetry" avg. press run 500-2M. Pub'd 2 poetry titles 1999; expects 2 poetry titles 2000. 8½x5½; avg. price, paper: $9.95. Publishes 20% of poetry manuscripts submitted. Reporting time: up to 3 months. Payment: negotiable. Interested in new or unpub'd poets: yes. Simultaneous submissions accepted: yes. Recently published poets: Ernesto Cardenal, Luz Maria Umpierre, Henry Noyes, William Everson. Submission quantity: 5-20. Special interests: Serious work dealing with themes of liberation, spirituality. No end line rhymes, no cute stuff.

NEW ENGLAND REVIEW, Middlebury College, Middlebury College, Middlebury, VT 05753, 802-443-5075, fax 802-443-2088, e-mail nereview@middlebury.edu, www.middlebury.edu/~nereview. Stephen Donadio, Editor. 1978. circ. 2M. 4/yr. Pub'd 80 poems 1999; expects 80 poems 2000, 80 poems 2001. sub. price: $23 individual, $40 institution; sample: $7. 184pp; 7x10; Rights purchased: first publication, and reprint option in subsequent editions of the magazine, in any form. Publishes 1% of poems submitted. Deadlines: must be postmarked between Sept. 1 and May 31. Reporting time: 8-12 weeks. Payment: $10 per page, $20 minimum, plus 2 copies. Interested in new or unpub'd poets: yes/yes. Simultaneous submissions accepted: yes, if stated. Recent contributors: Debora Greger, Reginald Shepherd, Alfred Corn, Brigit Pegeen Kelly, Charles Wright. Submission quantity: no more than 6. Special interests: We are very interested in translations from throughout the world.

New Hope International (see also AABYE (formerly New Hope International Writing); NEW HOPE INTERNATIONAL REVIEW), 20 Werneth Avenue, Gee Cross, Hyde SK14 5NL, United Kingdom, 0161-351 1878, newhope@iname.com, www.nhi.clara.net/nhihome.htm. Gerald England. 1970. "Study magazine first - individual collections published only after editor conversant with author's work. Details of any special anthologies are announced in the magazine. Guidelines available for IRC." avg. press run 500-1M. Pub'd 3 poetry titles 1999; expects 3 poetry titles 2000, 3 poetry titles 2001. size A5; avg. price, paper: $15 cash; non-sterling charges not accepted. 36-80pp; Publishes .5% of poetry manuscripts submitted. Reporting time: up to 6 months (usually not more than 5 weeks). Payment: large discount on copies. Interested in new or unpub'd poets: no. Simultaneous submissions accepted: no. Recently published poets: B.Z. Niditch, Steve Sneyd, Albert Russo, John Elsberg, Gillian Bence-Jones. Submission quantity: write first. Special interests: all styles from haiku to longpoems published.

NEW HOPE INTERNATIONAL REVIEW, New Hope International, 20 Werneth Avenue, Gee Cross, Hyde, Cheshire SK14 5NL, United Kingdom, 061-351-1878, newhope@iname.com. Gerald England. 1986. "We are interested in anything that is innovative or unusual." circ. 1M. 2-3/yr. Pub'd 10 poems 1999; expects 20 poems 2000, 20 poems 2001. sub. price: £13 for 3 issues. 60pp; size A5; Rights purchased: 1st British serial rights. Publishes less than 1% of poems submitted. Deadlines: submit to Aabye—some poems will be used in NHIR. Reporting time: up to 6 months but usually within 6 weeks. Payment: copies. Interested in new or unpub'd poets: yes. Simultaneous submissions accepted: no. Recent contributors: John Elsberg, Bill Meaddon, Neca Stoller, Patricia Prime, Dan Pugh. Submission quantity: no more than 6.

New Issues Poetry & Prose, Western Michigan University, 1201 Oliver Street, Kalamazoo, MI 49008, 616-387-2592 or 616-387-8185, Fax 616-387-2562, newissues-poetry@wmich.edu, www.umich.edu/newissues. Herbert Scott. 1996. "New Issues Poetry Prize, $1,000 and publication for a first book of poems. Deadline: Nov. 30. 2000 Judge: C.D. Wright. The Green Rose Prize in Poetry, $1,000 and publication for a book of poems by an established poet. Deadline: Sept. 30. Send SASE for guidelines, or visit our website" avg. press run 1.5M. Pub'd 6 poetry titles 1999; expects 6-7 poetry titles 2000, 7 poetry titles 2001. 6×8½; avg. price, cloth: $22; paper: $14. 72pp; We publish 1 of 250 manuscripts recieved. Reporting time: 3 months. Payment: poet receives 10% of press run in lieu of royalties. Interested in new or unpub'd poets: yes. Simultaneous submissions accepted: yes. Recently published poets: Patricia Jabbeh Wesley, Julie Moulds, Malena Morling, Gladys Cardiff, Deanna Lundin. Submission quantity: 48-72 pages. Special interests: We are looking for diverse, fresh voices. We do not favor any school or region in our national competition.

THE NEW LAUREL REVIEW, 828 Lesseps Street, New Orleans, LA 70117, 504-947-6001. Lee Meitzen Grue, Editor; Lenny Emmanuel, Poetry Editor. 1971. "We read in the fall. Do not read in the summer. Submit 3 poems. Next issue: New Poets." circ. 500. 1/yr. Pub'd 40 poems 1999; expects 34 poems 2000. sub. price: $10 individuals, $12 institutions, $15 foreign; sample: $8. 125pp; 6×9; Rights purchased: poets retain rights after publication. Publishes 10% of poems submitted. Deadlines: winter months open, we don't read submission during June, July, and August. Reporting time: 2-3 months usually. Payment: 1 issue in which they appear and discount on extras. Interested in new or unpub'd poets: yes. Simultaneous submissions accepted: reluctantly, must be informed of acceptance elsewhere. Recent contributors: Jaime Gil de Biema, Julie Kane, Katharine Soniat, Robert Cooperman, Len Roberts. Submission quantity: 3. Special interests: We use translations, songs, articles on jazz and folklore, as well as poetry and short fiction. We have a special section each issue on visual art, featuring the work of one artist, also an interview with, or article on the artist. Well-crafted work that has something to say always interests us. We would like our magazine's arrival to be an exciting event in the lives of our readers.

NEW LETTERS, University of Missouri, Kansas City, MO 64110, 816-235-1168, Fax 816-235-2611, www.umkc.edu/newsletters/. James McKinley, Editor. 1971 (Predecessor, *University Review,* 1934). "*New Letters* does not read manuscripts between May 15 and October 15, does occasionally publish special issues. Annual 'New Letters Awards': $1,000 fiction; $1,000 poetry; $1,000 the essay—send SASE or see website for more details and deadlines." circ. 2.5M. 4/yr. Pub'd 215 poems 1999; expects 263 poems 2000, 225 poems 2001. sub. price: $17; sample: $5. 140pp; 6×9; Rights purchased: first publication rights only. Publishes 1-2% of poems submitted. Deadlines: none. Reporting time: 2-4 months. Payment: small, plus 2 contributors' copies. Interested in new or unpub'd poets: yes. Simultaneous submissions accepted: no. Recent contributors: Galway Kinnell, Lisel Mueller, Linda Gregg, Jorie Graham, David Ray. Submission quantity: up to 6. Special interests: Translations, personal essays.

NEW METHODS JOURNAL (VETERINARY), PO Box 22605, San Francisco, CA 94122-0605, 415-664-3469. AHT Lippert, Editor. 1976. "Magazine is available to consumers. Policies on poetry not firm.

Reading: Prefer not to be rushed. Do: Send typed, double-spaced with one inch margins. Send SASE for return of work. May not return otherwise. Don't: Send hand-written submissions. Sometimes too hard to read. Special Issues: None yet on poetry. Generally used to break up the articles... Contests: May have one someday. Also we have been approached with funds by some individuals to have their work published in *New Methods*. In the past, this was a firm policy to say no. However, with our limited funds and therefore limited space for quality poems, we have decided that if we are interested in someone's work but unable to afford space and they are interested in at least paying for costs, we would publish more poetry and prose. I hope that this is understood and does not come off as mercenary." circ. 5.6M. Irregular. Pub'd 12 poems 1999; expects 12 poems 2001. sub. price: $29 (additional cost outside of U.S.A., all monies must be in U.S. funds); sample: $2.90. 4pp; 9×11; Rights purchased: none. Publishes 10% of poems submitted. Deadlines: none, unless we have a specific theme with a deadline. Reporting time: 4 weeks. Payment: none. Interested in new or unpub'd poets: yes, with SASE only for return. Simultaneous submissions accepted: yes, don't over supply us. It could be unfair to both of us. Submission quantity: no more than 3. Special interests: Since readers may not be reading publication because of poetry, make sure that your submission has something to do with animals and that it is not too out there. English only.

THE NEW MOON REVIEW, 148 Eighth Avenue #417, New York, NY 10011. Jerry Oleaf, Editor. 1991. "We can use all types of poetry whether its sonnets influenced by Keats or Zen poetry influenced by Basho, provided it's good quality. Include SASE." circ. 250. 2-3/yr. Pub'd 40 poems 1999; expects 40 poems 2000, 70 poems 2001. 32pp; 5½×8½; Reporting time: 3 weeks. Payment: in copies. Interested in new or unpub'd poets: yes. Simultaneous submissions accepted: yes. Recent contributors: Yuki Hartman, Janine Pommy Vega, Daniela Gioseffi.

NEW MUSE OF CONTEMPT, Broken Jaw Press, Box 596 Stn A, Fredericton, NB E3B 5A6, Canada, www.brokenjaw.com. Joe Blades. 1987. "Submissions of pithy poetry (esp. visual/concrete poetry, found poetry and homolinguistic text translations) welcome by post if accompanied by an SASE with Canadian postage (not USA postage) or International Postal Reply Coupons." circ. 200-500. 2/yr. Pub'd 1 poem 1999; expects 1 poem 2000. sub. price: $12; sample: $6. 52pp; 5½×8½; Rights purchased: first serial. Publishes 1% of poems submitted. Reporting time: 1-12 months. Payment: copies. Interested in new or unpub'd poets: yes. Simultaneous submissions accepted: no. Recent contributors: R.M. Vaughan, Adeena Navasick, Hugh Hazelton, Joe Blades.

New Native Press, PO Box 661, Cullowhee, NC 28723, 828-293-9237. Thomas Rain Crowe, Publisher; Nan Watkins, Managing Editor. 1979. "No unsolicited manuscripts considered with the exception of translation work." avg. press run 1M. Pub'd 2 poetry titles 1999; expects 1 poetry title 2000, 1 poetry title 2001. 5½×8; avg. price, paper: $9.95. 80pp; Payment: varies (usually 1/3 of run), 50% discount on additional copies. Interested in new or unpub'd poets: no. Simultaneous submissions accepted: no. Recently published poets: Ken Wainio, John Lane, Philip Daughtry, Meschach McLachlan, Danielle Truscott. Special interests: Special interests at this point in *translation*! Press will be focusing on publishing translation work of marginalized and endangered languages only, after 1998. Poetry only.

NEW ORLEANS REVIEW, Loyola University, Box 195, New Orleans, LA 70118, 504-865-3597. 1968. circ. 1M. 4/yr. Pub'd 50 poems 1999; expects 50 poems 2000, 50 poems 2001. sub. price: 4 issues - domestic $18 indiv, $21 instit, foreign $32; sample: $9 domestic, $15 foreign. 120-200pp; 9×6; Rights purchased: 1st North American Serial. Publishes 2% of poems submitted. Deadlines: none. Reporting time: 3 months. Payment: copies, negotiable. Interested in new or unpub'd poets: yes. Simultaneous submissions accepted: yes. Recent contributors: Mark Halliday, Angela Ball, D.C. Berry, Michael Harper, Yusef Komunyaaka. Submission quantity: 3-5. Special interests: Experimental poetry.

THE NEW PRESS LITERARY QUARTERLY, 6539 108th Street #E6, Forest Hills, NY 11375-2214, 718-459-6807; Fax; 718-275-1646. Evie-Ivy Biber, Poetry Editor. 1984. "We hold weekly poetry readings and workshops in NYC. Send SASE or call 718-229-6782 for details. Reading fee $2 for one to three poems, $4 for four to six poems maximum six poems per author per submission" circ. 2M. 4/yr. Pub'd 120 poems 1999; expects 150 poems 2000, 150 poems 2001. sub. price: $15; sample: $5.50. 40-48pp; 8½×11; Rights purchased: first time publication. Publishes 10% of poems submitted. Deadlines: July, 1. Reporting time: 4 months. Payment: 2 copies, annual poetry contest for submissions with $5 entry, $100 first prize, $75 second prize, 5 2-yr subscriptions as 3rd prizes. Interested in new or unpub'd poets: yes. Simultaneous submissions accepted: no. Recent contributors: Allen Ginsberg, Lawrence Ferlinghetti, Gina Bergamino, Joe Malone, Margueritte. Submission quantity: 1-6. Special interests: Occasionally we publish concrete poetry, and will publish rhymed and lyrical poetry as well as free verse. Maximum length for poetry: 100 lines. We are now accepting poetry in Spanish, Italian, French and Portugese, with their respective English translations. All poetry must be original and previously unpublished. Translators who are not the original authors must be credited, therefore, please include their names with your submissions.

THE NEW RENAISSANCE, An International Magazine of Ideas & Opinions, Emphasizing Literature

& The Arts, 26 Heath Road #11, Arlington, MA 02474-3645. Frank Finale. 1968. "All poetry submissions are tied into our awards programs: 1st award presented Fall 1996. Current subscribers. How to submit poems (see How many poems..etc) w/$10 ($11.50 foreign) entry fee. All others submit poems with $15 ($16.50 foreign) entry fee. Allow 4-6 months. Poems without entry fee returned *unread*." circ. 1.3M. 2/yr. Pub'd 25 poems 1999; expects 52 poems 2000, 50+ poems 2001. sub. price: $24/3 issues USA, $26/3 issues Canada; all others $32/3 issues; sample: $10 USA; $10.30 Canada; $11.60 all others. 144-184pp; 6×9; Rights purchased: all, but poets can re-market own work. Publishes about 15-18%, occasionally 25% of poems submitted. Deadlines: submissions open 2001: 1/2/01 to 6/30/01 only. Reporting time: 5-6 months when heavily oversubmitted. Payment: $20-$50, more for the *occasional* long poem. Interested in new or unpub'd poets: yes, if the poet feels they are as good as, or better than, the work we are currently publishing. Simultaneous submissions accepted: prefer not to. Recent contributors: Ann Struthers, Daniel Tobin, Marian Steele, Ralph Salisbury, Philip Murray. Submission quantity: 4-6, tops; for long poems 1 only. Special interests: Especially interested in translations. We've published poems from the Swedish, Bulgarian, Hungarian, Russian (Cyrilliac alphabets), Spanish, Turkish, Arabic, Greek, Italian, Flemish, Dutch, German, Polish, Hungarian, etc.; light poems , satire, long poems only occasionally. (Submit only one long poem if it is more than 3½ double-spaced typed pp.) Not especially interested in experimental poetry but try us if you think you have something that's really good. It may be a long shot, but we publish long shots occasionally.

New Rivers Press, Inc., 420 N. 5th Street, Suite 1180, Minneapolis, MN 55401, 612-339-7114. Robert Alexander, Creative Director. 1968. "New Rivers has a strong reputation for publishing work of quality, originality, and excellence, often by new poets—we probably publish more first books than any other small press publisher. We also pride ourselves on being eclectic, so our list is a strong but widely varied one. We lean more towards open forms and free verse than formalism, but we have published poets, like Charles Molesworth, who are very traditional in their use of forms. Our editorial decisions are *always* based on what we perceive to be a strong committed sense of voice and subject, which in the best poetry, are always unique and idiosyncratic. This means that a good deal of the poetry we publish has substantial political and social content because our writers are very often committed individuals, but we never publish anything merely because it is political and/or social. We publish more books by women, for instance, than most feminist publishing houses, but the reason is always based on quality rather than position." avg. press run 750-1M. Pub'd 5 poetry titles 1999; expects 5 poetry titles 2000, 5 poetry titles 2001. 6×9; avg. price, paper: $12.95. 96pp; Publishes 3-5% of poetry manuscripts submitted. Reporting time: 6 months. Payment: 100 free copies, or in the case of Minnesota Voices Project poetry winners $500; all NRP authors receive 15% royalties on list for second and subsequent printings. Interested in new or unpub'd poets: contact New Rivers for guidelines. Simultaneous submissions accepted: no. Recently published poets: Orval Lund, Marie Harris, Pamela Gemin, Susan Steger Welsh, Richard Broderick. Submission quantity: 5-10 and query with SASE.

THE NEW SOUTHERN SURREALIST REVIEW, Burning Llama Press, 82 Ridge Lake Drive, Columbia, SC 29209-4213. 1996. circ. 100-200. Irregular. sub. price: $10/3 issues (make checks payable to Keith Higginbotham); sample: $4. Pages vary; 8½×11.

New Spirit Press/The Poet Tree (see also POEMS THAT THUMP IN THE DARK/SECOND GLANCE), 82-34 138 Street #6F, Kew Gardens, NY 11435, 718-847-1482. Ignatius Graffeo, Editor. 1991. "Chapbook submissions should not be overly personal, profane or violent. Qualities we look for are honesty, originality, imagination, coherent theme, universal, metaphorical." avg. press run 150. Pub'd 20 poetry titles 1999; expects 20 poetry titles 2000, 30 poetry titles 2001. 5½×8½; avg. price, paper: $4; other: magazine $6. 20pp; Publishes 5% of poetry manuscripts submitted. Reporting time: 3 weeks. Payment: copies only. Interested in new or unpub'd poets: yes. Simultaneous submissions accepted: yes. Recently published poets: Mark Larson, Mary Winters, Gina Tabasso, H. Edgar Hix, William Harryman. Submission quantity: 20. Special interests: "Good, non-gimmicky, charismatic, qualitative verse."

NEW STONE CIRCLE, 1185 E 1900 N Road, White Heath, IL 61884. Karen Singer. 1994. circ. 100. 1-2/yr. Pub'd 30 poems 1999. sub. price: $8; sample: $4.50. 50pp; 5½×8½; Rights purchased: one-time rights. Publishes 5% of poems submitted. Deadlines: we read all year, contest deadline June 1. Reporting time: 3-6 months. Payment: 1 copy. Interested in new or unpub'd poets: yes. Simultaneous submissions accepted: yes, but tell us - no for contest. Recent contributors: Robert Cooperman, Chris Green, Janet Baker, Lois Marie Harrod. Submission quantity: 1-5.

NEW THOUGHT JOURNAL, 2520 Evelyn Drive, Kettering, OH 45409, Ph/Fax 937-293-9717; E-mail: ntjmag@aol.com. 1994. circ. 5M. 4/yr. sub. price: $15 for 4 issues; sample: $6 covers p/h. 40pp; 8½×11.

New World Press, 20 Driftwood Trail, Half Moon Bay, CA 94019-2349, 650-726-5939; Fax 415-921-3730. Noni Ph.D Howard, Publisher and Editor. 1974. "Please send nothing by mail without first calling my phone number for a personal inquiry" avg. press run 1.2M copies. Expects 2 poetry titles 2000, -1-3 poetry titles 2001. 9×6; avg. price, paper: $10. 100-200pp; Publishes less than 10% of poetry manuscripts submitted. Reporting time: 60 days. Payment: negotiable. Interested in new or unpub'd poets: no. Simultaneous submissions accepted: yes. Recently published poets: Jennifer Stone, Adrian Marcus, Evelyn Hickey. Submission quantity: 5 poems. Special interests: Poems can by any subject, but must have a strong universal appeal.

THE NEW WRITER, PO Box 60, Cranbrook, Kent TN17 2ZR, England, 01580-212626. Abi Hughes-Edwards. 1996. circ. 1.5M. 10/yr. Pub'd 60 poems 1999. sub. price: £45.50; sample: £3. 48pp; 8¼×11¾; Rights purchased: 1st British. Deadlines: none. Reporting time: 4-6 weeks. Payment: £3 per poem. Interested in new or unpub'd poets: yes. Simultaneous submissions accepted: yes. Recent contributors: Sue Butler, Kenneth C. Steven, Mario Petrucci, Linda Lamus, Mark Granier. Submission quantity: up to 10. Special interests: contemporary.

NEW WRITING, PO Box 1812, Amherst, NY 14226-7812, http://members.aol.com/newwriting/maga-zine.html. Sam Meade, Richard Lynch, Co-Editor. 1991. "Contest. Agency" circ. varies. Irregular. Pub'd 5 poems 1999; expects 8 poems 2000, 10 poems 2001. sub. price: free; sample: free. Rights purchased: 1st time. Publishes 3% of poems submitted. Payment: depends on quality of submission. Interested in new or unpub'd poets: yes. Simultaneous submissions accepted: yes. Submission quantity: 5-8.

●**Newcomb Publishers, Inc.**, 4812 North Fairfax Drive, Arlington, VA 22203, 703-524-1397. 6×9.

NEWSLETTER INAGO, Inago Press, PO Box 26244, Tucson, AZ 85726-6244, 520-294-7031. Del Reitz, Editor, Publisher. 1979. "Poems should be kept to 50 lines or less (shorter preferred). Copyright is retained by authors at all times except for the right of use in annual 'Best of Issue' numbers of *NI*, when contributors copies are again sent - and for use in periodic anthologies, approximately every 5 years, in book or audio tape (means permitting, both) production. Poets and subscribers will be notified. Redistrubution/resale by publisher approval only." circ. 200. 12/yr. Pub'd 200 poems 1999; expects 300 poems 2000, 200 poems 2001. sub. price: $17.50 U.S., $22.50 Canada, £21 U.K.; sample: $3.50 U.S. & Canada, U.K. £8. 4pp; 8×10½; Rights purchased: none. Publishes 20% of poems submitted. Deadlines: none. Reporting time: immediately. Payment: contributors copies. Interested in new or unpub'd poets: yes. Simultaneous submissions accepted: yes. Recent contributors: Steve Fay, Joshua Bodwell, Mark Petry, Susan Marshall, Askold Skalsky. Submission quantity: 10-15 with SASE or International Postal Coupons. Special interests: Theme poetry is discouraged since the widest range possible of a poet's output is desired for the issue in which s/he is featured. All subjects and styles will be considered although use of 'fecund old anglosaxonisms' should be used sparingly.

NEWSLETTER (LEAGUE OF CANADIAN POETS), 54 Wolseley Street 3rd Floor, Toronto, Ontario M5T IA5, Canada, 416-504-1657, Fax; 416-504-0096. Jan Horner. 1966. circ. 600. 6/yr. sub. price: $30; sample: $2. 32pp Museletter, 12pp Newsletter; 8½×11; Rights purchased: rights remain with poet. Payment: none. Interested in new or unpub'd poets: no.

Nextstep Books, 1070 Carolan Avenue #116, Burlingame, CA 94010, e-mail nextstep@nub.ml.org. 1998. 5½×8½.

Nicolin Fields Publishing, Inc., 3 Red Fox Road, North Hampton, NH 03862-3320, 603-964-1727, Fax 603-964-4221, nfp@nh.ultranet.com, www.PublishingWorks.com, and www.NicolinFields.com. 1994. avg. press run 100. Pub'd 1 poetry title 1999. 6×9; avg. price, paper: $10. 100pp; Publishes 1-3% of poetry manuscripts submitted. Reporting time: 4-6 weeks. Payment: standard. Interested in new or unpub'd poets: yes. Simultaneous submissions accepted: yes. Recently published poets: Sasha Wolfe. Submission quantity: 10.

NIGHTSHADE, 577 Central Avenue, Box 4, Jefferson, LA 70121-1400, e-mail fullmoon@eudoramail.com or haunted@rocketmail.com; Websites www.members.xoom.com/blackie, www.eclecticity.com/zines/, www.spa-ceports.com/~haunted/, www2.cybercities.com/z/zines/. Sharida Rizzuto, Harold Tollison, Ann Hoyt. 1983. circ. 800-1M. 2/yr. Pub'd 60 poems 1999; expects 60 poems 2000, 60 poems 2001. sub. price: $15.80; sample: $7.90. 100pp; 8½×11; Rights purchased: one-time, first serial, or second serial rights. Publishes 30-35% of poems submitted. Deadlines: always open to submissions. Reporting time: 2-6 weeks. Payment: free copies. Interested in new or unpub'd poets: yes. Simultaneous submissions accepted: yes. Recent contributors: Leilah Wendell, Richard David Behrens, Hay C. Day, George Chadderon. Submission quantity: 1-5. Special interests: Experimental, longpoems, light verse, satire, avant garde, beat, death, free verse, short poetry, surrealist, eclectic, horror, occult.

NIGHTSUN, English Department, Frostburg S. University, Frostburg, MD 21532, 301-687-4221. Douglas DeMars. 1981. circ. 500-1M. Pub'd 26 poems 1999; expects 50 poems 2000, 50 poems 2001. sub. price: $5 + $1.50 p/h; sample: $5 + $1.50 p/h. 60pp; 5½×8½; Rights purchased: rights revert to authors after publication. Publishes 1% of poems submitted. Deadlines: June 1. Reporting time: 2-3 months. Payment: author's copy. Interested in new or unpub'd poets: yes. Simultaneous submissions accepted: no. Recent contributors: Philip Dacey, Linda Paston, Marge Piercy, Diane Wakoski, Walter McDonald. Submission quantity: 3-5.

Nightsun Books, 823 Braddock Road, Cumberland, MD 21502-2622, 301-722-4861. Ruth Wilex. 1987. "Please inquire before submitting manuscripts!" avg. press run 300. Pub'd 1 poetry title 1999; expects 1 poetry title 2000, 2 poetry titles 2001. 5½×8½; avg. price, cloth: $6; paper: $5. 50pp; Publishes 5% of poetry manuscripts submitted. Reporting time: 4 months. Payment: varies, inquire. Interested in new or unpub'd poets: yes. Simultaneous submissions accepted: yes. Recently published poets: Jim Ralston, Frank Fleckenstein, Jorn Bramann. Submission quantity: 10.

NIMROD INTERNATIONAL, 600 South College Avenue, Tulsa, OK 74104-3126. Ivy Dempsey, William Epperson, Manly Johnson, Ruth Weston. 1956. "Ruth G. Hardman Award given annually: 1st prize $2000, 2nd $1000. Either a substantial effort in a single poem or a sequence of related poems is required; 1800 words maximum. Send business-size SASE for prize rules. Deadline for submissions—April 30. Previous judges: Mark Doty, Henry Taylor, and W.S. Merwin. Winners and judges are flown to Tulsa in October for a reading and reception." circ. 4M. 2/yr. Pub'd 70 poems 1999; expects 70 poems 2000, 70 poems 2001. sub. price: $17.50/yr; $30/2 yr.; Outside US - $19/$33; sample: $10. 160pp; 6×9; Rights purchased: 1st refusal. Publishes 1% of poems submitted. Deadlines: Ruth G. Hardman Award—submissions Jan. 1 to April 30. Reporting time: 3 months or more. Payment: Ruth G. Hardman Awards—1st prize $2000, 2nd $1000; 2 copies of issue. Interested in new or unpub'd poets: yes. Simultaneous submissions accepted: yes. Recent contributors: Ruth Schwartz, Lucia Getsi, George O'Connell, Patricia Traxler, Jeffrey Levine. Submission quantity: 3-6. Special interests: Quality.

nine muses books, 3541 Kent Creek Road, Winston, OR 97496, 541-679-6674; E-mail mw9muses@teleport.com. 1987. "nine muses is an author's collective. We recommend to other poets to consider doing the same" avg. press run 500. Pub'd 1 poetry title 1999; expects 4 poetry titles 2000, 2 poetry titles 2001. 5½×8½; avg. price, paper: $5-10. 65pp; Payment: author owns books. Interested in new or unpub'd poets: no. Recently published poets: Valenza, David, waterman, Hureaux, raphael. Submission quantity: No submission except by invitation.

96 INC, PO Box 15559, Boston, MA 02215. Julie Anderson, Andrew Dawson. 1992. circ. 3M. 1/yr. Pub'd 30 poems 1999. sub. price: $15 for all mailings, newsletters and announcements of readings and special events.; sample: $7.50. 60pp; 8½×11; Rights purchased: all rights revert to author. Publishes 2% of poems submitted. Deadlines: none. Reporting time: 6 months to 1 year. Payment: 4 copies of magazine. Interested in new or unpub'd poets: yes. Simultaneous submissions accepted: yes. Recent contributors: Dana Elder, Gary Duehr, Eugene Gloria, Jennifer Barber, Richard Fein.

Ninety-Six Press, Furman University, Greenville, SC 29613, 864-294-3156. Gilbert Allen, William Rogers. 1991. "Ninety-Six Press publishes books of poetry by authors from its region. The press reviews manuscripts only by invitation. No unsolicited manuscripts." avg. press run 500. Pub'd 1 poetry title 1999; expects 1 poetry title 2000, 1-2 poetry titles 2001. 6×9; avg. price, paper: $10. 50-70pp; Payment: copies. Recently published poets: William Aarnes, Bennie Lee Sinclair, Dorothy Perry Thompson, Starkey Flythe, Claire Bateman.

Nite-Owl Press (see also NITE-WRITER'S INTERNATIONAL LITERARY ARTS JOURNAL), 137 Pointview Road, Suite 300, Pittsburgh, PA 15227-3131, 412-885-3798. John A Thompson, Sr., Editor, Publisher; Bree Ann Orner, Assoc. Editor. 1993. "Send your emotions that erupt like a volcano and stain the page" avg. press run 100. Pub'd 1 poetry title 1999; expects 4 poetry titles 2000, 4 poetry titles 2001. 8½×11; avg. price, paper: $6. 30-50pp; Publishes 25% of poetry manuscripts submitted. Reporting time: within 2 weeks. Payment: must purchase copy. Interested in new or unpub'd poets: yes. Simultaneous submissions accepted: yes, if stated. Recently published poets: Lyn Lifshin, Simon Perchik, Richard King Perkins II, Frank J. Yourison, Dale Wallace. Submission quantity: 3-5. Special interests: Street people poetry, prison poetry and senior citizen's that still have a voice.

NITE-WRITER'S INTERNATIONAL LITERARY ARTS JOURNAL, Nite-Owl Press, 137 Pointview Road, Suite 300, Pittsburgh, PA 15227-3131, 412-885-3798, email NiteWrite2@aol.com. John A Sr. Thompson, Exec. Editor-Publisher; Bree Ann Orner, Assoc. Editor. 1993. circ. 100+. 4/yr. Expects 100 poems 2000, 100+ poems 2001. sub. price: $20. 30-50pp; 8½×11; Rights purchased: 1st serial rights. Publishes 25% of poems submitted. Deadlines: read all year. Reporting time: as time permits (usually within 2 weeks). Payment: none, must purchase copy in which work appears. Interested in new or unpub'd poets: yes. Simultaneous submissions accepted: yes. Recent contributors: Janet Nesler, Carol Frances Brown, Dawne C. Bauer, Louise Banks. Submission quantity: 3-5. Special interests: Street people poetry, prison poetry, and senior citizens that still have a voice.

THE NOCTURNAL LYRIC, PO Box 115, San Pedro, CA 90733-0115. Susan Moon, Editor. 1987. "We need *bizarre* poetry, horror poetry, and poems about death." circ. 500. 4/yr. Pub'd 50 poems 1999; expects 50 poems 2000, 50 poems 2001. sub. price: $10; sample: $3. 40pp; 5½×8½; Rights purchased: just the right to print it once. Publishes 15% of poems submitted. Deadlines: none. Reporting time: 6-8 months. Payment: discount coupons on subscriptions. Interested in new or unpub'd poets: yes! Simultaneous submissions accepted: yes. Recent contributors: Steve Zimmerman, Mike Catalano, Jennifer Berry. Submission quantity: 1-5. Special interests: We prefer poems that are short (approx. 20 lines and under) over longer poems. We do print longer ones, but only 1 or 2 per issue.

●NOON, 1369 Madison Avenue, PMB 298, New York, NY 10128, noonannual@yahoo.com. 2000. circ. 300. 1/yr. sub. price: $9. 200pp.

THE NORTH AMERICAN REVIEW, Univ. Of Northern Iowa, Cedar Falls, IA 50614, 319-273-6455. Vince Gotera. 1815. "We are interested in all types of poetry—free verse, formal, experimental, traditional—as long as it 'works.'" circ. 4M. 6/yr. Pub'd 20 poems 1999; expects 20 poems 2000, 50 poems 2001. sub. price: $22; sample: $5. 48pp; 8⅛×10⅞ (ABP Standard); Rights purchased: 1st N.A. serial. Publishes .2% of poems submitted. Reporting time: 4-6 weeks. Payment: 50¢ per line, $20 minimum. Interested in new or unpub'd poets: yes. Simultaneous submissions accepted: NO. Submission quantity: 3-5.

NORTH COAST REVIEW, Poetry Harbor, PO Box 103, Duluth, MN 55801-0103. Patrick McKinnon, Liz Minette, Ellie Schoenfeld. 1992. "Interested mostly in narrative free verse. Welcome work from all levels" circ. 1M. 2/yr. Pub'd 100 poems 1999; expects 100 poems 2000, 70 poems 2001. sub. price: $19.95/4 issues, $59 lifetime; sample: $4.95. 56pp; 7×8½; Rights purchased: one-time NA. Publishes 20% of poems submitted. Deadlines: 7/5 and 1/5. Reporting time: 1-6 months. Payment: $10 plus copies. Interested in new or unpub'd poets: yes. Simultaneous submissions accepted: yes. Recent contributors: Louis Jenkins, Ruth Burman, Mark Vinz, Ethna McKiernan, Bill Holm. Submission quantity: 3-6pp. Special interests: Regional poetry: MN, WI, UP of Michigan and ND.

NORTH DAKOTA QUARTERLY, UND Press, University of North Dakota, PO Box 7209, Grand Forks, ND 58202, 701-777-3322. Jay Meek, Poetry Editor. 1910. "Special issues are announced in advance. Recent special issues of *North Dakota Quarterly* include the Hemingway Centennial and the Bioregion of the Red River Valley. Other special issues include Nature Writing and the Columbus Quincentenary; Hemingway, Malraux, and the Spanish Civil War; and Yugoslav literature." circ. 750. 4/yr. Pub'd 80 poems 1999; expects 80 poems 2000, 80 poems 2001. sub. price: $25 individual, $30 institutional; sample: $8. 175pp; 6×9; Rights purchased: first US. Publishes 5% of poems submitted. Deadlines: we read manuscripts throughout the year. Reporting time: 4-6 weeks. Payment: copies, one-year subscription. Interested in new or unpub'd poets: yes. Simultaneous submissions accepted: no. Recent contributors: Richard Broderick, Adrian Louis, Diane Glancy, Susan Yuzna, Robert Wrigley. Submission quantity: 3-5. Special interests: We are open to the best work submitted by emerging and established writers. *North Dakota Quarterly* on occasion publishes translations from such writers as Catullus, Jammes, and Neruda.

North Stone Press (see also THE NORTH STONE REVIEW), PO Box 14098, Minneapolis, MN 55414. James Naiden, Editor; Allen Topper, Associate Editor; Anne Duggan, Associate Editor; Jack Jarpe, Assistant Editor. 1971. "Query first with SASE, not reading until 2001" avg. press run 500-1M. Pub'd 2 poetry titles 1999. 5½×8½; avg. price, cloth: $6-$9; paper: $10-$15. 30-65pp; Publishes 1 out of 500 poetry manuscripts. Reporting time: 2 months. Payment: copies, royalty paid only after costs of book are received by sales. Simultaneous submissions accepted: no. Recently published poets: August Kleinzahler, Bill Holm, David Ignatow, John Engman, Robert Bly. Submission quantity: optional, more than 1. Special interests: We'll consider anything to do with contemporary literature and life.

THE NORTH STONE REVIEW, North Stone Press, PO Box 14098, Minneapolis, MN 55414. James Naiden, Editor; Allen Topper, Associate Editor; Anne Duggan, Associate Editor; Jack Jarpe, Assistant Editor. 1971. "We're not reading unsolicited work until 2001—we're overloaded at present. We are interested in book reviews and entertain queries with SASE." circ. 1.5M. 2/yr. Pub'd 100 poems 1999. sub. price: $20/2 issues; sample: $10. 200-300pp; 8½×5½; Rights purchased: 1st rights with publication. Publishes 1 out of 200 poems submitted. Deadlines: none, but we have enough material until 1996. Reporting time: 2-6 weeks. Payment: 2 copies of given issue. Interested in new or unpub'd poets: not until 1995. Simultaneous submissions accepted: we hope that if we accept a poem it's not appearing elsewhere, too. Recent contributors: David Ignatow, Ralph J. Mills Jr., Robert Bly, Bill Holm, Sigrid Bergie. Submission quantity: no more than 10. Special interests: Contemporary poetry; query otherwise with SASE.

NORTHEAST, 1310 Shorewood Drive, La Crosse, WI 54601-7033. John Judson. 1962. "Please read us before submitting." circ. 400-500. 1/yr. sub. price: $33 for complete sub., includes 1 *NE* and all Juniper Press works for that year; $38 for institutions; sample: $3. 48-60pp; size varies; Rights purchased: 1st NA serial. Publishes probably 2% of poems submitted. Deadlines: no submissions June through August. Reporting time: 6-12 weeks. Payment: copies of magazine. Interested in new or unpub'd poets: yes. Simultaneous submissions accepted: prefer not. Recent contributors: W.R. Moses, Lisel Mueller, Bruce Cutler, Mary Kay Rummel, John Glowney. Submission quantity: no more than 5.

NORTHERN CONTOURS, PO Box 618, Quincy, CA 95971, 916-283-3402. Cindy Robinson. 1994. "Submissions arriving sans SASE will be recycled. I'm amazed at the number of submissions I receive from poets and writers out of our geographical preference." circ. 500. 1/yr. Pub'd 25 poems 1999; expects 50 poems 2000, 50 poems 2001. sub. price: $14; sample: $6. 96pp; 5½×8; Rights purchased: 1st American Serial Rights.

Publishes 1% of poems submitted. Deadlines: varies, please inquire. Reporting time: 1 week to 8 months. Payment: copies and discounts. Interested in new or unpub'd poets: yes. Simultaneous submissions accepted: yes. Recent contributors: Grace Grafton, Chris Olander, Leonard Cirino, Dennis Saleh, Kate Hulbert. Submission quantity: 6. Special interests: Interested in poetry from Northern California and Northwestern Nevada poets only. Open as to style and subject matter, though no 'greeting card' or other sentimental rhyming verse, please.

NORTHRIDGE REVIEW, c/o CSUN, 18111 Nordoff Street, Mail Stop 8248, Northridge, CA 91330-8261, E-mail 102504.1176@compuserve.com. Luisa Villani. 1980. "purchase a sample copy" circ. 400. 2/yr. Pub'd 60 poems 1999. sub. price: $14; sample: $4. 100pp; 8×5; Deadlines: 10/15 and 3/15. Simultaneous submissions accepted: no. Recent contributors: Tony Barnstone, Robert Arroyo, Lynn Root.

NORTHWEST REVIEW, 369 P.L.C., University of Oregon, Eugene, OR 97403, 503-346-3957. John Witte. 1957. "Advise to Authors: Persist! We're better able over time to understand an author's intents (and will, within the constraints of the time allowed us, make suggestions for revisions). Further, editors who read a large volume of submissions appreciate, and are naturally kindly disposed toward, authors who submit clear, error-free material for consideration." circ. 1.2M. 3/yr. Pub'd 60 poems 1999; expects 80 poems 2000, 80 poems 2001. sub. price: $20; sample: $3.50. 130pp; 6×9; Rights purchased: one-time, rights returned on request. Publishes 4% of poems submitted. Deadlines: ongoing. Reporting time: 8-10 weeks. Payment: 3 copies. Interested in new or unpub'd poets: yes. Simultaneous submissions accepted: no. Recent contributors: Madeline DeFrees, William Stafford, Alan Dugan, Richard Eberhart, Olga Broumas. Submission quantity: 6-8. Special interests: We are eager to consider writing from any and all genres and perspectives. The sole criterion for acceptance of material for publication in *Northwest Review* is that of excellence.

NORTHWOODS JOURNAL, A Magazine for Writers, Northwoods Press, Goose River Press, PO Box 298, Thomaston, ME 04861-0298, 207-345-0998, Fax 207-354-8953, cal@americanletters.org, www.american-letters.org. Robert W. Olmsted. 1986. "Do not submit without requesting submission guidelines." circ. 500. 4/yr. Pub'd 20 poems 1999; expects 30 poems 2000, 40 poems 2001. sub. price: $12.50, free to members of Conservatory of American Letters; sample: $8.45 ppd. 56pp; 5½×8½; Rights purchased: First American Serial. Publishes 85% of poems submitted. Deadlines: March 1 for spring, June 1 for summer, Sept. 1 for fall, Dec. 1 for winter. Reporting time: 48 hours if excellent or terrible, 2 weeks after deadline for vast majority. Payment: $4 per page or more. Interested in new or unpub'd poets: Very much. Simultaneous submissions accepted: absolutely NOT. Submission quantity: whatever can be afforded.

Northwoods Press (see also NORTHWOODS JOURNAL, A Magazine for Writers), PO Box 298, Thomaston, ME 04861-0298, 207-354-0998, Fax 207-354-8953, cal@americanletters.org, www.americanlet-ters.org. Robert W. Olmsted. 1972. "We have a published 15 point program for poetry, available for 2 stamps SASE. Poets should read it before submitting anything." avg. press run 350-500. Pub'd 1 poetry title 1999; expects 3 poetry titles 2000, 3 poetry titles 2001. 5½×8½; avg. price, cloth: $42.95; paper: $13.95; other: $100 collector's edition. 80pp; Publishes approx. 5% of poetry manuscripts submitted. Reporting time: 1 day to 1 month. Payment: minimum advance $250, minimum royalty 10% from first sale. Interested in new or unpub'd poets: yes. Simultaneous submissions accepted: no. Recently published poets: Joe Cardillo, Ted Grieder, Lynette Seator, Sylvia Relation, Vernon Schmid. Submission quantity: submit complete organized manuscript. Special interests: nothing previously published is considered.

NORTHWORDS, The Stable, Long Road, Avoch, Ross-shire IV9 8QR, Scotland, e-mail northwords@de-mon.co.uk. Angus Dunn, Editor. 1991. "Strong Scottish bias; please read magazine before submission" circ. 500. 3/yr. Pub'd 150 poems 1999; expects 150 poems 2000, 150 poems 2001. sub. price: £9 UK, £12 overseas; sample: £3 UK, £4 overseas. 64pp; size B5; Rights purchased: First publication only. Publishes 10% of poems submitted. Deadlines: on going. Reporting time: 6-8 weeks. Payment: £6-£20. Interested in new or unpub'd poets: yes. Simultaneous submissions accepted: no. Recent contributors: Thomas Land, Alan Warner, Gordon Meade, Robert Davidson, Michel Faber. Submission quantity: 5-12. Special interests: Fringe poetry: lyric poetry, Scots Gaelic, Irish Gaelic, Scots language.

Norton Coker Press, PO Box 640543, San Francisco, CA 94164-0543, 415-922-0395. 1988. avg. press run 150. Pub'd 2 poetry titles 1999; expects 3 poetry titles 2000, 6 poetry titles 2001. 5×7; avg. price, paper: $8. 44pp; Recently published poets: Lawrence Fixel, Will Inman, Ruth Taylor, Elizabeth Hurst, Jim Watson-Gove.

NOSTALGIA, A Sentimental State of Mind, PO Box 2224, Orangeburg, SC 29116. Connie Martin, Editor. 1986. "90% of material is selected through contest (2 per year) and entry fee reserves future edition. No sexual references, no profanity. Contest deadline June 30 and December 31 every year. No long poetry." circ. 1M. 2/yr. Pub'd 26 poems 1999; expects 30 poems 2000, 30 poems 2001. sub. price: $8; sample: $5. 24pp; 5½×8½; Rights purchased: rights revert to author upon publication. Deadlines: contest deadlines: June 30 and December 31 each year. Reporting time: 4-6 weeks. Payment: Average $750 per year. Interested in new or unpub'd poets: yes. Simultaneous submissions accepted: preferably not. Recent contributors: Arlene E. Paul, Charlie Owsley,

Joanne Childers, Barbara Jo Gauthier, Barbara J. Mayer. Submission quantity: 3. Special interests: I do not enjoy long poems, no profanity or sexual references but romance o.k. Prefer non-rhyme, but some rhyme o.k., prefer modern prose.

NOSTOC MAGAZINE, Arts End Books, Box 162, Newton, MA 02468. Marshall Brooks, Editor. 1973. "Not currently reading unsolicited mss., query first." circ. 300. 2/yr. Pub'd 25 poems 1999; expects 25 poems 2000, 25 poems 2001. sub. price: $10/4 issues; sample: $5. 40pp; size varies; Rights purchased: 1st North American. Publishes 10%-15% of poems submitted. Deadlines: none. Modest cash payment. Interested in new or unpub'd poets: yes. Simultaneous submissions accepted: no. Recent contributors: Len Krisak, Herschel Silverman, Bern Porter, Les Whitten. Special interests: Our interests are broad and diverse. Interested in translations.

NOTRE DAME REVIEW, English Dept., Creative Writing, University of Notre Dame, Notre Dame, IN 46556, 219-631-6952, Fax 219-631-4268. John Matthias, Poetry Editor. 1995. circ. 2M. 2/yr. Pub'd 70 poems 1999; expects 70 poems 2000, 70 poems 2001. sub. price: $15 individuals, $20 institutions; sample: $6. 115pp; 6×9; Rights purchased: 1st North American. Publishes 5% of poems submitted. Deadlines: Sept. to March. Reporting time: 3-4 months. Payment: variable. Interested in new or unpub'd poets: yes. Simultaneous submissions accepted: yes. Recent contributors: Seamus Heaney, Denise Levertov, Czeslaw Milosz. Submission quantity: 1-5.

NOVA EXPRESS, PO Box 27231, Austin, TX 78755, E-mail lawrence@bga.com. Lawrence Person, Editor. 1987. "Interested in science fiction, fantasy, horror. Nothing cute or cliched" circ. 750. 2/yr. Pub'd 2 poems 1999. sub. price: $12/4 issues; sample: $4. 48pp; 8½×11; Rights purchased: one time rights. Publishes 10% of poems submitted. Deadlines: irregular. Reporting time: 1-3 months. Payment: 2 contributor copies, plus a four issue subscription. Interested in new or unpub'd poets: yes. Simultaneous submissions accepted: no. Recent contributors: Alison Wimsatt, Don Webb, Robert Frazier, Holly Day, Mark McLaughlin.

●**Nova House Press,** 33 Lowry's Lane, Rosemont, PA 19010, tgavin@ea.pvt.k12.pa.us. 1998. 5½×8.

NOW AND THEN, PO Box 70556, East Tennessee State University, Johnson City, TN 37614-0556, 423-439-5348; fax 423-439-6340; e-mail woodsidj@etsu.edu. Linda Parsons. Address poetry submissions to: 2909 Fountain Park Blvd., Knoxville, TN 37917. 1984. "Regional Appalachian poetry. Special issues pre-announced. Send for free writer's guidelines and list of upcoming theme issues." circ. 1.5M. 3/yr. Expects 6 poems 2000, 20 poems 2001. sub. price: $20; sample: $5. 44pp; 8½×11; Rights purchased: all rights. Publishes a very small % of poems submitted. Deadlines: for each issue: Nov. 1, March 1, July 1. Reporting time: 5 months. Payment: 2 contributor's copies, $10 per poem. Interested in new or unpub'd poets: yes. Simultaneous submissions accepted: yes. Recent contributors: Jeff Daniel Marion, Michael McKee, Lynn Powell, Marilyn Kallet, Bill Brown. Submission quantity: up to 5. Special interests: All work must be done by or about Appalachians, but it can be utterly contemporary.

NOW HERE NOWHERE, Gravity Presses (Lest We All Float Away), Inc., 27030 Havelock, Dearborn Heights, MI 48127, 313-563-4683, e-mail kingston@gravitypresses.com. 1998. circ. 150. 4/yr. sub. price: $20; sample: $5.50. 48pp; 7×8½.

Now It's Up To You Publications, 157 S. Logan, Denver, CO 80209, 303-777-8951. Tom Parson. 1980. "I'm working now with handset letterpress printing, focusing on Paul Hunter's third book of poems, *It Loves Me It Loves Me Not.* Ongoing postcard format series, and I'm open to considering projects of various sizes and formats. I hope for poetry that does carry what is needed between people, the intervention of language in the real world." avg. press run 300-500 broadsides and chapbooks, 1M postcards. Pub'd 2-4 poetry titles 1999; expects 2-4 poetry titles 2000, 2-4 poetry titles 2001. avg. price, paper: $2-$4; other: 50¢/postcard (sets of 12 cards/$5); $2-$5 broadside (set of 6/$7). Postcards/broadsides 1p, chapbooks 24pp; Publishes 5% of poetry manuscripts submitted. Reporting time: largely unable to respond—sorry. Payment: 10% of copies, or flexible depending on the project involved. Interested in new or unpub'd poets: yes. Simultaneous submissions accepted: yes—it's nice to know what's going on, however. Recently published poets: Paul Hunter, Chris Woods, Maurice Kenny, Marilyn Krysl, Susan Tichy. Submission quantity: 4-10, or what you have that's ready to offer. Special interests: Previous efforts have included considerable attention to Seattle and NW poetry (through miscellaneous community-wide groupings such as *Poetry Exchange*'s monthly calendar; Red Sky Poetry Theatre's development of performance and talk art in weekly featured readings and open mics; and the annual Bumbershoot literary arts festival and small press bookfair). Since moving to Denver in 1983, I still feel the necessity of an actual local and regional context for poetry, while sensing the potentials of a much wider audience. Open to all sizes and styles; limited only by the technical demands of the letterpress and my own procrastinations. Interest in the intersections between poet and reader; the surreal and the real; the actual need for things to be said, and to be heard; language to fit a specific context—individual private sentiment or the need to address enormous political and military atrocities—all this leads me to point out that the poet and then the publisher only take it into print; it's up to others to take it from here.

NUTHOUSE, PO Box 119, Ellenton, FL 34222. Dr. Ludwig VonQuirk, Chief of Staff. 1993. circ. 100+. 6-10/yr. Pub'd 15 poems 1999; expects 20 poems 2000, 20 poems 2001. sub. price: $10 for 11 issues, checks payable to Twin Rivers Press; sample: $1. 12pp; 5½×8½; Rights purchased: one time rights. Publishes 25% of poems submitted. Reporting time: 1 month. Payment: contributor's copy. Interested in new or unpub'd poets: yes. Simultaneous submissions accepted: yes. Recent contributors: Holly Day, Kenneth Leonhardt, Don Webb, Daveed Gartenstein-Ross, Paul Weinman. Submission quantity: 1-2. Special interests: Humor and satire.

NYX OBSCURA MAGAZINE, PO Box 5554, Atlanta, GA 30307-0554, 704-684-6629; nyxobscura@aol.com. 1990. circ. 1.5M. 2/yr. sub. price: $10; sample: $5 + p/h. 40pp.

O

O.ARS, Inc., 21 Rockland Road, Weare, NH 03281, 603-529-1060. Don Wellman, Cola Franzen, Irene Turner. 1981. "Publishes anthologies only, each thematic, concerned with language, visual thought and translation. Advise familiarity with previous pubs." avg. press run 750. Pub'd 1 poetry title 1999. 7×10; avg. price, paper: $5. 90pp; Publishes 10% of poetry manuscripts submitted. Reporting time: 2-4 weeks. Payment: copies only. Interested in new or unpub'd poets: yes. Simultaneous submissions accepted: no. Recently published poets: Charles Berstein, Andrew Levy, Rosmarie Waldrop. Submission quantity: 5-10 pages.

OASIS, Oasis Books, 12 Stevenage Road, London SW6 6ES, United Kingdom. Ian Robinson. 1969. "Occasional special issues devoted to particular areas of writing (ie prose, translation) or countries (ie Greece, Slovenia)" circ. 500. 3/yr. sub. price: $30; sample: $5. 16pp; 5½×8¼; Rights purchased: none. Publishes 2% of poems submitted. Deadlines: none. Reporting time: 1 month. Payment: copies. Interested in new or unpub'd poets: yes, but queries and brief samples first. Simultaneous submissions accepted: occasionally. Recent contributors: Lee Harwood, Martin Anderson, Andrea Moorhead, Spencer Selby, Michael Heller. Submission quantity: 6. Special interests: translations, experimental poetry.

Oasis Books (see also OASIS; Shearsman Books), 12 Stevenage Road, London, SW6 6ES, United Kingdom. Ian Robinson, Editor. 1969. "Publication usually results from prolonged period of negotiations and it's very often as a result of our seeking out authors, rather that the other way around. Strong bias towards translations too, 50% of our titles have been translated material. Poetry now in fact is in decline for us. Leaning more towards prose." avg. press run 300-500. Pub'd 2 poetry titles 1999; expects 4 poetry titles 2000, 4 poetry titles 2001. 5½×8¼; avg. price, paper: £2-£4.95. 16-40pp; Publishes a very small % of poetry manuscripts submitted. Reporting time: 1 month. Payment: 25 copies. Interested in new or unpub'd poets: yes, but only after seeing samples of work. No use sending a complete ms. Simultaneous submissions accepted: no, usually not but occasionally. Recently published poets: Tomas Transtromer, Gunnar Harding, John Ash, Gustaf Sobin, Carl Rakosi. Submission quantity: 6-8. Special interests: Translations, longpoems, sequences, prose poetry, fiction.

Oasis In Print, PO Box 314, Clarkdale, GA 30111, 770-943-3377. 1996. 5½×8½.

Oberlin College Press (see also FIELD: Contemporary Poetry and Poetics), 10 N. Professor Street, Oberlin College, Oberlin, OH 44074-1095, 440-775-8408, Fax 440-775-8124, E-mail oc.press@oberlin.edu. David Walker, Co-Editor; David Young, Co-Editor. 1969. "Many people don't include sufficient return postage—we cannot respond to those submissions. Contact us for details of annual Field Poetry Prize for previously unpublished manuscripts." avg. press run 1.5M. Pub'd 2 poetry titles 1999. 5¼×8½; avg. price, cloth: $22.95; paper: $14.95. 100pp; Publishes .25%-.50% of poetry manuscripts submitted. Reporting time: 2 months. Payment: $1,000 *Field* Poetry Prize winner, 10% royalty on cloth sales, 7.5% royalty on paper. Interested in new or unpub'd poets: yes. Simultaneous submissions accepted: no. Recently published poets: Miroslav Holub, Marcia Southwick, Franz Wright, Russell Edson, Atilla Jozsef. Submission quantity: 5-8. Special interests: Translations must include proof of rights to translate.

OBJECT PERMANENCE, Flat 3/2, 16 Ancroft Street, Glasgow G20 7HU, Scotland, 0141-332-7571. 1994. circ. 250-270. Published every 4-5 months. sub. price: £9 surface mail; sample: £3. 68pp; 5.8×8.3.

OBLATES, 9480 N. De Mazenod Drive, Belleville, IL 62223-1160, 618-398-4848. Christine Portell, Managing Editor; Mary Mohrman, Manuscripts Editor. 1943. "We need poems which inspire, uplift and motivate on themes related to Christian values in everyday life. Length: 16 line average. We use well-written, perceptive, traditional verse. Avoid heavy allusions, clever rhyme schemes, and "heavy" modern verse. We prefer a reverent, inspirational tone. All submissions must be typed and double-spaced. No reprints considered at this time. Include a SASE with all correspondence. All material submitted to *Oblates* is on speculation until accepted for publication by the Missionary Association of Mary Immaculate. We have been receiving more submissions; we buy only what we will use in 3 years.'' circ. 500M. 6/yr. Pub'd 12 poems 1999; expects 12 poems 2000, 12 poems 2001. sample price: sample copy and writer's guidelines sent free with 2 first class stamps and SAE. 20pp; 8½×5¼; Rights purchased: 1st North American serial rights. Percent of submitted poems we publish varies greatly. Deadlines: poetry may be submitted at any time (seasonal material should be submitted 6-8 months in advance). Reporting time: 2 months. Payment: $30. Interested in new or unpub'd poets: yes, we always look for quality. Simultaneous submissions accepted: yes, if so noted. Recent contributors: Claire Puneky, Joy Lee Holman, Dorothy O'Connor, Dorthy H. Bizer. Submission quantity: no more than 3, prefer 1 or 2. Special interests: Christmas and seasonal poems are especially welcome.

OBSIDIAN II: BLACK LITERATURE IN REVIEW, Dept. of English, Box 8105, NC State University, Raleigh, NC 27695-8105, 919-515-3870. Gerald Barrax. 1975. ''We accept creative works in English by Black writers, with scholarly critical studies by all writers on Black Literature in English'' circ. 400. 2/yr. Pub'd 50-60 poems 1999; expects 50-60 poems 2000, 50-60 poems 2001. sub. price: $12; sample: $6. 130pp; 6×9; Rights purchased: rights accrue to author on publication. Publishes 20% of poems submitted. Deadlines: Spring issue Feb. 30, Summer May 30, Winter Oct. 30. Reporting time: 3-4 months. Payment: 2 copies of publication. Interested in new or unpub'd poets: yes. Simultaneous submissions accepted: no. Recent contributors: Gerald Early, Akua Lezli Hope, Wanda Coleman, Marilyn Waniek, Cornelius Eady. Submission quantity: 3-5.

OF UNICORNS AND SPACE STATIONS, PO Box 200, Bountiful, UT 84011-0200. Gene Davis, Senior Editor. 1994. ''5'' circ. 200. 2/yr. Pub'd 6 poems 1999; expects 6 poems 2000, 6 poems 2001. sub. price: $16/2 years; sample: $4. 60pp; 5½×8½; Rights purchased: one-time. Publishes 10% of poems submitted. Reporting time: 3 months. Payment: $5. Interested in new or unpub'd poets: yes. Simultaneous submissions accepted: yes. Submission quantity: 3. Special interests: Fixed form poetry given preference.

OFF OUR BACKS, 3600 20th Street, #201, San Francisco, CA 94110-2351, 415-546-0384. 1984. circ. 45M. 6/yr. sub. price: $34.95. 48pp.

Off the Cuff Books, 191 Sickles Avenue, San Francisco, CA 94112-4046, email suavd@sunsite.unc.edu. 1996.

OFF THE ROCKS, 921 W. Argyle #1W, Chicago, IL 60640, E-mail offtherock@aol.com. 1980. circ. 500+. 1/yr. 42pp; 8×12.

OFFICE NUMBER ONE, 1708 South Congress Avenue, Austin, TX 78704, 512-445-4489. Carlos B. Dingus, Editor. 1989. ''I want classical *limericks*. 2 verses of 3 anapests, 2 verses of 2 anapests, 1 verse of 3 anapest. Or haiku—both should be satirical. Quatrains, sonnets'' circ. 2M. 3/yr. Pub'd 10 poems 1999; expects 10 poems 2000, 10 poems 2001. sub. price: $8.84/6 issues; sample: $2. 12pp; 8½×11; Rights purchased: 1st time. Publishes 10% of poems submitted. Deadlines: continuous. Reporting time: 3-6 weeks. Payment: sample copies or 23¢ per poem, sometimes both. Interested in new or unpub'd poets: sure. Simultaneous submissions accepted: yes. Recent contributors: Hal Johnson, Frank Finuty, Gerald George, F.L. Light. Submission quantity: be expedient/short poems can be grouped on single page. Special interests: If you have a really great short poem, I can use it. I want poems that have rhyme and meter, otherwise it's prose. If it's prose, use complete sentences and correct punctuation. But as I say, I want limericks and haiku. Preferably several all related to a single theme. Stop sending pathetic, sad, or violent stuff.

THE OHIO REVIEW, 344 Scott Quad, Ohio University, Athens, OH 45701, 740-593-1900. Wayne Dodd, Editor. 1959. ''We do not read during the months of June, July, August. All manuscripts will be returned unread during that time.'' circ. 3.5M. 2/yr. Pub'd 75 poems 1999; expects 75 poems 2000, 75 poems 2001. sub. price: $16; sample: $6 (current issue will be sent). 208pp; 6×9; Rights purchased: 1st North American serial only. Publishes less than 1% of poems submitted. Deadlines: none. Reporting time: 30 days. Payment: minimum $25. Interested in new or unpub'd poets: yes. Simultaneous submissions accepted: no. Recent contributors: Stanley Plumly, Rita Dove, Sandra Agricola, Charles Wright, Jane Miller. Submission quantity: maximum of 5.

Ohio State University Press, 1050 Carmack Road, Columbus, OH 43210, 614-292-6930. David Citino. 1957. ''Plese write for complete poetry competition guidelines for the OSU Press/The *Journal* Award in Poetry'' avg. press run 1.5M. Pub'd 2 poetry titles 1999; expects 1 poetry title 2000, 1 poetry title 2001. avg. price, cloth: $12.95; paper: $6.95. 48-96pp; Reporting time: varies. Payment: varies. Interested in new or unpub'd poets: yes. Recently published poets: Richard Hague, David Citino, Walter McDonald, Robert Cording, Albert Goldbarth.

OLD CROW, PO Box 403, Easthampton, MA 01027-0403. John Gibney. 1991. ''Include bio-blurb and SASE'' circ. 500. 2/yr. Pub'd 70 poems 1999; expects 80 poems 2000, 75 poems 2001. sub. price: $10 + $2 p/h make check or money order payable to John Gibney; sample: $5 + $1 p/h. 100pp; 5⅜×8⅜; Publishes less than 1% of poems submitted. Deadlines: 3/15, 8/15. Reporting time: 6-8 weeks. Payment: free copy. Interested in new or unpub'd poets: yes. Simultaneous submissions accepted: yes. Recent contributors: Michael Ventura, Sam Cherubin, Elmar Shenkel, Patricia Martin, Christopher Jones. Submission quantity: no limit.

THE OLD RED KIMONO, Humanities, Floyd College, Box 1864, Rome, GA 30162, 404-295-6312. Jon Hershey, Jeffery Mack, Ed Sharp. 1972. "Best times to submit: October 1 through March 1. Must have SASE." circ. 1.2M. 1/yr. Pub'd 50 poems 1999. sample price: $3. 72pp; 8½×11; Rights purchased: 1st publication. Publishes 10% of poems submitted. Deadlines: March 1. Reporting time: 1 month. Payment: 2 copies. Interested in new or unpub'd poets: yes. Simultaneous submissions accepted: no. Recent contributors: Peter Huggins, John Morrison, Ruth Moon Kempher, Jack Stewart, Valerie Gilreath. Submission quantity: 5 or fewer. Special interests: *ORK* is looking for submissions of 3-5 short poems. Poems should be very concise and imagistic. Nothing sentimental or didactic. Mss read October 1 - March 1.

The Olive Press Publications, PO Box 99, Los Olivos, CA 93441, Tel/Fax 805-688-2445. Lynne Norris. 1978. avg. press run 1.5M. Expects 1 poetry title 2000. 6×9, 5½×8½, 8½×11; avg. price, paper: $10. 100pp; Interested in new or unpub'd poets: no. Recently published poets: Jake Copass. Special interests: History, cowboy, western.

OM, Box #181, 4505 University Way, NE, Seattle, WA 98105, 206-322-6387, davidlasky@yahoo.com. 1993. circ. 1M. 2/yr. sample price: $1. 24pp; size varies.

Ommation Press (see also MATI; SALOME: A Journal for the Performing Arts), 5548 North Sawyer, Chicago, IL 60625. Effie Mihopoulos, Editor. 1975. "Clean copy for submissions accompanied by SAE with *sufficient* return postage. Prefer complete ms to queries." avg. press run 500-1M. Expects 1 poetry title 2000, 1 poetry title 2001. 8½×11, 5×9; avg. price, paper: $4-$8. 40-120pp; Publishes 1 poetry manuscript annually. Reporting time: as soon as possible. Payment: copies, 50 chapbooks. Interested in new or unpub'd poets: yes. Simultaneous submissions accepted: yes (but please note so). Recently published poets: Lyn Lifshin, Cornelius Eady, Vincent Katz, Michael Cadnum, M.S. Robbins. Submission quantity: complete manuscript. Special interests: Experimental poetry, very open to submissions by women, but like poetry of all types, no particular preference.

ON SPEC, PO Box 4727, Edmonton, AB T6E 5G6, Canada, 403-413-0215; email onspec@earthling.net. Barry Hammond. 1989. "Doesn't use much rhyming poetry and no religious poems" circ. 1.75M. 4/yr. Pub'd 6 poems 1999; expects 6 poems 2000, 6 poems 2001. sub. price: $18CDN, $18US; sample: $7CDN, $7US. 112pp; 5×8; Rights purchased: First North American Serial Rights. Publishes 2% of poems submitted. Deadlines: May 31/Aug 31/Nov 30/Feb 28. Reporting time: 3-5 months. Payment: $20 CDN per poem and 1 contributor copy. Interested in new or unpub'd poets: not full length manuscripts but samples of up to 6 poems. Simultaneous submissions accepted: yes. Recent contributors: Sandra Kasturi, Barbarba Colebrook Peace, K.V. Skene, Alice Major. Submission quantity: up to max. of 6. Special interests: SF with emphasis on science, speculative poetry.

ONE TRICK PONY, Banshee Press, PO Box 11186, Philadelphia, PA 19136-6186. Louis McKee. 1997. circ. 400. 2/yr. sub. price: $10/3 issues; sample: $5. 60pp; 5½×8½; Rights purchased: 1st NA and reprint permission. Publishes 5%-10% of poems submitted. Deadlines: on-going. Reporting time: 2-4 weeks. Payment: copies. Interested in new or unpub'd poets: yes. Simultaneous submissions accepted: no. Recent contributors: Elaine Terranova, Len Roberts, William Heyen, Afra M. Weaver, Eileen D'Angelo. Submission quantity: 3-5.

ONIONHEAD, 115 North Kentucky Avenue, Lakeland, FL 33801, 941-680-2787. Susan Crawford, Editor; Dot D. Davis, Editor; Brenda Patterson, Editor. 1988. "Annual *WORDART* Poetry Competition. Send SASE for app. TBA deadline." circ. 250. 4/yr. Pub'd 100 poems 1999; expects 100 poems 2000, 100 poems 2001. sub. price: $8; sample: $3. 40pp; 5½×8½; Rights purchased: 1st North American serial rights and first electronic rights. Publishes 5% of poems submitted. Deadlines: we read continuously. Reporting time: 10 weeks. Payment: 1 copy. Interested in new or unpub'd poets: yes. Simultaneous submissions accepted: no. Recent contributors: Lyn Lifshin, Jessica Freeman, B.Z. Niditch, Peter Layton. Submission quantity: 3-8.

ONTHEBUS, Bombshelter Press, Bombshelter Press, P.O. Box 481270, Bicentennial Station, Los Angeles, CA 90048. Jack Grapes. 1989. "We will publish previously published poems and simultaneous submissions if properly notified. Cover letters with brief bio preferred. SASE a must. Poets should see a copy of magazine before submitting and read our guidelines" circ. 3M. 2/yr. Pub'd 500 poems 1999; expects 500 poems 2000, 500 poems 2001. sub. price: $28 for 3 issues; sample: $11. 275pp; 8½×5½; Publishes 5% of poems submitted. Deadlines: no submissions read November thru February or June thru August. Reporting time: 1-12 months. Payment: 1 copy, $ if available. Interested in new or unpub'd poets: yes. Simultaneous submissions accepted: yes, but let me know (also accept previously published work). Recent contributors: Charles Bukowski, Ernesto Cardenal, Stephen Dobyns, Ai, Norman Dubie. Submission quantity: no more than 6—10 page max. all poems. Special interests: mainstream contemporary poetry and prose, translations, essays, book reviews, interviews.

Oolichan Books, PO Box 10, Lantzville, B.C., V0R 2H0, Canada, 604-390-4839. Ron Smith, Poetry Editor. 1975. "Prefer letters of enquiry with writing sample and SASE." avg. press run 500. Pub'd 2 poetry titles 1999; expects 2 poetry titles 2000, 2 poetry titles 2001. 5½×8½, 6×9; avg. price, paper: $9.95; other: $30 signed and numbered limited special editions (cloth). 64pp; Publishes 1% of poetry manuscripts submitted. Reporting time: 2 months minimum. Payment: 10%. Interested in new or unpub'd poets: yes. Simultaneous submissions accepted: yes. Recently published poets: John O'Neill, George McWhirter, Ralph Gustafson, Jamie Reid, Joe Rosenblatt. Submission quantity: 10-15. Special interests: Contemporary verse. Canadian writers.

Open Hand Publishing Inc., PO Box 22048, Seattle, WA 98122, 206-323-2187. 1981. avg. press run 2M. 5½×8½; avg. price, paper: $12.95. 96pp; Publishes .5% of poetry manuscripts submitted. Reporting time: 4 weeks. Interested in new or unpub'd poets: no manuscripts being accepted at this time. Recently published poets: E.E. Miller, Zoe Anolesey, Pat Andrus, Tamera Medison-Shaw.

Open University of America Press, 3916 Commander Drive, Hyattsville, MD 20782-1027, 301-779-0220 phone/Fax, openuniv@aol.com. Mary Rodgers, Dan Rodgers. 1965. "We buy poems and small sets of poems outright (price negotiable). We use pre-copyrighted, pre-published work in our Open University of America publications with author's name cited" avg. press run 500. Pub'd 4 poetry titles 1999; expects 4 poetry titles 2000, 4 poetry titles 2001. 6×9, 8½×11; avg. price, cloth: $15; paper: $10. 150pp; Publishes 1% of poetry manuscripts submitted. Reporting time: 3-4 weeks, 2-3 weeks for single poems. Payment: by contract. Interested in new or unpub'd poets: yes. Simultaneous submissions accepted: no. Recently published poets: John Tormento, Emebeat Bekele, Raphael Flores, Mary Rodgers. Submission quantity: optional, 1-10. Special interests: We are specialty publishers for distance education emphasizing the literary aspect of pedagogy. We promote Catholic life and culture, K-Ph.D. humanistic teaching, open learning, Christian morality.

OPUS LITERARY REVIEW, Poetic Page, PO Box 71192, Madison Heights, MI 48071-0192, 313-548-0865. Denise Martinson, Editor, Publisher. 1993. "SASE & enough postage a must. Only the very best poetry" Pub'd 50 poems 1999; expects 50 poems 2000, 50 poems 2001. sub. price: $10; sample: $5 postpaid. Rights purchased: first rights. Publishes 20% of poems submitted. Deadlines: ongoing. Reporting time: 1 month. Payment: 1 copy. Interested in new or unpub'd poets: yes. Simultaneous submissions accepted: no. Recent contributors: Lifshin, Speers, Grey, King, Winters.

ORACLE POETRY, Rising Star Publishers, PO Box 7413, Langley Park, MD 20787. 1989. circ. 500. 4/yr. sub. price: $25, $30 institutions; sample: $5. 50pp; 5½×8½.

ORBIS, 27 Valley View, Primrose, Jarrow, Tyne & Wear NE32 5QT, England, +44 (0)191 489 7055; fax/modem +44 (0)191 430 1297; e-mail Mshields12@aol.com; mikeshields@compuserve.com. Mike Shields. 1968. "One per sheet (A4 or Quarto). Name and address on each sheet. Enclose IRC, *not* American postage! Annual 'Rhyme International' Competition for traditional poetry closes Sept. 30 each year and pays c. £1600/$2500 in prizes." circ. 1M. 4/yr. Pub'd 150-200 poems 1999. sub. price: $28; sample: $2. 80pp; 5¾×8¼; Rights purchased: first. Publishes 1% or less of poems submitted. Deadlines: none. Reporting time: 1-2 months. Payment: £5/$10 per acceptance, additional cash prizes available totalling £50/$75 per issue. Interested in new or unpub'd poets: yes. Simultaneous submissions accepted: no. Recent contributors: Dana Gioia, Seamus Heaney, Lyn Lifshin, Marge Piercy, Richard Wilbur. Submission quantity: 5. Special interests: Willing to consider most forms, but wildly experimental work, unoriginal traditional poetry, or undistinguished haiku unlikely to be accepted.

Orchises Press, PO Box 20602, Alexandria, VA 22320-1602, 703-683-1243. Roger Lathbury. 1983. "Prefer to seek out poetry rather than have it submitted; in any event, the chances of an over the transom acceptance are small and have diminished as last year we received more than a hundred unsolicited ms." avg. press run 1M. Pub'd 5 poetry titles 1999; expects 5 poetry titles 2000, 3 poetry titles 2001. 5×8½; avg. price, cloth: $21.95; paper: $12.95. 80pp; Publishes .5% of poetry manuscripts submitted. Reporting time: 2 weeks. Payment: after Orchises recoups cost of publication, 36%. Interested in new or unpub'd poets: we'll look, but prefer to ask for MS. Recently published poets: L.S. Asekoff, Christopher Buckley, Denise Duhamel, C.K. Williams. Special interests: Prefer poets whose work has been published nationally (*New Yorker, APR*, etc.).

Original Plus (see also JOURNAL OF CONTEMPARARY ANGLO-SCANDINAVIAN POETRY), 11 Heatherton Park, Bradford on Tone, Taunton, Somerset TA4 1EU, England, 01823-461725; e-mail smithsssj@aol.com. 1998. 5¾×8.

OSIRIS, Box 297, Deerfield, MA 01342, e-mail moorhead@k12s.phast.umass.edu. Andrea Moorhead. 1972. "*Osiris* is an international, multi-lingual journal interested in publishing contemporary poetry. Translators please make sure you have secured permission from the publisher and/or poet." circ. 1M. 2/yr. Pub'd 40-50 poems 1999. sub. price: $12 individuals and institutions; sample: $3. 40pp; 6×9; Rights purchased: none. Publishes 15% of poems submitted. Deadlines: work is read throughout the year. Reporting time: 4-6 weeks. Payment: 5 copies. Interested in new or unpub'd poets: yes. Simultaneous submissions accepted: no. Recent contributors: Robert Marteau, Madeleine Gagnon, D.G. Jones, Ingrid Swanberg, Flavio Ermini. Submission quantity: 3-8. Special interests: French, English and German poetry and translations from *other* languages.

Osric Publishing (see also THE WHITE CROW; H.A.K.T.U.P.!), PO Box 4501, Ann Arbor, MI 48106. Christopher Herdt. 1993. "No book-length manuscripts. No previously published poems, only new work please" avg. press run 200. Pub'd 2 poetry titles 1999; expects 2 poetry titles 2000, 2 poetry titles 2001. 5½x8½; avg. price, other: chapbooks $2. 32pp; Publishes 10% of poetry manuscripts submitted. Reporting time: 2 months. Payment: contributor's copies. Interested in new or unpub'd poets: yes. Simultaneous submissions accepted: yes. Recently published poets: Kenneth Pobo, B. Chown, Eileen Bell, Delia DeSantis. Submission quantity: 1-5.

Otherwind, 541 Lakeview Avenue, Ann Arbor, MI 48103-9704, 313-665-0703. Pat Smith, Editor. 1986. avg. press run 500. Pub'd 1 poetry title 1999; expects 1 poetry title 2000, 1 poetry title 2001. 6×9; avg. price, paper: $8. 96pp; Publishes 1% of poetry manuscripts submitted. Interested in new or unpub'd poets: no. Simultaneous submissions accepted: no. Recently published poets: David Matlin, Robert Kelly.

OTTER, Parford Cottage, Chagford, Newton Abbot TQ13 8JR, United Kingdom. C. Southgate, M. Beeson, R. Skinner, E. Pryor. Address poetry submissions to: Little Bystock, Richmond Road, Exeter, United Kingdom. 1988. "Authors should have (and indicate) an association with Devon, England." circ. 400. 3/yr. Pub'd 100 poems 1999. sub. price: £6.50; sample: £2.25 (convert to dollars and add $2 for US). 48pp; 5¾x8; Rights purchased: First British Serial Rights, copyright remaining with author. Publishes 25% of poems submitted. Reporting time: 6-8 weeks. Payment: 1 complimentary copy per poem. Interested in new or unpub'd poets: yes. Simultaneous submissions accepted: no. Recent contributors: Lawrence Sail, Ronald Tamplin, Harry Guest, Jane Beeson, Anne Born. Submission quantity: not more than 6. Special interests: Poems in strict forms welcomed.

OUT YOUR BACKDOOR: The Magazine of Informal Adventure and Cheap Culture, 4686 Meridian Road, Williamston, MI 48895, 517-347-1689; jp@glpbooks.com; www.glpbooks.com/oyb. 1989. "We like immediate, action-oriented poetry—relevant, pithy, boldly revealing, much experience, still in the activity depicted of the author. With practical things as subject, no sentiment or abstraction" circ. 5M. 2/yr. Pub'd 5 poems 1999; expects 5 poems 2000. sub. price: $8/4 issues; sample: $4. 48-64pp; 8×10½; Rights purchased: one-time. Publishes 1% of poems submitted. Payment: depends. Interested in new or unpub'd poets: yes. Simultaneous submissions accepted: yes. Recent contributors: Victor Vicente, Mimi Mayers, Jim Harrison, Terry Wooten, David Lee. Submission quantity: up to 10. Special interests: We've recently run poetry about mountain biking, yard farm scenes, and unusual news events, as relates to the outdoors experientially, not socially or politically.

OUTERBRIDGE, College of Staten Island, 2800 Victory Boulevard, Staten Island, NY 10314, 212-390-7654, 7779. Charlotte Alexander. 1975. "We like and seek crafted, professional poems, usually in groups of 3 to 5, submitted in clean copies folded together (not each separately!). We publicize theme issues or features through newsletters (to date: urban, rural, Southern, childhood, and outsider have been done; plans for: interdisciplinary, and immigrant, migrant experiences). We dislike multiple submissions, and don't read in July and August. As an annual we must build slowly and selectively" circ. 500-1M. 1/yr. Pub'd 37 poems 1999; expects 30 poems 2000, 45 poems 2001. sub. price: $6; sample: $6. 100-120pp; 5½x8½; Rights purchased: 1st. Publishes 6-7% of poems submitted. Deadlines: ongoing except July/August. Reporting time: 2 months. Payment: 2 copies. Interested in new or unpub'd poets: yes. Simultaneous submissions accepted: no. Recent contributors: Will Keeney, Walter McDonald, Naomi Rachel, Kim Roberts, Marilyn McComas. Submission quantity: 3-5. Special interests: We resist the very experimental longpoems, as well as poetry that has sacrificed art and craft to the cause of social protest. We try to be national, varied and reasonably eclectic.

OUTPOSTS POETRY QUARTERLY, Hippopotamus Press, 22, Whitewell Road, Frome, Somerset BA11 4EL, United Kingdom. Roland John, Editor. 1943. circ. 1.9M. 4/yr. Pub'd 180 poems 1999; expects 200 poems 2000, 360 poems 2001. sub. price: £14 or $24 (postage paid) for 1 year, £26 or $50 (postage paid) for 2 years; sample: $7. 80pp; size A5; Rights purchased: none. Publishes 2% of poems submitted. Deadlines: none. Reporting time: 2 weeks, 4 weeks non-UK. Payment: yes. Interested in new or unpub'd poets: yes. Simultaneous submissions accepted: yes. Recent contributors: Ted Hughes, Elizabeth Bartlett, Lotte Kramer, Peter Dale, Roy Fuller. Submission quantity: no more than 5. Special interests: Open to all kinds of poetry including translations.

Outrider Press, 937 Patricia Lane, Crete, IL 60417-1375, 708-672-6630 (voice), fax 708-672-5820, e-mail outriderPr@aol.com, www.outriderpress.com. Phyllis I. Nelson, President. 1988. "Produces handmade, handbound, blank page books, 50-300 pp, suitable for journals or personal poetry, as well as archival manuscript boxes. Our 2001 anthology will accept short fiction (to 2,500 words) and poetry (single-spaces, 1 page) on the theme of 'romantic love.' Send SASE for guidelines and entry forms. Deadlines for manuscripts-1/31/01." avg. press run 500. Pub'd 1 poetry title 1999. 5½x8½; avg. price, paper: $12; other: $9-$50 hand-bound, blank page books. Under 50pp; Percentage of poetry manuscripts published varies. Reporting time: 6 months. Payment: varies. Interested in new or unpub'd poets: yes. Simultaneous submissions accepted: yes. Recently published poets: Lyn Lifshin, Cynthia Gallaher, David Lloyd, James Wheldon, Alison Koffler. Submission quantity: 3-6.

THE OVAL MAGAZINE, 22 Douglass Street, Brooklyn, NY 11231. Henry Eckert. 1995. "The Oval sponsors an annual poetry and fiction contest. Send a SASE for details" circ. 225. 2/yr. Expects 25 poems 2000, 50 poems 2001. sub. price: $5; sample: $3. 72pp; 5½×8½; Rights purchased: one-time rights. Publishes 5-10% of poems submitted. Deadlines: year round. Reporting time: 2 months. Payment: copies. Interested in new or unpub'd poets: yes. Simultaneous submissions accepted: yes. Submission quantity: 6-8.

OVERLAND, PO Box 14146, Melbourne 3000, Australia. poetry editor General editor. 1954. circ. 2.4M. 4/yr. Pub'd 57 poems 1999; expects 54 poems 2000, 60 poems 2001. sub. price: $Aust 32 (local), $Aust 50 (foreign), $Aust 80 (airmail); sample: by arrangement. 88pp; 7¼×9¾; Rights purchased: first publication only. Publishes 3% of poems submitted. Reporting time: 3 months. Payment: $AUS40 minimum. Interested in new or unpub'd poets: yes. Recent contributors: Dorothy Hewett, M. Morgan, C. Wallace-Crabbe, G. Thomasetti. Submission quantity: few. Special interests: Include SASE, Australian writers preferred.

OWEN WISTER REVIEW, PO Box 3625, Laramie, WY 82071-3625, 307-766-4027; owr@uwyo.edu. Editor vary each year. 1978. "We don't read over summer. Submissions should be accompanied with *brief* autobiographical statement and SASE our submission season is from Aug-Dec 15. Write for guidelines" circ. 300-500. 1/yr. Pub'd 60 poems 1999; expects 58 poems 2000, 60 poems 2001. sub. price: $8.20; sample: $5. 120pp; 6×9; Rights purchased: all rights revert on publication. Publishes 10% of poems submitted. Deadlines: Augest 1 to December15. Reporting time: 6 weeks to 4 months. Payment: 1 contributor copy+ 10% discount on additional copies. Interested in new or unpub'd poets: yes. Simultaneous submissions accepted: yes. Recent contributors: Walt McDonald, Dianel Blane, Deb Park, Susan Richardson. Submission quantity: 5 max. Special interests: Do not use overly academic work; prefer *living* poetry.

Owl Creek Press, 2693 S.W. Camano Drive, Camano Island, WA 98292, 308-387-6101. Rich Ives. 1979. avg. press run 1M. Pub'd 2 poetry titles 1999; expects 4 poetry titles 2000, 3 poetry titles 2001. 5½×8½; avg. price, cloth: $17; paper: $12. 64pp; Publishes 1% of poetry manuscripts submitted. Reporting time: 2-4 months. Payment: 10% of copies first printing, cash prize awards, additional payment for additional printings. Interested in new or unpub'd poets: no. Simultaneous submissions accepted: yes. Recently published poets: Naomi Lazard, Laurie Blauner, Sandra McPherson, David Baker, John Morgan. Special interests: Translations.

OXYGEN, 537 Jones Street, PMB 999, San Francisco, CA 94102, 415-776-9681. Richard Hack. 1991. "We have published poems from 1/2 of a page to 18 pages in length. Will discuss excerpts from even longer mss." circ. 300. 1/yr. Pub'd 40 poems 1999; expects 40 poems 2000, 40 poems 2001. sub. price: $18, $25 institutions and foreign 4 issues; sample: $5. 100pp; 5½×8½; Rights purchased: all rights belong to author; mag is copyrighted and has ISSN. Publishes 1% of poems submitted. Reporting time: 2 weeks to 2 months. Payment: 2 copies of issue. Interested in new or unpub'd poets: definitely! Simultaneous submissions accepted: Yes! Recent contributors: Hafiz, Laurie Neighbors, Victor Martinez, Christine Bruckner, Robert Anbian. Submission quantity: 1-10. Special interests: Lyric drive. Political invective. Devotional poetry. Cosmic flow, good satire. Translations (include original). No 'experimental' poetry unless it is vivid. Light verse also.

Oyez, PO Box 5134, Berkeley, CA 94705. 1964. 5½×8½.

OYSTER BOY REVIEW, 191 Sickles Avenue, San Francisco, CA 94112-4046, Email oyster-boy@sunsite.unc.edu; www.sunsite.unc.edu/ob. 1994. circ. 250. 3/yr. sub. price: $12; sample: $4. 60pp; 6½×11.

O!!Zone (see also O!!ZONE, A LITERARY-ART ZINE), 1266 Fountain View Drive, Houston, TX 77057, 713-784-2802. Harry Burrus. 1993. "We don't want what you'd find in *APR* or *Poetry*." avg. press run 50-300. Pub'd 2-3 poetry titles 1999. 8½×11; avg. price, paper: $10; other: limited editions more. 90-120pp; Reporting time: ASAP. Payment: copies. Interested in new or unpub'd poets: yes. Simultaneous submissions accepted: yes. Recently published poets: Guy Beining, Laura Ryder, Anna Leonessa, David H. Stone, Dave Wright. Submission quantity: 6-8. Special interests: Collage writing as well as collage art, photos, the surreal. Not retro surreal Visual poetry is primary focus.

O!!ZONE, A LITERARY-ART ZINE, O!!Zone, 1266 Fountain View Drive, Houston, TX 77057, 713-784-2802. Harry Burrus, Publisher & Editor. 1993. "Don't want *APR*, *Poetry* or academic-type material. Always include cover letter, Visual poetry and college have a place here" circ. 500. 2-4/yr. Pub'd 150-200 poems 1999. sample price: varies. 80-100pp; 8½×11; Rights purchased: none. Deadlines: none. Reporting time: ASAP. Payment: copy of publication. Interested in new or unpub'd poets: yes. Simultaneous submissions accepted: yes. Recent contributors: Anthony Zautra, Spencer Selby, Laura Ryder, Pat Prime, Harl Ristan. Submission quantity: 6-8. Special interests: Want to see the surreal, erotic, sensual. A concern for the language and the visual.

OZ-STORY, 1516 Cypress Avenue, San Diego, CA 92103-4517. David Maxine. 1994. "All material must be related to or have to do with the land of OZ and its characters as created by Frank Baum." circ. 1.2M. 1/yr. Pub'd 4 poems 1999; expects 4 poems 2000, 5 poems 2001. sub. price: $14.95; sample: $14.95. 128pp; 8½×11;

Rights purchased: 1st publication rights. Publishes 25% of poems submitted. Deadlines: November 1, 1997. Reporting time: 1-2 months. Payment: 25¢ per line. Interested in new or unpub'd poets: yes. Simultaneous submissions accepted: no. Recent contributors: Ruth Berman, L. Frank Baum, Ruth Plumly Thompson, Eric Shanower. Submission quantity: 1-5. Special interests: Primarily light verse, children's verse.

P

P & K Stark Productions, Inc., 17125C W. Bluemound Road, Ste. 171, Brookfield, WI 53005, 414-543-9013. 1990. 6×9.

PABLO LENNIS, Etaoin Shrdlu Press, Fandom House, 30 N. 19th Street, Lafayette, IN 47904. John Thiel, General Editor. 1976. "No negative commentary, rhyme and meter required, short length is best, fantasy and science fiction only" circ. 100. 12/yr. Pub'd 32 poems 1999; expects 21 poems 2000. sub. price: $20-$25 overseas; sample: $2. 26pp; 8½×11; Rights purchased: right to print it the first time only. Publishes 80% of poems submitted. Deadlines: none, poems published as an opening occurs. Reporting time: immediately. Payment: 1 issue plus any reader response. Interested in new or unpub'd poets: sure. Simultaneous submissions accepted: no. Recent contributors: Dan Morton, Paul A. Crenshaw, Andrea Jarmai, Phonacelle Shapel, C.S. Thompson. Submission quantity: whatever he cares to. Special interests: Fantasy and science fiction poetry only.

PACIFIC COAST JOURNAL, French Bread Publications, PO Box 23868, San Jose, CA 95153, e-mail paccoastj@bjt.net. Stillson Graham, Editor. 1991. "French Bread Awards, every Sept. 1: Deadline" circ. 200. 4/yr. Pub'd 70-80 poems 1999; expects 80-100 poems 2000, 80-100 poems 2001. sub. price: $10; sample: $2.50. 48pp; 5½×8; Rights purchased: one-time. Publishes 5% of poems submitted. Deadlines: on going. Reporting time: 4 months. Payment: 1 copy. Interested in new or unpub'd poets: yes. Simultaneous submissions accepted: yes, if they let us know. Recent contributors: Janet Kuypers, Joan Payne Kincaid, Duane Locke, Michael Meinhoff, Donald Ryburn. Submission quantity: 4-6. Special interests: Experimental, visual poetry, poetry on the creative process.

PACIFIC ENTERPRISE, PO Box 1907, Fond du Lac, WI 54936-1907, 920-922-9218; rudyled@vbe.com. Frank Scotello. 1998. circ. 5M. 6/yr. sub. price: $19.95; sample: $3. 32pp; 8⅜×10⅞; Rights purchased: first rights. Publishes 25% of poems submitted. Reporting time: 4-6 weeks. Payment: 2 copies. Interested in new or unpub'd poets: yes. Simultaneous submissions accepted: yes. Recent contributors: Eileen Tabios, Jon Pineda, Jo Jo Sayson. Submission quantity: 3-5.

THE PACIFIC REVIEW, Department of English, Calif State University, San Bernardino, CA 92407, 714-880-5824. Rotating editors. 1982. "Mss. will be read only between September and February 1. Deadline is now Feb. 1" circ. 1M. 1/yr. Pub'd 30 poems 1999. sub. price: $7; sample: $5 (libraries $6.50). 104pp; 6×9; Rights purchased: 1st. Publishes 10% of poems submitted. Deadlines: Feb. 1. Reporting time: 2 months. Payment: in copies. Interested in new or unpub'd poets: yes, if so indicated. Recent contributors: Bin Ramki, Victor Martinez, Orlando Ramirez, Bruce Bond, Wyatt Prunty. Submission quantity: up to 5 individual mss. Special interests: *The Pacific Review* welcomes all submissions, in various genres/media/forms, while being particularly receptive to works/writers from and of Southern California.

PAGAN AMERICA, Crescent Moon, PO Box 393, Maidstone, Kent ME14 5XU, United Kingdom. Jeremy Robinson. 1992. "Non-rhyming poetry preferred. SAE and International Reply Coupon essential. Do not send whole manuscript" circ. 200. 2/yr. Pub'd 40 poems 1999; expects 40 poems 2000, 40 poems 2001. sub. price: $17; sample: $6. 80pp; 5⅞×8¼; Publishes 3% of poems submitted. Deadlines: Dec. 1, June 1. Reporting time: 3 months. Payment: complimentary copy of magazine. Interested in new or unpub'd poets: yes. Simultaneous submissions accepted: yes. Recent contributors: Peter Redgrove, D.J. Enright, Jeremy Reed, Elisabeth Bletsoe. Submission quantity: 6.

PAGAN PRIDE, Golden Isis Press, PO Box 4263, Chatsworth, CA 91313. Gerina Dunwich. 1996. "The Pagan Poets Society is a distinguished literary circle for poets who identify themselves and their work as 'Pagan.' Contributors must be members of the Pagan Poets Society" 2/yr. sub. price: free with membership in the Pagan Poetry Society; membership $13/1 year, $25/2 years, $100/lifetime; sample: $5 (checks payable to Gerina Dunwich). 20pp; 5½×8½; Rights purchased: First North American Serial Rights; rights revert to author upon publication. Publishes 25% of poems submitted. Reporting time: 2 weeks. Payment: free subscription, free listing in the P.P.S. directory, discounts on books and services. Interested in new or unpub'd poets: new poets. Simultaneous submissions accepted: yes. Recent contributors: Gerina Dunwich, Lee Prosser, Kathleen Kmen,

Reed Dunwich. Submission quantity: no limit.

●**Painted Leaf Press,** PO Box 2480, Times Square Station, New York, NY 10108-2480. 1997. "No unsolicited submissions accepted." 6×9.

Palanquin Press, English Department, University of South Carolina-Aiken, Aiken, SC 29801, 803-648-6851 x3208; fax 803-641-3461; email phebed@aiken.edu; email scpoet@scescape.net. 1988. 6×9.

Palladium Communications, 320 South Main Street, PO Box 8403, Ann Arbor, MI 48107-8403, 734-668-4646; FAX 734-663-9361. Carol Shepherd, Publisher. 1991. "We are a *special-interest-only* mixed media house for pan-American works which 'speak to the deep relationship of person to place, and communicate landscape and culture similarities and differences, to other people in other places on the planet.' Examples: poetry on exile/diaspora/immigration/Nueva Onda experience. We fully finance one title per year at most, mostly we joint venture titles which meet our mission, editorial, and involvement requirements. Submissions: 'one page query letter only, with a paragraph on who will buy a copy of your work and your resume of previous publications or releases. No unsolicited manuscripts or tapes, we simply pitch them in the trash.' SASP for confirmation of receipt. We request samples or demos if interested." avg. press run 1000 units print/CD, 500 units cassette. Expects 1 poetry title 2001. 6×9; avg. price, cloth: $35; paper: $15.95; other: music CD, spoken work: we anticipate $15.95. 100pp; Publishes less than 2% of poetry manuscripts submitted. Reporting time: 3 months. Payment: We pay royalties quarterly. If we finance a publication, author royalties are approximately 10% of net revenue collected. On joint ventures, consultations and subsidy projects we retain a royalty percentage of net ranging from 10-50%. Interested in new or unpub'd poets: Experienced writers in other genres with poetry mss which fit our focus, see additional comments. Simultaneous submissions accepted: See our strict guidelines in additional comments. Recently published poets: Galeano Dominguez, Edgar. Submission quantity: none. Special interests: bilingual editions of unusual projects meeting our objectives.

PALO ALTO REVIEW, 1400 West Villaret, San Antonio, TX 78224, 210-828-2998. Ellen Shull, Editor; Bob Richmond, Editor. 1992. "Write for guidelines and SASE" circ. 700. 2/yr. Pub'd 16 poems 1999; expects 16 poems 2000, 16 poems 2001. sub. price: $10; sample: $5. 60pp; 8½×11; Rights purchased: 1st NA. Publishes 2% of poems submitted. Deadlines: July 1, December 1. Reporting time: 6-8 weeks. Payment: 2 copies. Interested in new or unpub'd poets: yes. Simultaneous submissions accepted: yes. Recent contributors: Wendy Bishop, Diane Glancy, Michael Smith, Lyn Lifshin, Ruth Daigon. Submission quantity: 5-7. Special interests: We are open to most types.

PANDALOON, c/o Small Potatoes Press, PO Box 210977, Milwaukee, WI 53221, 800-642-9050, 414-294-2051, Fax 414-294-2053, email pandaloon@azml.com. 1997. "Light, accessible, inclusive" circ. 200. 12/yr. Pub'd 50 poems 1999; expects 150 poems 2000, 150 poems 2001. sub. price: $12; sample: $1 w/ SASE. 16pp; 4×7; Rights purchased: 1st North American. Publishes 10% of poems submitted. Deadlines: monthly. Reporting time: 2 months. Payment: 2 copies. Interested in new or unpub'd poets: yes. Simultaneous submissions accepted: no. Recent contributors: Kenneth Ellsworth, Deborah Bryne, Leonard Cirino, M. Tolman-Flannery, William Olson. Submission quantity: 3-5.

THE PANHANDLER, The Panhandler Press, English Dept., Univ. Of West Florida, Pensacola, FL 32514-5751, 904-474-2923. Laurie O'Brien, Editor. 1976. "We read continuously. Please limit submission to 6-7 poems. Annual chapbook competition: Submit 24-30 page manuscript between September 1 and December 15. Two manuscripts chosen for publication in special chapbook issue. $100 and 50 copies to winners. $15 reading fee includes winning chapbooks issue." circ. 500. 2/yr plus chapbook. Pub'd 100 poems 1999; expects 100 poems 2000, 100 poems 2001. sub. price: $10 includes yearly chapbook; sample: $5. 70pp; 6×9; Rights purchased: 1st North American. Publishes 5% of poems submitted. Deadlines: continuous. Reporting time: 3-6 months. Payment: copies. Interested in new or unpub'd poets: yes. Simultaneous submissions accepted: yes, please inform of simultaneous submission and acceptance elsewhere. Recent contributors: Walter McDonald, David Kirby, Victor Gischler, Yvonne Sapia. Submission quantity: 3-6. Special interests: Some translations. Maximum length 2-3 pp.; we like regional voices (ANY) and poems with serio-comic perspective.

Panjandrum Books (see also PANJANDRUM POETRY JOURNAL), 6156 Wilkinson Avenue, North Hollywood, CA 91606, 818-506-0202. Dennis Koran, Editor; David Guss, Associate Editor. 1971. "Always send SSAE; reading fee $5" avg. press run 500-1.5M. Pub'd 3 poetry titles 1999; expects 2 poetry titles 2000, 3 poetry titles 2001. size varies; avg. price, cloth: $16.95; paper: $8; other: Hd signed-$40. 80-120pp; Publishes .5%-1% of poetry manuscripts submitted. Reporting time: 4-6 weeks. Payment: by contract with terms negotiable. Interested in new or unpub'd poets: query first with SASE and a few samples. Recently published poets: Artaud, Eshleman, Jarry, Bador, Bruce. Submission quantity: query first. Special interests: Translation (esp. European), surrealism, dada, experimental poetry, regional poetry, longpoems.

PANJANDRUM POETRY JOURNAL, Panjandrum Books, 6156 Wilkinson Avenue, North Hollywood, CA 91606. Dennis Koran, Editor; David Guss, Associate Editor. 1971. "Always include SSAE." circ. 2M. Pub'd 50 poems 1999; expects 50 poems 2000, 50 poems 2001. sub. price: $20 instit. (3 issues); sample: varies with issue ordered as sample, plus shipping. 100-140pp; 5½×8½; Publishes .5%-1% of poems submitted. Reporting time: 4-6 weeks. Payment: 2 copies of issue. Interested in new or unpub'd poets: query first with SSAE and a few samples. Simultaneous submissions accepted: no. Recent contributors: Artaud, Eshleman, Jarry, Bador, Bruce. Submission quantity: no more than 10 poems. Special interests: Translations (esp. European), surrealism, experimental, dada.

THE PANNUS INDEX, BGB Press, Inc., 160 King Street, Northampton, MA 01060-2336, 413-584-4776; Fax 413-584-5674; www.javanet.com/~stout/pannus. Leonard Cirino. 1995. "poetry submisssions must pertain to theme of issue" circ. 500+. 2/yr. Pub'd 25 poems 1999; expects 30 poems 2000. sub. price: $12, $18 foreign; sample: $8. 120pp; 6¾×10¼; Publishes 15% of poems submitted. Deadlines: see guidelines. Reporting time: 4 months. Payment: comp. Interested in new or unpub'd poets: yes. Simultaneous submissions accepted: yes. Recent contributors: Richard Kostelanetz, Duane Locke, Alan Britt, Paul Roth. Special interests: translations, satire, anachronistic verse.

PANOPTICON, PO BOX 142, York Harbor, ME 03911-0142, E-mail jmoser41@portland.maine.edu. J. Moser, R. Moser. 1995. "Poets should maripulate language-make it do things. Poems, shouldn't simply communicate a concept, but rather should be richly layered with potential meaning." circ. 100-300. 4+. Pub'd 10 poems 1999; expects 40 poems 2000, 40 poems 2001. sub. price: $8; sample: $1. 20pp; 5×7; Rights purchased: all rights revert back to authors. Publishes 15% of poems submitted. Deadlines: open. Reporting time: 1 month. Payment: comp. copy of issue appeared in. Interested in new or unpub'd poets: yes. Simultaneous submissions accepted: yes. Recent contributors: Matt Jasper, David Castleman, Lyn Lifshin, John Grey, Randy Moser. Special interests: Prefers short, concise poems no longer than 50 lines in length.

THE PAPER BAG, The Paper Bag Press, PO Box 268805, Chicago, IL 60626-8805, 312-285-7972. Michael H. Brownstein. 1988. "We are interested in images, not poetry that would work better as fiction. No four letter words." circ. 200. 4/yr. Expects 125 poems 2001. sub. price: $12; sample: $3. 30pp; 8½×6; Rights purchased: none. Publishes 10% of poems submitted. Deadlines: none. Reporting time: 2 minutes to 8 weeks. Payment: contributors copy. Interested in new or unpub'd poets: yes. Simultaneous submissions accepted: no. Submission quantity: no limit. Special interests: Good imagery.

The Paper Bag Press (see also THE PAPER BAG), PO Box 268805, Chicago, IL 60626-8805, 312-285-7972. Michael H. Brownstein. 1988. avg. press run 200-300. Pub'd 4 poetry titles 1999; expects 4 poetry titles 2000, 4 poetry titles 2001. 8½×6; avg. price, paper: $3; other: $3. 20pp; Publishes 5% of poetry manuscripts submitted. Reporting time: 2 minutes to 8 weeks. Payment: contributor's copy. Interested in new or unpub'd poets: definitely. Simultaneous submissions accepted: no. Recently published poets: Martha Vertreace. Submission quantity: unlimited.

PAPER WASP: A Journal of Haiku, 7 Bellevue Terrace, St. Lucia, Queensland 4067, Australia, 61-7-33713509; Fax 61-7-33715527. Jacqui Murray, Ross Clark, John Knight, Jan Bostek. 1994. "SASE plus I.R.C.!" circ. 100. 4/yr. Pub'd 350 poems 1999; expects 350 poems 2000, 350 poems 2001. sub. price: $US26 airmail; sample: $US5. 20pp; 6×8½; Publishes 25% of poems submitted. Reporting time: 4-6 months. Interested in new or unpub'd poets: yes. Simultaneous submissions accepted: no. Recent contributors: Cornelis Vleeskons, Pat Prime, F. Matthew Blaine, Jan Bostok, Jim Kacian. Submission quantity: 2-10.

PAPERPLATES, 19 Kenwood Avenue, Toronto, ON M6C 2R8, Canada. Bernard Kelly, publisher. 1991. "Note that American stamps are not useable in Canada." 4/yr. Pub'd 25 poems 1999. 40pp; 8½×11; Rights purchased: first serial. Publishes 15% of poems submitted. Reporting time: 3-4 months. Payment: copies. Interested in new or unpub'd poets: yes. Simultaneous submissions accepted: no. Recent contributors: Outram, Lifshin, Sutherland. Submission quantity: 5.

PAPYRUS, Papyrus Literary Enterprises, Inc., 102 LaSalle Road, PO Box 270797, West Hartford, CT 06127, e-mail gwhitaker@imagine.com. Ginger Whitaker, Senior Editor. 1994. "Preferably submit on 3.5 inch disk with hard copy" circ. 2M. 4/yr. Expects 7 poems 2000, 21 poems 2001. sub. price: $8; sample: $2.20. 24pp; 8½×11; Rights purchased: one time. Publishes 25% of poems submitted. Deadlines: 2 months before end of quarter. Reporting time: 3 weeks. Payment: copies; occasionaly will pay veteran poet. Interested in new or unpub'd poets: yes. Simultaneous submissions accepted: no. Recent contributors: Robert Parham, Margaret Bristow, Frank Van Zant, James E. Cherry, Lenard D. Moore. Submission quantity: 3 at the most. Special interests: short works preferred; discourages experimental poetry, ethnic, U.S.-oriented, African-American preferred.

Papyrus Literary Enterprises, Inc. (see also PAPYRUS), 102 LaSalle Road, PO Box 270797, West Hartford, CT 06127, 203-233-7478, e-mail gwhitaker@imagine.com, http://www.readersndex.com/papyrus. 1994. 6×9.

●**PARADOXISM,** 200 College Road, University of New Mexico, Gallup, NM 87301, 505-726-8194, Fax 505-863-7532, smarand@unm.edu, www.gallup.unm.edu/~smarandache/. 1990. circ. 500. 1/yr. 52pp; size digest; Deadlines: do not submit mss. in the summer. Simultaneous submissions accepted: no.

PARA*PHRASE, Cosmic Trend, Sheridan Mall, Box 47014, Mississauga, Ontario L5K 2R2, Canada. George LeGrand, Jiri Jirasek. 1989. "Ask for free information on our anthology schedules and submission fees. Do not send us postal stamps, they are no good in Canada. Send $1 for postage" circ. 200. 1-2/yr. Pub'd 16 poems 1999; expects 16 poems 2000, 16 poems 2001. sub. price: $6 (for 4 issues); sample: $2. 20pp; 7×8½; Publishes 20% of poems submitted. Deadlines: none. Reporting time: 1 month. Payment: 1 free copy. Interested in new or unpub'd poets: yes. Simultaneous submissions accepted: yes. Recent contributors: Charles David Rice, Joanna Nealon, Susan Benischek. Submission quantity: 5-10. Special interests: We publish the 'spill-over' from our anthologies and other thematically related material. Send $ for a sample newsletter.

Pariah Press (see also HEELTAP/Pariah Press), 604 Hawthorne Avenue East, St. Paul, MN 55101-3531. Richard D. Houff. 1992. "Keep it thematic" avg. press run 100. Pub'd 1 poetry title 1999; expects 1 poetry title 2000, 2 poetry titles 2001. 5½×8½; avg. price, cloth: $14; paper: $4. 24pp. Publishes 5% of poetry manuscripts submitted. Reporting time: post in Jan., report Sept. Payment: 50 copies. Interested in new or unpub'd poets: yes. Simultaneous submissions accepted: yes. Recently published poets: Cheryl Townsend, Christopher Jones, R. Esterhouse, Lillian Oglethorpe, Paul Dickinson. Submission quantity: no more than 24.

Paris Press, Inc., 1117 West Road, Williamsburg, MA 01096, 413-628-0051. Jan Freeman. 1993. "We are interested in feminist work that is daring and beautiful. Highest literary quality desired. Contributors should send resumes and SASEs. Distributed by consortium and SPD" avg. press run 1.5M. Pub'd 1 poetry title 1999; expects 1 poetry title 2000, 1 poetry title 2001. 6×9; avg. price, paper: $12.95. 80pp; Publishes 1% of poetry manuscripts submitted. Reporting time: 3-6 months. Payment: standard royalty. Interested in new or unpub'd poets: yes. Simultaneous submissions accepted: no. Recently published poets: Ruth Stone, Jan Freeman. Submission quantity: 20. Special interests: Feminist, translations, experimental poetry.

PARIS/ATLANTIC, The American University of Paris, 31, avenue Bosquet, 75007 Paris, France, 33-1-01 40 62 05 89; fax 33-1-01 45 51 89 13. circ. 1.5M. 2/yr. sample price: sufficient postage. 80-100pp.

PARNASSUS LITERARY JOURNAL, Kudzu Press, PO Box 1384, Forest Park, GA 30298-1384. Denver Stull, Editor. 1975. "We currently have about 12 months backlog. We are a non-profit journal dedicated to the promotion of good poetry. We welcome all poets and all forms of poetry on any subject. We ask, however, that you keep it clean. No smut; no four letter words. An occasional contest is held—nothing spectacular or big bucks. But money is money. Also pay a small fee for best poem of the issue. Seldom accept anything longer than 24 lines. No oversize envelopes and no more than 3 poems! SAE's without sufficient postage will not be returned, submissions with postage due not accepted. Do not send your life's work." circ. 200+. 3/yr. Pub'd 350 poems 1999; expects 350 poems 2000, 350 poems 2001. sub. price: $18 for US and Canada, $25 overseas, make checks payable to Denver Stull; sample: $3. 64pp; 5½×8½; Rights purchased: first rights. Publishes 10% of poems submitted. Deadlines: 1 Mar., 1 June, 1 Aug., 1 Dec. Reporting time: 30 days. Payment: copy. Interested in new or unpub'd poets: yes. Simultaneous submissions accepted: yes. Recent contributors: Diana Rubin, Ruth Schuler, Carol Hamilton, Jean Calkins. Submission quantity: no more than 3.

PARNASSUS: Poetry in Review, 205 West 89th Street, Apartment 8F, New York, NY 10024, 212-362-3492, fax 212-875-0148, e-mail parnew@aol.com. Herbert Leibowitz, Editor; Ben Downing, Managing Editor. 1972. "*Parnassus* publishes a few unsolicated poems per year" circ. 1.75M. 2/yr. Pub'd 15-30 poems 1999. sub. price: $22 individuals, $46 institutions; sample: $10-$15. 350pp; 6×9¼; Publishes 0.5% of poems submitted. Deadlines: none. Reporting time: 1-6 weeks. Payment: $25 a page. Interested in new or unpub'd poets: yes. Simultaneous submissions accepted: yes. Recent contributors: Anne Carson, Richard Howard, Rita Dove, Jorie Graham, Albert Goldbarth. Submission quantity: maximum 5.

PARTING GIFTS, March Street Press, 3413 Wilshire Drive, Greensboro, NC 27408-2923. Robert Bixby. 1988. "Send anything as long as it's your best. I'm interested in a broad range of work." circ. 100. 2/yr. Pub'd 50 poems 1999; expects 50 poems 2000, 50 poems 2001. sub. price: $12; sample: $6. 72pp; 5½×7½; Rights purchased: first N.A. serial. Publishes 3% of poems submitted. Deadlines: none (January is best time to submit). Reporting time: usually 24 hours. Payment: 1 copy. Interested in new or unpub'd poets: yes. Simultaneous submissions accepted: no. Recent contributors: Lyn Lifshin, Elizabeth Kerlikowske, John Grey, Stu Dybek, Eric Torgersen, Kelly Cherry. Submission quantity: 3-5.

Partisan Press (see also BLUE COLLAR REVIEW), PO Box 11417, Norfolk, VA 23517, e-mail redart@pilot.infi.net. Al Markowitz, Editor; Mary Franke, Co-Editor. 1993. "Best to see issue before submitting: Contest: Working Peoples Poetry Competition - $15 per entry, prize $100 and subscription. Deadline May 1st." avg. press run 100. Pub'd 3 poetry titles 1999; expects 3 poetry titles 2000, 3 poetry titles 2001. 5½×8½; avg. price, paper: $5. 30-60pp; Publishes 10% of poetry manuscripts submitted. Reporting time: 3-6 weeks. Payment: 40 copies out of run of 100. Interested in new or unpub'd poets: yes. Simultaneous submissions accepted: yes. Recently published poets: Robert Edwards, Mary Franke, Katherine Kirkpatric, Sonia Sanchez, Virgil Suarez.

PARTISAN REVIEW, 236 Bay State Road, Boston, MA 02215, 617-353-4260. William Phillips,

Editor-in-Chief. 1934. "Manuscript must have a SASE- Allow 2 months before inquiring about submission-Name + address on each poem." circ. 8M. 4/yr. Expects 20-40 poems 2000. sub. price: $22; sample: $7.50 including postage. 160pp; 6×9; Rights purchased: first serial. Deadlines: anytime. Reporting time: 2-3 months. Payment: $50. Interested in new or unpub'd poets: yes. Simultaneous submissions accepted: no. Recent contributors: Derek Walcott, Seamus Heaney, Adam Zagajewski, Zbigniew Herbert, Ted Hughes. Submission quantity: 4-10. Special interests: Translations.

PASSAGER: A Journal of Remembrance and Discovery, 1420 N. Charles Street, Baltimore, MD 21201-5779, 301-625-3041. Kendra Kopelke, Rebecca Childers, Mary Azreal, Ebby Malmgren, Kathleen Fantom Shemer. 1989. "We have an annual poetry contest for new writer over age 50. Send SASE for details. Theme issues" circ. 500. 2/yr. Expects 2500 poems 2000. sub. price: $18; overseas US $28; libraries/institutions $36; sample: $4. 32pp; 8×8; Publishes 1% of poems submitted. Deadlines: Sept - May. Reporting time: 3 months. Payment: 2 copies of issue. Interested in new or unpub'd poets: yes. Simultaneous submissions accepted: yes. Submission quantity: 3-5. Special interests: Memory, no light verse.

PASSAGES NORTH, English Dept., N. Michigan Univ., 1401 Presque Isle Avenue, Marquette, MI 49855, 906-227-1203, 906-227-1795, Fax 906-227-1096. Kate Myers Hanson, Editor. 1979. "High quality contemporary poetry. Best times to send are September-December, January-March. Clean, clear manuscripts. No more than 4 poems preferred." circ. 1.5M. 1/yr. Pub'd 80 poems 1999; expects 80 poems 2000, 80 poems 2001. sub. price: $13/yr, $25/2 yrs; sample: $13. 225pp; 5½×8½; Rights purchased: 1st N. American rights revert to author upon publication. Publishes 5% of poems submitted. Deadlines: September-May. Reporting time: 3 months. Payment: 2 copies. Interested in new or unpub'd poets: yes. Simultaneous submissions accepted: yes. Recent contributors: William Olsen, Nancy Eimers, Lisa Lewis, Beckion Fritz Goldberg, Tony Hoogland. Submission quantity: 4. Special interests: No greeting card, "pop" verse, or song lyrics.

PASSAIC REVIEW (MILLENNIUM EDITIONS), c/o Ah! Sunflower Theater, PO Box 732, Spring Lake, NJ 07762. Richard Quatrone, Editor. 1979. "We may publish your work as it is sent; send clear copies" circ. 100. 2-6/yr. Pub'd 10 poems 1999; expects 100 poems 2000, 100 poems 2001. sub. price: $10; sample: $2 + 75¢ postage. Pages vary; 7×8½; Rights purchased: none. Publishes 3% of poems submitted. Deadlines: open. Reporting time: immediate to indefinite. Payment: 1 complimentary copy. Interested in new or unpub'd poets: yes. Simultaneous submissions accepted: yes, if so indicated. Recent contributors: Thuy-Duong Nguyen, Ronald Baatz, Robert Quatrone. Submission quantity: no limit. Special interests: Do not send offical 'soviet poetry' the ubiquitous, homogeneous, passionless stuff that clogs the veins, mind, and heart. Send real work. Erotic work welcomed.

Passeggiata Press, Inc., 222 West 'B' Street, Pueblo, CO 81003-3404, 719-544-1038, Fax 719-546-7889, e-mail Passeggia@aol.com. Donald E. Herdeck, Editor-Publisher. 1997. "Don't send full ms. unless we ask for it." avg. press run 500-1M. Pub'd 2 poetry titles 1999; expects 2 poetry titles 2000, 2 poetry titles 2001. 6×9, 5½×8½, 8½×11; avg. price, cloth: $22; paper: $12; other: some deluxe editions—$25 and up. 80-120pp; Publishes 5% of poetry manuscripts submitted. Reporting time: 15 weeks. Payment: small advance, usually 5% of est. net sales, 7.5% royalties overall. Interested in new or unpub'd poets: no. Simultaneous submissions accepted: yes. Recently published poets: Nina Iskrenko, Otto Orban, Lyubomir Levcher, Fan Chengda, Hilary Tham. Submission quantity: 10-20. Special interests: We publish poetry by some non-Western writers, and translations of same (from Arabic, Hindi, French (West African), Creole, etc.). We're happy to consider bi-lingual editions of poetry in original language, with facing English texts.

PASSION, Crescent Moon, PO Box 393, Maidstone, Kent ME14 5XU, United Kingdom. Jeremy Robinson. 1994. "SAE and International Reply Coupons essential. Non-rhyming poetry preferred. Do not send whole manuscript" circ. 200. 4/yr. Pub'd 40 poems 1999; expects 40 poems 2000, 40 poems 2001. sub. price: $17; sample: $4. 50pp; 5⅞×8¼; Publishes 3% of poems submitted. Reporting time: 3 months. Payment: to be negotiated. Interested in new or unpub'd poets: yes. Simultaneous submissions accepted: yes. Recent contributors: Peter Redgrove, Elisabeth Bletsoe, Jeremy Reed, D.J. Enright.

THE PATERSON LITERARY REVIEW, Passaic County Community College, College Boulevard, Paterson, NJ 07505-1179, 201-684-6555. Maria Mazziotti Gillan, Editor. 1979. "Prefer to read Oct-March. Please include SASE. Order one issue to determine type of work published. One issue $12." circ. 1M. 1/yr. Pub'd 300 poems 1999; expects 300 poems 2000, 300 poems 2001. sub. price: $12; sample: $12. 200pp; 6×9; Rights purchased: first rights, rights revert to contributor after publication. Publishes 5% of poems submitted. Deadlines: no summer submissions please, accept summissions from October-March. Reporting time: 6 months or less. Payment: contributor's copies. Interested in new or unpub'd poets: yes. Simultaneous submissions accepted: yes. Recent contributors: Marge Piercy, David Ray, Laura Boss, William Stafford, Sonia Sanchez, Ruth Strne. Submission quantity: 5. Special interests: Prefer clear, direct, powerful work, narrative poetry.

Path Press, Inc., PO Box 2925, Chicago, IL 60690-2925, 312-663-0167. Herman C. Gilbert, Executive Vice President. 1969. "We publish poetry and books by, for, and about Black American and Third World peoples" avg. press run 2M. Pub'd 2 poetry titles 1999; expects 3 poetry titles 2000, 3 poetry titles 2001. 5½×8½, varies; avg. price, cloth: $9.95; paper: $5.95. 74pp; Publishes less than 5% of poetry manuscripts submitted. Reporting time: 60-90 days. Payment: royalty contract 10%, no advance. Interested in new or unpub'd poets: yes. Simultaneous submissions accepted: yes. Recently published poets: Zack Gilbert. Submission quantity: entire manuscript.

●**Pathwise Press (see also BATHTUB GIN)**, PO Box 2392, Bloomington, IN 47402, 812-323-2985, charter@bluemarble.net, www.home.bluemarble.net/charter/btgin.htm. Christopher Harter. 1997. avg. press run 100-150. Pub'd 1 poetry title 1999; expects 2 poetry titles 2000, 2 poetry titles 2001. 5½×8½; avg. price, paper: $3. 36pp; Reporting time: 1-2 months. Payment: author receives large amount of gratis copies up front, 10% royalties on sales over initial 100. Interested in new or unpub'd poets: yes. Simultaneous submissions accepted: yes. Recently published poets: John Gohmann. Submission quantity: 10.

THE PATRIOT, Runaway Publications, PO Box 1172, Ashland, OR 97520, 503-482-2578. James L. Berkman, Publisher. 1984. "Do not accept unsolicited manuscripts. Each issue printed in limited edition and individually numbered and hand signed by the author." circ. 100. 1/yr. Pub'd 1 poem 1999; expects 1 poem 2000, 1 poem 2001. sub. price: $10; sample: $10. 8pp; 5½×8½; Rights purchased: negotiable. Payment: negotiable.

PAVEMENT SAW, Pavement Saw Press, PO Box 6291, Columbus, OH 43206, 614-263-7115, baratier@megsinet.net, www.pavementsaw.org. David Baratier, Editor. 1994. "Five poems, clean photocopy (prefer type quality). One page prose or 1-2 pages short fiction, acceptable also. *Pavement Saw* seeks poetry, prose, and short fiction which elevates the ordinary. The work should not merely startle, but rather employ academic structural techniques to indirectly encourage its readers to search for resolutions within their own experience and context of the work. Juxtaposition for tension, caesura's, colons, and the like permeate the issue. Peruse a copy for further indications of style and content. *Pavement Saw* rarely accepts previously published material, simultaneous submissions, and letterless mass submissions. Named emotion and greeting cards will be returned in flaming envelopes. There is one featured writer each issue - #2 Gian Lomardo, #3 Sean Killian #4 Sandra Kohler. These 'features' are chosen through the best of the regular submissions recieved. We are one of U.S. journals who devote a third of each issue to the prose-poem, short-short fiction, letter boundaries. Guidelines are printed in issue #5." circ. 500. 1/yr. Pub'd 60 poems 1999; expects 60 poems 2000, 60 poems 2001. sub. price: $10/2 issues; sample: $4. 80pp; 6×9¼; Rights purchased: 1st American. Publishes less than 1% of poems submitted. Deadlines: we read year round. Reporting time: 1-4 months. Payment: 2 copies. Interested in new or unpub'd poets: yes. Simultaneous submissions accepted: no. Recent contributors: Simon Perchik, Ruth Anderson Barrett, Stephen Ellis, Pamela Steed Hill, Virgil Suarez. Submission quantity: 5 with cover letter. Special interests: Poetry about work and labor, minimalist prose, experimental poetry.

Pavement Saw Press (see also PAVEMENT SAW), PO Box 6291, Columbus, OH 43206, baratier@megsinet.net, www.pavementsaw.org. David Baratier, Editor. 1994. "Full lengths books are usually chosen from authors published in *Pavement Saw* or from the yearly *Transcontinental* first book award. Chapbooks are chosen through a competion, anonymously, the 1999 judge was Ruth Anderson Barnett." avg. press run 300-500 chapbooks; 1M full length books. Pub'd 4 poetry titles 1999; expects 7 poetry titles 2000, 6 poetry titles 2001. 6×9, 8×9; avg. price, cloth: $75; paper: $12. 64-372pp, chapbooks 40pp; Publishes less than 1% of poetry manuscripts submitted. Reporting time: query before sending for guidelines or contest rules. Payment: 10% royalty plus copies. Interested in new or unpub'd poets: yes. Simultaneous submissions accepted: yes. Recently published poets: Robert Grenier, Simon Perchik, Shelley Stenhouse, Gordon Massman, Errol Miller. Submission quantity: query. Special interests: Poetry about work & labor, experimental in prose/poems/short fiction mixtures. Letters.

Paycock Press (see also GARGOYLE), 3938 Colchester Road, Apt. 364, Baltimore, MD 21229-5010, Fax; 410-644-5195; e-mail atticus@radix.net. Richard Peabody. 1976. "Press is in hiatus. these days serving only to umbrella *Gargoyle*" avg. press run 1M. 5½×8½, varies; avg. price, paper: $7.95. 64pp; Reporting time: fast. Payment: 10% of press run plus 50/50 split on sales if/when we break even. Interested in new or unpub'd poets: no. Simultaneous submissions accepted: no. Recently published poets: Tina Fulker, Harrison Fisher, George Myers Jr., Richard Peabody, Carlo Parcelli. Submission quantity: 5.

PEAKY HIDE, PO Box 1591, Upland, CA 91785. 1996. "Send SASE for upcoming theme issues—as they do vary" circ. less than 200. 4/yr. Pub'd 180-300 poems 1999. sub. price: $17; sample: $5. 48pp; size varies; Rights purchased: all rights revert to authors/artists upon publication. Publishes 35-40% of poems submitted. Reporting time: 1-2 months. Payment: 1 copy of issue in which work appears, other copies available at reduced price (generally $4 each). Interested in new or unpub'd poets: yes, very much so. Simultaneous submissions accepted: no. Recent contributors: Ann Erickson, Jen Hofer, Errol Miller, Carol Dorf, BZ Niditch. Submission quantity: 3-5. Special interests: experimental poetry, some visual poetry.

PEARL, Pearl Editions, 3030 E. Second Street, Long Beach, CA 90803, 562-434-4523 phone/Fax or

714-968-7530, mjohn5150@aol.com, www.pearlmag.com. Joan Jobe Smith, Marilyn Johnson, Barbara Hauk. 1987. "Prefer poems up to 35 lines with lines no longer than 10 words. Cover letters are welcome. Each issue contains a 15 page section featuring the work of a single writer (usually a poet). Featured poets include: Robert Peters, Lisa Glatt, Donna Hilbert, Gerald Locklin. We also sponsor an annual book contest judged by one of the better known poets we have published (2000 judge, Dorianne Laux, '99 judge, Ed Ochester). Contest submission period: May 1-July 15. Prize: $1,000, publication, 25 copies. Guidelines available for SASE, or visit website" circ. 600. 2/yr. Pub'd 150 poems 1999; expects 150 poems 2000, 150 poems 2001. sub. price: $18 (2 issues)+ 1 poetry book; sample: $7. 128pp; 5½×8½; Rights purchased: first serial rights. Publishes 5% of poems submitted. Deadlines: Submissions accepted Sept. - May only. Reporting time: 6-8 weeks. Payment: 1 copy. Interested in new or unpub'd poets: yes. Simultaneous submissions accepted: yes. Recent contributors: Ron Koertge, Fred Voss, Donna Hilbert, Gerald Locklin, Lisa Glatt. Submission quantity: 3-6. Special interests: We are interested in accessible, humanistic poetry that communicates and is related to real life. Humor and wit are welcome, along with the ironic and serious. No taboos stylistically or subject-wise. Our purpose is to provide a forum for lively, readable poetry that reflects a wide variety of contemporary voices, viewpoints, and experiences and that speaks to *real* people about *real* life in direct, living language, from the profane to the sublime.

Pearl Editions (see also PEARL), 3030 E. Second Street, Long Beach, CA 90803, 562-434-4523 phone/Fax or 714-968-7530, mjohn5150@aol.com, www.pearlmag.com. Joan Jobe Smith, Marilyn Johnson, Barbara Hauk. 1989. "We only publish solicited authors and the winner of our annual poetry book contest. Submission period: May 1 to July 15. Guidelines available for SASE, or visit website." avg. press run 500. Pub'd 3 poetry titles 1999; expects 3 poetry titles 2000, 2 poetry titles 2001. 5½×8½; avg. price, paper: $10. 64pp; Publishes less than 1% of poetry manuscripts submitted. Reporting time: 4-5 months. Payment: $1,000 + 25 copies (contest winner), 25 copies (solicited authors). Interested in new or unpub'd poets: yes (contest only). Simultaneous submissions accepted: yes (contest only). Recently published poets: Lisa Glatt, Donna Hilbert, David Hernandez, Denise Duhamel, Robert Perchan. Submission quantity: 48-64 (contest).

Pearl River Press (see also PEARL RIVER REVIEW), 32 Cambridge Avenue, Gulfport, MS 39507-4213. 1996. 6×9.

PEARL RIVER REVIEW, Pearl River Press, 32 Cambridge Avenue, Gulfport, MS 39507-4213. 1996. circ. 500. 2/yr. sub. price: $15; sample: $7.50. 50pp; 6×9.

Pecan Grove Press, Academic Library, Box AL, 1 Camino Santa Maria, San Antonio, TX 78228-8608, 210-436-3441. Palmer H. Hall, Karen Narvarte. 1988. avg. press run 500. Pub'd 7 poetry titles 1999; expects 6 poetry titles 2000. 8½×5½, 9×6; avg. price, paper: $10. 74-112pp; Publishes 2% of poetry manuscripts submitted. Reporting time: 1-4 months. Payment: 10 copies. When book breaks even 50/50 division after shipping/handling. Interested in new or unpub'd poets: yes. Simultaneous submissions accepted: yes, if the poet notifies us. Recently published poets: Triniad Sanchez, Edward Byrne, Gqyn McVay, Beth Simon, James Hoggard. Submission quantity: complete manuscript.

PEGASUS, Pegasus Publishing, PO Box 61324, Boulder City, NV 89006-1324. M.E. Hildebrand. 1986. "*Pegasus*, a quarterly, is devoted to original poetry. In sharing your experience, make a lasting impression by using fresh imagery." circ. 200. 4/yr. Pub'd 250 poems 1999; expects 250 poems 2000, 250 poems 2001. sub. price: $18, int'l add $5 postage; sample: $5 includes postage. 32pp; 5½×8½; Rights purchased: one-time rights. Publishes 10-15% of poems submitted. Deadlines: none. Reporting time: 2 weeks. Payment: publication is payment. Interested in new or unpub'd poets: yes. Simultaneous submissions accepted: no. Recent contributors: Elizabeth Perry, Robert K. Johnson, R. Nikolas Macioci, John Grey. Submission quantity: 3-5. Special interests: All styles and forms are considered.

THE PEGASUS REVIEW, PO Box 88, Henderson, MD 21640-0088, 410-482-6736. Arthur Bounds. 1980. "Magazine done in calligraphy, thematic, bi-monthly. Poetry - not more than 24 lines, the shorter the better; fiction - short short (about 2½ pages would be ideal); essays and cartoons. A SASE is a must. No SASE, no return. Beginners and seasoned writers welcomed. A sample copy will help understand magazine format" circ. 130. 6/yr + special issues. Pub'd 60 poems 1999; expects 75 poems 2000, 80 poems 2001. sub. price: $10; sample: $2.50. 10-12pp; 6½×8½; Rights purchased: one time rights. Publishes 35% of poems submitted. Deadlines: 1 month prior to upcoming theme. Reporting time: 6-12 weeks. Payment: 2 contributor's copies; occasional book awards. Interested in new or unpub'd poets: yes. Simultaneous submissions accepted: yes. Submission quantity: 3-5. Special interests: All material should follow the guide lines closely overall, brevity is the key if guidelines indicate no longer than 24 lines - don't submit 28 lines. It will be rejected, as with any publication guidelines they are indicated for a specific purpose. Above all for all writers - read, write and revise. They all work hand in hand. Join a local writers workshop and be active in it. Continue to market your work. Above all - perserve!

Pella Publishing Co (see also THE CHARIOTEER), 337 West 36th Street, New York, NY 10018,

212-279-9586. Leandros Papathanasiou, President & Publisher. 1976. avg. press run 1.5M. Expects 2 poetry titles 2000, 3 poetry titles 2001. 5½x8½; avg. price, paper: $12. 80-160pp; Publishes 3% of poetry manuscripts submitted. Reporting time: 4-6 weeks. Payment: standard. Interested in new or unpub'd poets: no. Simultaneous submissions accepted: no. Recently published poets: Seferis, Ritsos, Pagoulatiou, Anagnostakis, spanias. Submission quantity: 3. Special interests: Translations from the Greek only.

PEMBROKE MAGAZINE, UNCP, Box 1510, Pembroke, NC 28372-1510, 919-521-4214 ext 433. Shelby Stephenson, Editor. 1969. circ. 500. 1/yr. sub. price: $8; sample: $8. 275pp; 6x9; Reporting time: 1-3 months. Payment: 1 copy. Interested in new or unpub'd poets: yes. Simultaneous submissions accepted: no. Recent contributors: Allison Funk, Robert Morgan, A.R. Ammons, Daphne Athas, Jared Carter. Submission quantity: 3-5.

PEMMICAN, Pemmican Press, 9534 132nd Avenue NE, Kirkland, WA 98033-5212. Robert Edwards. 1992. "SASE required, no previously published work" circ. 300. 1/yr. Pub'd 40 poems 1999; expects 40 poems 2000, 40 poems 2001. sub. price: $5; sample: $4. 70pp; 7x8½; Rights purchased: 1st North American Serial Rights. Publishes 5-10% of poems submitted. Deadlines: none. Reporting time: 1 week to 1 month. Payment: 1 copy. Interested in new or unpub'd poets: yes. Simultaneous submissions accepted: yes, if notified. Recent contributors: Sherman Alexie, Adrian Louis, Olga Cabral, Margaret Randall, Luis Rodriguez. Submission quantity: 5-7. Special interests: We welcome: translations, political, feminist, experimental, prose poems.

Pemmican Press (see also PEMMICAN), 9534 132nd Avenue NE, Kirkland, WA 98033-5212. Robert Edwards. 1992. avg. press run 300. Pub'd 2 poetry titles 1999; expects 2 poetry titles 2000, 2 poetry titles 2001. 5½x8½; avg. price, paper: $5. 50pp; Reporting time: 1 month. Payment: varies. Interested in new or unpub'd poets: no. Simultaneous submissions accepted: yes. Recently published poets: Lyle Daggett, Prairie Miller, Gary David, Leif Halvorson, Sherman Alexie. Submission quantity: 5-7. Special interests: I am especially interested in seeing political poetry.

PEN & INK WRITERS JOURNAL, Baker Street Publications, 577 Central Avenue, Box 4, Jefferson, LA 70121-1400, E-mail editor@inforspacemail.com, publisher@mailexcite.com, www.zines.freeservers.com, www.members.theglobe.com/zines/default.html, www2.cybercities.com/z/zines/. Sharida Rizzuto, Editor; Harold Tollison, Associate Editor; Ann Hoyt, Assistant Editor. 1983. "This publication covers the writers market and writing. Poetry included should be about the craft of writing or drawing/painting. All submissions must be double-spaced and typewritten" circ. 1M. 3/yr. Pub'd 15-18 poems 1999. sub. price: $15/3 issues; sample: $5. 40-50pp; 5½x8½; Rights purchased: one-time rights, first serial rights, or second serial rights. Publishes 30% of poems submitted. Deadlines: always open to submissions. Reporting time: 2-6 weeks. Payment: free copies only. Interested in new or unpub'd poets: yes. Simultaneous submissions accepted: yes. Recent contributors: Holly Day, Peter Layton, Gregory E. Harrison, George Chaddevdou, John Youril. Submission quantity: 1-5. Special interests: We are willing to look at any type of poetry. No length requirements.

Pen-Dec Press (see also EX FILLAPIO IN PENUSIO; LIONESS EGGS RAGING; STUFFWAX BEEZER), 2526 Chatham Woods, Grand Rapids, MI 49546. Jim DeWitt, Editor. 1978. "No unsolicited mss. Poetry only: juiced, with zip. Must include letter of purpose and brief bio, SASE" Expects 1 poetry title 2000, 1 poetry title 2001. 5½x8½; avg. price, paper: $6. 24pp; Publishes 1% of poetry manuscripts submitted. Reporting time: 3 months. Interested in new or unpub'd poets: yes. Simultaneous submissions accepted: yes. Recently published poets: Phyllis Settles, Vicki Denardo, Cassius.

Pendragonian Publications (see also PENNY DREADFUL: Tales and Poems of Fantastic Terror; SONGS OF INNOCENCE), PO Box 719, New York, NY 10101-0719, mmpendragon@aol.com. Michael Pendragon, Editor & Publisher. 1995. "Our first anthology, *The Bible of Hell*, will print later this year (for release on 12/25/00). This is a themed, multi-author collection and will most likely be closed to submissions by the time this *Directory* publishes. I will consider single-author publications for future projects: query with proposition and samples." Pub'd 1 poetry title 1999. 5½x8½; avg. price, paper: $10. 200+pp; Publishes 2% of poetry manuscripts submitted. Reporting time: up to 1 year. Payment: 1 copy. Interested in new or unpub'd poets: yes. Simultaneous submissions accepted: yes. Recently published poets: Robert Pinsky, Lee Clark, Scott Urban, Charlee Jacob, James S. Dorr. Submission quantity: open. Special interests: Romantic, Bardic, prophetic, rhymed, metered verse.

Peninhand Press, 3665 Southeast Tolman, Portland, OR 97202. Tom Janisse. 1979. "We currently only print unpublished poems read at poetry readings in Portland, Oregon for a local and Northwest audience; and physicians who write medical poems" avg. press run 500. Expects 1 poetry title 2000, 1 poetry title 2001. 5½x8½; avg. price, paper: $3. 30pp; Publishes 15% of poetry manuscripts submitted. Reporting time: 6 months. Payment: copies. Interested in new or unpub'd poets: yes. Simultaneous submissions accepted: no. Recently published poets: Kelly Sievers, Michael Stine, Bob McFarlane. Submission quantity: 3-5.

PENNINE PLATFORM, 7 Cockley Hill Lane, Kirkheaton, Huddersfield HD5 OHH, West Yorkshire,

England, 0937-584674. Dr.K.E. Smith. 1966. "Concrete poetry too difficult to reproduce; tendency to print poems of social and religious comment on human conditions and political suffering. Preference for form of one kind or another. Poems should be accurately presented, unsloppily, so that experiment is not confused with error." circ. 250. 2/yr. Pub'd 80 poems 1999; expects 80 poems 2000, 80 poems 2001. sub. price: £8 UK, £12 abroad...sterling, £17 abroad...currency, £25 if by check... not in sterling; sample: £4. 48pp; size A5; Rights purchased: none, copyright remains with contributor. Publishes 10% of poems submitted. Deadlines: none. Reporting time: within 4 months. Payment: 1 free copy of magazine. Interested in new or unpub'd poets: yes. Simultaneous submissions accepted: no. Recent contributors: Pauline, Kirk, Anna Adams, Bill Headdon, B.W. Beynon, John Ward. Submission quantity: 6 or less. Special interests: Translations welcome, longpoems difficult because of space, local poems welcome (places, etc.), lightverse should be formally and otherwise good, agitprop discouraged.

PENNY DREADFUL: Tales and Poems of Fantastic Terror, Pendragonian Publications, PO Box 719, New York, NY 10101-0719, mmpendragon@aol.com. Michael M. Pendragon, Editor and Publisher. 1996. "Poems should fall within the Literary Horror genre. Publishes poetry short stories and artwork which celebrate the darker aspects of Man, the World, and their Creator. Poems should not exceed 5 pages, short stories should be between 500 and 3,500 words. We're looking for Literary Horror in the tradition of Poe, M.R. James, Shelley, and LeFanu. Dark, disquieting tales/poems designed to challenge the reader's perceptions of human nature, morality, and Man's place within the Darkness. Submit 3 to 5 poems." circ. 250. 3/yr. Pub'd 75 poems 1999; expects 200 poems 2000, 200 poems 2001. sub. price: $12; sample: $5. 140pp; 5½x8½; Rights purchased: one-time rights. Publishes 5% of poems submitted. Deadlines: open. Reporting time: 3 months or longer. Payment: 1 copy. Interested in new or unpub'd poets: yes. Simultaneous submissions accepted: yes. Recent contributors: Scott Thomas, Tamara Latham, Dennis Saleh, Louise Webster, Kevin N. Roberts. Special interests: Rhyme and meter are particulary encouraged.

PENNY-A-LINER, Redrosebush Press, PO Box 2163, Wenatchee, WA 98807-2163, 509-662-7858. 1991. circ. 1M+. 3/yr. sub. price: $18; sample: free. 44pp; 8½x11.

PenRose Publishing Company, Inc., PO Box 620, Mystic Island, NJ 08087, 609-296-1401. Roger E. Egan, Editor in Chief. 1992. "We welcome divergent and provocative material. We will decline manuscripts that do not need miminum literary stadards or are patently offensive to any group" avg. press run 750. Pub'd 1 poetry title 1999; expects 2 poetry titles 2000, 3 poetry titles 2001. 6x9; avg. price, paper: $13.95. 80pp; Publishes 10% of poetry manuscripts submitted. Reporting time: 2 months. Payment: all revenues return to author after production & fulfillment expenses; author owns inventory. Interested in new or unpub'd poets: yes. Recently published poets: Roswita Davis, Ruth Parks, Roger Egan. Submission quantity: 20.

Pentland Press, Inc., 5122 Bur Oak Circle, Raleigh, NC 27612, 919-782-0281. Carol A. Mitchell, Publisher. 1993. avg. press run 1000. Pub'd 3 poetry titles 1999; expects 3 poetry titles 2000, 5 poetry titles 2001. 6x9, 5½x8½; avg. price, cloth: $24.95; paper: $12.95. 50-100pp; Publishes 50% of poetry manuscripts submitted. Reporting time: 6-8 weeks. Payment: quarterly. Interested in new or unpub'd poets: yes. Simultaneous submissions accepted: no. Recently published poets: David Lindamood, Thomas Amherst Perry, Osman Turkay, Phyllis Aldcroft Kolseth, Ralph S. Stevens. Submission quantity: complete manuscript or collection. Special interests: English language only.

PERCEPTIONS, 73 Eastcombe Avenue, London, England SE7 7LL, England. Temi Rose. 1982. circ. 300. 3/yr. Pub'd 400 poems 1999. sub. price: $15; sample: $5. 40pp; 4¼x5½; Rights purchased: none. Publishes 25% of poems submitted. Deadlines: none. Reporting time: 3 months. Payment: 1 copy. Interested in new or unpub'd poets: yes. Simultaneous submissions accepted: yes. Recent contributors: Rama Rao, Camincha, Mary Gowland. Submission quantity: 3-10.

PEREGRINE, Amherst Writers & Artists Press, Inc., PO Box 1076, Amherst, MA 01004, 413-253-7764 phone/fax; e-mail awapress@javanet.com; www.javanet.com/~awapress. Nancy Rose, Managing Editor. 1981. "*Peregrine* has provided a forum for national and international writers for more than 18 years and is committed to finding excellent work by new writers as well as established authors. We seek poetry that is fresh, imaginative, human, and memorable. Annual contest: The Peregrine Prize, and The Best of the Nest. #10 SASE for guidelines." circ. 1M. 1/yr. Pub'd 20 poems 1999; expects 20 poems 2000, 20 poems 2001. sub. price: $20/3 years; sample: $8 postpaid. 100pp; 6x9; Rights purchased: first North American (no buy). Publishes 1-5% of poems submitted. Deadlines: April 1 each year for that year's issue. Reporting time: 4-6 months, October through April reading period. Payment: copies upon publication. Interested in new or unpub'd poets: yes. Simultaneous submissions accepted: yes. Recent contributors: Catherine Strisik, George Kalamaras, Fran Harris, Bill Brown, Barbara Ganzel. Submission quantity: 3-5 maximum (3 for contest).

PERIPHERAL VISION, Apartado 240, Portalegre, 7300, Portugal. Ken Schroeder. 1998. circ. 100-200. 2-4/yr. Pub'd 40 poems 1999; expects 40 poems 2000, 80 poems 2001. sub. price: $6. 40-50pp; size A4; Rights purchased: we don't buy anything. Publishes 25% of poems submitted. Deadlines: continuous. Reporting time:

fast. Payment: copies. Interested in new or unpub'd poets: yes. Simultaneous submissions accepted: yes. Recent contributors: Mark Terrill, Vasco Camara Pastana, Irma Garbarino, Thomas Michael McDade, Ana de Ceres. Submission quantity: no limit. Special interests: experimental, prose poetry, beat, haiku, long poems, anything.

PERSEPHONE, c/o John Cobb, 40 Avon Hill Street, Cambridge, MA 02138. 1995. circ. 500. 1/yr. sub. price: $15/2 years; sample: $6. 96pp; 7×9.

Persephone Press (see also Scots Plaid Press), 600 Kelly Road, Carthage, NC 28327, 910-947-2587; Fax 910-947-5112. Mary Belle Campbell, Founder, Consulting Editor; Tom Tolnay, Editor, Publisher. 1987. *"Query* with bio/vita, SASE, list of publications. Send no ms., no more than 2 page sample. Winners read last Sat. in June in Southern Pines, Weymouth Center, NC. Ask for NC Writers Network guidelines" avg. press run 250-500-1000. Pub'd 3 poetry titles 1999; expects 6 poetry titles 2000, 2 poetry titles 2001. 6×9; avg. price, cloth: $25-$95; paper: $10-$24. 32-64-128pp; Publishes 3% of poetry manuscripts submitted. Reporting time: 1 day to 6 months. Payment: 80% of run as royalties in advance; no advances. Interested in new or unpub'd poets: no (in little magazines at least). Simultaneous submissions accepted: yes. Recently published poets: Mary Snotherly, Gladys Hughes, Maureen Sutton, Diana Pinckney, Susan Meyers. Submission quantity: well-organized ms with theme - 24-30. Poems submit: 3 copies, 2 blind for Persephone Award Series. Special interests: long poems, narrative poems, family, or regional ethnic poems with feminist or Jungian psychology overtones.

Perugia Press, PO Box 108, Shutesbury, MA 01072, E-mail perugia@mindspring.com. Susan Kan. 1997. "Send preliminary submission of 10 poems, plus bio and cover letter describing whole manuscript" avg. press run 500. Pub'd 1 poetry title 1999; expects 1 poetry title 2000, 1 poetry title 2001. 6×9; avg. price, paper: $11.95. 88pp; Reporting time: 1 month. Payment: negotiable. Interested in new or unpub'd poets: yes. Simultaneous submissions accepted: yes. Recently published poets: Almitra David, Gail Thomas, Janet E. Aalfs, Catherine Anderson. Submission quantity: 10 poems or 10 pages, whichever is fewer. Special interests: Publishes first or second books by women, choosing lyrical over experimental.

The Petrarch Press, PO Box 488, Oregon House, CA 95962, 916-692-0828. Peter Bishop, Linda Kaplan. 1985. "Generally the press has printed only poetry which has withstood the many tests of many centuries; however, we are open to the possibility of publishing a contemporary poet if the material and terms are aacceptable to us." avg. press run 150. Expects 2 poetry titles 2000, 3 poetry titles 2001. 6¼×9½; avg. price, cloth: $90. 40pp; Reporting time: 2-3 weeks. Payment: varies. Interested in new or unpub'd poets: no. Simultaneous submissions accepted: yes. Recently published poets: Rilke, Whitman, Shakespeare, Dickenson, Milton. Submission quantity: varies. Special interests: We are not interested in experimental poetry.

Philomel Books, 345 Hudson Street, New York, NY 10014, 212-414-3610. Patricia Lee Gauch, Editorial Director; Michael Green, Editor. 1980. "We are a children's lit. imprint. Mostly we take anthologies, although we have seriously considered poems around a theme, and 1 poem picturebook" avg. press run 10M. Pub'd 2 poetry titles 1999; expects 2 poetry titles 2000, 2 poetry titles 2001. size varies; avg. price, cloth: $15.95. 40pp; Publishes 1% of poetry manuscripts submitted. Reporting time: 3 months (hopefully). Payment: 5% of 10%. Interested in new or unpub'd poets: no. Simultaneous submissions accepted: no. Recently published poets: Edna St. Vincent Millay, XJ Kennedy, Herman Melville, Nancy White Carlstrom, Langston Hughes. Submission quantity: 25 poems in focused topic form.

Phony Lid Publications (see also PICK POCKET BOOKS), PO Box 2153, Rosemead, CA 91770, e-mail phonylid@fyuocuk.com, www.fyuocuk.com. Teresa Turner. Address poetry submissions to: PO Box 3441, Quartz Hill, CA 93586. 1998. avg. press run 100. Pub'd 12 poetry titles 1999; expects 6 poetry titles 2000, 6 poetry titles 2001. 5½×4¼; avg. price, paper: $3. 24pp; Publishes 5% of poetry manuscripts submitted. Reporting time: 2 months. Payment: 25% print run. Interested in new or unpub'd poets: yes. Simultaneous submissions accepted: no. Recently published poets: Todd Moore, Stan Coldrum, David Rowe, Joy Lustig, Trey Pool. Submission quantity: 5.

●Piano Press, PO Box 85, Del Mar, CA 92014-0085, pianopress@aol.com, www.pianopress.iuma.com. Elizabeth C. Axford, M.A. 1999. "'The Art of Music' Annual Writing Contest includes poetry, deadline June 30th, SASE for entry form and contest rules, winning poems published in annual anthology, winners receive 5 copies of chapbook and a medal." avg. press run 500-1M. Expects 1 poetry title 2000, 1 poetry title 2001. 8½×11; avg. price, paper: $9.95. 60-100pp; Reporting time: 3 months. Payment: 5 copies of chapbook. Interested in new or unpub'd poets: yes. Simultaneous submissions accepted: yes. Recently published poets: Elizabeth C. Axford, Katherine Dines. Submission quantity: 1-3. Special interests: Music-related poetry only.

Picaro Press, 272 Road 6Rt, Cody, WY 82414, www.picaro.com. 1998.

PICK POCKET BOOKS, Phony Lid Publications, PO Box 2153, Rosemead, CA 91770, e-mail phonylid@fyuocuk.com, www.fyuocuk.com. Teresa Turner. Address poetry submissions to: PO Box 3441, Quartz Hill, CA 93586. 1998. "Disposable verse, adventures from the edge, frenzies of vice and other tales of degradation'' circ. 500. 2/yr. Pub'd 50+ poems 1999; expects 50+ poems 2000, 50+ poems 2001. sub. price: none; sample: $3 previous, $5 current. 36pp; 5½×4¼; Rights purchased: first serial. Publishes 5% of poems submitted. Deadlines: none. Reporting time: 2 months. Payment: copies. Interested in new or unpub'd poets: yes. Simultaneous submissions accepted: no! Recent contributors: Alan Catlin, C. Mulrooney, Errol Miller, Todd Moore, Marie Kazalia. Submission quantity: up to 5.

PIG IRON, Pig Iron Press, 26 North Phelps Street, PO Box 237, Youngstown, OH 44501, 216-747-6932; fax 216-747-0599. Jim Villani. 1974. "Send SASE for current theme and deadline." circ. 1M. 1/yr. Pub'd 50 poems 1999; expects 150 poems 2000, 100 poems 2001. sub. price: $12.95; sample: $6. 128pp; 8½×11; Rights purchased: 1st serial. Publishes 2% of poems submitted. Deadlines: continuing. Reporting time: 6 months. Payment: $5/poem. Interested in new or unpub'd poets: yes. Simultaneous submissions accepted: no. Recent contributors: Tod Gilmartin, Juanita Hall, Frank Polite, George Peffer, Nancy Bizzari. Submission quantity: 5. Special interests: 1995—The Family: Tradition and Potential; 1996—Jazz Tradition; 1997—Frontier: Custom and Archetype; 1998—Years of Rage: 1960s.

Pig Iron Press (see also PIG IRON), 26 North Phelps Street, PO Box 237, Youngstown, OH 44501, 216-747-6932; fax 216-747-0599. Jim Villani. 1974. "Sponsors the Kenneth Patchen Competition. Awards, bi-annually, to the selected poetry ms., paperback publication. Reading fee: $10." avg. press run 1M. Pub'd 1 poetry title 1999; expects 2 poetry titles 2000, 2 poetry titles 2001. 5½×8½; avg. price, paper: $12.95. 80pp; Publishes 2% of poetry manuscripts submitted. Reporting time: 6 months. Payment: 10%; no advance; report annually. Interested in new or unpub'd poets: no. Simultaneous submissions accepted: no. Recently published poets: Tom Gilmartin, Juanita Hall, Frank Polite, George Peffer, Nancy Bizzari. Submission quantity: 5.

PIKEVILLE REVIEW, Humanities Department, Pikeville College, Pikeville, KY 41501, 606-432-9612. Elgin M. Ward, Editor. 1987. circ. 500. 1/yr. Pub'd 25 poems 1999. sub. price: $4; sample: $3. 112pp; 5½×8½; Rights purchased: 1st Serial. Publishes 10% of poems submitted. Deadlines: March 31. Reporting time: 4 months. Payment: copies. Interested in new or unpub'd poets: yes. Simultaneous submissions accepted: no. Recent contributors: Michelle Bouisseau, Naton Leslie, Simon Perchik, Jim Wayne Miller, Karl Patten. Submission quantity: 3-5.

Pinched Nerves Press, 1610 Avenue P, Apt. 6-B, Brooklyn, NY 11229. 1989. 4¼×11.

Pinchgut Press, 6 Oaks Avenue, Cremorne, Sydney, N.S.W. 2090, Australia, 02-9908-2402. Marjorie Pizer. 1948. "Australian poems." avg. press run 500. Pub'd 1 poetry title 1999; expects 1 poetry title 2000, 1 poetry title 2001. avg. price, paper: $8-$17 Aust. 32-87pp; Publishes a very small % of poetry manuscripts submitted. Reporting time: fairly immediate. Payment: 10% retail price. Interested in new or unpub'd poets: not at the moment.

PINE ISLAND JOURNAL OF NEW ENGLAND POETRY, PO Box 317, West Springfield, MA 01090. Linda Porter, Editor. 1998. "Cover letter with bio. preferred with first-time submissions. Limited to poets currently residenced in New England. Up to 30 lines, haiku and other forms welcome, no horror, no erotica, no previously published material" circ. 200. 2/yr. Pub'd 87 poems 1999; expects 100 poems 2000, 100 poems 2001. sub. price: $10; sample: $5. 45pp; 5½×8; Rights purchased: First rights only, rights revert to author. Publishes 20% of poems submitted. Deadlines: reading is ongoing, please be sure that seasonal subjects are submitted *before* the season covered. Reporting time: 2-4 weeks. Payment: $1 per poem, plus 1 copy. Interested in new or unpub'd poets: yes. Simultaneous submissions accepted: no. Recent contributors: Doug Holder, Evelyn Lang, Larry Kimmel, Carol Purington, John Tagliabus. Submission quantity: 3-5.

PINYON POETRY, Dept. of Languages, Lit., & Comm., Mesa State College, 1100 North Ave., Grand Junction, CO 81502-2647, 970-248-1740. Randy Phillis, Al Learst. 1996. "Name and address on each poem. We read slower in the summer. Each issue we run 8-12 pages of a featured poet." circ. 200. 2/yr. Pub'd 100 poems 1999. sub. price: $8; sample: $3.50. 48pp; 5½×8½; Publishes 5% of poems submitted. Deadlines: none. Reporting time: 8-12 weeks, slower in summer. Payment: copies. Interested in new or unpub'd poets: yes. Simultaneous submissions accepted: no. Recent contributors: Mark Cox, Barry Spacks, H.A. Maxson, Wendy Bishop, Marjorie Maddox. Submission quantity: 3-5. Special interests: No bias other than quality, though we appreciate a strong voice.

THE PIPE SMOKER'S EPHEMERIS, 20-37 120th Street, College Point, NY 11356-2128. Tom Dunn, Editor. 1964. circ. 5M. 2/yr. Expects 20-25 poems 2000. 100pp; 8½×11; Rights purchased: none. Publishes 75% of poems submitted. Reporting time: immediately. Payment: copies of journal. Interested in new or unpub'd poets: yes. Simultaneous submissions accepted: yes. Submission quantity: no limit. Special interests: Looking for poetry related to pipes, pipe smoking, cigars, tobacco.

Pittore Euforico (see also ME MAGAZINE), PO Box 182, Bowdoinham, ME 04008, 207-666-8453. Carlo Pittore. 1978. "I only publish friends, when we CLICK. The poem must connect with me. They must come in and hit me. No guaranteed response without SASE." avg. press run 1M-2M. Pub'd 1 poetry title 1999. 8½×11.

Publishes 1% of poetry manuscripts submitted. Interested in new or unpub'd poets: yes, absolutely & preferably. Simultaneous submissions accepted: sure. Recently published poets: Bern Porter, Mark Melnicove, Roland Legiardi-Laura, Carlo Pittore, Steve Petroff. Submission quantity: 1-10. Special interests: Poems should be about *ME*—if for ME Magazine, but I might publish anything that overwhelms me.

The Place In The Woods (see also READ, AMERICA!), 3900 Glenwood Avenue, Golden Valley, MN 55422, 612-374-2120. Roger Hammer, Editor and Publisher. 1980. "Material can be exotic, not erotic. Free verse is fine. Writers 'into' their feelings to the exclusion of others need not submit" avg. press run 100. Pub'd 1 poetry title 1999; expects 2 poetry titles 2000, 2 poetry titles 2001. 8½x11; avg. price, cloth: $20; paper: $10. 80-100pp; Publishes 10% of poetry manuscripts submitted. Reporting time: 1 week to 1 month. Payment: buy all rights, royalty with each printing. Interested in new or unpub'd poets: yes (w/SASE). Simultaneous submissions accepted: no. Recently published poets: Donna Bauman, Kathryn Smitley. Submission quantity: 3. Special interests: Minority (any special cultural group - disabled, teen-age, prison, refugee, Asian, teacher) writing that communicates on issues of importance to the minority and the 'mainstream' culture, using poetry as both an art form and communications tool for better understanding and empathy.

PLAIN BROWN WRAPPER (PBW), 130 West Limestone, Yellow Springs, OH 45387, 513-767-7416. 1988. "Poems sent on a floppy disc in MacWrite will get special treatment." circ. 80 + several computer bulletin boards. 4/yr. Pub'd 3-400 poems 1999. 5-600pp; Rights purchased: none. Publishes 50% of poems submitted. Deadlines: May 1, August 1, November 1, February 1. Reporting time: 1-2 weeks. Payment: none, free copy. Interested in new or unpub'd poets: somewhat. Simultaneous submissions accepted: yes. Recent contributors: Cheryl Townsend, Marie Markoe, Lyn Lifshin, Danielle Willis, Marion Cohen. Submission quantity: 5 or 6. Special interests: I will print anything I consider to be first-rate.

Plain View Press, Inc., PO Box 33311, Austin, TX 78764, (512) 441-2452. Susan Bright. 1976. "We do not solicit manuscripts" avg. press run 2M. Pub'd 7 poetry titles 1999; expects 7 poetry titles 2000, 7 poetry titles 2001. size varies; avg. price, paper: $12.95. Pages vary; Reporting time: varies. Payment: varies. Interested in new or unpub'd poets: no. Simultaneous submissions accepted: yes. Recently published poets: Karla Andersdatter, Margo La Gattutaca, Lee Meitzen Grue, Betty Sue Flowers, Susan Bright. Submission quantity: 10. Special interests: We publish poetry, prose, and some non-fiction by women and literary work by men that is of interest to us.

THE PLASTIC TOWER, PO Box 702, Bowie, MD 20718. Carol Dyer, Roger Kyle-Keith. 1989. "We like all styles and subjects - there are no taboos! Also looking for artwork and freelance reviews" circ. 200. 4/yr. Pub'd 150 poems 1999; expects 150 poems 2000, 150 poems 2001. sub. price: $8; sample: $2.50. 48pp; 5½x8½; Rights purchased: 1st Serial. Publishes 5% of poems submitted. Reporting time: 5 months. Payment: copies. Interested in new or unpub'd poets: yes. Simultaneous submissions accepted: yes. Submission quantity: 3-5.

Playground Books, 26 Fox Hunt Drive #190, Bear, DE 19701-2534. 1994.

PLEASANT LIVING, Brandylane Publishers, PO Box 261, White Stone, VA 22578, 804-435-6900. 1989. circ. 15M. 6/yr. sub. price: $15; sample: free. 40pp; 8½x11.

Pleasure Boat Studio, 8630 NE Wardwell Road, Bainbridge Island, WA 98110-1589, 360-452-8686 tel/fax, email pbstudio@pbstudio.com, www.pbstudio.com. Jack Estes. 1996. "Pleasure Boat Studio is a publisher, in trade paperback editions, of the best poetry, fiction, and non-fiction (in English language original and translation) that it can find." avg. press run 1M-3M. Pub'd 2 poetry titles 1999; expects 2 poetry titles 2000, 2 poetry titles 2001. 6x9, 5½x8½; avg. price, paper: $12.95. 36-104pp; Pleasure Boat Studio is a small press. Chances of publication with us are correspondingly small. Reporting time: 2 months to query, 2 months to manuscript, if invited. Payment: standard royalty contract. Interested in new or unpub'd poets: Yes, but their work will have to compete with the work of the poets who have published widely and well. Simultaneous submissions accepted: We'd rather not. Recently published poets: William Slaughter, Frances Driscoll, Michael Daley, Edward Harkness. Submission quantity: Query with sample (6-12 poems) and cover letter. But read what we publish before doing so. Special interests: Contemporary poetry, free verse, open form.

Pleasure Dome Press (Long Island Poetry Collective Inc.) (see also XANADU), Box 773, Huntington, NY 11743. 1976. size varies.

PLEIADES MAGAZINE-Philae-Epic Journal-Thoughts Journal, Box 357, 6677 W. Colfax Avenue, Suite D, Lakewood, CO 80214, 303-237-1019. 1983; Philae founded 1947; Thoughts Magazine 1996. "*Pleiades* usually gives helpful suggestions on the art of writing poetry, with listed examples, and reference material." circ. 1.2M. 2/yr. Pub'd 45-30 poems 1999. sub. price: $9; sample: $3. 75pp; 8½x11; Rights purchased: rights remain with author. Publishes 60% of poems submitted. Deadlines: Sept. (for Fall-Winter Issue), April (for Spring-Summer Issue). Reporting time: 2 weeks. Payment: copies & trophies (sometime cash). Interested in new or unpub'd poets: yes. Simultaneous submissions accepted: no. Recent contributors: Rochelle, Morgan, Lucas, Livingston, Zapletal, numerous others. Submission quantity: 2. Special interests: Poets are asked to define poetry from prose and verse. We ask you to indicate what your efforts are. Many persons write what they call poetry, when in reality it is nothing more than an attempt at letter writing.

Plinth Books, Box 271118, W. Hartford, CT 06127-1118. James Finngan. 1995. "Query first w/short sample of book" avg. press run 500. Expects 2 poetry titles 2000, 3 poetry titles 2001. 6×9; avg. price, cloth: $22; paper: $12. 72pp; Publishes 1% of poetry manuscripts submitted. Reporting time: 3. Interested in new or unpub'd poets: yes, but query first. Simultaneous submissions accepted: yes, but query first. Submission quantity: 10-12pp.

PLOPLOP, Geekspeak Unique Press, PO Box 11443, Indianapolis, IN 46201, 317-630-9216. John Clark, Editor; Kit Andis, Contributing Editor; Deborah Sellers, Co-Editor. 1991. "Upcoming issues on Max Ernst, Kenneth Patchen, Henry Miller" circ. 300-500. 2/yr. sub. price: $10; sample: $4. 50pp; 8½×11; Rights purchased: none. Reporting time: 2-8 weeks. Payment: copy. Interested in new or unpub'd poets: yes. Simultaneous submissions accepted: yes. Recent contributors: Wanda Coleman, Antler, Richard Kostelanetz, Kit Andis, Hal Sirowitz. Special interests: Beat, DADA, Surrealisme, Outsider, Art Brut, Auant-Garde, Experimental, Andy Kaufman, Automatic, Spontaneous.

PLOUGHSHARES, Emerson College, 100 Beacon Street, Boston, MA 02116, 617-824-8753. David Daniel, Poetry Editor. 1971. "In the past we announced specific themes, but we no longer restrict submissions to thematic topics. Read an issue or two before submitting" circ. 6M. 3/yr. Pub'd 120 poems 1999; expects 120 poems 2000, 120 poems 2001. sub. price: $21/3 issues (domestic), $26/3 issues (foreign); $24/3 issues (institutional) Add $5/yr for international.; sample: $8. 224pp; 5½×8½; Rights purchased: 1st American serial. Publishes 1% of poems submitted. Deadlines: August 1 to March 31 (postmark dates). Reporting time: 3-5 months. Payment: $50/per poem minimum, $25/page per poem; $250 max per author. Interested in new or unpub'd poets: yes. Simultaneous submissions accepted: yes. Recent contributors: Charles Simic, George Starbuck, Al Young, Ellen Bryant Voigt, Frank Bidart. Submission quantity: 1-3.

THE PLOWMAN, Box 414, Whitby, Ontario L1N 5S4, Canada, 905-668-7803. Tony Scavetta. 1988. circ. 15M. 2/yr. Pub'd 400 poems 1999; expects 350 poems 2000, 350 poems 2001. sub. price: $10; sample: free. 20pp; tabloid; Rights purchased: none. Publishes 75% of poems submitted. Reporting time: 1 week. Payment: 20% royalties. Interested in new or unpub'd poets: yes. Simultaneous submissions accepted: yes. Recent contributors: J.C. Mastor, E.E. Martin, A. Cook, J. Binns, S. Cunningham, M. Hoffman. Submission quantity: 5.

Pluma Productions, 1977 Carmen Avenue, Los Angeles, CA 90068, email pluma@earthlink.net. 1992. 5½×8½.

PLUME, 15 Bolehill Park, Hove Edge, Brighouse, W. Yorks HD6 2RS, England, 01484-717808; email plumelit@aol.com or literature@plume.fsbusiness.co.uk. Steve Hobson. 1996. "Annual competition, closing date Feb. 1st, details supplied on receipt of SAE/IRC" circ. 200. 2/yr. sub. price: £6.50 (+ £.50 p/h); sample: £2 + £.50 p/h. 50pp; 5¾×8¼; Rights purchased: 1st Brit. serial. Publishes 10% of poems submitted. Reporting time: 6 weeks. Payment: negotiable. Interested in new or unpub'd poets: yes. Simultaneous submissions accepted: no. Recent contributors: Tessa Biddington, Brendan McMahon, Lee Grenfell. Submission quantity: 4 maximum. Special interests: Magazine mainly in English language, but submissions in French welcomed.

Pocahontas Press, Inc., PO Drawer F, Blacksburg, VA 24063-1020, 703-951-0467; 800-446-0467. Mary C. Holliman, President. 1984. "At this time we are doing only books, not magazines or newsletters" avg. press run 500. Pub'd 1 poetry title 1999; expects 1 poetry title 2000, 1 poetry title 2001. 5½×8½; avg. price, paper: $5.95. 80pp; Publishes 10% or less of poems submitted. Reporting time: 6 weeks to 3 months. Payment: 10% royalty, no advance. Interested in new or unpub'd poets: yes, in future but am currently over-extended. Simultaneous submissions accepted: yes, but I prefer to know that fact on submission, and will wait on other publishers' decision before making my own. Recently published poets: Cecil J. Mullins, Mildred Nash, Sedney Farr, Elaine Emans, Rita Riddle. Submission quantity: 3-5. Special interests: Spanish translations (I would publish in both languages), Chinese; Appalachian or Northeast regions—especially but not limited to those. Poetry is a sideline to my publications for young adults, and the histories and memories for adults.

POEM, Huntsville Literary Association, c/o English Department, University of Alabama, Huntsville, AL 35899. Nancy F. Dillard, Editor; Olga Lavan, Assistant Editor. 1967. "In continuous publication since 1967, *Poem* welcomes all submissions of good poetry. We are open to traditional as well as non-traditional forms and we have no bias as to length so long as the work has the expected compression and intensity of good poetry. We have no bias as to subject matter or theme; however, we generally favor poems that are about inspired sentiments earned from within the poem itself. We favor poems that have a high degree of verbal and dramatic tension, and that transpire from the particular to the universal. We welcome equally submissions from established poets as well as from less known and beginning poets. We do not accept translations or previously published works, nor do we consider simultaneous submissions. We have no requirements as to format, except that we prefer to see a sample of three to five poems at a submission and we require that all submissions be accompanied by a self-addressed, stamped envelope for response or return of manuscript. We generally respond within a month. We are a non-profitmaking organization and can pay only in copy to contributors. Sample copies are available at $5. Thank you for your interest.'' circ. 500. 2/yr. Pub'd 180 poems 1999; expects 180 poems 2000, 180 poems 2001. sub. price: $15; sample: $5. 70pp; 4½×7⅓; Rights purchased: copyright reverts. Publishes 10% of poems submitted. Reporting time: 1 month. Payment: copy. Interested in new or unpub'd poets: yes. Simultaneous submissions accepted: no. Recent contributors: Ronald Wallace, Mordecai Marcus, Michael McFee, Stephen Lang, Charles Edward Eaton. Submission quantity: 3-5. Special interests: Do not publish translations, prose poems.

POEMS & PLAYS, Department of English, Middle Tennessee State University, Murfreesboro, TN 37132, 615-898-2712. Gaylord Brewer, Editor. 1993. ''We read Oct 1.-Jan. 15 for spring issue. To enter the Tennessee Chapbook Prize, send 20-24 pages with SASE and $10 (for reading fee and copy of next issue)'' circ. 750. 1/yr. Pub'd 40 poems 1999; expects 40 poems 2000, 40 poems 2001. sub. price: $10/2 issues; sample: $6. 80+pp; 6×9; Rights purchased: 1st publication. Publishes 2-3% of poems submitted. Deadlines: Jan. 15. Reporting time: 1-2 months. Payment: 1 copy. Interested in new or unpub'd poets: yes. Recent contributors: Charles Bukowski, Stephen Dobyns, David Kirby, Vivian Shipley, Billy Collins. Submission quantity: 4-6 for regular submission; 20-24 pages for chapbook contest ($10 fee).

POEMS THAT THUMP IN THE DARK/SECOND GLANCE, New Spirit Press/The Poet Tree, 82-34 138 Street #6F, Kew Gardens, NY 11435, 718-847-1482. 1993. circ. 500. 2/yr. sub. price: $20; sample: $6. 72pp; 5½×8½.

POET LORE, The Writer's Center, 4508 Walsh Street, Bethesda, MD 20815-6006, 301-654-8664. Elizabeth Poliner, Executive Editor; Geraldine Connolly, Executive Editor. 1889. ''John Williams Andrews Narrative Poetry Contest—annual, $350 first prize. Rose Lefcowitz Prizes—annual, awarded to the best poem and best critical prose to appear in a volume of the magazine, $150 each.'' circ. 650. 4/yr. Pub'd 120 poems 1999; expects 120 poems 2000, 120 poems 2001. sub. price: $15 indiv., $24 instit.; sample: $4. 80pp; 6×9; Rights purchased: 1st serial. Publishes 10% of poems submitted. Deadlines: none. Reporting time: 12 weeks. Payment: 2 copies. Interested in new or unpub'd poets: yes. Simultaneous submissions accepted: no. Recent contributors: Walter McDonald, Yehuda Amichai, Enid Shomer, Cornelius Eady, Linda Pastan. Submission quantity: 3-5. Special interests: *Poet Lore* publishes original poems of all kinds. The editors continue to welcome narrative poetry and original translations of works by contemporary world poets. *Poet Lore* also publishes reviews of poetry collections. Typewritten, double-spaced manuscripts are requested. The name and address of the author should appear on each page, and a self-addressed, stamped envelope should be included with each group of submissions.

POETALK, Bay Area Poets Coalition, PO Box 11435, Berkeley, CA 94712-2435, 510-272-9176. Dale Hermann. 1974. ''We often publish one poem from each new contributor, but you must show some effort and talent. We may suggest revisions—if you do not want us to do that, *say so in a cover letter with each submission. Enclose SASE for return or comments, SASP for immediate response. We cannot tell you the status of your submission until the next meeting of our quarterly Editorial Board, so be patient. We try to both encourage and maintain high quality. Yearly contest & rules advertised in the Fall. Note: you do not have to be a member or subscriber to submit poetry. Place name and address on every sheet''* circ. 500. 6/yr. Pub'd 600 poems 1999; expects 600 poems 2000, 600 poems 2001. sub. price: $15 membership (includes yearly anthology); $6 subscription (write for foreign rates); sample: free (SASE, business size) 54¢ postage required. 24pp; 7×8½ (folded, printed both sides); Rights purchased: none. Publishes 20-30% of poems submitted. Deadlines: read all year; Editorial Board meets 6 times yearly. Reporting time: 2-4 months. Payment: copy of issue with their poem. Interested in new or unpub'd poets: absolutely. Simultaneous submissions accepted: yes, also works previously published—give us credit-line for prior publisher so we can print it. Recent contributors: Selima Soss, M.P.A. Shaffer, Tim Nuveen, Victor Claude Pirtle, Robert C. Boyce. Submission quantity: Open; not accepted without SASE with sufficient postage. Special interests: Prefer free verse, but would welcome well-done rhyme and blank verse; no pre-20th-century language or syntax. Have occasionally published poems in two languages, one of which must be English.

Poetic License Press, PO Box 85525, Westland, MI 48185-0525, 734-326-9368; FAX 734-326-3480; e-mail steveblo30@aol.com. Carol A. Belding, Owner; Editor. 1996. ''Policy on poetry subject submissions. PLP will publish poetry of all subject matter, with the exception of anything we determine (in our sole discretion) to be unacceptable.'' avg. press run 250. Pub'd 1 poetry title 1999; expects 1 poetry title 2000, 2 poetry titles 2001. 5½×8½; avg. price, paper: $6. 50pp; Publishes 10% of poetry manuscripts submitted. Payment: Pre press work-authors have sole ownership. If we publish, royalty & payment arrangements are set on an individual basis. Interested in new or unpub'd poets: Always include SASE, submissions cannot be returned without SASE. Simultaneous submissions accepted: yes. Submission quantity: 1-5.

Poetic Page (see also OPUS LITERARY REVIEW), PO Box 71192, Madison Heights, MI 48071-0192, 313-548-0865. Denise Martinson. 1989. ''We will read manuscripts. Poets *MUST* send SASE. We also have bi-monthly contests—winners appear inside. (Most books are invitational.)" avg. press run unlimited. Expects 5+ poetry titles 2000, 4+ poetry titles 2001. avg. price, paper: $6. 40pp; Reporting time: on request. Payment: no longer give royalties. Simultaneous submissions accepted: yes. Recently published poets: Alice Mackenzie-Swaim, Marian Ford Park, Phil Eisenberg, Patricia Lawrence, Lyn Lifshin. Submission quantity: 6-10, to see what type and style they do. Special interests: Prefer well-written poetry only.

POETIC SPACE: Poetry & Fiction, PO Box 11157, Eugene, OR 97440. Don Hildenbrand, Editor; Thomas Strand, Fiction Editor. 1983. "Prefer original, fresh work-non-traditional. SASE necessary, name & address on each page, no sloppy manuscripts." circ. 500-600. 2/yr plus one chapbook (poetry and fiction). Pub'd 100 poems 1999; expects 100 poems 2000, 100+ poems 2001. sub. price: $7/2 issues, $13.50/4 issues, $5 anthology, 1987-1991; sample: $3. 30-40pp; 8½×11; Rights purchased: rights revert to writer after publication, reserve right to publish in Poetic Space Anthology. Publishes 15% of poems submitted. Deadlines: none. Reporting time: 1-3 months. Payment: 1 copy + more, if postage paid (limit 3). Interested in new or unpub'd poets: yes. Simultaneous submissions accepted: no. Recent contributors: Albert Huffsticklen, Paul Weinman, Lyn Lifshin, Simon Perchik, Sherman Alexie. Submission quantity: 6-8. Special interests: Latin American Poetry, Native American Poetry, Poetry of Political and Social Protest, poetry in translation, feminist, gay.

Poetical Histories, 27 Sturton Street, Cambridge CB1 2QG, United Kingdom, 0223-327455. Peter Riley. 1986. "I normally publish only British modernist texts." avg. press run 150-200. Pub'd 6 poetry titles 1999; expects 6 poetry titles 2000, 6 poetry titles 2001. octavo; avg. price, paper: £3.50. 8pp; Publishes 10% of poetry manuscripts submitted. Reporting time: 2 weeks. Payment: none. Interested in new or unpub'd poets: write first with example. Recently published poets: J.H. Prynne, Nicholas Moore, John James, Denise Riley.

POETRY, 60 West Walton Street, Chicago, IL 60610, 312-255-3703. Joseph Parisi, Editor. 1912. "*Poetry* has no special manuscript needs, no special requirements as to form or genre; we examine in turn all work received and accept that which seems best. We can accept nothing which has been previously published or accepted for publication, anywhere, in any form, either in this country or abroad. We regret that the size of our staff does not permit us to give individual criticism. Submissions should be limited to four poems or fewer, typed single spaced. Manuscripts are usually reported on within twelve weeks from the day of receipt. All manuscripts must be accompanied by a stamped, self-addressed envelope. Stamps alone are not sufficient. Writers living abroad must enclose a self-addressed envelope together with enough postage in international reply coupons for at least sea mail return. Manuscripts should contain the author's name and address on every page. Payment is made on publication at the rate of $2 per line. *Poetry* is copyrighted for the protection of its contributors. The author, the author's agents or heirs, and no one else, will be given transfer of copyright when they request it for purposes of republication in book form. Several prizes, awarded annually, are announced every November for the best verse printed in *Poetry* during the preceding year. Only verse already published is eligible for consideration and no formal application is necessary. The Modern Poetry Association is the non-profit corporation which publishes *Poetry*. All contributions to the Association are deductible for income tax purposes." circ. 8M. 12/yr. Pub'd 311 poems 1999; expects 300 poems 2000, 300 poems 2001. sub. price: individuals $30, $38 outside USA; institutions $33, $41 outside USA; sample: $3.50 plus $1.50 postage. 64pp; 5½×9; Rights purchased: copyright is returned to the author on request. Publishes less than 1% of poems submitted. Deadlines: none, poems are considered throughout the year. Reporting time: 12 weeks. Payment: $2 per line on publication. Interested in new or unpub'd poets: yes. Simultaneous submissions accepted: no. Recent contributors: W.S. Merwin, Gary Soto, Adrienne Rich, A.R. Ammons, Mona Van Duyn. Submission quantity: 4 or fewer.

POETRY AND AUDIENCE, School of English, Cavendish Road, University of Leeds, Leeds Yorkshire, LS2 9JT, England. M. Tranter, A. Goody. 1953. "The magazine has a history of publishing established poets alongside the best of new poetry received. We read and select 2 months before publishing date, i.e. October and April each year" circ. 400+. 2/yr. Pub'd 60 poems 1999; expects 60 poems 2000, 60 poems 2001. sub. price: overseas £3 per issue, inland £1.50/issue; sample: £2 + 25% p/p. 32-52pp; quarto; Rights purchased: none. Publishes 15% of poems submitted. Deadlines: April/October. Reporting time: 1 month. Payment: none. Interested in new or unpub'd poets: yes. Simultaneous submissions accepted: no. Recent contributors: Carol Ann Duffy, Ian Duhig, Mark Jarman. Submission quantity: 2-4. Special interests: Short lyric, translations, prose poems, satire, black humour and creative writing in any genre.

•POETRY & PROSE ANNUAL, PO Box 541, Manzanita, OR 97130, www.poetryproseannual.com. Sandra Claire Foushee, Editor. 1996. circ. 1M. 1/yr. sub. price: $15. 88pp; 7×8½; Rights purchased: First & Second, then rights revert to author. Publishes a variable % of poems submitted. Deadlines: March 21. Reporting time: 6 weeks - 6 months. Payment: 2 copies. Interested in new or unpub'd poets: yes. Simultaneous submissions accepted: if notified should the poem be accepted elsewhere. Recent contributors: Mary Crow, Carlos Reyes, Renate Wood, Mary Legato Brownell, Tom Crawford. Submission quantity: 200 lines.

The Poetry Connection (see also THE POETRY CONNECTION), 13455 SW 16 Court #F-405, Pembroke Pines, FL 33027, 954-431-3016. 1988. "Chapbook publishing/Greeting card directory. Magic Circle (poetry/reading/publicity/distribution service)" Special interests: Magic Circle (publicity/distribution service).

THE POETRY CONNECTION, The Poetry Connection, 13455 SW 16 Court #F-405, Pembroke Pines, FL 33027, 305-431-3016. Sylvia Shichman, Editor, Publisher & Director. 1988. *"The Poetry Connection* is a monthly newsletter in flyer format and service...whereby poetry, songwriting, greeting card and performing artists publications/organizations listings and contests and poetry flyers are distributed to editors and publishers...helping poets to get published. Provides assistance in getting poetry published...plus info on writing for greeting card companies...plus info on poetry contests with cash awards! (Large SASE info)! *The Poety Connection* has a huge active mailing list of poets, writers, and songwriters of about 10,000 names and more...available for rental! *The Magic Circle* is a publicity/distribution service...wherby a bio and one poem is sent directly to editors and publishers... helping poets to get published. Please enclose a large SASE for information. Sample issue...$7/1 year membership is $20. A 1 year membership for *The Magic Circle* is $30 (50 copies) or $60 (100 copies). Please make all checks payable to: Sylvia Shichman, Editor!" 12/yr. sub. price: $20 Poetry Connection, $30 Magic Circle (50 copies), $60 combined service (100 copies); sample: (Sample - $5) plus $2 for postage. 8½x11; Special interests: All kinds of poetry.

●**THE POETRY CONSPIRACY**, PO Box 818, Cardiff, CA 92007. 1979. "We do not accept poetry via Fax or e-mail." circ. 500. 11/yr. Pub'd 143 poems 1999; expects 143 poems 2000, 143 poems 2001. sub. price: $15; sample: $2. 16pp; 7x8½.

POETRY DEPTH QUARTERLY, 5836 North Haven Drive, North Highlands, CA 95660, 916-331-3512, e-mail poetdpth@aol.com, www.angelfire.com/biz/PoetsGuild/guide.html. 1995. "Cover letter *required* with short 3-10 line biography. All poems must be in English, typewritten and presented exactly as you would like them to appear. Due to the page size, only 52 characters will fit across the page, including spaces. Poems of any length are considered, but each work must be the original property of the submitting poet. Your name and address must appear on each page submitted. For non e-mail submissions: include an SASE. Publication sponsors an annual Open Poetry Contest (with multiple winners)." circ. 200. 4/yr. sub. price: $18.50, $35/2 years, $45/3 years; add $10 a year for foreign postage or $2.50 per issue; sample: $5. 35-60pp; 5½x8½; Simultaneous submissions accepted: no. Recent contributors: Jane Blue, Taylor Graham, Simon Perchik, Ken Hoffman, Danyen Powell. Submission quantity: 3-5.

POETRY EAST, Dept. of English, DePaul Univ., 802 West Belden Avenue, Chicago, IL 60614, 312-325-7487. Richard Jones, Editor. 1980. "We suggest that authors request a sample copy ($8) before making submissions. We have no restrictions on the type of poetry or fiction that we publish. We have produced several theme issues in the past—among them, Political Poetry, Poetry and the Visual Arts, and recent American Surrealist Poetry." circ. 1.5M. 2/yr. Pub'd 150 poems 1999; expects 150 poems 2000, 150 poems 2001. sub. price: $20; sample: $8. 200pp for single issue, 300pp for double issue; 5½x8½; Rights purchased: we copyright every issue, rights revert to author upon publication. Publishes 5-15% of poems submitted. Deadlines: 6 months before publication of issue. Reporting time: 2-3 months. Payment: in author's copies. Interested in new or unpub'd poets: yes. Simultaneous submissions accepted: no. Recent contributors: Thomas McGrath, Gerald Stern, Mary Oliver, Cid Corman, Charles Bukowski. Submission quantity: 5-10. Special interests: *Poetry East* is especially interested in translations. In the past we have included features on Swedish, Finnish, French, and Italian poets. We are also interested in contemporary art.

THE POETRY EXPLOSION NEWSLETTER (THE PEN), PO Box 4725, Pittsburgh, PA 15206. Arthur C. Ford. 1985. "We use all subject matter except vulgarity. Guidelines must be adhered to." circ. 850. 4/yr. Pub'd 75 poems 1999; expects 80 poems 2000. sub. price: $20; sample: $4. 10-15pp; 8½x11; Rights purchased: one-time. Publishes 10-15% of poems submitted. Deadlines: 2 weeks prior to beginning of quarter (March, June, August, December). Reporting time: 2-4 weeks. Payment: copy. Interested in new or unpub'd poets: yes. Simultaneous submissions accepted: yes. Recent contributors: Floriana Hall, Rochelle H. Mehr, Bart Anello, Winnie Fitzpatrick, Dr. H. Graham. Submission quantity: 5 max. Special interests: We are versatile, poetry must be honest with a fresh approach to language usage!

POETRY FLASH, 1450 Fourth Street #4, Berkeley, CA 94710, 510-525-5476, Fax 510-525-6752. Joyce Jenkins, Editor; Richard Silberg, Associate Editor. 1972. "We seek quality and energy" circ. 22M. 6/yr. Pub'd 15 poems 1999; expects 20 poems 2000, 25 poems 2001. sub. price: $16 individuals, $16 institutions; sample: one copy (one time) free on request. 48pp; 11½x15, tabloid; Rights purchased: none, rights revert back to poet on publication. Publishes 2% of poems submitted. Deadlines: ongoing. Reporting time: 4 months. Payment: 2 year subscription. Interested in new or unpub'd poets: yes, but almost everything we have received from such poets is unpublishable or inappropriate for the *Poetry Flash*, we seek high quality submissions. Simultaneous submissions accepted: yes. Recent contributors: Dan Bellm, Bob Holman, Forrest Hamer, Linda McCarriston, Joanne Kyger. Submission quantity: 5 maximum. Special interests: We are interested in translations of poets who may be visiting the West from other countries. Contributors should realize that the *Poetry Flash* is primarily a review, and though we welcome poems, and have made a commitment to publish them, the fact that we publish fewer poems increases the competition. We would like to receive more high quality cutting-edge, experimental poems than we have in the past. Our perspective is Western, but our editorial allegiance is to poetry itself, not a geographical region.

Poetry Harbor (see also NORTH COAST REVIEW), PO Box 103, Duluth, MN 55801-0103. Patrick McKinnon, Ellie Schoenfeld, Liz Minette. 1992. "Query before sending. Include SASE" avg. press run 300. Expects 1 poetry title 2000, 1 poetry title 2001. 8½×7; avg. price, paper: $4.95. 28pp; Publishes 5% of poetry manuscripts submitted. Reporting time: 1-9 months. Payment: 50% discount + $100 honoraria. Interested in new or unpub'd poets: no. Simultaneous submissions accepted: no. Recently published poets: Warren Woessner, Nancy Fitzgerald, Francine Sterle. Submission quantity: query first. Special interests: Narrative imagist.

Poetry Ireland (see also POETRY IRELAND REVIEW), Bermingham Tower, Upper Yard, Dublin Castle, Dublin 2, Ireland. Biddy Jenkinson. 1981. "Always include an SASE or IRC" avg. press run 1.1M. Pub'd 4 poetry titles 1999; expects 4 poetry titles 2000, 4 poetry titles 2001. 6×8; avg. price, paper: US$8 + pp; other: IR £5.99. 136pp; Publishes 5%-10% of poetry manuscripts submitted. Reporting time: 3 months max. Payment: poets in complimentary copies, articles and reviews by arrangement IR £10 per contributor or 1 year subscription. Interested in new or unpub'd poets: yes. Simultaneous submissions accepted: no. Recently published poets: Ciaran Carson, Michael Longley, Tony Curtis, Nuela Ni Dhoruhnaill. Submission quantity: 3-5. Special interests: Lyric Poetry, Translation, Good Poetry!

POETRY IRELAND REVIEW, Poetry Ireland, Bermingham Tower, Upper yard, Dublin Castle, Dublin 2, Ireland, 6714632 + 353-1, fax 6714634 + 353-1. Biddy Jenkinson. 1981. "Essential to send SASE for return" circ. 1,100. 4/yr. Pub'd 300 poems 1999; expects 300 poems 2000, 300 poems 2001. sub. price: airmail IRT 44.00, US$70; surface IRT 24.00, US$50; sample: IR £5.99. 136pp; 6×8; Rights purchased: none. Publishes 10% of poems submitted. Deadlines: submissions accepted at anytime. Reporting time: 3 months max. Payment: IR £10 or 1 yrs subscription. Interested in new or unpub'd poets: yes. Simultaneous submissions accepted: no. Recent contributors: Seamus Heaney, Derek Mahon, Allen Ginsberg, Eavan Boland, Nuela NiDhomhnaill. Submission quantity: up to 6.

POETRY KANTO, Kanto Gakuin University, Kamariya Minami 3-22-1, Kanazawa-Ku, Yokohama 236-8502, Japan. William Elliott, Katsumasa Nishihara. 1984. "No pornography, usually poems up to 20-25 lines, *must submit SAE with postal reply coupons.*" circ. 700. 1/yr. Pub'd 50 poems 1999; expects 50 poems 2000, 50 poems 2001. 50-60pp; 7×10; Rights purchased: none. Publishes about 10% of poems submitted. Deadlines: we read all year, but prefer Nov-Feb, *query before submitting.* Reporting time: normally 1 month. Payment: 3 copies. Interested in new or unpub'd poets: yes. Simultaneous submissions accepted: no. Recent contributors: Nuala ni Dhomhnaill, W.D. Snodgrass, Michael Hamburger, Harry Guest, Christopher Middleton. Submission quantity: 3-5. Special interests: Some poems we solicit; others welcome. However, we distribute the magazine in connection with the annual Aug. Kanto Poetry Center Conference. *Special issues are common. Query first.*

THE POETRY MISCELLANY, English Dept. Univ of Tennessee, Chattanooga, TN 37403, 615-755-4213, 624-7279. Richard Jackson, Co-Editor; Michael Panori, Co-Editor; Richard Seehus, Assistant Editor. 1971. "Nothing special—summer is slower though. Send tranlations (with originals) to John DuVal, Translation Workshop, University of Arkansas, Fayetteville. We look at all types—I suppose the one question we ask, assuming first the language is interesting, is: 'What's at stake here?'" circ. 650. 1/yr. Pub'd 20 poems 1999; expects 20 poems 2000, 20 poems 2001. sub. price: $5; sample: $2. 12pp; tabloid; Rights purchased: rights revert to author on publication. Publishes 1% of poems submitted. Deadlines: none. Reporting time: 6 months. Payment: as grants allow. Interested in new or unpub'd poets: yes. Simultaneous submissions accepted: no. Recent contributors: William Matthews, Laura Jensen, Marvin Bell, Tomaz Salamun, Charles Simic. Submission quantity: 3-5.

POETRY MOTEL, Suburban Wilderness Press, PO Box 103, Duluth, MN 55801-0103. 1984. "Send your best stuff—we are eclectic in our taste and consider *everything*. Cover letter with a list of accomplishments is preferred. Urge you to sample an issue first, though" circ. 900. Published every 260 days. Pub'd 100 poems 1999; expects 100 poems 2000, 100 poems 2001. sub. price: $19.95/3 issues, $99 lifetime sub.; sample: $7.95. 52pp; 7×8½; Rights purchased: none. Percent of poems published varies. Deadlines: none. Reporting time: 1 week to never. Payment: varies. Interested in new or unpub'd poets: definitely. Simultaneous submissions accepted: sure. Recent contributors: Todd Moore, Julie Otten, Ron Androla, Patrick McKinnon, Tony Moffeit. Submission quantity: 3-5. Special interests: Narrative, imagistic, rhythmic.

POETRY NEW YORK: A Journal of Poetry and Translation, PO Box 3184, Church Street Station, New York, NY 10008. Burt Kimmelman, Tod Thilleman, Emmy Hunter. 1985. "We favor translations (submit with originals)" circ. 700. 1/yr. Pub'd 40 poems 1999. sample price: $7. 65pp; 6×9; Rights purchased: none. Publishes 5% of poems submitted. Deadlines: only submit between Sept. 1 thru May 1. Reporting time: 4 months. Payment: 1 copy. Interested in new or unpub'd poets: yes. Simultaneous submissions accepted: no. Recent contributors: Taggart, Heller, Weatherly, Amichai, Sanders. Submission quantity: 3-5. Special interests: Translations, experimental poetry.

161

POETRY NOTTINGHAM INTERNATIONAL, 71 Saxton Avenue, Heanor, Derbyshire DE75 7PZ, England. Cathy Grindrod. 1946. "Self-addressed envelope and 3 International Reply Coupons essential. The cost of the magazine in England is low, but the Bank charges £3 to exchange US dollars (charging the same to exchange 10 as 10,000). It would greatly assist the Editor if payment for single copies or yearly subscriptions could be made in sterling." circ. 300. 4/yr. Pub'd approx 480 poems 1999. sub. price: £17 sterling; sample: £2 sterling or $5 US. 56pp; 8¼×6; Rights purchased: none, poet retains copyright. Publishes 10% of poems submitted. Deadlines: none, submissions accepted at anytime. Reporting time: reply dispatched within 2 months; thereafter, allow time for mail to U.S.A. Payment: complimentary copy. Interested in new or unpub'd poets: yes. Simultaneous submissions accepted: no. Recent contributors: Leslie Palmer, GAy Brewer, Len Krisak, Ma Schaffner, Mary K. Herbert. Submission quantity: 5 or 6. Special interests: No long poems. Traditional forms accepted. Musical/rhythmic/lyrical literary qualities appreciated, also humour and a light touch with heavy issues.

POETRY NOW, Sacramento's Literary Calendar and Review, 1631 K Street, Sacramento, CA 95814, 916-441-7395, e-mail spc@quiknet.com, www.tomatoweb.com/spc. Heather Hutcheson, Managing Editor. 1994. "We are looking for fresh poems and have an annual contest. The deadline is typically Oct. 15th. Winners receive $100 and are published in *Poetry Now*" circ. 1500 + website. 12/yr. Pub'd 150-175 poems 1999. sub. price: $25; sample: $3. 8pp; 11×14; Rights purchased: none. Publishes 40% of poems submitted. Deadlines: on-going reading. Reporting time: 1-3 months. Payment: none. Interested in new or unpub'd poets: yes. Simultaneous submissions accepted: yes. Recent contributors: Joan Swift, Dan Bellm, Molly Fisk, Dennis Schmitz, Donna Hanelin. Submission quantity: 3-5.

POETRY NZ, 37 Margot Street, Epsom, Auckland 3, New Zealand, 64-9-524-5656. Alistair Paterson. 1990. "Each issue features 1 poet whose portrait appears on cover. *Poetry NZ* accepts new, unpublished work of the highest standard not only from established writers but also from talented new writers. Writers whose work is not accepted for publication *always* receive suggestions from the editor." circ. 1M. 2/yr. Pub'd 90 poems 1999; expects 92 poems 2000, 98 poems 2001. sub. price: $35, $16.50 US. 92pp; 6×8; Rights purchased: none. Publishes 10-12% of poems submitted. Deadlines: none. Reporting time: 4 weeks. Payment: NZ$25 per issue. Interested in new or unpub'd poets: yes. Simultaneous submissions accepted: no. Recent contributors: Wanda Coleman, Charles Bukowski, Kapka Kassabova, Tom Clark, Jan Kemp. Submission quantity: up to 20. Special interests: Translations, experimental poetry, regional poetry, longpoems, light verse, satire, etc.

The Poetry Project (see also THE POETRY PROJECT NEWSLETTER; THE WORLD), St. Mark's Church, 131 East 10th Street, New York, NY 10003, 212-674-0910, e-mail poproj@artomatic.com. Ed Friedman. 1966. "Most of our material is solicited" avg. press run 800. Pub'd 1 poetry title 1999; expects 1 poetry title 2000, 1 poetry title 2001. 6×9; avg. price, paper: $7. 130pp; Publishes 5% of poetry manuscripts submitted. Reporting time: 6 months. Payment: none. Simultaneous submissions accepted: no. Recently published poets: John Ashbery, Bernadette Mayer, Amiri Baraka, Alice Notley, John Yau. Submission quantity: 5 pages. Special interests: experimental poetry.

THE POETRY PROJECT NEWSLETTER, The Poetry Project, St. Mark's Church, 131 East 10th Street, New York, NY 10003, 212-674-0910, poproj@artomatic.com. 1966. circ. 4M. 5/yr. Pub'd 2 poems 1999; expects 2 poems 2000, 2 poems 2001. sub. price: $20; sample: $5. 32pp; 8½×11; Rights purchased: none. Publishes 2% of poems submitted. Payment: copies. Interested in new or unpub'd poets: no. Simultaneous submissions accepted: no. Recent contributors: Claudia Rankire, Prageeta Sharma, David Trinidad, Kimberly Lyons. Submission quantity: 5.

POETRY REVIEW, 22 Betterton Street, London WC2H 9BU, England. Peter Forbes. 1912. "Most issues have a theme but submissions needn't be tailored too closely to them" circ. 5M. 4/yr. Pub'd 100 poems 1999; expects 100 poems 2000, 100 poems 2001. sub. price: $56 individuals, $66 institutions, all airmail; sample: $10 surface, $15 airmail. 96pp; 240×170mm, copy size 198×147mm; Rights purchased: 1st U.K. serial rights. Publishes 1% of poems submitted. Deadlines: submissions accepted at anytime. Reporting time: up to 3 months. Payment: £40 per poem. Interested in new or unpub'd poets: yes, but previous study of *Poetry Review* is strongly advised. Simultaneous submissions accepted: no. Recent contributors: Mark Halliday, Billy Collins, James Tate, Carolyn Kizer, Mark Levine. Submission quantity: no more than 4. Special interests: Good fat poems preferred; short lines anathema.

POETRY USA, National Poetry Association Publishers, 934 Brannan Street, 2nd floor, San Francisco, CA 94103, 415-552-9261; FAX 415-552-9291; E-mail gamuse@slip.net, http://www.slip.net.gamuse. 1985. "Sample copies $4. Special sections: young people's poetry, poetry of the homeless, prison poetry." circ. 3M. 3-4/yr. Pub'd 350 poems 1999. sub. price: $10, $15 outside U.S.; sample: $4 ppd. 24-36pp; 11×17; Rights purchased: all rights revert to the author upon publication. Publishes 5% of poems submitted. Deadlines: March 21, June 21, Sept. 21, Dec. 21. Reporting time: 2-6 months. Payment: 2 copies. Interested in new or unpub'd poets: yes. Simultaneous submissions accepted: yes. Recent contributors: Anne Waldman, Ivan Arguelles, James Broughton, Diane di Prima, Jake Berry. Submission quantity: 3. Special interests: Submission: send no more than three poems, SASE, and e-mail address. *Poetry USA*, published by the National Poetry Association based in San Francisco, is a quarterly journal that aims to provide a common space for the diversity of voices that make up the American experience. Each issue usually includes poems from all over the country, and often includes sections from young people, poeple without a home, and people in prison. Our preference tends to be for shorter poems (under 50 lines, please) accessible to the non-literary general public. Poets from the community are invited to serve as guest editors, choosing different themes for each issue. *Poetry USA* was reorganizing during 1994 and 1995, and the summer 1996 issue marks the beginning of full output once again. The National Poetry Association, an all-volunteer organization founded in 1975, is committed to promoting the written, spoken and visual use of language in new and traditional ways.

POETRY WALES, Poetry Wales Press, Ltd., First Floor, 2 Wyndham Street, Bridgend, CF31 1EF, Wales. Robert Minhinnick. Address poetry submissions to: 11 Park Avenue, Porthcawl CF36 3EP, Wales. 1965. "Prefer typewritten submissions, accompanied by SAE if it's required to be returned." circ. 1M. 4/yr. Pub'd 200 poems 1999; expects 200 poems 2000, 200 poems 2001. sub. price: £18 (payment in sterling, or add $ equivalent of £s for bank charges); sample: £3 + postage. 72pp; 177×248mm; Publishes 5-10% of poems submitted. Reporting time: 1-2 months. Payment: by arrangement. Interested in new and unpub'd poets: yes. Simultaneous submissions accepted: no. Recent contributors: Dannie Abse, R.S. Thomas, J.P. Ward, Deryn Rees-Jones, Sheenagh Pugh. Submission quantity: 1-10. Special interests: Translations, regional poetry, longpoems, satire.

Poetry Wales Press, Ltd. (see also POETRY WALES), First Floor, 2 Wyndham Street, Bridgend CF31 1EF, Wales. Amy Wack, Mick Felton. 1981. "Submissions must be typed and accompanied by SAE if poet wishes it to be returned." Pub'd 6 poetry titles 1999; expects 8 poetry titles 2000, 6 poetry titles 2001. size varies; avg. price, cloth: £10.95; paper: £5.95. 64-120pp; Publishes 50% of poetry manuscripts submitted. Reporting time: 6 weeks. Payment: 10% royalty, 6 monthly. Interested in new or unpub'd poets: yes. Simultaneous submissions accepted: no. Recently published poets: Duncan Bush, Dannie Abse, Sheenagh Pugh, J.P. Ward, Tim Liardet. Submission quantity: 10-30. Special interests: Translations, experimental poetry, regional poetry, longpoems.

POETS AT WORK, Jessee Poet Publications, Box 113, VAMC, 325 New Castle Road, Butler, PA 16001. Jessee Poet. 1985. "Do include SASE; do keep submissions to 20 or fewer lines; continuous contest; some free, some 2 for a buck, some one buck." circ. 300+. 6/yr. Pub'd 1800 poems 1999. sub. price: $20; sample: $3.50. 36-40pp; 8½×11; Rights purchased: none. Publishes nearly 100% of poems submitted. Deadlines: none. Reporting time: about 2 weeks. Payment: none, I publish too many poets to pay them. Interested in new or unpub'd poets: yes, if they become subscribers. Simultaneous submissions accepted: yes and previously published poetry. Recent contributors: Ann Gasser, Ralph Hammond, William Middleton, Warren Jones, Dr. Karen Springer. Submission quantity: about 5. Special interests: I use all forms and themes written in good taste.

POET'S FANTASY, 227 Hatten Avenue, Rice Lake, WI 54868, 715-234-2205. Gloria Stoeckel, Publisher, Editor. 1991. "Cash contest each issue" circ. 250. 4/yr. Pub'd 120 poems 1999; expects 200 poems 2000, 260 poems 2001. sub. price: $20, $30 overseas; sample: $5; $8 overseas. 40-48pp; 8½×11; Rights purchased: first N. American. Publishes 95% of poems submitted. Deadlines: none. Reporting time: 2 weeks. Payment: $3 off coupon on publication. Interested in new or unpub'd poets: yes. Simultaneous submissions accepted: yes. Recent contributors: Edward J. McFadden, William J. White, Bernard Hewitt (Australia), Jim DeWitt, Steven Dupliji (Ukraine). Submission quantity: up to 5. Special interests: Sonnets, haiku, light verse, long poems, regional poems, short poems, inspirational.

POETS ON THE LINE, PO Box 020292, Brooklyn, NY 11202-0007, 212-766-4109. Linda Lerner. 1995. "For now, no unsolicited ms. Nos. 9&10 came out 1/2000 (double millennium issue) and will be the last regular issue to come out. There may be an occasional special issue of *POTL*, no plans as of yet. In this issue are: W.D. Ehrhart, Lynne Savitt, Kell Robertson, Philip Levine, Julia Vinograd and others." 2/yr. Pub'd 15-20 poems 1999. 31pp; Payment: none. Interested in new or unpub'd poets: no. Simultaneous submissions accepted: no. Recent contributors: W.D. Ehrhart, Enid Dame, Donald Lev, Tony Moffeit, Lawrence Ferlinghetti. Special interests: Consider Poets *On the Line* a continuing anthology. The idea is to produce a living body of work, that grows as new work is added. The poems published reflect the tastes of the editor. This is an attempt to publish those poems I consider unique in their individuality which pay no adherence to schools or current fads.

POET'S PARK, 2745 Monterey Highway #76, San Jose, CA 95111-3129, 408-578-3546; http://www.soos.com/poetpark. Richard Soos. 1992. "Poetry only accepted via e-mail. Only 1 poem please: soos@soos.com" circ. unlimited. Publishes 5% of poems submitted. Reporting time: 1-2 weeks. Interested in new or unpub'd poets: yes. Simultaneous submissions accepted: yes. Recent contributors: Hans Ebner, David Chorlton, Tony Moffeit, Galway Kinnell, Will Inman. Submission quantity: 1. Special interests: Current interest is in good, *modern* poetry.

POETS' ROUNDTABLE, 826 South Center Street, Terre Haute, IN 47807, 812-234-0819. Esther Alman,

President-Editor. 1939. *"Poets' Roundtable* is a bulletin published for the working poets. It contains news, notes, contest listings which are of value to them. Poems are included, but only as space permits. We are not an *open* market, but for members only" circ. 2M. 6/yr. Pub'd 50 poems 1999; expects 50 poems 2000, 50 poems 2001. sub. price: $10-membership; sample: free. 10pp; 8½x11; Simultaneous submissions accepted: no, but we prefer reprints.

POETS' VOICE, J. Mark Press, Box 500901, Malabar, FL 32950, website www.worldtv3.com/jmark.htm. 1965. circ. 1M. 4/yr. sub. price: $4; sample: free with SASE. 12pp; 7x8½.

POETS'PAPER, TWO RIVERS REVIEW, PO Box 85, Easton, PA 18044-0085, 610-559-3887; Irregular@enter.net. Carole J. Heffley, Editor. 1997. "Submissions open January 2-June 30, 2000 only" circ. 500. 2/yr. Pub'd 300 poems 1999; expects 155 poems 2000, 155 poems 2001. sample price: $5. 20pp; 11x17; Rights purchased: first-time rights. Publishes 60% of poems submitted. Deadlines: June 30, 2000. Reporting time: 4-8 weeks. Payment: none. Interested in new or unpub'd poets: yes. Simultaneous submissions accepted: no. Recent contributors: BG Thurston, Shirley Drake Jordan, Will Inman, T. Kilgore Splake. Submission quantity: 3. Special interests: interested in haiku, short verse, form as well as free verse.

POETSWEST LITERARY JOURNAL, 1011 Boren Avenue #155, Seattle, WA 98104, 206-682-1268, bjevans@postalzone.com. J. Glenn Evans. 1988. "Mainly publish poems chosen to read at Poets West reading series held quarterly at the Frye Art Museum in Seattle - only have space for 4 or 5 poems in addition to this. There is a $6 reading fee for 6 poems of less than 60 lines each. Price includes attend. at reading and copy of *PoetsWest Literary Journal* which retails for $5." circ. 200. 4/yr. Pub'd 170 poems 1999; expects 170 poems 2000, 170 poems 2001. sub. price: $17; sample: $5. 80pp; 5½x8½; Rights purchased: one time, rights revert to author. Publishes 15% of poems submitted. Deadlines: Jan. 2, Mar. 2, June 2, Oct. 1. Reporting time: 2 months. Payment: 1 copy. Interested in new or unpub'd poets: yes, but only if they are selected as a reader, they can come to Seattle, WA for reading at own expense. Simultaneous submissions accepted: yes. Recent contributors: Madeline De Frees, J. Glenn Evans, Arthur Ginsberg, Christine R. Swanberg, Joan Swift. Submission quantity: 6 each. Special interests: Only good poetry - previously published is not a problem with us. A good poem deserves repeated readings.

Point Riders Press, PO Box 2731, Norman, OK 73070. Frank Parman, Co-Editor; Arn Henderson, Co-Editor. 1974. "We discourage unsolicited submissions because we are temporarily inactive. Do not send unsolicited manuscripts." avg. press run 500. Pub'd 2 poetry titles 1999; expects 1 poetry title 2000, 1 poetry title 2001. 6x9, 5½x8½; avg. price, paper: $7. 64pp; Publishes less than 5% of poetry manuscripts submitted. Reporting time: 6 months. Payment: 10% of print run. Interested in new or unpub'd poets: only from Great Plains Region residents or poems about Great Plains area/people. Simultaneous submissions accepted: yes. Recently published poets: Jim Linebarger, Carter Revard, Ann Weisman, George Economou, Gar Bethel. Submission quantity: no unsolicited mss. Special interests: We are interested in work that is from or about the Great Plains region only. Poets should read our *Point Riders Great Plains Poetry Anthology* to see the kind of work we do.

Polar Bear Productions & Company, PO Box 311 Brook Street, Solon, ME 04979, 207-643-2795. 1991. 4½x7.

Poltroon Press, PO Box 5476, Berkeley, CA 94705, 510-845-8097. 1974. 6x9.

The Porcupine's Quill, Inc., 68 Main Street, Erin, Ontario N0B 1T0, Canada, 519-833-9158. John Metcalf. 1974. "We still do, of course, receive unsolicited manuscripts. Return envelope and postage are appreciated" avg. press run 500. Pub'd 4 poetry titles 1999; expects 3 poetry titles 2000, 3 poetry titles 2001. 6x9; avg. price, cloth: $20; paper: $7.95. 64pp; Publishes 1% of poetry manuscripts submitted. Reporting time: 2 months. Payment: 5% royalty usual. Interested in new or unpub'd poets: no, no unsolicited manuscripts. Simultaneous submissions accepted: no. Recently published poets: Robert Finch, Jane Urquhart, Robin Skelton, Irving Layton, Louis Dudek. Special interests: Canadian poets.

PORTALS, Redrosebush Press, PO Box 2163, Wenatchee, WA 98807-2163, 509-662-7858. 1991. circ. 1M+. 4/yr. sub. price: $15; sample: free. 44pp; 8½x11.

Portals Press, 4411 Fountainebleau Drive, New Orleans, LA 70125, 504-821-7723; E-mal jptravis@world-net.att.net. 1992. 5½x8½.

Bern Porter Books, 50 Salmond Road, Belfast, ME 04915, 207-338-3763. Bern Porter, Chairman of Board. 1911. "Poetry used in State of Maine Festivals; used in tape form world-wide; used in publication, *Bern Porter International*. SASE required, otherwise not returned. Distributed by Mark Melnicove, 216 Cedar Grove Road, Dresden, ME 04342" avg. press run 5M. Pub'd 61 poetry titles 1999; expects 83 poetry titles 2000, 79 poetry titles 2001. 5½x7, 8½x11; avg. price, cloth: $12.50; paper: $6; other: $75 (limited, signed, handmade). 42pp; Publishes 2% of poetry manuscripts submitted. Reporting time: 2 weeks. Payment: 10% of retail sale. Interested in new or unpub'd poets: either or both. Simultaneous submissions accepted: yes. Recently published poets: Pablo Picasso, Ivan Groll, Antoine Artaud, James Joyce, Kenneth Patchen. Submission quantity: 20. Special interests: 1) Classic literary only preferred. 2) Experimental, visual accepted. 3) Hand-made editions in less than 10 copies a specialty. 4) Translations considered. 5) A true international flavor expected, required.

BERN PORTER INTERNATIONAL, 50 Salmond Street, Belfast, ME 04915-6111, bpinternational@hotmail.com. Bern Porter. 1997. "Vanguard, experimental, visual—international flavor." 6/yr. Expects 92 poems 2000, 105 poems 2001. sub. price: $10; sample: $2.50. 12pp; 8½×11; Rights purchased: standard. Publishes 20% of poems submitted. Reporting time: 3 weeks. Payment: standard per line. Interested in new or unpub'd poets: yes. Simultaneous submissions accepted: yes. Submission quantity: 3-5.

PORTLAND REVIEW, PO Box 347, Portland, OR 97207-0347, 503-725-4533. Barbara Mann, Editor. 1955. "Work that is typed, clean, and comes with a title page & SASE. Write for 'themes.'" circ. 300. 3/yr. Pub'd 50 poems 1999. sub. price: $23; sample: $3 ($1 p/h) back issues, $6 ($1 p/h) current issues. 100pp; 6×9; Rights purchased: copy will remain within the rights of the author. Publishes 5% of poems submitted. Deadlines: Sept. 1, Jan. 1, March 1. Reporting time: 2 months. Payment: complimentary copy of magazine. Interested in new or unpub'd poets: of course. Simultaneous submissions accepted: yes. Recent contributors: James DePriest, Lyn Lifshin, William Stafford, Thom Gunn, Lucinda Parker. Submission quantity: 3-5 poems per submission. Special interests: light verse, satire, experimental poems.

Portmanteau Editions, PO Box 665, Somers, NY 10589. Harry H. Barlow, Jennifer M. Thornton. 1987. "Publishing schedule filled. We continue to publish poetry; however, because of the worldwide moolah shortage we can't consider new proposals or manuscripts at present."

The Post-Apollo Press, 35 Marie Street, Sausalito, CA 94965, 415-332-1458, fax 415-332-8045. Simone Fattal, Editor. 1982. "Not receiving/reading new work at this time due to full publishing schedule" avg. press run 1M. Pub'd 2 poetry titles 1999; expects 2 poetry titles 2000, 2 poetry titles 2001. avg. price, paper: $10. 100pp; Reporting time: 6 months. Payment: no advance royalties. Interested in new or unpub'd poets: no. Simultaneous submissions accepted: no. Recently published poets: Lyn Hejinian, Fanny Howe, Tom Raworth.

POSTCARD, PO Box 444, Tivioli, NY 12583. Jenny Fowler. 1995. "*Postcard* considers: short fiction, poetry, paragraphs, b/w art (no larger than 8x5") from people of all ages. Written works may be handwritten legibly or typed. Due to microcosmic format, shorter pieces are preferred. Translations also welcome. Please send SASE with sufficient postage for a response" circ. 200. 2/yr. Pub'd 6-12 poems 1999; expects 6-12 poems 2000, 6-12 poems 2001. sub. price: $3; sample: spare change. 7-12pp; 4¼x5½; Rights purchased: none. Deadlines: none. Reporting time: about 2 months. Payment: copies. Interested in new or unpub'd poets: yes. Simultaneous submissions accepted: yes. Submission quantity: up to 6.

Pot Shard Press, PO Box 215, Comptche, CA 95427, 707-937-2058. 1997. 9×6.

Potes & Poets Press Inc., 181 Edgemont Avenue, Elmwood, CT 06110, 203-233-2023; e-mail potepoet@home.com. Peter Ganick, Editor. 1980. "Potes & Poets now publishes *Abacus*, a 12-20 pp magazine devoted to the writing of one author per issue. In 1990, issue number fifty will be passed. We also publish perfectbound books and have 32 to our list now. We prefer language poetry, experimental texts, and feminist writings. Most of our publications are from manuscripts we have solicited from the authors. Some authors we have published: Charles Bernstein, Jackson Mac Low, Dennis Barone, Bruce Andrews, Carla Harryman, leslie Scalapino, Rachel Blau DuPlessis, Norma Cole and many others. Our books are distributed by Inland Book Company, Small Press Distribution, Small Press Traffic, and in the UK, Paul Green." avg. press run 500-650. Pub'd 4 poetry titles 1999; expects 2 poetry titles 2000, 4 poetry titles 2001. 8½×11; avg. price, paper: $10-$18. 72-110pp; Publishes 2% of poetry manuscripts submitted. Reporting time: within 3 months. Payment: 10% of edition, no monetary payment. Interested in new or unpub'd poets: yes. Simultaneous submissions accepted: yes. Recently published poets: Sheila E. Murphy, Andrew Lery, Leslie Scalapino, Martine Bellen, Rachel Blau DuPlessis.

POTOMAC REVIEW, PO Box 354, Port Tobacco, MD 20677, website www.meral.com/potomac. Hilary Tham, Poetry Editor. 1994. "Up to half of each issue pivots on a cross-cutting theme, e.g., Up from the Underground Railroad or The Lure of Trails. Write (w/SASE) for a look ahead, or check website." circ. 1.7M. 4/yr. Pub'd 120 poems 1999; expects 120 poems 2000, 120 poems 2001. sub. price: $18; sample: $4. 128pp; 5½x8½; Rights purchased: First North American. Publishes 5% of poems submitted. Deadlines: only for annual contest: Jan. 1-Mar. 31. Reporting time: 12 weeks on outside. Payment: complimentary copy ($300 + publication for contest winner). Interested in new or unpub'd poets: yes. Simultaneous submissions accepted: yes. Recent contributors: Moshe Dor, Leszek Szaruga, Vladimir Levchev, Miles David Moore, Virgil Suarez. Submission quantity: 3. Special interests: We're regionally rooted—with an international reach (Spring 2000 theme was Translation from the Inside Out). Our 'challenging diversity' of styles and subjects precludes porno and other extremes.

POTPOURRI: A Magazine of the Literary Arts, PO Box 8278, Prairie Village, KS 66208, 913-642-1503, Fax 913-642-3128, e-mail potpourrpub@aol.com. Terry Hoyland, Poetry Editor. 1989. "*Potpourri*'s Annual

National Poetry Month award- Submit for 1999: Jan.1,1999 through March 31,1999 First place: $100;honorable mentions second place $50 each. Potpourris' Council on national Literatures Award for poetry for 1999 closing date: Aug.31,1999. Theme: must express in a positive way our multi-cultural heritage and/or our nations history. First place $350. Honorable Mentions (2) $150 each. Ongoing reading, prefer seasonal poetry 3-6 months prior, one poem per page, name and address of author on each page, SASE, 12pt. type" circ. 3.5M. 4/yr. Pub'd 245 poems 1999; expects 250 poems 2000, 260 poems 2001. sub. price: $16; sample: $4.95 with 9 X 12 envelope. 80pp; 8×10¾; Rights purchased: One time. Publishes 5% of poems submitted. Deadlines: ongoing. Reporting time: 8 weeks. Payment: copies. Interested in new or unpub'd poets: yes. Simultaneous submissions accepted: yes, prefer to be informed. Recent contributors: David Ray, Robert Parham, Carol Hamilton, Robert Cooperman, Alan Britt. Submission quantity: 3. Special interests: Open as far as design and space in magazine permit.

THE POTTERSFIELD PORTFOLIO, PO Box 40, Station A, Sydney, Nova Scotia B1P 6G9, Canada, www.pportfolio.com. Susan Goyette, Poetry Editor. 1979. circ. 1M. 3/yr. Pub'd 56 poems 1999; expects 60 poems 2000. sub. price: $17 Canadian, $26 US and overseas (in U.S. dollars); sample: $6. 64pp; 8½×11; Rights purchased: first Canadian serial rights. Publishes 5% of poems submitted. Deadlines: none. Reporting time: 3 months. Payment: contributors copy/$5 per page to a max of $25. Interested in new or unpub'd poets: yes. Simultaneous submissions accepted: no. Recent contributors: Steven Heighton, Karen Connelly, Beth Simon, David Zieroth, Matt Robinson. Submission quantity: maximum 6.

POW-WOW, 577 Central Avenue #4, Jefferson, LA 70121-1400, e-mail: horizons@altavista.net or blueskies@discoverymail.com; Websites www.freeyellow.com/members2/oldwest/index.htm/, www2.cybercities.com/z/zines/. Sharida Rizzuto, Harold Tollison, Elaine Wolfe. 1983. circ. 300. 2/yr. Pub'd 38-40 poems 1999. sub. price: $13.80; sample: $6.90. 80pp; 8½×11; Rights purchased: one-time rights, first serial rights, or second serial rights. Publishes 30-35% of poems submitted. Recent contributors: Elaine Wolfe, Jay Stone, Mary White Cloud, Jim Story.

PRAIRIE FIRE, 423-100 Arthur Street, Winnipeg MB R3B 1H3, Canada, 204-943-9066, fax 942-1555. Melanie Cameron, Robert Budde. 1978. *"Prairie Fire* is concerned primarily with the contemporary writing of Canada. Please use Canadian stamps or IRC for your SASE. Guidelines are available on request with SASE." circ. 1.5M. 4/yr. Pub'd 30 poems 1999; expects 50 poems 2000, 50 poems 2001. sub. price: $25 Can. $30 US $35 Fgr, institutions add $10 per annum; sample: $9.95. 192pp; 9×6; Rights purchased: first, rights revert to author after publication. Publishes 2% of poems submitted. Deadlines: do not accept poetry May-August. Reporting time: 5+ months. Payment: $20 and up (rates available). Interested in new or unpub'd poets: yes. Simultaneous submissions accepted: no. Recent contributors: George Amabile, E.D. Blodgett, D.G. Jones, Patrick Lane, Patricia Young. Submission quantity: 6. Special interests: Regional poetry, longpoems.

THE PRAIRIE JOURNAL OF CANADIAN LITERATURE, Prairie Journal Press, PO Box 61203 Brentwood P.O., 217, 3630 Brentwood Road N.W., Calgary, Alberta T2L 2K6, Canada. A. Burke, Literary Editor. 1983. "We have done poetry issues on North America, also regional. Please no cowboys or sagebrush (tumbling tumbleweed). Contemporary, not necessarily regional. Canadian authors given priority." circ. 500+. 2/yr. Expects 25 poems 2000. sub. price: $6, $12 institutions; sample: $3. 40-60pp; 7×8½; Rights purchased: first N.A. serial rights. Publishes 25% of poems submitted. Deadlines: none. Reporting time: 2 weeks. Payment: copies and honoraria. Interested in new or unpub'd poets: yes. Simultaneous submissions accepted: no. Recent contributors: Mary Melfi, Catherine Mamo, Ronald Kurt, Fred Cogswell, Art Cuelho, Lorna Crozier. Submission quantity: 5. Special interests: Longpoem (if particularly strong writing), region as reflection of poet's self.

Prairie Journal Press (see also THE PRAIRIE JOURNAL OF CANADIAN LITERATURE), PO Box 61203 Brentwood P.O., 217, 3630 Brentwood Road N.W., Calgary, Alberta T2L 2K6, Canada. A. Burke. 1983. "We like doing anthologies whenever we have sufficient material. Collections of more than one author sell better than books by unknown writers. Canadian poets have priority." avg. press run 500+. Expects 1 poetry title 2000. 7×8½; avg. price, paper: $3 Canadian. 40-60pp; Publishes 25% of poetry manuscripts submitted. Reporting time: 2 weeks. Payment: copies. Interested in new or unpub'd poets: yes. Simultaneous submissions accepted: no. Recently published poets: John V. Hicks, Mary Melfi, Monty Reid, Sid Marty, Mick Burrs. Submission quantity: 5, no book-length submissions until solicited. Special interests: Contemporary free verse, regional in spirit not location.

PRAIRIE SCHOONER, 201 Andrews Hall, Univ. of Nebraska, Lincoln, NE 68588-0334, 402-472-0911. Hilda Raz, Editor. 1926. "Typed copies preferred; enclose SASE. $500 Strousse/ *Prairie Schooner* poetry award: annual; $500 Slote award to beginning writers: annual; $1,000 Stanley Award for poetry; $500 Strousse Award for poetry, $1,000 Larry Levis Prize for Poetry . The Jane Geske Award for work published in *Prairie Schooner*. These prizes are awarded to previous year's contributor's only" circ. 3.1M. 4/yr. Pub'd 172 poems 1999; expects 180 poems 2000, 180 poems 2001. sub. price: $22; sample: $5. 200pp; 6×9; Rights purchased: each issue is registered (for copyright) in name of *Prairie Schooner*, copyright released on request. Publishes

4% of poems submitted. Deadlines: Manuscripts are read from September through May only. Reporting time: 3-4 months. Payment: copies, reprints, and prizes. Interested in new or unpub'd poets: yes. Simultaneous submissions accepted: no. Recent contributors: Ha Jin, Marge Piercy, Sherman Alexie, Linda Pastan, Reginald Shepherd. Submission quantity: 4-8. Special interests: Read the magazine to discover the kind of poetry we publish.

PRAIRIE WINDS, Dakota Wesleyan University, DWU Box 536, Mitchell, SD 57301, 605-995-2814. Rebecca Cruse, Editor-in-Chief. 1946. "Include full name on all pages of submissions. Poetry of all styles except pornography welcome. Contact our office with any questions." circ. 500. 1/yr. Pub'd 60 poems 1999. sub. price: $4; sample: $4. 70-100pp; 7½x9¼; Rights purchased: none. Publishes 8% of poems submitted. Deadlines: Dec. 5. Reporting time: 2 months from deadline. Payment: 1 copy each. Interested in new or unpub'd poets: yes. Simultaneous submissions accepted: no. Recent contributors: Jeanne Emmons, James C. Van Oort, Mary Winters, Michael Richard. Submission quantity: 5-10.

Prakalpana Literature (see also PRAKALPANA SAHITYA/PRAKALPANA LITERATURE), P-40 Nandana Park, Calcutta-700034, West Bengal, India, (91) (033) 478-2347. Vattacharja Chandan, Dilip Gupta. 1974. "Generally from the poems published in our mags-*Prakalpana Sahitya/Prakalpana Literature* and *Kobisena*, we select poems for our future bilingual anthology of Sarbangin (=all out) poetry. So first we invite from new or unpublished poets, in English or in Bengali: only really avant garde, experimental poems that expose the pictures inherent in alphabets, using definitely visual and mathematical signs and dimensions with sonorous effects in words—that is Sarbangin poetry, for our mag. IRC/SASE is a must for queries. Submissions not returnable." avg. press run 500. 5½x8½; avg. price, other: price is fixed when a book is published. 56pp; Reporting time: 6 months. Payment: none. Simultaneous submissions accepted: no. Submission quantity: 3. Special interests: The selected Sarbangin poems are published in original with their translations into Bengali/English.

PRAKALPANA SAHITYA/PRAKALPANA LITERATURE, Prakalpana Literature, P-40 Nandana Park, Calcutta-700034, West Bengal, India, (91) (033) 478-2347. Vattacharja Chandan. 1977. "We invite from interested contributors in English or in Bengali: only really avant garde, experimental poems that expose the pictures inherent in alphabets, using definitely visual and mathematical signs and dimensions with sonorous effects in words—that is Sarbangin poetry. And from the poems published in our magazine, we select poems for our future bilingual anthology of Sarbangin poetry. IRC/SASE is a must for queries. MS not returnable." circ. 1M. 1/yr. sub. price: 6 rupees; sample: 20 rupees. Overseas: 6 IRCs or exchange of little mags. 120pp; 5x7; Rights purchased: none. Publishes 10% of poems submitted. Deadlines: none. Payment: 1 copy. Interested in new or unpub'd poets: yes. Simultaneous submissions accepted: no. Recent contributors: Dikip Gupta, Susan Smith Nash, Vattacharja Chandan, Narak Dar, Shyamali Mukherjee Bhattacharjee. Submission quantity: 4. Special interests: The selected Sarbangin poems are published in original with their translations into Bengali/English.

●**PRECHELONIAN, Blue Night Press,** 1003 Lakeway, Kalamazoo, MI 49001. 1991. 1/yr. sub. price: n/a; sample: $5. 25pp; 5½x8½.

Preludium Publishers (see also LIFTOUTS), 1414 South 3rd Street, No. 102, Minneapolis, MN 55454-1172, 612-321-9044, Fax 612-305-0655. Barry Casselman. 1971. "Preludium Publishers does not at this time accept unsolicited manuscripts of poetry." Expects 1-5 poetry titles 2001. Payment: to all authors published. Simultaneous submissions accepted: no. Special interests: Experimental poetry in English, and translations of new poetry from around the world.

PrePress Publishing of Michigan, 709 Sunbright Avenue, Portage, MI 49024-2759, 616-323-2659. 1992. 6x9.

PRESS, 2124 Broadway, Suite 323, New York, NY 10023, 212-579-0873. Daniel Roberts. 1995. circ. 10M. 4/yr. Expects 100 poems 2000, 100 poems 2001. sub. price: $24. 150pp; digest size; Rights purchased: one-time. Publishes 5% of poems submitted. Deadlines: on going. Reporting time: 4-6 weeks. Payment: minimum $50/poem. Interested in new or unpub'd poets: yes. Simultaneous submissions accepted: no. Recent contributors: Philip Levine, Charles Bukowski, Edward Hirsch, Paul Muldown, David Wagoner.

Press Here, PO Box 4014, Foster City, CA 94404, 415-571-9428, e-Mail WelchM@aol.com. Michael Dylan Welch, Editor & Publisher. 1989. "Press Here publishes books of poetry, primarily haiku and related forms. Queries appreciated before sending manuscripts. Books have won Merit Book Awards from the Haiku Society of America. Manuscripts preferred only by those published in the leading haiku magazines, but open to all possibilities—surprise the editor with quality and creativity. Especially interested in books of criticism on or about haiku or small-book-length interviews with established haiku poets. Also interested in concrete poetry." avg. press run 200-500. Pub'd 2 poetry titles 1999; expects 3 poetry titles 2000, 3 poetry titles 2001. 5½x8½; avg. price, paper: $4-$8. 28-96pp; Publishes 5% of poetry manuscripts submitted. Reporting time: usually 1-4 weeks for queries, 2-6 months for manuscripts (query first, please). Payment: usually in copies. Interested in new or unpub'd poets: yes, if the poet is *very* confident of the manuscript. Simultaneous submissions accepted:

yes, if indicated. Recently published poets: Lee Gurga, Anita Virgil, William Higginson, Michael Dylan Welch, Sono Uchida. Submission quantity: whatever you think will constitute a book. Special interests: Prefer books of, on, or about haiku, senryu, tanka, haibun, or renku, as well as concrete poetry.

The Press of Appletree Alley, Box 608 138 South Third Street, Lewisburg, PA 17837. John Wheatcroft. 1982. "The Press of Appletree Alley aims to achieve a highly professional standard of letterpress printing and to create distinctive designs in the publication of modern poetry and works of literary merit of any era." avg. press run 125. Pub'd 1 poetry title 1999; expects 1 poetry title 2000, 1 poetry title 2001. 6¼x9½; avg. price, cloth: $150 limited edition. 64pp; Payment: copies only. Interested in new or unpub'd poets: no. Simultaneous submissions accepted: no. Recently published poets: William Matthews, Bruce Smith, Molly Peacock, Colette Inez, Louis Simpson.

Press-Tige Publishing Company Inc. (see also WRITER'S MONTHLY GAZETTE), 291 Main Street, Catskill, NY 12414, 518-943-1440 X10. Kelly O'Donnell, Editor. 1972. "Contests (poetry) in our *Writer's Gazzette Newsletter* which is once a month. No morbid, death poems *please*" avg. press run 350. Pub'd 100 poetry titles 1999; expects 100 poetry titles 2000, 100 poetry titles 2001. 5¼x6¼; avg. price, cloth: $22.95; paper: $11.95; other: $8.50. 2pp; Publishes 60% of poetry manuscripts submitted. Reporting time: 1 month. Payment: 18%. Interested in new or unpub'd poets: yes. Simultaneous submissions accepted: yes. Recently published poets: Donna Keller, Laura Comito, Mary Santulli, Sara Montanye, Martha Reidda. Submission quantity: 10. Special interests: Light verse, ok, free verse, rhyming, children's, humorous, nature, environmental, inspirational.

Prickly Pear Press, 1402 Mimosa Pass, Cedar Park, TX 78613, 512-331-1557. Dave Oliphant. 1973. "No unsolicited mss." avg. press run 500. 6x9; avg. price, cloth: $13.95; paper: $9.95; other: $5. 64pp; Payment: copies. Interested in new or unpub'd poets: no. Simultaneous submissions accepted: no. Recently published poets: Joseph Colin Murphey, Dwight Fullingim, Rebecca Gonzales, Charles Behlen, William Barney. Special interests: Native Texas poets.

PRIMAVERA, PO Box 37-7547, Chicago, IL 60637-7547, 773-324-5920. Editorial Board. 1974. "Always include a self-addressed stamped envelope. PRIMAVERA reads manuscripts all year. We are interested in quality literature; while the magazine emphasizes the experiences of women, we reject trite confessional works and "feminist" diatribes. No simultaneous submissions." circ. 1M. 1/yr. Pub'd 30 poems 1999; expects 30 poems 2000, 30 poems 2001. sub. price: $10; sample: $5. 128pp; 8½x5½; Rights purchased: 1st North American. Publishes 1% of poems submitted. Deadlines: continuous. Reporting time: 1 week to 4 months. Payment: 2 copies. Interested in new or unpub'd poets: yes. Simultaneous submissions accepted: no. Recent contributors: Pamela Gemin, Simone Muench, Erika Krause, Stephanie Dickinson, Diane Seuss-Braleeman. Submission quantity: 5-6. Special interests: We publish work that reflects the experiences of women.

PRIME, 7116 Helen C. White Hall, Madison, WI 53706, 688-262-3262. 1992. "Our focus is writing by students of color" circ. 500. 1/yr. Pub'd 20 poems 1999; expects 20 poems 2000, 20 poems 2001. sub. price: $10; sample: $5. 36pp; 4¼x5½; Rights purchased: none. Publishes 10% of poems submitted. Deadlines: March, yearly. Reporting time: 1 month. Payment: none. Interested in new or unpub'd poets: yes. Simultaneous submissions accepted: yes. Submission quantity: 5. Special interests: All types, genres ok.

PRINCETON ARTS REVIEW, 102 Witherspoon Street, Princeton, NJ 08540, 609-924-8777. 1996. circ. 400. 2/yr. sub. price: $10; sample: $6. 80pp; 5½x8½.

Princeton University Press, 41 William Street, Princeton, NJ 08540, 609-258-4900. Robert E. Brown. 1905. "Lockert Library of Poetry in Translation: Manuscripts of poetry in translation will be accepted for review throughout the year. Please include a copy of the poems in their original language as well as any introductory material such as scholarly preface or foreword, and notes, if they are available. Manuscripts will be judged with several criteria in mind: the ability of the poetry to stand on its merits simply as poetry in English; fidelity to the tone and spirit of the original, rather than literal accuracy; and the importance of the translated poet to the literature of his or her time and country. Please send your manuscript to Lockert Library of Poetry in Translation, Princeton University Press, at the above address" avg. press run 400 cloth, 1M paper. Pub'd 2 poetry titles 1999; expects 2 poetry titles 2000, 2 poetry titles 2001. 6⅛x9¼; avg. price, cloth: $35; paper: $14.95. 100pp; Publishes less than 1% of poetry manuscripts submitted. Reporting time: 2½ months. Payment: varies with the individual. Interested in new or unpub'd poets: no. Simultaneous submissions accepted: yes, if the poet notifies us he or she is doing so, this is acceptable. Recently published poets: Faiz Ahmed Faiz. Submission quantity: At least 30. Special interests: translations.

PRISM INTERNATIONAL, E462-1866 Main Mall, University of British Columbia, Vancouver BC V6T 1Z1, Canada, 604-822-2514, fax 604-822-3616, e-mail prism@interchange.ubc.ca, www.arts.ubc.ca/prism. Andrea MacPherson, Poetry Editor. 1959. "1996 1st year for anual Poetry prize $500. Annual fiction contest with prizes totaling $3,000. Translations should come with a copy of the original work" circ. 1.25M. 4/yr. Pub'd 80 poems 1999; expects 80 poems 2000, 80 poems 2001. sub. price: $20 indiv., $28 libraries, Canadians add G.S.T., outside Canada pay US funds.; sample: $5.50. 96pp; 6×9; Rights purchased: 1st North American serial ($40 Can. per printed page). Publishes 1-5% of poems submitted. Deadlines: send anytime. Reporting time: 3-4 months. Payment: $40 Can. per printed page, upon publication + 1-year subscription; selected author receive an additional $10/printed page for publication on the World Wide Web. Interested in new or unpub'd poets: yes. Simultaneous submissions accepted: no. Recent contributors: Di Brandt, Billie Livingston, John Kinsella, rob mclennan, Pain Not Bread. Submission quantity: 5. Special interests: *Prism International* looks for poetry with clear movement and rhythm, and vivid imagery. We accept different kinds of poems, ranging from simple and grounded, to elegant and formal. We are also interested in translation. Above all, *Prism* seeks originality and clarity in poetry.

Proof Press (see also RAW NERVZ HAIKU), 67 Court Street, Aylmer, QC J9H 4M1, Canada, E-mail: dhoward@aix1.uottawa.ca. 1994. 5½×8½, 3½×4-1/9.

PROOF ROCK, Proof Rock Press, PO Box 607, Halifax, VA 24558. Don R. Conner, Editor; Serena Fusek, Poetry Editor. 1982. "We want to wake up our passive audience. Dare to find something new under the sun" circ. 300. 2/yr. Pub'd 120 poems 1999; expects 120 poems 2000, 120 poems 2001. sub. price: $5; sample: $3. 40pp; 5½×8½; Rights purchased: 1st North American. Publishes 15% of poems submitted. Deadlines: we accept submissions year round. Reporting time: 30 days, usually sooner. Payment: copies only. Interested in new or unpub'd poets: yes. Simultaneous submissions accepted: yes. Recent contributors: Lifshin, Locklin, Craig, Arguelles, Faucher. Submission quantity: up to 6. Special interests: Adventure, contemporary, erotica, experimental, fantasy, humor/satire.

Proper PH Publications (see also CONFLICT OF INTEREST), 4701 East National Road, Springfield, OH 45505-1847, 330-630-5646 phone/Fax; E-mail phartney@aol.com. 1994. 11×17.

THE PROSE POEM: An International Journal, English Department, Providence College, Providence, RI 02918, 401-865-2292. Peter Johnson, Editor; Brian Johnson, Assistant Editor. 1992. "Please do not send verse poems. Have a general idea of what a prose poem is. Subscribe to the journal." circ. 1M. 1/yr. Pub'd 40-70 poems 1999. sub. price: $8; sample: $8. 100-150pp; 6×9; Rights purchased: revert to author. Publishes 1-5% of poems submitted. Deadlines: December 1 to March 1 (We will not be reading again until Dec. 1 of 2001). Reporting time: 1-3 months. Payment: 2 copies. Interested in new or unpub'd poets: yes. Simultaneous submissions accepted: no. Recent contributors: Robert Bly, Russell Edson, David Ignatow, C.D. Wright, Charles Simic. Submission quantity: 3-5. Special interests: We look for good translations of contemporary poets.

PROSODIA, New College of California/Poetics, 766 Valencia Street, San Francisco, CA 94110, 415-437-3479, Fax 415-437-3702. 1990. circ. 500. 1/yr. sub. price: $8. 120pp; 6×9.

●Prospect Press (see also SPARROWGRASS POETRY NEWSLETTER), 609 Main Street, PO Box 162, Sistersville, WV 26175, 304-652-1920, Fax 304-652-1148, www.tinplace.com/prospect. Helen McInnis. 1997. avg. press run 500-750. Pub'd 5 poetry titles 1999; expects 7 poetry titles 2000, 15 poetry titles 2001. 6×9; avg. price, cloth: $16.95; paper: $9.95. 96pp; Publishes 75% of poetry manuscripts submitted. Reporting time: 4-6 weeks. Payment: 5% and up, subsidy/self-published authors receive all proceeds. Interested in new or unpub'd poets: yes. Simultaneous submissions accepted: yes. Recently published poets: June Owens, Douglas Johnson, Carol Petersen, Margaret Hellewell, Diana Rubin. Submission quantity: 40 pages.

Protean Press, 287-28th Avenue, San Francisco, CA 94121, fax 415-386-4980. 1984. avg. press run 60. Expects 9 poetry titles 2000, 2 poetry titles 2001. size varies; avg. price, other: $300. 15-20pp; Publishes 0% of poetry manuscripts submitted. Payment: varies. Interested in new or unpub'd poets: no. Simultaneous submissions accepted: no. Recently published poets: Terry Ehret, Susan Herron Sibbet, Jennifer Futernick, Margaret Kaufman, Jeanne Lohmann.

Protean Publications, 34 Summerfield Crescent, Flat 4, Edgbaston, Birmingham B16 OER, England. Paul Lester. 1980. "Deals with poetry, graphics, short stories and cultural and literary criticism." avg. press run 200-300. Pub'd 1 poetry title 1999; expects 2 poetry titles 2000. 4×6; avg. price, paper: 60p to £1. Reporting time: 6-8 weeks. Payment: by arrangement. Interested in new or unpub'd poets: depending on quality. Simultaneous submissions accepted: yes. Submission quantity: 6.

PROVINCETOWN ARTS, Provincetown Arts Press, 650 Commercial Street, Provincetown, MA 02657, 508-487-3167. Christopher Busa. 1985. circ. 8M. 1/yr. Pub'd 24 poems 1999; expects 30 poems 2000, 35 poems 2001. sub. price: $10; sample: $10. 184pp; 9×12; Rights purchased: 1st time publication, rights revert to author on publication. Publishes 3% of poems submitted. Deadlines: reading between Aug & Dec each year. Reporting time: 2 months. Payment: $25-$300. Interested in new or unpub'd poets: yes. Simultaneous submissions accepted: no. Recent contributors: Susan Mitchell, Mark Doty, Michael Klein, Martha Rhode, Maigin Cruz-Bernal. Submission quantity: 1-3.

Provincetown Arts Press (see also PROVINCETOWN ARTS), PO Box 35, 650 Commercial Street,

Provincetown, MA 02657, 508-487-3167; FAX 508-487-8634. Christopher Busa, Editorial Director. avg. press run 1.5M. Pub'd 2 poetry titles 1999; expects 2 poetry titles 2000, 2 poetry titles 2001. 6×8; avg. price, cloth: $35; paper: $10. 70pp; Publishes 1% of poetry manuscripts submitted. Reporting time: 4-6 months. Payment: $500 advance, 10% royalties. Interested in new or unpub'd poets: yes. Simultaneous submissions accepted: yes. Recently published poets: Michael Klein, Martha Rhodes, Anne-Marie Lesine, Ellen Dudley.

PSYCHOPOETICA, Department of Psychology, University of Hull, Hull HU6 7RX, United Kingdom, website www.fernhse.demon.co.uk/eastword/psycho. Geoff Lowe, Trevor Millum. 1980. "Thoughtful presentations welcomed." circ. 350. 2/yr plus occasional special anthologies. Pub'd 200 poems 1999; expects 200 poems 2000, 200 poems 2001. sub. price: $16 (plus postage); sample: $5. 60+pp; 8¼×11½ (A4); Publishes 8% of poems submitted. Deadlines: none. Reporting time: within 1 month-6 weeks. Payment: none. Interested in new or unpub'd poets: yes. Simultaneous submissions accepted: yes. Recent contributors: Peter Bakowski, John Brander, Jenni Collins, Rod Farmer, John Mingay. Submission quantity: up to 5. Special interests: Psychologically-based poetry.

PTOLEMY/BROWNS MILLS REVIEW, PO Box 252, Juliustown, NJ 08042, 609-893-0896. David Vajda. 1979. circ. 100-250. 1-2/yr. sub. price: $4; sample: $1-$2. 16pp; 5½×8½; Publishes 5-10% of poems submitted. Reporting time: immediate to a year. Payment: copies. Interested in new or unpub'd poets: if quality, YES! Simultaneous submissions accepted: no. Recent contributors: Edward Lynskey, Dan Raphael, Jesse Glass Jr. Submission quantity: at least 5.

Puckerbrush Press (see also THE PUCKERBRUSH REVIEW), 76 Main Street, Orono, ME 04473-1430, 207-866-4868. Constance Hunting, Editor, Publisher. 1971. "I simply publish what I like." avg. press run 250-500. Pub'd 2 poetry titles 1999; expects 2 poetry titles 2000. 6×9; avg. price, paper: $9.95. 60-80pp; Publishes at most 10% of poetry manuscripts submitted. Reporting time: 1 month. Payment: 10% retail copy. Interested in new or unpub'd poets: yes. Simultaneous submissions accepted: yes. Recently published poets: Deborah Pease, Mark Rutter, Harvena Richter, Patricia Ranzoni. Submission quantity: 12-15. Special interests: Translations, experimental poetry, longpoems.

THE PUCKERBRUSH REVIEW, Puckerbrush Press, 76 Main Street, Orono, ME 04473-1430. Constance Hunting, Editor, Publisher. 1978. "Just send, with SASE." circ. 250-300. 1-2/yr. Pub'd 20 poems 1999; expects 40 poems 2000. sub. price: $11; sample: $2. 100+pp; 8½×11; Rights purchased: none. Publishes 10% or less of poems submitted. Deadlines: none. Reporting time: 4 weeks. Payment: copies. Interested in new or unpub'd poets: yes. Simultaneous submissions accepted: yes. Recent contributors: Lee Sharkey, Patricia Ranzoni, Lacey Kellett, James Laughlin, David Gordon. Submission quantity: 4-5. Special interests: Translations, experimental poetry, regional poetry, longpoems, light verse, satire, etc.

Pudding House Publications (see also PUDDING MAGAZINE: The International Journal of Applied Poetry), 60 North Main Street, Johnstown, OH 43031, 740-967-6060, pudding@johnstown.net, www.puddinghouse.com. Jennifer Bosveld, Publisher-Editor. 1979. "Chapbooks considered continuously for a $10 reading fee. Include ample postage on a SASE. Sample books and magazines are $8.95 postpaid. Annual National Looking Glass Chapbook Competition deadlines June 30 and Sept. 30. $10 entry fee. Individual poems may be previously published but not as a whole. Include credits" avg. press run 400. Pub'd 12 poetry titles 1999; expects 32 poetry titles 2000, 36 poetry titles 2001. 5½×8½; avg. price, paper: $8.95; other: varies. 28pp; Publishes less than 1% of poetry manuscripts submitted. Reporting time: 2 weeks, sometimes overnight. Payment: 20 free copies and discount on additional copies plus 10 to reviewers of author's choice. Interested in new or unpub'd poets: yes. Simultaneous submissions accepted: no. Recently published poets: David Rigsbee, Kurt Brown, Charlie Rossiter, Christopher Millis, Vivian Shipley. Submission quantity: 10-50 for a chapbook, prefer 24-28 pages. Special interests: Poetry that reflects intense human conditions, felt experience, 'virtual journalism poetry' and more. Wide open really.

PUDDING MAGAZINE: The International Journal of Applied Poetry, Pudding House Publications, 60 North Main Street, Johnstown, OH 43031, 740-967-6060, pudding@johnstown.net, www.puddinghouse.com. Jennifer Bosveld, Editor; Doug Swisher, Associate Editor; Steve Abbott, Associate Editor; Jim Bosveld, Associate Editor; Ben Rader, Associate Editor. 1979. "We love to discover new talent. Free verse, experimental, and avant-garde especially requested. Looking for the wildly different and the subtly profound. We recommend: Reflections of intense human situations; Concrete images and specific detail; Artful expressions of unique situations; or the shock of recognition in things perhaps felt before (or almost felt) but never spoken. No trite comparisons, please. No cliches. No strictly religious verse or sentimentality. Mini-Articles: By poets who share their craft in the human services; About applied poetry experiences either from clients/patients or from psychiatrists, teachers, or other professionals and paraprofessionals who put the art of poetry to use helping others. Offers chapbook competitions annually, 1-on-1 editor tutorials and editor workshops, and writers accommodations at their bed and breakfast for writers on-site" circ. 2M. Irregular. Pub'd 250 poems 1999. sub. price: $18.95/3 issues; sample: $7.95. 45-95pp; 5½×8½; Rights purchased: 1st time w/permission to reprint. Publishes way less than 1% of poems submitted. Deadlines: continuous. Reporting time: usually overnight, unless we're traveling. Payment: 1 copy, 4 copies and $10 to featured poet. Interested in new or unpub'd poets: yes, eager, we've discovered exciting new voices. Simultaneous submissions accepted: no. Recent contributors: William Abraham Howard Jr., Rose M. Smith, Wilma Elizabeth McDaniel, Ron Moran, John Unland. Submission quantity: 2-6 unless chapbook. Special interests: Experimental poetry, popular culture, quirky characters, social justice, human services, poetry or writing therapy, with a highly artistic orientation, "virtual journalism"; also seek dense poetic short short stories or flash fiction.

PUERTO DEL SOL, Box 3E, New Mexico State University, Las Cruces, NM 88003, 505-646-2345. Kathleen West. 1961. "Send your best poems (not the one or two you wrote about the Southwest) typed, enclose SASE" circ. 1M. 2/yr. Pub'd 59 poems 1999; expects 60 poems 2000, 60 poems 2001. sub. price: $10; sample: $7. 200pp; 6×9; Rights purchased: none. Publishes 3-5% of poems submitted. Deadlines: accept submissions Sept. 1 to March 1. Reporting time: 1-2 months. Payment: copies right now. Interested in new or unpub'd poets: yes. Simultaneous submissions accepted: yes. Recent contributors: J.B. Goodenough, Walter McDonald, Walter Bargen, D.E. Stewart, Sheila Murphy. Submission quantity: around 5. Special interests: The best poems we can find, preferrably combining emotional depth with interesting language. Anything real (not exercises). Sympathetic to southwestern poetry but must be good. Interested in translations from the Spanish (accompanied by the originals) but both the original and the translation must be good poems.

PULSAR POETRY MAGAZINE, 34 Lineacre, Grange Park, Swindon, Wiltshire SN5 6DA, United Kingdom, 01793-875941, e-mail david.pike@virgin.net. David Pike, Editor. 1994. "Not keen on religious poetry. Refer herd-hitting or humorous work. Realism modern poetry, no glorious sunsets etc." circ. 300. 4/yr. Pub'd 75 poems 1999; expects 100 poems 2000. sub. price: $30; sample: free. 32pp; 5¾×8¼; We publish 1 in 30 poems submitted. Reporting time: 6 weeks max. Payment: none, but free copy of edition containing their work. Interested in new or unpub'd poets: yes. Simultaneous submissions accepted: no. Recent contributors: Merryn Williams, Wincey Willis, Virgil Suarez, Liz Atkin, Lachlan Robertson. Submission quantity: 6. Special interests: Like to recieve poetry from all over the globe, must be readable and in English with review postage paid. Also, will include black and white issustrations, if they are good. Send me poetry books and magazines to review. Annual Poetry Competition with cash prizes.

The Purchase Press, PO Box 5, Harrison, NY 10528, 914-967-4499. John Guenther. 1980. "Quality is our only consideration." avg. press run 300. Pub'd 1 poetry title 1999; expects 1 poetry title 2000. 6×9; avg. price, paper: $10. 64pp; Reporting time: 30 days. Payment: negotiated with author. Interested in new or unpub'd poets: yes. Simultaneous submissions accepted: yes. Recently published poets: Rainer Maria Rilke. Submission quantity: no specific number.

PURPLE, 213 Country Club Drive, Cape Girardeau, MO 63701-3339. 1997. circ. 300. 2/yr. 40pp.

Purple Finch Press, PO Box 758, Dewitt, NY 13214, 315-445-8087. Nancy Benson. 1992. "We are not considering unsolicited manuscripts at this time. Poetry of high literary quality, excellent images, sound blending with sensee, sensitive poetry, human nature, feelings, nature" avg. press run 500-2M. Pub'd 1 poetry title 1999; expects 2 poetry titles 2000, 3 poetry titles 2001. 5½×8½; avg. price, cloth: $11; paper: $20. 100pp; Publishes 20% of poetry manuscripts submitted. Reporting time: 2 months. Payment: 4-7.5% of net price. Interested in new or unpub'd poets: yes. Simultaneous submissions accepted: yes. Recently published poets: Nancy Keats. Submission quantity: 10. Special interests: Innovative language, similes, metaphors, catching musical moments in space in literary language.

THE PURPLE MONKEY, 200 East Redbud Road, Knoxville, TN 37920. W. Brian Ellis, Scott Gilbert. 1993. "Submissions should include a brief bio; we do not want to see art without craft" circ. 100. 4/yr. Pub'd 30 poems 1999; expects 45 poems 2000, 60 poems 2001. sub. price: $10; sample: $2.50. 30-40pp; 5½×8½; Rights purchased: First North American Serial. Publishes 15% of poems submitted. Deadlines: read continuosly. Reporting time: 2-5 months. Payment: 1 copy. Interested in new or unpub'd poets: yes. Simultaneous submissions accepted: yes. Recent contributors: Jeff Daniel Marion, Ted Kooser, Lyn Lifshin, Susan O'Dell Underwood. Submission quantity: up to 5.

PURPLE PATCH, 25 Griffiths Road, West Bromwich, B71 2EH, England. Geoff Stevens. 1976. "2 IRC's or $1 bill required for air mail replies to U.S.A. Xerox copies preferred from outside U.K." circ. 200. 3/yr. Pub'd 140 poems 1999; expects 160 poems 2000, 140 poems 2001. sub. price: £5.60 for 3, includes 100th issue (2001); sample: £1.50, $5 bill. 24+pp; 5¾×8½; Rights purchased: 1st British serial rights. Publishes 5% of poems submitted. Deadlines: anytime. Reporting time: 1 month. Payment: none. Interested in new or unpub'd poets: yes. Simultaneous submissions accepted: yes. Recent contributors: R.K. Avery, Sam Smith, R.G. Bishop, Maureen Weldon, John Hirst. Submission quantity: 2-6 preferred. Special interests: Considers any, but overlong and poor rhymes discouraged. Not too keen on haiku. Likes descriptive poems that give a real sense of place and/or feeling. Nostalgia also welcome. Would encourage untutored promise.

Pygmy Forest Press, PO Box 7097, Eureka, CA 95502-7097, 707-268-1274. Leonard Cirino, Editor & Publisher. 1987. "Prefer Steven, Roethke to Williams/Olson—esp. like Berryman, Lowell, Sexton, etc.

Thematic chapbooks. Like Brigit Pegeen Kelly, also Hayden Carruth, William Bronk, John Haines, and Patricia A. Smith'' avg. press run 200. Pub'd 3 poetry titles 1999; expects 3 poetry titles 2000, 3 poetry titles 2001. 5½×8½; avg. price, cloth: $25; paper: $6-$12. 32-80pp; Publishes 3-5% of poetry manuscripts submitted. Reporting time: immediate to 1 month. Payment: author provides camera-ready copy and pays 50-75% of printing costs, will receive like in copies. Interested in new or unpub'd poets: yes. Simultaneous submissions accepted: yes. Recently published poets: Kenn Mitchell, C.L. Cyndian, Michael McIrvin, Tom Lombardo, Joanne Lowery. Submission quantity: 10-15. Special interests: Translations interested, regional poetry welcome, rural, women's issues, prison/asylum experience. Long poems up to 28 pages for a single chapbook.

Pyx Press (see also MAGIC REALISM), Box 922648, Sylmar, CA 91392-2648. C. Darron Butler, Editor. 1990. "Query first with sample poems. No unsolic. submissions. Poets we publish generally appear first in *Shillelagh* or *Magic Realism*'' avg. press run 200. Pub'd 1 poetry title 1999; expects 3 poetry titles 2000, 2 poetry titles 2001. avg. price, other: chapbook $7. 28pp; Publishes 2% of poetry manuscripts submitted. Reporting time: up to 6 months. Payment: generally copies only for poetry. Interested in new or unpub'd poets: yes. Simultaneous submissions accepted: no. Recently published poets: Rafael Cadenas.

Q

QRL POETRY SERIES, Quarterly Review of Literature Press, Princeton University, 26 Haslet Avenue, Princeton, NJ 08540, 921-6976. R. Weiss, Editor; T. Weiss, Editor. 1943. "Only one manuscript with SASE per reading period. Rejected manuscripts may be revised and re-submitted. To encourage support, a subscription is requested with each submission. Send SASE for details.'' circ. 3-5M. 4-6/yr. Pub'd 5 books of poems 1999; expects 5 books of poems 2000, 5 books of poems 2001. sub. price: 2 volumes paper $20, single $12, $20 institutional & hardback per volume; sample: $10. 250-350pp; 5½×8½; Rights purchased: all book rights. Deadlines: May and October only. SASE must be sent for guidelines. Reporting time: 1-3 months. Payment: $1,000 award for each chosen manuscript + 100 copies. Interested in new or unpub'd poets: yes. Simultaneous submissions accepted: yes. Recent contributors: Dannie Abse, Joan Aleshire, Eugenio de Andrade, David Keller, Peter Stambler. Submission quantity: between 60-100 pages. Special interests: *QRL* considers books of poetry, poetic plays, a book of translations of one poet, a single long poem of 30 pages or more. Send SASE for guidelines and entry information.

QUADRANT MAGAZINE, PO Box 1495, Collingwood, Vic. 3066, Australia, (03) 417-6855. Les Morray. 1956. circ. 8M. 10/yr. Pub'd 220 poems 1999; expects 220 poems 2000, 220 poems 2001. sub. price: $A45. 88pp; size A4; Rights purchased: first serial rights. Publishes 10% of poems submitted. Payment: $40. Interested in new or unpub'd poets: yes. Simultaneous submissions accepted: no. Recent contributors: Les Murray, Bruce Daw, Alan Gould, Hal Colebatch, Edith Speers.

QUARTER AFTER EIGHT, Ellis Hall, Ohio University, Athens, OH 45701. 1993. circ. 1M. 1/yr. sub. price: $10; sample: $10. 300pp; 6×9.

Quarterly Committee of Queen's University (see also QUEEN'S QUARTERLY: A Canadian Review), Queen's University, Kingston, Ontario K7L 3N6, Canada, e-mail qquarter@post.queensu.ca, website http://info.queensu.ca/quarterly. B. Castel, Editor. 1893. avg. press run 3.5M. Pub'd 40 poetry titles 1999. 6×9; avg. price, paper: $6.50. 1 page; Publishes a very small % of poetry manuscripts submitted. Reporting time: 8-12 weeks. Payment: upon publication. Interested in new or unpub'd poets: yes. Simultaneous submissions accepted: no. Recently published poets: Katie Campbell, Sue Nevill, Evelyn Lau, Raymond Souster. Submission quantity: 6 (max). Special interests: Canadian poetry.

Quarterly Review of Literature Press (see also QRL POETRY SERIES), Princeton University, 26 Haslet Avenue, Princeton, NJ 08540, 609-921-6976, fax 609-258-2230, e-mail qrl@princeton.edu. R. Weiss, T. Weiss. 1943. "Please see manuscript guidelines. Submission May and November only. Number of pages: 60 to 100 pages. Must include SASE. A subscription should accompany submission.'' avg. press run 3M-5M. Pub'd 5 poetry titles 1999; expects 5 poetry titles 2000, 5 poetry titles 2001. 5½×8½; avg. price, cloth: $20 (4-6 titles within 1 Vol.); paper: $12; other: 2 volume subscription (8-12 titles): $20. 60-100pp; Reporting time: 1-2 months. Payment: $1,000 prize for each winning manuscript + 100 copies. Interested in new or unpub'd poets: yes. Simultaneous submissions accepted: yes, but a subscription must accompany each manuscript. Recently published poets: Stambler, Szymborska, So Chongju, Dannie Abse, Jane Hirshfield. Submission quantity: an entire book. Special interests: Poetic play, long poem, poetry translation of 1 poet, a book of miscellaneous poems.

QUARTERLY WEST, 200 South Central Campus Drive, Room 317, University of Utah, Salt Lake City, UT

84112, 801-581-3938. Heidi Blitch, Poetry Editor. 1976. "Summer is a good time to send poems. Around Christmas and at the beginning of summer are bad times." circ. 1.7M. 2/yr. Pub'd 63 poems 1999; expects 60 poems 2000, 60 poems 2001. sub. price: $12; sample: $7.50. 224pp; 6×9; Rights purchased: usual. Publishes less than 1% of poems submitted. Deadlines: we read year-round. Reporting time: 1-4 months. Payment: $25-$100 depending upon funds available. Interested in new or unpub'd poets: yes, both. Simultaneous submissions accepted: yes. Recent contributors: Larry Levis, Philip Levine, Lucia Perillo, Lisa Steinman, Miroslav Holub. Submission quantity: 3-4. Special interests: We welcome translations and poems that point toward new directions in poetry.

QUARTZ HILL JOURNAL OF THEOLOGY, 43543 51st Street West, Quartz Hill, CA 93536, 661-722-0891, 661-943-3484, E-mail robin@theology.edu. R.P. Nettelhorst. 1993. "*Quartz Hill Journal of Theology* is the official journal of Quartz Hill School of Theology, a ministry of Quartz Hill Community Church. Quartz Hill Community Church is associated with the southern Baptist. We accept as our doctrinal statement *The Baptist Faith and Message*, adopted by the SBC in 1963" circ. 200. 4/yr. Pub'd 6 poems 1999; expects 24 poems 2000, 24 poems 2001. sub. price: $20; sample: $5. 100pp; 8½×11; Rights purchased: FNASR. Publishes 50% of poems submitted. Reporting time: 30 days. Payment: 1 contributors copy. Interested in new or unpub'd poets: yes. Simultaneous submissions accepted: no. Recent contributors: Abbott Small, Ron Patterson, Dennis Knotts, William Beyer, Eric Ray. Submission quantity: 3. Special interests: Poems of any style, though especially interested in humor and satire as long as they are consistent with our nature as a religious journal.

QUEEN OF ALL HEARTS, 26 South Saxon Avenue, Bay Shore, NY 11706, 516-665-0726. Joseph Tusiani. 1950. "We can only accept Marian poetry; i.e., with Mary, Mother of Christ as basic theme." circ. 2M. 6/yr. Pub'd 25 poems 1999; expects 30 poems 2000, 30 poems 2001. sub. price: $20; sample: $3.50. 48pp; 7¾×10¾; Rights purchased: publishing rights only. Publishes 5% of poems submitted. Deadlines: 4 months previous. Reporting time: 3-4 weeks. Payment: free subscription + 6 complimentary copies. Interested in new or unpub'd poets: yes. Simultaneous submissions accepted: rarely. Recent contributors: Donato Coco, Tom Riley, Vivian Walsh, Nathan Cervo, Neil C. Fitzgerald. Submission quantity: 1-3. Special interests: short poems.

QUEEN'S QUARTERLY: A Canadian Review, Quarterly Committee of Queen's University, Queen's University, Kingston, Ontario K7L 3N6, Canada, 613-545-2667, e-mail qquarter@post.queensu.ca, website http:/info.queensu.ca/quarterly. Joan Harcourt, Poetry and Fiction Editor. 1893. circ. 3.5M. 4/yr. Pub'd 40 poems 1999. sub. price: $20 Canada, $25 U.S.; sample: $6.50. 160pp; 6×9; Rights purchased: 1st North American. Publishes a very small % of poems submitted. Deadlines: none. Reporting time: 4 weeks. Payment: upon publication. Interested in new or unpub'd poets: yes. Simultaneous submissions accepted: no. Recent contributors: Al Purdy, Michael Penny, Chad Norman, Anne LeOressay. Submission quantity: 6 (max). Special interests: Canadian poetry.

Quilted Walls Micropress, 426 N. Main Street, Herkimer, NY 13350. 1994. 5×8.

R

Rabeth Publishing Company, 201 S. Cottage Grove, Kirksville, MO 63501, 660-665-5143, e-mail qurabeth@kvmo.net. Elizabeth Quigley, Editor. 1990. "Rabeth Publishing Company was established to help new authors get their work published. The author will be carefully considered." avg. press run 500. Expects 2-3 poetry titles 2000. 5½×8½, 6×9; avg. price, cloth: $14; paper: $9.95; other: $4.95 saddle-stitched. 60-120pp; Publishes (if not offensive morally) 100% of poetry manuscripts submitted. Reporting time: 2 weeks. Payment: negotiable. Interested in new or unpub'd poets: yes. Simultaneous submissions accepted: yes. Recently published poets: Jane Finley Wilson, Cherlene Calhoun, Brenda J. Haliburton, David Bernatchez, Jackie D. Norman. Submission quantity: 5-8. Special interests: We publish any poetry written in good taste. Does not need to be religious, but may be. We need poetry for children, special days; longpoems are OK. We can also take facts and put them into poetry for anniversaries, birthdays and special occasions.

RADIANCE, The Magazine For Large Women, PO Box 30246, Oakland, CA 94604, 510-482-0680, E-mail info@radiancemagazine.com, www.radiancemagazine.com. Alice Ansfield. 1984. "We are a magazine geared to large women—we focus on self-esteem. We encourage our readers to feel good about themselves whatever their weight. We have articles on physical and emotional well-being, (without promotion of dieting/surgery, etc.), spirituality, cultural and historical views of body size, media, book reviews, ads...we are a quarterly magazine." circ. 15M. 4/yr. Pub'd 60 poems 1999. sub. price: $25 US; sample: $5 for writers only. 60pp; 8½×11; Rights purchased: 1 time. Publishes 10% of poems submitted. Deadlines: April 1, July 1, Oct. 1, Jan.1.

Reporting time: 2-4 months. Payment: $10-$15 plus contributor's copy. Interested in new or unpub'd poets: yes. Simultaneous submissions accepted: yes. Recent contributors: Anna Balint, Lonnie Hull DuPont. Submission quantity: as many as desired. Special interests: We welcome poetry on women and body image, self-esteem, growth, eating and food, and spirituality. Prefer well-crafted, unrhymed poetry. *Not* preachy.

RAFTERS, Calder Square PO Box 10929, State College, PA 16805-0929, 814-867-4073; mdu103@psu.edu. 1996. circ. 500. 4/yr. sub. price: $17; sample: $3.50 + p/h. 114pp; 6×9.

RAG MAG, Black Hat Press, Box 12, Goodhue, MN 55027, 651-923-4590. Beverly Voldseth Allers, Editor & Publisher. 1982. "Don't bother sending only 1 poem. No horrific, sadistic, pornographic stuff." circ. 300. 2/yr. Pub'd 100 poems 1999; expects 100 poems 2000, 100 poems 2001. sub. price: $10; sample: $4. 112pp; 6×9; Rights purchased: first only. Publishes 33% of poems submitted. Deadlines: end of May, nothing read during June, July, Aug. Reporting time: varies. Payment: 1 copy. Interested in new or unpub'd poets: yes. Simultaneous submissions accepted: yes. Recent contributors: Robert Bly, Tom Hennen, Karen Herseth Wee, Spencer Reece, Stephanie Pershing Buehler. Submission quantity: 6-8. Special interests: Alive & interesting.

RAG SHOCK, Lunar Offensive Publications, 1910 Foster Avenue, Brooklyn, NY 11230-1902. 1994. "Poetry to 100 lines. Include SASE. *Rag Shock* seeks the unprintable" circ. 1.5M. 1/yr. sub. price: $5; sample: $5. 144pp; 8½×10; Publishes 5-10% of poems submitted. Reporting time: 3 weeks. Payment: 1 copy for paper mss, 2 copies for IBM/DOS/ASCII diskette. Interested in new or unpub'd poets: yes. Simultaneous submissions accepted: yes. Submission quantity: 5 or less. Special interests: Need authors to go over their edges, into the realms of the disturbing and disturbed.

RAIN CITY REVIEW, 7215 SW LaView Drive, Portland, OR 97219, 503-771-1907. Brian Christopher Hamilton, Editor; Douglas Spangle, Senior Editor; Kelly Lenox Allan, Associate Editor; Tracy Burkholder, Associate Editor. 1993. "We prefer slightly darker, edgier work than most magazines - work with strong emotional connections that takes risks, and is afraid of nothing. Our tastes are very diverse" circ. 400-800. 2/yr. Pub'd 105 poems 1999; expects 90 poems 2000, 90 poems 2001. sub. price: $13 postpaid; sample: $7 postpaid. 100pp; 5½×8½; Rights purchased: First N. American Serial. Publishes 15% of poems submitted. Reporting time: 1-5 months. Payment: 1-3 copies. Interested in new or unpub'd poets: yes. Simultaneous submissions accepted: yes. Recent contributors: Kate Braverman, Judith Berke, Sharon Doubiago, Donald Rawley. Submission quantity: 4-5. Special interests: We are interested in seeing far more essays and translations.

THE RAINTOWN REVIEW, PO Box 370, Pittsboro, IN 46167-0370, hmpeditor@hotmail.com. Harvey Stanbrough. 1998. "Please send for a sample copy and/or guidelines before you submit work. Our favorite poetry is blank verse (unrhymed, loose iambic pentameter). End rhyme is neither a crime nor a requirement. If you say things in a new way and are serious about the craft of poetry and its application, your work will find a home here." circ. 2.5M. 2-4/yr. Pub'd 160 poems 1999; expects 160 poems 2000, 160 poems 2001. sub. price: $24/4 issues; sample: $6.50 ppd. 58pp; 8½×5½; Rights purchased: first or one-time rights. Publishes 5% of poems submitted. Deadlines: none. Reporting time: 1 month. Payment: 1 contributor's copy, otherwise by arrangement with poet. Interested in new or unpub'd poets: yes. Simultaneous submissions accepted: yes (and previously published works). Recent contributors: William Baer, Robin Tatum, Thomas Downing, Fredrick Zydek, Virginia Artrip Snyder. Submission quantity: up to 4.

RALPH'S REVIEW, 129 Wellington Avenue, #A, Albany, NY 12203-2637, e-mail rcpub@juno.com. R. Cornell. 1988. "I read all that I receive. Just send any poems. Send SASE. Up to 20 lines" circ. 100. 4/yr. Pub'd 25 poems 1999; expects 15 poems 2000, 30 poems 2001. sub. price: $15; sample: $2. 25pp; 8½×11; Rights purchased: First North American Serial Rights. Publishes 50-60% of poems submitted. Deadlines: open. Reporting time: 2-4 weeks. Payment: 1 copy. Interested in new or unpub'd poets: yes. Simultaneous submissions accepted: yes. Recent contributors: Kim Laico, Holly Day, John Grey, R. Cornell. Submission quantity: 2-5. Special interests: No rape, racial, anti-life.

RAMBUNCTIOUS REVIEW, Rambunctious Press, Inc., 1221 West Pratt Blvd., Chicago, IL 60626. R. Goldman, N. Lennon, E. Hausler. 1984. "Yearly poetry contest with cash prizes. Write for details, include SASE" circ. 600. 1/yr. Pub'd 20 poems 1999; expects 20 poems 2000, 20 poems 2001. sub. price: $12/3 issues; sample: $4. 48pp; 7×10; Rights purchased: 1st publication. Publishes 10% of poems submitted. Deadlines: none, but we do not accept submissions from June 1 to August 31. Reporting time: 9 months. Payment: 2 copies. Interested in new or unpub'd poets: yes. Simultaneous submissions accepted: yes. Recent contributors: Maureen Flannery, B.Z. Niditch, Hugh Fox, Glenna Holloway. Submission quantity: 1-5.

Rarach Press, 1005 Oakland Drive, Kalamazoo, MI 49008, 616-388-5631. L.R. Hanka. 1981. "I am more akin to the self-publishers. I publish only occasionally—at most one book per year and that only material that I have a personal attachment to. These are poems by my friends or poems I have translated or similar things. They are further a vehicle for my artwork and primarily bibliophilia hand-bound and hand-printed with original etchings or wood engravings. I do not solicit manuscripts" avg. press run 50. Pub'd 1 poetry title 1999; expects 1 poetry title 2000, 1 poetry title 2001. size highly variable; avg. price, cloth: $100; other: hand-bound $400 and up.

14-100pp; Reporting time: at leisure. Interested in new or unpub'd poets: no. Simultaneous submissions accepted: no. Recently published poets: Rilke, Hanka, Popkes, Armstrong, Mitchell, Delp.

THE RATIONAL FEMINIST, 10500 Ulmerton Road #726-202, Largo, FL 34641. Molly Gill. 1984. "Readable, legible, no vulgarity, no diversity or multi." circ. 100. 6-10/yr. Pub'd 12 poems 1999; expects 12 poems 2000, 12 poems 2001. sub. price: suggested donation for mv ministry $25; sample: $3 suggested donation, $5 outside USA. 16-27pp; 8½×14, 8½×11; Rights purchased: all vol. Publish 20 out of 365 poems submitted. Deadlines: May 15, July 15, Oct. 15, Dec. 15. Reporting time: 3 weeks. Interested in new or unpub'd poets: yes. Simultaneous submissions accepted: yes. Submission quantity: 3 max. Special interests: Western culture only.

RATTAPALLAX, 532 La Guardia Place, Suite 353, New York, NY 10012, 212-560-7459, e-mail rattapallax@hotmail.com. 1998. "Each issue includes a CD featuring the poets reading their accepted poems" circ. 2M. 2/yr. Pub'd 110 poems 1999; expects 110 poems 2000, 110 poems 2001. sub. price: $14; sample: $7.95. 128pp; 6×9; Rights purchased: First American serial rights. Publishes 1% of poems submitted. Deadlines: Dec. 1 and June 1. Reporting time: 2 months. Payment: none. Interested in new or unpub'd poets: yes. Simultaneous submissions accepted: no. Recent contributors: Bill Kushner, James Ragan, Karen Swenson, Ron Price, Mark Nickels. Submission quantity: 3-5 poems.

RATTLE, 13440 Ventura Boulevard #200, Sherman Oaks, CA 91423, 818-788-3232, fax 818-788-2831. Lee Stellasue, Poetry Editor. 1993. "Cover letter, bio and SASE" circ. 4M. 2/yr. Pub'd 250 poems 1999. sub. price: $16; sample: $8. 196pp; 6×9; Rights purchased: all published work returns to the author. Publishes 10% of poems submitted. Reporting time: 2-4 months. Payment: 2 copies. Interested in new or unpub'd poets: yes. Simultaneous submissions accepted: yes. Recent contributors: Dorianne Laux, Sam Hamill, Philip Levine, Edward Hirsch, Diane Wakoski. Submission quantity: 5.

THE RAVEN CHRONICLES, 1634 11th Avenue, Seattle, WA 98122, 206-323-4316, ravenchr@speakeasy.org, www.speakeasy.org/ravenchronicles. Tiffany Midge, Jody Aliesan. 1991. "Special themes some issues, check out our website" circ. 1M. 3/yr. Pub'd 50-60 poems 1999; expects 30-50 poems 2000. sub. price: $20, $30 foreign; sample: $4. 48-72pp; 8½×11; Rights purchased: 1st serial rights/pub rights. Publishes 5% of poems submitted. Deadlines: year round. Reporting time: 3-6 months. Payment: $5-$40. Interested in new or unpub'd poets: yes. Simultaneous submissions accepted: yes. Recent contributors: Diane Glancy, Margaret Randall, David Lloyd Whited, Anita Endrezze. Submission quantity: 5-10 once a year. Special interests: International poetry, cross-cultural issues.

●**Ravenwood Publishing,** PO Box 601551, Sacramento, CA 95860, 916-974-0764, Fax 916-972-9312, www.ravenwoodpub.com. 1997. 6×9.

Raw Dog Press, 151 S. West Street, Doylestown, PA 18901, 215-345-6838, www.freeyellow.com/members/rawdog/. Gerry R. Fabian, Editor. 1977. "Raw Dog Press has moved away from chapbooks and into specialty poetry. What we publish are poetry postcards. We also do bookmarks and poetry labels. Poetry should be short. What will work for us are short poems 3-7 lines that are understated and humorous and are universal statements of life! We welcome new poets and detest second-rate poems from 'name' poets." avg. press run 100. Pub'd 1 poetry title 1999; expects 1 poetry title 2000, 1 poetry title 2001. 4×6; avg. price, paper: $8. 12-15pp; Publishes 10% of poetry manuscripts submitted. Reporting time: 1 day to 1 month - no more than that! Payment: usually in copies although small cash prizes when money is available. Interested in new or unpub'd poets: yes. Simultaneous submissions accepted: no. Recently published poets: R. Gerry Fabian, John Grey, Wes Patterson, Chris Harter. Submission quantity: 3-5. Special interests: Once again, short poetry that is to the point. Our subject matter is open but humor always has an inside track. After humor, we tend to like a positive approach. Any poet worth his or her salt should invest $8 to buy a copy of *Post Poems* and see what we publish. In a nutshell, those poets who know what we want eventually publish here; those poets who deal in one-time submissions rarely hit the mark. We will bend over backward to help a poet and the ones who we publish speak very well of us. They become Raw Dog's literary ambassadors.

RAW NERVZ HAIKU, Proof Press, 67 Court Street, Aylmer, QC J9H 4M1, Canada, E-mail: dhoward@aix1.uottawa.ca. 1994. circ. 250. 4/yr. sub. price: $20; sample: $6. 52pp; 5½×8½.

THE RAW SEED REVIEW, 780 Merion Greene, Charlottesville, VA 22901. Sam Taylor. 1998. circ. 500. 2/yr. Expects 100 poems 2000, 100 poems 2001. sub. price: $14; sample: $7. 80pp; 6×9; Rights purchased: first. Publishes 5% of poems submitted. Deadlines: year round. Reporting time: 1-16 weeks. Payment: 1-2 copies. Interested in new or unpub'd poets: only if they've read an issue. Simultaneous submissions accepted: with notification. Recent contributors: Elisabeth Murawski, Jim Grabill, Martin Nakell, Duane Locke. Submission quantity: 3-6. Special interests: We would like to see more translations.

RAZOR WIRE, PO Box 8876, University Station, Reno, NV 89507, 702-847-9311, fax 702-847-9335, e-mail shaungrif@aol.com. Shaun T. Griffin, Editor. 1989. "Poetry published in *Razor Wire* is read at Razor Wire

Poetry/Art Show, opening day.'' 1/yr. Pub'd 30-50 poems 1999; expects 30-50 poems 2000, 30-50 poems 2001. sub. price: $6; sample: inquire. 50pp; 5×8; Rights purchased: rights revert to author immediately after publication. Publishes 30% of poems submitted. Deadlines: March 1. Reporting time: 2 months. Payment: copy(ies). Interested in new or unpub'd poets: yes. Simultaneous submissions accepted: yes. Recent contributors: Billy Weyer, Stephen Fogarty, Michael Smith, Joseph Morfin, James Stewart. Submission quantity: 5-15. Special interests: Not receiving enough translations (send original and translation). *Razor Wire* is open to all forms, well written.

READ, AMERICA!, The Place In The Woods, 3900 Glenwood Avenue, Golden Valley, MN 55422, 612-374-2120. Roger Hammer. 1982. ''Do not send erotic or ''navel contemplation'' pieces.'' circ. 10M. 4/yr. Pub'd 20 poems 1999; expects 30 poems 2000, 40 poems 2001. sub. price: $25; sample: $7.50. 16pp; 8½×11; Rights purchased: all. Publishes 20% of poems submitted. Deadlines: varies. Reporting time: 1 week to 1 month. Payment: $10 per item. Interested in new or unpub'd poets: Definitely. Simultaneous submissions accepted: no. Submission quantity: up to 3. Special interests: Light or profound, but MUST be understandable!

Reality Street Editions, 4 Howard Court, Peckham Rye, London SE15 3PH, United Kingdom, 0171-639-7297. Ken Edwards, Wendy Mulford. 1993. ''In 1993, Reality Studios (London) merged with Street Editions (Cambridge) under the joint imprint Reality Street Editions. Four titles a year will be published. Unfortunately, unsolicited submissions cannot be considered.'' avg. press run 300-400. Pub'd 1 poetry title 1999; expects 4 poetry titles 2000, 4 poetry titles 2001. avg. price, paper: $10-$15. 48-96pp; Payment: copies and/or flat fee. Interested in new or unpub'd poets: no. Simultaneous submissions accepted: no. Recently published poets: Allen Fisher, Tom Raworth, Fanny Howe, Sarah Kirsch, Denise Riley.

REALM OF DARKNESS, 577 Central Avenue, Box 4, Jefferson, LA 70121-1400, e-mail: fullmoon@eduora-mail.com or haunted@rocketmail.com; Websites www.members.xoom.com/blackie, www.spaceports.com/~haunted/, www.eclecticity.com/zines/, www2.cybercities.com/z/zines/, www.dreamers.dynip.com/zines/. Sharida Rizzuto, Harold Tollison, Ann Hoyt. 1983. ''Definitely on the dark side. Devoted to macabre poetry'' circ. 300. 2/yr. Pub'd 80 poems 1999. sub. price: $13.80; sample: $6.90. 80pp; 8½×11; Rights purchased: One-time first or second serial rights. Publishes 30-40% of poems submitted. Deadlines: Always open to submissions. Reporting time: 2-6 weeks. Payment: free copies. Interested in new or unpub'd poets: yes. Simultaneous submissions accepted: yes. Recent contributors: Kim Elizabeth, Leilah Wendell, Rose Dalton, Lucinda MacGregor, Gregory E. Harrison. Submission quantity: 1-5. Special interests: We are willing to look at any type of poetry.

REALM OF THE VAMPIRE, 577 Central Avenue, Box 4, Jefferson, LA 70121-1400, e-mail fullmoon@eudoramail.com, haunted@rocketmail.com, gothic@imaginemail.com; Websites www.eclecticity.com/zines/, www.freez.com/vampires, www.members.xoom.com/blackie, www.spaceports.com/~haunted/, www2.cybercities.com/z/zines/. Sharida Rizzuto, Editor; Harold Tollison, Associate Editor; Ann Hoyt, Assistant Editor. 1983. ''This publication is devoted to vampirism in literature, legend, and film. All submissions must be double-spaced and typewritten.'' circ. 500. 2+3. Pub'd 30-40 poems 1999; expects 40 poems 2000, 40 poems 2001. sub. price: $15.80, newsletter - $9; sample: $7.90 - $3. 40pp for newsletter, 100pp for journal; 8×11; Rights purchased: one-time rights, first serial rights, second serial rights, or simultaneous rights. Publishes 35% of poems submitted. Deadlines: always open to submissions. Reporting time: 2-6 weeks. Payment: free copies. Interested in new or unpub'd poets: yes. Simultaneous submissions accepted: yes. Recent contributors: Leilah Wendell, Jo Ellen Nokles, Lisa M. Rames, Kim Elizabeth, William Kopecky. Submission quantity: 1-5. Special interests: We are willing to look at any type of poetry. No length requirements.

RED BRICK REVIEW, PO Box 6527, Syracuse, NY 13217. Sean Thomas Dougherty, Editor. 1991. ''Always include SASE and not postcards. Annual poetry contest, deadline January 1 to February 14, Prize $100 plus publication'' circ. 1M. 1/yr. sub. price: $5; sample: $3. 64pp; 6×9; Rights purchased: First rights. Publishes 5% of poems submitted. Deadlines: March 1. Reporting time: 3 months. Payment: copies. Interested in new or unpub'd poets: yes. Simultaneous submissions accepted: no. Recent contributors: Charles Simic, Thylias Moss, Suzanne Proul, Gary Soto, Patricia Smith. Submission quantity: no more than 5. Special interests: Translation, regional poems.

Red Candle Press (see also **CANDELABRUM POETRY MAGAZINE**), 9 Milner Road, Wisbech, PE13 2LR, England, tel: 01945 581067. M.L. Mr. McCarthy. 1970. ''We publish *Candelabrum Poetry Magazine*. Traditional-type metrical and rhymed verse is our special interest. Any subject, except racism, sexism, or pornography. We've published Philip Higson's translations of Maurice Rollinat's French poems. We do not give advice to beginners.'' Expects 1 poetry title 2000. 5½×8. Publishes 5% of poetry manuscripts submitted. Payment: we publish and distribute free, as a service to poets, copyright stays with the author. Interested in new or unpub'd poets: we have published some such poets. Simultaneous submissions accepted: no, absolutely not. Recently published poets: Henry Fischer, Eric Martin, Marjory Doyne, David Hill, Alice Evans. Submission quantity: 3-6. Special interests: Any subject, other than racist, sexist or ageist, but traditional-type poetry is specially welcome.

176

Red Cedar Press (see also RED CEDAR REVIEW), 17C Morrill Hall, Michigan State University, E. Lansing, MI 48824, 517-355-9656, rcreview@msu.edu. Meg McClure, Poetry Editor. 1963. avg. press run 700. Pub'd 2 poetry titles 1999; expects 2 poetry titles 2000, 2 poetry titles 2001. avg. price, paper: $5. 90pp; Publishes 1% of poetry manuscripts submitted. Reporting time: 3 months. Payment: 2 copies. Interested in new or unpub'd poets: yes. Simultaneous submissions accepted: no. Recently published poets: Diane Wakoski, Lyn Lifshin, Carol Cavallaro, Lee Kottner. Submission quantity: 5 poems.

RED CEDAR REVIEW, Red Cedar Press, 17C Morrill Hall, English Dept., Michigan State Univ., E. Lansing, MI 48824, 517-355-9656, rcreview@msu.edu. Douglas Dowland, Meg McClure. 1963. "Reporting time for poetry submitted June, July, August—4 months. SASE required. No simultaneous submissions please." circ. 700. 2/yr. Expects 15 poems 2000. sub. price: $10; sample: $3. 80pp; 8½×5½; Rights purchased: none. Publishes 1% of poems submitted. Deadlines: none. Reporting time: 1-2 months, 4 months during summer. Payment: 2 copies of *RCR* issue in which they appear. Interested in new or unpub'd poets: yes. Simultaneous submissions accepted: no. Recent contributors: Lyn Lifshin, Carol Cavallaro, Jean Battlo, Lee Kottner, Diane Wakoski. Submission quantity: no more than 5. Special interests: All poetry forms acceptable, but haiku and long poems not preferred. Particular interest in experimental poetry, satire, and focused poetry.

Red Dragon Press, 433 Old Town Court, Alexandria, VA 22314, 703-683-5877. 1993. "$5 reading fee for poetry" avg. press run 500. Pub'd 3 poetry titles 1999; expects 5 poetry titles 2000, 5 poetry titles 2001. 5⅜×8½; avg. price, paper: $10.95. 64pp; Publishes 8% of poetry manuscripts submitted. Reporting time: 6 months. Payment: none, no royalties. Interested in new or unpub'd poets: yes. Simultaneous submissions accepted: yes. Recently published poets: Laura Qa, Dee Snyder, Grace Cavalieri, George Karos, James Kerns. Submission quantity: 1-5 or up to 5 pages. Special interests: Innovative, progressive and experimental poetry and prose.

Red Dust, PO Box 630, Gracie Station, New York, NY 10028, 212-348-4388. 1963. "Non-linear poetic texts/need not be 'poetry.'" avg. press run 300-500. Pub'd 3 poetry titles 1999; expects 4 poetry titles 2000, 3 poetry titles 2001. 8½×5½; avg. price, paper: $6.95; other: short works priced at $6.95. Short works 27pp; Reporting time: 2 months. Payment: 10% on retail price after advance $100-$300; for short works no payment, 30 free copies and further copies at 30% discount. Red Dust claims no rights, no percentage given. Interested in new or unpub'd poets: money is short, I leave decision to poets. Simultaneous submissions accepted: yes. Recently published poets: Francis Ponge, Geoffrey O'Brien, Meena Alexander, Maya Khosla, Bert Stern. Submission quantity: 10 xeroxed with SASE. Special interests: Poetic texts and translations.

Red Hen Press, PO Box 902582, Palmdale, CA 93590, Fax 818-831-6659, E-mail redhen@vpg.net. Kate Gale. 1995. "No rhyming poems" avg. press run 1M. Pub'd 2 poetry titles 1999; expects 2 poetry titles 2000, 2 poetry titles 2001. 5½×8½; avg. price, paper: $11.95. 64pp; Publishes 5% of poetry manuscripts submitted. Reporting time: 4-6 months. Payment: 10%. Interested in new or unpub'd poets: yes. Simultaneous submissions accepted: yes. Recently published poets: Dr. Ben Saltman, Ricardo Means Ybarra, Dr. Angela Ball, Marlene Pearson. Submission quantity: 5. Special interests: Translations are fine. No religious poetry, nothing that will also work in *Reader's Digest*.

RED LAMP, 5 Kahana Court, Mountain Creek, Queensland 4557, Australia, evans-baj@hotmail.com. 2/yr.

Red Moon Press (see also FROGPOND: Quarterly Haiku Journal), PO Box 2461, Winchester, VA 22604-1661, 540-722-2156, redmoon@shentel.net. Jim Kauan, Editor-in-Chief. 1978. "Primarily a haiku publisher, but we do consider other projects" avg. press run 500. Pub'd 8 poetry titles 1999; expects 8 poetry titles 2000, 8 poetry titles 2001. 5½×8½; avg. price, paper: $12-15. 32-160pp; Publishes 5% of poetry manuscripts submitted. Reporting time: 1-2 months. Payment: varies. Interested in new or unpub'd poets: no. Simultaneous submissions accepted: no. Recently published poets: Dee Evetts, Tom Smith, Cor van den Heuvel, Ban'ya Natsuishi. Submission quantity: 5-10. Special interests: very open to translation projects.

RED OWL, 35 Hampshire Road, Portsmouth, NH 03801-4815, 603-431-2691; redowlmag@juno.com. 1995. "Try and stay upbeat..." circ. 200. 2/yr. Pub'd 250 poems 1999; expects 250 poems 2000, 250 poems 2001. sub. price: $20; sample: $10. 70pp; 8½×11; Publishes 10% of poems submitted. Deadlines: In the spring I need poems about autumn, and vice versa. Reporting time: 2 weeks - 2 months. Payment: 1 copy. Interested in new or unpub'd poets: yes. Simultaneous submissions accepted: yes. Recent contributors: Christine Delea, John Grey, Albert Huffstickler, Robert D. Spector, Dawn Zapletal. Submission quantity: 2-4. Special interests: Fewer than twenty-five lines. If it looks good on paper—and you like the way is reads, then you have a good shot, and aim for the future...

RED ROCK REVIEW, English Dept J2A/Com. College S. NV, 3200 E. Cheyenne Avenue, N. Las Vegas, NV 89030, www.ccsn.nevada.edu/departments/english/redrock.htm. Tina D. Eliopulos, Poetry Editor. 1996. "We do not accept poems that exceed 80 lines." 2/yr. Pub'd 49 poems 1999. sub. price: $9.50. 120pp; 6½×9½; Rights purchased: We reserve first N. American serial rights only; all other rights revert to author and artist upon publication. Publishes 10% of poems submitted. Reporting time: 2 months. Payment: unsolicited writers receive 2 copies, solicited writers' payments are negotiable. Interested in new or unpub'd poets: yes. Simultaneous submissions accepted: no. Recent contributors: Alberto Rios, Naomi Shihab Nye, Stephen Liu, Steve Orlen, Dianna Henning. Submission quantity: no more than 4. Special interests: We enjoy all forms, but we pay particular attention to those works that treat the southwest landscape.

RED WHEELBARROW, 21250 Stevens Creek Blvd., De Anza College, Cupertino, CA 95014, Fax 408-864-5629, rsplitter@earthlink.net. Randolph Splitter. 1976. "Submission time: September-December" circ. 500. 1/yr. Pub'd 30 poems 1999; expects 30 poems 2000, 30 poems 2001. sub. price: $5; sample: $5. 100pp; 6×9; Rights purchased: first printing, then reverts back to writer. Publishes 5-10% of poems submitted. Deadlines: December 31. Reporting time: 3-6 months. Payment: 2 copies. Interested in new or unpub'd poets: yes. Simultaneous submissions accepted: yes. Recent contributors: Lyn Lifshin, Robert Cooperman, Ed Kleinschmidt, Walter Griffin, Chitra Divakaruni. Submission quantity: 3-5. Special interests: We print all kinds of poems in open and closed forms. We like precise writing, emotional honesty, diverse voices.

REDEMPTION, PO Box 54063, Vancouver, BC V7Y 1B0, Canada, 604-264-9109; Fax 604-264-8692; Redemption@pacificgroup.net. 1993. circ. 500+. 4/yr. sub. price: $15; sample: $5. 22pp; 8½×11.

REDOUBT, Faculty of Communication, PO Box 1, Belconnen, ACT 2616, Australia, 06-201-5270; fax 06-201-5300. Gillian Ferguson, Maureen Bettle. 1988. "Short poetry preferred (up to 30 lines). Do enclose SASE and shor biographical note" circ. 300. 2/yr. Pub'd 60 poems 1999. sub. price: $16; sample: free (depends on issue). 140pp; 6¾×9¾; Publishes 10% of poems submitted. Deadlines: none. Reporting time: average 4 months. Payment: according to funds available. Interested in new or unpub'd poets: yes. Simultaneous submissions accepted: yes. Submission quantity: no more than six.

Redrosebush Press (see also PENNY-A-LINER; PORTALS), PO Box 2163, Wenatchee, WA 98807-2163, 509-662-7858. 1991. 6×9.

REFLECT, 1317 Eagles Trace Path #D, Chesapeake, VA 23320-9461, 757-547-4464. W. S. Kennedy, Editor and Publisher. 1979. "We have become a vehicle for presentation of the newly-emerging *Spiral Back-To-Beauty Movement*. Study, therefore, of copies of *Reflect* is needed before submitting. For instance, we use the new fiction form: spiral fiction, which has four rules....study of *Reflect* is necessary to learn these rules." 4/yr. Pub'd 160 poems 1999; expects 240 poems 2000. sub. price: $8; sample: $2. 48pp; 5½×8½; Rights purchased: first rights. Publishes 40% of poems submitted. Deadlines: March 12, June 12, Sept. 12, Dec. 12. Reporting time: try to answer in 1 month. Payment: 1 free copy of the magazine in which any contributor's work appears. Interested in new or unpub'd poets: yes. Simultaneous submissions accepted: no. Recent contributors: Ruth Wildes Schuler, B.Z. Niditch, Stan Proper, Susan Tanaka, Marikay Brown. Submission quantity: 4-6; single-space all poems. Make checks/money orders to W.S. Kennedy (not to Reflect). Special interests: The criterion here is beauty (the one requirement of any art). All forms are considered with that standard in mind.

REFLECTIONS, PO Box 1197, Roxboro, NC 27573, 336-599-1181, e-mail furbisd@piedmont.cc.nc.us. 1999. "Will consider all accessible forms of poetry, including traditional forms. Send two copies of ms, one with name and address and one without. Send bio information in brief cover letter" circ. 500. 1/yr. sub. price: $7; sample: $6. 128pp; 5½×8½; Reporting time: 3 months. Payment: copy of publication with their work. Simultaneous submissions accepted: no. Submission quantity: up to 5.

Regent Press, 6020-A Adeline, Oakland, CA 94608, 415-548-8459. Mark Weiman. 1978. avg. press run 500. Pub'd 1 poetry title 1999. 5½×8½; avg. price, paper: $10.95. 250pp; Payment: 15%. Interested in new or unpub'd poets: no. Recently published poets: Claire Burch.

THE REJECTED QUARTERLY, PO Box 1351, Cobb, CA 95426, E-mail bplankton@juno.com. Daniel Weiss. 1998. 4/yr. Pub'd 5-10 poems 1999. sub. price: $20; sample: $5. 40pp; 8½×11; Rights purchased: 1st rights. Publishes 5% of poems submitted. Reporting time: 1-2 months. Payment: $5. Interested in new or unpub'd poets: yes. Simultaneous submissions accepted: no. Submission quantity: 1-5.

Relief Press, 245 Teaneck Road, Ridgefield Park, NJ 07660-2003, 201-641-3003. Ronnie L. Smith. 1995. "Our first title Mary Diane Hausman's A Born-Again Wife's First Lesbian Kiss has been very well received. More titles to come" avg. press run 2M-3M. Pub'd 1 poetry title 1999; expects 1 poetry title 2000, 1 poetry title 2001. 5½×8½; avg. price, paper: $9.95. 70+pp; Interested in new or unpub'd poets: Solicited MS only. Recently published poets: Mary Diane Hausman. Special interests: feminist, lesbian.

RENDITIONS, Research Centre for Translation, Chinese University of Hong Kong, Chinese University of Hong Kong, Shatin, NT, Hong Kong, 26-097-400, 26-097-407; fax 26-035-149; e-Mail renditions@cuhk.hk. Eva Hung, Editor. 1973. circ. 900. 2/yr. Pub'd 14 poems 1999; expects 10 poems 2000. sub. price: US $25. 160pp; 10¼×7½; Publishes less than 10% of poems submitted. Reporting time: 3 months. Payment: honoraria and 2 copies. Recent contributors: Gu Cheng, Shu Ting, Zheng Min, Chen Dong Dong. Special interests: Translations from Chinese ONLY with accompanying original texts.

178

Research Centre for Translation, Chinese University of Hong Kong (see also RENDITIONS), Research Centre for Translation, Chinese University of Hong Kong, Shatin, NT, Hong Kong, 852-26097700/7407; e-Mail renditions@cuhk.hk. 1986. 5½x8½.

RESPONSE: A Contemporary Jewish Review, PO BOX 250892, New York, NY 10025-1506. Pearl R. Gluck, Poetry Editor. 1966. "Jewish themes." circ. 1.6M. 4/yr. Pub'd 12 poems 1999; expects 25 poems 2000, 30 poems 2001. sub. price: $20 indiv., $36 instit., $12 students; sample: $6. 120pp; 6x9; Publishes 25% of poems submitted. Deadlines: submitted any time. Reporting time: 6-8 weeks. Payment: 3 complimentary issues/poem. Interested in new or unpub'd poets: absolutely. Simultaneous submissions accepted: no. Recent contributors: Peter Nickowitz, Mary Leader, Joshua Weiner. Submission quantity: 3-5. Special interests: Translations, experimental poetry.

Reyes Investment Enterprise Ltd., PO Box 3418, Maraval, Trinidad & Tobago, 809-638-3756; 809-657-3657. 1988. 5½x8½.

RFD, PO Box 68, Liberty, TN 37095, 615-536-5176. Corbeau. 1974. "We occasionally produce a poetry feature (every year or so), but generally we look for shorter poems." circ. 3.4M. 4/yr. Pub'd 45 poems 1999; expects 60 poems 2000, 70 poems 2001. sub. price: $20 2nd Class mailing, $32 1st Class, $25 foreign; sample: $6.50. 72pp; 8½x11; Rights purchased: authors retain rights. Publishes 15% of poems submitted. Deadlines: Winter Nov. 1, Spring Feb. 1, Summer May 1, Fall Aug. 1. Reporting time: 2-9 months. Payment: 1 copy of issue published in. Interested in new or unpub'd poets: yes. Simultaneous submissions accepted: yes. Recent contributors: John Soldo, Louie Crew, James Broughton, Keith Hale, Frederick Raborg Jr. Submission quantity: 1-5. Special interests: Experimental poetry, light verse, satire. Also poems relating to rural, gay, men's, or alternative themes.

Rhiannon Press, 1105 Bradley Avenue, Eau Claire, WI 54701, 715-835-0598. Peg Lauber. 1977. "We do not accept unsolicited manuscripts; we solicit those we want to apply. We have begun an annual Wisconsin Women's Chapbook Series." avg. press run 250. Pub'd 1 poetry title 1999; expects 1 poetry title 2000, 1 poetry title 2001. 5½x8½; avg. price, paper: $6. 30pp; Reporting time: 1 month average. Payment: 40 copies to author in lieu of royalties. Interested in new or unpub'd poets: no. Simultaneous submissions accepted: no. Recently published poets: Laurel Speer, Ingrid Swanberg, Betsy Adams, Margaret Kaminsky, Denise Sweet. Submission quantity: 5. Special interests: Women's poetry, especially women's Midwestern poetry.

RHINO: THE POETRY FORUM, PO Box 554, Winnetka, IL 60093, website www.artic.edu/~ageorg/rhino. Deborah Nodler Rosen, Kathleen Kirk, Helen Degen Cohen, Alice George. 1976. "We invite poems which exhibit passion and love affair with language" circ. 1M. 1/yr. Pub'd 70 poems 1999. sub. price: $6; sample: $5. 100pp; 5½x8½; Publishes 5% of poems submitted. Deadlines: 4/1-10/1. Reporting time: 2-3 months. Payment: 2 copies. Interested in new or unpub'd poets: yes. Simultaneous submissions accepted: yes. Recent contributors: Barry Silesky, Richard Jones, Maureen Seaton, Susan Terris, Rustin Larson. Submission quantity: 3-5. Special interests: Short/shorts, innovations in form, translations, occasional essays *on* poetry, Midwestern poets.

Rhizome, PO Box 265, Greensboro, PA 15338. 1989. "Formerly The Post-Industrial Press" avg. press run 1M-2M. Expects 1 poetry title 2000, 2-3 poetry titles 2001. 6x9; avg. price, paper: $5-$7. 50-100pp; Reporting time: immediately. Payment: negotiable. Interested in new or unpub'd poets: inquire. Simultaneous submissions accepted: no.

RHYME TIME POETRY NEWSLETTER, Hutton Publications, PO Box 2907, Decatur, IL 62524. Linda Hutton, Editor. 1981. circ. 100. 4/yr. Pub'd 100 poems 1999; expects 125 poems 2000, 150 poems 2001. sub. price: $24; sample: $4. 44-50pp; 5½x8½; Rights purchased: one-time rights only. Publishes 30% of poems submitted. Deadlines: year-round, except for contests with specific deadlines. Reporting time: 1 month. Payment: copies. Interested in new or unpub'd poets: yes. Simultaneous submissions accepted: yes. Recent contributors: Judy Barnes, Donna Edsall, Marian Poe. Submission quantity: 3-4. Special interests: No more than 16 lines; seasonal poetry always welcome, as is humorous poetry. No avant-garde, or sugary poetry accepted.

THE RIALTO, PO Box 309 Aylsham, Norwich NR11 6LN, England. Michael Mackmin. 1984. "Always include SAE or international reply coupon, overseas contributors note IRC essential. We enjoy reading good poems. Always type. Contributors should read the magazine first. Ask your library. *No unsolicited prose.*" circ. 1.5M. 3/yr. Expects 200 poems 2000. sub. price: £16 sterling; sample: £6 sterling. 48pp; size A4; Rights purchased: rights stay with poet. Publishes 1% of poems submitted. Reporting time: up to 3 months. Payment: £20 sterling. Interested in new or unpub'd poets: yes. Simultaneous submissions accepted: no. Recent contributors: Carol Ann Duffy, Peter Redgrove, Roy Fisher, Les Murray, George Szirtes. Submission quantity: about 4. Special interests: Some bias towards writers in Eastern UK.

Ridgeway Press of Michigan, PO Box 120, Roseville, MI 48066, 313-577-7713, Fax to M.L. Liebler 810-294-0474, E-mail milliebler@aol.com. M.L. Liebler. 1973. "No unsolicited manuscripts. Ridgeway has recently started a *small* chapbook series (12-16 page books) but we are currently overcommitted" avg. press run 300-1M. Pub'd 3 poetry titles 1999; expects 3 poetry titles 2000, 3 poetry titles 2001. 5½×8½, 6×9; avg. price, cloth: $20; paper: $10. 36-65pp; Publishes less than 5% of poetry manuscripts submitted. Payment: 50 copies of each edition. Interested in new or unpub'd poets: not at this time, we are over committed. Simultaneous submissions accepted: no. Recently published poets: Linda Nemec Foster, Edward Sanders, Faye Kicknosway, Barry Wallenstein, Terry Blackhawk. Submission quantity: 3-5 when we are reading. Special interests: Imagistic poetry, surrealist, urban, and labor poetry.

Rising Star Publishers (see also ORACLE POETRY), PO Box 7413, Langley Park, MD 20787.

Rising Tide Press New Mexico, PO Box 6136, Santa Fe, NM 87502-6136, 505-983-8484, fax 505-983-8484. 1991. ''We are only interested in extending the limits of English language construction'' Pub'd 2 poetry titles 1999; expects 2 poetry titles 2000, 2 poetry titles 2001. 5⅜×8½; avg. price, cloth: $12.95. 150pp; Payment: yes. Interested in new or unpub'd poets: no. Recently published poets: Stanley Berne, Arlene Zekowski. Special interests: Prose poetry only.

RIVER CITY, University of Memphis, Department of English, Memphis, TN 38152, 901-678-4591. Thomas Russell, Editor. 1980. ''Unsolicited poetry is not considered during June, July, and August. Please do not submit during those months. *River City* fiction contest awards $2,000 1st Place, $500 for Second, $300 for Third. The deadline is January 20, 2000. Send SASE for guidelines'' circ. 1M. 2/yr. Pub'd 40 poems 1999; expects 55 poems 2000, 46 poems 2001. sub. price: $12, $24/3 years; sample: $7. 100pp; 7×10; Rights purchased: 1st North American serial rights. Publishes 20% of poems submitted. Deadlines: Mid-March for summer issue, end of October for winter issue. Reporting time: 2 weeks-3 months. Payment: 2 copies. Interested in new or unpub'd poets: yes. Simultaneous submissions accepted: no. Recent contributors: Phillip Levine, Donald Justice, Marge Piercy, Marvin Bell, Adrienne Rich. Submission quantity: no more than 5. Special interests: On rare occasions we publish translations, and would like essays ranging from personal to scholarly.

RIVER KING POETRY SUPPLEMENT, PO Box 122, Freeburg, IL 62243. Wayne Lanter, Editor; Donna Biffar, Associate Editor. 1995. circ. 4.4M. 3/yr. Pub'd 150 poems 1999; expects 150 poems 2000, 150 poems 2001. sub. price: free; sample: free. 8pp; 11×17½; Rights purchased: 1 time. We publish 1 out of 15 poems submitted. Deadlines: none. Reporting time: 1 month. Payment: 10 copies. Interested in new or unpub'd poets: yes. Simultaneous submissions accepted: no. Recent contributors: Philip Dacey, Ken McCullough, Philip Miller, John Knoepfle, R.G. Bishop. Submission quantity: 5-6.

●**THE RIVER REVIEW/LA REVUE RIVIERE**, University of Maine-Fort Kent, 25 Pleasant Street, Fort Kent, ME 04743, 207-834-7542, river@maine.edu. 1995. circ. 750. 1/yr. sub. price: $6 US, $8.50 Canada; sample: $5 US. 150pp; 6×9.

RIVER STYX, 634 North Grand Blvd., 12th Floor, St. Louis, MO 63103-1002, 314-533-4541. Michael Castro, Senior Editor; Quincy Troupe, Senior Editor; Richard Newman, Editor. 1975. ''Manuscripts will not be returned without SASE. Please do not send us opaque, private poetry. *River Styx* International Poetry Contest. Deadline: May 31st. Past judges include Marilyn Hacker, Philip Levine, Molly Peacock, Mark Doty, and Naomi Shihab Nye.'' circ. 3M. 3/yr. Pub'd 70 poems 1999. sub. price: $20 individuals, $28 institutions; sample: $7. 108pp; 6×9; Rights purchased: none. Publishes less than 1% of poems submitted. Deadlines: May-November. Reporting time: 5 months maximum. Payment: contributor's copy + $8/page. Interested in new or unpub'd poets: yes. Simultaneous submissions accepted: yes, if so notified. Recent contributors: Louis Simpson, Rodney Jones, Naomi Shihab Nye, Catherine Bowman, Andrew Hudgins. Submission quantity: 3-5.

RIVERSIDE QUARTERLY, 1101 Washington Street, Marion, AL 36756-3213. Sheryl Smith, Poetry Editor. Address poetry submissions to: 515 Saratoga #2, Santa Clara, CA 95050. 1964. ''Max. length about 50 lines (one *RQ* page). No special verse preferences, though didactic or 'uplifting' verse is shunned, excoriated, and vomited upon.'' circ. 1.1M. Irregular. Pub'd 15 poems 1999; expects 25 poems 2000, 40 poems 2001. sub. price: $8/4 issues; sample: $2.50. 68pp; 8½×5½; Rights purchased: all rights revert to contributors on publication. Publishes 5% of poems submitted. Deadlines: none. Reporting time: 10 days. Payment: 4 copies. Interested in new or unpub'd poets: yes. Simultaneous submissions accepted: yes. Recent contributors: Denise Dumars, Thomas Kretz, Judy Kronenfeld, Edward Mycue, Virginia Smith. Submission quantity: 6 maximum.

Riverstone, A Press for Poetry, 7571 East Visao Drive, Scottsdale, AZ 85262. Margaret Holley. 1992. ''We are a chapbook press only. Our books are offset-printed and perfect bound. Please submit in May or June only up until June 30th deadline. $8 reading fee. Any style. The annual contest is our only submission time. No further guidelines.'' avg. press run 300. Pub'd 1 poetry title 1999; expects 1 poetry title 2000, 1 poetry title 2001. 5½×8½; avg. price, paper: $5; other: sample copy $5. 20-32pp; Publishes 1% of poetry manuscripts submitted. Reporting time: 2 months from contest deadline. Payment: contest winner receives $100 and 50 free copies. Interested in new or unpub'd poets: yes. Simultaneous submissions accepted: yes. Recently published poets: Cathleen Calbert, Margo Stever, Gary Myers, Anita Barrows, Martha Vertreace. Submission quantity: 20-32 pages with title page, acknowledgments, contents.

RIVERWIND, General Studies, Hocking College, Nelsonville, OH 45764, 614-753-3591. J.A. Fuller, Poetry Editor. 1975. "We focus mainly on Appalachian Writers (Ohio, W. Virginia, Kentucky, etc.) or issues." circ. 400. 1/yr. Expects 80-100 poems 2000. sub. price: $5; sample: $2.50. 112-156pp; 7×7; Rights purchased: 1st North American serial rights. Publishes 10% of poems submitted. Deadlines: We do not read in the summer. Reporting time: 1-3 months. Payment: 2 copies. Interested in new or unpub'd poets: yes. Simultaneous submissions accepted: no. Recent contributors: Richard Hague, Roy Bentley, Larry Smith, Phillip Arnold, Betsy Brown. Submission quantity: 3-6. Special interests: We enjoy reading and publishing a variety of quality works. Since we have recently shifted from being a national to a regional publication, we favor "Appalachian" writers (Ohio, W. Virginia, Kentucky, etc.), but read and publish work from all parts of US and the world.

THE ROANOKE REVIEW, English Dept., Roanoke College, Salem, VA 24153, 540-375-2367. Robert R. Walter, Associate Professor of English. 1968. circ. 200-300. 2/yr. Pub'd 40-60 poems 1999; expects 40-60 poems 2000, 40-60 poems 2001. sub. price: $9; sample: $3. 48-60pp; 6×9; Rights purchased: first serial. Publishes 5-10% of poems submitted. Deadlines: none. Reporting time: 10-12 weeks max. Payment: copies only (3). Interested in new or unpub'd poets: yes. Simultaneous submissions accepted: no.

THE ROCKFORD REVIEW, PO Box 858, Rockford, IL 61105, e-mail dragonldy@prodigy.net. David Ross, Editor. 1971. "SASE" circ. 740. 3/yr. Pub'd 75 poems 1999; expects 75 poems 2000, 75 poems 2001. sub. price: $18 (includes monthly newsletter *Write Away*); sample: $5. 52pp; 5¼×8½; Rights purchased: 1st NA serial. Publishes 5-10% of poems submitted. Deadlines: we read year-round. Reporting time: 6-8 weeks. Payment: 1 copy, consideration for $25 editor's choice; guest of honor at annual reading/reception. Interested in new or unpub'd poets: yes. Simultaneous submissions accepted: yes. Recent contributors: Marie Asner, Winnie Fitzpatrick, Cindy Guentherman, Baloian, Tom Chandler. Submission quantity: up to 5. Special interests: Focus on the human condition! Satire, experimental poetry.

ROMANTIC HEARTS, PO Box 450669, Westlake, OH 44145-0612, 216-979-9793; D.Krauss@genie.com. 1996. 6/yr. sub. price: $22; sample: $4. 24pp; 8½×11.

THE ROMANTIST, The F. Marion Crawford Memorial Society, Saracinesca House, 3610 Meadowbrook Avenue, Nashville, TN 37205. Steve Eng, Associate Editor. 1977. "We are closed to poetry through 2005. Lyrical verse with musical quality, images, and no trite poeticisms. Almost no unrimed poetry is accepted for publication" circ. 300 (limited and numbered). 1/yr. Pub'd 15 poems 1999. 160pp; 8½×11; Rights purchased: all rights, but permit subsequent publication at no charge to poet provided mention is made that the original pub. was in *The Romantist*. Publishes 15% of poems submitted. Deadlines: full through 1996. Reporting time: 1 month. Payment: tear sheet or copy of the issue at 1/2 price. Interested in new or unpub'd poets: no distinction. Simultaneous submissions accepted: no. Recent contributors: Donald Sidney-Fryer, Joey Froehlich, E. Richard Rabbit, Michael Fantina, Margo Skinner. Submission quantity: 3 maximum. Special interests: Fantasy (fairy, elf), horror, science-fiction.

Ronsdale Press, 3350 West 21st Avenue, Vancouver, B.C. V6S 1G7, Canada, 604-738-4688, toll free 888-879-0919, Fax 604-731-4548. Ronald B. Hatch, Director. 1988. "Authors must be Canadian citizens or landed immigrants" avg. press run 1M. Pub'd 4 poetry titles 1999; expects 3 poetry titles 2000, 3 poetry titles 2001. 6×9; avg. price, cloth: $24.95CAN; paper: $11.95 CAN. 75pp; Publishes 10% of poetry manuscripts submitted. Reporting time: 1 month to 6 weeks. Payment: 10% or books in lieu. Interested in new or unpub'd poets: yes. Simultaneous submissions accepted: yes, with a statement to that effect from author. Recently published poets: Inge Israel, Florence Treadwell, John Donlan, Harold Rhenisch, Kevin Roberts. Submission quantity: enough for 50 pages. Special interests: Dual-language editions, experimental, regional.

ROOM, 38 Ferris Place, Ossining, NY 10562-2818. John Perlman. 1987. "Room will publish single author chapbooks when and if a ms. so impresses the editor that he would be remissin returning the work. Requests for copies will be honored" circ. 150. sub. price: gratis. Pages vary; 5½×8; Publishes 1% of poems submitted. Reporting time: asap. Payment: copies and mailings. Interested in new or unpub'd poets: yes. Simultaneous submissions accepted: NO. Recent contributors: DiPalma, Taggart, Murphy, Wellman, Dent. Submission quantity: no more than 20.

ROOM OF ONE'S OWN, PO Box 46160, Station D, Vancouver, British Columbia V6J 5G5, Canada. 1975. circ. 500. 4/yr. Expects 60 poems 2000. sub. price: $22.50 ($25US foreign) indiv, $25 ($30US foreign) instit; sample: $7 Canadian ($7 US foreign). 128pp; 5½×8½; Rights purchased: 1st only. Publishes 10% of poems submitted. Deadlines: anytime. Reporting time: 9 months. Payment: $35 (Can.) on publication. Interested in new or unpub'd poets: yes. Simultaneous submissions accepted: no. Recent contributors: Sharon Nelson, Lorna Crozier, Ronnie Brown, Adele Wiseman, Lynn Crosbie. Submission quantity: up to 6. Special interests: Feminist literary.

Rose Alley Press, 4203 Brooklyn Avenue NE #103A, Seattle, WA 98105, 206-633-2725. David D. Horowitz. 1995. "We do not accept or read any manuscripts submitted to us. We contact poets whom we wish to publish." avg. press run 1M. Pub'd 1 poetry title 1999; expects 1 poetry title 2000, 1 poetry title 2001. 5½×8½, though this may vary slightly; avg. price, paper: $5.95-$9.95. 28-96pp; Payment: 10 complimentary copies and 15% of any profits after printing and marketing expenses. Interested in new or unpub'd poets: no. Recently published poets: Victoria Ford, William Dunlop, Michael Spence, David D. Horowitz, Douglas Schuder. Special interests: We prefer formal verse to free verse but will consider the latter as part of a larger collection. We like rhyme and meter; conciseness and precision; integrated form and theme; and line breaks resonant with meaning. We like urbanity, not snobbery; earthiness, not crudity; profundity, not pretension; and wit, not glibness.

Rose Shell Press, 15223 Coral Isle Court, Fort Meyers, FL 33919-8434, 941-454-6546. Rochelle Holt, Publisher. 1992. "Formerly Merging Media owned by D.C. Erdmann, 1978-1992. Anyone who has not purchased at least one Merging Media or Rose Shell Press title should not submit queries. We have a more personal relationship with our writers which comes from having known them as discriminating and literate buyers of aesthetic books by women and sensitive men." avg. press run 250-500. Pub'd 5 poetry titles 1999; expects 3 poetry titles 2000, 3 poetry titles 2001. 5×8; avg. price, paper: $10. 48pp; Publishes 90% of poetry manuscripts submitted. Reporting time: 2 weeks. Payment: 90% copies. Interested in new or unpub'd poets: send SASE for author-as-produer details. Simultaneous submissions accepted: not at this time; we are the final serious interest of the aspiring or experienced writer. Recently published poets: Geraldine Little, Susan Sheppard, Ruth Moon Kempher, Lili Bita, Rochelle Lynn Holt. Submission quantity: 5 with SASE. Special interests: Open now to poets and writers only on author/producer basis. Send SASE. We also trade logos; write for details.

ROSEBUD, PO Box 459, Cambridge, WI 53523, 608-423-9690. John C. Smelcer. 1993. "We favor good imagery and strong emotional content that fit the four or five rotating themes of each issue" circ. 12M. 4/yr. Expects 15 poems 2000, 20 poems 2001. sub. price: $24/4 issues; sample: $6.95. 136pp; 7×10; Rights purchased: 1st or 2nd. Publishes 5% of poems submitted. Deadlines: ongoing. Reporting time: 14 months. Payment: $45. Interested in new or unpub'd poets: yes. Simultaneous submissions accepted: yes. Recent contributors: Allen Ginsbero, Louis Simpson, Seamus Heaney, X.J. Kennedy, Philip Levine. Submission quantity: 2-5.

Roth Publishing, Inc., 175 Great Neck Road, Great Neck, NY 11021, 516-466-3676. 1976.

THE ROUND TABLE: A Journal of Poetry and Fiction, PO Box 18673, Rochester, NY 14618. Alan Lupack, Barbara Tepa Lupack. 1984. "Our issues will include poetry and fiction based on or alluding to the Arthurian legends." Irregular. Pub'd 20-25 poems 1999; expects 20-25 poems 2000, 20-25 poems 2001. sub. price: varies; sample: $7.50. 64pp; 8½×5½; Rights purchased: 1-time. Publishes less than 10% of poems submitted. Reporting time: varies, we try for 2 months; usually longer, especially for poems under serious consideration. Payment: 5 copies of chapbook. Interested in new or unpub'd poets: yes, if the poems are of high quality. Simultaneous submissions accepted: yes, but expect poets to inform us immediately if a poem is accepted elsewhere. Recent contributors: Kathleene West, Marilyn Coffey, Paul Scott, Wendy Mnookin, Norvus Lacy. Submission quantity: more than 1 or 2. Special interests: We are now publishing almost exclusively works based on the Arthurian legends, including volumes of Arthurian works by one author instead of annual issue of *The Round Table*.

Rowan Mountain Press, PO Box 10111, Blacksburg, VA 24062-0111, 540-961-3315, Fax 540-961-4883, e-mail faulkner@bev.net. 1988. "Invited mss. only." avg. press run 200. Pub'd 1 poetry title 1999; expects 1 poetry title 2000, 1 poetry title 2001. 5½×8½; avg. price, paper: $6. 75pp; Payment: 10% of press run. Interested in new or unpub'd poets: no. Simultaneous submissions accepted: no. Recently published poets: Bennie Lee Sinclair, Harry Dean, Philip Paradis, Rev. Norman M. Bowman. Submission quantity: invited mss only. Special interests: Appalachian region, Scottish.

Rowhouse Press (see also JACK MACKEREL MAGAZINE), PO Box 23134, Seattle, WA 98102-0434. Greg Bachar, Editor. 1992. avg. press run varies. Pub'd 2 poetry titles 1999; expects 3-4 poetry titles 2000, 7-8 poetry titles 2001. size varies; avg. price, paper: $5; other: $5 chapbooks. Pages vary; Reporting time: 2-4 weeks. Payment: copies. Interested in new or unpub'd poets: yes. Recently published poets: William D. Waltz, David Berman, Katie J. Kurtz, Ann Miller, Carl Faucher. Submission quantity: 3-5; 12-14 for chapbook series.

RUBBER DUCKY MAGAZINE, PO Box 799, Upper Montclair, NJ 07043, 201-783-0029. 1992. circ. 500. 4/yr. sub. price: $8; sample: $2. 20pp; 8×11.

Runaway Publications (see also THE PATRIOT), PO Box 1172, Ashland, OR 97520, 503-482-2578. James L. Berkman, Publisher. 1977. "Do not accept unsolicited manuscripts" avg. press run 100. Pub'd 1 poetry title 1999; expects 1 poetry title 2000, 1 poetry title 2001. 5½×8½; avg. price, paper: $10. 12pp; Payment: negotiable.

The Runaway Spoon Press, Box 3621, Port Charlotte, FL 33949-3621, 941-629-8045. Bob Grumman. 1987. "My press is in its second decade and slowing down. I'm no longer as open to new authors as I once was. I'm definitely not interested in the kind of thing commercial and academic presses publish.'' avg. press run 100. Pub'd 5 poetry titles 1999; expects 6 poetry titles 2000, 6 poetry titles 2001. 8½×5½; avg. price, paper: $5 ppd. 48pp; Publishes 2% of poetry manuscripts submitted. Reporting time: 1-2 weeks. Payment: 25 copies of first 100, 10% royalty thereafter. Interested in new or unpub'd poets: yes. Simultaneous submissions accepted: yes. Recently published poets: John M. Bennett, Karl Kempton, G. Huth, LeRoy Gorman, Stephen-Paul Martin. Submission quantity: 3-5. Special interests: Burstnorm poetry (If you don't know what that is, you probably shouldn't submit to the Runaway Spoon Press).

●**Rutledge Books, Inc.**, 107 Mill Plain Road, Danbury, CT 06811, 203-778-5925, Fax 203-798-7272, info@rutledgebooks.com, www.rutledgebooks.com. 1949. 5½×8½.

S

S Press, 527 Hudson Street, PO Box 20095, New York, NY 10014. 1982. ''We no longer publish a journal. Books appear sporadically'' avg. press run 750. Pub'd 2 poetry titles 1999; expects 2 poetry titles 2000, 2 poetry titles 2001. 6×9; avg. price, cloth: $10; paper: $10. 70pp; Publishes 5% of poetry manuscripts submitted. Reporting time: 2-4 weeks. Interested in new or unpub'd poets: no. Simultaneous submissions accepted: no. Recently published poets: William J. Austin.

Sachem Press, PO Box 9, Old Chatham, NY 12136, 518-794-8327. L. Hammer, S.A. Jaeger. 1980. ''We prefer to see an entire manuscript rather than samples.'' avg. press run 1M. Expects 1 poetry title 2001. 5½×8¼; avg. price, cloth: $17; paper: $9.95. 85pp; Reporting time: 3-6 months. Payment: negotiable. Interested in new or unpub'd poets: yes, those with magazine publication. Simultaneous submissions accepted: yes. Recently published poets: Vallejo, Ritsos, Sahtouris, Hammer, Rilke. Submission quantity: entire book. Special interests: Translations, poem sequences, prose-poems.

St. Andrew Press, PO Box 329, Big Island, VA 24526, 804-299-5956. Ray A. Buchanan. 1986. ''The St. Andrew Press is especially interested in doing thematic chapbooks on hunger, peace, justice, spirituality, Christian Community and related areas. We also are interested in book/cassette kits of music and related readings, etc.'' avg. press run 1M. Expects -1 poetry titles 2000, 1-2 poetry titles 2001. 5½×8½; avg. price, paper: $7.50; other: $9.95. 64-72pp; Reporting time: 1 month (4 weeks). Payment: negotiable. Interested in new or unpub'd poets: yes. Simultaneous submissions accepted: yes, if so marked. Submission quantity: 6-8.

St. Andrews Press, c/o St. Andrews College, Laurinburg, NC 28352-5598, 919-277-5310. Dan Auman, Director & Managing Editor. 1969-70. ''Always query'' avg. press run 500. Pub'd 6 poetry titles 1999; expects 7 poetry titles 2000, 7 poetry titles 2001. 5½×8½; avg. price, paper: $10; other: $5 chapbooks. 80pp; Publishes 2% of poetry manuscripts submitted. Reporting time: 4-6 months. Payment: 50 copies in lieu of royalty. Interested in new or unpub'd poets: yes—letter of inquiry required. Simultaneous submissions accepted: yes. Recently published poets: Barry Gifford, Charles Fort, Joseph Bathanti, Lenard Moore, David Rigsbee. Submission quantity: none. Special interests: Any local, national or international works.

ST. JOSEPH MESSENGER, PO Box 288, Jersey City, NJ 07303, 201-798-4141. Sister Mary Kuiken. 1898. ''Poems should be contemporary, clear, concise, blithe, beautiful, meaningful'' circ. 15M. 2/yr. Pub'd 25 poems 1999; expects 24 poems 2000, 30 poems 2001. sub. price: $5; sample: free. 16pp; 8½×11; Rights purchased: first and second, will release rights on request. Publishes 25% of poems submitted. Deadlines: can be submitted year round. Reporting time: 14 days. Payment: min. $5, max. $20-$25. Interested in new or unpub'd poets: yes. Simultaneous submissions accepted: yes. Recent contributors: Tom Walsh, Nancy Hyle, Michael Silverman, Anita Phillips, Bto. Franklin Cullen. Submission quantity: max 5. Special interests: Light verse, satire.

SALAMANDER, 48 Ackers Avenue, Brookline, MA 02146. 1992. circ. 1M. 2/yr. Pub'd 80 poems 1999; expects 80 poems 2000, 80 poems 2001. sub. price: $12; sample: $3. 80pp; 5½×8½; Rights purchased: none. Publishes 5% of poems submitted. Deadlines: we read year round. Reporting time: 4 months. Payment: 2 copies of mag. Simultaneous submissions accepted: prefer not. Recent contributors: Heather Reid, Martha Rhodes, Reetika Vazirani, Michael Collins, Phillis Levin. Submission quantity: approx. 5. Special interests: Translations.

THE SALEM JOURNAL, 577 Central Avenue, Box 4, Jefferson, LA 70121-1400, e-mail: fullmoon@eudora-mail.com or haunted@rocketmail.com; Websites www.eclecticity.com/zines/, www2.cybercities.com/z/zines/, www.members.xoom.com/blackie, www.spaceports.com/~haunted/, www.dreamers.dynip.com/zines/. Sharida Rizzuto, Harold Tollison, Lucinda MacGregor. 1983. ''Historical publication for witchcraft, voodoo, left-hand path, ancient Egyptian, Native American, Hermetic and other systems of magic'' circ. 1.2M. 2/yr. Pub'd 50 poems 1999. sub. price: $13.80; sample: $6.90. 80pp; 8½×11; Rights purchased: One-time rights, first or second time rights. Publishes 30-35% of poems submitted. Deadlines: always open to submissions. Reporting time: 2-6 weeks. Payment: free copy only. Interested in new or unpub'd poets: yes. Simultaneous submissions accepted: yes. Recent contributors: Richard Davignon, Ruth Wildes Schuler, Richard David Behrens, John Grey, Lucinda, MacGregor. Submission quantity: 1-5.

SALMAGUNDI, Skidmore College, Saratoga Springs, NY 12866, 518-584-5000. Robert Boyers, Peggy Boyers. 1965. circ. 5M-8M. 4/yr. Pub'd 50 poems 1999; expects 50 poems 2000, 75 poems 2001. sub. price: $15; sample: $5. 200pp; 5½×8½; Rights purchased: 1 time publication. Publishes 1% of poems submitted. Deadlines: before May 1 and after Oct. 15. Reporting time: 3-6 months. Payment: none. Interested in new or unpub'd poets: yes. Simultaneous submissions accepted: no. Recent contributors: Barry Goldensohn, Frank Bidart, Robert Pinsky, C.K. Williams, Karen Mulhollen. Submission quantity: 3-5. Special interests: *Not* especially interested in regional or light poetry.

Salmon Run Press, PO Box 672130, Chugiak, AK 99567-2130, 907-688-4268. John Smelcer, Editor-in-Chief. 1991. ''We sponsor an annual National Poetry Book contest in which we select one collection (48-96pg) for publication and national distribution. Print run is usually 500-1000. Deadline is Dec. 30th of each year. $10 reading fee required'' avg. press run 500-1000. Pub'd 3 poetry titles 1999. 6×9, 5½×8½; avg. price, paper: $10. 68-96pp; Publishes 1-2% of poetry manuscripts submitted. Reporting time: 1-3 months. Payment: 10% plus copies. Simultaneous submissions accepted: yes. Recently published poets: X.J. Kennedy, Molly Peacock, Ursula K. Le Guin, Philip Levine, Denise Duhamel. Submission quantity: 3-5.

SALOME: A Journal for the Performing Arts, Ommation Press, 5548 N. Sawyer, Chicago, IL 60625, 312-539-5745. Effie Mihopoulos. 1975. ''Include self-addressed stamped envelope with sufficient return postage.'' circ. 500. Irregular. Expects 20 poems 2000, 200-250 poems 2001. sub. price: $12; sample: $4 postcards and older issues, $8 current sample. 60-120pp; 8½×11; Publishes 85% of poems submitted. Deadlines: none. Reporting time: as soon as possible. Payment: contributor's copy. Interested in new or unpub'd poets: yes. Simultaneous submissions accepted: yes (please note so). Recent contributors: Ted Berrigan, Jessie T. Ellison, M.S. Robbins, Ed Orr, Lyn Lifshin. Submission quantity: up to 10. Special interests: must be about the performing arts.

SALT HILL, English Department, Syracuse University, Syracuse, NY 13244-1170. Erin Lambert, Poetry Editor. 1994. circ. 1M. 2/yr. Pub'd 50 poems 1999; expects 50 poems 2000, 70 poems 2001. sub. price: $15; sample: $8. 120-150pp; 5½×8½; Rights purchased: First North American. Publishes 5% of poems submitted. Deadlines: we read year round. Reporting time: 2-6 months. Payment: two copies. Interested in new or unpub'd poets: yes. Simultaneous submissions accepted: yes. Recent contributors: Bei Dao, Heather McHugh, Bill Knott, Jean Valeatine, Michael Burkard. Special interests: Interested in: prose and poetry of exceptional quality expressing a wide array of interests and concerns.

SALT LICK, Salt Lick Press, 1900 West Highway 6, Waco, TX 76712-0682. James Haining. 1939. ''Open. No particular bias toward content, form, length of submission. We print the best work we receive.'' circ. 1M. Irregular. Expects 40 poems 2000. sample price: $10 + postage. 64+pp; 8½×11; Rights purchased: all rights released after publication. Publishes 1-2% of poems submitted. Deadlines: none. Reporting time: 2-5 weeks. Payment: copies. Interested in new or unpub'd poets: yes. Simultaneous submissions accepted: yes. Recent contributors: Gerald Burns, Robert Trammel, Michael Lally, Julie Siegel, Robert Creeley. Submission quantity: 6-8.

Salt Lick Press (see also LUCKY HEART BOOKS; SALT LICK), 1900 West Hwy 6, Waco, TX 76712-0682. James Haining. 1969. ''Open. No bias toward content, form, length of submission. We print the best work we receive.'' avg. press run 1000. Pub'd 1 poetry title 1999; expects 1 poetry title 2000. 8½×11; avg. price, paper: $12. 64pp; Publishes 1-2% of poetry manuscripts submitted. Reporting time: 2-5 weeks. Payment: copies. Interested in new or unpub'd poets: yes. Simultaneous submissions accepted: yes. Recently published poets: Michael Lally, Robert Trammell, Gerald Burns, David Searcy, Robert Creeley. Submission quantity: 6-8. Special interests: Translations, experimental poetry, regional poetry, longpoems, light verse, satire, etc.

San Diego Poet's Press, c/o Kathleen Iddings, PO Box 8638, La Jolla, CA 92038, 858-457-1399. Kathleen Iddings, Editor & Publisher. 1981. ''This non-profit press was originated in 1982 to further the literary arts. Present Editor/Publisher/Poet Kathleen Iddings was an originator of the press. After this press published five anthologies, the American Book Series was established in 1989 for publishing a winner's first book of poetry. The winner is awarded $500. To date, six winning poets are published, as well as other poets who were not entering the contest. Watch *Small Press Review* and other poetry magazines for future contests and/or anthology announcements. They are not held every year.'' avg. press run 500. Expects 2 poetry titles 2000, 6 poetry titles 2001. 5½×8½; avg. price, cloth: $20; paper: $10. 75-100pp; Reporting time: 1 month. Payment: contest winners $500 plus publishing of manuscript; others, books. Interested in new or unpub'd poets: no. Simultaneous submissions accepted: yes. Recently published poets: Joan LaBombard, Kevin Griffith, Charles Atkinson, Lynne Hugo deCourcy, Michael Cleary. Submission quantity: 6. Special interests: Any poet may submit work throughout the year only if their individual poems are being widely accepted in fine publications.

San Diego State University Press, San Diego State University, San Diego, CA 92182, 619-594-6220. 6×9.

Sandberry Press, PO Box 507, Kingston 10, Jamaica, West Indies, fax 809-968-4067, phone 809-929-8089. Pamela Mordecai, Managing Editor; Sonia Chin, Consulting Editor; Martin Mordecai, Associate Editor; Rachel Mordecai, Editor. 1986. "Ms according to our specifications. Untidy or illegible m/s will be returned. Do not accept responsibility for "only" copies submitted" avg. press run 1M-5M. Pub'd 1 poetry title 1999; expects 3 poetry titles 2000, 3+ poetry titles 2001. 8½×5½, 6×9, 8½×11; avg. price, cloth: $12; paper: $9. 56-64pp; Publishes 10% of poetry manuscripts submitted. Reporting time: 3 months. Payment: 10% net receipts; payments calculated to 31 Dec., made 28 Feb. Interested in new or unpub'd poets: yes, but only poets from Caribbean. Simultaneous submissions accepted: no. Recently published poets: Jane King, Pamela Mordecai, Dennis Scott, Judith Hamilton, Elaine Savory. Submission quantity: up to 30 short poems. Special interests: Caribbean poetry; children's books—poetry and prose with Black/Caribbean focus.

SANDHILLS REVIEW (formerly ST. ANDREWS REVIEW), 2200 Airport Road, Pinehurst, NC 28374, 910-695-2756; FAX 910-695-3875. Stephen E. Smith. 1970. "Single-space all long poems." circ. 300-500. 2/yr. Pub'd 10 poems 1999; expects 10 poems 2000, 10 poems 2001. sub. price: $14; sample: $8.50. 120pp; 6×9; Publishes 10% of poems submitted. Deadlines: none. Reporting time: 3 months. Payment: 1 copy. Interested in new or unpub'd poets: yes. Simultaneous submissions accepted: yes. Recent contributors: Carolyn Kizer, Judith Sherwin, Martin Robbins, Rob Martin. Submission quantity: 3-5. Special interests: Any.

SANTA BARBARA REVIEW, PO Box 808, Summerland, CA 93067, 805-969-0861; E-mail jtaeby@West.net. P.S. Leddy. 1993. circ. 1M. 1/yr. Pub'd 50 poems 1999; expects 50 poems 2000, 50 poems 2001. sub. price: $10; sample: $10 + $2.50 p/h. 240pp; 6×9; Rights purchased: one-time. Publishes 20% of poems submitted. Deadlines: April. Reporting time: 2-3 months. Payment: 2 copies. Interested in new or unpub'd poets: yes. Simultaneous submissions accepted: no. Recent contributors: David R. Cook, Colin Sacks, Laurel Speer, Karen Fiser. Submission quantity: no more than 5.

Saqi Books Publisher, 26 Westbourne Grove, London W2 5RH, England, 071-221-9347, FAX 071-229-7692. 1983. 5¼×8; avg. price, cloth: £15/$22; paper: £4.95/$7.95. 168pp; Recently published poets: Mahmud Darwish, Samih al-Qasim, Adonis, Abdullah al-Udhari, Chris Abani. Special interests: We have published several poetry titles to-date (out of a total of forty titles):-*Victims of a Map* which is a bilingual (Arabic-English) anthology of contemporary Arabic poetry. The three poets in the anthology are Mahmud Darwish, Samih al-Qasim and Adonis. *Classical Poems by Arab Women* by Abdullah al-Udhari, *Kalakuta Republic* by Chris Abani.

Sarabande Books, Inc., 2234 Dundee Road, Suite 200, Louisville, KY 40205. Sarah Gorham, Editor-in-chief. 1994. "The majority of our poetry titles will come through invitation and through our national competition, The Kathryn A. Morton Prize in Poetry. Guidelines and our required entry form are available from November 1 through February 1 of each year. Please send a business sized SASE. Deadline for contest is February 15. Outside of our contest, we consider unsolicited material in September only. Writers must query first with a ten-page sample of poetry and a SASE, postmarked in September" avg. press run 1200-1500 paper, 300 hard. Pub'd 4 poetry titles 1999; expects 5 poetry titles 2000, 4 poetry titles 2001. 6×9; avg. price, cloth: $20.95; paper: $12.95. 80pp; Publishes less than 1% of poetry manuscripts submitted. Reporting time: 3-6 months. Payment: average 10%; winner of Kathryn A. Morton prize receives $2000. Interested in new or unpub'd poets: yes. Simultaneous submissions accepted: yes. Recently published poets: Sharon Bryan, Dick Allen, Michael Burkard, Belle Waring, Afaa Michael Weaver. Submission quantity: 10-postmarked during month of September. Special interests: Poetry of the highest artistic quality.

Saskatchewan Writers Guild (see also GRAIN), Box 1154, Regina, Saskatchewan S4P 3B4, Canada, 306-244-2828, grain.mag@sk.sympatico.ca. Sean Virgo, Poetry Editor. 1969. 6×9.

Saturday Press, Inc., PO Box 43548, Upper Montclair, NJ 07043, 973-256-5053. 1975. "We are not reading mss. now. We sponsor two publishing categories: 1) the Eileen W. Barnes Award competition to publish a first book of poems by a woman over 40. The contest is open nationwide, held in 1982, 1984, 1990, so far. Guest judges have included Maxine Kumin and Colette Inez. 2) the Invited Poets Series is open to men or women who have published at least one book. Not reading new submissions this year." avg. press run 750-1M. 5½×8½, 6×9; avg. price, paper: $5.00 to $7.00. 64-80pp; Publishes less than 1% of poetry manuscripts submitted. Reporting time: queries 2 weeks. Payment: individual arrangement. Interested in new or unpub'd poets: yes, but not reading mss at this time. Recently published poets: Colette Inez, Janice Thaddeus, Ghita Orth, Charlotte Mandel, Anneliese Wagner. Special interests: We have a special, but not exclusive, interest in women's poetry. We are open to any style, any subject. The criterion is excellence.

Savant Garde Workshop, PO Box 1650, Sag Harbor, NY 11963-0060, 516-725-1414; website www.savantgarde.org. Artemis Smith, Artistic Director. 1964. avg. press run 1M. Pub'd 2 poetry titles 1999. 6×9; avg. price, other: $100 perfectbound in multicolor author-signed laminate. 100pp; Publishes 1% of poetry manuscripts submitted. Reporting time: 3 weeks. Payment: varies. Interested in new or unpub'd poets: yes. Simultaneous submissions accepted: no. Recently published poets: Artemis Smith, Billie Taulman, John E. Beck, Marinelle Ringer. Submission quantity: complete manuscript. Special interests: Experimental poetry, longpoems, satire, philosophy, mathematics, and graphic poetry, too.

SCANDINAVIAN REVIEW, 15 East 65 Street, New York, NY 10021, 212-879-9779. 1913. *"SR* only publishes poetry in English translation from the Scandinavian languages, mostly from the juried competition for the ASF Translation Prize for which the postmark deadline is June 1; request a set of rules first.'' circ. 5M. 3/yr. sub. price: $15, $20 foreign; sample: $4. 96-104pp; 6×9¼; Rights purchased: as a non-profit organization, ASF requests a fees waiver generally. Publishes 1% of poems submitted. Deadlines: none. Reporting time: 3-6 months. Payment: $10-$15. Simultaneous submissions accepted: yes. Recent contributors: Pentii Saarikoski, Lassi Nummi, Stein Steinnov, Ivan Malinowski, Asger Schnack. Submission quantity: several. Special interests: Translations.

●**Scarlet Tanager Books,** PO Box 20906, Oakland, CA 94610, 510-763-3874. 1999. 6×9.

Scars Publications (see also CHILDREN, CHURCHES AND DADDIES, A Non Religious, Non Familial Literary Magazine), Attn: Janet Kuypers, 8830 West 120th Place, Palos Park, IL 60464-1137, E-mail ccandd@aol.com, www.members.aol.com/scarspub/scars.html. Janet Kuypers, Editor. 1993. ''SASE necessary. We print a magazine, CC+D; we print annual chapbooks and books, datebooks and wall calendars; we print 'the burning', 'god eyes', and 'poetry sampler', mini poem books. Contact us for more information. We also run calender/book/chapbook contests'' avg. press run varies. Pub'd 6 poetry titles 1999; expects 12 poetry titles 2000, 12 poetry titles 2001. 5½×8; avg. price, cloth: $11.95; paper: $5. 24-200pp; Publishes 20% of poetry manuscripts submitted. Reporting time: about 1 week; SASE necessary. Payment: none. Interested in new or unpub'd poets: yes. Simultaneous submissions accepted: yes. Recently published poets: Cheryl Townsend, Mary Winters, C. Ra McGuirt, John Sweet, Ben Ohmart. Submission quantity: as many as you want. Special interests: We look for very narrative poetry, sometimes with a feminist bent, though we are not limited. We want work to actually pull us in to your story, kicking and screaming. Make us feel like we're there. Permanent address: 8830 West 120th Place, Palos Park Illinois 60464, attn: Janet Kuypers. Electronic submissions (e-mail or tet format, Macintosh prefered) appreciated. Issues available in print (paid only), electronic format, and on the internet at above address.

SCAVENGER'S NEWSLETTER, 833 Main Street, Osage City, KS 66523-1241, 913-528-3538; E-mail foxscav1@jc.net. 1984. ''I use science fiction/fantasy/horror/mystery-related poetry 10 lines and under as filler. Writing related poetry is a possibility, when it's original in theme and not self-indulgent. Because the amount of poetry used is limited, I've been subject to recurrent overstock. Currently reading selectively'' circ. 1M. 12/yr. Pub'd 24 poems 1999; expects 24 poems 2000, 24 poems 2001. sub. price: $17; sample: $2.50. 28pp; 8½×7; Rights purchased: one time rights. Publishes 10% of poems submitted. Reporting time: 2 weeks to 1 month. Payment: $2 per poem on acceptance. Interested in new or unpub'd poets: yes. Simultaneous submissions accepted: yes (if they let me know they are simultaneous). Recent contributors: Rick Kennett, K.S. Hardy, Dan Crawford, Mike Allen, Jared Pratt. Submission quantity: 3-4.

Score (see also SCORE), 1015 NW Clifford Street, Pullman, WA 99163-3203. Craig Hill, Pullman Editor; Selby Spencer, San Francisco Editor. 1983. *"Score* is more than a magazine; though its focus is the visual poem, its other activities - broadsides, chapbooks, color xerox, postcards - encourage good work of any media, modus operandi, or genre. If curious, query.'' avg. press run 200. Pub'd 2 poetry titles 1999; expects 2 poetry titles 2000, 2 poetry titles 2001. size varies; avg. price, paper: $8. 24-30pp; Publishes 15% of poetry manuscripts submitted. Reporting time: 2 hours to 3 months. Payment: 25-50 copies to each contributor for books. Interested in new or unpub'd poets: yes, most certainly. Simultaneous submissions accepted: yes, as long as I'm informed (as are the other editors). Recently published poets: Bruce Andrews, Pete Spence, Aldon Nielsen, Stephen-Paul Martin, Daniel Davidson. Submission quantity: 4-6. Special interests: As stated above, we will consider any genre of any medium or mode. Our only requirement is that the work works and makes us work.

SCORE, Score, 1015 NW Clifford Street, Pullman, WA 99163-3203. Craig Hill, Selby Spencer. 1983. circ. 150-250. 1/yr. Pub'd 40-60 poems 1999. sub. price: $10; sample: $10. 50pp; 8½×11; Rights purchased: none. Publishes 5-10% of poems submitted. Deadlines: none. Reporting time: 2 hours to 2 months. Payment: 2 copies. Interested in new or unpub'd poets: yes, indeed. Simultaneous submissions accepted: yes, if all concerned are ''in the know'' Recent contributors: Bruce Andrews, Joe Keppler, Stephen-Paul Martin, Larry Eigner, Johanna Drucker. Submission quantity: 4-6. Special interests: Experimental poetry, focussing on visual/concrete works, sound texts, scores for language performance.

Scots Plaid Press (see also Persephone Press), 600 Kelly Road, Carthage, NC 28327, 910-947-2587; Fax 910-947-5112. 1987. 6×9, 5½×8½.

SCP NEWSLETTER, PO Box 4308, Berkeley, CA 94704. 1975. circ. 18M. 4 journals, 4 newsletters published per year. sub. price: $25/year; sample: free. 40pp single journals; 60pp for double journals; 8½×11.

THE SCRIBIA, PO Box 68, Grambling State University, Grambling, LA 71245, 318-644-2072; hoytda@alpha0.gram.edu. 1966. circ. 800. 1/yr. sub. price: cops; sample: cops. 72pp; 5½×8½.

Scripta Humanistica, 1383 Kersey Lane, Potomac, MD 20854, 301-294-7949; 301-340-1095. 6½×8½.

SCRIVENER, McGill University, 853 Sherbrooke Street W., Montreal, P.Q. H3A 2T6, Canada, 514-398-6588. Emily Barton, Daphne Brunelle. 1980. "Don't submit less than 5 poems. Can't read in the summer. Include SASE; name and address on each page. No U.S. stamps" circ. 500. 1/yr. Pub'd 14 poems 1999; expects 15 poems 2000, 20-25 poems 2001. sub. price: $7 + $2 p/h; sample: same. 100pp; 8×8½; Rights purchased: 1st N.A. serial rights. Publishes 5% of poems submitted. Reporting time: 4-6 weeks for acknowledgement, longer for acceptance/rejection. Payment: 1 copy. Interested in new or unpub'd poets: yes. Simultaneous submissions accepted: yes. Recent contributors: B.Z. Niditch, Lyn Lifshin, Simon Perchik, Paul Harrison, David Henderson. Submission quantity: 5-10. Special interests: We're open, but no hate literature!

Second Aeon Publications, 19 Southminster Road, Roath, Cardiff, Wales CF23 5AT, Great Britain, 029-2049-3093, peter.finch@dial.pipex.com. Peter Finch. 1967. "Publishes at least one item per year in editors interest area. Latest is a reprint of the 1970 edition of *For Jack Kerouac*—poems on his death, enlarged and reedited." avg. press run 200-1M. Pub'd 1 poetry title 1999; expects 1 poetry title 2000, 1 poetry title 2001. size A4; avg. price, paper: £2. 60pp; Publishes 1% of poetry manuscripts submitted. Reporting time: 2 weeks. Payment: by arrangement. Interested in new or unpub'd poets: no. Simultaneous submissions accepted: no. Recently published poets: Bob Cobbing, John Tripp, Iain Sinclair, William Wantling. Special interests: Experimental and sound poetry.

Second Coming Press, PO Box 31249, San Francisco, CA 94131. A.D. Winans. 1972. "Second Coming has published over 26 books and anthologies since 1972 - with the bulk of them coming from 1975 to the present. Query first. Anthologies usually involve work previously appearing in S.C. books and magazines, or solicited work. Write for author-title list." avg. press run 1M. Pub'd 1 poetry title 1999; expects 2 poetry titles 2000. 5½×8½, anthologies 6×9; avg. price, cloth: $15; paper: $4.95-$6.95; other: $3 chapbooks, $5 quality spineback. 64-96pp, anthologies 196-220pp; Publishes 5% or less of poetry manuscripts submitted. Reporting time: 1-2 months. Payment: 10% of print run, though we have given 10% of royalties in addition to print run; occasionally given a token $50 advance. Interested in new or unpub'd poets: no. Simultaneous submissions accepted: no. Recently published poets: Roy Schneider, Jack Micheline, Terry Kennedy, Gene Fowler, Lynne Savitt. Submission quantity: complete manuscript (seldom print book larger than 96 pages). Special interests: We do not publish books of translation, experimental poetry, nor single long-poem books, nor light verse. We are open to serious poetry, including political, and interested in good humor and satire. We will send a package of 5 books of poetry for an examination of what we are doing and looking for - for only $20.00 (including postage and handling). This source must be quoted as your reference source for this bargain package.

SEEMS, c/o Lakeland College, Box 359, Sheboygan, WI 53082-0359. Karl Elder, Editor. 1971. "In its third printing, *What Is The Future of Poetry?* (Seems #14), essays by twenty-two contemporary poets, including P. Dacey, S. Dunn, W. Heyen, W. Matthews, L. Stryk, and P. Zimmer, has been praised by poets and critics all over the country. Order a copy—if you don't like it, send it back, and we'll mail you your $5.00." circ. 350. Irregular. Expects 27 poems 2000, 15 poems 2001. sub. price: $16/4 issues; sample: $4. 40pp; 8½×7; Rights purchased: 1st North American serial rights. Publishes less than .5% of poems submitted. Deadlines: continuous. Reporting time: 1-4 months. Payment: copy of the issue. Interested in new or unpub'd poets: yes. Simultaneous submissions accepted: no. Recent contributors: Kim Bridgford, William Greenway, William Heyen, Mary MacGowan, Terry Savoie. Submission quantity: 3-5. Special interests: Quickfictions: narrative poems, prose poems—any membrane melding poetry and fiction—and sequences of poems. Also free verse, blank verse, syllabics, and one-of-a-kind forms.

SENECA REVIEW, Hobart & William Smith Colleges, Geneva, NY 14456, 315-781-3392; Fax 315-781-3348; senecareview@hws.edu. Deborah Tall, Editor. 1970. circ. 1M. 2/yr. Pub'd 85 poems 1999; expects 85 poems 2000, 85 poems 2001. sub. price: $11, $20/2 years, $28/3 years; sample: $5. 100pp; 8½×5½; Rights purchased: 1st serial. Publishes 1% of poems submitted. Deadlines: between Sept. 1 and May 1 annually. Reporting time: 8-12 weeks. Payment: 2 copies and a 2-year subscription. Interested in new or unpub'd poets: yes. Simultaneous submissions accepted: no. Recent contributors: Seamus Heaney, Rita Dove, Heather McHugh, Anne Carson, Yusef Komunyakaa. Submission quantity: 3-5. Special interests: We publish a great number of translations and are always happy to receive submissions of them.

SEPIA, Knill Cross House, Higher Anderton Road, Millbrook, Nr Torpoint, Cornwall, England. Colin David

Webb. 1977. "No verse, no traditional, no genre." circ. 100. 3/yr. Pub'd 80 poems 1999; expects 80 poems 2000, 80 poems 2001. sub. price: $10; sample: $2. 32pp; 6×8½; Rights purchased: none. Publishes 10% of poems submitted. Deadlines: none. Reporting time: 10 days. Payment: free copy of the issue they appear in. Interested in new or unpub'd poets: yes. Simultaneous submissions accepted: yes. Recent contributors: Jacques Du Lumiere, Maramoto Jenge, Charles Bukowski, Steve Walker. Submission quantity: 6. Special interests: Experimental, satire, translations, gutsy poems all welcome.

Serena Bay Books, PO Box 1655, Cooper Station, New York, NY 10276, 212-260-5580. Celeste Ewers, Editor. 1992. avg. press run 1M-3M. 5½×8½; avg. price, paper: $7.95. 80pp; Reporting time: 2 months. Payment: varies. Interested in new or unpub'd poets: yes. Simultaneous submissions accepted: yes. Submission quantity: Complete ms. with SASE and bio.

SERIE D'ECRITURE, Burning Deck Press, 71 Elmgrove Avenue, Providence, RI 02906. 1986. "Translations from French only." circ. 500. 1/yr. sub. price: $16/2 years; sample: $10. 64pp; 5½×8½; Payment: copies. Recent contributors: Jacqueline Risset, Emmanuel Hocquard, Jean Daive, Paol Keineg.

Seven Buffaloes Press (see also BLACK JACK & VALLEY GRAPEVINE; THE AZOREAN EXPRESS), Box 249, Big Timber, MT 59011. Art Coelho. 1973. "A lot of the time a poet sends a stamp with an envelope, but he or she might have from 8-10 pages of poems - and one stamp won't cover that. Four pages for one stamp; nine pages for the second ounce is a good rule of thumb. I am doing a yearly anthology issue on the Southern Appalachian Mountains." Pub'd 100 poetry titles 1999; expects 100 poetry titles 2000, 100 poetry titles 2001. 5½×8½. Publishes 10% of poetry manuscripts submitted. Reporting time: 1 day-2 weeks. Payment: copies. Interested in new or unpub'd poets: yes. Simultaneous submissions accepted: no. Recently published poets: Jim Wayne Miller, Simon Ortiz, Laurel Speer, Steven Levi, Bob Warden. Submission quantity: 4-12. Special interests: I publish rural poetry, farm and ranch, especially material from the Southern Appalachian region. In the case of the Appalachias I publish Hill and Holler poems. In other words my focus is on land and people themes; heritage, the working man, The American Indian and The American Hobo. Poets with a Dustbowl heritage.

SEWANEE REVIEW, Univ. of the South, 735 University Avenue, Sewanee, TN 37383-1000, 931-598-1246. George Core, Editor, Poetry Editor. 1892. "Include cover letter and SASE with sufficient postage. Do not apply for the Aiken Taylor prize (not a contest but an award)" circ. 3.2M. 4/yr. Pub'd 53 poems 1999; expects 50 poems 2000, 50 poems 2001. sub. price: $26 instit., $20 indiv.; sample: $7.25. 192pp; 6×9; Rights purchased: first serial. Publishes less than .1% of poems submitted. Deadlines: none. Reporting time: 3-6 weeks. Payment: approx. 60¢ per line. Interested in new or unpub'd poets: yes. Simultaneous submissions accepted: no. Recent contributors: Neal Bowers, Robert Cording, Anthony Hecht, Mark Jarman, Gladys Swan. Submission quantity: 6 or less. Special interests: We do not publish translations and rarely publish long poems.

SFEST, LTD., PO Box 1238, Simpsonville, SC 29681. M.T. Nowak. 1990. circ. 500. 4/yr. Pub'd 100 poems 1999. sub. price: $20; sample: $5. 50-100pp; 8½×11; Rights purchased: none. Publishes 10% of poems submitted. Reporting time: max. 4 weeks. Payment: complimentary copy. Interested in new or unpub'd poets: yes. Recent contributors: Conti, Lanciani, Lifshin, Diodurio. Submission quantity: 5.

SHADES OF DECEMBER, PO Box 244, Selden, NY 11784, E-mail eilonwy@innocent.com; www2.crosswinds.net/new-york/~shadesof12. Alexander Danner, Editor; Brandy L. Straus, Editor. 1998. circ. 200. 4/yr. sub. price: $10; sample: $2.75. 52pp; 5½×8½; Rights purchased: first NA serial rights. Deadlines: rolling. Reporting time: 2 weeks (electronic), 4-6 weeks by mail. Payment: 2 copies. Simultaneous submissions accepted: if noted. Recent contributors: Hank Ballenger, Sharron Belson. Submission quantity: 3-5.

Shadowlight Press, PO Box 746, Biglerville, PA 17307, e-mail bobmedcalfjr@blazenet.net. Jr. Robert R. Medcalf. 1981. "Always send SASE." avg. press run 50-100. Expects 10 poetry titles 2001. 8½×11; avg. price, other: $6 chapbook, $4 broadside (money order only made out to Robert R. Medcalf, Jr.). Chapbook 16pp, broadside 1pp; Publishes 10-20% of poetry manuscripts submitted. Reporting time: 2 weeks-2 months. Payment: $2-5/anthologies, $25/broadsides. Interested in new or unpub'd poets: yes. Simultaneous submissions accepted: yes. Submission quantity: 3-5. Special interests: Poetry of the imagination.

THE SHAKESPEARE NEWSLETTER, English Department, Iona College, New Rochelle, NY 10801. John W. Mahon, Thomas A. Pendleton. 1951. "Poems must be short (15 lines or less), make a striking print about S. and/or his plays, characters, or poems. No parodies of sonnets. Poet should know the character of the periodical to which he submits. S/he will have a better chance of success." circ. 2.5M. 4/yr. Pub'd 3 poems 1999; expects 4 poems 2000, 4 poems 2001. sub. price: indiv. $12, instit. $12, $14 foreign; sample: $3 + 50¢ postage. 20pp; 8½×11; Rights purchased: none. Publishes (if they are excellent for the *Newsletter*) 100% of poems submitted. Deadlines: anytime. Reporting time: 1-2 months. Payment: none. Interested in new or unpub'd poets: yes. Simultaneous submissions accepted: no. Recent contributors: Michael Palma. Submission quantity: 1. Special interests: Poems which show or give new insights on what oft is thought but n'er so well expressed. (Alexander Pope).

Shaolin Communications, PO Box 58547, Salt Lake City, UT 84158, 801-595-1123. Sifu Richard O'Connor. 1993. "Enjoy poetry plus artwork or photography that enhances mood or setting" avg. press run 1M. Pub'd 1 poetry title 1999; expects 1 poetry title 2000, 1 poetry title 2001. 8½×11; avg. price, cloth: $27.88; paper: $14.88. 115pp; Reporting time: 6 weeks. Payment: varied. Interested in new or unpub'd poets: yes. Simultaneous submissions accepted: yes. Recently published poets: T.S. Coyote, Master Zhen Shen-Lang. Submission quantity: 4. Special interests: Several topics of interest to us: Native Americans, Utah, religious issues, lyrics to songs, parenting, martial arts, Taolsm Buddhism.

SHARING & CARING, Halbar Publishing, 289 Taylor Street, Wills Point, TX 75169-9732. 1994. circ. 100+. 4/yr. sub. price: $55; sample: $9. 80pp; 8½×11.

SHATTERED WIG REVIEW, 425 E. 31st, Baltimore, MD 21218, 301-243-6888. Sonny Bodkin. 1988. circ. 500. 2/yr. Pub'd 40 poems 1999. sub. price: $9; sample: $4. 80pp; 8½×8½; Publishes 20% of poems submitted. Deadlines: none. Reporting time: 1-2 months. Payment: 1 copy. Interested in new or unpub'd poets: yes. Simultaneous submissions accepted: yes. Recent contributors: John M. Bennett, Little Mary Ann, Mary Winters, Chris Toll, Carl Watson. Submission quantity: no less than 2, no more than 5. Special interests: Prose poetry and concrete poetry, experimental poetry, satire.

Shearsman Books (see also Oasis Books), c/o Oasis Books, 12 Stevenage Road, London SW6 6ES, United Kingdom. Tony Frazer. Address poetry submissions to: Lark Rise, Fore Street, Kentisgeare, Cullompton, Devon EX15 2AD, United Kingdom. 1981. "Manuscripts are solicited by editor so far. Best of all, is to write first to editor and publisher, Tony Frazer, c/o the above address in U.K." avg. press run 300. Pub'd 4 poetry titles 1999; expects 5 poetry titles 2000, 1 poetry title 2001. 4½×6½; avg. price, paper: £1.50p. 10-80pp; Publishes a very small % of poetry manuscripts submitted. Reporting time: 2 months. Payment: copies only. Interested in new or unpub'd poets: in theory, yes; but most work accepted is solicited by editor. Simultaneous submissions accepted: no. Recently published poets: Gustaf Sobin, Martin Anderson, Philip Crick, Simon Perchik, Kjell Espmark. Submission quantity: 6-8. Special interests: Translations, longpoems, 'experimental' poetry, prose (essays, etc., non-fiction).

The Sheep Meadow Press, PO Box 1345, Riverdale-on-Hudson, NY 10471, 212-548-5547. Stanley Moss, Publisher, Editor-in-Chief. 1976. "All manuscripts should be sent with SASE" avg. press run 2M. Pub'd 4 poetry titles 1999; expects 14 poetry titles 2000, 8 poetry titles 2001. 8½×5½, 6×9; avg. price, cloth: $14.95; paper: $10.95. 100pp; Reporting time: 6 months. Payment: 10%. Interested in new or unpub'd poets: yes. Simultaneous submissions accepted: yes. Recently published poets: Alberto Rios, Cleopatra Mathis, Mary Kinzie, Mark Rudman, Stanley Kunitz. Submission quantity: manuscript. Special interests: Poems, prose poems, prose, translations.

SHENANDOAH, Troubadour Theater, 2nd Floor, Washington and Lee University, Lexington, VA 24450-0303, 540-463-8765. R.T. Smith, Editor. 1950. circ. 1.3M. 4/yr. Pub'd 96 poems 1999; expects 96 poems 2000, 96 poems 2001. sub. price: $22 individual, $25 institution; sample: $8. 150pp; 6×9; Rights purchased: first serial. Publishes less than 1% of poems submitted. Deadlines: Sept. to May. Reporting time: 3 weeks. Payment: $2.50/line. Interested in new or unpub'd poets: yes. Simultaneous submissions accepted: no. Recent contributors: Reynolds Price, Mary Oliver, Henry Taylor, W.S. Merwin, Marilyn Hacker. Submission quantity: 5 minimum.

Shenango River Books, PO Box 631, Sharon, PA 16146, 412-342-3811. Jeanne Mahon, Poetry Editor; Kevin Berland, Poetry Editor. 1994. avg. press run 600. Expects 2 poetry titles 2000. 5⅜×8½; avg. price, paper: $8. 64pp; Reporting time: no submissions, invitation only. Interested in new or unpub'd poets: no. Simultaneous submissions accepted: no. Recently published poets: John Swinton, Douglas Wiesen.

Sherman Asher Publishing, PO Box 2853, Santa Fe, NM 87504, 505-984-2686, FAX 505-820-2744, e-mail sapublish@att.net, www.shermanasher.com. Nancy Fay. 1995. "Well crafted work, look at recent publications to see our standards. Always include SASE for a response. Download guideline updates from our website" avg. press run 1M. Pub'd 3 poetry titles 1999; expects 4 poetry titles 2000, 3 poetry titles 2001. size varies; avg. price, paper: $13. Pages vary; Publishes less than 2% of poetry manuscripts submitted. Reporting time: 2 months. Payment: in copies. Interested in new or unpub'd poets: yes, we solicit for anthologies through *P&W* ads. Simultaneous submissions accepted: yes. Recently published poets: Mary McGinnis, Penny Harter, Judyth Hill, Alvaro Cardona-Hine, Marjorie Agosin. Submission quantity: 3.

SHIRIM, 4611 Vesper Avenue, Sherman Oaks, CA 91403-5615. Rabbi Marc Steven Dworkin. 1982. "*Shirim,* the first Jewish poetry journal in the U.S., publishes poetry that reflects the life styles, emotions, and attitudes of Jewish living. In addition, we sponsor an annual Jewish poetry conference at Hebrew Union College in Los Angeles" circ. 250. 2/yr. Pub'd 35 poems 1999. sub. price: $7; sample: $4. 36pp; 5¼×8½; Publishes 10% of poems submitted. Deadlines: continual. Reporting time: 2 months. Payment: copies. Interested in new or unpub'd poets: yes. Simultaneous submissions accepted: no. Recent contributors: Yehuda Amichai, Irving Layton, Deena Metzger, Robert Mezey, Karl Shapiro. Submission quantity: 5 poems. Special interests: All poems are published in English, and we are very interested in translations if the translator has the rights to the poem. No previously published poetry in English will be considered.

SHORT FUSE, PO Box 90436, Santa Barbara, CA 93190. Holden. 1983. circ. 500+. 6/yr. sub. price: $9, free to institutionalized persons; sample: $1. 20pp; Reporting time: 1 week. Payment: copies. Interested in new or unpub'd poets: yes. Simultaneous submissions accepted: yes. Recent contributors: Lyn Lifshin, Richard Kostelanetz, Bob Zorak, John M. Bennett, Colin Cross. Submission quantity: at least 3.

SHRIKE, 13 Primrose Way, Alperton, MDDX HA0 1DS, United Kingdom, 44-081-998-5707. 1995. circ. 100. 1/yr. sub. price: £4; sample: £2. 36pp; 5×8.

SICILIA PARRA, Legas, c/o Modern Foreign Languages, St. John's University, Jamaica, NY 11439-0002, 718-331-0613. 1979. circ. 2M. 2/yr. sub. price: $20; sample: $10. 20pp; 8½×11.

SIDEWALKS, PO Box 321, Champlin, MN 55316. Tom Heie. 1991. "Prefer accessible over abstruse, highly personal stuff; well-crafted work." circ. 300. 2/yr. Pub'd 43 poems 1999; expects 45+ poems 2000. sub. price: $9; sample: $6. 60-70pp; 5½×8½; Rights purchased: rights revert after publication. Publishes +/-10% of poems submitted. Deadlines: May 31, Dec. 31. Reporting time: 3-5 weeks after deadline. Payment: 1 copy. Interested in new or unpub'd poets: yes. Simultaneous submissions accepted: no. Recent contributors: Michael Dennis Browne, Robert Cooperman, Kenneth Pobo, William Reichard. Submission quantity: 3-5.

Signal Books, 7117 Tyndall Court, Raleigh, NC 27615, 919-870-8505 phone/fax; gtkach@worldnet.att.net. D. McMillan. 1985. avg. press run 500. Expects 2 poetry titles 2000, 2 poetry titles 2001. avg. price, paper: $9. 100pp; Publishes 2% of poetry manuscripts submitted. Reporting time: 2 weeks. Payment: standard industry contracts. Simultaneous submissions accepted: yes. Submission quantity: at least 20.

Signature Books, Attn: Boyd Payne, 564 West 400 North, Salt Lake City, UT 84116, 801-531-1483, fax 801-531-1488. Gary James Bergera. 1981. "Not accepting any submissions until further notice" avg. press run 1M. Pub'd 1 poetry title 1999; expects 1 poetry title 2000, 1 poetry title 2001. 6×9; avg. price, cloth: $24.95; paper: $10.95. 100pp; Publishes less than 1% of poetry manuscripts submitted. Reporting time: 6 months. Payment: 8% semi-annual. Recently published poets: Alex Caldiero, Kathy Evans, Susan Elizabeth Howe, Marilyn Bushman-Carlton, Lisa Bickmore.

Signpost Press Inc. (see also THE BELLINGHAM REVIEW), Mail Stop 9055, WWU, Bellingham, WA 98225, 360-650-3209. Robin Hemley, Editor. 1975. "Not accepting mss. at present. Many of our chapbooks have been winners in poetry chapbook competitions. The 1986 winner was *When She Was The Good-Time Girl* by Katharyn Machan Aal. This chapbook and the previous winners, *Living And Sinning For Them* by Paul Shuttleworth; *On The Line* by Jim Daniels, 1980; *Traveling* by Nancy King, 1981; *The Other Woman* by Linda Mizejewski, 1982; are available from the Signpost Press Inc. for $2 or $3 each—postpaid if payment accompanies order. We are not currently sponsoring a competition but will consider queries between October 15 and February 15." avg. press run 500. Expects 1 poetry title 2000, 2 poetry titles 2001. 5½×8½; avg. price, cloth: $12; paper: $3 for chapbooks, $8 for books. 24-68pp; Reporting time: 2-3 months. Payment: varies. Interested in new or unpub'd poets: yes. Simultaneous submissions accepted: yes. Recently published poets: Judy Collins, Joseph Green, Richard Martin, Sheila Farr, Kate Thompson. Submission quantity: poet should query first.

SILHOUETTE MAGAZINE, PO Box 53763, Baton Rouge, LA 70892, 504-358-0617. 1995. "Upcoming '98 themes: Armageddon, Revelations, crossroads, chainletters and superstitions" circ. 250. 4/yr. Pub'd 20 poems 1999; expects 30 poems 2000, 30+ poems 2001. sub. price: $15; sample: $3. 8½×11; Rights purchased: none. Publishes 55% of poems submitted. Deadlines: 21st every month. Reporting time: 6-8 weeks. Payment: publication. Interested in new or unpub'd poets: yes. Simultaneous submissions accepted: yes. Recent contributors: William Ashante Hobbs III, Erica Smith, Rufus Young, Bryan Ryan, Cassandra Wilder. Submission quantity: no limit. Special interests: spirituality.

Silver Mountain Press, Casilla 6572 Torres Sofer, Cochabamba, Bolivia. 1993. "The production schedule for this year and next is already set. No unsolicited mss." 5½×8½.

THE SILVER WEB, PO Box 38190, Tallahassee, FL 32315. Ann Kennedy. 1989. circ. 2M. 2/yr. Pub'd 10-12 poems 1999. sub. price: $12; sample: $5.95 + $1.25 p/h. 80+pp; 8½×11; Rights purchased: first time, or reprint rights, or one time rights - negotiable. Publishes less than 10% of poems submitted. Reporting time: 4-6 weeks. Payment: $10-$20. Interested in new or unpub'd poets: yes. Simultaneous submissions accepted: yes. Recent contributors: Glenna Halloway, Jessica Amanda Salmonson, John Grey, Holly Day, Simon Perchik. Submission quantity: up to 5. Special interests: Poems must use standard poetic conventions whether free verse of rhyming, no genre cliches.

SILVER WINGS/MAYFLOWER PULPIT, PO Box 1000, Pearblossom, CA 93553-1000, 805-264-3726. Jackson Wilcox. 1983. "Poems of 16 lines or less are given preference. No profanity. Poems should be typed, double space and fully identified with address on page. SASE. Required for return of rejected poems" circ. 250. 6/yr. Pub'd 5 poems 1999; expects 70 poems 2000, 70 poems 2001. sub. price: $10; sample: $2. 12-32pp; 5½×8½; Rights purchased: first. Publishes 10% of poems submitted. Deadlines: Feb. 15, May 15, Aug. 15, Nov. 15. Reporting time: 1 week to 3 months. Payment: 1 copy. Interested in new or unpub'd poets: yes. Simultaneous submissions accepted: not if we know it. Recent contributors: Mary Ann Henn, C. David Hay, Ruth Parks, Abbott Small, June Tompkins. Submission quantity: 3 or less. Special interests: Our interest is really Christian inspirational poetry. The best poems reflect a spiritual experience or message. The editor is a Christian evangelical. Haikus welcome.

SILVERFISH REVIEW, Silverfish Review Press, PO Box 3541, Eugene, OR 97403, 503-344-5060. Rodger Moody, Editor. 1979. "write for information about annual poetry book-length competition (SASE)" circ. 500. 2/yr. Pub'd 20 poems 1999; expects 20 poems 2000, 20 poems 2001. sub. price: $8 individuals, $12 institutions; sample: $4 plus $1.50 p/h. 48pp; 5½×8½; Rights purchased: rights revert to author. Publishes 5% of poems submitted. Deadlines: none. Reporting time: 1-16 weeks. Payment: 2 copies plus 1-year subscription and small payment when funding permits. Interested in new or unpub'd poets: yes. Simultaneous submissions accepted: no. Recent contributors: Lauren Mesa, Dorothy Barresi, Ivan Arguelles, Robert Ward, Floyd Skloot. Submission quantity: 5. Special interests: Beginning with Issue #11, *SR* will showcase translations from Latin America and Europe as well as continue to publish poems written in English. *SR* is also interested in reading long poems.

●**Silverfish Review Press (see also SILVERFISH REVIEW),** PO Box 3541, Eugene, OR 97403, 503-344-5060. Rodger Moody, Editor. 1979. "Write for information about annual poetry book-length competition (SASE)." 5½×8½, 6×9. Reporting time: 1-16 weeks. Payment: $1,000 to winner of annual poetry book contest (for author who has yet to publish a book). Interested in new or unpub'd poets: yes. Simultaneous submissions accepted: no.

SIMPLY WORDS, 605 Collins Avenue #23, Centerville, GA 31028, E-mail simplywords@hotmail.com. 1991. 4/yr. sub. price: $18.50; sample: $5. 25pp; 8×11.

Singing Horse Press, PO Box 40034, Philadelphia, PA 19106. Gil Ott, Editor. 1976. "Read the books and query first. No blind submissions." avg. press run 1M. Pub'd 2 poetry titles 1999; expects 2 poetry titles 2000, 2 poetry titles 2001. avg. price, paper: $9.50. 64pp; Reporting time: varies. Payment: author receives 10% of total press run, other by arrangement. Simultaneous submissions accepted: no. Recently published poets: Rosmarie Waldrop, David Miller, Asa Benveniste, Rachel Blau DuPlessis, Harryette Mullen.

SINISTER WISDOM, PO Box 3252, Berkeley, CA 94703, 510-532-5222. 1976. "Lesbian-feminist magazine, no homophobic or heterosexually-oriented poetry. 2 copies of each submission must be sent with SASE. #59 Love and Romance, $60 Mixed-Race, #61 Women in Prison." circ. 3M. 3/yr. Pub'd 50-75 poems 1999; expects 50-100 poems 2000, 50-100 poems 2001. sub. price: $20, $25 foreign; sample: $6.50 (pp). 128-144pp; 5×8; Rights purchased: all rights remain with contributor. Publishes 10-15% of poems submitted. Deadlines: February 1, June 1, October 1. Reporting time: 6-9 months. Payment: 2 copies. Interested in new or unpub'd poets: yes. Simultaneous submissions accepted: prefer not. Recent contributors: Jamie Lee Evans, Judith Witherow, Chrystos, Terri Jewell, Donna Allegra. Submission quantity: 1-5. Special interests: Poetry relevant to themes and/or lesbian experience, by lesbians only.

SITUATION, 10402 Ewell Avenue, Kensington, MD 20895-4025. Mark Wallace. 1992. circ. 150. 3/yr. Expects 60 poems 2000. sub. price: $10; sample: $3. 24pp; 7×8½; Publishes 33% of poems submitted. Reporting time: 3 months. Payment: none. Interested in new or unpub'd poets: yes. Simultaneous submissions accepted: yes. Recent contributors: Charles Bernstein, Rodrigo Toscano, Cydney Chadwick, Susan Schultz, Joan Retallack. Submission quantity: 6-8. Special interests: Experimental poetry.

69 FLAVORS OF PARANOIA, 2816 Rio Vista Court, Farmington, NM 87401-4557. 1996. circ. 200. 6/yr. sub. price: $16; sample: $3.50. 51pp; 5½×8½.

SKYLARK, 2200 169th Street, Purdue University Calumet, Hammond, IN 46323, 219-989-2273, Fax 219-989-2165, poetpam49@yahoo.com. Cathy Michniewicz, Poetry Editor. 1972. "Do not read in summer. Each poem should have the name and address of the poet accompanying it, along with the statement that the poem has not been previously published. No submissions returned without SASE's. Special theme: Education. Length: up to 45 lines acceptable but prefer 21 lines. Poems should be carefully proofread." circ. 800-1M. 1/yr. Pub'd 80 poems 1999; expects 80 poems 2000, 80 poems 2001. sub. price: $8; sample: $6.50 back issues. 100pp; 8½×11; Rights purchased: first rights. Publishes 20% of poems submitted. Deadlines: April 30. Reporting time: 3-6 months (do not read from May 1 to November 1). Payment: 1 copy per poem published. Interested in new or unpub'd poets: yes. Simultaneous submissions accepted: no. Recent contributors: liony batista, Joyce Brown, Joanne Clarkson, Jane McClellan, Dave McCullom. Submission quantity: 3-6. Special interests: All styles considered, but want to see more prose poems. Willing to consider well-constructed experimental poetry.

SKYWRITERS, Stained Glass Press, 245 Spring Street, SW, Concord, NC 28025. 1995. circ. 100. 4/yr. sub. price: $20; sample: free or $5. 40pp; 4×6.

SLANT: A Journal of Poetry, University of Central Arkansas, PO Box 5063, Conway, AR 72035-5000, 501-450-5107. James Fowler. 1987. "We use traditional and 'modern' poetry, even experimental, moderate length, any subject on approval of the Board of Readers. Our purpose is to publish a journal of fine poetry from all regions. No haiku, no translations. No previously published poems, no multiple submissions." circ. 175. 1/yr. Pub'd 72 poems 1999; expects 70 poems 2000, 72 poems 2001. sub. price: $10; sample: $10. 120pp; 6×9; Rights purchased: first N. American serial rights. Publishes 5% of poems submitted. Deadlines: November 15 for annual spring publication. Reporting time: 3-4 months from deadline. Payment: 1 copy on publication. Interested in new or unpub'd poets: yes. Simultaneous submissions accepted: no. Recent contributors: Sean Brendan-Brown, Linda Casebeer, Ethan Gilsdorf, Askold Skalsky, Luisa Villani. Submission quantity: up to 5 of moderate length. Special interests: We would like to see more formal and narrative poetry.

Slapering Hol Press, 300 Riverside Drive, Sleepy Hollow, NY 10591-1414, 914-332-5953. Stephanie Strickland, Co-Editor; Margo Stever, Co-Editor. 1988. "Please check *Poets & Writers* or other writers' journals for deadlines" avg. press run 400. Pub'd 1 poetry title 1999; expects 1 poetry title 2000, 1 poetry title 2001. 6×9; avg. price, paper: $8. 32pp; Payment: chapbooks pay $500 plus 20 copies. Interested in new or unpub'd poets: yes. Simultaneous submissions accepted: yes. Recently published poets: Dina Ben-Lev, Rachel Loden, Pearl Karrer, Lynn McGee, Paul-Victor Winters. Submission quantity: 24 pages.

SLEUTH JOURNAL, Baker Street Publications, 577 Central Avenue, Box 4, Jefferson, LA 70121-1400, E-mail sherlockian@mailcity.com, blackie@taskcity.com, www2.cybercities.com/z/zines, www.wbs.net/home-pages/b/l/a/blackkie.html. Sharida Rizzuto, Editor; Harold Tollison, Ann Hoyt. 1983. "This publication covers the entire mystery genre. All submissions must be double-spaced and typewritten" circ. 800. 2/yr. Pub'd 20-28 poems 1999. sub. price: $15.80; sample: $7.90. 100pp; 8½×11; Rights purchased: one-time rights, first serial rights, or second serial rights. Publishes 30% of poems submitted. Deadlines: always open to submissions. Reporting time: 2-6 weeks. Payment: negotiable. Interested in new or unpub'd poets: yes. Simultaneous submissions accepted: yes. Recent contributors: Julia Buonocore,Chadderon, George/Beltran, Margarita Perez, Harrison, Gregory E. Submission quantity: 1-5. Special interests: We are willing to look at any type of poetry. No length requirements.

SLIGHTLY WEST, The Evergreen State College, CAB 320, Olympia, WA 98505, 360-866-6000 x6879. Sarah Dougherty, Editor; Melia Luoto, Editor. 1985. "Please do not submit during Summer—submissions have to go through a change in management." circ. 1M. 2/yr. Pub'd 18 poems 1999; expects 34 poems 2000, 30 poems 2001. sub. price: $5; sample: $2.50. 50pp; 6×9; Rights purchased: single publishing; all rights are returned to contributors. Publishes 10% of poems submitted. Deadlines: late October and late February—call or write office for exact date. Reporting time: 3 months at the most. Payment: in copies. Interested in new or unpub'd poets: definitely interested. Simultaneous submissions accepted: yes. Recent contributors: Jeannette Allee, Scott Caughron, S.R. Duncan, Lyn Lifshin, Christy Soto. Submission quantity: no more than 4. Special interests: Concrete poetry about real experiences.

SLIPSTREAM, Slipstream Productions, Box 2071, New Market Station, Niagara Falls, NY 14301, 716-282-2616 (after 5 p.m., E.S.T.). Dan Sicoli, Robert Borgatti, Livio Farallo. 1980. "Always include a SASE with any submission; like contemporary urban feel to poems, do not use nature poetry; query for needs as we may be reading for a theme issue. ISSN 0749-0771. There is an annual poetry chapbook contest with a December 1 deadline. Send up to 40 pages of poetry, a SASE for return of your manuscript, and a $10 reading fee. Winner receives $1,000 cash award and 50 copies and all entrants receive a copy of the winning manuscript and a one issue subscription of *Slipstream*" circ. 500. 1/yr. Pub'd 150 poems 1999; expects 200 poems 2000, 150 poems 2001. sub. price: $15; sample: $6. 80pp; 7×8½; Rights purchased: one time use, previously unpublished. Publishes less than 10% of poems submitted. Deadlines: continuous. Reporting time: 2 weeks to 2 months. Payment: 1 copy at the moment. Interested in new or unpub'd poets: yes. Simultaneous submissions accepted: yes, if acknowledged. Recent contributors: Robert Cooperman, Gerald Locklin, Ed Taylor Jr., Patti Couch. Submission quantity: 3-6. Special interests: We like fresh writing that demands attention. No line length limit. All subjects, nothing taboo. Writing which is vital and on the cutting edge stands best chance for acceptance. Check out a sample issue. Query for themes and needs.

Slipstream Productions (see also SLIPSTREAM), Box 2071, New Market Station, Niagara Falls, NY 14301. Dan Sicoli, Co-Editor; Robert Borgatti, Co-Editor; Livio Faralco, Co-Editor. 1981. avg. press run 500. Pub'd 1 poetry title 1999; expects 1 poetry title 2000, 2 poetry titles 2001. avg. price, paper: $6. 40pp; Publishes less than 10% of poetry manuscripts submitted. Reporting time: 2 weeks to 2 months. Payment: $1,000 to contest winner. Interested in new or unpub'd poets: most poetry chapbooks published are solicited unless selected as winner of chapbook contest. Simultaneous submissions accepted: yes. Recently published poets: Gerald Locklin, Leslie Anne Mcilroy, Renny Christopher, Alison Pelegrin, Laurie Mazzaferro. Submission quantity: up to 5.

A Slow Tempo Press, 1345 North 40th Street, Lincoln, NE 68503-2109, 402-466-8689; slowtemp@aol.com. David McCleery. 1989. "By invitation only" avg. press run 500. Pub'd 2 poetry titles 1999; expects 2 poetry titles 2000. 6×9; avg. price, paper: $11. 72pp; Reporting time: 3 months. Payment: ask. Interested in new or unpub'd poets: no. Simultaneous submissions accepted: no. Recently published poets: William Kloefkorn, Nancy Peters Hastings, Twyla Hansen, Don Welch.

THE SMALL POND MAGAZINE OF LITERATURE aka SMALL POND, PO Box 664, Stratford, CT 06615, 203-378-4066. Napoleon St. Cyr, Editor. 1964. "Do's: Name and address on each page or poem. SASE a must. Don'ts: No translations, no handwritten copy. We don't have special issues, special themes, or contests." circ. 300. 3/yr. Pub'd 45 poems 1999; expects 45 poems 2000, 45 poems 2001. sub. price: $10; sample: $4, $2.50 random back issue. 42pp; 5½×8½; Rights purchased: all. Publishes 1-1.5% of poems submitted. Deadlines: none. Reporting time: 15-45 days. Payment: 2 copies of issue. Interested in new or unpub'd poets: yes. Simultaneous submissions accepted: no. Recent contributors: Robert Chute, Richard Kostelanetz, Simon Perchik, Nancy Means Wright, Marvin Solomon. Submission quantity: 3-8. Special interests: No longer use poems under 8 lines; 3-4 page limit on length. Otherwise open to any style, content, form.

Smiling Dog Press, 9875 Fritz, Maple City, MI 49664, 616-334-3695. 1989.

The Smith (subsidiary of The Generalist Assn., Inc.), 69 Joralemon Street, Brooklyn, NY 11201-4003. Harry Smith, Editor, Publisher; Michael McGrinder, Associate Editor. 1964. "Book program is extremely limited at current time—only 3-5 books per year, and we already have projects on hand. Do not send complete ms. Unable to accept certified or registered mail. SASE, please!" avg. press run 1M. Pub'd 1 poetry title 1999; expects 3 poetry titles 2000, 3 poetry titles 2001. 6×9; avg. price, cloth: $17.95; paper: $10.95. 88pp; Publishes 5% of poetry manuscripts submitted. Reporting time: 3 months. Payment: $500 as an advance against royalties. Interested in new or unpub'd poets: yes. Simultaneous submissions accepted: yes. Recently published poets: Menke Katz, Karen Swenson, Glenna Luschei, David Rigsbee, Lloyd Van Brunt. Submission quantity: 7-10.

Gibbs Smith, Publisher, 1877 East Gentile Street, PO Box 667, Layton, UT 84041, 801-544-9800; Fax 801-544-5582; E-mail info@GibbsSmith.com. Christopher Merrill, Consulting Editor; Gail Yngve, Editor. 1969. "Submit *only* during the month of April; all other manuscripts will be returned unread. Include SASE and a $15 reading fee" avg. press run 1.5M. Pub'd 1 poetry title 1999; expects 1 poetry title 2000, 1 poetry title 2001. 4¼×6¾ to 11×11; avg. price, paper: $9.95. 64pp; Reporting time: 3 months. Payment: $500 prize for winning manuscript + a royalty rate of 7% net. Interested in new or unpub'd poets: yes. Simultaneous submissions accepted: yes. Recently published poets: Norman Stock, H.L. Hix, Angie Estes, Catherine Bowman. Submission quantity: a full-length manuscript which may fit into a 64-page format.

SMOKE, Windows Project, Liver House, 96 Bold Street, Liverpool L1 4HY, England. Dave Ward. 1974. circ. 500. 2/yr. Pub'd 50 poems 1999. sub. price: £3/6 issues incl. postage; sample: 50p plus post. 24pp; size A5; Rights purchased: none, copyright stays with poet;. Publishes 1.28% of poems submitted. Reporting time: as soon as possible. Interested in new or unpub'd poets: yes. Simultaneous submissions accepted: yes. Recent contributors: Douglas Dunn, Alison Brackenbury, Matt Simpson, Lorena Cassady, Roger McGough. Submission quantity: 6.

The Snail's Pace Press, Inc., 85 Darwin Road, Cambridge, NY 12816, 518-677-5208, snail@poetic.com. Darby Penney, Editor; Ken Denberg, Editor. 1990. "Poetry and poetry in translation. We publish 3 chapbooks annually of contemporary poetry. A $10 reading fee is required. The editor especially welcomes chapbooks from women, people of color, and members of ethnic and cultural minorities." Expects 2 poetry titles 2000, 3 poetry titles 2001. 5¼×8¼; avg. price, paper: $6. 36pp; Publishes 10% of poetry manuscripts submitted. Reporting time: 4 months. Payment: $50 and 50 copies. Interested in new or unpub'd poets: yes. Simultaneous submissions accepted: no. Recently published poets: Grace Bauer, Barry Ballard. Submission quantity: 24-32 mss. pages.

SNAKE NATION REVIEW, 110 #2 West Force, Valdosta, GA 31601, 912-249-8334. William Fuller, Poetry Editor. 1989. "Spring Contest $100, $75, $50; Fall Editor's Choice for Poetry $100." circ. 1M. 4/yr. Pub'd 60 poems 1999; expects 80 poems 2000, 150 poems 2001. sub. price: $20; sample: $6 (includes mailing). 110pp; 6×9; Rights purchased: First rights. Publishes 20% of poems submitted. Deadlines: July 1, February 1, September 1. Reporting time: 3-6 months. Payment: prize money or 2 copies. Interested in new or unpub'd poets: yes. Simultaneous submissions accepted: yes, with prompt notification. Recent contributors: David Kirby, Judith Cofer, Van Broch, Constance Alexander. Submission quantity: 6-8. Special interests: Anything well-written.

SNAKE RIVER REFLECTIONS, 1863 Bitterroot Drive, Twin Falls, ID 83301, 208-734-0746, e-mail wjan@aol.com. 1990. circ. 250+. 10/yr (monthly, except Oct. & Dec.). Expects 100-130 poems 2000. sub. price: $7.50; sample: 75¢. 12pp; 5½×8½; Rights purchased: first rights. Publishes 10% of poems submitted. Deadlines: 3rd Saturday of each month; not published October or December. Reporting time: 3 weeks.

Payment: 1 copy. Interested in new or unpub'd poets: yes. Simultaneous submissions accepted: no. Recent contributors: Tom McFadden, C. David Hay, Mary Winters, Diane Krueger. Submission quantity: 15 max.

SNOWY EGRET, PO Box 9, Bowling Green, IN 47833. Karl Barnebey, Publisher; Philip Repp, Editor. 1922. "We publish only nature poetry or poetry that explores the psychological and spiritual connections between human beings and the natural world. Send #10 SASE for writer's guidelines." circ. 500. 2/yr. Pub'd 12 poems 1999; expects 18 poems 2000, 18 poems 2001. sub. price: $12/1 year, $20/2 years; sample: $8. 52pp; 8½×11; Rights purchased: first rights, one-time reprint rights. Publishes less than 5% of poems submitted. Deadlines: none. Reporting time: 1 month. Payment: $4 minimum, $4 full page. Interested in new or unpub'd poets: yes. Simultaneous submissions accepted: no. Recent contributors: Conrad Hilberry, Judith Nutter, Patricia Hooper, Jared Carter. Submission quantity: up to 5.

SO TO SPEAK, 4400 University Drive, MS 2D6, Fairfax, VA 22030-4444, sts@gmu.edu, www.gmu.edu/org/sts. Rebecca Knotts, Poetry Editor. 1991. "We run a poetry contest in the fall (postmark deadline Oct. 16) and a short fiction contest in the spring. We are especially interested in writing that takes risks. We are very interested in protecting a space for women, in remembering the past, and publishing for the future." circ. 1.3M. 2/yr. Pub'd 30 poems 1999. sub. price: $11; sample: $6. 120pp; 5×8; Rights purchased: first time publication. Publishes 10% of poems submitted. Deadlines: Autumn issue Oct. 10, Spring issue March 30. Reporting time: 3-4 months. Payment: 2 copies. Interested in new or unpub'd poets: yes! Simultaneous submissions accepted: yes. Recent contributors: Joan Retallack, Carolyn Forche, Heather Fuller, Jenn McCreary, Elizabeth Treadwell. Submission quantity: 3-5. Special interests: We publish experimental poetry and poetry from emerging writers.

SO YOUNG!, PO Box 141489, Coral Gables, FL 33114, 305-662-3928; FAX 305-661-4123. Julia Busch. 1996. "Light, philosophical, metaphysical, humorous, romantic, no heavy panting or flagwaving." circ. 1M. 6/yr. Pub'd 6-8 poems 1999; expects 6-8 poems 2000, 6-8 poems 2001. sub. price: $35 USA, $42 Canada; sample: same. 12pp; 8½×11; Rights purchased: First serial, one time. Publishes 20% of poems submitted. Reporting time: 2 days - 1 month. Payment: copies of newsletter. Interested in new or unpub'd poets: yes. Simultaneous submissions accepted: yes. Recent contributors: Sheryl L. Nelms, William Vernon, Lyn Lifshin. Submission quantity: up to 6. Special interests: up-beat, inspirational.

●**Soft Skull Press,** 100 Suffolk Street, Basement, New York, NY 10002, 212-673-2502, Fax 212-673-0787, sander@softskull.com, www.softskull.com. 1992. 5×8.

SOJOURNER, THE WOMEN'S FORUM, 42 Seaverns Avenue, Jamaica Plain, MA 02130-1109, 617-524-0415. Lee Varon, Denise Bergman. 1975. "By women, for women." circ. 45M. 11/yr. Expects 48 poems 2001. sub. price: $26; sample: $5. 52pp; 11×17; Rights purchased: first only. Publishes 10% or less of poems submitted. Deadlines: 1st of month. Reporting time: 2 months. Payment: subscription, 2 copies, $15. Interested in new or unpub'd poets: yes. Simultaneous submissions accepted: yes. Recent contributors: Lyn Lifshin, Michele Leavitt, Wendy Mrookin, Ellen Bass, Elana Dykewomon. Submission quantity: 3 maximum.

SOLO, 5146 Foothill, Carpinteria, CA 93013, berrypress@aol.com. Glenna Luschei, Founding Editor & Editor-in-Chief; David Oliveira, Co-Editor; Jackson Wheeler, Co-Editor. 1996. circ. 1M. 2/yr. Pub'd 60 poems 1999; expects 60 poems 2000, 60 poems 2001. sub. price: $16/2 issues; sample: $9. 130pp; 6×9; Rights purchased: negotiable. Publishes 75% of poems submitted. Deadlines: July and August. Reporting time: 1 month. Payment: copies only. Interested in new or unpub'd poets: sorry. Simultaneous submissions accepted: no. Recent contributors: Robert Creeley, Ron Koertge, Sherman Alexie, Fred Chappell, Carol Muske. Submission quantity: 5. Special interests: Sometimes we publish translations, prefer work previously never translated.

SOLO FLYER, 2115 Clearview NW, Massillon, OH 44646. David B. McCoy. 1979. "Three or more 4-page flyers will be published a year; each by an individual author. All styles of poetry using capitalization and punctuation will be considered. Like to publish poems that have a common theme Send up to 10 poems at a time, and include a SASE" circ. 100. 3/yr. Pub'd 12 poems 1999. sample price: free with SASE. 4pp; 5¼×8½; Publishes 5-10% of poems submitted. Deadlines: reading year-round—none. Reporting time: 1-3 months. Payment: 20-25 copies. Interested in new or unpub'd poets: yes. Simultaneous submissions accepted: yes. Recent contributors: Timothy Russell, Robert Miltner, Neil Carpathios. Submission quantity: up to 10. Special interests: Prose poetry.

SONAR MAP, PO Box 25243, Eugene, OR 97402, Voice/fax: 541-688-1523; eleg-sci@efn.org. 1996. circ. 2M. 4/yr. sub. price: $10; sample: trade for reviews. 24pp; 8¼×10¾.

SONGS OF INNOCENCE, Pendragonian Publications, PO Box 719, New York, NY 10101-0719, mmpendragon@aol.com. Michael Pendragon, Editor & Publisher. 1999. "*Songs of Innocence* is one of the foremost publications in the bourgeoning Romantic Renaissance, and seeks works reflecting the pieces of original Romantic Era: Blake, Shelley, Byron, Keats, Wordsworth, Coleridge, Poe, Whitman, et al. Themes should include mythical, Pagan, metaphysical, spiritual elements. Verses which include rhyme, meter, etc. are preferred." circ. 250. 3/yr. Pub'd 75 poems 1999; expects 200 poems 2000, 200 poems 2001. sub. price: $12; sample: $5. 100pp; 5½×8½; Rights purchased: one time. Publishes 5% of poems submitted. Deadlines: open. Reporting time: 3 months or longer. Payment: 1 copy. Interested in new or unpub'd poets: yes. Simultaneous submissions accepted: yes. Recent contributors: Louise Webster, Kevin N. Roberts, Tamara Latham, John Light, Joan Board. Special interests: Romantic poetry, long poems, up to 5 pages.

SONORA REVIEW, Dept. of English, University of Arizona, Tucson, AZ 85721, 520-626-8383. Kate Bertine, Michelle Roop. 1980. "Submissions read year round, though summer months are slower. Include SASE! Remember, our staff is all volunteers; we'll get to your poems as quickly as we can." circ. 800. 2/yr. Pub'd 40 poems 1999; expects 40 poems 2000, 40 poems 2001. sub. price: $12; sample: $6. 120pp; 6×9; Rights purchased: 1st U.S. serial. Publishes 1% of poems submitted. Deadlines: July for Fall issue, Dec. for Spring issue. Reporting time: 3-6 months. Payment: 2 copies. Interested in new or unpub'd poets: yes. Simultaneous submissions accepted: yes. Recent contributors: Jane Miller, Michael Burkard, Lisa Russ Spaar, Jack Heflin, Mark Doty. Submission quantity: 1-10. Special interests: We have recently produced special features on writing from various ethnic and oral traditions, and new voices from the Southwest. We are generally open to experimental and offbeat work.

SOUNDINGS EAST, English Dept., Salem State College, Salem, MA 01970, 978-542-6205. Paul Tuttle, Poetry Editor. 1973. "We have a 'Feature Poet' section in most issues. Usually, we invite a poet who has not yet published a book of poetry to submit 8-10 poems. We enjoy showcasing new talent." circ. 2M. 2/yr. Pub'd 30-35 poems 1999; expects 30-35 poems 2000, 30-35 poems 2001. sub. price: $10; sample: $3. 64pp; 5½×8½; Rights purchased: rights revert to authors. Publishes 10% of poems submitted. Deadlines: Fall November 20, Spring April 20. Reporting time: 7 months. Payment: 2 copies. Interested in new or unpub'd poets: yes. Simultaneous submissions accepted: yes. Recent contributors: Robert Cooperman, Debra Allbery, Martha Ramsey, Dionisio Martinez, "Incarcerated poets" Submission quantity: 3-4. Special interests: Free verse, serious and light. Don't print much rhymed poetry unless it's of unusually good quality. Keep poetry to 2 pages and under per poem.

THE SOUNDS OF POETRY, 2076 Vinewood, Detroit, MI 48216-5506. Jacqueline Sanchez, Publisher & Editor. 1983. "New poets should include a brief bio, typed. Do not send handwritten poetry." circ. 200. 3/yr. Pub'd 100 poems 1999; expects 150 poems 2000, 175 poems 2001. sub. price: $10; sample: $5. 20-36pp; 5½×8½; Rights purchased: none. Publishes 50% of poems submitted. Deadlines: accepting submissions beginning October 2000 for 2002/2003. Reporting time: 2 weeks to 1 year. Payment: copies only. Interested in new or unpub'd poets: yes. Simultaneous submissions accepted: no. Recent contributors: Bernard Hewitt, Carole Friend, Tumika Patrice Cain, Beverly Austin-Mayfield, Rod Farmer. Submission quantity: 5. Special interests: Gutsey satire, do *not* want poems about flowers. Would like to see poetry by truckers, motorcyclist and more international poets, including poems in Spanish.

SOUTH CAROLINA REVIEW, English Dept, Clemson Univ, Clemson, SC 29634-1503, 803-656-3151. Wayne Chapman, Editor. 1968. "We take any good poetry, not restricting ourselves to a specific category. Send a SASE for return of manuscript and a stamped self-addressed postcard for acknowledgement. Manuscripts received during June, July, August, and December are returned unread." circ. 600. 2/yr. Pub'd 35 poems 1999; expects 50 poems 2000, 40 poems 2001. sub. price: $10 + $2 s/h; sample: $10. 200-208pp; 9×6; Rights purchased: first serial rights. Publishes 3% of poems submitted. Deadlines: we do not read May-August or December. Reporting time: 6-9 months. Payment: copies. Interested in new or unpub'd poets: rarely accepted. Simultaneous submissions accepted: no. Recent contributors: Ron Rash, Pattiann Rogers, Claire Bateman, Rita Ann Higgins, Paul Muldoon. Submission quantity: 4-6 is usually adequate. Special interests: We generally prefer poems of a page or less, although we do publish longer ones on occasion. Please no chapbooks.

SOUTH DAKOTA REVIEW, University of South Dakota, 414 East Clark, Vermillion, SD 57069, 605-677-5184/5966. Brian Bedard, Editor; Eileen Sullivan, Assistant Editor. 1963. circ. 500. 4/yr. Pub'd 50 poems 1999; expects 50 poems 2000, 50 poems 2001. sub. price: $22, $36/2 years; international: $30, $45/2 years; sample: $7. 150-180pp; 6×9; Rights purchased: first and reprint. Publishes 6%-10% of poems submitted. Deadlines: any time. Reporting time: time varies; usually 6-10 weeks, longer occasionally. Payment: copies and a one year subscription. Interested in new or unpub'd poets: yes, but some experience needed, competition is keen. Simultaneous submissions accepted: no. Recent contributors: Twyla Hansen, Walter McDonald, Linda Hasselstrom, Joanne Lowery, Diana Henning. Submission quantity: 4-6. Special interests: Have published all kinds, but lean toward poems of 10-30 lines with original delineation of a place/a person in a place. Always pleased by third-person point of view if the poem is otherwise good also.

THE SOUTHERN CALIFORNIA ANTHOLOGY, Master of Professional Writing Program, WPH 404/Univ. of Southern Calif., Los Angeles, CA 90089-4034, 213-740-5775. 1983. "Material will not be returned without SASE." circ. 1M. 1/yr. Pub'd 24 poems 1999; expects 26 poems 2000, 25 poems 2001. sub. price: $9.95; sample: $5. 140pp; 5½×8½; Rights purchased: none, rights revert to author. Publishes 10% of poems submitted. Deadlines: January 15. Reporting time: 3 months. Payment: 3 copies. Interested in new or unpub'd poets: yes. Simultaneous submissions accepted: no. Recent contributors: Donald Hall, James Merrill, Denise Levertov, James Ragan, W.S. Merwin. Submission quantity: maximum of 5. Special interests: Open to all forms.

SOUTHERN HUMANITIES REVIEW, 9088 Haley Center, Auburn Univ., Auburn, AL 36849, 334-844-9088, www.auburn.edu/english/shr/home.htm. Dan Latimer, Virginia M. Kouidis, Co-Editors. 1967. "$50 Theodore Christian Hoepfner Prize annually for best *published* poem. Reading slows in summer. We rarely print a poem over 2pp long. Send submission in #10 business envelope. No e-mail submissions." circ. 700. 4/yr. Pub'd 40 poems 1999; expects 40 poems 2000, 40 poems 2001. sub. price: $15 U.S., $20 foreign; sample: $5 U.S.; $7 foreign. 100pp; 6×9; Publishes less than 2% of poems submitted. Reporting time: 60-90 days. Payment: 2 copies, $5 extra copies (we no longer give off prints). Interested in new or unpub'd poets: yes. Simultaneous submissions accepted: no. Recent contributors: Eamon Grennan, Donald Hall, Brendan Galvin, Mary Ruefle, Robert Morgan. Submission quantity: no more than 3-5. Special interests: Translations are encouraged. Include originals and permission from copyright holder.

SOUTHERN INDIANA REVIEW, Liberal Arts Department, Univ. of Southern Indiana, Evansville, IN 47712, 812-464-1735. fax 812-465-7152. email tkramer@evansville.net. Matthew E. Graham, Poetry Editor. 1994. "Submit October through December" circ. 350. 1/yr. Pub'd 14 poems 1999; expects 15 poems 2000, 15 poems 2001. sub. price: $10; sample: $10. 150pp; 6×9; Publishes 10% of poems submitted. Deadlines: Dec. 31. Reporting time: 2 months. Payment: copy of magazine. Interested in new or unpub'd poets: yes. Simultaneous submissions accepted: yes. Recent contributors: Liam Rector, Richard Newman, Allison Joseph, Leslie Adrienne Miller. Submission quantity: 3. Special interests: Poems that portray the Midwest or are written by Midwestern poets.

THE SOUTHERN JOURNAL, Appalachian Log Publishing Company, PO Box 20297, Charleston, WV 25362, 304-722-6866. 1991. circ. 5M. 12/yr. sub. price: $15; sample: $1.50. 33pp; 8½×11.

SOUTHERN POETRY REVIEW, Advancement Studies Dept., Central Piedmont Community College, Charlotte, NC 28235, 704-330-6002. Ken McLaurin, Editor; Lucinda Grey, Managing Editor; Paul Newman, Associate Editor; Shelley Crisp, Associate Editor; Martin Settle, Associate Editor; Christopher Davis, Managing Editor; Stella Hastie, Associate Editor; Mary Kratt, Associate Editor; Julie Townsend, Associate Editor; Kristina Wright, Associate Editor; Lynne Shrum, Associate Editor. 1958. "The best of what comes in, according to our views, we accept. Annual contest: The Guy Owen Prize ($500) Deadline is normally May 1. Write for details. We don't read during the summer." circ. 1M-1.2M. 2/yr. Pub'd 90 poems 1999; expects 90 poems 2000, 90 poems 2001. sub. price: $8; sample: $3. 80pp; 6×9; Rights purchased: 1st, but copyright reverts. Publishes 2% of poems submitted. Deadlines: we read continuously except during the summer. Reporting time: 4-6 months. Payment: 1 copy. Interested in new or unpub'd poets: yes. Simultaneous submissions accepted: no. Recent contributors: Betty Adcock, Linda Pastan, Diane Wakoski, Dabney Stuart, David Ray. Submission quantity: 3-5. Special interests: No special interests. We do serve as a natural outlet for poets in the south, in part due to the title, but the magazine is in no way regional.

THE SOUTHERN REVIEW, 43 Allen Hall, Louisiana State University, Baton Rouge, LA 70803, 225-388-5108. James Olney, Editor; Dave Smith, Editor. 1965 new series (1935 original series). "Poems selected with careful attention to craftsmanship and technique and to the seriousness of subject matter. Poetry length preferred: 1-4 pages." circ. 3.1M. 4/yr. Pub'd 98 poems 1999; expects 80 poems 2000, 80 poems 2001. sub. price: $25 ind., $50 inst.; sample: $8 ind., $16 inst. 250pp; 6¾×10; Rights purchased: 1st American serial rights only. Publishes 1% of poems submitted. Deadlines: We do not read unsolicited mss. in June, July, or August. Reporting time: 6 weeks. Payment: $20 per page. Interested in new or unpub'd poets: yes. Simultaneous submissions accepted: no. Recent contributors: Charles Wright, Brigit Pegeen Kelly, A.R. Ammons, Mary Oliver, Yusef Komunyakaa. Submission quantity: 4 or 5.

Southern Star Publishing, 4 Timberline Trail #D, Ormond Beach, FL 32174-4977. 1994. 4.3×7, 5×8.

SOUTHWEST JOURNAL, 577 Central Avenue, Box 4, Jefferson, LA 70121-0517, e-mail: horizons@alta-vista.net or blueskies@discoverymail.com; Websites www.freeyellow.com/members2/oldwest/index.htm/ or www2.cybercities.com/z/zines/. Sharida Rizzuto, Harold Tollison, Ann Hoyt, Elaine Wolfe. 1988. "We are interested in anything and everything about the Old West" circ. 300-500. 2/yr. Pub'd 20 poems 1999; expects 20 poems 2000, 20 poems 2001. sub. price: $13.80; sample: $7.90. 80pp; 8½×11; Rights purchased: one-time rights, first or second time rights. Publishes 40% of poems submitted. Deadlines: always open to submissions. Reporting time: 2-6 weeks. Payment: copy. Interested in new or unpub'd poets: yes. Simultaneous submissions accepted: yes. Recent contributors: Arthur Knight, John Youril, Lucinda MacGregor. Submission quantity: 1-5. Special interests: We are willing to look at any type of poetry.

SOUTHWEST REVIEW, Southern Methodist University, 307 Fondren Library W., Box 750374, Dallas, TX 75275-0374, 214-768-1037. Willard Spiegelman. 1915. "It is hard to describe the *Southwest Review*'s preference in poetry in a few words. We always suggest that potential contributors read several issues of the magazine to see for themselves what we like. But some things may be said: We demand very high quality in our poems; we accept both traditional and experimental writing, but avoid unnecessary obscurity and private symbolism; we place no arbitrary limits on length, but find shorter poems easier to fit into our format than longer ones. We have no specific limitations as to theme. All submissions should be typed neatly on white paper and accompanied by a stamped, self-addressed envelope. The *Southwest Review* does not consider simultaneous submissions. The *Southwest Review* is published quarterly. We send the poet three gratis contributor's copies of the issue. Also, SASE or IRC are necessary for a reply; only unpublished manuscripts are considered; we offer a $200 cash prize annually for the best poem that appeared in the magazine in the previous year (the Elizabeth Matchett Stover Memorial Award)." circ. 1.5M. 4/yr. Expects 48 poems 2000. sub. price: $24; sample: $6. 144pp; 6×9; Rights purchased: 1st North American serial. Publishes 6% of poems submitted. Deadlines: none. Reporting time: 1 month. Payment: depends. Interested in new or unpub'd poets: yes. Simultaneous submissions accepted: no. Recent contributors: Richard Foerster, Edward Hirsch, Jessica Hornik, Laurence Lieberman, Mary Jo Salter. Submission quantity: up to 5. Special interests: Traditional and experimental writing, but avoid unnecessary obscurity and private symbolism; we place no arbitrary limits on length, but find shorter poems easier to fit into our format than longer ones. We have no specific limitations as to theme.

SOU'WESTER, Southern Illinois University, Edwardsville, IL 62026-1438. Fred W. Robbins, Editor. 1960. "Advice to poets: Read poetry past and present. Have something to say and say it in your own voice. We look for poems of high quality that move the reader and take some risk. Poetry is a very personal thing for many editors. When all else fails, we may rely on gut reactions, so take whatever hints you're given to improve your poetry, and keep submitting." circ. 300. 2/yr. Pub'd 68 poems 1999; expects 68 poems 2000, 68 poems 2001. sub. price: $10; $18 2 years; sample: $5. 120pp; 6×9; Rights purchased: All; rights released upon publication, when requested. Publishes 2% of poems submitted. Deadlines: none. Reporting time: 2-4 months. Payment: 2 copies of issue; 1 year subscription. Interested in new or unpub'd poets: yes. Simultaneous submissions accepted: yes. Recent contributors: R.T. Smith, Ronald Wallace, Jennifer Atkinson, Frederick Zydek, Michael Strelow. Submission quantity: 3-5. Special interests: We will be pleased to see long poems.

THE SOW'S EAR POETRY REVIEW, The Sow's Ear Press, 19535 Pleasant View Drive, Abingdon, VA 24211-6827, 540-628-2651, richman@preferred.com. Larry Richman, Managing Editor. 1989. "Annual contest, deadline September/October, First prize $1,000, $2 fee per poem or $10/year subscription waived for entering 5 poems. No tabu subjects or forms of poetry. Seek reviews, interviews with poets, articles which give insight into poets or poetry. Seek b&w art. Chapbook contest accepts ms March-April. SASE for guidelines or by e-mail. First prize $1,000." circ. 600. 4/yr. Pub'd 55 poems 1999; expects 125 poems 2000, 125 poems 2001. sub. price: $10; sample: $5. 32pp; 8½×11; Rights purchased: First American Serial. Publishes 5% of poems submitted. Deadlines: none. Reporting time: 3-4 months. Payment: 2 copies. Interested in new or unpub'd poets: yes, we feature an unpublished poet several times a year. Simultaneous submissions accepted: yes. Recent contributors: Penelope Scambly Schott, R.T. Smith, Susan Terris, Madeline Tiger, Richard Hague. Submission quantity: 3-5. Special interests: No restrictions, but we do each issue feature a few writers from Bristol and environs. We welcome good political poetry. Our committee is made up of poets with very different tastes and ideas, so just about anything goes.

The Sow's Ear Press (see also THE SOW'S EAR POETRY REVIEW), 19535 Pleasant View Drive, Abingdon, VA 24211-6827, e-mail richman@preferred.com. 1989. 6×9.

SPACE AND TIME, 138 West 70th Street 4-B, New York, NY 10023-4432. Linda D. Addison, Poetry Editor. 1966. "Please make sure your poem has a strong fantasy or science fiction element - fanciful metaphors are not, on their own, enough." circ. 2M. 2/yr. Pub'd 10 poems 1999; expects 10 poems 2000, 10 poems 2001. sub. price: $10; sample: $5 + 1.50 p/h. 48pp; 8½×11; Rights purchased: 1st North American serial only. Publishes 1% of poems submitted. Deadlines: open. Reporting time: 2-3 months maximum. Payment: 2 contributor copies on publication + $5 minimum. Interested in new or unpub'd poets: yes. Simultaneous submissions accepted: no. Recent contributors: Richard Kostelanetz, Charlee Jacob, Corinne De Winter, Joey Froehlich, Catherine Mintz. Submission quantity: 1-5. Special interests: Would particularly like to see narrative poems with fresh story lines.

SPARROW, 103 Waldron Street, West Lafayette, IN 47906. Felix Stefanile, Selma Stefanile. 1954. "For the indefinite future we plan to publish only in the field of the contemporary sonnet, based upon the great English and Italian traditions, and shall consider no other type of writing for publication. We invite the submission of four or five pieces at a time. Usual rules for submission apply—typed copy, SASE for return." circ. 500-1.5M. 1/yr. Pub'd 100 poems 1999. sub. price: $6; sample: $5. 100pp; 8½×11; Rights purchased: first serial rights. Publishes 5-10% of poems submitted. Deadlines: we do not read from Oct. through Dec. Reporting time: within 6 weeks. Payment: $3 a poem, plus copy (1). Interested in new or unpub'd poets: yes. Simultaneous submissions accepted: absolutely not. Recent contributors: X.J. Kennedy, Dana Gioia, Dessa Crawford, Robert Mezey, Katherine McAlpine. Submission quantity: 4-5.

●**SPARROWGRASS POETRY NEWSLETTER, Prospect Press,** 609 Main Street, PO Box 193,

Sistersville, WV 26175, 304-652-1449; Fax 304-652-1148; www.tinplace.com/spfpoetry. Helen McInnis. 1993. "Two contests each year, summer and winter, with cash prizes: $100, $50, $25. $2 entry fee per poem in each contest." circ. 1M. 4/yr. Pub'd 40 poems 1999; expects 45 poems 2000, 50 poems 2001. sub. price: $21.95; sample: $4.50. 6pp; 8½×11; Rights purchased: require 1 time only. Publishes 5% of poems submitted. Deadlines: varies per contest. Reporting time: 6 months (for contest winners). Payment: $100, $50, $25 to top three contest winners. Interested in new or unpub'd poets: no. Simultaneous submissions accepted: yes. Recent contributors: June Owens, Douglas Johnson, Margaret Hellewell, Jane Pierretz, Marjorie Millinson. Submission quantity: up to 5 per contest. Special interests: for contests, maximum 20 lines per poem, all subjects and types welcome.

SPEAK UP, PO Box 100506, Denver, CO 80250, 303-715-0837, Fax 303-715-0793, speakupres@aol.com, www.speakuppress.org. 1999. "Teen literary journal" circ. 1M. 1/yr. sub. price: $10; sample: $8. 64pp; 5½×8½; Publishes 5% of poems submitted. Payment: 2 copies. Interested in new or unpub'd poets: yes. Simultaneous submissions accepted: yes. Submission quantity: no more than 5. Special interests: only accept poetry from young people 13-19 years old.

SPIDER, PO Box 300, Peru, IL 61354, 815-224-6656, Fax 815-224-6615. 1994. "SASE is required for response" circ. 92M. 12/yr. Pub'd 14 poems 1999; expects 15 poems 2000, 14 poems 2001. sub. price: $35.97; sample: $5. 34pp; 8×10; Rights purchased: First publication rights in the English language. Publishes 1% of poems submitted. Reporting time: approx. 3 months. Payment: up to $3 per line. Interested in new or unpub'd poets: only their best efforts. Simultaneous submissions accepted: yes - please indicate that poem is a simultaneous submission. Recent contributors: Constance Levy, Lilian Moore, Mary Quattlebaum, Isabel Joshlin Glaser, Michael Spooner. Submission quantity: No more than 5.

SPILLWAY, Tebot Bach, Box 7887, Huntington Beach, CA 92615-7887, 714-968-0905. Mifanwy Kaiser, Editor; J.D. Lloyd, Assistant Editor. 1993. 2/yr. Pub'd 160 poems 1999; expects 160 poems 2000, 160 poems 2001. sub. price: $14; sample: $10 postpaid. 176pp; 6×9; Rights purchased: 1st time. Deadlines: read year-round. Reporting time: 6 months. Payment: 1 copy. Interested in new or unpub'd poets: yes. Simultaneous submissions accepted: yes. Recent contributors: Richard Jones, Susan Terris, John Balabon, Eleanor Wilner, Charles Harper Webb. Submission quantity: 6 max. or 10 pages max.

SPIN, c/o Postal Agency, Ngakawav, Buller, New Zealand, 006495768577. L.H. Kyle. 1986. "Winter (July) issue features haiku & short poetry" circ. 150. 3/yr. Pub'd 150 poems 1999; expects 150 poems 2000, 150 poems 2001. sub. price: $US15, includes airmail p/h outside New Zealand; sample: $US3. 60pp; 5¾×8¼; Publishes 50% of poems submitted. Deadlines: 1 month before publication. Reporting time: 4 months max., usually less. Payment: nil. Interested in new or unpub'd poets: yes. Simultaneous submissions accepted: no. Recent contributors: Catherine Mair, Ruewyn Alexander, Leonardo Alishan, Philip A. Waterhouse, John Allison. Submission quantity: 6. Special interests: Interested in excellence in a variety of forms.

SPINNING JENNY, Black Dress Press, PO Box 213, Village Station, New York, NY 10014, website www.blackdresspress.com. C.E. Harrison, Editor. 1994. circ. 1M. 1/yr. Expects 30 poems 2000, 60 poems 2001. sub. price: $12; sample: $6. 96pp; 5½×9¼; Rights purchased: copyright to each published poems remains with the author. *SJ* has the right to distribute/sell each poem only in the original form of the magazine. Publishes 5% of poems submitted. Deadlines: none. Reporting time: 8 weeks. Payment: complimentary contributors copies. Interested in new or unpub'd poets: yes. Simultaneous submissions accepted: yes, though we do not publish previously published work. Recent contributors: Denise Duhamel, Matthew Lippman, m loncar, Renee Sedliar, Michael Morse. Submission quantity: 3-6. Special interests: experimental poetry.

The Spinning Star Press, 1065 E. Fairview Blvd., Inglewood, CA 90302, 213-464-3024. Bob Starr, Madeliene Sophie Gary, Carl Tate. 1986. "Due to some changes in policies, there may be a slowdown of poems published, but we plan to get a book of poetry out soon." 5½×8½. Recently published poets: Bob Starr, Carl Tate, Madeliene Sophie Gary, Alberta Haywood, Nat Dove.

SPIRIT TALK, Spirit Talk Press, PO Box 390, Browning, MT 59417, 406-338-2882; E-mail blkfoot4@3rivers.net. 1993. circ. 10M. 4/yr. sub. price: $25; sample: $4.95. 64pp; 8½×11.

Spirit Talk Press (see also SPIRIT TALK), PO Box 390, Browning, MT 59417, 406-338-2882; E-mail blkfoot4@3rivers.net. 1992. 8½×11.

THE SPIRIT THAT MOVES US, The Spirit That Moves Us Press, Inc., PO Box 720820-DB, Jackson Heights, Queens, NY 11372-0820, 718-426-8788, msklar@mindspring.com. Morty Sklar, Editor & Publisher; Marcela Bruno, Technical Editor. 1975. "We are in limbo at present. Query with SASE first, for theme and deadlines. No queries or submissions by e-mail. Send what *you* like best. We announce themes and deadlines in *Poets & Writers Magazine, Small Press Review* and many other places. Over 95% of what we publish is unsolicited." circ. 1.5M. Irregular. Pub'd 75 poems 1999; expects 50 poems 2000, 50 poems 2001. sub. price: $12 per volume. A volume could be in one year or two years. Our anthologies are part of the subscriptions;

sample: $6 ppd for *The Spirit That Moves Us Reader* (reg. $9), or *Free Parking: 15th Anniversary Collection*. 202pp; 5½×8½; Rights purchased: 1st printing, and reprints for anthologies. Publishes recently 2% of poems submitted. Deadlines: query first for theme. Reporting time: 3 months after deadline date. Payment: cloth copy or 2 paperbacks, also a 40% discount off paper, and 25% discount off extra cloth. Interested in new or unpub'd poets: yes. Simultaneous submissions accepted: yes, if we are informed about it. Recent contributors: Julia Alvarez, Darryl Holmes, Barbara Unger, Jaime Manrique, Rudy Kikel. Submission quantity: 3-5. Special interests: Work which expresses feeling. We're open to all styles.

The Spirit That Moves Us Press, Inc. (see also **THE SPIRIT THAT MOVES US**), PO Box 720820-DB, Jackson Heights, Queens, NY 11372-0820, 718-426-8788, msklar@mindspring.com. Morty Sklar, Editor & Publisher; Marcela Bruno, Technical Consultant. 1974. "We are in limbo at present. No e-mail queries or submissions. Query first for themes (with SASE) for anthologies. We announce themes and deadlines in *Poets & Writers Magazine, Small Press Review* and many other places. Our *Editor's Choice* series. Sample copy is $10 for #II or #III (reg. $15 with postage), and $7 for #I (501pp). $11 for *Patchwork of Dreams* (reg. $15)" avg. press run 2.1M. Pub'd 1 poetry title 1999; expects 1 poetry title 2000, 1 poetry title 2001. 5½×8½ pa, 6×9 cl; avg. price, cloth: $14; paper: $7.75. 132pp; Publishes 1.5% of poetry manuscripts submitted. Reporting time: 1 month book mss; 3 months after deadline for anthologies. Payment: cash, single authors; cash plus 1 cloth, collections; also 40% discount on paperbacks and 25% discount on extra clothbounds. Interested in new or unpub'd poets: yes. Simultaneous submissions accepted: yes, if notified about it. Recently published poets: Bob Jacob, Julia Alvarez, Rudy Kikel, Jaime Manrique, Barbara Unger. Submission quantity: 3-5 for anthologies, the whole ms for single-author books. Special interests: Work which expresses feeling. We're open to all styles.

SPITBALL: The Literary Baseball Magazine, 5560 Fox Road, Cincinnati, OH 45239-7271, 513-541-4296. Mike Shannon, Editor; William J. McGill, Poetry Editor. 1981. "We usually have 1 or 2 theme issues per year; writing poems for them is often a good way to break into *Spitball*. We did special issues in 1986 on 'Baseball Cards' and 'Roger Maris & NY Baseball'; in 1987 on 'Ballparks' and 'Blacks in Baseball'. Anyone interested in upcoming special issues can find out the topics by sending us a SASE. Our contest devoted to 'Casey at the Bat' was a huge success, and our special issues in which we printed the winning parodies and reviews of the runnersup has made a very significant contribution to the 'Casey' literary tradition. A $6 payment must accompany submissions from writers submitting to *Spitball* for the first time. In return, you will receive a sample copy. The $6 is a one-time charge. Once you have paid it, you may submit material as often as you like at no charge." circ. 1M. 2/yr. Pub'd 40 poems 1999. sub. price: $12; sample: $6. 96pp; 5½×8½; Rights purchased: 1st North American serial and reprint in *Spitball* anthologies. Publishes 10% of poems submitted. Reporting time: rejections usually within 1 week; 3 months max. Payment: copies. Interested in new or unpub'd poets: of course. Simultaneous submissions accepted: no, absolutely not! Recent contributors: Tim Peeler, Robert L. Harrison, Jim Palana, Robert Lord Keyes, Jim Daniels. Submission quantity: several if possible - no limit. Special interests: Throughout 1994 we are running a Babe Ruth Centennial Poetry Contest to celebrate the 100th anniversary of the Babe's birth (Feb. 6, 1895). Winning poems receive publication in *SB*, public readings, and a nice prize for author. More details for SASE. Deadline: 12/31/94.

THE SPITTING IMAGE, PO Box 20400 Tompkins Square Stn., New York, NY 10009. Julia Solis. 1994. circ. 500. 1-2/yr. Pub'd 7 poems 1999; expects 15 poems 2000, 15 poems 2001. sample price: $6.50. 80pp; 7×8½; Publishes less than 1% of poems submitted. Reporting time: 2 months. Payment: contributors copy. Interested in new or unpub'd poets: yes. Simultaneous submissions accepted: yes. Recent contributors: Richard Kostelanetz, Bob Flanagan, Jack Skelley, Tom Whalen. Submission quantity: 5 max. Special interests: We prefer highly unusual, absurd or experimental poetry. Nothing sentimental or political.

SPLIT SHIFT, Split Shift, 2461 Santa Monica Blvd. #C-122, Santa Monica, CA 90404. 1996. circ. 750. 150pp; 5×8.

Split Shift (see also **SPLIT SHIFT**), 2461 Santa Monica Blvd. #C-122, Santa Monica, CA 90404. 5×8.

Spoon River Poetry Press, PO Box 6, Granite Falls, MN 56241. David R. Pichaske. 1976. "We are not really open to unsolicited submissions, as it's all I can do to serve the poets I know and admire and have already published. And I'm tending increasingly to the large, hb collected poems type of books" avg. press run 750. Expects 3 poetry titles 2000. 5½×8½, 6×9; avg. price, cloth: $11.95; paper: $5.95. Hardback 144-288pp; paperback 64-80pp; Reporting time: soon unless I'm undecided or a grant is pending. Payment: large numbers of freebies, balance at 40% discount. Interested in new or unpub'd poets: no. Simultaneous submissions accepted: no. Recently published poets: John Knoepfle, Ralph J. Mills Jr., Leo Dangel, David Lee, Tim Geiger. Submission quantity: complete mss.

SPOON RIVER POETRY REVIEW, Department of English 4240, Illinois State University, Normal, IL 61790-4241, 309-438-7906, 309-438-3025. Lucia Getsi, Editor. 1976. "*SRPR* has no bias but excellence. We like poems that engage the reader at more than a ho-hum level. We do not read during the summer. We do run $1,000 Editors' Prize Contest - annual deadline April 15." circ. 1.5M. 2/yr. Pub'd 170 poems 1999; expects

200 poems 2000, 170 poems 2001. sub. price: $15 ($18 institutions); sample: $10. 128pp; 5½×8½; Rights purchased: we copyright with reversion of rights to poets. Publishes 1% of poems submitted. Deadlines: none, but we do not accept submissions May 1-Sept. 1. Reporting time: 2 months. Payment: copies. Interested in new or unpub'd poets: maybe. Simultaneous submissions accepted: reluctantly. Recent contributors: Dave Smith, Stuart Dybek, Susan Holahan, Bin Ramke, Leslie Adrienne Miller. Submission quantity: 3-5. Special interests: Translations.

SPORT LITERATE, Honest Reflections on Life's Leisurely Diversions, PO Box 577166, Chicago, IL 60657, 765-496-6524; sportlit@aol.com; www.avalon.net/~librarian/sportliterate. Jennifer Richter. 1995. "Publishing special 'Sportsmanship' issue in 2000. Consult web page for info. and guidelines." circ. 1.5M. 4/yr. Pub'd 15 poems 1999; expects 15 poems 2000, 15 poems 2001. sub. price: $15; sample: $5.75. 156pp; 5½×8½; Rights purchased: 1st time; revert back to poet. Publishes 5% of poems submitted. Deadlines: none. Reporting time: 2-3 months. Payment: 3 copies. Interested in new or unpub'd poets: yes. Simultaneous submissions accepted: yes, please inform us. Recent contributors: Norman German, Marilyn Kallet, Antonio Vallone, Wayne Zade. Submission quantity: no more than 5. Special interests: Open to all forms.

SPOUT, Spout Press, PO BOX 581067, Minneapolis, MN 55458-1067. John Colburn, Michelle Filkins, Chris Watercott. 1989. "Submissions should include SASE; it is helpful to have the authors's name and address on each poem" circ. 200+. 2-3/yr. Pub'd 60 poems 1999; expects 60 poems 2000, 60 poems 2001. sub. price: $12; sample: $4. 40pp; 8½×11; Publishes 10% of poems submitted. Deadlines: continuous. Reporting time: 1-3 months. Payment: copy of magazine. Interested in new or unpub'd poets: yes. Simultaneous submissions accepted: yes. Recent contributors: Jennifer Willoughby, Jeffrey Little, Emily Graves, John M. Bennett. Submission quantity: up to 6. Special interests: We frequently publish the experimental and surreal; rarely publish light verse or satire.

Spout Press (see also SPOUT), 28 W. Robie Street, St. Paul, MN 55107. 1996. 5½×8½.

SPSM&H, Amelia Press, 329 'E' Street, Bakersfield, CA 93304, 661-323-4064. Frederick A. Raborg, Jr., Editor. 1986. "*SPSM&H* usues only sonnets, traditional or experimental. We enjoy translations accompanied by copies of the original. We look for intensity, for the active voice rather than the passive, and please remember that Shakespeare wrote Shakespeare best. We will use the occasional erotic piece, but nothing salacious or pornographic. We enjoy furthering the efforts to understand ethnic problems and the gay/lesbian lifestyles, but those sonnets ought to enhance rather than demean, and further understanding and social acceptance." circ. 600. 4/yr. Pub'd 100 poems 1999; expects 120 poems 2000, 120 poems 2001. sub. price: $18; sample: $6. 44pp; 5½×8½; Rights purchased: 1st North American serial rights. Publishes 5% of poems submitted. No specific deadlines, ongoing consideration. Reporting time: 1-2 weeks. Payment: 2 'best of issue' poets each receive $14 on publication; no other payment. Interested in new or unpub'd poets: yes. Simultaneous submissions accepted: no. Recent contributors: Margaret Ryan, Harold Witt, Robert Wolfkill, Leonard Helie, Michael J. Bugeja. Submission quantity: 3-6. Special interests: We enjoy the use of satire and wit in sonnets, i.e. what Updike did with the form in *Midpoint* and, if it will help, know that the editor's favorite Shakespearean sonnet is #29. If you have a Laura or Larry in your life, please imitate Petrarch with surety and not with sappy vomiturition. Sidney did some nice things, of course, but please do not go rococo on him. Do not humiliate Hopkins, and awful Mason belongs in a...jar somewhere, not in *SPSM&H*. If your experimental efforts are sound enough, I'd accept them in double dactyls if necessary. Know the forms represented by the magazine's title, *SPSM&H*, in other words, and use that form which best fits your effort. *SPSM&H* translates to Shakespeare, Petrarch, Sidney, Milton & Hopkins. We also use sonnet sequences (see Katherine McAlpine's work in our Summer 89 issue), essays about the form, and we would consider even fiction which, in some interesting way, employs the form. Romantic or nature artwork, for which we pay a modest honorarium, is always considered—black and white only, any medium. We also use a few reviews and welcome books of, or about, the sonnet form.

The Square-Rigger Press, 1201 North 46th Street, Seattle, WA 98103-6610, 206-548-9385. 1973. 1¾×1-3/16, 1¼×2⅜.

Stained Glass Press (see also SKYWRITERS), 245 Spring Street, SW, Concord, NC 28025. 1994.

STAND MAGAZINE, School of English, Univeristy of Leeds, Leeds LS2 9JT, England. Rodney Pybus. 1952. "Enclose two International Reply Coupons with submission." circ. 4.5M. 4/yr. Pub'd 70 poems 1999; expects 80 poems 2000, 80 poems 2001. sub. price: $49.50; sample: $5. 120pp; 6-1/10×8; Rights purchased: copyright remains with authors. Publishes 5% of poems submitted. Deadlines: none. Reporting time: up to 2 months. Payment: £25 ($40) per poem or page of poems. Interested in new or unpub'd poets: yes. Simultaneous submissions accepted: no. Recent contributors: Jon Sulkin, Judith Kazantizis, Bernard O'Donoghue, Don Bogen, Ken Smith. Submission quantity: no more than 6 at one time. Special interests: Translations considered.

STAPLE, Tor Cottage, 81 Cavendish Road, Matlock, Derbyshire DE4 3HD, United Kingdom. Bob Windsor, Donald Measham. Address poetry submissions to: Gilderoy East, Upperwood Rd., Matlock Bath, DE4 3PD,

United Kingdom. 1982. "Biennial Open Poetry Competition is now annual. *Staple First Editions* series is rested. We do insist on first use of material." circ. 600. 4/yr. sub. price: £14 overseas (sterling only surface mail; £17.50 airmail); sample: £2 (sterling only surface mail, £3 airmail). 96pp; size A5; Rights purchased: none, beyond initial publication. Publishes 2% of poems submitted. Deadlines: early March, July, December. Reporting time: up to 3 months. Payment: £5 (or free subscription in first instance, overseas writers); £10 longer pieces. Interested in new or unpub'd poets: yes, particularly welcome. Simultaneous submissions accepted: reluctantly. Recent contributors: Ruth Sharman, U.A. Fanthorpe, Alison Spritzler-Rose, Donna Hilbert, Jennifer Olds. Submission quantity: prefer not more than 6. Special interests: Mainstream: emphasis on craft. No editorial hang-ups.

THE STAR BEACON, PO Box 117, Paonia, CO 81428, 970-527-3257, e-mail earthstar@tripod.net, http://earthstar.tripod.com/. 1987. "Not interested in vulgar language or erotica" circ. 500+. 12/yr. Pub'd 30 poems 1999; expects 8 poems 2000, 8 poems 2001. sub. price: $20; sample: $1.50. 12pp; 8½×11; Publishes 50% of poems submitted. Reporting time: 2 weeks. Payment: copies. Interested in new or unpub'd poets: yes. Simultaneous submissions accepted: yes. Recent contributors: Jean York, Merry Browne, Joan Hansen, Ethan Miller. Submission quantity: 1-5. Special interests: New Age themes, particularly space, angels and ET's.

Star Publications, PO Box 2144, Eureka Springs, AR 72632, 816-523-8228, Fax 501-981-1515, damon-dave@hotmail.com. 1977.

●**Star Rising Publishers/Allisone Press**, PO Box 3790, Sedona, AZ 86340, 877-249-6894 phone/Fax, allisone@ureach.com, www.allisonepress.com. 1997. 5½×8½.

Starbooks Press/FLF Press, 2516 Ridge Avenue, Sarasota, FL 34235, 941-957-1281, Fax 941-955-3829, starxxx@gte.net. Patrick J. Powers, Ed. Consultant. Address poetry submissions to: PO Box 2737, Sarasota, FL 34230. 1980. avg. press run 1M. 5½×8½; avg. price, paper: $7.95. 64pp; Reporting time: 2 months. Payment: negotiable. Interested in new or unpub'd poets: yes. Simultaneous submissions accepted: yes. Recently published poets: Leon del Ciervo, Edmond Miller. Submission quantity: 3. Special interests: Florida locale appreciated but not necessary.

STARBURST, Creative Arts & Science Enterprises, 341 Miller Street, Abilene, TX 79605-1903. Charles J. Palmer, Jacqueline Palmer. 1989. "Poetry: 32 lines or less. Any subject suitable for a general reading audience. $5 gift certificate if used." circ. 2M. 3/yr. Pub'd 100 poems 1999; expects 100 poems 2000, 100 poems 2001. sub. price: $21; sample: $7. 46pp; 8½×11; Rights purchased: none, author retains all rights. Publishes 8% of poems submitted. Deadlines: Jan. 31, April 30, July 31, Oct. 31. Reporting time: 90 days. Payment: winners of contest, cash and awards 90 days. Interested in new or unpub'd poets: yes. Simultaneous submissions accepted: yes. Recent contributors: M.L. Kiser, Ribert Mazur, E.J. Berlinski, Diana Kwiatkowski-Rubin, Michael Santiago. Submission quantity: no limit (1-10 is average).

STARGREEN, PO Box 380406, Cambridge, MA 02238, 617-868-3981. Patrick Smith, Editor. 1993. "Please include short bio, cover letter, and appropriate SASE. No outside submissions were published, but will publish in '97-98" circ. 500-1M. Irregular. sub. price: $10; sample: $2. 30pp; 5½×8½; Rights purchased: none. Publishes 0-5% of poems submitted. Deadlines: none. Reporting time: quickly. Payment: copies. Interested in new or unpub'd poets: why not? Simultaneous submissions accepted: why not? Recent contributors: Patrick Smith. Submission quantity: 5 max.

StarMist Books, Box 12640, Rochester, NY 14612. Beth Boyd, President. 1986. "No pornography." avg. press run 500. Pub'd 2 poetry titles 1999; expects 2-4 poetry titles 2000, 2-4 poetry titles 2001. 5½×8½; avg. price, paper: $6. 75pp; Reporting time: 2 weeks. Payment: negotiable. Interested in new or unpub'd poets: accepting by invitation only. Simultaneous submissions accepted: no. Recently published poets: Jani Johe Webster, Virginia Johe. Submission quantity: 2-3. Special interests: Interested in serious poetry, dealing with genuine feeling.

State Street Press, PO Box 278, Brockport, NY 14420, 716-637-0023. Judith Kitchen, Stan Sanvel Rubin, Bruce Bennett, Linda Allardt. 1981. "We sponsor a yearly contest, with a $10 entry fee, for which we send an existing chapbook. Poems should work as a collection—should be accompanied by SASE, sealed envelope containing name, address, any acknowledgements, etc. Author's name should NOT appear on the manuscript." avg. press run 400. Pub'd 4 poetry titles 1999; expects 5 poetry titles 2000, 4 poetry titles 2001. avg. price, paper: $6. 24pp; Publishes 2% of poetry manuscripts submitted. Reporting time: 4 months. Payment: authors receive free copies, can buy at cost, sell at a profit. Interested in new or unpub'd poets: yes, although most of our poets have been publishing in journals—we are a first collection. Simultaneous submissions accepted: yes. Recently published poets: Naomi Shihab Nye, Dionisio Martinez, Patricia Hooper, Joe Survant, Jan Beatty. Submission quantity: 20-24. Special interests: We have a variety of tastes and have printed both highly formal poetry, prose poetry, etc. We do want to see a collection that works thematically as a book, not merely a collection of unrelated poems.

Station Hill Press, Station Hill Road, Barrytown, NY 12507, 914-758-5840. 1978. avg. press run 2M. Pub'd 3 poetry titles 1999; expects 3 poetry titles 2000, 3 poetry titles 2001. 5¾×8¾, 5½×8½, 6×9, 7×10; avg. price, cloth: $29.95; paper: $9.95. 96pp; Reporting time: no guarantee except by written arrangement. Payment: percentage of gross or net income. Simultaneous submissions accepted: yes. Recently published poets: Edmond Jabes, Robert Kelly, Pierre Joris. Special interests: Translations, experimental poetry.

Steam Press/LAD Publishing, 5455 Meridian Mark, Suite 100, Atlanta, GA 30342, 404-257-1577; FAX 256-5475. Stan Cohen, David Bottoms. 1990. "Our initial efforts are to establish a series based on the collaborations of authors and artists in synergistic, beautiful volumes. Our participants include David Bottoms, Stan Cohen, Glenn Goldberg, Gary Stephan, Ed Ruscha. The books are issued in limited signed editions and trade paperback." avg. press run 550. Pub'd 1 poetry title 1999; expects 2 poetry titles 2000, 2-4 poetry titles 2001. 8×10; avg. price, cloth: $750.00; paper: $16. 40-80pp; Interested in new or unpub'd poets: no.

THE WALLACE STEVENS JOURNAL, The Wallace Stevens Society Press, Clarkson University, Box 5750, Potsdam, NY 13699-5750, 315-268-3987, serio@clarkson.edu, www.wallacestevens.com. Joseph Duemer. 1977. "We only publish poems that relate to Wallace Stevens—tributes to the master or reflections of his influence in theme or style. We are somewhat flexible on this." circ. 600. 2/yr. Pub'd 10-12 poems 1999. sub. price: $25 for individuals ($45 2-years), $32 for institutions, $37 for foreign; sample: $3 (postage. 120pp; 6×9; Rights purchased: none. Publishes 5% of poems submitted. Deadlines: none. Reporting time: 4-6 weeks. Payment: 1 copy of journal. Interested in new or unpub'd poets: yes. Simultaneous submissions accepted: no. Recent contributors: Stanley Plumly, Robert Pinsky, Albert Goldbarth. Submission quantity: 1-3.

The Wallace Stevens Society Press (see also THE WALLACE STEVENS JOURNAL), Box 5750 Clarkson University, Potsdam, NY 13699-5750, 315-268-3987, Fax 268-3983, serio@clarkson.edu, www.wallacestevens.com. John N. Serio, Series Editor. 1992. avg. press run 800. Expects 1 poetry title 2001. 6×9; avg. price, paper: $14.95. 88pp; Publishes 5% of poetry manuscripts submitted. Reporting time: 6-8 weeks. Payment: 10%. Interested in new or unpub'd poets: no. Simultaneous submissions accepted: no. Recently published poets: John Allman. Submission quantity: whole manuscript.

Still Waters Poetry Press, 459 S. Willow Avenue, Absecon, NJ 08201-4633. Shirley Lake, Editor. 1989. "We sponsor 2 annual contests: Women's Words (poems, essays) and Winter Poetry (query for current deadlines). We appreciate letter quality, neat, clean manuscripts. (Chapbooks only!)" avg. press run 300. Pub'd 5 poetry titles 1999; expects 5 poetry titles 2000, 5 poetry titles 2001. 5½×8½; avg. price, paper: $5; other: $3 (pamphlets). 28-44pp; Reporting time: 1 month; no report if SASE is not included with submission/correspondence. Payment: 10% of press run, discounts to author on additional copies, 10% royalty on 2nd and subsequent press runs. Interested in new or unpub'd poets: yes. Simultaneous submissions accepted: yes, provided we are so notified. Recently published poets: Madeline Tiger, Lynne H. deCourcy, Kate Abbe, Charles Rafferty, Susan Cavanaugh. Submission quantity: Author should query about this, including a brief description of the work and a brief biographical note. Special interests: We have a special interest in modern lyric poetry, rooted in everyday life on American soil, with strong well-earned closure. No restrictions on theme, subject, form or style. Short essays on poetic craft always welcome.

STONE SOUP, The Magazine By Young Writers and Artists, Box 83, Santa Cruz, CA 95063, 831-426-5557, Fax 831-426-1161, e-mail editor@stonesoup.com, www.stonesoup.com. Gerry Mandel, Editor. 1973. "We publish poetry by children through age 13 only. Most of the poems we reject are formula poems of some kind, such as haiku, cinquain, acrostics, or limericks. Most of the poems we publish are free verse, based on observation or experience. We look for language that is innovative and beautiful." circ. 20M. 6/yr. Pub'd 15 poems 1999; expects 15 poems 2000, 15 poems 2001. sub. price: $32; sample: $5.50. 48pp; 7×10; Rights purchased: all. Publishes .5% of poems submitted. Deadlines: none. Reporting time: 4 weeks. Payment: 2 copies and $25 plus certificate. Interested in new or unpub'd poets: yes. Simultaneous submissions accepted: no. Submission quantity: no limit.

Story Line Press, Three Oaks Farm, PO Box 1240, Ashland, OR 97520-0055, 541-512-8792, Fax 541-512-8793, mail@storylinepress.com, www.storylinepress.com. Robert McDowell. 1985. "Story Line Press is a non-profit 501C3 corporation and is generously funded by the Nicholas Roerich Museum of New York. In our first ten years of operation we published forty volumes of poetry by noted American and British poets. We will continue to do so as we expand our list to include fiction, non-fiction and plays." avg. press run 2M. Pub'd 9 poetry titles 1999; expects 9 poetry titles 2000, 9 poetry titles 2001. 6×9, 5½×8½; avg. price, cloth: $20; paper: $14. 80-192pp; Publishes a very small % of poetry manuscripts submitted. Reporting time: 3-6 months. Payment: depends, cash advance or payment in 10% of run; standard royalties. Interested in new or unpub'd poets: only for the annual Nicholas Roerich Poetry Prize. Simultaneous submissions accepted: no. Recently published poets: Rita Dove, Louis Simpson, Mark Jarman, Annie Finch, Richard Wilbun. Special interests: As the press has grown out of *The Reaper* magazine, our first love is narrative poetry. However, we consider all styles.

STORYBOARD, Division of English, University of Guam, Mangilao, GU 96923, E-mail jtalley@uog9.uog.edu. Jeannine E. Talley. 1991. circ. 200. 1/yr. Pub'd 32 poems 1999; expects 32 poems 2000, 32 poems 2001. sub. price: $7.50; sample: $4. 100pp; 5½×8½; Deadlines: open. Reporting time: 3-6 months. Payment: 2 copies. Interested in new or unpub'd poets: yes. Simultaneous submissions accepted: yes. Submission quantity: 3-5.

STOVEPIPE: A Journal of Little Literary Value, Sweet Lady Moon Press, PO Box 1076, Georgetown, KY 40324, troyteegarden@worldradio.org. Troy Teegarden. 1995. "Really enjoy personal letters included with poetry submissions. We like to know something about the poets we are publishing. Rhymed poetry is not preferred." circ. 250. 4/yr. Pub'd 55 poems 1999; expects 55 poems 2000, 55 poems 2001. sub. price: $10; sample: $2 or trade. 28pp; 8½×5½; Publishes 5% of poems submitted. Deadlines: always accepting submissions. Reporting time: 1 month (usually less). Payment: 1-year subscription. Interested in new or unpub'd poets: yes. Simultaneous submissions accepted: yes, very reluctantly, and must be stated somewhere. Recent contributors: John Sweet, Robin Merrill, Richard Taylor, J. Todd Dockery, Jeff Worley. Submission quantity: 3-5.

STROKER, c/o Trantino, RR 2 Box 280, Harveys Lake, PA 18618-9503. Irving Stettner. 1974. "Publish just good work." circ. 600. 3-4/yr. sub. price: $15 for 3 issues, $29 for 6 issues, $48 for 12 issues; sample: $5.25. 48pp; 5½×8½; Rights purchased: none. Publishes 10% of poems submitted. Deadlines: none. Reporting time: 4-6 weeks. Payment: contributor copies. Interested in new or unpub'd poets: yes. Simultaneous submissions accepted: yes. Recent contributors: William Joyce, Pat McKinnon, Christian Mauldin, Ron Papandrea, Danny Dellinger. Special interests: No special interest.

STRUGGLE: A Magazine of Proletarian Revolutionary Literature, PO Box 13261, Detroit, MI 48213-0261. Tim Hall, Editor. 1985. "Send SASE. Especially interested in poems of protest against the neo-conservative and liberal assault of world capital on the workers & poor countries. Also against aggressive wars, racism and ethnic cleansing. Solidarity with the oppressed and their rebellions, poems of the workers' movement against concessions, of the black people's struggle in the U.S., of the struggles of working women against sexism and exploitation, of the struggles and life of the homeless and the poor in general. Poetry critical of any facet of the oppression of modern capitalist life, including cultural life. Poetry reflecting struggle, fight-back. Do not like vagueness, lack of passion, pointless obscurity." 4/yr. Pub'd 75-80 poems 1999. sub. price: $10, $12 to institutions, $15 overseas, free to prisoners, trades ok; sample: $2.50 via mail. 36pp; 5½×8½; Rights purchased: none. Publishes 20% of poems submitted. Deadlines: none. Reporting time: 1-3 months, usually with a critique, time permitting. Payment: 2 copies. Interested in new or unpub'd poets: yes, (very). Simultaneous submissions accepted: yes, good poetry should be printed as many places as possible! Recent contributors: Cynthia Hatten, Luis Berriozabal, Howard L. Craft, Peter Dolack, Gilbert Gregory Gumbs. Submission quantity: up to 6 or 7. Special interests: We want poems and songs of rebellion against the rich. Various forms, humorous, satirical or serious, experimental or traditional. No more than 3 or 4 typewritten pages, double space—prefer shorter. Translations ok.

STUDENT LEADERSHIP JOURNAL, PO Box 7895, Madison, WI 53707-7895, 608-274-4823 X425, 413. Jeff Yourison, Editor. 1988. "We will read poetry any time. *Student Leadership* is the magazine of InterVarsity Christian Fellowship. *Student Leadership* is published for Christian college students; primarily for those attending secular colleges. Please do type, double-or triple-spaced, leave margins, and keep a copy for yourself. If you aren't sure how to make your poem 'right' for *Student Leadership*, take a look at several back issues to see what kinds of poetry we print. We are not impressed with cover letters that begin, 'I don't know what kind of poems you use, but I'm sending this along ...'We only print about a dozen poems a year. We have a small staff, so it may take several months before we get back to you about your manuscript. Be patient." circ. 8M. 4/yr. Pub'd 4 poems 1999; expects 4 poems 2000, 4 poems 2001. sub. price: $16; sample: $4. 32pp; 8×11; Rights purchased: first rights and reprint and onetime rights. Publishes 5% or less of poems submitted. Deadlines: none. Reporting time: 3-6 months. Payment: $20-$50. Interested in new or unpub'd poets: yes. Simultaneous submissions accepted: yes. Recent contributors: Luci Shaw, Brett Wilson, Mark Littleton, Steve Turner, Edgar Hix. Submission quantity: no more than 5. Special interests: We publish satire, light verse, experimental stuff, heavy traditional material - note, however, that *Student Leadership* is a quarterly magazine for college students, published during the academic year - targeted to Christian student leaders in secular ('non-Christian') schools. Most of what we print is mind-stretching, sometimes controversial, but always in a large Christian context.

Studia Hispanica Editors, Attn: Luis Ramos-Garcia, 2129 Folwell Avenue, St. Paul, MN 55108-1306, 612-574-9460. Dave Oliphant, Poetry Editor; Luis Ramos-Garcia, Poetry Editor (Bilingual). 1978. avg. press run 500. Pub'd 2 poetry titles 1999; expects 2 poetry titles 2000, 2 poetry titles 2001. 8×5½; avg. price, cloth: $25; paper: $9.95; other: $10. 150pp; Publishes 1% of poetry manuscripts submitted. Reporting time: 1 month. Payment: none. Interested in new or unpub'd poets: no. Simultaneous submissions accepted: no. Recently published poets: Vassar Miller, Naomi Shihab Nye, Giulia Colaizzi, Jenaro Talens, Ana Rosetti. Submission quantity: 40-50. Special interests: We are interested in publishing bilingual anthologies. Our purpose is to translate American (well-established, with a poetic trajectory & a good amount of published work) poets into Spanish. We also translate Latin American & European poets (Spain) into English (this section is by invitation only, but serious inquiries will be answered).

STUDIO - A Journal of Christians Writing, 727 Peel Street, Albury, N.S.W. 2640, Australia. Paul Grover, Managing Editor. 1980. "Poetry contest is run alternate years." circ. 300. 4/yr. Pub'd 100 poems 1999; expects 100 poems 2000, 100 poems 2001. sub. price: $AUD45; sample: $AUD8 (air mail). 36pp; 14.5×21cm; Rights purchased: none, except future acknowlegement of first publication. Publishes 5% of poems submitted. Deadlines: none. Reporting time: 1 month for overseas members. Payment: free copy of magazine. Interested in new or unpub'd poets: yes. Simultaneous submissions accepted: yes. Recent contributors: Andrew Lansdown, Les Murray, Graham Cole, John Foulcher, Kevin Hart. Submission quantity: 3-6 poems.

STUDIO ONE, College of St. Benedict, St. Joseph, MN 56374. Editors change yearly. 1976. "Typed, double spaced preferred, no limits on subject of form" circ. 900. 1/yr. Pub'd 40 poems 1999; expects 40 poems 2000, 40 poems 2001. sub. price: free, availability is extremely limited; all contributors receive one complimentary copy, all others are asked to send enough postage. 70-100pp; 7½×10; Rights purchased: none. Publishes 10% of poems submitted. Deadlines: February. Reporting time: 1-2 months from deadline. Payment: 1 complimentary contributor's copy. Interested in new or unpub'd poets: yes. Simultaneous submissions accepted: yes. Recent contributors: Larry Schug, Bill Meissener, Jonathan Levant. Submission quantity: 3-5.

STUFFWAX BEEZER, Pen-Dec Press, 2526 Chatham Woods, Grand Rapids, MI 49546. 2000. "Lusts for b&w art, uses no fiction. Seeking outrageous musings." Irregular. Pub'd 30 poems 1999; expects 30 poems 2000, 30 poems 2001. sample price: $4. 24pp; 8½×5½; Publishes 15% of poems submitted. Interested in new or unpub'd poets: yes. Simultaneous submissions accepted: yes. Recent contributors: Phyllis Settles, Marion Smith, Cassius, Rachael Houseman. Submission quantity: 8-10.

The Subourbon Press (see also THE HUNTED NEWS), PO Box 9101, Warwick, RI 02889, 401-739-2279. Mike Wood. 1991. "The only guidelines I would suggest when submitting both for the magazine and the chapbook series are that I only look for honesty. Conceit shows. If you need to write it, I need to read it." avg. press run 150-200. Pub'd 1 poetry title 1999; expects 1 poetry title 2000, 1 poetry title 2001. avg. price, paper: $2. 25-30pp; Publishes 10% of poetry manuscripts submitted. Reporting time: 1 month. Payment: copies. Interested in new or unpub'd poets: yes. Simultaneous submissions accepted: yes. Recently published poets: Thomas Vaultonburg, Mike Blake, Steve Richmond, Charles Bukowski, Hal Sirowitz. Submission quantity: 15-20. Special interests: Minimalist poetry, narrative poetry, translations, prose poems.

SUB-TERRAIN, PO Box 1575, Bentall Centre, Vancouver, B.C. V6C 2P7, Canada, 604-876-8710. Paul Pitre, Poetry Editor. 1988. "We are not interested in traditional rhyming poetry, unless the convention is being utilized in some new manner, or to make comment on the style itself. We want material with some socio-economic or political analysis. Only those submissions with Canadian postage or IRCs on SAE will be returned or responded to." circ. 3M. 3/yr. Pub'd 50 poems 1999; expects 50 poems 2000, 50 poems 2001. sub. price: $15; sample: $5 to cover post. 48pp; 8½×11; Rights purchased: one time only, reverts to author. Publishes 5% of poems submitted. Deadlines: ongoing. Reporting time: 2-4 months. Payment: 5 copies. Interested in new or unpub'd poets: yes. Must send query letter and sample poems first. Simultaneous submissions accepted: yes, but only want to publish previously unpublished work. Recent contributors: Sean Brendan-Brown, Peter Layton, Tammy Armstrong, Lyle Neff, Sharon McCartney. Submission quantity: 3-5. Special interests: Experimental, long poems, satire.

Suburban Wilderness Press (see also POETRY MOTEL), PO Box 103, Duluth, MN 55801-0103. 1984. "We publish 30-40 broadsides per year as a supplement to our mag, *Poetry Motel*. There are no guidelines for submitting work. We are always looking for new talent." avg. press run 150. Pub'd 40 poetry titles 1999; expects 40 poetry titles 2000, 40 poetry titles 2001. 8½×11; avg. price, paper: $3. 1 page broadsides; Percent of poems published varies. Reporting time: 0-5 months. Payment: various. Interested in new or unpub'd poets: sure. Simultaneous submissions accepted: sure. Recently published poets: Will Inman, Joanne Makela, Michael K. Johnson, Gregory Lanier, Sally Love Saunders. Submission quantity: 3-6. Special interests: We tend toward work that tells a story or a piece of a story somehow. Tend to stay away from "intellectual excercise"—save it for school. We live out here with people who don't care about school.

SULFUR, 210 Washtenaw, Ypsilanti, MI 48197-2526, 313-483-9787. Clayton Eshleman. 1981. "People should read (not glance at) *Sulfur* before submitting. While *Sulfur* is 80-90% taken up by my regular contributors, it does publish the young and the unknown; i.e. we have received four General Electric Younger Writers Awards over the past six years." circ. 2M. 2/yr. Pub'd 100 poems 1999; expects 100 poems 2000, 100 poems 2001. sub. price: $14 indiv., $20 inst. (add $4 for out of US mailing); sample: $8. 256pp; 6×9; Rights purchased: none. Publishes 10-15% of poems submitted. Deadlines: none. Reporting time: 2-3 weeks. Payment: $35-45 per contributor and 2 copies of issue. Interested in new or unpub'd poets: yes, if they have *read* at least one issue! Simultaneous submissions accepted: no. Recent contributors: Jerome Rothenberg, Bei Dao, Antoine

Artaud, Gary Snyder, Rachel Blau DuPlessis. Submission quantity: only a few. Special interests: We are interested in poetry that road-tests the language.

The Sulgrave Press, 2005 Longest Avenue, Louisville, KY 40204, 502-459-9713, Fax 502-459-9715. 1988.

SULPHUR RIVER LITERARY REVIEW, PO Box 19228, Austin, TX 78760-9228, 512-292-9456. Jamer Michael Robbins. 1978. circ. 200. 2/yr. Pub'd 100 poems 1999; expects 100 poems 2000, 100 poems 2001. sub. price: $12; sample: $7. 130pp; 5½×8½; Publishes 1% of poems submitted. Deadlines: I work from a backlog. Reporting time: 1 month. Payment: 2 copies. Interested in new or unpub'd poets: yes. Simultaneous submissions accepted: yes, but I don't like them. Recent contributors: Lyn Lifshin, Brian Clements, Miles David Moore, Robert Cooperman, Taylor Graham. Submission quantity: 5-6. Special interests: Translations, experimental poetry.

Summer Stream Press, PO Box 6056, Santa Barbara, CA 93160-6056, 805-962-6540. David Duane Frost. 1978. "We shall release the first of a series entitled *Box Cars*, poems by six U.S. poets from over the country, ca 420 pages (average 70 text pages per poet). This will be distributed through normal channels and thus available to local book shops. The large run will be in PB with shorter runs in hardcover trade and library binding. The poets share a 15% royalty. We are not concerned with whether or not the poems have been or will be published elsewhere; we only need permission for this series and of course will copyright for the poet. We have simplified the contract as much as possible. Our aim in each *Box Cars* is to be representative of many parts of the country and different styles of poetry. For example, in the first book we feature a fine traditional poet from Berkeley, CA followed by a feminist free-verser from Florida; a humorist plus myself from New York and Califonia, who write structured verse (not necessarily in traditional forms); and a free-verser from Santa Paula who writes vibrant and powerful poetry. Each poet approaches poetry differently, and the contents include different points of view. I would like to stress that we offer a chance for traditional poets to get their work published and we shall include at least one of them in each book." avg. press run 5M. Expects 1 poetry title 2000, 1 poetry title 2001. 5½×8½; avg. price, paper: $19.95; other: $34.95. 450pp; Publishes 2% of poetry manuscripts submitted. Reporting time: 6 months to 1 year. Payment: 15%. Interested in new or unpub'd poets: yes. Simultaneous submissions accepted: yes. Recently published poets: Robert K. Johnson, Martha E. Bosworth, Ruthann Robson, Ed Engle Jr., Clarke D. Wells. Submission quantity: ca. 12.

THE SUN, A MAGAZINE OF IDEAS, 107 North Roberson Street, Chapel Hill, NC 27516, 919-942-5282. Sy Safransky, Editor. 1974. "We avoid traditional, rhyming poetry, limericks, haikus, epic-length. We're open to almost anything else, free verse, prose poems, short and long poems" circ. 40M. 12/yr. Pub'd 25 poems 1999; expects 25 poems 2000, 25 poems 2001. sub. price: $34; sample: $5. 48pp; 8½×11; Rights purchased: first- or one-time. Publishes 1% of poems submitted. Deadlines: none. Reporting time: 3 months. Payment: subscription, copies, $50-$200. Interested in new or unpub'd poets: yes. Simultaneous submissions accepted: reluctantly. Recent contributors: Red Hawk, Sybil Smith, Alison Luterman, Lou Lipsitz, Chris Bursk. Submission quantity: no more than 6.

Sun Dog Press, 22058 Cumberland Drive, Northville, MI 48167, 248-449-7448, Fax 248-449-4070, sundogpr@voyager.net. Al Berlinski, Editor. 1987. 6×9. Reporting time: 2 months. Payment: royalty on sales. Interested in new or unpub'd poets: yes. Simultaneous submissions accepted: yes. Recently published poets: Neeli Cherkovski, Linda Nemec Foster, Kathleen Ripley Leo, Steve Richmond, Irving Stettner. Submission quantity: query first. Special interests: Hard-edged and innovative poetry.

THE SUNDAY SUITOR POETRY REVIEW, 329 Hyde Street, Salinas, CA 93907-2033, 209-858-1453. Elizabeth Fuller, Editor & Publisher. 1996. "*Always* include SASE; theme contests in each issue, chapbook and personalized bookmark service; no erotica, overly religious, no experimental." circ. 350. 6/yr. Pub'd 400 poems 1999; expects 400 poems 2000, 400 poems 2001. sub. price: $17 US, $20 international; sample: $4 U.S., $7 international. 50pp; 5½×8½; Rights purchased: none. Publishes 50% of poems submitted. Deadlines: accepted all year. Reporting time: 1-3 weeks. Payment: 1 copy. Interested in new or unpub'd poets: both new and unpublished welcome! Simultaneous submissions accepted: yes. Recent contributors: Louise Jaffe, A.D. Winans, Douglas Johnson, John Grey, Taylor Graham. Submission quantity: 5. Special interests: Love/life affirming, nature, light verse, romance, haiku, sonnets. No poems over 40 lines, editor prefers short verse, imagery-intensive.

Sunflower University Press, 1531 Yuma, (Box 1009), Manhattan, KS 66502, 785-539-1888, fax 785-539-2233. 1977. 8½×11, 5½×8½, 6×9.

Sunlight Publishers, PO Box 640545, San Francisco, CA 94109, 415-776-6249. Joseph Kent. 1989. "Some bias toward poetic consciousness of an evolutionary nature and organic poetry in the modernist vein based on experience of the perceiver." avg. press run 700. Pub'd 2 poetry titles 1999. 6×9; avg. price, paper: $6.95. 64pp; Publishes 2% of poetry manuscripts submitted. Reporting time: 1 month. Payment: 10% royalty on all sales, paid twice yearly. Interested in new or unpub'd poets: yes. Simultaneous submissions accepted: no. Recently published poets: John Brander, Joseph Kent.

Sun-Scape Publications, a division of Sun-Scape Enterprises Ltd., 65 High Ridge Road, Suite 103, Stamford, CT 06905, 203-838-3775; FAX 203-838-3775; orders 1-800-437-1454; info@sun-scape.com; www.sun-scape.com. Barry Brodie, Mary Gretchen Limper, Megan MacQueen. 1975. "We are not currently accepting manuscripts." avg. press run 1M-2M. Pub'd 1 poetry title 1999; expects 1 poetry title 2000. 7×8½; avg. price, cloth: $17.95; paper: $13.95. 150pp; Interested in new or unpub'd poets: not at this time. Simultaneous submissions accepted: no. Recently published poets: Rolland G. Smith, Kenneth George Mills.

●**SUPERIOR POETRY NEWS**, PO Box 424, Superior, MT 59872. 1995. "Poetry 40 lines or less, emphasis on originality" circ. 75-100. 4/yr. sub. price: $5.50; sample: $2. 12-20pp; 5½×8½; Reporting time: immediately. Payment: 1 copy. Simultaneous submissions accepted: yes. Special interests: We want translations of poetry from any language.

Swallow's Tale Press (see also Livingston Press), c/o LU Press, Station 22, University of West Alabama, Livingston, AL 35470. Joe Taylor. 1983. "We solicit our poetry." avg. press run 1M. 5½×8½; avg. price, cloth: $25; paper: $10. 72pp; Publishes 1% of poetry manuscripts submitted. Reporting time: 4 months. Payment: copies. Interested in new or unpub'd poets: no. Simultaneous submissions accepted: yes. Recently published poets: Stephen Corey, Louis Phillips, B.H. Fairchild, Rennie McQuilkin. Submission quantity: 48 pgs.

Swamp Press (see also TIGHTROPE), 15 Warwick Avenue, Northfield, MA 01360-1105. Ed Rayher, Chief Editor. 1975. "For manuscripts, please send a querry letter with a small sample of your work (3-6 poems). We specialize in fine press production—letter press, illustrated books on fine paper—we treat the book as an art object." avg. press run 300. Pub'd 2 poetry titles 1999; expects 2 poetry titles 2000, 2 poetry titles 2001. size varies; avg. price, cloth: $25; paper: $5. 36pp; Publishes 1% of poetry manuscripts submitted. Reporting time: 8-12 weeks. Payment: 10% of press run. Interested in new or unpub'd poets: yes. Simultaneous submissions accepted: no. Recently published poets: Robert Bensen, Carol Montgomery. Submission quantity: 3. Special interests: We're open to just about anything.

SWEET ANNIE & SWEET PEA REVIEW, Sweet Annie Press, 7750 Highway F-24 West, Baxter, IA 50028, 515-792-3578, FAX 515-792-1310. Beverly A. Clark. 1995. "Prefer proofed material" circ. 100+. 4/yr. sub. price: $24; sample: $6. 40pp; 5×8; Reporting time: 4-6 months. Interested in new or unpub'd poets: yes. Simultaneous submissions accepted: prefer not. Submission quantity: any. Special interests: Women's issues, natural themes, outdoors - land, solitude, simplified living.

Sweet Annie Press (see also SWEET ANNIE & SWEET PEA REVIEW), 7750 Highway F-24 West, Baxter, IA 50028, 515-792-3578, FAX 515-792-1310. Beverly A. Clark, Editor & Publisher. 1995. "Prefer proofed material" avg. press run 1M or less. Pub'd 4 poetry titles 1999; expects 4 poetry titles 2000. 5×8; avg. price, paper: $6. 40+pp; Publishes 25% of poetry manuscripts submitted. Reporting time: 4-6 months. Payment: 1 copy. Interested in new or unpub'd poets: yes. Simultaneous submissions accepted: prefer not. Recently published poets: M. Wehler, L. Robiner, R. Reynolds, C. Bowman, A. Betterton. Submission quantity: any. Special interests: Women's issues, natural themes, outdoors-land, solitude, simplified living, etc.

Sweet Lady Moon Press (see also STOVEPIPE: A Journal of Little Literary Value), PO Box 1076, Georgetown, KY 40324, troyteegarden@worldradio.org. Troy Teegarden. 1995. avg. press run 100. Pub'd 4 poetry titles 1999; expects 4 poetry titles 2000, 4 poetry titles 2001. 8½×5½, 4¼×11; avg. price, paper: $3. 40pp; Publishes 5% of poetry manuscripts submitted. Reporting time: 1 month. Payment: varies. Interested in new or unpub'd poets: yes. Simultaneous submissions accepted: yes, reluctantly. Recently published poets: Richard Taylor, Jeff Worley, Brooke Salisbury, Robin Merrill, John Sweet.

SYCAMORE REVIEW, Department of English, Purdue University, West Lafayette, IN 47907, 765-494-3783. Rotating Editorship. 1988. "Include SASE with submission" circ. 1M. 2/yr. Pub'd 60 poems 1999; expects 60 poems 2000, 60 poems 2001. sub. price: $12, $14 foreign; sample: $7. 160pp; 6×9; Rights purchased: Purdue University acquires, First-Time, North American rights only. Publishes less than 5% of poems submitted. Deadlines: submissions read between Sept. and March 31 (The Academic Year). Reporting time: 4 months. Payment: 2 copies. Interested in new or unpub'd poets: yes. Simultaneous submissions accepted: yes. Recent contributors: Gray Jacobik, Kathleen Peirce, Thomas Fink, Charles Harper Webb, Maria Terrone. Submission quantity: 3-5. Special interests: We accept high quality poetry regardless of form or subject matter. We publish translations. We seek experimental work that does not use convention as a crutch.

SYMBIOTIC OATMEAL, PO Box 14938, Philadelphia, PA 19149. 1997. circ. 50-100. Irregular. sample price: $2. 16pp; 8½×11.

SYNCOPATED CITY, PO Box 2382, Providence, RI 02906, litik@aol.com. 1996. circ. 200. 4/yr. sub. price: $12; sample: $3. 60pp; 5½×8½.

T

●**TABOO: Journal of Education & Culture**, 637 West Foster Avenue, State College, PA 16801. 1995. circ. 300. 2/yr. sub. price: $40 ind., $60 inst. 150pp; 6×9.

TAKAHE, PO Box 13-335, Christchurch 1, New Zealand, 03-5198133. Victoria Broome, Bernadette Hall. 1989. "We believe that poetry is, among other things, the art of significant silence, it demands an active reader whose trust in language matches that of the writer." circ. 340. 3-4/yr. Pub'd 60 poems 1999; expects 45 poems 2000, 45 poems 2001. sub. price: $24NZ/4 issues within New Zealand, $32NZ/4 issues foreign countries; sample: $7.50NZ. 60pp; 8×11¾; Publishes 6-10% of poems submitted. Deadlines: End of Feb, June, Oct. Reporting time: 1-4 months. Payment: complimentary copy, plus small increment at editor's discretion. Interested in new or unpub'd poets: yes. Simultaneous submissions accepted: yes, if advised. Recent contributors: John Allison, John O'Connor, Jules Leigh Koch, David Gregory, David Eggleton. Submission quantity: up to 7 poems, typed on A4 paper (Ariel II jet or laser preferred.). Special interests: Translations, experimental poetry and longer poems are all of interest.

Talent House Press, 1306 Talent Avenue, Talent, OR 97540, talhouse@mind.net. 1992. "We sponsor a chapbook contest every spring with guidelines announced in small press publications like *Poets & Writers* and *Small Press Review*. Other projects vary but never stem from unsolicited mss." 5½×8½.

TALISMAN: A Journal of Contemporary Poetry and Poetics, Talisman House, Publishers, PO Box 3157, Jersey City, NJ 07303-3157, 201-938-0698. Edward Foster, Editor. 1988. circ. 1M. 2/yr. Pub'd 100 poems 1999; expects 100 poems 2000, 100 poems 2001. sub. price: $11/2 issues individual, $15/2 issues institutions; sample: $6. 268pp; 5½×8½; Rights purchased: First North American periodical rights, all rights revert to authors upon publication. Publishes 5% of poems submitted. Deadlines: none. Reporting time: 1 month. Payment: 1 copy of magazine. Interested in new or unpub'd poets: yes. Simultaneous submissions accepted: no. Recent contributors: Robert Creeley, Gustaf Sobin, Alice Notley, William Bronx, Rosmarie Waldrop. Submission quantity: 2-3. Special interests: Translations, experimental poetry.

Talisman House, Publishers (see also TALISMAN: A Journal of Contemporary Poetry and Poetics), PO Box 3157, Jersey City, NJ 07303-3157, 201-938-0698. Edward Foster. 1993. "Essentially concerned with innovative work" avg. press run 1M. Pub'd 2 poetry titles 1999; expects 3 poetry titles 2000, 3 poetry titles 2001. 5½×8½, 6×9; avg. price, paper: $12; other: $32, library binding. 150-200pp; Reporting time: 3 months. Payment: individually negotiated. Interested in new or unpub'd poets: no. Simultaneous submissions accepted: no. Recently published poets: Alice Notley, William Bronx, Stephen Jonas. Submission quantity: A few. Special interests: Experimental poetry.

TALKING RIVER REVIEW, Lewis-Clark State College, 500 8th Avenue, Lewiston, ID 83501, 208-799-2307, triver@lcsc.edu. 1994. "Up to 5 poems, any length or style; submit Sept. 1 - March 1; submit poetry/prose under separate cover" circ. 500. 2/yr. Pub'd 50 poems 1999; expects 50 poems 2000, 50 poems 2001. sub. price: $14; sample: $5. 140pp; 6×9; Rights purchased: First N.American, revert to author on publication. Publishes 2% of poems submitted. Reporting time: 3 months. Payment: 2 copies + 1 year subscription. Interested in new or unpub'd poets: yes. Simultaneous submissions accepted: yes, with notification. Recent contributors: Greg Pape, Pattiann Rogers, Christopher Buckley, Dorianne Laux, Stephen Dunn. Submission quantity: up to 5. Special interests: Long poems okay.

●**TAMBOURINE**, PO Box 790, Sausalito, CA 94966, 415-383-8447. Karla Andersdatter. 2000. "Include SASE if you want submissions returned" circ. 2.5M. 1/yr. sub. price: $15. 150pp; 5½×11; Rights purchased: one-time printing only. Publishes 10% of poems submitted. Deadlines: April 1st, submit by invitation only. Payment: in books. Interested in new or unpub'd poets: yes. Simultaneous submissions accepted: no. Recent contributors: Karla Andersdatter, Hugh Fox, CB Follett, Chris Swanberg, Sandy White. Submission quantity: 10. Special interests: West Coast writers - women.

●**TAMEME**, 199 First Street, Los Altos, CA 94022, www.tameme.org. 1999. 1/yr. sub. price: $14.95; sample: $14.95. 225pp.

TAMPA REVIEW, 401 W. Kennedy Boulevard, University of Tampa-19F, Tampa, FL 33606-1490. Don Morrill, Poetry Editor; Kathryn Van Spanckeren, Poetry Editor. 1988. "Submissions are read from September through December. Must send SASE for response. We look for quality, polished work, with fresh ideas, imagery and language." circ. 750. 2/yr. Pub'd 32 poems 1999; expects 32 poems 2000, 32 poems 2001. sub. price: $15; sample: $6. 72-96pp; 7½×10½; Rights purchased: First North American Serial Rights. Publishes about 4% of poems submitted. Deadlines: December 31 (submissions should be made from September through December). Reporting time: report January through March. Payment: $10 per printed page. Interested in new or unpub'd poets: yes. Simultaneous submissions accepted: no. Recent contributors: Peter Meinke, Naomi Nye, Richard Chess, W.S. Merwin, Pattiann Rogers. Submission quantity: 3-6. Special interests: Translations, experimental poetry, regional poetry, longpoems, light verse, satire, etc.

TANDEM, 13 Stephenson Road Barbourne, Worcester, WR1 3EB, England, 01705-28002. 1993. circ. 300. Published when funds allow. sub. price: £12, £15 overseas; sample: No. 3 (£3.00 + pp). 100pp; size A5.

TAPROOT, a journal of older writers, Fine Arts Center 4290, University at Stony Brook, Stony Brook, NY 11794-5410, 516-632-6635. Philip W. Quigg, Editor; Enid Graf, Associate Editor. 1974. circ. 1M. 2/yr. Pub'd 100 poems 1999. sub. price: $18; sample: $8. 100pp; 8½×11; Rights purchased: none. Publishes 65% of poems submitted. Deadlines: publication available for Taproot Workshop members only. Payment: none. Interested in new or unpub'd poets: no. Recent contributors: Elizabeth Drewes, Jacqueline Allison, Murielle Minard, Margaret Bishop Brehmer, Sigmund Weiss. Special interests: Senior citizens, memoirs, etc.

TAPROOT LITERARY REVIEW, Taproot Press Publishing Co., Box 204, Ambridge, PA 15003, 412-266-8476, E-mail taproot10@aol.com. Tikvah Feinstein, Editor; Marc Rosenberg, Amy Dobsch. 1987. "We like to publish quality work that is not workshop poetry, but also enjoy that variety. Especially seeking multi-national themes." circ. 500. 1-2/yr. Pub'd 40-70 poems 1999. sub. price: $7.50; sample: $4 + $1.50 stamps. 84-100pp; 6×9; Rights purchased: first rights only. Publishes 30% of poems submitted. Deadlines: December 31. Reporting time: 3 months or less. Payment: prize money for winners, copies for entrants, authors. Interested in new or unpub'd poets: very much open to new writers. Simultaneous submissions accepted: no. Recent contributors: Elizabeth Howkins, Elizabeth Curry, Rochelle Mass, Erin Garstka, Gail Ghai. Submission quantity: no more than 5. Special interests: When a special voice shines through the words, we publish it.

●Taproot Press Publishing Co. (see also TAPROOT LITERARY REVIEW), Box 204, Ambridge, PA 15003, taproot10@aol.com. Tikvah Feinstein, Editor & Publisher. 1985. "Seeking theme of celebrations, especially cultural, multicultural, groups." avg. press run 500. Pub'd 58 poetry titles 1999; expects 65 poetry titles 2000, 75 poetry titles 2001. 6×9; avg. price, paper: $6.95. 1 page; Publishes 30-35% of poetry manuscripts submitted. Reporting time: 3-5 months. Payment: books. Interested in new or unpub'd poets: yes. Simultaneous submissions accepted: no. Recently published poets: Lyn Lifshin, Ellen Hyatt, Lila Julius, Gregory Johnstone, Charles Cingolini. Special interests: No longer than 35 lines. Seeking the finest poems we can get. New poets welcome, old friends cherished.

TAR RIVER POETRY, Department of English, East Carolina University, Greenville, NC 27858-4353, 919-328-6041. Peter Makuck, Editor; Luke Whisnant, Associate Editor. 1978. "Interested in skillful use of figurative language. No flat statement poetry." circ. 700. 2/yr. Pub'd 100 poems 1999. sub. price: $10, $18/2 yrs; sample: $5.50. 64pp; 6×8¾; Rights purchased: we don't buy, but we expect 1st rights, copyright reverts to author after publication. Publishes 15% of poems submitted. Deadlines: none, but we do not consider submissions during summer (May thru August). Reporting time: 4-6 weeks. Payment: copies of issue. Interested in new or unpub'd poets: yes. Simultaneous submissions accepted: no. Recent contributors: Mark Jarman, Lawrence Lieberman, Brendan Galvin, Elizabeth Dodd, Deborah Cummins. Submission quantity: 4-6. Special interests: We seldom publish haiku or light verse or 'experimental poetry'.

Taurean Horn Press, PO Box 641097, San Francisco, CA 94164. Bill Vartnaw. 1974. "Please do not submit. I request mss only." avg. press run 500-2M. Expects 2 poetry titles 2000, 1 poetry title 2001. 6×9; avg. price, paper: $10.95. 72pp; Publishes 0% of poetry manuscripts submitted. Payment: books. Interested in new or unpub'd poets: no. Recently published poets: Paula Gunn Allen, Carol Lee Sanchez, Tom Sharp, Gail Mitchell.

TEAK ROUNDUP, West Coast Paradise Publishing, PO Box 2093, Sardis Sta. Main, Sardis, BC V2R 1A5, Canada, 604-545-4186, Fax 604-545-4194. Robert G. Anstey. 1994. "Subscribers only eligible for publication. Write (SASE) for guidelines" circ. 500. 4/yr. Pub'd 260-280 poems 1999; expects 260-280 poems 2000, 260-280 poems 2001. sub. price: $17 Can, $13 U.S., $24 overseas; sample: $5 Can, $3 U.S., $8 overseas. 56pp; 5½×8½; Rights purchased: one time only. Publishes 90% of poems submitted. Deadlines: 6 weeks before Mar/Jun/Sept/Dec. Reporting time: return mail, friendly and fastest in business. Payment: none. Interested in new or unpub'd poets: yes. Simultaneous submissions accepted: yes. Recent contributors: Perry Harrison, John Binns, Alice Cundiff, Joan Hamilton, George Kuhn. Submission quantity: 3-5.

Tears in the Fence (see also TEARS IN THE FENCE), 38 Hod View Stourpaine, Blandford Forum, Dorset DT11 8TN, United Kingdom. 1995. 4×8.

TEARS IN THE FENCE, Tears in the Fence, 38 Hod View, Stourpaine, Blandford Forum, Dorset DT11 8TN, England. 1985. circ. 1.5M. 3/yr. sub. price: £12, $20 cash including postage; sample: same. 112pp; 4×8.

Tebot Bach (see also SPILLWAY), Box 7887, Huntington Beach, CA 92615-7887, 714-968-0905. Mifanwy Kaiser. 1998. avg. press run 1M. Pub'd 1 poetry title 1999; expects 2 poetry titles 2000, 2 poetry titles 2001.

6×9; avg. price, paper: $13. 94pp; Reporting time: 6 months. Payment: contract. Interested in new or unpub'd poets: first full-length book only. Recently published poets: Robin Chapman, M.L. Liebler, Richard Jones. Submission quantity: query first with sample of 10-15 poems.

Tecolote Publications, 4918 Del Monte Avenue, San Diego, CA 92107. 1986. 5½×8½.

TEEN VOICES MAGAZINE, 515 Washington Street, 6th Floor, Boston, MA 02111-1759, 617-426-5505, fax 617-426-5577, e-mail womenexp@teenvoices.com, website www.teenvoices.com. Shannon Berning, Managing Editor. 1988. "Themes are outlined in T.O.C., 90% chance of publishing if themes are used" circ. 75M. 4/yr. Pub'd 48 poems 1999. sub. price: $19.95; sample: $5. 64pp; 8⅜×10⅞; Rights purchased: none. Publishes 25% of poems submitted. Deadlines: anytime. Reporting time: 6 months. Payment: 5 copies of magazine. Interested in new or unpub'd poets: yes. Simultaneous submissions accepted: yes. Submission quantity: whatever they like. Special interests: short poems preferred.

TEENS IN MOTION NEWS, PO Box 1264, Santa Clara, CA 95052, 408-244-3718. Pamela Costa, Editor; Karen Alvein, Editor. 1995. "All poems relating to teenagers looked at - especially written by teenager" circ. 2.5M. 11/yr. Pub'd 12 poems 1999; expects 33 poems 2000, 45 poems 2001. sub. price: $8.50; sample: free. 20pp; 8½×5½; Rights purchased: one time. Publishes 99% of poems submitted. Deadlines: 10th of month preceeding desired publication. Reporting time: 2 weeks. Payment: copy of subcription. Interested in new or unpub'd poets: no. Simultaneous submissions accepted: yes. Recent contributors: Pamela K. Daniels, P.K. Costa, Karen Alvein, George Slavich, Tara-Lynn Sacco. Submission quantity: 1-2 poems. Special interests: Any and all by teenagers.

The Teitan Press, Inc., PO Box 10258, Chicago, IL 60610, 773-929-7892; FAX 773-871-3315, e-mail teitanpr@aol.com Web Site: http://users.aol.com/teitanpr. Martin Starr. 1985. "We specialize in editions of the works of Aleister Crowley and his circle; as such, we are *only* interested in works of this nature" avg. press run 2M. Pub'd 1 poetry title 1999. 6×9; avg. price, cloth: $24.95. 200pp; Interested in new or unpub'd poets: no. Recently published poets: Aleister Crowley. Special interests: Poetry of Aleister Crowley (1875-1947).

Telephone Books, 109 Dunk Rock Rd., Guilford, CT 06437, 203-453-1921. Maureen Owen. 1971. "No unsolicited ms please" avg. press run 500-750. Pub'd 2-3 poetry titles 1999; expects 2-3 poetry titles 2000, 2-3 poetry titles 2001. size varies; avg. price, paper: $7.95; other: $10-signed. 50pp; Payment: copies. Interested in new or unpub'd poets: no. Simultaneous submissions accepted: no. Recently published poets: Susan Howe, Patricia Jones, Tom Weigel, Fanny Howe, Will Bennett. Special interests: Experimental.

THE TEMPLE, Tsunami Inc., PO Box 100, Walla Walla, WA 99362-0033, E-mail tsunami@innw.net. Charles Potts. 1995. "Query with SASE before submitting." circ. 8M. 4/yr. Pub'd 300 poems 1999; expects 350 poems 2000, 300 poems 2001. sub. price: $20; sample: $5. 80pp; 6×9; Rights purchased: none. Publishes 1% of poems submitted. Deadlines: quarterly. Reporting time: 2 weeks. Payment: copies. Interested in new or unpub'd poets: yes. Simultaneous submissions accepted: no. Recent contributors: Yan Li, John Oliver Simon, Stephen Thomas, Teri Zipf, Sharon Doubiago. Submission quantity: 3-5. Special interests: Spanish and Chinese.

Temporary Vandalism Recordings (see also FREEDOM ISN'T FREE), PO Box 6184, Orange, CA 92863-6184, e-mail tvrec@yahoo.com. Robert Roden, Barton M. Saunders. 1991. avg. press run 100. Pub'd 2 poetry titles 1999; expects 3 poetry titles 2000, 3 poetry titles 2001. 5½×8½; avg. price, paper: $5; other: $8. 40pp; Publishes 1% of poetry manuscripts submitted. Reporting time: 3-6 months. Payment: 5 copies; 50% of net sales. Simultaneous submissions accepted: yes. Recently published poets: Charles Ardinger, M. Jaime-Becerra, Alan Cohol. Submission quantity: 3-5.

Ten Penny Players, Inc. (see also WATERWAYS: Poetry in the Mainstream), 393 St. Paul's Avenue, Staten Island, NY 10304-2127, 718-442-7429, www.tenpennyplayers.org. Barbara Fisher, Co-Editor; Richard Spiegel, Co-Editor. 1975. "Ten Penny Players publishes books for and by child and young adult poets. The youths come through our own workshops and classes or through submission of their teachers - primarily special education units and alternative High Schools. Our emphasis is on NYC & NYS children, regular and special education. Books written for children are developed in house. We don't have funds to publish books that come through submissions from adult writers. We do print an on-line publication." avg. press run 200. Pub'd 3 poetry titles 1999; expects 4 poetry titles 2000, 3 poetry titles 2001. 8½×5½; avg. price, paper: $5. 54-150pp; Reporting time: 1 month. Payment: copies and honorariums to read their work at performance programs. Interested in new or unpub'd poets: only if they're under 16 years old. Simultaneous submissions accepted: yes. Submission quantity: 10. Special interests: We have an aversion to most haiku and rhymed poetry and prefer ground based, humanistic oriented work. Presently publishing 40 High School literary magazines a month over 1996-00 school year. Poetry chapbooks by young adults—800 separate volumes to date; one perfectbound anthology a year.

Tesseract Publications, PO Box 164, Canton, SD 57013-0164, 605-987-5070, ta-shi@dtgnet.com, http://members.tripod.com/~washrag/. Janet Leih, Maryanna Manfred. 1981. "Be sure to keep a copy of any poems submitted. Name and Address on every page, one poem to a page, include 55¢ SASE (if return of poems desired.) Include sufficient postage." avg. press run 300. Expects 1 poetry title 2000, 1 poetry title 2001. 5½×8½, or author's request; avg. price, cloth: $15; paper: $5. 60pp; Publishes 90% of poetry manuscripts submitted. Reporting time: 3 months. Payment: subsidy only. Interested in new or unpub'd poets: yes. Simultaneous submissions accepted: yes. Recently published poets: Helen Forelle, Gertrude Johnson, Rita Crom, Lois Bogue, Fern Stuefen. Submission quantity: manuscript of completed poems.

●TESTIMONIES, 90 Mcpadden Drive, Stratford, CT 06615, 203-378-1853; Fax 203-378-1082; agroves202@aol.com. 1996. circ. 30M. 4/yr. sub. price: $19; sample: free. 8pp; 8×11.

THE TEXAS REVIEW, Texas Review Press, English Department, Sam Houston State University, Huntsville, TX 77341-2146. Paul Ruffin, Editor; Melissa Morphew, Assistant Editor. 1976. "We are looking for poetry with precise imagery, good introduction, strong conclusion. Cloying confessional poetry will not work here. We will no longer read June through August. Mark submissions 'poetry.'" circ. 750-1M. 2/yr. Pub'd 80 poems 1999. sub. price: $20; 2 years $35; 3 years $50; sample: $5. 160pp; 6×9; Rights purchased: First North American Serial Rights, rights revert to author on publication. Publishes 1% of poems submitted. Deadlines: none. Reporting time: 2-6 months. Payment: copies plus 1 year subscription. Interested in new or unpub'd poets: yes. Simultaneous submissions accepted: no. Recent contributors: William Stafford, Donald Justice, Fred Chappell, W.S. Merwin, Richard Eberhart. Submission quantity: 4-5. Special interests: We have an especial fondness for regional poetry, poetry of character and place.

Texas Review Press (see also THE TEXAS REVIEW), English Department, Sam Houston State University, Huntsville, TX 77341-2146. 1976. "We do not read June-August" 6×9. Publishes 1% of poetry manuscripts submitted. Reporting time: 2-6 months. Payment: copies plus 1 year subscription. Simultaneous submissions accepted: no.

TEXAS YOUNG WRITERS' NEWSLETTER, PO Box 942, Adkins, TX 78101. Susan Currie, Editor. 1994. "Only writers ages 12-19 may submit poetry. You *must* enclose an SASE." circ. 300. 9/yr. Pub'd 18 poems 1999; expects 18 poems 2000, 18 poems 2001. sub. price: $10; sample: $1. 7pp; 8½×11; Rights purchased: First. Publishes 40% of poems submitted. Deadlines: none. Reporting time: 4 weeks. Payment: 2 copies. Interested in new or unpub'd poets: very. Simultaneous submissions accepted: no. Submission quantity: up to 5.

THALIA: Studies in Literary Humor, Dept of English, Univ of Ottawa, Ottawa K1N 6N5, Canada, 613-230-9505, Fax 613-565-5786. Jacqueline Tavernier-Courbin. 1978. circ. 500. 2/yr or 1 double issue. Pub'd 3 poems 1999. sub. price: $25 individuals, $27 libraries, discounts for 2 or 3 year subs.; sample: $8-$10 except for double issues. 75-125pp; 7×8½; Rights purchased: first publication rights belong to journal. Publishes 15-20% of poems submitted. Reporting time: variable. Payment: none. Interested in new or unpub'd poets: yes. Simultaneous submissions accepted: yes, but must know about it. Submission quantity: no more than 4. Special interests: Literary satire.

:THAT:, 1070 Easton Valley Road, Easton, NH 03580. 1992. circ. 250. 2/yr. sub. price: $5 per issue; sample: $5. 15pp; size varies.

THEECLECTICS, Creative With Words Publications (CWW), PO Box 223226, Carmel, CA 93922, fax 831-655-8627; e-mail cwwpub@usa.net; website http://members.tripod.com/~CreativeWithWords. Brigitta Geltrich. 1998. 2/yr. 16+pp; 8½×11.

THEMA, PO Box 8747, Metairie, LA 70011-8747. Gail Howard, Poetry Editor. 1988. "Each issue related to a unique central premise. Publication dates and themes (submission deadline in brackets): Sept. 2001, Safety in Numbers [11-1-00], Jan. 2002, What Sarah (or Edward) Remembered [3-1-01], May 2002, The Third One [7-1-01]." circ. 300. 3/yr. Pub'd 24 poems 1999; expects 24 poems 2000, 24 poems 2001. sub. price: $16; sample: $8. 180pp; 5½×8½; Rights purchased: one-time rights. Publishes 5% of poems submitted. Deadlines: 6 months before month of publication of specified issue. Reporting time: 5-6 months after submission deadline for specific issue. Payment: $10. Interested in new or unpub'd poets: yes. Simultaneous submissions accepted: no. Recent contributors: John Grey, Daniel Green, Kate Harris, Sue Walker. Submission quantity: 1-3. Special interests: All types of poetic form welcome. Poems should be thoughtfully constructed and carefully distilled.

Theytus Books Ltd., Green Mountain Road, Lot 45, RR #2, Site 50, Comp. 8, Penticton, B.C. V2A 6J7, Canada. Greg Young-Ing, Manager. 1980. "Theytus publishes *only* First Nation writers." avg. press run 2.5M. Pub'd 2 poetry titles 1999; expects 3 poetry titles 2000, 3 poetry titles 2001. 6×9; avg. price, paper: $12.95. 150pp; Publishes 30% of poetry manuscripts submitted. Reporting time: 1-4 months. Interested in new or unpub'd poets: yes. Simultaneous submissions accepted: yes. Recently published poets: Jeannette Armstrong, Beth Cuthand, Lee Maracle, Armand Garnet Ruffo. Submission quantity: 20 maximum.

THIN AIR, PO Box 23549, Flagstaff, AZ 86002, www.nau.edu/~english/thinair/taframes.html. 1995. "17/20/20" circ. 400-600. 2/yr. sub. price: $9; sample: $4. 80-100pp; 5½×8½; Rights purchased: all rights, but rights revert to author upon acknowledgement of *Thin Air* as original publisher. Publishes 5-10% of poems submitted. Deadlines: we read from Sept. to May. Reporting time: 2-3 months. Payment: publication and 2 contributor's copies. Interested in new or unpub'd poets: yes. Simultaneous submissions accepted: yes, but we must be notified. Recent contributors: Brigit Pegeen Kelly, James Harms, Vivian Shipley, Charles H. Webb. Submission quantity: 3-5.

THIN COYOTE, Lost Prophet Press, 2657 Grand Street NE, Minneapolis, MN 55418-2603, 612-781-6224, Fax 612-333-5800. 1992. circ. 200-300. 3/yr. sub. price: $15; sample: $5. 45pp; 8½×11.

THIRD COAST, Department of English, Western Michigan University, Kalamazoo, MI 49008-5092, 616-387-2675; Fax 616-387-2562; www.wmich.edu/thirdcoast. 1995. "Submission guidelines are posted on our website. Our poetry editors serve on a rotating basis, for two issues. Please address submissions to 'Poetry Editors.'" circ. 500. 2/yr. Pub'd 63 poems 1999; expects 60-70 poems 2000, 60-70 poems 2001. sub. price: $11; sample: $6. 150pp; 6×9; Rights purchased: first time rights. Publishes 3-5% of poems submitted. Deadlines: we read submissions year-round. Reporting time: 4-12 weeks. Interested in new or unpub'd poets: yes. Simultaneous submissions accepted: yes. Recent contributors: Lisa Sewell, Robin Behn, Scott Withiam, Chase Twichell, David Wojahn. Submission quantity: 3-5.

●**THE THIRD HOUSE,** PO Box 7377, FDR Station, New York, NY 10150, jeyrep@compuserve.com. 1999. circ. 500. 12/yr. sub. price: $10; sample: $1. 4pp; 8½×11.

13TH MOON, 1400 Washington Avenue, SUNY, English Department, Albany, NY 12222-0001, 518-442-4181. Judith Johnson. 1973. "No manuscripts read in June, July, and August. Work by women (only). We actively discourage submissions from writers who have not read a recent issue. Critical articles and book reviews on work of women poets actively sought." circ. 1.5M. 1 double-issue per year. Pub'd 60 poems 1999. sub. price: $10 for 1 double issue; sample: $10. 275pp; 6×9; Rights purchased: 1st North American serial. Publishes 2-5% of poems submitted. Reporting time: 2 weeks-6 months. Payment: copies. Interested in new or unpub'd poets: yes, if they are readers of the magazine. Simultaneous submissions accepted: no. Recent contributors: Carolyn Beard Whitlow, Josephine Jacobsen, Toi Derricotte, Alicia Ostriker, Kathleene West. Submission quantity: 3-5. Special interests: In general, formal, or narrative poetry will find a more sympathetic reading than the free-verse, first-person, present-indicative lyric—we are very interested in having more submissions from third world women.

THIS IS IMPORTANT, PO Box 69, Beatty, OR 97621, 541-533-2486. F.A. Nettelbeck. 1980. "We are the originators of the poetry pamphlet—the smaller the poem and closer to the point, the better. Reading-time span of our readership, approx. 1-3 minutes." circ. 1M. 4/yr. Expects 24-30 poems 2001. sub. price: $10; sample: $1. 8pp; 2¾×4¼; Rights purchased: none. Publishes 10% of poems submitted. Deadlines: none. Reporting time: immediate. Payment: 50 copies. Interested in new or unpub'd poets: yes. Simultaneous submissions accepted: yes. Recent contributors: Tom Clark, Robin Holcomb, W.S. Burroughs, Anselm Hollo, Allen Ginsberg. Submission quantity: no limit. Special interests: We will consider anything with guts or a mournful heart...Albert Ayler meets Hank Williams, Jr.; turn the set *off.*

Thistledown Press Ltd., 633 Main Street, Saskatoon, Sask. S7H 0J8, Canada, 306-244-1722. Patrick O'Rourke, Editor-in-Chief. 1975. "Thistledown Press publishes Canadian authors exclusively. Poets should obtain our guidelines for submission and familiarize themselves with some of our books before submitting. Poets should also have some history of publication in magazines and a list of publication credits before sending us a book-length manuscript. We do not accept unsolicited mss. Poets must query first." avg. press run 750. Pub'd 3 poetry titles 1999; expects 3 poetry titles 2000, 3 poetry titles 2001. 5½×8½; avg. price, paper: $13. 80pp; Publishes 3-5% of poetry manuscripts submitted. Reporting time: 12 weeks. Payment: 10% of retail price. Interested in new or unpub'd poets: no. Simultaneous submissions accepted: no. Recently published poets: John V. Hicks, Sherry Johnson, Charles Noble, Eva Tihanyi, David Day. Submission quantity: a sample of 10-15 poems. Special interests: Thistledown Press is only interested in publishing quality contemporary poetry that demonstrates a distinctiveness of voice and language.

Thorntree Press, 547 Hawthorn Lane, Winnetka, IL 60093, 708-446-8099. 1985. "We are a tax-deductible, not-for-profit press." avg. press run 1M. Pub'd 1-2 poetry titles 1999; expects 1-2 poetry titles 2000, 1-2 poetry titles 2001. 6×9; avg. price, paper: $5.95. Publishes 3 poets selected from the competition. Reporting time: uncertain. Payment: none. Interested in new or unpub'd poets: not at this time. Simultaneous submissions accepted: no. Recently published poets: Marcia Lee Masters, Glen Brown, Martin Marcus, Lydia Webster. Submission quantity: a titled 10-page sheaf of poems.

THOUGHTS FOR ALL SEASONS: The Magazine of Epigrams, 478 NE 56th Street, Miami, FL 33137-2621, 305-756-8800. Prof. Michel P. Richard, Editor-in-Chief. 1976. "Rhymed verse up to one page in length; original limericks, nonsense verse with good imagery; no haiku, please. Include SASE with submissions. Advertising rates are available on request." circ. 1M. Irregular, special issues. Pub'd 350 poems 1999; expects 350 poems 2000, 350 poems 2001. sub. price: $4.75 + $1.25 p/h; sample: $4.75 + $1.25 p/h.

84pp; 5½×8½; Rights purchased: none. Publishes 10% of poems submitted. Deadlines: none specified. Reporting time: 1 week. Payment: free copy of magazine; however, *Reader's Digest* has requested permission to reprint, they pay $50 per. Interested in new or unpub'd poets: yes. Simultaneous submissions accepted: encouraged. Recent contributors: David Lunde, William Barney, Deborah Smith Parker, Richard Alan Bunch, Jill Williams. Submission quantity: no limits. Special interests: Emphasis is primarily, but not exclusively, satirical. Pen and ink drawings (copies only, please) will be considered. (Magazine is illustrated).

THE THREEPENNY REVIEW, PO Box 9131, Berkeley, CA 94709, 510-849-4545. Wendy Lesser. 1979. circ. 10M. 4/yr. Pub'd 35-40 poems 1999; expects 35-40 poems 2000, 40-44 poems 2001. sub. price: $20, $35/2 years; sample: $7. 40pp; 11×17; Rights purchased: first serial. Publishes about .5% of poems submitted. Deadlines: none. Reporting time: 2 weeks to 2 months. Payment: $100/poem. Interested in new or unpub'd poets: yes. Simultaneous submissions accepted: no. Recent contributors: Thom Gunn, Louise Gluck, Frank Bidart, Czeslaw Milosz. Submission quantity: 5 or less. Special interests: Short poems, narrative poems, formal poetry (among others).

Threshold Books, 3108 Tater Lane, Guilford, VT 05301, 802-254-8300; Fax 802-257-2779. Edmund Helminski, Director. 1981. "Please do not request to submit a manuscript unless it coincides with our special interests." avg. press run 2M. Pub'd 2 poetry titles 1999; expects 1 poetry title 2000, 1 poetry title 2001. 5½×8½; avg. price, cloth: $18; paper: $10. 140pp; Publishes 1% of poetry manuscripts submitted. Reporting time: 2 months. Payment: 7% of cover price, paid every 6 months. Interested in new or unpub'd poets: no. Simultaneous submissions accepted: yes. Recently published poets: Rainer Maria Rilke, Jelaluddin Rumi, Yunus Emre, Rabia. Submission quantity: 5. Special interests: We are interested in poetry in translation, especially of well-known authors, mystical, especially Rumi.

Thunder Rain Publishing Corp., PO Box 1001, Livingston, LA 70754-1407, 225-686-2002, Fax 686-2285, rhi@thunder-rain.com, www.thunder-rain.com. Phyllis J. Green. 1996. "We collaborate with poets throughout the publication process" avg. press run 2M. Pub'd 1 poetry title 1999; expects 2-3 poetry titles 2000, 3-4 poetry titles 2001. 5½×8½; avg. price, cloth: $28; paper: $13.95. 72pp; Publishes 50% of poetry manuscripts submitted. Reporting time: 3-6 months. Payment: varies. Interested in new or unpub'd poets: yes. Simultaneous submissions accepted: yes. Recently published poets: Peter Tomassi, J. Kevin Wolfe, Ward Kelley, M.W. Anderson, L.C. Langford. Submission quantity: 3-5 poems.

Tia Chucha Press, PO Box 476969, Chicago, IL 60647, 773-377-2496. Luis J. Rodriguez, Director. 1989. "We read in the summer for next year's booklist—send before June 30th." avg. press run 1M. Pub'd 3 poetry titles 1999; expects 4 poetry titles 2000, 4 poetry titles 2001. 6×9; avg. price, paper: $10.95. 64pp; Publishes .05% of poetry manuscripts submitted. Reporting time: 6 weeks to 6 months. Payment: 10% royalty, 50% discount on books. Interested in new or unpub'd poets: yes. Simultaneous submissions accepted: yes—please let us know! Recently published poets: Kyoko Mori, Virgil Suarez, Melvin Dixon, Ricardo Sanchez, Sterling Plumpp. Submission quantity: no less than 48 pages. Special interests: Charged poetry; well-crafted but powerful, to reach a broader number of people, yet able to stand up to any of the "academics."

TIGER MOON, Tiger Moon, 3/677 Coconut Grove, Prasanthi Nilayam A.P. 515134, India, terry-tgrmoon@mailcity.com. Terry Kennedy. 1991. "We read every word. Be brave." Pub'd about 100 poems 1999; expects 100 poems 2000, 100 poems 2001. sub. price: $100; sample: $10. Rights purchased: first North American Serial. Publishes 90% of poems submitted. Deadlines: no deadline—we are always searching for those voices that are *brave* enough to tell the secrets. Reporting time: immediate reply. Payment: copies and money when available. Interested in new or unpub'd poets: very. Simultaneous submissions accepted: yes. Recent contributors: Virginia Smith, Roger Taus, Vincent Ferrini, Ambika Amranth, Madison Morrison. Submission quantity: sample ms. Special interests: We want personal narratives, poems, essays that are rooted in personal experiences.

Tiger Moon (see also TIGER MOON), 3/677 Coconut Grove, Prasanthi Nilayam A.P., India, terry-tgrmoon@mailcity.com. Terry Kennedy, Publisher. 1991. "Authors self-publish." avg. press run 1M. Pub'd 2 poetry titles 1999; expects 4 poetry titles 2000, 5 poetry titles 2001. size varies; avg. price, cloth: $19.99; paper: $24. 90-100pp; Publishes 90% of poetry manuscripts submitted. Reporting time: immediate. Payment: 50-50. Interested in new or unpub'd poets: yes. Simultaneous submissions accepted: yes. Recently published poets: Virginia Smith, Laughing Rainbow Woman, Ambika Amranth, Madison Morrison. Submission quantity: Entire ms. with SASE. Special interests: Devotional poetry that celebrates our common divinity, regional poetry, lyric poetry.

TIGHTROPE, Swamp Press, 15 Warwick Avenue, Northfield, MA 01360. Ed Rayher, Chief Editor. 1975. "We're very picky. Abstractions generally leave us cold. The image, the well-articulated line makes our day. We try to comment when possible" circ. 350. 2/yr. Pub'd 40 poems 1999; expects 40 poems 2000, 40 poems 2001. sub. price: $10; sample: $6. 36pp; size varies; Rights purchased: one-time. Publishes 1% of poems submitted. Reporting time: 8-12 weeks. Payment: varies, usually copies. Interested in new or unpub'd poets:

yes. Simultaneous submissions accepted: no. Recent contributors: Alan Catlin, Jane Elkington-Wohl, Robert F. White, Julie Juarez, Jami Wolf. Submission quantity: 3-6. Special interests: Poetry and graphic art.

Tilbury House, Publishers, 132 Water Street, Gardiner, ME 04345, 207-582-1899. Mark Melnicove, Editor. 1990. "Looking for book length manuscripts that cohere as a book. Not interested in random selections." avg. press run 1M. Pub'd 2 poetry titles 1999; expects 1 poetry title 2000, 2 poetry titles 2001. size varies; avg. price, cloth: $19.95; paper: $8.95. 100pp; Publishes less than 1% of poetry manuscripts submitted. Reporting time: 2 months. Payment: 8-10% royalties. Interested in new or unpub'd poets: yes. Simultaneous submissions accepted: yes. Recently published poets: Steve Kowit, Jane Cooper, Joan Larkin, Grace Paley, Robert Winner. Submission quantity: complete book of poems.

TIMBER CREEK REVIEW, c/o J.M. Freiermuth, 3283 UNCG Station, Greensboro, NC 27413, 336-334-6970. 1994. "Send list of little magazines you subscribe to and bio with cover letter. We do not publish the names of the magazines that have published you in the past." circ. 150-180. 4/yr. Pub'd 52 poems 1999; expects 50 poems 2000, 50 poems 2001. sub. price: $15 individuals, $16 institutions and Canada, $22 international; sample: $4.25. 76-84pp; 5½×8½; Rights purchased: one time. Publishes 8% of poems submitted. Deadlines: do not read December-January. Reporting time: 2 weeks to 4 months. Payment: 1 copy. Interested in new or unpub'd poets: no. Simultaneous submissions accepted: yes. Recent contributors: Patricia Prime, Randy W. Oakes, David Fedo, Robert Cooperman, Joanne Lowrey. Submission quantity: 3-6. Special interests: We read all poetry but 3-20 lines work best for us.

Timberline Press, 6281 Red Bud, Fulton, MO 65251, 573-642-5035. Clarence Wolfshohl, Editor, Publisher. 1975. "Timberline Press prints chapbooks that are hand letterpress editions. The book-making is of high quality, typographically reflecting the poetry printed. The process is slow; thus, the poet must be patient and not expect to see his book for some time if the ms is accepted." avg. press run 200. Pub'd 1 poetry title 1999; expects 2 poetry titles 2000, 2 poetry titles 2001. 5½×7, 6×9; avg. price, paper: $10-$12. 35pp; Publishes 5% of poetry manuscripts submitted. Reporting time: within 30 days. Payment: 50-50 split after production-promotion expenses. Interested in new or unpub'd poets: yes. Simultaneous submissions accepted: no. Recently published poets: Wally Swist, William Hart, Walter Bargen, Dan Stryk, LeRoy Gorman. Submission quantity: 5-10. Special interests: Regional poetry (Southwest/Midwest/Ozark). Poetry that shows a concern for the land. Would like to see some good light verse and satire.

TIME FOR RHYME, c/o Richard Unger, PO Box 1055, Battleford SK S0M 0E0, Canada, 306-445-5172. Richard W. Unger, Editor. 1995. "American and foreign poets submit with IRCs or with Canadian postage on SASE (US $1 enclosed is also acceptable). Canadians with sufficient postage on SASE for return if necessary. Will accept handwritten manuscripts from those without typewriter or computer but only if clearly written i.e. very legible. No profanity, porn—keep 'family viewing'. Must rhyme. Message should be clear." circ. 80. 4/yr. Pub'd 60 poems 1999; expects 55-63 poems 2000, 55-60 poems 2001. sub. price: $12 Cdn. for Canadians, $12US for Americans, $17.50 Cdn. for overseas; sample: same. 32pp; 4×5½; Rights purchased: First N.A. serial (reprint rights if poet assures me they did not sell rights). Publishes 1% of poems submitted. Deadlines: seasonal about a year in advance. Reporting time: as quickly as possible. Payment: 1 copy (will consider cash payments when financially viable). Interested in new or unpub'd poets: yes. Simultaneous submissions accepted: no. Recent contributors: Kenneth A. Elliott, B. O'Donnell, George Statham, Anthony Chalk, Elizabeth Symon. Submission quantity: 3-5. Special interests: Light verse certainly welcome. I don't care for abstract verse. Don't make me wonder if you were on drugs when you wrote it. Also don't try to impress me with a sophisticated vocabulary. Aim to communicate rather than impress. Will consider religious verse.

TIME HAIKU, 105, Kings Head Hill, London E4 7JG, England, 0181-529-6478. 1994. 2/yr. sub. price: £10 USA. 36pp; 5.8×8.3.

●**TIN HOUSE,** 2601 NW Thurman Street, Portland, OR 97210, tinhouselg@aol.com. Amy Bartlett. 1999. circ. 5M. 4/yr. Pub'd 50 poems 1999; expects 50 poems 2000, 50 poems 2001. sub. price: $24.95; sample: $12.95. 224pp; 7×9; Rights purchased: 1st serial and anthology. Publishes 10% of poems submitted. Reporting time: 3 months. Payment: $50 and up. Interested in new or unpub'd poets: yes! Simultaneous submissions accepted: yes. Recent contributors: Charles Simic, Marge Piercy, Les Murray, Evincy Troupe, Jill Bialosky. Submission quantity: 1-3.

TitleWaves Publishing, PO Box 288, Lihue, HI 96766-0288, orders 800-867-7323. 1989. 5½×8½, 8½×11.

Tombouctou Books, 1472 Creekview Lane, Santa Cruz, CA 95062, 408-476-4144. 1975. "We do not accept unsolicited mss" 5½×8½. Simultaneous submissions accepted: no.

Torchlight Publishing, PO Box 52, Badger, CA 93603. 1989. 6×9.

TORRE DE PAPEL, 111 Phillips Hall, The University of Iowa, Iowa City, IA 52242, 319-335-2245. Eduardo Guizar Alvarez. 1991. circ. 400. 3/yr. Pub'd 20-25 poems 1999. sub. price: $30; sample: $10. 110pp; 8¾×11½; Deadlines: same as other contributions: May 31, October 31, February 28. Reporting time: 2 months (may vary). Payment: none. Interested in new or unpub'd poets: yes. Simultaneous submissions accepted: yes. Recent contributors: Oscar Milano, Maria Soldira, Gabriel Perez. Submission quantity: at least 5 preferred. Special interests: We encourage experimental poetry, as well as translations from or into Spanish, English and Portuguese.

TOUCHSTONE LITERARY JOURNAL, PO Box 8308, Spring, TX 77387-8308. William Laufer, Poetry Editor; T.E. Walthen, Assitant Poetry Editor; Guida Jackson, Poetry Chapbook Editor. 1976. "We are looking for the non-traditional and the experimental. We also publish translations. Please include the original-language version and a brief bio of the poet. We do not answer any letter without SASE. With any submission, please include at least a 2-sentence bio for our Contributors Information page. We publish chapbook collections of prose and poetry. Send SASE for guidelines before submitting chapbooks" circ. 1M. 1/yr, plus chapbook supplements. Pub'd 50 poems 1999; expects 30 poems 2000, 30 poems 2001. sub. price: contribution: 1 book postage stamps; sample: same. 80pp; 5½×8½; Rights purchased: first. Publishes 5% of poems submitted. Deadlines: none. Reporting time: 6 weeks. Payment: 1 contributor's copy. Interested in new or unpub'd poets: yes. Simultaneous submissions accepted: yes. Recent contributors: Marvin Soleman, Sheila Murphy, Michael Johnson, Ann Alejandro, Lyn Lifshin. Submission quantity: about 5. Special interests: Translations, experimental poetry. If the work is well-crafted, we can handle up to 75 lines; average Mss run 15-30. We are humanist-oriented. Our readership is largely academic with broad interests. We are interested in collections, but query first, requesting guidelines.

TOWER, Tower Poetry Society, c/o McMaster University, 1280 Main Street W Box 1021, Hamilton, Ontario, L8S ICO, Canada. Joanna Lawson, Editor-in-Chief. 1950. "Poems should be titled and no more than 40 lines." circ. 250. 2/yr. Pub'd 100 poems 1999; expects 100 poems 2000, 100 poems 2001. sub. price: $8 Canada and US, $9.50 abroad plus $2 p/h (Can. funds); sample: $2+ $1p/h (Can. funds). 44pp; 5½×8½; Rights purchased: first publication. Publishes 20% of poems submitted. Deadlines: during months of February and August. Reporting time: about 1 month. Payment: none, 1 copy. Interested in new or unpub'd poets: yes. Simultaneous submissions accepted: no. Recent contributors: Tony Cosier, Ken Samberg, Jean McCallian, Helen Fitzgerald Dougher, G.W. Down. Submission quantity: 4.

Tower Poetry Society (see also TOWER), c/o McMaster University, 1280 Main Street W. Box 1021, Hamilton, Ontario, L8S 1CO, Canada. Joanna Lawson. 1950. "We do *not* publish chap books for poets. We only publish TOWER, twice a year." 5½×8½. Interested in new or unpub'd poets: yes. Simultaneous submissions accepted: no. Submission quantity: 4.

TRANSCENDENT VISIONS, 251 South Olds Boulevard, 84-E, Fairless Hills, PA 19030-3426, 215-547-7159. David Kime, Beth Greenspan. 1992. "Our zine is by and for psychiatric survivors/ex-mental patients. We publish reviews of various types of magazines but especially would like to review poetry zines, chapbooks, etc., by psychiatric survivors/ex-mental patients" circ. 200. 2/yr. Pub'd 100 poems 1999; expects 75 poems 2000, 75 poems 2001. sub. price: $4; sample: $2. 26pp; 8½×11; Rights purchased: none. Publishes 50% of poems submitted. Deadlines: none. Reporting time: 1 month. Payment: copy of issue. Interested in new or unpub'd poets: yes, we are interested in reading poetry by anyone who is a psychiatric survivor/ex-mental patient. Simultaneous submissions accepted: yes. Recent contributors: Chriss-Spike Quatrone, Paul Weinman, Jim DeWitt, Gloria Delvecchio, Arlene Hampton. Submission quantity: 5-8. Special interests: We enjoy all types of poetry but especially poems that are bizarre, twisted and loaded with vinegar.

Transcending Mundane, Inc., PO Box 1241, Park City, UT 84060-1241, 435-615-9609, Fax 435-649-5140, transmun@paracreative.com, www.paracreative.com. 1998. 5½×8½.

TRANSMOG, Route 6, Box 138, Charleston, WV 25311, E-Mail: far@medinah.atc.ucarb.com. Richey Forrest. 1991. circ. 200. 2-6/yr. Pub'd 150 poems 1999; expects 150 poems 2000, 150 poems 2001. sub. price: no subscriptions; sample: $1. 30pp; 8½×11; Rights purchased: none. Publishes 50% of poems submitted. Deadlines: flexible. Reporting time: 2-8 weeks. Payment: copy. Interested in new or unpub'd poets: yes. Simultaneous submissions accepted: yes. Recent contributors: John Bennett, Jake Berry, Michael Basinski, Bill Paulauskus, Paul Weinman. Submission quantity: 1-5. Special interests: Dislocational, surreal, absurd, dada, edge, 'other'ness but not blood 'n guts.

TRANSNATIONAL PERSPECTIVES, CP 161, CH-1211 Geneva 16, Switzerland. Rene Wadlow. 1974. "Poems on nature, understanding between peoples, no humor, multicultural reading public." circ. 5M. 3/yr. Pub'd 14 poems 1999. sub. price: $20; sample: free. 48pp; 29×20cm; Publishes 5% of poems submitted. Reporting time: 2 months. Payment: 5 or more copies of issue with poem. Interested in new or unpub'd poets: yes. Simultaneous submissions accepted: yes. Recent contributors: Nicola Beech Squirrel, Verona Bratesch, Timothy Hodor. Submission quantity: 5-7.

TRICYCLE: The Buddhist Review, 92 Vandam Street, New York, NY 10013-1007. 1991. circ. 50M. 4/yr. Pub'd 6 poems 1999; expects 6 poems 2000, 6 poems 2001. sub. price: $24; sample: $7.50. 104pp; 8½×11; Rights purchased: first. Publishes 2% of poems submitted. Reporting time: 3 months. Payment: varies.

Interested in new or unpub'd poets: yes. Simultaneous submissions accepted: no. Submission quantity: 5.

TRIQUARTERLY, Northwestern University Press, 2020 Ridge, Evanston, IL 60208-4302, 847-491-7614. Susan Hahn. 1964. circ. 5M. 3/yr. Pub'd 90 poems 1999. sub. price: $24; sample: $5. 256pp; 6×9¼; Rights purchased: 1st N.A. serial rights and non-exclusive reprint rights. Publishes 1% of poems submitted. Deadlines: no submissions read between April 1 and Sept. 30. Reporting time: 8-12 weeks. Payment: $1.50 per line. Interested in new or unpub'd poets: yes. Simultaneous submissions accepted: no. Recent contributors: Alice Fulton, Campbell McGrath, Carol Frost, David Wojahn. Submission quantity: 3-6. Special interests: Always interested in translations of contemporary poetry—if the translations are strong poems and not merely a document pointing back at an original poem.

Trout Creek Press, 5976 Billings Road, Parkdale, OR 97041, 503-352-6494; e-Mail Lfh42@AOL.COM. Laurence F. Hawkins. 1981. "Chapbooks are published as time and money allow — about two/year." avg. press run 500. Pub'd 4 poetry titles 1999; expects 5 poetry titles 2000, 4 poetry titles 2001. size varies; avg. price, paper: $4. 40pp; Publishes 4% of poetry manuscripts submitted. Reporting time: 2-3 months. Payment: varies. Interested in new or unpub'd poets: yes. Simultaneous submissions accepted: no. Recently published poets: Judson Crews, Connie Fox, Leslie Leyland Fields, Nathaniel Tarn, Sheila Nickerson. Submission quantity: Samples or entire manuscript. Special interests: Interested in all poetic forms.

Truly Fine Press, PO Box 891, Bemidji, MN 56601. Jerry Madson. 1973. "Query, funding concerns limits publishing schedule. Truly Fine Press is a statement of being through experimental writing and concretel language poetry. ALLA (art-language, language-art). Now only doing visual poetry" avg. press run ultra limited editions. size varies; avg. price, paper: varies. Under 32pp; Reporting time: 1 week to 6 months. Payment: copies. Interested in new or unpub'd poets: yes. Simultaneous submissions accepted: yes. Recently published poets: Jerry Madson, Erin Camelot O'Connor. Special interests: All forms of experimental poetry. Visual poetry only that gravitates toward art.

Truman State University Press, 100 East Normal Street, Kirksville, MO 63501, 660-785-7199, FAX 660-785-4480. Nancy Reschly, Poetry Editor. 1986. "See T.S. Eliot Prize information at www2.truman.edu/tsup" avg. press run 500. Pub'd 2 poetry titles 1999; expects 3 poetry titles 2000, 3 poetry titles 2001. 6×9; avg. price, cloth: $20; paper: $15. 80pp; Publishes 5% of poetry manuscripts submitted. Reporting time: 3 months. Payment: 5%-10%. Interested in new or unpub'd poets: no. Simultaneous submissions accepted: no. Recently published poets: Jim Barnes, Samuel Maio, William Baer, David Keplinger, H.L. Hix. Submission quantity: 60.

Tsunami Inc. (see also THE TEMPLE), PO Box 100, Walla Walla, WA 99362-0033, E-mail tsunami@innw.net. Charles Potts, Stephen Thomas, Travis Catsull. 1995. "Query first with SASE - always." avg. press run 1M. Pub'd 2 poetry titles 1999; expects 4 poetry titles 2001. 5½×8½; avg. price, paper: $10-$15. 64-80pp; Publishes 1% of poetry manuscripts submitted. Reporting time: 90 days. Payment: 10%. Interested in new or unpub'd poets: yes. Simultaneous submissions accepted: yes. Recently published poets: Sharon Doubiago, Amalio Madueno, Suzanne Lummis, dan raphael, Mark Sargent. Submission quantity: 5.

TUCUMCARI LITERARY REVIEW, 3108 W. Bellevue Avenue, Los Angeles, CA 90026. Troxey Kemper. 1988. "The established forms get preference. Poems that provoke thought are welcome—not doggerel and greeting card verse, not religious or inspirational" circ. 200. 6-8/yr. Pub'd 280 poems 1999; expects 290 poems 2000, 290 poems 2001. sub. price: $12; sample: $2 (includes postage). 40pp; 5½×8½; Rights purchased: one-time. Publishes 20%-33% of poems submitted. Deadlines: none. Reporting time: 2 weeks, sooner if rejected, later if accepted and SASE is returned with copy of magazine. Payment: 1 copy. Interested in new or unpub'd poets: yes. Simultaneous submissions accepted: yes. Recent contributors: William Middleton, Andy Peterson, Bobby S. Rivera, Ruth Daniels, Elizabeth Dabbs. Submission quantity: 3 or 4. Special interests: Regional poetry (West, Southwest), light verse, Native American subjects, letters to the editor taking strong positions, opinion pieces, nostalgia and memories.

TURNING THE TIDE: A Journal of Anti-Racist Action, Research & Education, PO Box 1055, Culver City, CA 90232-1055, 310-495-0299, e-mail part2001@usa.net. 1987. "1-2 poems each issue." circ. 10M. 4/yr. sub. price: $15 individuals, $25 institutions; sample: $4. 16pp; 11×17.

TURNING WHEEL, PO Box 4650, Berkeley, CA 94704. Susan Moon. 1980. "Please try to relate poetry to our themes. Themes of upcoming issues are described on editorial page" circ. 5M. 4/yr. Pub'd 15 poems 1999; expects 15 poems 2000, 15 poems 2001. sub. price: $35 membership, $20 low-income; sample: $6 by mail. 48pp; 8½×11; Rights purchased: one-time rights. Publishes 5% of poems submitted. Deadlines: revolving. Reporting time: 1-2 months. Payment: 2 copies of magazine, one year subscription. Interested in new or unpub'd poets: yes. Simultaneous submissions accepted: yes, but tell us if your poem is accepted elsewhere. Recent contributors: Noah de Lissovoy, Leslie Scalapino, Deena Metzger, Gary Snyder, Fanny Howe. Submission quantity: up to 3. Special interests: Humorous poetry is always welcomed, Buddhist poetry.

Turnstone Press, 607-100 Arthur Street, Winnipeg R3B 1H3, Canada, 204-947-1555, E-mail acquisitions@turnstonepress.mb.ca. 1976. "Only publish work by Canadian citizens or residents." avg. press run 500-1M. Pub'd 1 poetry title 1999; expects 1 poetry title 2000, 1 poetry title 2001. 5½×8½; avg. price, paper: $9.95. 80pp; Publishes .8% of poetry manuscripts submitted. Reporting time: 4 months. Payment: 10% royalty annually. Interested in new or unpub'd poets: yes. Simultaneous submissions accepted: query first before sending. Recently published poets: Di Brandt, David Arnason, Sylvia Legris, Catherine Hunter, Patrick Friesen. Submission quantity: 70-100 pages. Special interests: Longpoems, experimental poetry, regional poetry (Canadian Prairies).

●**TWINSWORLD,** 11220 St. Joe Road, Fort Wayne, IN 46835, twinworld1@aol.com. 1989. circ. 4M. 4/yr. sub. price: $20; sample: $3. 42pp; 7½×10.

2AM MAGAZINE, 2AM Publications, PO Box 6754, Rockford, IL 61125-1754. Gretta McCombs Anderson, Editor. 1986. "We read poetry submissions year-round. Prefer short poems (20-35 lines). Always include SASE for reply. Quality (as defined by the editor) is only real criteria for acceptance. We publish what we like, and we sometimes don't know what we like until we see it!" circ. 2M. 4/yr. Pub'd 12 poems 1999; expects 30 poems 2000, 16 poems 2001. sub. price: $19; sample: $5.95. 68pp; 8½×11; Rights purchased: one-time. Publishes 2-3% of poems submitted. Deadlines: open market. Reporting time: 8-10 weeks. Payment: 1/2¢ per word or $1 per poem minimum; plus 1 complimentary contributor's copy. Interested in new or unpub'd poets: yes. Simultaneous submissions accepted: no. Recent contributors: Peni Griffin, Wayne Allen Sallee, Robert Dunn, Kenn Amdahl, Denise Dumars. Submission quantity: no more than 5. Special interests: Prefer horror, fantasy or science fictional poetry but will consider finely crafted experimental and/or mainstream contemporary work.

2AM Publications (see also 2AM MAGAZINE), PO Box 6754, Rockford, IL 61125-1754. Gretta M. Anderson, Editor. 1986. "We plan to publish between one and three chapbooks annually. We're *very* selective. No reply unless SASE with enough postage is enclosed with submission or query" avg. press run 250. Pub'd 1 poetry title 1999; expects 1 poetry title 2000. 6×9; avg. price, cloth: $9.95; paper: $4.95. 50pp; Publishes less than 1% of poetry manuscripts submitted. Reporting time: 4 months. Payment: negotiable. Interested in new or unpub'd poets: no. Simultaneous submissions accepted: no. Recently published poets: Bruce Boston. Submission quantity: query with samples and SASE. Special interests: Rich in concrete imagery horror and epic fantasy or science fiction poetry only.

Two Dog Press, PO Box 307, Deer Isle, ME 04627, 207-348-6819; fax 207-348-6016; email human@twodogpress.com. Karen Kaiser. 1997. "We are moving away from poetry; a book has to be exceptional to catch our attention" avg. press run 1M. Pub'd 1 poetry title 1999. size varies; avg. price, cloth: $21; paper: $9.95. 160pp; Publishes 5% of poetry manuscripts submitted. Reporting time: 1 month. Payment: varies. Interested in new or unpub'd poets: only if work is about dogs. Simultaneous submissions accepted: no. Recently published poets: David Sutherland, Paul Kloppenborg, Doug Tanury. Submission quantity: 5. Special interests: Think Dogs!

TWO RIVERS REVIEW, POETS'PAPER, 215 McCartney Street, Easton, PA 18042, 610-559-3887; tworiversreview@juno.com; www.members.tripod.com/~tworiversreview/index.html. 1997. circ. 500. 2/yr. sub. price: $15; sample: $5. 50pp; 5½×8½.

2.13.61 Publications, PO Box 1910, Los Angeles, CA 90078, 213-969-8791. 1984. avg. press run 1M. Pub'd 2 poetry titles 1999; expects 2 poetry titles 2000, 1 poetry title 2001. 5½×8½; avg. price, paper: $11. 100pp; Recently published poets: Tricia Warden, Bill Shields, Ellyn Maybe.

Tyro Publishing, 194 Carlbert Street, Sault St. Marie, Ontario P6A 5E1, Canada, 705-253-6402, Fax 705-942-3625; tyro@sympatico.ca. George Hemingway. 1984. "We try to help writers get their work into print even though it may not be Tyro. We prefer double-spacing between verses" avg. press run 500. Pub'd 60 poetry titles 1999; expects 60 poetry titles 2000, 70 poetry titles 2001. 5½×8½; avg. price, paper: $7. 100pp; Publishes 40% of poetry manuscripts submitted. Reporting time: 2 weeks to 1 month. Payment: none. Interested in new or unpub'd poets: yes. Simultaneous submissions accepted: yes. Recently published poets: Nancy Fisher, Bruce Bedell, Gordon L. Stone. Submission quantity: 5.

U

ULITARRA, PO Box 195, Armidale, New South Wales 2350, Australia, +612 6772 9135. Michael Sharkey. 1992. "We run an annual poetry competition (prize $1000 AUS). To enter, purchase a copy of the first issue for each year. Closing date June 2. We prefer poems typed, double spaced. We have a 2 week turn around on average. We urge prospective contributors to purchase an issue to see the sort of poetry we publish. Submissions must be accompanied by a self-addressed envelope for return of manuscripts; Australian stamp, or International Reply Coupons should be enclosed." circ. 600. 2/yr. sub. price: $20AUS (oversea airmail rate: New Zealand $30AUS, others $40AUS); sample: $10AUS (Oversea airmail rate: New Zealdn $15AUS, others $20AUS). 180pp; 5⅞×8¼; Rights purchased: first. Payment: $60 AUS minimum. Interested in new or unpub'd poets: yes. Simultaneous submissions accepted: no. Recent contributors: Brian Henry, Knute Skinner, Geraldine McKenzie, Vera Newson, Michelle Taylor. Submission quantity: 2 or 3.

Ultramarine Publishing Co., Inc., PO Box 303, Hastings-on-Hudson, NY 10706, 914-478-2522. Christopher P. Stephens. 1965. "No unsolicited manuscripts please. We primarily distribute books for major authors where their title was dropped by a large house. As David Rosenberg's *Blues of the Sky* was dropped by Harpers and he obtained the books which we distribute for him" Expects 3 poetry titles 2000. 6×9; avg. price, cloth: $12.50; paper: $7.50. 100pp; Publishes a small % of poetry manuscripts submitted. Reporting time: 60 days. Payment: twice a year 6/30 & 12/31; we split with the author when they have obtained a supply of copies for a dropped title. Interested in new or unpub'd poets: no. Simultaneous submissions accepted: yes. Recently published poets: Tom Disch, David Rosenberg. Special interests: Serious poetry. We concentrate upon fiction; we have 225 titles in print. 17 are poetry and 173 are fiction.

UND Press (see also NORTH DAKOTA QUARTERLY), University of North Dakota, PO Box 7209, Grand Forks, ND 58202, 701-777-3321. 1910. 6×9.

THE UNDERGROUND, PO Box 14311, Milwaukee, WI 53214. 1995. 3/yr. sub. price: $5; sample: $2. 12pp; 8½×11; Reporting time: 4 weeks. Payment: 2 contributors copies. Interested in new or unpub'd poets: yes. Simultaneous submissions accepted: yes. Special interests: Subversive, experimental, unusual poetry preferred.

Underwhich Editions, PO Box 262, Adelaide Street Station, Toronto, Ontario M5C 2J4, Canada, 536-9316. Steven Smith, Paul Dutton. 1978. "Not accepting unsolicited mss." avg. press run 200-500. Expects 2 poetry titles 2000, 1 poetry title 2001. avg. price, paper: $10; other: $4. 20pp; Payment: 10% (copies or sales). Recently published poets: Gerry Shikatani, Lucas Mulder, Paul Dutton, John Riddell, Mari-Lou Rowley.

Unfinished Monument Press, 237 Prospect Street South, Hamilton, Ontario L8M 2Z6, Canada, 905-312-1779, Fax 905-312-8285, meklerdeahl@globalserve.net, www.meklerdeahl.com. James Deahl. 1978. avg. press run 1M. Pub'd 5 poetry titles 1999; expects 6 poetry titles 2000, 7 poetry titles 2001. 5½×8½; avg. price, paper: $7-15. 20-126pp; Reporting time: 6 months. Payment: 10% in cash or copies. Interested in new or unpub'd poets: not at this time. Simultaneous submissions accepted: yes. Recently published poets: Chris Faiers, Mark McCawley, Leslie Webb, Linda Rogers, Tanis MacDonald. Submission quantity: 5. Special interests: We like People's poetry and longpoems.

THE UNFORGETTABLE FIRE, 206 North 6th Street, Prospect Park, NJ 07508-2025. Jordan O'Neill, Editor. 1991. "Especially interested in poems from people of color and most importantly, for the contributor to stay close to the feminist/humanist view." circ. 5M. 2/yr. Expects 25-35 poems 2000. sub. price: $10; sample: $5. 25-30pp; 8½×11; Rights purchased: none. Publishes 50% of poems submitted. Reporting time: 4-6 weeks. Payment: free samples (contributor's copies). Interested in new or unpub'd poets: yes. Simultaneous submissions accepted: yes. Recent contributors: Elisavietta Ritchie, Mary Sue Koeppel, Lyn Lifshin. Submission quantity: 1-5. Special interests: We are interested in many types/styles of poetry; however, very long poems do pose a potential problem on occasion so we would like to suggest very long poems not be submitted.

THE UNIT CIRCLE, PO Box 20352, Seattle, WA 98102, 206-297-2650, E-mail zine@unitcircle.com, www.unitcircle.com. 1992. "We consistantly feature poets in our issues" circ. 500. Constant. Pub'd 9 poems 1999; expects 12 poems 2000, 16 poems 2001. Publishes 5% of poems submitted. Reporting time: 4 weeks. Payment: issues. Interested in new or unpub'd poets: yes. Simultaneous submissions accepted: yes. Recent contributors: Errol Miller, Randall Brock, Mary Winters, Kent Clair Chamberlain. Submission quantity: 5. Special interests: We are extremely interested in quality experimental poetry. We are open to long poems as well.

UNITED LUMBEE NATION TIMES, P.O. Box 512, Fall River Mills, CA 96028, 530-336-6701. 1979. circ. 2M. 3-4/yr. Pub'd 12 poems 1999; expects 12 poems 2000, 12 poems 2001. sub. price: $8/4 issues; sample: $2. 8-12pp; 11½×15; Rights purchased: none. Publishes 90% of poems submitted. Payment: none. Interested in new or unpub'd poets: not really, but will if they are Native American Indian. Simultaneous submissions accepted: yes. Recent contributors: Stanford Summers, Straght Arrow Armstrong, Jeremy Notafroids, Poha Ma Hepiwilson. Submission quantity: not over 2.

Uniting the World Press, Inc. (see also MOTHER EARTH JOURNAL: An International Quarterly), c/o National Poetry Association, 934 Brannan Street, #2ND-FL, San Francisco, CA 94103, 415-552-9261; fax 415-552-9271. Herman Berlandt, Editor; Publisher, Maureen Hurley, Co-Editor. 1990. "We invite poems from colleagues beyond our borders in good English translations" avg. press run 2M. Pub'd 4 poetry titles 1999; expects 4 poetry titles 2000, 4 poetry titles 2001. 11×15; avg. price, paper: $5; other: $3 for a sample copy. 40pp; Publishes 15% of poetry manuscripts submitted. Reporting time: 2 months. Payment: 2 copies. Interested in new or unpub'd poets: yes. Simultaneous submissions accepted: yes. Recently published poets: Yang Liax (China), Oaka Makoto (Japan), Niyi Osundare (Nigeria), Lawrence Ferlinghetti (USA), Homero Aridjis (Mexico). Submission quantity: 3. Special interests: The poet's perspective on the current political + ecological global crisis. Must come with a rough English translation.

Unity Books, 1901 NW Blue Parkway, Unity Village, MO 64065, 816-524-3550, fax 816-251-3552. 1889. Expects 1 poetry title 2000. 5½×8½. Recently published poets: James Dillet Freeman.

University Editions, Inc., 59 Oak Lane, Spring Valley, Huntington, WV 25704, 304-429-7204. Ira Herman, Mananging Editor. 1984. "University Editions was established in 1984 to publish paperback books for a general audience. University Editions does not limit consideration to 'academic' styles or subjects. University Editions will publish quality poetry collections of all types and on all subjects. We are interested in experimental, free verse, haiku, and rhymed poetry. University Editions welcomes new or unpublished poets. Most of the poets we publish have had some poems appear in magazines or quarterlies before submitting a collection to us. Some have published books previously, but most have not. A publishing history is helpful but not essential. Each submission will receive careful consideration, and the editor will comment on the work if time permits. Translations, bilingual editions, children's poetry, and regional poetry collections will also be considered. A self-addressed envelope or mailer sufficient to return the work should be included with each query or manuscript." avg. press run 500-1M. Pub'd 10 poetry titles 1999; expects 12 poetry titles 2000, 18 poetry titles 2001. 5½×8½; avg. price, cloth: $7; paper: $5. 40-150pp; Publishes 15-20% of poetry manuscripts submitted. Reporting time: 1 month for complete manuscripts, 1 week for queries. Payment: varies, depending on author and book; most are subsidized. Interested in new or unpub'd poets: yes, most of our poets have not published previously in book form. Simultaneous submissions accepted: yes. Recently published poets: Barry Kvkovich, Florence Berg, John R. Smith. Submission quantity: either send a small sampling of 10 or so, or send the complete manuscript. Submitting the complete manuscript may speed consideration for publication.

University of Illinois Press, 1325 South Oak Street, Champaign, IL 61820-6903, 217-333-0950. Laurence Lieberman. 1918. "We are not presently accepting unsolicited submissions. In addition to volumes by individual poets, we also publish thematic anthologies (recent volumes published of baseball poems and working-class poems) and invite submissions in this area." avg. press run 1.2M-1.5M. Pub'd 3 poetry titles 1999; expects 4 poetry titles 2000, 4 poetry titles 2001. avg. price, cloth: $17.95; paper: $11.95. 75-90pp; Publishes 25% of poetry manuscripts submitted. Reporting time: 2½ to 3 months. Payment: 7½%. Interested in new or unpub'd poets: no. Simultaneous submissions accepted: no. Recently published poets: Lynn Emanuel, Laura Mullen, Mark Doty, Sandra McPherson, Jean Garrigue. Submission quantity: 70-100 ms pp.

University of Massachusetts Press, Box 429, Amherst, MA 01004-0429, 413-545-2217. Address poetry submissions to: Juniper Prize, c/o Mail Room, University of Massachusetts, Amherst, MA 01003. 1964. avg. press run 1.3M. Pub'd 2 poetry titles 1999; expects 1 poetry title 2000, 2 poetry titles 2001. 5½×8½; avg. price, cloth: $20; paper: $9.95. 80pp; Publishes 2% of poetry manuscripts submitted. Reporting time: Award winner announced six months after submission deadline. Payment: Juniper Prize award of $1,000 on first printing in lieu of royalties. Interested in new or unpub'd poets: yes. Simultaneous submissions accepted: yes. Recently published poets: Henry Lyman, Karen Donovan, Mark Wunderlich, Martin Espada, Richard Jackson. Submission quantity: 50-55.

University of Missouri Press, 2910 LeMone Boulevard, Columbia, MO 65201-0001, 314-882-7641. Clair Willcox. 1958. "Publishing four poetry collections a year, the University of Missouri Press maintains an energetic and diverse poetry list that includes both veteran authors and those publishing first books. Poets interested in publication should first submit four to six sample poems, a table of contents for the entire manuscript, and a cover letter giving any further information about the poet's work or background that the writer believes will be helpful. This material should be addressed to Clair Willcox, Poetry Editor." Pub'd 4 poetry titles 1999; expects 4 poetry titles 2000, 4 poetry titles 2001. 64pp; Interested in new or unpub'd poets: yes. Simultaneous submissions accepted: yes. Recently published poets: Michael Blumenthal, Miller Williams, Kevin Stein, James Whitehead, Heather Ross Miller. Submission quantity: 4-6.

University of Pittsburgh Press, 127 North Bellefield Avenue, Pittsburgh, PA 15260, 412-624-4110. Ed Ochester. 1936. "First books should be sent *only* during March and April; manuscripts should not be sent to the Press until the poet has requested a copy of the rules governing the Agnes Lynch Starrett Poetry Prize competition for a first book: send SASE to: Starrett Prize, University of Pittsburgh Press, 127 N. Bellefield Avenue, Pittsburgh, PA 15260. Poets who have previously published a book of poems should send manuscripts during September and October *only*" avg. press run 2M. Pub'd 8 poetry titles 1999; expects 7 poetry titles 2000, 7 poetry titles 2001. avg. price, cloth: $19.95; paper: $10.95. 80pp; Publishes .006% of poetry manuscripts submitted. Reporting time: 6 months. Payment: 12½% on cloth net sales, 8% on paper net sales.

218

Interested in new or unpub'd poets: yes, but only through the Agnes Lynch Starrett Poetry Prize competition; those interested should write for the rules. Simultaneous submissions accepted: yes. Recently published poets: Sharon Doubiago, Maggie Anderson, Elton Glaser, Michael S. Weaver, Kathleen Peirce. Submission quantity: 48-100 pages. Special interests: No restrictions, except that we are not currently soliciting translations. Only work of the highest professional quality is accepted for publication.

University of Sydney Union, Level One, Manning House, University of Sydney, NSW 2006, Australia. 1884.

UNIVERSITY OF WINDSOR REVIEW, Department of English, University of Windsor, Windsor, Ontario N9B3P4, Canada, 519-293-4232 X2332; Fax 519-973-7050; uwrevu@uwindsor.ca. John Ditsky, Poetry Editor. 1965. "No special restrictions—just good quality." circ. 250. 2/yr. Pub'd 35-40 poems 1999; expects 35-40 poems 2000, 35-40 poems 2001. sub. price: $19.95 CDN. (+ 7% GST) and $19.95 U.S. per year; sample: $8 Cdn. and $7 U.S. per year. 100pp; 6×9; Rights purchased: one-time NAR. Publishes 5% of poems submitted. Deadlines: none. Reporting time: 1-2 weeks. Payment: $15 per contributor. Interested in new or unpub'd poets: either. Simultaneous submissions accepted: no. Recent contributors: Tom Wayman, Peter Wild, Roger Finch, Walter McDonald, Lyn Lifshin. Submission quantity: 5-10.

THE UNKNOWN WRITER, 5 Pothat Street, Sloatsburg, NY 10974, 914-753-8363; Fax 914-753-6562; E-mail rsidor@worldnet.att.net. D.S. Davis. 1995. "No love poems!" circ. 500. 3/yr. Pub'd 10 poems 1999; expects 5 poems 2000, 5 poems 2001. sub. price: $7; sample: $2.50. 48pp; 5½×8½; Rights purchased: one-time. Publishes 10% of poems submitted. Reporting time: 3 months. Payment: 2 sample copies. Interested in new or unpub'd poets: yes. Simultaneous submissions accepted: yes. Recent contributors: David Castleman, Satig Mestopian, Stepan Chapman. Submission quantity: 3.

UNMUZZLED OX, ZerOX Books, 43B Clark Lane, Staten Island, NY 10304, 781-448-3395, 212-226-7170, MAndreOX@aol.com. Michael Andre. 1971. circ. 20M. 2/yr. sub. price: $20; sample: $7. 140pp; 8½×5½; Rights purchased: 1st serial rights. Publishes 1% of poems submitted. Payment: copies. Recent contributors: Creeley, Ginsberg, Berrigan, Pound.

UNO MAS MAGAZINE, PO Box 1832, Silver Spring, MD 20915, Fax 301-770-3250, unomasmag@aol.com, http://www.unomas.com/. Ron Saah. circ. 3.5M. 4/yr. sub. price: $11; sample: $3.50. 50pp; 8½×11; Rights purchased: one-time publication. Publishes 30% of poems submitted. Payment: copies. Interested in new or unpub'd poets: yes. Simultaneous submissions accepted: yes. Recent contributors: Sparrow, Bill Shields, Richard Peabody. Submission quantity: 5 or less.

UNWOUND, Lindsay Wilson, PO Box 835, Laramie, WY 82073, Website www.fyuocuk.com/unwound.htm. Lindsay Wilson. 1998. "No SASE, no chance!" circ. 200. 2/yr. Pub'd 120 poems 1999. sub. price: $5; sample: $3. 44pp; 8½×7½ (legal folded in half); Rights purchased: none. Publishes 10% of poems submitted. Deadlines: none, nothing read March or September. Reporting time: 3 weeks-3 months. Payment: copies. Interested in new or unpub'd poets: yes. Simultaneous submissions accepted: no. Recent contributors: Leonard J. Cirino, John Sweet, Gerald Locklin, Dan Crocker, John Grey. Submission quantity: 3-6. Special interests: I am primarily concerned with poetry that is honest, identifiable and imagistically concerned. If I had to be there to understand it, don't send it.

URBAN GRAFFITI, Greensleeve Editions, PO Box 41164, Edmonton, AB T6J 6M7, Canada. 1993. circ. 250. 2/yr. sub. price: $10; sample: $4. 24pp; 7×11.

Urban Legend Press (see also THE URBANITE), PO Box 4737, Davenport, IA 52808. Mark McLaughlin, Editor. 1991. "Single-author collections" avg. press run 150-1M. Pub'd 1 poetry title 1999; expects 2 poetry titles 2000, 2 poetry titles 2001. 8½×11; avg. price, paper: $5; other: $2 chapbook. 32pp; Publishes less than 5% of poetry manuscripts submitted. Reporting time: 2-3 months. Payment: negotiable. Interested in new or unpub'd poets: no. Simultaneous submissions accepted: no. Recently published poets: Marni Griffin, Pamela Briggs, Rain Graves, Michael McCarty. Submission quantity: 3-5. Special interests: Special interests: surrealism in poetry, long poems, some experimental.

THE URBANITE, Urban Legend Press, PO Box 4737, Davenport, IA 52808. Mark McLaughlin, Editor. 1991. "Query first with SASE to receive guidelines" circ. 750-1M. 3/yr. Pub'd 10 poems 1999; expects 15 poems 2000, 15 poems 2001. sub. price: $13.50/3 issues; sample: $5. 60-92pp; 8½×11; Rights purchased: FNASR & non-exclusive rights for public readings. Publishes less than 5% of poems submitted. Deadlines: constantly reading. Reporting time: 2-3 months at most. Payment: $10 per poem. Interested in new or unpub'd poets: no. Simultaneous submissions accepted: no. Recent contributors: Marni Griffin, Pamela Briggs, Rain Graves, Michael McCarty. Submission quantity: 3-5. Special interests: Surrealism, long poems, some experimental.

URBANUS/RAIZIRR, PO Box 192921, San Francisco, CA 94119-2921. Peter Drizhal. 1987. "Unless you know your market, read an issue. Unfortunately, much of the poetry we receive seems like a shot in the dark—thematically and stylistically off base." circ. 1M. 2/yr. Pub'd 20 poems 1999; expects 30 poems 2000,

30 poems 2001. sub. price: $12/3 issues, $15/3 issues institutions; sample: $5 (postpaid). 64pp; 5½×8½; Rights purchased: 1st NAS. Publishes 1% or less of poems submitted. Deadlines: Our reading periods vary-please write for guidelines befor submitting. Reporting time: 4-12 weeks. Payment: $10/poem + 5 copies. Interested in new or unpub'd poets: yes. Simultaneous submissions accepted: no. Recent contributors: Chris Gilbert, Heather McHugh, Yusef Komunyakaa, Mark Jarman, Isabel Nathaniel. Submission quantity: 3-5. Special interests: We prefer modernist and post-modernist poetry; no longpoems.

Urthona Press, 62 LakeShore Drive, Asheville, NC 28804-2436. David Hopes, Lily Butch. 1995. avg. press run 750-1M. Pub'd 1 poetry title 1999. avg. price, cloth: $20; paper: $12. Pages vary; Publishes 10% of poetry manuscripts submitted. Reporting time: 2-3 months. Interested in new or unpub'd poets: yes. Simultaneous submissions accepted: yes. Recently published poets: Ann Dunn, David Hopes, Mary Parker. Submission quantity: 60 pages.

US1 Poets' Cooperative (see also US1 WORKSHEETS), PO Box 127, Kingston, NJ 08528-0127, 609-921-1489; fax 609-279-1513. 1973. "Fiction limited to 2500 words-double spaced; poetry, 5 limit, keep copy. Reading in Spring. Send SASE/card for notice." avg. press run 500. Pub'd 1 poetry title 1999. 5½×8½; avg. price, paper: $7; other: backissues: $4. 70pp; Publishes 10% of poetry manuscripts submitted. Reporting time: varies, 1 week if not reading. Send SASE/postcard. Payment: 1 copy. Interested in new or unpub'd poets: yes. Simultaneous submissions accepted: no. Recently published poets: Alicia Ostriker, David Keller, James Richardson, Frederick Tibbetts, Lois M. Harrod. Submission quantity: 5. Special interests: No light verse; some translations with poem in original.

US1 WORKSHEETS, US1 Poets' Cooperative, PO Box 127, Kingston, NJ 08528-0127, 609-921-1489; fax 609-279-1513. Address poetry submissions to: PO Box 127, Kingston, NJ 08528-0127. 1973. "Fiction, double-spaced; poetry, 5 limit, single or double-spaced, copy of each poem. Usually read early each year, but send a SAS-postcard and we will notify you of reading periods." circ. 500. 1/yr. Pub'd 35 poems 1999; expects 40-45-40-45 poems 2000. sub. price: $10 (2 double issues); sample: $5; (old format) $4). 70pp; 5½×8½; Rights purchased: all rights copyrighted for authors. Publishes 10% of poems submitted. Deadlines: irregular, best to query first. Reporting time: 1 week if not reading; 2-3 months, if reading. Payment: 1 copy. Interested in new or unpub'd poets: yes. Simultaneous submissions accepted: no. Recent contributors: Alicia Ostriker, David Keller, Lois M. Harrod, James Richardson, Frederick Tibbetts. Submission quantity: 5. Special interests: Not interested in light verse; we like complex poetry. Some poetry translations (limited); include poem in original language.

Utah State University Press, 871 East 900 North, Logan, UT 84322-7800, 801-797-1362; 800-239-9974; Fax 801-797-0313.

V

VACUITY, 1512 Canyon Run Road, Naperville, IL 60565. 1994. circ. 500. Erratic. 25-30pp; 8½×10.

Vanessapress, PO Box 82761, Fairbanks, AK 99708, 907-488-5079; jrb@mosquitonet.com. 1984. avg. press run 300. 6×9; avg. price, paper: $9.95. Less than 100pp; Publishes a variable % of poetry manuscripts submitted. Reporting time: 3 months. Payment: arranged. Interested in new or unpub'd poets: Only Alaskan women poets. Simultaneous submissions accepted: no. Recently published poets: Sheila Nickerson, Robin Hodson. Submission quantity: 10-15.

Vehicule Press, PO Box 125, Place du Parc Station, Montreal, Quebec H2W 2M9, Canada, 514-844-6073, FAX 514-844-7543, vpress@com.org. Michael Harris. 1973. "We publish *Canadian poets only*. We publish first books as well as books by established poets. Most titles published as a 'Signal Edition', an imprint of Vehicule Press edited by Michael Harris." avg. press run 500-1M. Pub'd 4 poetry titles 1999; expects 4 poetry titles 2000, 4 poetry titles 2001. 6×9; avg. price, paper: $9.95-$12.95. 64-136pp; Publishes 10% of poetry manuscripts submitted. Reporting time: 8 weeks. Payment: royalty in books or 10% of retail price. Interested in new or unpub'd poets: yes. Simultaneous submissions accepted: no. Recently published poets: Louise Fabiani, Stephanie Bolster, Terence Young, Peter Richardson, Bruce Taylor. Submission quantity: 65-75 poems, to allow for editing. Special interests: Canadian poetry.

Veracity Press, 3765 Motor, Box 702, Los Angeles, CA 90034, 310-820-8269; Veracity96@aol.com. 1995. 5½×8½.

VERANDAH, Faculty of Arts, Deakin University, 221 Burwood Highway, Burwood, Victoria 3125, Australia, 03-9244-6742. 1986. circ. 1M. 1/yr. sub. price: $10 (Aus). 96pp.

VERSE, Department of English, University of Georgia, Athens, GA 30602. Andrew Zawacki, Brian Henry. 1984. circ. 1M. 3/yr. Pub'd 120 poems 1999; expects 120 poems 2000, 150 poems 2001. sub. price: $18 individual, $30 institution; sample: $6. 128-256pp; 6×9; Rights purchased: copyright stays with author. Publishes 1% of poems submitted. Deadlines: none. Reporting time: 3-6 months. Payment: 2 copies + 1-year subscription. Interested in new or unpub'd poets: yes. Simultaneous submissions accepted: yes. Recent contributors: John Ashbery, James Tate, Tomaz Salamun, Heather McHugh, Lisa Jarnot. Submission quantity: 5 maximum. Special interests: We always look for good translations of contemporary poets.

VERVE, PO Box 630305, Simi Valley, CA 93063-0305. Marilyn Hochheiser, Editor; Virginia Anderson, Associate Editor; Ron Reichick, Editor & Publisher. 1989. "Open to any style poetry-high literacy, free verse, traditional. Subject must fit theme. Two-page limit, 36 or less lines has best chance for acceptance. Contests two times a year, deadlines April 1, Oct 1; cash prizes and publication awarded." circ. 700. 2/yr. Pub'd 60 poems 1999; expects 60 poems 2000, 60 poems 2001. sub. price: $12/4 issues; sample: $3.50. 40pp; 5½×8½; Rights purchased: first. Publishes 3% of poems submitted. Deadlines: March 1, August 1. Reporting time: 4-6 weeks after deadline. Payment: copy. Interested in new or unpub'd poets: yes. Simultaneous submissions accepted: no. Recent contributors: Marge Piercy, Denise Levertov, Quincy Troupe, Philip Levine, Carol Muske. Submission quantity: 5 max.

Vesta Publications Limited (see also WRITER'S LIFELINE), PO Box 1641, Cornwall, Ont. K6H 5V6, Canada, 613-932-2135, FAX 613-932-7735. Stephen Gill. 1974. "We ask the author to pay only for our printing for the first collection." avg. press run 1M. Pub'd 2 poetry titles 1999; expects 2 poetry titles 2000, 4 poetry titles 2001. 5×8; avg. price, cloth: $25; paper: $9.50. 75pp; Reporting time: 4 weeks. Payment: 10%. Interested in new or unpub'd poets: yes. Simultaneous submissions accepted: yes. Recently published poets: Richard Crum, Stephen Gill, Bluebell Phillips, Minette Crow, Asoka Weerasinghe. Submission quantity: 50-70. Special interests: We like to receive any poetry that is good.

Via God Publishing, PO BOx 996, Beverly Hills, CA 90213, 310-390-0843. 1989. 5⅜×8⅜. Interested in new or unpub'd poets: no.

VIGIL, 12 Priory Mead, Bruton, Somerset BA10 0DZ, United Kingdom, Bruton 813349. John Howard-Greaves. 1986. circ. 200. 2/yr. Expects 35 poems 2000. sub. price: £8, $10; sample: £3. 44pp; size A5; Publishes 20% of poems submitted. Deadlines: Prospective contributors should try samples of their work or inquire about forthcoming publication dates. Reporting time: 8 weeks. Payment: copies. Interested in new or unpub'd poets: yes. Simultaneous submissions accepted: no. Recent contributors: Teresinka Pereira, Nancy Ellis Taylor, Patricia Hannah, Richard Schmonsees, Sheila Jacob. Submission quantity: up to 6.

THE VINCENT BROTHERS REVIEW, 4566 Northern Circle, Riverside, OH 45424-5733. Kimberly Willardson, Editor; Michelle Whitley Turner, Associate Editor. 1988. "Read the magazine. Send SASE for guidelines, deadlines, details, etc. We do publish theme issues, send SASE for upcoming issues information" circ. 350. 3/yr. Pub'd 9 poems 1999; expects 60 poems 2000, 60 poems 2001. sub. price: $12; sample: $6.50. 96pp; 5×8; Rights purchased: one-time only. Publishes 5% of poems submitted. Deadlines: vary—send SASE for details. Reporting time: 2-3 months. Payment: 2 copies of magazine; $5 per poem used on 'Page Left' (back page). Interested in new or unpub'd poets: yes, if poems are of professional quality. Simultaneous submissions accepted: no! not for poetry. Recent contributors: Todd Fry, Kerri Brostrom, Marc Awodey, Robert Miltner, Paul Humphrey. Submission quantity: 6. Special interests: We prefer shorter forms. We've recently added a 'Page Left' (Back Page) feature to the magazine and we're seeking concrete poems, experimental poems, word plays, etc., for that feature. Make sure you're familiar with the 'Page Left' format before submitting.

Vincent Laspina (see also BATH AVENUE NEWSLETTER (BATH)), 1980 65th Street #3D, Brooklyn, NY 11204, 718-331-5960; Fax 718-331-4997; Laspina@msn.con, VLaspina@wow.con. 1986.

VINTAGE NORTHWEST, PO Box 193, Bothell, WA 98041, 206-821-2411. Volunteer Editorial Board. 1980. "We are a volunteer committee publishing the *Vintage Northwest* for the unpublished senior author. Submissions are welcome from anyone over 50 years of age. Limit per poem is 32 lines. They should be typed (if possible), double-spaced, with pages numbered. Your name and address should appear on each page and please include a self-addressed, stamped envelope. Include a $2 reading fee for each submission." circ. 1.5M. 2/yr. Expects 20 poems 2000. sub. price: we are unable to take subscriptions as we are only volunteers. We do have a mailing list if people desire to be on it. Mailed copies are $3.25 (includes postage); sample: $3.25 (includes postage). 72-80pp; 7×8½; Rights purchased: none. Publishes 25% of poems submitted. Deadlines: approx. January 1 and July 1. Reporting time: varies, up to 3 months. Payment: in copy for accepted poems. Interested in new or unpub'd poets: yes, both. Simultaneous submissions accepted: yes—two. Recent contributors: Jean Immerwahr, Ellen S. Rogers, Muriel Kovinow, Glen McKinney, George Behrend. Submission quantity: no more than 2 (reading fee of $2 per poem submitted). Special interests: We like light verse, satire, humorous, reminiscing, etc. We do not have room for long poetry. We do not accept purely religious or political poetry, travel is good, inspirational.

221

VIRGIN MEAT E-ZINE, 2325 West Avenue K-15, Lancaster, CA 93536, E-mail virginmeat@aol.com; www.members.aol.com/virginmeat/magazine/gothic.html. Steve Blum. 1986. "Sample copies are recommended. Not reading anything by anybody who has not e-mailed for recent guidelines" circ. 5M. 3/yr. sample price: $5. One 3.5 floppy disk; Publishes 5% of poems submitted. Reporting time: 6 months for poetry. Payment: 1 copy for each poem submitted. Interested in new or unpub'd poets: yes. Simultaneous submissions accepted: yes. Submission quantity: 3-8. Special interests: Poetry: free verse, dark and depressing. "Cryptic". No references to every day objects or things.

VIRGINIA LITERARY REVIEW, Box 413 Newcomb Hall Station, Charlottesville, VA 22904, Email dpk2c@virginia.edu. Anita Fee. 1979. "Experimental work as well as fresh approaches to more traditional forms" circ. 3M. 2/yr. Pub'd 300 poems 1999; expects 300 poems 2000, 300 poems 2001. sub. price: $12; sample: $2. 36pp; 6½×10½; Rights purchased: rights revert to the artists after first serial publication. Publishes 5-8% of poems submitted. Deadlines: Nov. 1, March 1. Reporting time: 2-3 months. Payment: 3 copies. Interested in new or unpub'd poets: yes. Simultaneous submissions accepted: no. Recent contributors: Simon Perchik, Errol Miller, M. Hoffman, Shelley Girdner, Robert Grey. Submission quantity: 3-5. Special interests: No melodramatic/sentimental verse.

THE VIRGINIA QUARTERLY REVIEW, One West Range, PO Box 400223, Charlottesville, VA 22904-4223, 804-924-3124. Gregory Orr. 1925. circ. 4.5M. 4/yr. Pub'd 60 poems 1999; expects 60 poems 2000, 60 poems 2001. sub. price: $18 individual, $22 institution; sample: $5. 224pp; 5½×8; Rights purchased: all. Publishes 5% of poems submitted. Deadlines: 3 months in advance. Reporting time: 6 months. Payment: $1 per line. Interested in new or unpub'd poets: yes. Simultaneous submissions accepted: no. Recent contributors: Dave Smith, Kathleen Norris, Charles Simic, Rita Dove, Mary Oliver. Submission quantity: 5 only.

VIRTUTE ET MORTE MAGAZINE, PO Box 63113, Philadelphia, PA 19114-0813, 215-671-6419 pager, 215-338-8234. Lynnea Ranalli, General Editor. 1992. "Keep under one page please. Select ones not printed elsewhere" circ. 250-500. 1/yr. Pub'd 20 poems 1999; expects 50 poems 2000, 50-100 poems 2001. sub. price: $16 4 issues; sample: $5. 100pp; 8½×11; Rights purchased: none. Publishes 99% of poems submitted. Deadlines: none. Reporting time: 1 week with SASE, 1 month without. Payment: discount subscription, pull-out sheet of page poem is on. Interested in new or unpub'd poets: yes. Simultaneous submissions accepted: yes. Recent contributors: Cheryl Townsend, Denise Riccardo, Alane Salvatore, Christopher Lane, Darren Bently. Submission quantity: 2. Special interests: Those written in Latin are a plus, (hence, to go with the title).

VISIONS-INTERNATIONAL, The World Journal of Illustrated Poetry, Black Buzzard Press, 1007 Ficklen Road, Fredericksburg, VA 22405. Bradley R. Strahan, Editor; Shirley G. Sullivan, Associate Editor. 1979. "We do special issues at least once a year and announce them in *SPR* and *Poets & Writers* and anywhere else that will print notices. If you want to know what our plans for specials are, query us with *SASE*. All submissions must have adequate postage and include SASE. All poems must be typed (readable copies are fine). Prefer poems under 60 lines. If you don't want us to give editing suggestions on your poems, tell us. (If we do it's a compliment!)" circ. 750. 3/yr. Pub'd 150 poems 1999; expects 150 poems 2000, 150 poems 2001. sub. price: $15/1 yr, $28/2 yrs., special rate for libraries only—3 yrs. $45; sample: $4.50 plus same postage as single copy. 48pp; 5½×8½; Rights purchased: first only, reverts to author upon publication. Publishes 1% of poems submitted. Deadlines: applicable only to special issues (query w/SASE). Reporting time: 3 days-3 weeks, unless we're out of the country. Payment: 1 copy + *only when we get a grant* $5-10 per poem. Interested in new or unpub'd poets: yes. Simultaneous submissions accepted: no. Recent contributors: Marilyn Hacker, Naomi Shihab Nye, Sharon Olds, Ai, Lawrence Ferlinghetti. Submission quantity: 3-6. Special interests: We strongly suggest getting a sample copy before sending us material (reading the magazine is worth a thousand words of explanation). Sample is only $4.50 (if you want current issue send $5.50). We're looking for poems that are well crafted but that live and breathe, poems that reach into us, poems that say things in a new and exciting way but are not stagey or selfconscious. We often publish translations, but want to see original language version with translation. We enjoy skillfully done humor but not "light verse". What we don't want to see is: dry academic exercises (emotionless word games),"concrete" poetry, very experimental stuff, collections of words and/or letters arranged (usually strangely) on paper and called "poetry", purely regional stuff, "God is in his heaven and all's right with the world" poems, children's poetry (however we are quite open to work written by young people), soppy sentimental verse. Don't send us anything sexist or racist—we'll burn it. No superpatriotism or "this is why I hate America" stuff either. No previously published work (except in very special cases—query first).

Vista Publishing, Inc., 422 Morris Avenue, Suite 1, Long Branch, NJ 07740, 732-229-6500, Fax 732-229-9647, czagury@vistapubl.com. 1991. avg. press run 1M. Pub'd 2 poetry titles 1999; expects 3 poetry titles 2000, 2 poetry titles 2001. 6×9; avg. price, paper: $12.95. 120pp; Reporting time: 8 weeks. Payment: varies based on project. Interested in new or unpub'd poets: yes. Simultaneous submissions accepted: yes. Submission quantity: 50. Special interests: Vista Publishing specializes in the works of nurse authors.

Voices From My Retreat, Box 1077, S. Fallsburg, NY 12779, 914-436-7455; 1-800-484-1255 ex. 2485.

Marian Butler. 1996. avg. press run 500. Pub'd 25 poetry titles 1999. 4×5; avg. price, paper: $7. 50pp; Publishes 10% of poetry manuscripts submitted. Reporting time: 2 months. Payment: copies. Interested in new or unpub'd poets: yes. Submission quantity: up to 3.

VOICES - ISRAEL, c/o Mark Levinson, PO Box 5780, Herzliya 46157, Israel, 09-9552411. Mark Levinson, Editor; Gretti Izak, Associate Editor; Luiza Carol, Associate Editor. 1972. *"Voices Israel* is the only magazine in Israel devoted entirely to poetry in English. It calls for the submission of intelligible and feeling poetry connected with the potentialities of the human spirit, and the dangers confronting it. It also seeks the peace of all mankind. Copyright to all poems in vested in the poets themselves; the only request of the Editorial Board are that if a poem is first printed in *Voices Israel,* that fact should be made known in any subsequent publications of it. No more than 4 poems to be submitted to each issue (one a year), preferably under 40 lines each, in 7 copies." circ. 350. 1/yr. Pub'd 126 poems 1999; expects 90 poems 2000, 100 poems 2001. sub. price: $15 postpaid; sample: $10 postpaid. 125pp; 6½×9¼; Rights purchased: copyright is vested in poet; we request first publication rights. Deadlines: March 1 each year. Reporting time: we report by end of December each year. Payment: none. Interested in new or unpub'd poets: yes. Simultaneous submissions accepted: no. Recent contributors: Blaga Dimitrova, Roger White, Alan Sillitoe, Eugene Dubnow, Gad Yaacobi. Submission quantity: no more than 4. Special interests: Poetry in general. Religion especially Jewish. Peace in general. Translations accepted, but must be by permission accompanied by original language poem. Light verse and satire accepted. All forms of poetry accepted, sonnets, haikus, etc. No long poems, under 40 lines preferred.

●**VOID,** PO Box 21, Milford, ME 04401-0021, Fax 207-945-0760, poet@angryrodent.com. Paul Bosse, Editor; George Bragdon, Editor; D.W. Brainerd, Editor; Corey Paradise, Editor. 1999. "Enclose SASE" circ. 200-300. 4/yr. Pub'd 12 poems 1999; expects 9 poems 2000, 32 poems 2001. sub. price: $8; sample: $1.50. 42pp; 5½×8½; Rights purchased: First. Publishes 25% of poems submitted. Deadlines: any time. Reporting time: 1-6 weeks. Payment: copies. Interested in new or unpub'd poets: yes. Simultaneous submissions accepted: no. Recent contributors: Larrilee, Katrina Spofford, Jerusha Blue. Submission quantity: no limit. Special interests: Poetry of 50 lines or less, preferably shorter. Counter-culture outlook, 21st century reverberations of Imagists and Beats. Send recorded spoken word, too, any format. Limited # cassettes or ads of music and spoken word produced with each issue.

VOLITION, PO Box 314, Tenants Harbor, ME 04860. Bonnie Lateiner. 1982. "Please inquire with editor before sending work as submission. Publication dates are erratic with a current long pause due to restructuring and relocation." circ. 400. 1/yr. Pub'd 5 poems 1999. sub. price: $12; sample: $4. 50pp; 7×8; Publishes 10% of poems submitted. Deadlines: ongoing as issues come out. Reporting time: 1 month. Payment: 3 copies of issue they contribute to. Interested in new or unpub'd poets: no. Simultaneous submissions accepted: no. Recent contributors: Beverly Dahlen, Rick London, Tom Clark, Anita Valerio, Lee Harwood, Tama Janowitz. Submission quantity: 3-5 pages.

THE VORTEX, 30-32 Macaw Avenue, PO Box 279, Belmopan, Belize, 501-8-23284. David Gorham. 1981. circ. 2.33M. 13/yr. sub. price: $15, $25/2 years; sample: $2. 12pp; 8½×11; Rights purchased: all. Reporting time: 2 months. Payment: subscription for a year, and 5 copies with poetry. Interested in new or unpub'd poets: yes. Simultaneous submissions accepted: yes. Submission quantity: 5 or less.

W

W.W. Norton, 500 Fifth Avenue, New York, NY 10110, 212-354-5500. Jill Bialosky, Editor. 1923. "If you would like us to consider your work, please submit 15 poems along with the following information: title, publisher and year of all previous book publications, if any; list of both commercial and non-commercial magazines in which your poems have appeared, specifying those poems which may be included in your manuscript; list of major poetry readings you have given and when and where they took place; list of grants and/or awards you have received. Although previous book publication is not required, work will not be considered unless the poet has been already published in quality literary magazines. Please be forewarned that no poems or manuscripts will be returned unless accompanied by a SASE." avg. press run 3M. Pub'd 6 poetry titles 1999; expects 6 poetry titles 2000, 6 poetry titles 2001. avg. price, cloth: $21; paper: $11. 64pp; Publishes 1% of poetry manuscripts submitted. Reporting time: 16 weeks. Payment: advances based on projected sales, 10% royalty based on publisher's catalog retail price (hardcover); 6% on paperback. Interested in new or unpub'd poets: yes, but must have published poems in quality literary magazines. Simultaneous submissions accepted: yes. Recently published poets: Ellen Bryant Voigt, Adrienne Rich, Joy Harjo, Sandra M. Gilbert, Alice Fulton. Submission quantity: 15 poems. Special interests: No light verse, no inspirational verse.

W.W. Publications (see also MINAS TIRITH EVENING-STAR), PO Box 373, Highland, MI 48357-0373, 813-585-0985 phone/Fax. Philip Helms. 1967. "J.R.R. Tolkien or middle-earth or fantasy, please." avg. press run 350+. Pub'd 160+ poetry titles 1999. 8½×11; avg. price, paper: $2-$6. 2pp; Publishes 65%-80% of poetry manuscripts submitted. Reporting time: 1 month, SASE please. Payment: free issues. Interested in new or unpub'd poets: yes. Simultaneous submissions accepted: yes. Recently published poets: Thomas M. Egan, Anne Etkin, Nancy C. Pope, Lee Garig, Marthe Benedict. Submission quantity: no more than 5. Special interests: Fantasy, Tolkien, middle-earth.

Warthog Press, 29 South Valley Road, West Orange, NJ 07052, 201-731-9269. Patricia Fillingham. 1979. "Not interested in poetry I can't understand." avg. press run 1M. Pub'd 2-3 poetry titles 1999. 5½×8½; avg. price, paper: $10. 64pp; Reporting time: 10 days to 1 month. Payment: copies. Interested in new or unpub'd poets: yes. Simultaneous submissions accepted: yes. Submission quantity: 5. Special interests: Any kind of poetry, rarely rhyming, that illuminates the world.

WASCANA REVIEW OF CONTEMPORARY POETRY AND SHORT FICTION, Department of English, University of Regina, Regina, Sask S4S 0A2, Canada, 584-4302. Kathleen Wall, Editor; Troni Grande, Poetry Editor. 1966. circ. 300-500. 2/yr. Pub'd 41 poems 1999; expects 45 poems 2000, 45 poems 2001. sub. price: $12 ($10 Canadian); sample: $5. 90pp; 9×5½; Rights purchased: first serial. Publishes 10% of poems submitted. Reporting time: 2-3 months. Payment: $10 per page. Interested in new or unpub'd poets: most certainly. Simultaneous submissions accepted: no. Recent contributors: Beth Goobie, Susanna Roxman, Robert Cooperman, Lea Littlewolfe, Gary Hyland. Submission quantity: 2-5.

WASHINGTON REVIEW, PO Box 50132, Washington, DC 20091-0132, 202-638-0515. Heather Fuller, Literary Editor; Ross Taylor, Associate Literary Editor. 1975. circ. 10M. 6/yr. Pub'd 10 poems 1999; expects 10 poems 2000, 10 poems 2001. sub. price: $12/yr, $20/2 years; sample: $2.50. 32pp; 11¼×16; Rights purchased: none. Publishes 2% of poems submitted. Deadlines: anytime. Reporting time: 2-3 months. Payment: 5 copies. Interested in new or unpub'd poets: yes. Simultaneous submissions accepted: no. Recent contributors: Ray DiPalma, Rod Smith, Lisa Jarnot, Melanie Neilson, Anselm Berrigan. Submission quantity: 5-10. Special interests: Our interests are eclectic, but favor experimental poetry and poetry by D.C. area poets.

Washington Writers' Publishing House, PO Box 15271, Washington, DC 20003, 202-543-1905, 703-527-5890. 1975. "We have an annual competition, limited to people who live and/or work in the Greater Washington area including Baltimore. Each accepted author is expected to become a working member of the cooperative press. Our annual competition is announced in the spring. (Reading period: June 1 to September 30.) Send SASE for guidelines." avg. press run 750. Pub'd 2 poetry titles 1999; expects 2 poetry titles 2000, 2 poetry titles 2001. 5½×8½; avg. price, paper: $10. 64-72pp; Publishes 3% of poetry manuscripts submitted. Reporting time: 2 months. Payment: 50 copies. Interested in new or unpub'd poets: yes, D.C. and Baltimore area poets only. Simultaneous submissions accepted: yes. Recently published poets: Naomi Thiers, Joseph Thackery, Patricia Garfinkel, Ned Balbo, Dan Johnson. Submission quantity: 50 pages of poetry; 3 copies of ms. Special interests: Each volume differs.

Water Mark Press, 138 Duane Street, New York, NY 10013, 212-285-1609. Coco Gordon. 1978. "Am discontinuing award format—will publish only writers whose work is exceptional and meaningful to me as an intermedia and visual artist, such as projected book of Ray Johnson's work." avg. press run 50-600. Expects 1 poetry title 2000, 1 poetry title 2001. size varies; avg. price, cloth: $40; paper: $20; other: $100-$3,000 deluxe editions. 20-96pp; Publishes 0% of poetry manuscripts submitted. Payment: authors copies. Interested in new or unpub'd poets: not at this time. Simultaneous submissions accepted: no. Recently published poets: Carolyne Wright, Kirk Robertson, Ann Deagon, Myra Sklarew, Diane Furtney. Special interests: Only poets with well-developed senses—tend toward human expression in most experimental ways of thinking—original and moving regardless of style or presentation.

Water Row Press (see also WATER ROW REVIEW), PO Box 438, Sudbury, MA 01776. Cisco Harland, Jr. 1985. "Frequently accepting contributions from new poets for our anthologies and chapbooks. See one of our publications to get the idea. No SASE means no return of manuscripts." avg. press run 500. Pub'd 3 poetry titles 1999; expects 5 poetry titles 2000, 10 poetry titles 2001. avg. price, paper: $8.95. 75-100pp; Publishes 5% of poetry manuscripts submitted. Reporting time: 4-6 weeks. Payment: details on request. Interested in new or unpub'd poets: yes. Simultaneous submissions accepted: no. Submission quantity: 6-10.

WATER ROW REVIEW, Water Row Press, PO Box 438, Sudbury, MA 01776. 1986. circ. 2.5M. 4/yr. sub. price: $24; sample: $6. 100pp; 6×9.

WATERWAYS: Poetry in the Mainstream, Ten Penny Players, Inc., Bard Press, 393 St. Paul's Avenue, Staten Island, NY 10304-2127, 718-442-7429, www.tenpennyplayers.org. Barbara Fisher, Co-Editor; Richard Spiegel, Co-Editor. 1978. "Prefer a query with SASE first as we do theme issues and don't want people wasting their time sending material that's wrong for us. We prefer typed material, no dot matrix and no puff pieces about the poet. If it's right for us we'll publish, if not it doesn't matter who else likes the material. We read year round. We do writing workshops and poetry readings at libraries and contributors sometimes are asked to participate. We don't publish poems of an explicit sexual nature or dealing wih gratuitous violence to people or animals. Some of our contributors are children and while they deal very sensibly with these themes, we find them abhorrent and don't want such submissions. Issues are frequently published on our website." circ. 100-200. 11/yr. Pub'd 500 poems 1999; expects 500 poems 2000, 500 poems 2001. sub. price: $25; sample: $2.25. 40pp; 7×4¼; Rights purchased: one-time publication only. Publishes 60% of poems submitted. Deadlines: the first of each month for the following month's issue. Reporting time: under 1 month. Payment: contributor's copies. Interested in new or unpub'd poets: yes. Simultaneous submissions accepted: yes. Recent contributors: Arthur Knight, Kit Knight, Ida Fasel, Albert Huffstickler, Will Inman. Submission quantity: up to 10. Special interests: We are very much a 'regional' New York press and are always up for things about the New York experience - city or state. We rarely publish rhyme unless it's up to Christina Rossetti standard and few of us are this century. Haiku rarely makes it with us; most translations aren't as fine poetry as the original and we'd rather not use them.

WAY STATION MAGAZINE, 1319 South Logan-MLK, Lansing, MI 48910-1340. Randy Glumm, Managing Editor; Francisco Gonzalez, Spanish submissions. 1989. "$5 processing fee promptly returned if work is rejected or withdraw prior to setting for print" circ. 1M+. 4/yr. Pub'd 50 poems 1999; expects 100 poems 2000, 200 poems 2001. sub. price: $18 for 4 issues; sample: $6 mail-includes postage. 60pp; 7×8½; Rights purchased: 1st time only—revert to author upon publication. Publishes 30% of poems submitted. Deadlines: year 'round. Reporting time: 30-90 days or sooner. Payment: 2 copies but with plans to pay $ in future. Interested in new or unpub'd poets: yes. Simultaneous submissions accepted: yes, but submittor must be patient. Recent contributors: Etheridge Knight, Diane Wakoski, Stuart Dybek, Doug Lawder, Charles Bukowski. Submission quantity: 3-5, each should be no more than 1 page. Special interests: We use English predominantly but some Spanish with translations also. All languages w/translations welcome. Could really use some top-notch cartoons.

WEBER STUDIES: Voices and Viewpoints of the Contemporary West, Weber State University, 1214 University Circle, Ogden, UT 84408-1214, 801-626-6473 or 6657. Brad Roghaar, Associate Editor; Sherwin W. Howard, Editor. 1984. "Cannont publish previously published work. We seek poetry that informs the culture and/or environment of the contemporary Western United States." circ. 1M-1.2M. 3/yr. Pub'd 50 poems 1999; expects 40 poems 2000, 40 poems 2001. sub. price: $30 institutions, $20 individuals; sample: $8. 120pp; 7½×10; Rights purchased: US copyright and electronic publication. Publishes 15% of poems submitted. Deadlines: 6 months review process, publication within 12-15 months from date of acceptance. Reporting time: 12-15 months. Payment: $10-15 per page ($50 minimum). Interested in new or unpub'd poets: yes. Simultaneous submissions accepted: no. Recent contributors: David Lee, Katharine Coles, Lance Henson, Matzii Dineltsoi, William Kloefkorn. Submission quantity: 3-5.

WEIRD POETRY, American Living Press, PO Box 901, Allston, MA 02134, 617-522-6196. 1993. "Currently not accepting submissions." circ. 500. 1/yr. sample price: $5. 50+pp; 5½×8½.

●**WEIRD TALES, DNA Publications, Inc.,** 123 Crooked Lane, King of Prussia, PA 19406. 1923. circ. 9M. 4/yr. sub. price: $16; sample: $5.

WELLSPRING, 8260 W. River Road #315, Brooklyn Park, MN 55444-2266, 612-566-6663; fax 612-566-9754. 1989. circ. 300. 2/yr. sub. price: $10; sample: $6. 40pp; 8½×11.

The Wellsweep Press, 1 Grove End Ho., 150 Highgate Road, London HW5 1PD, England, (0171)267-3525, e-mail ws@shadoof.demon.co.uk. John Cayley. 1988. "Our specialization is Chinese poetry (of all ages) in translation, but we strongly prefer to produce books devoted to the work of a single Chinese author. Submissions outside these criteria are unlikely to be considered." avg. press run 500. Pub'd 3 poetry titles 1999; expects 2 poetry titles 2000, 2 poetry titles 2001. 13cm X 20cm; avg. price, paper: $12. 96pp; Publishes 5% of poetry manuscripts submitted. Reporting time: can be 2 months. Payment: up to 6% royalty. Interested in new or unpub'd poets: not unless related to Chinese poetry in translation. Simultaneous submissions accepted: no. Recently published poets: Arthur Cooper, Graham Hartill, Du Mu, Duoduo, Ruan Ji. Submission quantity: 15.

Wesleyan University Press, 110 Mount Vernon Street, Middletown, CT 06457, 203-344-7918. 1957. "New poets submissions are evaluated, whereas manuscripts by established authors (at least one published book) are first read by editors at the press and then sent to outside consultants. We accept and consider submissions year round. There is no submission fee, but we need two copies of the ms., copies of any reviews of previous books, and an SASE so that we can return the ms." avg. press run 500 cloth, 1M paper. Pub'd 6 poetry titles 1999; expects 6 poetry titles 2000, 6 poetry titles 2001. 6×9, 5½×8½; avg. price, cloth: $22.50; paper: $10.95. 64pp; Publishes 1% of poetry manuscripts submitted. Reporting time: 3-5 months. Payment: dependent on author—average 5-7% pa, 8-10% cl. Interested in new or unpub'd poets: yes. Recently published poets: Paul Zweig, Thulani Davis, Ernesto Cardenal, Yusef Komunyakaa, Garret Kaoru Hongo. Submission quantity: 60-65 pages. Special interests: We are interested in all kinds of poetry. Our past and future lists include James Dickey, Charles Wright, Brenda Marie Osbey, Olga Broumas, Susan Howe, Brenda Hillman, Joy Harjo, James Tate. We are also very interested in poetry-in-translation.

West Anglia Publications, PO Box 2683, La Jolla, CA 92038, 858-457-1399. Helynn Hoffa, Editor; Wilma Lusk, Publisher. Address poetry submissions to: PO Box 8638, La Jolla, CA 92038. 1978. ''Query with letter indicating your publishing record, your background as a poet/writer, any awards, etc. Send a sample of 6 of your best poems. Include SASE or work is not returned.'' avg. press run 500. Pub'd 4 poetry titles 1999; expects 4 poetry titles 2000, 4 poetry titles 2001. 5½x8½; avg. price, paper: $10. 100pp; Publishes 5% of poetry manuscripts submitted. Reporting time: 1 month. Payment: usually in books. Interested in new or unpub'd poets: yes, query first with 6 poems. Simultaneous submissions accepted: yes. Recently published poets: Kathleen Iddings, John Theobold, Gary Morgan, Robert Winteringer. Submission quantity: 6. Special interests: Am more interested in *good* poetry than the length of poems or certain subjects. Generally not interested in *all* end rhyme, metered poetry, unless it is exceptionally well done, & is contemporary language (not thee and thou).

WEST BRANCH, Bucknell Hall, Bucknell University, Lewisburg, PA 17837, 570-577-1853. Paula Closson Buck, Editor; Joshua Harmon, Editor; Andrew Ciotola, Managing Editor. 1977. ''Poems are read year 'round; prefer cleanly typed, non-xeroxed copies. Interested in free verse and especially formal poetry, both traditional and innovative'' circ. 1M. 2/yr. Pub'd 75 poems 1999; expects 75 poems 2000, 75 poems 2001. sub. price: $10; sample: $3. 118-140pp; 5½x8½; Rights purchased: 1st North American serial. Deadlines: none. Reporting time: 6-10 weeks. Payment: 3 copies. Interested in new or unpub'd poets: yes. Simultaneous submissions accepted: yes. Recent contributors: Barbara Crooker, Harry Humes, Deborah Burnham, Cory Brown, Julia Kasdorf. Submission quantity: 3-6.

WEST COAST LINE: A Journal of Contemporary Writing and Criticism, 2027 EAA, Simon Fraser University, Burnaby, B.C. V5A 1S6, Canada. Miriam Nichols, Editor; Roger Farr, Managing Editor. 1990. ''Send mss. to Managing Editor'' circ. 500. 3/yr. Pub'd 48 poems 1999; expects 50 poems 2000, 50 poems 2001. sub. price: $25 individuals, $40 libraries; sample: $10. 128-144pp; 7x8; Rights purchased: first time only. Publishes 20% of poems submitted. Reporting time: 3-4 months. Payment: $8-$10/page. Interested in new or unpub'd poets: sure, but please read the journal before submitting. Simultaneous submissions accepted: no. Recent contributors: Lisa Robertson, Rita Wong, Bruce Andrews, Erin Moure, Ashok Mathur. Submission quantity: 5-6. Special interests: Experimental, longpoems, poetics, translations.

West Coast Paradise Publishing (see also TEAK ROUNDUP), PO Box 2093, Sardis Sta. Main, Sardis, B.C. V2R 1A5, Canada, 604-824-9528, Fax 604-824-9541. Yvonne Anstey. 1993. avg. press run 100. Pub'd 10 poetry titles 1999. 5½x8½; avg. price, paper: $10.95. 100pp; Publishes 80% of poetry manuscripts submitted. Reporting time: 2 weeks. Interested in new or unpub'd poets: yes. Simultaneous submissions accepted: yes. Recently published poets: George Kuhn, Robert G. Anstey, Jean Cox. Submission quantity: 5.

West End Press, PO Box 27334, Albuquerque, NM 87125. John Crawford. 1976. ''Politically 'left' writings or progressive content; interest in multicultural writing. Majority of those published are women'' avg. press run 1.5M-2M. Pub'd 4 poetry titles 1999; expects 4 poetry titles 2000, 4 poetry titles 2001. 5½x8½, 6x9; avg. price, paper: $8.95-$10.95. 48-120pp; Publishes 1% of poetry manuscripts submitted. Reporting time: 3 months maximum. Payment: 10% of copies or 6% cash. Interested in new or unpub'd poets: yes. Simultaneous submissions accepted: no. Recently published poets: Russell Leong, Adrian C. Louis, Olga Cabral, Michelle T. Clinton, CarolAnn Russell. Submission quantity: send sample poem(s) and letter of inquiry. Special interests: Increasingly restricted to Southwest geographical area. Have done several Spanish and English texts. Increasing numbers of Native American titles.

WESTERN HUMANITIES REVIEW, University of Utah, Salt Lake City, UT 84112, 801-581-6070. Richard Howard, Poetry Editor. 1947. circ. 1.5M. 4/yr. Pub'd 17 poems 1999; expects 17 poems 2000, 17 poems 2001. sub. price: $26 (institutions) $20 (individuals); sample: $6. 96pp; 6x9; Rights purchased: 1st North American serial, but we release them to author at his/her request. Publishes .1% of poems submitted. Deadlines: none. Reporting time: 2-4 months. Payment: $50 per poem. Interested in new or unpub'd poets: yes. Simultaneous submissions accepted: yes. Recent contributors: Debora Greger, Allen Grossman, Rachel Hadas, Timothy Liu, Bin Ramke. Submission quantity: no limit. Special interests: We suggest that contributors look at an issue before submitting.

WESTERN SKIES, 577 Central Avenue, Box 4, Jefferson, LA 70121-1400, e-mail: horizons@altavista.net or blueskies@discoverymail.com; Websites www.freeyellow.com/members2/oldwest/index.htm/, www2.cyberci-ties.com/z/zines/. Sharida Rizzuto, Harold Tollison, Elaine Wolfe, Rose Dalton. 1992. ''We are interested in anything and everything about the Old West'' circ. 500-800. 2/yr. Pub'd 40-50 poems 1999. sub. price: $15.80; sample: $7.90. 100pp; 8½x11; Rights purchased: one-time rights, first serial rights, or second serial rights. Publishes 30-35% of poems submitted. Deadlines: always open to submissions. Reporting time: 2-6 weeks.

Payment: negotiable. Interested in new or unpub'd poets: yes. Recent contributors: Lyndia Glover, Josephine Imlay, Arthur Winfield Knight, Matthew R. Story, Olivia Diamond. Submission quantity: 1-5. Special interests: We are willing to look at any type of poetry, no length requirements.

●**WeWrite Corporation**, PO Box 498, Rochester, IL 62563, 217-498-8458, Fax 217-498-7524, dpalmer@wewrite.net, www.wewrite.net. 1993. 5¼×8.

WEYFARERS, Guildford Poets Press, 9 White Rose Lane, Woking, Surrey GU22 7JA, England. Jeffery Wheatley, Margaret Pain, Martin Jones. 1972. "Each poem, however short, should be on a separate sheet with name and address. Unpublished work only. If return is required, S.A.E. or sufficient I.R.C.'s must be enclosed. Publish all kinds of poetry, serious and humorous, free verse and rhymed/metred, but mostly 'mainstream' modern. Normal maximum is 40 lines. No way-out experimentation, graphics, or hard porn or long poems. We feature the Surrey Poetry Centre Open Competition annually." circ. 300. 3/yr. Pub'd 120 poems 1999; expects 120 poems 2000, 120 poems 2001. sub. price: £4.50 (overseas £5.50 sterling or cash, or $15 cheque); sample: £1.60 (overseas, £2 sterling or cash, or $5 cheque). 32pp; 8×6; Rights purchased: 1st British serial rights. Publishes 9% of poems submitted. Deadlines: End-January, end-May, end-September; best earlier. Reporting time: maximum 4 months. Payment: none, apart from 1 free copy of issue concerned. Interested in new or unpub'd poets: yes. Simultaneous submissions accepted: no. Recent contributors: Susan Skinner, David Schaal, Mario Petrucci, Michael Henry. Submission quantity: up to 6. Special interests: See above—satire or humorous verse acceptable. We advise seeing a copy of our mag before submitting.

Wheat Forders/Trabuco Books, Box 6317, Washington, DC 20015-0317, 202-362-1588. Renee K. Boyle, Editor; E.S. Lawrence, Assistant Editor. 1974. "Submit camera ready copy since we accept or reject totally. Prepare for a cooperative arrangement—in this you guarantee that 100 copies will be purchased at retail by friends or an organization. Details on request." avg. press run 500. Pub'd 1 poetry title 1999. 5½×8½; avg. price, cloth: $10; paper: $5. Up to 112pp; Publishes 11% of poetry manuscripts submitted. Reporting time: 4-6 weeks. Payment: 12% paid quarterly. Interested in new or unpub'd poets: yes. Simultaneous submissions accepted: yes. Recently published poets: Whiteford Vanderbilt, John E.W. Boyle. Submission quantity: at least 25, but depends on length. Special interests: Prefer poetry dealing with the new world outlook in these various scenes that are shaping the new paradigm. Writers should be familiar with psychophysics, Jungian psychology, metahistory, and shape ideas in those art images. Much as Lucretius did in: *On the Nature of Things*. Now you see why we publish so few works. See Whiteford Boyles *Graffiti on the Wall of Time* 1983 as an example of what we are after. If we get a certain foundation grant, we may be looking for a poet to put into poetry the results of research. We have no interest in the scatological junk jejeume love lyrics or pseudo modern obscurantism. To be published here you have not only to say something, you have to have as well as something to say. Much of modern poetry is sheer clap-trap, an ego trip.

WHETSTONE, Barrington Area Arts Council, PO Box 1266, Barrington, IL 60011, 847-382-5626. Sandra Berris, Marsha Portnoy, Jean Tolle. 1983. "Include SASE. We read year round, but best time is Jan.-June." circ. 800. 1/yr. Pub'd 12 poems 1999; expects 15 poems 2000, 15 poems 2001. sub. price: $8.50 ppd; sample: $5 ppd., includes guidelines. 120pp; 5⅞×9; Rights purchased: rights revert to author, 1st NA serial. Publishes under 5% of poems submitted. Deadlines: none. Reporting time: 3-5 months. Payment: variable money and eligible for *The Whetstone Prize*, annual cash awards, totaled $750 in 1999. Interested in new or unpub'd poets: yes. Simultaneous submissions accepted: yes, but please inform. Recent contributors: Helen Reed, John Dickson, Jon Tribble, Shulamith Wechter Caine, Ted May. Submission quantity: 3-5. Special interests: We look for stories and poems that reflect a wide range of human experience and a variety of literary styles.

White Buck Publishing, 5187 Colorado Avenue, Sheffield Village, OH 44054-2338, 440-934-4454 phone/fax. Rebekka K. Nielson, Associate Publisher. 1996. "All manuscripts should be neatly typed, double-spaced, with title, author, and page number. One poem per page. Manuscripts should be edited for spelling, grammar, and punctuation prior to submission." avg. press run 500-3M. Pub'd 1 poetry title 1999; expects 2 poetry titles 2000, 4 poetry titles 2001. 5½×8½; avg. price, cloth: $29.95; paper: $9.95. 125pp; Publishes 2-5% of poetry manuscripts submitted. Reporting time: 4-6 months. Payment: CASE by CASE basis dependent upon individual circumstance. Interested in new or unpub'd poets: yes. Simultaneous submissions accepted: yes. Recently published poets: Jerry D. Babb. Submission quantity: 40-50 per manuscript, 3-5 for evaluation. Special interests: Favor traditional verse, will not review esotorie, enigmatic submissions, al submissions must contain a Christian theme.

THE WHITE CROW, Osric Publishing, PO Box 4501, Ann Arbor, MI 48106. Christopher Herdt. 1994. "We prefer poetry that will interest and engage the average intelligent reader, not just other poets. Please, no previously published poems, only new work" circ. 200. 4/yr. Pub'd 60 poems 1999; expects 50 poems 2000, 50 poems 2001. sub. price: $6; sample: $2. 32pp; 5½×8; Publishes 10% of poems submitted. Reporting time: 4 months. Payment: contributor's copies. Interested in new or unpub'd poets: yes. Simultaneous submissions accepted: yes. Recent contributors: B. Chown, Eileen Bell, Delia DeSantis, Kenneth Pobo. Submission quantity: 1-5.

White Pine Press, PO Box 236, Buffalo, NY 14201-0236, 716-672-5743. Peter Blue Cloud Marjorie Agosin, Christopher Merrill. 1973. "We do not accept any unsolicited American Poetry except as entries in our annual competition. Write for guidelines. Authors should send a note of inquiry before submitting poetry in translation" avg. press run 750-1.2M. Pub'd 3 poetry titles 1999; expects 6 poetry titles 2000, 4 poetry titles 2001. 5½×8½; avg. price, cloth: $20; paper: $12. 80-120pp; Publishes 1-5% of poetry manuscripts submitted. Reporting time: 1-3 months. Payment: copies. Interested in new or unpub'd poets: no. Simultaneous submissions accepted: no. Recently published poets: Deborah Gorlin, Tomaz Salamun, Pablo Neruda, John F. Deane.

White Plume Press, 2442 NW Market Street #370, Seattle, WA 98107-4137, 206-764-1299, E-mail bd72@scn.org. Gene Nelson. 1988. "At this point I am not looking for unsolicited mss." avg. press run 200. Expects 1 poetry title 2000, 1 poetry title 2001. 6×9; avg. price, paper: $5.95. 64pp; Publishes 0% of poetry manuscripts submitted. Reporting time: 30 days with SASE. Payment: varies. Interested in new or unpub'd poets: no. Simultaneous submissions accepted: yes. Recently published poets: Kyle Kimberlin. Submission quantity: up to 5.

White Urp Press (see also ABBEY), 5360 Fallriver Row Court, Columbia, MD 21044. 8½×11.

Who Who Who Publishing (see also THE EVER DANCING MUSE), PO Box 7751, East Rutherford, NJ 07073. John Chorazy, Editor. 1993. "No rhyming poetry" Pub'd 2 poetry titles 1999; expects 2 poetry titles 2000, 2 poetry titles 2001. 8½×5½. 20pp; Reporting time: 1-4 weeks. Interested in new or unpub'd poets: yes. Simultaneous submissions accepted: yes, if specified. Recently published poets: Lyn Lifshin, Duane Locke, Mary Winters, Errol Miller, BZ Niditch. Submission quantity: 3-5.

WHOLE NOTES, Whole Notes Press, PO Box 1374, Las Cruces, NM 88004, 505-541-5744. Nancy Peters Hastings. 1984. "In even-numbered years *Whole Notes* features an issue of 'Writing by Young People'." circ. 400. 2/yr. Pub'd 40 poems 1999; expects 50 poems 2000, 45 poems 2001. sub. price: $6; sample: $3. 28pp; 5½×8½; Rights purchased: copyright as serial. Publishes 5% of poems submitted. Deadlines: ongoing. Reporting time: 2-3 weeks. Payment: 2 copies. Interested in new or unpub'd poets: yes. Simultaneous submissions accepted: no. Recent contributors: Don Welch, Carol Oles, Keith Wilson, Roy Scheele, Dan Stryk. Submission quantity: 2-5. Special interests: We welcome all forms and especially translations.

Whole Notes Press (see also WHOLE NOTES), PO Box 1374, Las Cruces, NM 88004, 505-382-7446. Nancy Peters Hastings. 1988. "Whole Notes Press features a poetry chapbook series." avg. press run 400. Pub'd 1 poetry title 1999; expects 1 poetry title 2000, 1 poetry title 2001. 5½×8½; avg. price, paper: $3; other: $3 chapbook. 20-24pp; Publishes 1% of poetry manuscripts submitted. Reporting time: 1 month. Payment: author will receive 25 copies of the chapbook. Interested in new or unpub'd poets: yes. Simultaneous submissions accepted: no. Recently published poets: Glenna Luschei, Keith Wilson, Roy Scheele, Robert Dorsett, Dan Stryk. Submission quantity: 3-8. Special interests: Poems dealing with the natural world are always welcome.

WHOLE TERRAIN - REFLECTIVE ENVIRONMENTAL PRACTICE, 40 Avon Street, Antioch New England, Keene, NH 03431-3516, 603-357-3122 ex. 272. 1992. "We seek poems that are reflective of the issue's theme" circ. 3M. 1/yr. Pub'd 5 poems 1999. sub. price: $7; sample: $5. 72pp; 7½×10½; Publishes 25% of poems submitted. Deadlines: February 15th of each year. Reporting time: 4-6 weeks. Payment: none. Interested in new or unpub'd poets: yes. Simultaneous submissions accepted: yes. Recent contributors: David Rothenberg, Thomas McGrath, Pattiann Rogers, Sandy Fink, Howard Nelson. Submission quantity: 1-5.

WICKED MYSTIC, 532 LaGuardia Place #371, New York, NY 10012, 718-638-1533. Andre Scheluchin. 1990. "Please type poetry. Include SASE, bio" circ. 10M. 4/yr. Pub'd 100 poems 1999; expects 100 poems 2000, 100 poems 2001. sub. price: $24; sample: $6 (mention Dustbooks $5). 80pp; 8½×11; Rights purchased: one-time. Publishes 5% of poems submitted. Deadlines: none. Reporting time: 2 weeks-2 months. Payment: $5 and 1 copy for each poem. Interested in new or unpub'd poets: yes. Simultaneous submissions accepted: no. Recent contributors: Michael Arnzen, John Grey, Scott C. Holstad, Gregory Nyman, Wayne Edwards. Submission quantity: up to 10. Special interests: Free verse.

WIDENER REVIEW, Humanities Division, Widener Univ., Chester, PA 19013, 610-499-4341. 1984. circ. 250. 1/yr. Pub'd 38 poems 1999. sub. price: $5; sample: $4. 100-120pp; 5½×8½; Rights purchased: first serial. Publishes 5% of poems submitted. Deadlines: August 15-February 15. Reporting time: 3 months. Payment: 1 copy. Interested in new or unpub'd poets: yes. Simultaneous submissions accepted: no. Recent contributors: Walter McDonald, Walter Griffin, Louis McKee, Mitchell LesCarbeau, Gary Fincke. Submission quantity: 3-5.

WILD DUCK REVIEW, PO BOX 388, Nevada City, CA 95959-0388, 530-478-0134, Fax 530-265-2304, casey@wildduckreview.com. Casey Walker. 1994. circ. 8M. 3/yr. sub. price: $24; sample: $4. 40pp; 11×14; Rights purchased: All rights revert. Payment: none. Recent contributors: Gary Snyder, George Keithley, Jim Harrison, Jim Dodge, Jerry Martien.

WILD EARTH, PO Box 455, Richmond, VT 05477, 802-434-4077, fax 802-434-5980, e-mail info@wild-earth.org. Gary Lawless, Poetry Editor; Sheila McGrory-Klyza. 1991. "Short poems are favored" circ. 9M. 4/yr. Pub'd 10 poems 1999; expects 10 poems 2000, 10 poems 2001. sub. price: $25; sample: $2. ~108pp; 8½×11; Publishes 1% of poems submitted. Deadlines: varies. Reporting time: varies. Payment: none. Interested in new or unpub'd poets: yes. Recent contributors: Gary Snyder, Gary Lawless, Grace Deen, Wendell Berry. Special interests: Wilderness, conservation, wild lands, biodiversity, wild life, nature.

WILLIAM AND MARY REVIEW, Campus Center, PO Box 8795, Williamsburg, VA 23187-8795, 757-221-3290, fax 757-221-3451. Editorships rotate yearly. 1962. "We do not read mss. between May and the end of August" circ. 5M. 1/yr. Pub'd 20 poems 1999; expects 15 poems 2000, 15-20 poems 2001. sub. price: $5.50; sample: $5.50. 115pp; 6×9; Rights purchased: all. Publishes 1% of poems submitted. Deadlines: January 15. Reporting time: 2-3 months. Payment: 5 copies. Interested in new or unpub'd poets: yes. Simultaneous submissions accepted: yes. Recent contributors: Amy Clampitt, Robert Bly, Jay Parini, Alberto Rios, Robert Hershon. Submission quantity: 5 max. Special interests: Translations, experimental poetry, regional poetry.

WILLOW SPRINGS, Eastern Washington Univ., MS-1, 526 5th Street, Cheney, WA 99004-2431, 509-623-4349. Christopher Howell, Editor. 1977. "We tend to publish poems with some essential vision, a sense of craft no matter the form, and a non-imitative voice. We prefer a voice fully engaged in the power of telling, and the power of the imagination." circ. 1,700. 2/yr. Pub'd 49 poems 1999; expects 55 poems 2000, 55 poems 2001. sub. price: $10.50; sample: $5.50. 128pp; 6×9; Rights purchased: none. Publishes 3-5% of poems submitted. Deadlines: we read September 15 - May 15. Reporting time: 2-3 months. Payment: contributor copies, year's subscription. Interested in new or unpub'd poets: yes. Simultaneous submissions accepted: no. Recent contributors: Laura Kasischke, Elizabeth Kirschner, D. Nurkse, Donald Revell, Bruce Weigl. Submission quantity: 3-9. Special interests: Translations, long poems, poetry reviews.

WIND, PO Box 24548, Lexington, KY 40524, 606-885-5342. Leatha F. Kendrick. 1971. "No taboos; poems well-written with something to say; follows no special schools or poetic form; no light verse, but acceptance depends on whether it's good. Annual chapbook competitions: write for details" circ. 425. 2/yr. Pub'd 100 poems 1999; expects 100 poems 2000, 100 poems 2001. sub. price: $10 individual, $12 institutional, $15 foreign; sample: $4.50. 100pp; 8½×5½; Rights purchased: first only (and anthology). Publishes 1% of poems submitted. Deadlines: continuous. Reporting time: 2-8 weeks. Payment: 1 contributor's copy. Interested in new or unpub'd poets: yes. Simultaneous submissions accepted: no. Recent contributors: Susan Terris, Kim Bridgford, Ron Houchin, Diane Lockward, David Citino. Submission quantity: 3-6. Special interests: Memorable, well-crafted poems; not heavy on experimental poetry, or light verse, or long poems for.

WINDHOVER: A Journal of Christian Literature, PO Box 8008, UMHB, Belton, TX 76513, 817-939-4564. Donna Walker-Nixon. 1995. circ. 500. 1/yr. Pub'd 70 poems 1999. sub. price: $8; sample: $5. 148pp; 6×9; Rights purchased: First North America. Publishes 10% of poems submitted. Reporting time: 3 months. Payment: 2 copies. Interested in new or unpub'd poets: yes. Simultaneous submissions accepted: yes. Recent contributors: Robert Fink, Walter McDonald, Kelly Cherry, Marjorie Maddox, David Brendan Hopes. Submission quantity: 4-5.

Windows Project (see also SMOKE), Liver House, 96 Bold Street, Liverpool L1 4HY, England. 1974. "No new ms." avg. press run 250. size A5; avg. price, paper: £1. 40pp; Interested in new or unpub'd poets: merseyside poets *only*. Simultaneous submissions accepted: no. Recently published poets: Matt Simpson, Peggy Poole, Kit Wright, Paul Evans.

●**Wind's Errand**, 6077 Far Hills Avenue #279, Dayton, OH 45459, windserrand@macconnect.com. Mary S. Clark. 1997. avg. press run 500. avg. price, cloth: $15; paper: $10.

Windsong Press, PO Box 644, Delta Jct., AK 99737, 907-895-4179. Sharon Haney. 1981. avg. press run 1M. Expects 1 poetry title 2000. 5½×8½, 8½×11; avg. price, paper: $7.95. 100pp; Reporting time: 2 months. Payment: none to date. Interested in new or unpub'd poets: not at this time. Simultaneous submissions accepted: no. Special interests: regional, feminist, narrative.

Windstorm Creative, 7419 Ebbert Drive SE, Port Orchard, WA 98367-9753, www.windstormcreative.com. Cris Newport. 1989. "Poetry collections should be those one might consider revolutionary or cutting edge. Read several of our titles before submitting. We are not accepting new work until Sept. 2000" avg. press run 5M. Pub'd 1 poetry title 1999; expects 1 poetry title 2000, 5 poetry titles 2001. 5½×8½; avg. price, paper: $9.95. 120pp; Publishes 5% of poetry manuscripts submitted. Reporting time: 3 months. Payment: 10-15%. Interested in new or unpub'd poets: yes. Simultaneous submissions accepted: yes. Recently published poets: Rudy Kikel, Leslea Newman, Jack Rickard, Michael Hattersley. Submission quantity: 100 minimum.

Wineberry Press, 3207 Macomb Street, NW, Washington, DC 20008-3327, 202-363-8036; e-mail chfarnsworth@compuserve.com. Elisavietta Ritchie, President. 1983. "We are a *very* small, no profit shoestring press with one anthology, 4 chapbooks, a dozen poems on postcards and one fiction collection so far. We expect to do more of both but mostly by poets in greater Washington area. So we can't handle outside solicitations or submissions. [Sorry to sound so negative!]" avg. press run 500. Pub'd 1 poetry title 1999; expects 1 poetry title 2000, 1 poetry title 2001. 5½×8½; avg. price, paper: $3-6. 24-144pp; Publishes a very small % of poetry manuscripts submitted. Reporting time: ASAP. Payment: copies (as many as they need). Interested in new or unpub'd poets: no—we have published new poets but can't handle any more submissions. Simultaneous submissions accepted: no. Recently published poets: Judith McCombs, Beatrice Murphy, Maxine Combs, Elizabeth Follin-James, Elisabeth Stevens. Submission quantity: None right now. Special interests: Experimental poetry, regional poetry, longpoems, short stories.

WISCONSIN ACADEMY REVIEW, 1922 University Ave., Madison, WI 53705, 608-263-1692. Faith B. Miracle, Editor. 1954. "Poets must live in or have lived in Wisconsin and show this on accompanying resume or cover letter." circ. 1.5M. 4/yr. Pub'd 28 poems 1999; expects 20-24 poems 2000. sub. price: $16; sample: $2. 48-52pp; 8½×11; Rights purchased: 1st. Publishes 12% of poems submitted. Deadlines: continuing. Reporting time: 8-10 weeks. Payment: 3 copies of issue. Interested in new or unpub'd poets: yes. Simultaneous submissions accepted: no. Recent contributors: Ron Wallace, Sara Rath, David Graham, Jean Feraca, Margaret Benbow. Submission quantity: 4-8.

Wisdom Publications, Inc., 199 Elm Street, Somerville, MA 02144-3129, 617-776-7416; Fax 617-776-7841. 1975. 6×9.

THE WISHING WELL, PO Box 178440, San Diego, CA 92177-8440, 619-270-2779. Laddie Hosler, Editor. 1974. "We publish only poetry written by our members, and we don't pay for it. We publish most of the poems that are submitted to us." circ. 3M. 6/yr. Pub'd 16 poems 1999; expects 20 poems 2000, 20 poems 2001. 5-7 mo. membership: $60; 3-5 mo $35; $120 U.S.; $150 foreign (except Canada/Mexico); photo published $10 extra (optional); sample price: $5. 40pp; 7×8½; Rights purchased: none. Publishes (if member) 95% of poems submitted. Deadlines: Mar. 1, July 1, Nov. 1. Payment: none. Interested in new or unpub'd poets: only if they're W.W. members. Simultaneous submissions accepted: yes, only if they're W.W. members. Submission quantity: unlimited, but 1-3 preferred. Special interests: Experimental poetry, longpoems, light verse, satire, lesbian. MUST be original.

WITNESS, Oakland Community College, 27055 Orchard Lake Road, Farmington Hills, MI 48334, 734-996-5732. Peter Stine, Editor. 1987. circ. 2.8M. 2/yr. Pub'd 20 poems 1999; expects 20 poems 2000, 20 poems 2001. sub. price: $15; sample: $9. 192pp; 6×9; Rights purchased: First North American Serial Rights. Publishes 5% of poems submitted. Reporting time: 3 months. Payment: $10 per page. Interested in new or unpub'd poets: yes. Simultaneous submissions accepted: yes. Recent contributors: Mary Oliver, Alicia Ostriker, Linda Pastan, Mark Doty, Jim Daniels. Submission quantity: 4 max.

Wolf Angel Press, 1011 Babcock Street, Neenah, WI 54956, 920-722-5826; e-mails flaherty@uwosh.edu, newpok32@uwosh.edu, stevens@tcccom.net; www.english.uwosh.edu/wolfangel/. Doug Flaherty, Editor. 1996. "Chapbooks only. Poetry collections should contain 4-5 published poems" avg. press run 500. Expects 1 poetry title 2000, 4 poetry titles 2001. 5½×8½; avg. price, paper: $5. 24-32pp; Publishes 5% of poetry manuscripts submitted. Reporting time: 1 month. Payment: author subsidized. Interested in new or unpub'd poets: yes. Simultaneous submissions accepted: yes. Recently published poets: Jim Last, Karla Huston. Submission quantity: 15-20.

Wolfsong Publications, 3123 South Kennedy, Sturtevant, WI 53177, Fax 262-886-5809, E-mail wolfsong@wi.net. Gary C. Busha, Publisher, Editor. 1974. "Wisconsin and surrounding state writers have priority" avg. press run 200. Pub'd 2 poetry titles 1999; expects 2 poetry titles 2000, 2 poetry titles 2001. 5½×8½; avg. price, paper: $5; other: $12 signed. 26-36pp; Reporting time: 2 weeks max. Payment: 5 copies. Interested in new or unpub'd poets: yes, but query first. Simultaneous submissions accepted: no. Recently published poets: Robert Schuler, Mariann Ritzer, Doug Flaherty, Liz Hammond, Mike Koehler. Submission quantity: query first. Special interests: Nature themes priority, but open to most.

WOMAN POET, Women-in-Literature, Inc., PO Box 60550, Reno, NV 89506, 702-972-1671. Elaine Dallman, Editor-in-Chief. 1978. "Our publication, *Woman Poet*, is a series of regional poetry anthologies. Each anthology presents previously unpublished fine poetry by approximately 30 poets, some well-known and some previously undiscovered. Three women poets of national prominence are studied in detail through selections of their work, informative interviews, critical essays and biographic data to let the reader get close to the poets and their poems. Examining a sampling of our poetry is suggested. In 1995, we plan to publish individual poetry books. Watch for notices in *Poets & Writers* and *American Poetry Review*" circ. 4M. Irregular. Expects 55 poems 2001. sub. price: $12.95 plus $1.75 shipping and insurance per copy; sample: $12.95 + $1.75 shipping and insurance. 100-130pp; 8×9½; Rights purchased: 1st N.A. serial rights. Publishes 3% of poems submitted. Deadlines: watch for deadline notices in *Poets & Writers* and *American Poetry Review*. Reporting time: 3 weeks to 3 months. Payment: copies. Interested in new or unpub'd poets: yes. Simultaneous submissions accepted: no. Recent contributors: Lisel Mueller, Madeline DeFrees, Marilyn Hacker, Audre Lorde, Judith Minty. Submission quantity: 4-5. Special interests: We are looking for fine unpublished poetry of any length on any theme.

Women-in-Literature, Inc. (see also WOMAN POET), PO Box 60550, Reno, NV 89506. Elaine Dallman, Editor-in-Chief. 1978. "Our publication, *Woman Poet*, is a series of regional poetry anthologies. Each anthology presents previously unpublished fine poetry by approximately 30 poets, some well-known and some previously undiscovered. Three women poets of national prominence are studied in detail through selections of their work, informative interviews, critical essays and biographic data to let the reader get close to the poets and their poems. Examining a sample of our poetry is suggested. Beginning in 1994, we plan to publish individual poetry books. Watch for notices in *Poets & Writers* and *American Poetry Review*." avg. press run 4M. Expects 1 poetry title 2001. 8×9½; avg. price, cloth: $19.95 + p/h; paper: $12.95 + p/h. 100-130pp; Publishes 3% of poetry manuscripts submitted. Reporting time: 3 weeks to 3 months. Payment: copies. Interested in new or unpub'd poets: yes. Simultaneous submissions accepted: no. Recently published poets: Lisel Mueller, Madeline DeFrees, Marilyn Hacker, Audre Lorde, Judith Minty. Submission quantity: 4-5. Special interests: We are looking for fine unpublished poetry of any length on any theme.

WOMEN'S STUDIES QUARTERLY, The Feminist Press c/o City College, Convent Ave. & 138th St., New York, NY 10031, 212-360-5790. 1971. circ. 1.5M. 2/yr. sub. price: $30 individuals, $40 institutions, foreign $40 individual, $50 institution; sample: $13. 200-250pp; 5½×8½.

WOMENWISE, 38 South Main Street, Concord, NH 03301, 603-225-2739. Luita Spangler, Co-Editor. 1977. "We do not print anything we judge to be sexist, racist, anti-semitic, agist, classist, or homophobic. We are a feminist women's health quarterly thinking about the possible use of *quality* poetry" circ. 2.5M. 4/yr. Pub'd 12 poems 1999; expects 12 poems 2000, 12 poems 2001. sub. price: $10; sample: $3.50. 12pp; 11×19; Rights purchased: first N.A. Publishes 5-10% of poems submitted. Reporting time: varies. Payment: in subscription. Interested in new or unpub'd poets: yes. Simultaneous submissions accepted: no. Recent contributors: Lyn Lifshin, Marian Gleason, Elizabeth Sanders, B.A. Cantwell, Margaret Robison. Submission quantity: no more than 2.

●**Woodburn Avenue Books**, 6850 Regional Street, Suite 100, Dublin, CA 94568, 1-888-490-1099 ext. 7; krudolph@mediaone.net. Bob Swartzel. 1999. "Woodburn Avenue Books was established in 1999 to publish the works of Kenny Rudolph. Woodburn Avenue Books is not currently accepting unsolicited material but hopes to expand its roster of authors in the future." Expects 1 poetry title 2000, 1 poetry title 2001. avg. price, paper: $12.95.

WOODNOTES, 248 Beach Park Boulevard, Foster City, CA 94404, 415-571-9428, e-mail WelchM@aol.com. Michael Dylan Welch. 1989. "Submit any time—poems will be considered for next issue. We generally do not hold poems for future issues. Please be your own editor first before submitting your poetry. We currently publish only subscribers' poems. *Woodnotes* is published quarterly by the Haiku Poets of Northern California. HPNC also operates Two Autumns Press, which has published 9 books so far (about 2 each year for)—all on haiku." circ. 220. 4/yr. Pub'd 450 poems 1999; expects 550 poems 2000, 650 poems 2001. sub. price: $12; sample: $4. 44pp; 5½×8½; Rights purchased: none. Publishes 10% of poems submitted. Deadlines: every 3 months, exact date varies slightly. Reporting time: usually 2 weeks or less. Payment: none, but we give a $10 best-of-issue award. Interested in new or unpub'd poets: yes, but only if they are a subscriber. Simultaneous submissions accepted: no. Recent contributors: Yvonne Hardenbrook, Alexis Rotella, Helen K. Daure, Christopher Herold, Pat Shelly. Submission quantity: from 5-20, preferably about 12. Special interests: *Woodnotes* publishes haiku and related forms, including tanka, haibun, senryu, and sequences. We also publish articles and interviews about haiku.

THE WORCESTER REVIEW, 6 Chatham Street, Worcester, MA 01609, 603-924-7342, 978-797-4770. Rodger Martin, Managing Editor. 1973. "We like to keep at least 33% of each issue showcasing regional poets (N. England) but quality is still top consideration for publication. Reporting times can lengthen during printing sessions (Sept-Oct & May-June). Please be certain name appears on each page when submitting" circ. 1M. 1/yr. Pub'd 40 poems 1999; expects 40 poems 2000, 40 poems 2001. sub. price: $20; sample: $5. 150pp; 6×9; Rights purchased: first publication rights only. Publishes less than 10% of poems submitted. Deadlines: continuous. Reporting time: 6+ months. Payment: in copies and small honorarium; $10 per poem, $20 fiction if grant funded. Interested in new or unpub'd poets: yes. Simultaneous submissions accepted: if identified. Recent contributors: Mary Fell, Walter McDonald, Joan Connor, Robert Pinsky, May Swenson. Submission quantity: 3-5 max. Special interests: We are particularly interested in New England writers. We also have limited space for translations.

The Word Works, Inc., PO Box 42164, Washington, DC 20015. Karren L. Alenier, President; Robert Sargent, Member of the Board; J. H. Beall, Grants Manager; Hilary Tham, Editor-in-Chief; Miles David Moore, Program administrator, The Washington Prize. 1974. "The author, as stated in our bylaws, is encouraged to participate in the process of making the book. Additionally, authors must get involved with the distribution. Initially in making inquiries, the author might identify his/her market and state realistic numbers. The author might discuss readings that he or she does, where new opportunities exist, how available the author is to travel and his or her ability to do so on what resources. Word Works sponsors the Washington Prize, a major annual award for a book length manuscript ($1500). Word Works sponsors the Joaquin Miller Cabin Poetry Series each summer in Washington, DC. We emphasize Poet/Artist collaborations. Poets usually work with a visual artist on cover and book design. Some of the artists working on Word Works books have been: William Christenberry, Raya Bodnarchuk, Paloma Cernuda and Rosemary Covey.'' avg. press run 500. Pub'd 3 poetry titles 1999; expects 4 poetry titles 2000, 3 poetry titles 2001. 5½×8½; avg. price, paper: $10; other: $10-$35. 72pp; Publishes 1% of poetry manuscripts submitted. Reporting time: 3 months. Payment: 15% of the run. Interested in new or unpub'd poets: yes, but letter of inquiry first. Simultaneous submissions accepted: yes, but only if we are told that the manuscript is being sent elsewhere as well. Recently published poets: Enid Shomer, George Young, Nathalie Anderson, Ann Rae Jonas, Grace Cavalieri. Submission quantity: 5. Special interests: We are interested well-crafted poems in a cohesive book length manuscipt. Long poems, experiments in language, forms or free verse are acceptable. We are not currently reading translations, regional poems, satire. We are not particularly interested in categorical 'light verse' or politically pointed work.

Wordcraft of Oregon, PO Box 3235, La Grande, OR 97850, 503-963-0723, E-mail wordcraft@oregontrail.net, http://www.oregontrail.net/~wordcraft. David Memmott. 1984. ''There are two poetry imprints at Wordcraft of Oregon: Jazz Police Books (speculative poetry) and Ice River Press (regional poetry-Eastern Oregon)'' avg. press run 250-1M. Pub'd 1 poetry title 1999; expects 2 poetry titles 2000, 2 poetry titles 2001. 5½×8½; avg. price, paper: $9-12; other: $6 chapbooks. 40-100pp; Reporting time: 60 days. Payment: copies or percentage by arrangement. Interested in new or unpub'd poets: Query first. Simultaneous submissions accepted: no. Recently published poets: David Axelrod, George Venn, Thomas Madden, Dan Raphael, John Noto. Submission quantity: query first. Special interests: The press will not be reading in 2000.

Words & Pictures Press, 1921 Sherry Lane, Apt. #87, Santa Ana, CA 92705-7621, 714-544-7282; Fax 714-544-7430; E-mail publisher@earthlink.net. 1994. 5½×8½.

WORDS OF WISDOM, 3283 UNCG Station, Greensboro, NC 27413, 336-334-6970; e-mail wowmail@hoopsmail.com. 1981. ''Most poetry is used as filler material. Prefer humorous to blank thought. *Light verse to 20 lines has a good chance with this magazine.* Don't send poetry without cover letter. Published 60 poems out of 500 received. We read all types of poetry.'' circ. 150-180. 4/yr. Pub'd 50 poems 1999; expects 50 poems 2000, 50 poems 2001. sub. price: $15 individuals, $16 institutions and Canada, $24 international; sample: $4. 76-88pp; 5½×8½; Rights purchased: first serial rights/one-time rights. Publishes 8-10% of poems submitted. Deadlines: seasonal 3-6 months ahead of time. Reporting time: usually in 3 weeks to 4 months. Payment: 1 copy of magazine. Interested in new or unpub'd poets: no. Simultaneous submissions accepted: yes, but no reprints please. Recent contributors: Jill Williams, Taylor Graham, Zahida Asghar, Joseph S. Salemi, Bartlett Boswell. Submission quantity: 3-6. Special interests: Light verse, satire, limericks, oriental forms sometimes.

THE WORLD, The Poetry Project, St. Marks Church/The Poetry Project, 131 East 10th Street, New York, NY 10003, poproj@artomatic.com. 1966. circ. 750. 1/yr. Pub'd 35 poems 1999; expects 35 poems 2000, 50 poems 2001. sub. price: $25/4 issues; sample: $7. 128pp; 6×9; Publishes 5% of poems submitted. Reporting time: 6 months. Payment: 2 copies. Interested in new or unpub'd poets: no. Simultaneous submissions accepted: no. Recent contributors: John Ashbery, Amiri Baraka, Bernadette Mayer, Alice Notley. Submission quantity: 5.

World Peace University Publications, PO Box 20728, Portland, OR 97294-0728, 503-252-3639, fax 503-255-5216. 1986. 5⅜×8½.

World Wisdom Books, Inc., PO Box 2682, Bloomington, IN 47402, 812-332-1663, e-mail wwbooks@worldwisdom.com. 1981. 5½×8¼.

WORMWOOD REVIEW, PO Box 50003, Loring Station, Minneapolis, MN 55405-0003, 612-381-1229. 1995. circ. 100. 2-3/yr. sub. price: $15/4 issues; sample: $3. 20pp; 8½×11.

THE WRITE WAY, 810 Overhill Road, Deland, FL 32720, 904-734-1955. Ann Larberg. 1988. ''Annual poetry issue published every year in December. $1 reading fee for contests'' circ. 2M. 4/yr. Pub'd 12 poems 1999; expects 12 poems 2000, 12 poems 2001. sub. price: $6; sample: $2. 6-8pp; 8½×11; Rights purchased: 1st National. Publishes 50% of poems submitted. Deadlines: Feb. 15, May 15, Aug. 15, Nov. 15. Reporting time: 6-8 weeks. Payment: copies. Interested in new or unpub'd poets: yes. Simultaneous submissions accepted: yes. Submission quantity: 2-4. Special interests: Haiku, limericks.

WRITER TO WRITER, PO Box 2336, Oak Park, IL 60303. 1997. circ. 125. 2/yr. sub. price: $10; sample: $5. 32pp; 8½×11.

WRITER'S EXCHANGE, 616 Eagle Bend Road, Clinton, TN 37716, E-mail eboone@aol.com, www.users.aol.com/writernet. Gene Boone. 1986. ''*Writer's Exchange* sponsors a quarterly poetry contest. Poets can send SASE for rules/guidelines'' circ. 250-300. 4/yr. Pub'd 100+ poems 1999. sub. price: $12;

sample: $2. 40pp; 5⅓×8; Rights purchased: First North American Serial Rights only. Publishes 50% of poems submitted. Deadlines: none. Reporting time: 2-4 weeks. Payment: contributor's copy. Interested in new or unpub'd poets: yes. Simultaneous submissions accepted: no. Recent contributors: Mary Ann Henn, Sarah Jensen, Diane L. Krueger, Violet Wilcox. Submission quantity: 2-10.

WRITERS' FORUM, University of Colorado, PO Box 7150, Colorado Springs, CO 80933-7150, 719-262-4006. Victoria McCabe, Poetry Editor; C. Kenneth Pellow, Editor-in-Chief. Address poetry submissions to: 303-321-8654. 1974. "Poems must be verbally interesting and reveal authentic voice. We read between Sept. 1 and March 1 each year. Submit poems with cover letter (brief bio, and relevant publishing information) and SASE." circ. 1M. 1/yr. Pub'd 25 poems 1999; expects 28 poems 2000, 30 poems 2001. sub. price: $10 includes postage; sample: $7 (includes postage) for readers of *International Directory of Little Magazines & Small Presses.* 200pp; 5½×8½; Rights purchased: one time only. Publishes 1% of poems submitted. Deadlines: Sept. 1-March 1. Reporting time: 3-6 weeks. Payment: author's copy, other copies discounted. Interested in new or unpub'd poets: yes. Simultaneous submissions accepted: read, yes; acceptance, infrequent. Recent contributors: David Ray, Donald Axinn, Yusef Komunyakaa, William Stafford, Simon Ortiz. Submission quantity: 3-5. Special interests: We especially encourage poetry of or about the West with substance related to the life and cultures of the Trans-Mississippi region, but we are open to English-language poetry from anywhere, and we have no restrictions about length, genre, or novelty as long as the work is imaginative and not merely clever. The human experience probed and outered into memorable speech and not obscured, sentimentalized, or self-confined. We want passion with form. We consider but do not always encourage translations. We also will consider Spanish poetry by Chicano writers of the West and English and/or Spanish poetry by Native Americans.

WRITERS GAZETTE, 899 Williamson Trail, Eclectic, AL 36024-6131. Brenda Williamson. 1980. "Prefer poems to be 30 lines or less. Very rarely use long poems" circ. 2M. 4/yr. Pub'd 200 poems 1999; expects 200 poems 2000, 200 poems 2001. sub. price: $18; sample: $5. 28pp; 8½×11; Rights purchased: first, second, or one-time. Publishes 10% of poems submitted. Deadlines: none. Reporting time: 4-8 weeks. Payment: varies. Interested in new or unpub'd poets: yes. Simultaneous submissions accepted: yes. Submission quantity: 4.

WRITER'S GUIDELINES: A Roundtable for Writers and Editors, HC77 Box 608, Pittsburg, MO 65724. 1988. circ. 1M. 6/yr. sub. price: $18; sample: $4. 32pp; 8½×11.

Writers House Press (see also THE BAREFOOT POET: Journal of Poetry, Fiction, Essays, & Art), PO Box 52, Pisgah, IA 51564-0052, 712-456-2132; stmike-press@saint-mike.org. John-Paul Ignoutius, O.L.S.M, Publisher. 1982. "We are not accepting manuscripts at this time. We are NOT a Vanity press. No amount of money donated to us will convince us to publish your book. We publish the books we want to publish based on artistic considerations only. Before a contract offer is made, your manuscript will go through about seven months of readings and screenings by assistant editors, and an Editorial Committee. We will respond to your proposal in about 3 months. A contract offer usually takes about an additional 4 months after we get the complete manuscript. And PLEASE, send a proposal first. Poets should send a cover letter detailing the plan and theme of the book they wish to publish, accompanied by about 10 poems as an example. Include chapter division plans, artwork needed, manuscript text of any forward, preface or introduction. Please include ideas for the best market that you think your work will appeal, and any reviews you have received on this or any other manuscript. SASE is required. We also publish a magazine entitled *The Barefoot Poet: Journal of Poetry, Fiction, Essays & Art.* Writers House Press has been acquired by St. Michael's Press" avg. press run 100-1M. Expects 1 poetry title 2001. 4¼×5½; avg. price, cloth: $19.95-29.95; paper: $9.95-19.95; other: $6.95-9.95. 56-100pp; Publishes 10% of poetry manuscripts submitted. Reporting time: 3 minutes - 3 months in proposal. Payment: we are a "Co-publishing Royalty" House, royalty begins at 10% and escalates to 15%. Interested in new or unpub'd poets: yes. Simultaneous submissions accepted: yes. Submission quantity: 10. Special interests: translations and political themes. Not interested in light verse or haiku.

WRITERS IN PARADISE, 4615 Gulf Boulevard, Ste. 104, St. Pete Beach, FL 33706, E-mail writers.in.paradise@worldnet.att.net. 1998. circ. 250. 12/yr. sub. price: $20, $12/6 month sub.; sample: $3. 16-32pp; 8×11.

WRITERS INK, Writers Unlimited Agency, Inc, Writers Ink Press, PO Box 2344, Selden, NY 11784, 516-451-0478 phone/fax, axelrodthepoet@yahoo.com. David B. Axelrod, Series Editor. 1975. "We have reduced newsletter to Sometimely and converted to chapbook format. We solicit and publish 2 mss. per year. We have a long backlist and are now publishing by our request only." circ. 2M. 0-4/yr. Pub'd 2 poems 1999; expects 2 poems 2000, 2 poems 2001. sub. price: $6; No samples. 4-12pp; 5×7; Rights purchased: author retains rights. Deadlines: none. Reporting time: 2 weeks. Payment: copies & 50% of profit over costs. Interested in new or unpub'd poets: not at this time. Simultaneous submissions accepted: yes, but no unsol. mss. at this time. Recent contributors: Adam Fisher, George Wallace, Edward Stever, Marvin Levine, Paul Agostino. Special interests: We publish news of our conferences and workshops in newsletter as publicity arm of writers unlimited agency, inc. and our magazine has become a Chapbook series.

Writers Ink Press (see also WRITERS INK), 233 Mooney Pond, PO Box 2344, Selden, Long Island, NY 11784-2344, 516-451-0478 phone/Fax, axelrodthepoet@yahoo.com. Dr. David B. Axelrod. 1975. "We presently publish by invitation only, selecting from among students who take Writers Unlimited's poetry workshops or established authors internationally." avg. press run 500-800. Pub'd 2 poetry titles 1999; expects 3 poetry titles 2000, 3 poetry titles 2001. 5×7, 6×9; avg. price, cloth: $15-$20; paper: $8-$12; other: $50 folio art editions. Chapbooks 36-48pp, perfectbound 72-128pp; Publishes 3 poetry manuscripts per year but presently by invitation only. Payment: 100 copies to author. Interested in new or unpub'd poets: we will keep an "active" file of all materials for possible future publication and/or referal to readings and periodicals. Simultaneous submissions accepted: yes, but authors should so indicate. Recently published poets: George Wallace, Adam Fisher, Edward Stever, Marvin Levine, Paul Agostino. Submission quantity: send best 10 and we will file for possible contact; mss. are not returned so keep copies. Special interests: For more information on workshops held throughout the year in Selden, Long Island and other international locations, write press. SASE.

WRITERS' JOURNAL, PO Box 394, Perham, MN 56573-0394, 218-346-7921, fax 218-346-7924, e-mail writersjournal@wadena.net. 1980. circ. 26M. 6/yr. sub. price: $19.97; sample: $5. 64pp; 8⅝×11⅛.

WRITER'S LIFELINE, Vesta Publications Limited, PO Box 1641, Cornwall, Ont. K6H 5V6, Canada. Stephen Gill. 1974. "Short poems are preferred—no indecent words." circ. 2M. 3/yr. Expects 75 poems 2000. sub. price: $18; sample: $8 for 3 issues. 36pp; 5¼×8¼; Rights purchased: 1st. Publishes 60% of poems submitted. Reporting time: 4-6 weeks. Payment: copies. Interested in new or unpub'd poets: yes. Simultaneous submissions accepted: no. Recent contributors: Gene Boone, Stephen Gill, Margaret Coates, Barbara Foster, John B. Lee. Submission quantity: 3-6.

WRITER'S MONTHLY GAZETTE, Press-Tige Publishing Company Inc., PO Box 788, Leeds, NY 12451. Kelly O'Donnell, Editor. 1972. "Poetry contests monthly in Writer's Gazette, retreats for artists, sermonians. No morbid, death poems *please*. Only positive up-beat poems. Think positive, believe and have faith in which that, which is good, and expect a positve response. Never falter from your positive outlook. Inspirational, humorous, children's, nature, environmental, free and light verses, only." circ. 160M. 12/yr. Pub'd 22 poems 1999. sub. price: $60; sample: $6. 8-10pp; 8½×11; Rights purchased: first time rights. Publishes 60% of poems submitted. Deadlines: 15th of every month. Reporting time: 1 month. Payment: $25 and up. Interested in new or unpub'd poets: yes. Simultaneous submissions accepted: yes. Recent contributors: Donna Keller, Laura Comito, Mary Santulli, Sara Montanye, Martha Reidda. Submission quantity: 10.

Writers Unlimited Agency, Inc (see also WRITERS INK), PO Box 2344, Selden, NY 11784, 516-451-0478 phone/Fax, axelrodthepoet@yahoo.com. Dr. David B. Axelrod. 1975. "No unsolicited mss. We do co-publications with 3WS, World-Wide Writers Services. We are international in scope, Long Island based, not-for-profit service group Writers Unlimited Agency, Inc., hence, Writers Ink Press." avg. press run 800. Pub'd 3 poetry titles 1999; expects 3 poetry titles 2000, 3 poetry titles 2001. 5½×8½, 5×8; avg. price, cloth: $18; paper: $12; other: $10 chapbook. 40pp; Payment: varies. Interested in new or unpub'd poets: no. Simultaneous submissions accepted: no. Recently published poets: Adam Fisher, Edward Stever, George Wallace, Paul Agostino, Linda Opyr. Submission quantity: presently 10 but by invitation only. Special interests: Translations, Long Island work, student chapbook series in affil. with SUNY system.

WRITER'S WORKSHOP REVIEW, 511 West 24th Street, Vancouver, WA 98660, 360-693-6509. 1993. circ. 500. 12/yr. sub. price: $20; sample: $3. 20pp; 8½×11.

WRITER'S WORLD, 204 East 19th Street, Big Stone Gap, VA 24219, 703-523-0830, fax 703-523-5757. Diane L. Krueger. Address poetry submissions to: 17 Oswego Avenue, Rockaway, NJ 07866, 201-627-0439, fax 201-627-3314. 1990. "No reading fees, no negative style poetry, no untitled poetry" circ. 2.6M. 6/yr. Pub'd 50 poems 1999; expects 50 poems 2000, 50 poems 2001. sub. price: $15; sample: $4.50. 24pp; 8½×11; Rights purchased: Assume First NA Serial Rights, revert to author on publication. Publishes 15% of poems submitted. Deadlines: none. Reporting time: 1 month. Payment: front cover poem $5, all others 2 copies. Interested in new or unpub'd poets: yes. Simultaneous submissions accepted: no. Recent contributors: Bobbie Saunders, Joyce Carbone, Denise Martinson, William J. White, Arthur C. Ford, Sr. Submission quantity: 3-5. Special interests: Competition is fierce, shorter is better, open to all writers.

WRITES OF PASSAGE, PO Box 1935, Livingston, NJ 07039, 212-473-7564; wpusa@aol.com; http://www.writes.org. Laura Hoffman, Wendy Mass. 1994. "We publish poems by teenagers across the country. Teens should include poem/s, SASE, and a brief biography. We also publish essays and advice on writing and we produce a teacher's guide offering lesson plans and tips for teaching." circ. 3M. 2/yr. Pub'd 75 poems 1999; expects 75 poems 2000, 75 poems 2001. sub. price: $12; sample: $6. 96pp; 5½×8½; Rights purchased: rights revert to author upon publication except when published in conjunction with *Writes of Passage*. Publishes 8% of poems submitted. Deadlines: none, continual basis. Reporting time: 2 months. Payment: 2 published magazines. Interested in new or unpub'd poets: yes, we publish the work of teenagers. Simultaneous submissions accepted: yes. Submission quantity: no more than 5. Special interests: Subjects can be on anything; usually they are on teen-related issues.

WRITING FOR OUR LIVES, 647 N. Santa Cruz Ave., The Annex, Los Gatos, CA 95030, 408-354-8604. Janet M. McEwan. 1991. "Please send two SASE's. Women poets only please" circ. 600. 1/yr. Pub'd 42 poems 1999; expects 30 poems 2000, 30 poems 2001. sub. price: 2 issues $15.50 U.S., $21 overseas; sample: $6-$8, $9-$11 overseas. 80pp; 5¼×8¼; Rights purchased: first world-wide english language serial or one-time reprint. Publishes 5% of poems submitted. Deadlines: Aug. 15. Reporting time: varies. Payment: 2 copies, plus discount on copies and subscription. Interested in new or unpub'd poets: Yes. Simultaneous submissions accepted: yes. Recent contributors: April Fields, Joyce Brady, Kathy Abelson, Jennifer Crystal Fang-Chien, Joan Zimmerman. Submission quantity: up to 5.

WRITING ULSTER, U. of Ulster-Jordanstown, Shore Rd, Newtownabbey Co. Antrim, BT 370QB, Northern Ireland, 011-44-232-365131, fax 232-366824. W. Lazenbatt. 1990. 1/yr. Pub'd 5 poems 1999; expects 5 poems 2000, 5 poems 2001. sub. price: £5. 192pp; 6×9; Publishes 70% of poems submitted. Deadlines: Oct.-Dec. for publication following springtime. Reporting time: 8 weeks. Payment: none. Interested in new or unpub'd poets: yes. Simultaneous submissions accepted: no. Recent contributors: Brendan Kennelly, Paul Muldoon, Fred Johnston, Frank Ormsby, Dermot Bolger. Submission quantity: 2-3.

X

XANADU, Pleasure Dome Press (Long Island Poetry Collective Inc.), Box 773, Huntington, NY 11743, 516-248-7716. Mildred M. Jeffrey, Lois V. Walker, Weslea Sidon, Sue Kain. 1975. "*Xanadu* has no particular requirements regarding submissions of poetry." circ. 300. 1/yr. Pub'd 50 poems 1999; expects 55 poems 2000, 55 poems 2001. sub. price: $7 (includes p/h); sample: $5. 64pp; 5½×8½; Rights purchased: 1st and 1 anthology/reprint. Publishes 10% of poems submitted. Deadlines: No specific deadlines. Reporting time: 2-3 months. Payment: each contributor receives 1 copy. Interested in new or unpub'd poets: yes. Simultaneous submissions accepted: no. Recent contributors: Simon Perchik, John S. Brugaletta, Lyn Stefenhagens, Rane Arroyo, Anita Feng. Submission quantity: 3-5.

XAVIER REVIEW, Box 110C, Xavier University, New Orleans, LA 70125, 504-483-7481 Bonner, 483-7303 Skinner, Fax 504-485-7917. Thomas Bonner, Editor. 1980. "No submissions during summer months." circ. 300. 2/yr. Pub'd 40 poems 1999; expects 40 poems 2000, 40 poems 2001. sub. price: $10 individuals, $15 institutions; sample: $5. 85pp; 6×9; Rights purchased: none. Publishes 10-15% of poems submitted. Deadlines: April (Spring issue), October (Fall issue). Reporting time: 2 months. Payment: 2 copies of journal. Interested in new or unpub'd poets: yes. Simultaneous submissions accepted: no. Recent contributors: Lorenzo Thomas, Patricia Ward, Biljana Obradovic, Toi Derricott. Submission quantity: 3-5. Special interests: translations, regional poetry.

XCP: CROSS-CULTURAL POETICS, College of St. Catherine, 601 25th Avenue South, Minneapolis, MN 55454, website http://bfn.org/~xcp. Mark Nowak. 1997. "Include SASE with all correspondence" circ. 850. 2/yr. Pub'd 50 poems 1999. sub. price: $18 indivduals, $40 institutions, foreign add $5; checks payable to College of St. Catherine.; sample: $9. 175pp; 6×9; Rights purchased: rights revert to author on publication. Publishes 2% of poems submitted. Deadlines: ongoing, check website for special topic issues. Reporting time: 1-2 months. Payment: 2 copies. Interested in new or unpub'd poets: yes. Simultaneous submissions accepted: no. Recent contributors: Amiri Baraka, Gerald Vizenor, Forrest Gander, Diane Glancy, Juan Felipe Herrera.

Xenos Books, Box 52152, Riverside, CA 92517, 909-370-2229; E-mail info@xenosbooks.com; http://www.xenosbooks.com. Karl Kvitko. 1986. "Cannot publish single poems—only books." avg. press run 300-500. Expects 1-2 poetry titles 2000. 5½×8¼, 8½×11; avg. price, cloth: $23; paper: $13. 120pp; Publishes 1-2% of poetry manuscripts submitted. Reporting time: 1-3 months. Payment: copies. Interested in new or unpub'd poets: yes, prefer foreign languages with translations. Simultaneous submissions accepted: yes. Recently published poets: Vincente Huidobro, Alfedo de Palchi, Imre Oravecz, William Allen, Mario Azzopardi. Submission quantity: a whole book or portion thereof, not individual poems. Special interests: Translations, experimental poetry, longpoems.

XIB, Xib Publications, 930 24th Street, San Diego, CA 92102-2006. Tolek. 1991. "Prefer personal cover letter." circ. 500. 1-2/yr. Pub'd 80 poems 1999; expects 50 poems 2000, 80 poems 2001. sub. price: $10; sample: $5. 60pp; 6¾×8½; Rights purchased: one-time; revert to author. Publishes 2% of poems submitted. Reporting time: 2 weeks. Payment: 1 copy. Interested in new or unpub'd poets: yes. Simultaneous submissions accepted: yes. Recent contributors: Robert Nagler, Pat McKinnon, Lisa Glatt, Sheila Murphy. Submission quantity: up to 7.

Xib Publications (see also XIB), 930 24th Street, San Diego, CA 92102-2006. Tolek. 1991. "Chapbook acceptances are solicited from regular submissions to *xib* magazine." avg. press run 50. Pub'd 1 poetry title 1999; expects 2 poetry titles 2000, 2 poetry titles 2001. 5½x8½; avg. price, other: $2 saddle, card stock. 20pp; Publishes 1% of poetry manuscripts submitted. Reporting time: 2 weeks. Payment: 40 copies initially, more to suit demand (of market). Interested in new or unpub'd poets: yes. Simultaneous submissions accepted: yes. Recently published poets: Cheryl Townsend. Submission quantity: up to 7.

X-it Press, PO Box 3756, Erie, PA 16508. Bobby Star. 1993. "please avoid typos" avg. press run 75-100. 8x5; avg. price, paper: $2. 16-32pp; We publish 10% or less of poetry submissions. Reporting time: 1-17 weeks. Payment: 10%-50% of press run. Interested in new or unpub'd poets: yes. Simultaneous submissions accepted: yes. Recently published poets: Joe R, R.L. Nichols. Submission quantity: partial or whole manuscript. Special interests: prefer post-beat poesy.

X-RAY, PO Box 1103, Ventura, CA 93002, e-mail johnny@xraybookco.com. Johnny Brewton, Editor. 1989. "Send a SASE along with submission for guidelines information" circ. 226. 2/yr. Pub'd 25 poems 1999; expects 66 poems 2000, 66½ poems 2001. sub. price: none. 80pp; 7x8½; Publishes 25% of poems submitted. Deadlines: ongoing. Reporting time: 2 weeks. Payment: 1 copy. Interested in new or unpub'd poets: yes. Simultaneous submissions accepted: no. Recent contributors: Ruth Weiss, Wanda Coleman, Dan Fante, A.D. Winans. Submission quantity: 1-5. Special interests: Favor prose, free verse, found poetry-concrete poetry.

XTRAS, From Here Press, PO Box 2740, Santa Fe, NM 87504-2740, 505-438-3249. William J. Higginson, Penny Harter. 1975. "*Xtras* is a serial chapbook series; each issue features one or a related group of authors" circ. 200-500. 0-1/yr. Expects 50 poems 2001. 28-72pp; 5½x8½; Rights purchased: book rights. Deadlines: none. Reporting time: varies. Payment: substantial number of copies. Interested in new or unpub'd poets: no unsolicited work. Recent contributors: Elizabeth Searle Lamb, Ruth Stone, Dee Evetts. Submission quantity: chapbook mss. Special interests: Mainly contemporary poetry, renga, haiku and related, including translations.

Y

THE YALE REVIEW, Yale University, PO Box 208243, New Haven, CT 06520-8243. J.D. McClatchy. 1911. "All submissions must be typed and accompanied by stamped, self-addressed return envelopes" circ. 6M. 4/yr. Expects 20-30 poems 2001. sub. price: $65 institutions, $27 individuals; sample: $10 (includes postage and handling). 160pp plus 16-24pp front matter; 6⅜x9¼; Rights purchased: 1st North American serial. Publishes 2% of poems submitted. Deadlines: none. Reporting time: 1-2 months. Payment: $100. Interested in new or unpub'd poets: yes. Simultaneous submissions accepted: no. Recent contributors: May Swenson, Adrienne Rich, Anthony Hecht, W.S. Merwin, Brenda Shavghvessy. Submission quantity: 1-5.

Yale University Press, PO Box 209040, New Haven, CT 06520-9040, 203-432-0960. 1908. "The only poetry we publish is the annual winner of the Yale Series of Younger Poets competition. Rules Governing Competition: The Yale Series of Younger Poets competition is open to any American writer under forty years of age (at the time the manuscript is submitted) who has not previously published a volume of poetry. The winning manuscript is published by Yale University Press, and the author receives the usual royalties. If no manuscript submitted is, in the opinion of the judge, worthy of publication, no volume will be published. Individual criticism of manuscripts cannot be given. Contestants should address manuscripts and correspondence to the Editor, Yale Series of Younger Poets, Yale University Press, 92A Yale Station, New Haven, Connecticut 06520. No application form is required. Submissions will be accepted only during the month of February; manuscripts postmarked after February 28 will be returned to sender unread. *A submission fee of $8 must accompany the manuscript; make checks payable to Yale University Press*. Yale University Press will acknowledge receipt of all manuscripts by April 1. Announcement of the winner will be made in the public media. The format of the series calls for a manuscript of from 48-64 pages, with no more than one poem on a page. Illustrations are not accepted. Manuscripts must be typewritten, either single or double spaced, and only a face copy or a good photocopy should be submitted. There should be a title page bearing the author's full name, address, and telephone number, a table of contents, and a page of biographical data. Pages should be numbered consecutively throughout, beginning with the title page. Manuscripts must be submitted in final form; later revisions cannot be considered. All verse must be original. Acknowledgments should be included for all poems previously published in newspapers or periodicals. Poets who have had volumes of poetry privately printed, or printed in limited editions of no more than 300 copies, are eligible. A contestant may submit only one manuscript in one year's competition. An unsuccessful manuscript may be revised and resubmitted in subsequent years. Contestants may submit their manuscripts elsewhere simultaneously, but Yale University Press should be notified immediately if a manuscript is committed to another press. Since Yale University Press cannot be responsible for the loss of manuscripts while in its possession or in transit, each author should retain at least one duplicate copy of the manuscript submitted. A SASE for return of the manuscript if it is not selected should accompany the manuscript; otherwise it will not be returned. Postal regulations prohibit the use of metered return envelopes'' avg. press run 2.5M. Pub'd 1 poetry title 1999; expects 1 poetry title 2000, 1 poetry title 2001. avg. price, cloth: $14.95; paper: $7.95. 96pp; Publishes less than 1% of poetry manuscripts submitted. Reporting time: 4-5 months. Payment: usual royalties on net receipts. Interested in new or unpub'd poets: yes. Simultaneous submissions accepted: yes. Recently published poets: Carolyn Forche, Olga Broumas, Richard Kenney, Tom Bolt, Nicholas Samaras. Submission quantity: 48-64 pages. Special interests: First books of unpublished poets. There are no limitations on the kind of poetry or the subject matter, though translations are not acceptable.

Years Press, Dept. of ATL, EBH, Michigan State University, E. Lansing, MI 48824-1033. F. Richard Thomas, Editor, Publisher; Leonora H. Smith, Associate Editor. 1973. "Years Press publishes poetry chapbooks irregularly. Sending of your poetry mss is not recommended, because mss are usually solicited after hearing a reading. If you decide to send, please query with 3 poems only. We publish primarily local (Michigan and Indiana) poets.'' avg. press run 300-400. Pub'd 1 poetry title 1999; expects 2 poetry titles 2000, 2 poetry titles 2001. 7×8½; avg. price, paper: $5. 12-24pp; Publishes .1% of poetry manuscripts submitted. Reporting time: 1 month. Payment: 5 copies. Recently published poets: Roger Pfingston, Stephen Dunning, Lee Upton, Carol Morris, Alice Friman. Submission quantity: 3. Special interests: We are always interested in poems from Danish authors about the US or US authors about Denmark.

YEFIEF, PO Box 8505, Santa Fe, NM 87504. 1992. circ. 1.5M. Frequency varies according to scope of publication. Pub'd 30 poems 1999; expects 50 poems 2000, 50+ poems 2001. sub. price: $24.95 per volume; sample: write for price. 175-250+pp; 8¼×10½; Rights purchased: all rights. Publishes very small % of poems submitted. Reporting time: 8-12 weeks. Payment: 2 copies. Interested in new or unpub'd poets: yes, but see special interests. Simultaneous submissions accepted: yes. Recent contributors: Nicole Brossard, Simon Perchik, Michael Palmer, Noemi Alingodan-Medina. Submission quantity: 4-6. Special interests: Very interested in challenging and verging poetry.

Yellow Moon Press, PO Box 381316, Cambridge, MA 02238-0001, 617-776-2230; Fax 617-776-8246; E-mail ymp@tiac.net; web site www.yellowmoon.com. Robert B. Smyth, Editor. 1978. "We are not actively considering unsolicited manuscripts. I am mainly interested in material related to the oral tradition and the work of men that explores the changes men are faced with today - In particular the ideas of male imitation and values from ancient times as they relate to today's changing male roles, - feminism + the growing men's movement.'' Expects 3-4 poetry titles 2000. 6×9, 8½×11; avg. price, cloth: $12.95; paper: $10.95; other: chapbook saddle stitched: $3-$4. 32-48pp; Reporting time: 6-8 weeks. Payment: varies but in general is 10% of sales after production expenses. Interested in new or unpub'd poets: no. Simultaneous submissions accepted: no. Recently published poets: Elizabeth McKim, Ruth Stone, Robert Bly, Coleman Barks. Submission quantity: 10-15. Special interests: Men's poetry, New England poets.

YELLOW SILK: Journal Of Erotic Arts, PO Box 6374, Albany, CA 94706, 510-644-4188. Lily Pond, Editor. 1981. "We do not read new poetry June thru Aug. of every year. Name, address and phone on each page. SASE. Don't fold separately. Don't like dot matrix or all caps - hard to read - evaluate. Neatness counts. No previously published. Will consider excerpt/review new books. Don't query. Themes have included 'Music of Eros,' 'Wild Women,' 'Flowers,' and 'Eros & Spirituality'.'' 1/yr. Pub'd 85 poems 1999. sub. price: bookstores only; sample: $7.50. 300pp; 6×9; Rights purchased: 1 year following publication and non-exclusive anthology or reprint. Publishes 1-2% of poems submitted. Reporting time: 3 months. Payment: 3 copies and cash payments. Interested in new or unpub'd poets: currently prefer work by established authors. Simultaneous submissions accepted: no. Recent contributors: W.S. Merwin, Sharon Olds, Ivan Arguelles, Marge Piercy, Galway Kinnell. Submission quantity: 8ish. Special interests: Interested in all kinds of poetry from the haiku - "simple" to the surrealistic complex. Translations (with originals), very much. Erotic. No brutality. Gay and straight, men and women. Read the magazine. No trite or seemingly "greeting card" sentiments. No porn.

Z

●**ZAUM - The Literary Review of Sonoma State University,** English Department, SSU, 1801 E. Cotati Avenue, Rohnert Park, CA 94928, 707-664-2140. 1996. circ. 500. 1/yr. sub. price: $9.50; sample: $7.75 + p/h. 100pp; 7×12.

Zephyr Press, 50 Kenwood Street, Brookline, MA 02446, 617-713-2813. J. Kates, Co-Director; Leora Zeitlin,

Co-Director; Christopher Mattison, Managing Editor. 1980. avg. press run 2-3M. Pub'd 1 poetry title 1999; expects 2 poetry titles 2000, 2 poetry titles 2001. 6×9; avg. price, cloth: $25; paper: $14. 200pp; Publishes 5% of poetry manuscripts submitted. Reporting time: 2-12 weeks. Payment: 8-10% of publisher's net. Interested in new or unpub'd poets: will accept query. Simultaneous submissions accepted: yes. Recently published poets: Dmitry Prigov, Bulat Okudzhava, Anna Akhmatova, Bei Dao, Chen Dong Dong. Special interests: Translations; Slavic and Central East European, East Asian.

ZerOX Books (see also UNMUZZLED OX), 105 Hudson Street, #311, New York, NY 10013. 1971. "We publish 'reprints' in 'Xerox'" 8½×11.

Zerx Press, 725 Van Buren Place SE, Albuquerque, NM 87108, zerxpress@aol.com. Mark Weber. 1983. avg. press run 200-500. Pub'd 5 poetry titles 1999; expects 6 poetry titles 2000, 2+ poetry titles 2001. 5½×8½; avg. price, other: $3 chapbook. 44pp; Payment: 35 free copies. Recently published poets: Fred Voss, t.l. kryss, Joan Jobe Smith, Todd Moore, Catherine Lynn. Special interests: narrative 20th century American poetry.

ZINE-ON-A-TAPE, 35 Kearsley Road, Sheffield, S2 4TE, United Kingdom, www.andysav.free-online.co.uk/. Andrew Savage. 1985. "We prefer you to submit poetry on tape" circ. 100. 1/yr. Pub'd 10 poems 1999; expects 10 poems 2000, 10 poems 2001. sub. price: £3 or $8 postpaid. Rights purchased: none. Publishes 10% of poems submitted. Deadlines: none. Reporting time: 3 months. Payment: 1 complimentary copy. Interested in new or unpub'd poets: yes, but only on tape. Simultaneous submissions accepted: yes. Recent contributors: Paul Rance, Wil Walker, Andy Darlington, Steve Sneyd, Lovely Ivor. Submission quantity: 4. Special interests: Humorous poetry and poetry set to music or weird noises or animal sounds.

Zoland Books, 384 Huron Avenue, Cambridge, MA 02138, 617-864-6252; FAX 617-661-4998. Roland F. Pease, Jr. 1987. avg. press run 1.5M. Pub'd 2 poetry titles 1999; expects 3 poetry titles 2000, 3 poetry titles 2001. size varies; avg. price, cloth: cloth editions are very rare; paper: $9.95. 126pp; Publishes 1-5% of poetry manuscripts submitted. Reporting time: 3 months. Payment: varies. Interested in new or unpub'd poets: no. Simultaneous submissions accepted: yes. Recently published poets: William Corbett, Sam Cornish, Joseph Lease, Joel Sloman, Patricia Smith. Submission quantity: complete manuscript with self addressed return materials w/adequate postage.

Zombie Logic Press, 420 E. 3rd Street Box 319, Byron, IL 61010, email Dobe 1969@aol.com. 1997. 5½×8.

ZONE 3, PO Box 4565, Austin Peay State University, Clarksville, TN 37044, 931-221-7031/7891. David Till, Co-Editor; Malcolm Glass, Co-Editor. 1986. "The editors want poems that are deeply rooted in something other than the desire to be published: place, mind, heart, experience, rage, imagination, laughter..." circ. 1M. 2/yr. Pub'd 125 poems 1999; expects 125 poems 2000, 125 poems 2001. sub. price: $8/yr, $10 to libraries & institutions; sample: $4. 70pp; 6×9; Rights purchased: first rights only. Publishes 2% of poems submitted. Deadlines: July 1 for spring/summer, Jan. 1 for fall/winter. Reporting time: 1-5 months after deadline date. Payment: 5 copies. Interested in new or unpub'd poets: yes. Simultaneous submissions accepted: absolutely not. Recent contributors: Michael Burkard, Dave Etter, Ann Struthers, Gregory Orr, Coleman Barks. Submission quantity: 4-5. Special interests: Any of the subject index categories.

●ZOPILOTE, 824 S. Mill Avenue, Suite 219, Tempe, AZ 85281, zopilote@inficad.com, www.zopilote.com. Rosita Dinedo, Poetry Reviews; Cristina Gonzalez, Poetry Editor. 1993. 6/yr. Pub'd 42 poems 1999; expects 43 poems 2000, 44 poems 2001. sub. price: $18; sample: $3.50. 24pp; 8½×11½; Rights purchased: none. Publishes 70-80% of poems submitted. Deadlines: concurrent. Reporting time: 1-2 months. Payment: none at this time. Interested in new or unpub'd poets: yes. Simultaneous submissions accepted: yes. Recent contributors: Carlos Ramirez Jr., Luis Angel Viniegra, Aixa Mont, Araceli Collazd Mapa, Rod Ricardo Livingstone. Submission quantity: as many as they want, we would publish only 1 or 2. Special interests: No love, porno, sexual, racist, or any other subject not related to our publication's focus/subject. Short poetry recommended.

ZUZU'S PETALS: QUARTERLY ONLINE, PO Box 4853, Ithaca, NY 14852-4853, e-mail zuzu@zuzu.com, website http://www.zuzu.com. T. Dunn, Editor. 1992. circ. unlimited. 4/yr. Expects 100 poems 2000, 200 poems 2001. sample price: $5 for our print poetry sample. 200pp; Rights purchased: one time only. Publishes 5% of poems submitted. Deadlines: open. Reporting time: 2 weeks to 2 months. Payment: none, the magazine is free through the net. Interested in new or unpub'd poets: yes. Simultaneous submissions accepted: yes. Recent contributors: Max Greenberg, Paul F. Thurn, Linda Batt, Jean-Paul DeVellard, Gayle Elen Harvey. Submission quantity: it's up to the poet, we're flexible. Special interests: We prefer non-rhyming, narrative, experimental, or visual poetry but don't let that stop you from sending us other types of poetry. We're pretty openminded. Our main criteria is excellence and originality of thought, surrealism, explorations of popular culture, and personal mythology are especially welcome.

Regional Index

ALABAMA

Doctor Jazz Press, 119 Pintail Drive, Pelham, AL 35124, 205-663-3403
AURA LITERARY/ARTS REVIEW, HUC 135, 1530 3rd Avenue South, Birmingham, AL 35294, 205-934-3216
BIRMINGHAM POETRY REVIEW, English Department, University of Alabam-Birmingham, Birmingham, AL 35294, 205-934-8573
DREAMS AND NIGHTMARES, 1300 Kicker Road, Tuscaloosa, AL 35404, 205-553-2284, e-Mail dragontea@earth-link.net
KID'S WORLD, 1300 Kicker Road, Tuscaloosa, AL 35404, 205-553-2284
Livingston Press, Station 22, University of West Alabama, Livingston, AL 35470
Swallow's Tale Press, c/o LU Press, Station 22, University of West Alabama, Livingston, AL 35470
THE BLACK WARRIOR REVIEW, PO Box 862936, University of Alabama, Tuscaloosa, AL 35486-0027, 205-348-4518
Catamount Press, 2519 Roland Road SW, Huntsville, AL 35805, 205-536-9801
COTYLEDON, 2519 Roland Road SW, Huntsville, AL 35805, 205-536-9801
Huntsville Literary Association, c/o English Department, University of Alabama, Huntsville, AL 35899
POEM, c/o English Department, University of Alabama, Huntsville, AL 35899
LAUREATE LETTER, 899 Williamson Trail, Eclectic, AL 36024
WRITERS GAZETTE, 899 Williamson Trail, Eclectic, AL 36024-6131
ALABAMA LITERARY REVIEW, Smith 253, Troy State University, Troy, AL 36082, 334-670-3307;FAX 334-670-3519
NEGATIVE CAPABILITY, 62 Ridgelawn Drive East, Mobile, AL 36608, 205-460-6146
Negative Capability Press, 62 Ridgelawn Drive East, Mobile, AL 36608, 334-460-6146
RIVERSIDE QUARTERLY, 1101 Washington Street, Marion, AL 36756-3213
SOUTHERN HUMANITIES REVIEW, 9088 Haley Center, Auburn Univ., Auburn, AL 36849, 334-844-9088, www.auburn.edu/english/shr/home.htm

ALASKA

ALASKA QUARTERLY REVIEW, University of Alaska-Anchorage, 3211 Providence Drive, Anchorage, AK 99508, 907-786-6916
MOOSE BOUND PRESS JOURNAL/NEWSLETTER, PO Box 111781, Anchorage, AK 99511-1781, 907-333-1465 phone/FAX e-mail mbpress@alaska.net; Website http://www.alaska.net/~mbpress
Salmon Run Press, PO Box 672130, Chugiak, AK 99567-2130, 907-688-4268
JOURNAL OF ALASKA WOMEN, HCR 64 Box 453, Seward, AK 99664, 907-288-3168
Fireweed Press, PO Box 75418, Fairbanks, AK 99707-2136, 907-452-5070 or 907-488-5079
Vanessapress, PO Box 82761, Fairbanks, AK 99708, 907-488-5079; jrb@mosquitonet.com
Windsong Press, PO Box 644, Delta Jct., AK 99737, 907-895-4179
EXPLORATIONS, English Dept., Alaska Univ. Southeast, 11120 Glacier Highway, Juneau, AK 99801

ARIZONA

Riverstone, A Press for Poetry, 7571 East Visao Drive, Scottsdale, AZ 85262
FOREVER ALIVE, PO Box 12305, Scottsdale, AZ 85267-2305, 602-922-0300; fax 602-922-0800; e-Mail HERBBOWIE@AOL.COM
ZOPILOTE, 824 S. Mill Avenue, Suite 219, Tempe, AZ 85281, zopilote@inficad.com, www.zopilote.com
Bilingual Review/Press, Hispanic Research Center, Arizona State Univ., Box 872702, Tempe, AZ 85287-2702, 602-965-3867
BILINGUAL REVIEW/Revista Bilingue, Hispanic Research Center, Arizona State Univ., Box 872702, Tempe, AZ 85287-2702, 602-965-3867
HAYDEN'S FERRY REVIEW, Box 871502, Arizona State University, Tempe, AZ 85287-1502, 602-965-1243
IGNIS FATUUS REVIEW, 18 Yuma Trail, Bisbee, AZ 85603
SONORA REVIEW, Dept. of English, University of Arizona, Tucson, AZ 85721, 520-626-8383
NEWSLETTER INAGO, Inago Press, PO Box 26244, Tucson, AZ 85726-6244, 520-294-7031
THIN AIR, PO Box 23549, Flagstaff, AZ 86002, www.nau.edu/~english/thinair/taframes.html
Star Rising Publishers/Allisone Press, PO Box 3790, Sedona, AZ 86340, 877-249-6894 phone/Fax, allisone@ureach.com, www.allisonepress.com

ARKANSAS

Cedar Hill Publications, 3722 Highway 8 West, Mena, AR 71953, 501-394-7029
CEDAR HILL REVIEW, 3722 Highway 8 West, Mena, AR 71953, 501-394-7029
SLANT: A Journal of Poetry, University of Central Arkansas, PO Box 5063, Conway, AR 72035-5000, 501-450-5107
CRAZYHORSE, 2801 S. University, Dept. of English, Univ. of Arkansas-Little Rock, Little Rock, AR 72204, 501-569-3161
AQUATERRA, METAECOLOGY & CULTURE, 5473 Highway 23N, Eureka Springs, AR 72631
Bearhouse Publishing, 398 Mundell Rd., Eureka Springs, AR 72631-8906, 501-253-9351, E-mail tbadger@ipa.net
LUCIDITY, 398 Mundell Rd., Eureka Springs, AR 72631-9505, 501-253-9351, E-mail tbadger@ipa.net
Star Publications, PO Box 2144, Eureka Springs, AR 72632, 816-523-8228, Fax 501-981-1515, damon-dave@hotmail.com
NEBO, Department of English, Arkansas Tech University, Russellville, AR 72801, 501-968-0256

CALIFORNIA

LOS, 150 North Catalina Street #2, Los Angeles, CA 90004
AAIMS Publishers, 11000 Wilshire Boulevard, PO Box 241777, Los Angeles, CA 90024-9577, 213-968-1195, 888-490-2276, fax 213-931-7217, email aaims1@aol.com
Heat Press, PO Box 26218, Los Angeles, CA 90026, 213-482-8902, chpeditt@cdrewu.edu
TUCUMCARI LITERARY REVIEW, 3108 W. Bellevue Avenue, Los Angeles, CA 90026
Veracity Press, 3765 Motor, Box 702, Los Angeles, CA 90034, 310-820-8269; Veracity96@aol.com

LYNX EYE, 1880 Hill Drive, Los Angeles, CA 90041, 323-550-8522
god is DEAD, publications, 910 North Martel, Suite #207, Los Angeles, CA 90046, 213-850-0067
Bombshelter Press, P.O Box 481266, Bicentennial Station, Los Angeles, CA 90048, 213-651-5488
ONTHEBUS, Bombshelter Press, P.O. Box 481270, Bicentennial Station, Los Angeles, CA 90048
INTERNATIONAL OLYMPIC LIFTER, 3562 Eagle Rock Boulevard, Los Angeles, CA 90065-2827, 213-257-8762
AMNESIA, PO Box 661441, Los Angeles, CA 90066
Courtyard Publishing Company, 3725 May Street, Los Angeles, CA 90066
Pluma Productions, 1977 Carmen Avenue, Los Angeles, CA 90068, email pluma@earthlink.net
2.13.61 Publications, PO Box 1910, Los Angeles, CA 90078, 213-969-8791
BLACK LACE, PO Box 83912, Los Angeles, CA 90083, 310-410-0808, fax 310-410-9250, e-mail newsroom@blk.com
BLACKFIRE, PO Box 83912, Los Angeles, CA 90083, 310-410-0808, fax 310-410-9250, e-mail newsroom@blk.com
BLK, PO Box 83912, Los Angeles, CA 90083, 310-410-0808, fax 310-410-9250, e-mail newsroom@blk.com
BLK Publishing Company, PO Box 83912, Los Angeles, CA 90083, 310-410-0808, Fax 310-410-9250, newsroom@blk.com
KUUMBA, PO Box 83912, Los Angeles, CA 90083, 310-410-0808, fax 310-410-9250, e-mail newsroom@blk.com
THE SOUTHERN CALIFORNIA ANTHOLOGY, Master of Professional Writing Program, WPH 404/Univ. of Southern Calif., Los Angeles, CA 90089-4034, 213-740-5775
AMERICAN INDIAN CULTURE AND RESEARCH JOURNAL, 3220 Campbell Hall, Box 951548, Los Angeles, CA 90095-1548, 310-825-7315; Fax 310-206-7060; www.sscnet.ucla.edu/esp/aisc/index.html
Bleeding Heart Press, PO Box 15902, Beverly Hills, CA 90209-1902
THE BLIND HORSE REVIEW, PO Box 15902, Beverly Hills, CA 90209-1902
Via God Publishing, PO BOx 996, Beverly Hills, CA 90213, 310-390-0843
TURNING THE TIDE: A Journal of Anti-Racist Action, Research & Education, PO Box 1055, Culver City, CA 90232-1055, 310-495-0299, e-mail part2001@usa.net
INTERBANG, PO Box 1574, Venice, CA 90294, 310-450-6372
The Spinning Star Press, 1065 E. Fairview Blvd., Inglewood, CA 90302, 213-464-3024
SPLIT SHIFT, 2461 Santa Monica Blvd. #C-122, Santa Monica, CA 90404
Split Shift, 2461 Santa Monica Blvd. #C-122, Santa Monica, CA 90404
MUSHROOM DREAMS, 14537 Longworth Avenue, Norwalk, CA 90650-4724
JB Press, 1130 North Cabrillo, San Pedro, CA 90731, 310-832-7024
LUMMOX JOURNAL, PO Box 5301, San Pedro, CA 90733-5301, 562-439-9858, e-mail lumoxraindog@earthlink.net
Lummox Press, PO Box 5301, San Pedro, CA 90733-5301, 310-521-9642, e-mail lumoxraindog@earthlink.net
THE NOCTURNAL LYRIC, PO Box 115, San Pedro, CA 90733-0115
BLACK CROSS, 3121 Corto Place #2, Long Beach, CA 90803, 562-987-4305; wstien@csulb.edu
PEARL, 3030 E. Second Street, Long Beach, CA 90803, 562-434-4523 phone/Fax or 714-968-7530, mjohn5150@aol.com, www.pearlmag.com
Pearl Editions, 3030 E. Second Street, Long Beach, CA 90803, 562-434-4523 phone/Fax or 714-968-7530, mjohn5150@aol.com, www.pearlmag.com
INDEFINITE SPACE, PO Box 40101, Pasadena, CA 91114
Golden Isis Press, PO Box 4263, Chatsworth, CA 91313
PAGAN PRIDE, PO Box 4263, Chatsworth, CA 91313
NORTHRIDGE REVIEW, c/o CSUN, 18111 Nordoff Street, Mail Stop 8248, Northridge, CA 91330-8261, E-mail 102504.1176@compuserve.com
CROSSCURRENTS, A QUARTERLY, 24440 Valencia Blvd. #3101, Valencia, CA 91355-1811, 818-991-1694
Delta Press, 27460 Avenue Scott, Valencia, CA 91355, 661-294-2208
Beacon Light Publishing (BLP), PO Box 1612, Thousand Oaks, CA 91358, 805-583-2002, toll free 888-771-1197
MAGIC REALISM, PO Box 922648, Sylmar, CA 91392-2648
Pyx Press, Box 922648, Sylmar, CA 91392-2648
Creative Book Company, 13920 Roscoe Boulevard, Panorama City, CA 91402-4213, Fax 818-894-5282
SHIRIM, 4611 Vesper Avenue, Sherman Oaks, CA 91403-5615
Center Press, PO Box 17897, Encino, CA 91416-7897
LUZ EN ARTE Y LITERATURA, 5008 Hazeltine Avenue #16, Sherman Oaks, CA 91423
RATTLE, 13440 Ventura Boulevard #200, Sherman Oaks, CA 91423, 818-788-3232, fax 818-788-2831
Panjandrum Books, 6156 Wilkinson Avenue, North Hollywood, CA 91606, 818-506-0202
PANJANDRUM POETRY JOURNAL, 6156 Wilkinson Avenue, North Hollywood, CA 91606
Phony Lid Publications, PO Box 2153, Rosemead, CA 91770, e-mail phonylid@fyuocuk.com, www.fyuocuk.com
PICK POCKET BOOKS, PO Box 2153, Rosemead, CA 91770, e-mail phonylid@fyuocuk.com, www.fyuocuk.com
PEAKY HIDE, PO Box 1591, Upland, CA 91785
THE POETRY CONSPIRACY, PO Box 818, Cardiff, CA 92007
Piano Press, PO Box 85, Del Mar, CA 92014-0085, pianopress@aol.com, www.pianopress.iuma.com
La Jolla Poets Press, PO Box 8638, La Jolla, CA 92038, 619-457-1399
San Diego Poet's Press, c/o Kathleen Iddings, PO Box 8638, La Jolla, CA 92038, 858-457-1399
West Anglia Publications, PO Box 2683, La Jolla, CA 92038, 858-457-1399
HIP Inc., PO Box 13665, La Jolla, CA 92039-3665, 505-534-9476; skip@hippy.com; www.hippy.com
HIPPYLAND HIPPIE MAGAZINE, PO Box 13665, La Jolla, CA 92039-3665, 505-534-9476; skip@hippy.com; www.hippy.com
DREAM INTERNATIONAL QUARTERLY, 411 14th Street #H1, Ramona, CA 92065-2769
XIB, 930 24th Street, San Diego, CA 92102-2006
Xib Publications, 930 24th Street, San Diego, CA 92102-2006
OZ-STORY, 1516 Cypress Avenue, San Diego, CA 92103-4517
Tecolote Publications, 4918 Del Monte Avenue, San Diego, CA 92107
Libra Publishers, Inc., 3089C Clairemont Dr., Suite 383, San Diego, CA 92117, 619-571-1414
Junction Press, PO Box 40537, San Diego, CA 92164-0537, 619-702-4607
THE WISHING WELL, PO Box 178440, San Diego, CA 92177-8440, 619-270-2779
San Diego State University Press, San Diego State University, San Diego, CA 92182, 619-594-6220
THE PACIFIC REVIEW, Department of English, Calif State University, San Bernardino, CA 92407, 714-880-5824
Xenos Books, Box 52152, Riverside, CA 92517, 909-370-2229; E-mail info@xenosbooks.com; http://www.xenos-books.com

240

FREE LUNCH, PO Box 7647, Laguna Niguel, CA 92607-7647
SPILLWAY, Box 7887, Huntington Beach, CA 92615-7887, 714-968-0905
Tebot Bach, Box 7887, Huntington Beach, CA 92615-7887, 714-968-0905
THE EAR, Irvine Valley Coll., School of Humanities, 5500 Irvine Center Drive, Irvine, CA 92620, 714-541-5341
JACARANDA, English Department, California State Univ—Fullerton, Fullerton, CA 92634, 714-773-3163
Words & Pictures Press, 1921 Sherry Lane, Apt. #87, Santa Ana, CA 92705-7621, 714-544-7282; Fax 714-544-7430;
    E-mail publisher@earthlink.net
Canterbury Press, 5540 Vista Del Amigo, Anaheim, CA 92807, Fax 714-998-1929
CALIFORNIA QUARTERLY (CQ), CSPS/CQ, PO Box 7126, Orange, CA 92863, 805-543-8255, 949-854-8024,
    jspalley@aol.com
FREEDOM ISN'T FREE, PO Box 6184, Orange, CA 92863-6184
Temporary Vandalism Recordings, PO Box 6184, Orange, CA 92863-6184, e-mail tvrec@yahoo.com
ART/LIFE, PO Box 23020, Ventura, CA 93002, 805-648-4331
Art/Life Limited Editions, PO Box 23020, Ventura, CA 93002, 805-648-4331
X-RAY, PO Box 1103, Ventura, CA 93002, e-mail johnny@xraybookco.com
SOLO, 5146 Foothill, Carpinteria, CA 93013, berrypress@aol.com
VERVE, PO Box 630305, Simi Valley, CA 93063-0305
SANTA BARBARA REVIEW, PO Box 808, Summerland, CA 93067, 805-969-0861; E-mail jtaeby@West.net
Fithian Press, PO Box 1525, Santa Barbara, CA 93102, 805-962-1780, Fax 805-962-8835, e-mail dandd@danielpublish-
    ing.com
John Daniel and Company, Publishers, PO Box 21922, Santa Barbara, CA 93121, 805-962-1780, fax 805-962-8835, email
    dand@danielpublishing.com
Green River Press, PO Box 6454, Santa Barbara, CA 93160, 805-964-4475, Fax 805-967-6208, 75364.3643@compu-
    serve.com
Summer Stream Press, PO Box 6056, Santa Barbara, CA 93160-6056, 805-962-6540
Mille Grazie Press, PO Box 92023, Santa Barbara, CA 93190, 805-963-8408
SHORT FUSE, PO Box 90436, Santa Barbara, CA 93190
DRY CRIK REVIEW, PO Box 44320, Lemon Cove, CA 93244, 209-597-2512; fax 209-597-2103
AMELIA, 329 'E' Street, Bakersfield, CA 93304, 661-323-4064
Amelia Press, 329 'E' Street, Bakersfield, CA 93304, 661-323-4064
CICADA, 329 'E' Street, Bakersfield, CA 93304, 661-323-4064
SPSM&H, 329 'E' Street, Bakersfield, CA 93304, 661-323-4064
KALDRON, An International Journal Of Visual Poetry, PO Box 7164, Halcyon, CA 93421-7164, 805-489-2770; Website
    http://www.thing.net/~grist/l&d/kaldron.htm
The Olive Press Publications, PO Box 99, Los Olivos, CA 93441, Tel/Fax 805-688-2445
VIRGIN MEAT E-ZINE, 2325 West Avenue K-15, Lancaster, CA 93536, E-mail virginmeat@aol.com;
    www.members.aol.com/virginmeat/magazine/gothic.html
QUARTZ HILL JOURNAL OF THEOLOGY, 43543 51st Street West, Quartz Hill, CA 93536, 661-722-0891,
    661-943-3484, E-mail robin@theology.edu
SILVER WINGS/MAYFLOWER PULPIT, PO Box 1000, Pearblossom, CA 93553-1000, 805-264-3726
Red Hen Press, PO Box 902582, Palmdale, CA 93590, Fax 818-831-6659, E-mail redhen@vpg.net
Torchlight Publishing, PO Box 52, Badger, CA 93603
THE SUNDAY SUITOR POETRY REVIEW, 329 Hyde Street, Salinas, CA 93907-2033, 209-858-1453
Creative With Words Publications (CWW), PO Box 223226, Carmel, CA 93922-3226, Fax: 831-655-8627; e-mail:
    cwwpub@usa.net; http://members.tripod.com/~creativewithwords
THEECLECTICS, PO Box 223226, Carmel, CA 93922, fax 831-655-8627; e-mail cwwpub@usa.net; website
    http://members.tripod.com/~CreativeWithWords
Buddhist Text Translation Society, 1777 Murchison Drive, Burlingame, CA 94010-4504, phone/fax 415-692-9286, e-mail
    drbabtts@jps.net
Nextstep Books, 1070 Carolan Avenue #116, Burlingame, CA 94010, e-mail nextstep@nub.ml.org
New World Press, 20 Driftwood Trail, Half Moon Bay, CA 94019-2349, 650-726-5939; Fax 415-921-3730
TAMEME, 199 First Street, Los Altos, CA 94022, www.tameme.org
Backspace Ink, 561 Paloma Avenue, Pacifica, CA 94044-2438, 650-355-4640, FAX 650-355-3630, joski@ix.netcom.com
The Heyeck Press, 25 Patrol Court, Woodside, CA 94062, 650-851-7491; Fax 650-851-5039; heyeck@ix.netcom.com
OXYGEN, 537 Jones Street, PMB 999, San Francisco, CA 94102, 415-776-9681
GLB Publishers, 1028 Howard Street #503, San Francisco, CA 94103, 415-621-8307, www.GLBpubs.com
Mandala Publishing Group, 1585A Folsom Street, San Francisco, CA 94103-3728, 541-688-2258, 800-688-2218; Fax
    541-461-3478; E-mail gvs@efn.org
MOTHER EARTH JOURNAL: An International Quarterly, c/o National Poetry Association, 934 Brannan Street, 2nd
    Floor, San Francisco, CA 94103, 415-552-9261; fax 415-552-9271
POETRY USA, 934 Brannan Street, 2nd floor, San Francisco, CA 94103, 415-552-9261; FAX 415-552-9291; E-mail
    gamuse@slip.net, http://www.slip.net.gamuse
Uniting the World Press, Inc., c/o National Poetry Association, 934 Brannan Street, #2ND-FL, San Francisco, CA 94103,
    415-552-9261; fax 415-552-9271
CAVEAT LECTOR, 400 Hyde Street, Apt. 606, San Francisco, CA 94109, 415-928-7431
Sunlight Publishers, PO Box 640545, San Francisco, CA 94109, 415-776-6249
BLUEBOOK, 766 Valencia Street, San Francisco, CA 94110, 415-437-3450, Fax 415-626-5541
CLUTCH, 147 Coleridge Street, San Francisco, CA 94110
OFF OUR BACKS, 3600 20th Street, #201, San Francisco, CA 94110-2351, 415-546-0384
PROSODIA, New College of California/Poetics, 766 Valencia Street, San Francisco, CA 94110, 415-437-3479, Fax
    415-437-3702
Off the Cuff Books, 191 Sickles Avenue, San Francisco, CA 94112-4046, email suavd@sunsite.unc.edu
OYSTER BOY REVIEW, 191 Sickles Avenue, San Francisco, CA 94112-4046, Email oyster-boy@sunsite.unc.edu;
    www.sunsite.unc.edu/ob
THE BLOWFISH CATALOG, 2261 Market Street #284, San Francisco, CA 94114, 415-864-0880; fax 1-415-864-1858;
    e-Mail blowfish@blowfish. rom
Blowfish Press, 2261 Market Street #284, San Francisco, CA 94114, 415-864-0880; fax 1-415-864-1858; e-Mail
    blowfish@blowfish. com

ENTELECHY MAGAZINE, 2363 Jackson Street #4, San Francisco, CA 94115-1345, e-mail shorn@entelechy.org; website www.entelechy.org
Aspermont Press, 1251 Hayes Street, San Francisco, CA 94117
URBANUS/RAIZIRR, PO Box 192921, San Francisco, CA 94119-2921
HARMONY: Voices for a Just Future, PO Box 210056, San Francisco, CA 94121-0056, 415-221-8527
Protean Press, 287-28th Avenue, San Francisco, CA 94121, fax 415-386-4980
NEW METHODS JOURNAL (VETERINARY), PO Box 22605, San Francisco, CA 94122-0605, 415-664-3469
National Poetry Association Publishers, Fort Mason Center, Building D, Room 270, San Francisco, CA 94123, 415-776-6602
Jesus Pinata Press, PO Box 26692, San Francisco, CA 94126, E-mail elfool@aol.com
HAIGHT ASHBURY LITERARY JOURNAL, 558 Joost Avenue, San Francisco, CA 94127
Second Coming Press, PO Box 31249, San Francisco, CA 94131
Androgyne Books, 930 Shields, San Francisco, CA 94132, 415-586-2697
FOURTEEN HILLS: The SFSU Review, Creative Writing Dept., SFSU, 1600 Holloway Avenue, San Francisco, CA 94132, 415-338-3083, fax 415-338-0504, E-mail hills@sfsu.edu
City Lights Books, Attn: Bob Sharrard, Editor, 261 Columbus Avenue, San Francisco, CA 94133, 415-362-8193
Gay Sunshine Press, Inc., PO Box 410690, San Francisco, CA 94141, 415-626-1935; Fax 415-626-1802
H2SO4, PO Box 423354, San Francisco, CA 94142, 415-431-2135, h2so4@socrates.berkeley.edu
ISSUES, PO Box 424885, San Francisco, CA 94142-4885, 415-864-4800 X136
Meridien PressWorks, PO Box 640024, San Francisco, CA 94164, 415-928-8904
Norton Coker Press, PO Box 640543, San Francisco, CA 94164-0543, 415-922-0395
Taurean Horn Press, PO Box 641097, San Francisco, CA 94164
Anamnesis Press, PO Box 51115, Palo Alto, CA 94303-0688, 415-255-8366, Fax 415-255-3190, anamnesis@compuserve.com, website ourworld.compuserve.com/homepages/anamnesis/
Press Here, PO Box 4014, Foster City, CA 94404, 415-571-9428, e-Mail WelchM@aol.com
WOODNOTES, 248 Beach Park Boulevard, Foster City, CA 94404, 415-571-9428, e-mail WelchM@aol.com
The Infinity Group, PO Box 2713, Castro Valley, CA 94546, 510-581-8172; kenandgenie@yahoo.com
DARK REGIONS: The Years Best Fantastic Fiction, 30 Canyon View Drive, Orinda, CA 94563
THE GENRE WRITER'S NEWS, 30 Canyon View Drive, Orinda, CA 94563, 510-254-7442
Woodburn Avenue Books, 6850 Regional Street, Suite 100, Dublin, CA 94568, 1-888-490-1099 ext. 7; krudolph@mediaone.net
LEFT CURVE, PO Box 472, Oakland, CA 94604, E-mail: leftcurv@wco.com
RADIANCE, The Magazine For Large Women, PO Box 30246, Oakland, CA 94604, 510-482-0680, E-mail info@radiancemagazine.com, www.radiancemagazine.com
Regent Press, 6020-A Adeline, Oakland, CA 94608, 415-548-8459
Broken Shadow Publications, 472 44th Street, Oakland, CA 94609-2136, 510-450-0640
ANT ANT ANT ANT ANT, PO Box 16177, Oakland, CA 94610, www.home.earthlink.net/~antfive
Scarlet Tanager Books, PO Box 20906, Oakland, CA 94610, 510-763-3874
Burning Bush Publications, PO Box 9636, Oakland, CA 94613-0636, 510-482-9996, www.bbbooks.com
HIP MAMA, Attn: Ariel Gore, PO Box 9097, Oakland, CA 94613, 510-658-4508
CC. Marimbo Communications, PO Box 933, Berkeley, CA 94701-0933
GESAR-Buddhism in the West, 2910 San Pablo Avenue, Berkeley, CA 94702, 415-548-5407
Homeward Press, PO Box 2307, Berkeley, CA 94702, 412-526-3254
AGADA, 2020 Essex Street, Berkeley, CA 94703, 510-848-0965
New Earth Publications, 1921 Ashby Ave, Berkeley, CA 94703, 510-549-0176
SINISTER WISDOM, PO Box 3252, Berkeley, CA 94703, 510-532-5222
SCP NEWSLETTER, PO Box 4308, Berkeley, CA 94704
TURNING WHEEL, PO Box 4650, Berkeley, CA 94704
Oyez, PO Box 5134, Berkeley, CA 94705
Poltroon Press, PO Box 5476, Berkeley, CA 94705, 510-845-8097
YELLOW SILK: Journal Of Erotic Arts, PO Box 6374, Albany, CA 94706, 510-644-4188
BLUE UNICORN, 22 Avon Road, Kensington, CA 94707, 510-526-8439
Kelsey St. Press, 50 Northgate Avenue, Berkeley, CA 94708-2008, 510-845-2260; FAX 510-548-9185, e-mail kelseyst@sirius.com; www.kelseyst.com
Heyday Books, PO Box 9145, Berkeley, CA 94709, 510-549-3564, FAX 510-549-1889
THE THREEPENNY REVIEW, PO Box 9131, Berkeley, CA 94709, 510-849-4545
THE BERKELEY REVIEW OF BOOKS, 1731 10th Street, Apt. A, Berkeley, CA 94710, 415-528-8713
Creative Arts Book Company, 833 Bancroft Way, Berkeley, CA 94710, staff@creativeartsbooks.com
POETRY FLASH, 1450 Fourth Street #4, Berkeley, CA 94710, 510-525-5476, Fax 510-525-6752
Bay Area Poets Coalition, POETALK, PO Box 11435, Berkeley, CA 94712-2435, 510-272-9176
THE CHEROTIC (r)EVOLUTIONARY, PO Box 11445, Berkeley, CA 94712, 510-526-7858, FAX 510-524-2053, fmoore@eroplay.com
Five Fingers Press, PO Box 12955, Berkeley, CA 94712-3955
FIVE FINGERS REVIEW, PO Box 12955, Berkeley, CA 94712-3955
MINDFIELD MAGAZINE: Your Mental Weapons Manual, PO Box 14114, Berkeley, CA 94712-5114, 510-433-7945; mindfld@dnai.com; www.dnai.com/mindfld
POETALK, PO Box 11435, Berkeley, CA 94712-2435, 510-272-9176
BERKELEY POETRY REVIEW, 201 MLK Student Union, University of California, Berkeley, CA 94720
Cadmus Editions, PO Box 126, Belvedere Tiburon, CA 94920-0126
ZAUM - The Literary Review of Sonoma State University, English Department, SSU, 1801 E. Cotati Avenue, Rohnert Park, CA 94928, 707-664-2140
BARNABE MOUNTAIN REVIEW, PO Box 529, Lagunitas, CA 94938
Kosmos, 20 Millard Road, Larkspur, CA 94939
NEW AMERICAN WRITING, 369 Molino Avenue, Mill Valley, CA 94941, 415-389-1877 phone/Fax
The Feathered Serpent, 55 Galli Drive #C, Novato, CA 94949-5715, 415-499-8751
The Post-Apollo Press, 35 Marie Street, Sausalito, CA 94965, 415-332-1458, fax 415-332-8045
Arctos Press, PO Box 401, Sausalito, CA 94966, 415-331-2503, Fax 415-331-3092, runes@aol.com, http://members.aol.com/runes/index.html

TAMBOURINE, PO Box 790, Sausalito, CA 94966, 415-383-8447
GINOSKO, PO Box 246, Fairfax, CA 94978, 415-460-8436
Big Star Press, 1770 48th Avenue, #2-D, Capitola, CA 95010, 408-464-3625 ph/fax
RED WHEELBARROW, 21250 Stevens Creek Blvd., De Anza College, Cupertino, CA 95014, Fax 408-864-5629, rsplitter@earthlink.net
WRITING FOR OUR LIVES, 647 N. Santa Cruz Ave., The Annex, Los Gatos, CA 95030, 408-354-8604
Amethyst & Emerald, 1556 Halford Avenue, Suite 124, Santa Clara, CA 95051-2661, 408-296-5483; fax 408-249-7646
TEENS IN MOTION NEWS, PO Box 1264, Santa Clara, CA 95052, 408-244-3718
Greenhouse Review Press, 3965 Bonny Doon Road, Santa Cruz, CA 95060, 831-426-4355
Moving Parts Press, 10699 Empire Grade, Santa Cruz, CA 95060-9474, 408-427-2271
Tombouctou Books, 1472 Creekview Lane, Santa Cruz, CA 95062, 408-476-4144
STONE SOUP, The Magazine By Young Writers and Artists, Box 83, Santa Cruz, CA 95063, 831-426-5557, Fax 831-426-1161, e-mail editor@stonesoup.com, www.stonesoup.com
POET'S PARK, 2745 Monterey Highway #76, San Jose, CA 95111-3129, 408-578-3546; http://www.soos.com/poetpark
CAESURA, San Jose Museum of Art, 110 S. Market, San Jose, CA 95113, FAX 408-624-7432
French Bread Publications, PO Box 23868, San Jose, CA 95153, e-mail paccoastj@bjt.net
PACIFIC COAST JOURNAL, PO Box 23868, San Jose, CA 95153, e-mail paccoastj@bjt.net
Black Sparrow Press, 24 Tenth Street, Santa Rosa, CA 95401
LEAPINGS LITERARY MAGAZINE, 2455 Pinercrest Drive, Santa Rosa, CA 95403, E-mail 72144.3133@compuserve.com
GREEN FUSE POETRY, 3365 Holland Drive, Santa Rosa, CA 95404, 707-544-8303
Clamshell Press, 160 California Avenue, Santa Rosa, CA 95405
THE REJECTED QUARTERLY, PO Box 1351, Cobb, CA 95426, E-mail bplankton@juno.com
Pot Shard Press, PO Box 215, Comptche, CA 95427, 707-937-2058
Lost Coast Press, 155 Cypress Street, Fort Bragg, CA 95437
AHA Books, PO Box 767, Gualala, CA 95445, 707-882-2226
MEMO, PO Box 1497, Mendocino, CA 95460
GREEN EGG, 212 S. Main Street #22B, Willits, CA 95490-3535, 707-456-0332; Fax 707-456-0333; e-mail admin@greenegg.org
Pygmy Forest Press, PO Box 7097, Eureka, CA 95502-7097, 707-268-1274
THE KERF, 883 W. Washington Boulevard, Crescent City, CA 95531, 707-464-6867
A.R.A. JOURNAL, Dr. Ion Manea-Manoliu, 3328 Monte Vista Avenue, Davis, CA 95616, 916-758-7720
American Romanian Academy, University of California, Dept. of French & Italian, Davis, CA 95616, 916-758-7720
AMERICAS REVIEW, PO Box 72466, Davis, CA 95617
MOCKINGBIRD, PO Box 761, Davis, CA 95617
THE ACORN, PO Box 1266, El Dorado, CA 95623, theacorn@visto.com
POETRY DEPTH QUARTERLY, 5836 North Haven Drive, North Highlands, CA 95660, 916-331-3512, e-mail poetdpth@aol.com, www.angelfire.com/biz/PoetsGuild/guide.html
THE COMPLEAT NURSE, PO Box 597, Roseville, CA 95678-0597, 415-707-2129 phone/Fax, www.drybones.com
Dry Bones Press, PO Box 597, Roseville, CA 95678-0597, 415-707-2129 phone/Fax, jrankin@drybones.com, www.drybones.com
Hot Pepper Press, PO Box 39, Somerset, CA 95684
Konocti Books, 23311 County Road 88, Winters, CA 95694
POETRY NOW, Sacramento's Literary Calendar and Review, 1631 K Street, Sacramento, CA 95814, 916-441-7395, e-mail spc@quiknet.com, www.tomatoweb.com/spc
EKPHRASIS, PO Box 161236, Sacramento, CA 95816-1236, 916-451-3038, http://members.aol.com/ekphrasisl
Frith Press, PO Box 161236, Sacramento, CA 95816-1236, 916-451-3038, http://members.aol.com/ekphrasisl
FUCK DECENCY, 5960 S. Land Park Drive #253, Sacramento, CA 95822
Ravenwood Publishing, PO Box 601551, Sacramento, CA 95860, 916-974-0764, Fax 916-972-9312, www.ravenwood-pub.com
Heidelberg Graphics, 2 Stansbury Court, Chico, CA 95928-9410, 530-342-6582
WILD DUCK REVIEW, PO BOX 388, Nevada City, CA 95959-0388, 530-478-0134, Fax 530-265-2304, casey@wildduckreview.com
The Petrarch Press, PO Box 488, Oregon House, CA 95962, 916-692-0828
Asylum Arts, 5847 Sawmill Rd., Paradise, CA 95969, 530-876-1454, asyarts@sunset.net
NORTHERN CONTOURS, PO Box 618, Quincy, CA 95971, 916-283-3402
Bear Star Press, 185 Hollow Oak Drive, Cohasset, CA 95973, 530-891-0360, www.bearstarpress.com
UNITED LUMBEE NATION TIMES, P.O. Box 512, Fall River Mills, CA 96028, 530-336-6701
Coyote Publishing, PO Box 1854, Yreka, CA 96097, 916-842-5788

COLORADO

National Writers Press, 3140 S. Peoria Street, PMB 294, Aurora, CO 80014, 720-851-1944, Fax 303-841-2607, www.nationalwriters.com
THE BLOOMSBURY REVIEW, 1553 Platte Street, Suite 206, Denver, CO 80202, 303-455-3123, Fax 303-455-7039
HIGH PLAINS LITERARY REVIEW, 180 Adams Street, Suite 250, Denver, CO 80206, (303) 320-6828
DENVER QUARTERLY, University of Denver, Denver, CO 80208, 303-871-2892
Now It's Up To You Publications, 157 S. Logan, Denver, CO 80209, 303-777-8951
PLEIADES MAGAZINE-Philae-Epic Journal-Thoughts Journal, Box 357, 6677 W. Colfax Avenue, Suite D, Lakewood, CO 80214, 303-237-1019
THE CLIMBING ART, 6390 E. Floyd Dr., Denver, CO 80222-7638
LFW Enterprises, PO Box 370234, Denver, CO 80237-0234, 303-750-1040
SPEAK UP, PO Box 100506, Denver, CO 80250, 303-715-0837, Fax 303-715-0793, speakupres@aol.com, www.speakuppress.org
MurPubCo, 3335 Chisholm Trail #206, Boulder, CO 80301
MANY MOUNTAINS MOVING, 420 22nd Street, Boulder, CO 80302, 303-545-9942, Fax 303-444-6510
MOONRABBIT REVIEW, 2525 Arapahoe Avenue, Ste. E4-230, Boulder, CO 80302, 303-439-8860; Fax 439-8362; JHLee@ucsub.Colorado.edu
Dead Metaphor Press, PO Box 2076, Boulder, CO 80306, 303-417-9398

THE BOOMERPHILE, PO Box 17446, Boulder, CO 80308-0446, 303-444-3363, www.delphi.com/boomer
BOULDER HERETIC, PO Box 17446, Boulder, CO 80308-0446, 303-444-3363, danculberson@juno.com
Bardsong Press, PO Box 775396, Steamboat Springs, CO 80477, 970-870-1401, fax 970-879-2657
COLORADO REVIEW: A Journal of Contemporary Literature, 359 Eddy, English Dept., Colorado State University, Fort Collins, CO 80523, 303-491-5449
C & G Publishing, Inc., PO Box 5199, Greeley, CO 80634, 970-356-9622, ccgcook@aol.com
THE ELEVENTH MUSE, a publication by Poetry West, PO Box 2413, Colorado Springs, CO 80901
Arjuna Library Press, 1025 Garner Street, D, Space 18, Colorado Springs, CO 80905-1774
JOURNAL OF REGIONAL CRITICISM, 1025 Garner Street, Box 18, Colorado Springs, CO 80905-1774
WRITERS' FORUM, University of Colorado, PO Box 7150, Colorado Springs, CO 80933-7150, 719-262-4006
Paul Dilsaver, Publisher, PO Box 1621, Pueblo, CO 81002
Passeggiata Press, Inc., 222 West 'B' Street, Pueblo, CO 81003-3404, 719-544-1038, Fax 719-546-7889, e-mail Passeggia@aol.com
THE STAR BEACON, PO Box 117, Paonia, CO 81428, 970-527-3257, e-mail earthstar@tripod.net, http://earthstar.tripod.com/
Acclaim Publishing Co. Inc., PO Box 3918, Grand Junction, CO 81502-3918, 719-784-3712
PINYON POETRY, Dept. of Languages, Lit., & Comm., Mesa State College, 1100 North Ave., Grand Junction, CO 81502-2647, 970-248-1740

CONNECTICUT

IBIS REVIEW, PO Box 133, Falls Village, CT 06031, 203-824-0355
IPSISSIMA VERBA/THE VERY WORDS: Fiction & Poetry in the First Person, 32 Forest Street, New Britain, CT 06052, fax 860-832-9566; e-mail: ipsiverba@aol.com
The Book Department, 107 White Rock Drive, Windsor, CT 06095-4348
Potes & Poets Press Inc., 181 Edgemont Avenue, Elmwood, CT 06110, 203-233-2023; e-mail potepoet@home.com
Plinth Books, Box 271118, W. Hartford, CT 06127-1118
PAPYRUS, 102 LaSalle Road, PO Box 270797, West Hartford, CT 06127, e-mail gwhitaker@imagine.com
Papyrus Literary Enterprises, Inc., 102 LaSalle Road, PO Box 270797, West Hartford, CT 06127, 203-233-7478, e-mail gwhitaker@imagine.com, http://www.readersndex.com/papyrus
Curbstone Press, 321 Jackson Street, Willimantic, CT 06226, 203-423-5110; fax 203-423-9242; e-Mail TAYLORAL@EC-SUC.CTSTATEV.EDU
THE CONNECTICUT POETRY REVIEW, PO Box 818, Stonington, CT 06378
GaiaQuest, PO Box 3065, Branford, CT 06405, 203-481-8747 phone/fax, gaiaquest@snet.net
Telephone Books, 109 Dunk Rock Rd., Guilford, CT 06437, 203-453-1921
Higganum Hill Books, PO Box 666, Higganum, CT 06441, rcdebold@connix.com
Wesleyan University Press, 110 Mount Vernon Street, Middletown, CT 06457, 203-344-7918
Cider Mill Press, PO Box 211, Stratford, CT 06497
DIRIGIBLE, 101 Cottage Street, New Haven, CT 06511, email dirigibl@javanet.com
CONNECTICUT REVIEW, SCSU, 501 Crescent Street, New Haven, CT 06515, 203-392-6737, Fax 203-392-5748
THE YALE REVIEW, Yale University, PO Box 208243, New Haven, CT 06520-8243
Yale University Press, PO Box 209040, New Haven, CT 06520-9040, 203-432-0960
AMARANTH, PO Box 184, Trumbull, CT 06611, 203-452-9652
THE SMALL POND MAGAZINE OF LITERATURE aka SMALL POND, PO Box 664, Stratford, CT 06615, 203-378-4066
TESTIMONIES, 90 Mcpadden Drive, Stratford, CT 06615, 203-378-1853; Fax 203-378-1082; agroves202@aol.com
CONNECTICUT RIVER REVIEW: A National Poetry Journal, PO Box 4053, Waterbury, CT 06704-0053, http://pages.prodigy.net/mmwalker/cpsindex.html
Chicory Blue Press, Inc., 795 East Street North, Goshen, CT 06756, 860-491-2271, FAX 860-491-8619
Rutledge Books, Inc., 107 Mill Plain Road, Danbury, CT 06811, 203-778-5925, Fax 203-798-7272, info@rutledge-books.com, www.rutledgebooks.com
New Canaan Publishing Company Inc., PO Box 752, New Canaan, CT 06840, 203-966-3408 phone/Fax
Intertext, 149 Water Street #35, Norwalk, CT 06854
Hannacroix Creek Books, Inc, 1127 High Ridge Road #110, Stamford, CT 06905, 203-321-8674; Fax 203-968-0193; E-mail hcbbooks@aol.com
Sun-Scape Publications, a division of Sun-Scape Enterprises Ltd., 65 High Ridge Road, Suite 103, Stamford, CT 06905, 203-838-3775; FAX 203-838-3775; orders 1-800-437-1454; info@sun-scape.com; www.sun-scape.com

DELAWARE

Playground Books, 26 Fox Hunt Drive #190, Bear, DE 19701-2534
BLADES, Poporo Press, 335 Paper Mill Road, Newark, DE 19711-2254
Griffon House Publications, 1401 Pennsylvania Avenue, Suite 105, Wilmington, DE 19806, 302-656-3230

DISTRICT OF COLUMBIA

Washington Writers' Publishing House, PO Box 15271, Washington, DC 20003, 202-543-1905, 703-527-5890
AERIAL, P.O. Box 25642, Washington, DC 20007, 202-362-6418; aerialedge@aol.com
KEREM: Creative Explorations in Judaism, 3035 Porter Street, NW, Washington, DC 20008, 202-364-3006; fax 202-364-3806; e-mail srh@udel.edu; www.kerem.com
Wineberry Press, 3207 Macomb Street, NW, Washington, DC 20008-3327, 202-363-8036; e-mail chfarnsworth@compu-serve.com
CONSCIENCE, 1436 U Street NW, Washington, DC 20009
GARGOYLE, 1508 U Street NW, Washington, DC 20009, 202-667-8148; e-mail atticus@radix.net
Maisonneuve Press, PO Box 2980, Washington, DC 20013-2980, 301-277-7505; FAX 301-277-2467
Wheat Forders/Trabuco Books, Box 6317, Washington, DC 20015-0317, 202-362-1588
The Word Works, Inc., PO Box 42164, Washington, DC 20015
FOLIO: A Literary Journal of American University, Dept. of Literature, American University, Washington, DC 20016, 202-885-2971
JAMES WHITE REVIEW; A Gay Men's Literary Quarterly, PO Box 73910, Washington, DC 20056-3910, 612-339-8317
THE DESK, PO Box 50376, Washington, DC 20091

WASHINGTON REVIEW, PO Box 50132, Washington, DC 20091-0132, 202-638-0515

FLORIDA

Kings Estate Press, 870 Kings Estate Road, St. Augustine, FL 32086, 800-249-7485, kep@aug.com
Southern Star Publishing, 4 Timberline Trail #D, Ormond Beach, FL 32174-4977
KALLIOPE, A Journal of Women's Literature and Art, 3939 Roosevelt Blvd, Florida Community College at Jacksonville, Jacksonville, FL 32205, 904-381-3511
MUDLARK, English Department, University of N. Florida, Jacksonville, FL 32224, 904-620-2273, Fax 904-620-3940, E-mail mudlark@unf.edu, www.unf.edu/mudlark
Anhinga Press, PO Box 10595, Tallahassee, FL 32302, 850-521-9920; Fax 850-442-6323; info@anhinga.org; www.anhinga.org
INTERNATIONAL QUARTERLY, PO Box 10521, Tallahassee, FL 32302-0521, 904-224-5078
FATHOMS, PO Box 62634, Tallahassee, FL 32313
THE SILVER WEB, PO Box 38190, Tallahassee, FL 32315
LITERARY MOMENTS, PO Box 30534, Pensacola, FL 32503-1534, 850-857-0178
HALF TONES TO JUBILEE, English Dept., 1000 College Blvd., Pensacola Jr. College, Pensacola, FL 32504, 904-484-1000 ext. 1400
THE PANHANDLER, The Panhandler Press, English Dept., Univ. Of West Florida, Pensacola, FL 32514-5751, 904-474-2923
Desktop, Ink., PO Box 548, Archer, FL 32618-0548, 352-486-6570 phone/Fax; E-mail dktop@aol.com
THE WRITE WAY, 810 Overhill Road, Deland, FL 32720, 904-734-1955
Four Seasons Publishers, PO Box 51, Titusville, FL 32781, E-mail fourseasons@gnc.net
THE FLORIDA REVIEW, PO Box 25000, English Department, University of Central Florida, Orlando, FL 32816, 407-823-2038
POETS' VOICE, Box 500901, Malabar, FL 32950, website www.worldtv3.com/jmark.htm
The Poetry Connection, 13455 SW 16 Court #F-405, Pembroke Pines, FL 33027, 954-431-3016
THE POETRY CONNECTION, 13455 SW 16 Court #F-405, Pembroke Pines, FL 33027, 305-431-3016
CAYO, A MAGAZINE OF LIFE IN THE KEYS, P.O. Box 4516, Key West, FL 33040, 305-296-4286
SO YOUNG!, PO Box 141489, Coral Gables, FL 33114, 305-662-3928; FAX 305-661-4123
MANGROVE MAGAZINE, Dept. of English, Univ. of Miami, PO Box 248145, Coral Gables, FL 33124, 305-284-2182
THOUGHTS FOR ALL SEASONS: The Magazine of Epigrams, 478 NE 56th Street, Miami, FL 33137-2621, 305-756-8800
LATINO STUFF REVIEW, PO Box 440195, Miami, FL 33144, www.ejl@lspress.net
LS Press, Inc., PO Box 440195, Miami, FL 33144, 305-262-1777; fax 305-447-8586; www.ejl@lspress.net
J. Mark Press, Box 742-052, Boynton Beach, FL 33474-7902, website www.worldtv3.com/jmark.htm
TAMPA REVIEW, 401 W. Kennedy Boulevard, University of Tampa-19F, Tampa, FL 33606-1490
McGregor Publishing, 4532 W. Kennedy Blvd., Tampa, FL 33609-2042, 813-681-0092; FAX 813-254-2665; Toll-free 888-405-2665
WRITERS IN PARADISE, 4615 Gulf Boulevard, Ste. 104, St. Pete Beach, FL 33706, E-mail writers.in.paradise@world-net.att.net
Little Bayou Press, 1735 First Avenue North, St. Petersburg, FL 33713-8903, 813-822-3278
ONIONHEAD, 115 North Kentucky Avenue, Lakeland, FL 33801, 941-680-2787
4*9*1, PO Box 91212, Lakeland, FL 33804, stompdncr@aol.com, www.fournineone.com
Rose Shell Press, 15223 Coral Isle Court, Fort Meyers, FL 33919-8434, 941-454-6546
The Runaway Spoon Press, Box 3621, Port Charlotte, FL 33949-3621, 941-629-8045
JAPANOPHILE, 6602 14th Avenue W, Bradenton, FL 34209-4527
Japanophile Press, 6602 14th Avenue W, Bradenton, FL 34209-4527, 517-669-2109; E-mail japanlove@aol.com
NUTHOUSE, PO Box 119, Ellenton, FL 34222
New Collage Press, 5700 North Trail, Sarasota, FL 34234, 813-359-4360
Starbooks Press/FLF Press, 2516 Ridge Avenue, Sarasota, FL 34235, 941-957-1281, Fax 941-955-3829, starxxx@gte.net
NEW COLLAGE MAGAZINE, 5700 N. Tamiami Trail, Sarasota, FL 34243-2197, 813-359-4360
HARP-STRINGS, PO Box 640387, Beverly Hills, FL 34464
THE RATIONAL FEMINIST, 10500 Ulmerton Road #726-202, Largo, FL 34641
Company of Words Publishing, 2082 Shannon Lakes Blvd., Kissimmee, FL 34743-3648, 617-492-7930; FAX 617-354-3392; e-mail wordspub@aol.com; web page www.wordspublishing.com

GEORGIA

A MESSAGE FROM THE HEART NEWS/MAGAZINE, PO Box 373424, Decatur, GA 30037, 770-961-2900, Fax 770-961-1711, kphilli4@bellsouth.net, www.messengerp.com
Messenger Publishing Inc., PO Box 373424, Decatur, GA 30037, 770-961-2900, Fax 770-961-1711, kphilli4@bellsouth.net, www.messengerp.com
Oasis In Print, PO Box 314, Clarkdale, GA 30111, 770-943-3377
THE OLD RED KIMONO, Humanities, Floyd College, Box 1864, Rome, GA 30162, 404-295-6312
Coreopsis Books, 1384 Township Drive, Lawrenceville, GA 30243, 404-995-9475
PARNASSUS LITERARY JOURNAL, Kudzu Press, PO Box 1384, Forest Park, GA 30298-1384
FIVE POINTS, Georgia State University, University Plaza, Atlanta, GA 30303-3083, 404-651-0071, Fax 404-651-3167
L'OUVERTURE, PO Box 8565, Atlanta, GA 30306, 404-572-9141
JAMES DICKEY NEWSLETTER, 1753 Dyson Drive, Atlanta, GA 30307, 404-373-2989 phone/FAX
NYX OBSCURA MAGAZINE, PO Box 5554, Atlanta, GA 30307-0554, 704-684-6629; nyxobscura@aol.com
Bosck Publishing House, 1474 Dodson Drive, Atlanta, GA 30311, 404-755-8170
LULLWATER REVIEW, Box 22036, Emory University, Atlanta, GA 30322, 404-727-6184
MIDWEST POETRY REVIEW, PO Box 20236, Atlanta, GA 30325-0236, 404-350-0714
THE CHATTAHOOCHEE REVIEW, Georgia Perimeter College, 2101 Womack Road, Dunwoody, GA 30338-4497, 404-551-3019
Steam Press/LAD Publishing, 5455 Meridian Mark, Suite 100, Atlanta, GA 30342, 404-257-1577; FAX 256-5475
HABERSHAM REVIEW, PO Box 10, Demorest, GA 30535, 706-778-3000 Ex 132
THE CLASSICAL OUTLOOK, Department of Classics, The University of Georgia, Athens, GA 30602, 706-542-9257, fax 706-542-8503, mricks@arches.uga.edu

THE GEORGIA REVIEW, Univ. of Georgia, Athens, GA 30602-9009, 706-542-3481
VERSE, Department of English, University of Georgia, Athens, GA 30602
THE LANGSTON HUGHES REVIEW, Box 2006, Univ. of Georgia, Athens, GA 30612-0006, 401-863-1815
SIMPLY WORDS, 605 Collins Avenue #23, Centerville, GA 31028, E-mail simplywords@hotmail.com
ARTS & LETTERS JOURNAL OF CONTEMPORARY CULTURE, Georgia College & State University, Campus Box
    89, Milledgeville, GA 31061-0490, 912-445-1289, al@mail.gcsu.edu, http://al.gcsu.edu
ATLANTA REVIEW, PO Box 8248, Atlanta, GA 31106
BABYSUE, PO Box 8989, Atlanta, GA 31106, 404-320-1178
Depth Charge, 1352 Hardeman, 1st Floor, Macon, GA 31201, 708-733-9554;800-639-0008; fax 708-733-0928
SNAKE NATION REVIEW, 110 #2 West Force, Valdosta, GA 31601, 912-249-8334

GUAM

H & C NEWSLETTER, PO Box 24814 GMF, Barrigada, GU 96921-4814, 671-477-1961
STORYBOARD, Division of English, University of Guam, Mangilao, GU 96923, E-mail jtalley@uog9.uog.edu

HAWAII

TitleWaves Publishing, PO Box 288, Lihue, HI 96766-0288, orders 800-867-7323
HAWAII PACIFIC REVIEW, 1060 Bishop Street, Honolulu, HI 96813, 808-544-1107
HAWAI'I REVIEW, c/o Dept. of English, 1733 Donaghho Road, Honolulu, HI 96822, 808-956-3030
MANOA: A Pacific Journal of International Writing, English Department, University of Hawaii, Honolulu, HI 96822,
    956-3070, fax 956-7808, E-mail mjournal-l@hawaii.edu
BAMBOO RIDGE, Journal of Hawai'i Literature and Arts, PO Box 61781, Honolulu, HI 96839-1781
Bamboo Ridge Press, PO Box 61781, Honolulu, HI 96839-1781, 808-626-1481 phone/Fax, brinfo@bambooridge.com

IDAHO

SNAKE RIVER REFLECTIONS, 1863 Bitterroot Drive, Twin Falls, ID 83301, 208-734-0746, e-mail wjan@aol.com
Confluence Press, Inc., Lewis-Clark State College, 500 8th Avenue, Lewiston, ID 83501-2698, 208-799-2336
TALKING RIVER REVIEW, Lewis-Clark State College, 500 8th Avenue, Lewiston, ID 83501, 208-799-2307,
    triver@lcsc.edu
Limberlost Press, 17 Canyon Trail, Boise, ID 83716
Ahsahta, Boise State University, Department of English, Boise, ID 83725, 208-426-1999; orders 1-800-526-6522;
    www.bsubkst.idbsu.edu/
COLD-DRILL, 1910 University Drive, Boise, ID 83725, 208-426-3862
Cold-Drill Books, Dept. of English, Boise State University, Boise, ID 83725
FUGUE, Brink Hall, Room 200, Engl. Dept., University of Idaho, Moscow, ID 83844-1102, 208-885-6156
THE EMSHOCK LETTER, Randall Flat Road, PO Box 411, Troy, ID 83871, 208-835-4902

ILLINOIS

THE CREATIVE WOMAN, 126 East Wing Street #288, Arlington Heights, IL 60004, 708-255-1232; FAX 708-255-1243
Fort Dearborn Press, 245 Bluff Court (LBS), Barrington, IL 60010, 312-235-8500
WHETSTONE, Barrington Area Arts Council, PO Box 1266, Barrington, IL 60011, 847-382-5626
Airplane Books, PO Box 111, Glenview, IL 60025
BAYBURY REVIEW, 40 High Street, Highwood, IL 60040, e-mail baybury@flash.net
Bolchazy-Carducci Publishers, Inc., 1000 Brown Street, Wauconda, IL 60084, 847-526-4344; fax 847-526-2867
RHINO: THE POETRY FORUM, PO Box 554, Winnetka, IL 60093, website www.artic.edu/~ageorg/rhino
Thorntree Press, 547 Hawthorn Lane, Winnetka, IL 60093, 708-446-8099
AIM MAGAZINE, PO Box 1174, Maywood, IL 60153-8174
Celestial Otter Press, 237 Park Trail Court, Schaumburg, IL 60173
MAGIC CHANGES, 237 Park Trail Court, Schaumburg, IL 60173
GOTTA WRITE NETWORK LITMAG, 515 East Thacker Street, Hoffman Estates, IL 60194-1957, FAX 847-296-7631;
    e-mail Netera@aol.com
BRILLIANT STAR, Baha'i National Center, 1233 Central Street, Evanston, IL 60201
DAUGHTERS OF SARAH, 2121 Sheridan Road, Evanston, IL 60201
TRIQUARTERLY, Northwestern University Press, 2020 Ridge, Evanston, IL 60208-4302, 847-491-7614
WRITER TO WRITER, PO Box 2336, Oak Park, IL 60303
The Hosanna Press, 203 Keystone, River Forest, IL 60305, 708-771-8259
Outrider Press, 937 Patricia Lane, Crete, IL 60417-1375, 708-672-6630 (voice), fax 708-672-5820, e-mail
    outriderPr@aol.com, www.outriderpress.com
Lakes & Prairies Press, 15774 S. LaGrange Road #172, Orland Park, IL 60462-4766, website www.lakesprairies.com
CHILDREN, CHURCHES AND DADDIES, A Non Religious, Non Familial Literary Magazine, Attn: Janet Kuypers, 8830
    West 120th Place, Palos Park, IL 60464, E-ail ccandd96@aol.com, www.members.aol.com/scarspub/scras.html
Scars Publications, Attn: Janet Kuypers, 8830 West 120th Place, Palos Park, IL 60464-1137, E-mail ccandd@aol.com,
    www.members.aol.com/scarspub/scars.html
CHAOS FOR THE CREATIVE MIND, PO Box 633, Tinley Park, IL 60477
VACUITY, 1512 Canyon Run Road, Naperville, IL 60565
POETRY, 60 West Walton Street, Chicago, IL 60610, 312-255-3703
The Teitan Press, Inc., PO Box 10258, Chicago, IL 60610, 773-929-7892; FAX 773-871-3315, e-mail teitanpr@aol.com
    Web Site: http://users.aol.com/teitanpr
CHRISTIANITY & THE ARTS, PO Box 118088, Chicago, IL 60611, 312-642-8606
ACM (ANOTHER CHICAGO MAGAZINE), 3709 N. Kenmore, Chicago, IL 60613, 312-248-7665, www.anotherchicago-
    mag.com
LIBIDO: The Journal of Sex and Sensibility, PO Box 146721, Chicago, IL 60614, 773-275-0842
THE MUSING PLACE, 2700 Lakeview, Chicago, IL 60614, 312-281-3800
POETRY EAST, Dept. of English, DePaul Univ., 802 West Belden Avenue, Chicago, IL 60614, 312-325-7487
MATI, 5548 N. Sawyer, Chicago, IL 60625
Ommation Press, 5548 North Sawyer, Chicago, IL 60625
SALOME: A Journal for the Performing Arts, 5548 N. Sawyer, Chicago, IL 60625, 312-539-5745
THE PAPER BAG, PO Box 268805, Chicago, IL 60626-8805, 312-285-7972

The Paper Bag Press, PO Box 268805, Chicago, IL 60626-8805, 312-285-7972
RAMBUNCTIOUS REVIEW, Rambunctious Press, Inc., 1221 West Pratt Blvd., Chicago, IL 60626
THE BAFFLER, PO Box 378293, Chicago, IL 60637
CHICAGO REVIEW, 5801 South Kenwood, Chicago, IL 60637, 773-702-0887, chicago-review@uchicago.edu
PRIMAVERA, PO Box 37-7547, Chicago, IL 60637-7547, 773-324-5920
CORNERSTONE, 939 W. Wilson Avenue, Chicago, IL 60640, 773-561-2450 ext. 2080; fax 773-989-2076
OFF THE ROCKS, 921 W. Argyle #1W, Chicago, IL 60640, E-mail offtherock@aol.com
Tia Chucha Press, PO Box 476969, Chicago, IL 60647, 773-377-2496
Juggernaut, PO Box 3824, Chicago, IL 60654-0824, 773-583-9261
FISH STORIES, 3540 N. Southport Avenue #493, Chicago, IL 60657-1436, 773-334-6690
SPORT LITERATE, Honest Reflections on Life's Leisurely Diversions, PO Box 577166, Chicago, IL 60657,
765-496-6524; sportlit@aol.com; www.avalon.net/~librarian/sportliterate
LIGHT: The Quarterly of Light Verse, PO Box 7500, Chicago, IL 60680
Path Press, Inc., PO Box 2925, Chicago, IL 60690-2925, 312-663-0167
Zombie Logic Press, 420 E. 3rd Street Box 319, Byron, IL 61010, email Dobe 1969@aol.com
THE ROCKFORD REVIEW, PO Box 858, Rockford, IL 61105, e-mail dragonldy@prodigy.net
Mortal Press, 2315 North Alpine Road, Rockford, IL 61107-1422, 815-399-8432
2AM MAGAZINE, PO Box 6754, Rockford, IL 61125-1754
2AM Publications, PO Box 6754, Rockford, IL 61125-1754
CRICKET, PO Box 300, Peru, IL 61354, 815-224-6656
LADYBUG, the Magazine for Young Children, 315 5th Street, PO Box 300, Peru, IL 61354, 815-224-6656
SPIDER, PO Box 300, Peru, IL 61354, 815-224-6656, Fax 815-224-6615
SPOON RIVER POETRY REVIEW, Department of English 4240, Illinois State University, Normal, IL 61790-4241,
309-438-7906, 309-438-3025
University of Illinois Press, 1325 South Oak Street, Champaign, IL 61820-6903, 217-333-0950
NEW STONE CIRCLE, 1185 E 1900 N Road, White Heath, IL 61884
KARAMU, Department of English, Eastern Illinois Univ., Charleston, IL 61920, 217-581-6297
DRUMVOICES REVUE, Southern Illinois University, English Dept., Box 1431, Edwardsville, IL 62026-1431,
618-650-2060; Fax 618-650-3509
SOU'WESTER, Southern Illinois University, Edwardsville, IL 62026-1438
OBLATES, 9480 N. De Mazenod Drive, Belleville, IL 62223-1160, 618-398-4848
Knightraven Books, PO Box 100, Collinsville, IL 62234, 314-725-1111, Fax 618-345-7436
RIVER KING POETRY SUPPLEMENT, PO Box 122, Freeburg, IL 62243
INTUITIVE EXPLORATIONS, PO Box 561, Quincy, IL 62306-0561, 217-222-9082
NATURE SOCIETY NEWS, Purple Martin Junction, Griggsville, IL 62340, 217-833-2323, Fax 217-833-2123,
natsoc@adams.net, www.naturesociety.org
Hutton Publications, Po Box 2907, Decatur, IL 62524
MYSTERY TIME ANTHOLOGY, PO Box 2907, Decatur, IL 62524
RHYME TIME POETRY NEWSLETTER, PO Box 2907, Decatur, IL 62524
Brooks Books, 4634 Hale Dr, Decatur, IL 62526-1117, 217-877-2966
MAYFLY, 4634 Hale Drive, Decatur, IL 62526-1117
WeWrite Corporation, PO Box 498, Rochester, IL 62563, 217-498-8458, Fax 217-498-7524, dpalmer@wewrite.net,
www.wewrite.net
ILLINOIS ARCHITECTURAL & HISTORICAL REVIEW, 202 South Plum, Havana, IL 62644, 309-543-4644
Embassy Hall Editions, PO Box 665, Centralia, IL 62801-0665
THE GALLEY SAIL REVIEW, PO Box 665, Centralia, IL 62801-0665
CRAB ORCHARD REVIEW, Dept. of English, Southern Illinois University, Carbondale, IL 62901, 618-453-6833

INDIANA

THE RAINTOWN REVIEW, PO Box 370, Pittsboro, IN 46167-0370, hmpeditor@hotmail.com
Geekspeak Unique Press, PO Box 11443, Indianapolis, IN 46201, 317-849-6227; www.ploplop.com
PLOPLOP, PO Box 11443, Indianapolis, IN 46201, 317-630-9216
NANNY FANNY, 2524 Stockbridge Drive #15, Indianapolis, IN 46268-2670, 317-329-1436, nightpoet@prodigy.net
SKYLARK, 2200 169th Street, Purdue University Calumet, Hammond, IN 46323, 219-989-2273, Fax 219-989-2165,
poetpam49@yahoo.com
NOTRE DAME REVIEW, English Dept., Creative Writing, University of Notre Dame, Notre Dame, IN 46556,
219-631-6952, Fax 219-631-4268
TWINSWORLD, 11220 St. Joe Road, Fort Wayne, IN 46835, twinworld1@aol.com
BARNWOOD, PO Box 146, Selma, IN 47383
The Barnwood Press, PO Box 146, Selma, IN 47383
BATHTUB GIN, PO Box 2392, Bloomington, IN 47402, 812-323-2985
INNER VOICES: A New Journal of Prison Literature, PO Box 4500 #219, Bloomington, IN 47402
Pathwise Press, PO Box 2392, Bloomington, IN 47402, 812-323-2985, charter@bluemarble.net, www.home.bluemar-
ble.net/charter/btgin.htm
World Wisdom Books, Inc., PO Box 2682, Bloomington, IN 47402, 812-332-1663, e-mail wwbooks@worldwisdom.com
Frozen Waffles Press/Shattered Sidewalks Press; 45th Century Chapbooks, The Writer's Group, 329 West 1st Street #5,
Bloomington, IN 47403
INDIANA REVIEW, Ballantine Hall 465, Indiana Univ., 1020 E. Kirkwood Avenue, Bloomington, IN 47405,
812-855-3439
THE FORMALIST, 320 Hunter Drive, Evansville, IN 47711-2218
SOUTHERN INDIANA REVIEW, Liberal Arts Department, Univ. of Southern Indiana, Evansville, IN 47712,
812-464-1735. fax 812-465-7152. email tkramer@evansville.net
EVANSVILLE REVIEW, Univ. of Evansville, English Dept., 1800 Lincoln Avenue, Evansville, IN 47714, 812-488-1042
POETS' ROUNDTABLE, 826 South Center Street, Terre Haute, IN 47807, 812-234-0819
AFRICAN AMERICAN REVIEW, Indiana State University, Dept. of English, Terre Haute, IN 47809, 812-237-2968
SNOWY EGRET, PO Box 9, Bowling Green, IN 47833
Etaoin Shrdlu Press, Fandom House, 30 N. 19th Street, Lafayette, IN 47904
PABLO LENNIS, Fandom House, 30 N. 19th Street, Lafayette, IN 47904

SPARROW, 103 Waldron Street, West Lafayette, IN 47906
SYCAMORE REVIEW, Department of English, Purdue University, West Lafayette, IN 47907, 765-494-3783

IOWA

FLYWAY, 206 Ross Hall, Iowa State University, Ames, IA 50011, 515-294-8273, FAX 515-294-6814, flyway@iastate.edu
SWEET ANNIE & SWEET PEA REVIEW, 7750 Highway F-24 West, Baxter, IA 50028, 515-792-3578, FAX 515-792-1310
Sweet Annie Press, 7750 Highway F-24 West, Baxter, IA 50028, 515-792-3578, FAX 515-792-1310
THE NORTH AMERICAN REVIEW, Univ. Of Northern Iowa, Cedar Falls, IA 50614, 319-273-6455
THE BAREFOOT POET: Journal of Poetry, Fiction, Essays, & Art, PO Box 52, Pisgah, IA 51564-0052, 712-456-2132; stmike-press@saint-mike.org
Writers House Press, PO Box 52, Pisgah, IA 51564-0052, 712-456-2132; stmike-press@saint-mike.org
COMMON LIVES / LESBIAN LIVES, 1802 7th Ave. Ct., Iowa City, IA 52240-6436
THE IOWA REVIEW, 308 EPB, Univ. Of Iowa, Iowa City, IA 52242, 319-335-0462
TORRE DE PAPEL, 111 Phillips Hall, The University of Iowa, Iowa City, IA 52242, 319-335-2245
Urban Legend Press, PO Box 4737, Davenport, IA 52808
THE URBANITE, PO Box 4737, Davenport, IA 52808

KANSAS

Broken Boulder Press, PO Box 172, Lawrence, KS 66044-0172, E-mail paulsilvia@excite.com, website www.broken-boulder.com
FIRST INTENSITY, PO Box 665, Lawrence, KS 66044-0713, e-mail leechapman@aol.com
First Intensity Press, PO Box 665, Lawrence, KS 66044, e-mail leechapman@aol.com
GESTALTEN, PO Box 172, Lawrence, KS 66044-0172, www.brokenboulder.com
COTTONWOOD, 400 Kansas Union, Box J, University of Kansas, Lawrence, KS 66045, 785-864-2528
Cottonwood Press, 400 Kansas Union, Box J, Univ. of Kansas, Lawrence, KS 66045, 785-864-2528
POTPOURRI: A Magazine of the Literary Arts, PO Box 8278, Prairie Village, KS 66208, 913-642-1503, Fax 913-642-3128, e-mail potpourrppub@aol.com
Sunflower University Press, 1531 Yuma, (Box 1009), Manhattan, KS 66502, 785-539-1888, fax 785-539-2233
SCAVENGER'S NEWSLETTER, 833 Main Street, Osage City, KS 66523-1241, 913-528-3538; E-mail foxscav1@jc.net
THE MIDWEST QUARTERLY, Pittsburg State University, History Department, Pittsburg, KS 66762, 316-235-4369
CHIRON REVIEW, 702 North Prairie, St. John, KS 67576-1516, 316-549-6156, 316-786-4955, chironreview@hot-mail.com, www.geocities.com/soho/nook/1748
Chiron Review Press, 702 North Prairie, St. John, KS 67576-1516, 316-549-6156, chironreview@hotmail.com, www.geocities.com/soho/nook/1748

KENTUCKY

The Advocado Press, PO Box 145, Louisville, KY 40201, 502-459-5343
THE DISABILITY RAG & RESOURCE, PO Box 145, Louisville, KY 40201, 502-459-5343
THE AMERICAN VOICE, 332 West Broadway, #1215, Louisville, KY 40202, 502-562-0045
THE LOUISVILLE REVIEW, Spalding University, 851 S. 4th Street, Louisville, KY 40203, 502-585-9911
The Sulgrave Press, 2005 Longest Avenue, Louisville, KY 40204, 502-459-9713, Fax 502-459-9715
Sarabande Books, Inc., 2234 Dundee Road, Suite 200, Louisville, KY 40205
Green River Writers, Inc./Grex Press, 11906 Locust Road, Middletown, KY 40243, 502-245-4902
STOVEPIPE: A Journal of Little Literary Value, PO Box 1076, Georgetown, KY 40324, troyteegarden@worldradio.org
Sweet Lady Moon Press, PO Box 1076, Georgetown, KY 40324, troyteegarden@worldradio.org
APPALACHIAN HERITAGE, Appalachian Center, Berea College, Berea, KY 40404, 859-985-3140, jim-gage@berea.edu
CHAFFIN JOURNAL, Department of English, 467 Case Annex, Eastern Kentucky University, Richmond, KY 40475-3140
LIMESTONE: A Literary Journal, English Dept., Univ. of Kentucky, 1215 Patterson Office Tower, Lexington, KY 40506-0027
WIND, PO Box 24548, Lexington, KY 40524, 606-885-5342
THE LICKING RIVER REVIEW, Department of Literature and Language, Northern Kentucky University, Highland Heights, KY 41099
MEDUSA'S HAIRDO, 2631 Seminole Avenue, Ashland, KY 41102, 606-325-7203, medusashairdo@yahoo.com
PIKEVILLE REVIEW, Humanities Department, Pikeville College, Pikeville, KY 41501, 606-432-9612

LOUISIANA

DESIRE STREET, 257 Bonnabel Boulevard, Metairie, LA 70005-3738, 504-835-3419, Fax 504-834-2005, ager80@worldnet.att.net
Lycanthrope Press, PO Box 9028, Metairie, LA 70005-9028, 504-866-9756
THEMA, PO Box 8747, Metairie, LA 70011-8747
Manya DeLeon Booksmith, 940 Royal Street, Suite 201, New Orleans, LA 70116, 504-895-2357
THE NEW LAUREL REVIEW, 828 Lesseps Street, New Orleans, LA 70117, 504-947-6001
LOWLANDS REVIEW, 6109 Magazine, New Orleans, LA 70118
NEW ORLEANS REVIEW, Loyola University, Box 195, New Orleans, LA 70118, 504-865-3597
Acre Press, 3003 Ponce De Leon Street, New Orleans, LA 70119
FELL SWOOP, 3003 Ponce de Leon Street, New Orleans, LA 70119
MESECHABE: The Journal of Surre(gion)alism, 1539 Crete Street, New Orleans, LA 70119, 504-944-4823
BAKER STREET GAZETTE, 577 Central Avenue, Box 4, Jefferson, LA 70121-1400, E-mail sherlockian@mailcity.com, sherlockian@england.com, www2.cybercities.com/z/zines/
Baker Street Publications, 577 Central Avenue, Box 4, Jefferson, LA 70121-1400, E-mail sherlockian@mailcity.com, sherlockian@england.com, www2.cybercities.com/z/zines/
DAYS AND NIGHTS OF A SMALL PRESS PUBLISHER, 577 Central Avenue, Box 4, Jefferson, LA 70121-1400, e-mail popculture@popmail.com, publisher@mailexcite.com; www2.cybercities.com/z/zines/
THE HAUNTED JOURNAL, 577 Central Avenue, Box 4, Jefferson, LA 70121-1400, e-mail fullmoon@edoramail.com or haunted@rocketmail.com; www.spaceports.com/~haunted, www.eclecticity.com/zines/, www.members.xoom.com/black-ie or http://www.angelfire.com/la/hauntings/index.htm/, www2.cybercities.com/z/zines
HOLLYWOOD NOSTALGIA, 577 Central Avenue, Box 4, Jefferson, LA 70121-1400, e-mail: publisher@mailexcite.com

or blackie@talkcity.com; Websites www.home.talkcity.com/SunsetBlvd/blackie, www.wbs.net/homepages/b/l/a/blackie.htm/, www2.cybercities.com/z/zines/
HORIZONS, 577 Central Avenue, Box 4, Jefferson, LA 70121-1400, e-mail: horizons@altavista.net or publisher@mailexcite.com; Website www2.cybercities.com/z/zines/
HORIZONS BEYOND, 577 Central Avenue, Box 4, Jefferson, LA 70121-0517, e-mail fullmoon@eudoramail.com or haunted@rocketmail.com; Websites www.members.xoom.com/blackie, www2.cybercities.com/z/zines/, www.eclecticity.com/zines/, www.spaceports.com/~haunted/
IRISH JOURNAL, 577 Central Avenue, Box 4, Jefferson, LA 70121-1400, e-mail irishrose@cmpnetmail.com, rose.dalton@edmail.com; websites www.fortunecity.com/bally/harp/189/, www2.cybercities.com/z/zines/
JACK THE RIPPER GAZETTE, 577 Central Avenue, Box 4, Jefferson, LA 70121-1400, sherlockian@england.com, sherlockian@mailcity.com, www2.cybercities.com/z/zines/
JEWISH LIFE, 577 Central Avenue, Box 4, Jefferson, LA 70121-1400, E-mail publisher@jewishmail.com, jewishlife@newyorkoffice.com; www.world.up.co.il/jewishlife, www2.cybercities.com/z/zines/
MIXED BAG, 577 Central Avenue, Box 4, Jefferson, LA 70121-1400, e-mail: publisher@mailexcite.com, zines@theglobe.com, zines@rsnmail.com; Websites www.members.tripod.com/~literary/index.htm/, www.members.theglobe.com/zines/default.htm/, www2.cybercities.com/z/zines/, www.zines.freeservers.com
NIGHTSHADE, 577 Central Avenue, Box 4, Jefferson, LA 70121-1400, e-mail fullmoon@eudoramail.com or haunted@rocketmail.com; Websites www.members.xoom.com/blackie, www.eclecticity.com/zines/, www.spaceports.com/~haunted/, www2.cybercities.com/z/zines/
PEN & INK WRITERS JOURNAL, 577 Central Avenue, Box 4, Jefferson, LA 70121-1400, E-mail editor@inforspacemail.com, publisher@mailexcite.com, www.zines.freeservers.com, www.members.theglobe.com/zines/default.html, www2.cybercities.com/z/zines/
POW-WOW, 577 Central Avenue #4, Jefferson, LA 70121-1400, e-mail: horizons@altavista.net or blueskies@discoverymail.com; Websites www.freeyellow.com/members2/oldwest/index.htm/, www2.cybercities.com/z/zines/
REALM OF DARKNESS, 577 Central Avenue, Box 4, Jefferson, LA 70121-1400, e-mail: fullmoon@eduoramail.com or haunted@rocketmail.com; Websites www.members.xoom.com/blackie, www.spaceports.com/~haunted/, www.eclecticity.com/zines/, www2.cybercities.com/z/zines/, www.dreamers.dynip.com/z/zines/
REALM OF THE VAMPIRE, 577 Central Avenue, Box 4, Jefferson, LA 70121-1400, e-mail fullmoon@eudoramail.com, haunted@rocketmail.com, gothic@imaginemail.com; Websites www.eclecticity.com/zines/, www.freez.com/vampires, www.members.xoom.com/blackie, www.spaceports.com/~haunted/, www2.cybercities.com/z/zines/
THE SALEM JOURNAL, 577 Central Avenue, Box 4, Jefferson, LA 70121-1400, e-mail: fullmoon@eudoramail.com or haunted@rocketmail.com; Websites www.eclecticity.com/zines/, www2.cybercities.com/z/zines/, www.members.xoom.com/blackie, www.spaceports.com/~haunted/, www.dreamers.dynip.com/z/zines/
SLEUTH JOURNAL, 577 Central Avenue, Box 4, Jefferson, LA 70121-1400, E-mail sherlockian@mailcity.com, blackie@taskcity.com, www2.cybercities.com/z/zines, www.wbs.net/homepages/b/l/a/blackie.html
SOUTHWEST JOURNAL, 577 Central Avenue, Box 4, Jefferson, LA 70121-0517, e-mail: horizons@altavista.net or blueskies@discoverymail.com; Websites www.freeyellow.com/members2/oldwest/index.htm/ or www2.cybercities.com/z/zines/
WESTERN SKIES, 577 Central Avenue, Box 4, Jefferson, LA 70121-1400, e-mail: horizons@altavista.net or blueskies@discoverymail.com; Websites www.freeyellow.com/members2/oldwest/index.htm/, www2.cybercities.com/z/zines/
JOURNAL OF CURRICULUM THEORIZING, 4154 State Street Drive, New Orleans, LA 70125
Portals Press, 4411 Fountainebleau Drive, New Orleans, LA 70125, 504-821-7723; E-mail jptravis@worldnet.att.net
XAVIER REVIEW, Box 110C, Xavier University, New Orleans, LA 70125, 504-483-7481 Bonner, 483-7303 Skinner, Fax 504-485-7917
THE LOUISIANA REVIEW, Division of Liberal Arts, Louisiana State Univ., PO Box 1129, Eunice, LA 70535
Thunder Rain Publishing Corp., PO Box 1001, Livingston, LA 70754-1407, 225-686-2002, Fax 686-2285, rhi@thunder-rain.com, www.thunder-rain.com
NEW DELTA REVIEW, c/o Dept. of English, Louisiana State University, Baton Rouge, LA 70803-5001, 504-388-4079
THE SOUTHERN REVIEW, 43 Allen Hall, Louisiana State University, Baton Rouge, LA 70803, 225-388-5108
Gothic Press, 4998 Perkins Road, Baton Rouge, LA 70808-3043, 504-766-2906
SILHOUETTE MAGAZINE, PO Box 53763, Baton Rouge, LA 70892, 504-358-0617
Louisiana State University Press, Baton Rouge, LA 70893, 504-388-6294
THE SCRIBIA, PO Box 68, Grambling State University, Grambling, LA 71245, 318-644-2072; hoytda@alpha0.gram.edu
ELEMENTS, 2820 Houston Street, Alexandria, LA 71301, 318-445-5055

MAINE

PANOPTICON, PO BOX 142, York Harbor, ME 03911-0142, E-mail jmoser41@portland.maine.edu
ME MAGAZINE, PO Box 182, Bowdoinham, ME 04008, 207-666-8453
Pittore Euforico, PO Box 182, Bowdoinham, ME 04008, 207-666-8453
Coyote Books, PO Box 629, Brunswick, ME 04011
Clamp Down Press, PO Box 7270, Cape Porpoise, ME 04014, 207-967-2605
THE CAFE REVIEW, c/o Yes Books, 20 Danforth Street, Portland, ME 04101, e-mail seegerlab@aol.com, www.thecafereview.com
Tilbury House, Publishers, 132 Water Street, Gardiner, ME 04345, 207-582-1899
VOID, PO Box 21, Milford, ME 04401-0021, Fax 207-945-0760, poet@angryrodent.com
Puckerbrush Press, 76 Main Street, Orono, ME 04473-1430, 207-866-4868
THE PUCKERBRUSH REVIEW, 76 Main Street, Orono, ME 04473-1430
Goose River Press, 3400 Friendship Road, Waldoboro, ME 04572, 207-832-6665, Fax 207-832-5348, dbenner@ime.net
FLYING HORSE, PO Box 1029, Ellsworth, ME 04605-1029
BELOIT POETRY JOURNAL, 24 Berry Cove Road, Lamoine, ME 04605, 207-667-5598
Two Dog Press, PO Box 307, Deer Isle, ME 04627, 207-348-6819; fax 207-348-6016; email human@twodogpress.com
THE RIVER REVIEW/LA REVUE RIVIERE, University of Maine-Fort Kent, 25 Pleasant Street, Fort Kent, ME 04743, 207-834-7542, river@maine.edu
VOLITION, PO Box 314, Tenants Harbor, ME 04860
NORTHWOODS JOURNAL, A Magazine for Writers, PO Box 298, Thomaston, ME 04861-0298, 207-345-0998, Fax 207-354-8953, cal@americanletters.org, www.americanletters.org
Northwoods Press, PO Box 298, Thomaston, ME 04861-0298, 207-354-0998, Fax 207-354-8953, cal@americanletters.org,

www.americanletters.org
Bern Porter Books, 50 Salmond Road, Belfast, ME 04915, 207-338-3763
BERN PORTER INTERNATIONAL, 50 Salmond Street, Belfast, ME 04915-6111, bpinternational@hotmail.com
Alice James Books, University of Maine at Farmington, 98 Main Street, Farmington, ME 04938-1911
Polar Bear Productions & Company, PO Box 311 Brook Street, Solon, ME 04979, 207-643-2795

MARYLAND

POTOMAC REVIEW, PO Box 354, Port Tobacco, MD 20677, website www.meral.com/potomac
THE PLASTIC TOWER, PO Box 702, Bowie, MD 20718
FEMINIST STUDIES, c/o Women's Studies Program, University of Maryland, College Park, MD 20742, 301-405-7413
Open University of America Press, 3916 Commander Drive, Hyattsville, MD 20782-1027, 301-779-0220 phone/Fax, openuniv@aol.com
ORACLE POETRY, PO Box 7413, Langley Park, MD 20787
Rising Star Publishers, PO Box 7413, Langley Park, MD 20787
POET LORE, The Writer's Center, 4508 Walsh Street, Bethesda, MD 20815-6006, 301-654-8664
Gut Punch Press, PO Box 105, Cabin John, MD 20818
IBEX Publishers, PO Box 30087, Bethesda, MD 20824, 301-718-8188, FAX 301-907-8707
Scripta Humanistica, 1383 Kersey Lane, Potomac, MD 20854, 301-294-7949; 301-340-1095
SITUATION, 10402 Ewell Avenue, Kensington, MD 20895-4025
UNO MAS MAGAZINE, PO Box 1832, Silver Spring, MD 20915, Fax 301-770-3250, unomasmag@aol.com, http://www.unomas.com/
ABBEY, 5360 Fallriver Row Court, Columbia, MD 21044
White Urp Press, 5360 Fallriver Row Court, Columbia, MD 21044
BLACK MOON, 233 Northway Road, Reisterstown, MD 21136, 410-833-9424
THE BALTIMORE REVIEW, PO Box 410, Riderwood, MD 21139, 410-377-5265, Fax 410-377-4325, E-mail hdiehl@bcpl.net
The Galileo Press Ltd., 3637 Black Rock Road, Upperco, MD 21155-9322
Jungle Man Press, 211 W. Mulberry Street, 3rd Floor, Baltimore, MD 21201
PASSAGER: A Journal of Remembrance and Discovery, 1420 N. Charles Street, Baltimore, MD 21201-5779, 301-625-3041
Dolphin-Moon Press, PO Box 22262, Baltimore, MD 21203
BrickHouse Books, Inc., 541 Piccadilly Road, Baltimore, MD 21204, 410-828-0724, 830-2938
CELEBRATION, 2707 Lawina Road, Baltimore, MD 21216-1608, 410-542-8785, wsullivan@freewwweb.com
SHATTERED WIG REVIEW, 425 E. 31st, Baltimore, MD 21218, 301-243-6888
MARYLAND POETRY REVIEW, 99 Smithwood Avenue, Baltimore, MD 21228, http://marylandpoetry.org
Paycock Press, 3938 Colchester Road, Apt. 364, Baltimore, MD 21229-5010, Fax; 410-644-5195; e-mail atticus@radix.net
American Literary Press Inc./Noble House, 8019 Belair Road #10, Baltimore, MD 21236, 410-882-7700; fax 410-882-7703; e-mail amerlit@erols.com; www.erols.com/amerlit
Nightsun Books, 823 Braddock Road, Cumberland, MD 21502-2622, 301-722-4861
THE COOL TRAVELER, 196 Bowery Street, Frostburg, MD 21532-2255, 215-440-0592
NIGHTSUN, English Department, Frostburg S. University, Frostburg, MD 21532, 301-687-4221
THE PEGASUS REVIEW, PO Box 88, Henderson, MD 21640-0088, 410-482-6736
ECLIPSE, General Delivery, Brownsville, MD 21715-9999, E-mail Kiirenza@aol.com
ANTIETAM REVIEW, 41 S. Potomac Street, Hagerstown, MD 21740-5512, 301-791-3132

MASSACHUSETTS

THE MASSACHUSETTS REVIEW, South College, Univ. of Mass/Box 37140, Amherst, MA 01003-7140, 413-545-2689
Amherst Writers & Artists Press, Inc., PO Box 1076, Amherst, MA 01004, 413-253-7764 phone/fax; e-mail awapress@javanet.com
PEREGRINE, PO Box 1076, Amherst, MA 01004, 413-253-7764 phone/fax; e-mail awapress@javanet.com; www.javanet.com/~awapress
University of Massachusetts Press, Box 429, Amherst, MA 01004-0429, 413-545-2217
Adastra Press, 16 Reservation Road, Easthampton, MA 01027-1227
OLD CROW, PO Box 403, Easthampton, MA 01027-0403
BGB Press, Inc., 160 King Street, Northampton, MA 01060-2336, www.home.earthlink.net/~bgbpress
THE PANNUS INDEX, 160 King Street, Northampton, MA 01060-2336, 413-584-4776; Fax 413-584-5674; www.javanet.com/~stout/pannus
EDITION KEY SATCH(EL), 93 Main Street, Florence, MA 01062, 413-587-0776 phone/Fax, keysatch@quale.com
Perugia Press, PO Box 108, Shutesbury, MA 01072, E-mail perugia@mindspring.com
Little River Press, 10 Lowell Avenue, Westfield, MA 01085, 413-568-5598
PINE ISLAND JOURNAL OF NEW ENGLAND POETRY, PO Box 317, West Springfield, MA 01090
Paris Press, Inc., 1117 West Road, Williamsburg, MA 01096, 413-628-0051
THE DROPLET JOURNAL, 19 Pine Street, Great Barrington, MA 01230-1417, 413-232-0052; E-mail droplet@bcn.net
The Figures, 5 Castle Hill Avenue, Great Barrington, MA 01230-1552, 413-528-2552
Mad River Press, State Road, Richmond, MA 01254, 413-698-3184
Hard Press, Inc., PO Box 184, West Stockbridge, MA 01266, 413-232-4690
LINGO, PO Box 184, West Stockbridge, MA 01266, 413-232-4690
Haley's, PO Box 248, Athol, MA 01331, haleyathol@aolcom
OSIRIS, Box 297, Deerfield, MA 01342, e-mail moorhead@k12s.phast.umass.edu
Swamp Press, 15 Warwick Avenue, Northfield, MA 01360-1105
TIGHTROPE, 15 Warwick Avenue, Northfield, MA 01360
BUTTON, PO Box 26, Lunenburg, MA 01462, E-mail buttonx26@aol.com
NEOLOGISMS, Box 869, 1102 Pleasant Street, Worcester, MA 01602
THE WORCESTER REVIEW, 6 Chatham Street, Worcester, MA 01609, 603-924-7342, 978-797-4770
THE AMERICAN DISSIDENT, 1837 Main Street, Concord, MA 01742, enmarge@aol.com
Artifact Press, Ltd., 900 Tanglewood Drive, Concord, MA 01742, 978-287-5296; Fax 978-287-5299; hershey@tiac.net
Drum, 40 Potter Street, Concord, MA 01742
Water Row Press, PO Box 438, Sudbury, MA 01776

WATER ROW REVIEW, PO Box 438, Sudbury, MA 01776
Essex Press, PO Box 914, North Andover, MA 01845, sxpress@banet.net
Loom Press, Box 1394, Lowell, MA 01853
ABORIGINAL, PO Box 2449, Woburn, MA 01880
FC-Izdat Publishing, 3 Cottage Avenue, Winchester, MA 01890, 617-776-2262; vvv@tiac.net
BACKSPACE: A QUEER POETS JOURNAL, 25 Riverside Avenue, Gloucester, MA 01930-2552, e-mail bkspqpj@aol.com
Epona Publishing, 12 Clearview Avenue #1, Gloucester, MA 01930, http://kathywer.homepage.com/index.html
SOUNDINGS EAST, English Dept., Salem State College, Salem, MA 01970, 978-542-6205
Four Way Books, PO Box 607, Marshfield, MA 02050
APPALACHIA JOURNAL, 5 Joy Street, Boston, MA 02108, 617-523-0636
TEEN VOICES MAGAZINE, 515 Washington Street, 6th Floor, Boston, MA 02111-1759, 617-426-5505, fax 617-426-5577, e-mail womenexp@teenvoices.com, website www.teenvoices.com
PLOUGHSHARES, Emerson College, 100 Beacon Street, Boston, MA 02116, 617-824-8753
BAY WINDOWS, 631 Tremont Street, Boston, MA 02118, 617-266-6670, X211
Good Gay Poets Press, Box 277, Astor Station, Boston, MA 02123
COLLEGE ENGLISH, Dept. of English, U Mass/Boston, 100 Morrissey Boulevard, Boston, MA 02125-3393
SOJOURNER, THE WOMEN'S FORUM, 42 Seaverns Avenue, Jamaica Plain, MA 02130-1109, 617-524-0415
American Living Press, PO Box 901, Allston, MA 02134, 617-522-6196
ATELIER, 8 Holton Street, Allston, MA 02134-1337
WEIRD POETRY, PO Box 901, Allston, MA 02134, 617-522-6196
THE BOSTON BOOK REVIEW, 30 Brattle Street, 4th floor, Cambridge, MA 02138, 617-497-0344, BBR-info@BostonBookReview.org, www.BostonBookReview.org
THE HARVARD ADVOCATE, 21 South St., Cambridge, MA 02138, 617-495-0737
PERSEPHONE, c/o John Cobb, 40 Avon Hill Street, Cambridge, MA 02138
Zoland Books, 384 Huron Avenue, Cambridge, MA 02138, 617-864-6252; FAX 617-661-4998
BOSTON REVIEW, 30 Wadsworth Street, MIT, Cambridge, MA 02139, 617-253-3642, fax 617-252-1549
IBBETSON ST. PRESS, 33 Ibbetson Street, Somerville, MA 02143, e-mail p99264@hotmail.com
Ibbetson St. Press, 33 Ibbetson Street, Somerville, MA 02143, e-mail p99264@hotmail.com
Wisdom Publications, Inc., 199 Elm Street, Somerville, MA 02144-3129, 617-776-7416; Fax 617-776-7841
SALAMANDER, 48 Ackers Avenue, Brookline, MA 02146
EASTGATE QUARTERLY REVIEW OF HYPERTEXT, 134 Main Street, Watertown, MA 02172, 617-924-9044, Fax 617-924-9051, info@eastgate.com
Eastgate Systems Inc., 134 Main Street, Watertown, MA 02172, 617-924-9044, Fax 617-924-9051, info@eastgate.com
AGNI, Boston University, 236 Bay State Road, Boston, MA 02215, 617-353-7135
FAG RAG, Box 15331, Kenmore Station, Boston, MA 02215, 617-426-4469
Fag Rag Books, PO Box 15331, Boston, MA 02215
96 INC, PO Box 15559, Boston, MA 02215
PARTISAN REVIEW, 236 Bay State Road, Boston, MA 02215, 617-353-4260
STARGREEN, PO Box 380406, Cambridge, MA 02238, 617-868-3981
Yellow Moon Press, PO Box 381316, Cambridge, MA 02238-0001, 617-776-2230; Fax 617-776-8246; E-mail ymp@tiac.net; web site www.yellowmoon.com
Hermes House Press, 113 Summit Avenue, Brookline, MA 02446-2319, 617-566-2468
KAIROS, A Journal of Contemporary Thought and Criticism, 113 Summit Avenue, Brookline, MA 02446-2319
Zephyr Press, 50 Kenwood Street, Brookline, MA 02446, 617-713-2813
Arts End Books, Box 162, Newton, MA 02468
NOSTOC MAGAZINE, Box 162, Newton, MA 02468
THE NEW RENAISSANCE, An International Magazine of Ideas & Opinions, Emphasizing Literature & The Arts, 26 Heath Road #11, Arlington, MA 02474-3645
THE AUROREAN, A POETIC QUARTERLY, PO Box 219, Sagamore Beach, MA 02562-0219, 508-833-0805 phone/fax, phone before faxing
FLOATING ISLAND, PO Box 2347, Brewster, MA 02631, 508-896-4572
Floating Island Publications, PO Box 2347, Brewster, MA 02631, 508-896-4572
THE HIGHWAY POET, PO Box 1400, Brewster, MA 02631
PROVINCETOWN ARTS, 650 Commercial Street, Provincetown, MA 02657, 508-487-3167
Provincetown Arts Press, PO Box 35, 650 Commercial Street, Provincetown, MA 02657, 508-487-3167; FAX 508-487-8634
Garden St Press, PO Box 1231, Truro, MA 02666-1231, 508-349-1991

MICHIGAN

INKY TRAIL NEWS, 70 Macomb Place, #226, Mt. Clemens, MI 48043, e-mail inkytrails@prodigy.net
Ridgeway Press of Michigan, PO Box 120, Roseville, MI 48066, 313-577-7713, Fax to M.L. Liebler 810-294-0474, E-mail milliebler@aol.com
ALARM CLOCK, PO Box 1551, Royal Oak, MI 48068, 313-593-9677
OPUS LITERARY REVIEW, PO Box 71192, Madison Heights, MI 48071-0192, 313-548-0865
Poetic Page, PO Box 71192, Madison Heights, MI 48071-0192, 313-548-0865
Otherwind, 541 Lakeview Avenue, Ann Arbor, MI 48103-9704, 313-665-0703
Center for Japanese Studies, 202 S. Thayer Street, University of Michigan, Ann Arbor, MI 48104-1608, 734-998-7265, FAX 734-998-7982
THE J MAN TIMES, 2246 Saint Francis Drive #A-211, Ann Arbor, MI 48104-4828, E-mail TheJMan99@aol.com
AFFABLE NEIGHBOR, PO Box 3635, Ann Arbor, MI 48106
Affable Neighbor Press, PO Box 3635, Ann Arbor, MI 48106
H.A.K.T.U.P.!, PO Box 4501, Ann Arbor, MI 48106, haktup@osric.com; www.osric.com/haktup/
MIM NOTES: Offcial Newsletter of the Maoist Internationalist Movement, PO Box 3576, Ann Arbor, MI 48106
Osric Publishing, PO Box 4501, Ann Arbor, MI 48106
THE WHITE CROW, PO Box 4501, Ann Arbor, MI 48106
Palladium Communications, 320 South Main Street, PO Box 8403, Ann Arbor, MI 48107-8403, 734-668-4646; FAX 734-663-9361

MICHIGAN QUARTERLY REVIEW, 3032 Rackham Bldg., University of Michigan, Ann Arbor, MI 48109, 734-764-9265
Gravity Presses (Lest We All Float Away), Inc., 27030 Havelock, Dearborn Heights, MI 48127, 313-563-4683, e-mail mikeb5000@yahoo.com
NOW HERE NOWHERE, 27030 Havelock, Dearborn Heights, MI 48127, 313-563-4683, e-mail kingston@gravity-presses.com
THE MAC GUFFIN, Schoolcraft College, 18600 Haggerty Road, Livonia, MI 48152, 313-462-4400, ext. 5292 or 5327
Sun Dog Press, 22058 Cumberland Drive, Northville, MI 48167, 248-449-7448, Fax 248-449-4070, sundogpr@voyager.net
Poetic License Press, PO Box 85525, Westland, MI 48185-0525, 734-326-9368; FAX 734-326-3480; e-mail steveblo30@aol.com
SULFUR, 210 Washtenaw, Ypsilanti, MI 48197-2526, 313-483-9787
STRUGGLE: A Magazine of Proletarian Revolutionary Literature, PO Box 13261, Detroit, MI 48213-0261
THE SOUNDS OF POETRY, 2076 Vinewood, Detroit, MI 48216-5506
Lotus Press, Inc., PO Box 21607, Detroit, MI 48221, 313-861-1280, fax 313-861-4740, lotuspress@aol.com
THE BRIDGE: A Journal of Fiction and Poetry, 14050 Vernon Street, Oak Park, MI 48237, 313-547-6823
WITNESS, Oakland Community College, 27055 Orchard Lake Road, Farmington Hills, MI 48334, 734-996-5732
W.W. Publications, PO Box 373, Highland, MI 48357-0373, 813-585-0985 phone/Fax
THE DRIFTWOOD REVIEW, PO Box 700, Linden, MI 48451, E-mail midrift@aol.com
MINAS TIRITH EVENING-STAR, PO BOX 7871, Flint, MI 48507-0871, 813-585-0985 phone/Fax
Mayapple Press, PO Box 5473, Saginaw, MI 48603-0473, 517-793-2801, kerman@mayapplepress.com, www.mayapple-press.com
THE CENTENNIAL REVIEW, 312 Linton Hall, Mich. State Univ., E. Lansing, MI 48824-1044, 517-355-1905
Red Cedar Press, 17C Morrill Hall, Michigan State University, E. Lansing, MI 48824, 517-355-9656, rcreview@msu.edu
RED CEDAR REVIEW, 17C Morrill Hall, English Dept., Michigan State Univ., E. Lansing, MI 48824, 517-355-9656, rcreview@msu.edu
Years Press, Dept. of ATL, EBH, Michigan State University, E. Lansing, MI 48824-1033
Bennett & Kitchel, PO Box 4422, East Lansing, MI 48826
OUT YOUR BACKDOOR: The Magazine of Informal Adventure and Cheap Culture, 4686 Meridian Road, Williamston, MI 48895, 517-347-1689; jp@glpbooks.com; www.glpbooks.com/oyb
WAY STATION MAGAZINE, 1319 South Logan-MLK, Lansing, MI 48910-1340
Blue Night Press, 1003 Lakeway, Kalamazoo, MI 49001
LITERALLY HORSES, 116 Fellows Avenue, Kalamazoo, MI 49001, 616-345-5915
PRECHELONIAN, 1003 Lakeway, Kalamazoo, MI 49001
New Issues Poetry & Prose, Western Michigan University, 1201 Oliver Street, Kalamazoo, MI 49008, 616-387-2592 or 616-387-8185, Fax 616-387-2562, newissues-poetry@wmich.edu, www.umich.edu/newissues
Rarach Press, 1005 Oakland Drive, Kalamazoo, MI 49008, 616-388-5631
THIRD COAST, Department of English, Western Michigan University, Kalamazoo, MI 49008-5092, 616-387-2675; Fax 616-387-2562; www.wmich.edu/thirdcoast
PrePress Publishing of Michigan, 709 Sunbright Avenue, Portage, MI 49024-2759, 616-323-2659
THE LETTER PARADE, PO Box 52, Comstock, MI 49041
CLUBHOUSE, Your Story Hour, PO Box 15, Berrien Springs, MI 49103, (616) 471-9009
BIG SCREAM, 2782 Dixie S.W., Grandville, MI 49418, 616-531-1442
Nada Press, 2782 Dixie S.W., Grandville, MI 49418, 616-531-1442
Gearhead Press, 565 Lincoln, Northwest, Grand Rapids, MI 49504, 459-7861 or 459-4577
ANGELFLESH, PO Box 141123, Grand Rapids, MI 49514
Angelflesh Press, PO Box 141123, Grand Rapids, MI 49514
EX FILLAPIO IN PENUSIO, 2526 Chatham Woods, Grand Rapids, MI 49546
LIONESS EGGS RAGING, 2526 Chatham Woods, Grand Rapids, MI 49546
Pen-Dec Press, 2526 Chatham Woods, Grand Rapids, MI 49546
STUFFWAX BEEZER, 2526 Chatham Woods, Grand Rapids, MI 49546
THE BANNER, 2850 Kalamazoo SE, Grand Rapids, MI 49560, 616-224-0819
Smiling Dog Press, 9875 Fritz, Maple City, MI 49664, 616-334-3695
PASSAGES NORTH, English Dept., N. Michigan Univ., 1401 Presque Isle Avenue, Marquette, MI 49855, 906-227-1203, 906-227-1795, Fax 906-227-1096

MINNESOTA

Black Hat Press, Box 12, Goodhue, MN 55027, 651-923-4590
RAG MAG, Box 12, Goodhue, MN 55027, 651-923-4590
GREAT RIVER REVIEW, PO Box 406, Red Wing, MN 55066, Fax 612-388-2528, E-mail acis@pressenter.com
THE FIREFLY (A Tiny Glow In a Forest of Darkness), 300 Broadway #107, St. Paul, MN 55101
HEELTAP/Pariah Press, c/o Richard D. Houff, 604 Hawthorne Ave. East, St. Paul, MN 55101-3531
Pariah Press, 604 Hawthorne Avenue East, St. Paul, MN 55101-3531
Spout Press, 28 W. Robie Street, St. Paul, MN 55107
Studia Hispanica Editors, Attn: Luis Ramos-Garcia, 2129 Folwell Avenue, St. Paul, MN 55108-1306, 612-574-9460
Graywolf Press, 2402 University Avenue #203, St. Paul, MN 55114, 651-641-0077, 651-641-0036
Network 3000 Publishing, 3432 Denmark Avenue #108, St. Paul, MN 55123-1088, 612-452-4173
SIDEWALKS, PO Box 321, Champlin, MN 55316
Coffee House Press, 27 N. 4th Street, Minneapolis, MN 55401, 612-338-0125, Fax 612-338-4004, jim@coffeehouse-press.org
New Rivers Press, Inc., 420 N. 5th Street, Suite 1180, Minneapolis, MN 55401, 612-339-7114
KARAWANE, 402 S. Cedar Lake Road, Minneapolis, MN 55405, 612-381-1229, karawane@prodigy.net, http://pages.prodigy.net/fluffysingler
WORMWOOD REVIEW, PO Box 50003, Loring Station, Minneapolis, MN 55405-0003, 612-381-1229
Mid-List Press, 4324 12th Avenue South, Minneapolis, MN 55407-3218, 612-822-3733, Fax 612-823-8387, guide@midlist.org, www.midlist.org
THE EVERGREEN CHRONICLES, PO Box 8939, Minneapolis, MN 55408-8939, 612-823-6638; e-mail evgrnch-ron@aol.com
LIGHTNING & ASH, 3010 Hennepin Avenue South #289, Minneapolis, MN 55408

CONDUIT, 510 Eighth Avenue NE, Minneapolis, MN 55413
ARTWORD QUARTERLY, PO Box 760, Minneapolis, MN 55414-2411, 612-378-3261
North Stone Press, PO Box 14098, Minneapolis, MN 55414
THE NORTH STONE REVIEW, PO Box 14098, Minneapolis, MN 55414
Milkweed Editions, 1011 Washington Ave. S., Ste. 300, Minneapolis, MN 55415, 612-332-3192, Fax 612-215-2550, www.milkweed.org
Lost Prophet Press, 2657 Grand Street NE, Mineapolis, MN 55418-2603, 612-781-6224, Fax 612-333-5800
THIN COYOTE, 2657 Grand Street NE, Minneapolis, MN 55418-2603, 612-781-6224, Fax 612-333-5800
The Place In The Woods, 3900 Glenwood Avenue, Golden Valley, MN 55422, 612-374-2120
READ, AMERICA!, 3900 Glenwood Avenue, Golden Valley, MN 55422, 612-374-2120
MIP Company, PO Box 27484, Minneapolis, MN 55427, 763-544-5915, Fax 952-544-6077, mp@mipco.com, www.mipco.com
WELLSPRING, 8260 W. River Road #315, Brooklyn Park, MN 55444-2266, 612-566-6663; fax 612-566-9754
LIFTOUTS, 1414 S. 3rd Street-#102, Minneapolis, MN 55454, 612-321-9044, Fax 612-305-0655
Preludium Publishers, 1414 South 3rd Street, No. 102, Minneapolis, MN 55454-1172, 612-321-9044, Fax 612-305-0655
XCP: CROSS-CULTURAL POETICS, College of St. Catherine, 601 25th Avenue South, Minneapolis, MN 55454, website http://bfn.org/~xcp
SPOUT, PO BOX 581067, Minneapolis, MN 55458-1067
NORTH COAST REVIEW, PO Box 103, Duluth, MN 55801-0103
Poetry Harbor, PO Box 103, Duluth, MN 55801-0103
POETRY MOTEL, PO Box 103, Duluth, MN 55801-0103
Suburban Wilderness Press, PO Box 103, Duluth, MN 55801-0103
Holy Cow! Press, PO Box 3170, Mount Royal Station, Duluth, MN 55803, 218-724-1653 phone/Fax
KUMQUAT MERINGUE, PO Box 736, Pine Island, MN 55963-0736, e-mail moodyriver@aol.com; Website Http://www.geostar.com/kumquatcastle
MANKATO POETRY REVIEW, Box 53, Mankato State University, Mankato, MN 56001, 507-389-5511
Spoon River Poetry Press, PO Box 6, Granite Falls, MN 56241
THE BURNING CLOUD REVIEW, 225 15th Avenue N, St. Cloud, MN 56303-4531, E-mail ERhinerson@aol.com
Little Leaf Press, Inc., PO Box 187, Milaca, MN 56353, 1-877-548-2431, Fax 320-556-3585, littleleaf@maxminn.com, www.maxminn.com/littleleaf
STUDIO ONE, College of St. Benedict, St. Joseph, MN 56374
ASCENT, Department of English, Concordia College, Moorhead, MN 56562, E-mail Ascent@cord.edu
WRITERS' JOURNAL, PO Box 394, Perham, MN 56573-0394, 218-346-7921, fax 218-346-7924, e-mail writersjournal@wadena.net
Truly Fine Press, PO Box 891, Bemidji, MN 56601
LOONFEATHER: A magazine of poetry, short prose, and graphics, PO Box 1212, Bemidji, MN 56619, 218-751-4869
Loonfeather Press, PO Box 1212, Bemidji, MN 56619, 218-751-4869

MISSISSIPPI

MISSISSIPPI REVIEW, USM, Box 5144, Southern Station, Hattiesburg, MS 39406-5144, 601-266-4321
Pearl River Press, 32 Cambridge Avenue, Gulfport, MS 39507-4213
PEARL RIVER REVIEW, 32 Cambridge Avenue, Gulfport, MS 39507-4213

MISSOURI

THE LOWELL REVIEW, 3075 Harness Drive, Florissant, MO 63033-3711, E-mail rita@etext.org; website http://www.etext.org/Zines/LowellReview
RIVER STYX, 634 North Grand Blvd., 12th Floor, St. Louis, MO 63103-1002, 314-533-4541
BOULEVARD, 4579 Laclede Avenue, #332, St. Louis, MO 63108-2103, 215-568-7062
Neshui Publishing, 1345 Bellevue, St. Louis, MO 63117, 314-725-5562, e-mail info@neshui.com, website www.neshui.com
NATURAL BRIDGE, English Dept., Univ. of Missouri, 8001 Natural Bridge Road, St. Louis, MO 63121, E-mail natural@jinx.umsl.edu
CHARITON REVIEW, Truman University, Kirksville, MO 63501, 660-785-4499
Rabeth Publishing Company, 201 S. Cottage Grove, Kirksville, MO 63501, 660-665-5143, e-mail qurabeth@kvmo.net
Truman State University Press, 100 East Normal Street, Kirksville, MO 63501, 660-785-7199, FAX 660-785-4480
THE CAPE ROCK, English Dept, Southeast Missouri State, Cape Girardeau, MO 63701, 314-651-2500
PURPLE, 213 Country Club Drive, Cape Girardeau, MO 63701-3339
Unity Books, 1901 NW Blue Parkway, Unity Village, MO 64065, 816-524-3550, fax 816-251-3552
BkMk Press, University of Missouri-Kansas City, 5100 Rockhill, University House, Kansas City, MO 64110, 816-235-2558; FAX 816-235-2611; freemank@smtpgate.ssb.umkc.edu
NEW LETTERS, University of Missouri, Kansas City, MO 64110, 816-235-1168, Fax 816-235-2611, www.umkc.edu/newsletters/
Helicon Nine Editions, Box 22412, Kansas City, MO 64113, 816-753-1095, Fax 816-753-1016, helicon9@aol.com, www.heliconnine.com
THE LAUREL REVIEW, Department of English, Northwest Missouri State University, Maryville, MO 64468, 816-562-1265
THE GREEN HILLS LITERARY LANTERN, PO Box 375, Trenton, MO 64683, 660-359-3948 x324
University of Missouri Press, 2910 LeMone Boulevard, Columbia, MO 65201-0001, 314-882-7641
MOCCASIN TELEGRAPH, 5813 E. Saint Charles Road, Columbia, MO 65202-3025, 573-817-3301
AFRO-HISPANIC REVIEW, Romance Languages, Univ. of Missouri, 143 Arts & Science Building, Columbia, MO 65211, 573-882-5040 or 573-882-5041
THE MINNESOTA REVIEW, English Dept., Univ. of Missouri, 107 Tate Hall, Columbia, MO 65211
THE MISSOURI REVIEW, 1507 Hillcrest Hall, University of Missouri-Columbia, Columbia, MO 65211, 573-882-4474; Fax 573-884-4671; e-mail umcastmr@missouri.edu
Timberline Press, 6281 Red Bud, Fulton, MO 65251, 573-642-5035
LOST GENERATION JOURNAL, Route 5 Box 134, Salem, MO 65560, 314-729-2545; 729-5669
WRITER'S GUIDELINES: A Roundtable for Writers and Editors, HC77 Box 608, Pittsburg, MO 65724

MONTANA

THE AZOREAN EXPRESS, PO Box 249, Big Timber, MT 59011
BLACK JACK & VALLEY GRAPEVINE, Box 249, Big Timber, MT 59011
Seven Buffaloes Press, Box 249, Big Timber, MT 59011
Erespin Press, 304 Mountain View Lane, Laurel, MT 59044-2047
SPIRIT TALK, PO Box 390, Browning, MT 59417, 406-338-2882; E-mail blkfoot4@3rivers.net
Spirit Talk Press, PO Box 390, Browning, MT 59417, 406-338-2882; E-mail blkfoot4@3rivers.net
CORONA, Dept. of Hist. & Phil., Montana State Univ., PO Box 172320, Bozeman, MT 59717, 406-994-5200
CUTBANK, English Dept., University of Montana, Missoula, MT 59812
SUPERIOR POETRY NEWS, PO Box 424, Superior, MT 59872

NEBRASKA

The Backwaters Press, 3502 North 52nd Street, Omaha, NE 68104-3506, 402-451-4052
Lone Willow Press, PO Box 31647, Omaha, NE 68131-0647
THE NEBRASKA REVIEW, FA 212, University of Nebraska-Omaha, Omaha, NE 68182-0324, 402-554-3159
Merrimack Books, PO Box 80702, Lincoln, NE 68501-0702, e-mail wedwards@infocom.com
A Slow Tempo Press, 1345 North 40th Street, Lincoln, NE 68503-2109, 402-466-8689; slowtemp@aol.com
PRAIRIE SCHOONER, 201 Andrews Hall, Univ. of Nebraska, Lincoln, NE 68588-0334, 402-472-0911
Morris Publishing, 3212 E. Hwy 30, Kearney, NE 68847, 800-650-7888

NEVADA

PEGASUS, Pegasus Publishing, PO Box 61324, Boulder City, NV 89006-1324
RED ROCK REVIEW, English Dept J2A/Com. College S. NV, 3200 E. Cheyenne Avenue, N. Las Vegas, NV 89030,
   www.ccsn.nevada.edu/departments/english/redrock.htm
INTERIM, Department of English, University of Nevada, Las Vegas, Las Vegas, NV 89154-5011, 702-895-3172
ART:MAG, PO Box 70896, Las Vegas, NV 89170, 702-734-8121
WOMAN POET, PO Box 60550, Reno, NV 89506, 702-972-1671
Women-in-Literature, Inc., PO Box 60550, Reno, NV 89506
RAZOR WIRE, PO Box 8876, University Station, Reno, NV 89507, 702-847-9311, fax 702-847-9335, e-mail
   shaungrif@aol.com

NEW HAMPSHIRE

Hobblebush Books, 17-A Old Milford Road, Brookline, NH 03033, voice/fax 603-672-4317; E-mail shall@jlc.net; website
   http:www.jlc.net/~hobblebush/
O.ARS, Inc., 21 Rockland Road, Weare, NH 03281, 603-529-1060
WOMENWISE, 38 South Main Street, Concord, NH 03301, 603-225-2739
BONE & FLESH, PO Box 349, Concord, NH 03302-0349
WHOLE TERRAIN - REFLECTIVE ENVIRONMENTAL PRACTICE, 40 Avon Street, Antioch New England, Keene,
   NH 03431-3516, 603-357-3122 ex. 272
William L. Bauhan, Publisher, PO Box 443, Dublin, NH 03444-0443, 603-563-8020
The Ark, 176 Centre Street, East Sullivan, NH 03445-4111, 603-847-3028, anarkiss@mindspring.com
COBBLESTONE: Discover American History, 30 Grove Street, Suite C, Peterborough, NH 03458, 603-924-7209, Fax
   603-924-7380, custsvc@cobblestone.mv.com
:THAT:, 1070 Easton Valley Road, Easton, NH 03580
RED OWL, 35 Hampshire Road, Portsmouth, NH 03801-4815, 603-431-2691; redowlmag@juno.com
Kettle of Fish Press, PO Box 364, Exeter, NH 03833
Nicolin Fields Publishing, Inc., 3 Red Fox Road, North Hampton, NH 03862-3320, 603-964-1727, Fax 603-964-4221,
   nfp@nh.ultranet.com, www.PublishingWorks.com, and www.NicolinFields.com

NEW JERSEY

EXIT 13 MAGAZINE, P O Box 423, Fanwood, NJ 07023
LONG SHOT, PO Box 6238, Hoboken, NJ 07030
WRITES OF PASSAGE, PO Box 1935, Livingston, NJ 07039, 212-473-7564; wpusa@aol.com; http://www.writes.org
RUBBER DUCKY MAGAZINE, PO Box 799, Upper Montclair, NJ 07043, 201-783-0029
Saturday Press, Inc., PO Box 43548, Upper Montclair, NJ 07043, 973-256-5053
Warthog Press, 29 South Valley Road, West Orange, NJ 07052, 201-731-9269
THE EVER DANCING MUSE, PO Box 7751, East Rutherford, NJ 07073
Who Who Who Publishing, PO Box 7751, East Rutherford, NJ 07073
The Fire!! Press, 241 Hillside Road, Elizabeth, NJ 07208, 908-289-3714, Fax 908-688-9330, firepres@injersey.com
ST. JOSEPH MESSENGER, PO Box 288, Jersey City, NJ 07303, 201-798-4141
TALISMAN: A Journal of Contemporary Poetry and Poetics, PO Box 3157, Jersey City, NJ 07303-3157, 201-938-0698
Talisman House, Publishers, PO Box 3157, Jersey City, NJ 07303-3157, 201-938-0698
Hug The Earth Publications, 42 Greenwood Avenue, Pequannock, NJ 07440
THE PATERSON LITERARY REVIEW, Passaic County Community College, College Boulevard, Paterson, NJ
   07505-1179, 201-684-6555
Lincoln Springs Press, 40 Post Avenue, Hawthorne, NJ 07506-1809
THE UNFORGETTABLE FIRE, 206 North 6th Street, Prospect Park, NJ 07508-2025
Relief Press, 245 Teaneck Road, Ridgefield Park, NJ 07660-2003, 201-641-3003
BRAVO, THE POET'S MAGAZINE, 1081 Trafalgar Street, Teaneck, NJ 07666, 201-836-5922
John Edwin Cowen/Bravo Editions, 1081 Trafalgar Street, Teaneck, NJ 07666
HELLP!, PO Box 38, Farmingdale, NJ 07727
Hellp! Press, PO Box 38, Farmingdale, NJ 07727
Vista Publishing, Inc., 422 Morris Avenue, Suite 1, Long Branch, NJ 07740, 732-229-6500, Fax 732-229-9647,
   czagury@vistapubl.com
PASSAIC REVIEW (MILLENNIUM EDITIONS), c/o Ah! Sunflower Theater, PO Box 732, Spring Lake, NJ 07762
JOURNAL OF NEW JERSEY POETS, 214 Center Grove Road, County College of Morris, Randolph, NJ 07869,
   201-328-5471, e-mail szulauf@ccm.edu

THE LITERARY REVIEW, Fairleigh Dickinson University, 285 Madison Avenue, Madison, NJ 07940, 973-443-8564, Fax 973-443-8364
PTOLEMY/BROWNS MILLS REVIEW, PO Box 252, Juliustown, NJ 08042, 609-893-0896
PenRose Publishing Company, Inc., PO Box 620, Mystic Island, NJ 08087, 609-296-1401
Still Waters Poetry Press, 459 S. Willow Avenue, Absecon, NJ 08201-4633
A COMPANION IN ZEOR, 307 Ashland Ave., Egg Harbor Township, NJ 08234-5568, 609-645-6938, fax 609-645-8084, Klitman323@aol.com, www.simegen.com/sgfandom/rimonslibrary/cz
DEVIL BLOSSOMS, PO Box 5122, Seabrook, NJ 08302
Branch Redd Books, 9300 Atlantic Avenue, Apt. 218, Margate City, NJ 08402-2340
BRANCH REDD REVIEW, 9300 Atlantic Ave, Apt 218, Margate City, NJ 08402-2340
Marymark Press, 45-08 Old Millstone Drive, East Windsor, NJ 08520, 609-443-0646, www.experimentalpoet.com
US1 Poets' Cooperative, PO Box 127, Kingston, NJ 08528-0127, 609-921-1489; fax 609-279-1513
US1 WORKSHEETS, PO Box 127, Kingston, NJ 08528-0127, 609-921-1489; fax 609-279-1513
PRINCETON ARTS REVIEW, 102 Witherspoon Street, Princeton, NJ 08540, 609-924-8777
Princeton University Press, 41 William Street, Princeton, NJ 08540, 609-258-4900
QRL POETRY SERIES, Princeton University, 26 Haslet Avenue, Princeton, NJ 08540, 921-6976
Quarterly Review of Literature Press, Princeton University, 26 Haslet Avenue, Princeton, NJ 08540, 609-921-6976, fax 609-258-2230, e-mail qrl@princeton.edu
THE KELSEY REVIEW, Mercer County, Community College, PO Box B, Trenton, NJ 08690, 609-586-4800 ext. 3326, e-mail kelsey.review@mccc.edu
BLACK BOUGH, 188 Grove Street #1, Somerville, NJ 08876
THE HIGGINSVILLE READER, PO Box 141, Three Bridges, NJ 08887, 908-788-0514, hgvreader@yahoo.com

NEW MEXICO

Duende Press, Box 571, Placitas, NM 87043, 505-867-5877
Zerx Press, 725 Van Buren Place SE, Albuquerque, NM 87108, zerxpress@aol.com
La Alameda Press, 9636 Guadalupe Trail NW, Albuquerque, NM 87114
West End Press, PO Box 27334, Albuquerque, NM 87125
BLUE MESA REVIEW, Department of English, Humanities Building, Albuquerque, NM 87131, 505-277-6347, fax 277-5573, bluemesa@unm.edu
ATOM MIND, PO Box 22068, Albuquerque, NM 87154
PARADOXISM, 200 College Road, University of New Mexico, Gallup, NM 87301, 505-726-8194, Fax 505-863-7532, smarand@unm.edu, www.gallup.unm.edu/~smarandache/
69 FLAVORS OF PARANOIA, 2816 Rio Vista Court, Farmington, NM 87401-4557
American Canadian Publishers, Inc., PO Box 4595, Santa Fe, NM 87502-4595, 505-983-8484, fax 505-983-8484
Rising Tide Press New Mexico, PO Box 6136, Santa Fe, NM 87502-6136, 505-983-8484, fax 505-983-8484
From Here Press, PO Box 2740, Santa Fe, NM 87504-2740, 505-438-3249
Sherman Asher Publishing, PO Box 2853, Santa Fe, NM 87504, 505-984-2686, FAX 505-820-2744, e-mail sapublish@att.net, www.shermanasher.com
XTRAS, PO Box 2740, Santa Fe, NM 87504-2740, 505-438-3249
YEFIEF, PO Box 8505, Santa Fe, NM 87504
Burning Books, PO Box 2638, Santa Fe, NM 87505, Fax 505-820-6216, E-mail brnbx@nets.com
COUNTERMEASURES, Creative Writing Program, College of Santa Fe, St. Michael's Drive, Santa Fe, NM 87505
Katydid Books, 1 Balsa Road, Santa Fe, NM 87505
THE GENTLE SURVIVALIST, General Delivery, Arroyo Seco, NM 87514
Minor Heron Press, 5275 NDCBU, Taos, NM 87571, 505-758-1800
PUERTO DEL SOL, Box 3E, New Mexico State University, Las Cruces, NM 88003, 505-646-2345
WHOLE NOTES, PO Box 1374, Las Cruces, NM 88004, 505-541-5744
Whole Notes Press, PO Box 1374, Las Cruces, NM 88004, 505-382-7446

NEW YORK

ISRAEL HORIZONS, 114 W. 26th Street #1001, New York, NY 10001-6812, 212-868-0377; FAX 212-868-0364
CURARE, c/o Whalen, 20 Clinton Street #1G, New York, NY 10002, 212-533-7167
Soft Skull Press, 100 Suffolk Street, Basement, New York, NY 10002, 212-673-2502, Fax 212-673-0787, sander@softskull.com, www.softskull.com
THE ASIAN PACIFIC AMERICAN JOURNAL, 37 Saint Marks Place, New York, NY 10003-7801, 212-228-6718
CONJUNCTIONS, 21 East 10th Street #3E, New York, NY 10003-5924
DOWN UNDER MANHATTAN BRIDGE, 224 E. 11th Street #5, New York, NY 10003-7329, 212-388-7051, lizard.evny@msn.com
FROM THE MARGIN, 50 E. 1st Street, Storefront West, New York, NY 10003-9311
JEWISH CURRENTS, 22 E. 17th Street, Suite 601, New York, NY 10003, 212-924-5740
LITERAL LATTE, 61 East 8th Street, Suite 240, New York, NY 10003, 212-260-5532
LUNGFULL! MAGAZINE, 126 East 4th Street #2, New York, NY 10003, 212-533-9317, lungfull@interport.net
The Poetry Project, St. Mark's Church, 131 East 10th Street, New York, NY 10003, 212-674-0910, e-mail poproj@artomatic.com
THE POETRY PROJECT NEWSLETTER, St. Mark's Church, 131 East 10th Street, New York, NY 10003, 212-674-0910, poproj@artomatic.com
THE WORLD, St. Marks Church/The Poetry Project, 131 East 10th Street, New York, NY 10003, poproj@artomatic.com
CLWN WR, PO Box 2165 Church Street Station, New York, NY 10008-2165
POETRY NEW YORK: A Journal of Poetry and Translation, PO Box 3184, Church Street Station, New York, NY 10008
COVER MAGAZINE, 632 East 14th Street, #18, New York, NY 10009, 212-673-1152, Fax 212-253-7614
A GATHERING OF THE TRIBES, PO Box 20693, Tompkins Square, New York, NY 10009, 212-674-3778, Fax 212-674-5576, info@tribes.org, www.tribes.org
Hard Press, 632 East 14th Street, #18, New York, NY 10009, 212-673-1152
HOME PLANET NEWS, P.O. Box 415 Stuyvesant Station, New York, NY 10009, 718-769-2854
Home Planet Publications, PO Box 415 Stuyvesant Station, New York, NY 10009, 718-769-2854
THE SPITTING IMAGE, PO Box 20400 Tompkins Square Stn., New York, NY 10009
THE AMICUS JOURNAL, 40 West 20th Street, New York, NY 10011, 212-727-2700

Edgewise Press, 24 Fifth Avenue #224, New York, NY 10011, 212-982-4818, FAX 212-982-1364
Fouque Publishers, 150 Fifth Avenue, Suite 845, New York, NY 10011, 646-486-1061, Fax 646-486-1091, fouquepublishers@earthlink.net
THE NEW MOON REVIEW, 148 Eighth Avenue #417, New York, NY 10011
ASSEMBLING, Box 444 Prince Street, New York, NY 10012-0008
Assembling Press, Box 444 Prince Street, New York, NY 10012-0008
Black Thistle Press, 491 Broadway, New York, NY 10012, 212-219-1898
BOMB MAGAZINE, 594 Broadway, Suite 905, New York, NY 10012, 212-431-3943, FAX 212-431-5880
The Future Press, Box 444 Prince Street, New York, NY 10012-0008
GRAND STREET, 214 Sullivan Street #6C, New York, NY 10012, 212-533-2944
RATTAPALLAX, 532 La Guardia Place, Suite 353, New York, NY 10012, 212-560-7459, e-mail rattapallax@hot-mail.com
WICKED MYSTIC, 532 LaGuardia Place #371, New York, NY 10012, 718-638-1533
Box Turtle Press, 184 Franklin Street, New York, NY 10013
Green Bean Press, PO Box 237, Canal Street Station, New York, NY 10013, phone/fax 718-302-1955, e-mail gbpress@earthlink.net
Kaya Press, 373 Broadway, Suite E2, New York, NY 10013, 212-343-9503, Fax 212-343-8291, kaya@kaya.com, www.kaya.com
MUDFISH, 184 Franklin Street, New York, NY 10013, 212-219-9278
TRICYCLE: The Buddhist Review, 92 Vandam Street, New York, NY 10013-1007
Water Mark Press, 138 Duane Street, New York, NY 10013, 212-285-1609
ZerOX Books, 105 Hudson Street, #311, New York, NY 10013
Bank Street Press, 24 Bank Street, New York, NY 10014, 212-255-0692
Black Dress Press, PO Box 213, Village Station, New York, NY 10014, website www.blackdresspress.com
Philomel Books, 345 Hudson Street, New York, NY 10014, 212-414-3610
S Press, 527 Hudson Street, PO Box 20095, New York, NY 10014
SPINNING JENNY, PO Box 213, Village Station, New York, NY 10014, website www.blackdresspress.com
Blacfax, Midtown Station, PO Box 542, New York, NY 10018
THE CHARIOTEER, 337 West 36 Street, New York, NY 10018, 212-279-9586
Pella Publishing Co, 337 West 36th Street, New York, NY 10018, 212-279-9586
AMERICA, 106 West 56th Street, New York, NY 10019, 212-581-4640
THE NEW CRITERION, 850 Seventh Avenue, New York, NY 10019, 212-247-6980
AMERICAN LETTERS & COMMENTARY, 850 Park Avenue, Suite 5B, New York, NY 10021, fax 212-327-0706, e-mail rabanna@aol.com, www.amleters.org
THE HUDSON REVIEW, 684 Park Avenue, New York, NY 10021, 212-650-0020, fax 212-774-1911
SCANDINAVIAN REVIEW, 15 East 65 Street, New York, NY 10021, 212-879-9779
ARARAT, 55 E 59th Street, New York, NY 10022-1112
AUFBAU, 2121 Broadway, New York, NY 10023, 212-873-7400, fax 212-496-5736
PRESS, 2124 Broadway, Suite 323, New York, NY 10023, 212-579-0873
SPACE AND TIME, 138 West 70th Street 4-B, New York, NY 10023-4432
Helikon Press, 120 West 71st Street, New York City, NY 10023
PARNASSUS: Poetry in Review, 205 West 89th Street, Apartment 8F, New York, NY 10024, 212-362-3492, fax 212-875-0148, e-mail parnew@aol.com
BARK!, PO Box 738, New York, NY 10025
Maxima New Media, 2472 Broadway #195, New York, NY 10025, 212-439-4177, Fax 212-439-4178, e-mail aronst@ibm.net
RESPONSE: A Contemporary Jewish Review, PO BOX 250892, New York, NY 10025-1506
Midmarch Arts Press, 300 Riverside Drive, New York City, NY 10025, 212-666-6990
THE MANHATTAN REVIEW, c/o Philip Fried, 440 Riverside Drive, #45, New York, NY 10027
Red Dust, PO Box 630, Gracie Station, New York, NY 10028, 212-348-4388
WOMEN'S STUDIES QUARTERLY, The Feminist Press c/o City College, Convent Ave. & 138th St., New York, NY 10031, 212-360-5790
META4: Journal of Object Oriented Poetics (OOPS), c/o Jurado, 1793 Riverside Drive #3F, New York, NY 10034
Italica Press, Inc., 595 Main Street, #605, New York, NY 10044, 212-935-4230; fax 212-838-7812; inquiries@italica-press.com
Pendragonian Publications, PO Box 719, New York, NY 10101-0719, mmpendragon@aol.com
PENNY DREADFUL: Tales and Poems of Fantastic Terror, PO Box 719, New York, NY 10101-0719, mmpendragon@aol.com
SONGS OF INNOCENCE, PO Box 719, New York, NY 10101-0719, mmpendragon@aol.com
LILITH, 250 West 57th, #2432, New York, NY 10107, 212-757-0818
GRUE MAGAZINE, Hell's Kitchen Productions, PO Box 370, Times Square Station, New York, NY 10108, e-mail nadramia@panix.com
Painted Leaf Press, PO Box 2480, Times Square Station, New York, NY 10108-2480
W.W. Norton, 500 Fifth Avenue, New York, NY 10110, 212-354-5500
NOON, 1369 Madison Avenue, PMB 298, New York, NY 10128, noonannual@yahoo.com
THE THIRD HOUSE, PO Box 7377, FDR Station, New York, NY 10150, jeyrep@compuserve.com
FISH DRUM MAGAZINE, PO Box 966, Murray Hill Station, New York, NY 10156, www.fishdrum.com
CHELSEA, PO Box 773, Cooper Station, New York, NY 10276-0773
Serena Bay Books, PO Box 1655, Cooper Station, New York, NY 10276, 212-260-5580
Bard Press, 393 St. Paul's Avenue, Staten Island, NY 10304-2127, 718-442-7429
Ten Penny Players, Inc., 393 St. Paul's Avenue, Staten Island, NY 10304-2127, 718-442-7429, www.tenpennyplayers.org
UNMUZZLED OX, 43B Clark Lane, Staten Island, NY 10304, 781-448-3395, 212-226-7170, MAndreOX@aol.com
WATERWAYS: Poetry in the Mainstream, 393 St. Paul's Avenue, Staten Island, NY 10304-2127, 718-442-7429, www.tenpennyplayers.org
APHRODITE GONE BERSERK, 233 Guyon Avenue, Staten Island, NY 10306
CRIPES!, 110 Bement Avenue, Staten Island, NY 10310
AMERICAN TANKA, PO Box 120-024, Staten Island, NY 10312-0024, email editor@americantanka.com, website www.americantanka.com

OUTERBRIDGE, College of Staten Island, 2800 Victory Boulevard, Staten Island, NY 10314, 212-390-7654, 7779
FIRST DRAFT, 3636 Fieldston Road, Apt. 7A, Riverdale Bronx, NY 10463-2041, 718-543-5493
Blind Beggar Press, Box 437 Williamsbridge Station, Bronx, NY 10467, 914-683-6792
The Sheep Meadow Press, PO Box 1345, Riverdale-on-Hudson, NY 10471, 212-548-5547
The Purchase Press, PO Box 5, Harrison, NY 10528, 914-967-4499
THE ICONOCLAST, 1675 Amazon Road, Mohegan Lake, NY 10547-1804
ROOM, 38 Ferris Place, Ossining, NY 10562-2818
Portmanteau Editions, PO Box 665, Somers, NY 10589
Slapering Hol Press, 300 Riverside Drive, Sleepy Hollow, NY 10591-1414, 914-332-5953
Ultramarine Publishing Co., Inc., PO Box 303, Hastings-on-Hudson, NY 10706, 914-478-2522
THE SHAKESPEARE NEWSLETTER, English Department, Iona College, New Rochelle, NY 10801
CROSS CURRENTS, College of New Rochelle, New Rochelle, NY 10805-2339, 914-235-1439; fax: 914-235-1584; aril@ecunet.org
HEAVEN BONE MAGAZINE, PO Box 486, Chester, NY 10918, 914-469-9018
Heaven Bone Press, PO Box 486, Chester, NY 10918, 914-469-9018
Chicken Soup Press, Inc., PO Box 164, Circleville, NY 10919, 914-692-6320, fax 914-692-7574, e-mail poet@warwick.net
Lintel, 24 Blake Lane, Middletown, NY 10940, 212-674-4901
Avocet Press Inc., 19 Paul Court, Pearl River, NY 10965, 212-754-6300, email oopc@interport.net, www.avocetpress.com
THE UNKNOWN WRITER, 5 Pothat Street, Sloatsburg, NY 10974, 914-753-8363; Fax 914-753-6562; E-mail rsidor@worldnet.att.net
Roth Publishing, Inc., 175 Great Neck Road, Great Neck, NY 11021, 516-466-3676
APKL Publications, 42-07 34th Avenue #4-D, Long Island City, NY 11101-1115
Low-Tech Press, 30-73 47th Street, Long Island City, NY 11103, 718-721-0946
The Smith (subsidiary of The Generalist Assn., Inc.), 69 Joralemon Street, Brooklyn, NY 11201-4003
POETS ON THE LINE, PO Box 020292, Brooklyn, NY 11202-0007, 212-766-4109
BATH AVENUE NEWSLETTER (BATH), 1980 65th Street #3D, Brooklyn, NY 11204, 718-331-5960; Fax 718-331-4997; E-mail Laspina@msn.con, VLaspina@wow.con
KOJA, 7314 21 Avenue #6E, Brooklyn, NY 11204, email mikekoja@aol.com
Legas, PO Box 040328, Brooklyn, NY 11204
Vincent Laspina, 1980 65th Street #3D, Brooklyn, NY 11204, 718-331-5960; Fax 718-331-4997; Laspina@msn.con, VLaspina@wow.con
HANGING LOOSE, 231 Wyckoff Street, Brooklyn, NY 11217
Hanging Loose Press, 231 Wyckoff Street, Brooklyn, NY 11217
Brownout Laboratories, 103 East 4th Street, Brooklyn, NY 11218
Face to Face Press, 3322 12th Avenue, Suite 2, Brooklyn, NY 11218, 718-436-2331, Fax 419-828-4684, slevart@face2facepress.com, www.face2facepress.com
Malafemmina Press, 4211 Fort Hamilton Parkway, Brooklyn, NY 11219
Pinched Nerves Press, 1610 Avenue P, Apt. 6-B, Brooklyn, NY 11229
Lunar Offensive Publications, 1910 Foster Avenue, Brooklyn, NY 11230-1902
RAG SHOCK, 1910 Foster Avenue, Brooklyn, NY 11230-1902
THE BROWNSTONE REVIEW, 335 Court St. #114, Brooklyn, NY 11231-4335
THE OVAL MAGAZINE, 22 Douglass Street, Brooklyn, NY 11231
THE PIPE SMOKER'S EPHEMERIS, 20-37 120th Street, College Point, NY 11356-2128
THE SPIRIT THAT MOVES US, PO Box 720820-DB, Jackson Heights, Queens, NY 11372-0820, 718-426-8788, msklar@mindspring.com
The Spirit That Moves Us Press, Inc., PO Box 720820-DB, Jackson Heights, Queens, NY 11372-0820, 718-426-8788, msklar@mindspring.com
Black Spring Press, 63-89 Saunders Street #6G, Rego Park, NY 11374
BLACK SPRING REVIEW, 63-89 Saunders Street #6G, Rego Park, NY 11374
BLACKBOX, 77-44 Austin Street #3F, Forest Hills, NY 11375
Lion Press, Ltd., 108-22 Queens Boulevard, #221, Forest Hills, NY 11375, 718-271-1394
THE NEW PRESS LITERARY QUARTERLY, 6539 108th Street #E6, Forest Hills, NY 11375-2214, 718-459-6807; Fax; 718-275-1646
THE LEDGE, 78-44 80th Street, Glendale, NY 11385
New Spirit Press/The Poet Tree, 82-34 138 Street #6F, Kew Gardens, NY 11435, 718-847-1482
POEMS THAT THUMP IN THE DARK/SECOND GLANCE, 82-34 138 Street #6F, Kew Gardens, NY 11435, 718-847-1482
ARBA SICULA, c/o Modern Foreign Languages, St. John's University, Jamaica, NY 11439-0002
SICILIA PARRA, c/o Modern Foreign Languages, St. John's University, Jamaica, NY 11439-0002, 718-331-0613
CONFRONTATION, English Department, C.W. Post of Long Island Univ., Greenvale, NY 11548, 516-299-2720
QUEEN OF ALL HEARTS, 26 South Saxon Avenue, Bay Shore, NY 11706, 516-665-0726
FANTASTIC STORIES, PO Box 329, Brightwaters, NY 11718-0329, E-mail pwpubl@aol.com
Pleasure Dome Press (Long Island Poetry Collective Inc.), Box 773, Huntington, NY 11743
XANADU, Box 773, Huntington, NY 11743, 516-248-7716
FULLOSIA PRESS, 299-9 Hawkins Avenue, PMB 865, Ronkonkoma, NY 11779, Fax 631-588-9428, deanofrpps@aol.com, www.angelfire.com/bc2/FULLOSIAPRESS/
SHADES OF DECEMBER, PO Box 244, Selden, NY 11784, E-mail eilonwy@innocent.com; www2.crosswinds.net/new-york/~shadesof12
WRITERS INK, PO Box 2344, Selden, NY 11784, 516-451-0478 phone/fax, axelrodthepoet@yahoo.com
Writers Unlimited Agency, Inc, PO Box 2344, Selden, NY 11784, 516-451-0478 phone/Fax, axelrodthepoet@yahoo.com
Writers Ink Press, 233 Mooney Pond, PO Box 2344, Selden, Long Island, NY 11784-2344, 516-451-0478 phone/Fax, axelrodthepoet@yahoo.com
Irish Studies, 2592 N Wading River Road, Wading River, NY 11792-1404, 516-929-0224
TAPROOT, a journal of older writers, Fine Arts Center 4290, University at Stony Brook, Stony Brook, NY 11794-5410, 516-632-6635
The Bookman Press, PO Box 1892, Sag Harbor, NY 11963, 516-725-1115
Savant Garde Workshop, PO Box 1650, Sag Harbor, NY 11963-0060, 516-725-1414; website www.savantgarde.org
BEGINNINGS - A Magazine for the Novice Writer, PO Box 92-R, Shirley, NY 11967, 516-924-7826,

scbeginnings@juno.com, www.scbeginnings.com
LITERARY ROCKET, PO Box 672, Water Mill, NY 11976-0672, e-mail RocketUSA@delphi.com
Sachem Press, PO Box 9, Old Chatham, NY 12136, 518-794-8327
RALPH'S REVIEW, 129 Wellington Avenue, #A, Albany, NY 12203-2637, e-mail rcpub@juno.com
A & U AMERICA'S AIDS MAGAZINE, 25 Monroe Street, Suite 205, Albany, NY 12210, 518-426-9010, fax
    518-436-5354, mailbox@aumag.org
THE KOSCIUSZKO PORTFOLIO, 405 Madison Avenue, Albany, NY 12210
THE LITTLE MAGAZINE, English Department, State Univ. of New York at Albany, Albany, NY 12222, website
    www.albany.edu/~litmag.
13TH MOON, 1400 Washington Avenue, SUNY, English Department, Albany, NY 12222-0001, 518-442-4181
Press-Tige Publishing Company Inc., 291 Main Street, Catskill, NY 12414, 518-943-1440 X10
WRITER'S MONTHLY GAZETTE, PO Box 788, Leeds, NY 12451
ART TIMES, PO Box 730, Mount Marion, NY 12456-0730, 914-246-6944, email arttimes@alster.net
HUNGER, PO Box 505, Rosendale, NY 12472, 914-658-9273, hungermag@aol.com, www.hungermagazine.com
Hunger Press, PO Box 505, Rosendale, NY 12472, hungermag@aol.com, www.hungermagazine.com
Left Hand Books, Station Hill Road, Barrytown, NY 12507, 914-758-6478; FAX 914-758-4416
Station Hill Press, Station Hill Road, Barrytown, NY 12507, 914-758-5840
The Groundwater Press, PO Box 704, Hudson, NY 12534, 516-767-8503
BLU, PO Box 517, New Paltz, NY 12561, 1-800-778-8461; e-mail revcenter@hotmail.com; website www.revolution-
    center.org
POSTCARD, PO Box 444, Tivioli, NY 12583
Voices From My Retreat, Box 1077, S. Fallsburg, NY 12779, 914-436-7455; 1-800-484-1255 ex. 2485
Alms House Press, PO Box 218, Woodbourne, NY 12788-0218
The Snail's Pace Press, Inc., 85 Darwin Road, Cambridge, NY 12816, 518-677-5208, snail@poetic.com
The Greenfield Review Press/Ithaca House, PO Box 308, Greenfield Center, NY 12833-0308, 518-584-1728
CHRONICLES OF DISORDER, 20 Edie Road, Saratoga Springs, NY 12866-5425
SALMAGUNDI, Skidmore College, Saratoga Springs, NY 12866, 518-584-5000
BITTER OLEANDER, 4983 Tall Oaks Drive, Fayetteville, NY 13066-9776, FAX 315-637-5056, E-mail
    bones44@ix.netcom.com
Purple Finch Press, PO Box 758, Dewitt, NY 13214, 315-445-8087
THE COMSTOCK REVIEW, Comstock Writers' Group, Inc., 4958 St. John Drive, Syracuse, NY 13215
RED BRICK REVIEW, PO Box 6527, Syracuse, NY 13217
SALT HILL, English Department, Syracuse University, Syracuse, NY 13244-1170
Baba Yoga Micropress, 430 N. Main Street, Herkimer, NY 13350
Quilted Walls Micropress, 426 N. Main Street, Herkimer, NY 13350
BLUELINE, State University College, English Dept., Potsdam, NY 13676, 315-267-2043
THE WALLACE STEVENS JOURNAL, Clarkson University, Box 5750, Potsdam, NY 13699-5750, 315-268-3987,
    serio@clarkson.edu, www.wallacestevens.com
The Wallace Stevens Society Press, Box 5750 Clarkson University, Potsdam, NY 13699-5750, 315-268-3987, Fax
    268-3983, serio@clarkson.edu, www.wallacestevens.com
Birch Brook Press, PO Box 81, Delhi, NY 13753, 212-353-3326 editorial messages only, Phone & Fax orders & sales
    inquiries 607-746-7453, birchbrkpr@prodigy.net, www.birchbrookpress.com
Bright Hill Press, PO Box 193, Treadwell, NY 13846, Fax 607-746-7274; E-mail wordthurs@aol.com
MOODY STREET IRREGULARS: A Jack Kerouac Magazine, 2737 Dodge Road, East Amherst, NY 14051-2113
Moody Street Irregulars, Inc., 2737 Dodge Road, East Amherst, NY 14051-2113
The Edwin Mellen Press, PO Box 450, Lewiston, NY 14092, 716-754-2266
Mellen Poetry Press, PO Box 450, 415 Ridge Street, Lewiston, NY 14092-0450, 716-754-2266, Fax 716-754-4056, E-mail
    mellen@wzrd.com, www.mellenpress.com
ELF: ECLECTIC LITERARY FORUM (ELF MAGAZINE), PO Box 392, Tonawanda, NY 14150, 716-693-7006
White Pine Press, PO Box 236, Buffalo, NY 14201-0236, 716-672-5743
BUCKLE &, PO Box 1653, Buffalo, NY 14205
EARTH'S DAUGHTERS: Feminist Arts Periodical, PO Box 41, Central Park Station, Buffalo, NY 14215-0041,
    716-627-9825, http://bfn.org/~edaught
1812, Box 1812, Amherst, NY 14226-7812, http://1812.simplenet.com
NEW WRITING, PO Box 1812, Amherst, NY 14226-7812, http://members.aol.com/newwriting/magazine.html
SLIPSTREAM, Box 2071, New Market Station, Niagara Falls, NY 14301, 716-282-2616 (after 5 p.m., E.S.T.)
Slipstream Productions, Box 2071, New Market Station, Niagara Falls, NY 14301
State Street Press, PO Box 278, Brockport, NY 14420, 716-637-0023
SENECA REVIEW, Hobart & William Smith Colleges, Geneva, NY 14456, 315-781-3392; Fax 315-781-3348;
    senecareview@hws.edu
BOA Editions, Ltd., 260 East Avenue, Rochester, NY 14604, 716-546-3410
GERBIL: Queer Culture Zine, PO Box 10692, Rochester, NY 14610, 716-262-3966, gerbil@rpa.net
StarMist Books, Box 12640, Rochester, NY 14612
THE ROUND TABLE: A Journal of Poetry and Fiction, PO Box 18673, Rochester, NY 14618
ZUZU'S PETALS: QUARTERLY ONLINE, PO Box 4853, Ithaca, NY 14852-4853, e-mail zuzu@zuzu.com, website
    http://www.zuzu.com
EPOCH, 251 Goldwin Smith Hall, Cornell Univ., Ithaca, NY 14853, 607-255-3385

NORTH CAROLINA

THE GREENSBORO REVIEW, PO Box 26170, Dept. of English, Univ. of North Carolina-Greensboro, Greensboro, NC
    27402-6170, 336-334-5459, fax 336-334-3281, e-mail jlclark@uncg.edu, www.uncg.edu/eng/mfa
March Street Press, 3413 Wilshire Drive, Greensboro, NC 27408-2923
PARTING GIFTS, 3413 Wilshire Drive, Greensboro, NC 27408-2923
INTERNATIONAL POETRY REVIEW, Dept of Romance Languages, The University of North Carolina at Greensboro,
    Greensboro, NC 27412-5001, 336-334-5655
TIMBER CREEK REVIEW, c/o J.M. Freiermuth, 3283 UNCG Station, Greensboro, NC 27413, 336-334-6970
WORDS OF WISDOM, 3283 UNCG Station, Greensboro, NC 27413, 336-334-6970; e-mail wowmail@hoopsmail.com
THE JOURNAL OF AFRICAN TRAVEL-WRITING, PO Box 346, Chapel Hill, NC 27514

THE SUN, A MAGAZINE OF IDEAS, 107 North Roberson Street, Chapel Hill, NC 27516, 919-942-5282
REFLECTIONS, PO Box 1197, Roxboro, NC 27573, 336-599-1181, e-mail furbisd@piedmont.cc.nc.us
THE CAROLINA QUARTERLY, CB# 3520 Greenlaw Hall, Univ of N. Carolina, Chapel Hill, NC 27599-3520, 919-962-0244, fax 919-962-3520
AC, 306 Parham Street, Suite 200, Raleigh, NC 27601, 919-834-5433; Fax 919-834-2449; E-mail gstudios@mindspring.com
Alternating Crimes Publishing, 306 Parham St. Ste 200, Raleigh, NC 27601, 919-834-5433; fax 919-834-2449; e-mail 6studios@mindspring.com
Pentland Press, Inc., 5122 Bur Oak Circle, Raleigh, NC 27612, 919-782-0281
DeeMar Communications, PMB 320, 6325-9 Falls of Neuse Rd., Raleigh, NC 27615, 919-870-6423, postmaster@dee-mar.com, www.deemarcommunications.com, www.deemar.com
Signal Books, 7117 Tyndall Court, Raleigh, NC 27615, 919-870-8505 phone/fax; gtkach@worldnet.att.net
OBSIDIAN II: BLACK LITERATURE IN REVIEW, Dept. of English, Box 8105, NC State University, Raleigh, NC 27695-8105, 919-515-3870
Carolina Wren Press/Lollipop Power Books, 120 Morris Street, Durham, NC 27701, 919-560-2738
LIES MAGAZINE, 1308 Shawnee, Durham, NC 27701, 505-268-7316; email okeefine@aol.com; www.cent.com/abetting/
TAR RIVER POETRY, Department of English, East Carolina University, Greenville, NC 27858-4353, 919-328-6041
CRUCIBLE, English Department, Barton College, Wilson, NC 27893, 252-399-6456
SKYWRITERS, 245 Spring Street, SW, Concord, NC 28025
Stained Glass Press, 245 Spring Street, SW, Concord, NC 28025
MAIN STREET RAG, PO Box 25331, Charlotte, NC 28229-5331, 704-535-1918, E-mail mainstrag@mindspring.com
SOUTHERN POETRY REVIEW, Advancement Studies Dept., Central Piedmont Community College, Charlotte, NC 28235, 704-330-6002
THE MINDFULNESS BELL, 14200 Fountain Lane, Charlotte, NC 28278, 510-527-3751; e-mail parapress@aol.com
Longleaf Press, Methodist College, English Dept., 5400 Ramsey Street, Fayetteville, NC 28311, 910-822-5403
Persephone Press, 600 Kelly Road, Carthage, NC 28327, 910-947-2587; Fax 910-947-5112
Scots Plaid Press, 600 Kelly Road, Carthage, NC 28327, 910-947-2587; Fax 910-947-5112
St. Andrews Press, c/o St. Andrews College, Laurinburg, NC 28352-5598, 919-277-5310
Mount Olive College Press, Mount Olive College, 634 Henderson Street, Mount Olive, NC 28365
MOUNT OLIVE REVIEW, Department of Language and Literature, 634 Henderson Street, Mount Olive, NC 28365, 919-658-2502
PEMBROKE MAGAZINE, UNCP, Box 1510, Pembroke, NC 28372-1510, 919-521-4214 ext 433
SANDHILLS REVIEW (formerly ST. ANDREWS REVIEW), 2200 Airport Road, Pinehurst, NC 28374, 910-695-2756; FAX 910-695-3875
THE FUTURE PHATNESS, 4902 University Drive, Wilmington, NC 28403-2922, 910-793-3362; kingpsycho@visinton.net
Appalachian Consortium Press, University Hall, Appalachian State University, Boone, NC 28608, 704-262-2064, fax 704-262-6564
BurnhillWolf, 321 Prospect Street, SW, Lenoir, NC 28645, 704-754-0287; FAX 707-754-8392
Lorien House, Attn: David Wilson, PO Box 1112, Black Mountain, NC 28711, 828-669-6211
Celo Valley Books, 346 Seven Mile Ridge Road, Burnsville, NC 28714, 828-675-5918
New Native Press, PO Box 661, Cullowhee, NC 28723, 828-293-9237
GREEN PRINTS, "The Weeder's Digest", PO Box 1355, Fairview, NC 28730, 704-628-1902
En Passant Poetry Press, 2 Whirlaway Court, Hendersonville, NC 28792-8552
EN PASSANT/POETRY, 2 Whirlaway Court, Hendersonville, NC 28792-8552
Urthona Press, 62 LakeShore Drive, Asheville, NC 28804-2436

NORTH DAKOTA

NORTH DAKOTA QUARTERLY, University of North Dakota, PO Box 7209, Grand Forks, ND 58202, 701-777-3322
UND Press, University of North Dakota, PO Box 7209, Grand Forks, ND 58202, 701-777-3321

OHIO

THE KENYON REVIEW, Kenyon College, Gambier, OH 43022, 740-427-5208, Fax 740-427-5417, e-mail kenyonreview@kenyon.edu
Pudding House Publications, 60 North Main Street, Johnstown, OH 43031, 740-967-6060, pudding@johnstown.net, www.puddinghouse.com
PUDDING MAGAZINE: The International Journal of Applied Poetry, 60 North Main Street, Johnstown, OH 43031, 740-967-6060, pudding@johnstown.net, www.puddinghouse.com
PAVEMENT SAW, PO Box 6291, Columbus, OH 43206, 614-263-7115, baratier@megsinet.net, www.pavementsaw.org
Pavement Saw Press, PO Box 6291, Columbus, OH 43206, baratier@megsinet.net, www.pavementsaw.org
DIONYSIA, Box 1500, Capital University, Columbus, OH 43209, 614-236-6563
THE JOURNAL, OSU Dept. of English, 164 W. 17th Avenue, 421 Denney Hall, Columbus, OH 43210-1370, 614-292-4076, fax 614-292-7816, e-mail thejournal05@pop.service.ohio-state.edu
Ohio State University Press, 1050 Carmack Road, Columbus, OH 43210, 614-292-6930
Carpenter Press, PO Box 14387, Columbus, OH 43214
LOST AND FOUND TIMES, 137 Leland Ave, Columbus, OH 43214
Luna Bisonte Prods, 137 Leland Ave, Columbus, OH 43214, 614-846-4126
MID-AMERICAN REVIEW, Dept of English, Bowling Green State University, Bowling Green, OH 43403, 419-372-2725
GRASSLANDS REVIEW, PO Box 626, Berea, OH 44017
White Buck Publishing, 5187 Colorado Avenue, Sheffield Village, OH 44054-2338, 440-934-4454 phone/fax
FIELD: Contemporary Poetry and Poetics, 10 N. Professor Street, Oberlin College, Oberlin, OH 44074-1095, 440-775-8408, Fax 440-775-8124, oc.press@oberlin.edu
Oberlin College Press, 10 N. Professor Street, Oberlin College, Oberlin, OH 44074-1095, 440-775-8408, Fax 440-775-8124, E-mail oc.press@oberlin.edu
BLOOD & FEATHERS: Poems of Survival, 36495 Vine Street, Suite I, Willoughby, OH 44094-6347, 440-951-1875
Cleveland State Univ. Poetry Center, 1983 East 24th Street, Cleveland, OH 44115-2400, 216-687-3986; Fax 216-687-6943; poetrycenter@popmail.csuohio.edu
Kenyette Productions, 20131 Champ Drive, Euclid, OH 44117-2208, 216-486-0544

Legal Information Publications, 18221 East Park Drive, Cleveland, OH 44119-2019
ROMANTIC HEARTS, PO Box 450669, Westlake, OH 44145-0612, 216-979-9793; D.Krauss@genie.com
IMPETUS, 4975 Comanche Trail, Stow, OH 44224, 216-688-5210 phone/Fax, E-mail impetus@aol.com
Implosion Press, 4975 Comanche Trail, Stow, OH 44224, 216-688-5210 phone/Fax, E-mail impetus@aol.com
HIRAM POETRY REVIEW, Box 162, Hiram, OH 44234, 330-569-5330, Fax 330-569-5449
KALEIDOSCOPE: International Magazine of Literature, Fine Arts, and Disability, United Disability Services, 701 S. Main
    Street, Akron, OH 44311-1019, 330-762-9755, 330-379-3349 (TDD), Fax 330-762-0912, mshiplett@udsakron.org,
    pboerner@udsakron.org
LETHOLOGICA, 710 Arch Street, Salem, OH 44460, lethicon@juno.com, www.geocities.com/lethicon
ICON, KSU-TC, 4314 Mahoning Avenue NW, Warren, OH 44483, 330-847-0571
PIG IRON, 26 North Phelps Street, PO Box 237, Youngstown, OH 44501, 216-747-6932; fax 216-747-0599
Pig Iron Press, 26 North Phelps Street, PO Box 237, Youngstown, OH 44501, 216-747-6932; fax 216-747-0599
SOLO FLYER, 2115 Clearview NW, Massillon, OH 44646
ARTFUL DODGE, Department of English, College of Wooster, Wooster, OH 44691
The Ashland Poetry Press, Ashland University, Ashland, OH 44805, 419-289-5110, FAX 419-289-5329
Bottom Dog Press, c/o Firelands College of BGSU, Huron, OH 44839, 419-433-5560, http://members.aol.com/lsmithdog/
    bottomdog
Cambric Press dba Emerald House, 208 Ohio Street, Huron, OH 44839-1514, 419-433-5660; 419-929-4203
Miami University Press, English Dept., Miami University, Oxford, OH 45056, 513-529-5110, Fax 513-529-1392, E-mail
    reissja@muohio.edu
SPITBALL: The Literary Baseball Magazine, 5560 Fox Road, Cincinnati, OH 45239-7271, 513-541-4296
THE ANTIOCH REVIEW, PO Box 148, Yellow Springs, OH 45387, 937-767-6389
PLAIN BROWN WRAPPER (PBW), 130 West Limestone, Yellow Springs, OH 45387, 513-767-7416
NEW THOUGHT JOURNAL, 2520 Evelyn Drive, Kettering, OH 45409, Ph/Fax 937-293-9717; E-mail; ntjmag@aol.com
THE VINCENT BROTHERS REVIEW, 4566 Northern Circle, Riverside, OH 45424-5733
Wind's Errand, 6077 Far Hills Avenue #279, Dayton, OH 45459, windserrand@macconnect.com
CONFLICT OF INTEREST, 4701 East National Road, Springfield, OH 45505-1847, 330-630-5646 phone/Fax; E-mail
    PHartney@aol.com
Proper PH Publications, 4701 East National Road, Springfield, OH 45505-1847, 330-630-5646 phone/Fax; E-mail
    phartney@aol.com
THE OHIO REVIEW, 344 Scott Quad, Ohio University, Athens, OH 45701, 740-593-1900
QUARTER AFTER EIGHT, Ellis Hall, Ohio University, Athens, OH 45701
CONFLUENCE, PO Box 336, Belpre, OH 45714, 304-422-3112; e-mail dbprather@prodigy.net
RIVERWIND, General Studies, Hocking College, Nelsonville, OH 45764, 614-753-3591

OKLAHOMA

BYLINE, PO Box 130596, Edmond, OK 73013, 405-348-5591
Point Riders Press, PO Box 2731, Norman, OK 73070
MACHINEGUN MAGAZINE: New Lit. Quarterly, 601 S. Washington, Suite 281, Stillwater, OK 74074, E-mail
    chinaski00@aol.com
CIMARRON REVIEW, 205 Morrill Hall, Oklahoma State University, Stillwater, OK 74078-0135, 405-744-9476
NIMROD INTERNATIONAL, 600 South College Avenue, Tulsa, OK 74104-3126
Hawk Publishing Group, 6420 S. Richmond Avenue, Tulsa, OK 74136, 918-492-3854, fax 918-492-2120,
    wb@hawkpub.com, www.hawkpub.com

OREGON

LUNO, 31960 SE Chin Street, Boring, OR 97009, 503-663-5153
Trout Creek Press, 5976 Billings Road, Parkdale, OR 97041, 503-352-6494; e-Mail Lfh42@AOL.COM
CLACKAMAS LITERARY REVIEW, 19600 South Molalla Avenue, Oregon City, OR 97045
The Bacchae Press, c/o The Brown Financial Group, 10 Sixth Street, Astoria, OR 97103-5315, 503-325-7972; FAX
    503-325-7959; 800-207-4358; E-mail brown@pacifier.com
Gaff Press, PO Box 1024, 114 SW Willow Lane, Astoria, OR 97103, 503-325-8288; e-mail gaffpres@pacifier.com
COZY DETECTIVE MYSTERY MAGAZINE, 686 Jakes Court, McMinnville, OR 97128, 503-435-1212; Fax
    503-472-4896; e-mail papercapers@yahoo.com
Meager Ink Press, 686 Jakes Court, McMinnville, OR 97128, 503-435-1212; detectivemag@onlinemac.com
POETRY & PROSE ANNUAL, PO Box 541, Manzanita, OR 97130, www.poetryproseannual.com
HUBBUB, 5344 S.E. 38th Avenue, Portland, OR 97202, 503-775-0370
Peninhand Press, 3665 Southeast Tolman, Portland, OR 97202
PORTLAND REVIEW, PO Box 347, Portland, OR 97207-0347, 503-725-4533
MR. COGITO, 2518 NW Savier Street, Portland, OR 97210, rjdavies@gte.net, barbala@teleport.com
Mr. Cogito Press, 2518 N.W. Savier, Portland, OR 97210, 503-233-8131, 226-4135, rjdavies@gte.net
TIN HOUSE, 2601 NW Thurman Street, Portland, OR 97210, tinhouselg@aol.com
RAIN CITY REVIEW, 7215 SW LaView Drive, Portland, OR 97219, 503-771-1907
Irvington St. Press, Inc., 3439 NE Sandy Boulevard #143, Portland, OR 97232, E-mail; pdxia@aol.com
Blue Unicorn Press, Inc., PO Box 40300, Portland, OR 97240-3826, 503-775-9322
Far Corner Books, PO Box 82157, Portland, OR 97282
World Peace University Publications, PO Box 20728, Portland, OR 97294-0728, 503-252-3639, fax 503-255-5216
THE BEAR DELUXE, PO Box 10342, Portland, OR 97296, 503-242-1047, Fax 503-243-2645, bear@teleport.com
ICARUS WAS RIGHT, PO Box 13731, Salem, OR 97309-1731, 619-461-0497; icaruswas@pobox.com
Itidwitir Publishing, PO Box 13731, Salem, OR 97309-1731, 619-461-0497; icaruswas@pobox.com
CALYX: A Journal of Art and Literature by Women, PO Box B, Corvallis, OR 97330, 541-753-9384, Fax 541-753-0515,
    calyx@proaxis.com
Calyx Books, PO Box B, Corvallis, OR 97330, 541-753-9384, Fax 541-753-0515, calyx@proaxis.com
BIRTHKIT NEWSLETTER, PO Box 2672, Eugene, OR 97402, 503-344-7438
BRIDGES: A Journal for Jewish Feminists and Our Friends, PO Box 24839, Eugene, OR 97402, 541-343-7617, E-mail
    ckinberg@pond.net
MIDWIFERY TODAY, Box 2672, Eugene, OR 97402, 503-344-7438
SONAR MAP, PO Box 25243, Eugene, OR 97402, Voice/fax: 541-688-1523; eleg-sci@efn.org

NORTHWEST REVIEW, 369 P.L.C., University of Oregon, Eugene, OR 97403, 503-346-3957
SILVERFISH REVIEW, PO Box 3541, Eugene, OR 97403, 503-344-5060
Silverfish Review Press, PO Box 3541, Eugene, OR 97403, 503-344-5060
POETIC SPACE: Poetry & Fiction, PO Box 11157, Eugene, OR 97440
nine muses books, 3541 Kent Creek Road, Winston, OR 97496, 541-679-6674; E-mail mw9muses@teleport.com
THE PATRIOT, PO Box 1172, Ashland, OR 97520, 503-482-2578
Runaway Publications, PO Box 1172, Ashland, OR 97520, 503-482-2578
Story Line Press, Three Oaks Farm, PO Box 1240, Ashland, OR 97520-0055, 541-512-8792, Fax 541-512-8793, mail@storylinepress.com, www.storylinepress.com
Castle Peak Editions, PO Box 277, Murphy, OR 97533, 503-846-6152
Talent House Press, 1306 Talent Avenue, Talent, OR 97540, talhouse@mind.net
THIS IS IMPORTANT, PO Box 69, Beatty, OR 97621, 541-533-2486
The Blue Oak Press, HC10 Box 621, Lakeview, OR 97630-9704, 916-994-3397
CALAPOOYA, School of Arts and Sciences, Eastern Oregon University, La Grande, OR 97850, 541-962-3633
Wordcraft of Oregon, PO Box 3235, La Grande, OR 97850, 503-963-0723, E-mail wordcraft@oregontrail.net, http://www.oregontrail.net/~wordcraft

PENNSYLVANIA

TAPROOT LITERARY REVIEW, Box 204, Ambridge, PA 15003, 412-266-8476, E-mail taproot10@aol.com
Taproot Press Publishing Co., Box 204, Ambridge, PA 15003, taproot10@aol.com
THE AGUILAR EXPRESSION, 1329 Gilmore Avenue, Donora, PA 15033, 724-379-8019
LILLIPUT REVIEW, 282 Main Street, Pittsburgh, PA 15201
THE POETRY EXPLOSION NEWSLETTER (THE PEN), PO Box 4725, Pittsburgh, PA 15206
Latin American Literary Review Press, 121 Edgewood Avenue, 1st Floor, Pittsburgh, PA 15218-1513, 412-371-9023; FAX 412-371-9025
Nite-Owl Press, 137 Pointview Road, Suite 300, Pittsburgh, PA 15227-3131, 412-885-3798
NITE-WRITER'S INTERNATIONAL LITERARY ARTS JOURNAL, 137 Pointview Road, Suite 300, Pittsburgh, PA 15227-3131, 412-885-3798, email NiteWrite2@aol.com
University of Pittsburgh Press, 127 North Bellefield Avenue, Pittsburgh, PA 15260, 412-624-4110
Rhizome, PO Box 265, Greensboro, PA 15338
Jessee Poet Publications, Box 113, VAMC, 325 New Castle Road, Butler, PA 16001
POETS AT WORK, Box 113, VAMC, 325 New Castle Road, Butler, PA 16001
Shenango River Books, PO Box 631, Sharon, PA 16146, 412-342-3811
ALLEGHENY REVIEW, Box 32, Allegheny College, Meadville, PA 16335, 814-332-6553
X-it Press, PO Box 3756, Erie, PA 16508
TABOO: Journal of Education & Culture, 637 West Foster Avenue, State College, PA 16801
RAFTERS, Calder Square PO Box 10929, State College, PA 16805-0929, 814-867-4073; mdu103@psu.edu
Exhorter Publications International, 323 W. High Street, Elizabethtown, PA 17022-2141
FAT TUESDAY, 560, Manada Gap Road, Grantville, PA 17028, 717-469-7159
EXPERIMENTAL FOREST, 223 A. Bosler Avenue, Lemoyne, PA 17043, 717-730-2143, xxforest@yahoo.com, www.geocities.com/paris/salon/9699
Logodaedalus, PO Box 14193, Harrisburg, PA 17104
LOGODAEDALUS, PO Box 14193, Harrisburg, PA 17104
Camel Press, Box 212, Needmore, PA 17238, 717-573-4526
DUST (From the Ego Trip), Box 212, Needmore, PA 17238, 717-573-4526
Shadowlight Press, PO Box 746, Biglerville, PA 17307, e-mail bobmedcalfjr@blazenet.net
THE GETTYSBURG REVIEW, Gettysburg College, Gettysburg, PA 17325, 717-337-6770
MEDIPHORS, PO Box 327, Bloomsburg, PA 17815, e-mail mediphor@ptd.net, website www.mediphors.org
The Press of Appletree Alley, Box 608 138 South Third Street, Lewisburg, PA 17837
WEST BRANCH, Bucknell Hall, Bucknell University, Lewisburg, PA 17837, 570-577-1853
TWO RIVERS REVIEW, 215 McCartney Street, Easton, PA 18042, 610-559-3887; tworiversreview@juno.com; www.members.tripod.com/~tworiversreview/index.html
POETS'PAPER, PO Box 85, Easton, PA 18044-0085, 610-559-3887; Irregular@enter.net
Desk-Drawer Micropress, 209 W. Ann Street, Milford, PA 18337
STROKER, c/o Trantino, RR 2 Box 280, Harveys Lake, PA 18618-9503
MATCHBOOK, 242 North Broad Street, Doylestown, PA 18901, 215-489-7755, Fax 215-340-3965, www.matchbook-press.com
Raw Dog Press, 151 S. West Street, Doylestown, PA 18901, 215-345-6838, www.freeyellow.com/members/rawdog/
Alpha Beat Press, 31 Waterloo Street, New Hope, PA 18938, 215-862-0299
ALPHA BEAT SOUP, Alpha Beat Press, 31 Waterloo Street, New Hope, PA 18938
BOUILLABAISSE, 31 Waterloo Street, New Hope, PA 18938, 215-862-0299
COKEFISH, 31 Waterloo Street, New Hope, PA 18938
Cokefish Press, 31 Waterloo Street, New Hope, PA 18938
Nova House Press, 33 Lowry's Lane, Rosemont, PA 19010, tgavin@ea.pvt.k12.pa.us
WIDENER REVIEW, Humanities Division, Widener Univ., Chester, PA 19013, 610-499-4341
Black Bear Publications, 1916 Lincoln Street, Croydon, PA 19021-8026, BBReview@earthlink.net, http://home.earth-link.net/~BBReview
BLACK BEAR REVIEW, Black Bear Publications, 1916 Lincoln Street, Croydon, PA 19021, E-mail BBReview@earth-link.net, http://home.earthlink.net/~BBReview
TRANSCENDENT VISIONS, 251 South Olds Boulevard, 84-E, Fairless Hills, PA 19030-3426, 215-547-7159
The Aldine Press, Ltd., 304 South Tyson Avenue, Glenside, PA 19038
HELLAS: A Journal of Poetry & the Humanities, 304 South Tyson Avenue, Glenside, PA 19038, 215-884-1086
J & J Consultants, Inc., 603 Olde Farm Road, Media, PA 19063, 610-565-9692, Fax 610-565-9694, wjones13@juno.com, www.members.tripod.com/walterjones/
MAD POETS REVIEW, PO Box 1248, Media, PA 19063-8248
NEW ALTERNATIVES, 603 Ole Farm Road, Media, PA 19063, 610-565-9692, Fax 610-565-9694, wjones13@juno.com, www.members.tripod/walterjones
DWAN, Box 411, Swarthmore, PA 19081, e-mail dsmith3@swarthmore.edu

AMERICAN POETRY REVIEW, 1721 Walnut St., Philadelphia, PA 19103, 215-496-0439
HIDDEN OAK POETRY JOURNAL, PO Box 2275, Philadelphia, PA 19103, hidoak@att.net
Jewish Publication Society, 2100 Arch Street, Philadelphia, PA 19103-1308, 215-564-5925; Fax 215-564-6640
CASTAWAYS, c/o Derek Davis, 3311 Baring Street, Philadelphia, PA 19104
Singing Horse Press, PO Box 40034, Philadelphia, PA 19106
AXE FACTORY REVIEW, PO Box 40691, Philadelphia, PA 19107
Cynic Press, PO Box 40691, Philadelphia, PA 19107
VIRTUTE ET MORTE MAGAZINE, PO Box 63113, Philadelphia, PA 19114-0813, 215-671-6419 pager, 215-338-8234
Bloody Someday Press, 3721 Midvale Avenue, Philadelphia, PA 19129, 610-667-6687; FAX 215-951-0342; E-mail
    poettes@erols.com; website http://www.libertynet.org/bsomeday
Banshee Press, PO Box 11186, Philadelphia, PA 19136-6186
ONE TRICK PONY, PO Box 11186, Philadelphia, PA 19136-6186
ENIGMA, 402 South 25th Street, Philadelphia, PA 19146, 215-545-8496, sydx@att.net
SYMBIOTIC OATMEAL, PO Box 14938, Philadelphia, PA 19149
WEIRD TALES, 123 Crooked Lane, King of Prussia, PA 19406
Dufour Editions Inc., PO Box 7, Chester Springs, PA 19425-0007, 610-458-5005, FAX 610-458-7103

RHODE ISLAND

Lost Roads Publishers, 351 Nayatt Road, Barrington, RI 02806-4336, 401-245-8069
MERLYN'S PEN: Fiction, Essays, and Poems By America's Teens, Merlyn's Pen, Inc., PO Box 910, East Greenwich, RI
    02818-0964, 401-885-5175, www.merlynspen.com
The Brookdale Press, 566 E. Shore Rd., Jamestown, RI 02835, 203-322-2474
THE GODDESS OF THE BAY, PO Box 8214, Warwick, RI 02888, E-mail Belindafox@aol.com
THE HUNTED NEWS, PO Box 9101, Warwick, RI 02889, 401-739-2279
The Subourbon Press, PO Box 9101, Warwick, RI 02889, 401-739-2279
ITALIAN AMERICANA, University of Rhode Island, 80 Washington Street, Providence, RI 02903-1803
Burning Deck Press, 71 Elmgrove Avenue, Providence, RI 02906
Copper Beech Press, P O Box 2578, English Department, Providence, RI 02906, 401-351-1253
NEDGE, PO Box 2321, Providence, RI 02906
SERIE D'ECRITURE, 71 Elmgrove Avenue, Providence, RI 02906
SYNCOPATED CITY, PO Box 2382, Providence, RI 02906, litik@aol.com
HURRICANE ALICE, Dept. of English, Rhode Island College, Providence, RI 02908
THE ALEMBIC, Department of English, Providence College, Providence, RI 02918-0001
THE PROSE POEM: An International Journal, English Department, Providence College, Providence, RI 02918,
    401-865-2292
Majestic Books, PO Box 19097D, Johnston, RI 02919

SOUTH CAROLINA

NOSTALGIA, A Sentimental State of Mind, PO Box 2224, Orangeburg, SC 29116
Burning Llama Press, 82 Ridge Lake Drive, Columbia, SC 29209-4213
THE IMPLODING TIE-DYED TOUPEE, 82 Ridge Lake Drive, Columbia, SC 29209-4213
THE NEW SOUTHERN SURREALIST REVIEW, 82 Ridge Lake Drive, Columbia, SC 29209-4213
ILLUMINATIONS, English Dept., 66 George Street, College of Charleston, Charleston, SC 29424-0001
Ninety-Six Press, Furman University, Greenville, SC 29613, 864-294-3156
SOUTH CAROLINA REVIEW, English Dept, Clemson Univ, Clemson, SC 29634-1503, 803-656-3151
SFEST, LTD., PO Box 1238, Simpsonville, SC 29681
THE DEVIL'S MILLHOPPER, USC - Aiken, 471 University Parkway, Aiken, SC 29801-6399, Fax/Phone 803-641-3239
    e-mail Gardner@vm.sc.edu
The Devil's Millhopper Press (TDM Press), USC - Aiken, 471 University Parkway, Aiken, SC 29801-6399, phone/fax
    803-641-3239; e-Mail gardner@vm.sc.edu
Palanquin Press, English Department, University of South Carolina-Aiken, Aiken, SC 29801, 803-648-6851 x3208; fax
    803-641-3461; email phebed@aiken.edu; email scpoet@scescape.net
APOSTROPHE: USCB Journal of the Arts, 801 Carteret Street, Beaufort, SC 29902, 803-521-4158; FAX 803-522-9733;
    E-Mail ibfrt56@vm.sc.edu

SOUTH DAKOTA

Tesseract Publications, PO Box 164, Canton, SD 57013-0164, 605-987-5070, ta-shi@dtgnet.com, http://members.tri-
    pod.com/~washrag/
SOUTH DAKOTA REVIEW, University of South Dakota, 414 East Clark, Vermillion, SD 57069, 605-677-5184/5966
Astro Black Books, P O Box 46, Sioux Falls, SD 57101, 605-338-0277
PRAIRIE WINDS, Dakota Wesleyan University, DWU Box 536, Mitchell, SD 57301, 605-995-2814

TENNESSEE

ZONE 3, PO Box 4565, Austin Peay State University, Clarksville, TN 37044, 931-221-7031/7891
RFD, PO Box 68, Liberty, TN 37095, 615-536-5176
POEMS & PLAYS, Department of English, Middle Tennessee State University, Murfreesboro, TN 37132, 615-898-2712
Journey Books Publishing, 3205 Highway 431, Spring Hill, TN 37174, 615-791-8006
The F. Marion Crawford Memorial Society, Saracinesca House, 3610 Meadowbrook Avenue, Nashville, TN 37205
THE ROMANTIST, Saracinesca House, 3610 Meadowbrook Avenue, Nashville, TN 37205
CUMBERLAND POETRY REVIEW, Poetics, Inc., PO Box 120128 Acklen Station, Nashville, TN 37212, 615-373-8948
Nashville House, PO Box 111864, Nashville, TN 37222, 615-834-5069
SEWANEE REVIEW, Univ. of the South, 735 University Avenue, Sewanee, TN 37383-1000, 931-598-1246
THE POETRY MISCELLANY, English Dept. Univ of Tennessee, Chattanooga, TN 37403, 615-755-4213, 624-7279
NOW AND THEN, PO Box 70556, East Tennessee State University, Johnson City, TN 37614-0556, 423-439-5348; fax
    423-439-6340; e-mail woodsidj@etsu.edu
WRITER'S EXCHANGE, 616 Eagle Bend Road, Clinton, TN 37716, E-mail eboone@aol.com, www.users.aol.com/
    writernet
THE PURPLE MONKEY, 200 East Redbud Road, Knoxville, TN 37920

RIVER CITY, University of Memphis, Department of English, Memphis, TN 38152, 901-678-4591

TEXAS

Halbar Publishing, 289 Taylor Street, Wills Point, TX 75169-9732
SHARING & CARING, 289 Taylor Street, Wills Point, TX 75169-9732
ILLYA'S HONEY, PO Box 225435, Dallas, TX 75222
SOUTHWEST REVIEW, Southern Methodist University, 307 Fondren Library W., Box 750374, Dallas, TX 75275-0374, 214-768-1037
Browder Springs, PO Box 823521, Dallas, TX 75382, 214-368-4360
BOTH SIDES NOW, 10547 State Highway 110 North, Tyler, TX 75704-3731, 903-592-4263
DESCANT, English Department, TCU, Box 297270, Fort Worth, TX 76129
LIGHTHOUSE STORY COLLECTIONS, Lighthouse Publications, PO Box 48114, Watauga, TX 76148-0114
AMERICAN LITERARY REVIEW, Dept of English, University of North Texas, Denton, TX 76203-6827, 817-565-2127
WINDHOVER: A Journal of Christian Literature, PO Box 8008, UMHB, Belton, TX 76513, 817-939-4564
LUCKY HEART BOOKS, 1900 West Highway 6, Waco, TX 76712
SALT LICK, 1900 West Highway 6, Waco, TX 76712-0682
Salt Lick Press, 1900 West Hwy 6, Waco, TX 76712-0682
CONCHO RIVER REVIEW, English Department, Angelo State University, San Angelo, TX 76909, 915-942-2273, james.moore@angelo.edu
O!!Zone, 1266 Fountain View Drive, Houston, TX 77057, 713-784-2802
O!!ZONE, A LITERARY-ART ZINE, 1266 Fountain View Drive, Houston, TX 77057, 713-784-2802
Arte Publico Press, University of Houston, Houston, TX 77204-2090, 713-743-2841
GULF COAST, Dept. of English, University of Houston, Houston, TX 77204-3012
Black Tie Press, PO Box 440004, Houston, TX 77244-0004, 713-789-5119 fax
THE TEXAS REVIEW, English Department, Sam Houston State University, Huntsville, TX 77341-2146
Texas Review Press, English Department, Sam Houston State University, Huntsville, TX 77341-2146
BLUE VIOLIN, PO Box 1175, Humble, TX 77347-1175
TOUCHSTONE LITERARY JOURNAL, PO Box 8308, Spring, TX 77387-8308
GRAFFITI OFF THE ASYLUM WALLS, 1002 Gunnison Street #A, Sealy, TX 77474-3725
Ledero Press, U. T. Box 35099, Galveston, TX 77555-5099, 409-772-2091
CONTEXT SOUTH, Box 4504, Schreiner College, Kerrville, TX 78028, 512-896-7945
TEXAS YOUNG WRITERS' NEWSLETTER, PO Box 942, Adkins, TX 78101
Chili Verde, 736 E. Guenther Street, San Antonio, TX 78210, 210-532-8384
PALO ALTO REVIEW, 1400 West Villaret, San Antonio, TX 78224, 210-828-2998
Pecan Grove Press, Academic Library, Box AL, 1 Camino Santa Maria, San Antonio, TX 78228-8608, 210-436-3441
LONE STARS MAGAZINE, 4219 Flinthill, San Antonio, TX 78230-1619
CHACHALACA POETRY REVIEW, English Department, Univ. of Texas - Brownsville, Brownsville, TX 78520, 956-544-8239; Fax 956-544-8988; E-Mail mlewis@b1.utb.edu
Prickly Pear Press, 1402 Mimosa Pass, Cedar Park, TX 78613, 512-331-1557
Armadillo Books, PO Box 2052, Georgetown, TX 78627-2052, 512-863-8660
Double SS Press, PO Box 1450, Wimberley, TX 78676, 512-847-5173, Fax 512-847-9099, dorey@sspress.com, www.sspress.com
THE DIRTY GOAT, 2717 Wooldridge, Austin, TX 78703, 512-482-8229, E-mail jbratcher3@aol.com
Host Publications, Inc., 2717 Wooldridge, Austin, TX 78703-1953, 512-482-8229, Fax 512-482-0580, jbratcher3@aol.com
OFFICE NUMBER ONE, 1708 South Congress Avenue, Austin, TX 78704, 512-445-4489
ARTHUR'S COUSIN, 6811 Greycloud, Austin, TX 78745, 512-445-7065
NOVA EXPRESS, PO Box 27231, Austin, TX 78755, E-mail lawrence@bga.com
SULPHUR RIVER LITERARY REVIEW, PO Box 19228, Austin, TX 78760-9228, 512-292-9456
BORDERLANDS: Texas Poetry Review, PO BOX 33096, Austin, TX 78764, fax 512-499-0441; e-mail cemgilbert@earthlink.net; website http://www.fastair.com/borderlands
Plain View Press, Inc., PO Box 33311, Austin, TX 78764, (512) 441-2452
Alligator Press, PO Box 49158, Austin, TX 78765, 512-454-0496; Fax 512-380-0098; www.alligatorpress.com
ART-CORE, PO Box 49324, Austin, TX 78765
LIME GREEN BULLDOZERS (AND OTHER RELATED SPECIES), PO Box 4333, Austin, TX 78765
NERVE COWBOY, PO Box 4973, Austin, TX 78765, www.onr.com/user/jwhagins/nervecowboy.html
THE ADVOCATE, HCR 2, Box 25, Panhandle, TX 79068, 806-335-1715
IRON HORSE LITERARY REVIEW, Texas Tech University, English Dept., PO Box 43091, Lubbock, TX 79409-3091, 806-742-2500 X234
DREAM WHIP, PO Box 53832, Lubbock, TX 79453, 806-794-9263
Creative Arts & Science Enterprises, 341 Miller Street, Abilene, TX 79605-1903
STARBURST, 341 Miller Street, Abilene, TX 79605-1903

UTAH

OF UNICORNS AND SPACE STATIONS, PO Box 200, Bountiful, UT 84011-0200
Gibbs Smith, Publisher, 1877 East Gentile Street, PO Box 667, Layton, UT 84041, 801-544-9800; Fax 801-544-5582; E-mail info@GibbsSmith.com
Transcending Mundane, Inc., PO Box 1241, Park City, UT 84060-1241, 435-615-9609, Fax 435-649-5140, transmun@paracreative.com, www.paracreative.com
QUARTERLY WEST, 200 South Central Campus Drive, Room 317, University of Utah, Salt Lake City, UT 84112, 801-581-3938
WESTERN HUMANITIES REVIEW, University of Utah, Salt Lake City, UT 84112, 801-581-6070
Signature Books, Attn: Boyd Payne, 564 West 400 North, Salt Lake City, UT 84116, 801-531-1483, fax 801-531-1488
Shaolin Communications, PO Box 58547, Salt Lake City, UT 84158, 801-595-1123
Utah State University Press, 871 East 900 North, Logan, UT 84322-7800, 801-797-1362; 800-239-9974; Fax 801-797-0313
WEBER STUDIES: Voices and Viewpoints of the Contemporary West, Weber State University, 1214 University Circle, Ogden, UT 84408-1214, 801-626-6473 or 6657
DREAM NETWORK JOURNAL, PO Box 1026, Moab, UT 84532-3031, 435-259-5936; dreamkey@lasal.net; http:dreamnetwork.net

VERMONT

Five Corners Publications, Ltd., Old Bridgewater Mill, PO Box 66, Bridgewater, VT 05034-0066, 802-672-3868; Fax 802-672-3296; e-mail don@fivecorners.com

Goats & Compasses, PO Box 524, Brownsville, VT 05037, 802-484-5169

GREEN WORLD: News and Views For Gardening Who Care About The Earth, 12 Dudley Street, Randolph, VT 05060-1202, E-mail: gx297@cleveland.freenet.edu

THE ANTHOLOGY OF NEW ENGLAND WRITERS, PO Box 483, Windsor, VT 05089, 802-674-2315, newvtpoet@aol.com

LONGHOUSE, 1604 River Road, Guilford, VT 05301, e-mail poetry@sover.net; www.sover.net/~poetry

Longhouse, 1604 River Road, Guilford, VT 05301, e-mail poetry@sover.net; www.sover.net/~poetry

MINESHAFT, 16 Johnson Pasture Drive, Guilford, VT 05301

Threshold Books, 3108 Tater Lane, Guilford, VT 05301, 802-254-8300; Fax 802-257-2779

THE MARLBORO REVIEW, PO Box 243, Marlboro, VT 05344

WILD EARTH, PO Box 455, Richmond, VT 05477, 802-434-4077, fax 802-434-5980, e-mail info@wild-earth.org

GREEN MOUNTAINS REVIEW, Johnson State College, Johnson, VT 05656, 802-635-1350

Middlebury College, Middlebury College, Middlebury, VT 05753, 802-443-5075, Fax 802-443-2088, E-mail nereview@middlebury.edu

NEW ENGLAND REVIEW, Middlebury College, Middlebury, VT 05753, 802-443-5075, fax 802-443-2088, e-mail nereview@middlebury.edu, www.middlebury.edu/~nereview

VIRGIN ISLANDS

THE CARIBBEAN WRITER, RR 2, Box 10,000, Univ of Virgin Islands, Kingshill, St. Croix, VI 00850, 340-692-4152; fax 340-692-4026; e-mail ewaters@uvi.edu or qmars@uvi.edu

VIRGINIA

THE EDGE CITY REVIEW, 10912 Harpers Square Court, Reston, VA 20191, E-mail terryp17@aol.com

DEANOTATIONS, 11919 Moss Point Lane, Reston, VA 20194, 703-471-7907, fax 703-471-6446, e-mail blehert@aol.com, website www.blehert.com

Excelsior Publishing, PO Box 8122, Reston, VA 20195-2022, lsheet@alum-mit.edu, www.excelsiorpublishing.com

Great Western Publishing Company, PO Box 2355, Reston, VA 20195-0355

SO TO SPEAK, 4400 University Drive, MS 2D6, Fairfax, VA 22030-4444, sts@gmu.edu, www.gmu.edu/org/sts

BLACK BUZZARD REVIEW, 1007 Ficklen Road, Fredericksburg, VA 22045

CHANTEH, the Iranian Cross Cultural Qu'ly, PO Box 703, Falls Church, VA 22046, 703-533-1727

IDIOT WIND, PO Box 87, Occoquan, VA 22125, 703-494-1897 evenings

BOGG, 422 N Cleveland Street, Arlington, VA 22201

Bogg Publications, 422 North Cleveland Street, Arlington, VA 22201

BRUTARIAN, PO Box 25222, Arlington, VA 22202-9222, 703-360-2514

Gival Press, PO Box 3812, Arlington, VA 22203, 703-351-0079 phone/Fax, givalpress@yahoo.com, www.givalpress.com

Newcomb Publishers, Inc., 4812 North Fairfax Drive, Arlington, VA 22203, 703-524-1397

MINIMUS, 2245 N. Buchanan Street, Arlington, VA 22207

Red Dragon Press, 433 Old Town Court, Alexandria, VA 22314, 703-683-5877

Orchises Press, PO Box 20602, Alexandria, VA 22320-1602, 703-683-1243

Black Buzzard Press, 1007 Ficklen Road, Fredericksburg, VA 22405

VISIONS-INTERNATIONAL, The World Journal of Illustrated Poetry, 1007 Ficklen Road, Fredericksburg, VA 22405

Brandylane Publishers, PO Box 261, White Stone, VA 22578, 804-435-6900; Fax 804-435-9812

PLEASANT LIVING, PO Box 261, White Stone, VA 22578, 804-435-6900

FROGPOND: Quarterly Haiku Journal, PO Box 2461, Winchester, VA 22604, 540-722-2156, redmoon@shentel.net

Red Moon Press, PO Box 2461, Winchester, VA 22604-1661, 540-722-2156, redmoon@shentel.net

THE RAW SEED REVIEW, 780 Merion Greene, Charlottesville, VA 22901

ARCHIPELAGO, PO Box 2485, Charlottesville, VA 22902-2485, editor@archipelago.org, www.archipelago.org

CALLALOO, English Dept., Univ. of Virginia, PO Box 400121, Charlottesville, VA 22904-4121, 804-924-6637, Fax 804-924-6472, callaloo@virginia.edu

VIRGINIA LITERARY REVIEW, Box 413 Newcomb Hall Station, Charlottesville, VA 22904, Email dpk2c@virginia.edu

THE VIRGINIA QUARTERLY REVIEW, One West Range, PO Box 400223, Charlottesville, VA 22904-4223, 804-924-3124

IRIS: A Journal About Women, Box 323, HSC, University of Virginia, Charlottesville, VA 22908, 804-924-4500; iris@virginia.edu

WILLIAM AND MARY REVIEW, Campus Center, PO Box 8795, Williamsburg, VA 23187-8795, 757-221-3290, fax 757-221-3451

REFLECT, 1317 Eagles Trace Path #D, Chesapeake, VA 23320-9461, 757-547-4464

J-Mart Press, PO Box 8884, Virginia Beach, VA 23450, 757-498-4060 (phone/fax), e-mail jmartpress@aol.com

BLUE COLLAR REVIEW, PO Box 11417, Norfolk, VA 23517, 757-627-0952; e-mail redart@pilot.infi.net

Partisan Press, PO Box 11417, Norfolk, VA 23517, e-mail redart@pilot.infi.net

Brunswick Publishing Corporation, 1386 Lawrenceville Plank Road, Lawrenceville, VA 23868, 804-848-3865; Fax 804-848-0607; brunspub@jnent.com

THE HOLLINS CRITIC, PO Box 9538, Hollins University, VA 24020

THE LYRIC, 307 Dunton Drive SW, Blacksburg, VA 24060-5127

Rowan Mountain Press, PO Box 10111, Blacksburg, VA 24062-0111, 540-961-3315, Fax 540-961-4883, e-mail faulkner@bev.net

Pocahontas Press, Inc., PO Drawer F, Blacksburg, VA 24063-1020, 703-951-0467; 800-446-0467

ABSOLUTE MAGNITUDE, PO Box 2988, Radford, VA 24143-2988, 540-763-2925, dnapublications@iname.com

DNA Publications, Inc., PO Box 2988, Radford, VA 24143-2988, 540-763-2925, dnapublications@iname.com

DREAMS OF DECADENCE: Vampire Poetry and Fiction, PO Box 2988, Radford, VA 24143-2988, dnapublications@iname.com

THE ROANOKE REVIEW, English Dept., Roanoke College, Salem, VA 24153, 540-375-2367

THE SOW'S EAR POETRY REVIEW, 19535 Pleasant View Drive, Abingdon, VA 24211-6827, 540-628-2651, richman@preferred.com

The Sow's Ear Press, 19535 Pleasant View Drive, Abingdon, VA 24211-6827, e-mail richman@preferred.com
WRITER'S WORLD, 204 East 19th Street, Big Stone Gap, VA 24219, 703-523-0830, fax 703-523-5757
SHENANDOAH, Troubadour Theater, 2nd Floor, Washington and Lee University, Lexington, VA 24450-0303, 540-463-8765
St. Andrew Press, PO Box 329, Big Island, VA 24526, 804-299-5956
PROOF ROCK, Proof Rock Press, PO Box 607, Halifax, VA 24558
THE MASONIA ROUNDUP, 200 Coolwell Road, Madison Heights, VA 24572-2719

WASHINGTON

ARNAZELLA, 3000 Landerholm Circle SE, Bellevue, WA 98007, 206-641-2373
PEMMICAN, 9534 132nd Avenue NE, Kirkland, WA 98033-5212
Pemmican Press, 9534 132nd Avenue NE, Kirkland, WA 98033-5212
VINTAGE NORTHWEST, PO Box 193, Bothell, WA 98041, 206-821-2411
JACK MACKEREL MAGAZINE, PO Box 23134, Seattle, WA 98102-0434
Laocoon Books, PO Box 20518, Seattle, WA 98102, 206-323-7268; erotica@laocoonbooks.com
Rowhouse Press, PO Box 23134, Seattle, WA 98102-0434
THE UNIT CIRCLE, PO Box 20352, Seattle, WA 98102, 206-297-2650, E-mail zine@unitcircle.com, www.unitcircle.com
CITY PRIMEVAL, PO Box 30064, Seattle, WA 98103, 206-440-0791
FINE MADNESS, PO Box 31138, Seattle, WA 98103-1138
The Square-Rigger Press, 1201 North 46th Street, Seattle, WA 98103-6610, 206-548-9385
ENDING THE BEGIN, PO Box 4774, Seattle, WA 98104-0774, 206-726-0948
Headveins Graphics, PO Box 4774, Seattle, WA 98104-0774, 206-726-0948
POETSWEST LITERARY JOURNAL, 1011 Boren Avenue #155, Seattle, WA 98104, 206-682-1268, bjevans@postal-zone.com
OM, Box #181, 4505 University Way, NE, Seattle, WA 98105, 206-322-6387, davidlasky@yahoo.com
Rose Alley Press, 4203 Brooklyn Avenue NE #103A, Seattle, WA 98105, 206-633-2725
Kota Press, 2237 NW 62nd, Suite 2, Seattle, WA 98107, editor@kotapress.com, www.kotapress.com
KOTA PRESS POETRY JOURNAL, 2237 NW 62nd, Suite 2, Seattle, WA 98107, editor@kotapress.com, www.kotapress.com/framejournal.htm
White Plume Press, 2442 NW Market Street #370, Seattle, WA 98107-4137, 206-764-1299, E-mail bd72@scn.org
AMERICAN JONES BUILDING & MAINTENANCE, PO Box 9569, Seattle, WA 98109, 206-443-4693; von@singspeak.com
Missing Spoke Press, PO Box 9569, Seattle, WA 98109, 206-443-4693; von@singspeak.com
Pleasure Boat Studio, 8630 NE Wardwell Road, Bainbridge Island, WA 98110-1589, 360-452-8686 tel/fax, email pbstudio@pbstudio.com, www.pbstudio.com
LITRAG, PO Box 21066, Seattle, WA 98111-3066, www.litrag.com
L'Epervier Press, 1326 NE 62nd Street, Seattle, WA 98115
Floating Bridge Press, PO Box 18814, Seattle, WA 98118, 206-860-0508
CRAB CREEK REVIEW, 1115 35th Avenue, Seattle, WA 98122-5210, 206-772-8489; http://www.drizzle.net/nccr
Open Hand Publishing Inc., PO Box 22048, Seattle, WA 98122, 206-323-2187
THE RAVEN CHRONICLES, 1634 11th Avenue, Seattle, WA 98122, 206-323-4316, ravenchr@speakeasy.org, www.speakeasy.org/ravenchronicles
BELLOWING ARK, PO Box 55564, Shoreline, WA 98155, 206-440-0791
Bellowing Ark Press, PO Box 55564, Shoreline, WA 98155, 206-440-0791
Light, Words & Music, 16710 16th N.W., Seattle, WA 98177, 206-546-1498, Fax 206-546-2585; sisp@aol.com
Island Publishers, Box 201, Anacortes, WA 98221-0201, 206-293-3285/293-5398
THE BELLINGHAM REVIEW, Mail Stop 9053, WWU, Bellingham, WA 98225, 360-650-3209
Signpost Press Inc., Mail Stop 9055, WWU, Bellingham, WA 98225, 360-650-3209
Lockhart Press, Inc., Box 1366, Lake Stevens, WA 98258, fax 206-335-4818, ral@halcyon.com, www.ralockhart.com
Owl Creek Press, 2693 S.W. Camano Drive, Camano Island, WA 98292, 308-387-6101
Brooding Heron Press, Bookmonger Road, Waldron Island, WA 98297
Windstorm Creative, 7419 Ebbert Drive SE, Port Orchard, WA 98367-9753, www.windstormcreative.com
Copper Canyon Press, PO Box 271, Port Townsend, WA 98368
LIBERTY, PO Box 1181, Port Townsend, WA 98368, 360-379-0242
Chandelier Books, PO Box 7610, Tacoma, WA 98407-0610
MCS Publishing, 5212 Chicago SW #2, Tacoma, WA 98499, 253-984-1345
SLIGHTLY WEST, The Evergreen State College, CAB 320, Olympia, WA 98505, 360-866-6000 x6879
Blue Star Press, PO Box 645, Oakville, WA 98568, 360-273-7656
anabasis, PO Box 216, Oysterville, WA 98641, anabasis@willapabay.org
WRITER'S WORKSHOP REVIEW, 511 West 24th Street, Vancouver, WA 98660, 360-693-6509
PENNY-A-LINER, PO Box 2163, Wenatchee, WA 98807-2163, 509-662-7858
PORTALS, PO Box 2163, Wenatchee, WA 98807-2163, 509-662-7858
Redrosebush Press, PO Box 2163, Wenatchee, WA 98807-2163, 509-662-7858
WILLOW SPRINGS, Eastern Washington Univ., MS-1, 526 5th Street, Cheney, WA 99004-2431, 509-623-4349
Score, 1015 NW Clifford Street, Pullman, WA 99163-3203
SCORE, 1015 NW Clifford Street, Pullman, WA 99163-3203
FRONTIERS: A Journal of Women Studies, Women's Studies, PO Box 644007, Washington State University, Pullman, WA 99164-4007, 509-335-7268
HELIOTROPE: A Writer's Summer Solstice, PO Box 20037, Spokane, WA 99204-0037, 509-624-0418
GEORGE & MERTIE'S PLACE: A Microzine, PO Box 10335, Spokane, WA 99209-1335, 509-325-3738
Lost Horse Press, 9327 South Cedar Rim Lane, Spokane, WA 99224, 509-448-4047; e-mail losthorse@ior.com
THE TEMPLE, PO Box 100, Walla Walla, WA 99362-0033, E-mail tsunami@innw.net
Tsunami Inc., PO Box 100, Walla Walla, WA 99362-0033, E-mail tsunami@innw.net

WEST VIRGINIA

Mountain State Press, c/o University of Charleston, 2300 MacCorkle Avenue SE, Charleston, WV 25304-1099, 304-357-4767, mspl@newwave.net
TRANSMOG, Route 6, Box 138, Charleston, WV 25311, E-Mail: far@medinah.atc.ucarb.com

Appalachian Log Publishing Company, PO Box 20297, Charleston, WV 25362, 304-342-5789
THE SOUTHERN JOURNAL, PO Box 20297, Charleston, WV 25362, 304-722-6866
The Bunny & The Crocodile Press/Forest Woods Media Productions, Inc, PO Box 416, Hedgesville, WV 25427-0416, 304-754-8847
Aegina Press, Inc., 1905 Madison Avenue, Huntington, WV 25704, 304-429-7204; fax 304-429-7234
University Editions, Inc., 59 Oak Lane, Spring Valley, Huntington, WV 25704, 304-429-7204
Prospect Press, 609 Main Street, PO Box 162, Sistersville, WV 26175, 304-652-1920, Fax 304-652-1148, www.tinplace.com/prospect
SPARROWGRASS POETRY NEWSLETTER, 609 Main Street, PO Box 193, Sistersville, WV 26175, 304-652-1449; Fax 304-652-1148; www.tinplace.com/spfpoetry
KESTREL: A Journal of Literature and Art, PO Box 1797, Clarksburg, WV 26302-1797, 304-367-4815, Fax 304-367-4896, e-mail kestrel@mail.fscwv.edu
BIBLIOPHILOS, 200 Security Building, Fairmont, WV 26554, 304-366-8107

WISCONSIN

P & K Stark Productions, Inc., 17125C W. Bluemound Road, Ste. 171, Brookfield, WI 53005, 414-543-9013
SEEMS, c/o Lakeland College, Box 359, Sheboygan, WI 53082-0359
Wolfsong Publications, 3123 South Kennedy, Sturtevant, WI 53177, Fax 262-886-5809, E-mail wolfsong@wi.net
THE CREAM CITY REVIEW, PO Box 413, English Dept, Curtin Hall, Univ. of Wisconsin, Milwaukee, WI 53201, 414-229-4708
EMERGING VOICES, 1722 N. 58th Street, Milwaukee, WI 53208-1618, 414-453-4678
FIRST CLASS, PO Box 12434, Milwaukee, WI 53212, E-mail chriftor@execpc.com, www.execpc.com/~chriftor
Four-Sep Publications, PO Box 12434, Milwaukee, WI 53212, E-mail chriftor@execpc.com, www.execpc.com/~chriftor
THE UNDERGROUND, PO Box 14311, Milwaukee, WI 53214
PANDALOON, c/o Small Potatoes Press, PO Box 210977, Milwaukee, WI 53221, 800-642-9050, 414-294-2051, Fax 414-294-2053, email pandaloon@azml.com
ACORN WHISTLE, 907 Brewster Avenue, Beloit, WI 53511
BLOCK'S MAGAZINE, 1419 Chapin Street, Beloit, WI 53511, 608-364-4893
ROSEBUD, PO Box 459, Cambridge, WI 53523, 608-423-9690
MODERN HAIKU, PO Box 1752, Madison, WI 53701
FEMINIST VOICES NEWSJOURNAL, 1630 Bultman Road #106, Madison, WI 53704-3676, 608-251-9268
Mica Press, 113 Cambridge Road, Madison, WI 53704-5909, 608-246-0759; Fax 608-246-0756; E-mail jgrant@book-zen.com; website www.bookzen.com
Muse World Media Group, PO Box 55094, Madison, WI 53705, 608-238-6681
WISCONSIN ACADEMY REVIEW, 1922 University Ave., Madison, WI 53705, 608-263-1692
THE MADISON REVIEW, Dept of English, H.C. White Hall, 600 N. Park Street, Madison, WI 53706, 263-3303
PRIME, 7116 Helen C. White Hall, Madison, WI 53706, 688-262-3262
STUDENT LEADERSHIP JOURNAL, PO Box 7895, Madison, WI 53707-7895, 608-274-4823 X425, 413
ABRAXAS, PO Box 260113, Madison, WI 53726-0113, 608-238-0175, irmarkha@students.wisc.edu, www.litline.org/html/abraxas.html, www.geocities.com/Paris/4614
Ghost Pony Press, PO Box 260113, Madison, WI 53726-0113, 608-238-0175, irmarkha@students.wisc.edu, www.litline.org/html/abraxas.html, www.geocities.com/Paris/4614, www.thing.net/~grist/l&d/dalevy/dalevy.htm, www.thing.net/~grist/ld/saiz/saiz.htm
Wm Caxton Ltd, PO Box 220, Ellison Bay, WI 54210-0220, 414-854-2955
THE GLASS CHERRY, 901 Europe Bay Road, Ellison Bay, WI 54210-9643, 414-854-9042
The Glass Cherry Press, 901 Europe Bay Road, Ellison Bay, WI 54210, 414-854-9042
DOOR COUNTY ALMANAK, 10905 Bay Shore Drive, Sister Bay, WI 54234, 414-854-2742
Jackson Harbor Press, RR 1, Box 107AA, Washington Island, WI 54246
NORTHEAST, 1310 Shorewood Drive, La Crosse, WI 54601-7033
Rhiannon Press, 1105 Bradley Avenue, Eau Claire, WI 54701, 715-835-0598
POET'S FANTASY, 227 Hatten Avenue, Rice Lake, WI 54868, 715-234-2205
The Green Hut Press, 1015 Jardin Street East, Appleton, WI 54911, 414-734-9728
PACIFIC ENTERPRISE, PO Box 1907, Fond du Lac, WI 54936-1907, 920-922-9218; rudyled@vbe.com
Wolf Angel Press, 1011 Babcock Street, Neenah, WI 54956, 920-722-5826; e-mails flaherty@uwosh.edu, newpok32@uwosh.edu, stevens@tcccom.net; www.english.uwosh.edu/wolfangel/.

WYOMING

Calypso Publications, 5810 Osage Avenue #205, Cheyenne, WY 82009
OWEN WISTER REVIEW, PO Box 3625, Laramie, WY 82071-3625, 307-766-4027; owr@uwyo.edu
UNWOUND, Lindsay Wilson, PO Box 835, Laramie, WY 82073, Website www.fyuocuk.com/unwound.htm
High Plains Press, Box 123, Glendo, WY 82213, 307-735-4370, Fax 307-735-4590, 800-552-7819
Picaro Press, 272 Road 6Rt, Cody, WY 82414, www.picaro.com
CRONE CHRONICLES: A Journal of Conscious Aging, PO Box 81, Kelly, WY 83011, 307-733-5409

AUSTRALIA

BLAST, PO Box 3514, Manuka, Act. 2603, Australia
EDDIE THE MAGAZINE, PO Box 199, Newtown, N.S.W. 2042, Australia, phone 61-2-211-2339; fax 61-2-211-2331
Galaxy Press, 71 Recreation Street, Tweed Heads, N.S.W. 2485, Australia, (07) 5536-1997
HECATE, P.O. Box 99, St. Lucia, Queensland 4067, Australia
HOBO POETRY & HAIKU MAGAZINE, PO Box 166, Hazelbrook NSW 2779, Australia
IDIOM 23, Central Queensland University, Rockhampton, Queensland, 4702, Australia, 0011-079-360655
IMAGO, Queensland Univ Technology, School of Media and Journalism, PO Box 2434, Brisbane Q1D 4001, Australia, (07)864 2976, FAX (07)864 1810
LINQ, School of Humanities, James Cook Univ.-North Queensland, Townsville 4811, Australia, e-mail jcu.linq@jcu.edu.au
MEANJIN, 131 Barry Street, Carlton, Victoria 3053, Australia, 613-9344-6950
MICROPRESS YATES, 29 Brittainy Street, Petrie, Queensland 4502, Australia, 07-32851462; gloriabe@powerup.com.au
OVERLAND, PO Box 14146, Melbourne 3000, Australia

266

PAPER WASP: A Journal of Haiku, 7 Bellevue Terrace, St. Lucia, Queensland 4067, Australia, 61-7-33713509; Fax 61-7-33715527
Pinchgut Press, 6 Oaks Avenue, Cremorne, Sydney, N.S.W. 2090, Australia, 02-9908-2402
QUADRANT MAGAZINE, PO Box 1495, Collingwood, Vic. 3066, Australia, (03) 417-6855
RED LAMP, 5 Kahana Court, Mountain Creek, Queensland 4557, Australia, evans-baj@hotmail.com
REDOUBT, Faculty of Communication, PO Box 1, Belconnen, ACT 2616, Australia, 06-201-5270; fax 06-201-5300
STUDIO - A Journal of Christians Writing, 727 Peel Street, Albury, N.S.W. 2640, Australia
ULITARRA, PO Box 195, Armidale, New South Wales 2350, Australia, +612 6772 9135
University of Sydney Union, Level One, Manning House, University of Sydney, NSW 2006, Australia
VERANDAH, Faculty of Arts, Deakin University, 221 Burwood Highway, Burwood, Victoria 3125, Australia, 03-9244-6742

BELIZE

GORHAM, 30-32 Macaw Avenue, PO Box 279, Belmopan, Belize, 501-8-23284
THE VORTEX, 30-32 Macaw Avenue, PO Box 279, Belmopan, Belize, 501-8-23284

BOLIVIA

Silver Mountain Press, Casilla 6572 Torres Sofer, Cochabamba, Bolivia

CANADA

Aardvark Enterprises (A Division of Speers Investments Ltd.), 204 Millbank Drive S.W., Calgary, Alta T2Y 2H9, Canada, 403-256-4639
ABILITY NETWORK, PO Box 24045, Dartmouth, Nova Scotia B3A 4T4, Canada, 902-461-9009; FAX 902-461-9484; e-Mail: anet@fox.nstn.ca
THE AFFILIATE, 777 Barb Road, #257, Vankleek Hill, Ontario K0B 1R0, Canada, 613-678-3453
THE AMETHYST REVIEW, 23 Riverside Avenue, Truro, N.S. B2N 4G2, Canada, 902-895-1345
THE ANTIGONISH REVIEW, St Francis Xavier University, PO Box 5000, Antigonish, Nova Scotia B2G 2W5, Canada
ARIEL—A Review of International English Literature, The University of Calgary, 2500 University Drive NW, Calgary, Alberta T2N 1N4, Canada, 403-220-4657
Borealis Press Limited, 110 Bloomingdale Street, Ottawa, Ont. K2C 4A4, Canada, 613-798-9299, Fax 613-798-9747
BRICK, Box 537, Station Q, Toronto, ON M4T 2M5, Canada, www.brickmag.com
Broken Jaw Press, PO Box 596 Stn A, Fredericton, NB E3B 5A6, Canada, ph/fax 506-454-5127, jblades@nbnet.nb.ca, www.brokenjaw.com
CANADIAN LITERATURE, University of British Columbia, 167-1855 West Mall, Vancouver, B.C. V6T 1Z2, Canada, 604-822-2780
CANADIAN WOMAN STUDIES/les cahiers de la femme, 212 Founders College, York Univ., 4700 Keele Street, New York, Ontario M3J 1P3, Canada, 416-736-5356, fax 416-736-5765, e-mail cwscf@yorku.ca
THE CAPILANO REVIEW, 2055 Purcell Way, North Vancouver, B.C. V7J 3H5, Canada, 604-984-1712
Cosmic Trend, Sheridan Mall, Box 47014, Mississauga, Ontario L5K 2R2, Canada
Coteau Books, 401-2206 Dewdney Avenue, Regina, Sask. S4R 1H3, Canada, 306-777-0170; e-Mail coteau@coteau.uni-base.com
COUNTRY CHARM MAGAZINE, Box 696, Palmerston, ON N0G 2P0, Canada, 519-343-3059
THE DALHOUSIE REVIEW, Dalhousie University, Halifax, Nova Scotia B3H 3J5, Canada, 902-494-2541, fax 902-494-3561, email dalhousie.review@dal.ca
DESCANT, PO Box 314, Station P, Toronto, Ontario M5S 2S8, Canada
ELLIPSE, Univ. de Sherbrooke, Box 10, Faculte des Lettres et Sciences Humaines, Sherbrooke, Quebec J1K 2R1, Canada, 819-821-7238
EMPLOI PLUS, 1256 Principale N. St., Ste. #203, L'Annonciation, Quebec, J0T 1T0, Canada, 819-275-3293 phone/Fax
EVENT, Douglas College, PO Box 2503, New Westminster, B.C. V3L 5B2, Canada, 604-527-5293, Fax 604-527-5095, event@douglas.bc.ca
THE FIDDLEHEAD, Campus House, PO Box 4400, University of New Brunswick, Fredericton, NB E3B 5A3, Canada, 506-453-3501
FIRM NONCOMMITTAL: An International Journal of Whimsy, 5 Vonda Avenue, Toronto, ON M2N 5E6, Canada, e-mail firmnon@idirect.com; webhome.idirect.com/~firmnon
FREEFALL, Alexandra Writers Centre Society, 922 9th Avenue S.E., Calgary, AB T2G 0S4, Canada, fax 403-264-4730, e-mail awcs@writtenword.org, website www.writtenword.org/awcs
GRAIN, Box 1154, Regina, Sask. S4P 3B4, Canada, 306-244-2828, e-mail grain.mag@sk.sympatico.ca
THE GREAT IDEA PATCH, 110 Jeffery Street, Shelburne, ON L0N 1S4, Canada
GREEN'S MAGAZINE, Box 3236, Regina, Saskatchewan S4P 3H1, Canada
Greensleeve Editions, PO Box 41164, Edmonton, AB T6J 6M7, Canada
Guernica Editions, Inc., PO Box 117, Station P, Toronto, Ontario M5S 2S6, Canada, 416-658-9888, FAX 416-657-8885, guernicaeditions@cs.com
Hochelaga Press, 4982 Connaught Avenue, Montreal, BC H4V 1X3, Canada, 514-484-3186; Fax 514-484-8971; hochelaga@sympatico.ca
Insomniac Press, 393 Shaw Street, Toronto, ON, M6J 2X4, Canada, 416-536-4308
KICK IT OVER, Kick It Over Collective, PO Box 5811, Station A, Toronto, Ontario M5W 1P2, Canada
THE MALAHAT REVIEW, PO Box 1700, Stn. CSC, Victoria, British Columbia V8W 2Y2, Canada
NEW MUSE OF CONTEMPT, Box 596 Stn A, Fredericton, NB E3B 5A6, Canada, www.brokenjaw.com
NEWSLETTER (LEAGUE OF CANADIAN POETS), 54 Wolseley Street 3rd Floor, Toronto, Ontario M5T IA5, Canada, 416-504-1657, Fax; 416-504-0096
ON SPEC, PO Box 4727, Edmonton, AB T6E 5G6, Canada, 403-413-0215; email onspec@earthling.net
Oolichan Books, PO Box 10, Lantzville, B.C., V0R 2H0, Canada, 604-390-4839
PAPERPLATES, 19 Kenwood Avenue, Toronto, ON M6C 2R8, Canada
PARA*PHRASE, Sheridan Mall, Box 47014, Mississauga, Ontario L5K 2R2, Canada
THE PLOWMAN, Box 414, Whitby, Ontario L1N 5S4, Canada, 905-668-7803
The Porcupine's Quill, Inc., 68 Main Street, Erin, Ontario N0B 1T0, Canada, 519-833-9158
THE POTTERSFIELD PORTFOLIO, PO Box 40, Station A, Sydney, Nova Scotia B1P 6G9, Canada, www.pportfolio.com
PRAIRIE FIRE, 423-100 Arthur Street, Winnipeg MB R3B 1H3, Canada, 204-943-9066, fax 942-1555

THE PRAIRIE JOURNAL OF CANADIAN LITERATURE, PO Box 61203 Brentwood P.O., 217, 3630 Brentwood Road N.W., Calgary, Alberta T2L 2K6, Canada

Prairie Journal Press, PO Box 61203 Brentwood P.O., 217, 3630 Brentwood Road N.W., Calgary, Alberta T2L 2K6, Canada

PRISM INTERNATIONAL, E462-1866 Main Mall, University of British Columbia, Vancouver BC V6T 1Z1, Canada, 604-822-2514, fax 604-822-3616, e-mail prism@interchange.ubc.ca, www.arts.ubc.ca/prism

Proof Press, 67 Court Street, Aylmer, QC J9H 4M1, Canada, E-mail: dhoward@aix1.uottawa.ca

Quarterly Committee of Queen's University, Queen's University, Kingston, Ontario K7L 3N6, Canada, e-mail qquarter@post.queensu.ca, website http://info.queensu.ca/quarterly

QUEEN'S QUARTERLY: A Canadian Review, Queen's University, Kingston, Ontario K7L 3N6, Canada, 613-545-2667, e-mail qquarter@post.queensu.ca, website http://info.queensu.ca/quarterly

RAW NERVZ HAIKU, 67 Court Street, Aylmer, QC J9H 4M1, Canada, E-mail: dhoward@aix1.uottawa.ca

REDEMPTION, PO Box 54063, Vancouver, BC V7Y 1B0, Canada, 604-264-9109; Fax 604-264-8692; Redemption@pacificgroup.net

Ronsdale Press, 3350 West 21st Avenue, Vancouver, B.C. V6S 1G7, Canada, 604-738-4688, toll free 888-879-0919, Fax 604-731-4548

ROOM OF ONE'S OWN, PO Box 46160, Station D, Vancouver, British Columbia V6J 5G5, Canada

Saskatchewan Writers Guild, Box 1154, Regina, Saskatchewan S4P 3B4, Canada, 306-244-2828, grain.mag@sk.sympatico.ca

SCRIVENER, McGill University, 853 Sherbrooke Street W., Montreal, P.Q. H3A 2T6, Canada, 514-398-6588

SUB-TERRAIN, PO Box 1575, Bentall Centre, Vancouver, B.C. V6C 2P7, Canada, 604-876-8710

TEAK ROUNDUP, PO Box 2093, Sardis Sta. Main, Sardis, BC V2R 1A5, Canada, 604-545-4186, Fax 604-545-4194

THALIA: Studies in Literary Humor, Dept of English, Univ of Ottawa, Ottawa K1N 6N5, Canada, 613-230-9505, Fax 613-565-5786

Theytus Books Ltd., Green Mountain Road, Lot 45, RR #2, Site 50, Comp. 8, Penticton, B.C. V2A 6J7, Canada

Thistledown Press Ltd., 633 Main Street, Saskatoon, Sask. S7H 0J8, Canada, 306-244-1722

TIME FOR RHYME, c/o Richard Unger, PO Box 1055, Battleford SK S0M 0E0, Canada, 306-445-5172

TOWER, c/o McMaster University, 1280 Main Street W Box 1021, Hamilton, Ontario, L8S ICO, Canada

Tower Poetry Society, c/o McMaster University, 1280 Main Street W. Box 1021, Hamilton, Ontario, L8S 1CO, Canada

Turnstone Press, 607-100 Arthur Street, Winnipeg R3B 1H3, Canada, 204-947-1555, E-mail acquisitions@turnstonepress.mb.ca

Tyro Publishing, 194 Carlbert Street, Sault St. Marie, Ontario P6A 5E1, Canada, 705-253-6402, Fax 705-942-3625; tyro@sympatico.ca

Underwhich Editions, PO Box 262, Adelaide Street Station, Toronto, Ontario M5C 2J4, Canada, 536-9316

Unfinished Monument Press, 237 Prospect Street South, Hamilton, Ontario L8M 2Z6, Canada, 905-312-1779, Fax 905-312-8285, meklerdeahl@globalserve.net, www.meklerdeahl.com

UNIVERSITY OF WINDSOR REVIEW, Department of English, University of Windsor, Windsor, Ontario N9B3P4, Canada, 519-293-4232 X2332; Fax 519-973-7050; uwrevu@uwindsor.ca

URBAN GRAFFITI, PO Box 41164, Edmonton, AB T6J 6M7, Canada

Vehicule Press, PO Box 125, Place du Parc Station, Montreal, Quebec H2W 2M9, Canada, 514-844-6073, FAX 514-844-7543, vpress@com.org

Vesta Publications Limited, PO Box 1641, Cornwall, Ont. K6H 5V6, Canada, 613-932-2135, FAX 613-932-7735

WASCANA REVIEW OF CONTEMPORARY POETRY AND SHORT FICTION, Department of English, University of Regina, Regina, Sask S4S 0A2, Canada, 584-4302

WEST COAST LINE: A Journal of Contemporary Writing and Criticism, 2027 EAA, Simon Fraser University, Burnaby, B.C. V5A 1S6, Canada

West Coast Paradise Publishing, PO Box 2093, Sardis Sta. Main, Sardis, B.C. V2R 1A5, Canada, 604-824-9528, Fax 604-824-9541

WRITER'S LIFELINE, PO Box 1641, Cornwall, Ont. K6H 5V6, Canada

CZECH REPUBLIC

JEJUNE: america Eats its Young, PO Box 85, Prague 1, 110 01, Czech Republic, 42-2-96141082; Fax 42-2-24256243

ENGLAND

A.L.I., 20 Byron Place, Bristol, B58 1JT, England, E-mail: DSR@maths.bath.ac.uk

AMBIT, 17 Priory Gardens, London, N6 5QY, England, 0181-340-3566

AQUARIUS, Flat 4, Room B, 116 Sutherland Avenue, London W9, England

BB Books, 1 Spring Bank, Longsight Road, Copster Green, Blackburn, Lancs BB1 9EU, England, 0254 249128

THE BOUND SPIRAL, 72 First Avenue, Bush Hill Park, Enfield, Middlesex, EN1 1BW, England

CANDELABRUM POETRY MAGAZINE, 9 Milner Road, Wisbech PE13 2LR, England, tel: 01945 581067

Carrefour Press, Saddle Fold, Hawkins Lane, Rainow, Macclesfield, Cheshire, England

DANDELION ARTS MAGAZINE, Casa Alba, 24 Frosty Hollow, E. Hunsbury, Northants NN4 0SY, England, 01604-701730

Enitharmon Press, 36 St George's Avenue, London N7 OHD, England, 0171-607-7194; FAX 0171-607-8694

FENICE BROADSHEETS, 78 Cambridge Street, Leicester LE3 0JP, England, 547419

Fern Publications, Casa Alba, 24 Frosty Hollow, E. Hunsbury, Northants NN4 0SY, England, 01604-701730

GLOBAL TAPESTRY, Spring Bank, Longsight Road, Copster Green, Blackburn, Lancs BB1 9EU, England, 0254 249128

Guildford Poets Press, 9 White Rose Lane, Woking, Surrey, GU22 7JA, England

Hippopotamus Press, 22 Whitewell Road, Frome, Somerset BA11 4EL, England, 0373-466653

HQ POETRY MAGAZINE (The Haiku Quarterly), 39 Exmouth Street, Swindon, Wilshire, SN1 3PU, England

Interim Press, 3 Thornton Close, Budleigh Salterton, Devon EX9 6PJ, England, (0395) 445231

JAMES JOYCE BROADSHEET, School of English, University of Leeds, West Yorkshire LS2 9JT, England, 0113-233-4739

JOURNAL OF CONTEMPARARY ANGLO-SCANDINAVIAN POETRY, 11 Heatherton Park, Bradford on Tone, Taunton, Somerset TA4 1EU, England, 01823-461725; e-mail smithsssj@aol.com

K.T. Publications, 16, Fane Close, Stamford, Lincs., PE9 1HG, England, (07180) 754193

KRAX, 63 Dixon Lane, Leeds, Yorkshire LS12 4RR, England

LONDON REVIEW OF BOOKS, 28-30 Little Russell Street, London WC1A 2HN, England, 020-7209-1141, fax

020-7209-1151
The Menard Press, 8 The Oaks, Woodside Avenue, London N12 8AR, England
New Broom Private Press, 78 Cambridge Street, Leicester, England
THE NEW WRITER, PO Box 60, Cranbrook, Kent TN17 2ZR, England, 01580-212626
ORBIS, 27 Valley View, Primrose, Jarrow, Tyne & Wear NE32 5QT, England, +44 (0)191 489 7055; fax/modem +44 (0)191 430 1297; e-mail Mshields12@aol.com; mikeshields@compuserve.com
Original Plus, 11 Heatherton Park, Bradford on Tone, Taunton, Somerset TA4 1EU, England, 01823-461725; e-mail smithsssj@aol.com
PENNINE PLATFORM, 7 Cockley Hill Lane, Kirkheaton, Huddersfield HD5 OHH, West Yorkshire, England, 0937-584674
PERCEPTIONS, 73 Eastcombe Avenue, London, England SE7 7LL, England
PLUME, 15 Bolehill Park, Hove Edge, Brighouse, W. Yorks HD6 2RS, England, 01484-717808; email plumelit@aol.com or literature@plume.fsbusiness.co.uk
POETRY AND AUDIENCE, School of English, Cavendish Road, University of Leeds, Leeds Yorkshire, LS2 9JT, England
POETRY NOTTINGHAM INTERNATIONAL, 71 Saxton Avenue, Heanor, Derbyshire DE75 7PZ, England
POETRY REVIEW, 22 Betterton Street, London WC2H 9BU, England
Protean Publications, 34 Summerfield Crescent, Flat 4, Edgbaston, Birmingham B16 OER, England
PURPLE PATCH, 25 Griffiths Road, West Bromwich, B71 2EH, England
Red Candle Press, 9 Milner Road, Wisbech, PE13 2LR, England, tel: 01945 581067
THE RIALTO, PO Box 309 Aylsham, Norwich NR11 6LN, England
Saqi Books Publisher, 26 Westbourne Grove, London W2 5RH, England, 071-221-9347, FAX 071-229-7692
SEPIA, Knill Cross House, Higher Anderton Road, Millbrook, Nr Torpoint, Cornwall, England
SMOKE, Liver House, 96 Bold Street, Liverpool L1 4HY, England
STAND MAGAZINE, School of English, Univeristy of Leeds, Leeds LS2 9JT, England
TANDEM, 13 Stephenson Road Barbourne, Worchester, WR1 3EB, England, 01705-28002
TEARS IN THE FENCE, 38 Hod View, Stourpaine, Blandford Forum, Dorset DT11 8TN, England
TIME HAIKU, 105, Kings Head Hill, London E4 7JG, England, 0181-529-6478
The Wellsweep Press, 1 Grove End Ho., 150 Highgate Road, London HW5 1PD, England, (0171)267-3525, e-mail ws@shadoof.demon.co.uk
WEYFARERS, 9 White Rose Lane, Woking, Surrey GU22 7JA, England
Windows Project, Liver House, 96 Bold Street, Liverpool L1 4HY, England

FRANCE

FRANK: AN INTERNATIONAL JOURNAL OF CONTEMPORARY WRITING AND ART, 32 rue Edouard Vaillant, 93100 Montreuil Sous Bois, France, (33) 1 48596658, e-mail david@paris-anglo.com
Handshake Editions, Atelier A2, 83 rue de la Tombe-Issoire, Paris 75014, France, 4327-1767
PARIS/ATLANTIC, The American University of Paris, 31, avenue Bosquet, 75007 Paris, France, 33-1-01 40 62 05 89; fax 33-1-01 45 51 89 13

GERMANY

Expanded Media Editions, PO Box 190136, Prinz Albert Str. 65, 53AA3 Bonn 1, Germany, Germany, 0228/22 95 83, FAX 0228/21 95 07

GREAT BRITAIN

IOTA, 67 Hady Crescent, Chesterfield, Derbyshire S41 0EB, Great Britain, 01246-276532
Second Aeon Publications, 19 Southminster Road, Roath, Cardiff, Wales CF23 5AT, Great Britain, 029-2049-3093, peter.finch@dial.pipex.com

HONG KONG

RENDITIONS, Chinese University of Hong Kong, Shatin, NT, Hong Kong, 26-097-400, 26-097-407; fax 26-035-149; e-Mail renditions@cuhk.hk
Research Centre for Translation, Chinese University of Hong Kong, Research Centre for Translation, Chinese University of Hong Kong, Shatin, NT, Hong Kong, 852-26097700/7407; e-Mail renditions@cuhk.hk

INDIA

THE INDIAN WRITER, 1-A, 59 Ormes Road, Chennai 600010, India, 6261370, 6284421
JAFFE INTERNATIONAL, Kunnuparambil Buildings, Kurichy, Kottayam 686549, India, 91-481-430470; FAX 91-481-561190
Jaffe Publishing Management Service, Kunnuparambil Buildings, Kurichy, Kottayam 686549, India, phone/fax 91-481-430470
MANUSHI - a journal about women & society, C-174 Lajpat Nagar - I, New Delhi, New Delhi 110024, India, 6833022 or 6839158
Prakalpana Literature, P-40 Nandana Park, Calcutta-700034, West Bengal, India, (91) (033) 478-2347
PRAKALPANA SAHITYA/PRAKALPANA LITERATURE, P-40 Nandana Park, Calcutta-700034, West Bengal, India, (91) (033) 478-2347
TIGER MOON, 3/677 Coconut Grove, Prasanthi Nilayam A.P. 515134, India, terry-tgrmoon@mailcity.com
Tiger Moon, 3/677 Coconut Grove, Prasanthi Nilayam A.P., India, terry-tgrmoon@mailcity.com

IRELAND

THE BROBDINGNAGIAN TIMES, 96 Albert Road, Cork, Ireland, (214311227)
THE CELTIC PEN, 36 Fruithill Park, Belfast, BT11 8GE, Ireland, 01232-232608
Poetry Ireland, Bermingham Tower, Upper Yard, Dublin Castle, Dublin 2, Ireland
POETRY IRELAND REVIEW, Bermingham Tower, Upper yard, Dublin Castle, Dublin 2, Ireland, 6714632 + 353-1, fax 6714634 + 353-1

ISRAEL

VOICES - ISRAEL, c/o Mark Levinson, PO Box 5780, Herzliya 46157, Israel, 09-9552411

ITALY

LO STRANIERO: The Stranger, Der Fremde, L'Etranger, Via Chiaia 149, Napoli 80121, Italy, ITALY/81/426052

JAPAN

Abiko Literary Press (ALP Ltd.), 8-1-8 Namiki, Abiko, Chiba 270-1165, Japan, 011-81-471-69-7319
THE ABIKO QUARTERLY WITH JAMES JOYCE FW STUDIES, 8-1-8 Namiki, Abiko-shi, Chiba-ken 270-1165, Japan, 011-81-471-69-7319, alp@mil.net.ne.jp
BLUE BEAT JACKET, 1-5-54 Sugue-cho, Sanjo-shi, Niigata-ken 955-0832, Japan, 0256-32-3301
Blue Jacket Press, 1-5-54 Sugue-cho, Sanjo-shi, Niigata-ken 955-0832, Japan, 0256-32-3301
THE LONSDALE - The International Quarterly of The Romantic Six, Trash City 3rd Floor, 6-18-16 Nishi-Gotanda, Shinagawa-ku, Tokyo 141, Japan, 03(5434)0729
POETRY KANTO, Kanto Gakuin University, Kamariya Minami 3-22-1, Kanazawa-Ku, Yokohama 236-8502, Japan

MEXICO

Barking Dog Books, Centro De Mensajes, A.P. 48, Todos Santos, B.C.S. 23300, Mexico, fax 011-52-114-50288

NEW ZEALAND

POETRY NZ, 37 Margot Street, Epsom, Auckland 3, New Zealand, 64-9-524-5656
SPIN, c/o Postal Agency, Ngakawav, Buller, New Zealand, 006495768577
TAKAHE, PO Box 13-335, Christchurch 1, New Zealand, 03-5198133

NORTHERN IRELAND

WRITING ULSTER, U. of Ulster-Jordanstown, Shore Rd, Newtownabbey Co. Antrim, BT 370QB, Northern Ireland, 011-44-232-365131, fax 232-366824

PEOPLE'S REPUBLIC OF CHINA

CHINESE LITERATURE, 24 Baiwanzhuang Road, Beijing 100037, People's Republic of China, 892554
Chinese Literature Press, 24 Baiwanzhuang Road, Beijing 100037, People's Republic of China

PORTUGAL

PERIPHERAL VISION, Apartado 240, Portalegre, 7300, Portugal

SCOTLAND

CHAPMAN, 4 Broughton Place, Edinburgh EH1 3RX, Scotland, 0131-557-2207
NORTHWORDS, The Stable, Long Road, Avoch, Ross-shire IV9 8QR, Scotland, e-mail northwords@demon.co.uk
OBJECT PERMANENCE, Flat 3/2, 16 Ancroft Street, Glasgow G20 7HU, Scotland, 0141-332-7571

SWITZERLAND

TRANSNATIONAL PERSPECTIVES, CP 161, CH-1211 Geneva 16, Switzerland

TRINIDAD & TOBAGO

Reyes Investment Enterprise Ltd., PO Box 3418, Maraval, Trinidad & Tobago, 809-638-3756; 809-657-3657

UNITED KINGDOM

AABYE (formerly New Hope International Writing), 20 Werneth Avenue, Gee Cross, Hyde, Cheshire SK14 5NL, United Kingdom, 061-351-1878, newhope@iname.com
AVON LITERARY INTELLIGENCER, 20 Byron Place, Bristol, BS8 1JT, United Kingdom, 44-225-826105
BLITHE SPIRIT, Hill House Farm, Knighton, Powys LD7 1NA, United Kingdom, 0154-752-8542, Fax 0154-752-0685
BREAKFAST ALL DAY, 43 Kingsdown House, Amhurst Road, London E8 2AS, United Kingdom, 0171-923-0734
Crescent Moon, PO Box 393, Maidstone, Kent ME14 5XU, United Kingdom
DIALOGOS: Hellenic Studies Review, Dept. of Byzantine & Modern Greek, Attn: David Ricks, King's College, London WC2R 2LS, United Kingdom, fax 020-7848-873-2830
EUROPEAN JUDAISM, Leo Baeck College, 80 East End Rd., Sternberg Centre for Judaism, London N3 2SY, United Kingdom, 44-181-349-4525; Fax 44-181-343-2558; leo-baeck-college@mailbox.ulcc.ac.uk; www.lb-college.demon.co.uk
FIGMENTS, 14 William Street, Donaghadee, Co. Down NI BT21 0HP, United Kingdom, 01247-884267
Figments Publishing, 14 William Street, Donaghadee, Co. Down N.I. BT21 0HP, United Kingdom, 01247-884267
FIRE, Field Cottage, Old Whitehill, Tackley, Kidlington OXON OX5 3AB, United Kingdom
THE FROGMORE PAPERS, 42 Morehall Avenue, Folkestone, Kent CT19 4EF, United Kingdom
The Frogmore Press, 42 Morehall Avenue, Folkestone, Kent. CT19 4EF, United Kingdom
Kozmik Press, 134 Elsenham Street, London SW18 5NP, United Kingdom, 44-81-874-8218
LINKS, 'Bude Haven' 18 Frankfield Rise, Tunbridge Wells TN2 5LF, United Kingdom, 01892-539800
MAIN STREET JOURNAL, 29 Princes Road, Ashford, Middlesex TW15 2LT, United Kingdom, 44-171-378-8809
New Hope International, 20 Werneth Avenue, Gee Cross, Hyde SK14 5NL, United Kingdom, 0161-351 1878, newhope@iname.com, www.nhi.clara.net/nhihome.htm
NEW HOPE INTERNATIONAL REVIEW, 20 Werneth Avenue, Gee Cross, Hyde, Cheshire SK14 5NL, United Kingdom, 061-351-1878, newhope@iname.com
OASIS, 12 Stevenage Road, London SW6 6ES, United Kingdom
Oasis Books, 12 Stevenage Road, London, SW6 6ES, United Kingdom
OTTER, Parford Cottage, Chagford, Newton Abbot TQ13 8JR, United Kingdom
OUTPOSTS POETRY QUARTERLY, 22, Whitewell Road, Frome, Somerset BA11 4EL, United Kingdom
PAGAN AMERICA, PO Box 393, Maidstone, Kent ME14 5XU, United Kingdom
PASSION, PO Box 393, Maidstone, Kent ME14 5XU, United Kingdom
Poetical Histories, 27 Sturton Street, Cambridge CB1 2QG, United Kingdom, 0223-327455
PSYCHOPOETICA, Department of Psychology, University of Hull, Hull HU6 7RX, United Kingdom, website www.fernhse.demon.co.uk/eastword/psycho
PULSAR POETRY MAGAZINE, 34 Lineacre, Grange Park, Swindon, Wiltshire SN5 6DA, United Kingdom,

01793-875941, e-mail david.pike@virgin.net
Reality Street Editions, 4 Howard Court, Peckham Rye, London SE15 3PH, United Kingdom, 0171-639-7297
Shearsman Books, c/o Oasis Books, 12 Stevenage Road, London SW6 6ES, United Kingdom
SHRIKE, 13 Primrose Way, Alperton, MDDX HA0 1DS, United Kingdom, 44-081-998-5707
STAPLE, Tor Cottage, 81 Cavendish Road, Matlock, Derbyshire DE4 3HD, United Kingdom
Tears in the Fence, 38 Hod View Stourpaine, Blandford Forum, Dorset DT11 8TN, United Kingdom
VIGIL, 12 Priory Mead, Bruton, Somerset BA10 0DZ, United Kingdom, Bruton 813349
ZINE-ON-A-TAPE, 35 Kearsley Road, Sheffield, S2 4TE, United Kingdom, www.andysav.free-online.co.uk/

WALES

POETRY WALES, First Floor, 2 Wyndham Street, Bridgend, CF31 1EF, Wales
Poetry Wales Press, Ltd., First Floor, 2 Wyndham Street, Bridgend CF31 1EF, Wales

WEST INDIES

Sandberry Press, PO Box 507, Kingston 10, Jamaica, West Indies, fax 809-968-4067, phone 809-929-8089

271

Subject Index

The Place In The Woods
READ, AMERICA!
Starbooks Press/FLF Press
TAMPA REVIEW
Tesseract Publications
THE VINCENT BROTHERS REVIEW
WOMENWISE

ALASKAN

Ahsahta
Baker Street Publications
BRILLIANT STAR
ELF: ECLECTIC LITERARY FORUM (ELF MAGA-
ZINE)
Intertext
POW-WOW
WESTERN SKIES
Windsong Press

AMERICAN EXPERIENCE

AMERICAN JONES BUILDING & MAINTENANCE
American Literary Press Inc./Noble House
Art/Life Limited Editions
ART:MAG
AURA LITERARY/ARTS REVIEW
Baker Street Publications
BLOOD & FEATHERS: Poems of Survival
THE BOOMERPHILE
ELF: ECLECTIC LITERARY FORUM (ELF MAGA-
ZINE)
EXIT 13 MAGAZINE
FULLOSIA PRESS
Ghost Pony Press
IRIS: A Journal About Women
Lakes & Prairies Press
LEAPINGS LITERARY MAGAZINE
LUMMOX JOURNAL
MANY MOUNTAINS MOVING
THE MASONIA ROUNDUP
Missing Spoke Press
Mountain State Press
THE NEW PRESS LITERARY QUARTERLY
The Place In The Woods
READ, AMERICA!
Runaway Publications
SKYLARK
SPORT LITERATE, Honest Reflections on Life's Leisur-
ely Diversions
STUDENT LEADERSHIP JOURNAL
TAMPA REVIEW
THIS IS IMPORTANT
University of Massachusetts Press
THE VINCENT BROTHERS REVIEW
WESTERN SKIES
Writers House Press
WRITING ULSTER

AMERICAN SOUTH

CC. Marimbo Communications

AMERICAN WEST

THE ACORN
Ahsahta
Baker Street Publications
Blue Unicorn Press, Inc.
CC. Marimbo Communications
Confluence Press, Inc.
ELF: ECLECTIC LITERARY FORUM (ELF MAGA-
ZINE)
High Plains Press
LITERALLY HORSES
MIXED BAG
Point Riders Press
POW-WOW
RED ROCK REVIEW
Signature Books
THE SOUTHERN CALIFORNIA ANTHOLOGY
SOUTHWEST JOURNAL

TALKING RIVER REVIEW
TUCUMCARI LITERARY REVIEW
THE VINCENT BROTHERS REVIEW
WESTERN SKIES
WRITERS' FORUM

ANARCHIST

ASSEMBLING
BOTH SIDES NOW
Center Press
Cynic Press
Drum
FAG RAG
GLOBAL TAPESTRY
H2SO4
THE J MAN TIMES
KALDRON, An International Journal Of Visual Poetry
KICK IT OVER
LIMESTONE: A Literary Journal
LUMMOX JOURNAL
MESECHABE: The Journal of Surre(gion)alism
OXYGEN
POETRY MOTEL
SLIPSTREAM
SUB-TERRAIN
Suburban Wilderness Press
VOID
WICKED MYSTIC

ANIMALS

THE ACORN
American Literary Press Inc./Noble House
ASSEMBLING
Brunswick Publishing Corporation
Celestial Otter Press
CHIRON REVIEW
CONJUNCTIONS
ELF: ECLECTIC LITERARY FORUM (ELF MAGA-
ZINE)
LADYBUG, the Magazine for Young Children
LIGHTHOUSE STORY COLLECTIONS
LITERALLY HORSES
MAGIC CHANGES
NEW HOPE INTERNATIONAL REVIEW
NEW METHODS JOURNAL (VETERINARY)
THE NEW PRESS LITERARY QUARTERLY
Outrider Press
The Place In The Woods
RALPH'S REVIEW
READ, AMERICA!
RED OWL
SNOWY EGRET
THE VINCENT BROTHERS REVIEW
Washington Writers' Publishing House
Windsong Press

ANTHOLOGY

THE ANTHOLOGY OF NEW ENGLAND WRITERS
Arctos Press
BkMk Press
Broken Jaw Press
GaiaQuest
JACK MACKEREL MAGAZINE
Jackson Harbor Press
LUMMOX JOURNAL
Malafemmina Press
Ronsdale Press
Rowhouse Press
Slapering Hol Press
The Spirit That Moves Us Press, Inc.

APPLIED POETRY

Aegina Press, Inc.
ANT ANT ANT ANT ANT
ASSEMBLING
Center Press
CONTEXT SOUTH
Cynic Press

THE EVERGREEN CHRONICLES
KALDRON, An International Journal Of Visual Poetry
LEAPINGS LITERARY MAGAZINE
LIMESTONE: A Literary Journal
NEW HOPE INTERNATIONAL REVIEW
Pudding House Publications
PUDDING MAGAZINE: The International Journal of
   Applied Poetry
Savant Garde Workshop
StarMist Books
University Editions, Inc.

ART

A & U AMERICA'S AIDS MAGAZINE
ABRAXAS
ANT ANT ANT ANT ANT
Arjuna Library Press
ART-CORE
Art/Life Limited Editions
ART:MAG
ASSEMBLING
AURA LITERARY/ARTS REVIEW
Baker Street Publications
THE BAREFOOT POET: Journal of Poetry, Fiction,
   Essays, & Art
BLADES
THE BOOMERPHILE
BUTTON
CEDAR HILL REVIEW
Center Press
THE COOL TRAVELER
Cynic Press
DAYS AND NIGHTS OF A SMALL PRESS PUB-
   LISHER
ELF: ECLECTIC LITERARY FORUM (ELF MAGA-
   ZINE)
ENDING THE BEGIN
FIVE POINTS
Galaxy Press
THE GLASS CHERRY
The Glass Cherry Press
GRAIN
Headveins Graphics
HIP MAMA
The Hosanna Press
Interim Press
JACK MACKEREL MAGAZINE
JOURNAL OF REGIONAL CRITICISM
KALDRON, An International Journal Of Visual Poetry
KALEIDOSCOPE: International Magazine of Literature,
   Fine Arts, and Disability
LEAPINGS LITERARY MAGAZINE
LEFT CURVE
LUMMOX JOURNAL
LUZ EN ARTE Y LITERATURA
META4: Journal of Object Oriented Poetics (OOPS)
Mortal Press
NITE-WRITER'S   INTERNATIONAL   LITERARY
   ARTS JOURNAL
POETRY AND AUDIENCE
POETRY NOTTINGHAM INTERNATIONAL
PROVINCETOWN ARTS
RADIANCE, The Magazine For Large Women
Rarach Press
REFLECT
Rowhouse Press
SALT LICK
Salt Lick Press
Savant Garde Workshop
SCRIVENER
Shadowlight Press
Gibbs Smith, Publisher
SOUTH DAKOTA REVIEW
THE SOUTHERN CALIFORNIA ANTHOLOGY
Starbooks Press/FLF Press
University of Massachusetts Press
THE VINCENT BROTHERS REVIEW
Washington Writers' Publishing House

Writers House Press

ASIAN

AXE FACTORY REVIEW
Baker Street Publications
THE BAREFOOT POET: Journal of Poetry, Fiction,
   Essays, & Art
BRILLIANT STAR
Buddhist Text Translation Society
Copper Canyon Press
Cynic Press
ELF: ECLECTIC LITERARY FORUM (ELF MAGA-
   ZINE)
MANUSHI - a journal about women & society
MANY MOUNTAINS MOVING
THE NEW PRESS LITERARY QUARTERLY
Passeggiata Press, Inc.
The Place In The Woods
Press Here
READ, AMERICA!
The Wellsweep Press
WORDS OF WISDOM

ASIAN AMERICAN POETS

THE AMERICAN VOICE
ASSEMBLING
Assembling Press
Baker Street Publications
BAMBOO RIDGE, Journal of Hawai'i Literature and Arts
Bamboo Ridge Press
THE BAREFOOT POET: Journal of Poetry, Fiction,
   Essays, & Art
BRILLIANT STAR
Brunswick Publishing Corporation
Burning Bush Publications
Carolina Wren Press/Lollipop Power Books
City Lights Books
Cynic Press
ELF: ECLECTIC LITERARY FORUM (ELF MAGA-
   ZINE)
EPOCH
HIP MAMA
HURRICANE ALICE
KARAMU
Lakes & Prairies Press
LUMMOX JOURNAL
LUZ EN ARTE Y LITERATURA
MANY MOUNTAINS MOVING
MESECHABE: The Journal of Surre(gion)alism
NEW ENGLAND REVIEW
NEW HOPE INTERNATIONAL REVIEW
THE NEW PRESS LITERARY QUARTERLY
THE NORTH AMERICAN REVIEW
PASSAGER: A Journal of Remembrance and Discovery
Passeggiata Press, Inc.
The Place In The Woods
POETRY NOTTINGHAM INTERNATIONAL
READ, AMERICA!
The Snail's Pace Press, Inc.
SOUTH DAKOTA REVIEW
WEST COAST LINE: A Journal of Contemporary
   Writing and Criticism
West End Press
Writers House Press

ATHEISM

ASSEMBLING
THE BOOMERPHILE
LIMESTONE: A Literary Journal
WICKED MYSTIC

AUSTRALIAN

American Literary Press Inc./Noble House
Galaxy Press
THE NEW PRESS LITERARY QUARTERLY
TAMPA REVIEW
WRITING ULSTER

274

AVANT GARDE

A & U AMERICA'S AIDS MAGAZINE
AABYE (formerly New Hope International Writing)
ABRAXAS
Aegina Press, Inc.
AMELIA
AMERICAN LETTERS & COMMENTARY
American Literary Press Inc./Noble House
THE AMERICAN VOICE
ANT ANT ANT ANT ANT
Arjuna Library Press
ART-CORE
ASSEMBLING
AURA LITERARY/ARTS REVIEW
Baker Street Publications
BATHTUB GIN
BELOIT POETRY JOURNAL
BkMk Press
Black Sparrow Press
Black Tie Press
BLADES
Bloody Someday Press
BOUILLABAISSE
Burning Books
Burning Llama Press
THE CAPILANO REVIEW
THE CAROLINA QUARTERLY
CHIRON REVIEW
CHRONICLES OF DISORDER
Cleveland State Univ. Poetry Center
CLWN WR
CONDUIT
CONFRONTATION
CONTEXT SOUTH
CURARE
DAYS AND NIGHTS OF A SMALL PRESS PUB-
LISHER
Depth Charge
DIRIGIBLE
Drum
ELF: ECLECTIC LITERARY FORUM (ELF MAGA-
ZINE)
ENDING THE BEGIN
EPOCH
FOLIO: A Literary Journal of American University
FRANK: AN INTERNATIONAL JOURNAL OF CON-
TEMPORARY WRITING AND ART
Galaxy Press
THE GALLEY SAIL REVIEW
Ghost Pony Press
GINOSKO
GLOBAL TAPESTRY
GREAT RIVER REVIEW
THE HAUNTED JOURNAL
Headveins Graphics
HEAVEN BONE MAGAZINE
HIP MAMA
HIRAM POETRY REVIEW
H2SO4
THE IMPLODING TIE-DYED TOUPEE
Implosion Press
JACK MACKEREL MAGAZINE
JOURNAL OF REGIONAL CRITICISM
KALDRON, An International Journal Of Visual Poetry
KARAWANE
KOJA
LEAPINGS LITERARY MAGAZINE
LEFT CURVE
Left Hand Books
LOST AND FOUND TIMES
LOST GENERATION JOURNAL
Luna Bisonte Prods
THE MAC GUFFIN
MESECHABE: The Journal of Surre(gion)alism
META4: Journal of Object Oriented Poetics (OOPS)
MINESHAFT
MIXED BAG

Mortal Press
NEDGE
NEW AMERICAN WRITING
NEW HOPE INTERNATIONAL REVIEW
THE NEW PRESS LITERARY QUARTERLY
NIGHTSHADE
ON SPEC
PACIFIC COAST JOURNAL
Paris Press, Inc.
PEGASUS
PERIPHERAL VISION
PLAIN BROWN WRAPPER (PBW)
POETRY MOTEL
POETRY NOTTINGHAM INTERNATIONAL
The Poetry Project
THE POETRY PROJECT NEWSLETTER
Prakalpana Literature
PRAKALPANA SAHITYA/PRAKALPANA LITERA-
TURE
REALM OF THE VAMPIRE
Red Dragon Press
Rowhouse Press
Savant Garde Workshop
SCAVENGER'S NEWSLETTER
Second Coming Press
SKYLARK
SLIPSTREAM
THE SOUNDS OF POETRY
THE SOUTHERN CALIFORNIA ANTHOLOGY
THE SPITTING IMAGE
SPOUT
SPSM&H
Starbooks Press/FLF Press
Suburban Wilderness Press
TAMPA REVIEW
THIS IS IMPORTANT
Underwhich Editions
THE VINCENT BROTHERS REVIEW
VOID
VOLITION
Washington Writers' Publishing House
Water Row Press
WEST COAST LINE: A Journal of Contemporary
Writing and Criticism
Wineberry Press
WRITER'S EXCHANGE
WRITERS' FORUM
XIB
Xib Publications
ZUZU'S PETALS: QUARTERLY ONLINE

BASEBALL

Cynic Press
Drum
LIMESTONE: A Literary Journal
RED ROCK REVIEW
SPORT LITERATE, Honest Reflections on Life's Leisur-
ely Diversions

BEAT GENERATION

AABYE (formerly New Hope International Writing)
ABRAXAS
Aegina Press, Inc.
Alpha Beat Press
ALPHA BEAT SOUP
ARTHUR'S COUSIN
ART:MAG
ASSEMBLING
AURA LITERARY/ARTS REVIEW
Baker Street Publications
Black Sparrow Press
BLUE BEAT JACKET
Blue Jacket Press
THE BOOMERPHILE
BOUILLABAISSE
THE CAFE REVIEW
Center Press
CHIRON REVIEW

CHRONICLES OF DISORDER
City Lights Books
CONTEXT SOUTH
CURARE
Cynic Press
DAYS AND NIGHTS OF A SMALL PRESS PUB-
LISHER
DOWN UNDER MANHATTAN BRIDGE
Drum
ELF: ECLECTIC LITERARY FORUM (ELF MAGA-
ZINE)
GARGOYLE
Gay Sunshine Press, Inc.
Ghost Pony Press
THE GLASS CHERRY
The Glass Cherry Press
GLOBAL TAPESTRY
Golden Isis Press
THE HAUNTED JOURNAL
Implosion Press
THE J MAN TIMES
Lakes & Prairies Press
LUMMOX JOURNAL
MESECHABE: The Journal of Surre(gion)alism
MIXED BAG
THE NEW PRESS LITERARY QUARTERLY
NIGHTSHADE
PERIPHERAL VISION
PLAIN BROWN WRAPPER (PBW)
POETRY MOTEL
Second Coming Press
SLIPSTREAM
SONORA REVIEW
THE SPITTING IMAGE
STOVEPIPE: A Journal of Little Literary Value
Suburban Wilderness Press
THIS IS IMPORTANT
University Editions, Inc.
THE VINCENT BROTHERS REVIEW
VOID
Washington Writers' Publishing House
Water Row Press

BLACK

AFRICAN AMERICAN REVIEW
AFRO-HISPANIC REVIEW
American Literary Press Inc./Noble House
Baker Street Publications
BRILLIANT STAR
Brunswick Publishing Corporation
ELF: ECLECTIC LITERARY FORUM (ELF MAGA-
ZINE)
The Fire!! Press
KARAMU
Lotus Press, Inc.
LUMMOX JOURNAL
MESECHABE: The Journal of Surre(gion)alism
OBSIDIAN II: BLACK LITERATURE IN REVIEW
PASSAGER: A Journal of Remembrance and Discovery
The Place In The Woods
READ, AMERICA!
THE SOUTHERN REVIEW
STAPLE
Starbooks Press/FLF Press
University of Massachusetts Press
THE VINCENT BROTHERS REVIEW
Washington Writers' Publishing House

BRITISH

AABYE (formerly New Hope International Writing)
ELF: ECLECTIC LITERARY FORUM (ELF MAGA-
ZINE)
Helikon Press
NEW HOPE INTERNATIONAL REVIEW
ORBIS
Reality Street Editions
THE SOUTHERN REVIEW
STAPLE

Story Line Press
TAMPA REVIEW
Unfinished Monument Press

BROADSIDES

BATHTUB GIN
Black Sparrow Press
BOUILLABAISSE
DEANOTATIONS
Drum
Erespin Press
Ghost Pony Press
Greenhouse Review Press
Hug The Earth Publications
LOST AND FOUND TIMES
Lotus Press, Inc.
LUMMOX JOURNAL
Luna Bisonte Prods
Moving Parts Press
New Native Press
Now It's Up To You Publications
POETRY MOTEL
Second Coming Press
Gibbs Smith, Publisher
SUB-TERRAIN
Suburban Wilderness Press

BROTHERHOOD

KICK IT OVER
LUMMOX JOURNAL
SKYLARK
Starbooks Press/FLF Press
VOICES - ISRAEL

BUSINESS

THE BOOMERPHILE

CANADA/CANADIAN POETS

ALPHA BEAT SOUP
American Literary Press Inc./Noble House
THE AMERICAN VOICE
THE ANTIGONISH REVIEW
Baker Street Publications
BOGG
BRILLIANT STAR
Broken Jaw Press
THE CAPILANO REVIEW
THE CAROLINA QUARTERLY
Coteau Books
DAYS AND NIGHTS OF A SMALL PRESS PUB-
LISHER
ELF: ECLECTIC LITERARY FORUM (ELF MAGA-
ZINE)
EMPLOI PLUS
ENTELECHY MAGAZINE
EPOCH
THE HAUNTED JOURNAL
Insomniac Press
KRAX
LUZ EN ARTE Y LITERATURA
MESECHABE: The Journal of Surre(gion)alism
NEW ENGLAND REVIEW
THE NEW PRESS LITERARY QUARTERLY
NEWSLETTER (LEAGUE OF CANADIAN POETS)
NIGHTSHADE
Oolichan Books
OSIRIS
THE POTTERSFIELD PORTFOLIO
PRAIRIE FIRE
REALM OF THE VAMPIRE
Ronsdale Press
TAMPA REVIEW
Thistledown Press Ltd.
Underwhich Editions
Unfinished Monument Press
Vehicule Press
WEST COAST LINE: A Journal of Contemporary
Writing and Criticism

WRITERS' FORUM

CATHOLIC

American Literary Press Inc./Noble House
THE BAREFOOT POET: Journal of Poetry, Fiction,
   Essays, & Art
Cynic Press
OBLATES
POETRY NOTTINGHAM INTERNATIONAL
SILVER WINGS/MAYFLOWER PULPIT
Washington Writers' Publishing House
White Buck Publishing
Writers House Press

CELIBACY

CONJUNCTIONS
Cynic Press
Washington Writers' Publishing House
Writers House Press

CELTIC

Bardsong Press
Bloody Someday Press

CHILDREN

AABYE (formerly New Hope International Writing)
American Literary Press Inc./Noble House
Art/Life Limited Editions
THE BOOMERPHILE
BRILLIANT STAR
THE CAROLINA QUARTERLY
Creative With Words Publications (CWW)
Cynic Press
HIP MAMA
KID'S WORLD
LADYBUG, the Magazine for Young Children
LIGHTHOUSE STORY COLLECTIONS
LIMESTONE: A Literary Journal
LUZ EN ARTE Y LITERATURA
THE MASONIA ROUNDUP
NEW HOPE INTERNATIONAL REVIEW
NITE-WRITER'S INTERNATIONAL LITERARY
   ARTS JOURNAL
The Place In The Woods
READ, AMERICA!
Ronsdale Press
SPIDER
Ten Penny Players, Inc.
TEXAS YOUNG WRITERS' NEWSLETTER
Washington Writers' Publishing House

CHRISTIAN

AABYE (formerly New Hope International Writing)
American Literary Press Inc./Noble House
APKL Publications
Arjuna Library Press
THE BAREFOOT POET: Journal of Poetry, Fiction,
   Essays, & Art
Blue Unicorn Press, Inc.
CORNERSTONE
DAUGHTERS OF SARAH
FULLOSIA PRESS
ISSUES
THE J MAN TIMES
LIGHTHOUSE STORY COLLECTIONS
Mountain State Press
NEW HOPE INTERNATIONAL REVIEW
THE NEW PRESS LITERARY QUARTERLY
NITE-WRITER'S INTERNATIONAL LITERARY
   ARTS JOURNAL
OTTER
THE PATRIOT
POETRY AND AUDIENCE
POETRY NOTTINGHAM INTERNATIONAL
POET'S PARK
QUARTZ HILL JOURNAL OF THEOLOGY
Runaway Publications
St. Andrew Press

SILVER WINGS/MAYFLOWER PULPIT
STUDENT LEADERSHIP JOURNAL
STUDIO - A Journal of Christians Writing
TAMPA REVIEW
Washington Writers' Publishing House
White Buck Publishing
Windsong Press
Writers House Press

CLASSICAL

ASSEMBLING
BIBLIOPHILOS
Brunswick Publishing Corporation
Center Press
THE CLASSICAL OUTLOOK
Cynic Press
DIALOGOS: Hellenic Studies Review
ELF: ECLECTIC LITERARY FORUM (ELF MAGA-
   ZINE)
THE EVERGREEN CHRONICLES
Galaxy Press
THE MADISON REVIEW
Mortal Press
Mountain State Press
NEW HOPE INTERNATIONAL REVIEW
THE NEW PRESS LITERARY QUARTERLY
ORBIS
POETRY AND AUDIENCE
Ronsdale Press
THE SHAKESPEARE NEWSLETTER
SONGS OF INNOCENCE

COLLABORATIVE

ABRAXAS
From Here Press
Ghost Pony Press
Greenhouse Review Press
NEW HOPE INTERNATIONAL REVIEW
Underwhich Editions
Washington Writers' Publishing House
XTRAS

COMMUNIST

LEFT CURVE
STRUGGLE: A Magazine of Proletarian Revolutionary
   Literature

COMMUNITY

AMERICAN JONES BUILDING & MAINTENANCE
DAUGHTERS OF SARAH
KICK IT OVER
THE MASONIA ROUNDUP
Missing Spoke Press
OUT YOUR BACKDOOR: The Magazine of Informal
   Adventure and Cheap Culture

COMPUTERS

AABYE (formerly New Hope International Writing)
THE BAREFOOT POET: Journal of Poetry, Fiction,
   Essays, & Art
THE BOOMERPHILE
Celestial Otter Press
HIRAM POETRY REVIEW
MAGIC CHANGES
NEW HOPE INTERNATIONAL REVIEW
PACIFIC COAST JOURNAL
SCAVENGER'S NEWSLETTER
Washington Writers' Publishing House
WRITER'S EXCHANGE

CONCRETE

AABYE (formerly New Hope International Writing)
ABRAXAS
ASSEMBLING
BOGG
Broken Jaw Press
Burning Llama Press
THE CAPILANO REVIEW

Cleveland State Univ. Poetry Center
CLWN WR
CONTEXT SOUTH
Depth Charge
Drum
THE EVERGREEN CHRONICLES
Ghost Pony Press
HIRAM POETRY REVIEW
THE IMPLODING TIE-DYED TOUPEE
KALDRON, An International Journal Of Visual Poetry
KOJA
LIMESTONE: A Literary Journal
LOST AND FOUND TIMES
LUMMOX JOURNAL
Luna Bisonte Prods
NEW HOPE INTERNATIONAL REVIEW
THE NEW PRESS LITERARY QUARTERLY
NITE-WRITER'S INTERNATIONAL LITERARY ARTS JOURNAL
OWEN WISTER REVIEW
PEGASUS
PERIPHERAL VISION
Press Here
Savant Garde Workshop
SCORE
TAMPA REVIEW
Underwhich Editions
THE VINCENT BROTHERS REVIEW
Washington Writers' Publishing House
Wineberry Press

CONTEMPORARY

A & U AMERICA'S AIDS MAGAZINE
ABRAXAS
ACM (ANOTHER CHICAGO MAGAZINE)
Adastra Press
AFRICAN AMERICAN REVIEW
AGNI
THE AGUILAR EXPRESSION
ALASKA QUARTERLY REVIEW
AMELIA
AMERICAN JONES BUILDING & MAINTENANCE
American Literary Press Inc./Noble House
THE AMERICAN VOICE
Anhinga Press
ANTIETAM REVIEW
Arjuna Library Press
Art/Life Limited Editions
ART:MAG
The Ashland Poetry Press
ASSEMBLING
Assembling Press
AURA LITERARY/ARTS REVIEW
Baker Street Publications
THE BAREFOOT POET: Journal of Poetry, Fiction, Essays, & Art
BARNWOOD
The Barnwood Press
BELOIT POETRY JOURNAL
BkMk Press
Black Buzzard Press
Black Hat Press
Black Tie Press
THE BLACK WARRIOR REVIEW
BORDERLANDS: Texas Poetry Review
Bottom Dog Press
Brooding Heron Press
Brunswick Publishing Corporation
THE CAROLINA QUARTERLY
Center Press
CHELSEA
CHICAGO REVIEW
Chicory Blue Press, Inc.
City Lights Books
Cleveland State Univ. Poetry Center
CONDUIT
Confluence Press, Inc.
CONFRONTATION

CORNERSTONE
CRAB CREEK REVIEW
THE CREAM CITY REVIEW
DAYS AND NIGHTS OF A SMALL PRESS PUBLISHER
DEANOTATIONS
Manya DeLeon Booksmith
ELF: ECLECTIC LITERARY FORUM (ELF MAGAZINE)
THE EVERGREEN CHRONICLES
FIELD: Contemporary Poetry and Poetics
THE FLORIDA REVIEW
FOLIO: A Literary Journal of American University
FRANK: AN INTERNATIONAL JOURNAL OF CONTEMPORARY WRITING AND ART
From Here Press
Ghost Pony Press
GLOBAL TAPESTRY
GREAT RIVER REVIEW
GREEN MOUNTAINS REVIEW
Greenhouse Review Press
The Groundwater Press
THE HAUNTED JOURNAL
HIRAM POETRY REVIEW
HOLLYWOOD NOSTALGIA
HOME PLANET NEWS
The Hosanna Press
HUBBUB
INTERIM
Intertext
IRIS: A Journal About Women
IRON HORSE LITERARY REVIEW
JEWISH LIFE
THE JOURNAL
JOURNAL OF REGIONAL CRITICISM
KALDRON, An International Journal Of Visual Poetry
KARAMU
KRAX
THE LAUREL REVIEW
LEAPINGS LITERARY MAGAZINE
THE LEDGE
LEFT CURVE
THE LICKING RIVER REVIEW
LIMESTONE: A Literary Journal
Lintel
Loom Press
LOST AND FOUND TIMES
LUMMOX JOURNAL
Luna Bisonte Prods
LUZ EN ARTE Y LITERATURA
THE MAC GUFFIN
MANGROVE MAGAZINE
MID-AMERICAN REVIEW
Milkweed Editions
Mille Grazie Press
Missing Spoke Press
MR. COGITO
Mortal Press
MUDLARK
NANNY FANNY
NEDGE
NEOLOGISMS
NEW ENGLAND REVIEW
THE NEW PRESS LITERARY QUARTERLY
THE NEW RENAISSANCE, An International Magazine of Ideas & Opinions, Emphasizing Literature & The Arts
NIGHTSHADE
NIGHTSUN
NIMROD INTERNATIONAL
NITE-WRITER'S INTERNATIONAL LITERARY ARTS JOURNAL
Oberlin College Press
THE OHIO REVIEW
THE OLD RED KIMONO
Oolichan Books
ORBIS
OSIRIS

Paris Press, Inc.
PARNASSUS: Poetry in Review
PASSAGES NORTH
PEARL
PEGASUS
PENNINE PLATFORM
Pleasure Boat Studio
POETRY MOTEL
POETRY NOTTINGHAM INTERNATIONAL
Point Riders Press
POTPOURRI: A Magazine of the Literary Arts
The Press of Appletree Alley
PRISM INTERNATIONAL
PUDDING MAGAZINE: The International Journal of
    Applied Poetry
RAG MAG
RATTAPALLAX
RED ROCK REVIEW
Ridgeway Press of Michigan
RIVER CITY
Ronsdale Press
ROSEBUD
SALMAGUNDI
Savant Garde Workshop
Second Coming Press
SENECA REVIEW
SIDEWALKS
Signature Books
SKYLARK
SLIPSTREAM
Gibbs Smith, Publisher
The Snail's Pace Press, Inc.
SOJOURNER, THE WOMEN'S FORUM
THE SOUTHERN CALIFORNIA ANTHOLOGY
SOUTHERN INDIANA REVIEW
THE SOUTHERN REVIEW
THE SOW'S EAR POETRY REVIEW
SPIN
Starbooks Press/FLF Press
STOVEPIPE: A Journal of Little Literary Value
STUDENT LEADERSHIP JOURNAL
Suburban Wilderness Press
Summer Stream Press
SYCAMORE REVIEW
THIS IS IMPORTANT
Thistledown Press Ltd.
TOUCHSTONE LITERARY JOURNAL
University of Massachusetts Press
VERSE
THE VINCENT BROTHERS REVIEW
VISIONS-INTERNATIONAL, The World Journal of
    Illustrated Poetry
VOICES - ISRAEL
VOLITION
Warthog Press
Washington Writers' Publishing House
WATERWAYS: Poetry in the Mainstream
WEST COAST LINE: A Journal of Contemporary
    Writing and Criticism
Wineberry Press
THE WISHING WELL
Woodburn Avenue Books
WRITER'S EXCHANGE
WRITERS' FORUM
Writers House Press
XTRAS
Years Press
Zoland Books

CREATIVITY

American Living Press
Art/Life Limited Editions
Baker Street Publications
THE CAROLINA QUARTERLY
CONTEXT SOUTH
CORNERSTONE
THE CREATIVE WOMAN
ELF: ECLECTIC LITERARY FORUM (ELF MAGA-
ZINE)
Galaxy Press
HOLLYWOOD NOSTALGIA
JEWISH LIFE
JOURNAL OF REGIONAL CRITICISM
Mortal Press
NEW HOPE INTERNATIONAL REVIEW
NIGHTSHADE
PASSAGER: A Journal of Remembrance and Discovery
PEN & INK WRITERS JOURNAL
POETRY AND AUDIENCE
POET'S FANTASY
PUDDING MAGAZINE: The International Journal of
    Applied Poetry
St. Andrew Press
Savant Garde Workshop
SPORT LITERATE, Honest Reflections on Life's Leisur-
    ely Diversions
THE SUNDAY SUITOR POETRY REVIEW
TAMPA REVIEW
THE VINCENT BROTHERS REVIEW
WEYFARERS
WRITER'S EXCHANGE

CRITICISM

ABRAXAS
AFRICAN AMERICAN REVIEW
AXE FACTORY REVIEW
BAKER STREET GAZETTE
Baker Street Publications
BORDERLANDS: Texas Poetry Review
Manya DeLeon Booksmith
DIRIGIBLE
THE EVERGREEN CHRONICLES
From Here Press
GREEN MOUNTAINS REVIEW
THE HAUNTED JOURNAL
HORIZONS BEYOND
JEWISH LIFE
JOURNAL OF REGIONAL CRITICISM
KALEIDOSCOPE: International Magazine of Literature,
    Fine Arts, and Disability
Katydid Books
Lakes & Prairies Press
LIMESTONE: A Literary Journal
LUMMOX JOURNAL
LUZ EN ARTE Y LITERATURA
MIXED BAG
MUDLARK
NEOLOGISMS
THE NEW PRESS LITERARY QUARTERLY
NIGHTSHADE
OUTPOSTS POETRY QUARTERLY
PEN & INK WRITERS JOURNAL
SEWANEE REVIEW
SLEUTH JOURNAL
SOUTHERN INDIANA REVIEW
THE SOUTHERN REVIEW
TOUCHSTONE LITERARY JOURNAL
University of Massachusetts Press
THE VINCENT BROTHERS REVIEW
WEST COAST LINE: A Journal of Contemporary
    Writing and Criticism
WICKED MYSTIC
XAVIER REVIEW

CUBIST

Black Tie Press
FINE MADNESS
LOST GENERATION JOURNAL
LUMMOX JOURNAL
THE SPITTING IMAGE

CZECH

MESECHABE: The Journal of Surre(gion)alism
THE NEW PRESS LITERARY QUARTERLY

DANISH

ENTELECHY MAGAZINE
THE NEW PRESS LITERARY QUARTERLY
Years Press

DEATH/BEREAVEMENT

A & U AMERICA'S AIDS MAGAZINE
AABYE (formerly New Hope International Writing)
American Literary Press Inc./Noble House
The Ashland Poetry Press
Baker Street Publications
THE CAROLINA QUARTERLY
CURARE
DEANOTATIONS
FELL SWOOP
THE HAUNTED JOURNAL
HOLLYWOOD NOSTALGIA
THE J MAN TIMES
JEWISH LIFE
LUZ EN ARTE Y LITERATURA
NIGHTSHADE
THE NOCTURNAL LYRIC
Pendragonian Publications
PENNY DREADFUL: Tales and Poems of Fantastic
   Terror
REALM OF DARKNESS
REALM OF THE VAMPIRE
THE ROMANTIST
THE SALEM JOURNAL
SILVER WINGS/MAYFLOWER PULPIT
2AM MAGAZINE
Washington Writers' Publishing House
WATERWAYS: Poetry in the Mainstream
WICKED MYSTIC
Windsong Press

DISABLED

AABYE (formerly New Hope International Writing)
ABILITY NETWORK
ELF: ECLECTIC LITERARY FORUM (ELF MAGA-
   ZINE)
HIP MAMA
NEW HOPE INTERNATIONAL REVIEW
THE NEW PRESS LITERARY QUARTERLY
The Place In The Woods
SKYLARK
The Snail's Pace Press, Inc.

DRAMATIC

AABYE (formerly New Hope International Writing)
Bloody Someday Press
HOLLYWOOD NOSTALGIA
THE NEW PRESS LITERARY QUARTERLY
POETIC SPACE: Poetry & Fiction
RED WHEELBARROW
Ridgeway Press of Michigan
Savant Garde Workshop
THE VINCENT BROTHERS REVIEW
WICKED MYSTIC
Woodburn Avenue Books
Writers House Press

DUTCH

ENTELECHY MAGAZINE
THE NEW PRESS LITERARY QUARTERLY
ROOM

ECLECTIC

AC
Adastra Press
Alternating Crimes Publishing
AMERICAN LETTERS & COMMENTARY
American Literary Press Inc./Noble House
Anamnesis Press
AURA LITERARY/ARTS REVIEW
AXE FACTORY REVIEW
Baker Street Publications

BLACK MOON
Black Tie Press
Bloody Someday Press
CEDAR HILL REVIEW
Center Press
CRAB CREEK REVIEW
DAYS AND NIGHTS OF A SMALL PRESS PUB-
   LISHER
DEANOTATIONS
Depth Charge
ELF: ECLECTIC LITERARY FORUM (ELF MAGA-
   ZINE)
THE GALLEY SAIL REVIEW
THE GREENSBORO REVIEW
THE HAUNTED JOURNAL
HEAVEN BONE MAGAZINE
HOME PLANET NEWS
H2SO4
THE ICONOCLAST
JACK MACKEREL MAGAZINE
JEWISH LIFE
Lakes & Prairies Press
LEAPINGS LITERARY MAGAZINE
LIMESTONE: A Literary Journal
LUZ EN ARTE Y LITERATURA
THE MADISON REVIEW
MANGROVE MAGAZINE
Milkweed Editions
MIXED BAG
MOCKINGBIRD
Mortal Press
NIGHTSHADE
PASSAIC REVIEW (MILLENNIUM EDITIONS)
PEARL
PLAIN BROWN WRAPPER (PBW)
POETRY MOTEL
THE RIALTO
ROSEBUD
Rowhouse Press
Savant Garde Workshop
SILHOUETTE MAGAZINE
SKYLARK
The Snail's Pace Press, Inc.
Suburban Wilderness Press
TAPROOT LITERARY REVIEW
THE VINCENT BROTHERS REVIEW
VOID
Xib Publications
ZUZU'S PETALS: QUARTERLY ONLINE

ECOLOGY/ENVIRONMENT

THE AMICUS JOURNAL
Art/Life Limited Editions
ART:MAG
ASSEMBLING
Baker Street Publications
Black Bear Publications
BLACK BEAR REVIEW
BLUELINE
THE BOOMERPHILE
BORDERLANDS: Texas Poetry Review
BRILLIANT STAR
Celestial Otter Press
Confluence Press, Inc.
THE CREATIVE WOMAN
Cynic Press
GaiaQuest
GLOBAL TAPESTRY
GREEN FUSE POETRY
GREEN WORLD: News and Views For Gardening Who
   Care About The Earth
Hug The Earth Publications
KICK IT OVER
LEAPINGS LITERARY MAGAZINE
LUMMOX JOURNAL
MAGIC CHANGES
MESECHABE: The Journal of Surre(gion)alism
Milkweed Editions

MOCKINGBIRD
NEW HOPE INTERNATIONAL REVIEW
THE NORTH AMERICAN REVIEW
OTTER
PASSAIC REVIEW (MILLENNIUM EDITIONS)
Pocahontas Press, Inc.
POW-WOW
RALPH'S REVIEW
RED OWL
RFD
SOUTH DAKOTA REVIEW
STOVEPIPE: A Journal of Little Literary Value
TALKING RIVER REVIEW
THIS IS IMPORTANT
2AM MAGAZINE
University of Massachusetts Press
THE UNKNOWN WRITER
THE VINCENT BROTHERS REVIEW
VOID
Washington Writers' Publishing House
WESTERN SKIES
WRITERS' FORUM

EGYPT

Baker Street Publications
Golden Isis Press

ELEGIAC

THE EVERGREEN CHRONICLES
FINE MADNESS
THE FLORIDA REVIEW
GLB Publishers
HARP-STRINGS
NEW HOPE INTERNATIONAL REVIEW
POETRY AND AUDIENCE
SEWANEE REVIEW
THE SOUTHERN REVIEW
THE VINCENT BROTHERS REVIEW
Wind's Errand

EROTICA

A & U AMERICA'S AIDS MAGAZINE
AABYE (formerly New Hope International Writing)
AC
Alternating Crimes Publishing
ANT ANT ANT ANT ANT
ARTHUR'S COUSIN
ASSEMBLING
AXE FACTORY REVIEW
Black Tie Press
THE BOOMERPHILE
THE CAROLINA QUARTERLY
Center Press
CHIRON REVIEW
CHRONICLES OF DISORDER
CURARE
Cynic Press
DOWN UNDER MANHATTAN BRIDGE
Duende Press
THE EVERGREEN CHRONICLES
GARGOYLE
Gay Sunshine Press, Inc.
GLB Publishers
Golden Isis Press
HOLLYWOOD NOSTALGIA
H2SO4
HURRICANE ALICE
Implosion Press
JACK MACKEREL MAGAZINE
KOJA
Lakes & Prairies Press
Laocoon Books
LIMESTONE: A Literary Journal
LUMMOX JOURNAL
LUZ EN ARTE Y LITERATURA
MESECHABE: The Journal of Surre(gion)alism
META4: Journal of Object Oriented Poetics (OOPS)
MIP Company

Moving Parts Press
NEW HOPE INTERNATIONAL REVIEW
NITE-WRITER'S INTERNATIONAL LITERARY
    ARTS JOURNAL
PASSAIC REVIEW (MILLENNIUM EDITIONS)
PERIPHERAL VISION
PLAIN BROWN WRAPPER (PBW)
REALM OF THE VAMPIRE
RED OWL
Rowhouse Press
THE SALEM JOURNAL
SLIPSTREAM
THE SOUNDS OF POETRY
THE SPITTING IMAGE
Starbooks Press/FLF Press
SUB-TERRAIN
The Teitan Press, Inc.
THIS IS IMPORTANT
Washington Writers' Publishing House
WICKED MYSTIC
Windsong Press
YELLOW SILK: Journal Of Erotic Arts

ESSAYS

A & U AMERICA'S AIDS MAGAZINE
AABYE (formerly New Hope International Writing)
AXE FACTORY REVIEW
BAKER STREET GAZETTE
Baker Street Publications
THE BAREFOOT POET: Journal of Poetry, Fiction,
    Essays, & Art
BORDERLANDS: Texas Poetry Review
CONFLUENCE
CONTEXT SOUTH
Cynic Press
DIRIGIBLE
THE EVERGREEN CHRONICLES
FIVE POINTS
Galaxy Press
THE HAUNTED JOURNAL
H2SO4
HURRICANE ALICE
JACK MACKEREL MAGAZINE
JACK THE RIPPER GAZETTE
KALEIDOSCOPE: International Magazine of Literature,
    Fine Arts, and Disability
Katydid Books
LUMMOX JOURNAL
LUZ EN ARTE Y LITERATURA
THE MARLBORO REVIEW
MESECHABE: The Journal of Surre(gion)alism
MID-AMERICAN REVIEW
MIXED BAG
Mortal Press
MUDLARK
NEBO
NEW HOPE INTERNATIONAL REVIEW
PARNASSUS: Poetry in Review
PLAIN BROWN WRAPPER (PBW)
Rowhouse Press
THE SALEM JOURNAL
SEWANEE REVIEW
SLEUTH JOURNAL
SOUTHERN INDIANA REVIEW
SYCAMORE REVIEW
University of Massachusetts Press
THE VINCENT BROTHERS REVIEW
Woodburn Avenue Books
Writers House Press
XAVIER REVIEW
ZUZU'S PETALS: QUARTERLY ONLINE

ETHNIC

AFRICAN AMERICAN REVIEW
American Literary Press Inc./Noble House
ARARAT
Baker Street Publications
BkMk Press

Black Buzzard Press
BLADES
BORDERLANDS: Texas Poetry Review
BRILLIANT STAR
CALYX: A Journal of Art and Literature by Women
THE CAROLINA QUARTERLY
CHIRON REVIEW
City Lights Books
Cynic Press
HIP MAMA
IRIS: A Journal About Women
ISRAEL HORIZONS
ISSUES
JEWISH CURRENTS
JEWISH LIFE
KARAMU
LADYBUG, the Magazine for Young Children
LEAPINGS LITERARY MAGAZINE
MANY MOUNTAINS MOVING
MOCKINGBIRD
THE NEW PRESS LITERARY QUARTERLY
NIMROD INTERNATIONAL
THE NORTH AMERICAN REVIEW
PASSAGER: A Journal of Remembrance and Discovery
Passeggiata Press, Inc.
Pella Publishing Co
The Place In The Woods
Point Riders Press
READ, AMERICA!
SONORA REVIEW
The Spirit That Moves Us Press, Inc.
STUDENT LEADERSHIP JOURNAL
TUCUMCARI LITERARY REVIEW
THE VINCENT BROTHERS REVIEW
VISIONS-INTERNATIONAL, The World Journal of
  Illustrated Poetry
Washington Writers' Publishing House
THE WISHING WELL

EXPERIMENTAL

A & U AMERICA'S AIDS MAGAZINE
AABYE (formerly New Hope International Writing)
THE AGUILAR EXPRESSION
ALASKA QUARTERLY REVIEW
AMELIA
AMERICAN JONES BUILDING & MAINTENANCE
AMERICAN LETTERS & COMMENTARY
American Literary Press Inc./Noble House
American Living Press
THE AMERICAN VOICE
ANT ANT ANT ANT ANT
Arjuna Library Press
ARTHUR'S COUSIN
ART:MAG
ASSEMBLING
AURA LITERARY/ARTS REVIEW
Baker Street Publications
Bard Press
BATHTUB GIN
BELOIT POETRY JOURNAL
Black Tie Press
BLADES
Brunswick Publishing Corporation
Burning Books
Burning Deck Press
Burning Llama Press
THE CAPILANO REVIEW
THE CAROLINA QUARTERLY
Center Press
CHELSEA
CHIRON REVIEW
CHRONICLES OF DISORDER
Cleveland State Univ. Poetry Center
CLWN WR
COKEFISH
CONDUIT
CURARE
DAYS AND NIGHTS OF A SMALL PRESS PUB-

LISHER
DEANOTATIONS
Depth Charge
DIRIGIBLE
DOWN UNDER MANHATTAN BRIDGE
EARTH'S DAUGHTERS: Feminist Arts Periodical
ECLIPSE
ENDING THE BEGIN
ENTELECHY MAGAZINE
EPOCH
THE EVERGREEN CHRONICLES
FOLIO: A Literary Journal of American University
French Bread Publications
Ghost Pony Press
GINOSKO
GLB Publishers
Golden Isis Press
GREAT RIVER REVIEW
THE HAUNTED JOURNAL
HEAVEN BONE MAGAZINE
HIP MAMA
HIRAM POETRY REVIEW
HOLLYWOOD NOSTALGIA
HORIZONS BEYOND
H2SO4
THE IMPLODING TIE-DYED TOUPEE
Implosion Press
IRIS: A Journal About Women
THE J MAN TIMES
JACK MACKEREL MAGAZINE
JEWISH LIFE
THE JOURNAL
JOURNAL OF REGIONAL CRITICISM
KALDRON, An International Journal Of Visual Poetry
KARAMU
KOJA
LEAPINGS LITERARY MAGAZINE
LEFT CURVE
Left Hand Books
LETHOLOGICA
LIMESTONE: A Literary Journal
Lintel
THE LITTLE MAGAZINE
LOGODAEDALUS
LOST AND FOUND TIMES
LUMMOX JOURNAL
Luna Bisonte Prods
LUZ EN ARTE Y LITERATURA
THE MAC GUFFIN
THE MADISON REVIEW
MESECHABE: The Journal of Surre(gion)alism
META4: Journal of Object Oriented Poetics (OOPS)
MINESHAFT
Missing Spoke Press
MIXED BAG
Mortal Press
Moving Parts Press
NEDGE
NEW AMERICAN WRITING
NEW HOPE INTERNATIONAL REVIEW
NIGHTSHADE
NIMROD INTERNATIONAL
THE NORTH AMERICAN REVIEW
ON SPEC
OWEN WISTER REVIEW
PACIFIC COAST JOURNAL
Painted Leaf Press
PEGASUS
PERIPHERAL VISION
POETRY NOTTINGHAM INTERNATIONAL
The Poetry Project
THE POETRY PROJECT NEWSLETTER
Prakalpana Literature
PRAKALPANA SAHITYA/PRAKALPANA LITERA-
  TURE
Pudding House Publications
PUDDING MAGAZINE: The International Journal of
  Applied Poetry

Reality Street Editions
REALM OF DARKNESS
Red Dragon Press
Ronsdale Press
Rowhouse Press
The Runaway Spoon Press
THE SALEM JOURNAL
Savant Garde Workshop
SCAVENGER'S NEWSLETTER
SCORE
SIDEWALKS
SKYLARK
SLIPSTREAM
The Snail's Pace Press, Inc.
SONORA REVIEW
THE SOUTHERN CALIFORNIA ANTHOLOGY
THE SPITTING IMAGE
SPOON RIVER POETRY REVIEW
SPOUT
STOVEPIPE: A Journal of Little Literary Value
SUB-TERRAIN
TAMPA REVIEW
Telephone Books
THIS IS IMPORTANT
THE UNDERGROUND
Underwhich Editions
University Editions, Inc.
THE VINCENT BROTHERS REVIEW
VOLITION
Washington Writers' Publishing House
WEST COAST LINE: A Journal of Contemporary
   Writing and Criticism
Wineberry Press
THE WORLD
WRITERS' FORUM
Xenos Books
XIB
Xib Publications
ZUZU'S PETALS: QUARTERLY ONLINE

FAMILY

AABYE (formerly New Hope International Writing)
AMERICAN JONES BUILDING & MAINTENANCE
American Literary Press Inc./Noble House
Arctos Press
THE BAREFOOT POET: Journal of Poetry, Fiction,
   Essays, & Art
THE BOOMERPHILE
BRILLIANT STAR
THE CAROLINA QUARTERLY
Confluence Press, Inc.
DOWN UNDER MANHATTAN BRIDGE
THE GREAT IDEA PATCH
HIP MAMA
JEWISH LIFE
LADYBUG, the Magazine for Young Children
LEAPINGS LITERARY MAGAZINE
LIGHTHOUSE STORY COLLECTIONS
THE MASONIA ROUNDUP
Missing Spoke Press
MOOSE BOUND PRESS JOURNAL/NEWSLETTER
Mortal Press
Moving Parts Press
NEW HOPE INTERNATIONAL REVIEW
Outrider Press
SIDEWALKS
Signature Books
SILVER WINGS/MAYFLOWER PULPIT
THE SOUTHERN REVIEW
THE VINCENT BROTHERS REVIEW
Washington Writers' Publishing House
Writers House Press
Years Press

FANTASY

American Literary Press Inc./Noble House
Anamnesis Press
ART:MAG

Baker Street Publications
Black Tie Press
THE CAROLINA QUARTERLY
Cynic Press
DARK REGIONS: The Years Best Fantastic Fiction
DREAMS AND NIGHTMARES
ECLIPSE
GLB Publishers
Golden Isis Press
THE HAUNTED JOURNAL
HEAVEN BONE MAGAZINE
HORIZONS BEYOND
Journey Books Publishing
KID'S WORLD
KRAX
LEAPINGS LITERARY MAGAZINE
MINAS TIRITH EVENING-STAR
MIXED BAG
Mortal Press
NEW HOPE INTERNATIONAL REVIEW
THE NEW PRESS LITERARY QUARTERLY
NIGHTSHADE
THE NOCTURNAL LYRIC
NOVA EXPRESS
OF UNICORNS AND SPACE STATIONS
ON SPEC
OTTER
OZ-STORY
PABLO LENNIS
Pendragonian Publications
RALPH'S REVIEW
THE RATIONAL FEMINIST
REALM OF THE VAMPIRE
RED OWL
THE ROMANTIST
THE SALEM JOURNAL
Shadowlight Press
SONGS OF INNOCENCE
SPACE AND TIME
TALKING RIVER REVIEW
W.W. Publications
WICKED MYSTIC

FEMINIST

American Literary Press Inc./Noble House
THE AMERICAN VOICE
ASSEMBLING
Black Tie Press
BRIDGES: A Journal for Jewish Feminists and Our
   Friends
Broken Jaw Press
CALYX: A Journal of Art and Literature by Women
THE CAROLINA QUARTERLY
Chicory Blue Press, Inc.
CHIRON REVIEW
City Lights Books
Copper Canyon Press
Coteau Books
THE CREATIVE WOMAN
CURARE
Cynic Press
DAUGHTERS OF SARAH
DOWN UNDER MANHATTAN BRIDGE
EARTH'S DAUGHTERS: Feminist Arts Periodical
EPOCH
THE EVERGREEN CHRONICLES
FEMINIST VOICES NEWSJOURNAL
THE FLORIDA REVIEW
FRONTIERS: A Journal of Women Studies
GLB Publishers
Golden Isis Press
Good Gay Poets Press
H2SO4
HURRICANE ALICE
Implosion Press
IRIS: A Journal About Women
JEWISH CURRENTS
KARAMU

FREE VERSE

AABYE (formerly New Hope International Writing)
ABRAXAS
THE ACORN
ACORN WHISTLE
Adastra Press
Aegina Press, Inc.
THE AGUILAR EXPRESSION
Ahsahta
AMELIA
AMERICAN JONES BUILDING & MAINTENANCE
AMERICAN LETTERS & COMMENTARY
American Literary Press Inc./Noble House
THE AMERICAN VOICE
Amethyst & Emerald
THE ANTHOLOGY OF NEW ENGLAND WRITERS
Arjuna Library Press
ARTHUR'S COUSIN
The Ashland Poetry Press
ASSEMBLING
AURA LITERARY/ARTS REVIEW
BAKER STREET GAZETTE
Baker Street Publications
Bard Press
THE BAREFOOT POET: Journal of Poetry, Fiction,
    Essays, & Art
BATHTUB GIN
Bay Area Poets Coalition
BELLOWING ARK
BELOIT POETRY JOURNAL
BkMk Press
Black Buzzard Press
Black Tie Press
BLOOD & FEATHERS: Poems of Survival
Blue Unicorn Press, Inc.
BOGG
THE BOOMERPHILE
Brunswick Publishing Corporation
BYLINE
THE CAROLINA QUARTERLY
Carolina Wren Press/Lollipop Power Books
CEDAR HILL REVIEW
Center Press
CHARITON REVIEW
CHELSEA
CHIRON REVIEW
THE CLASSICAL OUTLOOK
Cleveland State Univ. Poetry Center
THE COMSTOCK REVIEW
CONDUIT
CONFLUENCE
Confluence Press, Inc.
CORNERSTONE
CRAB CREEK REVIEW
THE CREAM CITY REVIEW
Creative With Words Publications (CWW)
Cynic Press
DAYS AND NIGHTS OF A SMALL PRESS PUB-
    LISHER
DEANOTATIONS
EARTH'S DAUGHTERS: Feminist Arts Periodical
ELF: ECLECTIC LITERARY FORUM (ELF MAGA-
    ZINE)
En Passant Poetry Press
EN PASSANT/POETRY
ENTELECHY MAGAZINE
THE EVERGREEN CHRONICLES
FINE MADNESS
FOLIO: A Literary Journal of American University
French Bread Publications
From Here Press
Galaxy Press
Ghost Pony Press
THE GLASS CHERRY
The Glass Cherry Press
GLB Publishers
Golden Isis Press

GREAT RIVER REVIEW
Greenhouse Review Press
THE HAUNTED JOURNAL
Hippopotamus Press
HOLLYWOOD NOSTALGIA
HORIZONS BEYOND
The Hosanna Press
THE ICONOCLAST
Implosion Press
INTERBANG
Intertext
IRISH JOURNAL
IRON HORSE LITERARY REVIEW
ISRAEL HORIZONS
JACK THE RIPPER GAZETTE
Jackson Harbor Press
JEWISH LIFE
KALEIDOSCOPE: International Magazine of Literature,
    Fine Arts, and Disability
KARAMU
Kenyette Productions
KRAX
Lakes & Prairies Press
THE LAUREL REVIEW
LEAPINGS LITERARY MAGAZINE
LEFT CURVE
THE LICKING RIVER REVIEW
LIGHTHOUSE STORY COLLECTIONS
LIMESTONE: A Literary Journal
Lintel
THE LITERARY REVIEW
Longleaf Press
LOST GENERATION JOURNAL
Lotus Press, Inc.
LUMMOX JOURNAL
LUZ EN ARTE Y LITERATURA
THE MAC GUFFIN
MANGROVE MAGAZINE
MESECHABE: The Journal of Surre(gion)alism
Milkweed Editions
Missing Spoke Press
MIXED BAG
MOOSE BOUND PRESS JOURNAL/NEWSLETTER
Mortal Press
Mountain State Press
NANNY FANNY
NEDGE
NEW HOPE INTERNATIONAL REVIEW
THE NEW PRESS LITERARY QUARTERLY
THE NEW RENAISSANCE, An International Magazine
    of Ideas & Opinions, Emphasizing Literature & The
    Arts
NEWSLETTER INAGO
NIGHTSHADE
NIMROD INTERNATIONAL
NITE-WRITER'S   INTERNATIONAL   LITERARY
    ARTS JOURNAL
THE OHIO REVIEW
ORBIS
OUTPOSTS POETRY QUARTERLY
PACIFIC COAST JOURNAL
PARNASSUS LITERARY JOURNAL
PASSAGER: A Journal of Remembrance and Discovery
PEARL
PEGASUS
PEN & INK WRITERS JOURNAL
PERIPHERAL VISION
The Place In The Woods
Pleasure Boat Studio
POETALK
Poetic Page
POETRY AND AUDIENCE
POETRY MOTEL
POETRY NOTTINGHAM INTERNATIONAL
POTPOURRI: A Magazine of the Literary Arts
POW-WOW
PRAIRIE FIRE
THE PRAIRIE JOURNAL OF CANADIAN LITERA-

TURE
Prairie Journal Press
PUDDING MAGAZINE: The International Journal of
Applied Poetry
RALPH'S REVIEW
READ, AMERICA!
REALM OF DARKNESS
REALM OF THE VAMPIRE
RED WHEELBARROW
REFLECT
Ronsdale Press
ROSEBUD
THE SALEM JOURNAL
SALT LICK
Salt Lick Press
SCAVENGER'S NEWSLETTER
SCRIVENER
Second Coming Press
SENECA REVIEW
SEWANEE REVIEW
Shaolin Communications
SIDEWALKS
Signature Books
SKYLARK
SLEUTH JOURNAL
The Snail's Pace Press, Inc.
SONORA REVIEW
THE SOUNDS OF POETRY
THE SOUTHERN CALIFORNIA ANTHOLOGY
SOUTHERN INDIANA REVIEW
THE SOW'S EAR POETRY REVIEW
SPIN
THE SPITTING IMAGE
SPOON RIVER POETRY REVIEW
SPORT LITERATE, Honest Reflections on Life's Leisur-
ely Diversions
STAPLE
Starbooks Press/FLF Press
STOVEPIPE: A Journal of Little Literary Value
STUDIO - A Journal of Christians Writing
Suburban Wilderness Press
THE SUNDAY SUITOR POETRY REVIEW
TAMPA REVIEW
Telephone Books
Tesseract Publications
University Editions, Inc.
VERSE
THE VINCENT BROTHERS REVIEW
VOICES - ISRAEL
VOID
WATERWAYS: Poetry in the Mainstream
WESTERN SKIES
WHOLE NOTES
Whole Notes Press
Windsong Press
Woodburn Avenue Books
WRITER'S EXCHANGE
WRITERS' FORUM
Writers House Press
WRITING ULSTER

FRENCH

Copper Canyon Press
LOST GENERATION JOURNAL
MESECHABE: The Journal of Surre(gion)alism
THE NEW PRESS LITERARY QUARTERLY
OSIRIS
THE SOUNDS OF POETRY

FUTURIST

JACK MACKEREL MAGAZINE
KOJA
ON SPEC
RED OWL
Rowhouse Press
Savant Garde Workshop
Shadowlight Press

GAY

A & U AMERICA'S AIDS MAGAZINE
AMELIA
THE AMERICAN VOICE
ASSEMBLING
BAY WINDOWS
BLACK LACE
Black Sparrow Press
BOUILLABAISSE
Broken Jaw Press
Burning Bush Publications
CALYX: A Journal of Art and Literature by Women
Carolina Wren Press/Lollipop Power Books
CHIRON REVIEW
CICADA
City Lights Books
Copper Canyon Press
Cynic Press
DOWN UNDER MANHATTAN BRIDGE
THE EVERGREEN CHRONICLES
FAG RAG
Gay Sunshine Press, Inc.
GLB Publishers
Golden Isis Press
Good Gay Poets Press
HIP MAMA
KARAMU
Lakes & Prairies Press
Lintel
LUMMOX JOURNAL
MESECHABE: The Journal of Surre(gion)alism
MOCKINGBIRD
THE NEW PRESS LITERARY QUARTERLY
Now It's Up To You Publications
Painted Leaf Press
POETRY MOTEL
RFD
SPSM&H
Starbooks Press/FLF Press
Suburban Wilderness Press
THE WISHING WELL
WOMENWISE
WRITER'S EXCHANGE

GENERAL

ACORN WHISTLE
Adastra Press
Alternating Crimes Publishing
American Literary Press Inc./Noble House
ASSEMBLING
THE BELLINGHAM REVIEW
BkMk Press
BOULEVARD
Brunswick Publishing Corporation
THE CAROLINA QUARTERLY
Center Press
CONFRONTATION
Copper Canyon Press
CUMBERLAND POETRY REVIEW
John Daniel and Company, Publishers
FIELD: Contemporary Poetry and Poetics
Fithian Press
THE GALLEY SAIL REVIEW
Golden Isis Press
GREEN MOUNTAINS REVIEW
HAYDEN'S FERRY REVIEW
THE ICONOCLAST
ILLUMINATIONS
JEJUNE: america Eats its Young
THE KELSEY REVIEW
Kosmos
KRAX
Lakes & Prairies Press
LEAPINGS LITERARY MAGAZINE
Lorien House
LUZ EN ARTE Y LITERATURA
THE MADISON REVIEW

MANGROVE MAGAZINE
Mid-List Press
Minor Heron Press
MR. COGITO
Mortal Press
Oberlin College Press
OXYGEN
Path Press, Inc.
PINE ISLAND JOURNAL OF NEW ENGLAND
POETRY
POETRY AND AUDIENCE
POETRY MOTEL
THE PURPLE MONKEY
THE RAINTOWN REVIEW
RED ROCK REVIEW
SEWANEE REVIEW
SIDEWALKS
Signature Books
Signpost Press Inc.
SKYLARK
SLIPSTREAM
THE SOW'S EAR POETRY REVIEW
Suburban Wilderness Press
THE SUNDAY SUITOR POETRY REVIEW
THEMA
UNIVERSITY OF WINDSOR REVIEW
THE VINCENT BROTHERS REVIEW
VOICES - ISRAEL
Woodburn Avenue Books
WRITER'S EXCHANGE
WRITERS GAZETTE
Writers House Press

GEOGRAPHY

BORDERLANDS: Texas Poetry Review
EPOCH
EXIT 13 MAGAZINE
LUMMOX JOURNAL
NEW HOPE INTERNATIONAL REVIEW
POW-WOW

GEOLOGY

American Literary Press Inc./Noble House
BUTTON
EPOCH
FELL SWOOP

GERMAN

AUFBAU
Cynic Press
Intertext
THE NEW PRESS LITERARY QUARTERLY

GREAT BRITAIN

AABYE (formerly New Hope International Writing)
BOGG
GARGOYLE
KRAX
NEW HOPE INTERNATIONAL REVIEW
THE NEW PRESS LITERARY QUARTERLY
ORBIS
OTTER
POETRY NOTTINGHAM INTERNATIONAL
POETRY WALES
TAMPA REVIEW

GREAT LAKES

Jackson Harbor Press
SKYLARK

GREAT PLAINS

Coteau Books
Point Riders Press
POW-WOW
PRAIRIE FIRE
SKYLARK
TALKING RIVER REVIEW
Tesseract Publications

WESTERN SKIES

GREEK

Copper Canyon Press
THE NEW PRESS LITERARY QUARTERLY

GREEN

ASSEMBLING
BOTH SIDES NOW
THE FLORIDA REVIEW
LIMESTONE: A Literary Journal
SLIPSTREAM
THE VINCENT BROTHERS REVIEW

HAIKU

AABYE (formerly New Hope International Writing)
AMELIA
American Literary Press Inc./Noble House
ANT ANT ANT ANT ANT
ASSEMBLING
THE AUROREAN, A POETIC QUARTERLY
Baker Street Publications
BLADES
Brooks Books
BYLINE
CEDAR HILL REVIEW
CICADA
Confluence Press, Inc.
Cynic Press
DAYS AND NIGHTS OF A SMALL PRESS PUB-
LISHER
DEANOTATIONS
ENDING THE BEGIN
THE EVERGREEN CHRONICLES
FROGPOND: Quarterly Haiku Journal
From Here Press
THE GLASS CHERRY
The Glass Cherry Press
Golden Isis Press
Headveins Graphics
Hippopotamus Press
HOLLYWOOD NOSTALGIA
The Hosanna Press
ICON
INTERBANG
Jackson Harbor Press
JEWISH LIFE
KALEIDOSCOPE: International Magazine of Literature,
Fine Arts, and Disability
KARAMU
Kenyette Productions
LILLIPUT REVIEW
LIMESTONE: A Literary Journal
LUMMOX JOURNAL
LUZ EN ARTE Y LITERATURA
MAYFLY
META4: Journal of Object Oriented Poetics (OOPS)
MINESHAFT
MODERN HAIKU
NEW HOPE INTERNATIONAL REVIEW
THE NEW PRESS LITERARY QUARTERLY
NIGHTSHADE
NITE-WRITER'S INTERNATIONAL LITERARY
ARTS JOURNAL
OUTPOSTS POETRY QUARTERLY
OWEN WISTER REVIEW
PARNASSUS LITERARY JOURNAL
PEGASUS
PERIPHERAL VISION
PINE ISLAND JOURNAL OF NEW ENGLAND
POETRY
POETRY AND AUDIENCE
POETRY NOTTINGHAM INTERNATIONAL
POTPOURRI: A Magazine of the Literary Arts
POW-WOW
Press Here
REFLECT
The Runaway Spoon Press

THE SALEM JOURNAL
Shaolin Communications
SIDEWALKS
SILVER WINGS/MAYFLOWER PULPIT
SKYLARK
SOUTHERN INDIANA REVIEW
SPIN
STOVEPIPE: A Journal of Little Literary Value
STUDIO - A Journal of Christians Writing
THE SUNDAY SUITOR POETRY REVIEW
TAMPA REVIEW
Tesseract Publications
University Editions, Inc.
THE VINCENT BROTHERS REVIEW
VOID
THE VORTEX
WORDS OF WISDOM
WRITER'S EXCHANGE
XTRAS

HANDICAPPED

AABYE (formerly New Hope International Writing)
BRILLIANT STAR
Creative With Words Publications (CWW)
HURRICANE ALICE
KALEIDOSCOPE: International Magazine of Literature,
   Fine Arts, and Disability
MANY MOUNTAINS MOVING
NEW HOPE INTERNATIONAL REVIEW
THE NEW PRESS LITERARY QUARTERLY
The Place In The Woods
READ, AMERICA!
THE WISHING WELL

HAWAII

Ahsahta
BAMBOO RIDGE, Journal of Hawai'i Literature and Arts
Bamboo Ridge Press
HAWAII PACIFIC REVIEW
THE NEW PRESS LITERARY QUARTERLY

HISPANIC

AFRO-HISPANIC REVIEW
Ahsahta
Bilingual Review/Press
BILINGUAL REVIEW/Revista Bilingue
BRILLIANT STAR
Burning Bush Publications
CALYX: A Journal of Art and Literature by Women
Copper Canyon Press
EPOCH
HIP MAMA
HURRICANE ALICE
LOST AND FOUND TIMES
LUMMOX JOURNAL
Luna Bisonte Prods
LUZ EN ARTE Y LITERATURA
MESECHABE: The Journal of Surre(gion)alism
Minor Heron Press
THE NEW PRESS LITERARY QUARTERLY
THE NORTH AMERICAN REVIEW
Painted Leaf Press
The Place In The Woods
READ, AMERICA!
Serena Bay Books
The Snail's Pace Press, Inc.
SONORA REVIEW
TAMPA REVIEW
West End Press
WRITERS' FORUM
XAVIER REVIEW

HISTORY

THE ACORN
The Ashland Poetry Press
THE BAREFOOT POET: Journal of Poetry, Fiction,
   Essays, & Art
BIBLIOPHILOS

Blue Unicorn Press, Inc.
THE BOOMERPHILE
THE CHARIOTEER
Coteau Books
Cynic Press
Erespin Press
Galaxy Press
THE GALLEY SAIL REVIEW
Golden Isis Press
High Plains Press
JEWISH LIFE
LEAPINGS LITERARY MAGAZINE
LOST GENERATION JOURNAL
NEW HOPE INTERNATIONAL REVIEW
THE NEW PRESS LITERARY QUARTERLY
OXYGEN
Pella Publishing Co
The Place In The Woods
Pocahontas Press, Inc.
POETRY AND AUDIENCE
POW-WOW
READ, AMERICA!
THE SOUTHERN REVIEW
THE VINCENT BROTHERS REVIEW
THE VORTEX
WESTERN SKIES
Writers House Press

HORROR

American Literary Press Inc./Noble House
Anamnesis Press
Arjuna Library Press
Baker Street Publications
Cynic Press
DARK REGIONS: The Years Best Fantastic Fiction
DREAMS AND NIGHTMARES
ECLIPSE
FELL SWOOP
THE HAUNTED JOURNAL
MIXED BAG
NIGHTSHADE
THE NOCTURNAL LYRIC
NOVA EXPRESS
ON SPEC
Pendragonian Publications
PENNY DREADFUL: Tales and Poems of Fantastic
   Terror
RALPH'S REVIEW
REALM OF DARKNESS
REALM OF THE VAMPIRE
THE ROMANTIST
THE SALEM JOURNAL
Shadowlight Press
SPACE AND TIME
WICKED MYSTIC

HUMAN RIGHTS

AMERICAN JONES BUILDING & MAINTENANCE
ART:MAG
Baker Street Publications
Copper Canyon Press
Coteau Books
DAUGHTERS OF SARAH
HIP MAMA
Implosion Press
JEWISH LIFE
MANY MOUNTAINS MOVING
MESECHABE: The Journal of Surre(gion)alism
Missing Spoke Press
MR. COGITO
OXYGEN
The Place In The Woods
POETRY MOTEL
POW-WOW
READ, AMERICA!
Suburban Wilderness Press
THIS IS IMPORTANT
THE UNDERGROUND

VOICES - ISRAEL
WRITER'S EXCHANGE
Writers House Press

HUMANIST

American Literary Press Inc./Noble House
The Ashland Poetry Press
ASSEMBLING
AURA LITERARY/ARTS REVIEW
Baker Street Publications
Bottom Dog Press
Center Press
Confluence Press, Inc.
CRAB CREEK REVIEW
Cynic Press
DAYS AND NIGHTS OF A SMALL PRESS PUB-
LISHER
DOWN UNDER MANHATTAN BRIDGE
Erespin Press
GREAT RIVER REVIEW
KICK IT OVER
Lakes & Prairies Press
LEAPINGS LITERARY MAGAZINE
Lintel
LUCIDITY
Mortal Press
NEDGE
THE NEW RENAISSANCE, An International Magazine
of Ideas & Opinions, Emphasizing Literature & The
Arts
POETRY AND AUDIENCE
POETRY NOTTINGHAM INTERNATIONAL
Pudding House Publications
PUDDING MAGAZINE: The International Journal of
Applied Poetry
RADIANCE, The Magazine For Large Women
Savant Garde Workshop
SCAVENGER'S NEWSLETTER
THE SOUTHERN REVIEW
STAPLE
STUDIO - A Journal of Christians Writing
TOUCHSTONE LITERARY JOURNAL
University Editions, Inc.
VISIONS-INTERNATIONAL, The World Journal of
Illustrated Poetry
THE WISHING WELL
WRITER'S EXCHANGE

HUMOR

A & U AMERICA'S AIDS MAGAZINE
AABYE (formerly New Hope International Writing)
Acre Press
AMELIA
American Literary Press Inc./Noble House
The Ashland Poetry Press
THE AUROREAN, A POETIC QUARTERLY
Baker Street Publications
BELOIT POETRY JOURNAL
BLADES
BOGG
THE BOOMERPHILE
Center Press
CHIRON REVIEW
CICADA
THE CLASSICAL OUTLOOK
THE COMSTOCK REVIEW
Coteau Books
Creative With Words Publications (CWW)
THE CREATIVE WOMAN
Cynic Press
DAUGHTERS OF SARAH
DEANOTATIONS
THE EVERGREEN CHRONICLES
FINE MADNESS
Greenhouse Review Press
THE HAUNTED JOURNAL
HOLLYWOOD NOSTALGIA
THE ICONOCLAST

IDIOT WIND
INTERBANG
IRON HORSE LITERARY REVIEW
THE J MAN TIMES
JACK MACKEREL MAGAZINE
JACK THE RIPPER GAZETTE
JEWISH LIFE
KID'S WORLD
KRAX
LADYBUG, the Magazine for Young Children
THE LAUREL REVIEW
LIGHTHOUSE STORY COLLECTIONS
THE MASONIA ROUNDUP
Mortal Press
Moving Parts Press
NANNY FANNY
NEW HOPE INTERNATIONAL REVIEW
THE NEW PRESS LITERARY QUARTERLY
NIGHTSHADE
ORBIS
OZ-STORY
PARNASSUS LITERARY JOURNAL
PASSAGER: A Journal of Remembrance and Discovery
PEGASUS
The Place In The Woods
POETRY MOTEL
RALPH'S REVIEW
Raw Dog Press
READ, AMERICA!
RED OWL
Rowhouse Press
SCAVENGER'S NEWSLETTER
Second Coming Press
Signature Books
SILHOUETTE MAGAZINE
SKYLARK
SPSM&H
STOVEPIPE: A Journal of Little Literary Value
Suburban Wilderness Press
TAMPA REVIEW
Tesseract Publications
THOUGHTS FOR ALL SEASONS: The Magazine of
Epigrams
TUCUMCARI LITERARY REVIEW
THE VINCENT BROTHERS REVIEW
VOICES - ISRAEL
Woodburn Avenue Books
WRITER'S EXCHANGE

HUNGER

Baker Street Publications
CORNERSTONE
St. Andrew Press

IDAHO

COLD-DRILL
TALKING RIVER REVIEW
WESTERN SKIES

ILLINOIS

THE GALLEY SAIL REVIEW
KARAMU
SPOON RIVER POETRY REVIEW

ILLUSTRATED

American Literary Press Inc./Noble House
CONTEXT SOUTH
DOWN UNDER MANHATTAN BRIDGE
HIP MAMA
KRAX
Mortal Press
NEW HOPE INTERNATIONAL REVIEW
THE NEW PRESS LITERARY QUARTERLY
NITE-WRITER'S INTERNATIONAL LITERARY
ARTS JOURNAL
Shaolin Communications
TAPROOT LITERARY REVIEW
VOID

IMAGIST

A & U AMERICA'S AIDS MAGAZINE
AABYE (formerly New Hope International Writing)
Aegina Press, Inc.
AMELIA
Arjuna Library Press
Art/Life Limited Editions
ASSEMBLING
AXE FACTORY REVIEW
Baker Street Publications
Bard Press
BATHTUB GIN
BELLOWING ARK
Black Buzzard Press
Black Sparrow Press
Bloody Someday Press
Burning Llama Press
Center Press
CHARITON REVIEW
CICADA
Cleveland State Univ. Poetry Center
THE COMSTOCK REVIEW
CRAB CREEK REVIEW
Creative With Words Publications (CWW)
Cynic Press
DAYS AND NIGHTS OF A SMALL PRESS PUB-
LISHER
DOWN UNDER MANHATTAN BRIDGE
En Passant Poetry Press
EN PASSANT/POETRY
THE FLORIDA REVIEW
GARGOYLE
THE GLASS CHERRY
The Glass Cherry Press
THE HAUNTED JOURNAL
The Hosanna Press
THE IMPLODING TIE-DYED TOUPEE
Interim Press
THE J MAN TIMES
JEWISH LIFE
KARAMU
KARAWANE
Lakes & Prairies Press
THE LICKING RIVER REVIEW
THE MAC GUFFIN
MESECHABE: The Journal of Surre(gion)alism
META4: Journal of Object Oriented Poetics (OOPS)
Mortal Press
NEOLOGISMS
NEW HOPE INTERNATIONAL REVIEW
NIGHTSHADE
nine muses books
OUTPOSTS POETRY QUARTERLY
PERIPHERAL VISION
POETRY MOTEL
POETRY NOTTINGHAM INTERNATIONAL
REALM OF THE VAMPIRE
Red Dragon Press
ROSEBUD
SALT LICK
Salt Lick Press
SCAVENGER'S NEWSLETTER
SCRIVENER
Shadowlight Press
SKYLARK
THE SOUTHERN REVIEW
SPOUT
SPSM&H
Suburban Wilderness Press
THE SUNDAY SUITOR POETRY REVIEW
TAMPA REVIEW
Unfinished Monument Press
University Editions, Inc.
VERSE
THE VINCENT BROTHERS REVIEW
VOID
WATERWAYS: Poetry in the Mainstream
Wineberry Press
WRITERS' FORUM

INDIA

THE NEW PRESS LITERARY QUARTERLY
Passeggiata Press, Inc.

INSPIRATIONAL

A & U AMERICA'S AIDS MAGAZINE
American Literary Press Inc./Noble House
Amethyst & Emerald
THE AUROREAN, A POETIC QUARTERLY
Buddhist Text Translation Society
THE GALLEY SAIL REVIEW
ISSUES
LEAPINGS LITERARY MAGAZINE
LIGHTHOUSE STORY COLLECTIONS
Mortal Press
THE NEW PRESS LITERARY QUARTERLY
OBLATES
PARNASSUS LITERARY JOURNAL
POET'S FANTASY
POET'S PARK
RADIANCE, The Magazine For Large Women
SILHOUETTE MAGAZINE
SILVER WINGS/MAYFLOWER PULPIT
STUDENT LEADERSHIP JOURNAL
STUDIO - A Journal of Christians Writing
THE SUNDAY SUITOR POETRY REVIEW
Tesseract Publications
Vista Publishing, Inc.
WEYFARERS
WRITER'S EXCHANGE

INTERNATIONAL

American Literary Press Inc./Noble House
THE BAREFOOT POET: Journal of Poetry, Fiction,
Essays, & Art
Black Tie Press
Bloody Someday Press
THE BOOMERPHILE
BRILLIANT STAR
Brunswick Publishing Corporation
CONFLUENCE
THE COOL TRAVELER
Manya DeLeon Booksmith
THE FLORIDA REVIEW
From Here Press
HAWAII PACIFIC REVIEW
HIP MAMA
HOME PLANET NEWS
ILLUMINATIONS
IRIS: A Journal About Women
KALEIDOSCOPE: International Magazine of Literature,
Fine Arts, and Disability
LEFT CURVE
LUZ EN ARTE Y LITERATURA
MR. COGITO
NEW HOPE INTERNATIONAL REVIEW
THE NEW PRESS LITERARY QUARTERLY
ORBIS
OWEN WISTER REVIEW
PEGASUS
PERIPHERAL VISION
PRISM INTERNATIONAL
SEWANEE REVIEW
Shaolin Communications
The Snail's Pace Press, Inc.
STRUGGLE: A Magazine of Proletarian Revolutionary
Literature
TAMPA REVIEW
TAPROOT LITERARY REVIEW
THE VINCENT BROTHERS REVIEW
VOICES - ISRAEL
Writers House Press
XTRAS
Years Press

IRELAND/IRISH

Baker Street Publications
EXIT 13 MAGAZINE
GARGOYLE
Helikon Press
IRISH JOURNAL
THE NEW PRESS LITERARY QUARTERLY
THE ROMANTIST
SENECA REVIEW
THE SOUTHERN REVIEW
WRITING ULSTER

ISLAMIC

THE NEW PRESS LITERARY QUARTERLY

ITALIAN

THE COOL TRAVELER
HIP MAMA
ITALIAN AMERICANA
LUZ EN ARTE Y LITERATURA
THE NEW PRESS LITERARY QUARTERLY

JAPAN

AMERICAN TANKA
AXE FACTORY REVIEW
Center for Japanese Studies
Copper Canyon Press
Cynic Press
FISH DRUM MAGAZINE
Gay Sunshine Press, Inc.
Katydid Books
THE NEW PRESS LITERARY QUARTERLY
Press Here

JEWISH

AGADA
APKL Publications
AUFBAU
Baker Street Publications
BkMk Press
BRIDGES: A Journal for Jewish Feminists and Our
    Friends
Burning Bush Publications
Center Press
Copper Canyon Press
EUROPEAN JUDAISM
Galaxy Press
HIP MAMA
HURRICANE ALICE
ISRAEL HORIZONS
ISSUES
JEWISH CURRENTS
JEWISH LIFE
KEREM: Creative Explorations in Judaism
MANY MOUNTAINS MOVING
MIXED BAG
THE NEW PRESS LITERARY QUARTERLY
OXYGEN
VOICES - ISRAEL
Washington Writers' Publishing House

JUNGIAN

Arjuna Library Press
Cynic Press
Lockhart Press, Inc.
LUMMOX JOURNAL
THE NEW PRESS LITERARY QUARTERLY
NEWSLETTER INAGO
PENNINE PLATFORM
Red Dragon Press
Savant Garde Workshop
SOUTH DAKOTA REVIEW
Story Line Press
STUDIO - A Journal of Christians Writing
WRITERS' FORUM

LABOR

AMERICAN JONES BUILDING & MAINTENANCE
Missing Spoke Press
OXYGEN
Ridgeway Press of Michigan
STRUGGLE: A Magazine of Proletarian Revolutionary
    Literature
TALKING RIVER REVIEW
University of Massachusetts Press

LAISSEZ-FAIRE

AMERICAN JONES BUILDING & MAINTENANCE
BUTTON
Missing Spoke Press
PASSAGER: A Journal of Remembrance and Discovery

LANGUAGE

AABYE (formerly New Hope International Writing)
ABRAXAS
AMELIA
Art/Life Limited Editions
Bard Press
Burning Deck Press
THE CAROLINA QUARTERLY
CHIRON REVIEW
THE CLASSICAL OUTLOOK
CONDUIT
CONTEXT SOUTH
CRAB CREEK REVIEW
THE CREAM CITY REVIEW
Creative With Words Publications (CWW)
DIRIGIBLE
THE EVERGREEN CHRONICLES
FOLIO: A Literary Journal of American University
Galaxy Press
Ghost Pony Press
H2SO4
INDIANA REVIEW
JOURNAL OF REGIONAL CRITICISM
KALDRON, An International Journal Of Visual Poetry
THE MAC GUFFIN
MESECHABE: The Journal of Surre(gion)alism
META4: Journal of Object Oriented Poetics (OOPS)
NEW AMERICAN WRITING
NEW HOPE INTERNATIONAL REVIEW
THE NEW PRESS LITERARY QUARTERLY
nine muses books
OSIRIS
Passeggiata Press, Inc.
POETRY NOTTINGHAM INTERNATIONAL
Potes & Poets Press Inc.
Reality Street Editions
Savant Garde Workshop
SCORE
SCRIVENER
THE SPITTING IMAGE
THIS IS IMPORTANT
THE VINCENT BROTHERS REVIEW
WEST COAST LINE: A Journal of Contemporary
    Writing and Criticism

LESBIAN

ASSEMBLING
BAY WINDOWS
BRIDGES: A Journal for Jewish Feminists and Our
    Friends
Broken Jaw Press
Burning Bush Publications
Carolina Wren Press/Lollipop Power Books
Chicory Blue Press, Inc.
COMMON LIVES / LESBIAN LIVES
Copper Canyon Press
Coteau Books
DAUGHTERS OF SARAH
THE EVERGREEN CHRONICLES
FRONTIERS: A Journal of Women Studies
GLB Publishers

Golden Isis Press
HIP MAMA
HURRICANE ALICE
IRIS: A Journal About Women
KARAMU
Lakes & Prairies Press
MESECHABE: The Journal of Surre(gion)alism
Outrider Press
Painted Leaf Press
RED OWL
Relief Press
SINISTER WISDOM
SOJOURNER, THE WOMEN'S FORUM
Starbooks Press/FLF Press
WOMENWISE

LIBRARIES

JEWISH LIFE
The Place In The Woods
READ, AMERICA!

LIGHT VERSE

A & U AMERICA'S AIDS MAGAZINE
AMELIA
American Literary Press Inc./Noble House
Appalachian Consortium Press
BAKER STREET GAZETTE
Bay Area Poets Coalition
THE BOOMERPHILE
BRILLIANT STAR
BYLINE
THE CAROLINA QUARTERLY
THE CLASSICAL OUTLOOK
Creative With Words Publications (CWW)
Cynic Press
DAYS AND NIGHTS OF A SMALL PRESS PUB-
    LISHER
DEANOTATIONS
ENTELECHY MAGAZINE
THE GALLEY SAIL REVIEW
Golden Isis Press
THE HAUNTED JOURNAL
HOLLYWOOD NOSTALGIA
HORIZONS BEYOND
IRISH JOURNAL
JACK THE RIPPER GAZETTE
Jackson Harbor Press
JEWISH LIFE
KRAX
THE LAUREL REVIEW
LIGHTHOUSE STORY COLLECTIONS
LOST GENERATION JOURNAL
MIXED BAG
MOOSE BOUND PRESS JOURNAL/NEWSLETTER
Mortal Press
NANNY FANNY
NEW HOPE INTERNATIONAL REVIEW
THE NEW PRESS LITERARY QUARTERLY
NIGHTSHADE
NITE-WRITER'S   INTERNATIONAL   LITERARY
    ARTS JOURNAL
ORBIS
PARNASSUS LITERARY JOURNAL
PEN & INK WRITERS JOURNAL
The Place In The Woods
POETALK
POETRY AND AUDIENCE
POET'S FANTASY
POTPOURRI: A Magazine of the Literary Arts
POW-WOW
READ, AMERICA!
REALM OF DARKNESS
ROSEBUD
THE SALEM JOURNAL
SKYLARK
SLEUTH JOURNAL
STUDIO - A Journal of Christians Writing
THE SUNDAY SUITOR POETRY REVIEW

TAMPA REVIEW
Tesseract Publications
TEXAS YOUNG WRITERS' NEWSLETTER
THE VINCENT BROTHERS REVIEW
VOICES - ISRAEL
WORDS OF WISDOM

LIMERICKS

AMELIA
BRILLIANT STAR
Cynic Press
DEANOTATIONS
MOOSE BOUND PRESS JOURNAL/NEWSLETTER
THE NEW PRESS LITERARY QUARTERLY
TUCUMCARI LITERARY REVIEW
THE VINCENT BROTHERS REVIEW
VOICES - ISRAEL
WORDS OF WISDOM

LOGIC

LIMESTONE: A Literary Journal
Savant Garde Workshop

LONG POEMS

A & U AMERICA'S AIDS MAGAZINE
AABYE (formerly New Hope International Writing)
ABRAXAS
Adastra Press
Aegina Press, Inc.
AGNI
Ahsahta
American Literary Press Inc./Noble House
Arjuna Library Press
BAKER STREET GAZETTE
Baker Street Publications
Bard Press
BELLOWING ARK
BELOIT POETRY JOURNAL
BkMk Press
Black Tie Press
Bloody Someday Press
Bottom Dog Press
Brunswick Publishing Corporation
THE CAROLINA QUARTERLY
CHARITON REVIEW
CONDUIT
Copper Canyon Press
Coteau Books
Cynic Press
DAYS AND NIGHTS OF A SMALL PRESS PUB-
    LISHER
DEANOTATIONS
Depth Charge
DOWN UNDER MANHATTAN BRIDGE
EPOCH
FINE MADNESS
FIVE POINTS
THE FLORIDA REVIEW
Ghost Pony Press
GLB Publishers
GLOBAL TAPESTRY
THE GREAT IDEA PATCH
GREEN MOUNTAINS REVIEW
Greenhouse Review Press
HARP-STRINGS
THE HAUNTED JOURNAL
Hippopotamus Press
HOLLYWOOD NOSTALGIA
HORIZONS BEYOND
Interim Press
ISRAEL HORIZONS
JACK MACKEREL MAGAZINE
JACK THE RIPPER GAZETTE
Jackson Harbor Press
JEWISH LIFE
THE JOURNAL
Katydid Books
Lakes & Prairies Press

THE LAUREL REVIEW
Lintel
THE LITERARY REVIEW
Lockhart Press, Inc.
Longleaf Press
LUZ EN ARTE Y LITERATURA
THE MAC GUFFIN
THE MADISON REVIEW
MANY MOUNTAINS MOVING
Milkweed Editions
MINESHAFT
MIXED BAG
Mortal Press
NEDGE
NEW ENGLAND REVIEW
NEW HOPE INTERNATIONAL REVIEW
THE NEW PRESS LITERARY QUARTERLY
THE NEW RENAISSANCE, An International Magazine
of Ideas & Opinions, Emphasizing Literature & The
Arts
NIGHTSHADE
OSIRIS
OUTPOSTS POETRY QUARTERLY
PARNASSUS: Poetry in Review
THE PATRIOT
PERIPHERAL VISION
THE POETRY MISCELLANY
POET'S FANTASY
POW-WOW
PRAIRIE FIRE
THE PRAIRIE JOURNAL OF CANADIAN LITERA-
TURE
Prairie Journal Press
THE RAINTOWN REVIEW
Reality Street Editions
REALM OF DARKNESS
REALM OF THE VAMPIRE
Ronsdale Press
Rowhouse Press
Runaway Publications
THE SALEM JOURNAL
SALT LICK
Salt Lick Press
Savant Garde Workshop
SCRIVENER
SLEUTH JOURNAL
SLIPSTREAM
THE SOUTHERN CALIFORNIA ANTHOLOGY
SOUTHERN INDIANA REVIEW
Starbooks Press/FLF Press
Story Line Press
TALKING RIVER REVIEW
TAMPA REVIEW
Underwhich Editions
Unfinished Monument Press
Vehicule Press
WEST COAST LINE: A Journal of Contemporary
Writing and Criticism
WESTERN SKIES
WHOLE NOTES
Whole Notes Press
Wind's Errand
WRITERS' FORUM
Writers House Press
WRITING ULSTER

LORE

THE ACORN
Creative With Words Publications (CWW)
THE HAUNTED JOURNAL
IRISH JOURNAL
JEWISH LIFE
NEW HOPE INTERNATIONAL REVIEW
NIGHTSHADE
POW-WOW
RALPH'S REVIEW
THE SALEM JOURNAL
Starbooks Press/FLF Press

THE VINCENT BROTHERS REVIEW
WESTERN SKIES

LYRIC

AABYE (formerly New Hope International Writing)
ABRAXAS
ACORN WHISTLE
Adastra Press
AGADA
Ahsahta
AMELIA
AMERICAN LETTERS & COMMENTARY
American Literary Press Inc./Noble House
Arctos Press
The Ark
The Ashland Poetry Press
BELLOWING ARK
BELOIT POETRY JOURNAL
BkMk Press
Black Buzzard Press
Black Tie Press
BLUELINE
BRAVO, THE POET'S MAGAZINE
BYLINE
CHARITON REVIEW
THE CLASSICAL OUTLOOK
THE COMSTOCK REVIEW
CONTEXT SOUTH
Copper Beech Press
John Edwin Cowen/Bravo Editions
CRAB CREEK REVIEW
THE CREAM CITY REVIEW
THE CREATIVE WOMAN
Cynic Press
DEANOTATIONS
THE EVERGREEN CHRONICLES
FINE MADNESS
Ghost Pony Press
GREAT RIVER REVIEW
HARP-STRINGS
Hippopotamus Press
Huntsville Literary Association
INDIANA REVIEW
INTERBANG
Interim Press
KARAMU
Lakes & Prairies Press
LEAPINGS LITERARY MAGAZINE
Left Hand Books
THE LICKING RIVER REVIEW
Lintel
LOST GENERATION JOURNAL
Lotus Press, Inc.
LUZ EN ARTE Y LITERATURA
Milkweed Editions
Mortal Press
NEW ENGLAND REVIEW
THE NEW PRESS LITERARY QUARTERLY
THE NEW RENAISSANCE, An International Magazine
of Ideas & Opinions, Emphasizing Literature & The
Arts
nine muses books
OSIRIS
OUTPOSTS POETRY QUARTERLY
PARNASSUS: Poetry in Review
THE PATRIOT
Pendragonian Publications
PENNINE PLATFORM
PENNY DREADFUL: Tales and Poems of Fantastic
Terror
POEM
POETRY AND AUDIENCE
POETRY NOTTINGHAM INTERNATIONAL
POTPOURRI: A Magazine of the Literary Arts
Prairie Journal Press
RED WHEELBARROW
Runaway Publications
SENECA REVIEW

SEWANEE REVIEW
Shaolin Communications
SKYLARK
The Snail's Pace Press, Inc.
SONGS OF INNOCENCE
THE SOW'S EAR POETRY REVIEW
Story Line Press
STUDIO - A Journal of Christians Writing
TAMPA REVIEW
Telephone Books
Tesseract Publications
University of Massachusetts Press
Vehicle Press
VERSE
THE VINCENT BROTHERS REVIEW
VISIONS-INTERNATIONAL, The World Journal of
   Illustrated Poetry
WESTERN HUMANITIES REVIEW
WOMAN POET
Women-in-Literature, Inc.
WRITER'S EXCHANGE
WRITERS' FORUM

MARTIAL ARTS

Cynic Press
FELL SWOOP
JOURNAL OF REGIONAL CRITICISM

MATHEMATICS

LIMESTONE: A Literary Journal
Savant Garde Workshop

MEN

AC
Alternating Crimes Publishing
American Literary Press Inc./Noble House
BLOOD & FEATHERS: Poems of Survival
Coteau Books
Cynic Press
THE EVERGREEN CHRONICLES
GLB Publishers
Moving Parts Press
RFD
Ronsdale Press
Yellow Moon Press

METAPHYSICAL

American Literary Press Inc./Noble House
Amethyst & Emerald
Bloody Someday Press
Blue Unicorn Press, Inc.
BOTH SIDES NOW
Galaxy Press
THE GALLEY SAIL REVIEW
HEAVEN BONE MAGAZINE
THE ICONOCLAST
JEWISH LIFE
LUZ EN ARTE Y LITERATURA
META4: Journal of Object Oriented Poetics (OOPS)
NEW HOPE INTERNATIONAL REVIEW
Pendragonian Publications
THE SALEM JOURNAL
SONGS OF INNOCENCE
THE SOUTHERN REVIEW
STAPLE
THE VINCENT BROTHERS REVIEW
VOID
WRITER'S EXCHANGE

MIDWEST

Art/Life Limited Editions
BIBLIOPHILOS
BkMk Press
GREAT RIVER REVIEW
KARAMU
Kenyette Productions
Lakes & Prairies Press
THE LAUREL REVIEW

THE LICKING RIVER REVIEW
Outrider Press
POETRY MOTEL
POW-WOW
SKYLARK
SOUTHERN INDIANA REVIEW
Suburban Wilderness Press
Tesseract Publications
THE VINCENT BROTHERS REVIEW
WESTERN SKIES

MILITARY

FULLOSIA PRESS

MOTORCYCLES

GLB Publishers
OUT YOUR BACKDOOR: The Magazine of Informal
   Adventure and Cheap Culture

MONOGRAPHS

Brunswick Publishing Corporation
Intertext
STAPLE

MOVIES

Art/Life Limited Editions
BAKER STREET GAZETTE
Baker Street Publications
Galaxy Press
HOLLYWOOD NOSTALGIA
HURRICANE ALICE
JACK THE RIPPER GAZETTE
JEWISH LIFE
NIGHTSHADE
REALM OF THE VAMPIRE
THE SALEM JOURNAL
SLEUTH JOURNAL
Starbooks Press/FLF Press
THE VINCENT BROTHERS REVIEW

MUSIC

AABYE (formerly New Hope International Writing)
Art/Life Limited Editions
Burning Books
Celestial Otter Press
CHRONICLES OF DISORDER
DANDELION ARTS MAGAZINE
DOWN UNDER MANHATTAN BRIDGE
Drum
Galaxy Press
LUMMOX JOURNAL
MAGIC CHANGES
NEW HOPE INTERNATIONAL REVIEW
Piano Press
POETRY NOTTINGHAM INTERNATIONAL
REFLECT
Shaolin Communications
Starbooks Press/FLF Press
Underwhich Editions
Woodburn Avenue Books

MYSTERY

BAKER STREET GAZETTE
Baker Street Publications
Celestial Otter Press
THE GREAT IDEA PATCH
JACK THE RIPPER GAZETTE
KID'S WORLD
MAGIC CHANGES
MYSTERY TIME ANTHOLOGY
SLEUTH JOURNAL

MYSTICAL

Baker Street Publications
Black Tie Press
Blue Unicorn Press, Inc.
Center Press
Cynic Press

THE EVERGREEN CHRONICLES
THE GALLEY SAIL REVIEW
GINOSKO
THE HAUNTED JOURNAL
HEAVEN BONE MAGAZINE
IRISH JOURNAL
JACK MACKEREL MAGAZINE
JEWISH LIFE
JOURNAL OF REGIONAL CRITICISM
LUMMOX JOURNAL
LUZ EN ARTE Y LITERATURA
META4: Journal of Object Oriented Poetics (OOPS)
MIXED BAG
Mortal Press
PLAIN BROWN WRAPPER (PBW)
POETRY AND AUDIENCE
POET'S FANTASY
POW-WOW
REALM OF DARKNESS
Red Dragon Press
RED OWL
Rowhouse Press
THE SALEM JOURNAL
SILHOUETTE MAGAZINE
Taurean Horn Press
THE VINCENT BROTHERS REVIEW
VOID

NARRATIVE

A & U AMERICA'S AIDS MAGAZINE
ACORN WHISTLE
AGADA
American Literary Press Inc./Noble House
Appalachian Consortium Press
Arctos Press
The Ark
Baker Street Publications
THE BAREFOOT POET: Journal of Poetry, Fiction,
    Essays, & Art
Black Tie Press
Bottom Dog Press
BYLINE
CEDAR HILL REVIEW
Center Press
THE COMSTOCK REVIEW
CONDUIT
THE CREAM CITY REVIEW
DAYS AND NIGHTS OF A SMALL PRESS PUB-
    LISHER
DOWN UNDER MANHATTAN BRIDGE
En Passant Poetry Press
EN PASSANT/POETRY
EPOCH
THE EVERGREEN CHRONICLES
THE FLORIDA REVIEW
FOLIO: A Literary Journal of American University
Galaxy Press
THE GALLEY SAIL REVIEW
THE GLASS CHERRY
The Glass Cherry Press
HARP-STRINGS
The Hosanna Press
JEWISH LIFE
THE JOURNAL
Lakes & Prairies Press
THE LAUREL REVIEW
THE LICKING RIVER REVIEW
Lintel
THE LITERARY REVIEW
LOST GENERATION JOURNAL
MANGROVE MAGAZINE
MANKATO POETRY REVIEW
MOOSE BOUND PRESS JOURNAL/NEWSLETTER
Mortal Press
NEW ENGLAND REVIEW
THE NEW PRESS LITERARY QUARTERLY
THE NEW RENAISSANCE, An International Magazine
    of Ideas & Opinions, Emphasizing Literature & The

Arts
NEWSLETTER INAGO
PASSAGER: A Journal of Remembrance and Discovery
Pocahontas Press, Inc.
POET LORE
POETRY MOTEL
POW-WOW
RED WHEELBARROW
Ronsdale Press
ROSEBUD
THE SALEM JOURNAL
SCRIVENER
SIDEWALKS
SKYLARK
The Snail's Pace Press, Inc.
SONORA REVIEW
THE SOUTHERN REVIEW
SPACE AND TIME
Story Line Press
Suburban Wilderness Press
TALKING RIVER REVIEW
Tesseract Publications
VERSE
THE VINCENT BROTHERS REVIEW
VOLITION
WESTERN SKIES
WHOLE NOTES
Whole Notes Press
Wind's Errand
Wineberry Press
WOMAN POET
Women-in-Literature, Inc.
WRITERS' FORUM
Writers House Press
ZUZU'S PETALS: QUARTERLY ONLINE

NATIVE AMERICAN

ABRAXAS
Ahsahta
THE AMERICAN VOICE
THE AMICUS JOURNAL
Baker Street Publications
Black Bear Publications
BLACK BEAR REVIEW
BRILLIANT STAR
Broken Jaw Press
Burning Bush Publications
CALYX: A Journal of Art and Literature by Women
Carolina Wren Press/Lollipop Power Books
CHARITON REVIEW
Coteau Books
Creative With Words Publications (CWW)
CURARE
Cynic Press
EPOCH
THE GALLEY SAIL REVIEW
Ghost Pony Press
THE GLASS CHERRY
The Glass Cherry Press
Holy Cow! Press
HURRICANE ALICE
IRON HORSE LITERARY REVIEW
KARAMU
LUMMOX JOURNAL
MANY MOUNTAINS MOVING
MESECHABE: The Journal of Surre(gion)alism
Minor Heron Press
MOOSE BOUND PRESS JOURNAL/NEWSLETTER
NEDGE
THE NEW PRESS LITERARY QUARTERLY
THE NORTH AMERICAN REVIEW
Passeggiata Press, Inc.
The Place In The Woods
Pocahontas Press, Inc.
Point Riders Press
POW-WOW
READ, AMERICA!
RED OWL

RFD
THE SALEM JOURNAL
Shaolin Communications
SKYLARK
The Snail's Pace Press, Inc.
SOUTHWEST JOURNAL
TALKING RIVER REVIEW
Taurean Horn Press
THE VINCENT BROTHERS REVIEW
West End Press
WESTERN SKIES
THE WISHING WELL
WRITERS' FORUM
Yellow Moon Press

NATURE

AABYE (formerly New Hope International Writing)
THE ACORN
ACORN WHISTLE
Adastra Press
Ahsahta
American Literary Press Inc./Noble House
THE AMICUS JOURNAL
Arctos Press
Baker Street Publications
BLUELINE
BORDERLANDS: Texas Poetry Review
Celestial Otter Press
CONFLUENCE
Confluence Press, Inc.
Coteau Books
Cynic Press
GaiaQuest
THE GLASS CHERRY
The Glass Cherry Press
GREEN WORLD: News and Views For Gardening Who
  Care About The Earth
HARP-STRINGS
THE HAUNTED JOURNAL
Hug The Earth Publications
KARAMU
Konocti Books
LEAPINGS LITERARY MAGAZINE
LIGHTHOUSE STORY COLLECTIONS
THE LITERARY REVIEW
LUMMOX JOURNAL
MAGIC CHANGES
MANKATO POETRY REVIEW
Milkweed Editions
MOOSE BOUND PRESS JOURNAL/NEWSLETTER
Outrider Press
Pocahontas Press, Inc.
POW-WOW
Press Here
THE RATIONAL FEMINIST
RED OWL
RFD
ROOM
THE SALEM JOURNAL
SILVER WINGS/MAYFLOWER PULPIT
Gibbs Smith, Publisher
SNOWY EGRET
SOUTHWEST JOURNAL
THE SUNDAY SUITOR POETRY REVIEW
THE UNKNOWN WRITER
THE VINCENT BROTHERS REVIEW
WESTERN SKIES
WHOLE NOTES
Whole Notes Press
Wineberry Press
THE WISHING WELL
WRITER'S EXCHANGE

NEW AGE

American Literary Press Inc./Noble House
Blue Unicorn Press, Inc.
BOTH SIDES NOW
Celestial Otter Press

THE CREATIVE WOMAN
Cynic Press
FOLIO: A Literary Journal of American University
THE GLASS CHERRY
The Glass Cherry Press
Golden Isis Press
HEAVEN BONE MAGAZINE
KALDRON, An International Journal Of Visual Poetry
LUZ EN ARTE Y LITERATURA
MAGIC CHANGES
META4: Journal of Object Oriented Poetics (OOPS)
NIGHTSHADE
The Place In The Woods
POETRY MOTEL
READ, AMERICA!
SILHOUETTE MAGAZINE
SLIPSTREAM
Suburban Wilderness Press
VOID
XIB
Xib Publications

NEW ENGLAND

THE AUROREAN, A POETIC QUARTERLY
BIBLIOPHILOS
GaiaQuest
NEDGE
PINE ISLAND JOURNAL OF NEW ENGLAND
  POETRY
VOID
Zoland Books

NEW YORK SCHOOL

AXE FACTORY REVIEW
Baker Street Publications
Cynic Press
FELL SWOOP
NEDGE
NEW AMERICAN WRITING
THE NEW PRESS LITERARY QUARTERLY
The Poetry Project
SLIPSTREAM
THE WORLD

OBJECTIVIST/PROJECTIVIST

ASSEMBLING
Black Sparrow Press
CONTEXT SOUTH
Drum
EPOCH
THE GLASS CHERRY
The Glass Cherry Press
Lakes & Prairies Press
LIMESTONE: A Literary Journal
MESECHABE: The Journal of Surre(gion)alism
NEDGE
PASSAGER: A Journal of Remembrance and Discovery
ROOM
Taurean Horn Press
THE VINCENT BROTHERS REVIEW

OCCULT/MAGIC

American Literary Press Inc./Noble House
Arjuna Library Press
Baker Street Publications
BOTH SIDES NOW
Celestial Otter Press
CURARE
ECLIPSE
THE GALLEY SAIL REVIEW
Golden Isis Press
GRUE MAGAZINE
THE HAUNTED JOURNAL
HEAVEN BONE MAGAZINE
HORIZONS BEYOND
IRISH JOURNAL
KID'S WORLD
Lycanthrope Press

MAGIC CHANGES
META4: Journal of Object Oriented Poetics (OOPS)
MIXED BAG
NIGHTSHADE
nine muses books
Pendragonian Publications
PENNY DREADFUL: Tales and Poems of Fantastic Terror
REALM OF DARKNESS
REALM OF THE VAMPIRE
REFLECT
RFD
THE SALEM JOURNAL
SCAVENGER'S NEWSLETTER
Shadowlight Press
SONGS OF INNOCENCE
SPACE AND TIME
TALKING RIVER REVIEW
The Teitan Press, Inc.
2AM MAGAZINE
VOID
WICKED MYSTIC
Wineberry Press

OPEN FORM

ASSEMBLING
AURA LITERARY/ARTS REVIEW
Baker Street Publications
BLOOD & FEATHERS: Poems of Survival
Bloody Someday Press
Burning Llama Press
CURARE
Cynic Press
DAYS AND NIGHTS OF A SMALL PRESS PUBLISHER
DOWN UNDER MANHATTAN BRIDGE
EARTH'S DAUGHTERS: Feminist Arts Periodical
THE EVERGREEN CHRONICLES
THE FLORIDA REVIEW
THE HAUNTED JOURNAL
HAWAII PACIFIC REVIEW
HOLLYWOOD NOSTALGIA
THE IMPLODING TIE-DYED TOUPEE
JEWISH LIFE
JOURNAL OF REGIONAL CRITICISM
KARAMU
KID'S WORLD
LEAPINGS LITERARY MAGAZINE
LOST GENERATION JOURNAL
LUZ EN ARTE Y LITERATURA
MANGROVE MAGAZINE
MOOSE BOUND PRESS JOURNAL/NEWSLETTER
Mortal Press
NEDGE
NEOLOGISMS
THE NEW PRESS LITERARY QUARTERLY
NIGHTSHADE
THE NORTH AMERICAN REVIEW
ORBIS
PEGASUS
Pleasure Boat Studio
POW-WOW
REALM OF THE VAMPIRE
THE SALEM JOURNAL
Savant Garde Workshop
SIDEWALKS
SKYLARK
SLIPSTREAM
SPIN
SPINNING JENNY
STOVEPIPE: A Journal of Little Literary Value
Taurean Horn Press
Unfinished Monument Press
THE VINCENT BROTHERS REVIEW
WESTERN HUMANITIES REVIEW
WESTERN SKIES
WOMAN POET
Women-in-Literature, Inc.

ORGANIC

CONFLUENCE
DOWN UNDER MANHATTAN BRIDGE
GREEN WORLD: News and Views For Gardening Who Care About The Earth
Mortal Press
THE VINCENT BROTHERS REVIEW

ORIENTAL

AXE FACTORY REVIEW
THE BAREFOOT POET: Journal of Poetry, Fiction, Essays, & Art
Cynic Press
FISH DRUM MAGAZINE
Shaolin Communications

ORNITHOLOGY

Drum

PACIFIST

BOTH SIDES NOW
DAUGHTERS OF SARAH
HARMONY: Voices for a Just Future
KICK IT OVER
Lakes & Prairies Press
MESECHABE: The Journal of Surre(gion)alism
National Poetry Association Publishers
The Place In The Woods
Pocahontas Press, Inc.
READ, AMERICA!
VOICES - ISRAEL
WOMENWISE

PARENTS

DOWN UNDER MANHATTAN BRIDGE
HIP MAMA
LADYBUG, the Magazine for Young Children
NEW ALTERNATIVES
THE SOUTHERN REVIEW

PARODY

A & U AMERICA'S AIDS MAGAZINE
Acre Press
THE BAREFOOT POET: Journal of Poetry, Fiction, Essays, & Art
Black Tie Press
THE BOOMERPHILE
CRAB CREEK REVIEW
Creative With Words Publications (CWW)
Cynic Press
DEANOTATIONS
IDIOT WIND
KRAX
THE MASONIA ROUNDUP
NEW HOPE INTERNATIONAL REVIEW
ORBIS
THE RAINTOWN REVIEW
SCAVENGER'S NEWSLETTER
Second Coming Press
THE VINCENT BROTHERS REVIEW
Wind's Errand
WRITERS' FORUM
Writers House Press

PATRIOTIC

THE PATRIOT
Runaway Publications

PHILOSOPHICAL

THE AGUILAR EXPRESSION
Amethyst & Emerald
Arjuna Library Press
AXE FACTORY REVIEW
THE BAREFOOT POET: Journal of Poetry, Fiction, Essays, & Art
THE BOOMERPHILE
BORDERLANDS: Texas Poetry Review

PSYCHOLOGY

THE AGUILAR EXPRESSION
DOWN UNDER MANHATTAN BRIDGE
Galaxy Press
Red Dragon Press

QUATRAIN

DEANOTATIONS
THE EVERGREEN CHRONICLES
THE NEW PRESS LITERARY QUARTERLY
SEWANEE REVIEW
THE SOUTHERN REVIEW
THE SUNDAY SUITOR POETRY REVIEW
THE VINCENT BROTHERS REVIEW

REGIONAL

Adastra Press
Ahsahta
American Literary Press Inc./Noble House
Appalachian Consortium Press
Baker Street Publications
BkMk Press
Black Hat Press
BLUELINE
BORDERLANDS: Texas Poetry Review
Coteau Books
Fireweed Press
GREAT RIVER REVIEW
GREEN WORLD: News and Views For Gardening Who
  Care About The Earth
High Plains Press
Holy Cow! Press
IRON HORSE LITERARY REVIEW
Jackson Harbor Press
Konocti Books
LEAPINGS LITERARY MAGAZINE
MANKATO POETRY REVIEW
MIXED BAG
NEDGE
THE NEW PRESS LITERARY QUARTERLY
PEN & INK WRITERS JOURNAL
Pocahontas Press, Inc.
POETRY NOTTINGHAM INTERNATIONAL
Point Riders Press
POW-WOW
THE PRAIRIE JOURNAL OF CANADIAN LITERA-
  TURE
Prairie Journal Press
RAG MAG
Rowan Mountain Press
Signature Books
SKYLARK
SOUTH DAKOTA REVIEW
SPSM&H
Story Line Press
TALKING RIVER REVIEW
TUCUMCARI LITERARY REVIEW
WESTERN SKIES
Windsong Press
WRITERS' FORUM
XAVIER REVIEW

RELIGION

AABYE (formerly New Hope International Writing)
American Literary Press Inc./Noble House
AXE FACTORY REVIEW
THE BANNER
BOTH SIDES NOW
Buddhist Text Translation Society
CORNERSTONE
DAUGHTERS OF SARAH
ISRAEL HORIZONS
ISSUES
THE J MAN TIMES
KEREM: Creative Explorations in Judaism
LEAPINGS LITERARY MAGAZINE
NEW ALTERNATIVES

OBLATES
OXYGEN
POETRY AND AUDIENCE
POETRY NOTTINGHAM INTERNATIONAL
POET'S PARK
QUARTZ HILL JOURNAL OF THEOLOGY
Rabeth Publishing Company
St. Andrew Press
Signature Books
SILVER WINGS/MAYFLOWER PULPIT
STUDENT LEADERSHIP JOURNAL
STUDIO - A Journal of Christians Writing
VOICES - ISRAEL
VOID
White Buck Publishing
Writers House Press

REVIEWS

AFRICAN AMERICAN REVIEW
AURA LITERARY/ARTS REVIEW
BAKER STREET GAZETTE
BLOOD & FEATHERS: Poems of Survival
BORDERLANDS: Texas Poetry Review
THE CREAM CITY REVIEW
CUMBERLAND POETRY REVIEW
DIRIGIBLE
THE EVERGREEN CHRONICLES
FINE MADNESS
THE HAUNTED JOURNAL
HORIZONS BEYOND
H2SO4
IOTA
JACK MACKEREL MAGAZINE
THE JOURNAL
KALEIDOSCOPE: International Magazine of Literature,
  Fine Arts, and Disability
LEAPINGS LITERARY MAGAZINE
LOST GENERATION JOURNAL
LUMMOX JOURNAL
THE MARLBORO REVIEW
MID-AMERICAN REVIEW
MIXED BAG
MOCKINGBIRD
MODERN HAIKU
NEBO
NEW HOPE INTERNATIONAL REVIEW
NIGHTSHADE
OXYGEN
PEN & INK WRITERS JOURNAL
POET LORE
POETIC SPACE: Poetry & Fiction
POETRY AND AUDIENCE
PRAIRIE FIRE
Rowhouse Press
SEWANEE REVIEW
SLEUTH JOURNAL
SONGS OF INNOCENCE
SOUTHERN INDIANA REVIEW
SPINNING JENNY
TOUCHSTONE LITERARY JOURNAL
THE VINCENT BROTHERS REVIEW
ZUZU'S PETALS: QUARTERLY ONLINE

RHYME

A & U AMERICA'S AIDS MAGAZINE
THE ACORN
Aegina Press, Inc.
American Literary Press Inc./Noble House
The Ashland Poetry Press
BELLOWING ARK
BELOIT POETRY JOURNAL
BYLINE
CHARITON REVIEW
A COMPANION IN ZEOR
CRAB CREEK REVIEW
Cynic Press
DEANOTATIONS
THE FORMALIST

Galaxy Press
Golden Isis Press
Greenhouse Review Press
HARP-STRINGS
Helikon Press
INTERBANG
KRAX
LADYBUG, the Magazine for Young Children
THE LAUREL REVIEW
LEAPINGS LITERARY MAGAZINE
LIGHTHOUSE STORY COLLECTIONS
THE LITERARY REVIEW
LOST GENERATION JOURNAL
MOOSE BOUND PRESS JOURNAL/NEWSLETTER
Mortal Press
NANNY FANNY
NEDGE
NEW ALTERNATIVES
NEW HOPE INTERNATIONAL REVIEW
THE NEW PRESS LITERARY QUARTERLY
ORBIS
PARNASSUS LITERARY JOURNAL
PEGASUS
Pendragonian Publications
PENNY DREADFUL: Tales and Poems of Fantastic
   Terror
Poetic Page
POETRY AND AUDIENCE
POETRY NOTTINGHAM INTERNATIONAL
REFLECT
Rose Alley Press
SEWANEE REVIEW
SKYLARK
SONGS OF INNOCENCE
THE SOUTHERN REVIEW
SPSM&H
Story Line Press
THE SUNDAY SUITOR POETRY REVIEW
Tesseract Publications
TIME FOR RHYME
TUCUMCARI LITERARY REVIEW
THE VINCENT BROTHERS REVIEW

RITUAL

THE HAUNTED JOURNAL
THE SALEM JOURNAL

ROMANCE

American Literary Press Inc./Noble House
BLOOD & FEATHERS: Poems of Survival
KRAX
Shaolin Communications
THE SUNDAY SUITOR POETRY REVIEW
Tesseract Publications
Wind's Errand

ROMANIAN

BIBLIOPHILOS
THE NEW PRESS LITERARY QUARTERLY

RURAL

AABYE (formerly New Hope International Writing)
Baker Street Publications
KARAMU
LIGHTHOUSE STORY COLLECTIONS
LUMMOX JOURNAL
MIXED BAG
Nightsun Books
THE VINCENT BROTHERS REVIEW
WESTERN SKIES
WHOLE NOTES
Whole Notes Press

RUSSIAN

THE BAREFOOT POET: Journal of Poetry, Fiction,
   Essays, & Art
Gay Sunshine Press, Inc.
KOJA

MIP Company
THE NEW PRESS LITERARY QUARTERLY
Passeggiata Press, Inc.
Story Line Press
TAMPA REVIEW
Writers House Press

SARBANGIN

Prakalpana Literature
PRAKALPANA SAHITYA/PRAKALPANA LITERA-
   TURE

SATIRE

A & U AMERICA'S AIDS MAGAZINE
ABRAXAS
AMERICAN JONES BUILDING & MAINTENANCE
American Literary Press Inc./Noble House
American Living Press
ART:MAG
The Ashland Poetry Press
ASSEMBLING
AXE FACTORY REVIEW
Baker Street Publications
BATHTUB GIN
BELOIT POETRY JOURNAL
THE BOOMERPHILE
BORDERLANDS: Texas Poetry Review
THE CLASSICAL OUTLOOK
CRAB CREEK REVIEW
Creative With Words Publications (CWW)
Cynic Press
DAUGHTERS OF SARAH
DAYS AND NIGHTS OF A SMALL PRESS PUB-
   LISHER
DEANOTATIONS
EARTH'S DAUGHTERS: Feminist Arts Periodical
FINE MADNESS
THE GALLEY SAIL REVIEW
THE HAUNTED JOURNAL
HOLLYWOOD NOSTALGIA
IDIOT WIND
THE J MAN TIMES
JEWISH LIFE
THE LAUREL REVIEW
LEAPINGS LITERARY MAGAZINE
LUMMOX JOURNAL
THE MASONIA ROUNDUP
Missing Spoke Press
NEW HOPE INTERNATIONAL REVIEW
NIGHTSHADE
Nightsun Books
ORBIS
Pocahontas Press, Inc.
POETRY MOTEL
POETRY NOTTINGHAM INTERNATIONAL
REALM OF THE VAMPIRE
Ronsdale Press
The Runaway Spoon Press
SCRIVENER
Second Coming Press
Starbooks Press/FLF Press
Suburban Wilderness Press
TAMPA REVIEW
THOUGHTS FOR ALL SEASONS: The Magazine of
   Epigrams
THE UNDERGROUND
THE VINCENT BROTHERS REVIEW
Wind's Errand
THE WISHING WELL
WRITERS' FORUM
Writers House Press
ZUZU'S PETALS: QUARTERLY ONLINE

SCANDINAVIA

THE COOL TRAVELER
Cynic Press
FRANK: AN INTERNATIONAL JOURNAL OF CON-
   TEMPORARY WRITING AND ART

Hippopotamus Press
THE NEW PRESS LITERARY QUARTERLY
SOUTH DAKOTA REVIEW
Years Press

SCIENCE

Anamnesis Press
Drum
NEW HOPE INTERNATIONAL REVIEW
OF UNICORNS AND SPACE STATIONS
ON SPEC
PABLO LENNIS
Shadowlight Press

SCIENCE FICTION

Anamnesis Press
Arjuna Library Press
A COMPANION IN ZEOR
Cynic Press
DARK REGIONS: The Years Best Fantastic Fiction
DREAMS AND NIGHTMARES
ECLIPSE
GRUE MAGAZINE
HORIZONS BEYOND
Journey Books Publishing
KID'S WORLD
NEW HOPE INTERNATIONAL REVIEW
NOVA EXPRESS
OF UNICORNS AND SPACE STATIONS
ON SPEC
PABLO LENNIS
Pocahontas Press, Inc.
RED OWL
THE ROMANTIST
Shadowlight Press
SPACE AND TIME
Story Line Press
2AM MAGAZINE

SCOTTISH

AABYE (formerly New Hope International Writing)
CHAPMAN
Helikon Press
Jackson Harbor Press
NEW HOPE INTERNATIONAL REVIEW
THE NEW PRESS LITERARY QUARTERLY
Rowan Mountain Press

SEX

ARTHUR'S COUSIN
ART:MAG
ASSEMBLING
AXE FACTORY REVIEW
Black Tie Press
THE BOOMERPHILE
Center Press
Cynic Press
DEANOTATIONS
Gay Sunshine Press, Inc.
Ghost Pony Press
GLB Publishers
HURRICANE ALICE
Implosion Press
IRIS: A Journal About Women
JACK MACKEREL MAGAZINE
KOJA
Laocoon Books
LIMESTONE: A Literary Journal
MESECHABE: The Journal of Surre(gion)alism
MIP Company
NEW HOPE INTERNATIONAL REVIEW
OXYGEN
PASSAIC REVIEW (MILLENNIUM EDITIONS)
PLAIN BROWN WRAPPER (PBW)
RED OWL
Rowhouse Press
Shaolin Communications
SLIPSTREAM

THE SPITTING IMAGE
Starbooks Press/FLF Press
WICKED MYSTIC

SHAKESPEARE

THE NEW PRESS LITERARY QUARTERLY
THE SHAKESPEARE NEWSLETTER
SPSM&H

SHERLOCK HOLMES

BAKER STREET GAZETTE
Baker Street Publications
SLEUTH JOURNAL

SHORT POETRY

A & U AMERICA'S AIDS MAGAZINE
AABYE (formerly New Hope International Writing)
AC
THE ACORN
Ahsahta
Alternating Crimes Publishing
AMERICAN JONES BUILDING & MAINTENANCE
American Literary Press Inc./Noble House
ANT ANT ANT ANT ANT
THE ANTIGONISH REVIEW
ART-CORE
The Ashland Poetry Press
AURA LITERARY/ARTS REVIEW
AXE FACTORY REVIEW
BAKER STREET GAZETTE
Baker Street Publications
THE BAREFOOT POET: Journal of Poetry, Fiction, Essays, & Art
Bay Area Poets Coalition
BELLOWING ARK
BELOIT POETRY JOURNAL
Black Buzzard Press
Black Hat Press
Black Tie Press
BLOOD & FEATHERS: Poems of Survival
Blue Unicorn Press, Inc.
BOGG
THE BOOMERPHILE
BUTTON
BYLINE
THE CAROLINA QUARTERLY
CC. Marimbo Communications
Center Press
CHARITON REVIEW
CHIRON REVIEW
CICADA
THE CLASSICAL OUTLOOK
A COMPANION IN ZEOR
CONDUIT
Copper Beech Press
Coteau Books
CRAB CREEK REVIEW
Creative With Words Publications (CWW)
DAYS AND NIGHTS OF A SMALL PRESS PUBLISHER
DEANOTATIONS
DOWN UNDER MANHATTAN BRIDGE
EMPLOI PLUS
ENDING THE BEGIN
THE EVERGREEN CHRONICLES
FINE MADNESS
FULLOSIA PRESS
Galaxy Press
THE GREAT IDEA PATCH
Greenhouse Review Press
The Groundwater Press
THE HAUNTED JOURNAL
Headveins Graphics
HIP MAMA
Hippopotamus Press
HOLLYWOOD NOSTALGIA
HORIZONS BEYOND
Huntsville Literary Association

THE ICONOCLAST
Intertext
IRISH JOURNAL
THE J MAN TIMES
JACK THE RIPPER GAZETTE
Jackson Harbor Press
JEWISH LIFE
Journey Books Publishing
KALEIDOSCOPE: International Magazine of Literature, Fine Arts, and Disability
KARAMU
Katydid Books
KID'S WORLD
KRAX
LADYBUG, the Magazine for Young Children
Lakes & Prairies Press
THE LAUREL REVIEW
LETHOLOGICA
LIGHTHOUSE STORY COLLECTIONS
LILLIPUT REVIEW
Lintel
LOST AND FOUND TIMES
LOST GENERATION JOURNAL
LUMMOX JOURNAL
Luna Bisonte Prods
LUZ EN ARTE Y LITERATURA
THE MAC GUFFIN
THE MADISON REVIEW
MANGROVE MAGAZINE
MANY MOUNTAINS MOVING
THE MASONIA ROUNDUP
Missing Spoke Press
MIXED BAG
Mortal Press
NEW HOPE INTERNATIONAL REVIEW
THE NEW PRESS LITERARY QUARTERLY
NEWSLETTER INAGO
NIGHTSHADE
OWEN WISTER REVIEW
OXYGEN
PARNASSUS LITERARY JOURNAL
PEGASUS
PEN & INK WRITERS JOURNAL
PENNINE PLATFORM
POEM
POETALK
THE POETRY MISCELLANY
POETRY NOTTINGHAM INTERNATIONAL
POET'S FANTASY
POW-WOW
THE PRAIRIE JOURNAL OF CANADIAN LITERA-TURE
Press Here
PUDDING MAGAZINE: The International Journal of Applied Poetry
RAG MAG
THE RAINTOWN REVIEW
RALPH'S REVIEW
RAMBUNCTIOUS REVIEW
Raw Dog Press
REALM OF DARKNESS
REALM OF THE VAMPIRE
Red Dragon Press
REFLECT
Ridgeway Press of Michigan
THE SALEM JOURNAL
Savant Garde Workshop
SCRIVENER
SIDEWALKS
SLEUTH JOURNAL
SLIPSTREAM
THE SOUNDS OF POETRY
SOUTHERN INDIANA REVIEW
SPIN
SPORT LITERATE, Honest Reflections on Life's Leisurely Diversions
SPSM&H
Starbooks Press/FLF Press

STOVEPIPE: A Journal of Little Literary Value
STUDIO - A Journal of Christians Writing
THE SUNDAY SUITOR POETRY REVIEW
TAMPA REVIEW
Ten Penny Players, Inc.
Tesseract Publications
TEXAS YOUNG WRITERS' NEWSLETTER
THIS IS IMPORTANT
2AM MAGAZINE
THE UNKNOWN WRITER
THE VINCENT BROTHERS REVIEW
VISIONS-INTERNATIONAL, The World Journal of Illustrated Poetry
Vista Publishing, Inc.
VOICES - ISRAEL
VOID
WESTERN SKIES
Wineberry Press
WORDS OF WISDOM
WRITER'S EXCHANGE
WRITERS' FORUM
Writers House Press
XAVIER REVIEW
Years Press

SOCIAL AWARENESS

Adastra Press
AMERICAN JONES BUILDING & MAINTENANCE
American Literary Press Inc./Noble House
THE AMERICAN VOICE
Arctos Press
Assembling Press
AURA LITERARY/ARTS REVIEW
Baker Street Publications
THE BAREFOOT POET: Journal of Poetry, Fiction, Essays, & Art
BELOIT POETRY JOURNAL
Black Bear Publications
BLACK BEAR REVIEW
Blue Unicorn Press, Inc.
THE BOOMERPHILE
BORDERLANDS: Texas Poetry Review
BOTH SIDES NOW
BRILLIANT STAR
Burning Bush Publications
Center Press
Copper Canyon Press
CORNERSTONE
Coteau Books
CRAB CREEK REVIEW
DAYS AND NIGHTS OF A SMALL PRESS PUB-LISHER
DeeMar Communications
THE EVERGREEN CHRONICLES
HIP MAMA
HOME PLANET NEWS
Implosion Press
ISRAEL HORIZONS
JEWISH CURRENTS
JEWISH LIFE
KICK IT OVER
Lakes & Prairies Press
LEAPINGS LITERARY MAGAZINE
LUMMOX JOURNAL
LUZ EN ARTE Y LITERATURA
MANY MOUNTAINS MOVING
Missing Spoke Press
MR. COGITO
MIXED BAG
NEDGE
NEWSLETTER INAGO
PENNINE PLATFORM
Pocahontas Press, Inc.
POETRY MOTEL
POW-WOW
Pudding House Publications
PUDDING MAGAZINE: The International Journal of Applied Poetry

THE ANTIGONISH REVIEW
Arjuna Library Press
ARTHUR'S COUSIN
ART:MAG
AURA LITERARY/ARTS REVIEW
AXE FACTORY REVIEW
Baker Street Publications
Black Buzzard Press
Black Sparrow Press
Black Tie Press
BLADES
Burning Llama Press
CEDAR HILL REVIEW
Celestial Otter Press
CHIRON REVIEW
CHRONICLES OF DISORDER
City Lights Books
CLWN WR
CONDUIT
CONTEXT SOUTH
CURARE
DAYS AND NIGHTS OF A SMALL PRESS PUB-
   LISHER
DIRIGIBLE
DOWN UNDER MANHATTAN BRIDGE
EARTH'S DAUGHTERS: Feminist Arts Periodical
FINE MADNESS
GARGOYLE
GINOSKO
GLB Publishers
GRUE MAGAZINE
THE HAUNTED JOURNAL
HEAVEN BONE MAGAZINE
HORIZONS BEYOND
THE IMPLODING TIE-DYED TOUPEE
Intertext
IRISH JOURNAL
THE J MAN TIMES
JACK MACKEREL MAGAZINE
JEWISH LIFE
JOURNAL OF REGIONAL CRITICISM
KARAWANE
KRAX
LOST AND FOUND TIMES
LOST GENERATION JOURNAL
LUMMOX JOURNAL
Luna Bisonte Prods
LUZ EN ARTE Y LITERATURA
MAGIC CHANGES
MESECHABE: The Journal of Surre(gion)alism
MINESHAFT
MIXED BAG
Mortal Press
NEW HOPE INTERNATIONAL REVIEW
THE NEW RENAISSANCE, An International Magazine
   of Ideas & Opinions, Emphasizing Literature & The
   Arts
NIGHTSHADE
NOVA EXPRESS
POETRY MOTEL
THE RAINTOWN REVIEW
REALM OF DARKNESS
REALM OF THE VAMPIRE
Red Dragon Press
Ridgeway Press of Michigan
Ronsdale Press
Rowhouse Press
THE SALEM JOURNAL
SKYLARK
SLIPSTREAM
THE SPITTING IMAGE
SPOON RIVER POETRY REVIEW
SPOUT
Suburban Wilderness Press
THE UNDERGROUND
Unfinished Monument Press
THE VINCENT BROTHERS REVIEW
VISIONS-INTERNATIONAL, The World Journal of

Illustrated Poetry
VOID
VOLITION
Wineberry Press
XIB
Xib Publications
ZUZU'S PETALS: QUARTERLY ONLINE

SYMBOLIC

Arjuna Library Press
ART:MAG
Black Tie Press
Bloody Someday Press
Blue Unicorn Press, Inc.
DOWN UNDER MANHATTAN BRIDGE
THE EVERGREEN CHRONICLES
Galaxy Press
GINOSKO
HEAVEN BONE MAGAZINE
KARAMU
LOST GENERATION JOURNAL
META4: Journal of Object Oriented Poetics (OOPS)
Mortal Press
OXYGEN
PEGASUS
REALM OF THE VAMPIRE
Red Dragon Press
Ronsdale Press
STUDENT LEADERSHIP JOURNAL
THE SUNDAY SUITOR POETRY REVIEW
Taurean Horn Press
THE VINCENT BROTHERS REVIEW

THEORY

DIRIGIBLE
Galaxy Press
LIMESTONE: A Literary Journal
Savant Garde Workshop

THIRD WORLD

THE AMERICAN VOICE
ASSEMBLING
Baker Street Publications
THE BAREFOOT POET: Journal of Poetry, Fiction,
   Essays, & Art
Blind Beggar Press
BORDERLANDS: Texas Poetry Review
BRILLIANT STAR
CALYX: A Journal of Art and Literature by Women
City Lights Books
THE COOL TRAVELER
Cynic Press
EPOCH
HIP MAMA
Holy Cow! Press
H2SO4
Kenyette Productions
LEFT CURVE
Lotus Press, Inc.
MESECHABE: The Journal of Surre(gion)alism
MR. COGITO
Passeggiata Press, Inc.
Path Press, Inc.
RED OWL
St. Andrew Press
The Snail's Pace Press, Inc.
Writers House Press

TIBETAN

AXE FACTORY REVIEW
Cynic Press
FELL SWOOP
nine muses books

TRADITIONAL

AABYE (formerly New Hope International Writing)
American Literary Press Inc./Noble House
The Ashland Poetry Press

Baker Street Publications
BELLOWING ARK
BELOIT POETRY JOURNAL
THE CAROLINA QUARTERLY
Center Press
CHIRON REVIEW
Cleveland State Univ. Poetry Center
CONFRONTATION
Cynic Press
DEANOTATIONS
FOLIO: A Literary Journal of American University
THE FORMALIST
Galaxy Press
HARP-STRINGS
THE HAUNTED JOURNAL
HIRAM POETRY REVIEW
Huntsville Literary Association
LADYBUG, the Magazine for Young Children
THE LAUREL REVIEW
LEAPINGS LITERARY MAGAZINE
LIGHTHOUSE STORY COLLECTIONS
THE LITTLE MAGAZINE
THE MADISON REVIEW
MANKATO POETRY REVIEW
Mortal Press
NEW HOPE INTERNATIONAL REVIEW
NIGHTSHADE
ORBIS
PARNASSUS LITERARY JOURNAL
PEGASUS
PENNINE PLATFORM
POEM
POET'S PARK
THE RAINTOWN REVIEW
REALM OF THE VAMPIRE
RED WHEELBARROW
THE ROMANTIST
SEWANEE REVIEW
Gibbs Smith, Publisher
SONORA REVIEW
THE SOUTHERN REVIEW
SPSM&H
STAPLE
Story Line Press
Summer Stream Press
TAMPA REVIEW
Tesseract Publications
THE VINCENT BROTHERS REVIEW
VISIONS-INTERNATIONAL, The World Journal of
   Illustrated Poetry
WESTERN SKIES
White Buck Publishing
Wineberry Press
WRITERS' FORUM

TRANSLATION

AABYE (formerly New Hope International Writing)
ABRAXAS
AGADA
The Ark
ASSEMBLING
AXE FACTORY REVIEW
Baker Street Publications
THE BAREFOOT POET: Journal of Poetry, Fiction,
   Essays, & Art
BELOIT POETRY JOURNAL
BkMk Press
Black Buzzard Press
BLACK MOON
BLADES
BRANCH REDD REVIEW
Buddhist Text Translation Society
CALYX: A Journal of Art and Literature by Women
THE CAROLINA QUARTERLY
Carolina Wren Press/Lollipop Power Books
Center for Japanese Studies
THE CHARIOTEER
CHARITON REVIEW

CHELSEA
CICADA
City Lights Books
THE CLASSICAL OUTLOOK
CONDUIT
CONFLUENCE
CONFRONTATION
Copper Beech Press
Copper Canyon Press
CRAB CREEK REVIEW
THE CREAM CITY REVIEW
Cynic Press
DIALOGOS: Hellenic Studies Review
DIRIGIBLE
En Passant Poetry Press
EN PASSANT/POETRY
Erespin Press
THE EVERGREEN CHRONICLES
FIELD: Contemporary Poetry and Poetics
FINE MADNESS
FOLIO: A Literary Journal of American University
THE FORMALIST
FRANK: AN INTERNATIONAL JOURNAL OF CON-
   TEMPORARY WRITING AND ART
From Here Press
GARGOYLE
Gay Sunshine Press, Inc.
The Groundwater Press
THE HAUNTED JOURNAL
Hippopotamus Press
ILLUMINATIONS
Interim Press
ISRAEL HORIZONS
Italica Press, Inc.
Kosmos
LADYBUG, the Magazine for Young Children
Latin American Literary Review Press
THE LITERARY REVIEW
LUMMOX JOURNAL
LUZ EN ARTE Y LITERATURA
THE MARLBORO REVIEW
MID-AMERICAN REVIEW
MINESHAFT
MR. COGITO
Moving Parts Press
NATURAL BRIDGE
NEBO
THE NEW RENAISSANCE, An International Magazine
   of Ideas & Opinions, Emphasizing Literature & The
   Arts
NIGHTSHADE
Oberlin College Press
ORBIS
OSIRIS
OUTPOSTS POETRY QUARTERLY
PARNASSUS: Poetry in Review
Passeggiata Press, Inc.
Pella Publishing Co
PENNINE PLATFORM
Pocahontas Press, Inc.
POETRY NEW YORK: A Journal of Poetry and
   Translation
POETRY NOTTINGHAM INTERNATIONAL
Rarach Press
Reality Street Editions
REALM OF THE VAMPIRE
RENDITIONS
SALMAGUNDI
SENECA REVIEW
Serena Bay Books
SKYLARK
The Snail's Pace Press, Inc.
The Spirit That Moves Us Press, Inc.
THE SPITTING IMAGE
SYCAMORE REVIEW
TAMPA REVIEW
TOUCHSTONE LITERARY JOURNAL
VOICES - ISRAEL

The Wellsweep Press
WEST COAST LINE: A Journal of Contemporary
  Writing and Criticism
WHOLE NOTES
Whole Notes Press
WRITERS' FORUM
Writers House Press
Xenos Books
XTRAS

TRAVEL/TRANSPORTATION

AABYE (formerly New Hope International Writing)
Baker Street Publications
BLADES
THE COOL TRAVELER
ENTELECHY MAGAZINE
EXIT 13 MAGAZINE
OUT YOUR BACKDOOR: The Magazine of Informal
  Adventure and Cheap Culture
Pocahontas Press, Inc.
SPORT LITERATE, Honest Reflections on Life's Leisur-
  ely Diversions
THE VINCENT BROTHERS REVIEW
WORDS OF WISDOM

URBAN

Art/Life Limited Editions
Baker Street Publications
THE COOL TRAVELER
DOWN UNDER MANHATTAN BRIDGE
HOME PLANET NEWS
KICK IT OVER
THE LAUREL REVIEW
LUMMOX JOURNAL
OXYGEN
Ridgeway Press of Michigan
SLIPSTREAM
University of Massachusetts Press
THE VINCENT BROTHERS REVIEW
XIB
Xib Publications

VEGETARIAN

Buddhist Text Translation Society
CHIRON REVIEW
DOWN UNDER MANHATTAN BRIDGE
GLOBAL TAPESTRY
RFD
THE VINCENT BROTHERS REVIEW
VOICES - ISRAEL

VICTIMS

DOWN UNDER MANHATTAN BRIDGE
GLB Publishers
Writers House Press

VICTORIANA

BAKER STREET GAZETTE
Baker Street Publications
BIBLIOPHILOS
BUTTON
JACK THE RIPPER GAZETTE
THE NOCTURNAL LYRIC
SKYLARK
SLEUTH JOURNAL

VIET NAM

AXE FACTORY REVIEW
THE BAREFOOT POET: Journal of Poetry, Fiction,
  Essays, & Art
BkMk Press
Black Bear Publications
BLACK BEAR REVIEW
THE BOOMERPHILE
Cynic Press
DeeMar Communications
PASSAIC REVIEW (MILLENNIUM EDITIONS)
Rowan Mountain Press

SLIPSTREAM
2AM MAGAZINE
Writers House Press

VILLANELLE

AABYE (formerly New Hope International Writing)
BELLOWING ARK
THE CAROLINA QUARTERLY
THE COMSTOCK REVIEW
CONJUNCTIONS
Cynic Press
DEANOTATIONS
THE EVERGREEN CHRONICLES
HARP-STRINGS
Hippopotamus Press
Huntsville Literary Association
THE LAUREL REVIEW
THE LICKING RIVER REVIEW
NEW HOPE INTERNATIONAL REVIEW
PENNINE PLATFORM
POEM
THE RAINTOWN REVIEW
SEWANEE REVIEW
STAPLE
STUDIO - A Journal of Christians Writing
Tesseract Publications
THE VINCENT BROTHERS REVIEW
WRITERS' FORUM

VISIONARY

AMERICAN JONES BUILDING & MAINTENANCE
American Living Press
Anamnesis Press
APKL Publications
ART:MAG
DEANOTATIONS
DOWN UNDER MANHATTAN BRIDGE
GINOSKO
JEJUNE: america Eats its Young
Left Hand Books
LUZ EN ARTE Y LITERATURA
Missing Spoke Press
ON SPEC
The Place In The Woods
READ, AMERICA!
Red Dragon Press
Savant Garde Workshop
Shadowlight Press
THE VINCENT BROTHERS REVIEW

VISUAL

AABYE (formerly New Hope International Writing)
ABRAXAS
ANT ANT ANT ANT ANT
Arjuna Library Press
Art/Life Limited Editions
Baker Street Publications
Black Tie Press
BORDERLANDS: Texas Poetry Review
CLWN WR
DAYS AND NIGHTS OF A SMALL PRESS PUB-
  LISHER
ENDING THE BEGIN
French Bread Publications
THE HAUNTED JOURNAL
Headveins Graphics
HOLLYWOOD NOSTALGIA
IRISH JOURNAL
JEWISH LIFE
KALDRON, An International Journal Of Visual Poetry
KOJA
KRAX
LEFT CURVE
Left Hand Books
LOST AND FOUND TIMES
Luna Bisonte Prods
MESECHABE: The Journal of Surre(gion)alism
NEW HOPE INTERNATIONAL REVIEW

PACIFIC COAST JOURNAL
POW-WOW
The Runaway Spoon Press
Savant Garde Workshop
THE SUNDAY SUITOR POETRY REVIEW
Truly Fine Press
THE VINCENT BROTHERS REVIEW
WESTERN SKIES
WRITER'S EXCHANGE
XIB
Xib Publications
ZUZU'S PETALS: QUARTERLY ONLINE

WAR

BORDERLANDS: Texas Poetry Review
Lakes & Prairies Press
NITE-WRITER'S INTERNATIONAL LITERARY
    ARTS JOURNAL
Writers House Press

WELSH

Story Line Press

WESTERN

Baker Street Publications
BORDERLANDS: Texas Poetry Review
Coteau Books
Cynic Press
LITERALLY HORSES
Nashville House
Poetry Wales Press, Ltd.
POW-WOW
Gibbs Smith, Publisher
TALKING RIVER REVIEW
WESTERN SKIES

WOMEN

AC
Acre Press
Alternating Crimes Publishing
American Literary Press Inc./Noble House
THE AMERICAN VOICE
Amethyst & Emerald
ART:MAG
The Ashland Poetry Press
ASSEMBLING
BkMk Press
Black Hat Press
BLOOD & FEATHERS: Poems of Survival
Blue Unicorn Press, Inc.
BRIDGES: A Journal for Jewish Feminists and Our
    Friends
Broken Jaw Press
Burning Bush Publications
CALYX: A Journal of Art and Literature by Women
THE CAROLINA QUARTERLY
Carolina Wren Press/Lollipop Power Books
CEDAR HILL REVIEW
Chicory Blue Press, Inc.
Copper Canyon Press
Coteau Books
THE CREATIVE WOMAN
Cynic Press
DAUGHTERS OF SARAH
DeeMar Communications
DOWN UNDER MANHATTAN BRIDGE
EARTH'S DAUGHTERS: Feminist Arts Periodical
THE EVERGREEN CHRONICLES
FRONTIERS: A Journal of Women Studies
THE GLASS CHERRY
The Glass Cherry Press
GLB Publishers
High Plains Press
HIP MAMA
HURRICANE ALICE
Implosion Press
IRIS: A Journal About Women
JEJUNE: america Eats its Young

KALLIOPE, A Journal of Women's Literature and Art
KARAMU
Lakes & Prairies Press
LEAPINGS LITERARY MAGAZINE
Lotus Press, Inc.
LUMMOX JOURNAL
LUZ EN ARTE Y LITERATURA
MANUSHI - a journal about women & society
MANY MOUNTAINS MOVING
MESECHABE: The Journal of Surre(gion)alism
Minor Heron Press
Moving Parts Press
Nightsun Books
Outrider Press
Painted Leaf Press
Paris Press, Inc.
PARNASSUS: Poetry in Review
PASSAIC REVIEW (MILLENNIUM EDITIONS)
Passeggiata Press, Inc.
Perugia Press
The Place In The Woods
Plain View Press, Inc.
Pocahontas Press, Inc.
POETRY AND AUDIENCE
Prairie Journal Press
PRIMAVERA
RADIANCE, The Magazine For Large Women
RAG MAG
THE RATIONAL FEMINIST
READ, AMERICA!
Relief Press
Rhiannon Press
Ronsdale Press
Rose Shell Press
THE SALEM JOURNAL
Sandberry Press
Signature Books
SKYLARK
The Snail's Pace Press, Inc.
SOJOURNER, THE WOMEN'S FORUM
THE SOUTHERN REVIEW
Starbooks Press/FLF Press
University of Massachusetts Press
Vista Publishing, Inc.
West End Press
Windsong Press
Wineberry Press
THE WISHING WELL
WOMAN POET
Women-in-Literature, Inc.
WOMENWISE
WRITERS' FORUM
WRITING FOR OUR LIVES

WRITING

Baker Street Publications
THE BAREFOOT POET: Journal of Poetry, Fiction,
    Essays, & Art
BARNWOOD
Cynic Press
DAYS AND NIGHTS OF A SMALL PRESS PUB-
    LISHER
THE HAUNTED JOURNAL
JEWISH LIFE
Mortal Press
NEW HOPE INTERNATIONAL REVIEW
PACIFIC COAST JOURNAL
PAPYRUS
PASSAGER: A Journal of Remembrance and Discovery
PEN & INK WRITERS JOURNAL
POET'S FANTASY
SALT LICK
Salt Lick Press
SPORT LITERATE, Honest Reflections on Life's Leisur-
    ely Diversions
THE SUNDAY SUITOR POETRY REVIEW
WRITES OF PASSAGE

WRITING THERAPY

WRITER'S EXCHANGE

YOUTH

HIP MAMA
Kenyette Productions
Lakes & Prairies Press
LIGHTHOUSE STORY COLLECTIONS
MERLYN'S PEN: Fiction, Essays, and Poems By
    America's Teens
PASSAIC REVIEW (MILLENNIUM EDITIONS)
THE SOUTHERN REVIEW
Starbooks Press/FLF Press
Writers House Press
WRITES OF PASSAGE

ZEN

AXE FACTORY REVIEW
THE BOOMERPHILE
Buddhist Text Translation Society
BUTTON
CC. Marimbo Communications
Copper Canyon Press
Cynic Press
FISH DRUM MAGAZINE
Ghost Pony Press
THE GLASS CHERRY
The Glass Cherry Press
KID'S WORLD
LIMESTONE: A Literary Journal
LUMMOX JOURNAL
Lycanthrope Press
Press Here
ROOM
Shaolin Communications